CASES AND MATERIALS ON

LAND USE

Fifth Edition

By

Robert R. Wright

Donaghey Distinguished Professor of Law
University of Arkansas
Little Rock

Morton Gitelman

Distinguished Professor of Law
University of Arkansas
Fayetteville

AMERICAN CASEBOOK SERIES®

WEST PUBLISHING CO.
ST. PAUL, MINN., 1997

 *TEXT IS PRINTED ON 10% POST CONSUMER RECYCLED PAPER*

To Susan and Robin

Robert R. Wright

To Marcia

Morton Gitelman

A land of settled government,
A land of just and old renown,
Where freedom slowly broadens down
From precedent to precedent.

Alfred, Lord Tennyson

*

iii

Preface

Since the publication of the last edition of this casebook in 1990, land use law has been in the forefront of the public eye. The United States Supreme Court has taken more land use cases in the past decade than in many previous decades combined. Also, Congress and state legislatures have been active in writing and passing new legislation in the field. The central issue in land use litigation and legislation remains—the perennial problem of accommodating the interests of private property and the public interest in regulating the use of land for the health, safety and welfare of the people. In our society and under its constitutional principles the law recognizes both private and public rights in land. Our legal institutions have devoted much effort to striking a proper balance among those interests. As with many legal problems, that balancing is left ultimately to the courts. Therefore, this is a casebook in the traditional sense. The cases are important and the courts are far from unanimous in their views of where the balance should be struck. These materials probe the limits of such efforts from several different perspectives.

The first perspective to be explored will be familiar to students who have already studied property law and tort law—private law as it imposes limits on a property owner in the uses to which the property is put. The law of waste and of nuisance is presented from a functional approach, i.e., how these ancient common law institutions are used to control land uses. In this sense nuisance law, for example, is presented as the law of neighbors and neighborhoods. In the third chapter restrictive covenants and equitable servitudes are explored as private land use control devices. Also, some ancillary institutions such as easements and defeasible estates are briefly touched upon.

The bulk of the materials, beginning with Chapter IV, look at public regulation of land use. We begin with a look at the use of public planning of land use and what that means for communities and for land owners. Government planning has always engendered debate about basic political views of the nature of our society. Land use planning has at times been in the center of such debate. Consequently, the legal effects of public land use planning are far from fixed in this nation. Judicial views on this subject, though sparse, present some interesting perspectives on the utility of planning.

Chapter V, which has been considerably expanded for this edition, presents the central constitutional problem of how far government regulation of land use may go before it encounters constitutional restrictions on the taking of property for public use or purpose without just compensation. This area of land use law has seen a significant increase in litigation with several Supreme Court pronouncements. Yet the question of what constitutes a taking of property is not easily answered. The Supreme Court cases establish the basic constitutional considerations, but many state and lower federal decisions are necessary to help understand the contours of the words in our constitution. Defining "property" for example, or "public purpose" in the context of specific disputes is far from a dictionary task. The increasingly important area of remedies for landowners by way of suits for inverse condemnation or damages under Title 42, Section 1983 is given fuller treatment than in past editions. Also, in the mid-1990's state legislatures have studied and passed several different types of taking legislation, usually from the perspective of reaffirming and strengthening the rights of owners of private property. This chapter is crucial for students to develop the tools to probe what follows.

Chapter VI is devoted to application of the regulatory taking principles to the prevention and regulation of land development. In the past dozen years this area of land use law has burgeoned, clearly outstripping the historic staple of zoning law in the posing of difficult and important issues for judicial resolution. Here we encounter regulations which totally or nearly so prevent development of land for sake of the environment, to protect endangered species and open space, to preserve historic structures, to regulate urban growth. The cases dealing with these issues are timely, yet timeless. The clash between private property and public interest is most clearly evident. Also in this chapter regulation of development is taken up in such areas as sewer and water moratoria and subdivision regulation and exactions. The law of exactions is the subject of two recent Supreme Court decisions that have created a flurry of new cases in state courts. The chapter closes with a section devoted to public and private cooperation in land development. Very interesting current problems are presented which is, in many respects, the converse of the theme of public regulation—instead of looking at the limits of public interference with the private sector we look at the public involvement in land development in cooperation with the private sector.

The basics of zoning comprise the seventh chapter. Zoning, an institution dating back but eighty-five years, has been the primary vehicle used by municipal government to regulate the use of land. In terms of legal proceedings, many a new lawyer will find that appearing before planning commissions, boards of adjustment, city councils and other administrative and legislative bodies can be a regular part of the practice of law. Chapter VII should be seen as a basic education in the terminology, theory and practice of zoning law. Even in this basic chapter, however, new problem areas have emerged since the previous edition. Especially in the areas of citizen involvement by way of the referendum and initiative, intergovernmental conflicts and the applicability of antitrust law, new cases and disputes have occupied courts all across the land.

Chapter VIII, Zoning and Discrimination, was an important part of the previous edition and remains important in this edition. A number of newer cases have been included in the areas of single-family definitions, mobile home and group home regulation, exclusion of religious uses and private schools, and discrimination in housing. The previous materials on inclusionary zoning, the land use law equivalent of affirmative action in the field of employment have been revised minimally. The use of inclusionary devices has not spread to many states in recent years. Yet, the issues presented are of extraordinary interest and worthy of serious study.

The final chapter deals with aesthetic regulation and preservation of resources. In the area of aesthetics, sign regulations and architectural control of dwellings are problems of abiding interest and the number of cases on sign regulation seem to increase yearly. The problems of resource preservation, natural resources, the coastlines, agricultural land, beaches and streams and rivers are constantly being litigated.

ROBERT R. WRIGHT
MORTON GITELMAN

July, 1997

Summary of Contents

Table of Contents

Table of Cases

The principal cases are in bold type. Cases cited or discussed in the text are roman type. References are to pages. Cases cited in principal cases and within other quoted materials are not included.

*

CASES AND MATERIALS ON
LAND USE
Fifth Edition

*

Chapter I

LAND USE CONTROLS: AN HISTORICAL OVERVIEW

In his *Commentaries on the Laws of England,* Blackstone wrote that nothing "so generally strikes the imagination and engages the affections of mankind, as the right of property; or that sole and despotic dominion which one man claims and exercises over the external things of the world in total exclusion of the right of any other individual in the universe."[1] But the elevated position that property rights would be accorded by such a proposition did not exist in the late eighteenth century when Blackstone wrote and certainly does not exist today. There are external rights which existed then and which continue to exist today in a more modern form on behalf of other landowners and the public in general. While this should come as no surprise to anyone who has taken the basic property course, it flies in the face of the old idea that a landowner "has a right to do what he wants to do on his own land."

Someone advancing such a proposition could quote even further from Blackstone, somewhat out of context, to this effect:

> So great, moreover, is the regard of the law for private property, that it will not authorize the least violation of it; *no, not even for the general good of the whole community.*[2]

Blackstone was discussing the "absolute right inherent in every Englishman" which consisted of the free use, enjoyment and alienation of his property "without any control or diminution, *save only by the laws of the land.*"[3] While the concept of what is a permitted control or diminution has broadened as a result of problems created by increasing industrialization, urban growth, and population density, public controls on the private use of land have long existed. These controls or limitations on private rights are more obvious today because they have become

---

1. II W. Blackstone, Commentaries on the Laws of England 2 (1782).

2. I W. Blackstone, id. at 139. Emphasis supplied.

3. Id. at 138. Emphasis supplied.

1

more numerous and more refined in response to changing circumstances and social conditions.

The concept of private property ownership as an absolute, uncontrolled right possibly stemmed in part from the writings of John Locke. Locke's writings were influential on American thinkers of the eighteenth century, including Thomas Jefferson, and Locke viewed the ownership of land as an inherent or natural right. But Locke was speaking of the rights of Englishmen to acquire and hold title to land and to have the exclusive right to it and possession of it.[4] This principle was transferred quite readily into the American experience, as Jefferson drew heavily upon Locke's "life, liberty and property" trilogy, converting it into "life, liberty and the pursuit of happiness" in the Declaration of Independence with the latter alteration apparently intended to mean more, but certainly no less.[5] Thus did it become engrained in Anglo–American juristic thought that in an open society, each person had a right by virtue of being a person to acquire and hold real estate. This fundamental principle is no weaker today than it was in the time of Locke and Jefferson. But the right to acquire and hold title to land did not necessarily carry with it the right to *use* it in any and every way. At this point, the rights of adjoining landowners and the broader rights of the public in general enter the picture. It would be a mistake, however, to infer that a conflict of interests is the inevitable result or that the posture of the collective mass of the people acting through public agencies is essentially hostile to the rights of individual property owners. This picture of the "public interest" as being in conflict with the property rights of individual citizens is itself a misleading and largely erroneous one, as we shall see. But the first essential to an understanding of the situation is the realization that as civilized society emerged and took shape, certain limitations also developed in the natural course of events, and these limitations applied as much to land as to other aspects of life.

Richard T. Ely, a political economist, in his work Property and Contract in Their Relation to the Distribution of Wealth (N.Y.: The Macmillan Co., 1914), said:

> Furthermore, *Property is exclusive in its nature and not absolute.* A phrase is found in Roman law which, as a definition of property, is misleading. The phrase is, *"Dominium est jus utendi et abutendi re."* Some have said that it means that the right of

4. Locke's theory of property justified the ownership of property by the labor which went into its improvement. See Locke, Second Treatise * * * Of Civil Government in English Philosophers from Bacon to Mill 413 (Burtt ed. 1939). This aspect of his philosophy has not stood the test of time, while the concept of property ownership as an inherent right is very much a part of our legal heritage. Thus, the Arkansas Constitution of 1874, for example, in Article 2, Section 2 states that "acquiring,

possessing and protecting property" is an "inherent and inalienable" right, and states in Article 2, Section 22, that "the right of property is before and higher than any constitutional sanction."

5. The Bill of Rights to the U.S. Constitution returns, of course, to the "life, liberty, or property" language in the due process provision of the Fifth Amendment, and the language is repeated in the Fourteenth Amendment.

property carries with it the right to use or to abuse a thing, and so it has been actually claimed that property is the right to use or misuse a thing, and that the right of property carries with it the right to make a bad use of things. But such an idea comes from bad translation. *Abutendi* means to use up or consume a thing, not to abuse it * * *.

The right of property is an exclusive right, but it has never been an absolute right. In so far as the right of property existed it was an exclusive right, that is, it excluded others; but it was not a right without limitations or qualifications. Notice the distinction between *exclusive* and *absolute*.

The truth is, there are two sides to private property, *the individual side and the social side.* The social side of property finds illustration in the right of eminent domain and in the right of taxation. If there were no such thing as the social side of private property, how could the right of taxation exist? * * *

So also with the right of eminent domain. It is utterly incompatible with the absolute right of private property. *Moreover, this social side of private property is not to be regarded as something exceptional.* On the contrary, it is an essential part of the institution itself. It is just as much a part of private property, as it exists at the present time, as the individual side is a part of it. The two necessarily go together, so that if one perishes the other must perish. The social side limits the individual side, and as it is always present there is no such thing as absolute private property. An absolute right of property, as the great jurist, the late Professor von Ihering says, would result in the dissolution of society.

Vol. 1, pp. 135–137.

In this connection, long before the first faint light of English civilization, the earliest code of Roman law, the Twelve Tables, provided:

> Whoever sets a hedge around his land shall not exceed the boundary; in the case of a wall, he shall leave one foot; in the case of a house, two feet. If a grave or pit, the required depth. If a well, a path, an olive or fig tree, nine feet. Finally, whoever plants other trees shall leave a space of five feet between [his] property and his neighbor's. If there is litigation about boundaries, five feet.[6]

Limitations on the use of rural and urban land have been grist for the legislative mill for much, if not all, of our legal history. Through the centuries that saw the development of the common law in England dozens, if not hundreds, of statutes placed restrictions on the use of land. When highwaymen were abroad robbing innocent travelers, Parliament enacted a statute requiring property owners to cut down the high hedges along roadways to keep miscreants from "lurking to do hurt." When London suffered the great fire in the seventeenth century, the first set of

---

6. As quoted in Treasury of Law 71 (Nice ed. 1964). Nice states that the Twelve Tables were drafted by a commission in 451–450 B.C.

comprehensive building regulations was enacted in 1666 so that rebuilt London would be safer; a large administrative bureaucracy was established to examine building plans and issue permits. See T. F. Reddaway, The Rebuilding of London After the Great Fire (London: Edward Arnold & Co., 1940).

In colonial times on American shores land use regulations and limitations on the rights of owners were rampant. In the Dutch colonies in what is now New York, immigrants held very fragile title to land that was allotted to them; emerging communities could reallocate land freely. The English colonies also imposed affirmative and negative limitations on private property. In John F. Hart, Colonial Land Use Law and its Significance for Modern Takings Doctrine, 109 Harv. L. Rev. 1252 (1996) the author catalogs a wide variety of colonial laws and rules that regulated the use of land. In Kenney, Forest Legislation in America Prior to March 4, 1789 (Cornell Exp. Sta. Bull., 1916), the author reported at 361:

> * * * The writer soon found that forestry and timber problems had claimed the attention of colonial legislative bodies on many occasions during the seventeenth century, and that hundreds of such laws had been enacted previous to the establishment of the National Government. Long before the Federal Constitution became effective—on March 4, 1789—the legislatures of most of the colonies had realized that forest fires constituted a great menace to the welfare of the people, and modern trespass laws and regulations of the lumber industry have their forerunners in the legislation of the seventeenth and eighteenth centuries. The influence of American forests in the development of the spirit of opposition to Great Britain that culminated in the Revolution of 1776 has not been given its due importance by political and economic writers, nor has it been known that certain developments of forest regulation in the colonies were strikingly anticipatory of recent movements in national forest policy.

An excellent summary of some controls on land use in New York City, spanning three centuries, may be found in McGoldrick et al., Building Regulation in New York City (1944). The introduction to this volume states, at 3–4:

> One need not go very far into the countryside to find areas where one may build his home according to his own notions. But even the earliest experience in tiny New Amsterdam showed that fires from one person's badly built or neglected chimney could menace the homes and lives of his neighbors, and that, if people were to live in compact communities, some surrender of the individual's right to do as he pleases was essential to the protection of the lives and health of all.

> And so we find that three centuries in New York have produced a body of rules regarding buildings scattered among thousands of pages of statutes, local laws and departmental regulations and that

there are upwards of ten thousand public employees all or part of whose time is devoted to enforcing them. The development of these rules has been the product of experience, frequently harsh experience, which has demonstrated the need for such rules if life, health and property in a compact community are to be safe. * * *

Also see Theodore Steinberg, God's Terminus: Boundaries, Nature, and Property on the Michigan Shore, 37 Am. J. Legal Hist. 65 (1993).

After the American Revolution one of the first problems taken up by Congress was the question of public lands. A concise overview of our national policies in connection with the disposal of the public domain can be found in Public Land Law Review Commission, History of Public Land Law Development, pp. 765–773 (1968):

> American land policy from Independence to the end of the 19th century had four objectives inherited from the colonial period: (1) to produce revenue for the government; (2) to facilitate the settlement and growth of new communities; (3) to reward veterans of wars; and (4) to promote education, the establishment of eleemosynary institutions, and the construction of internal improvements by grants of land. Spokesmen for all four of these objectives were to clash over the relative importance of each and were to cause the adoption of measures that were inharmonious and incongruous with others.

> The need to refund the heavy debts contracted during the Revolution which went unpaid under the Confederation, induced Thomas Jefferson, the agrarian radical, Alexander Hamilton, the fiscal conservative, and Albert Gallatin, who represented a midway position between the views of the two, to agree to pledge the income from land sales for the retirement of the debt. The public lands were to be sold and the proceeds "appropriated toward sinking or discharging the debts * * * and * * * applied solely to that use." This solemn pledge of August 4, 1790, and of April, 1798, was to hold Congress to a revenue policy until the debt was retired. Land was to be sold in large tracts at competitive bidding on a wholesale basis and it was expected that the buyers would then retail it out to small farmers in the way that James Fenimore Cooper was retailing land on the New York frontier.

> Agrarian followers of Jefferson disliked the emphasis upon revenue in the disposal of the public lands. They agreed with him that "the small landholders are the most precious part of a State" and that "vast grants" or large ownerships tending toward "monopolies" were wrong. They wished to give the common man easy access to the public land and the chance to acquire ownership out of the capital they accumulated from cultivating it. This involved permitting settlers to search out attractive locations, to improve them, and after a few years to preempt them at the minimum price. Frontier settlers wanted no speculators buying at a competitive sale and therefore they demanded the right of preemption and wanted the public land reserved for farm makers. Failing that, they wanted

sales postponed as long as possible to give them time to accumulate the $200 for their quarter-section and to assure that settlers took up most of the land. At the same time they wanted no restrictions placed on the areas into which they might move and urged the speedy removal of the Indians from desirable areas and the rapid survey of the lands.

In addition to these advocates of a wide-open land system that would permit individuals to settle wherever they wished, there was another element of the population concerned with the business in land, timber, and minerals. No one has essayed a history of the land business but when one thinks of the number of speculators, land agents, landlookers, timber cruisers, dealers in land warrants, scrip, and tax titles, and lawyers who were absorbed in these frontier occupations, and of the fortunes that were made and lost in land speculation, it is easy to see that the influence of these classes was large. Persons engaged in the land business wanted no restrictions placed in their way of profit, no regulations such as were suggested by the Commissioner of the Land Office at one time, no investigations of their activities. On the positive side they favored legislation that would attract immigration, provide internal improvements and encourage statehood, and they joined with pioneer settlers in booster activities that would stimulate a demand for land and a rise in its value.

The third objective of using the public lands to reward veterans of past wars was pursued generously by Congress. Even if they had served only a few days, veterans of all wars through that with Mexico were given warrants they could exchange for land, first in military tracts, later anywhere there was public land open to entry. True, the maximum grant of 160 acres, which was given to officers as well as men, was small in comparison with the more generous bounties officers had received in the colonial period, but in a more democratic age the old disparities between ranks seemed less desirable. The great majority of the warrants were sold at well below the government-minimum price for land, thereby reducing the cost of land for speculators and such settlers as acquired them.

Very early the public land states began to exhibit disenchantment with Federal ownership, administration, and determination of policy concerning the public lands. They recalled that they were admitted into the Union "on an equal footing with the original states, in all respects, whatever," and yet were denied ownership of the ungranted land within their boundaries, whereas Massachusetts and all others of the Original Thirteen had retained the ungranted lands within their boundaries. Furthermore, the new states had been required to make a compact that they would not tax the newly granted lands for 5 years after they were sold. To win the acceptance of such compacts the new states were offered one thirty-sixth of the public lands within their borders for schools and smaller grants for other purposes. No state was content with such a bargain. Some tried to induce the Federal government to cede its lands to them; others strove to gain larger donations and over the course of years Congress did become increasingly liberal. School donations were increased from one section in each township to two and finally to four, large grants were given for agricultural colleges, and, most important, for the construction of roads, canals, and railroads, the dredging and improvement of navigable rivers, and for irrigation. The states having found a way of gaining ownership of a portion of the public lands came forth with many proposals for internal improvements, some dubious to say the least. Most questionable was the donation of the swamplands to the states which were expected to drain them—something that strict constructionists thought the Federal government lacked the power to do.

Grants for public schools, for roads, canals, and railroads could be justified, said those who always searched for specific authorization in the Constitution for any action they might favor, on the ground that they would enhance the value of the remaining lands and thereby bring to the government as great a return as if no land had been given away. By giving one half the land in alternate sections for internal improvements and raising the price of the reserved sections to the double-minimum there would be no loss. Congress, having found a nearly perfect rationalization for grants it wished to make, was willing to vote huge grants to the transcontinental railroads in 1862–71.

Through the granting process Congress was experimenting with bounties, subsidies to worthy objects that could not be achieved, at least not at that time, without Federal aid in the form of public lands. In voting these bounties it was slowly expanding its own vision of America's destiny and of the powers of the national government under the Constitution. It was the Federal government that built the National Road in Ohio, roughly Route 40 today, and made possible the Illinois and Michigan Canal, the predecessor of the Chicago Drainage Canal, and the most widely used Soo Canal. It was the Federal government that made possible early construction of the Union Pacific, the Northern Pacific, the Santa Fe, and the Southern Pacific Railroads. It was the Federal government that provided a source of funds for common schools in frontier communities and initiated moves for the establishment of the great state universities. These Federal land grants made necessary the creation of state and railroad land departments to sell these grants at the highest price obtainable if the purposes for which they were given were to be achieved. In the 1850's, then, Congress was relaxing its own emphasis upon revenue, was issuing great quantities of military bounty warrants and scrip that sold for less than $1.25 an acre, under western pressure was graduating the price of land in proportion to the length of time it had been on the market and was moving toward a policy of free grants; at the same time the states and the railroads were attempting to extract from their grants the greatest possible return. The incongruity was apparent to few at the time.

Having pledged the income from the sale of public lands to the retirement of the war debt it was natural that the public lands should be placed under the charge of the Treasury Department (they remained there until 1849 when they were transferred to the newly established Department of the Interior, where western influences were to be much stronger). It was also natural for Congress to ask of the brilliant Hamilton a plan for the sale of the lands which was partly incorporated in the first important land act of the new government in 1796. But Congress early showed its intention of determining land policies. It had no great liking for Executive leadership, whether it came from the President, as during the Jackson administration or, at a later date, from vigorous and energetic administrators of the Land Office like John Wilson and William E.J. Sparks. Commissioners of the General Land Office who irked Congress did not last long.

Outstanding American statesmen who have had a share in shaping our land policies have held very diverse views. In addition to Hamilton, Jefferson, and Gallatin in the early period, we have Madison and Monroe expressing grave constitutional doubts as to the use of Federal power to develop internal improvements, whereas John Quincy Adams reverted to Hamilton's and Gallatin's broad latitudinarian concept of Federal powers. Jackson and Calhoun both advocated the transfer of the public lands to the states when the income from the public domain was no longer essential for the central government. Cession of the lands would remove one of the principal nationalizing forces which Calhoun so greatly feared, and would at the same time win for him a political following in the newer states. Henry Clay wanted to retain the $1.25–an–acre price and distribute the surplus income to the states on the basis of their population, a position that was liked in the older and more populous states. Thomas Hart Benton, friend of the St. Louis barons of the fur trade and of claimants to huge land grants, preferred to cheapen the price of land by graduating it in relation to the length of time it had been on the market.

In the middle period, new statesmen like Stephen A. Douglas argued that the Nation with its new acquisitions on the Pacific should be bound together by railroads which could only be built with great donations of land. Andrew Johnson, Horace Greeley, and George W. Julian favored abandoning the revenue policy and granting free homesteads to all who would go west to make farms. They were responsible for banning all speculative purchasing of land in the five southern public land states from 1866 to 1876.

What of earlier objectives of Federal land policy after the adoption of the Homestead Act? The revenue concept was not abandoned. Land already offered and great acreages to be put up at auction in the future were available for purchase in any amount at $1.25 an acre, or at less cost if depreciated bounty warrants and scrip were used. In the event that a homesteader preferred to take title after 6 months on his claim he could commute the 160–acre entry to a cash entry by paying $200. The Desert Land Act of 1877 offered settlers arid land in tracts as large as 640 acres if they would conduct water on it and pay $1.25 an acre. The Timber and Stone Act of 1878 provided for the sale of 160 acres of land for its timber or stone for $2.50 an acre. Actually, the government received far more from land sales and mineral leases after the initiation of free lands than it did before. True, the income from public lands constituted a very small percentage of the gross government revenue in contrast to the earlier years when it amounted to as much as 48 percent in one year. Revenue was no longer a major objective, though there were those like Carl Schurz who felt that a fair price in relation to value should be paid for forest land.

Veterans of the Civil War were not to be rewarded by military bounties, though there was a strong bloc which favored the revival of the bounty acts of 1847 and 1855. But since all persons, including veterans, were entitled to free homesteads if they would live upon them and develop them, the bonus of an extra quarter-section would only play into the hands of speculators, as the earlier bounty warrants had done. Veterans were given the right to homestead on 160 acres of double-minimum priced land within the primary area of railroad land grants and some were able to make something out of the soldier's additional homestead rights which came to be one of the most valuable forms of scrip and one of the most abused. Later, veterans were given preference in the selection of homesteads in reclamation projects.

Congress continued to make grants to states, with increasing liberality. Notwithstanding, the newer states after 1860 did not receive as large a proportion of their land as did Florida, Louisiana, Michigan, Wisconsin or Arkansas which had been given their swamp and overflowed tracts by the Acts of 1849 and 1850. Furthermore, Congress was placing restrictions upon the price for which the land could be sold. In the case of the Omnibus States (Montana, North and South Dakota, Washington), the minimum price was $10 an acre. Thus while giving land directly to homesteaders the Federal government was requiring the states to withhold their place grants until they could sell at the minimum it established.

Equally difficult to reconcile with free lands were the grants to railroads. The colonization railroads advertised their lands extensively in Europe and in the older parts of the United States, and brought in many thousands of settlers to buy and develop their lands. At least one railroad recovered the full original cost of its construction from its land sales and some others did nearly as well.

* * *

Meantime the business of wholesale purchasing of public lands, subdividing them, laying out towns, and retailing lots and small farm tracts became one of the biggest businesses of the country and one on which many of its fortunes were founded. As population grew in the older areas and people swarmed to the new, the demand for land sent prices upward, revealing marvelous opportunities for profit by anticipating future land needs. Land speculation had been one of the early factors behind the establishment of the Colonies. Few of the founders from John Winthrop to George Washington had failed to accumulate land as an investment and few of them thought of a possible conflict of interest between their investments and the legislation or administrative practices they favored that made them possible. As the way was opened for the granting of land for canals, roads, and railroads few people saw anything wrong in favoring legislation that would enhance the value of their lands along the routes of proposed projects. Stephen A. Douglas, John Wentworth, Daniel Webster, and Samuel C. Pomeroy were just four of the members of Congress who supported legislation that promised them high returns on investments they had previously made. Those who had less capital and less political influence could anticipate the coming of settlers to their areas by buying an extra quarter-section, or at least by trying to control it through a claims association. People from high and low ranks indulged in land speculation. Not only did western settlers try to accumulate in proper and legal ways more land than they had the capital and physical energy to develop, but they were also ready to misuse the settlement laws and take advantage of their loopholes, of the dishonesty of local officers, and the cupidity of investigating agents. In some areas they were led to this type of conduct by the fact that the quantity of land they could legally obtain from the Federal government was not a large enough economic unit; in some instances they were bogus settlers acquiring land for large cattle companies or speculators.

The second of the early objectives was never discarded. Business interests in the newly developing western states were constantly trying to draw settlers to their communities and to prevent any action that might retard immigration, settlement, and development. Before 1902 many westerners had held that all public lands should be reserved for homesteaders and that none should be sold. In 1889 they had brought about the end of unlimited sales and in 1891 they secured legislation to halt cash sales, though commutation and desert land sales were still bringing in funds to the Treasury. Now they proposed to divert practically all income from these sales into a revolving fund for the construction of dams and reservoirs to provide water for the irrigation of arid lands. Reclamation soon grew into a mighty giant bringing to the semi-arid states both a farm population and the possibility of industrial development and urban growth.

Retrospectively, critics may see that many blunders were made in legislating for the administration and disposal of the public lands. * * * The inflexible government price of $1.25, maintained until 1854, caused buyers to seek out only the best land. Combined with the rapid opening of new areas to purchase and settlement, the inflexible price served to scatter settlement widely, delay the coming of social institutions, and push the frontier of settlement far into the Indian country with friction and wars resulting.

Classification and appraisal of the public lands was out of the question before 1870 but thereafter some progress might have been made with more constructive leadership. Homesteading might better have been confined to areas with sufficient rainfall, but banned in the semi-arid lands west of the 102d meridian and heavily forested regions of the Upper Lakes States, the Rocky Mountains and the Pacific Coast. Settlement laws, including the Homestead, Timber Culture, and Desert Land Acts and other measures ostensibly adopted for settlers, such as the Timber and Stone Act and the Forest Lieu Act should, after an initial but short period of trial, have been amended or repealed, as all succeeding Commissioners recommended. The preemption and the Timber Culture Acts were repealed in 1891 but Congress permitted the Timber and Stone Act to remain in operation, to the great and constant annoyance of the Commissioners. Registers, receivers, and surveyors general were responsible to the local and national political leadership which gave them their appointments, and too often if the local leaders were in the lumber business or in the livestock industry the conflicts of interest were commonly resolved in favor of the interests rather than the government. Establishment of great ownerships—partly corporate and partly individual—of timberlands, rangelands, and even farmlands were enabled, and at times there was cause for concern because the proportion of farms occupied by tenants was increasing rapidly.

Yet with all the poorly drafted legislation, the mediocre and sometimes corrupt land officials, the constant effort of settlers, monied speculators and great land companies to engross land for the unearned increment they might extract from it, the Federal land system seems to have worked surprisingly well, if we may judge by the results. Outside the cotton-growing South where the plantation system prevailed before 1860 and tenancy and sharecropping subsequently, suitable public land was being acquired by small owner operators and tenancy was less common. Disregarding the southern states, a total of 1,738,176 farms had been created in the public land states by 1880 and only in four states—California, Oregon, Colorado, and Nevada—did the farms average over 160 acres. Of these farms 1,381,406, 80 percent of the total, were owner operated. This is good evidence that the railroad grants, the land given to endow the states, and even the speculative purchases were being divided into single family farms. Except in Illinois and Iowa, tenancy seems to have been largely the result of ownership passing from one generation to another. By 1900 the public land states, still excluding the cotton South, boasted 2,404,968 farms, 70 percent of which were owner operated. It was still possible to say, as had been even more true in 1880, that the public domain had been so disposed of as to increase the class of small landowners, as Jefferson had desired.

Before the close of the 19th century many thoughtful people became aware of the value and future significance of the natural resources still held by the Federal government and of the need for giving more attention to the methods of managing and disposing of them. This was reflected in the greater care given to the framing of new land legislation. * * *

Another result of the greater appreciation of the value, uniqueness and diminishing amount of the public domain with its forests, wildlife, whitewater streams and scenic spots, was that some people began to question whether private ownership was superior to public ownership. The rapid depletion of the standing forests in the Lake States gave rise to the fear that in a generation or less, at the then rate of cutting, supplies would become so depleted as to compel reliance on other countries. Scientific forest management as practiced abroad attracted attention. Conservation was advocated both by preservationists who wanted to lock up certain resources such as Yosemite and Yellowstone so as to prevent any exploitation of their timber, minerals, or water power and to retain these great works of nature in public ownership for future generations, and by advocates of scientific management and use of the forests, minerals, and water power. The concept of permanent reservations was difficult for many to accept. Had not America's greatness rested upon the license to exploit without government interference? Yet a number of national parks were set aside and the Act of 1891, authorizing the President to establish forest reserves on the public domain, made possible considerable progress in developing a conservation program before the end of the century.

Theodore Roosevelt brought to the conservation movement strong national leadership, a dramatic ability to interest the public, and an understanding of Presidential powers and how to use them to advance the ends he favored. Most of the western forests of today were set aside in his administration. It was Gifford Pinchot who constantly needled the President to withdraw lands for national forests, to protect the government's rights to rich coal deposits, and retain water power sites in public ownership. Roosevelt and Pinchot made a team unmatched in American history for what they preserved for future generations. Conservation became the fifth, and to many the overwhelming, objective of American land policy.

A sixth objective has become in the 20th century quite basic in determining land policy. Instead of considering the economic value of land in terms of its best use either as rangeland or for forests, for watershed protection, recreation, preservation of wildlife, mining, industry or urban proliferation, the modern multiple-purpose objective takes all these factors into consideration and upon that broad base the future use of any particular tract may be determined.

Conservation had its advocates in all parts of the country but its support in the states in which there remained large amounts of public land was distinctly more tepid than elsewhere. Why, said West Coast lumbermen, were the public forests to be withheld from purchase and cutting when no such withholding had existed elsewhere? Why should the grazing lands be retained in Federal ownership and be managed by an agency quartered in Washington? Why should 86 percent of the entire acreage of Nevada, 66 percent of Utah, 64 percent of Idaho be retained in Federal ownership, kept off the local tax lists, the timber withheld from cutting, the rangelands denied to sheepmen or cattlemen who had no local property base, the power sites developed by public agencies and not subjected to local taxes? In the past the states had mismanaged and wastefully disposed of the Federal land which had been granted them but in recent decades it can be argued that most of them were managing their landed property as well as the Federal government was. These western states came to think of the extensive Federal lands within their borders, reserved or withdrawn from entry, as retarding their development, slowing down their progress, and keeping them in thralldom to a remote government not capable of understanding their needs. Too often, they forgot that substantial portions of the returns from minerals, lumbering, grazing, and water power development on the public lands were either flowing into reclamation development or the building of access roads and other improvements in their section.

Finally, in appraising the American land system the question that should be asked is not whether East and West have received their proportionate share of the public domain, or the income from it, or whether the western states have been treated in an unequal and niggardly fashion in not being granted all the land within their boundaries. The questions are: (1) whether land-hungry settlers have been able to establish themselves permanently on suitable land with secure titles to farms of efficient size; (2) whether the minerals, forests, and grazing resources have been efficiently used without undue waste; and (3) whether the long-run interests of a growing Nation have been foreseen and provided for.

The public lands have come to have different levels of interest for society as it has become more mature. At one time the government was concerned only with revenue and the public mainly with surface rights to good land for farms. Later it became important first to develop, then to conserve the natural resources of the land in timber, minerals, oil, and water. Nowadays the land as living space and play space has taken on new values. Our more mobile population, in which those who are East today are West tomorrow, tends to erase sectional attitudes once important.

———

For a discussion of some of the early land policies and practices in the United States and their effect on the social and economic development of the new nation, see Wright, The Relation of Law in America to Socio–Economic Change, 28 Ark.L.Rev. 440 (1975), and for an overview of early land settlement practices, see Clawson, The Land System of the United States (1968).

———

While legislation regulating land and other resources is not new, there is the constantly recurring and ever-increasing problem of how best to deal with these problems. Further, the enormity and complexity of the situation is compounded by modern environmental and ecological concerns. There is no longer a situation in which problems are sufficiently isolated to permit solution through the passage of legislation directed toward one well-defined issue.

As the student proceeds through this book, then, he should concern himself with such questions as what tools are available to him with respect to land use controls, the extent to which such tools are adequate and whether and how they should be expanded or could be improved, what new concepts and principles are evolving, what new methodology might be developed to cope more effectively with these problems, the interrelationship of land use controls and related environmental concerns, the effect of land use and environmental controls upon economic conditions and the relative scale of values which should be applied, the effects of zoning, including its exclusionary nature, the total scope of the problem and the extent to which other than local governmental units are or should be involved, the relative and appropriate position in the total scheme of things of legislative bodies, administrative agencies and courts, and finally changing concepts relative to land ownership and permissible limitations and regulations.

In the material which immediately follows, we will examine some common law and equitable devices which provide means of control on the use or abuse of land. Aside from understanding their general use and the rules which govern their application, the student should consider their effectiveness, their utilization in modern situations, and whether they might be expanded or applied to new problems or conditions.

Chapter II

JUDICIAL CONTROL OF LAND USE: NUISANCE, WASTE AND RELATED DOCTRINES

If the first chapter disengaged the reader of the assumption that legislative controls over the use of land were wholly a twentieth century phenomenon or that these somehow emerged in full bloom from the era of the Franklin Roosevelt administration and the recesses of the great depression, this chapter is intended to focus attention on yet another consideration which is essential to an understanding of the present-day situation. Today, we deal quite heavily with land use problems through means of statutes and ordinances and through regulations developed by governmental bodies to whom such authority has been entrusted. But this modern methodology should not obscure the fact that there are a number of historic, common law or equitable devices employed not by legislative or regulatory bodies but by courts as a means of controlling the activities of individuals with respect to the use of land. These arose in response to a different situation than that which most commonly troubles us today. These judge-made concepts were developed to govern situations in which the private rights of one individual impinged upon the rights of others. These were "after the fact" adjudications, for the most part, which determined in a limited context a dispute between individuals who possessed or asserted conflicting rights or in some instances between a single individual and either a large segment of individuals or the public in general. The aims and purposes involved were different from those which surround land use planning today. The ordered development of a geographical area and the various attributes of social engineering were not present. As in all lawsuits, there were sharply focused issues, and the object was to determine certain facts, apply the law and thereby settle the dispute in question. Nonetheless, the result was to control in a negative way the use of land by an individual or individuals. X could not do something on or with a piece of land because it would interfere with the rights of Y in one way or another in a situation in which law or equity accorded paramount importance to the rights of Y. Thus, in Hohfeldian terms, X had a duty not to interfere with the rights of Y.

Certainly reliance upon judicial interference is not an effective way to promote the rational development of a given geographical area. Yet this form of regulation and of limitation upon the uses to which a particular piece of land might be put is important to use not only as an historic method of control but also because these devices remain available today, although ordinances, statutes or regulations may render such actions unnecessary where a public nuisance results or where the activity in question amounts to a violation of the public interest as expressed in one of the ways mentioned. In many situations, however, the public interest is not at stake, and it is purely a matter of individual versus individual.

In this latter context, there is a common thread which joins together the material contained in this chapter—the conflicting rights of owners of interests in land with respect to one or more pieces of real estate. This problem will manifest itself in somewhat different ways. In one type of situation we are involved with two or more persons who possess an interest of one type or another in the *same* parcel of land. Usually one of them occupies and possesses the premises while the other or others do not. This situation presents a relational conflict in which controls are imposed upon the possessor for the benefit of a person or persons not in possession. Such problems involve landlords and tenants, life tenants and remaindermen, secured creditors and debtors (including mortgagors and lienors), possessors of the land holding legal title and purchasers holding equitable title under real estate sales contracts, conflicts between two or more tenants in common or between joint tenants, and conflicts between beneficiaries and trustees, covenantors and covenantees, and grantors and grantees. All of these are relational situations which provide the seeds for conflict over the use, abuse or misuse of the same piece of land. The doctrine which generally comes into play in this situation is that pertaining to the law of waste. Broadly speaking, it has been said:

> The proper test is whether or not the acts alleged to be waste have departed from the standard of conduct imposed upon the tenant by the terms of the instrument creating his estate, the custom of the community, the requirements of policy, and the standard of reasonableness.[1]

It is obvious that "the proper test" possesses an inherent flexibility which would seem to permit courts to weigh community considerations in determining the outcome of otherwise private litigation in which waste is asserted. This is implicit in taking into account community custom and policy requirements. It may be concluded that even in purely

---

1. 5 American Law of Property § 20.11 (Casner ed. 1952). The doctrines of the law of waste which are involved in most of these relational situations are reviewed by John H. Merryman at §§ 20.1–.14.

private lawsuits, there are broader considerations and perhaps wider ranging ramifications to be examined.

While the law of waste involves conflicts between parties holding interests in the same parcel or parcels, the law of nuisance involves conflicts between neighboring property owners. Nuisance litigation rests generally upon the ancient maxim to the effect that one property owner has a duty not to interfere with the use of the land of an adjoining or nearby owner—*sic utere tuo ut alienum non laedas.* Interference with the use of adjoining land could come in a variety of ways. A continuing trespass, for example, would be an interference which would be subject to relief both at law and in equity. But in the case of nuisance, the question of trespass does not arise, even though it may be argued that the invasion of sound waves, odors, smoke or gases amounts to a technical trespass. Generally speaking, if an activity or use of property is such as to unduly interfere with or prove substantially harmful to the use of nearby land or if it adversely and materially affects the health, morals, welfare or safety of the community or the health or safety of private persons, then such use or activity may be enjoined as constituting a nuisance. The limitation placed upon the landowner harboring or creating the nuisance may vary from a judicial declaration to cease such activity completely, to some modification which establishes legitimate parameters within which the use may continue on a limited basis not deemed to constitute excessive interference. In this latter situation courts usually justify these partial measures on the basis that they are sufficient to alleviate the evil complained of or that they are all that is reasonably required. This is referred to as "balancing the equities" or "balancing the hardships" and represents a judicial approximation of what is fair in adjusting the right of one landowner to make use of his land and the right of another landowner or the public generally to be free from harm emanating from such use.

Unlike waste, the law of nuisance (particularly in the case of a public nuisance or perhaps a nuisance *per se,* which are discussed later in this chapter), bears a certain kinship to the same power which forms the basis for the law of zoning—the power to regulate for the health, morals, safety and welfare of the community, which is usually simply referred to as the police power. In zoning, the interest in the protection of the community is manifested through legislative and administrative actions which at times result in judicial review. In nuisance cases in which a community interest is being protected or advanced, the action takes place in court and is generally based upon judge-made doctrines or occasionally upon legislative declarations that a certain activity is forbidden or constitutes a nuisance. A further parallel in nuisance cases (particularly private nuisances) can be drawn with regard to restrictive covenants. In the case of a nuisance, by operation of law, a burden is in effect imposed upon the use of a parcel of land. It is a negative right which is inherent in nearby property owners or in the public generally and which is somewhat parallel to the concept of an equitable servitude or reciprocal negative easement. These parallels or comparisons might be kept in mind as we move from judicial constraints to private land use controls through restrictive covenants and into consideration of the law of planning and zoning.

These judge-made controls which govern land disputes involving neighbors effectuate or enforce a form of private planning in the sense that a person cannot use his property without considering the effect upon nearby landowners or the public. There are other situations which also illustrate the impact of judge-made law. Court decisions pertaining to lateral support, adverse possession, redemption and possession by land purchasers and mortgagors in default, trade and agricultural fixtures, implied easements, tenant improvements, duties to repair, drainage of surface water, duties to fence, materialmen's liens, and equitable conversion, for example, also affect the way in which land is used. Some judicial decisions enlarge upon or interpret the common law of the past while some lend new dimensions to legislative enactments. The impact of courts is manifested in both instances.

From all of this it may be concluded that controls on the use of land are not merely the product of legislative enactments and that the impact of the judicial branch is of long standing and continuing importance. Nonetheless, the principal concern in courses on land use is with legal tools which can be employed over a substantial geographical area in an affirmative manner to accomplish public or private land planning goals. Judicial decisions are essentially negative in nature, and except for the law pertaining to equitable restrictions and, to a lesser degree, to nuisance problems, judge-made law is not crucial except to the extent that it interprets or develops land use regulatory devices and legislative enactments. As is apparent and has been alluded to earlier, judges do not initiate lawsuits and they consider only such issues as are raised in limited situations presented to them. Case law is normally a narrowly focused process which is both haphazard and hit or miss in dealing with this subject matter. Even in the cases which come before them, courts are often working with rules which are in actuality only broadly and sometimes vaguely stated standards of conduct which may lead to a different result in circumstances which differ only slightly, if at all, in the facts. Occasionally it may be desirable to have such suits brought in order to prevent waste, enjoin a nuisance or enforce a restrictive covenant. But even in such circumstances, lawyers and clients must face the possibility that the judge may be either unwilling or unequipped to understand the problems of community growth and patterns of living in the latter quarter of the twentieth century or may be overly steeped in the traditions of the nineteenth century, when natural resources were more readily available and seemed inexhaustible and when the laissez faire concept permeated the attitudes of the courts in dealing with all forms of economic wealth. A judge may not see the full panorama or explicitly recognize all that is at stake. He may view himself, in the traditional way, as the arbiter of a limited issue or set of issues affecting only the narrowly defined rights of the litigants. In such a situation he may overlook ramifications which can extend beyond the channelized issues before him.

In this chapter only brief note is taken of some of the obvious and rather direct judicial excursions into the land use field. Actually, much of the general law of property as it relates to the creation and transfer of interests, including the power of "dead hand" control over land, the protection of possession and other rights and interests against claims of third parties, and the termination of interests, importantly affects the use that can be made of land.[2] In this connection, in a landmark law review article in the Pennsylvania Law Review, one author observed that law "by the steady restraints of its abiding forms" molds society while at the same time it "fixes and preserves" it.[3] He concluded that it was an understatement to say that social life creates property law, but instead "an intimacy exists between them" in which each "gives form and life to the other."[4]

With these preliminary considerations in mind, some examination may be made of the regulatory effects of judge-made law on land ownership and use.

SECTION 1.   THE LAW OF WASTE

REPORT OF THE NEW YORK LAW REVISION
COMMISSION 389 et seq.

(1935).

When the ownership of land is divided between an owner of the possessory estate and an owner of future interest, a problem often arises

2. For a stimulating analysis along these lines, see Hunt, Federal and State Control of Land: A Synopsis, in McDougal and Haber, Property, Wealth, Land 70 (1948).

3. Philbrick, Changing Conceptions of Property in Law, 86 U.Pa.L.Rev. 691, 695 (1939). See also an interesting, more recent examination: Large, This Land is Whose Land? Changing Concepts of Land as Property, 1973 Wis.L.Rev. 1039. Professor Large provides a thought-provoking discussion of land ownership and limitations upon land use in the light of modern environmental concerns, state and federal legislation and other factors.

4. Id. In fact, law both reacts and interacts. "It has been both an agent of incipient social and economic change, and an agency to recognize the *fait accompli*." Thus: "Law's conservatism, in the real and best sense of the word, has been manifested in its ability to accomplish the purpose of assimilating change into the broader fabric of our life and institutions without disturbing

the basic framework or upsetting the momentum." Wright, The Law of Airspace 277, 278 (1968). (Reprinted from The Law of Airspace, by Robert R. Wright, copyright 1968 by The Bobbs–Merrill Company, Inc. Reprinted by permission. All rights reserved.) However, the problem in property law is often the difficulty of accomplishing reasoned, overdue change. As Holmes said, [property law] "is a matter of history that has not forgotten Lord Coke." Gardiner v. William S. Butler & Co., 245 U.S. 603, 605, 38 S.Ct. 214, 214, 62 L.Ed. 505 (1918). On the struggles of one jurisdiction in the field of property, see Fetters, The Entailed Estate: Ferment for Reform in Arkansas, 19 Ark.L.Rev. 275 (1966); Fetters, Destructibility of Contingent Remainders, 21 Ark. L.Rev. 145 (1967); Mochary, Reflections of An Arkansas Property Teacher Upon Reading Professor Leach's Property Law Indicted, 21 Ark.L.Rev. 567 (1968); Wright, Medieval Law in the Age of Space: Some "Rules of Property" in Arkansas, 22 Ark.L.Rev. 248 (1968); Comment, The Doctrine of Worthier Title, 21 Ark.L.Rev. 394 (1967).

as to the extent of the privilege of the owner of the possessory estate to "change" the premises over objection by the owner of the future interest. Similar problems can—and sometimes do—arise between co-tenants or mortgagor and mortgagee or vendor and vendee.

The law of waste is a part of the regulation of the relations between persons who simultaneously have interests in the same thing. Normally one of these persons has possession and the others are out of possession. Such a circumstance requires that the one in possession be forbidden such action as will diminish the market value of the other interests; and that he be required to act fairly in the maintenance of the property by the payment of current charges and the prevention of its deterioration. The regulation goes further and restricts, to some extent, the power of the person in possession to make "changes" in the premises. All of these detailed rules have a single underlying justification or objective which is to assure to each person, in such a split ownership, the accomplishment of his reasonable desires to the largest extent that is consistent with the reasonable protection of the other interests. This is the criterion by which any detail of the existing law of waste should be tested. The owner of the possessory interest is to be curtailed in his behavior only to the extent necessary for the reasonable protection of the other interests in the same thing. When a rule of law goes beyond this it has departed from the social justification for this part of our law.

The law of waste assumed large importance with the Statute of Marlborough in 1267 and this importance was increased by the Statute of Gloucester enacted eleven years later. The specific rules in this branch of the law were evolved under the conditions existing in England in the six centuries following 1250. Two aspects of these conditions require particular consideration. In the first place England, for this entire period of time, was predominantly an agricultural country. The vast majority of the ownerships split between two or more persons consisted of lands devoted to farm purposes. Hence the English law of waste consists largely of the rules applicable as between present and future owners of farm lands of the type found in England. In the second place, the English judicial interpretation of what constitutes "reasonable protection of the other interests" is bound to be an expression of the then existing social attitudes of that country. English society during those six centuries was relatively static. Particularly in its countryside, people expected and desired things to remain as they had been. Innovation or change was frowned upon.

The English law of waste which evolved under these conditions was highly regulatory of the conduct of the possessory owner. A tenant for years or for life was prohibited from changing arable land into woodland, or from converting meadow into arable land or from altering meadow into orchard. A cutting of wood, except within the narrow limits allowed for firewood or repairs, was waste, and if a house fell down and such a tenant rebuilt it larger than it was before, it was waste, because the lessor, when he regained the property, would have a bigger structure to keep in repair. The removal of a door or a window or a partition was forbidden. The genius of these rules was the assumed social desirability of things remaining as they had been.

About one hundred years ago, English cases began to show a reaction against these rigid rules. It was recognized that pulling down a barn which was no longer useful could not be injurious to the inheritance and hence was not waste. The erection of a new barn on a different and more convenient site was held to be a permissible change. Lands used for the growing of timber for sale were allowed to be used in the same manner by the life tenant. A tenant having a lease for nine hundred ninety-nine years was permitted to change store buildings into houses over the objection of his lessor. A tenant having a term of twenty-one years was permitted to erect the glass houses requisite for the transformation of a suburban farm into a market garden.

Thus the English courts, in the first five centuries of the evolution of the law of waste, evolved rigorous restriction of the partial owner in possession but, during the past century lessened these restrictions by a partial return to rules more conformable to the underlying social justification of this branch of the law.

Outside the State of New York, American decisions manifest two divergent trends which are clearly observable.

The first of these trends is not unique in this branch of law. Some judges and some states accept the detailed rules of the early English law without examination into the continued utilization of these rules in the country of their origin, without consideration of the utility of these rules under the conditions existent at the time of decision, and with no interest in the underlying social objective of the law of waste. Clark v. Holden, 73 Mass. (7 Gray) 8 (1856), decided in Massachusetts in 1856, concerned a life tenant who had permitted an original pasture to grow into a woodland and then later had cut the trees on it. The court held that the cutting of these trees could not be justified by showing it would have been good husbandry for an owner in fee simple to cut this timber and to clear the land for cultivation. Robertson v. Meadors, 73 Ind. 43 (1880), decided in Indiana in 1880, dealt with the behavior of a life tenant in thirty-one acres. The defendant sought to justify his timber cutting by showing that only six acres of the plot were sufficiently cleared to permit cultivation and that the cutting of further timber was necessary to make the plot reasonably productive. A demurrer to the answer was sustained. In Davenport v. Magoon, 13 Or. 3, 4 P. 299 (1884) a lessee was given express power "to alter" the premises to adapt them to business purposes other than those of a livery stable. The existing structure consisted of a one and one-half story building used for a livery stable. This building was 100 feet by 80 feet in size. The tenant proposed to tear down this building and to erect a two-story building to be used by Chinese. The proposed building was to be 100 feet by 95 feet in size. Under the lease the lessor had a duty to repair the structures on the property in case of fire. The court sustained the complaint of the lessor in an action seeking to enjoin the proposed conduct of the tenant stating that the lessor's burden under his covenant to repair would be heavier with the new building than with the old building. The unpopularity of the Chinese in that community is not mentioned by the court as a reason for its decision. Dooley v. Stringham, 4 Utah 107, 7 P. 405 (1885) enjoined a life tenant from tearing down an adobe dwelling house with the professed object of replacing this with a better building. The court's reasoning was that the adobe building had substantial value; therefore its removal was waste. "Whether appellant would ever replace it with a better, or as good a building, or any building, is beyond our province to inquire." Perhaps one of the best illustrations of the persistence of the early English rules is found in Klie v. Von Broock, 56 N.J.Eq. 18, 37 A. 469 (1897), decided in New Jersey in 1897. A tenant had acquired adjoining property and had opened a doorway some five by eight feet in size through the party wall separating the two structures. At the suit of his lessor he was compelled to wall up this opening and his offer to give security for the restoration of the wall at the end of the term was refused.

The second of these trends manifests a more penetrating understanding of the role of law in society. It shows a recognition of the power of changed conditions to alter the concept of waste. The underlying objective of the law of waste remains unchanged but the specific rules by which that objective is sought to be attained are greatly changed.

As might have been expected, this second trend found both its earliest and its most complete expression in timber cases. English farm lands possessed scant timber supplies. On a continent of virgin forests, timber often seemed more a public enemy than an asset to be rigorously conserved. This difference in conditions led to a complete difference of rule. In a note published in 1912 in the Lawyers Reports Annotated the prevailing American rule is well stated in the following language, 37 LRA (N.S.) 763 (1912):

> The rule established by the weight of authority in this country permits the tenant for life to cut timber for the purpose of clearing the land, provided the part cleared, with that already prepared for cultivation, as compared to the remainder of the tract, does not exceed the proportion of cleared to wooded land, usually maintained in good husbandry; and provided, further, that he does not materially lessen the value of the inheritance.

This twofold requirement of, first, no material decrease in the value of the inheritance, and second, the behavior characteristic of good husbandry, makes a regulation far more in conformity with the underlying objective of the law of waste than the specific restrictions evolved by the English courts in the middle ages. The decisions are also of more general significance since they embody a recognition of the power of changed conditions to alter the content of the concept of waste.

An early Massachusetts case manifests this same second trend on quite different facts. The owner of an estate for life took down some fences, laid out and filled in a new street across the land, dug cellars, erected wooden houses and regraded the parts near these houses with the dirt removed from the cellars. The defendant urged that none of these acts constituted waste and his contention was upheld. Here the land was in the stage of transition from farm land to suburban land. The change in conditions was a factor necessarily considered in determining whether change in use should be regarded as waste.

The abolition of slavery and the resultant change in the mode of operating southern plantations afforded another opportunity for the outcropping of this second trend. The needed reorganization of the plantation required the removal of some cabins and the cutting of considerable timber. Since all of these acts were in accord with "good husbandry" under the changed conditions of economic life, they were not waste when done by the owner of an estate for life. Similarly allowing a huge building to fall into decay was held not to be waste when the change in the mode of cultivation due to the abolition of slavery made the disappearance of the building no injury to the inheritance. In this last case the court gave clear expression to its attitude, Sherrill v. Connor, 107 N.C. 630, 12 S.E. 588 (1890):

> This Court can take notice of the fact that the barns formerly used at such establishments have often, if not generally, proven too large to be kept up by an owner who survived the war long enough to accommodate himself to, and arrange his business in relation to the changed condition as to labor and alterations in methods consequent upon emancipation. When it became necessary to build tenement-houses at suitable points for the accommodation of lessees of different sections of the estate, the negro cabin, the large smokehouse for the storage of bacon, and the large barn for the protection of all the stock needed, possibly to operate the entire farm, were no longer useful, and were often torn down, or suffered to fall into decay, and were replaced by others of a size suited to the new state of affairs. If it was proper when our ancestors were transplanted in America to look to the reason of the common law, and hold that under different conditions, in an undeveloped country, the clearing of land by a life-tenant should no longer be held per se to amount to waste, without regard to its effect upon the interest of an reversioner, there are reasons equally as potent for leaving a jury with explicit instructions to determine whether a prudent owner of the fee, if in possession in lieu of the life tenant, would have suffered the barn, or other building, unsuitable because of its great proportions, to his wants in the new state of society, to have fallen into decay rather than incur the cost of repair.

More recently the problem has arisen in a new form. The development of cities causes neighborhoods to change from a use predominantly residential to uses predominantly business or causes the obsolescence of a building at a much sooner date than could reasonably have been anticipated. When ownership of land thus affected is split into present and future interests, the owner of the possessory interest desires to change the premises to adapt them to new uses while the owner of the non-possessory interests often opposes such change. Such opposition can be motivated either by a sincere desire to receive the property in its original condition or by the questionable desire to establish a veto power which can be released for a consideration. Two cases illustrate this aspect of the second trend. The more important of these cases is Melms v. Pabst Brewing Co., 104 Wis. 7, 79 N.W. 738 (1899), decided in Wisconsin in 1899. An action for waste was brought by the owner of the reversion against the owner of the estate for life. The owner of the estate for life had destroyed a dwelling house and graded down the lot some twenty or thirty feet so as to make it available for business use. As a result of the growth of the city, this lot had been enveloped by factories on the lower level. The house was undesirable as a residence and business use of the elevated lot was impractical. The value of the plot was substantially enhanced. The complaint of the reversioner was dismissed, the court saying:

> In the absence of any contract * * * to use the property for a specified purpose, or to return it in the same condition in which it was received, a radical and permanent change of surrounding conditions, such as is presented in the case before us, must always be an important, and sometimes a controlling consideration upon the question whether a physical change in the use of the buildings constitutes waste.

The second of these two cases, Willing v. Chicago Auditorium, 277 U.S. 274, 48 S.Ct. 507, 72 L.Ed. 880 (1927), was decided upon a purely procedural point in 1927. This case merely decided that no declaratory judgment could be granted by Federal courts allowing a ninety-nine year lessee to replace an obsolescent building which cost originally some $2,000,000 by a modern building costing approximately $15,000,000. The case is important in that it shows a form in which the strength of this second trend is likely to be tested in the future.

Summarizing this second trend, we find a quite widespread recognition of the responsiveness of the content of the concept of waste to changes in conditions. This has resulted in the "good husbandry" relaxation as to timber cutting, the allowance of new construction when farm land becomes suited for the uses of city lots, the permitting of changes in structures to meet the needs created by the abolition of slavery and the refusal of judicial assistance as against physical changes in structures made desirable by a changed character of the neighborhood. The conflict between this second trend and the first trend described herein is obvious.

BISHOP OF WINCHESTER'S CASE

Court of Chancery, ante 1638.
1 Rolle, Abridgment, 380 (T, 3).

If a lessee for years, without impeachment of waste, about the end of his term, intends to cut down all the timber trees, an injunction lies out of a court of equity upon this matter, to stop the cutting down of the trees notwithstanding the agreement of the parties, because it is against the public good to destroy the trees, and the suit is to hinder and prevent it, and not to have damages after it is done.

VANE v. LORD BARNARD

Court of Chancery, 1716.
2 Vernon 738.

The defendant, on the marriage of the plaintiff his eldest son with the daughter of Morgan Randyll, and 10,000£ portion, settled (*inter alia*) Raby Castle on himself for life, without impeachment of waste, remainder to his son for life, and to his first and other sons in tail male.

The defendant, the Lord Barnard, having taken some displeasure against his son, got two hundred workmen together, and of a sudden, in a few days, stript the castle of the lead, iron, glass-doors, and boards, & c. to the value of 3000£.

The Court, upon filing the bill, granted an injunction to stay committing of waste, in pulling down the castle; and now, upon the hearing of the cause, decreed, not only the injunction to continue, but that the castle should be repaired, and put into the same condition it was in, in August, 1714; and for that purpose a commission was to issue to ascertain what ought to be repaired, and a master to see it done at the expense and charge of the defendant, the Lord Barnard; and decreed the plaintiff his costs.

Note

In the Bishop of Winchester's Case, the term, "without impeachment of waste," is employed. It has been noted that this phrase has seldom been used in the United States. Chafee and Re, Cases and Materials on Equity 702 n. 21 (5th ed. 1967), cites Clement v. Wheeler, 25 N.H. 361 (1852) as furnishing a lone example, although other cases have recognized the English doctrine. See also, Stevens v. Rose, 69 Mich. 259, 37 N.W. 205 (1888). The provision, if expressed in an instrument creating a life estate or an estate for years, shielded the tenant from legal liability for acts of waste, and apparently the provision was frequently employed in England around the time of the Bishop of Winchester's Case. But equity restrained tenants from such unconscionable acts as cutting "all the timber trees," as the Bishop's Case states, and from other wanton acts of destruction, as in Vane v. Lord Barnard. There was a tendency toward intervention by equity based on the absence of an adequate legal remedy and the necessity to protect the reversioner or remainderman. For a more detailed discussion on equitable waste, see Walsh, A Treatise on Equity 142–46 (1930). In commenting on the ambivalent position whereby the law denied a remedy and equity provided relief, Langdell argued that in such a situation either law or equity "*may* be wrong, and one of them *must* be; for the question depends entirely upon the legal effect to be given the words 'without impeachment of waste,' and that cannot depend upon the kind of court in which the question happens to arise." Langdell, Brief Survey of Equity Jurisdiction 4 (2d ed. 1908). He also observed that the practical effect was that there was an equitable remedy, even though none existed at law, and the result therefore was that the tenant had committed an act which in equity was a tort and at law was not. It would appear to be sounder to ignore the seeming contradiction and to conclude that in the value judgment of the time, as manifested with greater flexibility in the court of chancery, there was a point beyond which a tenant would not be permitted to go in perpetrating waste no matter what phraseology was employed, the reason being that the public interest entered into equity's consideration, while at law it did not. Moreover, the *basis* for equitable relief is different; it affords a remedy many times when none exists at law, and indeed this is why it originated. In 1 Ames, Cases in Equity Jurisdiction at 469 n. 2 (1904), a number of English cases are listed in which injunctions to restrain the commission of equitable waste were granted against a tenant not impeachable for waste.

CITY OF WHITE PLAINS v. GRIFFEN

Supreme Court, Westchester County, New York, 1938.
169 Misc. 706, 8 N.Y.S.2d 32, affirmed 255 App.Div. 1003, 8 N.Y.S.2d 462 (1938).

ALDRICH, JUSTICE. In this action brought by the City of White Plains as plaintiff for the foreclosure of various tax liens, the plaintiff seeks a temporary injunction restraining the defendant owners of the fee from removing or in any manner disturbing the top soil upon the premises affected by the action. The tax liens held by the plaintiff, the foreclosure of which is involved in the action, directly involve some $28,000, but it is conceded that the total unpaid tax liens upon the premises, all of which are held by the plaintiff, aggregate from $125,000 to $200,000, the defendants indicating the lower figure and the plaintiff the higher. The defendant owners are in default in the action and concededly have no defense. It appears that they have entered into an agreement with a contractor for the sale of certain top soil from the premises for the sum of 25¢ per cubic yard. Upon the argument counsel indicated that the expected revenue from the sale of the top soil would be some $15,000, or possibly running as high as $25,000. The contemplated removal, therefore, is of from 60,000 to 100,000 cubic yards of top soil. The Court is satisfied from the papers submitted that the property will be substantially damaged by the removal of this soil and to the extent of the damage the security of the plaintiff will be thereby impaired. The papers justify the conclusion that the cost of replacement of such soil would be many times the amount to be received by the owners. The claim of the opposing defendants that the property, after the removal, will be just as good as it is now, is not persuasive. That there will be substantial damage as the result of such removal is quite apparent. The plaintiff is entitled to the benefit of all its present security for the payment of the unpaid taxes, penalties, etc. It is a reasonable inference that with the premises substantially denuded of top soil the amount which the property may be reasonably expected to bring upon a sale will be materially reduced. The removal of top soil constitutes waste. Cosgriff v. Dewey, 164 N.Y. 1, at page 3, 58 N.E. 1, 79 Am.St.Rep. 620. § 981 of the Civil Practice Act, applicable to actions of this description, expressly authorizes a restraining order if the defendant commits waste upon "or does any other damage to" the property in question. Under that section the right to an injunction is not limited to what would be waste under other circumstances but covers "any other damage to the property." Thompson v. Manhattan Ry. Co., 130 N.Y. 360, at page 365, 29 N.E. 264, at page 265. That the contemplated removal of this top soil will constitute a damage to the property is clearly apparent. The plaintiff comes squarely within the provisions of the statute and is entitled to a temporary injunction accordingly.

The motion by the plaintiff for a temporary injunction restraining the defendants from the removal of or in any way interfering with the top soil upon the premises involved in the action is granted. The liability of the plaintiff for damages under § 820 of the Civil Practice Act to be limited to $15,000. Settle order on two hours' notice at chambers, White Plains.

Note

City of White Plains v. Griffen presents a situation in which the plaintiff was in effect acting on behalf of the people generally in seeking to prevent the lessening in value of the land involved. The City action avoided the diminution of the security for the tax indebtedness owing it. Courts generally have not hesitated to grant relief to persons not in possession who hold various kinds of security interests in the premises. The more common situation would involve a mortgagee whose security might be impaired, but as the above case indicates, others holding similar or related interests may seek and receive the aid in equity. Should equity intervene to protect such interests if the waste committed will not reduce the value of the land below the amount of the indebtedness? See, generally, 5 Powell, Real Property ¶ 644(2) at 56–44, 56–45 (1989).

HAUSMANN v. HAUSMANN

Appellate Court of Illinois, Fifth District, 1992.
231 Ill.App.3d 361, 172 Ill.Dec. 937, 596 N.E.2d 216.

JUSTICE CHAPMAN delivered the opinion of the court:

Charles Hausmann, the plaintiff, filed suit against his uncle, George Hausmann, the defendant, concerning real estate in which Charles held a remainder interest following George's life estate. In the first of two counts, Charles alleged that George had committed waste by failing to pay the 1986 real estate taxes due on the land and asked for a declaration of the parties' rights, an order directing future payment of taxes, and a reimbursement to Charles for the amount he had paid to redeem the property from sale for delinquent taxes. In Count II, Charles alleged that his uncle's failure to pay the taxes was intentional and was done in order to deprive Charles of his interest by having George's stepson purchase the land at the tax sale. Charles prayed for compensatory and punitive damages.

George Hausmann filed a counterclaim alleging that Charles had not repaid a loan of $5,000 on an unwritten agreement. George also claimed that Charles owed him an amount for rental and storage of personal property on the land in issue.

After a bench trial the court entered judgment for Charles on Count I of his complaint and awarded him $1,671.20 plus interest of $194.33. On Count II the court awarded Charles $7,500 in punitive damages.

On the counterclaim the court found for George and against Charles for the $5,000 claimed but found for Charles on the amount allegedly due for rental and storage.

On appeal Charles Hausmann contends that the trial court's award of the $5,000 was contrary to the manifest weight of the evidence and that the trial court erred in not entering an injunction against the defendant requiring him to pay real estate taxes on the land in the future. The defendant cross-appeals alleging the trial court erred in reconstituting the plaintiff's amended complaint, in granting punitive damages, in failing to find that the plaintiff's redemption of the 1986 taxes was a voluntary act, in stifling an attempted impeachment, and in entering judgment for Charles on the rental-and-storage issue. We affirm.

Esther Buckley, the plaintiff's grandmother, and the mother of the defendant, deeded her son, George Hausmann, a life estate interest in the property involved with a remainder upon George's death to her grandson, Charles Hausmann. George operated an asphalt business on this land from 1958 until January 1, 1988, when he sold the business to his wife, Ruby Hausmann, for $10.

In 1982 the plaintiff started a roofing business in the building located on the disputed land, and sometime that year George hired Charles to repair the roof on that building. Six months later 25% of the roof blew off, and Charles repaired it at an additional cost of $2,000. George testified that Charles at that time promised if the roof blew off again to repair it free of cost.

George testified that the roof was again damaged on the morning of April 22, 1984. According to George, Charles acknowledged that he had promised to repair the roof but claimed that he required an additional $5,000 for materials and insurance. George stated that he loaned Charles the $5,000 and Charles then repaired the roof. Charles, however, testified that he had borrowed the $5,000 on April 25 to finance an independent project, that the damage to the roof did not occur until April 27, and that the defendant agreed to forgive the $5,000 loan in exchange for Charles' repair of the roof.

* * *

In the fall of 1987 George Hausmann, allegedly acting on the advice of his attorney, did not pay the real estate taxes for the property in question. On October 26, 1987, the premises were subjected to sale for delinquent taxes. Prior to the sale, Stacy Stewart, the defendant's 19–year-old stepson, arranged to purchase the premises at the sale. For this purpose Stewart enlisted the aid of Roberta Quandt, a secretary in the firm of Martin Corbell, long-time attorney for the defendant. Quandt testified that she attended the sale and acquired the property for Stacy Stewart for $771.02 at a 0% interest rate.

On January 6, 1988, the defendant sent Charles a letter terminating his use of the premises and demanding rental of $5 a day for plaintiff's personal property not thereafter removed.

On January 26, 1988, Charles Hausmann redeemed the premises by paying $778.02 on the still delinquent 1986 real estate taxes.

Defendant did not pay the 1987 real estate taxes on the land when due in 1988, and when the premises were sold for delinquent taxes, Charles bid them in at 0% for $893.18 on November 21, 1988.

On February 18, 1988, plaintiff filed his original complaint.

* * *

The plaintiff also contends that, after finding the defendant committed waste on the land in question, the trial court erred by not entering an injunction against the defendant compelling him to pay future real estate taxes. Defendant counters that the trial court incorrectly recognized a cause of action on this count in that no Illinois court has ever found failure to pay real estate taxes to equal waste, thus this was not an equity matter and an equitable remedy such as an injunction would be improper.

We address first the defendant's contention as to whether or not there was a valid cause of action. Defendant correctly points out that no statute or case exists in Illinois specifically declaring the failure of a life tenant to pay property taxes to constitute waste. It has long been accepted, however, that a life tenant has a duty to pay real estate taxes assessed against the land during his life tenancy. (Huston v. Tribbetts (1898), 171 Ill. 547, 550, 49 N.E. 711, 711.) The issue then becomes, can a breach of this duty give rise to an action in waste?

Breach of this duty has been held in other jurisdictions to constitute waste. In Thayer v. Shorey (1934), 287 Mass. 76, 191 N.E. 435, the Supreme Court of Massachusetts, citing Wade v. Malloy, 16 Hun (N.Y.) 226, held that when a life tenant fails in his duty to pay taxes, an action of waste will lie against him. The Missouri Supreme Court in Farmers Mutual Fire & Lightning Insurance Co. v. Crowley (1945), 354 Mo. 649, 190 S.W.2d 250, stated that a life tenant has a duty to pay taxes, make ordinary repairs, and keep down interest on encumbrances and his failure to perform these duties falls under the extension of the rule which prohibits waste.

In Bond v. Lockwood, the Illinois Supreme Court cited the English common law definition of waste: "Any act or omission which diminished the value of the estate or its income, or increased the burdens upon it or impaired the evidence of title thereto, was considered waste." (Bond v. Lockwood (1864), 33 Ill. 212, 221.) More recently, "Waste occurs when someone who lawfully has possession of real estate destroys it, misuses it, alters it or neglects it so that the interest of persons having a subsequent right to possession is prejudiced in some way or there is a diminution in the value of the land being wasted." Pasulka v. Koob (1988), 170 Ill.App.3d 191, 209, 121 Ill.Dec. 179, 191, 524 N.E.2d 1227, 1239, citing 78 Am.Jur.2d Waste § 1 (1975).

Plaintiff argues that a life tenant's failure to perform his duty to pay the real estate taxes levied upon the land in which he holds his life tenancy, thereby subjecting the land to possible sale for delinquent taxes, may increase the burden upon the land, impair evidence of title, and prejudice the interests of persons with a subsequent right to possession, thereby giving rise to a cause of action in waste.

Defendant, on the other hand, asserts that such a finding is not particularly logical when considering the lengthy and detailed procedures, provided by the Revenue Act of 1939, which must be fulfilled before a divestiture of title in favor of a tax purchaser can occur. (Ill.Rev.Stat.1989, ch. 120, par. 705–752.1.) Waste, however, is more often a process, a series of acts or omissions, rather than a singular event. A structure need not completely collapse before a cause of action in waste will be found to exist. To hold otherwise would be to deny an adequate remedy until after the waste was completed, or nearly so. Such a ruling would belie the very nature of equity, which is fairness. Waste, when possible, should be arrested rather than allowed to run its full course.

Defendant also points out that waste is generally limited to physical damage to the property. (Metropolitan Life Insurance Co. v. W.T. Grant Co. (1944), 321 Ill.App. 487, 501, 53 N.E.2d 255, 262.) This, however, is merely a historical observation rather than a rule of law.

We hold that failure to pay real estate taxes on a life estate by the life tenant may give rise to a cause of action in waste. As such, an injunction would not be an improper remedy against said waste. (Wise v. Potomac National Bank (1946), 393 Ill. 357, 361, 65 N.E.2d 767, 769.) We disagree, however, with plaintiff's argument that Wise suggests that where damages have been awarded against a life tenant for waste an injunction should be entered as a matter of course. Wise merely describes an injunction under these circumstances as an appropriate remedy which may be granted. Absent a showing of an abuse of discretion on the trial court's part, we will not second-guess its decision not to enter an injunction on behalf of the plaintiff. Given that defendant was subjected to both actual and punitive damages, the trial court may have decided that an injunction was simply unnecessary. We find no abuse of discretion in the trial court's failure to issue an injunction against the defendant.

* * *

The defendant continues that the trial court erred in granting plaintiff the punitive damages prayed for in Count II of plaintiff's complaint. * * * Defendant also claims punitive damages were improper in that defendant acted in good faith and upon advice of counsel. This, however, is not borne out by the record. Defendant's attorney, Martin Corbell, expressly testified that at no time did he tell George Hausmann not to pay his taxes. In fact, the record tends to suggest that, contrary to George's claims of good faith, his failure to pay the taxes was little more than a thinly veiled attempt to divest the plaintiff of his interest in the land. Defendant's story that his 19–year-old stepson endeavored to gain title to the property with the aid of Quandt, an employee of defendant's attorney for over 38 years, without any help or encouragement from the defendant is at best improbable. Punitive damages may be awarded when tortious acts are committed with fraud, or when defendant acts willfully or with such gross negligence as to indicate a wanton disregard for the rights of others. (Kelsay v. Motorola, Inc. (1978), 74 Ill.2d 172, 186, 23 Ill.Dec. 559, 565, 384 N.E.2d 353, 359.) We find no error in the trial court's award of punitive damages. * * *

Defendant alleges that Charles' redemption of the 1986 real estate taxes was a voluntary act taken under no compulsion and did not, in and of itself, give rise to a legally enforceable cause of action against George. We find this contention completely without merit. It has already been established that the defendant had a duty to pay the real estate taxes, and that failure to do so gave rise to a valid cause of action for waste on behalf of the plaintiff. To suggest that the plaintiff, who took action to protect his interests and rights, was a volunteer whose actions liberated the defendant of all duties and obligations is untenable. The defendant failed in his duty. The plaintiff was compelled to act or risk possible divestment. The plaintiff is entitled to compensation. We refuse to hold that an individual must wait until the last possible moment, before moving to protect his rights, to avoid being labeled a volunteer.

* * *

For the foregoing reasons, the judgment of the trial court is affirmed.

Notes

1. Is nonpayment of property taxes really waste? Notice that the court upheld the denial of injunctive relief to Charles to compel George to pay future property taxes. Courts will normally issue injunctions to keep a life tenant who starts cutting trees from cutting in the future (refer back to the Bishop of Winchester's Case). Are trees different than taxes? Or is there a different policy explanation, e.g., in our modern, complex, many-layered world of taxation, failure to pay taxes in a particular situation might be completely innocent. Of course, the state of mind of the current possessor of Blackacre has never been a recognized factor in waste cases, which purport to look solely at the damage to the future interest holder.

2. How far and to whom should the right extend to seek relief against acts of waste? When does a person have rights which are too remote to permit suit? Although equity has traditionally permitted the holder of an indefeasibly vested future interest to enjoin waste, what rights if any should be extended to a person possessing only a defeasible or contingent future

interest? See Watson v. Wolff–Goldman Realty Co., 95 Ark. 18, 128 S.W. 581 (1910); Wise v. Potomac Nat'l Bank, 393 Ill. 357, 65 N.E.2d 767 (1946). In Sargent Lake Ass'n v. Dane, 116 N.H. 19, 351 A.2d 54 (1976) the court held that a developer who purchased a partly completed subdivision from the original grantor could be held liable for waste in not repairing a dam that controlled the waters in Sargent Lake; the court had some difficulty in sorting out the respective duties of the developer and the existing lot owners because the property owner's association did not come into existence until after the original grantor had sold many of the lots and the dam was not conveyed to the association until 1970. In a subsequent decision, Sargent Lake Ass'n v. Dane, 118 N.H. 720, 393 A.2d 559 (1978), the court affirmed the findings of a master who found that the period of permissive waste was 1970 to 1973 and the damages sustained by the plaintiffs in that period were $3,253, one half the cost of repairing the dam

In Union County v. Union County Fair Association, 276 Ark. 132, 633 S.W.2d 17 (1982), the issue was whether the holder of a possibility of reverter after a determinable fee could maintain an action for waste. There would be no forfeiture by the fair association "unless no Fair is held for a period of at least two consecutive years." The litigation was prompted by the association's plans to remove a grandstand to expand an area for the showing of cattle and hogs. The court stated:

> The issue then becomes whether the holder of a possibility of reverter may enjoin an act of waste which, in this case, is the proposed removal of the grandstand. In Watson v. Wolff–Goldman Realty Co., 95 Ark. 18, 128 S.W. 581 (1910), we held that a contingent remainderman may enjoin waste where the estate may become his at the termination of a life estate. However, the chancellor correctly noted in the present case there is no proof that the termination of the determinable fee is ever likely to occur. Instead, there is a possibility the determinable fee will endure forever, as distinguished from the remainder following the life estate in the Watson case, supra. The chancellor also found that the alleged waste could cause no serious damage to the property and denied the injunction. We affirm. The holder of a possibility of reverter can restrain an act of waste by the holder of a determinable fee only when it appears that there is a reasonable certainty that the fee will terminate and the waste would cause serious damage to the property.

3. Waste cases have probably, more often than not, involved the cutting of timber; and the timber cases in America, as we have seen, came to follow in large measure the "good husbandry" test—i.e., whether the act in question operated to benefit or diminish the value of the freehold. See 5 American Law of Property § 20.2, at 77 (Casner ed. 1952). In this context, and along the same line mentioned in the preceding paragraph, should the purchaser under a contract of sale, who has only the equitable title, be permitted to recover for timber cut by the vendor after the contract has been entered into but before the time for delivery of the deed? See Walker v. Dibble, 241 Ark. 692, 409 S.W.2d 333 (1966).

4. Reference should be had to Annot., Right of Contingent Remainderman to Maintain Action for Damages for Waste, 56 A.L.R.3d 677 (1974). This annotation presents a good discussion of the holdings in this regard.

The weight of authority denies a right of recovery because there is no immediate estate of inheritance, there is no existing interest in the property, and the contingency might not occur. Are these barriers to recovery reasonable in the light of modern rules of property? If the contingency did not occur, how could you avoid paying a remainderman for damages to which he was not entitled?

DELANO v. SMITH

Supreme Judicial Court of Massachusetts, 1910.
206 Mass. 365, 92 N.E. 500.

RUGG, J. This is an action of tort in the nature of waste. The defendants constituted the board of health in the city of Everett. The plaintiff was the mortgagee of certain real estate in that city, the buildings upon which consisted of one house of three tenements and a store and a stable. On or about the twenty-first day of December 1901, the defendants, acting as members of the board of health, leased of the mortgagor said premises "to be used as a contagious hospital." Occupation for that purpose began at once and continued until December 22, 1902, during which period forty-two persons sick with smallpox were treated, six of whom died. The plaintiff did not know of the lease nor of such occupation until after it had continued for several months. The defense is that the acts complained of were done under the authority of the lease given by the mortgagor. It is to be noted that the defendants did not proceed under Pub.Sts. c. 80, sec. 43, then in force (now R.L. c. 75, sec. 46, as amended by St.1906, c. 365, sec. 2). They undertook to perform the public duty incumbent upon them of providing a proper place for the treatment of persons suffering from smallpox by agreement with the mortgagor, and not by any exercise of the power delegated by the Commonwealth.

Whatever may be the law in other jurisdictions by statute or otherwise, "it has long been settled in this Commonwealth that, as to all the world except the mortgagee, mortgagor is the owner of the mortgaged lands, at least till the mortgagee has entered for possession." Dolliver v. St. Joseph Fire & Marine Ins. Co., 128 Mass. 315. Whether the mortgagee is in possession of the mortgaged premises or not, or whether his right to possession begins only with the breach of condition and there has been no breach, nevertheless he has such an interest in the property and its preservation as enables him to maintain an action in his own name for injury to it. Such right of action is founded not upon the right to present possession, but on title to the estate. He may maintain such an action, although he is a junior mortgagee and although the security remains ample for his protection. He has a right to his security unimpaired. The leading principles by which the rights of mortgagor and mortgagee may be worked out are clearly explained by Wells, J., in Gooding v. Shea, 103 Mass. 360. Cases which recognize a right of action in the mortgagee to recover damages for injury to his security are numerous. See, for example, James v. Worcester, 141 Mass. 361; Wilbur v. Moulton, 127 Mass. 509; Searle v. Sawyer, 127 Mass. 491;

Byrom v. Chapin, 113 Mass. 308, 311; Stewart v. Fingelstone, ante, 28; Ocean Accident & Guarantee Corp. v. Ilford Gas Co. [1905] 2 K.B. 493; Fidelity Trust Co. v. Hoboken & Manhattan Railroad, 1 Buch. 14. An action for such injury lies as well against the mortgagor, although rightfully in possession. The mortgagor is liable to the mortgagee for waste. The mortgagor in this respect stands to the mortgagee as a tenant to a landlord, or a tenant for life to a reversioner. Goodman v. Kine, 8 Beav. 379. King v. Smith, 2 Hare, 239. Page v. Robinson, 10 Cush. 99. Hutchins v. King, 1 Wall. 53. A lease made by the mortgagor after the rights of the mortgagee have become fixed cannot affect the latter in any way without his consent. Tilden v. Greenwood, 149 Mass. 567, 22 N.E. 45. Elmore v. Symonds, 183 Mass. 321, 67 N.E. 314.

The fundamental question, therefore, is whether upon the facts agreed it was permissible for the jury to find that waste had been committed. Under the conditions prevailing in this Commonwealth waste is an unreasonable or improper use, abuse, mismanagement or omission of duty touching real estate by one rightfully in possession which results in its substantial injury. It is the violation of an obligation to treat the premises in such having an underlying interest undeteriorated by any wilful or negligent act. Pynchon v. Stearns, 11 Met. 304. United States v. Bostwick, 94 U.S. 53, 24 L.Ed. 65. Townshend v. Moore, 4 Vroom 284. Turner v. Wright, 2 De.G., F. & J. 234, 246. 30 Am. & Eng. Encyc. of Law, (2d ed.) 255, and cases cited. Waste does not necessarily mean a subtraction of something from the corporal substance of the estate. Perhaps it may not always include change in material condition, though it is not necessary to decide that point in this case. Its early and frequent application was in an agricultural sense, where it means a damaging use not in accordance with good husbandry. Pratt v. Brett, 2 Madd. 62. Patterson v. Central Canada Loan & Savings Co., 29 Ont. 134, 137. It generally consists in some definite physical injury. This is shown by reference to the earlier definitions, as for instance that of Blackstone, who calls it a "spoil or destruction in houses, gardens, trees, or other corporeal hereditaments." 2 Black.Com. (Sharswood's ed.) 281.

On principle it follows that mere injury to the reputation of real estate or the supposed diminution of its value resting on whimsical or emotional grounds or arising from dictates of custom or taste do not constitute waste. These considerations have nothing to do with material substance, but depend upon evanescent or intangible preferences or prejudices. It is the commonly accepted view that smallpox is a contagious disease, spread through the instrumentality of germs, which although invisible to the naked eye are perniciously active and capable of causing loathsome and often fatal sickness. In Commonwealth v. Pear, 183 Mass. 242, 66 N.E. 719, is a statement of the judicial notice which the court will take of the horrors of smallpox. From the agreed facts the jury would have been warranted in finding that this building was filled in every nook and crevice with the microscopic germs of this dreaded disease. This might have been found to constitute an essential alteration in the qualities and condition of the house with reference to the purposes for which it was intended to be used, such as to constitute a definite injury. Inoculation with germs of glanders was held to be a "bodily injury" in H.P. Hood & Sons v. Maryland Casualty Co., ante, 223. Sowing the seeds of noxious weeds was restrained as waste in Pratt v. Brett, 2 Madd. 62. Impregnation of a building with the indiscernible but vital germs of a dangerous malady is closely analogous to the sowing of seeds of deleterious plants, and may be in its effect far more detrimental. It may be in fact even more harmful than to tear down or remove a part of the building. It is in principle the same general kind of damage as the more familiar instances of waste. The possibility of germination of the disease germs which, it might have been found, were deposited through the action of the defendants within the house in question was or might have been found to be waste, unless it is shown that they can be removed by disinfection or otherwise without material physical change in the building, so as to make it as safe for residence as before. Whether this can be done or not depends upon evidence. Hersey v. Chapin, 162 Mass. 176, 38 N.E. 442, while not decisive of the present case, seems to go upon the ground that the use of a building as a smallpox hospital might be an injury to the reversion. See also United States v. Bostwick, 94 U.S. 53, 24 L.Ed. 65.

A case like the present should be submitted to the jury under instructions which would permit the plaintiff to recover the diminution in the value of his property for every valuable use among ordinarily intelligent men arising from the occupancy for a smallpox hospital, provided the jury were satisfied that it was not reasonable and proper to let the building for this purpose, having reference to the probable effects upon its future growing out of the presence of disease-producing conditions, in view of the existing state of the art of disinfection or other way of rendering it healthful, and excluding all sentimental or fanciful notions affecting only its reputation.

From an examination of the record there appears to be ground for the view that the case was tried throughout upon the theory that recovery was sought and could be had for injury to the reputation of the estate apart from any physical waste, and that the stipulation and agreement, that, in the event of the ruling to the effect that the plaintiff could not recover being wrong, judgment should be entered for the plaintiff, was made and entered into under such a misapprehension as to render what has taken place a mistrial or to make it unjust to hold the parties to it in view of the present opinion. The declaration is broad enough to include damages of the nature which we have held may be recovered. Hence the entry should be: Judgment for the plaintiff for the sum found by the jury, unless within sixty days from the filing of the rescript the justice of the Superior Court before whom the trial occurred shall decide after hearing that under these circumstances justice requires a new trial and enter an order to that effect.

So ordered.

Notes

1. The idea of damages to the reputation of real estate is not confined to actions based on the law of waste. Can the owner of real property, a portion of which is condemned for high voltage power lines, claim that public fears (whether real or imaginary) that power lines cause cancer constitute an element of compensation damages? In Criscuola v. Power Authority of the State of New York, 81 N.Y.2d 649, 602 N.Y.S.2d 588, 621 N.E.2d 1195 (1993) the court said:

> The only issue before us centers on the claim for consequential damages, based on the claimants' assertion that "cancerphobia" and the public's perception of a health risk from exposure to electromagnetic emissions from power lines negatively impact upon the market value of their property and "will render the remainder valueless." They argue that they should not have to prove the "reasonableness" of this perception as a separate, additional component of diminished market value. We agree
> * * *

> The issue in a just compensation proceeding is whether or not the market value has been adversely affected * * * This consequence may be present even if the public's fear is unreasonable. Whether the danger is a scientifically genuine or verifiable fact should be irrelevant to the central issue of its market value impact.

> Although this issue is a matter of first impression in this Court, it has been well ventilated in sibling jurisdictions whose precedents offer some useful instruction. The Court of Appeals of Kansas summarized the three prevailing views as of 1981 in Willsey v. Kansas City Power & Light Co., 6 Kan.App.2d 599, 631 P.2d 268, supra. The Willsey court noted that the characterizations and labels attached to the varieties of test are inaccurate. Thus, the so-called "majority" view, in which evidence of the effect on market value of a fear of danger from power lines was unequivocally rejected, was actually followed by only four States in 1981 (id., 631 P.2d, at 273–274 [Ala, Fla, Ill, W Va]). In contrast, the "minority" view, in which such evidence is routinely admitted on a simple showing that the fear exists and affects market value, was followed by 11 States and the Sixth Circuit (id., 631 P.2d, at 274 [Ark, Cal, Ind, Iowa, La, NC, Ohio, Okla, SD, Va, Wash]). In these jurisdictions, the reasonableness of the fear is either assumed or deemed irrelevant or collateral to the market value issue and the considerations that customarily pertain to its just resolution. * * *

> Recently, Florida, California and Kansas reaffirmed that reasonableness is not a factor in determining whether consequential damages may be awarded for a diminution or elimination of market value due to a fear of health risks from exposure to power lines.

However, in Dixie Textile Waste Co. v. Oglethorpe Power Corp., 214 Ga.App. 125, 447 S.E.2d 328 (1994) the court held expert testimony regarding the public's fear of electric power lines inadmissible in a condemnation case.

Another case to consider is Barton v. New York City Comm'n on Human Rights, 140 Misc.2d 554, 531 N.Y.S.2d 979 (1988). A dentist subleased some of his office space for two nights a week to a young dentist who specialized in treating AIDS patients in need of dental treatment; when the lessor could not get the sublessee to stop soliciting AIDS patients for dental treatment, he evicted the sublessee, because of the potential fears of non-AIDS patients of the lessor. The human rights commission found that the lessor discriminated and awarded damages to the sublessee.

2. Converting the premises into a haven for smallpox sufferers would hardly constitute the usual type of situation involved, of course. More often today, alteration of the premises is governed by conditions specifically set forth in leases. What if the lessee in such an arrangement were allowed by the terms of the instrument to alter the premises to the extent necessary for use as a garage and planned to cut a fourteen foot doorway in the front of the building? Assuming that the lessee was permitted to sublet or assign the leased premises, could the lessor prevent the cutting of the doorway by alleging that this was in contravention of the provisions of the lease? Could the lessor successfully argue that the permission granted in the lease to make alterations for "use" of the premises was ambiguous and that a covenant against such alteration should be implied? Would it make any difference if the use contemplated by the parties at the time of entering into the lease was that the property would be used as a grocery store? See Turman v. Safeway Stores, Inc., 132 Mont. 273, 317 P.2d 302 (1957), noted in 19 Mont.L.Rev. 167 (1958). Cf. F.W. Woolworth Co. v. Nelson, 204 Ala. 172, 85 So. 449, 13 A.L.R. 820 (1920).

LYTLE v. PAYETTE–OREGON SLOPE IRRIGATION DIST.

Supreme Court of Oregon, 1944.
175 Or. 276, 152 P.2d 934, 156 A.L.R. 894.

[Plaintiff owned 128 acres of irrigable farm land. She alleged in her complaint that certain irrigation district assessments made by the defendant were invalid; that the district had foreclosed these assessments, purchased at the invalid sale and had gone into possession of the land. She sought damages for use and occupation and for waste. The trial court gave judgment on the pleadings against her. The Supreme Court reversed. Only a small part of the opinion is given.]

HAY, J. * * * The appellant contends that, while the district had possession of the property, it was guilty of ill husbandry, in that it failed to farm and cultivate the land, and thereby permitted it to become infested with noxious weeds. This, no doubt, should be regarded as waste, and, if respondents were responsible therefor, they would be liable. 3 Am.Jr., Appeal and Error, Section 1260; Hess v. Deppen, 125 Ky. 424, 101 S.W. 362, 15 Ann.Cas. 670. Waste is "a spoil or destruction in houses, gardens, trees or other corporeal hereditaments, to the disher-sion of him that hath the remainder or reversion." 2 Bla.Com. 281, cited with approval in Davenport v. Magoon, 13 Or. 3, 4 P. 299, 57 Am.Rep. 1. Ill husbandry, carried to such extent as materially injures the rights of the landlord or reversioner, constitutes waste. 67 C.J.S. Waste, Section 12. The infestation of the property with noxious weeds would certainly,

we think, materially injure the rights of the owner of the land. A trustee is under a duty to use such care and skill to preserve the trust property as a man of ordinary prudence would exercise in dealing with his own property. Restatement, Trusts, Sections 174, 176; Elliott v. Mosgrove, 162 Or. 507, 538, 91 P.2d 852. If the infestation of the land by weeds was the result of the respondents' mismanagement, judged by the standard of care and skill of a man of ordinary prudence, they would, we think, be liable. Restatement, Restitution, Section 74f. The measure of compensation is the diminution, caused by the waste, in the market value of the property or, in other words, as applied to the facts alleged in the complaint here, the difference between the market value of the land when free from weeds, and its market value when weed-infested. Winans v. Valentine, 152 Or. 462, 54 P.2d 106; 3 C.J.S. Agriculture, Section 28.
* * *

Notes

1. This case is representative of those in which the possessor is responsible for waste resulting from actions which constitute poor husbandry on his part. See 5 American Law of Property § 20.9, at 93 (Casner ed. 1952). Somewhat related are those cases in which the tenant is guilty of permissive waste in failing to repair the premises or otherwise protect the property in question against deterioration. Although the duty of the tenant may at times be nebulous and inexact, if a life tenant or tenant for years fails to fulfill his obligations to the extent that permissive waste results, most American courts will grant relief (although the burdens vary). See generally 5 American Law of Property § 20.12, at 99–102 (Casner ed. 1952); 5 Powell, Real Property ¶ 640, at 23 (1980).

2. Of course, although a tenant normally commits permissive waste when he fails to keep the premises in repair or commits acts of poor husbandry, he is not liable for normal depreciation. At times there may be differences as to what constitutes a positive duty to keep the premises in repair as opposed to what amounts to normal depreciation. There may also be differences over the adequacy of the repair or the form it takes. You might also have a peculiar melding of permissive waste and voluntary waste—in which the tenant in possession performed some affirmative act designed to keep a structure in repair, but the action taken was deemed to be inadequate (i.e., permissive waste) and at the same time created a situation in which the attractiveness or ultimate value of the premises was reduced (affirmative waste) as a result of the method of repair employed or the eventual appearance of the premises.

3. See the Annot., What Constitutes Waste Justifying Appointment of Receiver of Mortgaged Property, 55 A.L.R.3d 1041 (1974). Also see Gitelman, The Impact of the Statute of Gloucester on the Development of the American Law of Waste, 39 Ark.L.Rev. 669 (1986).

MELMS v. PABST BREWING CO.

Supreme Court of Wisconsin, 1899.
104 Wis. 7, 79 N.W. 738.

[Action was brought by Franz Melms and others, as reversioners. The waste claimed was the destruction of a dwelling house and the grading of the land to street level. The house was brick and cost about $20,000 when built in 1864. A brewery was situated on part of the premises. Previous litigation established that Pabst had acquired the brewery property in fee simple absolute but had only acquired a life estate pur autre vie in the homestead. The life estate was that of Mrs. Charles Melms, the widow of the man who built the house. The evidence showed that after the brewing company acquired the land, the general character of the area rapidly changed "so that soon after the year 1890 it became wholly undesirable and unprofitable as residence property. Factories and railway tracts increased in the vicinity, and the balance of the property was built up with brewing buildings, until the quarter of an acre homestead in question became an isolated lot and building, standing from 20 to 30 feet above the level of the street, the balance of the property having been graded down * * * for business purposes. The evidence shows * * * that, owing to these circumstances, the residence, which was at one time a handsome and desirable one, became of no practical value, and would not rent for enough to pay taxes and insurance thereon * * *." Since it was valuable as business property, Pabst removed the house and graded the property to street level under the belief at the time that it owned the homestead in fee simple. The trial court held for Pabst. The opinion of the Court, which provides an extensive review of the rules of waste, has been reduced substantially in length.]

WINSLOW, J. * * * That these acts would constitute waste under ordinary circumstances cannot be doubted. It is not necessary to delve deeply into the Year Books, or philosophize extensively as to the meaning of early judicial utterances in order to arrive at this conclusion. * * * But, while they are correct as general expressions of the law upon the subject, and were properly applicable to the cases under consideration, it must be remembered that they are general rules only, and, like most general propositions, are not to be accepted without limitation or reserve under any and all circumstances. Thus the ancient English rule which prevented the tenant from converting a meadow into arable land was early softened down, and the doctrine of meliorating waste was adopted, which, without changing the legal definition of waste, still allowed the tenant to change the course of husbandry upon the estate if such change be for the betterment of the estate. Bewes, Waste, p. 134, and cases cited. Again, and in accordance with this same principle, the rule that any change in a building upon the premises constitutes waste has been greatly modified, even in England; and it is now well settled that, while such change may constitute technical waste, still it will not be enjoined in equity when it clearly appears that the change will be, in effect, a meliorating change, which rather improves the inheritance than injures it. Doherty v. Allman, 3 App.Cas. 709; In re McIntosh, 61 Law J.Q.B. 164. Following the same general line of reasoning, it was early held in the United States that, while the English doctrine as to waste was a part of our common law, still that the cutting of timber in order to clear up wild land and fit it for cultivation, if consonant with the rules of good husbandry, was not waste, although such acts would clearly have been waste in England. Tied. Real Prop. (Eng.Ed.) § 74; Rice, Mod.Law Real Prop. §§ 160, 161; Wilkinson v. Wilkinson, 59 Wis. 557, 18 N.W. 527. These familiar examples of departure from ancient rules will serve to show that, while definitions have remained much the same, the law upon the subject of waste is not an unchanging and unchangeable code, which was crystallized for all time in the days of feudal tenures, but that it is subject to such reasonable modifications as may be demanded by the growth of civilization and varying conditions. And so it is now laid down that the same act may be waste in one part of the country while in another it is a legitimate use of the land, and that the usages and customs of each community enter largely into the settlement of the question. Tied. Real Prop. (Eng.Ed.) § 73. This is entirely consistent with, and in fact springs from, the central idea upon which the disability of waste is now, and always has been, founded, namely, the preservation of the property for the benefit of the owner of the future estate without permanent injury to it. This element will be found in all the definitions of waste, namely, that it must be an act resulting in permanent injury to the inheritance or future estate. * * *

There are no contract relations in the present case. The defendants are the grantees of a life estate, and their rights may continue for a number of years. The evidence shows that the property became valueless for the purpose of residence property as the result of the growth and development of a great city. Business and manufacturing interests advanced and surrounded the once elegant mansion, until it stood isolated and alone, standing upon just enough ground to support it, and surrounded by factories and railway tracks, absolutely undesirable as a residence, and incapable of any use as business property. Here was a complete change of conditions, not produced by the tenant, but resulting from causes which none could control. Can it be reasonably or logically said that this entire change of condition is to be completely ignored, and the ironclad rule applied that the tenant can make no change in the uses of the property because he will destroy its identity? Must the tenant stand by, and preserve the useless dwelling house, so that he may at some future time turn it over to the reversioner, equally useless? Certainly, all the analogies are to the contrary. As we have before seen, the cutting of timber, which in England was considered waste, has become in this country an act which may be waste or not, according to the surrounding conditions and the rules of good husbandry; and the same rule applies to the change of a meadow to arable land. The changes of conditions which justify these departures from early inflexible rules are no more marked nor complete than is the change of conditions which destroys the value of residence property as such, and renders it only useful for business purposes. Suppose the house in question had been so situated that it could have been remodeled into business property; would any court of equity have enjoined such remodeling under the circumstances here shown, or ought any court to render a judgment for damages for such an act? Clearly, we think not. * * * It is certainly true that a case involving so complete a change of situation as regards buildings has been rarely, if ever, presented to the courts, yet we are not without authorities approaching very nearly to the case before us. Thus, in the case of Doherty v. Allman, before cited, a court of equity refused an injunction preventing a tenant for a long term from changing storehouses into dwelling houses, on the ground that by change of conditions the demand for storehouses had ceased, and the property had become worthless, whereas it might be productive when fitted for dwelling houses. Again, in the case of Sherrill v. Connor, 107 N.C. 630, 12 S.E. 588, which was an action for permissive waste against a tenant in dower, who had permitted large barns and outbuildings upon a plantation to fall into decay, it was held that, as these buildings had been built before the Civil War to accommodate the operation of the plantation by slaves, it was not necessarily waste to tear them down, or allow them to remain unrepaired, after the war, when the conditions had completely changed by reason of the emancipation, and the changed methods of use resulting therefrom; and that it became a question for the jury whether a prudent owner of the fee, if in possession, would have suffered the unsuitable barns and buildings to have fallen into decay, rather than incur the cost of repair. This last case is very persuasive and well reasoned, and it well states the principle which we think is equally applicable to the case before us. In the absence of any contract, express or implied, to use the property for a specified purpose, or to return it in the same condition in which it was received, a radical and permanent change of surrounding conditions, such as is presented in the case before us, must always be an important, and sometimes a controlling, consideration upon the question whether a physical change in the use of the buildings constitutes waste. In the present case this consideration was regarded by the trial court as controlling, and we are satisfied that this is the right view. This case is not to be construed as justifying a tenant in making substantial changes in the leasehold property, or the buildings thereon, to suit his own whim or convenience, because, perchance, he may be able to show that the change is in some degree beneficial. Under all ordinary circumstances the landlord or reversioner, even in the absence of any contract, is entitled to receive the property at the close of the tenancy substantially in the condition in which it was when the tenant received it; but when, as here, there has occurred a complete and permanent change of surrounding conditions, which has deprived the property of its value and usefulness as previously used, the question whether a life tenant, not bound by contract to restore the property in the same condition in which he received it, has been guilty of waste in making changes necessary to make the property useful, is a question of fact for the jury under proper instructions, or for the court where, as in the present case, the question is tried by the court. Judgment affirmed.

Notes

1. The Melms case, which was also cited in the material at the beginning of this section, is the leading case on a change of circumstances in the surrounding area justifying what would otherwise amount to waste. This doctrine bears a similarity to that which we will take up later in the book in which the neighborhood changes so drastically that a restrictive covenant limiting a subdivision to a specific use (which is usually residential) becomes subject to being declared unenforceable. The underlying theory in the waste situation is essentially the same in that it should not constitute waste, generally speaking, to convert property from some use which is worthless or rapidly becoming worthless into some legitimate use of much greater value.

When can you be certain that an area has in fact changed sufficiently to justify taking action similar to that in the Melms case? Is it enough that there is an economic advantage to be gained or that the change is essential to the normal development of the land? Does it matter whether the tenant in possession is there on a long term basis or a short term basis? What if he is a life tenant, but is in his sixties or seventies?

3. Under the early common law rule, if a tenant removed or altered the premises or replaced an old structure with a new structure, it amounted to waste. It was called "ameliorating waste" where the land value increased. The modern rule is substantially more reasonable, as we have seen.

4. The law of waste as applied to minerals is a matter of substantial interest in oil and gas producing areas. A student note in 55 Ky.L.J. 118 (1955) set forth three theories as to the rights of adjoining landowners with respect to waste of oil and gas: (1) the surface owner owns the oil and gas in place beneath the surface (which presumably has its origin in Coke's maxim, *cujus est solum, ejus est usque ad coelum et ad inferos*); (2) the surface owner has no ownership or title in the minerals beneath the surface but only a paramount right to search for them and reduce them to possession (and presumably a right of exclusion as to others, as far as his own land surface is concerned); and (3) the theory that the surface owner has an interest in common with others and has correlative rights in the minerals. In support of the third theory, see Ohio Oil Co. v. Indiana, 177 U.S. 190, 20 S.Ct. 576, 44 L.Ed. 729 (1900). 1 Kuntz, Oil and Gas § 4.7 (1962) states that this does not mean that every landowner is entitled to a proportionate share but that owners have the right to a fair opportunity to extract the minerals. Kuntz indicates that the fairness of allocation ultimately involves determining what part of the common source could have been produced without waste in the absence of regulation. In Northern Natural Gas Co. v. State Corp. Comm'n of Kansas, 372 U.S. 84, 83 S.Ct. 646, 9 L.Ed.2d 601 (1963), the Court indicated that the state is not without alternative means of checking waste and a disproportionate or discriminatory taking. See also Justice Rutledge's dissent in Republic Natural Gas Co. v. Oklahoma, 334 U.S. 62, 93–94, 68 S.Ct. 972, 988–989, 92 L.Ed. 1212 (1948).

Of course, injunctive relief will lie to prevent operations which threaten to spoil the common source of supply. See 1 Kuntz, supra at § 4.5.

SECTION 2. THE LAW OF NUISANCE

A. SOME IMPORTANT BASIC CONSIDERATIONS

(1) Historical Aspects

Long before the modern era of "comprehensive" zoning, courts in the haphazard fashion of our case law and through loose doctrines of private and public nuisance were mitigating against the worst effects of unplanned development of English and American communities. Many thousands of discordant land uses have been reviewed by courts since the law of "nuisance" began to take shape soon after the Norman Conquest. The judge-made criteria for the resolution of land use conflicts show the vagueness and resultant flexibility which one would expect. They display the extreme difficulty of choosing, through the individualized method of the case law process, between clashing land uses that exist in bewildering variety.

In England, at first, such disputes were resolved in local and manorial courts. But after the law reforms of Henry II, in the latter part of the 12th Century, the king's courts began to encroach rapidly into land disputes in general and into nuisance disputes in particular. For private nuisances the royal courts at first gave the dual relief of damages and specific abatement through the assize of novel disseisin and through the assize of nuisance. The ancient overlappings and confusions between these two assizes no longer concern us. Suffice it to say that they were both superseded by trespass on the case, which afforded damages only, so that for specific abatement it became necessary for plaintiffs to petition the Chancery Court for injunctive relief. And today most private nuisance cases "sound" in equity for injunctions, though there may be an incidental prayer for damages.

Avoiding for the moment the difficult problem of drawing the lines of demarcation between "private" nuisances and "public" nuisances, we may look briefly into the ways *public nuisance* cases got into court in times past, and the ways in which they get there today.

A citizen apparently did not, at first, have any judicial remedy when he suffered damages because of a public nuisance. Rather rigorous rules of self-help abatement existed, particularly where the nuisance consisted in interfering with ready passage on a public highway. Presentment and indictment, as for other crimes, seemed to have been the sole early judicial weapon against the public nuisance. The earliest case suggesting that an individual could sue for a public nuisance was in 1535, (Y.B. 27 Hy. VIII 26, 27), but the doctrine that the individual plaintiff must show "special damages" was soon engrafted into the law and flourished like a sturdy weed. Today, if someone can prove "special damages" to the satisfaction of the court, he can not only collect the damages but may also be entitled to an injunction abating the public nuisance. In addition, the community through the municipal, county, or district attorney may also sue to abate the nuisance by injunction. Special statutes often set out conditions that must be met before the prosecuting authority can bring such an action.

(2) Public and Private Nuisances

Putting procedural matters aside, what in substance distinguishes a "private" nuisance from a "public" nuisance?

Public nuisances include a great many interferences with the comfort, moral standards, health, safety and convenience of the community. Included are activities which,

(1) Endanger the health or safety of a considerable number of people, such as discharging fumes from a white lead works or an open pit smelter, polluting a public water supply, or maintaining a breeding place for mosquitoes;

(2) Endanger the property of a considerable number of persons, such as storing explosives in a populous place or keeping diseased animals;

(3) Offend public morals, such as operating a house of prostitution, a gambling house, a disorderly saloon or an indecent exhibition;

(4) Interfere with the comfort of a considerable number of people particularly through odors, dust, smoke, sound or vibrations;

(5) Upset public convenience by obstructing a highway, navigable stream or bridge, or by creating a condition that makes travel unsafe or interferes with the use of a public square or park;

(6) Violate a criminal statute which declares the violation to be a public nuisance, such as permitting black currant plants to grow, failing to drain mosquito breeding waters, eavesdropping on a jury, being a common scold, placing advertising signs along a highway so as to obstruct the view, running dance marathons, using a shanty when fishing through the ice, and a rich variety of unrelated minor offenses.

At common law, a public nuisance was always a crime and punishable as such. Most of our states have enacted very broad criminal statutes, in addition to the specific kinds previously referred to, saying in effect that to maintain a public nuisance is a crime.

A private nuisance is an interference with the use or enjoyment of land, other than by direct physical invasion or trespass. Unlike a public nuisance, a private nuisance normally only affects a limited number of landowners and, perhaps more typically, involves a dispute between adjoining landowners.

Ambrose invades Bruce's exclusive right to possess land by physically going onto Bruce's land and cutting a tree. This direct invasion of Bruce's land space is a trespass for which Bruce had an action of trespass at common law, and for which he today can bring a civil action "sounding" in trespass. But suppose that Ambrose stays strictly on his own land, and there operates a lime kiln, a pig farm, a blasting operation or a dam, so that the smoke, stench, vibration, noise or water substantially interferes with Bruce in the use of his land? Even though there may be no technical trespass, there may be a legal wrong in the form of a private nuisance. In this age of science, invasion of A's land space by light rays, particulates of energy or molecules of dust or gas originating on B's land may constitute a direct physical invasion, a "trespass." But to our forefathers these were indirect invasions and the remedy "sounded" in nuisance, not in trespass. Consider Martin v. Reynolds Metals Co., 221 Or. 86, 342 P.2d 790 (1959), certiorari denied 362 U.S. 918, 80 S.Ct. 672, 4 L.Ed.2d 739 (1960): Plaintiffs alleged damages from fluoride gases and particulates which moved from defendants' aluminum reduction plant to plaintiffs' lands. A two-year statute of limitations barred a "nuisance" action. It was held that the action could be brought under the six-year statute of limitations for trespass actions. Here is some interesting language from the court's opinion:

> The view recognizing a trespassory invasion where there is no "thing" which can be seen with the naked eye undoubtedly runs counter to the definition of trespass expressed in some quarters. Restatement of Torts § 158, Comment h (1934); Prosser, Law of Torts § 13 (2d ed. 1955). It is quite possible that in an earlier day when science had not yet peered into the molecular and atomic world of small particles, the courts could not fit an invasion through unseen physical instrumentalities into the requirement that a trespass can result only from a direct invasion. But in this atomic age even the uneducated know the great and awful force contained in the atom and what it can do to a man's property if it is released. In fact, the now famous equation $E = mc^2$ has taught us that mass and energy are equivalents and that our concept of "things" must be reframed. If these observations on science in relation to the law of trespass should appear theoretical and unreal in the abstract, they become very practical and real to the possessor of land when the unseen force cracks the foundation of his house. The force is just as real if it is chemical in nature and must be awakened by the intervention of another agency before it does harm.

> If, then, we must look to the character of the instrumentality which is used in making an intrusion upon another's land we prefer to emphasize the object's energy or force rather than its size. Viewed in this way we may define trespass as any intrusion which invades the possessor's protected interest in exclusive possession, whether that intrusion is by visible or invisible pieces of matter or by energy which can be measured only by the mathematical language of the physicist.

> We are of the opinion, therefore, that the intrusion of the fluoride particulates in the present case constituted a trespass.[5]

---

5. Not only may noise, dust, lights, etc., constitute a nuisance, but these elements may under certain circumstances and in certain jurisdictions also constitute a "taking" of private property. See, e.g., United States v. Certain Parcels of Land in Kent

Notice that a nuisance may exist because of (1) an intentional act as in damming water; (2) negligence as in failing to keep pig pens reasonably clean; or (3) absolute liability imposed because Ambrose has engaged in an ultrahazardous use of his land. "Private nuisance" then does not really refer to a type of tortious conduct; it refers to the kind of property interest invaded by the wrongdoer.

A nuisance may be public and private at one and the same time. This is true where conduct constituting a public nuisance substantially interferes with the use of a privately owned tract of land. A house of prostitution next door to a home may sufficiently interfere with use of the land to constitute a private nuisance; it is also a public nuisance. The owner of adjoining land can sue to enjoin it; so can the district attorney. Jones obstructs a public highway and also bars access from Smith's land onto the highway. Here again what Jones does is both a public and a private nuisance. Or sometimes Ambrose's activities on his own land substantially affect a sufficient number of land occupiers in the neighborhood to constitute a public nuisance. At the same time his activities may constitute a private nuisance with respect to each neighbor individually.

In none of these cases of public nuisance interfering substantially with individual landowners should it be necessary to prove "special damages" to get private relief and some well-reasoned cases have indicated as much. On the other hand, where a public nuisance causes private injury other than damage to land, there are many cases insisting on proof of "special damage" (i.e., damage different in "kind" rather than "degree" from that sustained by the public generally) as a condition to relief for a private plaintiff. Thus, owners of a steamboat line were denied recovery for obstruction of a navigable stream on the ground that like everyone else they had only lost the use of the river.

Notice that from the point of view of land planning, of closing out or controlling discordant land uses, doctrines evolved in public as in private nuisance cases are in point. As indicated, these doctrines have been kept vague and general and accordingly flexible.

(3) The Duty Not to Interfere Substantially With Your Neighbor

The courts have long recognized that give and take in living is unavoidable in an organized society, since almost any use someone may make of his land will interfere to some extent with the free use and undisturbed enjoyment by others of neighboring land. Britton, writing around 1300 A.D., put it this way:

County, Mich., 252 F.Supp. 319 (W.D.Mich. 1966); Thornburg v. Port of Portland, 233 Or. 178, 376 P.2d 100 (1962); and Martin v. Port of Seattle, 64 Wash.2d 309, 391 P.2d 540 (1964), certiorari denied 379 U.S. 989, 85 S.Ct. 701, 13 L.Ed.2d 610 (1965). Cf.: Batten v. United States, 292 F.2d 144 (10th Cir.1961), 306 F.2d 580 (10th Cir.1962), certiorari denied 371 U.S. 955, 83 S.Ct. 506, 9 L.Ed.2d 502 (1963), rehearing denied 372 U.S. 925, 83 S.Ct. 718, 9 L.Ed.2d 731 (1963); and Mosher v. City of Boulder, 225 F.Supp. 32 (D.C.Colo.1964).

Sometimes the soil is subject to a servitude by law, although not by any man's appointment, or by the establishment of peaceable seisin, and as, for example, to the obligation that no one shall do anything in his own soil that may be a grievance or annoyance to his neighbor.

Britton 1, 140b, 56 (F.M. Nichols ed. 1901).

Since Britton wrote, Anglo–American courts have said over and over again that the occupancy of neighboring tracts of land by different individuals gives rise to probable conflicts of interests between them, and the interest of each must be reasonably limited so that the interest of the other may have reasonable play.[6]

Aside from statutory controls on land use, then, we have long had as an integral part of our jurisprudence the principle which undergirds the law of nuisance and which finds expression in the maxim, *sic utere tuo ut alienum non laedas,* to the effect that no one may use his property in such a way as to injure the person or property of another. This concept provides a balancing of the legitimate interests of adjoining landowners and was expressed by a New York court in this way: "As a general rule, an owner is at liberty to use his property as he sees fit, without objection or interference from his neighbor, provided such use does not violate an ordinance or statute. There is, however, a limitation to this rule; one made necessary by the intricate, complex, and changing life of today. The old and familiar maxim that one must so use his property as not to injure that of another (sic utere tuo ut alienum non laedas) is deeply imbedded in our law. An owner will not be permitted to make an unreasonable use of his premises to the material annoyance of his neighbor, if the latter's enjoyment of life or property is materially lessened thereby. This principle is aptly stated by Andrews, C.M., in Booth v. Rome, W. & O. T. R.R. Co., 140 N.Y. 267, 274, 35 N.E. 592, 594, 24 L.R.A. 105, 37 Am.St.Rep. 552 (1893), as follows: 'The general rule that no one has absolute freedom in the use of his property, but is restrained by the coexistence of equal rights in his neighbor to the use of his property, so that each, in exercising his right, must do no act which causes injury to his neighbor, is so well understood, is so universally recognized, and stands so impregnably in the necessities of the social state, that its vindication by argument would be superfluous. The maxim which embodies it is sometimes loosely interpreted as forbidding all use by one of his own property, which annoys or disturbs his neighbor in the enjoyment of his property. The real meaning of the rule is that one may not use his own property to the injury of any legal right of another.'" Bove v. Donner–Hanna Coke Corp., 236 App.Div. 37, 258 N.Y.S. 229, 231 (1932) (an excerpt of which appears subsequently in the book). The court goes on to state that this rule is "imperative, or life to-day in our congested centers would be intolerable and unbearable."

6. See 2 American Law of Property § 8.1–8.108 (Casner ed. 1952) (Supp.1977), by the late Professor Oliver S. Rundell on "Easements."

But these broad generalizations do not carry one very far in the solution of specific conflicts. Other guides which sound more specific, even though in fact they may not be, have been evolved for this reason.

(4) The Restatement's Guides to What is "Substantial" Harm

First, it is said that an essential element is proof of substantial harm, or threat of substantial harm, either to the land as such or to its use and enjoyment.

Next, it is said that the court must weigh the gravity of harm to the plaintiff against the utility of the defendant's use. This is elaborated in the Restatement of Torts 2d (1979) as follows:

§ 827.   Gravity of Harm—Factors Involved.

In determining the gravity of harm from an intentional invasion of another's interest in the use and enjoyment of land, the following factors are important:

(a) The extent of the harm involved;

(b) the character of the harm involved;

(c) the *social value* which the law attaches to the type of use or enjoyment invaded;

(d) the *suitability* of the particular use or enjoyment invaded *to the character of the locality;*

(e) the burden on the person harmed of avoiding the harm.

§ 828.   Utility of Conduct—Factors Involved.

In determining the utility of conduct that causes an intentional invasion of another's interest in the use and enjoyment of land, the following factors are important:

(a) the *social value* that the law attaches to the primary purpose of the conduct;

(b) the *suitability* of the conduct *to the character of the locality;* and

(c) the impracticability of preventing or avoiding the invasion. (Emphasis Supplied)

One of the things which you will observe in the nuisance cases which follow in this chapter is the obvious fact that there is no universal standard of "social value" or need. You will also observe that by focusing on the "suitability" of the use for the particular locality judges often find themselves acting something like planning commissions in evaluating facts about the character of the district. (Is there a role for cost-benefit economists and land use planners to play in nuisance actions as expert witnesses?)

Another thing revealed by these cases is that many courts in addition to balancing utility of use against gravity of harm also balance "hardships" or "equities" in determining whether to enjoin the nuisance or just grant judgment for damages.

Further, there is the question of whether nuisance relief should be granted where the plaintiff "came" or "moved" to an activity which was there first. American courts are divided on the point of whether relief should be granted or should be barred on the basis of acquiescence and estoppel. Some courts have held that this defense alone is not sufficient and that there must be other facts present in order to bar the plaintiff. This would seem to be the prevailing view, perhaps based on the idea that otherwise the alleged noxious activity would acquire something in the nature of an easement or servitude over surrounding land. On the other hand, a substantial number of cases have viewed "coming" or "moving" to the nuisance as an absolute defense because of the hardship to the defendant and the fact that the nuisance was self-created by the plaintiff in moving there. A distinction is to be made between a situation in which a plaintiff goes out into an undeveloped area and then sues to abate a noxious activity and a situation in which the noxious activity is gradually approached by the natural outgrowth of the community. The latter is not considered moving to the nuisance. See City of Fort Smith v. Western Hide & Fur Co., infra.

Somewhat related is the question of whether or not a prescriptive right to maintain a private nuisance can be acquired. The argument would be that the prescriptive right attached when the aggrieved land-owner failed to sue within the period of the statute of limitations. The difficulty is in establishing when the statute began to run. No cause of action lies until substantial harm exists or is imminent. Also, some courts state that there is a new cause of action with every day of continuance of the nuisance. Benton v. Kernan, 127 N.J.Eq. 434, 13 A.2d 825 (1940), modified 130 N.J.Eq. 193, 21 A.2d 755 (1941). Other courts call this a permanent nuisance from which the cause of action arises at first occurrence. In that situation, such harmful activity would almost always lead to litigation before the normally long statutory period expired. Consequently, the theoretical ability of a tortfeasor to obtain prescriptive rights to operate a private nuisance is seldom any more than theoretical. Prescriptive rights cannot be obtained in a public nuisance or one designated as a crime under the commonly accepted view.

(5) Nuisance Per Se and Nuisance Per Accidens

Courts have made much of two labels: *"nuisance per se"* and *"nuisance per accidens."* In the first category fall immoral activities, some extrahazardous practices, certain court-declared nuisances and clear violations of valid statutes declaring violations to be nuisances. Certain activities which in the haphazard process of the case law have been over and over again declared nuisances may ultimately be said to be *"nuisances per se."* Thus, as we will see, a funeral parlor in a residential area has been held to be a nuisance so often that today courts are apt to declare it a *nuisance per se* without spending much more time on the case than it takes to pin the label. Proof that a nuisance in fact (*per accidens*) exists takes more doing. Here the plaintiff must convince the court that the facts he has proved with respect to location, harm and other circumstances merit the relief sought. His case must stand on its own facts more or less unaided by precedent.

(6) Motive and Nuisance

A word about motive in nuisance cases is appropriate. Here one thinks immediately of the spite fence cases, where the objectionable use has no utility, is motivated by malice and fails entirely to offset the harm done with social values. The trend today is in the direction of declaring spite fences actionable nuisances. But in some states the legislature has had to intervene to overcome the effects of "absolute property rights" case law.

To the contrary, some courts acted in the late 19th and early 20th centuries to declare it to be an actionable nuisance to erect or maintain spite fences: E.g., Alabama in Norton v. Randolph, 176 Ala. 381, 58 So. 283 (1912); Michigan in Burke v. Smith, 69 Mich. 380, 37 N.W. 838 (1888); North Carolina in Barger v. Barringer, 151 N.C. 433, 66 S.E. 439 (1909); and Oklahoma in Hibbard v. Halliday, 58 Okl. 244, 158 P. 1158 (1916). Cases of this variety established the modern trend. Of course, as is implicit in the definition of a "spite fence," if it does in fact serve a useful purpose, it is legitimate whatever the inconvenience it may cause. See, e.g., De Mers v. Graupner, 186 Ark. 214, 53 S.W.2d 8 (1932). In such a situation, motivation for the fence is immaterial.

(7) Doctrinal Versus Functional Approach to Nuisance Cases

The cases which follow in this chapter give us an opportunity to see nuisance doctrines at work. But the cases have not been arranged along doctrinal lines. Instead we take up through them typical modern day land use conflicts which arise in the open country, on the rural-urban fringe and in older closely settled areas. Mostly we consider areas that are unzoned, although we also devote attention to some problems which arise in zoned areas.

(8) Supplementary References

The foregoing has quite obviously been a rather abbreviated examination of doctrines and problems which pertain to the law of nuisance. To develop a more thorough appreciation of the considerations involved, students should resort to additional textual analysis.[7]

Such a wide variety of uses have been attacked over the years as constituting nuisances that the specific subject-matter involved in the cases can almost be catalogued on an ad hoc basis. This impression is sustained by annotations appearing in the various volumes of the American Law Reports.

---

7. See, e.g., 6A American Law of Property §§ 28.22–.35 (Casner ed. 1954) (Supp. 1977), 5 Powell on Real Property 64–1–66 (Rohan, ed., 1988 Rev.), and Prosser and Keeton, The Law of Torts §§ 86–91 (5th ed. 1984).

With respect to the interplay of nuisance and zoning, an article written in 1955 concluded:

"Widespread use of zoning is liberalizing the application of nuisance doctrine in unzoned areas. Particularly is this true in the open country in or near solidly residential suburbs on the urban fringe and in older residential areas which have maintained their residential integrity. As this process of liberalization continues for unzoned areas, precedents are being built up which may make nuisance doctrine more valuable for the elimination of nonconforming uses in zoned area. Other points of contact in modern cases between nuisance and zoning suggest the need for greater attention to the nuisance-zoning dichotomy."[8]

Along this line, see Ellickson, Alternatives to Zoning: Covenants, Nuisance Rules, and Fines as Land Use Controls, 40 U.Chi.L.Rev. 681 (1973), in which the author argues that nuisance law is a neglected area which could be put to much greater use.

B. CONFLICTING USES IN OPEN COUNTRY

(1) Uses in Conflict With Agricultural, Livestock or Commercial Operations

HULBERT v. CALIFORNIA PORTLAND CEMENT CO.

Supreme Court of California, 1911.
161 Cal. 239, 118 P. 928.

[Capacity of defendant's mill was 3,000 barrels of cement a day, or around 900,000 barrels a year. The trial court's injunction restricted operations to 88,706 barrels per annum. The defendant is here asking the state supreme court to stay the operation of this injunction pending appeal. Limitations of space require the omission of much of the court's discussion of case law precedents, as well as the concurring opinion of Sloss, J.]

Melvin, J. * * * The salient facts shown by the petitioner are that the California Portland Cement Company is engaged in the manufacture of cement on property situated nearly two miles from the center of the city of Colton in the county of San Bernardino, but not within the limits of said city; that said manufactory is located at Slover Mountain, where the substances necessary to the production of Portland cement are quarried; that long before the surrounding country had been generally devoted to the production of citrus fruits, Slover Mountain had been known as a place where limestone was produced; that quarries of marble and limestone had been established there; that lime kilns had been operated upon said mountain for many years; that in 1891 the petitioner obtained title to said premises and commenced thereon the manufacture

8. Beuscher and Morrison, Judicial Zoning Through Recent Nuisance Cases, 1955 Wis.L.Rev. 440, 457. This article provides a helpful analysis with respect to points which might be considered in class.

of Portland cement; that the said corporation has expended upon said property more than eight hundred thousand dollars; that at the time when petitioner began the erection of the cement plant the land surrounding the plant was vacant and unimproved, except some land lying to the north, which had been planted to young citrus trees; that these trees were first planted about a year before the erection of the cement plant was commenced (but long after the lime kilns and the marble quarries had been operated); that subsequently, other orange groves had been planted in the neighborhood; that petitioner's plant on Slover Mountain has a capacity of three thousand barrels of cement per day; but that by the judgment of the superior court in two certain actions against petitioner entitled Lillie A. Hulbert, Administratrix etc. v. California Portland Cement Company, a Corporation, and Spencer E. Gilbert, plaintiff, v. the same defendant, the corporation aforesaid was enjoined from operating its plant in such a manner as to produce an excess of 88,706 barrels of finished cement per annum; that the regular pay-roll of the company includes the names of about five hundred men who are paid about thirty-five thousand dollars a month; that the fixed, constant monthly expenses for supplies and materials amount to thirty-five thousand dollars; that the California Portland Cement Company employs the best, most modern methods in its processes of manufacture, but that nevertheless there is an unavoidable escape into the air of certain dust and smoke; that petitioner has no other location for the conduct of its business at a profit; that the land of the Hulbert estate is located from fifteen hundred to twenty-five hundred feet from petitioner's cement works and that Spencer E. Gilbert's land is all within one thousand feet therefrom; that petitioner has diligently sought some means of preventing the escape of dust from its factories; that it has consulted the best experts and sought the best information obtainable, and that it is now and has been for a long time conducting experiments along the lines suggested by the most eminent engineering authorities upon this subject, and that as soon as any process can be evolved for preventing the escape of the dust, the petitioner will adopt such process in its works, and it is believed that a process now constructing with all diligence by petitioner will effectually prevent the escape of dust. Petitioner also alleges that it is easily possible to estimate the damages of the plaintiffs in money while it is utterly impracticable to estimate the damage in money which will be caused to the petitioner by the closing of the plant, and that stopping the plant pending the appeals will cause financial ruin to the chief stockholders of the petitioner, and that the elements of loss averred are irreparable on account of the disorganization of petitioner's working force, loss of market, and deterioration of machinery.

The learned judge of the superior court in deciding the cases in which petitioner here was defendant, described the method of manufacturing cement and the injury to the trees. He said, in part: "The output from these two mills at the present time is about 2500 barrels of cement every twenty-four hours, and to produce this there is fed into the various kilns of the defendant, during the time mentioned, about one and one-half millions pounds of raw mix, composed of limestone and clay, ground as fine as flour and thoroughly mixed. This raw mix is fed into the tops of kilns, wherein the temperature varies from 1800 to 3000 degrees Fahrenheit, and through which kilns the heated air and combustion gases pass at the rate of many thousands of feet per minute. The result of this almost inconceivable draft is to carry out, in addition to the usual products of combustion, particles of the raw mix, to the extent of probably twenty tons per day or more, the greater part of which, without question, is carried up into the air by the rising gases, and thereafter, through the action of the winds and force of gravity, distributed over the surrounding territory." Speaking of the premises of the plaintiffs he said that because of prevailing westerly winds and on account of the proximity of the mills said lands were almost continually subject to the deposit of dust. In this regard he said: "It is the fact, incontrovertibly established by both the testimony of witnesses and personal inspections made by the court that a well-nigh continuous shower of cement dust, emanating from defendant's cement mills and caused by their operation, is, and for some years past has been, falling upon the properties of the plaintiffs covering and coating the ground, filtering through their homes, into all parts thereof, forming an opaque semi-cemented encrustation upon the upper sides of all exposed flowers and foliage, particularly leaves of citrus trees, and leaving ineradicable, yet withal plainly discernible marks and evidence of dust, dusty deposits, and grayish colorings resulting therefrom, upon the citrus fruits. The encrustations above mentioned, unlike the deposits occasionally occurring on leaves because of the presence of undue amounts of road dust or field dust, are not dissipated by the strongest winds, nor washed off through the action of the most protracted rains. Their presence, from repeated observations, seems to be as continuous as their hold upon the leaves seems tenacious." The court further found that the deposit of dust on the fruit decreased its value; that the constant presence of dust on the limbs and leaves of the trees rendered the cultivation of the ground and the harvesting of the crop more costly than it would have been under ordinary conditions; and that said dust added to the usual and ordinary discomforts of life by its presence in the homes of the plaintiffs. The court also found that the operation of the old mill of the defendant corporation had occurred with the acquiescence of the plaintiffs and that the defendant had acquired a prescriptive right to manufacture the maximum quantity of cement produced annually by that factory.

In view of such facts solemnly found by the court after trial, we cannot say that there is reason for a suspension by this court of the injunction, even conceding that we have power under proper circumstances thus to prevent a disturbance of existing conditions, pending an appeal. We are not insensible to the fact that petitioner's business is a very important enterprise; that its location is peculiarly adapted for the manufacture of cement; and that great loss may result to the corporation by the enforcement of the injunction. Even if the officers of the corporation are willing to furnish a bond in a sum equal to the value of the properties of Gilbert and of the Hulbert estate here involved, we cannot, under plain principles of equity, compel these plaintiffs to have recourse to their action at law only and take from them the benefit of the injunctive relief accorded them by the chancellor below. To permit the cement company to continue its operations even to the extent of destroying the property of the two plaintiffs and requiring payment of the full value thereof would be, in effect, allowing the seizure of private property for a use other than a public one—something unheard of and totally unauthorized in the law. Hennessy v. Carmony, 50 N.J.Eq. 616, 25 A. 374; Sullivan v. Jones & Laughlin Steel Co., 208 Pa. 540, 57 A. 1065, 66 L.R.A. 712. Nor may we say, as petitioner urges us to declare, that cement dust is not a nuisance and therefore that the restraint imposed is illegal, even though this is one of the first cases, if not the very first, of its kind, in which the emission of cement dust from a factory has been enjoined, for we are bound by the findings of the court in this proceeding and may not consider their sufficiency or lack of it until we take up the appeals on their merits. The court has found that the plaintiffs in the actions tried were specially damaged by a nuisance maintained by the cement company. This entitles the plaintiffs not only to damages, but to such relief as the facts warrant, and the chancellor has determined that limiting the production in the manner selected is a proper form of protection to their rights. It is well settled in California that a nuisance which consists in pouring soot or the like upon the property of a neighbor in such manner as to interfere with the comfortable enjoyment of the premises is a private nuisance which may be enjoined or abated, and for which likewise, the persons specially injured may recover pecuniary damages. Code Civ.Proc., sec. 721; Fisher v. Zumwalt, 128 Cal. 493, 61 P. 82; Melvin v. E.B. & A.L. Stone Co., 7 Cal.App. 327, 94 P. 390; Judson v. Los Angeles Sub. Gas Co., 157 Cal. 168, 26 L.R.A., N.S., 183, 106 P. 581. The last-named case was one in which the operation of a gas factory does not constitute a nuisance per se. The manufacture in or near a great city of gas for illuminating and heating is not only legitimate but is very necessary to the comfort of the people. But in this, as in any other sort of lawful business, the person conducting it is subject to the rule *sic utere tuo ut alienum non laedas,* even when operating under municipal permission or under public obligation to furnish a commodity. Terre Haute Gas Co. v. Teel, 20 Ind. 131; Attorney–General v. Gaslight & Coke Co., L.R., 7 Ch.Div. 217; Sullivan v. Royer, 72 Cal. 248, 13 P. 655. Nor will the adoption of the most approved appliances and methods of production justify the continuance of that which, in spite of them, remains a nuisance. Evans v. Reading Chemical & Fertilizing Co., 160 Pa. 209, 28 A. 702; Susquehanna Fertilizer Co. v. Malone, 73 Md. 268, 25 Am.St.Rep. 595, 20 A. 900, 9 L.R.A. 737; Susquehanna Fertilizer Co. v. Spangler, 86 Md. 562, 63 Am.St.Rep. 533, 39 A. 270.

Petitioner contends for the rule that the resulting injuries must be balanced by the court and that where the hardship inflicted upon one party by the granting of an injunction would be very much greater than that which would be suffered by the other party if the nuisance were permitted to continue, injunctive relief should be denied. This doctrine of "the balance of hardship" and the associated rule that "an injunction is not of right but of grace" are the bases of petitioner's argument, and many authorities in support of them have been called to our attention. In petitioner's behalf are cited such cases as Richard's Appeal, 57 Pa.St. 105, 98 Am.Dec. 202, where an injunction which had been sought to restrain defendant from using large quantities of bituminous coal to plaintiff's damage was refused, and the plaintiff was remitted to his action at law, the court saying, among other things: "Whatever of injury may have or shall result to his, the plaintiff's property, from the defendant's works, by reason of a nuisance complained of, is only such as is incident to a lawful business conducted in the ordinary way and by no unusual means. Still there may be injury to the plaintiff, but this of itself may not entitle him to the remedy he seeks. It may not, if ever so clearly established, be a cause in which equity ought to enjoin the defendant in the use of a material necessary to the successful production of an article of such prime necessity as good iron; especially if it be very certain that a greater injury would ensue by enjoining than would result by refusal to enjoin." The same rule was announced in Dilworth's Appeal, 91 Pa.St. 247, a case involving the building of a powder house near plaintiff, and in Huckenstine's Appeal, 70 Pa.St. 102, 10 Am.Rep. 669. Petitioner admits that in the later case of Sullivan v. Jones & Laughlin Steel Co., 208 Pa.St. 540, 57 A. 1065, 66 L.R.A. 712, the supreme court of Pennsylvania reached a different conclusion, but contends that the opinion in that case merely defines the word "grace" as used in Huckenstine's Appeal, the real meaning of the expression "an injunction is a matter of grace" being that a high degree of discretion is exercised by a chancellor in awarding or denying an injunction. An examination of the case, however, shows that the court went very much further than a mere definition of the phrase "of grace." In that case the defendant had erected a large factory for the manufacture of steel on land purchased from one of the plaintiffs, but after many years defendant had commenced the use of "Mesaba" ore, which caused the emission of great quantities of fine dust upon the property of plaintiffs. The supreme court of Pennsylvania in reversing the decree of the lower court dismissing the bill went into the matter of "balancing injuries," and "injunctions of grace" very thoroughly and we may with propriety, I think, quote and adopt some of its language upon these subjects as follows: "It is urged that as an injunction is a matter of grace, and not of right, and more injury would result in awarding than refusing it, it ought not to go out in this case. A chancellor does act as of grace, but that grace sometimes becomes a matter of right to the suitor in its court, and, when it is clear that the law cannot give protection and relief—to which the complainant in equity is admittedly entitled—the chancellor can no more withhold his grace than the law can deny protection and relief, if able to give them. This is too often overlooked when it is said that in equity a decree is of grace, and not of right, as a judgment at law. In Walters v. McElroy et al., 151 Pa.St. 549, 25 A. 125, the defendants gave as one of the reasons why the plaintiff's bill should be dismissed, that his land was worth but little, while they were engaged in a great mining industry which would be paralyzed if they should be enjoined from a continuance of the acts complained of; and the principle was invoked that, as a decree in equity is of grace, a chancellor will never enjoin an act where, by so doing, greater injury will result than from a refusal to enjoin. To this we said: The phrase 'of grace,' predicated of a decree in equity, had its origin in an age when kings dispensed their royal favors by the hands of their chancellors; but although it continues to be repeated occasionally, it has no rightful place in the jurisprudence of a free commonwealth, and ought to be relegated to the age in which it was appropriate. It has been somewhere said that equity has its laws, as law has its equity. This is but another form of saying that equitable remedies are administered in accordance with rules as certain as human wisdom can devise, leaving their application only in doubtful cases to the discretion, not the unmerited favor or grace, of the chancellor. Certainly no chancellor in any English speaking country will at this day admit that he dispenses favors or refuses rightful demands, or deny that, when a suitor has brought his cause clearly within the rules of equity jurisprudence, the relief he asks is demandable *ex debito justitiae,* and needs not to be implored *ex gratia.* And as to the principle involved, that a chancellor will refuse to enjoin when greater injury will result from granting than from refusing an injunction, it is enough to observe that it has no application where the act complained of is in itself, as well as in its incidents tortious. In such case it cannot be said that injury would result from an injunction, for no man can complain that he is injured by being prevented from doing to the hurt of another that which he has no right to do. Nor can it make the slightest difference that the plaintiff's property is of insignificant value to him as compared with the advantages that would accrue to the defendants from its occupation. There can be no balancing of conveniences when such balancing involves the preservation of an established right, though possessed by a peasant only to a cottage as his home, and which will be extinguished if relief is not granted against one who would destroy it in artificially using his own land. Though it is said a chancellor will consider whether he would not do a greater injury by enjoining than would result from refusal and leaving the party to his redress at the hands of a court and jury, and if, in conscience, the former should appear, he will refuse to enjoin. Richard's Appeal, 57 Pa.St. 105, 98 Am.Dec. 202; that 'it often becomes a grave question whether so great an injury would not be done to the community by enjoining the business, that the complaining party should be left to his remedy at law.' Dilworth's Appeal, 91 Pa.St. 247; and similar expressions are to be found in other cases; 'none of them, nor all of them, can be authority for the proposition that equity, a case for its cognizance being otherwise made out, will refuse to protect a man in the possession and enjoyment of his property because that right is less valuable to him than the power to destroy it may be to his neighbor or to the public.' Evans v. Reading Chemical & Fertilizing Co., 160 Pa. 209, 28 A. 702. The right of a man to use and enjoy his property is as supreme as his neighbor's, and no artificial use of it by either can be permitted to destroy that of the other."

* * * We are convinced that upon reason and upon great weight of authority we should deny petitioner's prayer, considering the subject upon the assumption that we have power under the constitution in aid of our appellate jurisdiction in a proper case to suspend the operation of a prohibitory injunction pending an appeal.

Let the temporary order staying the operation of the injunction be dismissed and the petition be denied.

Notes

1. With the California court's refusal to balance hardships, compare §§ 933 and 936 of the Restatement of Torts 2d (1979). Comment (a) to section 933 says:

> The availability of an injunction against a tort * * * depends upon a comparative appraisal of all of the factors in the case. These factors include the relative adequacy to the plaintiff of an injunction and of the other remedies, plaintiff's laches or unclean hands, the relative hardship likely to result to defendant if an injunction should be granted and to plaintiff if it should be denied, the interests of third persons and of the public, and the practicability of framing and enforcing the order or judgment. * * *

And in Comment (c) under § 942 the Restatement says:

> The local community sometimes has a public interest at stake. For example, it will suffer loss of taxes and purchasing power of workers if an industrial plant that has been found to be a nuisance is ordered to be shut down or moved to another location.

For a discussion of the similar provisions of the 1939 Restatement in a nuisance case involving tough "balancing of hardship" problems, see Riter v. Keokuk Electro–Metals Co., 248 Iowa 710, 82 N.W.2d 151 (1957), which essentially embraces the restatement.

2. Other dramatic contests between farmers and country-located industries have involved ore reduction. Some were those involving two great open-air, roast-heap copper smelters in southeastern Tennessee. In Madison v. Ducktown Sulphur, Copper & Iron Co., 113 Tenn. 331, 83 S.W. 658 (1904), the court refused to enjoin "a great and increasing industry" with resulting heavy losses in employment, payrolls, taxes and local business. The court denied injunctive relief to farmers against the devastating effect on crops and other vegetation of sulphurous gases, pointing out that the defendants had spent $200,000 on ineffective experiments to reduce the nuisance. The farmers were relegated to their remedy for damages. Later, the State of Georgia sued on behalf of numerous Georgia landowners whose forests, crops and orchards were being destroyed by the fumes in five Georgia counties. The United States Supreme Court granted an injunction, saying, "It [Georgia] is not lightly to be required to give up quasi-sovereign rights for pay," and "this court has not quite the same freedom to balance the harm that will be done by an injunction against that of which the plaintiff

complains, that it would have in deciding between two subjects of a single political power." Georgia v. Tennessee Copper Co., 206 U.S. 230, 237–38, 27 S.Ct. 618, 619, 51 L.Ed. 1038 (1907). Experiments were conducted which led to new production processes and a substantial reduction of harmful fumes. See Georgia v. Tennessee Copper Co., 237 U.S. 474, 35 S.Ct. 631, 59 L.Ed. 1054 (1915), 240 U.S. 650, 36 S.Ct. 465, 60 L.Ed. 846 (1916), and 1 Haynes, American Chemical Industry, A History 263 (1954).

In several cases embattled farmers, at great expense and without marked success, sued ore reduction works claiming damage to cows and other farm animals due to ingestion of fluoride dusts which were carried from defendants' chimneys through the atmosphere and deposited on grass and other vegetation on plaintiffs' farms. See Arvidson v. Reynolds Metals Co., 125 F.Supp. 481 (W.D.Wash.1954), affirmed 236 F.2d 224 (9th Cir.1956), certiorari denied 352 U.S. 968, 77 S.Ct. 359, 1 L.Ed.2d 323 (1957), and Erekson v. United States Steel Corp., 260 F.2d 423 (10th Cir.1958). But see Reynolds Metals Co. v. Yturbide, 258 F.2d 321 (9th Cir.1958), where the attorney for the farmers successfully argued res ipsa loquitur from the law of negligence.

In the Arvidson case, supra, the federal district court said at pages 483, 486 and 488:

> Plaintiffs had the burden of establishing by a preponderance of the evidence that the market value of their farms was depreciated and/or that the physical condition and milk producing capacity of their cattle were damaged by fluorides emanating from defendants' plants. * * *

> [After summarizing the testimony of experts called by the company the court concluded:] I have reached the following basic conclusions on the factual issues of the case: Plaintiffs have not sustained the burden of producing a preponderance of credible evidence to establish (a) fluorine content in the forage on their lands in amounts above nontoxic limits; (b) substantial fluorine content in forage attributable to effluence from defendants' plants; or (c) that plaintiffs' lands or cattle sustained fluorine damages in particulars and amounts that can be determined with reasonable or any certainty.

> * * * The court is fully satisfied that the utility of defendants' plant operations and their importance to the economy and security of the nation far outweigh any injury to plaintiffs shown by the evidence. Consequently, neither a finding of nuisance nor granting of relief based thereon is justified. * * *

Almost four years after the district judge's decision, it was reported in The Washington Farmer:

> Cowlitz county dairymen have been retreating from the vicinity of Longview and Kelso ever since widespread fluorosis was diagnosed * * * in the mid–1940's.

> Five dairy farms remain within six miles of the factory complex, embracing an aluminum smelter and a pulp mill, just south of Longview. Not long ago there were about 2000 cows. There may be 100 cows left. * * *

Qualified observers say that what is happening and has happened in Cowlitz county is contributing to implications of vast importance to agriculture in Washington, when coexistence with industry becomes a problem in the future.[9]

In the case of Erekson v. United States Steel Corp., 260 F.2d 423 (10th Cir.1958), the farmers were required to attempt to prove their claims "cow by cow" and "sheep by sheep." There was no jury because plaintiffs had started out asking for an injunction and had shifted to damage claims later. Was this good strategy? Also, would it have sufficed in both the Arvidson and the Erekson cases if the plaintiffs had merely proven that even though scientists contended there were not enough fluorides to harm cattle, nevertheless prospective purchasers of farm lands *thought there were* and consequently the marketability of the farms and the values of the farm lands were greatly diminished. Which controls, the common man's assumption or the scientist's knowledge? See Everett v. Paschall, 61 Wash. 47, 111 P. 879 (1910) and Ferry v. City of Seattle, 116 Wash. 648, 200 P. 336 (1921), reversed 116 Wash. 648, 203 P. 40 (1922).

These ore reduction cases involved great expense. Thus, in the Erekson case, supra, an action that involved 300 claims of livestock owners, there were 260 witnesses, 6,622 pages of testimony, 1,267 exhibits, 100,000 chemical analyses of vegetation for fluorine, diagnoses for about 12,000 cattle and thousands of sheep. Counsel presented a special referee with brochures "summarizing" the evidence in 10,000 pages and the referee's report to the court was 347 pages long!

On liability for escaping gases or pollutants generally, see Annot., 54 A.L.R.2d 764 (1957) and 2 A.L.R.4th 1054 (1980).

3. The principal case and the ore reduction cases raise the question of how the offending plant can acquire "control" over the wide area adversely affected by its dust, particulates or gases? From the point of view of the company, which is the best approach?:

a. Operate the plant for a sufficient length of time to acquire a prescriptive right over the neighboring land?

b. Wait until there is trouble and then, as a condition of settlement of damage claims, take grants of "easements" or other rights to deposit dust?

c. Simply expect to be sued repeatedly by the same landowners and to pay judgments assessed for damages, as "rent" for the use of the land? From the point of view of the damaged landowners, is this in practical effect eminent domain for a private purpose?

d. Wait until a damage or injunction judgment has been obtained, appeal, and then work out a purchase and leaseback deal or an easement or covenant deal?

---

9. "Farm Retreat from Industry," The Washington Farmer 5 (June 19, 1958). See also a carefully prepared study finding "excessive fluorides in some areas" and recommending that agricultural enterprises less sensitive to fluorides than dairying be considered. Adams, Miller and Allmendinger, Air Pollution in Cowlitz County 6 (Wash. Ag.Exp.Sta.Circ. 352, Dec. 1959).

e. Purchase a large area around the plant before operations are begun and then lease or sell with protective covenants the land not needed for production?

4. Of course, many of these older cases might never have come about or might have taken a different turn if the situation had arisen during the 1970's or 1980's after the passage of modern air and water pollution statutes. Agency enforcement of pollution control laws provides a possible alternative on at least some occasions to expensive litigation by private landowners—except, of course, for damages already inflicted.

5. In Board of Health of Wayne Township v. Paterson Tallow Co., 1 N.J.Super. 397, 65 A.2d 112 (1948) the Board of Health sought an injunction to restrain the operation of the fat rendering plants on the ground that the odors emanating therefrom constituted a nuisance hazardous to the public health. After describing the company's efforts to deal with the odors, the court concluded:

> [T]he proofs do not clearly and convincingly establish that the defendant Paterson Tallow Company's plant is now being operated as a nuisance hazardous to the public health. The weight of the testimony indicates that although the plant is, with wholly apparent cause, undesirable from the neighbors' viewpoint, its present operation is not, in any real sense, a public health hazard. The installation of the plant's new equipment represents a bona fide attempt to increase the plant's odor control and undoubtedly beneficial results have resulted. Further plant improvements are being made and the company would be well advised not only to continue them, but also to increase their scope to the end that all basis for any complaints whatever by neighbors is effectively removed.

Odiferous industrial plants in the open country continue to plague the courts, raising the question whether there is any longer a place for stenchful industry to "hide." A rendering plant in rural rolling farming country was declared a nuisance, but the offender was given a chance to improve conditions by the installation of condensers. Greaser v. Robinson, 54 Montg. 347 (Pa.1938). In Utah, a rendering plant in a rural area was declared a nuisance, damages were given, but an injunction was denied because the embattled neighbors were so late in suing. Ludlow v. Colorado Animal By–Products Co., 104 Utah 221, 137 P.2d 347 (1943). But in Demont v. Abbas, 149 Neb. 765, 32 N.W.2d 737 (1948), the Nebraska court refused to anticipate that the building and operating of a rendering plant in a farming area would necessarily be a nuisance.

McCAW v. HARRISON

Court of Appeals of Kentucky, 1953.
259 S.W.2d 457.

DUNCAN, JUSTICE. Appellants, who own and operate a dairy farm on land located on each side of the Fayette and Jessamine county line, sought by this action to enjoin appellees from using their adjoining boundary for commercial cemetery purposes. The appeal is from a judgment which denies this relief. The question presented is largely one of fact, the determination of which requires a review of some rather morbid details referred to in the evidence.

Appellants' well, which is the main source of water for stock and family purposes, is located some five hundred feet from the property line of the proposed cemetery. The area embraced by the cemetery site and appellants' land is underlaid with cavernous limestone which contains sinkholes, crevices, channels, and fissures. The overburden of soil is shallow as indicated by rock-sounding maps filed by appellees. Therefore, the burial of bodies will necessarily be on or very close to the underlying rock.

For the appellants, the testimony of an eminent geologist, pathologist, an embalmer, and a cemetery manager indicates some possibility of contamination of the wells and springs in that area. These witnesses, each testifying as to facts within his particular field, describe the process of contamination as follows: (1) harmful disease germs and bacteria are present at death; (2) these organisms survive the embalming process because of the low pressures used to preserve as near as can be, the lifelike appearance of bodies; (3) the water in the area involved will reach these decaying and putrefied bodies because of the shallow overburden of soil and because of the manner of modern day burials; and (4) that the fissures, crevices, channels, and sinkholes in the underlying cavernous limestone will act as a channel and stream for the water carrying these harmful organisms into wells and springs in the area. These witnesses express the view that the contamination resulting from the disease germs and bacteria from the dead human bodies is a definite hazard to appellants' health.

On the other hand, a civil engineer, specializing in sanitary engineering, and a bacteriologist, who has for more than twenty-six years been a professor of bacteriology at the University of Kentucky, testifying for appellees, express the opinion that no contamination of appellants' water supply will result from the proposed use. These witnesses say that the combined factors of the virtual disinfection of the body by embalming, plus the barriers of the casket and vault, make it virtually impossible for the harmful organisms to get into the soil; that even should they reach the soil, they cannot travel a greater distance than fifty feet, which distance is usually considered as affording complete protection to wells and springs from contamination of decaying bodies.

A cemetery does not constitute a nuisance merely because it is a constant reminder of death and has a depressing influence on the minds of persons who observe it, or because it tends to depreciate the value of property in the neighborhood, or is offensive to the aesthetic sense of an adjoining proprietor. 10 Am.Jur., pages 498–499, section 16, Cemeteries. On the other hand, if the location or maintenance of a cemetery endangers the public health, either by corrupting the surrounding atmosphere, or water of wells or springs, it constitutes a nuisance. Nelson v. Swedish E.L. Cemetery Ass'n, 111 Minn. 149, 126 N.W. 723, 127 N.W. 626, 34 L.R.A.N.S., 565; McDaniel v. Forrest Park Cemetery Co., 156 Ark. 571, 246 S.W. 874; Sutton v. Findlay Cemetery Ass'n, 270 Ill. 11, 110 N.E. 315, L.R.A.1916B,1135; Hite v. Cashmere Cemetery Ass'n, 158 Wash. 421, 290 P. 1008.

The parties are in practical agreement concerning the legal principles which control the disposition of this appeal. Their disagreement concerns the question of whether or not the evidence is sufficient to indicate that the maintenance of this cemetery will sufficiently endanger the health of appellants and others so as to bring it within the rule which we have stated.

It hardly needs citation of authority to support the proposition that where the evidence is conflicting and the mind of the reviewing court has no more than a doubt concerning the finding of a Chancellor on a question of fact, the finding will not be disturbed. The evidence in this case deals with a highly technical subject, and although conflicting, does not preponderate greatly in favor of either side. We do not have such a clear conviction of error in the finding of the Chancellor as would justify a reversal.

The contention of appellants that a further hazard to the safety of the residents of the area will be created by possible traffic congestion resulting from slow-moving funeral processions is hardly worthy of note. Funeral processions are an inevitable incident of cemeteries regardless of their location, and to some extent always present a traffic problem. Without reviewing the evidence on this feature of the case, it is sufficient to say that we are not impressed with the argument that the maintenance of the cemetery should be enjoined because of the probability of traffic congestion and possibility of resulting accidents.

For the reasons indicated, the judgment of the lower court is affirmed.

Notes

1.   Cemetery use, whether in the open country or closer in, is not likely to be enjoined as a nuisance. See Jones v. Highland Memorial Park, 242 S.W.2d 250 (Tex.Civ.App.1951); cases cited in Annot., 87 A.L.R. 760 (1933), 50 A.L.R.2d 1324 (1956), and 14 Am.Jur.2d §§ 12–13 (1964). A comparison of the cemetery cases, where the complainant often loses, with the funeral parlor cases where the complainant who lives in a residential district always wins, is a fit subject for investigation by the social psychologist.

2.   What about obstructions into roads or navigable streams? It has been stated that "an obstruction placed anywhere within the street limits, even though not on the part of the street ordinarily used for travel, or placed in the air over a street, may constitute a nuisance." Sloan v. City of Greenville, 235 S.C. 277, 111 S.E.2d 573 (1959), and see Annot., 76 A.L.R.2d 896, 898 (1961). In Captain Soma Boat Line, Inc. v. City of Wisconsin Dells, 79 Wis.2d 10, 255 N.W.2d 441 (1977), a tour boat operation sued the city for overhead obstruction of a stream which ran into the Wisconsin River. It was alleged that a street bridge obstructed it at that point in violation of the Northwest Ordinance of 1787, the Wisconsin Constitution, common law, and a state statute declaring obstructions of navigable waters to be public nuisances. The boat line operator lost because, with knowledge of the situation, he had purchased some larger boats. The bridge was not an

obstruction to the boats up until then, and the court thought it unreasonable to tear down a public bridge for the benefit of this one entrepreneur.

(2) Uses in Conflict With Rural Residential Use

STATE EX REL. CUNNINGHAM v. FEEZELL

Supreme Court of Tennessee, 1966.
218 Tenn. 17, 400 S.W.2d 716.

[Twenty-six individuals brought suit in the name of the State to enjoin the Defendant from establishing a crematory in a "rural or rural residential" area. The Petitioners alleged that the proposed crematory would constitute a public or private nuisance. Defendant proposed to carry out his operation in a small building which had been converted from a garage and which had a large, protruding smokestack. The petition emphasized the mental anguish of people in the area at the thought that defendant would be burning "dead human bodies." It was alleged that this would "deprive the property owners of the quiet use and enjoyment of their property and endanger their lives and health either by actually rendering them sick mentally and/or physically." It was also contended that the ambulances on these narrow roads would create traffic hazards; that school children and churchgoers would be adversely affected; that dead bodies would have to be stored in the area due to the inadequacy of Defendant's operations; and that there would be pollution resulting from noxious odors, smells, and the emission of vapors. They alleged that no other such establishment was permitted in Tennessee. Defendant's demurrer was sustained by the trial court.]

WHITE, JUSTICE.

* * *

The question presented for determination by the Court is essentially this: Does a cause of action exist to enjoin, as a nuisance, a proposed cremation establishment in a rural or rural residential area under averments of the residents of the area that it will cause mental anguish, depressed feelings, physical discomfort and lower property values? We do not think so.

We believe that for an injunction suit to be sustained prior to the alleged nuisance coming into being, it must be sufficiently shown in the original bill or petition that the proposed establishment is a nuisance *per se;* that is, within itself.

"A nuisance at law or a nuisance per se is an act, occupation, or structure which is a nuisance at all times and under any circumstances, *regardless of location or surroundings.* Nuisances in fact or per accidens are those which become nuisances by reason of circumstances and surroundings and an act may be found to be a nuisance as a matter of fact where the natural tendency of the act is to create danger or inflict injury on person or property. 66 C.J.S. Nuisances § 3 (1950). (Emphasis supplied.)

"Other definitions are: any act or omission or use of property or thing which is of itself hurtful to the health, tranquility, or morals, or which outrages the decency of the community; that which *cannot* be so *conducted* or *maintained* as to be *lawfully carried on* or *permitted* to *exist;* and, as related to private persons, an act or use of property of a continuing nature, offensive to and legally injurious to health and property, or both. 39 Am.Jur., Nuisances, § 11 (1942)." (Emphasis supplied.)

It is perhaps misleading to define a nuisance per se as one which exists "at all times and under any circumstances, regardless of location or surroundings." Actually, a nuisance cannot exist without surrounding circumstances, because it is the surrounding circumstances that determine whether an injury is occasioned; and it is axiomatic that some injury must be occasioned or be at least imminent because of the alleged "nuisance."

There is, in at least one case in this State, an indication that the difference between a nuisance per se, and a nuisance per accidens is that in the former, injury in some form is certain to be inflicted, while in the latter, the injury is uncertain or contingent until it actually occurs. Pearce v. Gibson County, 107 Tenn. 224, 64 S.W. 33, 55 L.R.A. 477 (1901). This case held that where injury from a nuisance is not real and immediate and certain to occur, but only uncertain or contingent, the nuisance will not be enjoined anticipatory to its going into operation. C.J.S. indicates agreement with this case:

A *mere possibility* or *fear* of *future injury* from a structure, instrumentality, or business which is *not* a nuisance *per se* is not ground for injunction, and equity will not interfere where the apprehended injury is doubtful or speculative; reasonable probability, or even reasonable certainty, of injury, or a showing that there will necessarily be a nuisance, is required. 66 C.J.S., Nuisances § 113 (1950). (Emphasis supplied.)

Another Tennessee case sets forth the rule more generally: Injunctions will not issue "merely to relieve the fears or apprehensions of an applicant." Nashville, C. & St. L.R. v. Railroad & Public Utilities Comm., 161 Tenn. 592, 32 S.W.2d 1043 (1930). In Central Drug Store v. Adams, 184 Tenn. 541, 201 S.W.2d 682 (1947), it was said that

* * * [w]here a business is not a nuisance in and of itself, a court of equity will not anticipate that it will be operated injuriously to others and award an injunction to abate it. 184 Tenn. at 549, 201 S.W.2d at 685.

We do not say that an anticipatory nuisance is not enjoinable under any circumstances. If the injury anticipated is imminent and certain to occur, there may, in fact, be a proper case for immediate abatement, provided, of course the injury is recognized as otherwise actionable at law and equity. We do not say that mental disturbances or "psychic" injuries caused by a nuisance, public or private, are not such as may be actionable at law or equity. They can, in fact, be very real to the complainants. We do say, however, that allegations in the petition must be sufficient, in defining the circumstances and mode of operation surrounding the undertaking, to persuade the court, if they are proved, that injury is imminent and certain. We are convinced that proof of the alleged location of defendant's crematory and the alleged mode of operation and physical appearance of the same will be insufficient to foretell certain injury.

Our research has uncovered no case involving the attempted abatement of a human cremation establishment. Possibly the closest analogy would be the operation of a funeral parlor—at least as regards "psychic" injuries and lowered property values. In a zoning case, Qualls v. City of Memphis, 15 Tenn.App. 575 (1932), it was held alternatively that even though a funeral parlor was not a nuisance per se, it could become so with certain facts and circumstances present such as residences nearby, location on a narrow street, and a small lot. The case obviously involves an urban or suburban location, which is not an allegation in the instant case.

* * *

As regards funeral parlors or undertaking establishments, the majority rule in this country, according to an annotation in 39 A.L.R.2d 1000 (1955), is

> " * * * that if an undertaking establishment in a purely residential section causes from its normal operations, depressing feelings to families in the immediate neighborhood, and, as a constant reminder of death, appreciably impairs their happiness or weakens their powers of resistance and depreciates the values of their properties, such an establishment constitutes a nuisance."

In the cases that have ruled on this point of equity, the circumstances surrounding the so-called "nuisance" and the anticipated injuries alleged have not followed any exclusive pattern, so some of them merit closer examination. It will be noted that most of these cases rule on the basis of a *proposed* undertaking establishment; the injuries complained of are what *would* occur *if* the business is allowed to begin. * * *

We consider two cases which appear to follow the majority rule, but which apply a certain flexibility to the problem. In May v. Upton, 233 Miss. 447, 102 So.2d 339 (1958), it was stated that in an area "essentially" residential, a proposed funeral home should be enjoined as a nuisance but *each case turns on its own facts,* and where an examination of the circumstances, from the evidence presented, indicates otherwise, an injunction should not issue; in this case the funeral home was to be put on the boundary of residential and commercial areas and was *not* enjoined.

In Jack v. Torrant, 136 Conn. 414, 71 A.2d 705 (1950), it was the opinion of the court that certain factors regarding the residences in the area should be examined; their extent, kind and location. It is also indicated, as other cases indicate, that the depressed feelings and discomfort must be those that ordinary people sustain in living near an undertaking establishment.

Our holding in the instant case does not, perhaps, coincide precisely with some of the cases following the majority rule. We are not, however, in disagreement with what we think are two of the better reasoned cases aforementioned, i.e., May v. Upton, supra, and Jack v. Torrant, supra. Nevertheless, we are limited in the instant case to an examination of those factors alleged in the petition, proof of which would not indicate certain injury, either emotional or physical, to petitioners. Residences in a rural area are sparsely situated and there is no allegation in the bill that any residence is in close proximity to the proposed crematory, but that it is to be located in "an entirely rural area."

There is, of course, a minority rule, the gist of which is that mental suffering or depressed feelings are not actionable injuries where funeral parlors are proposed for residential areas. Stoddard v. Snodgrass, 117 Or. 262, 241 P. 73, 43 A.L.R. 1160 (1925), is a good example of this line of cases. In Dawson v. Laufersweiler, 241 Iowa 850, 43 N.W.2d 726 (1950), the court indicated, in dictum, that no injunction would issue in a strictly residential area; however, the case actually turned on the fact that the neighborhood was "in transition" from a residential to a commercial area. Bauman v. Piser Undertakers Co., 34 Ill.App.2d 145, 180 N.E.2d 705 (1962), apparently follows the minority rule, except that here the section of the street on which a mortuary was to be built was zoned for it, but the total area surrounding the site was predominantly residential.

* * *

Because we find the allegations in the petition insufficient, even if proved, to persuade us that a nuisance is sure to be created by the operation of a crematory in this particular location, we therefore, affirm the ruling of the trial court as set forth in a splendid memorandum opinion.

Affirmed.

Note

This case should be compared with the funeral home cases which appear later in the book, as well as with cases involving cemeteries. It has been suggested that these cases present an interesting study in the manner in which psychological reactions produce socio-economic situations which in turn affect the law. The statements of the Tennessee Court in State ex rel. Cunningham v. Feezell are illuminating in this regard. While the Court cites previous Tennessee case law for the proposition that injunctions will not issue for the purpose of calming the fears or apprehensions of the plaintiffs, the Court seems to concede that "mental disturbances or 'psychic' injuries caused by a nuisance" may produce a cause of action assuming (citing Jack v. Torrant, 136 Conn. 414, 71 A.2d 705 (1950)) "the depressed feelings and discomfort" are "those that ordinary people sustain." Would "ordinary people" be depressed or discomforted by the sight of an automobile junkyard extending for hundreds of yards along a major highway on the edge of a metropolitan area? Would "ordinary people" be adversely affected by unsightly conditions in residential areas or by urban blight or similar situations? Compare this line of thinking with case law relating to aesthetic zoning later in the book.

Is the problem of the funeral home and the crematory and similar establishments one that can be distinguished on the basis that certain controls, whether based on judge-made law or equitable principles or the police power, are justified where aesthetics (a sissy, snobbish notion?) blends into fear (which, though unreasonable, becomes reasonable if widely shared)? In the case of a junkyard, a guy (alive, with cigar) is just trying to make a buck; but no one likes death or taxes, and if Uncle Harry dies, plant him quick.

LEE v. BOWLES

Texas Court of Civil Appeals, 1965.
397 S.W.2d 923.

[Lee sought to enjoin Bowles and Pan American Speedway from establishing and operating an automobile race track and drag strip near his residence in a predominantly rural area, a few miles north of San Antonio. The lower court enjoined the operation of the drag strip but allowed the proposed race track. The trial court did this despite a jury finding that the race track alone constituted a nuisance because it found that the equities favored the race track operators and the community. Lee, the appellant, argued that the doctrine of balancing the equities would not apply and that both activities should be enjoined. Appellant owned a $100,000 home (bought in 1962) in a largely rural area with a few residences. Appellant acted promptly relative to preventing the race track, although by that time the appellees had expended or become obligated for over $100,000. Little construction had commenced, however, and appellees did not try to limit their obligations. The track was to be located 2,800 feet from appellant's home. There was traffic on a nearby road and highway and occasional nearby flights from Randolph Air Force Base, but appellant argued that the traffic would greatly increase and stated that the flights were too infrequent to bother him. There was expert testimony for appellant that the average noise level from the racers would double the average highway traffic noise level, that ordinary conversation could not be accomplished at more than one to four feet on appellant's patio during the races, that sleep would be difficult, and that traffic congestion would result.]

WHITE, JUSTICE

* * *

Appellant urges the doctrine of balancing the equities should not be applied in this case, as appellees did not show a public necessity for the race track, but rather a purpose of private profit. The track was planned in an unzoned area and the proposed operation was a lawful business. The case therefore involves the conflicting rights of two lawful owners.

The courts have consistently recognized that the abatement of a lawful place of business is a harsh remedy. The trial court properly heard evidence on the question of balancing the equities to determine if an injunction should be granted. Hindman v. Texas Lime Co., 157 Tex. 592, 305 S.W.2d 947 (1957), affirming Tex.Civ.App., 300 S.W.2d 112; Storey v. Central Hide & Rendering Co., 148 Tex. 509, 226 S.W.2d 615 (1950); Garland Grain Co. v. D–C Home Owners Improvement Ass'n., Tex.Civ. App., 393 S.W.2d 635, wr. ref., n.r.e.; Hill v. Villarreal, Tex.Civ.App., 383 S.W.2d 463, wr. ref. n.r.e.; Georg v. Animal Defense League, Tex.Civ. App., 231 S.W.2d 807, wr. ref. n.r.e.

Thirteen witnesses, including three State Representatives from Bex- ar County, the Sheriff of Bexar County, a San Antonio hotel manager, and a professional sports writer, testified that the proposed race track would be an asset and beneficial to San Antonio and Bexar County. There was evidence that automobile racing is the second most popular sport in the United States from the standpoint of number of paid spectators, and is gaining in popularity; that this track would help the economy of the area and stimulate tourist trade; that there were suffi- cient people in Bexar County interested in this sport to support a race track. Several residents in the immediate vicinity of the track testified it would stimulate growth in their area. A realtor testified appellees' land was suitable for a race track and that this was the highest and best use of this land. There was evidence that there was no other location in Bexar County that would not be within one-half mile of a residence and subject to the same objections raised by appellant.

Appellee Bowles testified the track would be operated in a manner so as to interfere as little as possible with appellant's home life. He said the track season would be five months, from May to late September and would operate primarily on Saturday nights, with the racing program ending by 10:00 p.m. He promised that Toepperwein Road would be paved before the track opened and the track parking lot would be paved if excessive dust was created. Officers would be hired to handle traffic congestion and the entire area would be kept free of debris.

The evidence showed that appellant's swimming pool and patio are on the opposite side of his house from the track site, and that the prevailing wind during the track season would blow from the residence toward the track. The noise level would be greatly diminished inside appellant's home.

* * *

Appellant urges that the doctrine of balancing the equities should be applied only where a public necessity is shown. In Storey v. Central Hide & Rendering Co., supra, the Court required a balancing of equities and quoted with approval 31 Tex.Jur. 448, which reads in part as follows: "According to the doctrine of 'comparative injury' or 'balancing of equities' the court will consider the injury which may result to the defendant and the public by granting the injunction as well as the injury to be sustained by the complainant if the writ be denied. If the court finds that the injury to the complainant is slight in comparison to the injury caused the defendant and the public by enjoining the nuisance, relief will ordinarily be refused. It has been pointed out that the cases in which a nuisance is permitted to exist under this doctrine are based on the stern rule of necessity rather than on the right of the author of the nuisance to work a hurt, or injury to his neighbor. The necessity of others may compel the injured party to seek relief by way of an action at law for damages rather than by a suit in equity to abate the nuisance."

In Storey the Supreme Court affirmed the action of the Court of Civil Appeals in reversing the trial court's action in permanently enjoining the operation of a rendering plant. This Court recently affirmed a trial court's balancing of the equities in favor of operation of a rendering plant. See Hill v. Villarreal, supra. The doctrine of balancing of the equities has been applied in other cases in which the public necessity has not been as dramatically shown and where private proprietary interests were involved. Hindman v. Texas Lime Co., supra, involved a plant manufacturing lime products; Georg v. Animal Defense League involved an animal shelter for stray dogs. In Lamb v. Kinslow, Tex.Civ.App., 256 S.W.2d 903, the rule was applied, but the trial court found that the equities were against the burning of cotton burrs by the gin. Fargason v. Economy Furniture, Inc., Tex.Civ.App., 356 S.W.2d 212, balanced the equities in favor of operation of a furniture plant; and in Garland Grain Co. v. D–C Home Owners Improvement Association, supra, the Court of Civil Appeals balanced the equities in favor of operation of a feed lot.

The evidence in this case justified a finding by the trial court that the public generally would benefit from the operation of this track, both from a standpoint of recreational value and as an economic asset. Further, there was no showing that the proposed location was unsuitable.

Appellant cites several out-of-state authorities involving race tracks. Sakler v. Huls, Ohio Com.Pl., 183 N.E.2d 152, and Shew v. Deremer, 203 N.E.2d 863, are opinions of Ohio trial courts wherein the trial court granted the injunctions against a race track. They therefore are not applicable in our case, where the chancellor has balanced the equities in favor of operation of the race track. In Kohr v. Weber, 402 Pa. 63, 166 A.2d 871 (1960), the trial court enjoined operation of a drag strip and the Supreme Court affirmed. In Hooks v. Inter. Speedways, Inc. (1965), 263 N.C. 686, 140 S.E.2d 387 the Court held that church officials alleged a cause of action to enjoin construction of a race track close to the eighty-year-old church, where evidence showed that church services would be disturbed. The only case cited by appellant wherein the chancellor's decision was reversed is Guarina v. Bogart, 407 Pa. 307, 180 A.2d 557, 93 A.L.R.2d 1165 (1962), where a drive-in theatre used public loud speakers in lieu of individual car speakers which could have been installed at a small cost. The Supreme Court reversed the case and, although not shutting down the theatre, required it to install car speakers.

Appellant urges that an abuse of discretion is shown in that the trial court enjoined appellees' operation of a drag strip, while refusing to enjoin a race track. It is seen, however, that appellee Bowles and his attorneys stated in open court that appellees had abandoned their intention to construct a drag strip and were willing to be enjoined from constructing same.

The balancing of equities was an issue to be determined by the chancellor in accordance with established equitable rules and principles. Hill v. Villarreal, supra. We have reviewed the record in this case and cannot say that the trial court abused its discretion in refusing to enjoin the proposed operation of the oval race track.

* * *

The judgment is affirmed.

Notes

1. On "balancing the equities," compare this case with the Spur Industries case reproduced in a later subsection, and consider (a) whether and the extent to which, if any, the Texas concept differs from the Arizona approach; and (b) whether it mattered that in Spur, the Arizona Court was dealing with the conflict between a rapidly developing residential development (even though somewhat out in the country) and a rural livestock operation, whereas the Texas Court of Civil Appeals was involved with the conflict between limited, though expensive rural housing and a commercial enterprise which was viewed as an "asset" by the local, political power structure. To add to the foregoing: (a) how much did it matter that the area involved in the Spur Industries case was developing into a residential area while the area near the Texas race track was largely rural with only scattered expensive homes; and (b) further, to what extent are the "equities" balanced differently when a major commercial interest, with widespread community support, runs head on into a single landowner with a nice home, (or even widely scattered landowners), or a livestock operation?

2. In all of these cases, students should follow the type of evidence introduced by the parties. Noise, dust, odors, smells, vapors, lights, traffic congestion, interruption of privacy and outdoor use, inability to sleep, impairment of health, diminution of property values, mental stress—these and similar elements are those which form the basis and the proof for nuisance allegations.

3. And, of course, in all of this, we must consider the problem of the race track, the crematory, the quarry, and other industrial or potentially objectionable commercial operations. The owners know they must go to the country or at least out on the fringe of the urban area, but the farther out they go, the more undesirable may be the location. The quarry may be limited by the location of the necessary raw materials; the race track cannot be so far out that it deters customers by the mileage involved; and the crematory (taking into account the fact that the Tennessee operation was quite primitive) cannot be too far away from its customers either. The conflict with individuals who purchase a few acres and build an expensive home designed for "country" living is not unusual.

4. Neither motorcycle nor automobile racing is normally regarded as amounting to a nuisance per se, and to obtain an injunction for an anticipated nuisance, one must establish to the court's satisfaction that it is apparent that a nuisance in fact will result. See, generally, Lykins v. Dayton Motorcycle Club, Inc., 33 Ohio App.2d 269, 294 N.E.2d 227 (1972), and Hooks v. International Speedways, Inc., 263 N.C. 686, 140 S.E.2d 387 (1965).

5. Compare Lee v. Bowles with the Indiana case that follows.

FRIENDSHIP FARMS CAMPS, INC. v. PARSON

Appellate Court of Indiana, First District, 1977.
172 Ind.App. 73, 359 N.E.2d 280.

ROBERTSON, CHIEF JUDGE.

Defendants-appellants Friendship Farms Camps, Inc. (Friendship) is appealing the awarding of damages to each of the plaintiffs-appellees, Parsons and Combs, as well as the trial court's granting of an injunction designed to abate a nuisance.

* * *

The record shows that Ronald Gabbard, his wife, and parents orally leased their 80 acres of rural property to Friendship Farms Camps, Inc. for use as a campground. Friendship Farms Camps, Inc. was organized and incorporated by Ronald Gabbard, his wife, and another primarily for the purpose of providing camping facilities on the Gabbard property.

Prior to 1972, youth day camps were held on the property, but beginning in 1972, a number of weekly high school marching band camps were held. The bands would arrive on Sunday afternoon and stay until Friday evening during which time they would practice both marching and playing music. During 1973 and 1974, the band camps use increased, and Friendship proposed to extend the 1975 program to include weekend band camps during football season.

The Parsons and the Combs, whose residences were located across the road from Friendship, brought an action against Friendship to abate an alleged nuisance and for damages. The essence of their testimony at trial was that during the summer months loud band music and electronically amplified voices could be heard from 7:00 or 8:00 A.M. until 9:00 or 10:00 P.M. which interfered with their sleep and use of their property during the evening hours. They had complained to Gabbard and asked that the band music be confined to an earlier hour. Gabbard made an effort to enforce quiet hours. However, the evening noise continued for the reason that the cooler period of the day was better for practice time.

The trial court awarded Parsons and Combs $600 each in damages and permanently enjoined Friendship from permitting music or the use of bull horns on its property between 5:00 P.M. and 8:00 A.M. on weekdays and any time during weekends.

* * *

Friendship's contention that actual physical sickness or illness must result before a nuisance may be found is without merit. This court has repeatedly stated that the essence of a private nuisance is the fact that one party is using his property to the detriment of the use and enjoyment of others. Stover v. Fechtman (1966), 140 Ind.App. 62, 222 N.E.2d 281; Cox v. Schlachter, supra. While injury to health is a factor to be considered in determining if one's property is being detrimentally used, it is not the only factor to be considered for our legislature has defined a nuisance as:

> "Whatever is injurious to health or indecent or offensive to the senses, or an obstruction to the free use of property, so as essentially to interfere with the comfortable enjoyment of life or property, is a nuisance and the subject of an action." IC 1971, 34–1–52–1 (Burns Code Ed.).

It is settled that noise, in and of itself, may constitute a nuisance if such noise is unreasonable in its degree. Muehlman v. Keilman (1971), 257 Ind. 100, 272 N.E.2d 591. Reasonableness is a question for the trier of fact. Muehlman v. Keilman, supra.

The evidence at trial shows that the proximity of the band music and amplified voices aggravated existing illnesses of Dr. Parsons and Mrs. Combs. Additionally, the noise interfered with sleep, required windows and doors to be kept closed on summer evenings, prohibited hearing television or conversing with another person in the same room, and made sitting outside unpleasant and visiting with others virtually impossible.

We are of the opinion that there was an adequate evidentiary foundation for the trial court's judgment.

Friendship further argues under this issue that the evidence is not sufficient to support the trial court's restrictive time limitations specified in the injunction. Friendship does not argue that the trial court had no authority to enjoin them but that a time limitation set at 8:30 P.M. should have been imposed.

As previously stated, noise as a nuisance is subject to a test of reasonableness, and reasonableness is to be decided by the trier of fact. Muehlman v. Keilman, supra. The record reveals that Parson and Combs complained that the noise interfered with their sleep, prevented them from entertaining friends, and prohibited relaxation.

We are of the opinion that the evidence and reasonable inferences to be drawn therefrom are sufficient to sustain the limited permanent injunction.

Friendship argues that the trial court's decision is contrary to law because there was no finding that its operations produced actual physical discomfort to persons of ordinary sensibilities, tastes, and habits and that the net effect of the injunction was to destroy the operation of a lawful and useful business.

Our previous discussion relating to the sufficiency of the evidence demonstrates that actual physical discomfort is not, necessarily, the sole ingredient of a nuisance. See: IC 1971, 34–1–52–1 (Burns Code Ed.).

As to whether the operation of a lawful and useful business is being destroyed, we agree that curtailment exists, but not its destruction.

It is the law in Indiana that a lawful and useful business is not to be destroyed unless the necessity for doing so be strong, clear, and urgent. Owen et al. v. Phillips et al. (1881), 73 Ind. 284. In the present case, the injunction granted by the trial court will not destroy Friendship's business operation. The evidence shows Friendship Farms may continue to conduct band camps during the weekdays within the specified time periods. Furthermore, the camping facilities operated by Friendship were shown to be amenable for uses other than band camps.

* * *

Friendship argues that the trial court's action prevented it from showing that the operation of its business promoted the interests of the surrounding area to an extent outweighing the private inconvenience resulting therefrom. Friendship relies upon Northern Indiana Public Service Co. v. W.J. & M.S. Vesey (1936), 210 Ind. 338, 200 N.E. 620, for the proposition that it is a defense to an action to enjoin a nuisance that the act promotes the public convenience and interest to such an extent as to outweigh the private inconvenience. In Northern Indiana Public Service Co., our Supreme Court refused to abate the operation of a gas plant because of the overriding public interest to be served by the continued production of gas for the community's use. While refusing to enjoin the gas plant, the court did award permanent damages.

We feel that in certain circumstances the continued operation of a nuisance creating business is necessary for the benefit and convenience of the community. In these limited situations, less injury would be occasioned by the continued operation of the nuisance than by enjoining it. However, the private injury suffered must be compensated by an award of permanent damages if appropriate.

We believe the trial court was correct in finding that this case does not present a situation where the social utility of the Friendship business greatly outweighed the private harm to the adjoining land owners. Therefore, no error existed in the trial court's ruling.

Friendship finally contends that the monetary damages are excessive and contrary to law. In support of this contention, Friendship argues that no evidence was presented showing a decrease in the fair rental values of the Parsons and Combs properties.

The proper measure of damages in cases of this posture, where the nuisance is found to be abatable, is the injury to the use of the property determined by the depreciation in the fair market rental value during the time the nuisance existed. Harrison v. Indiana Auto Shredders Co. (7th Cir.1975), 528 F.2d 1107; Cox v. Schlachter, supra; Davoust v. Mitchell (1970), 146 Ind.App. 536, 257 N.E.2d 332.

The trial court determined that the fair market rental value of the properties owned by Parsons and Combs depreciated in the amount of six hundred dollars ($600.00) as a result of the Friendship nuisance. Judgment was entered accordingly.

* * *

[Discussion of damages is omitted.]

Affirmed.

(3) Uses in Conflict With Part Time, Recreational Residences

CLARK v. WAMBOLD

Supreme Court of Wisconsin, 1917.
165 Wis. 70, 160 N.W. 1039.

This is an action in equity to enjoin the defendant from maintaining a nuisance consisting of pig pens and pig yards, immediately adjacent to plaintiff's premises on the east shore of Eagle lake in Waukesha county, Wisconsin. The plaintiff owns two acres of land on the shore of the lake, which he purchased in 1905, part of it being purchased from the defendant, and all of which he uses for summer residence purposes. The defendant owns a farm immediately east of the plaintiff's premises and also operates a feed mill thereon. For years before the commencement of this action he has made a business of raising pigs and selling them when about six weeks old, sometimes having eight or nine brood sows at a time. The yards or inclosures in which the pigs are bred are close to the feed mill and also near the plaintiff's property. The brood sows are fed largely with sweepings from the feed mill. There was much evidence to the effect that the pig pens and inclosures were kept in a filthy condition and that the odors arising therefrom and drifting over the plaintiff's premises were very offensive and continuous during the summer months. There was also considerable testimony to the effect that the pens and yards were kept in as clean and sanitary condition as reasonably possible and better than most farmers are accustomed to keep such places. The pig pens and inclosures existed and were in use in 1905, when the plaintiff purchased his property along the lake shore, and at that time the plaintiff bought of the defendant two small parcels along the east side of his property, on which pig pens were situated, in order to remove the pens and keep the defendant's hogs further away from his summer home. The defendant raised more pigs during the years beginning with 1911 or 1912 than before. The court found in substance that the pens and yards were kept in as clean and sanitary condition as can be expected; that there were no odors except such as necessarily exist around well kept pens and yards; and that the effect of such odors is not such as to materially interfere with the enjoyment of plaintiff's premises or materially impair their use by people of ordinary sensibilities. Judgment was entered dismissing the complaint without costs except clerk's fees, and the plaintiff appeals. * * *

WINSLOW, C.J. The raising of pigs is a perfectly lawful and respectable business. Doubtless it will remain so as long as the human palate craves the thin cut of juicy ham and the crisp slice of breakfast bacon. With all the marvelous advance in the science of animal husbandry which has taken place in recent years we have not yet produced the odorless pig. He may come at some future time in company with the voiceless cat and the flealess dog, but he is not yet in sight. Whenever he comes he will be welcome, but in the meantime pigs will be pigs, and we must put up as best we may with the odorous pig and his still more odorous pen.

Manifestly pigs cannot be raised in the city, hence they must be raised on the farm. If they are raised there under conditions as clean and sanitary as can reasonably be attained considering the characteristics of the animal and the necessity for confinement in close quarters, the fact that odors from those quarters are carried abroad on the summer breeze will not make an actionable nuisance.

It becomes one of those minor discomforts of life which must be borne in deference to the principle that one man's enjoyment of property cannot always be the controlling factor, but must be considered in connection with the reasonable and lawful use of other property by his neighbors.

The trial court in the present case has found upon sufficient evidence that the pens are kept with reasonable cleanliness and we do not find ourselves able to say that the clear preponderance of the evidence is against the finding. It follows that the judgment must be affirmed. Notwithstanding this result, it is not deemed improper to suggest to the respondent that insistence on extreme legal rights is not always good policy, to say nothing of good neighborliness. It is far better to make a friend of one's neighbor by foregoing, at his request, the exercise of some minor right which causes him discomfort, than to make an enemy of him by insisting upon the right simply because the law gives it. It does not appear that it would be difficult, or even inconvenient, to remove the pig yards which are nearest to the plaintiff's property to some other spot upon the farm. Good neighborliness strongly suggests that he ought to do so. A good neighbor is a great treasure. We can generally have such treasures if we are neighborly ourselves. The golden rule is just as good a rule of conduct now as it was nineteen hundred years ago. We are confident that if the defendant acts upon it in the present case he will in the end experience greater satisfaction from that action than he now experiences in the affirmance of this judgment.

By the Court.—Judgment affirmed.

Notes

1. While on the subject of pigs and pig pens, you may care to compare with the Wambold case, William Aldred's Case, 9 Co.Rep. 57b, 77 Eng.Rep. 816 (1610). William Aldred brought trespass on the case against Thomas Benton for erecting a hog sty on Benton's land, near William's house. The trial court found for William, but Benton moved in arrest of judgment, "that

the building of the house for hogs was necessary for the sustenance of man: and one ought not to have so delicate a nose, that he cannot bear the smell of hogs; for *lex non favet delicatorum votis"* * * * (the law does not favor the wishes of the dainty). But Benton's motion did not succeed, "for in a house four things are desired *habitio hominis* [habitation by man], *delectatio inhabitantis* [the pleasure of the inhabitant], *necessitas lumines* [necessary light], *et sulubritas aeris* [and wholesome air]." Have our standards of comfort in the home improved or declined in three centuries?

2. On the matter of protecting recreational living (without zoning), consider Schneider v. Fromm Laboratories, Inc., 262 Wis. 21, 53 N.W.2d 737 (1952), where the court, on behalf of four week-end and two permanent residents, refused to enjoin the keeping of between 400 and 900 dogs for the purpose of producing vaccine for dog, fox and horse diseases.

3. Attempts by recreational dwellers to keep out bathing beaches catering to the masses have not been successful. Watchung Lake v. Mobus, 119 N.J.L. 272, 196 A. 223 (1938); State ex rel. Warner v. Hayes Inv. Corp., 13 Wash.2d 306, 125 P.2d 262 (1942). Similarly an attempt to enjoin a public fishing site failed. Gableman v. Department of Conservation, 309 Mich. 416, 15 N.W.2d 689 (1944). Summer dwellers also failed to close up a year-around poultry farm in Wetstone v. Cantor, 144 Conn. 77, 127 A.2d 70 (1956). But shore owners on a 75–acre lake succeeded in enjoining "unreasonable" water skiing in Florio v. State ex rel. Epperson, 119 So.2d 305 (Fla.App.1960), noted in Annot., 80 A.L.R.2d 1117 (1961).

4. Contrasting somewhat with Clark v. Wambold is Mitchell v. Hines, 305 Mich. 296, 9 N.W.2d 547 (1943), which was an action to enjoin a piggery brought by owners of residences in a subdivision in the same general vicinity. The pigs were fed with garbage which was placed in an open field, with the unconsumed portion later being plowed under. Testimony showed that the odors during the spring, summer and fall of 1941 were quite revolting and were reoccurring in the spring of 1942 at the time of trial. The odor had not become objectionable until around 1940, and the plaintiffs and witnesses had lived in that area for from one to twenty-one years. The Michigan court stated that feeding garbage to pigs "is not a new custom nor are the premises where pigs are kept usually odorless." Pig-raising is a lawful business so long as it does not constitute a nuisance because of the means of operation. This was not considered to be a case where newcomers had moved to the nuisance. Said the court: "[R]ather we have a case where for some years the piggery was conducted on a small scale and was not objectionable. Then, either the increased size of the piggery or the condition of the fields through the continued dumping of garbage thereon, or both, created such odors that this suit resulted. The fact that the plaintiffs are home owners and that a residential district has expanded so that it is now in the immediate neighborhood of the piggery is not arguable. If the plaintiffs were farmers in a rural community and such a condition existed on an adjacent farm, they would still have grounds for complaint." The court concluded that the piggery was a private nuisance and should be enjoined because there was no proof as to how the odors from such a large-scale garbage-feeding operation could be controlled. Can this case be distinguished from Clark v. Wambold because the farm was on the fringe of the subdivision rather than in open country? Consider the language of the court.

Whatever the answer, the size of the operation and the methods employed quite obviously had a great deal to do with the decision.

C. CONFLICTING USES ON THE RURURBAN FRINGE

write

MAYKUT v. PLASKO

Brief Due Mon. Feb 4

Supreme Court of Connecticut, 1976.
170 Conn. 310, 365 A.2d 1114.

LONGO, ASSOCIATE JUSTICE.

The defendants, Martin and Mary Plasko, own a twenty-eight acre farm in Trumbull, a portion of which they used to raise corn. To reduce damage to their ripening corn caused by marauding birds, from time to time they used a mechanical noisemaking device known as a "corn cannon" which emitted a noise like a gunshot or explosion. They operated it from 7 a.m. to 8 p.m. and the device sounded at about five-minute intervals. The plaintiff lives in a residence located about 600 feet from the defendants' land, in one of the densely populated areas which border the farm on three sides. The plaintiff complained to the police about the noise of the corn cannon during the summer of 1970; and when he was again disturbed by the cannon in 1971, the plaintiff obtained an ex parte temporary injunction against its continued use. In August of 1972, the plaintiff brought the present action in Circuit Court. After a full hearing, the court granted a permanent injunction against the use of the cannon, and awarded the plaintiff damages in the amount of $25. The court also held that since the use of the cannon constituted a common-law nuisance, it was not necessary to consider claims made by the defendants that a permit for its use had been issued which was valid under the General Statutes and the zoning regulations of the town of Trumbull.

* * *

The law imposes upon every property owner a duty "to make a reasonable use of his own property so as to occasion no unnecessary damage or annoyance to his neighbor." Nailor v. C.W. Blakeslee & Sons, Inc., 117 Conn. 241, 245, 167 A. 548, cited in Herbert v. Smyth, 155 Conn. 78, 82, 230 A.2d 235, 237. Determining reasonableness "is essentially a weighing process, involving a comparative evaluation of conflicting interests in various situations." Restatement, 4 Torts § 826, p. 242, cited in O'Neill v. Carolina Freight Carriers Corporation, 156 Conn. 613, 617, 618, 244 A.2d 372, and Nair v. Thaw, 156 Conn. 445, 452, 242 A.2d 757. The appellate court found no indication that this weighing test had been applied, and therefore dissolved the permanent injunction. We have examined the record in this case and we find that the trial judge did apply the test set out above. Although a memorandum of decision cannot take the place of a finding, it may be consulted "to ascertain the ground on which the court acted." Ruggles v. Town Plan & Zoning Commission, 154 Conn. 711, 712, 226 A.2d 108. In its memorandum of decision, the trial court made explicit reference to the weighing test in the following manner: "Determining unreasonableness is essentially a weighing process, involving a comparative evaluation of conflicting interests." The facts outlined in that memorandum of decision and set out in the finding include a consideration not only of the interest of the plaintiff, but of the defendants also. The trial court did apply the proper test.

* * *

The trial and the appellate courts agreed that, if the existence of an enjoinable nuisance was properly found by the trial court, it was not necessary to consider the validity of General Statutes § 26–47a[10] and a provision and amendment of the zoning regulations of the town of Trumbull, both of which the defendants cite as the source of authorization for the use of the corn cannon. We agree with the trial and appellate courts, for "[a]ccording to the weight of authority * * * while what is authorized by law cannot be a public nuisance, it may nevertheless be a private nuisance, and the legislative authorization does not affect any claim of a private citizen for damages * * * or for an injunction." 58 Am.Jur.2d, Nuisances, § 230. This court follows that rule and has upheld the issuance of injunctions against the conduct on one's own property of an otherwise lawful activity. O'Neill v. Carolina Freight Carriers Corporation, 156 Conn. 613, 617, 244 A.2d 372; Nair v. Thaw, 156 Conn. 445, 451–52, 242 A.2d 757. That a municipality by its zoning regulations condones certain uses is no defense to an unreasonable use constituting a nuisance. Herbert v. Smyth, 155 Conn. 78, 83, 230 A.2d 235. The use of the corn cannon was a private nuisance, for it affected a few persons in relation to a right they enjoyed by virtue of their interest in land. 58 Am.Jur.2d, Nuisances, § 9; Prosser, Torts (3d Ed.) § 90. Because the fact that an act may otherwise be lawful does not prevent it from being a private nuisance, it is not necessary to consider the legislative and municipal provisions upon which the defendants seek to rely.

The trial court's conclusion that an enjoinable nuisance existed was arrived at according to law. As to the judgment of the Appellate Division, there is error, the judgment is set aside and the case is remanded to the

10. "[General Statutes] Sec. 26–47a. Use of Noise-making Devices to Repel Marauding Birds and Wildlife. Any provision of any general statute or municipal ordinance, which ordinance is adopted after June 21, 1967, to the contrary notwithstanding, any owner of land used for agricultural purposes may apply to the commissioner of environmental protection for a permit to use noise-making devices, of types approved by said commissioner, to scare or repel marauding birds or other wildlife to prevent the damage and destruction of crops and other property during such hours and such seasons of the year as are determined necessary by said commissioner, provided no permit shall be issued by said commissioner for the use of any such device except in respect to any one parcel of land of the applicant not less than five acres in area or for use within five hundred feet of any place of human habitation, except the dwelling of the applicant for such permit, unless written consent of all occupants, eighteen years of age or over, of places of human habitation within said five hundred feet is presented to said commissioner. No such device shall be used by any person before obtaining such permit. Said commissioner shall promulgate regulations concerning the type and use of such devices to insure public safety."

Appellate Division with direction to affirm the judgment of the Circuit Court.

* * *

Note

Consider the difference it makes that the city has moved to the country in a solid phalanx of residential subdivisions, as compared with topsy-like, mixed use growth through metes and bounds sales. See Beuscher and Morrison, Judicial Zoning through Recent Nuisance Cases, 1955 Wis.L.Rev. 440, 447–448. The existence of mixed uses and the complete lack of control of future development were factors in denying nuisance injunctions in the following fringe area cases:

Bell v. Brockman, 190 Okl. 583, 126 P.2d 78 (1942)—Filling station;

Roberts v. C.F. Adams & Son, 199 Okl. 369, 184 P.2d 634 (1947)— Gasoline bulk plant;

Menger v. Pass, 367 Pa. 432, 80 A.2d 702 (1951)—Tourist court. (See also Daniels v. Notor, 389 Pa. 510, 133 A.2d 520 (1957), and Annot., Tourist or Trailer Camp, Motor Court or Motel, as Nuisance, 24 A.L.R.2d 571 (1952));

Borough of McKees Rocks v. Rennekamp Supply Co., 344 Pa. 443, 25 A.2d 710 (1942)—Concrete block plant;

Perry Mount Park Cemetery Ass'n v. Netzel, 274 Mich. 97, 264 N.W. 303 (1936)—Cemetery attempt to enjoin auto salvaging;

On the other hand, even though a fringe area has developed into an unmixed residential neighborhood, reluctance to enjoin anticipated nuisances has caused courts to refuse injunctions in the following cases on a "let's wait and see how bad it's really going to be" basis:

Moore v. Baldwin County, 209 Ga. 541, 74 S.E.2d 449 (1953)—A convict labor camp; and,

Eddy v. Thornton, 205 Ark. 843, 170 S.W.2d 995 (1943)—Adding a saw mill to a lumber yard.

SPUR INDUS., INC. v. DEL E. WEBB DEVELOPMENT CO.

Supreme Court of Arizona, 1972.
108 Ariz. 178, 494 P.2d 700.

CAMERON, VICE CHIEF JUSTICE. From a judgment permanently enjoining the defendant, Spur Industries, Inc., from operating a cattle feedlot near the plaintiff Del E. Webb Development Company's Sun City, Spur appeals. Webb cross-appeals. Although numerous issues are raised, we feel that it is necessary to answer only two questions. They are:

1. Where the operation of a business, such as a cattle feedlot is lawful in the first instance, but becomes a nuisance by reason of a nearby residential area, may the feedlot operation be enjoined in an action brought by the developer of the residential area?

2. Assuming that the nuisance may be enjoined, may the developer
    of a completely new town or urban area in a previously agricul-
    tural area be required to indemnify the operator of the feedlot
    who must move or cease operation because of the presence of
    the residential area created by the developer?

The facts necessary for a determination of this matter on appeal are
as follows. The area in question is located in Maricopa County, Arizona,
some 14 to 15 miles west of the urban area of Phoenix, on the Phoenix–
Wickenburg Highway, also known as Grand Avenue. About two miles
south of Grand Avenue is Olive Avenue which runs east and west. 111th
Avenue runs north and south as does the Agua Fria River immediately
to the west. See Exhibits A and B below.

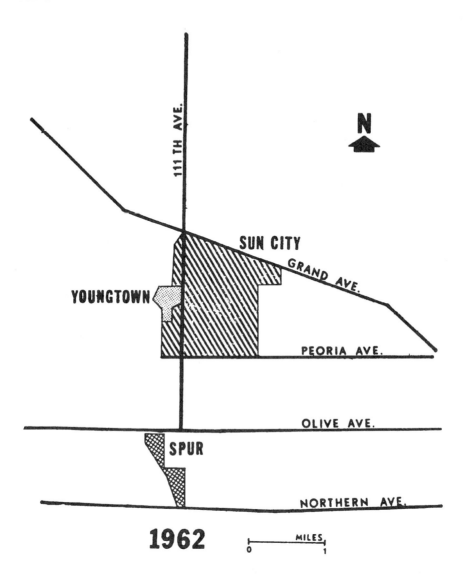

EXHIBIT A

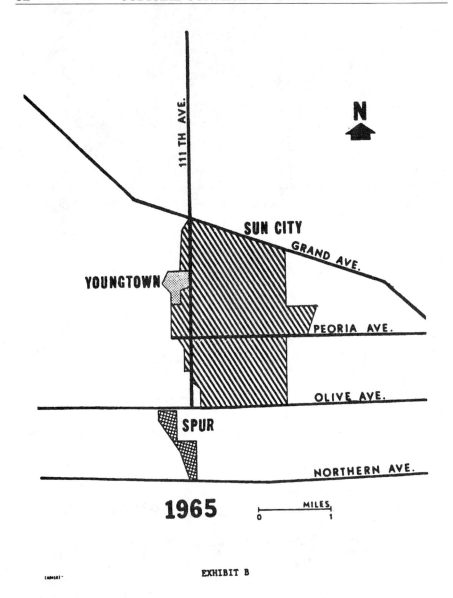

1965

EXHIBIT B

Farming started in this area about 1911. * * * By 1950, the only urban areas in the vicinity were the agriculturally related communities of Peoria, El Mirage, and Surprise located along Grand Avenue. Along 111th Avenue, approximately one mile south of Grand Avenue and 1½ miles north of Olive Avenue, the community of Youngtown was commenced in 1954. Youngtown is a retirement community appealing primarily to senior citizens.

In 1956, Spur's predecessors in interest, H. Marion Welborn and the Northside Hay Mill and Trading Company, developed feedlots, about ½ mile south of Olive Avenue, in an area between the confluence of the usually dry Agua Fria and New Rivers. The area is well suited for cattle

feeding and in 1959, there were 25 cattle feeding pens or dairy operations within a 7 mile radius of the location developed by Spur's predecessors. In April and May of 1959, the Northside Hay Mill was feeding
between 6,000 and 7,000 head of cattle and Welborn approximately 1,500
head on a combined area of 35 acres.

In May of 1959, Del Webb began to plan the development of an
urban area to be known as Sun City. For this purpose, the Marinette and
the Santa Fe Ranches, some 20,000 acres of farmland, were purchased
for $15,000,000 or $750.00 per acre. This price was considerably less
than the price of land located near the urban area of Phoenix, and along
with the success of Youngtown was a factor influencing the decision to
purchase the property in question.

By September 1959, Del Webb had started construction of a golf
course south of Grand Avenue and Spur's predecessors had started to
level ground for more feedlot area. In 1960, Spur purchased the property
in question and began a rebuilding and expansion program extending
both to the north and south of the original facilities. By 1962, Spur's
expansion program was completed and had expanded from approximately 35 acres to 114 acres. See Exhibit A above.

Accompanied by an extensive advertising campaign, homes were
first offered by Del Webb in January 1960 and the first unit to be
completed was south of Grand Avenue and approximately 2½ miles north
of Spur. By 2 May 1960, there were 450 to 500 houses completed or
under construction. At this time, Del Webb did not consider odors from
the Spur feed pens a problem and Del Webb continued to develop in a
southerly direction, until sales resistance became so great that the
parcels were difficult if not impossible to sell. * * *

By December 1967, Del Webb's property had extended south to
Olive Avenue and Spur was within 500 feet of Olive Avenue to the north.
See Exhibit B above. Del Webb filed its original complaint alleging that
in excess of 1,300 lots in the southwest portion were unfit for development for sale as residential lots because of the operation of the Spur
feedlot.

Del Webb's suit complained that the Spur feeding operation was a
public nuisance because of the flies and the odor which were drifting or
being blown by the prevailing south to north wind over the southern
portion of Sun City. At the time of the suit, Spur was feeding between
20,000 and 30,000 head of cattle, and the facts amply support the finding
of the trial court that the feed pens had become a nuisance to the people
who resided in the southern part of Del Webb's development. The
testimony indicated that cattle in a commercial feedlot will produce 35 to
40 pounds of wet manure per day, per head, or over a million pounds of
wet manure per day for 30,000 head of cattle, and that despite the
admittedly good feedlot management and good housekeeping practices by
Spur, the resulting odor and flies produced an annoying if not unhealthy
situation as far as the senior citizens of southern Sun City were
concerned. There is no doubt that some of the citizens of Sun City were

unable to enjoy the outdoor living which Del Webb had advertised and that Del Webb was faced with sales resistance from prospective purchasers as well as strong and persistent complaints from the people who had purchased homes in that area.

* * *

It is noted, however, that neither the citizens of Sun City nor Youngtown are represented in this lawsuit and the suit is solely between Del E. Webb Development Company and Spur Industries, Inc.

May Spur Be Enjoined?

The difference between a private nuisance and a public nuisance is generally one of degree. A private nuisance is one affecting a single individual or a definite small number of persons in the enjoyment of private rights not common to the public, while a public nuisance is one affecting the rights enjoyed by citizens as a part of the public. To constitute a public nuisance, the nuisance must affect a considerable number of people or an entire community or neighborhood. City of Phoenix v. Johnson, 51 Ariz. 115, 75 P.2d 30 (1938).

Where the injury is slight, the remedy for minor inconveniences lies in an action for damages rather than in one for an injunction. Kubby v. Hammond, 68 Ariz. 17, 198 P.2d 134 (1948). Moreover, some courts have held, in the "balancing of conveniences" cases, that damages may be the sole remedy. See Boomer v. Atlantic Cement Co., 26 N.Y.2d 219, 309 N.Y.S.2d 312, 257 N.E.2d 870, 40 A.L.R.3d 590 (1970), and annotation comments, 40 A.L.R.3d 601.

Thus, it would appear from the admittedly incomplete record as developed in the trial court, that, at most, residents of Youngtown would be entitled to damages rather than injunctive relief.

We have no difficulty, however, in agreeing with the conclusion of the trial court that Spur's operation was an enjoinable public nuisance as far as the people in the southern portion of Del Webb's Sun City were concerned.

§ 36–601, subsec. A reads as follows:

"§ 36–601. Public nuisances dangerous to public health

"A. The following conditions are specifically declared public nuisances dangerous to the public health:

"1. Any condition or place in populous areas which constitutes a breeding place for flies, rodents, mosquitoes and other insects which are capable of carrying and transmitting disease-causing organisms to any person or persons."

By this statute, before an otherwise lawful (and necessary) business may be declared a public nuisance, there must be a "populous" area in which people are injured:

" * * * [I]t hardly admits a doubt that, in determining the question as to whether a lawful occupation is so conducted as to constitute a nuisance as a matter of fact, the locality and surroundings are of the first importance. (citations omitted) A business which is not per se a public nuisance may become such by being carried on at a place where the health, comfort, or convenience of a populous neighborhood is affected. * * * What might amount to a serious nuisance in one locality by reason of the density of the population, or character of the neighborhood affected, may in another place and under different surroundings be deemed proper and unobjectionable. * * *." MacDonald v. Perry, 32 Ariz. 39, 49–50, 255 P. 494, 497 (1927).

It is clear that as to the citizens of Sun City, the operation of Spur's feedlot was both a public and a private nuisance. They could have successfully maintained an action to abate the nuisance. Del Webb, having shown a special injury in the loss of sales, had a standing to bring suit to enjoin the nuisance. Engle v. Clark, 53 Ariz. 472, 90 P.2d 994 (1939); City of Phoenix v. Johnson, supra. The judgment of the trial court permanently enjoining the operation of the feedlot is affirmed.

MUST DEL WEBB INDEMNIFY SPUR?

A suit to enjoin a nuisance sounds in equity and the courts have long recognized a special responsibility to the public when acting as a court of equity:

§ 104.   Where public interest is involved.

"Courts of equity may, and frequently do, go much further both to give and withhold relief in furtherance of the public interest than they are accustomed to go when only private interests are involved. Accordingly, the granting or withholding of relief may properly be dependent upon considerations of public interest. * * *." 27 Am. Jur.2d, Equity, page 626.

In addition to protecting the public interest, however, courts of equity are concerned with protecting the operator of a lawfully, albeit noxious, business from the result of a knowing and willful encroachment by others near his business.

In the so-called "coming to the nuisance" cases, the courts have held that the residential landowner may not have relief if he knowingly came into a neighborhood reserved for industrial or agricultural endeavors and has been damaged thereby:

"Plaintiffs chose to live in an area uncontrolled by zoning laws or restrictive covenants and remote from urban development. In such an area plaintiffs cannot complain that legitimate agricultural pursuits are being carried on in the vicinity, nor can plaintiffs, having chosen to build in an agricultural area, complain that the agricultural pursuits carried on in the area depreciate the value of their homes. The area being *primarily agricultural,* any opinion reflecting the value of such property must take this factor into account. The standards affecting the value of residence property in an urban setting, subject to zoning controls and controlled planning techniques, cannot be the standards by which agricultural properties are judged.

"People employed in a city who build their homes in suburban areas of the county beyond the limits of a city and zoning regulations do so for a reason. Some do so to avoid the high taxation rate imposed by cities, or to avoid special assessments for street, sewer and water projects. They usually build on improved or hard surface highways, which have been built either at state or county expense and thereby avoid special assessments for these improvements. It may be that they desire to get away from the congestion of traffic, smoke, noise, foul air and the many other annoyances of city life. But with all these advantages in going beyond the area which is zoned and restricted to protect them in their homes, they must be prepared to take the disadvantages." Dill v. Excel Packing Company, 183 Kan. 513, 525, 526, 331 P.2d 539, 548, 549 (1958). See also East St. Johns Shingle Co. v. City of Portland, 195 Or. 505, 246 P.2d 554, 560–562 (1952).

And:

* * * a party cannot justly call upon the law to make that place suitable for his residence which was not so when he selected it. * * *. Gilbert v. Showerman, 23 Mich. 448, 455, 2 Brown 158 (1871).

Were Webb the only party injured, we would feel justified in holding that the doctrine of "coming to the nuisance" would have been a bar to the relief asked by Webb, and, on the other hand, had Spur located the feedlot near the outskirts of a city and had the city grown toward the feedlot, Spur would have to suffer the cost of abating the nuisance as to those people locating within the growth pattern of the expanding city:

"The case affords, perhaps, an example where a business established at a place remote from population is gradually surrounded and becomes part of a populous center, so that a business which formerly was not an interference with the rights of others has become so by the encroachment of the population * * *." City of Ft. Smith v. Western Hide & Fur Co., 153 Ark. 99, 103, 239 S.W. 724, 726 (1922).

We agree, however, with the Massachusetts court that:

"The law of nuisance affords no rigid rule to be applied in all instances. It is elastic. It undertakes to require only that which is fair and reasonable under all the circumstances. In a commonwealth like this, which depends for its material prosperity so largely on the continued growth and enlargement of manufacturing of diverse varieties, 'extreme rights' cannot be enforced. * * *." Stevens v. Rockport Granite Co., 216 Mass. 486, 488, 104 N.E. 371, 373 (1914).

There was no indication in the instant case at the time Spur and its predecessors located in western Maricopa County that a new city would spring up, full-blown, alongside the feeding operation and that the developer of that city would ask the court to order Spur to move because of the new city. Spur is required to move not because of any wrongdoing on the part of Spur, but because of a proper and legitimate regard of the courts for the rights and interests of the public.

Del Webb, on the other hand, is entitled to the relief prayed for (a permanent injunction), not because Webb is blameless, but because of the damage to the people who have been encouraged to purchase homes in Sun City. It does not equitably or legally follow, however, that Webb, being entitled to the injunction, is then free of any liability to Spur if Webb has in fact been the cause of the damage Spur has sustained. It does not seem harsh to require a developer, who has taken advantage of the lesser land values in a rural area as well as the availability of large tracts of land on which to build and develop a new town or city in the area, to indemnify those who are forced to leave as a result.

Having brought people to the nuisance to the foreseeable detriment of Spur, Webb must indemnify Spur for a reasonable amount of the cost of moving or shutting down. It should be noted that this relief to Spur is limited to a case wherein a developer has, with foreseeability, brought into a previously agricultural or industrial area the population which makes necessary the granting of an injunction against a lawful business and for which the business has no adequate relief.

It is therefore the decision of this court that the matter be remanded to the trial court for a hearing upon the damages sustained by the defendant Spur as a reasonable and direct result of the granting of the permanent injunction. Since the result of the appeal may appear novel and both sides have obtained a measure of relief, it is ordered that each side will bear its own costs.

Affirmed in part, reversed in part, and remanded for further proceedings consistent with this opinion.

Notes

1. Does the decision of the Arizona Court amount in effect to a taking of private property for *private* use in contravention of the established eminent domain principle that upon payment of just compensation private property may be taken for *public* use? Or does the result render a certain portion of Spur's property unusable without indemnification, since the only payment by Webb is for the cost of Spur's moving "or shutting down" expenses? Does this decision, which the Court acknowledges "may appear novel," provide a reasonable solution to the problem of "moving to the nuisance" where the activity producing the nuisance is located in a somewhat isolated area? Or should this case be viewed as one in which there was not a true "moving to the nuisance" but as one in which the populated area gradually expanded to encompass or reach the area of the nuisance?

2. In Meat Producers, Inc. v. McFarland, 476 S.W.2d 406 (Tex.Civ.App. 1972), a cattle-feeding operation "of considerable magnitude" was emitting disagreeable odors and permanent damages were sought. At the time of trial, the operations had been suspended, but the Texas Court held it to be a nuisance anyway and granted damages. The plaintiff owned 645 acres adjacent to the Meat Producers' property, and he alleged that the odors had

reduced the market value of his property to $335 per acre. The jury found in his favor and assessed a diminution in value of $135 per acre. The defendant argued that any inconvenience from the feed lot was trivial because no one was living on the plaintiff's land when the feed lot was in operation or at the time of trial. The appellate court rejected that argument, saying that the injury is not limited to the actual use of the land. Testimony established that the highest and best use of the land was for residential purposes, "and since there was evidence that odors from the feed lot would substantially interfere with that use, we hold that there was evidence to support the finding that a nuisance existed." The argument that no physical disturbance of the land resulted was also rejected because a "nuisance is by definition a non-trespassory invasion" and it "may be by pollution of the air as well as by disturbance of the soil." Also rejected was the defendant's argument that if a feed lot cannot be operated in a rural area, there are few places where it can be operated inoffensively. The court stated: "For the purpose of determining liability for damages, interference with use of land may be unreasonable, even though utility of the activity causing such interference is great and the harm is relatively small, since it may be reasonable to continue a useful activity causing such interference if payment is made for the harm, but unreasonable to continue it without paying." Various other arguments of the defendant were also rejected. Compare this court's approach with that of the Arizona Court in Spur Industries. Do you think this court would have accepted a "coming to the nuisance" argument by defendant if the plaintiff had begun to develop his land for homesites? By paying permanent damages, is the feed lot operation in effect acquiring something in the nature of an easement or servitude with respect to the land of the plaintiff?

BOOMER v. ATLANTIC CEMENT CO., INC.

Court of Appeals of New York, 1970.
26 N.Y.2d 219, 309 N.Y.S.2d 312, 257 N.E.2d 870.

BERGAN, JUDGE.

Defendant operates a large cement plant near Albany. These are actions for injunction and damages by neighboring land owners alleging injury to property from dirt, smoke and vibration emanating from the plant. A nuisance has been found after trial, temporary damages have been allowed; but an injunction has been denied.

The public concern with air pollution arising from many sources in industry and in transportation is currently accorded ever wider recognition accompanied by a growing sense of responsibility in State and Federal Governments to control it. Cement plants are obvious sources of air pollution in the neighborhoods where they operate.

But there is now before the court private litigation in which individual property owners have sought specific relief from a single plant operation. The threshold question raised by the division of view on this appeal is whether the court should resolve the litigation between the parties now before it as equitably as seems possible; or whether, seeking promotion of the general public welfare, it should channel private litigation into broad public objectives.

A court performs its essential function when it decides the rights of parties before it. Its decision of private controversies may sometimes greatly affect public issues. Large questions of law are often resolved by the manner in which private litigation is decided. But this is normally an incident to the court's main function to settle controversy. It is a rare exercise of judicial power to use a decision in private litigation as a purposeful mechanism to achieve direct public objectives greatly beyond the rights and interests before the court.

Effective control of air pollution is a problem presently far from solution even with the full public and financial powers of government. In large measure adequate technical procedures are yet to be developed and some that appear possible may be economically impracticable.

It seems apparent that the amelioration of air pollution will depend on technical research in great depth; on a carefully balanced consideration of the economic impact of close regulation; and of the actual effect on public health. It is likely to require massive public expenditure and to demand more than any local community can accomplish and to depend on regional and interstate controls.

A court should not try to do this on its own as a by-product of private litigation and it seems manifest that the judicial establishment is neither equipped in the limited nature of any judgment it can pronounce nor prepared to lay down and implement an effective policy for the elimination of air pollution. This is an area beyond the circumference of one private lawsuit. It is a direct responsibility for government and should not thus be undertaken as an incident to solving a dispute between property owners and a single cement plant—one of many—in the Hudson River valley.

The cement making operations of defendant have been found by the court at Special Term to have damaged the nearby properties of plaintiffs in these two actions. That court, as it has been noted, accordingly found defendant maintained a nuisance and this has been affirmed at the Appellate Division. The total damage to plaintiffs' properties is, however, relatively small in comparison with the value of defendant's operation and with the consequences of the injunction which plaintiffs seek.

The ground for the denial of injunction, notwithstanding the finding both that there is a nuisance and that plaintiffs have been damaged substantially, is the large disparity in economic consequences of the nuisance and of the injunction. This theory cannot, however, be sustained without overruling a doctrine which has been consistently reaffirmed in several leading cases in this court and which has never been disavowed here, namely that where a nuisance has been found and where there has been any substantial damage shown by the party complaining an injunction will be granted.

The rule in New York has been that such a nuisance will be enjoined although marked disparity be shown in economic consequence between the effect of the injunction and the effect of the nuisance.

The problem of disparity in economic consequence was sharply in focus in Whalen v. Union Bag & Paper Co., 208 N.Y. 1, 101 N.E. 805. A pulp mill entailing an investment of more than a million dollars polluted a stream in which plaintiff, who owned a farm, was "a lower riparian owner". The economic loss to plaintiff from this pollution was small. This court, reversing the Appellate Division, reinstated the injunction granted by the Special Term against the argument of the mill owner that in view of "the slight advantage to plaintiff and the great loss that will be inflicted on defendant" an injunction should not be granted (p. 2, 101 N.E. p. 805). "Such a balancing of injuries cannot be justified by the circumstances of this case", Judge Werner noted (p. 4, 101 N.E. p. 805). He continued: "Although the damage to the plaintiff may be slight as compared with the defendant's expense of abating the condition, that is not a good reason for refusing an injunction" (p. 5, 101 N.E. p. 806).

Thus the unconditional injunction granted at Special Term was reinstated. The rule laid down in that case, then, is that whenever the damage resulting from a nuisance is found not "unsubstantial", viz., $100 a year, injunction would follow. This states a rule that had been followed in this court with marked consistency * * *

There are cases where injunction has been denied. McCann v. Chasm Power Co., 211 N.Y. 301, 105 N.E. 416 is one of them. There, however, the damage shown by plaintiffs was not only unsubstantial, it was non-existent. Plaintiffs owned a rocky bank of the stream in which defendant had raised the level of the water. This had no economic or other adverse consequence to plaintiffs, and thus injunctive relief was denied. Similar is the basis for denial of injunction in Forstmann v. Joray Holding Co., 244 N.Y. 22, 154 N.E. 652 where no benefit to plaintiffs could be seen from the injunction sought (p. 32, 154 N.E. 655). Thus if, within Whalen v. Union Bag & Paper Co., supra, which authoritatively states the rule in New York, the damage to plaintiffs in these present cases from defendant's cement plant is "not unsubstantial", an injunction should follow.

Although the court at Special Term and the Appellate Division held that injunction should be denied, it was found that plaintiffs had been damaged in various specific amounts up to the time of the trial and damages to the respective plaintiffs were awarded for those amounts. The effect of this was, injunction having been denied, plaintiffs could maintain successive actions at law for damages thereafter as further damage was incurred.

The court at Special Term also found the amount of permanent damage attributable to each plaintiff, for the guidance of the parties in the event both sides stipulated to the payment and acceptance of such permanent damage as a settlement of all the controversies among the parties. The total of permanent damages to all plaintiffs thus found was $185,000. This basis of adjustment has not resulted in any stipulation by the parties.

This result at Special Term and at the Appellate Division is a departure from a rule that has become settled; but to follow the rule literally in these cases would be to close down the plant at once. This court is fully agreed to avoid that immediately drastic remedy; the difference in view is how best to avoid it.[11]

One alternative is to grant the injunction but postpone its effect to a specified future date to give opportunity for technical advances to permit defendant to eliminate the nuisance; another is to grant the injunction conditioned on the payment of permanent damages to plaintiffs which would compensate them for the total economic loss to their property present and future caused by defendant's operations. For reasons which will be developed the court chooses the latter alternative.

If the injunction were to be granted unless within a short period—e.g., 18 months—the nuisance be abated by improved methods, there would be no assurance that any significant technical improvement would occur.

The parties could settle this private litigation at any time if defendant paid enough money and the imminent threat of closing the plant would build up the pressure on defendant. If there were no improved techniques found, there would inevitably be applications to the court at Special Term for extensions of time to perform on showing of good faith efforts to find such techniques.

Moreover, techniques to eliminate dust and other annoying by-products of cement making are unlikely to be developed by any research the defendant can undertake within any short period, but will depend on the total resources of the cement industry nationwide and throughout the world. The problem is universal wherever cement is made.

For obvious reasons the rate of the research is beyond control of defendant. If at the end of 18 months the whole industry has not found a technical solution a court would be hard put to close down this one cement plant if due regard be given to equitable principles.

On the other hand, to grant the injunction unless defendant pays plaintiffs such permanent damages as may be fixed by the court seems to do justice between the contending parties. All of the attributions of economic loss to the properties on which plaintiffs' complaints are based will have been redressed.

The nuisance complained of by these plaintiffs may have other public or private consequences, but these particular parties are the only ones who have sought remedies and the judgment proposed will fully redress them. The limitation of relief granted is a limitation only within the four corners of these actions and does not foreclose public health or other public agencies from seeking proper relief in a proper court.

---

11. Respondent's investment in the plant is in excess of $45,000,000. There are over 300 people employed there.

It seems reasonable to think that the risk of being required to pay permanent damages to injured property owners by cement plant owners would itself be a reasonable effective spur to research for improved techniques to minimize nuisance.

* * *

The damage base here suggested is consistent with the general rule in those nuisance cases where damages are allowed. "Where a nuisance is of such a permanent and unabatable character that a single recovery can be had, including the whole damage past and future resulting therefrom, there can be but one recovery" (66 C.J.S. Nuisances § 140, p. 947). It has been said that permanent damages are allowed where the loss recoverable would obviously be small as compared with the cost of removal of the nuisance (Kentucky–Ohio Gas Co. v. Bowling, 264 Ky. 470, 477, 95 S.W.2d 1).

The present cases and the remedy here proposed are in a number of other respects rather similar to Northern Indiana Public Service Co. v. W.J. & M.S. Vesey, 210 Ind. 338, 200 N.E. 620 decided by the Supreme Court of Indiana. The gases, odors, ammonia and smoke from the Northern Indiana company's gas plant damaged the nearby Vesey greenhouse operation. An injunction and damages were sought, but an injunction was denied and the relief granted was limited to permanent damages "present, past, and future" (p. 371, 200 N.E. 620).

Denial of injunction was grounded on a public interest in the operation of the gas plant and on the court's conclusion "that less injury would be occasioned by requiring the appellant [Public Service] to pay the appellee [Vesey] all damages suffered by it * * * than by enjoining the operation of the gas plant; and that the maintenance and operation of the gas plant should not be enjoined" (p. 349, 200 N.E. p. 625).

* * *

It was held that in this type of continuing and recurrent nuisance permanent damages were appropriate. See, also, City of Amarillo v. Ware, 120 Tex. 456, 40 S.W.2d 57 where recurring overflows from a system of storm sewers were treated as the kind of nuisance for which permanent depreciation of value of affected property would be recoverable.

* * *

Thus it seems fair to both sides to grant permanent damages to plaintiffs which will terminate this private litigation. The theory of damage is the "servitude on land" of plaintiffs imposed by defendant's nuisance. (See United States v. Causby, 328 U.S. 256, 261, 262, 267, 66 S.Ct. 1062, 90 L.Ed. 1206, where the term "servitude" addressed to the land was used by Justice Douglas relating to the effect of airplane noise on property near an airport.)

The judgment, by allowance of permanent damages imposing a servitude on land, which is the basis of the actions, would preclude future recovery by plaintiffs or their grantees (see Northern Indiana Public Serv. Co. v. W.J. & M.S. Vesey, supra, p. 351, 200 N.E. 620).

This should be placed beyond debate by a provision of the judgment that the payment by defendant and the acceptance by plaintiffs of permanent damages found by the court shall be in compensation for a servitude on the land.

Although the Trial Term has found permanent damages as a possible basis of settlement of the litigation, on remission the court should be entirely free to re-examine this subject. It may again find the permanent damage already found; or make new findings.

The orders should be reversed, without costs, and the cases remitted to Supreme Court, Albany County to grant an injunction which shall be vacated upon payment by defendant of such amounts of permanent damage to the respective plaintiffs as shall for this purpose be determined by the court.

JASEN, JUDGE (dissenting).

I agree with the majority that a reversal is required here, but I do not subscribe to the newly enunciated doctrine of assessment of permanent damages, in lieu of an injunction, where substantial property rights have been impaired by the creation of a nuisance.

* * *

The specific problem faced here is known as particulate contamination because of the fine dust particles emanating from defendant's cement plant. The particular type of nuisance is not new, having appeared in many cases for at least the past 60 years. (See Hulbert v. California Portland Cement Co., 161 Cal. 239, 118 P. 928 [1911].) It is interesting to note that cement production has recently been identified as a significant source of particulate contamination in the Hudson Valley. This type of pollution, wherein very small particles escape and stay in the atmosphere, has been denominated as the type of air pollution which produces the greatest hazard to human health. We have thus a nuisance which not only is damaging to the plaintiffs, but also is decidedly harmful to the general public.

I see grave dangers in overruling our long-established rule of granting an injunction where a nuisance results in substantial continuing damage. In permitting the injunction to become inoperative upon the payment of permanent damages, the majority is, in effect, licensing a continuing wrong. It is the same as saying to the cement company, you may continue to do harm to your neighbors so long as you pay a fee for it. Furthermore, once such permanent damages are assessed and paid, the incentive to alleviate the wrong would be eliminated, thereby continuing air pollution of an area without abatement.

* * *

This kind of inverse condemnation (Ferguson v. Village of Hamburg, 272 N.Y. 234, 5 N.E.2d 801) may not be invoked by a private person or corporation for private gain or advantage. Inverse condemnation should only be permitted when the public is primarily served in the taking or impairment of property. (Matter of New York City Housing Auth. v. Muller, 270 N.Y. 333, 343, 1 N.E.2d 153, 156; Pocantico Water–Works Co. v. Bird, 130 N.Y. 249, 258, 29 N.E. 246, 248.) The promotion of the interests of the polluting cement company has, in my opinion, no public use or benefit.

Nor is it constitutionally permissible to impose [a] servitude on land, without consent of the owner, by payment of permanent damages where the continuing impairment of the land is for a private use. (See Fifth Ave. Coach Lines v. City of New York, 11 N.Y.2d 342, 347, 229 N.Y.S.2d 400, 403, 183 N.E.2d 684, 686; Walker v. City of Hutchinson, 352 U.S. 112, 77 S.Ct. 200, 1 L.Ed.2d 178.) This is made clear by the State Constitution (art. I, § 7, subd. [a]) which provides that "[p]rivate property shall not be taken for *public use* without just compensation" (emphasis added). It is, of course, significant that the section makes no mention of taking for a *private* use.

In sum, then, by constitutional mandate as well as by judicial pronouncement, the permanent impairment of private property for private purposes is not authorized in the absence of clearly demonstrated public benefit and use.

I would enjoin the defendant cement company from continuing the discharge of dust particles upon its neighbors' properties unless, within 18 months, the cement company abated this nuisance.

* * *

Notes

1. The Boomer and Spur cases might be compared with some cases in which courts are not as eager to permit the nuisance-like activity to continue. In Mowrer v. Ashland Oil & Refining Co., 518 F.2d 659 (7th Cir.1975), seeping oil from a capped well was held to create a private nuisance despite the fact that the activity causing the seep was conducted with due care. In Associated Metals & Minerals Corp. v. Dixon Chemical & Research, Inc., 82 N.J.Super. 281, 197 A.2d 569 (1963), odors, dusts and fumes produced by defendant and causing a continuous invasion of adjacent property were held to produce a nuisance regardless of considerations of due care or negligence.

2. On the other hand, in Summers v. Acme Flour Mills Co., 263 P.2d 515 (Okl.1953), the court said that it had to be established that the mill was operated in an unreasonable manner in order to establish a nuisance produced by the airborne dust. See also, Riblet v. Ideal Cement Co., 54 Wash.2d 779, 345 P.2d 173 (1959). In that case, incidentally, the plaintiff had been bringing successful nuisance suits every two years against the previous owner of the defendant. The facts of the previous suits were binding against the current owner. A proliferation of lawsuits, of course, was one thing the Boomer majority sought to prevent.

3. One problem which periodically arises with land located on the urban fringe is that relating to ultrahazardous activities. Are these nuisances per se, as they almost certainly would be declared to be if they were located in a settled residential area? The rather dated but still useful American Law of Property § 28.27 (1954) referred to such activity, as well as malicious interference and activities intrinsically detrimental to health and welfare as "hybrid activities" which are not necessarily unreasonable "but which are always unreasonable in certain localities and under certain conditions." The burden is on the plaintiff to establish that the location and conditions are such that these should be enjoined or damages should be awarded or both. This leaves them as something less than nuisances per se, practically speaking, since the facts have to be proven to the court's satisfaction.

The cases illustrate the problem:

(a) In Hero Lands Co. v. Texaco, Inc., 310 So.2d 93 (La.1975), the question was whether the construction of a hazardous high pressure gas pipeline adjacent to and within fifteen feet of the Hero Lands tract gave rise to an action for damages which impaired the market value and full use of the Hero Lands property. It was concluded that this constituted a dangerous nuisance because it "involved inherent hazards and dangers which are well-known to the public and those purchasing land." Hero was said to have incurred $30,000 in damages.

(b) However, in Hays v. Hartfield L–P Gas, 159 Ind.App. 297, 306 N.E.2d 373 (1974), injunctive relief and damages were sought against Hartfield for the planned operation of a liquid propane bulk plant to be situated near Hays' property. The tank was 300 feet away from Hays' property and had to be set back substantially from a highway so as not to be a traffic hazard. Objection was also made as to anticipated annoyance from dust, noise, lights and odors. These properties were on the fringe of the town limits, but outside of its boundaries. Hays conceded that it was not a nuisance per se, and the court held that evidence was lacking to show that it was a nuisance in fact. There was no proof that it presented a hazard, said the court, and mere fear or apprehension of danger was not enough.

(c) More recent cases involve hazardous wastes, as for example in Wilson v. Key Tronic Corp., 40 Wash.App. 802, 701 P.2d 518 (1985), in which there had been the disposal of hazardous waste on adjoining land, and the plaintiff had had to haul water to his property for months resulting in disruption of family life. Damages were allowed for the annoyance, discomfort and mental anguish accompanying the situation. In Village of Wilsonville v. SCA Services, Inc., 86 Ill.2d 1, 55 Ill.Dec. 499, 426 N.E.2d 824 (1981) the court upheld a permanent injunction against a chemical waste dump and a trial court order for exhumation of all material from the site and reclamation of the land.

(d) In Daniel v. Kosh, 173 Va. 352, 4 S.E.2d 381 (1939), the plaintiff lived near a coal yard and railroad track. The defendant had for some years been unloading gasoline from tank cars into storage tanks for his gasoline business within 100 feet of plaintiff's home. As a result of this, the plaintiff's fire insurance carrier increased his insurance rates to approximately three and one-half times of what they had been. The plaintiff filed suit to enjoin the unloading of gasoline and recover damages. Relief was denied. The court stated that it knew of "no case in which it was held that a mere increase in the insurance rate entitles the plaintiff to redress either in equity or at law. * * * The authorities indeed are to the contrary." It also pointed out that certain other commercial activities, such as a beauty shop, a carpenter shop and a furniture repair shop would also increase the rates.

D. CONFLICTING USES IN OLDER SETTLED AREAS
(1) Residential Areas

MAHONEY v. WALTER

Supreme Court of Appeals of West Virginia, 1974.
157 W.Va. 882, 205 S.E.2d 692.

SPROUSE, JUSTICE:

This case is before the Court upon an appeal from the judgment of the Circuit Court of Marshall County in an action instituted by Raymond Mahoney and fifteen other residents and property owners in Mar–Win Place, a community in Marshall County. The plaintiffs sought to permanently enjoin Eugene A. Walter, Mary A. Walter and Cecil Walter, the defendants, from using their property for the purpose of operating a salvage yard. The defendants were permanently enjoined from operating the salvage yard by the Common Pleas Court of Marshall County, and this judgment was affirmed by an order of the Circuit Court of Marshall County. It is from the judgment of the circuit court that the defendants prosecute this appeal.

* * *

It is apparent from the evidence that Mar–Win Place has been an established community in Marshall County for a number of years and existed as the same type locality for a long time prior to the establishment of the defendants' salvage yard business in 1969. The evidence disclosed that Mar–Win Place is primarily a residential area but was unzoned as to commercial use. Some eight or ten businesses operate in the area including a beauty shop, television repair shop and a tax service. Among the businesses operating in the area, Trenton Construction Company is the largest. It is located on the northern-most edge of the community, but testimony reflected that, because of the topography of the land, the location of the business was neither unsightly nor objectionable. The owner of Trenton Construction Company testified that he had taken great pains to plant trees and foliage to conceal the business from view. The salvage yard was operated primarily as a means of obtaining used parts from wrecked and abandoned automobiles.

The evidence for the plaintiffs revealed the following facts: Approximately one hundred vehicles were stored at random upon the defendants' property. No precaution was taken to drain the vehicles of gasoline or other flammable materials; nor was precaution taken by the defendants to prevent entrance to the yard itself or to the trunks, hoods or interiors of the stored vehicles. A wooden fence had been erected across the front of the property, but no fence had been erected to the sides or rear of the storage area.

The salvage yard is located within a minimum distance of thirty feet to a maximum distance of three hundred feet from adjoining property owners. The yard is open for business six days a week from eight o'clock a.m. to five o'clock p.m. Work was occasionally performed in the yard on Sundays. A four-inch high pressure natural gas line traverses the entire width of the property. A number of wrecked and abandoned vehicles are stacked over the line, undrained of gasoline and other flammable materials. Several of the plaintiffs and their witnesses expressed fear that this situation presented a potential fire hazard.

According to some of the plaintiffs' witnesses a number of rats and snakes had been seen in the vicinity of the salvage yard. Others testified that there were a number of children in the area, and several of the witnesses had observed them playing in or near the salvage yard.

A witness for the plaintiff testified that the noise of the wreckers disturbed her and that she had heard cars being moved in the junk yard between ten and eleven o'clock p.m. Another indicated she was disturbed by the unsightly growth of high weeds in the salvage yard.

Six of the plaintiffs testified that their property values had diminished since the commencement of the operation of the salvage yard. A real estate appraiser in the area stated that he believed that the location of the salvage yard was a deteriorating factor in the value of the Mar–Win property. One plaintiff testified that she had planned to do extensive remodeling to her home but would not do so now because of the salvage yard. Other witnesses for the plaintiff testified that the salvage yard was unsightly, that it disturbed the natural and physical beauty of the neighborhood, and that it presented a threat to the health and safety of the residents of Mar–Win Place.

The principal defense witness, Cecil Walter, testified that the salvage yard could be suitably fenced to prevent entrance of children and to make it more attractive. No action in this respect has been taken by the defendants. Walter stated that he had operated salvage yards for a number of years and had never experienced a fire. He admitted a certain amount of noise was attached to the business of pressing and baling the wrecked cars and abandoned vehicles.

Two residents of Mar–Win testified for the defendants. Neither felt the neighborhood was exclusively residential. * * *

The trial court concluded that the location of the salvage yard is a threat to the health of the residents; that it destroys the natural beauty of the area; that it tends to destroy the residential quality of the area, causing a depreciation of property values; that it causes stress to the residents of the area and interferes with their comfort and enjoyment;

that its presence has a deleterious effect on the neighborhood; and that all of this constituted a nuisance which he permanently enjoined.

* * *

The sole issue, therefore, on this appeal is whether the trial court abused its discretion in finding the presence of the salvage yard in the Mar–Win community constituted a nuisance which should be completely enjoined.

* * *

The sole issue, therefore, on this appeal is whether the trial court abused its discretion in finding the presence of the salvage yard in the Mar–Win community constituted a nuisance which should be completely enjoined.

* * *

The appellant contends that the doctrine of the "balancing of conveniences" should be applied—that is, that when the injury to the defendant in losing its business location is so much greater than the inconvenience to the owners of nearby property, the permanent injunction should be denied or, at the very least, the injunction order should be tailored to permit the continued operation of the salvage yard with appropriate steps being taken to reduce the objectionable features. Considering the relative hardship imposed upon the parties either by granting or denying an injunction is a doctrine that has been in American law for some time. Restatement of Torts, Injunctions, Section 941. However, the balancing of convenience—the disparity of economic consequences is a comparatively new development. 22 Case W.L.Rev. 356; 43 Colo.L.Rev. 225. Under this doctrine, economic consequence to the business owner and the public is compared to the damage to the adjacent property owners who may be compensated by action and damage. The damage to the business owner is normally the loss of investment, loss of profit and the like. The damage to the public is the loss of economic stimuli such as loss of employment.

One of the chief problems with this doctrine is that it compares the general loss to the public, such as loss of jobs, while it only considers specific loss to the private land owner, i.e., the specific money damage to his property, notwithstanding he may be damaged in many general ways which cannot be translated into specific damages. Regardless of the judicial soundness of the doctrine of "balancing conveniences", there was no evidence in this case of a general public economic interest. The only economic interest to be balanced was the private economic interest of the business owner, that is, the loss of this specific locality where he could conduct his business. Admitting this can be, and probably is considerable, Mar–Win Place is not the only locality wherein this type of business can be conducted. The mobility of a business, that is, its adaptability to being conducted in various places rather than in one specific locality is one of the factors to be considered. Sanders v.

Roselawn Memorial Gardens, 152 W.Va. 91, 159 S.E.2d 784; Parkersburg Builders Material Company v. Barrack, 118 W.Va. 608, 191 S.E. 368.

Modern cases litigating alleged nuisances frequently involve the resolution of conflicting interests between business and private residences. This case falls within that pattern.

* * *

However, it is possible that the character of a locality or neighborhood can be altered by business actions carried on by local traditions. "In business and industrial districts the rights of residents have become modified to some extent by the use to which such districts are put." 58 Am.Jur.2d, Nuisances, Section 39, page 605.

It is clear that the type of locality has an important bearing on a reasonable use of a business property. * * *

This Court has previously applied law of nuisance to various phases of the automotive business. Martin v. Williams, supra; Parkersburg Builders Material Company v. Barrack, 118 W.Va. 608, 191 S.E. 368. We have said:

> "An automobile junk yard is not necessarily an objectionable place. The business of buying old automobiles, wrecking them and selling serviceable parts as such and junking the residue is an honorable and useful business. But an outdoor lay-out of a business of that kind necessarily is not pleasing to the view. Such business, therefore, should not be located in a community of unquestioned residential character.

> "Where, however, a section of a municipality is not a clearly established residential community a court of equity will not be warranted in excluding therefrom as a nuisance an automobile-wrecking business merely on the ground of unsightliness." Parkersburg Builders Material Company v. Barrack, supra at 613, 191 S.E. at 371.

The trial court in this proceeding was presented two basic considerations: (1) Did a nuisance exist; and (2) was it of such a nature as to require its complete abatement by a total permanent injunction. In arriving at its first conclusion, the court could properly consider the nature of the businesses; the type of locality in which the business is located; and the type of activities complained of.

While some testimony was conflicting, there was ample evidence upon which the court could conclude that Mar–Win Place was basically a residential area with some unoffensive businesses.

There is likewise evidence to sustain the court's finding that the area, in the immediate vicinity of the salvage yard, was exclusively residential. Facts concerning the activities complained of have been recited. The unsightliness of the yard itself, the noise necessitated by the preparing of the junked automobiles for removal, the possible danger of flammable materials, the possible danger to children from the unprotected nature of the area, and the prevalence of rodents and insects justified the trial court in finding that a nuisance existed regardless of whether the area was exclusively or primarily residential.

The defendants moved that the trial court grant a modified injunction abating the nuisance by permitting them to remedy objectionable features. The trial court overruled that motion and there is ample evidence to sustain this decision that the nuisance could not be abated in this manner.

* * *

Viewing the record as a whole, it is abundantly clear that the trial court had more than sufficient evidence upon which to make a finding that Mar–Win Place was a residential area; that the defendants were conducting their business in the residential area in such a manner as to constitute a nuisance; and that the nuisance could not be abated by anything short of an injunction requiring its removal. The court, having sufficient evidence on which to base its decision of fact and conclusions of law, it cannot be said to have abused its discretion.

* * *

Affirmed.

Notes

1. Parkersburg Builders Material Co. v. Barrack, 118 W.Va. 608, 191 S.E. 368 (1937), concurring opinion 118 W.Va. 608, 192 S.E. 291, 110 A.L.R. 1454 (1937), which is cited in the preceding case, is a leading decision on automobile junkyards. In that case the junkyard property was situated about a thousand feet from the city's eastern boundary near a few residences and several businesses. The court stated that an automobile junkyard was not a nuisance per se, but that it "is not pleasing to the view" and therefore, "should not be located in a community of unquestioned residential character." It did not view the area in question as an established residential area. The principal importance of the Parkersburg case lies in the aesthetic considerations which it took into account. The court pointed out that courts of equity abate nuisances based on noise or on conditions "offensive to the olfactory nerves" but have hesitated to abate nuisances based on visual offensiveness because of the difficulty in creating a standard of measurement. The court stated:

> Happily, the day has arrived when persons may entertain appreciation of the aesthetic and be heard in equity in vindication of their love of beautiful, without becoming objects of opprobrium. Basically, this is because a thing visually offensive may seriously affect the residents of a community in the reasonable enjoyment of their homes, and may produce a decided reduction in property values. Courts must not be indifferent to the truth that within essential limitations aesthetics has a proper place in the community affairs of modern society.

The court recognized that "equity should not be aroused to action merely on the basis of the fastidiousness of taste of complainants." The discussion of aesthetics amounted to dictum in the sense that the junkyard was not enjoined due to its location. But the basis of the holding in the principal case demonstrates the importance of the comments in Parkersburg. Both cases should be remembered in connection with material later on relating to zoning for aesthetic purposes.

2.   In the principal case, in which West Virginia did enjoin the junkyard, was consideration given to factors other than the unsightliness of the operation? In short, was the decision grounded solely on aesthetic considerations?

3.   In 1948 the California Court of Appeals (First District) abated an ugly wooden structure, surrounded by stacks of wooden and paper boxes and waste material, and located in the heart of an attractive residential area, not because it was unsightly, but because it was a fire hazard. People v. Oliver, 86 Cal.App.2d 885, 195 P.2d 926 (1948). And in 1951, the Iowa court was still saying in Livingston v. Davis, 243 Iowa 21, 50 N.W.2d 592 (1951): "That a thing is unsightly or offends the aesthetic sense does not ordinarily make it a nuisance or afford grounds for injunctive relief." And see a long dictum on aesthetics as a basis for nuisance injunctions in a case where the lower court's injunction requiring the screening of a junkyard in a mixed use neighborhood was annulled. Feldstein v. Kammauf, 209 Md. 479, 121 A.2d 716 (1956).

The typical case law lawyer's insistence on a reported case "on all fours on its facts" before he will go to court undoubtedly explains why the challenge of unaesthetic sights as nuisances has not been in the courts more frequently in recent years. In fact, this insistence may explain in large part the long lag in nuisance law between social change and case holdings. There may well have been a lack of new kinds of challenging case situations to stimulate the courts to change.

4.   Compare also with the principal case the earlier West Virginia case of Martin v. Williams, 141 W.Va. 595, 93 S.E.2d 835 (1956), annotated in 59 W.Va.L.Rev. 92 (1956). A used car lot on a busy highway was closed by injunction at the behest of homeowners most of whom lived in another municipality across the highway in a residential A zone. The court mentions this zoning but does not stress it. Aesthetics are discussed but the court does not rest the case on this basis. In fact, its statement in this regard is considerably weaker than in that of the Parkersburg case. Bright lights and noise as disturbers of quiet living are stressed. A vigorous dissent argues that a legitimate business should not be closed even though it may be somewhat disturbing. Also, see Farley v. Graney, 146 W.Va. 22, 119 S.E.2d 833 (1960).

5.   Notice in the principal case and in other cases in this chapter that the court's determination of how large or how small an area it will look at in evaluating the "character of the locality" may be crucial. See Restatement of Torts 2d § 827 (1979), and Beuscher and Morrison, Judicial Zoning through Recent Nuisance Cases, 1955 Wis.L.Rev. 440, 443–444.

6.   Although this chapter is concerned with the use of nuisance concepts in dealing with land use problems, it should be noted that the inadequacy of nuisance doctrines has been illustrated by the tendency of states to adopt planning and zoning statutes which are designed to include the rural-urban fringe.

LEW v. SUPERIOR COURT

Court of Appeal, First District, Division 4, California, 1993.
20 Cal.App.4th 866, 25 Cal.Rptr.2d 42.

PERLEY, ASSOCIATE JUSTICE.

Petitioners Albert G. Lew and B.K. Lew, owners of an apartment building in Berkeley, seek a peremptory writ of mandate to compel respondent superior court to set aside its judgment in favor of 75 plaintiffs in a consolidated small claims matter. We issued an alternative writ at the direction of the Supreme Court and, having considered the merits of the petition, now discharge the alternative writ and deny the petition.

PROCEDURAL AND FACTUAL BACKGROUND

Real parties (plaintiffs below and hereafter) are neighbors of a 36–unit HUD-insured section 8 (42 U.S.C.A. 1437 et seq.) apartment complex owned by petitioners located at 1615–1617 Russell Street, Berkeley, California. In August 1991, 66 actions were filed by plaintiffs in small claims court and consolidated for trial. According to the exemplar claim attached to the instant petition, plaintiffs contended that the defendants "allow illegal activity to occur on their property at 1615, & 1617 Russell St. which has caused me emotional and mental distress." Plaintiffs prevailed in small claims court, and petitioners appealed. The appeals were consolidated with nine others for a total of seventy five, and a trial de novo was held in superior court commencing on December 3, 1991.

At the trial de novo, several, although not a majority of the plaintiffs, testified. The other plaintiffs furnished affidavits setting forth their damages. Many plaintiffs signed a statement in the following form: "I have been confronted by the drug dealers, drug customers, and/or prostitutes that frequent and work around and from 1615–1617 Russell Street. On numerous occasions I have reported to the police the drug activity and other illegal activity coming from this property. [¶] Weekly I have lost many hours of sleep from the cars that burn rubber after each drug buy in the middle of the night, people fighting and yelling, sounds of gun shots, and the fear that grips me night and day for myself and my family's safety. [¶] Numerous times I have been confronted by dealers or buyers and I am now afraid to walk near this property and down my street. In fact, I often fear for my life day and night. This fear has permeated my home, my life, and my soul. [¶] I request your Honor award me $5,000 plus court costs for the suffering this property has caused me." Some of the plaintiffs drafted their own statements of damages or added individual examples of damage to the form. For example, Edgar Peterson, Jr., added to the form as follows: "Because of this illegal activity my child is unable to use our front yard and I even have to check the back yard since it has been intruded upon from time to time by people running from the police. He is learning to count by how many gunshots he hears and can't understand why he can't even enjoy our rose garden. . . . "

On May 14, 1992, respondent court issued a statement of decision and judgment in favor of the plaintiffs for damages totaling $218,325. The court found that at all relevant times, the property was "being used as a center for sale and distribution of drugs." It found that petitioners knew or should have known of the problems generated by their building and had failed to do what a reasonable person under the same or similar circumstances would have done. "While there was testimony of some efforts, including cooperation for a time with local police, the posting of 'no trespass' signs and the installation of new locks on some apartments, credible testimony indicated that a cooperative effort with the tenants and neighbors, a live-in manager, more secure fencing, and a key-card gate, as well as further efforts in cooperation with the City of Berkeley were strongly indicated. [¶] [Petitioners] reacted to the activity on the property by first denying that they were occurring, and then rejecting the notion that anything could be done to remedy the situation. While it is uncontradicted that [petitioners] lost money on the property as an investment, no evidence was presented that they were unable to discuss solutions with neighbors and tenants or to take ordinary steps to ensure the peaceful enjoyment of the apartments in the complex, as well as the vicinity of the property where drug traffic activities had established a pattern of affecting homes along defined routes."

Respondent court found for the plaintiffs on both a private and a public nuisance theory and awarded damages in each case in the amount sought by plaintiffs.

DISCUSSION

Relying on Martinez v. Pacific Bell (1990) 225 Cal.App.3d 1557, 275 Cal.Rptr. 878, and other cases refusing to hold defendants liable for the criminal acts of third persons, petitioners contend that a landlord should not be liable for damages resulting from criminal activity or tortious acts committed off of the landlord's property by drug dealers and their customers against third parties when neither the dealers, their customers, nor the third parties are the landlord's tenants.

In Martinez, the operator of a parking lot was assaulted by persons hanging about public telephone booths which were located near the lot and were used to conduct illegal drug transactions. After the operator was shot and robbed by unknown persons, he sued the telephone company to recover for his injuries on the ground, among others, that the telephone booth constituted a public nuisance. Although the court rejected the theory, it recognized that "a neighboring landowner might potentially receive normal nuisance remedies of injunction or damages for diminution in property value, which damage allegedly resulted from drug-related activities on another's nearby property." (Martinez v. Pacific Bell, supra, 225 Cal.App.3d at p. 1568, 275 Cal.Rptr. 878; see also Oscar v. University Students Cooperative Association (9th Cir.1991) 939 F.2d 808, neighbors of the building in which drug dealing allegedly occurred have valid cause of action for damages against owners under RICO and California law; Farmer v. Behmer (1909) 9 Cal.App. 773, 100

P. 901, neighbor of a house of prostitution can recover damages on a nuisance theory for interference with the use and enjoyment of his property.)

The Legislature has resolved any doubt as to the question of whether a so-called "drug house" is a nuisance through the enactment of section 11570 of the Health and Safety Code. That section, enacted in 1972, provides as follows: "Every building or place used for the purpose of unlawfully selling, serving, storing, keeping, manufacturing, or giving away any controlled substance, precursor, or analog specified in this division, and every building or place wherein or upon which those acts take place, is a nuisance which shall be enjoined, abated, and prevented, and for which damages may be recovered, whether it is a public or private nuisance."

Respondent court specifically found that the property was "being used as a center for sale and distribution of drugs." Thus, if the finding is supported by the evidence, the property is a nuisance by legislative definition. It is a nuisance in itself, a nuisance per se. (Cf. Farmer v. Behmer, supra, 9 Cal.App. 773, 778, 100 P. 901.) The fact that the immediate and specific injury plaintiffs suffered from this nuisance was due to the acts of third parties, rather than, for example, being due to noxious gases, is not relevant to the issue of whether the property qualifies as a nuisance under section 11570. That section does not require that the unlawful activity which makes the building a nuisance be conducted by the owner of the building, a tenant of the building, or a person entering with permission.

Petitioners take the position that the only remedy for a nuisance as defined by section 11570 is that which is provided by the sections following, i.e., section 11571 et seq. This remedy is an abatement action against "the owner, lessee, or agent of the building" maintained by a public official or by a citizen in his or her own name. (§ 11571.) It is a comprehensive scheme which includes sale of chattels used in maintaining the nuisance (§ 11581, subd. (a)) and may include closure of the premises for one year (§ 11581, subd. (b)(1)) and a civil penalty of up to $25,000.00 (§ 11581, subd. (b)(2)). Section 11573.5 provides that, under certain circumstances, the premises may be closed pending trial and provides for assistance to innocent tenants in that event. There is nothing in this statutory scheme for the abatement of "drug houses" that forecloses the lesser remedy of an action for damages in small claims court by a private party and, in fact, subdivision (f) of section 11573.5 provides that the remedies in that section "shall be in addition to any other existing remedies for nuisance abatement actions.... "

Civil Code section 3479 defines as a nuisance "[a]nything which is injurious to health, or is indecent or offensive to the senses, or an obstruction to the free use of property, so as to interfere with the comfortable enjoyment of life or property.... " An action may be maintained for damages "by any person whose property is injuriously affected, or whose personal enjoyment is lessened" by a nuisance as defined by section 3479. (Code Civ.Proc., § 731.) Section 11570 is significant in identifying a "drug house" as a nuisance because it makes clear that such a property qualifies as a nuisance within the broader Civil Code definition. We do not consider that it provides the sole remedy of an injured party. Not only has the Legislature so indicated in subdivision (f) of section 11573.5 but also it is long established law in California that one may maintain an action at law for damages for a nuisance without seeking an abatement thereof. (McIvor v. Mercer–Fraser Co. (1946) 76 Cal.App.2d 247, 254, 172 P.2d 758.) "Where the acts complained of amount to a nuisance, for which the person injured may have his action to abate the nuisance, he is not limited to that remedy, but may sue to recover the damages sustained by the wrongful acts of the defendant." (Will v. Sinkwitz (1871) 41 Cal. 588, 594.)

It has also been established that persons injured by a nuisance may seek damages in small claims court and that the small claims court has the power to consolidate numerous claims despite the fact that the issues may be complex and the ultimate judgment far in excess of the individual limits of a small claims judgment. (City and County of San Francisco v. Small Claims Division (1983) 141 Cal.App.3d 470, 190 Cal.Rptr. 340; see 26 U.S.F.L.Rev. 261.)

The important problem in this case relates to the fact that many of the acts which were injurious to the peace of mind of plaintiffs were committed off petitioners' property by persons who were not identified as tenants of the property and were not on petitioners' property. It bears emphasis that real parties did not seek to recover for the acts of these third parties but for the act of petitioners in maintaining their property as a nuisance. Although a nuisance and liability therefor may exist without negligence (Sturges v. Charles L. Harney, Inc. (1958) 165 Cal.App.2d 306, 318, 331 P.2d 1072), we need not determine whether it would ever be appropriate to impose liability upon owners whose property, without any fault of theirs, was a nuisance as defined by section 11570. Liability was imposed in this case on a theory of active fault on the part of petitioners in the management of their property.

Petitioners make the point that the damages suffered by plaintiffs are no different in kind from the damages suffered by the public at large but differ only in degree and are, therefore, not compensable. This principle, applicable to actions for public nuisances, does not apply in the instant case because the damages suffered affect the use and enjoyment of property. "The fact that a nuisance is public does not deprive the individual of his action in cases where, as to him, it is private and obstructs the free use and enjoyment of his private property. [Citations.]" (Fisher v. Zumwalt (1900) 128 Cal. 493, 496, 61 P. 82.)

* * *

The mental suffering which is the main component of the injuries alleged by plaintiffs is compensable under a nuisance theory. * * *

Petitioners did not attack the sufficiency of the evidence of damage at trial and do not do so in the instant petition. They do attack the finding of respondent court that their property was a hub of drug activity and the conclusion that petitioners did not act as a reasonable person in dealing with the problem that existed. Both attacks are without merit.

Sergeant Garen Nielsen testified that he had been the patrol sergeant for the area in which the property was located for one and one-half years and before that had been an undercover narcotics agent for the area for two and one-half years. He estimated that he had been to the property over 250 times on crime-related matters. He testified that the property is a hub or center for drug activity in the neighborhood, a place of "shelter and safety from the police." He had made two dozen arrests at the building and testified that, despite the fact that none of the dealers arrested lived there, they had easy access to the building and employed that access to thwart police efforts to apprehend them.

Weldon Rucker, the assistant city manager, called by the defense, also testified that he had known there was a drug problem at that location since he first became involved with the city's effort to control drugs in 1988. He described the drug operation there as "sophisticated" and the building as "like a fortress" for the sale of drugs. The property was so well known that citizens from other areas seeking to purchase drugs would engage a taxicab to be taken to Melrose Apartments to score.

Not only was there substantial evidence that the property was used in the sale of drugs and the harboring of drug dealers, the conclusion that petitioners did not take all reasonable measures available to them to control their property is supported by the evidence. Mr. Rucker testified that it was possible to clear up drug centers with the help of cooperative and aggressive management. Sergeant Nielsen suggested several specific steps that could be taken to meet the problem at that location. The steps that the court found could have been taken were not extraordinary, i.e., employment of "a live-in manager, more secure fencing, and a key-card gate." Under these circumstances, this court cannot say as a matter of law that petitioners acted reasonably in their efforts to meet the problem they knew existed on their property.

The alternative writ is discharged and the petition is denied.

Notes

1. What do you think of the strategy used by the neighbors in this case? Isn't it clear that seeking injunctive relief against the defendant would have been futile? In most nuisance cases the injunction is the weapon of choice for those who are offended by the defendant's land use; however, the Lew case is certainly an alternative approach for some kinds of nuisances.

2. In Essick v. Shillam, 347 Pa. 373, 32 A.2d 416 (1943) neighbors sought to enjoin the building of a supermarket as a nuisance. The court dissolved the trial court's injunction, stating in part: "Obviously, a commu-

nity grocery store in a residential district is not such a nuisance per se. It has been held that such stores do not detract from the residential character of the vicinity. * * * Because, however, the establishment here proposed is a supermarket, designed to attract patrons from other communities and having as an adjunct a parking lot for customers, the court below has placed it in the category of those enterprises which are nuisances as a matter of law when carried on in a residential area. No decision of an appellate court in this Commonwealth has been cited in support of this proposition, and it must be rejected."

In Bortz v. Troth, 359 Pa. 326, 59 A.2d 93 (1948), landowners sued to enjoin the erection and operation of a gasoline station. The case centered around the residential character of the neighborhood. The service station was to be built at the only non-commercial corner of a five-corner intersection. (See the map of the area which is included in these notes.) However, the Pennsylvania Court found that to allow the station would be to permit a commercial use to intrude into an exclusively residential area which was not in transition. The nearby commercial uses were not deemed to have altered the character of the residential district. Their proximity did not make it transitional. "To establish that principle as one of law will negative the existence of lines of demarcation dividing commercial, residential and exclusively residential districts. Commercial areas would be moved forward without restraint. * * * Fringe areas would advance so that block after block would steadily succumb to inroads of industrial enterprises."

BORTZ v. TROTH, 359 PA. 326, 59 A.2d 93 (1948)

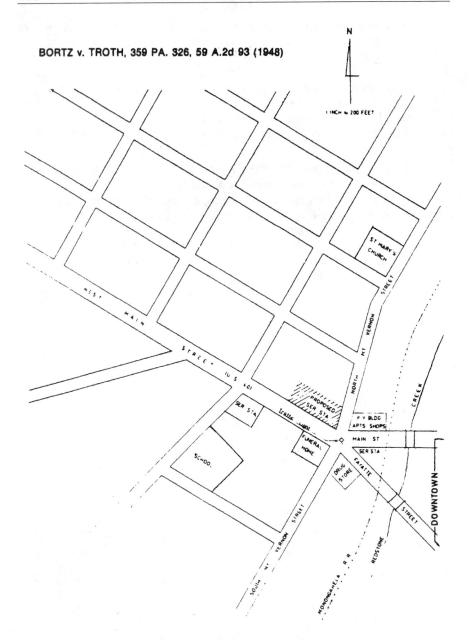

3.   By far, most of the cases testing whether an unzoned area was "exclusively residential," "predominantly residential" or "in transition" are those involving the proposed or actual operation of funeral parlors. If the area is exclusively residential or predominantly residential, the funeral home is almost sure to be enjoined. And there has been some judicial insistence that commercial invasion of a residential neighborhood must be considerable before a funeral home will be permitted. No one seems ever to have analyzed the funeral parlor cases in the light of the oft-repeated statement that a

mere breach of aesthetic standards is not a nuisance. A representative funeral parlor case follows.

POWELL v. TAYLOR

Supreme Court of Arkansas, 1954.
222 Ark. 896, 263 S.W.2d 906.

GEORGE ROSE SMITH, JUSTICE. This is a suit brought by six residents of Gurdon to enjoin the appellees from establishing a funeral home in a residential district within the city. The defendants intend to remodel a dwelling known as the Taylor place and to use it as a combined residence and undertaking parlor. The plaintiffs, who own homes nearby, objected to the proposal and offered to reimburse the defendants for the preliminary expenses already incurred. This effort to dissuade the defendants having failed, the present suit was filed. The chancellor denied relief upon the ground that the neighborhood is not exclusively residential.

On this particular subject the law has undergone a marked change in the past fifty years. Until about the end of the nineteenth century the only limitation upon one's right to use his property as he pleased was the prohibition against inflicting upon his neighbors injury affecting the physical senses. Hence the older cases went no farther than to exclude as nuisances, in residential districts, such offensive businesses as slaughter-houses, livery stables, blasting operations, and the like.

Today this narrow view prevails, if at all, in a few jurisdictions only. It is now generally recognized that the inhabitants of a residential neighborhood may, by taking prompt action before a funeral home has been established therein, prevent its intrusion. In 1952 the Supreme Court of Louisiana reviewed the more recent decisions in twenty-two States and found that nineteen prohibit the entry of a mortuary into a residential area, while only three courts adhered to the older view. Frederick v. Brown Funeral Homes, Inc., 222 La. 57, 62 So.2d 100. In a casenote the matter is summed up in these words: "The modern tendency to expand equity's protection of aesthetics and mental health has led the majority of jurisdictions to bar funeral homes or cemeteries from the residential sanctuaries of ordinarily sensitive people." 4 Ark.L.Rev. 483. These decisions rest not upon a finding that an undertaking parlor is physically offensive but rather upon the premise that its continuous suggestion of death and dead bodies tends to destroy the comfort and repose sought in home ownership.

We have already announced our preference for the view that permits the citizens of a residential district to make timely objection to its invasion by a funeral home. In Fentress v. Sicard, 181 Ark. 173, 25 S.W.2d 18, 19, we set aside the chancellor's injunction only because the neighborhood was changing to a business district, having already acquired drugstores, filling stations, grocery stores, etc. In that opinion we said, with reference to the proposed mortuary: "If the district of the location was an exclusively residential one, its intrusion therein would ordinarily constitute a nuisance, and could be prevented by injunction."

It is our conclusion in the case at bar that the neighborhood in question is so essentially residential in character as to entitle the appellants to the relief asked. The Taylor place is situated at the corner of Eighth and East Main Streets, and the testimony is largely directed to the area extending for two blocks in each direction, or a total of sixteen city blocks. In a relatively small city an area of this size may well be treated as a district in itself, else there might be no residential districts in the whole community. Gurdon is a city of the second class, having had a population of 2,390 in the year 1950. It is not shown to have adopted a zoning ordinance.

This square of sixteen blocks is bounded on the west by a public highway which is bordered by commercial establishments, their exact nature not being shown in detail. Otherwise the neighborhood is exclusively residential in appearance and almost so in its actual use. A seamstress living two doors east of the Taylor place earns some income by sewing at home. The couple in the house just south of the Taylor place rent rooms to elderly people and take care of them when they are ill. J.T. McAllister lives diagonally across the intersection from the Taylor place. He is in the wholesale lumber business and uses one room as an office, keeping books there and transacting business by telephone and with persons who call. A photograph of this home shows that there is no sign or anything else to indicate that business is carried on there. Farther up the street an eighty-year-old dentist has a small office in his yard and occasionally treats patients. The testimony discloses no other commercial activity within the area.

On the other hand, the residential quality of the neighborhood is convincingly shown. A real estate dealer describes it as the best residential section in Gurdon. Estimates as to the value of various homes range from $15,000 to $35,000. Many inhabitants of the area confirm its residential character and earnestly protest the entry of the mortuary. One, whose wife suffered a mental illness some years ago, says that he will be forced to move away if the funeral home is established. Another testifies that he will not build a home on his vacant lots across the street from the Taylor place if it is converted to a funeral parlor. A third testifies that she lost interest in buying the house next to the Taylor place when she learned of the defendants' plans. It is true that other witnesses state that they have no objection to the proposal, and the chancellor found that property values will not be adversely affected. But we regard the residential character of the vicinity as the controlling issue, and the evidence upon that question preponderates in favor of the appellants.

Reversed.

MILLWEE, JUSTICE (dissenting). As I read the opinion of the majority, it is now the law in Arkansas that the operation of a modest undertaking parlor in a mixed residential and business area of a city of the second class constitutes a nuisance per se and may be abated as such by injunction. This holding is so foreign to the traditional attitude of this court and the general legislative policy of this state that I must respectfully dissent.

While the majority conclude that the area in question here is "essentially" residential, they proceed to apply the so-called "modern rule", which is, in those jurisdictions which recognize it, only applicable when the affected area is "exclusively" or "purely" residential. Since this goes far beyond any of the authorities cited by the majority, I suppose it should be dubbed the "ultra modern rule". It is perfectly apparent from the detailed description of the majority that the area affected here is a mixed commercial and residential one and that the chancellor was eminently correct in holding that it was not "exclusively" residential. This determination by the chancellor is in my opinion fully supported by the great preponderance of the evidence.

Moreover, the majority failed to mention the fact that appellees' contemplated operation does not include the holding of funerals or the maintenance of noisy ambulances—factors which usually accompany the operation of a funeral home. Nor does the instant case contain factors presented by the proof in the cases relied on by the majority, such as the escape of noxious odors, the depreciation of values in surrounding properties, the ability of neighbors to see the taking in or carrying out of bodies or that they will be rendered more susceptible to contagious diseases. On the contrary, it is undisputed that the structure planned by appellees will greatly improve the beauty of the neighborhood, that there will be no noise from ambulances and no escape of odors or gases. It was further shown that within a radius of two blocks from appellees' property there is a nursing home, a dentist office, a real estate office, a lumber office, a seamstress place of business, service station, boat factory, lumber company office, church and a hospital. Two blocks away is the business district on Highway 53, and three and a half blocks away is a bulk gas plant. This could hardly be called a purely residential section.

In denying an injunction, the able chancellor stated in the decree: "The rule is well settled that no injunction should be issued in advance of the construction of a legal structure, or in advance of the operation of a legal business, unless it be certain that the same will constitute a nuisance; and, where the claim to relief is based on the use which is to be made of a lawful business, the Court will ordinarily not interfere by injunction in advance of actual operation.

"Since the funeral home in the instant case is not a nuisance per se and may be operated in such a manner as to not become a nuisance, the rule that Chancery Courts will not issue an injunction in advance of actual operation, but will leave the complainants to assert their rights thereafter, if the contemplated use results in a nuisance, is applicable and controlling in the case at bar."

Under our decisions it is difficult to see how the trial court could have reached any other conclusion. The rule which he declared has been consistently applied in numerous cases involving most every character of lawful business or operation. Among these are: a livery stable, Durfey v.

Thalheimer, 85 Ark. 544, 109 S.W. 519; a cotton gin, Swaim v. Morris, 93 Ark. 362, 125 S.W. 432; a filling station, Ft. Smith v. Norris, 178 Ark. 399, 10 S.W.2d 861; a cemetery, McDaniel v. Forrest Park Cemetery Co., 156 Ark. 571, 246 S.W. 874; a hide and fur business, Ft. Smith v. Western Hide and Fur Co., 153 Ark. 99, 239 S.W. 724; an ice plant, Bickley v. Morgan Utilities Co., Inc., 173 Ark. 1038, 294 S.W. 38; a tuberculosis sanatorium, Mitchell v. Deisch, 179 Ark. 788, 18 S.W.2d 364; a quarry and rock crusher, Jones v. Kelley Trust Co., 179 Ark. 857, 18 S.W.2d 356; a tabernacle, Murphy v. Cupp, 182 Ark. 334, 31 S.W.2d 396; a sawmill, Eddy v. Thornton, 205 Ark. 843, 170 S.W.2d 995; a bowling alley, Kimmons v. Benson, 220 Ark. 299, 247 S.W.2d 468.

In the McDaniel case, supra [156 Ark. 571, 246 S.W. 874], we adopted the following as a well settled rule: " 'The unpleasant reflections suggested by having before one's eyes constantly recurring memorials of death is not such a nuisance as will authorize the intervention of equity.' " In the Kimmons case, supra, we reaffirmed the rule that we would decline to enjoin the erection of a lawful business structure where there is a doubt that it would prove to be a nuisance. Certainly appellees are entitled to the benefit of that doubt by the great preponderance of the evidence in this case.

About the only businesses or operations which this court has seen fit to enjoin as nuisances per se are: a gaming house, Vanderworker v. State, 13 Ark. 700; a bawdy house, State v. Porter, 38 Ark. 637; and the standing of a stallion or jackass within the limits of a municipality, Ex parte Foote, 70 Ark. 12, 65 S.W. 706. To this select group must now be added the operation of a modest undertaking parlor, where no funerals are to be held, in an area of a city of the second class which is "essentially" but not "actually" or "exclusively" residential.

It should be a matter of common knowledge that there are scores of undertaking establishments located in residential, or mixed residential and commercial, areas of the smaller municipalities in this state with hundreds of thousands of dollars invested in them. Under the rule proclaimed today these enterprises are placed in a most precarious position. And in the future many citizens, such as the appellees, will be denied the privilege of pursuing a dignified and lawful calling in places where their services would be highly welcome and most sorely needed. I cannot agree to this rule.

McFADDIN, J., joins in this dissent.

Notes

1. Compare with this, however, the language of a case from the same jurisdiction only a few years later: "In addition to the above, we found in Fentress v. Sicard, 181 Ark. 173, 25 S.W.2d 18, and Blair v. Yancy et al., Ark.1958, 229 Ark. 745, 318 S.W.2d 589, dealing with funeral parlors and undertaking establishments, that the establishment of such businesses would not be prohibited simply because they might be offensive to adjoining property owners' senses and/or depreciate their property. Therefore, the use

of the land as a cemetery, not being a nuisance per se * * * does not constitute an invasion of appellee's property." North Hill Memorial Gardens v. Hicks, 230 Ark. 787, 326 S.W.2d 797 (1959). However, the Fentress case involved an area in transition to a business area, the Blair case involved a mortuary in a commercial zone, and the case quoted from involved a cemetery.

On the other hand, a minority of jurisdictions do not adhere to the rule stated in Powell v. Taylor. Those cases hold that funeral homes can only become nuisances per accidens as a result of the way in which they are operated. E.g.: Frederick v. Brown Funeral Homes, 222 La. 57, 62 So.2d 100 (1952).

2.   Compare also with the principal case Miller–Elston Mortuary, Inc. v. Paal, 261 Ark. 644, 550 S.W.2d 771 (1977), where the court reversed a trial court finding that a funeral parlor would be a nuisance in a predominantly residential area. The court, in reversing, noted that improper reliance was placed on testimony that allowing the funeral parlor, a black-owned business, to locate in an area which was becoming racially integrated, would discourage further integration.

3.   Some samples of language from court opinions serve to illustrate the attitude toward funeral parlors. In Smith v. Fairchild, 193 Miss. 536, 10 So.2d 172 (1942), the Court did not believe that several commercial operations in the area changed the neighborhood from "essentially" residential. The court quoted from Tureman v. Ketterlin, 304 Mo. 221, 263 S.W. 202, 43 A.L.R. 1155 (1924) to this effect: "An undertaking establishment stands on a different footing from that of the occasional corner grocery and oil filling station which have made their appearances there. The latter may offend the aesthetic sense of those living in their proximity; the former would destroy, in an essential respect, the comfort and repose of their home." "The constant going and coming of the hearse; * * * the not infrequent taking in and out of dead bodies; the occasional funeral with its mourners and funeral airs, held in the part of the house designed for a chapel; the unknown dead in the morgue, and the visits of relatives seeking to identify them; the thought of autopsies, of embalming; the dread, or horror, or thought, that the dead are or may be lying in the house next door, a morgue; the dread of communicable disease, not well founded, as we have seen, but nevertheless present in the mind of the normal layman—all of these are conducive to depression of the normal person; each of these is a constant reminder of mortality. These constant reminders, this depression of mind, deprive the home of that comfort and repose to which its owner is entitled." In Fraser v. Fred Parker Funeral Home, 201 S.C. 88, 21 S.E.2d 577 (1942), the Court referred to the need for preservation of the homes of the people as "places of ultimate retreat, security, or release from the cares and struggles for a living" and as having "distinct and necessary characteristics, one of which is cheer." Funeral homes injure this mental health and cheerfulness, said the Court. Indeed: "This is not a case of trying to balance the rights of a home owner with the rights simply of a business operator, and if it were we could not be unmindful that America's future is greatly determined by its homes, and that the 'strength of a nation, especially a republic is in the intelligent and well-ordered homes of the people.' " These two 1942 cases present an almost moralistic defense of good being threatened by evil.

4. For cases permitting the establishment of funeral parlors on the ground, among others, that commercial uses had sufficiently entered the area, see O'Connor v. Ryan, 159 S.W.2d 531 (Tex.Civ.App.1942) and Moss v. Burke and Trotti, Inc., 198 La. 76, 3 So.2d 281 (1941).

Displaying and selling tombstones in a residential section, even though the display was in the form of a mock graveyard, was not enjoined. Grubbs v. Wooten, 189 Ga. 390, 5 S.E.2d 874 (1940). But an injunction was given where stone cutting accompanied the monument sales business in City of Bethlehem v. Druckenmiller, 344 Pa. 170, 25 A.2d 190 (1942).

In Young v. St. Martin's Church, 361 Pa. 505, 64 A.2d 814 (1949), owners of "palatial dwelling houses" in an exclusively residential district failed in their efforts to prevent the establishment of a cemetery nearby. However, efforts to prevent operation of a mental sanitarium and a venereal disease clinic respectively in residential districts succeeded in Park v. Stolzheise, 24 Wash.2d 781, 167 P.2d 412 (1946) and Benton v. Pittard, 197 Ga. 843, 31 S.E.2d 6, 153 A.L.R. 968 (1944).

5. On the subject of permissible activities in a residential area, not involving funeral homes, what about one involving the razing of a nice home? In Eyerman v. Mercantile Trust Co., 524 S.W.2d 210 (Mo.App.1975), the court was confronted with a petition from neighbors to prevent the demolition of a home in a nice, old subdivision. The deceased owner had provided in her will that it be razed. The neighbors alleged that this would harm their property rights, violate the subdivision trust indenture, amount to a private nuisance and violate public policy. Neither the devisees nor the city were parties to the suit. (The devisees presumably could have brought an action for waste. The will may have contained a "no contest" provision.) The court declined to declare this to be a nuisance but enjoined the executor on the basis of public policy, perhaps partially because the subdivision had been designated a landmark by the City (and perhaps unconsciously drawing upon a related concept in the law of trusts).

Eyerman obviously is not a typical nuisance case. It is questionable whether it ought to be considered a nuisance case at all. But how else could the injunction be granted? Is public policy such a broad concept that an injunction can be granted on such a ground? What was actually proposed was an act of waste as to the heirs of the decedent. Where were they and why were they not in court? Does the holding of the majority bear a relationship to the doctrine in the law of trusts that a trust cannot be created to carry out an act such as this because it would be against public policy to enforce the trust?

6. Nuisance cases quite often hinge on the attitudes of judges toward a particular activity. "Halfway house" cases involving homes designed to help rehabilitate offenders and move them back gradually into society are an example. Two cases which are very similar, but reach different results, are Arkansas Release Guidance Foundation v. Needler, 252 Ark. 194, 477 S.W.2d 821 (1972) and Nicholson v. Connecticut Half–Way House, Inc., 153 Conn. 507, 218 A.2d 383 (1966). In Needler, the operation was enjoined, but in Nicholson, injunctive relief was denied. The Arkansas Supreme Court attempted to distinguish the earlier Connecticut decision on the basis that in Nicholson "there was only apprehension of decrease in property values and

no evidence of any actual decrease in values of nearby property" whereas in Needler there was "evidence relating to the operation of the halfway house reflecting significant decrease in property values in the mixed business and residential area * * * because of the nature of the occupants of the halfway house." This decrease was based, however, on fear and apprehension, and the Arkansas Court admits that Connecticut had said that equity should not interfere "simply because of fears and apprehensions existing without substantial reason." The Arkansas Court apparently concluded that the fear and apprehension was justified and that its effect on property values was substantial and significant. One distinguishing factor was that the halfway house in Nicholson had not yet gone into operation. Nonetheless, these cases help serve to illustrate how societal values may affect the outcome. This would seem to be true in the Eyerman case. The court was simply not going to permit something so outrageous as the razing of an expensive home.

PRAH v. MARETTI

Supreme Court of Wisconsin, 1982.
108 Wis.2d 223, 321 N.W.2d 182.

ABRAHAMSON, JUSTICE.

This appeal [presents] an issue of first impression, namely, whether an owner of a solar-heated residence states a claim upon which relief can be granted when he asserts that his neighbor's proposed construction of a residence (which conforms to existing deed restrictions and local ordinances) interferes with his access to an unobstructed path for sunlight across the neighbor's property. This case thus involves a conflict between one landowner (Glenn Prah, the plaintiff) interested in unobstructed access to sunlight across adjoining property as a natural source of energy and an adjoining landowner (Richard D. Maretti, the defendant) interested in the development of his land.

The circuit court concluded that the plaintiff presented no claim upon which relief could be granted and granted summary judgment for the defendant. We reverse the judgment of the circuit court and remand the cause to the circuit court for further proceedings.

According to the complaint, the plaintiff is the owner of a residence which was constructed during the years 1978–1979. The complaint alleges that the residence has a solar system which includes collectors on the roof to supply energy for heat and hot water and that after the plaintiff built his solar-heated house, the defendant purchased the lot adjacent to and immediately to the south of the plaintiff's lot and commenced planning construction of a home. The complaint further states that when the plaintiff learned of defendant's plans to build the house he advised the defendant that if the house were built at the proposed location, defendant's house would substantially and adversely affect the integrity of plaintiff's solar system and could cause plaintiff other damage. Nevertheless, the defendant began construction. The complaint further alleges that the plaintiff is entitled to "unrestricted use of the sun and its solar power" and demands judgment for injunctive relief and damages.[12]

After filing his complaint, the plaintiff moved for a temporary injunction to restrain and enjoin construction by the defendant. In ruling on that motion the circuit court heard testimony, received affidavits and viewed the site.

The record made on the motion reveals the following additional facts: Plaintiff's home was the first residence built in the subdivision, and although plaintiff did not build his house in the center of the lot it was built in accordance with applicable restrictions. Plaintiff advised defendant that if the defendant's home were built at the proposed site it would cause a shadowing effect on the solar collectors which would reduce the efficiency of the system and possibly damage the system. To avoid these adverse effects, plaintiff requested defendant to locate his home an additional several feet away from the plaintiff's lot line, the exact number being disputed. Plaintiff and defendant failed to reach an agreement on the location of defendant's home before defendant started construction. The Architectural Control Committee of the subdivision and the Planning Commission of the City of Muskego approved the defendant's plans for his home, including its location on the lot. After such approval, the defendant apparently changed the grade of the property without prior notice to the Architectural Control Committee. The problem with defendant's proposed construction, as far as the plaintiff's interests are concerned, arises from a combination of the grade and the distance of defendant's home from the defendant's lot line.

The circuit court denied plaintiff's motion for injunctive relief, declared it would entertain a motion for summary judgment and thereafter entered judgment in favor of the defendant.

* * *

The plaintiff presents three legal theories to support his claim that the defendant's continued construction of a home justifies granting him relief: (1) the construction constitutes a common law private nuisance; (2) the construction is prohibited by sec. 844.01, Stats.1979–80;[13] and (3)

---

12. As part of his amended answer to the complaint the defendant asserts that "the plaintiff's complaint fails to state a claim or cause of action against the defendant upon which relief can be granted and that the plaintiff is without legal or equitable rights with respect to his claim that he is entitled to the unrestricted use of the sun and its solar power and that the plaintiff's action is frivolous and without merit."

For a discussion of protecting solar access, see Note, Obtaining Access to Solar Energy: Nuisance, Water Rights, and Zoning Administration, 45 Bkyn.L.Rev. 357 (1979); Comment, Obstruction of Sunlight as a Private Nuisance, 65 Cal.L.Rev. 94 (1977); Comment, Solar Rights: Guarantee-

ing a Place in the Sun, 57 Ore.L.Rev. 94 (1977); Note, The Allocation of Sunlight; Solar Rights and the Prior Appropriation Doctrine, 47 U.Colo.L.Rev. 421 (1976).

13. Sec. 844.01, Stats.1979–80, provides:

"(1) Any person owning or claiming an interest in real property may bring an action claiming physical injury to, or interference with, the property or his interest therein; the action may be to redress past injury, to restrain further injury, to abate the source of injury, or for other appropriate relief.

(2) Physical injury includes unprivileged intrusions and encroachments; the injury may be surface, subsurface or su-

the construction interferes with the solar easement plaintiff acquired under the doctrine of prior appropriation.[14]

As to the claim of private nuisance the circuit court concluded that the law of private nuisance requires the court to make "a comparative evaluation of the conflicting interests and to weigh the gravity of the harm to the plaintiff against the utility of the defendant's conduct." The circuit court concluded: "A comparative evaluation of the conflicting interests, keeping in mind the omissions and commissions of both Prah and Maretti, indicates that defendant's conduct does not cause the gravity of the harm which the plaintiff himself may well have avoided by proper planning." The circuit court also concluded that sec. 844.01 does not apply to a home constructed in accordance with deed and municipal ordinance requirements. Further, the circuit court rejected the prior appropriation doctrine as "an intrusion of judicial egoism over legislative passivity."

We consider first whether the complaint states a claim for relief based on common law private nuisance. This state has long recognized that an owner of land does not have an absolute or unlimited right to use the land in a way which injures the rights of others. The rights of neighboring landowners are relative; the uses by one must not unreasonably impair the uses or enjoyment of the other.[15] VI-A *American Law of Property* sec. 28.22, pp. 64–65 (1954). When one landowner's use of his or her property unreasonably interferes with another's enjoyment of his or

prasurface; the injury may arise from activities on the plaintiff's property, or from activities outside the plaintiff's property which affect plaintiff's property.

(3) Interference with an interest is any activity other than physical injury which lessens the possibility of use or enjoyment of the interest.

(4) The lessening of a security interest without physical injury is not actionable unless such lessening constitutes waste."

We can find no reported cases in which sec. 844.01 has been interpreted and applied, and the parties do not cite any.

14. Under the doctrine of prior appropriation the first user to appropriate the resource has the right of continued use to the exclusion of others.

The doctrine of prior appropriation has been used by several western states to allocate water, *Paug-Vik v. Wards Cove,* 633 P.2d 1015 (Alaska 1981), and by the New Mexico legislature to allocate solar access, secs. 47–3–1 to 47–3–5, N.M.Stats.1978. See also Note, The Allocation of Sunlight: Solar Rights and the Prior Appropriation Doctrine, 47 Colo.L.Rev. 421 (1976).

15. In *Abdella v. Smith,* 34 Wis.2d 393, 399, 149 N.W.2d 537 (1967), this court

quoted with approval Dean Prosser's description of the judicial balancing of the reciprocal rights and privileges of neighbors in the use of their land: "Most of the litigation as to private nuisance has dealt with the conflicting interests of landowners and the question of the reasonableness of the defendant's conduct: The defendant's privilege of making a reasonable use of his own property for his own benefit and conducting his affairs in his own way is no less important than the plaintiff's right to use and enjoy his premises. The two are correlative and interdependent, and neither is entitled to prevail entirely, at the expense of the other. Some balance must be struck between the two. The plaintiff must be expected to endure some inconvenience rather than curtail the defendant's freedom of action, and the defendant must so use his own property that he causes no unreasonable harm to the plaintiff. The law of private nuisance is very largely a series of adjustments to limit the reciprocal rights and privileges of both. In every case the court must make a comparative evaluation of the conflicting interests according to objective legal standards, and the gravity of the harm to the plaintiff must be weighed against the utility of the defendant's conduct." Prosser, Law of Torts, sec. 89, p. 596 (2d ed. 1971) (Citations omitted).

her property, that use is said to be a private nuisance. *Hoene v. Milwaukee,* 17 Wis.2d 209, 214, 116 N.W.2d 112 (1962); *Metzger v. Hochrein,* 107 Wis. 267, 269, 83 N.W. 308 (1900). See also Prosser, *Law of Torts* sec. 89, p. 591 (2d ed. 1971).

The private nuisance doctrine has traditionally been employed in this state to balance the conflicting rights of landowners, and this court has recently adopted the analysis of private nuisance set forth in the Restatement (Second) of Torts. *CEW Mgmt. Corp. v. First Federal Savings & Loan Association,* 88 Wis.2d 631, 633, 277 N.W.2d 766 (1979). The Restatement defines private nuisance as "a nontrespassory invasion of another's interest in the private use and enjoyment of land." Restatement (Second) of Torts sec. 821D (1977). The phrase "interest in the private use and enjoyment of land" as used in sec. 821D is broadly defined to include any disturbance of the enjoyment of property.

* * *

Although the defendant's obstruction of the plaintiff's access to sunlight appears to fall within the Restatement's broad concept of a private nuisance as a nontrespassory invasion of another's interest in the private use and enjoyment of land, the defendant asserts that he has a right to develop his property in compliance with statutes, ordinances and private covenants without regard to the effect of such development upon the plaintiff's access to sunlight. In essence, the defendant is asking this court to hold that the private nuisance doctrine is not applicable in the instant case and that his right to develop his land is a right which is *per se* superior to his neighbor's interest in access to sunlight. This position is expressed in the maxim "cujus est solum, ejus est usque ad coelum et ad infernos," that is, the owner of land owns up to the sky and down to the center of the earth. The rights of the surface owner are, however, not unlimited. *U.S. v. Causby,* 328 U.S. 256, 260–1, 66 S.Ct. 1062, 1065, 90 L.Ed. 1206 (1946). See also 114.03, Stats.1979–80.

The defendant is not completely correct in asserting that the common law did not protect a landowner's access to sunlight across adjoining property. At English common law a landowner could acquire a right to receive sunlight across adjoining land by both express agreement and under the judge-made doctrine of "ancient lights." Under the doctrine of ancient lights if the landowner had received sunlight across adjoining property for a specified period of time, the landowner was entitled to continue to receive unobstructed access to sunlight across the adjoining property. Under the doctrine the landowner acquired a negative prescriptive easement and could prevent the adjoining landowner from obstructing access to light.[16]

---

16. Pfeiffer, Ancient Lights: Legal Protection of Access to Solar Energy, 68 ABAJ 288 (1982). No American common law state recognizes a landowner's right to acquire an easement of light by prescription. Comment, Solar Lights: Guaranteeing a Place in the Sun, 57 Ore.L.Rev. 94, 112 (1977).

Although American courts have not been as receptive to protecting a landowner's access to sunlight as the English courts, American courts have afforded some protection to a landowner's interest in access to sunlight. American courts honor express easements to sunlight. American courts initially enforced the English common law doctrine of ancient lights, but later every state which considered the doctrine repudiated it as inconsistent with the needs of a developing country. Indeed, for just that reason this court concluded that an easement to light and air over adjacent property could not be created or acquired by prescription and has been unwilling to recognize such an easement by implication. *Depner v. United States National Bank,* 202 Wis. 405, 408, 232 N.W. 851 (1930); *Miller v. Hoeschler,* 126 Wis. 263, 268–69, 105 N.W. 790 (1905).

Many jurisdictions in this country have protected a landowner from malicious obstruction of access to light (the spite fence cases) under the common law private nuisance doctrine.[17] If an activity is motivated by malice it lacks utility and the harm it causes others outweighs any social values. VI–A Law of Property sec. 28.28, p. 79 (1954) This court was reluctant to protect a landowner's interest in sunlight even against a spite fence, only to be overruled by the legislature. Shortly after this court upheld a landowner's right to erect a useless and unsightly sixteen-foot spite fence four feet from his neighbor's windows, *Metzger v. Hochrein,* 107 Wis. 267, 83 N.W. 308 (1900), the legislature enacted a law specifically defining a spite fence as an actionable private nuisance. Thus a landowner's interest in sunlight has been protected in this country by common law private nuisance law at least in the narrow context of the modern American rule invalidating spite fences. See, *e.g., Sundowner, Inc. v. King,* 95 Idaho 367, 509 P.2d 785 (1973); Restatement (Second) of Torts, sec. 829 (1977).

This court's reluctance in the nineteenth and early part of the twentieth century to provide broader protection for a landowner's access to sunlight was premised on three policy considerations. First, the right of landowners to use their property as they wished, as long as they did not cause physical damage to a neighbor, was jealously guarded. *Metzger v. Hochrein,* 107 Wis. 267, 272, 83 N.W. 308 (1900).

Second, sunlight was valued only for aesthetic enjoyment or as illumination. Since artificial light could be used for illumination, loss of sunlight was at most a personal annoyance which was given little, if any, weight by society.

Third, society had a significant interest in not restricting or impeding land development. *Dillman v. Hoffman,* 38 Wis. 559, 574 (1875). This

---

17. In several of the spite fence cases, courts have recognized the property owner's interest in sunlight. *Hornsby v. Smith,* 191 Ga. 491, 500, 13 S.E.2d 20 (1941) ("the air and light no matter from which direction they come are God-given, and are essential to the life, comfort, and happiness of everyone"); *Burke v. Smith,* 69 Mich. 380, 389, 37 N.W. 838 (1888) ("the right to breathe the air and enjoy the sunshine, is a natural one"); *Barger v. Barringer,* 151 N.C. 433, 437, 66 S.E. 439 (1909) ("light and air are as much a necessity as water, and all are the common heritage of mankind").

court repeatedly emphasized that in the growth period of the nineteenth and early twentieth centuries change is to be expected and is essential to property and that recognition of a right to sunlight would hinder property development.

* * *

Considering these three policies, this court concluded that in the absence of an express agreement granting access to sunlight, a landowner's obstruction of another's access to sunlight was not actionable. *Miller v. Hoeschler, supra,* 126 Wis. at 271, 105 N.W. 790; *Depner v. United States National Bank, supra,* 202 Wis. at 410, 232 N.W. 851. These three policies are no longer fully accepted or applicable. They reflect factual circumstances and social priorities that are now obsolete.

First, society has increasingly regulated the use of land by the landowner for the general welfare. *Euclid v. Ambler Realty Co.,* 272 U.S. 365, 47 S.Ct. 114, 71 L.Ed. 303 (1926); *Just v. Marinette,* 56 Wis.2d 7, 201 N.W.2d 761 (1972).

Second, access to sunlight has taken on a new significance in recent years. In this case the plaintiff seeks to protect access to sunlight, not for aesthetic reasons or as a source of illumination but as a source of energy. Access to sunlight as an energy source is of significance both to the landowner who invests in solar collectors and to a society which has an interest in developing alternative sources of energy.[18]

Third, the policy of favoring unhindered private development in an expanding economy is no longer in harmony with the realities of our society. *State v. Deetz,* 66 Wis.2d 1, 224 N.W.2d 407 (1974). The need for easy and rapid development is not as great today as it once was, while our perception of the value of sunlight as a source of energy has increased significantly.

Courts should not implement obsolete policies that have lost their vigor over the course of the years. The law of private nuisance is better suited to resolve landowners' disputes about property development in the 1980's than is a rigid rule which does not recognize a landowner's interest in access to sunlight. As we said in *Ballstadt v. Pagel,* 202 Wis.

18. State and federal governments are encouraging the use of the sun as a significant source of energy. In this state the legislature has granted tax benefits to encourage the utilization of solar energy. See Ch. 349, 350, Laws of 1979. See also Ch. 354, Laws of 1981 (eff. May 7, 1982) enabling legislation providing for local ordinances guaranteeing access to sunlight.

The federal government has also recognized the importance of solar energy and currently encourages its utilization by means of tax benefits, direct subsidies and government loans for solar projects. Energy Tax Act of 1978, Nov. 9, 1978, P.L. 95–618, 92 Stat. 3174, relevant portion codified at 26 U.S.C.A. sec. 44(c) (1982 Supp.); Energy Security Act, June 30, 1980, P.L. 96–294, 94 Stat. 611, relevant portion codified at 12 U.S.C.A. sec. 3610 (1980); Small Business Energy Loan Act, July 4, 1978, P.L. 95–315, 92 Stat. 377, relevant portion codified within 15 U.S.C.A. secs. 631, 633, 636, and 639 (1982 Supp.); National Energy Conservation Policy Act, Nov. 9, 1978, P.L. 95–619, 92 Stat. 3206, relevant portion codified at 42 U.S.C.A. secs. 1451, 1703–45 (1982 Supp.); Energy Conservation and Production Act, Aug. 14, 1976, P.L. 94–385, 90 Stat. 1125, relevant portion codified at 42 U.S.C.A. sec. 6881 (1977).

484, 489, 232 N.W. 862 (1930), "What is regarded in law as constituting a nuisance in modern times would no doubt have been tolerated without question in former times." We read *State v. Deetz,* 66 Wis.2d 1, 224 N.W.2d 407 (1974), as an endorsement of the application of common law nuisance to situations involving the conflicting interests of landowners and as rejecting *per se* exclusions to the nuisance law reasonable use doctrine.

* * *

Yet the defendant would have us ignore the flexible private nuisance law as a means of resolving the dispute between the landowners in this case and would have us adopt an approach, already abandoned in *Deetz,* of favoring the unrestricted development of land and of applying a rigid and inflexible rule protecting his right to build on his land and disregarding any interest of the plaintiff in the use and enjoyment of his land. This we refuse to do.[19]

Private nuisance law, the law traditionally used to adjudicate conflicts between private landowners, has the flexibility to protect both a landowner's right of access to sunlight and another landowner's right to develop land. Private nuisance law is better suited to regulate access to sunlight in modern society and is more in harmony with legislative policy and the prior decisions of this court than is an inflexible doctrine of non-recognition of any interest in access to sunlight across adjoining land.

We therefore hold that private nuisance law, that is, the reasonable use doctrine as set forth in the Restatement, is applicable to the instant case. Recognition of a nuisance claim for unreasonable obstruction of access to sunlight will not prevent land development or unduly hinder the use of adjoining land. It will promote the reasonable use and

19. Defendant's position that a landowner's interest in access to sunlight across adjoining land is not "legally enforceable" and is therefore excluded *per se* from private nuisance law was adopted in *Fontainebleau Hotel Corp. v. Forty-Five Twenty-Five, Inc.,* 114 So.2d 357 (Fla.App.1959), *cert. den.* 117 So.2d 842 (Fla.1960). The Florida district court of appeals permitted construction of a building which cast a shadow on a neighboring hotel's swimming pool. The court asserted that nuisance law protects only those interests "which [are] recognized and protected by law," and that there is no legally recognized or protected right to access to sunlight. A property owner does not, said the Florida court, in the absence of a contract or statute, acquire a presumptive or implied right to the free flow of light and air across adjoining land. The Florida court then concluded that a lawful structure which causes injury to another by cutting off light and air—whether or not erected partly for spite—does not give rise to a cause of action for damages or for an injunction. See also *People ex rel. Hoogasian v. Sears, Roebuck & Co.,* 52 Ill.2d 301, 287 N.E.2d 677 (1972).

We do not find the reasoning of *Fontainebleau* persuasive. The court leaped from rejecting an easement by prescription (the doctrine of ancient lights) and an easement by implication to the conclusion that there is no right to protection from obstruction of access to sunlight. The court's statement that a landowner has no right to light should be the conclusion, not its initial premise. The court did not explain why an owner's interest in unobstructed light should not be protected or in what manner an owner's interest in unobstructed sunlight differs from an owner's interest in being free from obtrusive noises or smells or differs from an owner's interest in unobstructed use of water. The recognition of a *per se* exception to private nuisance law may invite unreasonable behavior.

enjoyment of land in a manner suitable to the 1980's. That obstruction of access to light might be found to constitute a nuisance in certain circumstances does not mean that it will be or must be found to constitute a nuisance under all circumstances. The result in each case depends on whether the conduct complained of is unreasonable.

Accordingly we hold that the plaintiff in this case has stated a claim under which relief can be granted. Nonetheless we do not determine whether the plaintiff in this case is entitled to relief. In order to be entitled to relief the plaintiff must prove the elements required to establish actionable nuisance, and the conduct of the defendant herein must be judged by the reasonable use doctrine.

The defendant asserts that even if we hold that the private nuisance doctrine applies to obstruction of access to sunlight across adjoining land, the circuit court's granting of summary judgment should be affirmed.

Although the memorandum decision of the circuit court in the instant case is unclear, it appears that the circuit court recognized that the common law private nuisance doctrine was applicable but concluded that defendant's conduct was not unreasonable. The circuit court apparently attempted to balance the utility of the defendant's conduct with the gravity of the harm. Sec. 826, Restatement (Second) of Torts (1977). The defendant urges us to accept the circuit court's balance as adequate. We decline to do so.

The circuit court concluded that because the defendant's proposed house was in conformity with zoning regulations, building codes and deed restrictions, the defendant's use of the land was reasonable. This court has concluded that a landowner's compliance with zoning laws does not automatically bar a nuisance claim. Compliance with the law "is not the controlling factor, though it is, of course, entitled to some weight." *Bie v. Ingersoll,* 27 Wis.2d 490, 495, 135 N.W.2d 250 (1965). The circuit court also concluded that the plaintiff could have avoided any harm by locating his own house in a better place. Again, plaintiff's ability to avoid the harm is a relevant but not a conclusive factor. See secs. 826, 827, 828, Restatement (Second) of Torts (1977).

* * *

The judgment of the circuit court is reversed and the cause remanded for proceedings not inconsistent with this opinion.

CECI, J., not participating.

CALLOW, J. dissents [The long dissent is not reproduced due to space limitations.]

Notes

1. In his dissent, Justice Callow argued that the law of private nuisance could not be extended to protect light and air if the obstruction served a useful purpose. He argued that "spite fence" cases are predicated on malice and that the facts of this case do not fit that requirement. He viewed

the majority opinion as being in error in dismissing certain rules as being out of date. He thought that policy decisions of this nature should be left to the legislature. He pointed out that the defendant was in conformity with zoning regulations, building codes, deed restrictions and that his use of the land to build a home was reasonable. He viewed the plaintiff's solar system as "an unusually sensitive use." He argued that there was no notice by Prah to Maretti relative to the solar collector. He also points out in an interesting footnote that "Mr. Prah could have avoided this litigation by building his own home in the center of his lot instead of only ten feet from the Maretti lot line and/or by purchasing the adjoining lot for his own protection. Mr. Maretti has already moved the proposed location of his home over an additional ten feet to accommodate Mr. Prah's solar collector, and he testified that moving the home any further would interfere with his view of the lake on which the property faces." With regard to this last point, could it not be urged that Prah in effect moved to the nuisance and should be estopped to complain? What do you think about the other points made by the dissenting justice? Is Wisconsin now in the position of being the only American jurisdiction that recognizes to a limited degree the English doctrine of ancient lights?

Compare with the Prah case Sher v. Leiderman, 181 Cal.App.3d 867, 226 Cal.Rptr. 698 (1986) where the court ruled against the owner of a passive solar home holding that the neighbors' trees were not a private nuisance. In County of Westchester v. Town of Greenwich, Connecticut, 76 F.3d 42 (2d Cir.1996) a county in New York brought an action against the Connecticut city and several landowners to obtain a prescriptive easement along a runway approach to the county airport and have the landowners' trees cut as a public nuisance. The court found for the landowners, quoting the trial judge's statement: "If normally unobjectionable land use such as growing trees can be transformed into an 'unreasonable' activity by the act of building an airport that lacks the necessary property rights for full operation, then there would be no reason for airports to ever bother paying for property rights beyond those needed for the the land the airport actually occupies, because the airports could acquire the air easements they needed without cost by bringing nuisance suits against any landowner whose property contained structures blocking, or threatening to block, the airport's runways' clear zones."

2. In Prah v. Maretti, the Wisconsin Court commented approvingly on the fact that solar collectors can provide an important alternative source of energy. In Rose v. Chaikin, 187 N.J.Super. 210, 453 A.2d 1378 (1982), the court thought less of the operation by defendants of a privately owned windmill. The defendants had built the windmill in "an effort to save on electric bills and conserve energy." The noise from the windmill was alleged by plaintiffs to produce "stress-related symptoms, together with a general inability to enjoy the peace of their homes." The court found that the noise levels "are of such a nature that they would be offensive to people of normal sensibilities and, in fact, have unreasonably interfered with plaintiffs' use and enjoyment of their properties." There were certain natural sounds in the area (—the ocean, sea gulls, the wind and distant, occasional boat traffic—), but the windmill produced unnatural sounds which were more or less constant. Witnesses testified that the plaintiffs suffered from nervous-

ness, dizziness, loss of sleep and fatigue and that the sounds interfered with normal home activities such as reading, eating, watching television and general relaxation. The court enjoined the windmill, rejecting a counterclaim by defendants objecting to plaintiffs' heat pump. On the question of the windmill's value as an alternative energy source, the court stated:

When consideration is given to the social utility of the windmill and the availability of reasonable alternatives, the conclusion supporting an injunction is the same. Defendants' purpose in installing the windmill was to conserve energy and save on electric bills. Speaking to the latter goal first, clearly the court can take judicial notice that alternative devices are available which are significantly less intrusive. Evid.R. 9(1). As to its social utility, a more careful analysis is required. Defendants argue that the windmill furthers the national need to conserve energy by the use of an alternative renewable source of power. See, generally, Wind Energy Systems Act of 1980, 42 U.S.C.A., §§ 9201–13, and Public Utility Regulatory Policies Act of 1978, 16 U.S.C.A., § 824a–3. The social utility of alternate energy sources cannot be denied; nor should the court ignore the proposition that scientific and social progress sometimes reasonably require a reduction in personal comfort. Protokowitz v. Lesofski, supra 69 N.J.Super. at 443, 174 A.2d 385; Annotation, "Nuisance—Operation of Air Conditioner," 79 A.L.R.3d 320, 328 (1977). On the other hand, the fact that a device represents a scientific advance and has social utility does not mean that it is permissible at any cost. Such factors must be weighed against the quantum of harm the device brings to others. Sans v. Ramsey Golf & Country Club, supra, 29 N.J. at 448–49, 149 A.2d 599.

(2) Commercial and Industrial Areas

BOVE v. DONNER–HANNA COKE CORP.

Supreme Court of New York, Appellate Division, 1932.
236 App.Div. 37, 258 N.Y.S. 229, motion denied
236 App.Div. 775, 258 N.Y.S. 1075 (1932).

[Plaintiff built a house, the front of which was later converted into a grocery store on two lots in Buffalo, N.Y. Later the defendant's coke plant was built across the street. The plant operates 24 hours a day. Coke is heated to around 2000° F. and is taken out of the ovens and run under a "quencher" causing a tremendous cloud of steam, carrying with it minute particles of coke and some gas. Plaintiff claims a private nuisance and sues to enjoin it. The trial court refused the injunction. Plaintiff appealed. On appeal the trial court was affirmed. Only a small part of the opinion is given.]

* * *

It is true that the appellant was a resident of this locality for several years before the defendant came on the scene of action, and that, when the plaintiff built her house, the land on which these coke ovens now stand was a hickory grove. But in a growing community changes are inevitable. This region was never fitted for a residential district; for years it has been peculiarly adapted for factory sites. This was apparent when plaintiff bought her lots and when she built her house. The land is low and lies adjacent to the Buffalo river, a navigable stream connecting with Lake Erie. Seven different railroads run through this area. Freight tracks and yards can be seen in every direction. Railroads naturally follow the low levels in passing through a city. Cheap transportation is an attraction which always draws factories and industrial plants to a locality. It is common knowledge that a combination of rail and water terminal facilities will stamp a section as a site suitable for industries of the heavier type, rather than for residential purposes. In 1910 there were at least eight industrial plants, with a total assessed valuation of over a million dollars, within a radius of a mile from plaintiff's house.

With all the dirt, smoke and gas which necessarily come from factory chimneys; trains and boats, and with full knowledge that this region was especially adapted for industrial rather than residential purposes, and that factories would increase in the future, plaintiff selected this locality as the site of her future home. She voluntarily moved into this district, fully aware of the fact that the atmosphere would constantly be contaminated by dirt, gas and foul odors; and that she could not hope to find in this locality the pure air of a strictly residential zone. She evidently saw certain advantages in living in this congested center. This is not the case of an industry, with its attendant noise and dirt, invading a quiet, residential district. It is just the opposite. Here a residence is built in an area naturally adapted for industrial purposes and already dedicated to that use. Plaintiff can hardly be heard to complain at this late date that her peace and comfort have been disturbed by a situation which existed, to some extent at least, at the very time she bought her property, and which condition she must have known would grow worse rather than better as the years went by.

Today there are twenty industrial plants within a radius of less than a mile and three-quarters from appellant's house, with more than sixty-five smokestacks rising in the air, and belching forth clouds of smoke; every day there are 148 passenger trains, and 225 freight trains, to say nothing of switch engines, passing over these various railroad tracks near to the plaintiff's property; over 10,000 boats, a large portion of which burn soft coal, pass up and down the Buffalo river every season. Across the street, and within 300 feet from plaintiff's house, is a large tank of the Iroquois Gas Company which is used for the storage of gas.

The utter abandonment of this locality for residential purposes, and its universal use as an industrial center, becomes manifest when one considers that in 1929 the assessed valuation of the twenty industrial plants above referred to aggregated over $20,000,000, and that the city in 1925 passed a zoning ordinance putting this area in the third industrial district, a zone in which stockyards, glue factories, coke ovens, steel furnaces, rolling mills and other similar enterprises were permitted to be located.

One has only to mention these facts to visualize the condition of the atmosphere in this locality. It is quite easy to imagine that many of the things of which the plaintiff complains are due to causes over which the defendant has no control. At any rate, if appellant is immune from the annoyance occasioned by the smoke and odor which must necessarily come from these various sources, it would hardly seem that she could consistently claim that her health has been impaired, and that the use and enjoyment of her home have been seriously interfered with solely because of the dirt, gas and stench which have reached her from defendant's plant.

It is very true that the law is no respecter of persons, and that the most humble citizen in the land is entitled to identically the same protection accorded to the master of the most gorgeous palace. However, the fact that the plaintiff has voluntarily chosen to live in the smoke and turmoil of this industrial zone is some evidence, at least, that any annoyance which she has suffered from the dirt, gas and odor which have emanated from defendant's plant is more imaginary and theoretical than it is real and substantial.

I think that the trial court was amply justified in refusing to interfere with the operation of the defendant's coke ovens. No consideration of public policy or private rights demands any such sacrifice of this industry. * * *

Notes

1. Compare Nussbaum v. Lacopo, 27 N.Y.2d 311, 317 N.Y.S.2d 347, 265 N.E.2d 762 (1970) where the plaintiff who lived in a home abutting the thirteenth hole of defendant's golf course, and was hit by a stray golf ball while sitting on his patio sued, alleging nuisance and negligence. The court said:

> The design of the course was not such as to create a cause of action in nuisance or in negligence. "To constitute a nuisance, the use must be such as to produce a tangible and appreciable injury to neighboring property, or such as to render its enjoyment especially uncomfortable or inconvenient." (Campbell v. Seaman, 63 N.Y. 568, 577). But not every intrusion will constitute a nuisance. "Persons living in organized communities must suffer some damage, annoyance and inconvenience from each other. * * * If one lives in the city he must expect to suffer the dirt, smoke, noisome odors and confusion incident to city life" (Campbell v. Seaman, 63 N.Y. 568, 577, supra). So, too, one who deliberately decides to reside in the suburbs on very desirable lots adjoining golf clubs and thus receive the social benefits and other not inconsiderable advantages of country club surroundings must accept the occasional, concomitant annoyances (Patton v. Westwood Country Club Co., 18 Ohio App.2d 137, 247 N.E.2d 761 [1969]).

> Nuisance imports a continuous invasion of rights, and the occasional—"once or twice a week"—errant golf ball that was found on plaintiff's property does not constitute sufficient impairment of plaintiff's rights (see Bohan v. Port Jervis Gas–Light Co., 122 N.Y. 18, 25–26, 25 N.E. 246, 247–248). There were only, according to plaintiff and his wife, a few golf balls, which were found in the *bushes* and *fence area* of

plaintiff's backyard. These minimal trespasses would not warrant the granting of an injunction and cannot sustain a recovery for plaintiff's injuries.

2. See, along this line, City of Milwaukee v. Milbrew, Inc., 240 Wis. 527, 3 N.W.2d 386, 141 A.L.R. 277 (1942); Storey v. Central Hide & Rendering Co., 148 Tex. 509, 226 S.W.2d 615 (1950); and Louisville Refining Co. v. Mudd, 339 S.W.2d 181 (Ky.1960).

CITY OF FORT SMITH v. WESTERN HIDE & FUR CO.

Supreme Court of Arkansas, 1922.
153 Ark. 99, 239 S.W. 724.

McCULLOCH, C.J. Appellee is engaged in the business of buying and selling hides and furs, the business being operated in its own building situated near the center of the business district in the city of Fort Smith. Appellee has been operating the business at that place for the past ten years.

This is an action in chancery, instituted by the city of Fort Smith against appellee, to restrain the further operation of said business at the place mentioned on the ground, as alleged in the complaint, that the method in which the business is operated constitutes a public nuisance.

It is alleged in the complaint that appellee's place of business is situated in a thickly populated section of the city and is a great annoyance to the people in that neighborhood and to passers-by, for the reason that the storage of hides in the house gives off offensive odors and attracts flies, and affects the comfort and endangers the health of the people of the city living near that locality. The complaint, in other words, states facts relative to the manner in which the business is conducted sufficient to constitute the maintenance of a public nuisance.

Appellee, in the answer, denied the allegation of the complaint with respect to the method in which the business was operated, and denied that offensive odors arose from the place of business, or that flies were attracted there any more than is the case at other places of business during warm weather.

There was a trial of the issues before the court upon oral testimony, reduced to writing and made a part of the record, and the decree dismissed the complaint for want of equity.

The distinction between a public and private nuisance lies merely in the extent of the injury or annoyance which results therefrom. If injury results only to a few, on account of the peculiar circumstances, the nuisance is private, and the remedy is confined to those who suffer from the effects of the nuisance. If, on the other hand, the injury or annoyance is sufficient in extent to become common to all persons who may come within its influence, it is of a public nature, and the remedy is by action on the part of the municipality to abate the nuisance, either by police interference under an ordinance, or by suit in equity to restrain the maintenance of the nuisance. Harvey v. Dewoody, 18 Ark. 252; Town of Lonoke v. C.R.I. & P. R. Co., 92 Ark. 546, 123 S.W. 395; Gus Blass Dry Goods Co. v. Reinman & Wolfort, 102 Ark. 287, 143 S.W. 1087. * * *

There were numerous witnesses in the case for the city and for appellee. The city introduced eight witnesses, all of whom gave testimony which tended to show that the operation of the business by appellee was a nuisance, that noxious odors arose from the building, particularly that part where hides were stored, and that in warm weather there was an accumulation of flies about the place. Most of these witnesses were people who lived in the immediate neighborhood and were engaged in business of various kinds.

One of the witnesses operated a baker shop and lunch room, and he testified that the odors from appellee's place of business were so offensive inside of the shop that waiting customers would not remain in the room, but would stand on the outside so that they could get relief from the odors.

One of the witnesses—Mr. Miller—was a commissioner of the city and a member of the district board of health, and he testified that he visited appellee's place of business several times and found that the odors from the place were very offensive. He testified that he visited the place for the purpose of making an investigation and that he could detect the odors a considerable distance from the house.

Appellee introduced ten or twelve witnesses in addition to the manager and owner, whose testimony tended to some extent to overcome the charge that offensive odors constantly arose from the building, at least to the extent claimed by witnesses for the city. These witnesses were more or less definite in their statements, but none of them disputed the fact that there were peculiar odors arising more or less from the place of business. Many of the witnesses said that these odors were noticeable but were not offensive. Some of the witnesses stated that the odors arose on account of the disinfectants used and that these were not offensive odors, at least not so to them.

Mr. Davidson, the manager of the business, stated that there were odors going out from the hides, but that such an odor as that was not offensive. He admitted, however, that sometimes hides were bought which were partially decomposed and that it was necessary to put them down in salt in order to stop decomposition. He testified that all the fresh hides purchased were salted to prevent decomposition.

A careful consideration of the testimony leaves no escape from the conclusion that the place of business maintained by appellee was offensive to those who came into the immediate neighborhood. There were bad odors which were easily detected, and which were sufficient to constantly annoy those who were engaged in business in the locality or who came there for any purpose.

It is conceded that the operation of a hide and fur business is not a nuisance per se, but the contention is that the operation in the manner in which it is carried on in the locality where the place of business is situated constitutes a nuisance, and we are of the opinion that the preponderance of the evidence sustains this contention.

The case affords, perhaps, an example where a business established at a place remote from population is gradually surrounded and becomes part of a populous center, so that a business which formerly was not an interference with the rights of others has become so by the encroachment of the population. Under these circumstances, private rights must yield to the public good, and a court of equity will afford relief, even where a thing, originally harmless under certain circumstances, has become a nuisance under changed conditions.

Appellee pleads a license from the city in bar of the right to abate the nuisance, but the fact that the city granted a license to operate a hide and fur business does not imply that it could be operated in a manner so as to constitute a public nuisance, or to bar the city from suppressing the nuisance. Durfey v. Thalheimer, supra; Wilder v. Little Rock, 150 Ark. 439, 234 S.W. 479.

The decree is therefore reversed, and the cause remanded, with directions to enter a decree in favor of the city of Fort Smith, according to the prayer of the complaint, restraining appellee from maintaining a nuisance.

SUNDOWNER, INC. v. KING

Supreme Court of Idaho, 1973.
95 Idaho 367, 509 P.2d 785.

SHEPARD, JUSTICE.

This is an appeal from a judgment ordering partial abatement of a spite fence erected between two adjoining motels in Caldwell, Idaho. This action is evidently an outgrowth of a continuing dispute between the parties resulting from the 1966 sale of a motel. See: King v. H.J. McNeel, Inc., 94 Idaho 444, 489 P.2d 1324 (1971).

In 1966 Robert Bushnell sold a motel to defendants-appellants King. Bushnell then built another motel, the Desert Inn, on property immediately adjoining that sold to the Kings.

The Kings thereafter brought an action against Bushnell (H.J. McNeel, Inc.) based on alleged misrepresentations by Bushnell in the 1966 sale of the motel property. See: King v. H.J. McNeel, Inc., supra. In 1968 the Kings built a large structure, variously described as a fence or sign, some 16 inches from the boundary line between the King and Bushnell properties. The structure is 85 ft. in length and 18 ft. in height. It is raised 2 ft. off the ground and is 2 ft. from the Desert Inn building. It parallels the entire northwest side of the Desert Inn building, obscures approximately 80% of the Desert Inn building and restricts the passage of light and air to its rooms.

Bushnell brought the instant action seeking damages and injunctive relief compelling the removal of the structure. Following trial to the court, the district court found that the structure was erected out of spite and that it was erected in violation of a municipal ordinance. The trial court ordered the structure reduced to a maximum height of 6 ft.

The Kings appeal from the judgment entered against them and claim that the trial court erred in many of its findings of fact and its applications of law. The Kings assert the trial court erred in finding that the "sign" was in fact a fence; that the structure had little or no value for advertising purposes; that the structure cuts out light and air from the rooms of the Desert Inn Motel; that the structure has caused damage by way of diminution of the value of the Desert Inn Motel property; that the erection of the structure was motivated by ill-feeling and spite; that the structure was erected to establish a dividing line; and that the trial court erred in failing to find the structure was necessary to distinguish between the two adjoining motels.

We have examined the record at length and conclude that the findings of the trial court are supported by substantial although conflicting evidence. The trial court had before it both still and moving pictures of the various buildings. The record contains testimony that the structure is the largest "sign" then existing in Oregon, Northern Nevada and Idaho. An advertising expert testified that the structure, because of its location and type, had no value for advertising and that its cost, i.e., $6,300, would not be justified for advertising purposes. * * *

* * *

The pivotal and dispositive issue in this matter is whether the trial court erred in requiring partial abatement of the structure on the ground that it was a spite fence. Under the so-called English rule, followed by most 19th century American courts, the erection and maintenance of a spite fence was not an actionable wrong. These older cases were founded on the premise that a property owner has an absolute right to use his property in any manner he desires. See: 5 Powell on Real Property, ¶ 696, p. 276 (1949 ed. rev'd 1968); Letts v. Kessler, 54 Ohio St. 73, 42 N.E. 765 (1896).

Under the modern American rule, however, one may not erect a structure for the sole purpose of annoying his neighbor. Many courts hold that a spite fence which serves no useful purpose may give rise to an action for both injunctive relief and damages. See: 5 Powell, supra, ¶ 696, p. 277; IA Thompson on Real Property, § 239 (1964 ed.). Many courts following the above rule further characterize a spite fence as a nuisance. See: Hornsby v. Smith, 191 Ga. 491, 13 S.E.2d 20 (1941); Barger v. Barringer, 151 N.C. 433, 66 S.E. 439 (1909); Annotation 133 A.L.R. 691.

One of the first cases rejecting the older English view and announcing the new American rule on spite fences is Burke v. Smith, 69 Mich. 380, 37 N.W. 838 (1888). Subsequently, many American jurisdictions have adopted and followed *Burke* so that it is clearly the prevailing modern view. See: Powell, supra, ¶ 696 at p. 279; Flaherty v. Moran, 81

Mich. 52, 45 N.W. 381 (1890); Barger v. Barringer, supra; Norton v. Randolph, 176 Ala. 381, 58 So. 283 (1912); Bush v. Mockett, 95 Neb. 552, 145 N.W. 1001 (1914); Hibbard v. Halliday, 58 Okla. 244, 158 P. 1158 (1916); Parker v. Harvey, 164 So. 507 (La.App.1935); Hornsby v. Smith, supra; Brittingham v. Robertson, 280 A.2d 741 (Del.Ch.1971). Also see the opinion of Mr. Justice Holmes in Rideout v. Knox, 148 Mass. 368, 19 N.E. 390 (1889).

In *Burke* a property owner built two 11 ft. fences blocking the light and air to his neighbors' windows. The fences served no useful purpose to their owner and were erected solely because of his malice toward his neighbor. Justice Morse applied the maxim *sic utere tuo ut alienum non laedas,* and concluded:

"But it must be remembered that no man has a legal right to make a malicious use of his property, not for any benefit or advantage to himself, but for the avowed purpose of damaging his neighbor. To hold otherwise would make the law a convenient engine, in cases like the present, to injure and destroy the peace and comfort, and to damage the property of one's neighbor for no other than a wicked purpose, which in itself is, or ought to be, unlawful. The right to do this cannot, in an enlightened country, exist, either in the use of property, or in any way or manner. There is no doubt in my mind that these uncouth screens or 'obscurers' as they are named in the record, are a nuisance, and were erected without right, and for a malicious purpose. What right has the defendant, in the light of the just and beneficient principles of equity, to shut out God's free air and sunlight from the windows of his neighbor, not for any benefit or advantage to himself, or profit to his land, but simply to gratify his own wicked malice against his neighbor? None whatever. The wanton infliction of damage can never be a right. It is a wrong, and a violation of right, and is not without remedy. The right to breath the air, and to enjoy the sunshine, is a natural one; and no man can pollute the atmosphere, or shut out the light of heaven, for no better reason than that the situation of his property is such that he is given the opportunity of so doing, and wishes to gratify his spite and malice towards his neighbor." 37 N.W. at 842.

We agree both with the philosophy expressed in the *Burke* opinion and with that of other jurisdictions following what we feel is the better-reasoned approach. We hold that no property owner has the right to erect and maintain an otherwise useless structure for the sole purpose of injuring his neighbor. The trial court found on the basis of substantial evidence that the structure served no useful purpose to its owners and was erected because of the Kings' ill-will and enmity toward their neighboring competitor. We therefore hold that the trial court did not err in partially abating and enjoining the "sign" structure as a spite fence.

* * *

The judgment of the trial court is affirmed. Costs to respondent.

* * *

Notes

1. Since the easement for light and air concept in English property law has not been generally accepted in the United States in the absence of a showing of absolute necessity, the "spite fence" rule becomes important as a means of dealing with situations of this type. However, if the alleged spite fence served a useful or necessary purpose of the landowner who erected it, injunctive relief would be denied.

2. Nuisance concepts sometimes provide the basis for administrative action or legislation. In Great Lakes Motorcycle Dealers Ass'n, Inc. v. City of Detroit, 38 Mich.App. 564, 196 N.W.2d 787 (1972), the plaintiffs brought a class action to enjoin the erection and enforcement of signs prohibiting the operation of motorcycles on certain streets in the city. The number of these vehicles with the accompanying noise had grown to the point that citizen complaints led the city to accept petitions requesting that they be barred from certain streets. Such signs had been erected over approximately 237 blocks. Although finding that the city had a legitimate interest in regulating traffic so as to eliminate noise and excessive speed, the court held that the blanket exclusion of all such vehicles exceeded reasonable limitations. Said the court: "While some motorcycle riders may well drive vehicles which are excessively noisy at speeds in excess of the posted limits, there is certainly no valid basis for applying the 'Hell's Angels' conception of the motorcycle rider to all motorcycle users." Maybe not, but there are not many little old ladies whipping around on motorcycles.

3. Another example of nuisance concepts undergirding legislative or administrative action of the city is illustrated in City of Chicago v. Birnbaum, 49 Ill.2d 250, 274 N.E.2d 22 (1971), in which it was proper for the city to order the demolition of buildings which were in a hazardous condition and constituted a danger to surrounding property. The evidence showed that the condition of the buildings could not be remedied by repair without major reconstruction. It was appropriate, said the Illinois Supreme Court, for the city to take action under its police power to abate such nuisances, despite the defendant's claim that this deprived him of his property without just compensation.

4. Commercial signs that are not subject to spite fence allegations are sometimes the target of nuisance actions based on other grounds. Frandsen v. Mayer, 155 N.W.2d 294 (N.D.1967), although it reversed the granting of injunctive relief by the trial judge, stated that under proper circumstances the sign could be enjoined either as a nuisance per accidens or as a public nuisance. Here, the plaintiffs were alleging that the sign was so located that it caused motorists to miss their motel or not to know whether it was a motel, thereby harming business. The court felt that evidence to show harm caused by the sign was lacking.

(3) Areas Adjoining Parks or Recreational Facilities

In City of Newport News v. Hertzler, 216 Va. 587, 221 S.E.2d 146 (1976), a public park was involved. Hertzler and 31 others alleged that the park had been opened when it was incomplete, unregulated and unsupervised. They complained of erosion of the shore caused by speeding boats launched from the park, health hazards caused by debris, human excrement and stench, annoyance from parties, lack of toilets, lights, trash containers and telephones, and lack of supervision. The trial court granted an injunction which was reversed on appeal. The Virginia Court stated that most of the complaining came from Hertzler and rather cavalierly dismissed his complaints—e.g., (in response to Hertzler's observing human excrement in the park and his viewing a male urinating), this was "not sufficient * * * to show that sanitary facilities were needed or that, if installed, they would be used." The impression provided by this case is that a court will not be inclined to shut down a public park except in an extreme situation.

Certainly, public parks or open space do not represent the only basis for nuisance allegations with regard to public facilities. In Vincent v. Salt Lake County, 583 P.2d 105 (Utah 1978), it was alleged that damages to a privately owned garage had resulted from a leaking county storm drain. The drain had been installed in a subdivision in 1957, and the plaintiffs had constructed their home approximately two years later. The garage wall began to crack in 1971 and widened in 1972. The county stated that an inspection showed no corollary between the drain and the cracks. However, the county failed to reveal that the inspection revealed some unsealed joints in the drain, some of which were grouted at that time. Additional cracks and the eventual sagging of the garage ensued in subsequent years. It was not until August, 1974, when the plaintiffs hired a contractor that they discovered the source of the problem. In affirming a money judgment against the county, the Utah Supreme Court treated the leaking drain as a latent defect unknown to plaintiffs until shortly before they filed suit. The court sustained a trial court instruction that a "nuisance is a condition, not an act or failure to act on the part of the person responsible for the condition."

Can you use "self-help" to abate a nuisance? In State ex rel. Herman v. Cardon, 112 Ariz. 548, 544 P.2d 657 (1976), the State and Gila County, Arizona, sued property owners abutting a highway to recover damages because they had destroyed 29.5 feet of the concrete along the highway which interfered with access to property on which they operated a service station. (The curb had been constructed prior to the time they acquired their lots.) The Arizona Supreme Court stated that public highways were "ways common and free to all persons" and that "a person who suffers injury through a nuisance, here interference with the right of access, may abate it without resort to legal proceedings provided he can do so without bringing about a breach of the peace." The court quoted from Prosser, Law of Torts § 90, p. 605 (4th ed. 1971) to this effect: "Summary abatement of a private nuisance by self-help is open only to those whose interests in the enjoyment of land are interfered with, or in other words, to those to whom it is a nuisance." The court added: "We can conceive of no legal reason why the sovereignty [sic] is immune from this legal principle."

Also, on highways, see State ex rel. State Highway Comm'n v. Johns, 507 S.W.2d 75 (Mo.App.1974), in which an injunction was granted against the encroachment of a building into a street even though the traveled portion of the street was unaffected. The court quoted from cases stating that "any permanent structure or purpresture which materially encroaches upon a public street and impedes travel is a nuisance per se, and may be abated, notwithstanding space is left for the passage of the public."

The Model Airspace Act, adopted by the American Bar Association, provides for a situation in which the state may join with private persons in the joint development and multiple use of the highway rights of way. This would lead to privately owned structures being placed on rights of way or possibly over highways or under elevated highways. This same Act provides that while the state possesses the right to make full use of the airspace over or under a right of way, the residual rights of the owners in fee cannot be additionally burdened without just compensation. See, e.g., 60 Okl.Stat.Ann. §§ 811, 813 (Supp.1974–75). See also, Wright, The Model Airspace Act: Old and New Law for Contemporary Land Use Problems, 1972 Law and the Social Order (Ariz.St.L.J.) 529.

E.   NUISANCES IN ZONED AREAS

GREEN v. CASTLE CONCRETE CO.

Supreme Court of Colorado, 1973.
181 Colo. 309, 509 P.2d 588.

[Castle Concrete conducted a mining operation at Snyder Quarry which was enjoined as a public and a private nuisance. Castle was in compliance with state statutes and zoning laws. The issue is whether the operation of a limestone quarry permitted by zoning can be deemed a public nuisance. A further issue is whether the evidence will support a finding of a private nuisance. Castle had been quarrying in the general area for some years and had begun in 1969 to acquire new land, including the Snyder Quarry. Around $250,000 had been invested in land acquisitions. Although a road had been improved preparatory to the quarry operations, little if any of the actual operations had begun when suit was commenced. Seven residents with homes over a mile east of the area filed suit. Their asserted class action was dismissed and only the individual claims remained. Some testimony and a portion of the lower court's opinion dealt with ecological and environmental considerations, but the trial court ruled that this evidence was not considered in granting the injunction. Judicial notice was taken of the value of tourism and the economic loss which might result. Castle argued on appeal that (1) the authority of the trial court was exceeded in enjoining the operations as a public nuisance, and (2) that the finding of a private nuisance was not supported by the evidence.]

DAY, JUSTICE.

* * *

I.

Taking up first the question of the public nuisance, this court very recently discussed the law of public nuisance as pronounced in Robinson Brick Co. v. Luthi, 115 Colo. 106, 169 P.2d 171. See Hobbs v. Smith, Colo., 493 P.2d 1352, wherein the following was quoted from *Robinson Brick:*

> " 'Where the legislative arm of the government has declared by statute and zoning resolution what activities may or may not be conducted in a prescribed zone, it has in effect declared what is or is not a *public nuisance*. What might have been a proper field for judicial action prior to such legislation becomes improper when the law-making branch of government has entered the field. None of the numerous cases cited appears to go so far as to approve the enjoining of a business operating under valid legislative zoning authority.' "(Emphasis added.)

This court then held that, notwithstanding such a ruling on public nuisance:

> * * * It is now the generally accepted rule that regardless of compliance with zoning ordinances or regulations, both business and residential uses may be enjoined *if they constitute a nuisance to an adjoining property owner or resident.* [Citations] (Emphasis added.)

Hobbs and Board of County Commissioners v. Thompson, Colo., 493 P.2d 1358, are authority for the proposition that, when the question of public nuisance versus publicly authorized activities forms the issue, the courts will defer to the legislative branch of government with constitutional or other relevant limitations. Furthermore, in the most recent case of Western Paving Construction Co. v. Board of County Commissioners, Colo., 506 P.2d 1230, the court stated:

> In addition, when the matter is permitted by right in the zone created and either through an environmental concern or a change of circumstances the use is incompatible with prior usage, the proper procedure is to amend the zoning resolution. * * *

II.

An examination of the record on the propriety of a finding of a private nuisance reveals substantial infirmities and its failure to support the court's judgment. Comment (g) of the Restatement, Torts § 822, pointing up the requirement that there must be a "substantial invasion" to create a cause of action in nuisance, states:

> "By substantial invasion is meant an invasion that involves more than slight inconvenience or petty annoyance. The law does not concern itself with trifles, and therefore there must be a real and appreciable interference with the present usability of a person's land before he can have a cause of action under the rule here stated. * * * "

Additionally, a reading of the record convinces us that there is not sufficient substantial, competent evidence to support a finding of private nuisance. See Ryan v. Pitkin Iron Corp., 10th Cir., 444 F.2d 717; Haskell v. Denver Tramway Co., 23 Colo. 60, 46 P. 121. The record is devoid of any proof that the quarry has been or *will in fact* be a nuisance. Speculation as to the future harmful effects of blasting and from dust pollution are not based on any actual occurrences other than a test blast. Other blasting complained of was in connection with building the road which would not reoccur. The defendant has not been given an opportunity to show that it can use methods which will remedy the anticipatory nuisance. Plaintiffs have fallen short of discharging the evidentiary burden necessary to entitle them to an injunction on any of the bases asserted. We have stated in other relevant opinions that in such circumstances the trial court should be reversed. See Mowry v. Jackson, 140 Colo. 197, 343 P.2d 833; Hawkins v. Elston, 58 Colo. 400, 146 P. 254; Davis v. Pursel, 55 Colo. 287, 134 P. 107.

It should be noted that our decision is merely a holding that broad injunctive powers may not be used in advance to prohibit lawful business activity which may not be a nuisance. To do so would be unreasonably harsh on the defendant. Withholding of injunctive relief on the basis of the present status of operations preserves to the complaining party the right to enjoin the activity if it in fact proves to be a nuisance. Haskell v. Denver Tramway Co., supra. For example, in Turner v. Spokane, 39 Wash.2d 332, 235 P.2d 300, an injunction was denied, as it was found that the testimony did not establish that there was such certainty and imminence of the apprehended annoyance and damage as would warrant injunctive relief. This was upheld on appeal, although it was recognized that an injunction might be proper in a later case upon a showing that after the quarry had been in operation it did in fact constitute a nuisance.

Thus, should future blasting, dust, or other considerations become a substantial interference, it would be on new grounds and a decision based on the present status would not be a bar to the plaintiffs or any other persons seeking injunctive relief.

It has been evident to county and state authorities for some years that quarry operations in at least two adjacent areas have been continuing and that large limestone formations abound in this area. Yet no move has been made by the legislature or county or city officials to rezone the area, set it aside for parks and recreation, or to compensate the owners for the taking. Solutions for problems of the magnitude anticipated here may suggest legislative and not judicial action.

We feel compelled to state that, although the goal of creating an aesthetically pleasing environment is clearly laudable, it is equally clear that where the accomplishment of this goal entails the restructuring of societal rights and priorities it cannot be fairly or justly done through a judicially sanctioned private condemnation without compensation under the guise of abating a nuisance. In our populous society, the courts cannot be available to enjoin an activity solely because it causes some aesthetic discomfort or annoyance. Given our myriad and disparate tastes, life styles, mores, and attitudes, the availability of a judicial remedy for such complaints would cause inexorable confusion.

The judgment is reversed, and the cause is remanded with directions to vacate the injunction and dismiss the complaint.

KELLEY and GROVES, JJ., concur in the result.

PRINGLE, C.J., dissents.

GROVES, JUSTICE (concurring in the result):

I concur in the result under the evidence in this case. I do not join in the proposition—if it is the ruling of the majority opinion—that under no circumstances can courts enjoin a legislatively permitted public nuisance.

KELLEY, J., joins in this concurrence.

PRINGLE, CHIEF JUSTICE (dissenting):

I respectfully dissent. The majority opinion today announces the rule that any activity operating under a valid legislative zoning authority can never be declared a public nuisance by the courts. I cannot agree. The welfare, the safety, and the health of the public, including its right to a decent environment, transcends, in my view, the right to engage in a zone permitted business, and where that business is so conducted as to detrimentally affect the public health, welfare, and safety, including the public's right to a decent environment, and thus become a danger to them, then it becomes a public nuisance subject to control by the courts.

Notes

1. Robinson Brick Co. v. Luthi, which is cited in the majority opinion, is reproduced in the first edition of Beuscher and Wright, at page 98. In this case, the plaintiff operated a large greenhouse and the defendant mined clay for bricks. The county zoning ordinance did not permit clay mining, but the defendant's activities antedated the ordinance and constituted a non-conforming use. The Colorado Court held that the state had "pre-empted the field of public nuisance as it relates to this case." Nominal damages were allowed in connection with the private nuisance. (Plaintiff testified that the dust from these operations spoiled his plants growing in the open and caused the need for more cleansing of plants in the greenhouse.)

2. See also Dudding v. Automatic Gas Co., 145 Tex. 1, 193 S.W.2d 517 (1946). Admittedly, the nuisance injunction has been less than successful in eliminating non-conforming uses from zoned areas. On this, see, Noel, Retroactive Zoning and Nuisances, 41 Colum.L.Rev. 457 (1941), and Willis, The Elimination of Nonconforming Uses, 1951 Wis.L.Rev. 685 (1951). Among the cases see, Oklahoma City v. Dolese, 48 F.2d 734 (10th Cir.1931) (failure to remove non-conforming coal yard); Firth v. Scherzberg, 366 Pa. 443, 77 A.2d 443 (1951) (motor terminal); City of Akron v. Chapman, 160 Ohio St. 382, 116 N.E.2d 697 (1953) (reliance solely on retroactive zoning provisions of ordinance and not on nuisance failed to succeed in removal of junk yard). For cases more favorable to the removal or abatement of objectionable nonconforming uses, see Eaton v. Klimm, 217 Cal. 362, 18 P.2d

678 (1933); Malm v. Dubrey, 325 Mass. 63, 88 N.E.2d 900 (1949); and Civic Ass'n of Dearborn Township, Dist. No. 3 v. Horowitz, 318 Mich. 333, 28 N.W.2d 97 (1947) (street carnival can continue, but only if cleaned up).

JONES v. RUMFORD

Supreme Court of Washington, 1964.
64 Wash.2d 559, 392 P.2d 808.

[Only that portion of the opinion relating to the subject at hand is excerpted.]

RUMMEL, JUDGE pro tem.

The plaintiff, respondent here, brought this action to enjoin the defendants from operating a chicken breeding plant, and for damages for alleged depreciation in value of his property, for impairment of the use of his property, and for invasion of his privacy. He contended that the defendants' breeding plant constituted a nuisance because of the existence of offensive odors, flies, insects and rodents, all caused by the plant.

* * *

The plaintiff has his home on a 2–acre plot next door to the chicken plant. The walls of the plant are 4 feet from his line. Prior to the building of this plant, both parties signed a petition which caused the area to be zoned to permit agricultural pursuits, including poultry raising.

It is the contention of the defendants, now appellants, that because their operation is in an area zoned for agriculture they should not be liable for damages unless they operate their plant in an unreasonable manner. They assert that in any case the plaintiff is estopped to complain, for the reason that he stood by without objection while defendants invested a very substantial sum in the construction of their plant. However, this latter contention is eliminated because of the positive testimony of the plaintiff that the defendant assured him before the building was constructed "that you would never know a chicken coop was there." If believed by the court, such a representation by the defendant would eliminate his contention that the plaintiff is now estopped.

In connection with the question of nuisance, defendants argue that what is permitted by law cannot be a nuisance per se. They cite Hardin v. Olympic Portland Cement Co., 89 Wash. 320, p. 325, 154 P. 450, p. 451 (1916), which contains this language:

"* * * a lawful business is never a nuisance *per se,* but may become a nuisance by reason of extraneous circumstances, such *as being located in an inappropriate place, or conducted or kept in an improper manner.* * * *

"No one has a right, however, to pursue a lawful business, if thereby he injures his neighbor *(except such injuries as the public* *must suffer in common in order to permit lawful enterprises to operate)* without compensating such for the damages actually sustained. * * * " (Italics ours.)

The defendants further quote from Bruskland v. Oak Theater, Inc., 42 Wash.2d 346, p. 350, 254 P.2d 1035, p. 1037 (1953), as follows:

" * * * The rule of law deducible from the statute and these cases is that, when proper authority authorizes the operation of a lawful business in a certain area, such business does not constitute a nuisance in a legal sense, but it may become such *if it is conducted in such an unreasonable manner* that it substantially annoys the comfort or repose of others or essentially interferes with the enjoyment of property in violation of RCW 7.48.010 and 7.48.120. * * * " (Italics ours.)

Defendants contend that if the area was zoned for agriculture, and if the trial court found that they had used all modern techniques to control the odor but had been unable to do so, they could not have been maintaining a nuisance. These points of argument, however, fail to take into account the principle of law that, even if a person conducts a plant in the best manner which is practicable with a sound operation, he may still be using his property in an unreasonable manner. Not only is this conception of nuisance recognized in the excerpts quoted by the defendants, but it is amplified in Riblet v. Spokane–Portland Cement Co., 41 Wash.2d 249, p. 254, 248 P.2d 380, p. 382 (1952), where it is said:

"Our basic point of inquiry relates to the general theory of the law of nuisance. This appears primarily to be based upon generally accepted ideas of right, equity and justice. The thought is inherent that not even a fee-simple owner has a totality of rights in and with respect to his real property."

In so far as the law of nuisance is concerned, rights as to the usage of land are relative. The general legal principle to be inferred from court action in nuisance cases is that one landowner will not be permitted to use his land so unreasonably as to interfere unreasonably with another landowner's use and enjoyment of his land:

"The crux of the matter appears to be reasonableness. Admittedly, the term is a flexible one. It has many shades and varieties of meaning. In a nuisance case, the fundamental inquiry always appears to be whether the use of certain land can be considered as reasonable in relation to all the facts and surrounding circumstances.

"Application of the doctrine of nuisance requires a balancing of rights, interests, and convenience. * * * "

* * *

An aerial photograph of the neighborhood, entered as an exhibit, reveals that the building of the defendants looms up as a much larger structure than the houses and outbuildings on the lands of the surrounding neighbors. The character of the neighborhood is not that of a typical farming community, but rather that of a residential area so common on the fringes of cities, neighborhoods where the residents are not primarily engaged in farming but rather are supplementing their incomes from other occupations by raising vegetables and a few chickens or farm animals.

In addition to the testimony of himself and his wife, the plaintiff presented 12 neighbors as witnesses, all of whom testified to an almost unbearable situation regarding odors and flies. The location of each of their properties is noted on a rough sketch of the neighborhood, and reveals that the properties of these witnesses constituted almost a solid ring around and adjacent to the property of the defendants. This testimony was of very substantial character and volume.

[The trial court's award of damages was affirmed.]

Notes

1. In Rockenbach v. Apostle, 330 Mich. 338, 47 N.W.2d 636 (1951), the question was whether an undertaking establishment could be maintained in a residential district which permitted funeral homes subject to certain requirements. These requirements had been met, but the nuisance question remained. The Michigan Supreme Court stated:

> The weight of authority is to the effect that an ordinance which allows the establishment or maintenance of a funeral home or undertaking establishment in a district zoned either for residential or commercial purposes is permissive only, and not controlling as to whether such undertaking establishment would constitute a nuisance which might be enjoined by an equity court. However, proof of the existence of such a zoning ordinance is admissible as evidence of the character of the district, and bearing on the question of nuisance. A nuisance will not be upheld solely on the ground that it has been permitted by municipal ordinance. Sweet v. Campbell, supra; Williams v. Blue Bird Laundry Co., 85 Cal.App. 388, 259 P. 484; Fendley v. City of Anaheim, 110 Cal.App. 731, 294 P. 769; Kosich v. Poultrymen's Service Corp., 136 N.J.Eq. 571, 43 A.2d 15; Perrin's Appeal, 305 Pa. 42, 156 A. 305, 79 A.L.R. 912; White v. Old York Road Country Club, 318 Pa. 346, 178 A. 3. * * *

2. For non-funeral parlor cases announcing the doctrine that a permitted use under zoning may be a nuisance, see Beane v. H.K. Porter, Inc., 280 Mass. 538, 182 N.E. 823 (1932) (drop forge hammers); Reid v. Brodsky, 397 Pa. 463, 156 A.2d 334 (1959) (a taproom restaurant that attracted delinquents into a resident area zoned "commercial"); and Harris v. Skirving, 41 Wash.2d 200, 248 P.2d 408 (1952) (garbage dump). A nuisance was found to exist in an "unclassified zone" in Turner v. City of Spokane, 39 Wash.2d 332, 235 P.2d 300 (1951) (rock quarry).

3. But compare Union City v. Southern Pacific Co., 261 Cal.App.2d 277, 67 Cal.Rptr. 816 (1968), which relies on a provision of the California Civil Code in stating that no activity which is conducted under the express authority of a statute can be held to be a nuisance.

4. General considerations of this problem may be found in Beuscher and Morrison, Judicial Zoning through Recent Nuisance Cases, 1955 Wis. L.Rev. 440, 455–457, as follows:

> "Weight Given by Courts in Nuisance Cases to Zoning
> Findings About Character of the District

> "Typically where a zoning ordinance has characterized a district, the court in a nuisance case will agree that the finding is entitled to attention. Then the court will make its own determination, sometimes in conflict with that of the legislative arm. Thus a lower Pennsylvania court permitted a dump to continue as a non-conforming use in a district zoned Class A Residential, pointing out that there was open land around the dump and that zoning land residential does not make it residential in fact.

> "Nuisance Doctrine as a Basis for Private
> Enforcement of Zoning Ordinances

> "Where a zoning ordinance does not expressly authorize private individuals to sue to enforce it by injunction, the question has come up whether such an individual can sue on a nuisance theory arguing either, (1) the violation of the zoning ordinance is a nuisance per se, or (2) it is a common law nuisance in fact.

> "In Hopkins v. MacCulloch, owners of adjacent property sued to enjoin the defendants' grocery store and cafe. The defendant had been a non-conforming user, but by tearing down the original store and re-building it he had become an illegal user under the zoning ordinance. His use was declared to be a nuisance mainly because the zoning ordinance said so, and an injunction was granted. But in another case actual proof that the violation of the ordinance was a common law nuisance was required as a prerequisite to injunctive relief to a private plaintiff. In addition, the individual plaintiff must show that he is damaged by the violation. * * *

> "Other Points of Contact Between Nuisance and Zoning

> "Occasionally nuisance cases are used in construing zoning restrictions against noxious uses. There have also been some attempts to invalidate particular spot zoning amendments, on the ground that the spot use would constitute a nuisance. And finally, ordinances barring single uses as nuisances continue to come before the courts. Quite a number of these enactments have fallen under the judicial axe, but none of them fell, so far as we could find, because they constituted invalid noncomprehensive zoning."

See also, Comment, Zoning and the Law of Nuisance, 29 Fordham L.Rev. 749 (1961).

5. In People ex rel. Hoogasian v. Sears, Roebuck & Co., 52 Ill.2d 301, 287 N.E.2d 677 (1972) the plaintiffs sought to enjoin the continued construction of the Sears Tower, a 110 story, 1350 foot high office building in downtown Chicago:

Plaintiffs alleged that if construction was allowed to continue the building would interfere with television reception in certain areas. This interference would occur because the broadcasting antennas of Chicago television stations are lower than the contemplated structure which would cause the signals that emanate from these antennas to abnormally reflect from defendant's building thereby allegedly producing distortions on television screens in these areas.

The principal issue in this case is whether defendant has a legal right to use the air space above its property subject only to legislative limitation, or stated conversely, whether an individual or class of individuals has the right to limit the use of such property on the basis that interference with television reception constitutes an actionable nuisance.

* * *

In effect we have competing legitimate commercial interests, both of concern to the public. (See: Richmond Bros., Inc. v. Hagemann (Mass. 1971), 268 N.E.2d 680.) The responsibility in this case for inadequate television reception in certain areas rests more with the broadcaster's choice of location than with the height of defendant's building. Therefore disruption of television signals initiated by totally independent third parties over which defendant has no control cannot be the basis for enjoining the full legal use and enjoyment of defendant's property.

* * *

Considering the foregoing, it is clear to us that absent legislation to the contrary, defendant has a proprietary right to construct a building to its desired height and that completion of the project would not constitute a nuisance under the circumstances of this case. * * *

6. If the Sears case seems somewhat far out in terms of nuisances in zoned areas, let us turn to something more commonplace—billboards. In General Elec. Co. v. Maurice Callahan & Sons, Inc., 2 Mass.App.Ct. 124, 309 N.E.2d 209 (1974), an action was brought to enjoin the erection and maintenance of two billboards. One of the arguments advanced by the defendant was that the billboards were not a nuisance at common law and the plaintiff had no remedy. The court rejected this argument because the plaintiff was basing his action on a statute which allowed restraint of the erection of a billboard or sign which violated any rule or regulation of a statutory board. The billboards violated the rules, and the landowner was not required to exhaust his administrative remedies before suing to enjoin. A final argument was that the adoption of a new zoning ordinance by the city permitting billboards in the area involved rendered the case moot. But the new ordinance also contained a limitation on the size of billboards, and these were about twice that size.

7. Shifflett v. Baltimore County, 247 Md. 151, 230 A.2d 310 (1967) involved another old favorite—junkyards. Testimony adduced at the trial established what everyone knows—that junkyards are incompatible with residential use. They were not deemed to be nuisances per se, but "courts in other jurisdictions have found * * * that the elimination of junkyards which enjoy the status of a non-conforming use in a residential neighborhood is a reasonable exercise of the police power, because of their nature or the

manner in which they are conducted, if the time given for the elimination of the non-conforming use is adequate." The court upheld a zoning ordinance requiring that the junkyards be eliminated within two years of the effective date of the ordinance. Obviously, the junkyards were considered to have nuisance-like characteristics. Moreover, in a residential district, should not a junkyard be regarded as a nuisance per se?

8. What about the operation of a gravel pit in an area zoned for residential use? In City of Cloquet v. Cloquet Sand and Gravel, Inc., 312 Minn. 277, 251 N.W.2d 642 (1977), the gravel pit operators had never secured a conditional use permit to operate in a residential area as required by ordinance, but the trial court held that they need not comply with that requirement because the city was not uniformly enforcing its ordinance. But independent of the ordinance, the court held that defendant's activities, including an excavation that produced a drop-off of 75 to 90 feet, constituted a nuisance. The trial court ordered erection of a fence, the smoothing out of the land contours when the operation ceased, and ordered them to cease operating until the order was complied with. The Minnesota Supreme Court affirmed.

9. Some alleged nuisances in zoned areas present First Amendment considerations. For example, what about statutes or ordinances requiring the licensing and thereby allowing the prohibition of theatrical performances and concerts? See Town of West Greenwich v. Stepping Stone Enterprises, Ltd., 122 R.I. 132, 416 A.2d 659 (1979). In Havurah v. Zoning Board of Appeals, 177 Conn. 440, 418 A.2d 82 (1979), the appellant was a religious organization which argued that sleeping accommodations were essential to its religious fellowship. A zoning board of appeals had concluded that unrestricted overnight lodging was a residential use unrelated to the right to worship. See also Napro Development Corp. v. Town of Berlin, 135 Vt. 353, 376 A.2d 342 (1977) involving an adult book store. The Supreme Court of Vermont was cautious to employ the concept of public nuisance in a situation which might intrude on free speech or expression. See also, on adult book stores, Commonwealth v. Van Emburg, 467 Pa. 445, 359 A.2d 178 (1976), and on adult movies, Commonwealth v. MacDonald, 464 Pa. 435, 347 A.2d 290 (1975). Statutes or ordinances regulating such activities have commonly been attacked as being constitutionally vague.

10. What if you have something as beneficial to the public as a nursing home for handicapped children, whose property has been rezoned, but the rezoning has been held invalid? In Schubach v. Silver, 461 Pa. 366, 336 A.2d 328 (1975), neighboring property owners brought suit to enjoin it as a nuisance based upon the earlier decision on the zoning.

F. NUISANCE DOCTRINE AND ENVIRONMENTAL REGULATION

POTTOCK v. CONTINENTAL CAN CO.

Court of Chancery of Delaware, 1965.
42 Del.Ch. 296, 210 A.2d 295.

[Plaintiff operated a junkyard which "has larger commercial implications than one might infer" normally. Defendant operated an adjacent manufacturing plant which ejected soot into the air, and Plaintiff claimed that this constituted a nuisance which caused him special injury. If Plaintiff was correct, said the Court, this could constitute both a public and private nuisance. Defendant based his affirmative defenses on the state air pollution act arguing that the Plaintiff had failed to exhaust his administrative remedies and that he had an adequate remedy at law. The Court stated that this posed a basic issue as to whether the remedies provided in the air pollution act precluded the exercise of jurisdiction by the Court.]

SEITZ, CHANCELLOR:

* * *

Our Supreme Court in duPont v. duPont, 32 Del.Ch. 413, 85 A.2d 724, construed our Constitution as prohibiting the legislature from depriving this court of its so-called traditional jurisdiction (that existing in 1792) unless an equivalent remedy was provided and also unless that remedy was expressly or by necessary implication made exclusive. The parties tacitly concede that the granting of injunctive relief against nuisances was part of equity's traditional jurisdiction. I shall assume, without deciding, that the administrative remedy with its appeal provision fulfills the "equivalent remedy" requirement of our Constitution, as to the nuisance aspect of this case. However, nowhere in the Air Pollution Act is there any language that expressly provides or by necessary implication requires a holding that the remedy therein created was intended to be exclusive. Thus, this constitutional prerequisite to the abrogation of equity jurisdiction in this area has not been met.

But defendant argues that the nuisance issue should be made subject to the doctrine of primary administrative jurisdiction. This judicially created doctrine is based, inter alia, on the presumed expertise of an agency specifically assigned by law to deal with a particular subject matter. It is true that under the doctrine of primary administrative jurisdiction the court, instead of dismissing the case, may in a proper case retain jurisdiction. Nevertheless, the court must give some significance to the issue or issues submitted to an administrative agency under the primary jurisdiction doctrine. If it does not then the commission's action is meaningless. Since the doctrine does require the court to attach legal significance to a commission's findings, its application would constitute a limitation on the full exercise of this court's traditional constitutional jurisdiction in favor of an administrative agency. This can only be done where the statutory remedy meets the constitutional standard. Here the lack of language of exclusiveness in the Act creating the Authority prevents the court from applying the doctrine.

Defendant places great reliance on the opinions of this court in Schofield v. Material Transit (Air Pollution Authority), (Del.Ch.), 206 A.2d 100 and Tollin v. Diamond State Telephone Company (Public Service Commission), 39 Del.Ch. 350, 164 A.2d 254. In those cases the court stayed proceedings seeking equitable relief in this court and in effect required the plaintiffs to bring their complaints before the administrative agencies indicated. In doing so the court relied upon the doctrine of primary administrative jurisdiction. See 3 Davis, Administrative Law Treatise, § 19.01, et seq. Thus, the court in those cases did, in effect, require the plaintiffs to proceed before administrative agencies which could take cognizance of their basic claims and process them. Apparently no contention was made in either of those cases that in view of the traditional equitable relief sought and the language of the statutes creating such agencies, this court lacked the power to apply the principle of primary administrative jurisdiction because of the interpretation placed upon the constitutional provision creating the Court of Chancery. I therefore reluctantly conclude that these cases are not binding precedent in this type of case where a party sees fit, as here, to insist upon proceeding in this court.

It follows that the existence of the Air Pollution Act does not provide an adequate remedy at law within the constitutional test applicable to the court's jurisdiction. By the same reasoning the doctrine of primary administrative jurisdiction may not be invoked to deprive a party of his full rights in this court.

I therefore conclude that the second and eighth affirmative defenses are without merit as a matter of law.

An appropriate order may be presented.

Notes

1. The Pottock case was back before the Delaware Chancery Court a few months later for a decision on the merits. (This is reported in 42 Del.Ch. 360, 211 A.2d 622 (1965).) In this opinion the junkyard sounds a bit less special. In any event, the Court held that earlier a nuisance had existed and plaintiff could collect damages but that the use of "soot-off" had eliminated any substantial harm and that injunctive relief should be denied. The fact that the junkyard was a non-conforming use in a manufacturing zone seemed to play a part in the decision, along with the observation that much of the "material on which the soot falls is already dirty and often rusting."

2. On the question of statutorily created administrative remedies as opposed to remedies available in equity or at common law, see Annot., Right to Maintain Action to Enjoin Public Nuisance as Affected by Existence of Pollution Control Agency, 60 A.L.R.3d 665 (1974). Most courts which have considered the allegation have held that the creation of an administrative body to control pollution without any evidence that the legislature intended to divest the courts of their common law jurisdiction over nuisance actions is insufficient to preclude the courts from enjoining a pollution-producing activity as a public nuisance. Certainly, the existence of such administrative remedies should not be viewed as eliminating the right of a complaining party to seek injunctive relief and damages. Pollution acts should properly be viewed as creating another avenue of approach to the solution of these problems. See, e.g., Illinois v. City of Milwaukee, 406 U.S. 91, 92 S.Ct. 1385, 31 L.Ed.2d 712 (1972); J.D. Jewell, Inc. v. Hancock, 226 Ga. 480, 175 S.E.2d 847 (1970); and State v. Dairyland Power Coop., 52 Wis.2d 45, 187 N.W.2d 878 (1971). Cf.: Commonwealth v. Glen Alden Corp., 418 Pa. 57, 210 A.2d

256 (1965); State ex rel. Norvell v. Arizona Public Serv. Co., 85 N.M. 165, 510 P.2d 98 (1973).

3.   In the Pottock case the Delaware Chancery Court did not reach the question of the comparative economic importance of the plaintiff's junkyard (with "larger commercial implications than one might infer" from the description) as opposed to Continental Can's manufacturing plant. The economic question and the question of relative hardship is not reached. Yet, as has been indicated previously, this can amount to an important question. In the Spur Industries case, supra, for example, the Arizona Court was arriving at a balancing of the relative hardships in a somewhat novel way. Numerous cases manifest this problem. In Koseris v. J.R. Simplot Co., 82 Idaho 263, 352 P.2d 235 (1960), there was a conflict between owners of a two-acre tract on which was located a cinder block building used to store small articles and the operators of a large chemical phosphate fertilizer plant which hired over 1,000 people and had an annual payroll of about one and a quarter million dollars. The problem stemmed from the emission of dust and fumes from the plant. The Idaho Supreme Court stated that the "comparative benefits and hardships should be weighed in determining whether injunction is the appropriate remedy" and that the court must weigh the gravity of harm to the plaintiffs against the utility and reasonableness of defendant's conduct. The Idaho Court quoted from York v. Stallings, 217 Or. 13, 341 P.2d 529, a 1959 Oregon case, to this effect: "This court heretofore has accepted the balancing doctrine in cases involving the public convenience. In [a prior Oregon case], this court stated: ' * * * sometimes a court of equity will decline to raise its restraining arm and refuse to issue an injunction * * * even though an admitted legal right has been violated, when it appears that * * * the issuance of an injunction would cause serious public inconvenience or loss without a correspondingly great advantage to the complainant.' " The Idaho Court concluded that injunctive relief should not prohibit Simplot Company from "conducting its lawful business; nor prohibit the emission of dust and fumes beyond the quantity that may be emitted upon reasonable control thereof by installation of up-to-date systems of control; nor beyond what is inherent in the industry when conducted consonant with modern methods." It was then held that the trial court erred in not permitting the introduction of evidence along those lines, along with any contradictory evidence which the plaintiff might wish to offer in rebuttal.

4.   In City of Milwaukee v. Illinois and Michigan (Milwaukee II), 451 U.S. 304, 101 S.Ct. 1784, 68 L.Ed.2d 114 (1981) the Court considered whether a federal common law nuisance action to abate pollution of Lake Michigan would lie after Congress allegedly preempted the cause of action by passage of the Federal Water Pollution Control Act. The majority opinion held that the Act had preempted the plaintiffs' claims under common law:

* * *

Federal common law is a "necessary expedient," Committee for the Consideration of the Jones Falls Sewage System v. Train, 539 F.2d 1006, 1008 (C.A.4 1976) (en banc), and when Congress addresses a question previously governed by a decision rested on federal common law the need for such an unusual exercise of lawmaking by federal courts disappears. This was pointedly recognized in Illinois v. Milwaukee [Milwaukee I] itself, 406 U.S., at 107, 92 S.Ct., at 1394 ("new federal laws and new federal regulations may in time pre-empt the field of federal common law of nuisance"), and in the lower court decision extensively relied upon in that case, Texas v. Pankey, 441 F.2d 236, 241 (C.A.10 1971) (federal common law applies "[u]ntil the field has been made the subject of comprehensive legislation or authorized administrative standards") (quoted in Illinois v. Milwaukee, supra, at 107, n. 9, 92 S.Ct., at 1395, n. 9).

* * *

We conclude that, at least so far as concerns the claims of respondents, Congress has not left the formulation of appropriate federal standards to the courts through application of often vague and indeterminate nuisance concepts and maxims of equity jurisprudence, but rather has occupied the field through the establishment of a comprehensive regulatory program supervised by an expert administrative agency. The 1972 amendments to the Federal Water Pollution Control Act were not merely another law "touching interstate waters" of the sort surveyed in Illinois v. Milwaukee, 406 U.S., at 101–103, 92 S.Ct., at 1391–1392, and found inadequate to supplant federal common law. Rather, the amendments were viewed by Congress as a "total restructuring" and "complete rewriting" of the existing water pollution legislation considered in that case.

5. In Marshall v. Consumers Power Co., 65 Mich.App. 237, 237 N.W.2d 266 (1975), the plaintiff sought to enjoin the construction of a nuclear power plant to be built by the defendant on the shore of a river slightly over a mile from plaintiff's residence. The complaint alleged that the plant would constitute a "private and/or public nuisance" and would violate Michigan's environmental protection act, as well as constitute a common law nuisance. It was alleged that steam fog and icing would result in the winter, that hazardous driving conditions would result, that plaintiff's premises would receive accumulations of ice, that plaintiff's health would be jeopardized, that there would be anxiety to plaintiff over a possible nuclear accident, that his insurance would be cancelled, and that the emergency core cooling system would not work. A major question for the Michigan court was whether the Atomic Energy Act preempted state common law remedies under the law of nuisance. The court concluded that the rights and interests involved were sufficiently dissimilar that a state court has the power to proceed and also that state courts are the place to assert state-protected rights. A federal permit to build the power plant was viewed as strictly that and as not doing away with the right of the state court to entertain nuisance allegations. However, the court concluded that it was not a nuisance per se and that the question of nuisance per accidens would have to await its construction and operation.

6. Also consider Ohio v. Wyandotte Chemicals Corp., 401 U.S. 493, 91 S.Ct. 1005, 28 L.Ed.2d 256 (1971). There, original jurisdiction in a suit to abate interstate pollution was refused by the Supreme Court. In a footnote in State of Illinois v. City of Milwaukee, supra, the Supreme Court stated that Wyandotte "was based on the preoccupation of that litigation with

public nuisance under Ohio law, not the federal common law which we now hold is ample basis for federal jurisdiction * * *." Commenting on this "cryptic footnote," the Michigan court stated: "It [the Supreme Court] felt that a state court has as compelling a claim to adjudicate the controversy and that the case would be decided under the common law of nuisance. The Court stressed the value of 'close supervision of the technical performance of local industries' by state courts. In Illinois v. Milwaukee, however, the Court held that Federal common law governed such suits. * * * In any case, Federal common law would be enforced with reference to state standards."

7. The problem as to preemption of the federal common law continued after Milwaukee II in other cases. Illinois v. Outboard Marine Corp., 680 F.2d 473 (7th Cir.1982) held that the Federal Water Pollution Control Act displaced the federal common law remedy for nuisances resulting from a discharge of pollutants into navigable waters before 1972 as well as after 1972 (—in other words, it applied retroactively). In Middlesex County Sewerage Authority v. National Sea Clammers Association, 453 U.S. 1, 101 S.Ct. 2615, 69 L.Ed.2d 435 (1981), the Supreme Court extended the doctrine of Milwaukee II to coastal waters. But the Court said, "we need not decide whether a cause of action may be brought under federal common law by a private plaintiff seeking damages." 451 U.S. at 21, 101 S.Ct. at 2627. In Illinois v. Milwaukee, 731 F.2d 403 (7th Cir.1984), it was held that the federal water pollution laws preempt a state nuisance claim based on interstate water pollution, as well as a federal claim.

However, the question arose again in International Paper Co. v. Ouellette, 479 U.S. 481, 107 S.Ct. 805, 93 L.Ed.2d 883 (1987). A paper company's mill on the New York side of Lake Champlain was discharging effluents into the lake through a pipe that ended just short of the Vermont border. Property owners in Vermont sued in Vermont state court based on the Vermont common law of nuisance. The case was removed to federal district court in Vermont, which held that the Act's savings clause preserves actions to redress interstate water pollution under the law of the State where the injury occurred, and the Court of Appeals affirmed. The savings clause said that the Act would not be construed as impairing the rights of the States with respect to their waters and further that there would be no restriction of any right which any person might have under statute or common law to seek enforcement of any effluent standard or limitation or to seek other relief. The federal district court interpreted this to mean that an action to control water pollution could be brought under the law of the State where the injury occurred (i.e., Vermont). The Supreme Court, however, adopted an interpretation followed by the Seventh Circuit in the last Illinois v. Milwaukee case, cited above. ("Milwaukee III.") This was that the savings clause could preserve state nuisance law only as to discharges occurring within the source State, which meant that a claim could be filed against International Paper under the New York common law, but not under Vermont common law. The Supreme Court thus held that the court must apply the law of the State in which the "point source" is located. Justice Powell, for the Court, stated:

* * *

An interpretation of the saving clause that preserved actions brought under an affected State's law would disrupt this balance of interests. If a New York source were liable for violations of Vermont law, that law could effectively override both the permit requirements and the policy choices made by the source State. The affected State's nuisance laws would subject the point source to the threat of legal and equitable penalties if the permit standards were less stringent than those imposed by the affected State. Such penalties would compel the source to adopt different control standards and a different compliance schedule from those approved by the EPA, even though the affected State had not engaged in the same weighing of the costs and benefits. This case illustrates the problems with such a rule. If the Vermont court ruled that respondents were entitled to the full amount of damages and injunctive relief sought in the complaint, at a minimum IPC would have to change its methods of doing business and controlling pollution to avoid the threat of ongoing liability. In suits such as this, an affected state court also could require the source to cease operations by ordering immediate abatement. Critically, these liabilities would attach even though the source had complied fully with its state and federal permit obligations. The inevitable result of such suits would be that Vermont and other States could do indirectly what they could not do directly—regulate the conduct of out-of-state sources.

Application of an affected State's law to an out-of-state source also would undermine the important goals of efficiency and predictability in the permit system. The history of the 1972 amendments shows that Congress intended to establish "clear and identifiable" discharge standards. See S.Rep. No. 92–414, p. 81 (1971), 2 Leg.Hist. 1499. As noted above, under the reading of the saving clause proposed by respondents, a source would be subject to a variety of common-law rules established by the different States along the interstate waterways. These nuisance standards often are "vague" and "indeterminate." The application of numerous States' laws would only exacerbate the vagueness and resulting uncertainty. The Court of Appeals in *Milwaukee III* identified the problem with such an irrational system of regulation:

"For a number of different states to have independent and plenary regulatory authority over a single discharge would lead to chaotic confrontation between sovereign states. Dischargers would be forced to meet not only the statutory limitations of all states potentially affected by their discharges but also the common law standards developed through case law of those states. It would be virtually impossible to predict the standard for a lawful discharge into an interstate body of water. Any permit issued under the Act would be rendered meaningless." 731 F.2d, at 414.

It is unlikely—to say the least—that Congress intended to establish such a chaotic regulatory structure.

* * *

Our conclusion that Vermont nuisance law is inapplicable to a New York point source does not leave respondents without a remedy. The CWA precludes only those suits that may require standards of effluent control that are incompatible with those established by the procedures set forth in the Act. The saving clause specifically preserves other state

actions, and therefore nothing in the Act bars aggrieved individuals from bringing a nuisance claim pursuant to the law of the *source* State.
* * *

IPC asks the Court to go one step further and hold that all state-law suits also must be brought in source-state *courts*. As petitioner cites little authority or justification for this position, we find no basis for holding that Vermont is an improper forum. Simply because a cause of action is preempted does not mean that judicial jurisdiction over the claim is affected as well; the Act pre-empts laws, not courts. In the absence of statutory authority to the contrary, the rule is settled that a district court sitting in diversity is competent to apply the law of a foreign State.

8. What about federal air pollution statutes? In New England Legal Foundation v. Castle, 666 F.2d 30 (2d Cir.1981), the court did not reach the question of whether the Federal Clean Air Act preempts federal common law actions.

9. Environmental regulation by the federal and state governments has given rise to a large number of cases which run across several areas of law. Nuisance law forms part of the basis for the enforcement of these regulations. Thus, in Pottawattamie County v. Iowa Dept. of Environmental Quality, Air Quality Comm'n, 272 N.W.2d 448 (Iowa 1978), the state agency had brought suit against two counties for violating the rules on emissions of "fugitive dust" caused by truck travel to and from a rock quarry. The Iowa Supreme Court held that the section of the statutes presenting an articulated standard for determining a nuisance in connection with the fugitive dust rule was not unconstitutionally vague since it had been applied numerous times and refined by case law. The counties further contended that the rule could only be applied to public nuisance situations. The Iowa Supreme Court disagreed, stating:

> The same circumstances may create both a public and private nuisance. The facts may create a nuisance to the general population and also a nuisance to individual plaintiffs. Park v. Chicago & S.W.R. Co., 43 Iowa 636, 638 (1876); Ozark Poultry Products, Inc. v. Garman, 251 Ark. 389, 472 S.W.2d 714, 715–716 (1971). The elements of public nuisance are: (1) unlawful or antisocial conduct that (2) in some way injures (3) a substantial number of people. State ex rel. Turner v. Younker Brothers, Inc., 210 N.W.2d at 564. The determination of private nuisance rests upon whether there has been 'an actionable interference with a person's interest in the private use and enjoyment of his land.' Patz v. Farmegg Products, Inc., 196 N.W.2d at 560.

10. See also such cases as National Wood Preservers, Inc. v. Commonwealth, 489 Pa. 221, 414 A.2d 37 (1980), involving water pollution; Sundell v. Town of New London, 119 N.H. 839, 409 A.2d 1315 (1979), where riparian and littoral owners sued a town which operated a sewage treatment plant which discharged nutrient-laden effluent into a brook; Filisko v. Bridgeport Hydraulic Co., 176 Conn. 33, 404 A.2d 889 (1978), involving a nuisance caused by water pollution; and City of Bridgeton v. B.P. Oil, Inc., 146 N.J.Super. 169, 369 A.2d 49 (1976), involving an oil spill and holding that a

person who stores pollutant or ultra-hazardous substances is strictly liable for damages caused by such substances.

G. TRESPASS OR NUISANCE

There has been so much nuisance litigation in recent years that it could well form the subject of a much longer chapter or a separate book. Space does not permit consideration of all of the questions that arise. One, however, that is of some significance is the interplay of nuisance and trespass law. This issue is not new. For example, in Ivester v. City of Winston–Salem, 215 N.C. 1, 1 S.E.2d 88 (1939), the plaintiffs alleged that they were entitled to damages from the defendant city because of a taking resulting from the maintenance by the city of an incinerator and abattoir close to their property. This produced noxious odors, smoke, fumes and falling ashes. It was alleged that this was a nuisance which resulted in a substantial diminution in the value of their property and that they were entitled to just compensation. The North Carolina Supreme Court regarded this as a suit to recover damages for loss produced by a continuing nuisance and allowed it to proceed.

It may not matter that much, but as noted earlier, there was also a trespass involved in the form of the particles which passed over onto the land of the plaintiffs. The same may be said of the smoke and odors. See, however, Maddy v. Vulcan Materials Co., 737 F.Supp. 1528 (D.Kan. 1990). The federal court held that Kansas would adopt the modern view that an indirect or intangible invasion can constitute a trespass when there has been an infringement of the owner's exclusive possessory interest. But, held the court, in this case where the plaintiffs brought a trespass action for the passage of airborne contaminants across their property, they did not show damages that would have implicated their right to exclusive possession.

The trespass versus nuisance question, it would seem, should not preclude a landowner from recovering for a taking no matter whether the actions complained of result from a pure trespass or from a continuing nuisance. But it does in cases involving airports and aviation. The majority view in the United States is that continuing-trespasses by low flying aircraft which interfere with the landowner's use of his property may result in a taking for which compensation can be recovered in an inverse condemnation suit. But if the planes do not pass through the airspace of the plaintiff, he cannot recover. Why should this be so? Why should not the result in the Ivester case, involving a continuing nuisance, also apply to aircraft passing through nearby airspace? The noise does not just go down; it flows out like the ripples produced by a pebble tossed in a pond. The answer is that the maxim, *cujus est solum ejus est usque ad coelum,* enunciated by Lord Coke, meant that a landowner owned the space above his land up to the heavens. Thus, to take his land (airspace), there had to be a trespass. See generally, R. Wright, The Law of Airspace (1968).

Some fairly recent cases have made substantial inroads on this obviously irrational rule. Two of these cases are Thornburg v. Port of

Portland, 233 Or. 178, 376 P.2d 100 (1962) and Martin v. Port of Seattle, 64 Wash.2d 309, 391 P.2d 540 (1964). In essence, those cases hold that noise may constitute a nuisance and that the nuisance produced can effectively take what might be called an easement for noise. The cases, particularly Thornburg, point out the absurdity of making a distinction as to whether the noise comes down from above or from some other direction. A landowner, as was stated by a Florida appeals court decision which adheres to the same view, "has a right to be free from unreasonable interference caused by the noise, and if such noise and/or intense vibration produced by low flying aircraft deprived such owner of an essential element in his relationship to his land, compensation therefor should be made by the public authority responsible" for it. City of Jacksonville v. Schumann, 199 So.2d 727 (Fla.App.1967). The Schumann case viewed this as also being the view of the United States Supreme Court in United States v. Causby, 328 U.S. 256, 66 S.Ct. 1062, 90 L.Ed. 1206 (1946) and Griggs v. Allegheny County, 369 U.S. 84, 82 S.Ct. 531, 7 L.Ed.2d 585 (1962). However, that is not clear from those cases.

A sensible approach is also illustrated by the Supreme Court of New Hampshire in Ferguson v. City of Keene, 111 N.H. 222, 279 A.2d 605 (1971). There, the plaintiff sued the defendant city based on the use of an area behind the plaintiff's house as a warm-up or holding area for jet planes prior to take-off. Noise, dust and some property damage were alleged, and damages were sought based on this nuisance. Although the court did not get into the trespass versus nuisance question directly, as in the cases mentioned previously, it sustained the verdict for the diminution in value produced by the nuisance. Obviously, if aircraft on the ground can produce a nuisance, the question of trespass when the aircraft are in the air should not be permitted to bar recovery.

Chapter III

PRIVATE LAW DEVICES
TO ASSURE LAND
DEVELOPMENT PLANS

SECTION 1. GUIDEPOSTS IN
A SEMANTIC JUNGLE

From the previous chapter it is obvious that one cannot efficiently achieve planned land development by relying on the happenstance processes of nuisance law. It is also clear that plans alone are not enough. There must be legally enforceable means to implement or protect plans. In subsequent chapters we deal with legislative and administrative controls designed to accomplish public land use planning. In this chapter we deal with so-called "private" land use restrictions. These involve typically "a right in the land of another." That is, someone not the owner of land is put in a position in which he can compel the owner to carry out or to refrain from carrying out specified activities on his land.

The variety of private law devices available to accomplish land use goals is substantial. The lawyer is faced with a problem of knowledgeable choice. And once he has chosen the device he intends to use he must know how to create the selected relationship. Then, regardless of the selection he has made, he is faced by a formidable challenge to be extraordinarily careful in his writing, because what he writes may bind the land for many years. This chapter attempts to set up enough guideposts so that a lawyer can at least begin to make intelligent choices.

First, it may help to outline typical functional situations in which the lawyer operates in this area of the law. The list is by no means complete; it is illustrative only. Later, we will turn to a more detailed problem in order to raise many of the questions dealt with in this chapter, but first, the outline:

A. Private Arrangements to Implement Private Plans

    1. Two or more landowners want to assure that their lands will be kept in open space uses, will be developed for large lot

residential use only, or will be subject to a building development scheme.

2. A public utility wants to acquire a right of way across private land for its poles, wires or pipes.

3. Two or more neighbors want to establish a common driveway, or an access way across the land of one or to preserve a scenic view over the land of one for the benefit of another.

4. To implement a subdivision building scheme:

a. A subdivider wants unilaterally to declare how the land is to be used, that it is to be subject to architectural controls, building setbacks, and the like; or

b. The subdivider wishes to enter into an agreement with each lot buyer under which the buyer agrees to the building scheme for the lot he is buying and the subdivider agrees to it for all of the unsold lots; or

c. The subdivider wants each lot buyer to agree that the lot being purchased is subject to the building scheme.

B. Adaptation of Private Land Planning Tools to Public Planning Ends

1. A city and a developer wish to agree that slum-cleared land will be redeveloped in accordance with a plan made by the city.

2. A city wants to approve a subdivision plat but only on condition that the land will be developed or used in specified ways, subject to access, setback, lot size or other restrictions.

3. A city is willing to approve an amendment rezoning X's land from residential to commercial but only after X has formally agreed that the land will actually be used for only one of many "permitted" commercial purposes.

4. A unit of government wants to acquire from landowner a right preserving an open area, permitting public use, public access to a lake, or similar uses.

5. A unit of government is selling forest land which it owns to a private company. It wants to assure the cutting of sizeable trees only and other desired forestry practices.

[These last five situations suggest that the line between "private" law and "public" law may not always be easy to draw.]

A More Specific Problem

To raise questions, intrigue and perhaps help organize your interest in the subject matter of this chapter, here is a specific and fairly detailed problem:

Andrew Developer is our client. He has purchased a 40 acre tract of land. We have previously handled the title checking and conveyancing problems for this purchase. Now he wants us to do the legal work necessary to carry out and maintain the plans he has for a subdivision development of the tract, to be known as Sunrise Hills Addition. Our client has decided on the general layout and design of the subdivision—the size and arrangement of lots and blocks, the location and width of streets, and similar arrangements. He has employed Speedy Engineers to follow this site plan in surveying and monumenting the lots, in marking off streets and blocks, and in drawing an accurate map or plat of Sunrise Subdivision. This survey and map may have to meet detailed standards of accuracy and monumenting fixed either by local ordinance or by state statute.

Having submitted the preliminary site plan informally to the local planning commission, Developer knows that in order to get the final plat formally approved so that it can be recorded, he is going to have to:

(1) Dedicate all land needed for streets to the city;

(2) Provide minimum building line set-backs of 25 feet from the street for all lots, 5 feet for side yards and a minimum rear yard area of 30 feet;

(3) Restrict all lots abutting on Hudson Street, a major thorough-fare, so that there will be no access from these lots onto that street; and

(4) Give a small area to the city for park purposes.

In addition and on his own initiative Developer wishes to assure exterior architectural control over all houses to be built in the subdivision; permit single family residential use only; prevent redivision of lots into smaller lots and reserve a 5 foot strip to the rear of each lot for utility pipes, poles and wires. He also wants trustees elected by the lot owners to administer and enforce the restrictions.

The area is zoned, "R–1, Residential," but Developer does not wish to rely on the "whims of the local politicians" who may amend the ordinance at some future date, and besides several of the desired restrictions are not included in the zoning ordinance.

How can "suggested" and volunteered planning ends like those above listed be legally assured?

The Tool of Dedication

First, consider the tool of *"dedication."* This will make it possible for Developer to convey to the city, in trust for the public, the land needed for streets and sidewalks and the public park. Should we also use the device of dedication to achieve an easement of nonaccess for all lots abutting on Hudson Street and possibly also a building line "easement" for front, side and rear yards? The platting statutes will probably tell fairly precisely how dedications can be accomplished in the particular state. But in absence of statute so-called common law dedication is available to accomplish the desired transfers for the public purposes stated. For every dedication there is involved an offer by the dedicator and an acceptance, either formal or *de facto,* by the governmental unit.

We will want to be sure that any dedication offers are duly accepted. Otherwise we will have merely created a unilateral offer to dedicate which will continue in force until revoked or until accepted, perhaps much later. It will be well for us to brush up on local case law on dedications and read a good text on the subject. (For example, see McQuillin on Municipal Corporations (3d ed. rev. 1983), sections 33.01 and following.) We will want to be in a position to advise our client just when the dedication becomes legally effective, so that he can know when his responsibilities for the street and park land end.

There is a great deal of case law on the question of when a dedication becomes legally effective, but mostly the cases involve failures to follow detailed requirements of the dedication statutes. In any event we will not have time to explore fully the subject of dedications in this course. One unusual case to consider, however, is St. Charles Parish School Bd. v. P & L Investment Corp., 674 So.2d 218 (La.1996) where the court held that a school board was entitled to use the property of an adjoining private landowner because of a "tacit" dedication; the court also examined and rejected arguments that the board obtained the right by prescription or servitude.

Other Tools

Next, and before leaping to the conclusion that all the rest of our client's problems can be taken care of by a neat package of "restrictive covenants" copied from the nearest form book, it will be well if we try to find our way through the jungle of legal semantics into which his problems plunge us. As a non-lawyer our client is thinking quite simply about imposing "restrictions" on the land.

Unfortunately, as lawyers, with the possibility of future judicial scrutiny of our work in mind, we cannot be as uninhibited in our approach to Developer's problems. Having read a few of the cases in this chapter, you will likely agree that this is most assuredly and unfortunately true.

Just to list the concepts that plague us as we work with our client's problems is enough to forewarn the uninitiated to proceed with great caution:

(1) *Easement*—affirmative, negative, appurtenant, in gross, express, implied and prescriptive—as distinguished from license and equitable servitude;

(2) *Defeasible estate*—on condition subsequent with right of entry or determinable fee with a possibility of reverter, as distinguished from covenant;

(3) *Covenants* that run in equity as distinguished from those that run at law and those that do not run at all;

(4) *Equitable servitude*—appurtenant, or in gross, as distinguished from mere contract rights and easements;

(5) *Conveyance* and *grant* distinguished from contract.

Legal writers have had a field day in this heaven of concepts, but they have only infrequently descended to the functional level of our client's real life problems.

Conveyance and Grant Distinguished From Contract

The case materials which follow introduce the student to the subtleties of *defeasible estates, restrictive covenants* and *equitable servitudes.* But before looking into these cases it is well to point out that typically easements and defeasible estates are created by language of transfer—of grant, reservation or conveyance. Covenants, leading to equitable servitudes, are created by language of promise—of contract. Normally a conveyance or grant purports to change the relationship not just between the parties but as to other persons generally. If a lot owner conveys a five-foot utility easement at the rear of his lot to a public utility company, then to all the world the company owns this easement and by recording the instrument of grant it can give notice of its rights to the world.

On the other hand, a contract typically purports to change the legal relationships of the parties only. So if lot owner merely *promises* that his lot will be restricted by a five-foot utility easement, we have presented the problem with which courts have wrestled for centuries: How can a third person (a subsequent purchaser or user of the lot, for instance) be bound or burdened by a promise to which he was not a party? During a period when contracts generally were not assignable, the English *law* courts, beginning with Spencer's Case, 5 Coke 16a, 77 Eng.Rep. 72 (1583), worked out some rules usually treated under the subject heading, "real covenants running with the land."

The Development of Equitable Restrictions Called Equitable Servitudes

Any doctrine permitting a man to be held on a promise he never made is likely to be sharply circumscribed. This has happened in *law* actions for damages brought on covenants alleged to run with the land. The promise must be under "seal," it must "touch and concern" the land, it must "run with" the land, and there must be "privity of estate." If any of these requirements is lacking then the burden of the promise cannot run at *law* even though the benefit of it may.

But as a practical matter these law action limitations and the great gloss of case law that has been built up around each do not concern us in the usual case. Developer is not interested in bringing damage actions; he wants an arrangement that will give him or other lot owners standing in court *to enjoin* violations of the restrictive promises. Therefore, we are primarily interested in the limitations which the courts in *equity* cases have worked out for the "running of the burden" of restrictive covenants; that is, the extent to which subsequent purchasers or users can by injunction be prevented from acting in violation of the promise in which they had no part. In another case, however, our client may be interested in covenants under which monetary assessments can be imposed on lot owners for community purposes, and here the "running of burdens" at law would be of importance. See Neponsit Property Owners' Ass'n v. Emigrant Ind. Savings Bank, infra.

In general, equity has been willing to find the remedy at law inadequate in restrictive covenant cases and has required the subsequent purchaser or user to fulfill the burden of the promise where the intention that the burden pass to him is clear and where he took *with notice of the promise*. For those with notice it was unconscionable to do what the promise said should not be done. By making such promises recordable, a way of giving notice to all (i.e., constructive notice through recordation) was found. Liability of the successors of the promisor was based on the combined grounds of inadequacy of legal remedy and equitable estoppel. The liability was therefore non-contractual in nature and was thought to be unlike the liability of one to whom the burden of a covenant has run at law. The peculiar requirements respecting seal, privity, running and touching and concerning have no relation to it.

There is no unanimity in the cases about whether equity is enforcing a contractual promise or is merely recognizing an incorporeal property interest (an equitable servitude), which the courts themselves have molded out of typical equitable considerations of fairness and conscience. It is usual today to say that promissory restrictions impose on the land "equitable servitudes." But these interests being equitable may not have the quality of the easement at law, namely that they may be owned or enforced by anyone, whether he owns or possesses land in the subdivision or not.

More specifically, in terms of our hypothetical problem, we will want to look to the time when Developer no longer has any lots of his own, but when out of pride of business reputation or otherwise he desires to enforce the restrictions. Further, note the non-access restriction on the lots abutting the street and that the set-back, side yard and rear yard restrictions on all the lots are intended as much or more for the benefit of the community as a whole as for the individual lot owners in the subdivision. It seems only sensible, therefore, to try to arrange matters so that the local municipality as well as lot owners will have a standing in a court of equity at least as to those restrictions which the city has demanded as a condition to plat approval. This means, among other things, that we should give careful consideration to the possibility of granting "easements" for those restrictions which we are sure will fit that category using promissory restrictions for the rest. And for the rest of the restrictions we may want to create an agency of some kind charged with the duty of overseeing and enforcing the restrictions.

In framing our covenants there are important drafting caveats to be kept in mind. Some of these will develop from the cases in this chapter.

SECTION 2. THE USE OF EASEMENTS

In a study prepared for the Outdoor Recreation Resources Review Commission in 1962, entitled "Land Acquisition for Outdoor Recreation—Analysis of Selected Legal Problems," Norman Williams, Jr., an able lawyer-planner, prepared some material which bears directly upon the easement device and legal problems which may arise in connection with its application in land use situations. The following excerpts are taken from pages 88 to 92 of ORRRC Study 16 by Mr. Williams:

Summary of Technical Problems in Easement Law

Among the technical legal problems which arise in easement law, and which may be of relevance in the present context, are the following:

1. Whether new types of easements can be created or whether the content of easements is a closed category.

2. The distinction between appurtenant easements and easements in gross.

3. In the case of appurtenant easements, what will be accepted as a dominant tenement, and whether such an easement can be severed from the dominant tenement.

4. In the case of easements in gross, whether these are or can be made assignable.

5. The various possibilities of automatic termination of the easement rights, without notice and without compensation.

6. The various administrative difficulties which result from split ownership.

In discussing these legal problems, it is assumed that we are dealing with appurtenant easements and easements in gross as they occurred at common law, without statutory modification or clarification.

The Creation of New Easements

While there is some old authority to the effect that easements are a closed category, it is quite clear in the mid–20th century that new types of easements can be created, and in fact are being created and enforced all the time.

* * *

Easements—Appurtenant and in Gross

The basic distinction in easement law is between appurtenant easements and easements in gross. Appurtenant easements, the more familiar type, are easements which are connected with and attached to the ownership of nearby land. The characteristic case is the right of way across one piece of land, possessed by the owner of another piece of land, usually nearby. In this case, the land subject to the right of way is known as the servient tenement; and the land adjacent, whose owner gets the benefit of the right of way, is known as the dominant tenement. The principal characteristic of an appurtenant easement is that there must be a dominant tenement. If there is no dominant tenement—as, for example, in the case of a right of way owned by somebody not having other land nearby—the right is known as an easement in gross. In any given case, if there is any doubt as to which type a given easement is, there is a strong presumption in law in favor of an easement appurtenant.

Appurtenant Easements

Several technical legal problems arising in connection with an appurtenant easement may be relevant to conservation easements.

A scenic easement along a highway is a typical example of an appurtenant easement, for the right to limit land use in the strip adjacent to the right of way is clearly appurtenant to the ownership of the highway itself. A conservation easement, however, will involve a somewhat different situation. Normally there will not be any publicly owned land, immediately adjacent or nearby, which can serve as the dominant tenement. If there does happen to be, in most cases it would be difficult to prove that the open area was acquired as an incident thereto. The only likely possibility here is a road.[1] If a road does happen to be available, about the only instance in which the open area can be argued to be "appurtenant" to the road is in the case of the typical scenic easement.

The argument might conceivably be made that conservation easements could be regarded as appurtenant to all the land in the community on the ground that they increase the value and desirability of all such land. This seems too thin a basis, however, on which to hang a major program.

Appurtenant easements are the most common form of easements and the requirement of a dominant tenement is the principal legal characteristic of an appurtenant easement. If there is no dominant tenement—and no overall statutory scheme spelling out the nature of the new right—legal trouble may ensue. Again, a case illustrates the type of problem which might arise in dealing with appurtenant easements. The Greater Pittsburgh Airport was apparently owned by Allegheny County. In a proceeding[2] by the United States to condemn a clearance easement covering an area outside the airport, the pleadings were apparently rather confused. As a result, it was not altogether clear why the Federal Government was the agency which was interesting itself in protecting the approaches to this airport. In this situation the lower court refused to grant condemnation of the clearance easement. This

---

1. Compare the famous covenant case of London County Council v. Allen, (1914) 3 K.B. 642.

2. United States v. 64.88 Acres of Land in Allegheny County, 144 F.Supp. 29 (W.D.Pa.1956), reversed 244 F.2d 534 (3d Cir.1957).

court was bothered by the fact that there was no indication of what the Federal Government's legal interest in the Greater Pittsburgh Airport was. Was the Government leasing the airport or part thereof? Was the Air Force using it? It was held that the United States did not have the power to condemn an interest in air space in such "helter-skelter fashion."[3] The court assumed that such an easement "must be attached to"[4] (i.e. appurtenant to) some property owned by the Government and, since the Government agency seeking to condemn the easement apparently had not shown that it had any legal interest in the airport, condemnation was refused. While this decision was based upon a lack of statutory authority, the difficulty here arose directly from the traditional requirement of a dominant tenement in connection with an appurtenant easement.

This lower court decision was reversed on appeal by the Third Circuit Court of Appeals. In this opinion the court referred to clearance easements as follows:

> * * * the claimed right of clearance is merely a provision for assuring that space shall be unoccupied and vision unobstructed above a designated altitude. Unquestionably, this is in aid of navigation.[5]

The circuit court was not worried about the Government's legal basis for seeking these particular easements on the ground that the Federal Government clearly could act to promote and protect avigation in interstate commerce. Moreover, the court invoked the rule that there will be no judicial review of the extent of land, or the type of estate, needed. The court also said:

> We do not know of any constitutional doctrine which restricts the government's taking of easements in private land to those easements which are appurtenant to a neighboring tract owned or controlled by the United States.[6]

True enough, but stating the issue in terms of constitutional law rather misses the point of the lower court opinion. The confusion noted in the opinion below involved the problem of statutory authorization in relation to common law precedent.

Because of the difficulties[7] which may arise from this requirement of a dominant tenement, easements appurtenant are not an appropriate legal vehicle to use in a broad program of acquiring conservation easements.

3. 144 F.Supp. at 35.
4. 144 F.Supp. at 35.
5. 244 F.2d at 535–36.
6. Id. at 536.
7. As an additional minor point, the rights inherent in an appurtenant easement normally pass with the ownership of the dominant tenement, and, as a corollary, it is usually considered legally impossible to sever these rights from the ownership of the dominant tenement. See for example Cadwalader v. Bailey, 17 R.I. 495, 23 A. 20 (1891) * * *. Conceivably this might create some problems; a situation might arise where it would be desirable to assign the dominant and servient tenements to different public agencies.

Easements in Gross

Conservation easements must normally be either the lesser type of easement, i.e., easements in gross, or some wholly new form of legal right and interest. If such easements are considered as easements in gross, in the traditional form—without special statutory definition—several types of legal problems may arise.

In the first place, there was an old rule, primarily in England, that easements in gross are not recognized at all; i.e., an easement must be attached to a dominant tenement. It is difficult to believe that this would ever be a serious obstacle to a new program. Remembering that the first legal challenge may involve a hard case, however, where the court might be looking for some basis for invalidating the program, one cannot be 100 percent sure. Moreover, there is another old doctrine that negative easements must be appurtenant, so that there is no such thing as a negative easement in gross. It seems unlikely that this is a correct statement of the law today. Nevertheless the statement might cause difficulty.[8]

Moreover, even where they are recognized, easements in gross are generally regarded as a rather limited and weak form of legal interest in land—rather a poor thing, at best—for several reasons. Easements in gross are not favored in law; in case of any doubt the presumption is that an easement is appurtenant. Moreover, major questions arise on their assignability and on the possibility of their termination. These problems raise a real question as to whether so important a program should be based upon a rather thin reed.

One of the classical legal controversies is whether easements in gross are or can be made assignable. In olden days, unquestionably such easements were regarded as personal to the grantee, and so could not be assigned or inherited; and there is distinguished recent authority to support this rule, at least as to the assignment of the benefit.[9] Other cases, particularly more recently, have tended to hold that an easement in gross is assignable. This remains to some extent an open question as of this moment.

This question of the assignability of an easement in gross is not merely of academic interest; it may be of some practical importance in connection with conservation easements. We are concerned here with a change in the use of the land. If a conservation easement falls within the legal category of an easement in gross, and if the benefit, i.e., the right to enforce the easement rights, cannot be assigned, very real problems may arise. For example, what happens to such easements in the case of an annexation proceeding, or even a consolidation? Or, supposing a regional planning authority develops, it might be logical to have the easements

---

8. See 2 American Law Property, sec. 8.12 (1962 Supp.)

9. Clark, Real Covenants and Interests Running with the Land (2d ed. 1947), pp. 67–79, argues strongly against the assigna-bility of the benefits of an easement in gross. Compare Comment, Assignability of Easements in Gross, 32 Yale L.J. 813 (1923, by Professor Nance).

assigned to that authority, and help to put it in business. Perhaps a public agency would somehow be exempt from such a rule; but it would clearly be undesirable to have any open question on the assignability of such interests.

An examination of 20th-century case law on the assignability of the benefit of an easement in gross reveals sharply divergent trends. In the States where such an easement is clearly accepted and valid, it is often recognized that this question is really a matter of intent. If the arrangement creating the easement was such as to make it obvious that assignment was intended, the easement will be held assignable. For example, in an old New Jersey case, the Standard Oil Company obtained easements through an agent for a pipeline right of way; and he promptly assigned to the company the easements, which had been made out in his name.[10] As the court recognized, no one could ever have thought of these easements as appurtenant to a dominant tenement. Similarly, it would make no sense at all to assume that the benefit of the easement was intended for the agent and not for the oil company, his principal. In this situation the easement was held assignable. Similarly, in a New York decision[11] the court held that the intent was clearly to create an assignable easement in gross. Like most rules of easement law, the rule against the assignment of easements in gross can thus most sensibly be regarded as a rule of interpretation, which can always be taken care of by sufficiently clear language in the grant.

Unfortunately, it is not always that simple. It would be unwise to assume that this is a problem which can safely be ignored. As indicated above, there is a sharp split in the authority on the point. On one hand a substantial group of 20th–century cases have held that easements in gross cannot be assigned.[12] And several decisions, in this century, even contain statements that there is no way in which an easement in gross can be made assignable.[13]

On the other hand, a substantial group of cases have held that an easement in gross can be assigned. In a recent New Jersey case, a lower court noted that:

10. Standard Oil Co. v. Buchi, 72 N.J.Eq. 492, 66 A. 427 (Ch.1907).

11. Gould v. Wilson, 115 N.Y.S.2d 177 (Sup.Ct.1952).

12. See for example Waller v. Hildebrecht, 295 Ill. 116, 128 N.E. 807 (1920); Stockdale v. Yerden, 220 Mich. 444, 190 N.W. 225 (1922); Morgan v. McLoughlin, 6 Misc.2d 434, 163 N.Y.S.2d 51 (Sup.Ct.1957), affirmed sub nom. Morgan v. Glen Cove, 6 App.Div.2d 704, 174 N.Y.S.2d 890 (2d Dept. 1958), affirmed mem. 5 N.Y.2d 1041, 158 N.E.2d 498 (1959); Field v. Morris, 88 Ark. 148, 114 S.W. 206 (1908); Wooldridge v. Smith, 243 Mo. 190, 147 S.W. 1019 (1912); Saratoga State Waters Corp. v. Pratt, 227 N.Y. 429, 125 N.E. 834 (1920). See also: Thompson, Real Property, §§ 932–33 at 732–41 (1961 Repl.).

13. See for example Eastman v. Piper, 68 Cal.App. 554, 567, 229 P. 1002, 1007 (1924) ("for easements in gross (strictly speaking they are not easements) are not assignable nor inheritable, and they cannot be made so by any terms in the grant."); Rubel Bros. v. Dumont Coal & Ice Co., 111 Misc. 658, 182 N.Y.S. 204 (Sup.Ct.1920), reversed 200 App.Div. 135, 192 N.Y.S. 705 (1922), quoted in footnote 1. See also: Thompson, Real Property, §§ 932–33 at 732–41 (1961 Repl.).

* * * In recent years * * * there has been a growing tendency to recognize the right to transfer easements in gross and to protect them as assignable interests in real estate.[14]

The Restatement of Property states flatly that commercial easements in gross are assignable.[15] In this situation, all that can be said for sure is that the law is unclear, in a state of flux.

* * *

Enforcement Against Subsequent Purchasers

The converse of the above problem is how to bind subsequent purchasers of the fee to respect the rights under the easement. Technically, this is known in law as the assignment of the burden.

The problem of notice is a real one with conservation easements. Frequently, perhaps normally, there would not be any conspicuous physical evidence of such an easement and there is always the danger that subsequent purchasers would not understand the obligations they were assuming. The National Park Service's experience with scenic easements indicates that this danger is a real one.

This is one problem which has a simple solution. Clearly, such easements should be recorded, as the cases indicate that in many instances they are. A statute authorizing the acquisition of such easements should specifically require that they be recorded. If they are, under general doctrines of law, this provides sufficient notice to bind subsequent purchasers. Moreover, if, as recommended below, the rights under the conservation easement are spelled out in some detail, this should serve to inform the landowners adequately regarding their obligations.

Termination of Easements

Easements may be perpetual, or for a stated term of years, but they are also subject to termination by operation of law. Another serious problem is raised by the possibility of sudden and automatic termination of easements by rule of law, with no compensation to the holder of the easement.

The possibility of such adventitious termination is one of the major problems in a related field of law, that of restrictive covenants. The courts, in exercising their discretion in granting equitable remedies,

14. Weber v. Dockray, 2 N.J.Super. 492, 496, 64 A.2d 631, 633 (1949). For discussion of the assignability of an easement in gross to a municipality, see Poull v. Mockley, 33 Wis. 482 (1873) and Pinkum v. Eau Claire, 81 Wis. 301, 51 N.W. 550 (1892). Also see Thompson, Real Property § 315 (1961 Repl.).

15. Restatement, Property, sec. 499 (1944). See also Florida Blue Ridge Corp. v. Tennessee Electric Power Co., 106 F.2d 913 (5th Cir.1939), certiorari denied 309 U.S. 666, 60 S.Ct. 591, 84 L.Ed. 1013 (1940); Johnston v. Michigan Consolidated Gas Co., 337 Mich. 572, 60 N.W.2d 464 (1953); Atlantic Mills v. New York Central R.R., 126 Misc. 349, 214 N.Y.S. 123 (Sup.Ct.1926); and Callahan v. Martin, 3 Cal.2d 110, 43 P.2d 788 (1935), involving a California statute setting forth a presumption that easements in gross are assignable, unless otherwise indicated.

reserve the right not to enforce a covenant in cases where a change of conditions in the neighborhood has in effect already frustrated the purpose of the covenant.[16] Since covenants are often interpreted as creating negative easements, the possibility exists that this rule of law might be carried over to apply to other easements. Thus far it apparently has not been, but there is an analogous rule in easement law. If an easement is dependent upon special circumstances and exists for a particular purpose, and if that purpose can no longer be carried out, the easement is automatically extinguished. As one authoritative study stated this problem in a related field, that of highway easements:

> Assuming that an easement was acquired and that because of changing conditions the land is no longer required, in many jurisdictions the land would revert to the former owner or abutting owner. The State's financial investment would be forfeited.[17]

A few cases will illustrate the principle. The construction of a freeway in Providence on an embankment over the bed of the former street and with fences cutting off access to adjacent lots, clearly eliminated the usefulness of an easement of access to the former street. The court held in such circumstances that:

> * * * the purpose for which the easement was intended was now impossible of accomplishment and had therefore become extinguished.[18]

Similarly, a small private road led from a group of homes along the shore of a peninsula in Tidewater, Virginia to a public road which ran along the center of the peninsula. The public road was closed at the time of the construction of a large oil refinery on the peninsula. The residents could get out to the main road by other roads, ranging from a half mile longer to 2 miles. The court held that since the private road now ran into a dead end, the former easement for the private road simply ceased to exist.[19]

Consider, then, the possibilities if the normal rules of easement law are assumed to apply to conservation easements. Under the above rule, judges might well decide that the purpose of maintaining open space by conservation easements—particularly in the case of a quasiscenic easement with no public right of entry—has been destroyed by additional residential developments nearby, or perhaps by a group of billboards on nearby property not covered by the easement. The easement may then

---

16. See for example City of Little Rock v. Joyner, 212 Ark. 508, 206 S.W.2d 446 (1947); Downs v. Kroeger, 200 Cal. 743, 254 P. 1101 (1927); Bickell v. Moraio, 117 Conn. 176, 167 A. 722 (1933); and cf.: Paschen v. Pashkow, 63 Ill.App.2d 56, 211 N.E.2d 576 (1965).

17. See Highway Research Board, Condemnation of Property for Highway Purposes. A Legal Analysis (Special Reports 32 and 33, 1958), part 1, p. 9.

18. Kilmartin Realty Inc. v. Silver Spring Realty Co., 90 R.I. 103, 155 A.2d 247, 249 (1959). For a discussion of extinction of easements generally, see Thompson, Real Property §§ 440–449 at 753–804 (1961 Repl.).

19. Hudson v. American Oil Co., 152 F.Supp. 757 (E.D.Va.1957), affirmed 253 F.2d 27 (4th Cir.1958).

simply be released, as having failed of its real purpose. Clearly this would be a most undesirable way to terminate conservation easements.

A related problem involves the doctrine of merger. Under traditional doctrines of law, if both the fee ownership and an easement in a given lot come under the same ownership, the two legal estates are merged into one, and the easement disappears into and is swallowed up by the larger (fee) estate. In our situation, the practical consequences are clear. If a governmental agency should come into possession of land on which the same agency already owned a conservation easement—for example, by tax foreclosure proceedings—under this doctrine the easement would presumably be extinguished at that point. If the easement were to continue in existence, it would have to be reinstituted at the time the land were sold off, by specific provision to that effect. This would not be unreasonable or particularly difficult, but it would have to be remembered.

A related problem involves the case of an easement acquired by a governmental agency and then forgotten by the agency and the public alike. There should be some way to terminate the Government's rights in such a situation. Normally, adverse possession does not run against the Government. The enabling law should therefore make adverse possession applicable, if such a situation continues for a fairly long period—say 10 to 20 years.

Problems of Administration and Enforcement in Divided Ownership

Finally, and more generally, there are the inevitable administrative difficulties in enforcing the respective rights of the parties in a situation where a single tract of land is in effect in split ownership. Inevitably there is a clash of interests and the possibility of confusion, which may be mitigated—but not prevented—if the mutual rights are defined as clearly as possible.

Several problems should be noted. First, it is clearly impossible to foresee all the problems of conflicting land use which may arise in such a situation. Therefore, if what the Government owns are certain specified rights acquired from the fee owner, the fee owner remains in substantial control of the situation; any right not explicitly granted remains in his hands.[20] The owner of the servient tenement, i.e., the fee owner, is likely to hold the whip hand in any unforeseen situation.

Moreover, there are very real practical problems on the effective enforcement of the rights under such an easement, as the National Park Service has found out. As indicated above, the courts are normally reluctant to issue injunctions in advance against threatened violations of

---

20. This is analogous to the problem of prohibitory use zoning regulations; anything not specifically prohibited in such a district goes in as of right. See for example Matter of Gamelli v. Murdock, 273 App.Div. 1019, 79 N.Y.S.2d 277 (1948), affirmed mem. 298 N.Y. 664, 82 N.E.2d 401 (1948); Murphy Motor Sales v. First Nat. Bank of St. Johnsbury, 122 Vt. 121, 165 A.2d 341, 82 A.L.R.2d 985 (1960).

contract or property rights.[21] In what types of situations will an injunction lie to protect the rights under such an easement? Moreover, once the damage is done, how is it possible to prove damages? Assuming a typical case, where the farmer cuts down trees covered by a scenic or a conservation easement, what damage can the Government prove and how can the damage be evaluated? One practical solution here would seem to be to insert a liquidated damages clause, although this might run up the cost of the easement to the Government.

Some interesting cases on easements in recent years include:

a. Hillary Corp. v. United States Cold Storage, Inc., 250 Neb. 397, 550 N.W.2d 889 (1996). A landowner was held to have an implied easement for railway access across adjoining property because a predecessor in interest possessed an implied easement and did not intend to abandon it; therefore the current owner obtained it with the conveyance to it.

b. Compare Universal Motor Fuels, Inc. v. Johnston, 260 Kan. 58, 917 P.2d 877 (1996) where the court held when the landowner's predecessor conveyed all highway access rights to the state department of transportation, reserving access rights over three portions of the property to themselves and their successors or assigns, no contractual promise was created binding the department to recognizing such access rights forever.

c. Gilder v. Mitchell, 668 A.2d 879 (Me.1995). The owners of a servient estate who unilaterally relocated an easement across their property lost a case where the owner of the dominant estate successfully argued that the reservation of a right to relocate the easement in the deed was personal to the original grantor and could not be exercised by the owners of the servient estate.

d. Peterson v.Beck, 537 N.W.2d 375 (S.D.1995). A golf club was held to have an implied easement to utilize a parking lot located between the golf club and a supper club. Even though the golf club could not establish adverse possession, this did not preclude the finding of an implied easement.

e. Warburton v. Virginia Beach Fed. Savings & Loan Ass'n, 899 P.2d 779 (Utah App.1995). After a developer failed and the bank foreclosed, purchasers of lots sued the bank for easement rights to use the country club. The court held that language in the deeds granting purchasers membership in the country club did not convey an easement.

SECTION 3. DEFEASIBLE ESTATES VERSUS COVENANTS

One ill-advised way to restrict land use is through the well-established historical device of the defeasible fee. A defeasible fee may be a fee simple determinable or a fee simple upon condition subsequent. In either

---

21. See 43 C.J.S. Injunctions §§ 17–21 (1945). [Now, 1978, with 1990 Cum.Supp.].

event, unlike the fee simple absolute, the fee may automatically terminate or be subject to a power of termination at some undetermined future date. In both situations there is a potential for the forfeiture or loss of title and its reinvestiture in the grantor who created the estate. In Hagaman v. Board of Educ. of Woodbridge Twp., 117 N.J.Super. 446, 285 A.2d 63 (1971), the Appellate Division of the New Jersey Superior Court provided an excellent and well-documented summary of the pertinent points of law relating to defeasible fees. Here are the basic rules abstracted from that opinion:

(1) "In determining the meaning of a deed, prime consideration is [given to] the intent of the parties."

(2) "An estate in fee simple determinable is an estate in fee simple which automatically determines upon the occurrence of a given event. The grantor retains a possibility of reverter upon the occurrence of the stated event. * * * Generally, the intent to create such an estate is indicated by the use of words denoting duration of time such as 'while,' 'during,' 'so long as.' * * * 'The absence of some one of these phraseologies makes it likely that a court will find a covenant, a trust, or some other type of interest less drastic in its sanctions.' "

(3) "However, ' * * * particular forms of expression standing alone and without resort to the purpose of the instrument in question are not determinative * * *.' Words of limitation merely stating the purpose for which the land is conveyed usually do not indicate an intent to create an estate in fee simple determinable although other language in the instrument, the amount of consideration and the circumstances surrounding the conveyance may indicate such an intent. When a conveyance contains only a clause of condition or of covenant, such clause does not usually indicate an intent to create a fee simple determinable."

(4) "An estate in fee simple subject to a condition subsequent is an estate in fee simple which upon the occurrence of a given event gives to the grantor or his successor in interest the right to reenter and terminate the estate. Upon the occurrence of the given event, the forfeiture of the estate is not automatic. The intent to create such an estate may be indicated by the use of such words as 'on condition that,' 'provided that.' "

(5) "However, such language is not necessarily determinative. Generally, an intent to create a fee simple subject to a condition subsequent is established when the conveyance contains one of the above phrases and a provision that if the given event occurs the grantor may enter and terminate or has a right to re-enter. * * * A mere statement of the use to which the conveyed land is to be devoted is not sufficient to create an estate in fee simple subject to a condition subsequent. * * * Absent clear intention to create a fee simple subject to a condition subsequent, a conveyance with words of condition may be found to create a covenant, a trust, or a mere precatory expression."

(6) "Language in an instrument which is alleged to create a fee simple determinable or a fee simple subject to a condition subsequent is

strictly construed. 'A recognized rule of construction indicates that an instrument, when a choice exists, is to be construed against rather than in favor of a forfeiture.' "

(7) "If a choice is between an estate in fee simple determinable and an estate on condition subsequent, the latter is preferred."

(8) "Where it is doubtful whether a clause in a deed is a covenant or a condition, the former is preferred."

(9) "When a condition in a deed is relied upon to defeat an estate, it should be strictly construed and its violation must be clearly established."

(10) [Implicit from the foregoing, but not a direct quote:] The law abhors a forfeiture. Equity abhors forfeitures.

A leading New Jersey case, on which the court in the Hagaman case relied, is Oldfield v. Stoeco Homes, Inc., 26 N.J. 246, 139 A.2d 291 (1958).

With the foregoing basic rules in mind, let us examine some other cases on the subject.

CITY OF IDAHO SPRINGS v. GOLDEN SAV. & LOAN ASS'N

Colorado Court of Appeals, 1970.
29 Colo.App. 119, 480 P.2d 847.

COYTE, JUDGE.

* * *

The City of Idaho Springs, a second-class city, filed the initial complaint in this suit seeking to quiet title in itself to a certain tract of land located in Clear Creek County. Prior to this suit, the City had determined that a municipal swimming pool was necessary. However, it lacked the proper amount of funds to adequately construct and maintain such a pool. In 1955, the City, in accordance with C.R.S.1953, 139–32–2, had an election to determine whether to sell this particular tract of land to Frank Overturf by warranty deed, subject to the following provision:

> * * * provided, however, that the real property described herein, together with the improvements thereon, shall be used perpetually and solely for the purpose (sic) of the operation of a swimming pool, which said restriction shall run with the land hereby conveyed and in the event of any breach thereof, said property shall forthwith revert to the said party of the first part, its successors and assigns.

The electorate authorized the sale and conveyance and the property was conveyed in accordance therewith.

Defendant Frank Overturf then conveyed the property to Overturf's Park, Inc., which in turn executed a deed of trust to defendant Golden Savings and Loan. Upon default in payment, Golden Savings and Loan foreclosed its deed of trust on the property and acquired a public trustee's deed in January of 1966.

The property was not being used as a swimming pool and, therefore, plaintiff filed suit to enforce the reversion clause contained in the deed and to reaffirm its title to the property. Defendant Golden Savings and Loan Association answered, generally denying the validity of plaintiff's claimed interest, and affirmatively counterclaimed to quiet title in itself to the property in question.

* * *

The sole issue raised by this appeal is the question of whether or not a second-class city may convey property with a possibility of reverter.

Since the trial court based its decision upon C.R.S.1953, 139–32–2 (reenacted as C.R.S.1963, 139–32–2) as interpreted by Centennial Properties v. Littleton, 154 Colo. 191, 390 P.2d 471, a full discussion of this case is necessary.

In *Centennial,* supra, the City of Littleton executed a "warranty deed," conveying a certain tract of land to defendant, title to which would automatically revert to the City after ninety-nine years. Holding this "reversion" to be void, the Supreme Court noted that under the applicable statute, C.R.S.1953, 139–32–2, cities and towns (not home rule cities) had the power " * * * to sell and dispose * * * "of real property, but did not have the power to lease property owned by the city. It further held that plaintiff could not convey real property and at the same time retain a present vested interest in the property. Accordingly, the present vested interest retained by the city was declared to be void and title was quieted in the grantee.

The question here, however, is whether a city may properly convey real property, yet retain a possibility of reverter to it. As defined in School District, etc. v. Russell, 156 Colo. 75, 396 P.2d 929, a possibility of reverter is merely the *possibility* that the land will come back to the grantor. Frank Overturf and his successors held a fee simple determinable estate, which would last as long as the land was used for the purpose specified in the conveying instrument.

The holder of a bare possibility of reverter does not have a present "vested" interest or "estate" in the land. United States v. 2,184.81 Acres of Land, 45 F.Supp. 681. This being so, the City upon delivery of its deed conveyed the entire legal title to the property in question.

The instrument here is in fact a warranty deed granting defendants a fee simple determinable estate in the property so long as it remains in use as a swimming pool. At the time of conveyance, the City of Idaho Springs parted with all present interest in the property, United States v. 2,184.81 Acres of Land, supra, retaining only the possibility of regaining title at some indefinite time in the future, if the specified condition under which the property was conveyed should cease to exist.

For this reason, we conclude that there was full compliance with the statute and that the possibility of reverter contained in the warranty deed was valid and enforceable. Judgment is reversed with directions to enter judgment quieting title in the plaintiff in accordance with this opinion.

SILVERSTEIN, C.J., and ENOCH, J., concur.

Notes

1. Unlike this case, defeasible fees are more commonly employed by private persons rather than by governmental units. They are often related to religion or liquor, although in different ways. One of the classic examples of the fee simple determinable is the conveyance "for as long as St. Paul's Church shall stand." Whether a determinable fee or a fee simple upon condition subsequent, the language often provides for automatic reverter or a right of entry for condition broken in the event "vinous, spirituous or fermented liquors" are sold, or if the premises are used for gambling or some "immoral purpose." (See, e.g., Northwestern Improvement Co. v. Lowry, 104 Mont. 289, 66 P.2d 792, 110 A.L.R. 605 (1937), in which the question was whether a tax deed wiped out the restrictive covenants, and it was held that it did not. The covenants did not rise to the level of a defeasible fee.) Deeds or wills containing such provisions might be compared to the preoccupation of medieval landowners with benefiting the Church in some manner that would avoid some time in purgatory or otherwise expiate their sins. Provisions against "demon rum" should set well with the Almighty. The problem is that in the absence of statutory limitations, the result is to cloud land titles, promote litigation, deter alienability, and permit the dead hand to rule from the grave. Yet such provisions do not violate the Rule against Perpetuities, nor do restrictive covenants, as revealed in McKinnon v. Neugent, 225 Ga. 215, 167 S.E.2d 593 (1969). In that case, a statute which limited enforceability of covenants in zoned areas to 20 years did not render invalid restrictive covenants which were to run for 25 years.

2. In connection with the tax deed problem in the Lowry case, mentioned in the preceding note, consider the following cases from other jurisdictions:

In Hayes v. Gibbs, 110 Utah 54, 169 P.2d 781 (1946), a general plan of restricted development was found to exist, and the court held that while the authorities "are not uniform on the subject * * * ordinarily a tax sale does not divest easements charged upon the property sold." (169 P.2d at 786.) In Schlafly v. Baumann, 341 Mo. 755, 108 S.W.2d 363 (1937), the Missouri statute was interpreted to mean that a tax sale buyer of a residential lot subject to deed restrictions acquired the lot subject to such restrictions since it was assessed on the basis of the enhanced value produced by the restrictions. In Alamogordo Improvement Co. v. Prendergast, 43 N.M. 245, 91 P.2d 428 (1939), the New Mexico court upheld the power of the seller of lots subject to a restriction against the sale of liquor to enforce the restriction against a tax sale purchaser on the theory that the lot was increased in value by the restriction and that this was considered in assessing the lot for tax purposes.

Whether a tax deed wipes out an equitable servitude imposed by a restrictive covenant may be dependent on judicial interpretation of local tax statutes. Some statutes are "in personam" in that they impose liability on the landowner rather than on the land itself. In that situation, nonpayment results in the sale of the owner's interest only, and the purchaser at the tax sale obtains a derivative title—that is, a title which is encumbered only to the same extent as the delinquent taxpayer. Most states have "in rem" statutes in which the encumbrance attaches to the land itself and the tax sale gives rise to a new title freed of all encumbrances. These statutes often allow room for judicial interpretation. Some statutes expressly save "easements" existing at the time of sale and this term may in its context be held broad enough to include equitable servitudes. See Halpin v. Poushter, 59 N.Y.S.2d 338 (Sup.Ct.1945). Several states expressly provide that restrictions imposed by covenants running with the land survive the tax sale and tax deed. See Wis.Stat. § 75.14(4) (1989), which codified the prior holding in Doherty v. Rice, 240 Wis. 389, 3 N.W.2d 734 (1942).

There is an ancillary—perhaps basic—policy issue involved here: Should other lot owners in a subdivision have to pay delinquent taxes on a lot in order to maintain the restriction and thereby prevent destruction of the restricted character of the neighborhood?

On this subject generally, see 2 American Law of Property § 9.40 at 451–52 (1952).

3. Putting aside the tax deed question, which is only ancillary to this discussion, consider the preceding principal case in the light of the case which follows. Are these cases that clearly distinguishable as to the language used and the intent involved?

BARNETT v. COUNTY OF WASHOE

Supreme Court of Nevada, 1970.
86 Nev. 730, 476 P.2d 8.

MOWBRAY, JUSTICE:

The narrow issue presented for our consideration on this appeal calls for our interpretation of the habendum clause set forth in the original deed that conveyed the property known as the Washoe County Golf Course to Washoe County.

1. THE FACTS

In 1935, Messrs. Harlan L. Heward and Leo F. Schmitt and Country Club, Inc., owners of the property in question, deeded it to the County. The deed contained the following provision:

"This deed is made subject to the additional *covenant,* that the premises hereby conveyed shall be used and operated for golf and golfing purposes, and that in the event any use is made of said premises for other or contrary purposes, the title to the premises hereby conveyed shall revert to the Grantors herein, their heirs and successors, as their respective interest shall then appear." (Emphasis added.)

The County completed the golf course in 1936. It has been in continuous use since that time.

On March 31, 1936, Harlan L. Heward conveyed to the corporation, Country Club, Inc., (1) all his interest in an adjoining parcel of property (designated Parcel A) that was owned by Messrs. Heward, Schmitt, and the corporation and (2) his interest in the property upon which the golf course was situated (designated Parcel B).

In 1940, the appellant-plaintiff, Phillip Barnett, as beneficiary of a deed of trust, acquired Parcel A by foreclosure. The interest in the Golf Course was inadvertently omitted at that time, but the deed was corrected in 1953 to reflect the transfer to Barnett of whatever interest remained in Parcel B. Three years later, in 1943, Mr. Barnett sold Parcel A to Edward P. Waltz. Twenty-nine years later, in February 1969, Mr. Barnett commenced the present action in district court seeking a declaratory judgment decreeing that "the plaintiff [Barnett] have a reversionary right in and to the real property [Golf Course] * * * "The trial judge rejected Barnett's claim; hence, this appeal. We agree with the ruling of the district judge, and we affirm the judgment of the lower court.

2. A COVENANT VS. A CONDITION SUBSEQUENT

A clause in a deed imposing a restrictive use on the grantee will be considered as a covenant rather than a condition subsequent when that can reasonably be done. A condition and restriction must be interpreted in the light of the deed as a whole in order to ascertain the interest of the parties. Tamalpais Land & Water Co. v. Northwestern Pac. R.R. Co., 73 Cal.App.2d 917, 167 P.2d 825 (1946); Rosecrans v. Pacific Elec. Ry. Co., 21 Cal.2d 602, 134 P.2d 245 (1943).

If the meaning of the deed is not clear, the court may resort to established rules of construction to aid in the ascertainment of the grantor's intention by extrinsic means, where such intention cannot otherwise be ascertained. Davis v. Moore, 387 P.2d 483 (Okl.1963); Brown v. Huckabaa, 264 Ala. 660, 89 So.2d 180 (1956); Koff v. Frank, 22 Misc.2d 551, 194 N.Y.S.2d 753 (1959). The district judge did so in the instant case by receiving into evidence the written offer of the donor-grantor offering the land to the County[22] and the acceptance of that offer

---

22.

"March 13th, 1935.

"Golf Committee of the Reno Chamber of Commerce
Reno, Nevada
City Council of the City of Reno,
Reno, Nevada.
Board of County Commissioners of Washoe County, Nevada, Reno, Nevada.
Gentlemen:

I hereby offer to donate to you, or to such public agency as you may designate, the West 54.75 acres of what is known as the Reno Golf Course, as said area is de-

scribed upon that certain plat which is attached to and made a part of this letter.

The terms of the offer are as follows:

1. That upon said acreage, together with other available or purchasable acreage, *there be constructed* an eighteen hole standard municipal or public golf course.

2. That said golf course *be constructed* prior to August 1st, 1936. I state to you that the two parties to whom I have outstanding commitments have approved the making of this offer and have agreed to join in the execu-

as reflected in the minutes of the Washoe County Commissioners' meeting of May 1, 1935.[23]

In his written decision, the district judge, in commenting on the donor-grantor's offer and its acceptance by the County, stated:

"It is noted in passing that neither the letter proposal nor the resolution contained any reference to any reversionary rights. The language of the offer ' * * * I will place in escrow a gift deed conveying *clear title* to the described and platted acreage * * * '[emphasis added] is clear and convincing evidence of the intention of all parties concerned. There appears no other evidence herein which would authorize the duly elected Commissioners at that time to accept the grant on any other basis than as proposed. The additional language, at most, appears to be an afterthought—included in case the golf course was not constructed in accordance with the proposal. Emphasis is on the actual prompt *construction* of the golf course— with use of land as such automatically and necessarily following construction and being so understood.

"The County's acceptance of subject deed was not without assumption of affirmative obligation, as well as consequent direct benefit which enured to the grantors.

"In this connection the Court finds that the County of Washoe has faithfully and fully performed all the terms and conditions of Deed for more than 30 years without interruption, developing the subject property to the point where today it is an enviable landmark which has been used and enjoyed by its rightful beneficiaries, the citizens of Washoe County and the public at large. The County's full performance of the subject covenant to date, coupled with every apparent indication of continuous use of the property for golf purposes for an indefinite period of time, plus continuous expenditure of substantial amounts of public funds to improve and maintain the property has clearly earned the County the right to *clear title* to this property as against Plaintiff's assertion of a mere 'naked' alleged, reversionary interest." (Emphasis in original.)

We agree with the ruling of the district judge.

A condition involving a forfeiture shall be strictly interpreted against the party for whose benefit it was created. As the court said in Gramer v. City of Sacramento, 2 Cal.2d 432, 41 P.2d 543, 545 (1935):

---

tion of any and all necessary conveyances.

As soon as you have acquired other necessary acreage and are prepared to commence construction, I will place in escrow a *gift deed* conveying *clear title* to the described and platted acreage, to such public corporation or agency as you may designate. (Emphasis supplied)

"Sincerely yours,

HLH:M"

23. "IT IS FURTHER RESOLVED: That Washoe County accept the offer of Harlan L. Heward donating to said County 54.75 acres of land to be used for the purpose and subject to the conditions stated in such offer, dated March 13, 1935, a copy of which is attached hereto annexed."

* * *'' * * * Such conditions [conditions subsequent] are not favored in law because they tend to destroy estates, and no provision in a deed relied on to create a condition subsequent will be so interpreted, if the language of the provision will bear any other reasonable construction. * * *'' * * *

Particularly is this so when the grantee is a governmental agency. As the court declared in PCK Properties, Inc. v. City of Cuyahoga Falls, 112 Ohio App. 492, 176 N.E.2d 441, 444 (1960):

"A review of the many leading cases in the various states leads to the conclusion that there is a common judicial aversion toward the termination of estates or their forfeiture upon the exercise of rights of re-entry, where the grantor [sic] is a public entity such as a state, county or municipal corporation. There appears to be an expressed reluctance to hold that either a determinable fee, or an estate upon condition subsequent, has been created."

A parallel case to the instant one is Savanna School Dist. v. McLeod, 137 Cal.App.2d 491, 290 P.2d 593, 594 (1955), where land to be used for a public school was deeded to a school district with the following habendum clause:

" 'Said land is hereby conveyed to said party of the second part for public school purposes only, and it is expressly understood and agreed that as a consideration for this conveyance said party of the second part shall build and maintain a public school building on said land, and that the title and ownership of said land shall revert to said parties of the first part upon a failure by said party of the second part to erect and maintain a building thereon to be used exclusively for public school purposes.' " See also Hawe v. Hawe, 89 Idaho 367, 406 P.2d 106 (1965); Bornholdt v. Southern Pac. Co., 327 F.2d 18 (9th Cir.1964), and Alamo School Dist. v. Jones, 182 Cal.App.2d 180, 6 Cal.Rptr. 272 (1960).

Although the word "covenant" was not used in the Savanna habendum clause, and no extrinsic evidence, such as the original donor-grantor's offer, was received, as it was in this case, the California court concluded that a covenant only was intended by the parties and that "the use of said [school] building for said school purposes for a period of forty-five years constituted a full performance by plaintiff [school district] of all the terms and provisions of said [the questioned] deed; * * *"

In the instant case, the County has continuously operated the Golf Course for 34 years. We hold that the language of the habendum clause in the deed conveying the property to the County for a golf course may be reasonably interpreted as a covenant to install and operate a golf course by the County for the use and enjoyment of the general public; that the covenant has been met and satisfied; and that therefore the appellant, Barnett, has no reversionary interest in the Washoe County Golf Course. The judgment of the district court is affirmed.

* * *

Notes

With respect to the use of conditions subsequent or limitations to impose "restrictions" on a subdivision:

1. The following is quoted from Melli, Subdivision Control in Wisconsin, 1953 Wis.L.Rev. 391, 450–51:

The use of conditions as a means of enforcing restrictions should be avoided if possible. A condition provides that in case of violation of a restriction, the title reverts to the original grantor. Although such provisions are frequently inserted in deeds and are even recommended by attorneys, there are a number of disadvantages to their use:

(a) The condition is a very drastic remedy since it usually provides that the owner gets no compensation for improvements he has made.

(b) It may create a flaw in the title to the property because of the difficulty of determining if there has ever been a violation of the condition.

(c) It may defeat its own purpose because the court may find that reversion of title to the grantor is the only remedy provided and a suit for an injunction by other property owners cannot be maintained. This specific problem apparently has not come up in Wisconsin, but in one case where the instrument setting up the restrictions contained a condition the court allowed a suit for an injunction without even discussing whether it was the proper remedy. Schneider v. Eckhoff, 188 Wis. 550, 206 N.W. 838 (1926).

2. As we will see, injunctions for the enforcement of restrictive covenants may be refused because of a change in neighborhood conditions. Does the same doctrine apply to rights of entry based on conditions subsequent? See Clark, Real Covenants and Other Interests which "Run with Land" 198 (2d ed. 1947).

3. The Uniform Act Relating to Reverter of Realty, approved by the Commissioners on Uniform Laws in 1944, reads in part as follows:

Section 1. (Conditions, Restrictions, Reverter.) Every condition [restrictive covenant] limitation or possibility of reverter affecting the title or use of real property shall be limited to a term not exceeding [thirty] years after the effective date of the instrument creating it notwithstanding any provision in that instrument. This section shall not affect any condition, restrictive covenant, limitation or possibility of reverter existing on the effective date of this act or contained in a grant from the state or in any gift or devise for public, charitable, religious or educational purposes, neither shall it affect any lease present or future or any easement, right of way, mortgage, or trust, or any communication, transmission or transportation line, right to take minerals, or charge for support during the life of a person or persons [or any restrictive covenant without right of reentry or reverter].

(Note: If the first bracket—"restrictive covenant"—is included, the final bracketed material is omitted, and vice-versa.)

Charles Ascher commented in Urban Redevelopment: Problems and Practices 260 (Woodbury ed. 1953) that if restrictive covenants are included by use of the first bracket, community schemes are imperiled. Do you agree?

SECTION 4. RESTRICTIVE COVENANTS

A. REAL COVENANTS

When is a covenant personal in nature, so that it only involves the persons who entered into the covenant, and when is it a covenant that serves to bind successive owners of the land involved? That is the problem that centers around the question of real covenants which "run with the land." A real covenant runs with the land in the sense that it is affixed to the title and is enforceable against the holder of the title even if he is a remote grantee and not the original covenantor. In that sense it takes on the qualities of an appurtenant easement.

For a covenant to run with the land and thus continue to impress its requirement against successive titleholders, it must be intended by the original covenantor and covenantee that it not be merely a personal promise and that it continue to be effective as a burden on the title long after the original parties are gone. But intent alone is not enough. It must also be shown that the covenant was intended to "touch and concern" the land—that is, relate to it and affect it as opposed to relating only to the parties agreeing to it. Further, there must be privity of estate between the party seeking to enforce it and the party who is to be bound by it. A real covenant thus becomes an incident to the ownership of the particular land involved, adheres to the title, and derives its vitality from the land itself. That is the result of these ancient requirements of real covenants.

When the Restatement of Property was drafted, conflicting views over the requirements and nature of real covenants surfaced through the opinions of such scholars as Judge Charles Clark, former dean at Yale, and Dean and Professor Oliver S. Rundell of Wisconsin. These contrasting views are manifested in Clark, Covenants and Interests Running with Land (2d ed. 1947), and Rundell, Judge Clark on the American Law Institute's Law of Real Covenants: A Comment, 53 Yale L.J. 312 (1944). How strictly these ancient requirements should be applied in the modern context formed much of the basis for disagreement, and the case which follows is a leading case which grapples with this problem.

NEPONSIT PROPERTY OWNERS' ASS'N v. EMIGRANT INDUSTRIAL SAV. BANK

Court of Appeals of New York, 1938.
278 N.Y. 248, 15 N.E.2d 793, 118 A.L.R. 973.

LEHMAN, J. The plaintiff, as assignee of Neponsit Realty Company, has brought this action to foreclose a lien upon land which the defendant owns. The lien, it is alleged, arises from a covenant, condition or charge contained in a deed of conveyance of the land from Neponsit Realty Company to a predecessor in title of the defendant. The defendant purchased the land at a judicial sale. The referee's deed to the defendant and every deed in the defendant's chain of title since the conveyance of the land by Neponsit Realty Company purports to convey the property subject to the covenant, condition or charge contained in the original deed. The answer of the defendant contains, in addition to denials of some of the allegations of the complaint, seven separate affirmative defenses and a counterclaim. The defendant moved for judgment on the pleadings, dismissing the complaint pursuant to rule 112 of the Rules of Civil Practice. The plaintiff moved to dismiss the counterclaim pursuant to rule 109, subdivision 6, and to strike out the affirmative defenses contained in the answer pursuant to rule 103, as well as pursuant to rule 109, subdivision 6, of the Rules of Civil Practice. The motion of the plaintiff was granted and the motion of the defendant denied. The Appellate Division unanimously affirmed the order of the Special Term and granted leave to appeal to this court upon certified questions.

* * *

It appears that in January, 1911, Neponsit Realty Company, as owner of a tract of land in Queens county, caused to be filed in the office of the clerk of the county a map of the land. The tract was developed for a strictly residential community, and Neponsit Realty Company conveyed lots in the tract to purchasers, describing such lots by reference to the filed map and to roads and streets shown thereon. In 1917, Neponsit Realty Company conveyed the land now owned by the defendant to Robert Oldner Deyer and his wife by deed which contained the covenant upon which the plaintiff's cause of action is based.

That covenant provides:

"And the party of the second part for the party of the second part and the heirs, successors and assigns of the party of the second part further covenants that the property conveyed by this deed shall be subject to an annual charge in such an amount as will be fixed by the party of the first part, its successors and assigns, not, however exceeding in any year the sum of four ($4.00) Dollars per lot 20 X 100 feet. The assigns of the party of the first part may include a Property Owners' Association which may hereafter be organized for the purposes referred to in this paragraph, and in case such association is organized the sums in this paragraph provided for shall be payable to such association. The party of the second part for the party of the second part and the heirs, successors and assigns of the party of the second part covenants that they will pay this charge to the party of the first part, its successors and assigns on the first day of May in each and every year, and further covenants that said charge shall on said date in each year become a lien on the land and shall continue to be such lien until fully paid. Such charge shall be payable to the party of the first part or its successors or assigns, and shall be devoted to the maintenance of the roads, paths, parks, beach, sewers and such other public purposes as shall from time to time be determined by the party of the first part, its successors or assigns. And the party of the second part by the acceptance of this deed hereby expressly vests in the party of the first part, its successors and assigns, the right and power to bring all actions against the owner of the premises hereby conveyed or any part thereof for the collection of such charge and to enforce the aforesaid lien therefor.

These covenants shall run with the land and shall be construed as real covenants running with the land until January 31st, 1940, when they shall cease and determine.''

Every subsequent deed of conveyance of the property in the defendant's chain of title, including the deed from the referee to the defendant, contained, as we have said, a provision that they were made subject to covenants and restrictions of former deeds of record.

There can be no doubt that Neponsit Realty Company intended that the covenant should run with the land and should be enforceable by a property owners association against every owner of property in the residential tract which the realty company was then developing. The language of the covenant admits of no other construction. Regardless of the intention of the parties, a covenant will run with the land and will be enforceable against a subsequent purchaser of the land at the suit of one who claims the benefit of the covenant, only if the covenant complies with certain legal requirements. These requirements rest upon ancient rules and precedents. The age-old essentials of a real covenant, aside from the form of the covenant, may be summarily formulated as follows: (1) it must appear that grantor and grantee intended that the covenant should run with the land; (2) it must appear that the covenant is one "touching" or "concerning" the land with which it runs; (3) it must appear that there is "privity of estate" between the promisee or party claiming the benefit of the covenant and the right to enforce it, and the promisor or party who rests under the burden of the covenant. Clark on Covenants and Interests Running with Land, p. 74. Although the deeds "contained a provision to the effect that the covenants ran with the land, such provision in the absence of the other legal requirements is insufficient to accomplish such a purpose." Morgan Lake Co. v. New York, N.H. & H.R.R. Co., 262 N.Y. 234, 238, 186 N.E. 685, 686. In his opinion in that case, Judge Crane posed but found it unnecessary to decide many of the questions which the court must consider in this case.

The covenant in this case is * * * an affirmative covenant to pay money for use in connection with, but not upon, the land which it is said is subject to the burden of the covenant. Does such a covenant "touch" or "concern" the land? These terms are not part of a statutory definition, a limitation placed by the State upon the power of the courts to enforce covenants *intended* to run with the land by the parties who entered into the covenants. Rather they are words used by courts in England in old cases to describe a limitation which the courts themselves created or to formulate a test which the courts have devised and which the courts voluntarily apply. Cf. Spencer's Case, Coke, vol. 3, part 5, 16a; Mayor of Congleton v. Pattison, 10 East 130. In truth such a description or test so formulated is too vague to be of much assistance and judges and academic scholars alike have struggled, not with entire success, to formulate a test at once more satisfactory and more accurate. * * *

* * * It has been often said that a covenant to pay a sum of money is a personal affirmative covenant which usually does not concern or touch the land. Such statements are based upon English decisions which hold in effect that only covenants, which compel the covenanter to submit to some *restriction on the use* of his property, touch or concern the land, and that the burden of a covenant which requires the covenanter to do an affirmative act, even on his own land, for the benefit of the owner of a "dominant" estate, does not run with his land. Miller v. Clary, 210 N.Y. 127, 103 N.E. 1114, L.R.A.1918E, 222, Ann.Cas.1915B, 872. In that case the court pointed out that in many jurisdictions of this country the narrow English rule has been criticized and a more liberal and flexible rule has been substituted. In this State the courts have not gone so far. We have not abandoned the historic distinction drawn by the English courts. * * * Guaranty Trust Co. of New York v. New York & Queens County Ry. Co., 253 N.Y. 190, 204, 170 N.E. 887, 892, opinion by Cardozo, Ch. J.

Both in that case and in the case of Miller v. Clary, supra, the court pointed out that there were some exceptions or limitations in the application of the general rule. Some promises to pay money have been enforced, as covenants running with the land, against subsequent holders of the land who took with notice of the covenant. Cf. Greenfarb v. R.S.K. Realty Corp., 256 N.Y. 130, 175 N.E. 649; Morgan Lake Co. v. New York, N.H. & H.R.R. Co., supra. It may be difficult to classify these exceptions or to formulate a test of whether a particular covenant to pay money or to perform some other act falls within the general rule that ordinarily an affirmative covenant is a personal and not a real covenant, or falls outside the limitations placed upon the general rule. At least it must "touch" or "concern" the land in a substantial degree, and though it may be inexpedient and perhaps impossible to formulate a rigid test or definition which will be entirely satisfactory or which can be applied mechanically in all cases, we should at least be able to state the problem and find a reasonable method of approach to it. It has been suggested that a covenant which runs with the land must affect the legal relations—the advantages and the burdens—of the parties to the covenant, as owners of particular parcels of land and not merely as members of the community in general, such as taxpayers or owners of other land. Clark, op. cit. p. 76, Cf. Professor Bigelow's article on The Contents of Covenants in Leases, 12 Mich.L.Rev. 639; 30 Law Quarterly Review, 319. That method of approach has the merit of realism. The test is based on the effect of the covenant rather than on technical distinctions. Does the covenant impose, on the one hand, a burden upon an interest in land, which on the other hand increases the value of a different interest in the same or related land?

Even though we accept that approach and test, it still remains true that whether a particular covenant is sufficiently connected with the use of land to run with the land, must be in many cases a question of degree. A promise to pay for something to be done in connection with the promisor's land does not differ essentially from a promise by the promisor to do the thing himself, and both promises constitute, in a substantial sense, a restriction upon the owner's right to use the land, and a burden upon the legal interest of the owner. On the other hand, a covenant to perform or pay for the performance of an affirmative act disconnected with the use of the land cannot ordinarily touch or concern the land in any substantial degree. Thus, unless we exalt technical form over substance, the distinction between covenants which run with land and covenants which are personal, must depend upon the effect of the covenant on the legal rights which otherwise would flow from ownership of land and which are connected with the land. The problem then is: Does the covenant in purpose and effect substantially alter these rights?

* * *

Looking at the problem presented in this case from the same point of view and stressing the intent and substantial effect of the covenant rather than its form, it seems clear that the covenant may properly be said to touch and concern the land of the defendant and its burden should run with the land. True, it calls for payment of a sum of money to be expended for "public purposes" upon land other than the land conveyed by Neponsit Realty Company to plaintiff's predecessor in title. By that conveyance the grantee, however, obtained not only title to particular lots, but an easement or right of common enjoyment with other property owners in roads, beaches, public parks or spaces and improvements in the same tract. For full enjoyment in common by the defendant and other property owners of these easements or rights, the roads and public places must be maintained. In order that the burden of maintaining public improvements should rest upon the land benefitted by the improvements, the grantor exacted from the grantee of the land with its appurtenant easement or right of enjoyment a covenant that the burden of paying the cost should be inseparably attached to the land which enjoys the benefit. It is plain that any distinction or definition which would exclude such a covenant from the classification of covenants which "touch" or "concern" the land would be based on form and not on substance.

Another difficulty remains. Though between the grantor and the grantee there was privity of estate, the covenant provides that its benefit shall run to the assigns of the grantor who "may include a Property Owners' Association which may hereafter be organized for the purposes referred to in this paragraph." The plaintiff has been organized to receive the sums payable by the property owners and to expend them for the benefit of such owners. Various definitions have been formulated of "privity of estate" in connection with covenants that run with the land, but none of such definitions seems to cover the relationship between the plaintiff and the defendant in this case. The plaintiff has not succeeded to the ownership of any property of the grantor. It does not appear that it ever had title to the streets or public places upon which charges which are payable to it must be expended. It does not appear that it owns any other property in the residential tract to which any easement or right of enjoyment in such property is appurtenant. It is created solely to act as the assignee of the benefit of the covenant, and it has no interest of its own in the enforcement of the covenant.

The arguments that under such circumstances the plaintiff has no right of action to enforce a covenant running with the land are all based upon a distinction between the corporate property owners association and the property owners for whose benefit the association has been formed. If that distinction may be ignored, then the basis of the arguments is destroyed. * * *

The corporate plaintiff has been formed as a convenient instrument by which the property owners may advance their common interests. We do not ignore the corporate form when we recognize that the Neponsit Property Owners Association, Inc., is acting as the agent or representative of the Neponsit property owners. As we have said in another case: when Neponsit Property Owners Association, Inc., "was formed, the property owners were expected to, and have looked to that organization as the medium through which enjoyment of their common right might be preserved equally for all." Matter of City of New York, Public Beach, Borough of Queens, 269 N.Y. 64, 75, 199 N.E. 5, 9. Under the conditions thus presented we said: "it may be difficult, or even impossible, to classify into recognized categories the nature of the interest of the membership corporation and its members in the land. The corporate entity cannot be disregarded, nor can the separate interests of the members of the corporation" (p. 73, 199 N.E. page 8). Only blind adherence to an ancient formula devised to meet entirely different conditions could constrain the court to hold that a corporation formed as a medium for the enjoyment of common rights of property owners owns no property which would benefit by enforcement of common rights and has no cause of action in equity to enforce the covenant upon which such common rights depend. Every reason which in other circumstances may justify the ancient formula should not be applied in this case. In substance if not in form the covenant is a restrictive covenant which touches and concerns the defendant's land, and in substance, if not in form, there is privity of estate between the plaintiff and the defendant.

We have considered the other contentions of the defendant and especially the defense that the alleged lien based upon the covenant set forth in the complaint constitutes an interest in land and is unenforceable under the provisions of sections 242 and 259 of the Real Property Law, Cons.Laws, ch. 50. We find the defense insufficient.

The order should be affirmed, with costs, and the certified questions answered in the affirmative. * * *

Notes

1. It must be clear from the instruments involved that any charge sought to be recovered by the property owners' association from the landowners in a subdivision is required by covenants running with the land. Thus, in Woodland Beach Property Owners' Ass'n v. Worley, 253 Md. 442, 252 A.2d 827 (1969), the association (Woodland) sought to enforce the annual charge against a lot owner who had failed to pay it. Pursuant to its charter and by-laws, Woodland had improved certain beaches and parks for the use and enjoyment of the property owners and had imposed a small fee to be paid each year by each lot owner. The Maryland Court of Appeals stated:

> The facts as alleged and as appear in the exhibits indicate that Woodland was obligated to maintain the areas in question, and no obligation was placed upon the lot owners to contribute any part of the expense of such maintenance. In some developments, the title instruments impose a specific charge on the individual lots as covenants running with the land to provide for such maintenance. See Wehr v. Roland Park Co., 143 Md. 384, 387–388, 122 A. 363, 364–365 (1923), but the title instruments in the instant case do not purport to impose such a charge. On the contrary, the obligation to maintain is placed upon Woodland, without any provision giving Woodland the right to collect any sum, equitable or otherwise, from the lot owners. It is clear to us that under these circumstances we should not imply *the existence* of such a covenant and charge on the land.

In line with the Woodland Beach case is Cummings v. Dosam, Inc., 273 N.C. 28, 159 S.E.2d 513 (1968), which invalidated for vagueness restrictions referring to "this Tract and adjoining Tracts being acquired by grantee." The Woodland Beach case required that restrictive covenants be strictly construed, but in Friedberg v. Riverpoint Bldg. Committee, 218 Va. 659, 239 S.E.2d 106 (1977), the court followed the same rule but stated that if it was apparent from the entire instrument that the restrictions must carry a particular meaning by necessary implication, then a use which was denied implicitly must be deemed to be as clearly forbidden as if it had been expressly denied. See similarly, Long v. Branham, 271 N.C. 264, 156 S.E.2d 235 (1967); but compare Lochwood Meadows, Inc. v. Buck, 416 S.W.2d 623 (Tex.Civ.App.1967) (a restriction against a fence or wall would not prohibit a hedge); and Sine v. Western Travel, Inc., 19 Utah 2d 61, 426 P.2d 9 (1967) (restriction against a motel did not prevent construction of a restaurant having no physical connection with a motel on adjacent, unrestricted land). Also see Big Sky Hidden Village Owners Association, Inc. v. Hidden Village, Inc., 276 Mont. 268, 915 P.2d 845 (1996) where the court held that adjoining tracts to the condominium development that were included in the developer's planned unit development plan, were not subject to the restrictions in the original condominium declaration.

The strict construction rule on restrictive covenants often manifests itself in connection with loose statements in the restrictions. Thus, the words "residential purposes" generally do not suffice to exclude multiple family dwellings. See, e.g., Shermer v. Haynes, 248 Ark. 255, 451 S.W.2d 445 (1970), and Houk v. Ross, 34 Ohio St.2d 77, 296 N.E.2d 266 (1973).

2. Compare also with Neponsit, Phillips v. Smith, 240 Iowa 863, 38 N.W.2d 87 (1949), where a covenant in deeds to summer resort lots to pay $6.00 a year to the owner of Bluff Park Resort was said to run with the land. But the covenant was held to be "dependent" upon the carrying out of the duty to maintain the resort area. The owner of Bluff Park Resort allowed his horses and pigs to roam at will through the development and did little to maintain it. The action to establish and foreclose liens for the annual assessment failed. See also Nassau County v. Kensington Ass'n, 21 N.Y.S.2d 208 (Sup.Ct.1940). And compare Harrison–Rye Realty Corp. v. Crigler, 61 N.Y.S.2d 191 (1945), affirmed 272 App.Div. 939, 72 N.Y.S.2d 417 (1947), appeal granted 272 App.Div. 976, 73 N.Y.S.2d 636 (1947), affirmed 298 N.Y. 602, 81 N.E.2d 331 (1948) with Harrison–Rye Realty Corp. v. New Rochelle Trust Co., 177 Misc. 776, 31 N.Y.S.2d 1005 (Sup.Ct.1941) reaching opposite results on the same monetary assessment covenant. And see Annot., 23 A.L.R.2d 520 (1952). In Tentindo v. Locke Lake Colony Ass'n, 120 N.H. 593, 419 A.2d 1097 (1980) the court held assessments could not be imposed on lot owners whose membership in the owner's association was involuntary; the association was created by the developer to take over management of common areas, and the deeds of the plaintiff lot owners provided only that an annual $15 premium was to be paid to the developer for benefits provided. Also see Holiday Pines Prop. Owners Ass'n, Inc. v. Wetherington, 596 So.2d 84 (Fla.App.1992).

3. Sometimes the dispute over liability for monetary assessments is between a lot owner and the developer of a sizeable community. Can the development company write the covenants so as to result in lower annual assessments for the lots it retains while purchasers must pay a higher assessment? On this question, see Kell v. Bella Vista Village Property Owners Ass'n, 258 Ark. 757, 528 S.W.2d 651 (1975). In large scale retirement communities the problem of inflationary costs of maintenance is especially critical because there may be large numbers of non-resident lot owners scattered around the country who are years away from building their retirement dream homes and who will vote against any increase in maintenance assessments; this group usually outnumbers the current residents who have an interest in raising the assessments to keep the community pleasant and well-maintained.

4. For an overall discussion, see Lundberg, Restrictive Covenants and Land Use Control: Private Zoning, 34 Mont.L.Rev. 199 (1973).

5. Many cases deal with the scope of the activity intended to be barred or encouraged:

    a. In 1898 grantors covenanted that "they will erect or maintain no
        building or structure of such a character as to interrupt or interfere

with the view [of the sea] over said parcel. * * * " In 1957 they used the parcel for parking cars and buses which blocked the view of the sea. Is there a violation of the covenant? Was the intention to bar structures or to protect the view? Leavitt v. Davis, 153 Me. 279, 136 A.2d 535 (1957) refused an injunction. There is a strong dissent with which an annotator in 1959 Duke L.Rev. 310 agrees.

b. A covenant restricts land to "dwelling house" use. Does this mean a single family house or will a large multiple-family apartment be permitted? See Minister, Reformed Protestant Dutch Church v. Madison Avenue Building Co., 214 N.Y. 268, 108 N.E. 444 (1915). Would a fraternity or boarding house be permitted? Hooker v. Alexander, 129 Conn. 433, 29 A.2d 308 (1942) and Seeley v. Phi Sigma Delta House Corp., 245 Mich. 252, 222 N.W. 180 (1928). (A similar problem is encountered in connection with zoning definitions of a "dwelling house," "single-family dwelling," and the like, which will be discussed at greater length in a later chapter.) What if a deed restricts the use of land to "not more than one residence" to be built on each tract and provides that "the said premises shall be used for residence purposes only" and the defendant wants to erect a duplex on the premises? In Houk v. Ross, 34 Ohio St.2d 77, 296 N.E.2d 266 (1973), the court interpreted the restriction in the "manner which least restricts the free use of the land" and held that this language only prevented construction of more than one residence buildings and did not prohibit a multiple-family dwelling. A similar case is Burns v. Wood, 492 S.W.2d 940 (Tex.1973). In Shermer v. Haynes, 248 Ark. 255, 451 S.W.2d 445 (1970), the use was limited to "residential purposes only" and the Arkansas court held that this did not operate to limit use to single-family residences and that a covenant requiring a minimum of 1200 square feet of living area did not prohibit construction of an apartment complex where the covenant did not require 1200 square feet in each unit or each single residence. Compare Cash v. Catholic Diocese of Kansas City–St. Joseph, 414 S.W.2d 346 (Mo.App.1967), in which the restriction limiting the lots for use for "detached single family dwellings only" was held to exclude a proposed building to be used as a residence by nuns who taught at a parochial school.

c. The covenant provides that "All lots . . . shall be used exclusively for residential purposes and no commercial enterprise shall be constructed or permitted on any of said property." In Yogman v. Parrott, 142 Or.App. 544, 921 P.2d 1352 (1996) the court held that the owner of a vacation home in the subdivision did not violate the covenant by renting out the home to groups of up to 10 people for short periods of time when the owner was not in occupancy; renting was not regarded as commercial activity by the court, looking to the use of the property. In modern condominium developments the covenants are usually quite specific on the issue of whether an owner can rent his unit.

6. There are 728 lot owners in a restricted subdivision. Must they all be joined as parties in a declaratory judgment action involving the construc-

tion of the restrictive covenants? See Lozoff v. Kaisershot, 11 Wis.2d 485, 105 N.W.2d 783 (1960).

B. EQUITABLE SERVITUDES

Despite some relaxation of the requirements of a real covenant in cases such as Neponsit, the basic requisites for enforcement of a covenant at law remain with us. Equity, of course, by its very nature is different, and the principles or maxims which it has developed often lead to a different result. We see this difference quite vividly in the enforcement of "servitudes" in equity in situations in which the law courts would not enforce a covenant because it did not run with the land, touch or concern the land, or lacked privity.

TULK v. MOXHAY

English High Court of Chancery, 1848.
2 Phillips 774, 41 Eng.Rep. 1143.

In the year 1808 the Plaintiff, being then the owner in fee of the vacant piece of ground in Leicester Square, as well as of several of the houses forming the Square, sold the piece of ground by the description of "Leicester Square Garden or Pleasure Ground, with the equestrian statute then standing in the centre thereof, and the iron railing and stone work round the same," to one Elms in fee: and the deed of conveyance contained a covenant by Elms, for himself, his heirs, and assigns, with the Plaintiff, his heirs, executors, and administrators, "that Elms, his heirs, and assigns should, and would from time to time, and at all times thereafter at his and their own costs and charges, keep and maintain the said piece of ground and Square Garden, and the iron railing round the same in its then form, and in sufficient and proper repair as a Square Garden and Pleasure Ground, in an open state, uncovered with any buildings, in neat and ornamental order; and that it should be lawful for the inhabitants of Leicester Square, tenants of the Plaintiff, on payment of a reasonable rent for the same, to have keys at their own expense and the privilege of admission therewith at any time or times into the said Square Garden and Pleasure Ground."

The piece of land so conveyed passed by divers mesne conveyances into the hands of the Defendant, whose purchase deed contained no similar covenant with his vendor: but he admitted that he had purchased with notice of the covenant in the deed of 1808.

The Defendant having manifested an intention to alter the character of the Square Garden, and asserted a right, if he thought fit, to build upon it, the Plaintiff, who still remained owner of several houses in the Square, filed this bill for an injunction; and an injunction was granted by the Master of the Rolls, to restrain the Defendant from converting or using the piece of ground and Square Garden, and the iron railing round the same, to or for any other purpose than as a Square Garden and Pleasure Ground in an open state, and uncovered with buildings.

On a motion, now made, to discharge that order,

Mr. R. Palmer, for the Defendant, contended that the covenant did not run with the land, so as to be binding at law upon a purchaser from the covenantor, and he relied on the dictum of Lord Brougham C. in Keppell v. Bayley (2 M. & K. 547), to the effect that notice of such a covenant did not give a Court of Equity jurisdiction to enforce it by injunction against such purchaser, inasmuch as "the knowledge by an assignee of an estate, that his assignor had assumed to bind others than the law authorized him to affect by his contract,—had attempted to create a burthen upon property which was inconsistent with the nature of that property, and unknown to the principles of the law—could not bind such assignee by affecting his conscience." * * *

The LORD CHANCELLOR (without calling upon the other side.)

That this Court has jurisdiction to enforce a contract between the owner of land and his neighbor purchasing a part of it, that the latter shall either use or abstain from using the land purchased in a particular way, is what I never knew disputed. Here there is no question about the contract: the owner of certain houses in the Square sells the land adjoining, with a covenant from the purchaser not to use it for any other purpose than as a Square Garden. And it is now contended, not that the vendee could violate that contract, but that he might sell the piece of land, and that the purchaser from him may violate it without this Court having any power to interfere. If that were so, it would be impossible for an owner of land to sell part of it without incurring the risk of rendering what he retains worthless. It is said that, the covenant being one which does not run with the land, this Court cannot enforce it; but the question is, not whether the covenant runs with the land, but whether a party shall be permitted to use the land in a manner inconsistent with the contract entered into by his vendor, and with notice of which he purchased. Of course, the price would be affected by the covenant, and nothing could be more inequitable than that the original purchaser should be able to sell the property the next day for a greater price, in consideration of the assignee being allowed to escape from the liability which he had himself undertaken.

That the question does not depend upon whether the covenant runs with the land, is evident from this, that if there was a mere agreement and no covenant, this Court would enforce it against a party purchasing with notice of it; for if an equity is attached to the property by the owner, no one purchasing with notice of that equity can stand in a different situation from the party from whom he purchased. There are not only cases before the Vice–Chancellor of England, in which he considered that doctrine as not in dispute; but looking at the ground on which Lord Eldon disposed of the case of the Duke of Bedford v. The Trustees of the British Museum (2 M. & K. 552), it is impossible to suppose that he entertained any doubt of it. * * *

With respect to the observations of Lord Brougham in Keppell v. Bayley, he never could have meant to lay down, that this Court would not enforce an equity attached to land by the owner, unless under such circumstances as would maintain an action at law. If that be the result of his observations, I can only say that I cannot coincide with it.

I think the cases cited before the Vice–Chancellor and this decision of the Master of the Rolls perfectly right, and, therefore, that this motion must be refused with costs.

LONDON COUNTY COUNCIL v. ALLEN

English Court of Appeal, King's Bench Division.
L.R. (1914) 3 K.B. 642, Ann.Cas.1916C 932.

SCRUTTON, J. read the following judgment:—In this case the London County Council, on January 24, 1907, entered into an indenture with one Morris Joseph Allen, a builder, describing himself as "the owner in fee simple of certain land," by which he "doth hereby for himself, his heirs and assigns, and other the persons claiming under him, and so far as practicable to bind the land and hereditaments herein mentioned into whosoever hands the same may come, covenant and agree with the council that he and they will not erect or place, or cause or permit to be erected or placed, any building, structure, or other erection upon the land shewn by green colour on the said plan, without the previous consent in writing of the council so to do, and that on every conveyance, sale, charge, mortgage, lease, assignment, or other dealing with the land herein mentioned or any part thereof he will give notice of the aforesaid covenant in every conveyance, transfer, mortgage, charge, lease, assignment, or other document by which such dealing is effected." The plots coloured green were two plots intended to be reserved for the making of roads. On plot No. 1, in July, 1911, three houses were build by Mrs. Allen; on plot No. 2 a wall was built by Allen. The London County Council thereupon issued a writ claiming a mandatory injunction to pull down the houses and wall respectively. Thereupon it was alleged that as to plot No. 1 the legal estate was in one Norris as mortgagee, and the equity of redemption in Mrs. Allen, who had taken title from Mr. Allen and Willcocks, his mortgagee, who had no notice of the restrictive covenant; and it was contended (1) by way of demurrer that as the London County Council were not neighbouring landowners, or grantors of the plot in question, a covenant by Allen in their favour was only a personal covenant, and could not affect the land when in the hands of assigns of Allen, whether they had notice of the covenant or not. It was said that to affect them the right must be in the nature of a negative easement; that an easement required both a dominant and a servient tenement; and that as the council had no land to which the benefit of the covenant could attach, there could be no dominant tenement, and therefore no negative easement binding on a servient tenement, but only an easement in gross, which did not bind assigns of the land. (2) It was alleged that the defendants Mrs. Allen and Norris could prove they were purchasers for value of the legal estate without notice of the covenant, and therefore not bound by it. Avory J. found on the second contention as a fact that Mrs. Allen and Norris had not satisfied him they had not notice, actual or constructive, of the covenant. On the first contention he said: "It was contended before me that this restrictive covenant, being in the nature of a negative easement, the action would not lie except at the suit of a covenantee who was at the time of the covenant in possession of land which required protection, and that the plaintiffs were not at the time in possession of any such land. But having regard to the powers vested in the London County Council under ss. 7 and 9 of the London Building Act, 1894, and to the admission made in the argument before me that the conditions imposed in this case were not ultra vires, I think this contention fails." He apparently treated the duty and interest of the county council in the matter of new streets as sufficient to make the covenant bind the land in the hands of assigns from Allen. This Court determined to decide the first contention before hearing argument on the second, and we have now to decide on the first contention.

Counsel on each side agreed that the burden of this covenant would not run with the land at law, so as to bind assigns, for the reason stated in the notes to Spencer's Case (1 Sm.L.C., 11th ed., at p. 88) that "there appears to be no authority which has decided, apart from the equitable doctrine of notice" (by which is meant, as hereinafter explained, the doctrine identified with the case of Tulk v. Moxhay (2 Ph. 774)) "that the burden of a covenant will run with land in any case except that of landlord and tenant." This opinion appears to be justified by the judgments of the Court of Appeal in Austerberry v. Oldham Corporation, 29 Ch.D. 750, especially that of Lindley L.J. at p. 781 and of Fry L.J. at p. 784.

The question then is whether it is essential to the doctrine of Tulk v. Moxhay, supra, that the covenantee should have at the time of the creation of the covenant, and afterwards, land for the benefit of which the covenant is created, in order that the burden of the covenant may bind assigns of the land to which it relates. It is clear that the covenantee may sue the covenantor himself, though the former has parted with the land to which the covenant relates: Stokes v. Russell, 3 T.R. 678. To answer the question as to the assigns of the covenantor, and the land in their hands, requires the investigation of the historical growth of the doctrine of Tulk v. Moxhay, supra. Though the covenantee in that case did hold adjacent land, there is no trace in the judgment of Lord Cottenham of the requirement that the covenantee should have and continue to hold land to be benefited by the covenant. I read Lord Cottenham's judgment as proceeding entirely on the question of notice of the covenant, and on the equitable ground that a man purchasing land with notice that there was a covenant not to use it in a particular way would not be allowed to violate the covenant he knew of when he bought the land. Lord Cottenham states the question, "Whether a party shall be permitted to use the land in a manner inconsistent with the contract entered into by his vendor and with notice of which he purchased," and answers it: "If there was a mere agreement and no covenant, this Court would enforce it against a party purchasing with notice of it; for if an equity is attached to the property by the owner, no one purchasing with notice of that equity can stand in a different situation from the party from whom he purchased."

Up to 1881, when counsel in Haywood v. Brunswick Permanent Benefit Building Society, 8 Q.B.D. 403 stated (at p. 405) that Tulk v. Moxhay, supra, had been applied in fifteen cases, I cannot trace, nor could counsel before us discover, that Tulk v. Moxhay, supra, had been based on anything but notice of the covenant by the assignee. In the case cited, in which the Court of Appeal refused to extend the doctrine to an affirmative covenant to repair, Lindley L.J. said (at p. 410): "The result of these cases is that only such a covenant as can be complied with without expenditure of money will be enforced against the assignee on the ground of notice." Brett L.J. said (at p. 408): "That case" Tulk v. Moxhay, supra "decided that an assignee taking land subject to a certain class of covenants is bound by such covenants if he has notice of them, and that the class of covenants comprehended within the rule is that covenants restricting the mode of using the land only will be enforced." Cotton L.J., after citing Lord Cottenham that "No one purchasing with notice of that equity can stand in a different situation from the party from whom he purchased," said (at p. 409): "This lays down the real principle that an equity attaches to the owner of the land." Meanwhile in De Mattos v. Gibson, 4 De G. & J. 276, p. 282, in 1858, Knight Bruce L.J. had put the principle as applying to all property thus: "Reason and justice seem to prescribe that, at least as a general rule, where a man, by gift or purchase, acquires property from another, with knowledge of a previous contract, lawfully and for valuable consideration made by him with a third person, to use and employ the property for a particular purpose in a specified manner, the acquirer shall not, to the material damage of the third person, in opposition to the contract and inconsistently with it, use and employ the property in a manner not allowable to the giver or seller," resting the matter on knowledge of the previous contract, that is notice. * * * [The court then reviews numerous English cases and continues.]

I think the result of this long chain of authorities is that, whereas in my view, at the time of Tulk v. Moxhay, supra, and for at least twenty years afterwards, the plaintiffs in this case would have succeeded against an assign on the ground that the assign had notice of the covenant, since Formby v. Barker, 1903, 2 Ch. 539, In re Nisbet and Potts' Contract, 1905, 1 Ch. 391; 1906, 1 Ch. 386, and Millbourn v. Lyons, 1914, 1 Ch. 34; 2 Ch. 231, three decisions of the Court of Appeal, the plaintiffs must fail on the ground that they have never had any land for the benefit of which this "equitable interest analogous to a negative easement" could be created, and therefore cannot sue a person who bought the land with knowledge that there was a restrictive covenant as to its use, which he proceeds to disregard, because he is not privy to the contract. I think the learned editors of Dart on Vendors and Purchasers, 7th ed., vol. ii, p. 769, are justified by the present state of the authorities in saying that "the question of notice to the purchaser has nothing whatsoever to do with the question whether the covenant binds him, except in so far as the absence of notice may enable him to raise the plea of purchaser for valuable consideration without notice." If the covenant does not run with the land in law, its benefit can only be asserted against an assign of the land burdened, if the covenant was made for the benefit of certain land, all or some of which remains in the possession of the covenantee or his assign, suing to enforce the covenant. It may be, if the matter is considered by a higher tribunal, that tribunal may see its way to revert to what I think was the earlier doctrine of notice, or at any rate to treat it as co-existing with the later refinement of "an equitable interest analogous to a negative easement" binding on persons who are ignorant of it. The remarks of Lord Selborne in Earl of Zetland v. Hislop, 7 App.Cas. 427, at pp. 446, 447, are not favourable to the too rigid development or enforcement of the latter alternative; and the observations of Lord Macnaghten (p. 32), Lord Davey (p. 35) and Lord Lindley (p. 36), in Noakes & Co. v. Rice [1902] A.C. 24, seem to suggest that the doctrine of Tulk v. Moxhay, supra, may well be reconsidered and put on a proper footing. For I regard it as very regrettable that a public body should be prevented from enforcing a restriction on the use of property imposed for the public benefit against persons who bought the property knowing of the restriction, by the apparently immaterial circumstance that the public body does not own any land in the immediate neighbourhood. But, after a careful consideration of the authorities, I am forced to the view that the later decisions of this Court compel me so to hold.

In my opinion, therefore, the demurrer of Mr. Norris and of Mrs. Allen succeeds. The action against Mr. Norris must be dismissed with costs. I regret that I do not see my way to depriving Mrs. Allen of her costs, as, whatever may be her equitable rights, I am not at all favourably impressed with her conduct as a good citizen. I see no reason for interfering with the judgment against Mr. Allen in respect of plots No. 1 or No. 2, and his appeal must be dismissed with costs.

[Kennedy L.J. concurred in Scrutton's analysis of the cases. Buckley, L.J. in his own elaborate opinion placed a different interpretation on Tulk v. Moxhay and other earlier cases, but concurred in the result.]

Notes

1. Tulk v. Moxhay was the landmark case which provided the foundation on which equity erected a set of rules governing the enforcement of negative or restrictive covenants based on the concept of notice. See generally 5 R. Powell, Real Property ¶ 671 (1990). To what extent did the London County Council case limit or modify Tulk v. Moxhay? Should the London County Council case be followed in the United States or not? Recall that easements in gross have been accepted in the United States, but not in England. Under those circumstances should you have to have land benefited? Consider these questions in conjunction with such later cases as Van Sant v. Rose and Kent v. Koch.

2. Subsequent to the London County Council case, Parliament passed a statute as follows:

    (1) Where—

(b) * * * An owner of any land has entered into a covenant with the local authority concerning the land for purposes of any of the provisions of said act; the authority shall have power to enforce the covenant against the persons deriving title under the covenantor, notwithstanding that the authority are not in possession of or interested in any land for the benefit of which the covenant was entered into, in like manner and to the like extent as if they had been possessed of or interested in such land. Sec. 78 Housing Act, 1935; 25 & 26 Geo. 5, c. 40.

The 1935 statute is no longer in force. It has been replaced by section 37 of the Town and Country Planning Act of 1962, which states that "An agreement made * * * with any person interested in land may be enforced by the local planning authority against persons deriving title under that person in respect of that land, as if the local planning authority were possessed of adjacent land and as if the agreement had been expressed to be made for the benefit of such land."

3. Suppose the London County Council had exacted from M.J. Allen a "dedication" of "public rights" in the two plots colored green describing rights just as they were described in the "covenants" involved in this case. Would the court then have granted the injunction requiring Mrs. Allen to tear the houses down?

4. In a 1979 statute the Wisconsin legislature provided in Wis.Stat. § 236.293 (1957):

"Restrictions for Public Benefit. Any restriction placed on land by covenant, grant of easement or in any other manner, which was required by a public body or which names a public body or public utility as grantee, promisee or beneficiary vests in the public body or public utility the right to enforce the restriction at law or in equity against anyone who has or acquires an interest in the land subject to the restriction. The restriction may be released or waived in writing of the public body or public utility having the right of enforcement."

Was this legislation necessary, in your opinion?

5. Before you assume that London County Council could not happen on this side of the Atlantic, consider One Twenty–Five Varsity Road Ltd. v. Township of York, 23 Dom.L.Rep.2d 465 (Ontario Ct. of App.1960). The developer at the insistence of the township covenanted for himself, successors and assigns not to remove a ridge of earth or to build on two lots unless neighbors consented. They did not consent. Held: The burden of the covenant did not run and the township could not enforce it against a purchaser with notice. For a critical review of the holding see Rickerd, Use of Restrictive Covenants in Agreements Entered into as a Condition to Approval of a Plan of Subdivision, 19 Faculty L.Rev. 159 (1961). The reviewer suggests various alternatives including the "annexation" of the covenant to one of the streets owned by the township. What do you think? Shouldn't it be enough to suggest that the local unit was merely asserting its police power? The fact that this assertion was dressed in the clothes of a "private" covenant should not blind us to the essence of the transaction.

VAN SANT v. ROSE

Supreme Court of Illinois, 1913.
260 Ill. 401, 103 N.E. 194.

[In 1904, plaintiff deeded a lot to the defendant. The deed contained a restrictive covenant prohibiting erection of an apartment building on the lot. After deeding the land, plaintiff owned no other land in the neighborhood. Defendant conveyed the land through an intermediary to his wife, the co-defendant. Now almost 19 years later his wife is proposing to erect an apartment building on the lot and plaintiff sues to enjoin. Injunction was granted and on appeal this was affirmed. Only a small part of the opinion is given.]

FARMER, J.

* * *

True, a bill to enjoin the breach of restrictive covenants cannot be maintained by one having no connection with or interest in their enforcement, but we cannot agree that complainants had no interest. They were the original covenantees and by their conveyance of the property reserved an interest in it. They conveyed the property subject to that interest. They had a right to reserve such interest, and this right was not dependent upon the covenantees having other property in the vicinity that would be affected by a breach of the covenants or that they should in any other manner sustain damages thereby. This court has held, in harmony with the prevailing rule in other jurisdictions, that the right to enjoin the breach of restrictive covenants does not depend upon whether the covenantee will be damaged by the breach, but the mere breach is sufficient ground for interference by injunction. Bispham's Principles of Equity,—4th ed.—par. 461; Consolidated Coal Co. v. Schmisseur, 135 Ill. 371; Hartman v. Wells, 257 Ill. 167, 100 N.E. 500. It would seem inconsistent, then, to say, as the covenantees had no other land in the neighborhood they had no interest in the performance of the covenants. The only purpose their having other land in the vicinity could serve would be to show that they would be injuriously affected,—that is, damaged,—by a violation of the contract. But as their right does not necessarily depend upon their being damaged by the breach, it would seem it would not necessarily depend upon their owning other land in the vicinity. Bispham, in the paragraph above referred to, says it is no answer to an action of this kind to say the breach will inflict no injury upon the complainant or even that it would be a positive benefit. * * *

Notes

1. See, in connection with this case, Clark, Real Covenants and Other Interest Which "Run with Land" 181–82 (2d ed. 1947). The Van Sant case represents the minority view, while the majority view and traditional approach is represented by the next case, Kent v. Koch. After reading Kent v. Koch, consider which you think is the *better* view. Which position would you

adopt if you were on the supreme court of a state deciding the question for the first time in that jurisdiction?

2. See Merrionette Manor Homes Imp. Ass'n v. Heda, 11 Ill.App.2d 186, 136 N.E.2d 556 (1956), allowing a homeowners' association to enforce a covenant and stating that Illinois law "is not so strictly defined as to require in all cases that the one seeking enforcement must show some right or beneficial interest in the land affected * * *."

KENT v. KOCH

Court of Appeals of California, 1958.
166 Cal.App.2d 579, 333 P.2d 411.

[Defendant was restrained by the trial court from constructing a green fiberglass fence on his premises contrary to a "Declaration of Restrictions, Conditions, Covenants and Agreements." The declaration had been recorded by the plaintiffs in 1936, at which time the plaintiff had begun a large housing development consisting of a number of subdivision units. As each subdivision unit was opened, a declaration of restrictions was recorded, and each declaration, subsequent to subdivision 1, purported to benefit not only the property within that subdivision unit but all of the property within the entire development tract, which was known as "Kent Woodlands." Plaintiffs controlled building applications at first, but then an architectural supervising committee, provided for in declarations other than the subdivision 1 declaration, was appointed by plaintiffs from property owners (none from subdivision 1 owners), and this committee controlled applications. Defendant's property is located in subdivision 1, and plaintiffs have sold all their lots in that subdivision. But plaintiffs had retained "Parcel A," which was an entrance to Kent Woodlands. Defendant, having been turned down in his application to build the green fiberglass fence by the architectural committee, proceeded to file suit. The trial court held that the defendant's lot was subject to the restrictions; that plaintiffs owned a parcel in subdivision 1 known as parcel A as well as other lots in the general tract, Kent Woodlands; and that sales had been in accordance with a general plan of restrictions designed to benefit all lots in the overall tract. After setting out the text of the declaration pertaining to subdivision 1, the appellate court reached the following decision, having earlier stated that the question which was "determinative of the appeal" was the plaintiffs' right to complain in light of the fact that they owned no lots in subdivision 1.]

BRAY, J.

A mere perusal of said agreement shows that it did not intend to make the restrictions for the benefit of any property other than that referred to in it, namely, the lots shown on the map of subdivision 1. It expressly says that it is for the direct benefit of "each and every lot shown on said recorded map." Time and again it refers to "said lots" meaning the lots shown on that map. There is not the slightest ambiguity in the document. It is impossible to read into such clear language any intent to make the restrictions applicable to any other property. Plaintiffs contend that the last line of paragraph 12 above quoted shows such intention. On the contrary it strongly indicates that the restrictions are for the benefit of subdivision 1 lots only. That sentence instead of stating that plaintiffs would subject the new units (the adjoining and contiguous property) to be opened by them to the same restrictions as required of subdivision 1, or would make any restrictions upon the new units applicable to subdivision 1 lots, merely states that plaintiffs will restrict the sale and use of such property "in such a way as, in their opinion shall not impair the value or desirability of the property shown on said map, for residential purposes." This language discloses that plaintiffs intended the new units to be completely independent of the first unit, except only that they would be restricted in such manner as in plaintiffs' opinion not to impair the desirability for residential purposes of the lots in subdivision 1.

It is well settled in this state that restrictive covenants made for the benefit of other property retained by the grantor can not be enforced by the grantor after he no longer owns any of the property benefited. In Blodgett v. Trumbull, 1927, 83 Cal.App. 566, 257 P. 199, the grantors deeded to the plaintiff a certain lot subject to certain conditions and restrictions in the deed. Although these were not made for the benefit of the adjoining lots which belonged to the grantors, the court held (83 Cal.App. at page 571, 257 P. at page 202): " * * * the grantors did reserve for themselves, their successors, or assigns the right to enjoin, abate, or remedy by appropriate proceedings any breach of any of the restrictions. The right so reserved would be enforceable, in the absence of fraud, while the defendant Trumbull [the surviving grantor] remained owner of the adjoining lots; but after she had parted with the property which would derive benefit from a continuance of the restrictions, she would have no standing, in a court of equity at least, to complain of a breach." In Townsend v. Allen, 114 Cal.App.2d 291, at page 297, 250 P.2d 292, at page 296, 39 A.L.R.2d 1108, the court stated: "However, it does not follow that the grantor retains said right of enforcement even though he has disposed of all land he had retained without making any such restriction. The contrary is shown by cases relating to building and occupation restrictions on subdivisions in which cases the right of enforcement of grantor is considered lost when he has lost all interest in the property to be benefited. In Firth v. Marovich, 160 Cal. 257, 260, 116 P. 729, 731 [Ann.Cas.1912D, 1190] it is said (obiter): 'It is not open to question that building restrictions of the kind contained in the deed * * * are valid and enforceable at the suit of the grantor *so long as he continues to own any part of the tract for the benefit of which the restrictions were exacted.*' " (Emphasis ours.)

In Marra v. Aetna Construction Co., 1940, 15 Cal.2d 375, 378, 101 P.2d 490, 492 the court said: "The doctrine of equitable servitudes has been invoked chiefly in cases where uniform building restrictions have been imposed pursuant to a general plan for improving an entire tract or real estate subdivision * * *. It is true, however, that a servitude cannot exist in gross, but must be appurtenant to other benefited property."

* * *

It must be remembered in construing the declaration of restrictions that "any provisions of an instrument creating or claimed to create such a servitude will be strictly construed, any doubt being resolved in favor of the free use of the land." Wing v. Forest Lawn Cemetery Ass'n, 1940, 15 Cal.2d 472, 479, 101 P.2d 1099, 1103, 130 A.L.R. 120; Werner v. Graham, 181 Cal. 174, 181, 183 P. 945. Thus, plaintiffs having disposed of all the lots in subdivision 1, do not have any property to be benefited by the enforcement of the restrictions and have no standing in a court of equity. Actually, plaintiffs do own a small portion of subdivision 1. However, admittedly this "parcel," so-called on the map, is too small for residence purposes and was reserved for the special purpose of parking for the tract office which adjoins it, as an entrance to the tract, and as a location for the tract's signboard. It is obvious that this parcel would in nowise be benefited by the enforcement of the restrictions. Blodgett v. Trumbull, supra, 83 Cal.App. 566, 571, 257 P. 199, points out that after a grantor has parted with the property which would derive benefit from a continuance of the restrictions, such grantor has no standing in court to enforce the restrictions.

Restrictions in a deed cannot be enforced by one lot owner in a tract against another lot owner between whom there is neither privity of contract nor privity of estate. "The leading case on this subject, and the one that is determinative of this appeal, is Werner v. Graham, 181 Cal. 174, 183 P. 945. In that case, among other things, it was specifically held that such servitudes will be enforced only when part of a general plan expressed in the deed, and when the deed expressly provides such restrictions are for the benefit of the other lots in the tract. In other words, unless specifically stated to be for the benefit of other lot owners, such covenants or restrictions are enforceable only as between the original parties to the deed, or their heirs or assigns." Fees v. Williams, 212 Cal. 688, 690, 300 P. 30, 31; see also Townsend v. Allen, 114 Cal.App.2d 291, 297, 250 P.2d 292, 39 A.L.R.2d 1108.

Plaintiffs' contention that the provision in paragraph 12 to the effect that plaintiffs will restrict the use of property in the units other than subdivision 1 gives them, as owners of property in the other subdivisions, a right to enforce the restrictions on subdivision 1, is answered by Werner v. Graham, supra, 1919, 181 Cal. 174, 183 P. 945, which the court says in Wing v. Forest Lawn Cemetery Ass'n, supra, 15 Cal.2d 472, 480, 101 P.2d 1099, 130 A.L.R. 120, "has oft been cited as the leading case in this state defining the manner in which an equitable servitude may be established." There restrictive conditions were placed in a deed of one lot in a tract which the owner was subdividing according to a map on file. No express statement was included to the effect that they were for the benefit of the other lots in the tract. In selling these other lots the grantor placed similar restrictions in the deeds thereto. The court held that the failure to state in the deed that the restrictions were for the benefit of the other lots in the tract, although most probably the grantor intended them to be, made the restrictions unenforceable by owners of any other lots. It said (181 Cal. at pages 183–184, 183 P. at page 949): "It is undoubted that, when the owner of a subdivided tract conveys the various parcels in the tract by deeds containing appropriate language imposing restrictions on each parcel as part of a general plan of restrictions common to all the parcels and designed for their mutual benefit, mutual equitable servitudes are thereby created in favor of each parcel as against all the others. The agreement between the grantor and each grantee in such a case as expressed in the instruments between them is both that the parcel conveyed shall be subject to restrictions in accordance with the plan for the benefit of all the other parcels and also that all other parcels shall be subject to such restrictions for its benefit. In such a case the mutual servitudes spring into existence as between the first parcel conveyed and the balance of the parcels at the time of the first conveyance. As each conveyance follows, the burden and the benefit of the mutual restrictions imposed by preceding conveyances as between the particular parcel conveyed and those previously conveyed pass as an incident of the ownership of the parcel, and similar restrictions are created by the conveyance as between the lot conveyed and the lots still retained by the original owner." Of this character is Alderson v. Cutting, 163 Cal. [503], 504, 126 P. 157, Ann.Cas.1914A, 1.

"The difference between such a case and the one at bar is that here there is no language in the instruments between the parties— that is, the deeds—which refers to a common plan of restrictions, or which expresses or in any way indicates any agreement between grantor and grantee that the lot conveyed is taken subject to any such plan."

"While the decisions in other states upon the question now before us are in conflict, it is recognized by the law writers that the majority view is to the effect that such restrictions and conditions as those now before us can be enforced only by the owner of a part of the land for the benefit of which the restrictions and conditions were created." Young v. Cramer, 38 Cal.App.2d 64, 68, 100 P.2d 523, 525.

See also Alexander v. Title Ins. & Trust Co., 48 Cal.App.2d 488, 492, 119 P.2d 992, 994, where the court stated, referring to the evidence, "It discloses a situation in which the reversionary right is held by an entity which is not the owner of the land in the same tract and cannot claim that its right as a landowner would be adversely affected as to use or value by removal of the restriction. It is held by a corporation as trustee for the syndicate which has disposed of all the property in the tract under restrictions as to use. These obviously had as their basis the benefit to be conferred on other property in the same tract." Just as in our case. Both parties cite Los Angeles University v. Swarth, 9 Cir., 1901, 107 F. 798, 54 L.R.A. 262. There the complainants and others owned large tracts of land adjoining the city of Los Angeles. They joined in a deed to Los Angeles University, a corporation, of 7½ acres of land.

The deed provided that the land was to be used exclusively as a campus for the university proposed to be located thereon, and that if prior to a certain date the land was not so used title would revert to the grantors. The court held (at page 806): "In general terms, the benefit of a condition in a grant is reserved to the grantor and his heirs without regard to the ownership of other property; but, where the grant contains a restriction in the nature of a covenant that has relation to a benefit to adjoining property, the restriction can only be enforced in favor of the title to such adjoining property", and that as the complainants failed to show ownership in the land they could not maintain the action to restrain the defendant from using the lands for drilling for oil. The court stated that it was alleged in the complaint that the complainants and the others who had conveyed the land relied upon certain representations that the land would be used exclusively for university purposes to the benefit of the adjoining lands owned by the complainant and others. It then stated that as the complainants had no interest in these adjoining lands, they were no longer interested in the benefit arising from the restriction in the deed and therefore were not in a position to maintain the action. This case upholds the principles we have heretofore discussed and in no way supports the contention that mere ownership of adjoining lands gives the right to enforce restrictions in a deed that does not provide that the restrictions are for the benefit of those adjoining lands.

As plaintiffs have no interest in any property to be benefited by the restrictions, they may not maintain this action.

The judgment is reversed.

PETERS, P.J., and FRED B. WOOD, J., concur.

Notes

1. If you represented a real estate developer who wished to sell all of the lots in his subdivision but wished, in the interest of maintaining his business reputation as the developer of high quality subdivisions, to be able to enforce a covenant against landowners in the subdivision, is there any way you could draft a covenant to assure the developer of this right?

2. For an extended discussion of standing to enforce restrictive covenants, see Annot., Who May Enforce Restrictive Covenant or Agreement as to Use of Real Property, 51 A.L.R.3d 556 (1973). On whether an adjacent lot owner in a separate subdivision has standing to sue, see Corn Ins. Agency v. Darby Builders, 254 Ark. 1004, 497 S.W.2d 260 (1973). Enforcement is discussed, infra, in a separate subsection. And see Haldeman v. Teicholz, 197 A.D.2d 223, 611 N.Y.S.2d 669 (1994); Jones v. Herald, 881 P.2d 116 (Okl. App.1994).

3. Charles Ascher in Urban Redevelopment: Problems and Practices 226, 237–238 (Woodbury ed. 1953) commented:

Experience has shown that neither maintenance nor enforcement can be left as responsibility of one or more property owners. In the early years, the developing agency may legitimately take a leading role; indeed it has an obligation to protect the integrity of the scheme against ill-considered acts of the purchasers, however innocent of purpose, until they have time to understand the intentions of the developer. Moreover, in the early years, the developing agency usually has substantial financial interests to protect in unsold land or purchase-money obligations.

But as these financial interests become less and as the attention and energies of the developing agency are focused elsewhere, its readiness to incur expense and trouble on behalf of the scheme weakens. * * *

Effective administration involves some cost and will make claim upon community funds that many residents would prefer to see spent in activities that seem more immediately gratifying, but there is now more than a generation of experience to prove that controls cannot be left to a committee of volunteers. [Copyright 1953 by the University of Chicago. All rights reserved. Published 1953 by the University of Chicago Press. Composed and printed by Kingsport Press, Inc., Kingsport, Tennessee, U.S.A.]

Can Mr. Ascher's concern be met by having local governmental units administer private restrictive covenants? See Susman, Municipal Enforcement of Private Restrictive Covenants: An Innovation in Land–Use Control, 44 Texas L.Rev. 741 (1966).

SANBORN v. McLEAN

Supreme Court of Michigan, 1925.
233 Mich. 227, 206 N.W. 496, 60 A.L.R. 1212.

WIEST, J. Defendant Christina McLean owns the west 35 feet of lot 86 of Green Lawn subdivision, at the northeast corner of Collingwood avenue and Second boulevard, in the city of Detroit, upon which there is a dwelling house, occupied by herself and her husband, defendant John A. McLean. The house fronts Collingwood avenue. At the rear of the lot is an alley. Mrs. McLean derived title from her husband and, in the course of the opinion, we will speak of both as defendants. Mr. and Mrs. McLean started to erect a gasoline filling station at the rear end of their lot, and they and their contractor, William S. Weir, were enjoined by decree from doing so and bring the issues before us by appeal. Mr. Weir will not be further mentioned in the opinion.

Collingwood avenue is a high-grade residence street between Woodward avenue and Hamilton boulevard, with single, double and apartment houses, and plaintiffs who are owners of land adjoining, and in the vicinity of defendants' land, and who trace title, as do defendants, to the proprietors of the subdivision, claim that the proposed gasoline station will be a nuisance per se, is in violation of the general plan fixed for use of all lots on the street for residence purposes only, as evidenced by restrictions upon 53 of the 91 lots fronting on Collingwood avenue, and that defendants' lot is subject to a reciprocal negative easement barring a use so detrimental to the enjoyment and value of its neighbors. Defendants insist that no restrictions appear in their chain of title and they purchased without notice of any reciprocal negative easement, and

deny that a gasoline station is a nuisance per se. We find no occasion to
pass upon the question of nuisance, as the case can be decided under the
rule of reciprocal negative easement.

This subdivision was planned strictly for residence purposes, except
lots fronting Woodward avenue and Hamilton boulevard. The 91 lots on
Collingwood avenue were platted in 1891, designed for and each one sold
solely for residence purposes, and residences have been erected upon all
of the lots. Is defendants' lot subject to a reciprocal negative easement?
If the owner of two or more lots, so situated as to bear the relation sells
one with restrictions of benefit to the land retained, the servitude
becomes mutual, and, during the period of restraint, the owner of the lot
or lots retained can do nothing forbidden to the owner of the lot sold.
For want of a better descriptive term this is styled a reciprocal negative
easement. It runs with the land sold by virtue of express fastening and
abides with the land retained until loosened by expiration of its period of
service or by events working its destruction. It is not personal to owners
but operative upon use of the land by any owner having actual or
constructive notice thereof. It is an easement passing its benefits and
carrying its obligations to all purchasers of land subject to its affirmative
or negative mandates. It originates for mutual benefit and exists with
vigor sufficient to work its ends. It must start with a common owner.
Reciprocal negative easements are never retroactive; the very nature of
their origin forbids. They arise, if at all, out of a benefit accorded land
retained by restrictions upon neighboring land sold by a common owner.
Such a scheme of restrictions must start with a common owner; it
cannot arise and fasten upon one lot by reason of other lot owners
conforming to a general plan. If a reciprocal negative easement attached
to defendants' lot it was fastened thereto while in the hands of the
common owner of it and neighboring lots by way of sale of other lots
with restrictions beneficial at that time to it. This leads to inquiry as to
what lots, if any, were sold with restrictions by the common owner
before the sale of defendants' lot. While the proofs cover another avenue
we need consider sales only on Collingwood.

December 28, 1892, Robert J. and Joseph R. McLaughlin, who were
then evidently owners of the lots on Collingwood avenue, deeded lots 37
to 41 and 58 to 62 inclusive, with the following restrictions:

> No residence shall be erected upon said premises, which shall
> cost less than $2,500 and nothing but residences shall be erected
> upon said premises. Said residences shall front on Helene (now
> Collingwood) avenue and be placed no nearer than 20 feet from the
> front street line.

July 24, 1893, the McLaughlins conveyed lots 17 to 21 and 78 to 82,
both inclusive, and lot 98 with the same restrictions. Such restrictions
were imposed for the benefit of the lands held by the grantors to carry
out the scheme of a residential district, and a restrictive negative
easement attached to the lots retained, and title to lot 86 was then in the
McLaughlins. Defendants' title, through mesne conveyances, runs back

to a deed by the McLaughlins dated September 7, 1893, without restrictions mentioned therein. Subsequent deeds to other lots were executed by the McLaughlins, some with restrictions and some without. Previous to September 7, 1893, a reciprocal negative easement had attached to lot 86 by acts of the owners, as before mentioned, and such easement is still attached and may now be enforced by plaintiffs, provided defendants, at the time of their purchase, had knowledge, actual or constructive, thereof. The plaintiffs run back with their title, as do defendants, to a common owner. This common owner, as before stated, by restrictions upon lots sold, had burdened all the lots retained with reciprocal restrictions. Defendants' lot and plaintiff Sanborn's lot, next thereto, were held by such common owner, burdened with a reciprocal negative easement, and when later sold to separate parties, remained burdened therewith and right to demand observance thereof passed to each purchaser with notice of the easement. The restrictions were upon defendants' lot while it was in the hands of the common owners, and abstract of title to defendants' lot showed the common owners and the record showed deeds of lots in the plat restricted to perfect and carry out the general plan and resulting in a reciprocal negative easement upon defendants' lot and all lots within its scope, and defendants and their predecessors in title were bound by constructive notice under our recording acts. The original plan was repeatedly declared in subsequent sales of lots by restrictions in the deeds, and while some lots sold were not so restricted the purchasers thereof, in every instance, observed the general plan and purpose of the restrictions in building residences. For upward of 30 years the united efforts of all persons interested have carried out the common purpose of making and keeping all the lots strictly for residences, and defendants are the first to depart therefrom.

When Mr. McLean purchased on contract in 1910 or 1911, there was a partly built dwelling house on lot 86, which he completed and now occupies. He had an abstract of title which he examined and claims he was told by the grantor that the lot was unrestricted. Considering the character of use made of all the lots open to a view of Mr. McLean when he purchased, we think he was put thereby to inquiry, beyond asking his grantor whether there were restrictions. He had an abstract showing the subdivision and that lot 86 had 97 companions; he could not avoid noticing the strictly uniform residence character given the lots by the expensive dwellings thereon, and the least inquiry would have quickly developed the fact that lot 86 was subjected to a reciprocal negative easement, and he could finish his house and, like the others, enjoy the benefits of the easement. We do not say Mr. McLean should have asked his neighbors about restrictions, but we do say that with the notice he had from a view of the premises on the street, clearly indicating the residences were built and the lots occupied in strict accordance with a general plan, he was put to inquiry, and had he inquired he would have found of record the reason for such general conformation, and the benefits thereof serving the owners of lot 86 and the obligations running with such service and available to adjacent lot owners to prevent a departure from the general plan by an owner of lot 86.

While no case appears to be on all fours with the one at bar the principles we have stated, and the conclusions announced, are supported by Allen v. City of Detroit, 167 Mich. 464, 133 N.W. 317, 36 L.R.A., N.S., 890; McQuade v. Wilcox, 215 Mich. 302, 183 N.W. 771, 16 A.L.R. 997; French v. White Star Refining Co., 229 Mich. 474, 201 N.W. 444; Silberman v. Uhrlaub, 116 App.Div. 869, 102 N.Y.S. 299; Boyden v. Roberts, 131 Wis. 659, 111 N.W. 701; Howland v. Andrus, 80 N.J.Eq. 276, 83 A. 982.

We notice the decree in the circuit directed that the work done on the building be torn down. If the portion of the building constructed can be utilized for any purpose within the restrictions it need not be destroyed.

With this modification the decree in the circuit is affirmed, with costs to plaintiffs. * * *

Notes

1. Sanborn v. McLean is a leading case on the equitable interposing of servitudes or reciprocal negative easements based upon a common building scheme. In Ruffinengo v. Miller, 579 P.2d 342 (Utah 1978), the court stated: "It has long been established that if a general scheme for building or development is intended by the original grantor, subsequent grantees may bring action against each other to enforce restrictive covenants, and such intent may be shown by the acts of the grantor and the attendant circumstances." Ruffinengo was allowed to make such a showing over an objection by Miller that he had successfully defended an almost identical lawsuit brought by two other subdivision landowners a short time before, the court stating that he was not in privity with them, not a party, and that there was no collateral estoppel. See also Friedberg v. Riverpoint Bldg. Committee, 218 Va. 659, 239 S.E.2d 106 (1977), upholding a covenant requiring prior approval of construction plans where it applied to all lots as a part of a uniform plan of development. See generally also, Hamrick v. Herrera, 744 S.W.2d 458 (Mo.App.1987); Taylor v. Melton, 130 Colo. 280, 274 P.2d 977 (1954); Fitzwater v. Walker, 281 So.2d 790 (La.App.1973); La Fetra v. Beveridge, 124 N.J.Eq. 24, 199 A. 70 (1938), and Annot., 4 A.L.R.2d 1364 (1949).

2. A common scheme of development sometimes has to run too many hurdles to prevail. In G.L. Cline and Son, Inc. v. Cavalier Bldg. Corp., 213 Va. 557, 193 S.E.2d 693 (1973), it was held that there was no common scheme developed by a common grantor and that there was no violation of a setback requirement in written restrictive covenants where construction was begun before the effective date of the covenants. See also Ross v. Harootunian, 257 Cal.App.2d 292, 64 Cal.Rptr. 537 (1967), in which a deed restriction did not state that it was part of a general building plan for a tract development and thus no building scheme would be enforced. A somewhat similar case is Fournier v. Kattar, 108 N.H. 424, 238 A.2d 12 (1968). The problem stems from the use of deeds containing restrictions as opposed to

filing a plat and restrictive covenants. In Clark v. Guy Drews Post of the American Legion, 247 Wis. 48, 18 N.W.2d 322 (1945), a plat was recorded without restrictions indicated on the plat. A number of deeds were conveyed with restrictions for residential use only. The American Legion's deed contained no restrictive provision of that type. No general scheme of development was found, and the covenants in the other deeds were deemed to be personal covenants. An examination of the record in the case revealed that the subdivider's officer testified that a residential development plan was intended; this was well-known to the townspeople; purchasers were verbally informed of the residential nature of the development; there had been compliance sufficient to indicate a general scheme; all deeds except four contained the restrictions; and even the last deed contained restrictions. The message is thus clear as to the gamble involved in depending on the common scheme of development rule.

3. A Problem of Record Notice: Developer creates and records a subdivision of 100 lots. The first lot sold is lot 89. The deed recites that the buyer will use the lot for single family residential purposes. It also contains a covenant by Developer that all remaining lots in the subdivision shall also be restricted to single family residences. The deed is recorded. In selling other lots, including lot 25 purchased by your client, no mention is made of the restrictions, either orally or in the instruments of conveyance. Your client knew nothing about the restriction when he purchased. Now he wants to build a four-family apartment building on his lot. Neighbors are protesting and threatening an injunction action. Will you advise him to fight it, and, if so, what are his chances of success?

See Lowes v. Carter, 124 Md. 678, 93 A. 216 (1915) and IV American Law of Property § 17.24 at 601 (1952).

4. Suppose restrictions imposed by a developer are not identical for all lots. Is it possible nevertheless for the court to find and enforce a general building scheme? See Thodos v. Shirk, 248 Iowa 172, 79 N.W.2d 733 (1956) and Grange v. Korff, 248 Iowa 118, 79 N.W.2d 743 (1956). Compare Bein v. McPhaul, 357 S.W.2d 420 (Tex.Civ.App.1962). In Frey v. Poynor, 369 P.2d 168 (Okl.1962), 26 out of 280 lots were not restricted, yet a building scheme was found to exist. But failure to restrict 40% of the lots was fatal to the existence of a building scheme. In re Congregation of St. Rita, 130 So.2d 425 (La.App.1961). See Thompson, Real Property § 3164 at 131–143 (1962). In Arthur M. Deck & Associates v. Crispin, 888 S.W.2d 56 (Tex.App.1994) the court held that disparate treatment of some lots did not preclude enforcement of the restrictions because of the unique circumstances of the case (when a set of 1940 single-family only covenants was amended in 1993, two lots were exempted; the court was convinced that those two lots with condominiums on them were physically different).

5. Sometimes a developer acquires a large tract of land which he subdivides piecemeal, one manageable area at a time. Instead of restricting the whole tract in one fell swoop, he restricts each subdivision as he creates it. One of the ablest subdividers in the country, J.C. Nichols of Kansas City, now deceased, strongly urged this procedure. See Urban Land Institute, Community Developer's Handbook (1954 ed.). But suppose the restrictions imposed upon each subdivision are not uniform one set with the other? Do

lot owners in subdivision 1 have any standing to enforce restrictions on subdivision 2, etc.? Thus, in Gammons v. Kennett Park Development Corp., 30 Del.Ch. 525, 61 A.2d 391 (1948), Developer acquired a 640 acre tract and created a series of subdivisions, imposing different restrictions upon each. There was nothing in the deeds restricting the first and later subdivisions to suggest a uniform plan for the entire 640 acres. Held: The owner of a lot in subdivision A of the tract had no standing to protest the release, modification or termination of restrictions in accordance with provisions applicable to subdivision B of the tract. Also see Griffin v. Tall Timbers Development, Inc., 681 So.2d 546 (Miss.1996) where the court held covenants giving the original developer of a subdivision the right to form a property owners' association ran with the land and therefore a successor developer had the right to form an association. Compare Holiday Pines Prop. Owners Ass'n, Inc. v. Wetherington, 596 So.2d 84 (Fla.App.1992).

6. Consider the following cases:

In Hagan v. Sabal Palms, 186 So.2d 302 (Fla.App.1966), a situation was involved in which land was subdivided by a common owner who then sold to different grantees imposing in each deed a restriction limiting the land to use for dwelling purposes. It was held that any grantee might enforce the restrictions against any other grantee on either the basis of mutuality of covenant and consideration or on the basis that reciprocal negative easements had been created. It was considered immaterial as to whether the covenant was one running with the land. The court stated that in a common scheme of development, as here, the burden followed the benefit and became incident to the ownership of the lots.

In Maxwell v. Land Developers, 485 S.W.2d 869 (Tenn.App.1972), the court felt that the restrictions were ambiguous, but stated: "If, however, the seventeen previously executed deeds contained restrictions inserted for the purpose of carrying out a general plan of development of the entire tract, including the remainder thereof retained by the grantor, and the various grantees relied upon this general plan of development and purchased in reliance on the restrictions being made applicable to the entire tract, any party who purchased the remainder of the tract with *actual* knowledge of the general plan of development, and the prior purchases * * * would take the land so purchased subject to those restrictions."

In Steuart Transportation Co. v. Ashe, 269 Md. 74, 304 A.2d 788 (1973), it is emphasized that the establishment of a uniform plan of development "is a matter of intention of the parties." The court found that the similarity in the method of development and applicability of the provisions indicated an intention to continue a uniform plan; that the plat and dedicatory supplement indicated a uniform plan; and that the plan became operative with the first deed.

In Evans v. Pollock, 793 S.W.2d 14 (Tex.App.1989) the court rejected a claim by property owners that all the property in the subdivision was subject to a covenant for residential use. The court held that the residential restriction did not apply to all of the subdivision property at the time the original owners established the subdivision and that a reciprocal negative easement could not be imposed where the restriction did not apply to all subdivision property.

7. As the principal case indicates, building development plans have formed the basis for an extension of the concept of notice. If a subsequent taker of land took it with what courts consider as constituting notice of a certain scheme of development, then he is as bound by the use limitations as much as if his land were specifically burdened by a restrictive covenant contained in the deed. However, it is touch and go as to what circumstances will establish that a common development scheme exists. Some of the factors involved which may establish a building scheme and circumstances which may tend to refute the existence of a common plan of development are discussed in 5 Powell, Real Property ¶ 672 (1990). Generalizations are somewhat difficult, and some of the cases do not mesh too well when the decisions are compared. Some of the elements to be considered, however, are the intent of the original grantor or developer as measured by the circumstances surrounding the development and by his conduct; a fair uniformity of application of essentially similar restrictions; the number percentage of lots which are burdened; a fairly compact and definable area which is affected; and the absence of any substantial variations in the area. With respect to the intent of the developer and the evidentiary circumstances surrounding the development, if the purchasers were shown a map or plat of an entire tract and the developer indicated that he intended to put the entire tract on the market and that he would insert similar restrictions in deeds for lots to be sold later on, and if there were reliance demonstrated by actual development in accordance with the restrictions and substantial uniformity in restrictions imposed by deeds executed by the developer, this evidence would point toward a common building scheme and would be important in establishing the existence of such a development scheme.

WARREN v. DETLEFSEN

Supreme Court of Arkansas, 1984.
281 Ark. 196, 663 S.W.2d 710.

HICKMAN, JUSTICE.

Mike Detlefsen and others filed suit to enjoin the construction of two duplexes in the Warren Subdivision 3 in El Dorado, Arkansas. This subdivision is one of three adjoining residential neighborhoods which were part of a development by the Warrens through their partnership, the Warren Construction Company. The chancellor held that the Warrens should be enjoined from building the duplexes based on the restrictive covenants contained in the deeds of the appellees and the representations made by the Warrens concerning the development of the three subdivisions. In finding that these were enforceable restrictive covenants for single family use, the chancellor relied on the language in the deeds that the property was to be used for residential purposes, and that "carport" was used singularly in the deeds. Those factors coupled with the oral representations of the Warrens led the chancellor to conclude the restrictive covenants were enforceable. We find no error under these facts.

The chancellor received into evidence deeds to the lots which the Warrens had sold in each of the three units. In Unit One, there are nine lots, with five of the deeds containing covenants restricting use to "residential purposes only" and requiring a minimum of fourteen hundred square feet. One deed recites similar language except it requires a minimum of twelve hundred square feet. One deed states that the lot can be "used only for residential purposes" and requires a minimum cost of $30,000. Two deeds contain no covenants.

Unit Two consists of 21 lots with three of the deeds restricting use to "residential purposes only," "the dwelling," and require a minimum of fourteen hundred square feet. Four deeds are restricted to "residential purposes only," "the residence dwelling," and a minimum of fourteen hundred square feet. Four deeds contain this same language except the area is reduced to a minimum of twelve hundred square feet. Eight deeds in Unit Two contain no covenants.

In Unit Three, 20 lots had been sold at the time of trial. Of those, 11 deeds contain the restriction "for residential purposes only," "the residence dwelling," and require a minimum of twelve hundred square feet. One deed is restricted to "residential purposes only," "the residence," and requires a minimum of fourteen hundred square feet.

In promoting the development, the Warrens did not make a distinction between the three units, selling the area as a single neighborhood. There are no visible boundaries or divisions between the units. The Warrens, through Warren Construction Company, are the grantors, the developers, and the builders of the subdivisions. The Warrens displayed a master plat of the entire development on the wall of their office for prospective purchasers to view. This master plat was not recorded.

The Warrens argue that the chancellor erred in allowing witnesses to testify concerning oral representations allegedly made by them at the time the appellees were considering purchasing lots and homes within the units. This concerned the type of homes being built and the general scheme or plan of development which the Warrens intended to pursue. Testimony reflected that the Warrens had discussed these intentions with the prospective buyers, assuring them that only single family homes would be constructed, that no apartments would be constructed and that no mobile homes would be placed in any of the three units. Further, the appellees testified that they relied on these statements, at least in part, in deciding to purchase from the Warrens. At least one witness said he was told no duplexes would be built. Generally, duplexes were not mentioned.

While parol evidence is generally inadmissible to vary or contradict the language of a restrictive covenant, *Linder Corp. v. Pyeatt*, 222 Ark. 949, 264 S.W.2d 619 (1954), such evidence is admissible to establish a general building plan or scheme of development and improvement. Such plan or scheme can be proven by express covenant, by implication from a field map, or by parol representation made in sales brochures, maps, advertising, or oral statements upon which the purchaser relied in making his decision to purchase. 20 Am.Jur.2d *Covenants* § 175. This general scheme is shown by the deeds and by the oral statements of the

Warrens. Seven of the nine deeds in Unit One are restricted to residential use. Thirteen of 21 deeds in Unit Two are restricted to residential use. In Unit Three, 12 of the 20 deeds contain similar restrictions. Mrs. Warren testified that she and Mr. Warren intended to insert the restrictions in all deeds in the three units. She also testified that they were aware that the prospective purchasers were relying on their oral representations in deciding whether or not to buy. The subdivisions, themselves, consisted of single-family dwellings only at the time the appellees purchased their lots and homes. Both Warrens testified that the economy dictated they change their plans and build the duplexes rather than single family residences.

The Warrens argue that the chancellor erred in finding that the restrictions contained in the deeds of the appellees were the proper basis for enjoining the construction of the duplexes. They contend that the wording of the restrictions does not limit their development to single family dwellings, but rather, that multi-family use was permissible, citing *Shermer v. Haynes,* 248 Ark. 255, 451 S.W.2d 445 (1970). There, we held that covenants which restrict use to "residence" or "dwelling" purpose alone, generally do not have the effect of forbidding the erection or maintenance of multiple family dwellings. However, the chancellor in this case had testimony and facts of a total building and selling scheme which indicate single residence purposes only. Further, the testimony reflects that the oral representations, combined with the express covenants, were the basis of the purchasers' decisions to buy lots in the neighborhood. The homes in the units display a uniformity of development, further indication of the general plan and scheme.

These restrictions are enforceable against the lots retained by the Warrens in the three units as a reciprocal negative easement. When the grantor places an express restriction in deeds to his grantees within the particular development, the restriction attaches to the lots retained to prevent their use in a manner detrimental to the enjoyment and value of neighboring lots sold with the restriction. 20 Am.Jur.2d *Covenants* § 173. The Warrens had the restrictions placed in their grantees' deeds, and the chancellor's findings support a conclusion that the Warrens intended to bind all the lots sold within the three units.

Finally, the Warrens challenge the standing of homeowners in Units One and Two to seek enforcement of the restrictions against the lots retained by the Warrens in Unit Three. They argue that these first two subdivisions are legally separate subdivisions and, as such, the owners within them can not have the restrictions enforced in the third, separate subdivision. However, in the negotiations leading to the purchase, the Warrens represented that the development would consist of some 350 homes, all being single family dwellings. The buyers were shown a master plat which depicted the three subdivisions as a single development, with only a line distinguishing the boundaries of each unit. Otherwise, there are no visible boundaries or divisions between the units. The buyers relied upon these factors in making their decision to purchase. Also, at least two of the appellees were homeowners in Unit Three.

* * *

Affirmed.

Note

Subsequent to the decision in the principal case, the Arkansas Supreme Court stated in Knowles v. Anderson, 307 Ark. 393, 398–399, 821 S.W.2d 466, 469 (1991):

> The Chancellor's conclusion that a restrictive covenant may be enforced based solely on a general plan of development in the absence of restrictions in the grantee's chain of title is unsupported by the case law and contrary to the [Arkansas] statute [providing for recordation or restrictive covenants which would be binding on subsequent purchasers]. * * *
>
> [T]here must be restrictions in the grantee's chain of title *and* a general plan of development before a restrictive covenant is enforceable.

The court then distinguished the Detlefsen case as follows:

> The fact that [oral] representations of a general restrictive development scheme were made coupled with the restrictions shown in each of the deeds to the grantees led the Chancellor to conclude that the developer's retained land should also be restricted. As we were not concerned with a subsequent purchaser seeking to avoid a restrictive covenant of which he had no actual knowledge, there was no need to refer to the Statute. Indeed, the Statute is wholly inapplicable to a reciprocal negative easement situation, as it arises not by operation of law but as a purely equitable remedy based on the contractual relationship between the common grantor and his grantees.

Is that a sufficient explanation of the difference between a reciprocal negative easement based on a general scheme of development, on the one hand, and a recorded set of restrictive covenants which are contained in the chain of title to each in the subdivision? Is the reciprocal negative easement applied solely as an equitable remedy to bind the hands of the common grantor as to retained lots? Is there no kinship between the reciprocal negative easement and the recorded restrictive covenant? Certainly, for purposes of notice they are different, because there is nothing in the chain of title that reveals the limitation in either the Detlefsen or similar cases. Does Knowles v. Anderson unduly constrict the concept of the reciprocal negative easement based on a general scheme of development?

C. THE NATURE OF THE INTEREST CREATED: PROPERTY OR CONTRACT?

REMILONG v. CROLLA

Supreme Court of Wyoming, 1978.
576 P.2d 461.

GUTHRIE, CHIEF JUSTICE.

Appellants prosecute this appeal from a judgment ordering them to remove certain trailers and mobile homes from lands which they own and permanently enjoining them and their successors or assigns from placing, or allowing the placement of, any such trailers or mobile homes upon these lands.

Appellants Remilongs were the original owners of the lands now owned and occupied by appellees Crollas and sold them the tract which they now own and where their home is located, but appellants retained a portion thereof, being an adjoining tract to which this injunctive action was applied. The tract which the Remilongs retained contains 2.9 acres. The adjoining tract sold to the Crollas is one containing approximately .88 acres upon which is located a house which Remilongs sold to Crollas for the sum of $50,000. Crollas assert that a condition of the purchase was that Remilongs would remove all the trailers or mobile homes from the tract which they retained and claim that the fact they have now moved trailers thereon greatly diminishes the value of the lands purchased and that these lands were purchased in reliance upon such promise and agreement. Additionally, they claim damages in the sum of $10,000. * * *

This matter presents two questions upon which our decision must be based, i.e., does an oral contract creating a restrictive covenant come within the statute of frauds? If such agreement is within the prohibition of the statute of frauds, may the effect thereof be avoided by the application of an equitable or promissory estoppel?

It is apparent that if the answer to this first question is in the negative, this judgment should be summarily affirmed. We do not find that this may be so answered, however.

Appellees concede an existent conflict of judicial opinion in this area,[24] and cite authority sustaining their position that such an agreement does not come within the statute. However, in our view, and after examining such authorities, it appears that these opinions are "result oriented" and that the logic upon which they are based is at least questionable. It may be suggested that these opinions ignore certain realities as to the possible effect of such restrictions upon the use,

---

24. This writer deems it would serve no good purpose to set out at any length the several ways in which these contracts were treated and the various results flowing therefrom, but commends the reader to an examination of 5 Powell on Real Property, § 671, p. 144, et seq. (1976); 7 Thompson on Real Property, § 3169, p. 175, et seq. (1962 Repl.); 20 Am.Jur.2d Covenants, Conditions, Etc., § 172, p. 731, et seq.; Annotation 5 A.L.R.2d 1316, 1318.

enjoyment, and value of the lands to which they are attached and that the courts may have been more interested in relieving what appeared to be onerous situations than in a proper application of the law. * * *

This court has not heretofore considered the question of whether a restrictive covenant is within the statute of frauds, although an easement for an irrigation ditch has been held to be an interest in real estate within the statute, Linck v. Brown, 55 Wyo. 100, 96 P.2d 909, 911. An agreement restricting the use of land is described in many cases and considered to be a negative easement, Huggins v. Castle Estates, Inc., 36 N.Y.2d 427, 369 N.Y.S.2d 80, 330 N.E.2d 48; Bennett v. Charles Corporation, W.Va., 226 S.E.2d 559, 563; Putnam v. Dickinson, N.D., 142 N.W.2d 111, 124; Fort Dodge, Des Moines & Southern Railway v. American Community Stores Corporation, 256 Iowa 1344, 131 N.W.2d 515, 521. When its establishment is sought in equity it has been treated or described as an equitable estate or interest in land, Turner v. Brocato, 206 Md. 336, 111 A.2d 855, 861, and cited authorities. However, it is not necessary herein to categorize the nature of the interest created by a restrictive covenant because its real effect upon the use, enjoyment and value of the property to which it may be attached is obvious. A statement appearing in Wiley v. Dunn, 358 Ill. 97, 192 N.E. 661, 663, is most applicable in this case:

> " ' * * * The policy of the law requires that everything which affects the title to real estate shall be in writing, and that nothing shall be left to the frailty of human memory or as a temptation to perjury. * * * ' " (Quoting from Stephens v. St. Louis Union Trust Co., 260 Ill. 364, 103 N.E. 190, 193; and cited with approval in Corbridge v. Westminster Presbyterian Church and Society, 18 Ill.App.2d 245, 151 N.E.2d 822, 831.)

This view is consistent with Crosby v. Strahan's Estate, supra, and only serves to implement and strengthen that holding. It may be more desirable, instead of categorizing such restrictive covenant as an equitable interest, equitable servitude, or a negative easement, to frankly recognize that such covenant does affect the title, use, and estate, and recognize it independently for what it is. At best, it could probably be classified as creating a type of equitable ownership or servitude. It would appear of particular importance that such restrictive covenants be classified as interests in land without reference to particular terminology because of their increasing importance and use in our modern-day society. We would then hold that this asserted agreement creating a restrictive covenant upon appellants' land was within the prohibition of the statute of frauds, Frank v. Visockas, 356 Mass. 227, 228–229, 249 N.E.2d 1; Cottrell v. Nurnberger, 131 W.Va. 391, 47 S.E.2d 454, 456, 5 A.L.R.2d 1298; Droutman v. E.M. & L. Garage, Inc., 129 N.J.Eq. 545, 20 A.2d 75, 76; Annotation 5 A.L.R.2d 1316, 1320–1322; 5 Powell on Real Property, § 672, pp. 152–153 (1976); A.L.I. Restatement of the Law, Property, § 522, p. 3165 (1944). This does not, however, dispose of this case.

In defense of their judgment, appellees raise another proposition, i.e., if the statute of frauds does apply to this case appellants should not be allowed to rely upon it because of fraud or equitable or promissory estoppel, and the trial court apparently recognized that in its findings.

This case poses the direct question of whether equitable, or particularly promissory, estoppel may be used to defeat the statute of frauds and result in the creation of a restrictive covenant, a negative covenant, or equitable servitude upon the lands of the Remilongs. In Crosby v. Strahan's Estate, supra, this court examined and cited with approval authorities which expressed the view that the statute of frauds was an expression of "fixed legislative policy of the state" and that it was "absolutely necessary to preserve the title to real property from the chances, the uncertainty, and the fraud attending the admission of parol testimony." It further enunciated the caveat that the court should not be tempted to turn aside from its plain provisions merely because of the hardship of a particular case.

Since this is the first case before us involving the avoidance of the statute of frauds to effect the creation of such restrictive covenants, and realizing their increased use, their importance and necessity to present-day society, and the potential number of land titles which could conceivably be affected, this question must be approached with the greatest of caution.

Many authorities, in applying the principle of promissory estoppel, to avoid the provisions of this statute suggest that the purpose of the statute is to prevent suborned perjury in apparent recognition that this was at least one purpose which the statute of frauds no longer subserved. England partially repealed the statute of frauds because this necessity had been removed. See 68 Harv.L.Rev. 383 (1954). It is for this reason your writer finds helpful the application of the rules set out in many cases which involve the application of estoppel in cases which arise other than under paragraph 5 of our statute.

Some courts have met this problem squarely and held they would not by adoption of the doctrine of promissory estoppel avoid the legislative action embraced in the statute of frauds, Tanenbaum v. Biscayne Osteopathic Hospital, Inc., Fla., 190 So.2d 777, 779. If a contract is clearly within the statute, to apply this doctrine of promissory estoppel is to repeal the statute, Sinclair v. Sullivan Chevrolet Company, 45 Ill. App.2d 10, 195 N.E.2d 250, 253, affirmed 31 Ill.2d 507, 202 N.E.2d 516. The rule has been recognized that the defense of the statute cannot be raised unless there is a misrepresentation that the requirements of the statute had been complied with or there had been a promise to make a written memorandum, 21 Turtle Creek Square, Ltd. v. New York State Teachers' Retirement System, 5 Cir. 432 F.2d 64, 65, certiorari denied 401 U.S. 955, 91 S.Ct. 975, 28 L.Ed.2d 239.

Although this court has recognized the almost universal rule that restrictions upon the use of lands are not favored, we have also recognized that equity does have a role to play in limited circumstances,

Kindler v. Anderson, Wyo., 433 P.2d 268, 271; Metcalf v. Hart, 3 Wyo. 513, 27 P. 900, 31 Am.St.Rep. 122, affirmed 31 P. 407; Vogel v. Shaw, 42 Wyo. 333, 294 P. 687, 75 A.L.R. 639; Forde v. Libby, 22 Wyo. 464, 143 P. 1190. We speak of limited circumstances because the declared legislative policy encompassed in the statute of frauds should be departed from only when such action is necessary to "avoid the fraud, and accomplish what justice and good conscience demand," Metcalf v. Hart, supra, 27 P. at 913. Also, see Roberts Construction Company v. Vondriska, Wyo., 547 P.2d 1171, 1181. To accomplish the purposes of the statute of frauds, it may be necessary for a court to uphold oral agreements, Tucker v. Owen, 4 Cir., 94 F.2d 49, 52.

In light of the fact that appellees could easily have avoided this problem by placing all commitments in writing, they bear a heavy burden to show why the court should come to their rescue, but they have sustained such burden in this case. The trial court's findings that the appellants' promise to remove all the trailers from the remaining property and not permit the further placement of trailers thereon, that the appellants took affirmative action in removing all such trailers at that time, and that the appellees relied thereon, were sustained by the evidence. This is sufficient to apply the doctrine of promissory estoppel, Hanna State & Savings Bank v. Matson, 53 Wyo. 1, 77 P.2d 621, 625, wherein this court cites § 90, Restatement of Contracts, and Vogel v. Shaw, supra. See also § 217A, Restatement of the Law Second, Contracts 2d, Tentative Drafts Nos. 1–7 (Revised and Edited 1973); cf., Pickett v. Associates Discount Corporation of Wyoming, Wyo., 435 P.2d 445, 447.

* * *

For the reasons stated above, the judgment is affirmed.

Notes

1. It is obvious from the cases that courts encounter difficulty in attempting to decide whether they have under consideration a creature of contract law or a property interest. Clearly, whatever the contract ramifications, under the weight of modern authority, what we call today an "equitable servitude" is a property interest, cognizable and enforceable in equity, which burdens one piece of land to the benefit of another. According to 2 Nichols, Eminent Domain § 5.15(1) Rev.3d ed. 1989, a restrictive covenant constitutes property in the constitutional sense for which compensation must be made if the land in question is taken. These are in the nature of equitable easements, and when land is taken for a public use which will ultimately result in a violation of the restrictions, the landowners who were benefitted by the restrictions are entitled to compensation.

2. Consider the "contract" theory as opposed to the "equitable servitude" theory from the point of view of:

(A) Notice through recordation.

(B) Statute of Frauds.

(C) Parol Evidence Rule.

(D) Restrictions "in gross" as distinguished from restrictions "appurtenant."

(E) Rights of subsequent purchasers to sue prior purchasers and vice versa.

See II American Law of Property § 9.25, at 404 (1952).

3. In Westhampton, Inc. v. Kehoe, 227 Ga. 642, 182 S.E.2d 430, 433 (1971), the Georgia court adopted the holding of a trial court that "generally, oral restrictions as to the use of land are valid and enforceable." In that case the purchasers had relied upon the oral representations of the developer as to the quality and size of homes in the subdivision.

MORLEY v. JACKSON REDEVELOPMENT AUTHORITY

Supreme Court of Mississippi, 1994.
632 So.2d 1284

En Banc.

SULLIVAN, JUSTICE, for the Court:

The Jackson Redevelopment Authority (JRA) filed this suit to acquire Morley and Laurence's (owners) property on October 23, 1989, in Hinds County Special Court of Eminent Domain. The owners removed the action to the United States District Court for the Southern District of Mississippi, Jackson Division, and filed an answer on December 20, 1989. The District Court remanded to the state court for failure of complete diversity of citizenship among the parties. Standard Life Insurance Company was also joined as a party to the suit, as it claimed an interest in a restrictive covenant on the property. The trial court held that Standard Life had no compensable interest in the property and granted summary judgment against it, but granted Standard Life leave to appeal. The trial court also granted summary judgment for JRA on the question of public use and necessity. After discovery and a number of pretrial motions and hearings on those motions, the case went to trial on April 17, 1990. The jury awarded the owners $500,000 and the owners have appealed. * * *

The owners purchased the King Edward Hotel property from Standard Life Insurance Company in 1981 for $450,000. The owners had been involved in a number of real estate investments over the years and had a special interest in purchasing historical properties such as the King Edward.

The King Edward Hotel was built in 1923 on a lot of 69,159 square feet in downtown Jackson bounded by West Capitol, Mill and Pearl Streets. The property actually consists of three separate structures. The main hotel tower has 12 floors containing approximately 224,040 square feet of space. Adjacent to the hotel tower is a convention center containing approximately 7,842 square feet and a three-story parking garage which once housed an automobile dealership. The King Edward is on the National Register of Historic Places due to its excellent architectural design and the fact that for many years it served as the center of social and political activity in Jackson.

The King Edward today is a blight on the Jackson skyline. Last occupied in 1967, the building now is home only to a group of pigeons that enter through the numerous broken windows and mark the hotel with great mounds of disease-carrying excrement. Almost all of the witnesses at the trial agreed that the main tower was structurally sound. An expert engineer called by JRA created the most doubt on the soundness of the structure by testifying that two of the 1300 to 1400 steel columns in the building had been exposed and begun to corrode. He stated that tests would have to be made on more of the columns in order to determine the extent of possible corrosion in other parts of the building frame. The owners' expert architect, however, thought that the only reason those columns were deteriorating was the fact that the roof over both of them had holes in it, allowing moisture to seep into those columns. It was generally agreed also that any renovation of the hotel would require "gutting" the entire building, which meant removing all of the finishing material in the hotel and using only the existing structural frame and the facade of the building. Further measures necessary for a renovation were the addition of another stairwell to meet current building codes, removal of asbestos, and removal of the large accumulations of pigeon droppings.

* * *

When the Standard Life Insurance Company sold the King Edward property to Morley and Laurence in 1981, it inserted a covenant, which reads:

> Subject, however, to the following covenants and restrictions, which shall be taken to be covenants running with the land and binding upon the Grantees, their heirs, administrators, executors, assigns and successors in Title: The property shall be used as offices, a hotel, apartments, commercial rental property or a combination of these. No part of the property shall be converted for use as a home for the elderly, a nursing home or as low rent, government subsidized housing.

JRA argues that restrictive covenants such as this are not compensable property interests in an eminent domain action, and that even if they are, this particular one is not compensable because the dominant estate is not identified, no proposed violation of the covenant has been shown and even if a violation is shown, damages are too speculative to allow. Standard Life's position is that their interest is a compensable property interest which has a value which may be determined by the effect on the market value of its own property if it is taken. The owners object to any holding that would diminish their recovery.

State courts are in disagreement over the question of whether compensation is due for the taking of a restrictive covenant and the United States Supreme Court has never decided the question. The majority of states have found such interests to be property for the purposes of the Fifth Amendment and their own takings clauses and thus subject to the due compensation principle. States which deny compensation generally find that restrictive covenants are not interests in land, but merely personal rights not covered by the takings clause. See, Annotation, 4 A.L.R.3rd 1137 (1965); Law of Real Property ¶ 679[4] (Supp.1988). Many opinions which find such interests not compensable mention public policy reasons for the decisions, including the fear that recognition by the public that restrictive covenants are property interests would result in greater costs for government to acquire property and widespread proliferation of the covenants in order to thwart attempts by the sovereign to take property for public use. Stoebuck, Condemnation of Rights the Condemnee Holds in Lands of Another, 56 Iowa L.Rev. 293, 306–307 (1970); Anderson v. Lynch, 188 Ga. 154, 3 S.E.2d 85 (Ga.1939).

We view as better reasoned those opinions that find such interests to be interests in real property for which due compensation must be paid upon a taking by the exercise of eminent domain powers.

These courts take a different view of the meaning of property. For example, in finding the taking of a right to assess fees against a parcel of property a right for which compensation was due, one federal appeals Court quoted an earlier U.S. Supreme Court decision:

> It is conceivable that the [term "property"] was used in its vulgar and untechnical sense of the physical thing with respect to which the citizen exercises rights recognized by law. On the other hand, it may have been employed in a more accurate sense to denote the group of rights inhering in the citizen's relation to the physical thing, as the right to possess, use and dispose of it. In point of fact, the construction given the phrase has been the latter.

Adaman Mutual Water Company v. United States, 278 F.2d 842, 845 (9th Cir.1960) (quoting United States v. General Motors Corp., 323 U.S. 373, 377–380, 65 S.Ct. 357, 359–361, 89 L.Ed. 311 (1945)).

In a similar description of the scope of what constitutes "property" for purposes of the takings clause, Professor Stoebuck wrote:

> For every burden on your land, someone else enjoys a corresponding benefit or right. Physicists tell us that matter may not be destroyed—altered in form or transformed into energy, but not destroyed. And so with the interests in land; they may be redistributed, but the totality of absolute ownership will always exist somewhere, though scattered among the state and various individuals.... If your land is burdened by private restrictions known as restrictive covenants, servitudes, or negative easements [your neighbor] still has a property interest, though of a negative rather than positive sort. Matter has simply been altered in form.

Stoebuck, Condemnation of Rights the Condemnee Holds in Lands of Another, 56 Iowa L.Rev. 293, 293 (1970).

Both Professor Stoebuck and the Court in Adaman note that restrictive covenants have more in common with other interests accepted as property than not. Restrictive covenants generally must be created by a deed, be properly recorded, pass the Statute of Frauds and, once created, they run with the land. They, therefore, have more in common with real property than with property outside that rubric. Adaman, 278 F.2d at 849; Stoebuck 56 Iowa L.Rev. at 305. "Because the transfer of these rights and duties are subject to legal principles different from those which concern the passing of other interests, a unique, direct connection with the land is established. This connection justifies the distinction [between property and other rights]." Adaman, 278 F.2d at 849. The Adaman Court finally compared restrictive covenants to easements, which universally require compensation when taken, and concluded, "[b]oth interests are directly connected to the land and we are unable to find a distinction between them which will justify dissimilar treatment at the hands of the condemning authority." Id. at 849.

Clearly, Standard Life kept one of the "bundle of rights" which made up the complete estate when they sold the King Edward to Morley and Laurence. For this reason JRA's argument that only where the dominant estate is mentioned in the instrument containing the covenant may the owner of the dominant estate be entitled to compensation [is] unpersuasive. The "stick" Standard Life kept is the right of Morley and Laurence or their successors in title to build housing for the elderly, a nursing home, or government subsidized housing on the property. In order for the owners or their successors to use the property for any of these purposes, they would have to buy this right back from Standard Life. Would any prudent buyer seeking to purchase the property for one of those uses do so without purchasing this right? Would they not want, indeed, need a deed showing that Standard Life had sold the rights back to the owners? Certainly. To do otherwise would be to buy a lawsuit. Without a repurchase of the rights, the title to the property would be unmarketable.

Therefore, this Court finds that the restrictive covenant in favor of Standard Life is an interest in land subject to the due compensation principle under Section 17 of our Constitution.

Having found the restrictive covenant is an interest in land subject to compensation, it is necessary to discuss the method of calculating that compensation.

We have heretofore strictly adhered to the "unit rule." We set out the basis and application of the rule in Lennep v. Mississippi State Highway Commission, 347 So.2d 341 (Miss.1977), quoted in Mississippi State Highway Commission v. Daughtrey–Hughes, Inc., 375 So.2d 413, 414 (Miss.1979).

It is clear that the legislature intended for the unit valuation method to be applied in determining compensation in eminent domain cases. Mississippi Code Annotated, Section 11–27–5 (1972). We have consistently followed the statutory mandate and use the unit valuation method for determining compensation where property sought to be condemned involves a leasehold interest. In Lee v. Indian Creek Drainage District, 246 Miss. 254, 148 So.2d 663, 666 (1963), we stated Where there are different interests or estates in the property acquired by condemnation, the proper course is to ascertain the entire compensation to be awarded as though the property belonged to one person and then apportion this sum among the different parties according to their respective rights.

Accord, State Highway Comm. v. Rankin County Board of Ed., 531 So.2d 612 (Miss.1988).

Nichols' The Law of Eminent Domain, Sackman (3rd Ed.1990) points out the difficulty of valuation of restrictive covenants by the traditional unit rule:

There is no doubt a property may be restricted by means of a covenant running with the land to a use which is quite consistent with its highest and best use on the date of the condemnation. Thus, a servient tenement will have a value at least in theory equaling its value as unencumbered. Yet, the restriction imposed in favor of one or more other properties may be of substantial value to those properties. Thus, the "unit rule" has no application.

Id. at s 12.05[4][h], p. 129.

The proper method of valuation is the difference between the market value of the dominant estate before and after the taking. Standard Life urges the Court to adopt this view.

However, that view is fundamentally incompatible with the reality that the covenant gives Standard Life an interest in the King Edward property. The unit rule requires that in this case, a value be assessed on the fee simple interest in the King Edward, then that amount be apportioned among the owners and Standard Life, according to their respective interests.

JRA insists that any damages to Standard Life's covenant are purely speculative and thus should not be compensable. However, Standard Life's covenant is plainly being extinguished. We recently stated that:

Because our constitution requires "due compensation" the presumption is that the construction will be of such character as to do the most injury to the remaining property of the landowner. 4 Nichols, The Law of Eminent Domain § 14.15, pp. 14–327 thru–329 (Rev. 3d Ed.1990). This view is a function of the policy imperative that compensation and damages be payable once and for all and not piecemeal. One policy imperative of the before-and-after rule for more than half a century has been that the landowner's entire right and the Commission's entire liability will be resolved in a single action. That rule gives the landowner substantial incentive to discover and show all special damages.

King v. Miss. State Highway Commission, 609 So.2d 1251, 1254 (Miss. 1992) (footnote omitted).

Although we made these statements in an inverse condemnation case, the rationale applies equally to the facts in this case. The lower court was presented with ample evidence that the restrictive covenant had value. Therefore, it erred in granting summary judgment against Standard Life.

AFFIRMED IN PART; REVERSED IN PART AND REMANDED TO THE SPECIAL COURT OF EMINENT DOMAIN OF HINDS COUNTY, MISSISSIPPI.

Notes

1.   The so-called minority view on compensation for a restrictive covenant has some strong adherents. Consider the following statements from the case of Arkansas State Highway Comm'n v. McNeill, 238 Ark. 244, 381 S.W.2d 425 (1964):

The McNeills own a residence in Crestview Estates, an addition to Fort Smith. The Crestview bill of assurances provides that property in the addition shall be used only for residential purposes. The highway department does not propose to take any of the appellees' land. It is, however, acquiring a tract that is comprised of eleven lots within the addition and that abuts the appellees' north boundary line. When the interchange is completed the area behind the McNeills' home will be a busy highway instead of a quiet residential district. Expert witnesses testified that this transition will diminish the value of the plaintiffs' property by $10,000 or more. * * *

Does the fact that the proposed interchange will violate the restrictive covenant render the appellant liable for the decrease in the market value of the McNeills' property? This problem has arisen in some twenty jurisdictions, with the decisions about equally divided between the allowance of compensation and its denial. The cases are discussed in Nichols, Eminent Domain (3d Ed.), § 5.73, and in a Comment, 53 Mich.L.Rev. 451. When compensation is allowed it is ordinarily measured by the diminution in market value. United States v. Certain Land in City of Augusta, D.C.Maine, 220 F.Supp. 696; United States v. 11.06 Acres, D.C.Mo., 89 F.Supp. 852; Town of Stamford v. Vuono, 108 Conn. 359, 143 A. 245; Johnstone v. Detroit, G.H. & M.R.R., 245 Mich. 65, 222 N.W. 325, 67 A.L.R. 373. The American Law Institute indicates that compensation may be proper in some instances, but it refuses to express an opinion about the correct measure of damages. Restatement, Property, § 566.

Many of the decisions denying compensation are discussed in Anderson v. Lynch, 188 Ga. 154, 3 S.E.2d 85, 122 A.L.R. 1456. The courts seem to have had some difficulty in finding a sound basis for refusing an award, some saying that the plaintiff has no property interest in the land being taken, others that the restrictive covenant does not confer a property right, and still others that the public power of eminent domain should not be impaired by private contract. * * *

In those jurisdictions where, as here, compensation would be denied in the absence of a restriction, the decisions approving an award on the basis of the restriction alone are, in our opinion, demonstrably wrong. We need not, however, adopt the somewhat dubious reasons that have been given for the denial of compensation. We think the problem is essentially a simple one in causation.

It seems almost too plain for argument that the reduction in the value of the McNeills' property is attributable not to the breach of the restriction but rather to the fact that a highway is about to pass through a residential district. Suppose, for example, that this addition, Crestview Estates, had been developed in exactly the same way that it was actually developed, as a residential district, but without any such restriction in the bill of assurances. If the interchange had then been constructed the McNeills' damage, as far as the pleadings and proof indicate, would have been the same to the penny as if the restriction had existed. Yet it would not have been compensable. Thus it is illogical to permit a recovery upon the theory that the breach of covenant is the proximate cause of the injury.

Another illustration to demonstrate the fallacy in the decisions allowing compensation: Assume the existence of a purely residential area that is in part restricted and in part unrestricted. If a highway should be constructed just within the restricted section the landowners on that side of the highway would receive compensation while those on the other side, although suffering identical damage, would be without a remedy. Under such a rule it is evident that whenever the owners of property in an unrestricted neighborhood learn that a throughway is coming in their direction it is to their advantage to enter into an agreement imposing restrictions. In that way, by merely signing a piece of paper which they may destroy at will, they are able to pluck valuable causes of action from the thin air.

We do not deny the existence of a property right in the appellees. It may be that the restrictive covenant gave added value to their land when they bought it. But it is not the breach of the covenant alone that is causing their damage. This same tract, instead of being taken for a highway, might have been condemned by the city as a site for a public park. That too would have involved a breach of covenant, but the value of the appellees' property might actually have been enhanced. Thus there is no logical basis for attributing the appellees' present damage to the naked breach of covenant. Even without the restriction their injury would still have occurred. We cannot permit an irrelevant clause in the bill of assurances to create a fictitious cause of action.

2. Also consider these comments by the Supreme Court of California in Southern California Edison Co. v. Bourgerie, 9 Cal.3d 169, 107 Cal.Rptr. 76, 79, 507 P.2d 964, 967 (1973):

We need not contemplate in depth the somewhat esoteric dialogue on the appropriate characterization of a building restriction. One writer has perceptively declared that the 'no-property-interest argument is less the motivation for denial of compensation than it is a rationalization for a result desired for other reasons' (Stoebuck, op. cit. supra, 56 Iowa

L.Rev. at p. 306). An objective analysis reveals the real basis for the decisions which deny compensation for the violation of building restrictions by a condemner relates to pragmatic considerations of public policy rather than abstract doctrines of property law, and it is upon these issues of policy that jurisdictions choose between the minority and majority views. * * * Denial of compensation has been justified upon the ground that the cost of constructing public projects will be substantially increased if compensation must be provided by a condemner for the violation of a restriction. In addition, it is asserted that a condemner might be required to join a large number of landowners as defendants in cases where the benefit of the restriction runs to numerous lots, and that this could result in inhibiting the condemner's ability to acquire essential property. Finally, it has been suggested that landowners might 'pluck valuable causes of action from the thin air' by entering into agreements imposing restrictions whenever condemnation proceedings are on the horizon. (Arkansas State Highway Comm'n v. McNeill, 238 Ark. 244, 381 S.W.2d 425, 427 (1964).) We find these reasons for denying compensation to be unpersuasive. Conceding the possibility that the cost of condemning property might be increased somewhat by awarding compensation for the violation of building restrictions, we cannot conclude that such increases will significantly burden exercise of the power of eminent domain. As a practical matter some takings would result in negligible damage to the owners * * *; if the character of the improvement were such that damage to some landowners would result * * *, it is likely that only those immediately adjoining or in close proximity to the improvement would suffer substantial injury, even in highly restricted areas.

See also: Horst v. Housing Auth., 184 Neb. 215, 166 N.W.2d 119, 121 (1969) ("We therefore hold that lawful covenants restricting the use of land and binding upon successors in title constitute an interest in the land, and property in the constitutional sense. Where the taking of the land by eminent domain permits a use violative of the restrictions and extinguishes such interest, there is a taking of the property of the owners of the land for whose benefit the restrictions were imposed, and such owner is entitled to compensation for the damage * * * "); Meredith v. Washoe County School District, 84 Nev. 15, 435 P.2d 750 (1968) ("The basic question, then, is whether an equitable servitude, or easement, such as here, a restrictive covenant, is deemed to be 'property' in a constitutional sense, for which just compensation must be paid. To a 'majority' of jurisdictions this has been the question and has been answered in the affirmative."); Moschetti v. Tucson, 9 Ariz.App. 108, 449 P.2d 945 (1969); Staninger v. Jacksonville Expressway Auth., 182 So.2d 483 (Fla.App.1966); and State v. Reece, 374 S.W.2d 686 (Tex.Civ.App.1964). Compare Burma Hills Development Co. v. Marr, 285 Ala. 141, 229 So.2d 776 (1969), in which after considering the statement of the "majority" and "minority" views, Alabama decided to adhere to the minority.

3. On the Bourgerie case, supra note 2, see Note, Restrictive Covenants in Eminent Domain Proceedings, 7 Loyola (L.A.) L.Rev. 327 (1974). The notewriter believes that this case reflects a trend on the part of the California court to permit compensation for other interests currently not

compensable and to increase the remedies of local residents in environmentally disruptive situations. See also Note, Nuisance Damages as an Alternative to Compensation of Land Use Restrictions in Eminent Domain, 47 So.Cal.L.Rev. 998, 1052 (1974), which argues that the Bourgerie decision and other California cases have "opened the door" for payment of nuisance damages.

4. In Harris County Flood Control District v. Glenbrook Patiohome Owners Ass'n, 933 S.W.2d 570 (Tex.App.1996) the court held that the homeowners association had a cause of action in inverse condemnation for a taking of its property right to collect assessment fees for the period of time from when the government entity purchased 20 homes to widen a bayou until the entity brought an action to condemn the covenants. (The flood control district refused to pay the monthly fees required by the covenants after it purchased the homes.)

D. ENFORCEMENT

Problems relating to enforcement are diverse. The basic rule is that any person owning a lot in the subdivision may enforce the restrictive covenants against any other landowner in the subdivision. Each lot is at one and the same time both a dominant and servient tenement; each lot is burdened by the covenants and each is benefited.

But a variety of questions may arise relative to enforcement. Some of those questions arise in relation to termination, such as whether the change of conditions and circumstances in the subdivision and its environs would render it inequitable to enforce the covenants. Some questions relate to the propriety of enforcing the covenants. Has there been such a waiver of them in similar situations that it would not be equitable to enforce them in this one? Has there been laches on the part of the plaintiff? Should principles of equitable estoppel apply?

Sometimes the issue is the validity of the covenants themselves. Are they even-handed in their operation, and are they reasonable? Are they constitutional?

Some cases involve rather unusual arguments insofar as the typical restrictive covenant situation is concerned. In Quadro Stations, Inc. v. Gilley, 7 N.C.App. 227, 172 S.E.2d 237 (1970), about four acres adjoining property which was sold was restricted from use in the sale of petroleum products for a period of 25 years. The court held this not to be unreasonable as to the area involved, and, it did not accept the argument of the defendants that the covenant was illegal as being in restraint of trade. The same issue arose in Webster v. Star Distributing Co., Inc., 241 Ga. 270, 244 S.E.2d 826 (1978), in which the lease of the Websters contained a restrictive covenant limiting the use of the premises to professional dry cleaning and laundering, but prohibited coin-operated laundering, while Star's lease limited use to coin-operated laundering and dry cleaning. When Star began engaging in "drop-off" laundry business, the Websters sued. The covenant was upheld as not being in restraint of trade.

Standing may sometimes also be a factor. In Nonnenmann v. Lucky Stores, Inc., 53 Ill.App.3d 509, 10 Ill.Dec. 714, 368 N.E.2d 200 (1977), the plaintiff had violated the covenants (although not the zoning which accompanied annexation of the subdivision) by building apartment houses on two lots in the subdivision. The court held that he still had standing to seek injunctive relief based upon the defendant's violation of the covenants. Probably not all courts would have permitted him to come into equity under the circumstances.

The single-family classification often gives rise to enforcement questions, as some of the cases later on will illustrate, as does the vague "residential use" classification. In Hanley v. Misischi, 111 R.I. 233, 302 A.2d 79 (1973), a landowner was not permitted to construct a street across her lot to give access to houses to be constructed on a new plat because the proposed street was not a single family home and was not of benefit or incidental to residential use in the subdivision.

The cases which follow illustrate some of the conflicts which arise in connection with single family limitations.

BROWNFIELD SUBDIVISION, INC. v. McKEE

Supreme Court of Illinois, 1975.
61 Ill.2d 168, 334 N.E.2d 131.

WARD, JUSTICE.

Acting on the complaint of Brownfield Subdivision, Inc., a not-for-profit corporation, and E.J. Buras, the plaintiffs, the circuit court of Champaign County entered an order of injunction prohibiting the defendants, Robert and Mary Ann Collenberger, from occupying what was described as a sectional home in the Brownfield subdivision as a residence. The ground for the order was the court's finding that the structure was a mobile home, a type of structure prohibited in the subdivision by an applicable restrictive covenant. The appellate court affirmed (19 Ill.App.3d 374, 311 N.E.2d 194), and we granted a petition for leave to appeal filed by the defendants.

The restrictive covenant provides in part:

"No building shall be erected on any lot except a one family dwelling house, a garage and one service building and used exclusively as such. Buildings shall be permanent structures of an attractive design. Duplexes may be built on Lots 34, 35, 36, 37 and 38.

"No structure of a temporary character, trailer, basement, tent, shack, mobile home or garage shall be used on any Lot, at any time, as a residence, either temporarily or permanently."

The Collenbergers purchased a structure described as an "Armor Home" and a lot in the Brownfield subdivision from Rex McKee, another defendant, who is the president of Illinois Mobile Homes, Inc. A retail installment contract was used by the parties in the sale of the structure. It described the Armor Home as a mobile home and provided that title should remain vested in the seller until full payment was made. The Collenbergers were given a certificate of title which also referred to the Armor Home as a mobile home and stated its year of manufacture, its style or model and its serial number.

The Armor Home here is 52 feet long, 24 feet wide and has a total living area of 1,460 feet. It is manufactured in two separate sections which, when joined, provide three bedrooms, a living room, dining room, kitchen, a utility room and 1½ baths. The sections are built upon detachable running gears, i.e., upon undercarriages, springs, axles, wheels and hitches, which are designed to permit their removal at the location where the structure is to be installed.

Prior to installing the Armor Home on their lot, the Collenbergers constructed a concrete foundation 52 feet long, 24 feet wide and 36 inches deep. Stacks of concrete blocks were placed on top of the foundation. Then, three steel I-beams were placed on top of the stacks. When the two sections were delivered at the lot, they were set on jacks which had been placed on the four corners of the foundation. Workmen then removed the detachable running gears from the two sections and lowered the two sections onto the I-beams. The sections were fastened together by angle irons and 16–penny nails.

After the sections were connected, a mason cemented the ends of the beams and the stacks of concrete blocks to the foundation. The mason also built a perimeter wall of building blocks which was cemented to the foundation. However, the bottom of the Armor Home was not cemented, welded or attached in any way to the I-beams or to the perimeter wall. The structure simply rested on the three I-beams. After the sections were joined aluminum enamel siding was installed on the sides of the structure. A family room was added connecting the Armor Home to a previously constructed garage.

Robert Collenberger testified that he knew of the covenant's restrictions when he bought the lot. He said that although the Armor Home after installation could be transported to another location by reattaching the running gear to the bottom of each section, the structure would first have to be dismantled. This would require removing the aluminum siding, removing the bolts from the angle irons and the nails connecting the two sections, removing the shingles from the roof and disconnecting all the utilities.

Rex E. McKee testified that he sold the sectional home to the Collenbergers. He said that there is a difference between a double-wide mobile home and a sectional home. A double-wide home is two mobile homes constructed so that they may be fitted together to make a large mobile home, and it is portable, he said. A sectional home is designed to be a single dwelling with a single roof, and though it is constructed in two sections, it is not portable, he testified. He said that in his opinion the Collenberger's house was a permanent single house and not a mobile home.

He did admit, on cross-examination, that he had advertised the Armor Home as a "double wide mobile home." * * *

Warren Huddleston, the president of Countryside Mobile Homes, Inc., testified that the difference between mobile homes and sectional homes is that a mobile home's running gear is designed to be a permanent part of the unit. He said that a sectional home's running gear is designed to be detached, that is, it is designed to be removed from the housing unit when the unit is placed on a foundation. He stated that the Collenbergers' house in his opinion is a permanent family dwelling and not a mobile home.

The defendants' contention is that their Armor Home is a sectional home and therefore not a mobile home. This contention relies upon the testimony of Rex McKee and Warren Huddleston that sectional homes and mobile homes have important differences. The defendants alternatively argue that even if the structure was a mobile home, it became a permanent structure when it was placed in the foundation.

* * *

There is authority that modular and sectional homes are considered to be in the mobile-home category. B. Hodes and G. Roberson, The Law of Mobile Homes 4 (3d ed. 1974) states:

* * *

"4. A *Modular Unit* is a factory fabricated transportable building unit designed to be used by itself or to be incorporated with similar units at a building site into a modular structure to be used for residential, commercial, educational or industrial purposes.

"5. A *Sectional Home* is a dwelling made of two or more modular units factory fabricated and transported to the home site where they are put on a foundation and joined to make a single house."

We consider the structure here must be deemed to be within the prohibitory language of the covenant, "no structure of a temporary character, trailer * * *."

It was advertised as a double-wide mobile home in the installment contract under which it was purchased. Photographs in evidence show it to have the superstructure and appearance of a mobile home. In Hodes and Roberson, The Law of Mobile Homes, which we have cited, it is said that sectional homes are regarded as within the mobile-homes category. There was a concrete foundation here but the structure was in no way attached to it or to the three I-beams on which the structure simply rested. The structure can be transported to another location after the two sections have been separated and the removable undercarriages reattached to the bottoms of the sections. One of the exhibits (an article from a trade journal) attached to the defendants' brief in this court refers to a modular unit's portability as a difference from and an advantage over the conventional home.

The majority of courts considering the question have held that removing the wheels or running gear of a mobile home and placing it on a permanent foundation does not convert the home into a permanent structure. In addition to Timmerman v. Gabriel and Town of Manchester v. Phillips, which we described above, such holdings include: Town of Brewster v. Sherman (1962), 343 Mass. 598, 180 N.E.2d 338; Town of Greenland v. Hussey (1970), 110 N.H. 269, 266 A.2d 122; Bullock v. Kattner (Tex.Civ.App.1973), 502 S.W.2d 828; Jones v. Beiber (1960), 251 Iowa 969, 103 N.W.2d 364. See also City of Astoria v. Nothwang (1960), 221 Or. 452, 351 P.2d 688.

There is some contrary authority: Anstine v. Zoning Board of Adjustment (1963), 411 Pa. 33, 190 A.2d 712; Lescault v. Zoning Board of Review (1960), 91 R.I. 277, 162 A.2d 807; In re Willey (1958), 120 Vt. 359, 140 A.2d 11. However, we consider the position taken in the majority of holdings is to be preferred.

For the reasons given, the judgment of the appellate court is affirmed.

Judgment affirmed.

Notes

1. The problem of mobile homes, modular units, sectional units, prefabricated homes and the like are problems of the modern era and the high cost of single family units of the traditional type. The law wrestles with these problems in the context of zoning ordinances as well as in regard to restrictive covenants. Socio-economic considerations, as well as legal principles and interpretations, are involved whether the courts mention them or not.

2. The two cases most relied upon in the preceding case were Timmerman v. Gabriel, 155 Mont. 294, 470 P.2d 528 (1970) and Town of Manchester v. Phillips, 343 Mass. 591, 180 N.E.2d 333 (1962), both of which are in accord. The covenant in Timmerman prohibited trailers and temporary structures, and the structure and its installation were similar to the Armor Home in the Brownfield Subdivision case. The structure was described as a "double wide mobile home" composed of two structures built similar to a trailer house, which when bolted together formed a house 20 feet by 50 feet with 1,000 square feet of floor space. These units had been hauled to a subdivision, put on concrete blocks and bolted together. The wheels, springs, axles and the like were removed and taken away. A septic tank, propane tank and power line were installed, and a water system was attached to a well on the premises. Trees and landscaping followed. The Montana Court felt that this was insufficient to convert the structure into a permanent home of a single family variety, that you still had trailers involved, and that the covenant was violated. The Massachusetts case involved a zoning ordinance, but it was involved with essentially the same type of situation and reached the same result. "It looks like a trailer, has the qualities of a trailer superstructure, and has been built as a trailer." 343 Mass. at 596, 180 N.E.2d at 337.

3. A related situation was considered in Lawrence v. Harding, 225 Ga. 148, 166 S.E.2d 336 (1969). The restrictive covenant provided that a "building" with metal siding or metal roofing was prohibited. The mobile home was placed on a permanent foundation, was completely enclosed, had an attached porch, had concrete underpinnings, had a metal roof, and had a septic tank, gas line, water line, and electric lines. It was held to be a building for purposes of the restrictive covenant and thus violative of the covenant. The Georgia Court, by holding it to be a "building", declined to accept the argument of the defendants that if the covenants had sought to forbid mobile homes, they could have so stated. While the reasoning process may be different from that in the preceding cases, the result was the same— the mobile home or "building" or whatever had to go.

4. Aside from the question of mobile homes or modular structures, what about condominiums? When many sets of restrictive covenants were drafted, the concept of the condominium involving ownership of airspace and joint ownership of common areas was unknown. Yet as far as ownership of the condominium itself is concerned, it is arguably a single unit in the sense that it is an owned dwelling housing a single family. In Callahan v. Weiland, 291 Ala. 183, 279 So.2d 451 (1973), the Alabama Supreme Court was confronted with a situation involving deed restrictions which prevented maintaining an apartment house on the premises. Callahan wanted to construct a ten-story condominium on five lots in the subdivision. The provision also stated that "a single dwelling house with necessary outbuildings" was all that could be erected. The court held the proposed condominium to be an apartment house within the intent of the provisions since condominiums were unknown when the restrictions were written. The Alabama court was fully aware of the difference between a condominium and an apartment house but felt that any multi-unit dwelling was contrary to the intent of the restrictions. On this subject generally, see Annot., Use of Property for Multiple Dwellings as Violating Restrictive Covenant Permitting Property to Be Used for Residential Purposes Only, 99 A.L.R.3d 985 (1980); Annot., Erection of Condominium as Violation of Restrictive Covenant Forbidding Erection of Apartment Houses, 65 A.L.R.3d 1212 (1975); and Annot., Zoning or Building Regulations as Applied to Condominiums, 71 A.L.R.3d 866 (1976).

5. Enforcement cases quite often deal with definitions. In Turner v. England, 628 S.W.2d 213 (Tex.App.1982), the question was whether a concrete slab was a "structure" which the covenants prohibited. The concrete slab was actually a tennis court. After stating the settled law in Texas that restrictive covenants are to be strictly construed, and after citing cases from Utah, Pennsylvania and Massachusetts to the effect that tennis courts are not prohibited structures, the court held that a concrete slab for a tennis court would not violate the restrictive covenants.

6. Can or should the public get involved in how the covenants are enforced? In Home Builders Ass'n of Greater St. Louis v. City of St. Peters, 868 S.W.2d 187 (Mo.App.1994) the court upheld a city ordinance that required any new residential subdivision be encumbered by an indenture containing several minimum requirements, including that any subdivision have at least three subdivision managers, that subdivisions with covenants must assess a fee sufficient to enforce the covenants, and that each developer

at the outset of his subdivision establish a trust account at a bank, deposit at least $2,000 in the account, and that after ten or more lots are sold a majority of the lot owners, other than the developer, may require the trustee of the trust account to reimburse them for the costs of enforcing covenants not enforced by the subdivision managers. What policy considerations do you discern behind such an ordinance?

HOFFMAN v. COHEN

Supreme Court of South Carolina, 1974.
262 S.C. 71, 202 S.E.2d 363.

LITTLEJOHN, JUSTICE: This class action was instituted by the respondent, Ralph Hoffman, as Trustee, for a declaratory judgment holding that the proposed construction of a high-rise condominium apartment building, containing 62 dwelling units, upon certain lands owned by him in the Forest Dunes Subdivision of Myrtle Beach would not violate the restrictive covenants imposed upon that subdivision by its original developer. The defendants-appellants are lot owners in the subdivision and were made parties individually and as representatives of all other lot owners.

The issues were referred to the Master in Equity for Horry County, who recommended that the court declare that such a condominium is permissible under the applicable restrictions. His recommendation was accepted by the circuit court and incorporated into its order, from which this appeal is prosecuted by the defendants.

The Forest Dunes Subdivision was originally developed by Myrtle Beach Farms Company in 1941. It fronts on the Atlantic Ocean approximately 1900 feet, with a depth, running back to U.S. Highway No. 17, of approximately 1550 feet. A map of the subdivision indicates that there are approximately 185 lots, nearly all of which have a width of 75 feet and a depth of 150 feet. All but three of the 20 lots which front on the Atlantic Ocean have a width of 75 feet and a depth of approximately 260 feet. The property upon which the respondent proposes to build the condominium is composed of two beach-front lots, each 75 feet by 260 feet, plus an adjoining area designated "reserved", which is slightly larger than one of the platted lots. They lie in the southeastern corner of the subdivision, facing the strand and fronting on the ocean. It is uncontradicted that all deeds executed by the developer to all lots in Forest Dunes, including those owned by the respondent, contain the same restrictive covenants which provide in pertinent part as follows:

"a. No lot shall be subdivided and no residence or building, including porches and projections of any kind, shall be erected so as to extend beyond, over or across any of the building lines relating to said lot.

* * *

"c. This property shall be used for residential purposes only and any residence erected on the lot herein conveyed is to cost not less than Six Thousand ($6,000.00) Dollars or to be built according to plans and specifications approved by grantor hereof in writing by its proper officers.

* * *

"g. No lot shall be subdivided, or its boundary lines changed except with written consent of the grantor endorsed on the deed of conveyance thereof.

"h. The conditions, limitations, and restrictions hereinabove made shall be deemed covenants running with the land binding on both the grantor and grantee, their heirs, successors and assigns."

Single-family residences are the rule in the subdivision, the principal exception being a two-story building containing five separate dwelling units constructed upon the lot which lies immediately to the north of the respondent's property.

The respondent proposes to construct a building estimated to cost $3,000,000.00. The first floor would be partially underground and used for parking; the main, or ground floor, would have two apartments and a recreation room, manager's quarters and service areas. Above that would be 15 floors composed of four apartment units each. There would be two elevators in the building. Common facilities for the unit owners include a lobby, a recreation room, parking garage, elevators, hallways, foyer, utility rooms, swimming pool, shuffleboard courts and other related recreational facilities.

The appellants submit four questions for our determination. Under the view we take, we need answer only one basic inquiry: Would the proposed condominium violate the restrictions quoted hereinabove? We think that it would and, accordingly, reverse the order of the trial court.

Restrictive covenants are contractual in nature. The cardinal rule of construction in interpreting any contract is to ascertain and give effect to the intention of the parties. Such intent should, as nearly as possible, be gleaned from the instrument itself. Nance v. Waldrop, 258 S.C. 69, 187 S.E.2d 226 (1972).

The respondent asserts that the language in the restrictions in question is unambiguous. Because multi-family dwellings, including condominiums, clearly constitute a permissible use, his argument continues, there is no room for construction and no need to resort to matters outside the restrictions themselves. We disagree. We cannot say that reasonable men could not differ as to the meaning of the language employed.

The respondent argues that conventional apartment-type buildings are permitted under the restrictions and that the only difference between a conventional apartment house and a condominium-type of apartment building lies in the fact that normally an apartment building has one owner, whereas a condominium-type apartment building has many owners. He further urges that some three owners have built two living units on their lots and that one has built five units on his lot. The question of whether a conventional apartment-type building would be permitted in this subdivision is not before the Court at this time, but we cannot agree that there are no basic differences between a conventional apartment building and a condominium apartment building. We think that the building of 62 dwelling units on what amounts to approximately three building lots is entirely inconsistent with the overall scheme of the subdivision. Though a condominium is not strictly speaking a commercial project, it involves congestion and many of the undesirable characteristics incident to a commercial undertaking such as a hotel. It is common knowledge that beach residences, especially apartments (conventional or condominium), are often rented to temporary guests at least a part of the year. When so used in a building of this type, the property would become a commercial-type operation, inconsistent, we think, with the whole tenor of the restrictions.

The respondent correctly relies upon Sprouse v. Winston, 212 S.C. 176, 46 S.E.2d 874 (1948), for the proposition that restrictive covenants are to be construed most strictly against the grantor and persons seeking to enforce them. However, it was also held therein that "the rule will not be applied to defeat the obvious purpose of the restriction" and, before giving it effect, "the court will have recourse to every aid, rule, or canon of construction to ascertain the intention of the parties * * *." See also Edwards v. Surratt, 228 S.C. 512, 90 S.E.2d 906 (1956).

In construing covenants the circumstances surrounding their origin are proper considerations for a court when the language used is susceptible of more than one reasonable interpretation. * * * The concept of condominiums is relatively new to South Carolina; in fact, it was only eleven years ago that the "Horizontal Property Act" was enacted by our legislature. See 11 S.C.Code § 57–494 et seq. (Cum.Supp.1971). It is a virtual certainty that the question of whether condominiums should be permitted on this property was not even considered by the developer in 1941 when these restrictions were whelped. * * *

The Forest Dunes Subdivision is now a rather fully developed subdivision consisting almost exclusively of single-family residences. So far as the record shows no contest has been made concerning those lots whereon more than one residential unit has been constructed. The houses that have been constructed therein are rather substantial in size, with an average value of approximately $50,000.00.

The evidence warrants the conclusion that a general building scheme or plan of development founded on these restrictions has evolved in the area here in question. The [appellants] in this action and their predecessors in title have obviously relied upon the restrictions in buying and developing the property. The circumstances surrounding the inception of the restrictions and the developments subsequent thereto enforce the argument that the restrictions as drawn were designed and intended to prevent such uses as the [respondent proposes to make of his lots]. Nance v. Waldrop, supra.

Reversed.

Moss, C.J., and Lewis, J., concur.

Bussey and Brailsford, JJ., dissent.

Bussey, Justice (dissenting): Being of the view that the issues in this cause were correctly decided below, I most respectfully dissent. Prior to July 7, 1970, the particular area of Myrtle Beach was zoned as "single family residential" by the City of Myrtle Beach. On that date, the city amended its zoning ordinance, over the objection of at least some of the appellants in this proceeding, so as to permit condominiums in the area. It is true that Forest Dunes Subdivision has developed basically, but not exclusively, as a single family residence neighborhood, there having been some violations of the zoning ordinance. It is clearly inferable that it so developed because of the zoning ordinance rather than because of anything contained in the restrictive covenants.

As I see it, the appellants, in essence, are asking the Court to do what the city has declined to do: to-wit: keep the area zoned for "single family residence" purposes. They correctly concede that the phrase "for residential purposes only" does not limit the use of these lots to single family dwellings because such phrase has been almost universally interpreted to designate the character of the use and not the quantity, and that such phrase alone would not ordinarily limit the number of units on a lot so long as they are used as residences. 26 C.J.S. Deeds § 164(3)(c), p. 1121; 14 A.L.R.2d 1403.

Appellants argue, however, that the proposed use of the lots is not residential in character, but commercial, and that the use of the word "residence" in the singular, rather than the plural, in two places in the restrictions has the effect of limiting the use of the lots to "single family residential use." No in point authority is cited for either of these contentions.

With the possible exception of Nance v. Waldrop, 258 S.C. 69, 187 S.E.2d 226, which I conceive to be clearly distinguishable factually, none of the authorities cited in the majority opinion are, I think, in point or supportive of the result reached. In my view, there is nothing in the restrictions that can soundly be construed as precluding the construction of an apartment building in the area, or limiting the size thereof.

Although condominiums were not known in South Carolina at the time the restrictions were written, apartment buildings certainly were. It seems clear to me that the proposed condominium is not nearly so commercial in its characteristics as would be an apartment building of the same size. Had the developer intended or contemplated restricting the lots to use for the purpose of "single family residences" or to either prohibit or limit the size of apartment buildings, it would have been relatively simple to so expressly state. The construction placed upon a contract by the parties themselves is, of course, entitled to weight, but the development of the area as primarily one of single family residences perforce the zoning ordinance of the City of Myrtle Beach throws no light whatever on the intention of the parties.

The weight of well reasoned authority is in accord with the following language from 26 C.J.S. Deeds § 163, p. 1102:

"The court may not limit a restriction in a deed, nor, on the other hand, will a restriction be enlarged or extended by construction or implication beyond the clear meaning of its terms, *even to accomplish what it may be thought the parties would have desired had a situation which later developed been foreseen by them at the time when the restriction was written.*" (Emphasis added.) See Forest Land Co. v. Black, 216 S.C. 255, 57 S.E.2d 420.

It is still the settled rule in this jurisdiction that restrictions as to the use of real estate should be strictly construed and all doubts resolved in favor of free use of the property, subject, however, to the provision that this rule of strict construction should not be applied so as to defeat the plain and obvious purpose of the instrument. It follows, of course, that where the language of the restrictions is equally capable of two or more different constructions that construction will be adopted which least restricts the use of the property. McDonald v. Welborn, 220 S.C. 10, 66 S.E.2d 327; Maxwell v. Smith, 228 S.C. 182, 89 S.E.2d 280; Cothran v. Stroman, 246 S.C. 42, 142 S.E.2d 368; Baltz, Inc. v. R.V. Chandler & Co., 248 S.C. 484, 151 S.E.2d 441; Edwards v. Surratt, 228 S.C. 512, 90 S.E.2d 906. Neither the appellants nor the majority opinion point to any language in the restrictions expressing a "plain and obvious purpose" to restrict the use of lots in the area to "single family residences only," and no such plain and obvious purpose being reflected in the restrictions, there is no occasion for us to refrain from applying the rule of strict construction.

In conclusion, the proposed condominium is basically and fundamentally residential in nature and there is, I submit, nothing in the record to indicate that it has or will come to have such commercial aspects as constitute a violation of the restriction that the property be used for "residential purposes only." Certainly, the provision of certain minimal facilities for the joint use of the various owners of the condominium units does not make the project a commercial one. Estimated cost of the individual two and three bedroom units ranges from sixty thousand dollars to one hundred thousand dollars per unit. There is no evidence in the record that the rental of any of these units is contemplated. While some rentals will no doubt occur, the very cost of the units suggests the likelihood that any rentals will be minimal.

BRAILSFORD, J., concurs.

Notes

1. Consider this: The covenants provided that no lot could be subdivided. In a condominium, there is a division of ownership with each landowner holding title to the airspace which constitutes his living area and with common ownership in such areas as the walls, the roof, the foundation, the

elevators, stairs, recreation rooms, and so on. Could it be said that the nature of a condominium in and of itself produces divided ownership and thus "subdivides" the total landspace parcel? See Wright, The Law of Airspace 87–98 (1968).

2. Note that the City of Myrtle Beach had zoned this area so as to permit multiple-family dwellings, including condominiums. The question of conflicts or inconsistencies between zoning regulations and restrictive covenants is considered, infra. Recall this case when you arrive at that material.

3. If you owned a large lot in an exclusive residential area, which lot was irregularly shaped and situated on rugged terrain, and the area was limited by restrictive covenants to single-family dwellings, could you build a cluster of condominium townhouses on the property which were separated by an airspace in between each townhouse? Assume that the townhouses are quite attractive and that each sells at a price comparable to houses in the area. Assume also that this particular construction can make the most effective use of the land in question. What is the answer?

McDONALD v. CHAFFIN

Court of Appeals of Tennessee, Middle Section, 1975.
529 S.W.2d 54.

[Trustees of the West Meade Church of Christ purchased property in the West Meade Farms subdivision subject to the restrictive covenants filed of record. The covenants provided that only "a private dwelling house, or improvement in connection therewith" could be erected on the premises and specifically excluded certain uses, such as apartment houses and business structures and places "of public gathering." The plaintiffs, owners of property in the subdivision, alleged that defendants were using the property for church services and sought injunctive relief. Defendants admitted that they had met on the premises "in a private religious gathering." The Chancellor enjoined the defendants from using their property as a church on the basis that the premises were not being used as a private dwelling and were being used as a place of public gathering. The defendants appealed, alleging a violation of the First Amendment to the United States Constitution.]

DROWOTA, JUDGE.

Restrictive covenants are to be strictly construed. That is, they are to be read without the drawing of unnecessary implications and will not be taken to preclude that which is not plainly prohibited. *Shea v. Sargent*, 499 S.W.2d 871, 873 (Tenn.1973). But in reading the covenant we should give the words a fair and reasonable meaning in order to effectuate its purpose. *Hamilton v. Broyles*, 57 Tenn.App. 116, 415 S.W.2d 352 (1966).

We agree that any use of the subject property as a church building would constitute a violation of the applicable restrictive covenant. Such use is not for residential purposes, and we take judicial notice that such use would ordinarily entail regular public gatherings. This result is mandated by the plain meaning of the covenant and is consistent with the "complete accord" reached by the many other courts that have considered the question of the applicability to churches of covenants restricting property to residential use. See Annot., 13 A.L.R.2d 1239.

There is no bill of exceptions in this case and we find no proof in the record to contradict the Chancellor's finding that the building on the subject property was in fact used as a church and not as a residence, or that the worship services were public gatherings. It was conceded by appellants in oral argument that no one resides in the structure. Thus we are not faced with any issue involving the applicability of such restrictive covenants to persons conducting private religious worship services in their homes.

The remaining question is whether federal constitutional restrictions exist on the power of the Chancery Court to enforce the restrictive covenant in this case. The restrictive covenant here involved was expressly incorporated by reference into the deed conveying the property to defendants. As such the restriction originated purely in private conduct. It is not clear whether judicial enforcement of the private agreement, *in such a case as this,* ought to trigger constitutional restrictions designed to restrain action by the federal and state governments. Of course, the agreement rests upon state law recognizing the validity of such limitations on land use and requires for its effectiveness enforcement by the state. See *Shelley v. Kraemer,* 334 U.S. 1, 68 S.Ct. 836, 92 L.Ed. 1161 (1948) (court enforcement of a restrictive covenant excluding persons of designated race or color from the ownership or occupancy of real property constitutes state action).

Assuming, *arguendo,* the presence of state action, we find that court enforcement of the restrictive covenant does not violate the first amendment. Enforcement of a facially neutral restriction on the use of land for other than residential purposes works only an incidental or indirect burden on appellants no different from that borne by other property owners and does not rise to the level of a violation of their rights of assembly or free exercise of religion. See *Braunfeld v. Brown,* 366 U.S. 599, 81 S.Ct. 1144, 6 L.Ed.2d 563 (1961). In this circumstance, churches are on the same plane as other property owners with respect to the use of land. Because of the incidental nature of the restriction, we are not obligated to find a "compelling" state interest to support the restriction. Compare *Braunfeld v. Brown,* supra, with *Sherbert v. Verner,* 374 U.S. 398, 83 S.Ct. 1790, 10 L.Ed.2d 965 (1963).

We are not here faced with a situation in which persons are effectively restricted from establishing a place of worship due to a pervasive system of restrictive covenants or zoning throughout the area. Nor are we confronted with an attempt to secure the assistance of the state in the discriminatory enforcement of restrictions as between religions. The first amendment does not preclude reasonable regulation of the time, place, or manner of the exercise of constitutionally protected activities. *Jones v. Opelika,* 316 U.S. 584, 62 S.Ct. 1231, 86 L.Ed. 1691 (1942).

* * *

Affirmed.

SHRIVER, P.J., and TODD, J., concur.

Notes

1. Restrictive covenants, which expressly or by necessary implication exclude churches, have been upheld in the vast majority of cases. See, e.g., Hall v. Church of the Open Bible, 4 Wis.2d 246, 89 N.W.2d 798 (1958). This would also apply if an existing residence were altered in such a way as to provide for the conduct of church services. Matthews v. First Christian Church, 355 Mo. 627, 197 S.W.2d 617 (1946). For a discussion of some of the cases, see Note, Restrictive Covenants as a Device to Control Religious Uses, 12 Syracuse L.Rev. 347 (1961). Such a covenant has been enforced even though the zoning ordinance expressly permits churches. Abrams v. Shuger, 336 Mich. 59, 57 N.W.2d 445 (1953).

Sometimes the exclusion of churches is inadvertent as where a hasty draftsman writes "single family residential use only" without realizing that if the people who come to live in the new neighborhood later want a church there, releases will have to be obtained from possibly dozens of lot owners. Moreover, some of the owners may be infants, mental incompetents or absentee landlords. For a case which gets into this subject along with questions of changed conditions and acquiescence, see City of Houston v. Emmanuel United Pentecostal Church, 429 S.W.2d 679 (Tex.Civ.App.1968). Also see Fitzwilliam v. Wesley United Methodist Church, 882 S.W.2d 343 (Mo.App.1994) where the words "residential use" in the restrictions were interpreted to allow a church that had purchased a lot with a house on it in the subdivision to tear down the house and put in a parking lot. A very similar case is Bagko Development Co. v. Damitz, 640 N.E.2d 67 (Ind.App. 1994) which interpreted "residential purposes" to allow a Little League practice field.

2. Occasional cases challenge such covenants as being violative of the First Amendment as did the principal case. In West Hill Baptist Church v. Abbate, 24 Ohio Misc. 66, 261 N.E.2d 196 (1969), a restrictive covenant was challenged on that basis. This court compared covenants to zoning and concluded that this was simply "private zoning or zoning by contract." It concluded that if a zoning ordinance is unconstitutional, then a restrictive covenant in the same area and to the same effect would be unconstitutional. It cited Shelley v. Kraemer with regard to state action and concluded that enforcement of the covenants against the church would violate the religious freedom guaranteed by the First Amendment. But unlike the Shelley case, which held it to be invalid to exclude people on the basis of race, this type of covenant does not seek to keep people out on any basis. It simply limits the *uses* in the subdivision. Moreover, it is fallacious to equate zoning (—a public exercise of the police power—) with private restrictive covenants which are a matter of contract and are non-discriminatory use limitations. The Abbate

case was contrary to prior Ohio case law. Cleveland Baptist Association v. Scovil, 107 Ohio St. 67, 140 N.E. 647 (1923).

3. Shelley v. Kraemer invalidated a racial restrictive covenant. The unenforceability and invalidity of racial restrictive covenants does not serve to invalidate the other covenants because they are severable. See, e.g., Skinner v. Henderson, 556 S.W.2d 730 (Mo.App.1977).

4. Enforcement of restrictive covenants to enjoin the building of a church can fail for reasons similar to those involving other, non-church situations. In Pinetree Estates Homeowners Association v. First United Lutheran Church, 241 Ga. 228, 244 S.E.2d 856 (1978), the homeowners were unable to enforce restrictive covenants against the church because they could not show that the church and any one of them had a common grantor bound by the covenants. The homeowners contended that the church had constructive notice. Could not the argument of the common scheme of development have been applied on behalf of the homeowners? The court does not discuss it.

5. Only rarely do courts have to consider whether a covenant is violative of public policy and thus unenforceable. One interesting case along this line is Davidson Bros., Inc. v. D. Katz & Sons, Inc., 274 N.J.Super. 159, 643 A.2d 642 (1994). The court found that a covenant prohibiting the use of the property for a supermarket was contrary to public policy because to enforce the covenant would reduce the necessary shopping services available to a large population of disadvantaged persons in New Brunswick, New Jersey.

ROFE v. ROBINSON

Supreme Court of Michigan, 1982.
415 Mich. 345, 329 N.W.2d 704.

LEVIN, JUSTICE.

This action concerns the enforceability of deed restrictions. Plaintiffs and defendants are property owners in the Hickory Knolls Subdivision. The deed restrictions provide that all buildings in the subdivision are to be restricted to residential, single-family use. Defendants, however, seek to construct three one-story office buildings on two of the lots in this subdivision. The front of these buildings would face plaintiffs' adjoining lots. Defendants, under the zoning ordinance, are required to build a six-foot wall along the border separating office use from residential use. Defendants' proposed site plans provide for parking along this wall. Plaintiffs brought this action seeking a permanent injunction enjoining defendants from developing their lots as office sites.

The trial court upheld the restrictions and issued the permanent injunction plaintiffs requested. The Court of Appeals reversed, finding a change in the character of the subdivision. We reverse the decision of the Court of Appeals, 99 Mich.App. 404, 298 N.W.2d 609, and remand for consideration of the issues the Court of Appeals found unnecessary to address.

I

Hickory Knolls Subdivision is triangular and consists of 45 lots. The subdivision is bounded by Telegraph Road on the east, Franklin Road on the west, and Hickory Grove Road on the south. Lots 1 through 12 are accessible only from Telegraph Road and comprise the eastern side of the triangle. Each of lots 1 to 12 is vacant, except lot 2. Until 1971, no commercial development occurred on any of the lots in the subdivision. However, in 1971, the residence on lot 2 was converted to office use. There has been no objection by the residents of the subdivision to the use of the building on lot 2 as an office.

In 1956, the subdivision was zoned for single-family residential use. In 1968, Bloomfield Township changed the zoning on lots 1 to 12 to the 0–1 classification, limiting construction to office buildings and prohibiting the construction of single-family residences.

* * *

Across from the Hickory Knolls Subdivision, on the other side of Telegraph Road, is the Hickory Grove Subdivision, a residential area. There is a berm separating this subdivision from Telegraph Road. The area along Telegraph Road north of Franklin Road is zoned for office development and consists of several office buildings. The land along Telegraph Road south of Hickory Grove Road is vacant for some distance.

Plaintiffs argue that the deed restrictions should be enforced because the restrictions constitute a valuable property right and because there have been no changes in the subdivision to render enforcement of the restrictions inequitable.

Defendants contend that the restrictions are unenforceable because it is illegal (due to the rezoning) and impractical to build residences on lots 7 and 8. Defendants further contend that the character of the subdivision has changed so that it is inequitable to enforce the restrictions, citing factors such as rezoning, the use of the building on lot 2 as an office, the evolution of Telegraph Road, and the condemnation of 54 feet of lots 7 and 8 for the widening of Telegraph Road. We are not persuaded by these arguments.

II

Deed restrictions are property rights. The courts will protect those rights if they are of value to the property owner asserting the right and if the owner is not estopped from seeking enforcement.

Defendants argue that it is impractical to build residences on lots 7 and 8. They contend that a residence cannot be economically built or sold and that the deed restrictions will require the lots to remain permanently vacant and useless. Plaintiffs' witness testified that there is always a market for any property with appropriate price adjustments and lots 1 through 12 could be sold as residential lots.

Economic impracticability does not itself justify lifting building restrictions. Plaintiffs purchased their property, in apparent reliance on the deed restrictions, and defendants were on notice of the restrictions when they purchased their lots. This Court has long recognized that such restrictions create valuable property rights. "The right, if it has been acquired, to live in a district uninvaded by stores, garages, business and apartment houses is a valuable right." In *Cooper v. Kovan,* 349 Mich. 520, 530–531, 84 N.W.2d 859 (1957), this Court said:

> "Home owners seek, by purchasing in areas restricted to residential building, freedom from noise and traffic which are characteristic of business areas. How much in dollars the peace and quiet of this neighborhood is worth, or how much the contemplated major business invasion would diminish that value, would be hard to establish. But it is clear in our mind that residential restrictions generally constitute a property right of distinct worth."

The change in zoning does not support defendants' challenge to the validity of the deed restriction. If, as the defendants contend, the property as restricted is substantially valueless regardless of the zoning, then it is the deed restriction and not the zoning which brought about the loss of value.

Even if the zoning were relevant, it is well established in this state that a change in zoning cannot, by itself, override prior restrictions placed in deeds. Zoning laws determine property owners' obligations to the community at large but do not determine the rights and obligations of parties to a private contract. These are separate obligations, both of which may be enforceable.

Defendants next argue that the character of the subdivision has changed so that enforcement of the restrictions would be inequitable. In support of this claim, defendants cite factors such as rezoning, the use of lot 2 for business purposes, and the evolution and widening of Telegraph Road. However, the restrictions will not be lifted unless the character of the subdivision has changed in such a way as to subvert the original purpose of the restrictions. Because the character of the subdivision has not so changed, defendants are not entitled to relief on these grounds.

A change in zoning is not sufficient evidence of a change in the character of an area to require lifting residential restrictions. In *Brideau v. Grissom,* 369 Mich. 661, 668, 120 N.W.2d 829 (1963), this Court said that "[t]he change in the zoning ordinance cannot operate to destroy the obligations involved in the restrictions. * * * Such change is only a factor to be considered in determining whether a change of circumstances has occurred that an equity court will not enforce the restriction." In *Brideau,* this Court found the restriction to be enforceable in spite of the zoning change, because this Court was "unable to say that the original plan of development [had] been subverted by a change in the character and usage of the neighborhood." A change in zoning is thus only relevant if it is indicative of a change in the character of the area. Rezoning itself is not such a change.

We are also unpersuaded that use of one of the 45 lots for office purposes so changes the character of the subdivision as to render the restrictions inequitable. This structure was built as a residence and previously used as such, although now it is used for business purposes. The use of this building for office purposes has not materially changed the character of the subdivision. The subdivision has remained substantially residential.

Likewise, the evolution and widening of Telegraph Road does not justify lifting the restrictions. The widening of Telegraph Road has not changed the character of the subdivision. The subdivision is still substantially residential. Similarly, the evolution of Telegraph Road into a business district has not rendered enforceability of the restrictions inequitable, because the subdivision has not lost its character as a residential area. "The fact that substantial changes in the character of the neighborhood outside of the subdivision have taken place does not make it inequitable to enforce the restrictions." Furthermore, as this Court said in *Redfern Lawns Civic Ass'n. v. Currie Pontiac Co.*, 328 Mich. 463, 470, 44 N.W.2d 8 (1950), "there must of necessity be a dividing line somewhere".

Although there has been a change in the character of Telegraph Road, this change has not subverted the purpose of the residential restrictions so as to render enforcement of the restrictions inequitable.

We therefore reverse the decision of the Court of Appeals and remand for consideration of the issues regarding laches, waiver, and interpretation of the deed restrictions, which it found unnecessary to consider.

WILLIAMS, C.J., and KAVANAGH, COLEMAN, RYAN and FITZGERALD, JJ., concur.

RILEY, J., not participating.

[The extensive footnotes of the court have been omitted.]

Notes

1. Compare the language in Rice v. Heggy, 158 Cal.App.2d 89, 322 P.2d 53 (1958): "Appellants stress the point that some of the property in question has been rezoned * * * since the making of the deed restrictions, and argue that this rezoning should override the restrictions. The contention is untenable and such rezoning by no means compelled the trial court to declare that appellants were entitled to construct multiple unit dwellings which would violate the deed restrictions." Does this mean that the deed restrictions take precedence or that the more restrictive of the two, whether zoning or the covenants, takes precedence?

2. In Grubel v. MacLaughlin, 286 F.Supp. 24 (D.V.I.1968), the court held that "the obligation of the plaintiffs under the restrictive covenant to use their land for residential purposes only has been extinguished by the zoning regulation which makes that use unlawful. Since * * * the zoning regulation is valid, it necessarily follows that the restrictive covenant in the plaintiffs' deed is unenforceable * * *." That does not find support in more

than a handful of cases. The general rule is that zoning regulations do not supersede or vitiate lawful restrictive covenants in situations in which the restrictive covenants are more restrictive. See generally Allen v. Axford, 285 Ala. 251, 231 So.2d 122 (1969); G.M.L. Land Corp. v. Foley, 20 A.D.2d 645, 246 N.Y.S.2d 338 (1964), affirmed 14 N.Y.2d 823, 251 N.Y.S.2d 472, 200 N.E.2d 455 (1964). A zoning ordinance, in and of itself, does not render null and void an otherwise valid restrictive covenant or building limitation. Lamica v. Gerdes, 270 N.C. 85, 153 S.E.2d 814 (1967). See generally, Church, The Effect of Private Restrictive Covenants on Exercise of the Public Powers of Zoning and Eminent Domain, 1963 Wis.L.Rev. 321.

3. In City of Harrisburg v. Capitol Housing Corp., 117 Pa.Cmwlth. 408, 543 A.2d 620 (1988), a redevelopment contract was incorporated into a vendor's deed restricting the use of the land in question to "residential private housing" for a period of forty years. Because of that, it was held that a proposed conveyance of the apartment building on the land to a nontaxable, governmental entity (the Pennsylvania Higher Education Assistance Agency) would violate such restriction and the sale was enjoined. The Commonwealth Court stated that the state agency did not have the authority to override a land use restriction incorporated into a deed.

BROWN v. MORRIS
Supreme Court of Alabama, 1966.
279 Ala. 241, 184 So.2d 148.

Per Curiam.

[The Browns, plaintiffs, and the defendants, Morris and Pierson, owned lots in the same subdivision. Restrictive covenants had been written in deeds in 1956 by Lookout Land Company and duly recorded. The Browns acquired title in 1961 and Morris and Pierson in 1964. The Lookout Land covenants restricted the lots to "residential purposes" and buildings on each lot to "one detached single family dwelling." There were minimum cost and size, setback, and minimum area requirements as to lots. The defendants were constructing their building on land zoned in 1948 for business purposes, part of which was not on land in the subdivision. Defendants argued, among other things, that there were houses that violated the location requirements of the restrictions. That part of the opinion is omitted, but the court rejected it, distinguishing between locational deviations and restrictions as to the type and character of buildings. Only that part of the opinion dealing with the zoning conflict is reproduced.]

* * *

Appellees here contend that the property upon which appellees were constructing their building, contrary to the restrictions in their deed, was zoned by the City of Gadsden for commercial use some years before the land was subdivided and the present restrictions placed thereon.

The restrictions placed on the property by the owners when it was subdivided are more restrictive than those prescribed by the zoning ordinance. The ordinance permits the property to be used for a single-family residence in addition to business use. Private restrictions subsequent to valid zoning restrictions, may be more but not less restrictive. Under such circumstances, the restrictions here at issue will prevail. Bluett v. Cook County, 19 Ill.App.2d 172, 153 N.E.2d 305; Connelly v. Morris, 125 N.E.2d 765 (Ohio Com.Pl.).

It has been held by this court in McKee v. Club–View Heights, 230 Ala. 652, 654, 162 So. 671 (1, 2), 673, as follows:

> "It is well settled by the repeated decisions of this court that the owner of land, in making a sale thereof, may retain an easement or impose a servitude in the land sold, and, when not in restraint of trade, may retain in himself certain uses, which would otherwise pass to the grantee. 'Such retention, or limitation of the use, being a condition upon which the estate is acquired, attaches as an infirmity in the estate itself, and as a privilege or easement in the estate of the grantor, in whose favor the limitation is imposed.' Webb v. Robbins, 77 Ala. 176, 183. The grantee in accepting the deed containing such conditions or covenants accepts the title encumbered thereby, and is bound as though he had signed the conveyance, and 'he cannot complain, for he purchased and paid for only a qualified use.' Morris & Morris v. Tuscaloosa Manufacturing Co., 83 Ala. 565, 571, 3 So. 689, 691."

Also, in Thrasher v. Bear, 239 Ala. 438, 440, 195 So. 441, 443, we observed:

> "The respective rights of the parties in such premises to enforce building restrictions against another grantee is based on the fact that such scheme constitutes a part of the consideration. Vol. 4, Thompson on Real Property, §§ 3399, 3441; 18 C.J. p. 397, § 463."

Also, we said in Scheuer v. Britt, 218 Ala. 270, 118 So. 658:

> "In such cases the equitable right to enforce such mutual covenants is rested on the fact that the building scheme forms an inducement to buy, and becomes a part of the consideration. The buyer submits to a burden upon his lot because of the fact that a like burden is imposed on his neighbor's lot, operating to the benefit of both, and carries a mutual burden resting on the seller and the purchasers. * * * "

We hold that the trial court erred in denying relief to complainants and in dismissing their bill of complaint, as amended. On remandment of this cause, the trial court upon finality of this opinion will forthwith enter a decree enjoining the respondents, their agents, servants or employees, their heirs and successors, sublessees or assigns from erecting upon said property, described in the bill of complaint, any building other than a one-family residence as provided in the restrictions and the deeds to said property, and from using said property for any other purpose.

The decree of the trial court is reversed and the cause remanded for compliance with this opinion.

Note

Unlike Rofe v. Robinson, this case involved a situation in which the land had been zoned commercial prior to imposition of the restrictive covenants. The result is the same. There is nothing to prevent a developer from imposing more restrictive limitations upon the use of his land than those imposed by the local government. Basically, restrictive covenants do not supersede zoning, nor does zoning by itself vitiate the restrictive covenants. Probably a fair approximation of the majority view is that if the covenant is less restrictive, the ordinance will prevail and if the covenant is more restrictive, the covenant will prevail. Neither is superseded nor eliminated; the more restrictive prevails.

As Rofe v. Robinson indicates, however, a carefully considered zoning amendment that is less restrictive than the covenants is some indication that the conditions in the restricted area may have changed to the point that the covenants should no longer be enforced in equity.

E. ALTERATION AND TERMINATION

HEFFNER v. LITCHFIELD GOLF CO.

Supreme Court of South Carolina, 1972.
258 S.C. 447, 189 S.E.2d 3.

BRAILSFORD, JUSTICE: This is an appeal from an order of the circuit court denying an injunction against the proposed construction of tennis courts on two lots owned by the respondent, Litchfield Golf Company, Inc., hereinafter called Litchfield.

In 1969 the appellant purchased from Litchfield lot number 33, section E, as shown on the recorded plat of Litchfield Golf Club and subdivision. The recorded plat contained no restrictions on land use within the subdivision, which consists of 580 lots laid out with maximum exposure to the eighteen hole golf course and related facilities. However, all conveyances of lots within the subdivision, including the conveyance to appellant, have contained identical provisions, twenty in number, which impose limitations on the use of the lot conveyed. The first provision restricts the lot to residential use. The twentieth provision, at the heart of the case, reads:

> It is understood and agreed that these covenants, conditions and restrictions are made solely for the benefit of the Grantor and Grantee herein and may be changed at any time by mutual consent in writing of the parties hereto, their heirs, successors or assigns.

Lots 30, 31 and 32 of section E had been sold by Litchfield before the appellant purchased lot 33. These four lots front on serpentine Eagle Avenue which meanders between the eighth and ninth holes, the clubhouse area, the fifth, sixth and seventh holes, the practice range and the tennis court area. A total of thirty-three lots front on this street.

Twenty-eight of these, including lots 30–33, abut directly on the golf course. Lot 30 is the westernmost of the four lots, and it is bounded by the tennis court area on the west. Sometime after the appellant completed construction of an expensive home on his lot, Litchfield reacquired lots 30 and 31 and made known its intention to expand the club's tennis court area by utilizing lots 30 and 31. The appellant, whose home is separated from the existing courts by lots 30–32, each fronting one hundred feet on Eagle Avenue, contends that these lots are burdened with restrictions which preclude the intended use.

Because of the express limitation contained in the above quoted provision of the indenture, appellant has no standing to enforce the restrictive covenants imposed upon lots 30 and 31 on the occasion of their original sale by Litchfield. Litchfield and the grantees in that deed reserved to themselves the right to modify the restrictions imposed on the use of the lots, and Litchfield presently stands simultaneously as original grantor and as successor to the original grantees of those lots. Hence, the covenant, as such, does not bar the intended use of the premises by Litchfield.

Appellant's suit must fail unless it is supported by the doctrine of reciprocal negative easements by implication, which has been expounded in a number of our decisions * * *.

* * *

Mutuality of covenant and consideration, which are essential to the existence of a general scheme of development enforceable, inter se, by the purchasers of lots in a subdivision, may be implied only when the common grantor manifests his intention to subject the parcels conveyed to common restrictions for the benefit of all grantees. By the express terms of the twentieth provision, uniformly included in the Litchfield deeds, the benefit of the restrictions in each is limited to the parties thereto, who reserve the right to modify or abrogate by mutual assent. This directly precludes an implication that the grantor intended to create restrictions for the benefit of all purchasers in the subdivision. By near unanimous authority, no enforceable general scheme of development is inferable in the face of a provision of this tenor. See the cases collected at 19 A.L.R.2d 1274, 1282 (1951), and 4 A.L.R.3d 570, 573 (1965); 26 C.J.S. Deeds § 167(2) at 1145 (1956); 20 Am.Jur.2d, Covenants, Conditions, and Restrictions, Sec. 178 (1965); Humphrey v. Beall, 215 N.C. 15, 200 S.E. 918 (1939); Brighton by the Sea, Inc. v. Rivkin, 201 App.Div. 726, 195 N.Y.S. 198 (1922).

* * *

Affirmed.

Moss, C.J., and Lewis, Bussey and Littlejohn, JJ., concur.

Notes

1. Regardless of whether both parties have the power to release the lots from the restriction or the subdivider reserves the right to release

remaining lots from the burden, the courts generally have been quick to say that there is no general plan and the restriction may not be enforced. See Suttle v. Bailey, 68 N.M. 283, 361 P.2d 325 (1961); and Maples v. Horton, 239 N.C. 394, 80 S.E.2d 38 (1954). And see Bride v. Finegan, 226 Md. 356, 174 A.2d 70 (1961) refusing to find a general development plan where covenants said the subdivider must consent to further subdivision of parcels. In Brighton by the Sea v. Rivkin, 201 App.Div. 726, 195 N.Y.S. 198 (1922), the plaintiff, who owned 10 blocks of land, developed it by erecting 300 dwellings. The deeds to each lot, including the one to the defendant, bound the grantee not to conduct any trade or business on the lot. But the grantor was not bound by the covenants in these deeds to restrict all of the lots in like manner. Further, power to alter or modify or annul any of the restrictions by agreement with the owner of the particular lot was expressly reserved in the grantor. The grantor sought to enjoin defendant from conducting a business on her lot without grantor's consent. The court said: "The provisions reserving grantor control over the restrictions prevented any mutuality of covenant and consideration between the grantees, and marked the covenant as being for the benefit of the grantor." The court held that there should be no interim decree of specific performance, and that whether one should ultimately issue or not should await full trial of the action so the court could determine whether specific performance was "equitable" under all the circumstances. In Baldwin v. Barbon Corp., 773 S.W.2d 681 (Tex.App.1989) the court held that a developer who had expressly reserved the right to amend or alter the covenants was authorized to remove residential restrictions on some of the lots (he still owned several lots in the subdivision).

2. It is not uncommon to find a provision in the restrictive covenants stating that provisions in them may be amended or modified by a writing signed by a substantial percentage of the lot owners in the subdivision (normally anywhere from 60% to 75%). Of course, these are sometimes written in an ambiguous way. See Pearce v. Scarcello, 920 S.W.2d 643 (Mo.App.1996). The original covenants required wooden shingles on roofs. Seven houseowners replaced their shingles with non-wooden material, after a majority of the homeowners filed amended covenants with the Recorder of Deeds. The court said the covenant had not been properly amended and ordered the removal of the shingles. Poor drafting creates most of the ambiguity problems; for example, the covenants state that they are to run for 30 years, after which time they shall be automatically extended for 10 year periods unless a majority of the owners record an agreement to change the covenants. This fairly common language creates a problem of interpretation, i.e., can the owners modify the covenants during the first 30 years, or only during the 10 year periods? In several cases the courts have said that the covenants cannot be changed during the initial period, even though that may not be what the grantor contemplated. See, e.g., Boyles v. Hausmann, 2 Neb.App. 388, 509 N.W.2d 676 (Neb.App.1993) and Kauffman v. Roling, 851 S.W.2d 789 (Mo.App.1993).

If restrictive covenants serve to create an interest in land, how can that interest be violated or limited by a majority vote of the landowners? Once a property interest has been created, even if there is only one dissenter to some change affecting that interest, is it not a taking of his property to make the change? Obviously, the concept that the change may be made, based upon provisions in the restrictive covenants, draws upon their contractual heritage.

3. In Finucan v. Coronet Homes, Inc., 259 S.C. 142, 191 S.E.2d 5 (1972), the South Carolina Supreme Court reversed a lower court ruling that held that owners of lots in the original 1957 subdivision had no standing to enforce covenants pertaining to a 1960 addition to the subdivision. The 1957 subdivision had 38 lots in it, and the covenants were subject to change by a majority of the lot owners. The 1960 addition had identical restrictive covenants, and the court believed that the 1960 plat plus the original 38 lots constituted one subdivision, and that change could be effected only by a majority of the entire (1957 and 1960) subdivision.

WEST ALAMEDA HEIGHTS HOMEOWNERS ASS'N v. BOARD OF COUNTY COMMISSIONERS OF JEFFERSON COUNTY

Supreme Court of Colorado, 1969.
169 Colo. 491, 458 P.2d 253.

[This was a class action by the homeowners association and certain individuals to enjoin the construction of two large shopping facilities on the property in question by Woolworth and Safeway. The covenants restricted the use of the land to residential, and the trial court declared the covenants null and void. The subdivision was a large one of over 350 lots, only 80 to 85 of which were undeveloped. The only commercial uses were a service station and a garden center located on land originally reserved in the plat for commercial use. Apartments were on other land set aside for commercial purposes. The proposed shopping facilities would be on residential land as restricted by the covenants. The action was precipitated by an application by George Newton, the original developer, to re-zone part of the blocks retained by him which front on a four-lane highway. Outside of the subdivision and close by, there had been extensive commercial development. The trial court invalidated the covenants on the basis that the character of the area had changed and that the subject land was not suitable for residential use and thus enforcement of the covenants would not be equitable.]

DAY, JUSTICE.

* * *

QUESTION TO BE DETERMINED: DO THE FACTS OF THIS CASE AND THE LAW APPLICABLE THERETO JUSTIFY THE TRIAL COURT IN RULING THAT THE COVENANTS RESTRICTING TO RESIDENTIAL USE BLOCKS 13, 14 *and* 15 NO LONGER APPLY?

We answer the question in the negative and hold that the covenants are valid and enforceable.

The pertinent rule of law applicable to this case is most recently set out in Zavislak v. Shipman, 147 Colo. 184, 362 P.2d 1053, wherein this court adopted the language of McArthur v. Hood Rubber Co., 221 Mass. 372, 109 N.E. 162, as follows:

" ' * * * When the purpose for which the restriction was imposed has come to an end, and where the use of the tract of land for whose benefit it was established has so utterly changed that no party to the bill could be heard to enforce it in equity or would suffer any damage by its violation, * * * a proper case is made out for equitable relief. * * * ' "

Parties plaintiffs and defendants all rely on our pronouncement in *Zavislak*. The court, in striking down the covenants, attempted to apply the same rule of law. We hold, however, that the court misconceived and misapplied the rule to changes and developments outside of and beyond the subdivision itself. This is made evident by the court's reference to the changed traffic patterns on Wadsworth and Alameda and the development of Villa Italia Shopping Center and other developments east of the Alameda and Wadsworth intersection.

The true test here, however, as to whether the purpose of the restrictions has come to an end, is the development of the subdivision which is the subject of the covenants subsequent to their creation. Thus the courts look to whether the original purposes of insuring maintenance of residential character for the subdivision has been abandoned or changed by acquiescence or passiveness of the subdivision residents.

Newton, in planning the property with the restrictions which he imposed, intended to insure the maintenance of the residential character for the subdivision. That purpose has continued to the present time, and the effect of it is demonstrated by what has happened to land outside of its perimeter over which the West Alameda Heights residents had no control. It is undisputed that in the subdivision wherein the covenants did control no change of the use contemplated when the plat was filed has occurred. Only the property originally platted for use of commercial enterprises thereon has been occupied as such.

Another test announced in the *Zavislak* case is whether the parties would suffer any damage by the removal of the covenant. Touching on this phase the testimony of the individual plaintiffs was that their property would be subject to substantial decrease in value. One of plaintiffs' witnesses—a professional land planner—depicted the foreseeable increase in traffic to and from the proposed shopping facility with concomitant increase in noise, fumes, and hazard to children. The Traffic and Safety Engineer for Jefferson County stated that although he probably could control increased traffic through the residential area by the use of traffic signals and one-way streets, he candidly admitted that such a traffic pattern would inconvenience the homeowners as much as it might deter shoppers from driving through the area. There was testimony as to the present pleasant aspects of the neighborhood, undisturbed by the commercial activity beyond the borders.

Contrariwise, the defendants did not prove that the purpose of the protective covenants had come to an end; that the land use within the tract had changed from what it was intended to be at the time the plat was filed; and that no person would suffer any damage by its violation. The evidence therefore is contrary to the court's finding that plaintiffs will suffer no damage from commercial use of the subject property.

Cases are numerous from other jurisdictions wherein covenants have been sought to be removed because subject lands would be more valuable for commercial than for residential purposes, and wherein there were conditions such as the presence of commercial uses nearby, heavy street traffic on the perimeter of the tract, and some commercial property within a primarily residential subdivision. But the weight of authority supports the view that *changes outside* of the tract will not warrant the lifting of restrictive covenants affecting property within the subdivision if the covenants are still a benefit to the owners of the property under the restrictions. Robertson v. Nichols, 92 Cal.App.2d 201, 206 P.2d 898; Batman v. Creighton, 101 So.2d 587 (Fla.App.); Cawthon v. Anderson, 211 Ga. 77, 84 S.E.2d 66; Redfern Lawns Civic Ass'n, et al. v. Currie Pontiac Co., 328 Mich. 463, 44 N.W.2d 8; Weinstein v. Swartz, 3 N.J. 80, 68 A.2d 865; Chuba v. Glasgow, 61 N.M. 302, 299 P.2d 774; Frey v. Poynor, 369 P.2d 168 (Okla.); Pitts v. Brown, 215 S.C. 122, 54 S.E.2d 538; Bullock v. Steinmil Realty, Inc., 1 Misc.2d 46, 145 N.Y.S.2d 331, aff'd 3 A.D.2d 806, 161 N.Y.S.2d 602.

Normal growth and change and the possibility of encroachment of commercial uses, we can infer, were contemplated when the covenants and the master plan of development were created by the original owner and platter. There would be no need for the covenants to protect the subdivisions from inroads of commercial expansion if it were not expected that such might take place. As long as the original purpose of the covenants can still be accomplished and substantial benefit will inure to the restricted area by their enforcement, the covenants stand even though the subject property has a greater value if used for other purposes. See 4 A.L.R.2d 1111.

A comment in Cowling v. Colligan, 158 Tex. 458, 312 S.W.2d 943, appeals to us:

> "The reasoning of the courts is that if because of changed conditions outside the restricted area one lot or tract were permitted to drop from under the protective cover of residential-only restrictions, the owner of the adjoining lot would then have an equal claim on the conscience of the court, and, in due course, all other lots would fall like tenpins, thus circumventing and nullifying the restriction and destroying the essentially residential character of the entire area."

In the case of protective covenants, it has sometimes been held that changes within the affected area may result in modification or removal of the covenant because the changes were within the control of those entitled to enforce the covenant. In other words, the doctrines of abandonment, estoppel and waiver are applicable. *See* Thodos v. Shirk, 248 Iowa 172, 79 N.W.2d 733; Mechling v. Dawson, 234 Ky. 318, 28

S.W.2d 18; Greer v. Bornstein, 246 Ky. 286, 54 S.W.2d 927; Tull v. Doctors Bldg. Inc., 255 N.C. 23, 120 S.E.2d 817. However, as to changes in conditions occurring outside the area restricted, the parties affected have no control whatever, and the doctrines of waiver, abandonment and estoppel are not applicable. Here, the problem presents itself as to whether the outside conditions affect the entire subdivision in a way that the restrictive purposes of the protective covenants would be defeated. As stated in Thodos v. Shirk, supra:

> "In both cases the factual situation largely governs as to whether or not equity will refuse to enforce the restrictions for the reason that by so doing the result would be oppressive and inequitable without any appreciable value to other property in the restricted area. It has been said that in order for this equitable defense of change of conditions to arise, there must be a change in the character of the surrounding neighborhood sufficient to make it impossible any longer to secure in substantial degree the benefits sought to be realized through the performance of the building restriction."

The construction of Villa Italia Shopping Center and of other commercial properties outside of West Alameda Heights, but in close proximity to it, have not changed the residential character of the subdivision. If the changed conditions outside the tract have made the particular property held by the owner since the original platting less desirable for residential use than it previously was, this is not to say that the whole tract has been made unfit for residential use. On the contrary, the evidence shows that the subdivision is a residential area of high quality, with expensive homes and quiet streets. The construction of commercial facilities nearby are all the more reason why the covenants for West Alameda Heights must be strictly enforced. The covenants have no meaning if external forces and pressures result in their removal.

The judgment is reversed and the cause remanded to the trial court with directions to enter a permanent injunction as prayed for in the complaint.

HODGES, GROVES and LEE, JJ., concur.

Notes

1. In Redfern Lawns Civic Ass'n v. Currie Pontiac Co., 328 Mich. 463, 44 N.W.2d 8 (1950), cited in the principal case, the Michigan court said: "The only equitable consideration in the case at bar appears to be the undesirability of using the lots in question for resident purposes. On this point it may be observed that there must of necessity be a dividing line somewhere. The original subdividers made no provision for possible business lots along Grand River avenue. It is inevitable that all lots on the fringe of a residential district may, with the changes of the surrounding neighborhood, become a buffer between the residential area and a business or commercial area. It is one of the factors inherent in considering the nature and value of such property. To lift the restriction under consideration here on the lots in question would only cut down this desirable residential area and create

another buffer area. To permit the dividing line to be moved in the case at bar thereby creating another buffer district, now composed of both residences and vacant property, does not present sufficiently strong equitable considerations."

2. In comparison with the principal case, see City of Little Rock v. Joyner, 212 Ark. 508, 206 S.W.2d 446 (1947), in which the Arkansas court ruled that in a situation in which the conditions surrounding the property in question had so changed that the usefulness of the area for residential purposes had been substantially impaired or perhaps even destroyed by the development of the business district, the court would decree cancellation of the restrictive covenants. The theory was that enforcement of a restrictive covenant may be rendered inequitable, oppressive and unfair where the nature of the neighborhood has changed substantially. Clearly, the implication is that changes in the unrestricted area which *surrounds* the restricted area are of some consequence. What if a restrictive covenant prohibits conducting a business on the premises, the land is situated across the street from a fully developed residential area, and the landowners in the latter area assert that if the restriction is removed, they will suffer grave and irreparable injury? Should the covenant be cancelled? See Storthz v. Midland Hills Land Co., 192 Ark. 273, 90 S.W.2d 772 (1936). What are the considerations involved?

3. There have been a good many of these change of character cases in recent years, and the problem usually comes from the effect of the commercialization of nearby property on border or buffer lots (as illustrated by the principal case). What if reasonable minds might differ on whether a change in character has occurred? In Semachko v. Hopko, 35 Ohio App.2d 205, 301 N.E.2d 560 (1973), the court stated that "reasonable minds can come to different conclusions whether there was a substantial change in the character of the neighborhood * * * so as to nullify the deed restrictions * * *. Under such circumstances, a court of equity will not enforce such restriction." Do you agree? In Albino v. Pacific First Fed. Sav. and Loan Ass'n, 257 Or. 473, 479 P.2d 760 (1971), the Oregon court said that in order to refuse to enforce the restrictions "the effect of the change upon the restricted area" must be "such as to 'clearly neutralize the benefits of the restrictions to the point of defeating the object and purpose of the covenant'" and that it is not enough that because of external changes the restricted residential area may now be more valuable for commercial purposes. In Inabinet v. Booe, 262 S.C. 81, 202 S.E.2d 643 (1974), it was stated that the changes must be "so radical as to practically destroy the essential objectives and purposes of the agreement." See similarly, Murphey v. Gray, 84 Ariz. 299, 327 P.2d 751 (1958); Eilers v. Alewel, 393 S.W.2d 584 (Mo.1965); and Paschen v. Pashkow, 63 Ill.App.2d 56, 211 N.E.2d 576 (1965).

4. Consider:

(a) Whether restrictive covenants in an older area of the city can ever be effectively used in the battle against urban blight and for urban reconditioning.

(b) The implications of "changes in the neighborhood" cases for the lawyer who is sitting down to draft a set of restrictions for a current development.

(c) The effect in change of neighborhood cases of such factual elements as (1) consent by a majority of lot owners in the subdivision to the change; (2) previous uncontested violations; (3) a showing that owing to changes outside the subdivision the restrictions no longer enhance the market value of the restricted land; (4) a showing, such as was made in the principal case, that the buffer lots have suffered greatly in value to the protection of the lots farther in; (5) the plaintiff has himself violated the covenant. These elements suggest other grounds sometimes used by courts when refusing to enforce covenants by injunction: (1) estoppel; (2) "unclean hands"; (3) acquiescence; (4) waiver; (5) abandonment; (6) laches. How do these concepts differ? Would you prepare and prove your case, for a client who wants to break the covenant, in the same way regardless of whether you were stressing change in neighborhood or any one of the six other "grounds" just listed? See 5 Powell, Real Property ¶ 679 (1990) and 2 American Law of Property §§ 9.38–9.39 (1952).

(d) Assuming a sufficient change in the neighborhood has occurred, is it appropriate to refuse to enforce restrictions piecemeal at only some places in the subdivision? See Tull v. Doctors Bldg. Inc., 255 N.C. 23, 120 S.E.2d 817 (1961) where the court refused to consider changes outside the subdivision and where it refused to approach nonenforcement on a piecemeal basis. The case is critically reviewed by Kinsey, Restrictive Covenants—Effect of Change of Conditions on Enforcement, 41 N.C.L.Rev. 147 (1962).

(e) Whether, if a court refuses to enforce a restriction by injunction because of a change in the neighborhood, this also bars action on the covenant at law for damages.

See on most of these and other points, II American Law of Property § 9.39 (1952); Annot., Incidental Use of Dwelling for Business or Professional Purposes as Violation of Covenant Restricting Use to Residential Purposes, 21 A.L.R.3d 641 (1968); and Annot., Restrictive Covenant Limiting Land Use to "Private Residence" or "Private Residential Purposes": Interpretation and Application, 43 A.L.R.4th 71 (1986).

5. How long will a restrictive covenant endure, assuming no express time limitation, no change in the character of the neighborhood or other reason for denial of judicial enforcement? The rule against restraints on alienation is chiefly concerned with limitations on *estates* in land, not with promises respecting the use of land. See Restatement of Property § 394 (1944). And the same can be said of the Rule against Perpetuities. A comment under section 399 of the Restatement says that any "undesirable freezing of a locality into a mode of use unsuited to social interests" can be prevented by rules developed in equity without calling on the Rule against Perpetuities. The common assumption that covenants are limited to 25, or 30, or 99 years or some other magical period is not justified as a matter of case law. There are so-called "clearing statutes" in some states. In Wisconsin, for example, Wis.Stat.Ann. § 893.15(5) (1966) limits such restrictions to 60 years, unless renewed by fresh recording. Some states limit the duration to 20 or 30 years. Ga.Code Ann. § 29–301 (1980) and Minn.Stat.Ann. § 500.20 (1947). See also N.Y.Law Revision Commissioners Report 691–780 (1951). And recall the Uniform Act Relating to Reverter of Realty previously noted. Clearing statutes are discussed in Ascher, Urban Redevelopment:

Problems and Practices 258–260 (1953), and Clark, Real Covenants and Other Interests Which "Run with Land" 199 (2d ed. 1947).

6. But quite apart from the maximum legal life of a restriction on the use of land, there is the practical problem of the draftsman—should he impose on the land a restriction for the indefinite future? Or should he place an express time limitation on the restriction? Or should he provide for a community association and either give it power to renew the restriction at the end of a designated period by affirmative action, or power to permit the restriction automatically to renew itself by non-action? Note the technique suggested in the FHA outline of protective covenants. The nature of the restriction is of major importance in considering questions like this. Imposing the "wrong kind" of restrictions on land for the indefinite future has often brought criticism of all restrictions and explains the movement for clearing statutes. Yet a lot owner may want the "right kind" of restrictions to continue indefinitely. The resolution of this conundrum may lie not in clearing statutes or even in case law, but in governmental administrative or judicial review procedures yet uninvented. One other thing about clearing statutes: When does the clearing period start? If it starts with the imposition of restrictions on the particular lot, then it may happen that restrictions expire on your lot long before they do on your neighbor's.

In England and in at least one American state, statutes provide for special actions for removal of restrictions imposed by covenants. The English statute permits an action in the Lands Tribunal and discharge or modification of a restrictive covenant on (1) a showing of change in character of the property or the neighborhood, or (2) a showing that the proposed discharge or modification will not injure the persons entitled to the benefit of the restriction. Volume 7 of the Planning and Compensation Reports of the Land Tribunal (1957) reports numerous cases on discharge and modification of covenants under Subsection (1) of section 84 of the Law of Property Act of 1925. See Preston and Newsom, Restrictive Covenants Ch. 7 (3d ed. 1960); N.Y.Real Property Actions & Proc.Law § 1951 (McKinney 1979); and Abbott, Statutory Provisions for the Modification and Discharge of Restrictive Covenants Affecting Freehold Lands, 18 Faculty L.Rev. 141 (1958). See also an article in 110 Solicitors' Journal 521 (1966) on The Law Commission and Restrictive Covenants.

An annotation discussing the validity and effect of *contractual* provisions relating to the revocation or modification of covenants is found in Annot., 4 A.L.R.3d 570 (1965). These contractual provisions may place the power to revoke or modify in the original owner or subdivider, the grantees or lot owners, or revocation or modification may be dependent on the happening of certain described occurrences. The annotator notes a trend toward the vesting of such powers in the owners or toward allowing the lot owners to participate with the developer in this process.

A Note on Community Associations as Private Governments

The popularity of condominium developments, retirement communities, planned unit developments and even new towns has created a number of legal issues, some of which have already been touched on in this chapter. All of these modern types of large scale residential developments utilize restrictive covenants to set the parameters of land uses, and most of them rely on a property owners association or community association to govern the rules created by the covenants, and to make new rules through a procedure set forth in the covenants. Frequently, conflict arises where the association is seeking to enforce the covenant against one owner. In some respects, especially in larger covenant-ruled communities, the association takes on the role of a private government with many powers; and, in running the association, the question of such niceties as "constitutional rights" is often invoked. In an article in the Wall Street Journal, Sept. 22, 1994, p. 1, Mitchell Pacelle, a staff reporter for the newspaper, reports on a number of disputes between owners and associations and also on the spread of this sort of private government: "About 100,000 of the roughly 300,000 dwelling units in Montgomery County, an affluent expanse of suburban Washington that includes Rockville, are ruled by community associations, including nearly all newly built homes.[25] * * * [An owner's] yard and home are very much the business of the association, a private, government-like body that enforces strict rules about everything from paint and storm doors to sandboxes and birdhouses." Lawyers who are consulted on disputes between owners and associations often turn to the the Community Associations Institute in Alexandria, Virginia an organization that provides publications and a great deal of information. See the Institute website, http://www.caionline.com/.

Many of the disputes over covenant enforcement stem from antagonisms among neighbors and only occasionally are those antagonisms strong enough that a client will invest in legal fees and court costs in an attempt to challenge the association. However, the number of people willing to do so is growing steadily. The lawyer's role in these battles should go beyond counseling about the law of covenants; he or she should look to the real issues of life that led to the standoff and be willing to counsel clients thoughtfully about matters other than legalities.

One case that generated much comment was Nahrstedt v. Lakeside Village Condominium Association, Inc., 8 Cal.4th 361, 33 Cal.Rptr.2d 63, 878 P.2d 1275 (1994). A homeowner in a 530–unit condominium complex sued to prevent the association from enforcing a restriction against the keeping of animals in any unit in the development. She alleged that the restriction was unreasonable as applied to her because she kept her three cats indoors, they made no noise, and were in no way a nuisance; she also sought damages for invasion of privacy and emotional distress. The intermediate appellate court divided, as did the California Supreme Court. The majority opinion in the supreme court wrote an extensive guide to the history of associations, now called "common interest developments" in California.[26] The opinion concluded that as a matter of policy it would be unwise for courts to review restrictions on a case-by-case "as applied" basis because that "would impose substantial litigation costs on the owners through their homeowners associa-

25. Various estimates place the number of persons living in dwellings ruled by covenants, nationwide, at 25 to 30 million.

26. The California statute governing common interest developments is Cal.Civ. Code § 1350 et seq. Of some interest is the fact that several legislators have complained that the act is complicated and difficult for associations to follow; on Feb. 20, 1997, a Resolution, SR 10 was introduced to create a working group to review the act, to be composed of "representatives of common interest development owners, community association boards, management companies, and other practitioners."

tion, which would have to defend not only against owners contesting the application of the [covenants] to them, but also against owners contesting any case-by-case exceptions the homeowners association might make. In short, it is difficult to imagine what could more disrupt the harmony of a common interest development than the course proposed by the dissent." The dissenting opinion stressed the values of pet ownership, the fact that the plaintiff's cats were never outside her unit (they were only discovered by neighbors peering into her window), and said this about the underlying issues of private government:

> Our true task in this turmoil is to strike a balance between the governing rights accorded a condominium association and the individual freedom of its members. To fulfill that function, a reviewing court must view with a skeptic's eye restrictions driven by fear, anxiety, or intolerance. In any community, we do not exist in vacuo. There are many annoyances we tolerate because not to do so would be repressive and place the freedom of others at risk.

> In contravention, the majority's failure to consider the real burden imposed by the pet restriction unfortunately belittles and trivializes the interest at stake here. Pet ownership substantially enhances the quality of life for those who desire it. When others are not only undisturbed by, but completely unaware of, the presence of pets being enjoyed by their neighbors, the balance of benefit and burden is rendered disproportionate and unreasonable, rebutting any presumption of validity. Their view, shorn of grace and guiding philosophy, is devoid of the humanity that must temper the interpretation and application of all laws, for in a civilized society that is the source of their authority. As judicial architects of the rules of life, we better serve when we construct halls of harmony rather than walls of wrath.

The court remanded the case to the court of appeals to determine whether the covenant was reasonable, "not by reference to facts that are specific to the objecting homeowner, but by reference to the common interest development as a whole." The court also said that the recorded covenant is presumed reasonable "and will be enforced uniformly against all residents of the common interest development unless the restriction is arbitrary, imposes burdens on the use of lands it affects that substantially outweigh the restriction's benefits to the development's residents, or violates a fundamental public policy."

Some other cases in the same vein are Hidden Harbour Estates v. Basso, 393 So.2d 637 (Fla.App.1981) (the court drew a distinction between association rules in the recorded covenants and those imposed by the association board of directors, according more judicial review to rules not in the covenants); Noble v. Murphy, 34 Mass.App.Ct. 452, 612 N.E.2d 266 (1993).In Woodmoor Improvement Association v. Brenner, 919 P.2d 928 (Colo.App. 1996) the court held that a homeowner could keep his satellite dish despite a covenant against outside aerials or antennas, because the architectural committee of the association had approved his plans, thus creating an estoppel against the association. Also see, Uriel Reichman, Residential Private Governments: An Introductory Survey, 43 U. Chi. L. Rev. 253 (1976); Robert G. Natelson, Consent, Coercion, and "Reasonableness" in Private

Law: The Special Case of the Property Owners Association, 51 Ohio State L. J. 41 (1990); Comment, Beyond Nahrstedt: Reviewing Restrictions Governing Life in a Property Owner Association, 42 UCLA L. Rev. 837 (1995).

Are homeowners in condominiums immune from those who would assert constitutional rights, if doing so would violate a covenant? This interesting question was presented in a New Jersey case, Guttenberg Taxpayers and Rentpayers Association v. Galaxy Towers Condominium Association, 296 N.J.Super. 101, 686 A.2d 344 (1995) affirmed, after remand 297 N.J.Super. 309, 688 A.2d 108 (1996). The covenant in this case seemed to bar distribution of political literature in a three-building, 1015 unit condominium complex. The plaintiffs sought a declaratory judgement and injunction to allow distribution of information about an upcoming school board election by slipping literature under doors. The plaintiffs alleged that the condominium complex was in essence the functional equivalent of a company town, citing Marsh v. Alabama, 326 U.S. 501, 66 S.Ct. 276, 90 L.Ed. 265 (1946). The court remanded to the trial court for a full hearing, stating that the case involved balancing of property rights and free speech rights. The trial court held for the plaintiffs, finding that they had no meaningful alternative method of access to the large number of registered voters who lived in the complex (mailing literature could not be accomplished in time to provide information about the election). The injunction was affirmed without opinion. Also see David J. Kennedy, Residential Associations as State Actors: Regulating the Impact of Gated Communities on Nonmembers, 105 Yale L.J. 761 (1995).

In the planned community or new town situation, where the only government is the association, the issue of incorporation is frequently raised. The movement to incorporate may be based on democratic ideals or it may be fueled by economic concerns (a desire to relieve the burden of assessments by securing state turnback revenues). The largest new town in America, Columbia, Maryland has been caught up in this issue. See Michael Janofsky, Citizens Debate Change in a Maryland Suburb, New York Times, Feb. 26, 1995, p. 11.

MORRIS v. NEASE

Supreme Court of Appeals of West Virginia, 1977.
160 W.Va. 774, 238 S.E.2d 844.

[In 1972, Dr. Nease opened his chiropractic clinic. Some of his neighbors sued to close his clinic based upon a restrictive covenant from the early 1900's limiting the use to "dwelling or residential purposes, or purposes of like nature" and which also provided that the covenant would run with the land. The trial court issued a permanent injunction. On appeal, Dr. Nease argued that the restrictions had been nullified due to changes in the character of the neighborhood. He also raised other equitable defenses such as acquiescence.]

NEELY, JUSTICE:

* * *

West Virginia recognizes the commonly accepted legal proposition that changes in a neighborhood's character can nullify restrictive covenants affecting neighborhood property. See Wallace v. St. Clair, 147 W.Va. 377 at 397, 127 S.E.2d 742 at 755 (1962). Technically, there is a distinction between changes which occur within the restricted neighborhood itself and changes in the surrounding, unrestricted area. The "problem of *change of conditions* arises where the complainant's and defendant's lots lie within a restricted subdivision, but the area surrounding the restricted subdivision has been so changed by the acts of third persons that the building scheme for the subdivision has been frustrated through no fault of the lot owners themselves." 2 American Law of Property 445–446 (A.J. Casner ed. 1952, emphasis added) [hereinafter cited as 2 American Law of Property]. When, however, the change in the neighborhood's character is a result of "violations within the subdivision itself, a problem of *abandonment* rather than change of conditions is involved." 2 American Law of Property 446 (emphasis added).

Some of the evidence in this case concerns the complainants' own violations of the restrictive covenants. This evidence properly goes to the question of abandonment, since the complainants' property clearly lies within the restricted area. Other evidence concerns non-residential uses of near-by property, some of which may lie within, and some outside, the restricted area. This evidence could show either abandonment or change of conditions, depending on the exact location of the property having the non-residential use. We will consider all the evidence relating to the changing character of the neighborhood here, and we will refrain from drawing technical distinctions between abandonment and change of conditions. Regardless of how it is characterized or labeled, the fundamental issue of this case is the viability of restrictive covenants in a changing neighborhood.

The evidence shows that a substantial amount of commercial property is located a short distance from Dr. Nease's clinic. Twenty-seventh Street, the nearest cross street to his Third Avenue clinic, has a maintenance company, a brokerage company, a repair shop, and a beauty shop, all within two blocks of Third Avenue. Another beauty shop is located on Twenty-eighth Street within half a block of Third Avenue. The 2800 block of Third Avenue itself has a service station, a laundry, and a church, while the 2600 block, has an antique shop, a church, and a ball field.

These properties significantly change the original residential character of the neighborhood. It does not follow, however, that the entire neighborhood is perforce released from the burden of the restrictive covenants. On the contrary, every effort must be exerted to protect the unchanged portions of residential neighborhoods when businesses begin to encroach on the fringes. The obvious danger is that restrictions throughout an entire area can eventually be destroyed through succeeding block-by-block changes in the neighborhood's character:

> [A]s soon as the border lots are freed, the next tier of lots is put in the same position as that in which the border lots were originally.

Thus by a step-by-step process the restrictions must be relaxed until the plan is totally defeated. [2 American Law of Property 446]

To guard against such an eventuality courts in a majority of jurisdictions have evolved the rule that "if the benefits of the original plan for a restricted subdivision can still be realized for the protection of interior lots, the restrictions should be enforced against the border lots, notwithstanding the fact that such lot owners are deprived of the most valuable use of their lots." 2 American Law of Property 447. West Virginia has adopted the essence of this salutary rule by holding that "changed conditions of the neighborhood will not be sufficient to defeat the right [to enforce restrictive covenants] unless the changes are 'so radical as practically to destroy the essential objects and purposes of the agreement.' " Wallace v. St. Clair, 147 W.Va. 377 at 399, 127 S.E.2d 742 at 757 (1962). Based on the evidence thus far discussed, we can say that the non-residential uses of property in the complainants' neighborhood have not destroyed the essential objects and purposes of the restrictive covenants and that the benefits of the original plan can still be realized for that portion of the neighborhood which retains its residential character. In this respect we note that protection against covenant violations can be afforded to an area as small as one block. See Wallace v. St. Clair, 147 W.Va. 377 at 399, 127 S.E.2d 742 at 756 (1962).

There are additional changes affecting the character of the neighborhood which remain to be considered. These changes have occurred in the block where the complainants reside and the chiropractic clinic is located. On a corner property at one end of the block is the Highlawn United Methodist Church. The evidence shows that the church building was constructed in compliance with neighborhood setback requirements, and with the permission of the property owners in the 2700 block of Third Avenue. The church blends well with the character of the neighborhood; nonetheless, it is a non-residential use. Another change in the neighborhood is the shift in the use of many properties from single-family occupancy to multi-family occupancy, apparently in violation of the applicable restrictive covenants. This change for the most part stems from the conversion into apartment units of garage-stable facilities formerly used by servants or guests. The evidence shows that a number of such apartment units existed in the 2700 block of Third Avenue, and that these units were in various stages of occupancy including unoccupied but available for rent, occupied by extended family members related to the main dwelling's owners, and occupied by unrelated tenants. In addition, at least one main house on the block was divided into two rental units. Despite these significant departures from the neighborhood plan of limiting the occupancy of each lot to single families, the 2700 block of Third Avenue has retained the residential character which was also an important and essential part of the original plan. Even the church, which represents the most drastic change in the block, complements the residential character of the area in a manner that business enterprises do not. Accordingly, we find that the changes in the neighborhood's character, both in the 2700 block of Third Avenue and in the nearby area, have not been so radical that the restrictive covenants involved here are nullified.

Having found Dr. Nease's arguments concerning the neighborhood's changing character to be unconvincing, we turn now to the personal equitable defenses he raised in this proceeding. The foremost among these defenses is acquiescence, which may be described as follows:

> "The equitable defense of acquiescence arises where the complainant has acquiesced in the violation of the same type of restriction by third parties. Where the complainant has failed to enforce a similar equitable servitude against third parties, he has debarred himself from obtaining equitable relief against the defendant for subsequent violations of the same character. The reason for allowing this defense of acquiescence is the belief that the complainant, by his conduct in failing to seek enforcement against similar violations by third parties, has induced the defendant to assume that the restrictions are no longer in effect. Thus, acquiescence by the complainant to the violations of dissimilar restrictions cannot be a bar to enforcement where the restrictions are essentially different so that abandonment of one would not induce a reasonable person to assume that the other was also abandoned. Likewise, failure to sue for prior breaches by others where the breaches were noninjurious to the complainant cannot be treated as an acquiescence sufficient to bar equitable relief against a more serious and damaging violation."
> [2 American Law of Property 441–442, footnotes omitted]

This defense is recognized in West Virginia. See syl. pt. 4, Wallace v. St. Clair, 147 W.Va. 377, 127 S.E.2d 742 (1962). In analyzing this defense, we must compare Dr. Nease's covenant violations with other violations in the same neighborhood in which the complainants have acquiesced. The violations outside the 2700 block of Third Avenue are too remote to be considered injurious to the complainants' interests. Accordingly, these violations do not provide the basis for the defense of acquiescence. Likewise, the apparent violations in the 2700 block itself, such as the rental of garage apartments and the construction of a church, are not so similar in character to Dr. Nease's clinic, or so injurious to the complainants, that they entitle Dr. Nease to raise the defense of acquiescence. There is one significant violation, however, which we find to be critical to Dr. Nease's defense of acquiescence, namely the use of Dr. Nease's property by his predecessor in title before Dr. Nease established his clinic.

The evidence shows that the property Dr. Nease purchased was divided into five rental units, four in the main structure and one in an outbuilding. There is a very fine line between residential and commercial use in this instance, and Dr. Nease could fairly have assumed that the neighborhood acquiesced in a commercial use of 2703 Third Avenue. This assumption was warranted, we believe, by the fact that in this particular neighborhood the operation of five rental units on one lot is essentially a commercial undertaking. Although the character of Dr.

Nease's business differs from that of the preceding business at the same location, the similarities between the businesses are sufficient in our view to entitle Dr. Nease to raise the defense of acquiescence. Both businesses brought added traffic into the neighborhood and resulted in other minor disruptions which are out of the ordinary. Furthermore, it would appear that both businesses resulted in about the same injury to the complainants. In any case it does not seem that the clinic is a significantly more serious and damaging covenant violation than the five-unit rental property.

We can only judge the similarities between Dr. Nease's clinic and the preceding use of the same property on the basis of the record before us. The record indicates that Dr. Nease rehabilitated his property in such a manner that it harmonizes well with other dwellings on the block. In addition there was testimony that Dr. Nease did not conduct a high-volume practice. Furthermore, the discreet sign which identifies the clinic is placed on the building itself, rather than at the curb, where it would call more attention to the commercial character of the property. In short, Dr. Nease's commercial use of the property appears to be restrained and dignified, and we note that the complainants have acquiesced in only such a use. Should Dr. Nease significantly alter the character of his clinic, or should some other less restrained business move into the property, the complainants would have cause to reexamine the situation and take whatever action they deem appropriate to protect their interests.

We need not consider the other errors assigned by Dr. Nease because our decision with respect to the defense of acquiescence is dispositive of the case. Accordingly, for the foregoing reasons, the judgment of the Circuit Court of Cabell County is reversed.

Reversed.

Notes

1. As noted earlier, the "change in circumstances" cases take on a variety of shapes and colors. In Laney v. Early, 292 Ala. 227, 292 So.2d 103 (1974), it was held that the construction of an interstate highway which might divide the subdivision and detract from its appearance was not enough to destroy the basis of the restriction and did not establish such a change of condition as to render enforcement inequitable. In Circle Square Co. v. Atlantis Development Co., 267 S.C. 618, 230 S.E.2d 704 (1976), a covenant restricting land to "semi-residential" use was enforced despite the fact that a shopping and business area had been constructed in the restricted area.

In connection with the American Law Institute's current work on the Restatement of Property, 3d (Servitudes), close attention is being given to the issue of modification or termination of servitudes due to changed circumstances. In preliminary drafts the operative language has changed considerably from the first version that would have allowed courts to terminate servitudes rather freely, to the latest draft (Tentative Draft No. 6 1997) that uses the following language:

§ 7.10   Modification and Termination of Servitudes Because of Changed Conditions

When a change has taken place since the creation of a servitude that makes it impossible as a practical matter to accomplish the purpose for which a servitude was created, a court may modify the servitude to permit the purpose to be accomplished. If a modification is not practicable, a court may terminate the servitude. * * *

Also see, generally, Tentative Drafts 1–5, Restatement of the Law Third, Property (Servitudes); James L. Winokur, Ancient Strands Rewoven, or Fashioned Out of Whole Cloth?: First Impressions of the Emerging Restatement of Servitudes, 27 Conn. L. Rev. 131 (1994).

2.   As the principal case indicates, other defenses are sometimes employed, such as acquiescence, waiver and laches. In Underwood v. Webb, 544 S.W.2d 187 (Tex.Civ.App.1976), a violation on two lots in a 493 lot development was considered insufficient to eliminate the restriction. In Hargroder v. City of Eunice, 341 So.2d 463 (La.App.1976), there was no waiver of the limitation to residential use by the erection of numerous storage sheds in violation of the restriction. On the other hand, if landowners stand by for an unreasonable length of time while erection of the violating structure takes place, laches may preclude them from suing. Weinstein v. Tariff, 356 Mass. 738, 255 N.E.2d 595 (1970). Estoppel may also apply, as it did in Kelly v. Lovejoy, 172 Mont. 516, 565 P.2d 321 (1977), where the landowners purchased their land knowing that their neighbors were keeping horses in violation of the restrictions. (It was also deemed that they acquiesced in the horses being there.)

3.   There may also be termination based on relative hardship, although the covenant will be enforced if the community benefits derived are deemed to be greater. Gaskin v. Harris, 82 N.M. 336, 481 P.2d 698 (1971).

4.   The question of the monetary value of the property with and without the restrictions may enter in, as it did in Hunter v. Pillers, 464 S.W.2d 939 (Tex.Civ.App.1971), in which the appraised value of residential property of $52,800 was lowered to $7,800 due to the construction of an interstate highway adjacent to the land and the owner had an offer to sell at $85,000 if the restrictions were cancelled.

5.   Duration of the restrictive covenants is obviously a problem (which leads to "change in circumstances" cases), and in states in which no statutory provisions limit the duration and the covenants themselves do not limit the duration, the indefinite duration of the restrictions is not deemed unreasonable and unenforceable per se. See Moore v. Smith, 443 S.W.2d 552 (Tex.1969). It is a better practice in such states to provide for automatic expiration of the covenants after a period of years, such as 25, or to provide for automatic extension for successive periods after that unless cancelled by a majority of the landowners. Care to avoid ambiguities in drafting is essential, however, as illustrated by Leaver v. Grose, 563 P.2d 773 (Utah 1977).

6.   If there is a division of a benefited estate, is the covenant destroyed? See Old Dominion Iron & Steel Corp. v. Virginia Elec. and Power Co., 215 Va. 658, 212 S.E.2d 715 (1975).

In Zile, Private Restrictions on Residential Subdivisions: Some Drafting Suggestions, 32 Wis.Bar Bull. 26 (1959), may be found some valuable comments on considerations which enter into the preparation of documents of this type. Reference should be had, in that connection, to the 1959 Wis.L.Rev., containing discussion of the description of the area and the establishment of a general plan or scheme, the legal effect and enforcement of private restrictions, the definition of "building" or "structure" and problems associated with man-made objects primarily in the ground rather than above it, the type of dwelling to be allowed, the building location, the lot size, the dwelling size, height restrictions, cost considerations, building materials, architectural or design control, temporary structures, time for completion of construction, utility easements, miscellaneous restrictions, lifetime of restrictions and renewal provisions, substantive regulatory provisions, amending procedures, and land use problems and concepts generally. A more detailed discussion of these concepts and provisions and a summation of this material is contained in Beuscher, Land Use Controls—Cases and Materials, at 134a–134k (4th ed. 1966). Generally speaking, some of the aspects to be considered and properly developed in such a drafting process are these:

A. The area should be clearly described by use of the subdivision name (assuming the entire area is to be restricted); otherwise, the area must be described specifically by lots and blocks or in metes and bounds.

B. The intent to establish a general plan of development should be clearly expressed.

C. Certain words (such as "structure," "family" and "building") should be defined at the outset and later used as defined.

D. The general nature of the land use should be specified, as for example, "for residential purposes only," perhaps excluding also all but single-family residential uses or exempting from the exclusion certain named professional businesses.

E. The buildings permissible on each lot should be stated, as for example, a dwelling house with attached garage. Some statement may be desired to make it clear that churches, etc., are not excluded.

F. The type of dwelling may be specified—as, for example, a dwelling for a single family.

G. Setback lines from streets, sides of the lot, and the rear boundary should be provided for. In this connection, it must be determined whether only minimal requirements are to be provided or whether it is deemed desirable to have all houses a uniform distance from the street. Corner lots, irregular lots and lots with unusual topography must be considered, along with the desired size of yards. Aesthetic considerations may also enter into the provisions, and it may be well to provide that interior side yard lines or rear yard lines are inapplicable where lots are consolidated.

H. Provision should be made so that a minimum lot size is maintained (as through provisions against the division of single, unconsolidated lots). This is somewhat tricky, however, as, for example, the prohibition should not prevent the division of three regular lots into two lots (each of which would be larger than a single lot).

I. Provision should be made for a minimum building size, which presumably would bear some relationship to the lot size. The reference might be to the total square footage of inside living space, or to ground floor area (making provision for a larger ground floor area in the case of one-story dwellings than in the case of two-story dwellings), etc. Garages, breezeways, porches, carports, attics and utility rooms should (or for the most part would be) excluded from such computation. If such words as "living area" or "ground floor space" are employed, these should be clearly defined in the definitions section. Depending upon the area of the country, some provision may be made with respect to basements (which would usually be less common in the South and Southwest, for example, than in the East or Middle West).

J. Height limitations may be desirable, depending upon the type of development involved. This might be expressed either in feet or in stories. Chimneys, TV antennas or the like would normally be excluded from consideration in situations in which the height is measured in feet. In hilly areas, split levels may present some particular problems both as to height provisions measured in feet and in number of stories.

K. In addition to provisions pertaining to size, it may be desirable to provide for structures costing a minimum amount in order to preserve the high quality of the area. This opens something of a Pandora's box, however, unless dealt with clearly. The cost figure might be based on the evaluation of the structure by the lending agency or the sales price of the contractor or the builder's cost. A greater difficulty arises from the tendency of real estate to appreciate in dollar value over a long period of time, with the result that a new "$30,000 house" of today may amount essentially to what would have been classified as a new "$15,000 house" only a relatively few years ago. This is probably a continuing trend. If cost figures are used, it may be desirable to accelerate them in accord with some recognized price index on building costs, such as that published by the Bureau of Standards, but that may create or lead to more difficulty than is merited. Another consideration on cost figures is whether the architects' fee, legal fees, landscaping costs and the like are included.

L. Provisions relating to building materials may be desirable. For example, a sanction against pre-fabricated homes might be inserted; or it might be provided that a given percentage of the outside walls must be covered with brick or stone; exposed cement blocks, stucco or plywood exteriors or fake siding might be prohibited; and buildings moved onto the lot from elsewhere might be ruled out. Other provisions (perhaps taken care of by city codes) might be added to require insulation in the outer walls and roof, to require certain types of foundations, or to require the use of certain grades or types of lumber or other construction or engineering specifications.

M. Architectural or design control provisions may be desirable—as, for example, providing for plans to be approved in advance in writing by the developer or by a subsequently elected committee of property owners in the area. Such provisions, of course, require specificity if they are to be effective and if confusion is to be avoided.

N. Limitations on occupancy or use, other than as dwellings, may be desirable.

O. Occasionally, the developer may wish to provide that construction work must be completed within a given period of time, although this would normally be left to private contract.

P. Unsightly fences and signs in many instances will be prohibited, although decorative fences (and this must be clearly defined) may serve a useful purpose and thus be permitted. Location, height, materials and the like are aspects to be considered in connection with "decorative" fences.

Q. The developer may wish to provide for limitations on highway or street access or which direction houses built on corners will face. Normally, these considerations would be of little or no import, however.

R. Various provisions relating to utilities usually are provided. It may be desirable to provide altogether for underground utilities (or for a portion of the utilities to be underground). Minimally, some provision should be made which will confine the utilities to a given area (such as a five-foot easement for utility purposes over the rear of each lot).

S. It may be desirable to incorporate some provisions relating to landscaping, yards, the alteration of natural flow of ground water, the preservation of trees, or the like.

T. Enforcement provisions are not essential, but it may be desirable (due to the natural reluctance or inertia of people in acting) to designate a person, persons or a committee empowered to act on behalf of all property owners in enforcing the building scheme. This would be in addition to, and not in limitation of, the right of any individual property owner to take action unilaterally; or it could be exclusive. The former would seem to be preferable.

U. Provisions might shorten the statute of limitations. The end result would be to force offended property owners to act within a somewhat more reasonable period of time or be barred.

V. Provisions causing the restrictions to expire after a given time might be desirable. As an alternative, it might be provided that the restrictions would be automatically extended unless a majority of the owners abolished or modified them in writing (with the same being filed of record). Such provisions might be varied in several other ways. Of course, a change in conditions in the area or the changed nature of the neighborhood may lay the basis for terminating the restrictions through an adjudication that it would be inequitable to enforce them.

W. An amending procedure should be provided for in order that a majority or more of the property owners may make such modifications when necessary. Presumably, the "majority" (or whatever figure might be used) would be a majority of the owners of lots in the subdivision. Moreover, the "owner" should normally be defined as the holder of the fee simple title, not the lessee. The statement might be made that amendments would be in keeping with the general plan of development and could not be such as to alter the basic scheme.

X. A severability clause might be inserted, although its insertion or deletion is probably of little legal consequence. Invalidation of one of the provisions would normally leave the general plan unaffected anyway, and if the invalidation destroyed the general plan, then the severability clause could not save what was left.

Restrictive covenants designed to promote an ordered, desired development of a given land area are of no value unless they are observed and unless they are enforced when violated. The developer should take pains, therefore, to call the covenants to the attention of lot purchasers—not just so they will observe them, but also in order that they will make an effort to see that others observe them. A separate printed sheet containing the covenants and delivered at the time of sale would be helpful.

Chapter IV

THE PLANNING PROCESS AND THE COMPREHENSIVE PLAN

SECTION 1. BACKGROUND AND ORGANIZATION FOR PLANNING

In a book published in 1943, Walter Lippmann observed that people "who formulate the laws and administer them are men, and, being men, there is an enormous disparity between the simplicity of their minds and the real complexity of any large society."[1]

This, of course, is the problem with planning of any kind on any scale of any size. To do much beyond planning a neighborhood subdivision or an isolated area calls for more information, facts, projections and estimations than most people have the time, patience or wisdom to digest and translate into what might be called "the long view." Men of vision have too often been rare commodities in America when it came to the growth and development of our cities, and in fact, until relatively recent times, public planning itself has been a commodity little used or demanded. As we have become an urban nation, however, and as the crisis of our cities has developed into perhaps the overwhelming domestic problem of the latter part of the twentieth century, our attitudes have changed and the planning process has become a central theme of urban life.

This chapter deals with the device which is basic to urban planning. It may be known as "the master plan," or "the comprehensive plan," "the development plan," or the municipal or city plan, or in some statutes or cases, just "the plan."[2] Whatever the nomenclature, the

---

1. Lippmann, The Good Society 28 (1943).

2. See the landmark article, Haar, In Accordance with a Comprehensive Plan, 68 Harv.L.Rev. 1154 (1955). Professor Haar points out that the master plan is a long-term outline of a projected, general form of development, while zoning is simply a tool employed to implement the broader plan, but he observes that unfortunately, in many instances, zoning has proceeded without any master plan and courts have re-

263

device itself is supposedly long range and comprehensive in nature, looking toward the future growth and development of the area involved and seeking to project into time a concept under which the community may be developed in an orderly and desirable fashion and through which the needs, aspirations and welfare of its members may be better served.[3] If it is prepared properly, it will be based on all the best evidence available—economic statistics, growth patterns, living patterns, prevalent social and physical conditions, anticipated trends bearing upon the total socioeconomic picture, potential factors for change within the community, transportation problems, community objectives, increasing or diminishing industrialization, and other factors which may be appropriate to a knowledgeable consideration. By its very nature, the plan will be visionary; in some of its aspects, it will almost surely prove to be in error; but its success will in the long run be measured by how close it comes to hitting the mark and to serving the best interests of the community and by how much it does in fact provide the guide to the future. The worst of all plans will generally prove better than none at all, for we have already been through that phase in America and many of our older cities are Exhibit A for planning proponents. The better plans, however, will serve to revitalize the older and poorer areas of our cities and to assure that the newer areas do not suffer from the errors of the past. There is no panacea; no master plan meets that criteria. What it represents is the application of knowledge and common sense in an attempt to confront tomorrow's problems today.

The problems and objectives of planning have been detailed in many forms by a variety of competent people with varying backgrounds. As an introduction to this subject, we have selected some excerpts which illustrate both a brief history of the problem and some of the considerations which enter in. The first which we have extracted is rather dated today, but it points up the problem with some of the older concepts and the urban difficulties which were clearly evident about 50 years ago. It is from a report entitled, "Our Cities—Their Role in the National Economy," which was published in 1937 by the Urbanism Committee to the

quired none. Id., at 1156, 1157. Professor Haar also explored the master plan concept in detail in Haar, The Master Plan: An Impermanent Constitution, 20 Law & Contemp.Prob. 353 (1955), listing an extensive and detailed appendix of relevant provisions of state statutes then in effect. Id., at 378–418. For an exploration of a particular aspect of the master plan, see Nelson, The Master Plan and Subdivision Control, 16 Maine L.Rev. 107 (1964). Somewhat the contrary to Haar's support of a master plan which would be in effect prior to the enactment of the zoning ordinance is expressed in 1 Rathkopf, The Law of Zoning and Planning § 9–6 (3d ed. 1959). Rathkopf apparently favors the reasoning of the New Jersey court that zoning need not await the

preparation of a master plan. See Angermeier v. Borough of Sea Girt, 27 N.J. 298, 142 A.2d 624 (1958).

3. The Standard City Planning Enabling Act promulgated by the Department of Commerce in 1928, provided, in part, in §§ 6, 7: "The plan shall be made with the general purpose of guiding and accomplishing a coordinated, adjusted, and harmonious development of the municipality and its environs which will * * * best promote health, safety, morals, order, convenience, prosperity, and general welfare, as well as efficiency and economy in the process of development." Modern statutes are still somewhat inclined to echo this language.

National Resources Committee, these particular excerpts coming from pages 43 and 48:

Both physically and socially the cities of the United States bear the imprint of private ownership of land and the absence of a sound long-term land policy. Our traditional procedure of settling communities by allotting homesteads to those that wanted them, and our time-sanctioned method of allowing their subdivision into uniform small lots which were sold to private owners to use, by and large, as their means, their tastes, and their needs dictated, have produced the characteristic features of the typical American city with its stereotyped, monotonous gridiron block pattern. * * *

A survey of 144 planned communities undertaken by this committee indicates the unmistakable success of planning. The industries involved recognize the value of the city plan as do the real-estate people. Such communities are comparatively free from overcrowding of buildings and of people. The residents of the better planned communities enjoy greater efficiency, greater safety, a more healthful environment, and, in great measure, live a more satisfying life. A high degree of social cohesion and community spirit is evident and a greater degree of self-sufficiency is found. Large departures from the plan are the exception. Unforeseen change is a much greater threat to a city plan than physical deterioration. The borders of the planned community are its weakest points; they should be protected from unsuitable development by such physical buffers as "green belts" and land acquisition on a generous scale. Except where all the homes are rented by an industrial company, they tend to become occupied by persons working elsewhere.

That there is a direct relationship between the definiteness and continuity of governmental policy and the success of a city plan can scarcely be doubted. Under conditions of long-time unified control, intelligent planning may confidently be expected to be effective as a tool in the hands of those working for community welfare to prevent many of the ills and conflicts of purposes and interests otherwise likely to occur in the development and continued existence of future new and enlarged communities. It is quite clear, however, that constant vigilance and continuous readaptation to changing conditions are essential elements in every form of social control of the urban structure, whether it be desired to obtain a more adequate urban existence through building regulation, zoning, planning, taxation, a rational land policy, or a combination of these devices. Until the Nation as a whole recognizes that land is a public utility instead of a speculative commodity, not much prospect exists either of obtaining adequate housing for the population or for reconstructing cities to make them fit for human living. * * *

———

A recognition of the historical setting for our urban difficulties and some of the major land use problems in urban areas were explored by

Charles M. Haar and Lloyd Rodwin in Urban Land Policies: United
States, Housing and Town and Country Planning (Bull. 7 U.N.1953) in
this discussion:

Most feudal vestiges and tenures in the United States were swept
away with the Revolution. The next century and a half witnessed a
radical experiment in a free land system within a market economy. The
great release of energy and development that has characterized United
States expansion from a colony to its present position is partly a
consequence. A nation without a city of 50,000 in 1790 zoomed to a
population of more than 150 million. Primitive areas were developed;
resources discovered and harnessed; millions of immigrants were absorbed. New towns burgeoned, older cities expanded; and an agricultural
economy was transformed into an industrial workshop and commercial
entrepot for the world. A building industry emerged that, for all its
limitations, could produce more than a million homes a year plus
sufficient non-residential structures to serve the greatest concentration
of economic activities in the world. Today this land system serves more
than 232 cities over 50,000 population, 18 over 500,000, and 5 over a
million. More than half of the total population lives in 168 metropolitan
areas.

But this system of land holding and land commerce had its imperfec-
tions. Contemporary urban land policies in the United States are the
result of recognized inadequacies in the operation of this market system
and in its institutional framework. These policies control, guide and on
occasion even eliminate the market mechanism; or they attempt to
change the institutional structure. But the advantages of the entrepreneurial economy and the resulting strong attachments have led to
solutions that try primarily to correct maladjustments or control abuses
of the market mechanism, rather than to eliminate its essential features.
Similar loyalties shape the approach to major institutional difficulties.
Understanding this background is the key to an analysis of urban land
problems and policies in the United States, and to assessing the possible
application of this experience to other countries.

Major urban land problems and the market mechanism

In the process of breaking through frontiers, providing a haven for
immigrants, altering the dominant patterns of economic life and transforming cities from small distributing centres for farm products into
great nuclei of commercial activity, modern services and industrial
production, many land problems emerged. Some of the more important
of these are enumerated below.

Congestion. Unplanned growth has resulted in the overburdening of
street and transportation systems as well as other public facilities.

Slums and blighted areas. With increasing income and rising standards of demand, large areas of housing are below accepted minimum
social standards in the United States today. There are also many
districts whose repair and maintenance costs are often higher than

present or prospective rental income; actual repairs are minimal and depreciation is accelerated.

Inadequate open space. Insufficient and badly distributed open land and park and playground space throughout the urban residential areas have contributed to the inferior quality and depreciation of neighborhoods.

Disorganized land uses. Distribution of land use has been haphazard. Poor location of homes and places of work causes long daily journeys; and the mixture of incompatible commercial, industrial and residential uses impairs efficiency and hastens decay.

High land costs in central areas. Acquisition problems, demolition costs and speculative or inflated valuations of land often make prohibitive the cost of reducing excessively high population densities, or of converting land to new, less intense, more desirable use.

Premature and abortive subdivisions. Much peripheral land outside city limits and beyond the reach of municipal regulation was developed too early or failed to find a market. This land is now frozen out of use because of archaic street patterns, heavy tax charges and complicated title and acquisition problems.

Housing shortage and building cycles. Low income families are repeatedly confronted with a shortage of suitable accommodation at rents they can afford. Other segments of the population are periodically confronted with steep price rises following periods of acute housing shortage, or decline of values after overbuilding.

Imperfect patterns of tenure. Home ownership is the socially compulsive ideal. The typical house built in the United States is for sale. The average builder operates with relatively limited capital and finds it more profitable and less risky to sell rather than to rent. But many low and middle income families cannot, or at any rate should not, face the financial risks and immobility which ownership entails.

Inflexible physical patterns. The society is characterized by considerable population mobility, technological change and rapid development, but once physical land patterns have been established, they are relatively inflexible. Adjustments to change or to new social or physical needs are difficult, costly and sometimes impossible.

Stratified social patterns. Within the cities, population is often distributed according to economic status, as well as common ethnic or national origins. Some of these patterns have become fixed, often artificially. Breakdown of these rigidities is considered desirable; but the proper heterogeneous patterns which will encourage diverse groups to live together peacefully are largely unknown, and are only now in the process of investigation.

Economic theorists, on the basis of certain assumptions, can show that the free or perfect market achieves an efficient distribution of goods and services. But the urban land market is neither free nor perfect. Lack of knowledge has resulted in inefficiency, overproduction, and other misjudgments. Even if a better free market mechanism existed, the social results would be discouraging. The inadequate income of some groups has handicapped the widespread production of houses of better standards with sufficient open space and amenities. Still other impediments have been the limited mechanization of the home-building industry, the restrictions of building and zoning codes, the violent fluctuations of the economy with its sudden surges and halts in economic and urban growth, the discrepancies between costs to the entrepreneur and to society, and the relative inflexibility of physical patterns. Government assistance was required and often obtained. Some notable policies have been introduced, and some successes achieved. Other problems still defy final solution. Unless they materialize, some unsatisfactory physical patterns may endure for generations. * * *

The Haar and Rodwin excerpt refers to the history of population growth in the United States in rather sweeping terms. A closer look at the history of our land system may provide some useful background for understanding the role of planning and the police power in relation to American values and attitudes about land. Surely one of the most dramatic aspects of that history is the disposal of the public domain. Roughly three-fourths of the continental United States was part of the federal domain and during the nineteenth century public land policies centered on disposal of this domain. Refer back to Chapter I.

Many in the planning movement advocate recapturing public ownership of land as the best means of achieving meaningful control of land development; their model is the European tradition of public ownership with leasing to private developers. In a small way the American experiment with urban renewal in the 1950–1970 period had, in part, that goal. However, the thrust of the thinking today is quite different. Consider the following excerpt from Commentary on Article 6, Land Banking, Model Land Development Code, Official Draft, pp. 253–263 (1974):

> The term "land banking" is one that appears frequently in the literature of land use law, economics and planning. Although the term is not always used uniformly, in general we may define it as follows:

> A system in which a governmental entity acquires a substantial fraction of the land in a region that is available for future development for the purpose of controlling the future growth of the region.

> * * *

> Canada and a number of European countries, notably Sweden and the Netherlands, have used land banking extensively, and it has been widely acclaimed as a means of encouraging orderly urban

growth. The technique has acquired a substantial number of proponents in this country as well.

Until recently support for land banking in the United States has been primarily academic. However, in 1974 Congress passed the Housing and Community Development Act of 1974 which authorizes the use of federal funds for land banking. * * * The availability of federal money is likely to quicken state and local interest in land banking.

Proponents of land banking have relied primarily on two basic arguments: (1) that it will have an anti-inflationary effect on land prices, and (2) that it will permit more rational patterns of development rather than urban sprawl.

* * *

The other prominent argument in support of land banking—that it will promote more rational and efficient development patterns—also goes back at least to the 1930's, when land banking was promoted as a device to provide green belts around urban areas. Buttenheim and Cornick, "Urban Land Reserves," 14 Journal of Land & Public Utility Economics 254–65 (1938). See also National Resources Committee, "Our Cities: Their Role in the National Economy" (1937).

In recent years Professor John Reps has been one of the most persuasive advocates of land banking as a means of controlling urban sprawl:

"The proposed method of directing urban expansion would promote contiguous development rather than the wasteful, discontinuous pattern which now prevails and which results very largely from the whimsical characteristics of the peripheral land market. In order to find land on which to build, the developer must often leapfrog over near-in tracts which are held off the market for one reason or another. The expense of public services and facilities becomes unnecessarily high, and the cost to individuals in time and money is increased by this useless and unessential dispersal. The proposed system would normally place on the market only land contiguous to the existing network of services, but it could also be employed to create new towns or detached satellites where this is found desirable."

J. Reps, "The Future of American Planning: Requiem or Renascence?" 1967 Planning 47, 52.

The late Professor Charles Abrams also suggested large scale land acquisition in the path of urban development as a means of preventing sprawl and ensuring planned growth.

"State land renewal agencies should be organized for the main function of acquiring vacant land outside city boundaries. The state agency would have power to acquire large areas, improve them with streets and utilities, and resell them for private development according to a prearranged plan. Land essential for schools, parks and other public uses would be preserved. The state and Federal governments would contribute the essential subsidies for acquisition and improvement, and the land would be resold at market value."

"U.S. Housing: A New Program," as printed by the Tamiment Institute, New York, based on a speech delivered by Abrams before the National Housing Conference in June, 1957.

Land banking may also play an important role in the conservation of natural resources. The need for more efficient patterns of urban growth is highlighted by long term projections of declining supplies of fuels and other natural resources. See, e.g., D.H. Meadows, et al., The Limits of Growth 56–59 (1972). The random pattern which follows free market speculation in land is not conducive to the construction of mass transit facilities. Land banking may be able to direct growth in directions which facilitate more economical patterns of transportation and urban services.

The National Commission on Urban Problems recommended that state governments enact legislation enabling appropriate governmental agencies to acquire land in advance of development for the following purposes: (a) assuring the continuing availability of sites needed for development; (b) controlling the timing, location, type and scale of development; (c) preventing urban sprawl; and (d) reserving to the public gains in land values resulting from the action of government in promoting and servicing development. National Commission on Urban Problems, Building the American City 251 (1968).

* * *

In 1974 Congress responded by providing specific legislative authority in the Community Development Act of 1974 for the allocation of funds under the special revenue sharing program for "community development" grants to local governments for "the acquisition of real property * * * which is (a) blighted, deteriorated, deteriorating, undeveloped or inappropriately developed from the standpoint of sound community development and growth; (b) appropriate for rehabilitation or conservation activities; (c) appropriate for the preservation or restoration of historic sites, the beautification of urban land, the conservation of open spaces, natural resources, and scenic areas, the provision of recreational opportunities, or the guidance of urban development; (d) to be used for the provision of public works, facilities, and improvements eligible for assistance under this title; or (e) to be used for other public purposes." 42 U.S.C.A. 5305(a)(1) (1974). This statutory authority appears sufficiently broad to permit the use of federal funds for any type of land banking authorized under this Article 6.

Will Land Banking Work?

Opponents of land banking argue that it cannot really achieve the purposes claimed for it. Sylvan Kamm, author of a highly critical study of land banking, argues that it is impossible to achieve both better quality development and lower land prices.

The essence of orderly development is that varying land uses will support each other and there will be no wastage of land through scatteration. Given such a pattern the functional utility of all parcels will be increased—an increase which would be reflected in price.

S. Kamm, "Land Banking: Public Policy Alternatives and Dilemmas" 11 (Urban Institute Paper No. 112–28, 1970).

Kamm also discounts the experience with land banking in Sweden, arguing that in Sweden the powerful and financially self-sufficient central cities dominate the metropolitan areas, and that Sweden has traditionally accepted strong, centralized planning and extensive government ownership of land. Id. at 15–17. See also Shirley Passow, "Land Reserves and Teamwork in Planning Stockholm," 36 J. of The American Institute of Planners 179 (1970); National Academy of Sciences and National Academy of Engineering, Urban Growth and Land Development 32–33 (1972).

Other students of land banking have expressed doubt about its political feasibility in the United States:

> "Too many are making too much from the appreciation of land values in areas of urban growth. And more importantly, there is a general sense that this idea would establish more public control over land development than the public wants." Kermit Parsons et al., Public Land Acquisition for New Communities and the Control of Urban Growth: Alternative Strategies (1973).

Will It Work Too Well?

Land banking, like any other powerful governmental program, presents the dangers of abuse. Governmental officials could manipulate the program to favor friends and injure enemies much as other governmental programs have occasionally been abused in the past. The Code assumes that the existing penalties for abuse of governmental power will be appropriate to deal with possible abuses of the land banking power and that no special provision needs to be added to this Code to deal with such possibilities.

* * *

Notes

1. While substantial attention is devoted here to the concept of land banking, a practical problem remains with regard to the cost involved. Land banking would be a rather expensive practice which would not be feasible in most local communities and which neither the federal nor various state governments would probably be willing to fund to any substantial extent at the present time. This is a major problem in addition to the problem of whether it could accomplish its purpose, or the question of whether the process might lead to abuse by government officials. See A.L. Strong, Land Banking (Johns Hopkins Univ. Press 1979). For another view of public land

acquisition to effectuate land use policies, see Reps, Public Land, Urban Development Policy, and the American Planning Tradition, in Clawson (ed.), Modernizing Urban Land Policy (1973).

2. Although the terminology of land banking is not often encountered in current literature, the concept is alive and well. Several states have successfully established land purchase or development rights acquisition programs funded by public bond issues. For example, in New York in 1986, a 1.45 billion dollar Environmental Quality Bond Act was approved by voters and the governor proposed an additional 2 billion dollar program in 1990 (which failed at the polls). California voters approved a 775 million dollar program to acquire open space in 1988; Florida spends nearly 100 million dollars annually to preserve rivers and coastline, and Massachusetts committed 105 million dollars in 1988–89 for land acquisition. Other states with sizeable programs include New Jersey and Connecticut. For some discussion of the New York program, see Vaccaro v. Jorling, 151 A.D.2d 34, 546 N.Y.S.2d 470 (1989). Most of the money spent under these programs is for acquisition of environmentally sensitive areas and open space. Some money is used for municipal park acquisition and restoration of historic sites and buildings.

3. Not strictly speaking in the realm of land banking, but closely related, is the federal program to allow conversion of abandoned railroad right of way into hiking or nature trails. The program is administered by the Interstate Commerce Commission and is based on the notion that the railroad right of way should be preserved for future transportation needs of the nation, but in the interim, public use of the right of way should be permitted. Landowners adjacent to railroad right of way frequently object to nature trails and claim a right of reverter. The program has been upheld in the courts. See Glosemeyer v. Missouri–Kansas–Texas R.R., 879 F.2d 316 (8th Cir.1989), cert. denied , 494 U.S. 1003, 110 S.Ct. 1295, 108 L.Ed.2d 473 (1990); Barney v. Burlington Northern Railroad Co., Inc. 490 N.W.2d 726 (S.D.1992); Preseault v. I.C.C., 494 U.S. 1, 110 S.Ct. 914, 108 L.Ed.2d 1 (1990) (the long history of this case in the federal claims court and the Court of Appeals for the Federal Circuit is traced in Preseault v. United States, 100 F.3d 1525 (Fed.Cir.1996)). Also see, Comment, Rails to Trails: Converting America's Abandoned Railroads Into Nature Trails, 22 Akron L.Rev. 645 (1989).

SECTION 2. THE PLANNERS

In most states, by statute, planning studies and the preparation of a comprehensive plan are prerequisites to the enactment of implementing legislation, such as subdivision regulations or zoning ordinances. In some states, statutes now make planning by municipalities compulsory. The question naturally arises as to who is to do the planning. This section provides some material sketching the history of the planning profession followed by material relating to the legal status of planners.

A. HISTORY OF THE PLANNING PROFESSION

W.I. Goodman (ed.), Principles and Practice of Urban Planning, pp. 19–28 (Int'l City Managers' Ass'n, 1968):[4]

1900–1930: The Partial Recovery of a Planning Function

It would be pleasant to recount a simple tale in which, after the dark ages of the 19th century, urban planning emerged from bondage, gradually gathered to itself a panoply of techniques, powers, and ideals, and finally became totally equipped to grant cities a comprehensive salvation. To describe such a process of linear, cumulative development would indeed be heartwarming—but inaccurate. In fact, the American planning movement after 1900 followed a path that was to lead it into serious irrelevance thirty years later. The recovery of an adequate planning function was not to be an easy task.

In 1900, the centennial year of Washington, D.C., the annual meeting of the American Institute of Architects was held in the capital city. Several important papers dealt with the beautification of areas containing the principal government buildings. These plans came to the attention of Senator James McMillan. As chairman of the Committee on the District of Columbia, McMillan was instrumental in obtaining a Senate authorization to prepare plans for the District's park system. The subcommittee responsible for the work immediately constituted a Senate Park Commission, the members of which were Daniel Burnham, Charles McKim, Augustus Saint–Gaudens, and Frederick Law Olmsted, Jr. The old Columbian Exposition team had been reconvened.

* * *

This earliest manifestation of the rebirth of planning is usually called the City Beautiful Movement. Since the only available models were the Columbian Exposition and the Washington Plan of 1902, the content of the plans was invariably restricted to three elements: civic centers, thoroughfares, and parks. Boulevards and parkways were the design elements that tied together the schemes for impressive public buildings and open spaces. As the leading practitioner of the Movement, Daniel Burnham, asserted in his San Francisco plan report, "A city plan must ever deal mainly with the direction and width of its streets."

* * *

The City Beautiful Movement was the beginning of comprehensive planning. Professionals like Burnham saw that there was a need to relate buildings to each other and to their sites. In emphasizing the three-dimensional quality of urban planning, they reasserted the vitality of one part of the colonial planning tradition. Hereafter, city planning would no longer be equivalent to a street map.

The Movement had inspirational value in popularizing and dramatizing the need for city planning. Furthermore, it was not completely blind to the interconnections between physical planning and the socio-

---

4. This material was prepared by James G. Coke. Reprinted with permission of the International City Managers' Association.

political aspects of urban life. In the Plan of Chicago, Burnham recognized the problem of the slum neighborhood and warned that the city might soon be forced to provide public housing as a matter of simple justice.

Despite these undeniable contributions to the revitalization of a planning function, the City Beautiful Movement quickly revealed certain deficiencies. To begin with, beautification and adornment had limited practicability for most cities. In light of other demands upon the municipal treasury, the benefits hardly seemed worth the high costs involved. A more serious defect was the lack of legitimation of any public control over the private actions that were decisive in setting the quality of the urban environment. The early planners merely avoided the issue when they made "planning" coterminous with parks, boulevards, and civic centers. This choice of a focus had two unintended consequences. It made sure that the claims of the policy did not become an issue, since the achievement of these limited goals required public investment, rather than controls. At the same time, the choice created a special upper-middle class constituency for planning. By nature suspicious of governmental controls, particularly at the local level, this group would respond enthusiastically to an all-rewarding objective like beautification through public investment.

* * *

An event in 1911 foretold the direction in which city planning would go in the next two decades. Two years before, the first national Conference on City planning was convened at the call of the New York Committee on Congestion of Population. The Committee represented those who were primarily interested in housing and thus was anchored in one of the two groups that kept planning alive during the 19th century. The theme of the 1909 Conference was using planning to deal with social problems. The papers dealt more with economics than aesthetics. They called for an urban planning process based upon a type of research alien to the City Beautiful leaders. * * *

The City Beautiful Movement established two aspects of local planning that remain in common use today: the professional consultant and the quasi-independent planning commission composed of leading citizens. The consultant system emerged quite naturally. There was no separate planning profession; the emphasis was upon the production of a one-shot plan; and the architects and landscape architects who became planners were accustomed to the client-consultant relationship. Given these conditions, there was really no alternative method for providing a professional staff. However, the exclusive reliance on consultants became more and more dysfunctional for effective planning.

* * *

Planning as an official function of local government became established almost as quickly as the consultant system. Although the first City Beautiful plans were prepared under private auspices by civic organizations, there was early recognition of the need for placing responsibility under public authority. Cities turned to a familiar device: the appointment of prestigious citizens to an unpaid commission. The first city planning commissions were in Hartford (1907) and Milwaukee (1908).

* * *

During the 1920's, city planning became increasingly popular. Although there were some changes in emphasis, the general trend was to move in the directions chartered by the City Beautiful Movement. Cities continued to show little inclination to add planners to the full-time municipal bureaucracy; in 1929 only 46 cities had planning budgets of more than $5,000. Thus the itinerant consultants grew in numbers and prestige. Semi-independent planning commissions multiplied, as this way of organizing the local planning function became imbedded in the enabling statutes of state after state. The U.S. Department of Commerce gave additional sanction to the use of planning commissions in its 1928 model law, A Standard City Planning Enabling Act. Because the leadership of most local planning commissions rested in the hands of Chambers of Commerce and well-to-do citizens, their plans paid no attention to slums or poverty. Through their decisions and actions physical layout remained supreme.

The major changes in local planning during the twenties were (1) the addition of engineers and lawyers to the ranks of the planning profession, (2) the beginnings of state and metropolitan planning, and (3) the rapid rise and immense popularity of zoning. This last change was the most important of all. Zoning became to planning what the sacraments are to the Bible—a visible sign of grace.

A separate planning profession had been slowly emerging since 1909, when Harvard's School of Landscape Architecture offered the first university course in city planning. A decade later, the Harvard curriculum included principles of city planning, practice and design, principles of construction, and planting design. Eight other educational institutions were offering some instruction in city planning. The course work was, like Harvard's, usually offered by landscape architecture faculties. * * *

The hallmark of the 1920's was the widespread acceptance of comprehensive zoning. Building upon a limited legal base that had allowed municipalities to control "public nuisances," lawyers like Edward Bassett and Alfred Bettman began to develop zoning as a method for effectuating a community plan. In 1913, the New York Heights of Buildings Commission, chaired by Bassett, adopted a report that laid the foundation for the 1916 New York City ordinance, the first comprehensive zoning ordinance to be enacted by an American city. This new technique received a great deal of publicity. The National Planning Conferences had lengthy papers and discussions on zoning each year from 1916 through 1925, and again from 1928 through 1931, when the emphasis shifted to the administration of zoning ordinances. * * *

In sum, local planning on the eve of the Great Depression had attained status and self-identity. American cities had recovered a planning function. Yet the relevance of most planning programs to basic urban problems seemed questionable. Organization for planning was in the hands of quasi-independent commissions composed of business executives, realtors, and the high priests of the economic order—lawyers, architects, and engineers. For the most part, these lay leaders looked upon planning as a citizens' effort, to be "sold" to recalcitrant politicians. Lacking funds for a permanent staff of any size, the commissions employed consultants to prepare a "Master Plan." In due course, the Plan would be presented, and anyone at all acquainted with the field could anticipate the sections of the report: (1) streets, (2) transit and transportation, (3) parks and recreation, (4) civic appearance, and (5) zoning. These headings had almost become stereotypes. Except for zoning and transit, the scope of the plans went little beyond the framework developed by Burnham and his contemporaries. If the politicians could be induced to adopt the recommended zoning ordinance, planning was completed. The commission could think of little else to do, other than advocate the bromide that the Master Plan should be kept up-to-date. * * *

The Depression experience provided a powerful impetus toward a redefinition of local planning. When it was seen that the Unseen Hand did not necessarily assure continued high levels of economic activity, the nation's attention became focused on creating new institutional structures and coordinating their activities with old ones. Planning could not escape these questions of administration and organization. Many of its leaders saw that if planning were to be more than the civic New Year's resolution, it had to become anchored in the ongoing political process. The establishment of the American Society of Planning Officials in 1934 was an early organizational expression of the new concern with planning policy. ASPO was to serve as the vehicle through which public officials and professionals could discuss common concerns. * * *

In reviewing the ferment of the 1930's, it seems clear that the Urbanism Committee of the National Resources Committee was a major force in stimulating the new outlook on local planning. Composed primarily of students of public administration, the Committee accepted two major premises for making planning effective. First, it saw that there is a direct relationship between the definiteness and continuity of governmental policy and the success of the city plan. Second, it called attention to the fact that physical planning has no meaning apart from a matrix of social and economic factors. * * *

Following World War II, there was a dynamic expansion of local planning in the directions pointed out in the 1930's. Budgets grew and so did staff resources. The rise of the resident planning staff began at the end of the Depression. Some consultants, like Nolen and Bartholomew, encouraged cities with which they had contracts to hire the consultant's professionals in residence as permanent staff after the consulting job had been completed. The growing number of planning schools increased the supply of trained professionals. While only four schools offered graduate degrees in city planning in 1940, there were 19 professional degree programs a decade later. University curricula not only made more planners available, but also expanded the expertise of those entering the field. * * *

Vastly more sophisticated methods of analysis became commonplace. A comparison of Stuart Chapin's textbook Urban Land Use Planning with, say, the 1929 edition of Nolen's book shows how strongly planning now relies upon the disciplines of economics, sociology, and geography for its analytic tools. Planning techniques have been most highly refined in the model building and computer technology applied since 1955 by the massive transportation studies in Chicago, Detroit, Philadelphia, Pittsburgh, and other large cities.

Planning is now considered a governmental function at all levels— municipal, metropolitan, and state. No doubt the federal grants first authorized under Section 701 of the Housing Act of 1954 acted as powerful leverage in stimulating small cities and metropolitan areas to organize planning agencies. However, the pressures of urban growth would probably, in time, have been as compelling as the availability of money. In large cities, particularly, the governmental character of planning has been interpreted to mean an integration of the planning function into the administrative structure. Planning departments have replaced several quasi-independent commissions. This has made it easier for elected chief executives to adopt planning as part of their political platforms and to use the planning agency for objectives far broader than physical development.

* * *

From this perspective, it is easy to account for the popularity of local planning in the late 1920's. The end result of the line of development that began in 1900 was a type of planning that did little violence to the concepts on which 19th century city development had proceeded. The planning activity of the 1920s did not challenge the view of land as a speculative commodity, but simply imposed a few ground rules under which speculation was to be carried on. It did not ask local government to become a positive instrument of the public welfare, but assumed that public powers would continue to be exercised as the handmaiden of private development. Finally, the planning activities of the 1920's were seen as an instrument in the economic competition among cities. To have a master plan or a zoning ordinance was a badge of modernity and "progress." Concern with the quality of urban development, apart from sheer quantity, was a retrograde notion. To be bigger meant, *ipso facto,* to be better, and planning marched forward under the watchword "Grow or Die."

Since 1930, the major trends in planning have interposed a set of ideas that challenged the older ideology. Those who are concerned with effective guidance of urban development are asking the polity to adjust to new conditions by accommodating more extensive public interest claims on private actions. Some cities are experimenting with new combinations of public and private activities through such devices as non-profit development corporations. Some are attempting to integrate social and physical planning. There is a search for satisfactory alternatives to the traditional practice of zoning and subdivision control.

Yet, anyone familiar with American local politics must recognize the power of the older ideas. Urban land is not completely recognized as a community resource; the capabilities and intentions of municipal governments are viewed with suspicion; growth is in itself admirable; and many people are, at base, anticity. As a result, two traditions of local planning exist side-by-side in the United States. One rests upon the foundations of the 1920s, the other upon the alternatives first posed in the 1930s. The latter is the more vital and timely, for it provides the concepts through which the urban polity is overcoming the conditions that, for more than a century, vitiated attempts to create a more satisfactory urban environment.

B. THE LEGAL STATUS OF PLANNERS

NEW JERSEY CHAPTER, AMERICAN INSTITUTE OF PLANNERS v. NEW JERSEY STATE BD. OF PROFESSIONAL PLANNERS

Supreme Court of New Jersey, 1967.
48 N.J. 581, 227 A.2d 313, appeal dismissed, certiorari denied
389 U.S. 8, 88 S.Ct. 70, 19 L.Ed.2d 8 (1967).

FRANCIS, J. In this declaratory judgment proceeding the Chancery Division of the Superior Court declared unconstitutional a portion of section 11 of the professional planners licensing act, L.1962, c. 109; N.J.S.A. 45:14A–11. The condemned portion exempted duly licensed professional engineers, licensed land surveyors and registered architects of this State from the requirement, imposed by the statute on all other persons, to take and pass an examination for a planner's license, and it directed the State Board of Professional Planners (which was created by the same statute) to issue such a license on application therefor and payment of fee by any such exempted person. The trial court also held that the invalid portion of section 11 was severable, and not so intimately connected with the statute as to indicate that the Legislature would not have adopted the remainder without it. The Board was restrained from issuing licenses to persons who sought to qualify under the offending exemption. An appeal was taken to the Appellate Division, where the restraint was continued until final judgment. Thereafter, before the matter was reached for argument there, all parties moved for certification pursuant to R.R. 1:10–3, and we granted the motion.

The action was instituted by the New Jersey Chapter, American Institute of Planners, an unincorporated association of the State of New Jersey. The association is a professional society created to study and advance the art and science of city, regional, state and national planning.
* * *

Prior to 1962 unsuccessful attempts were made under the sponsorship of the American Institute of Planners to obtain passage by the Legislature of a so-called professional planners licensing act. The proposal encountered opposition from other established professional groups, principally engineers, land surveyors and architects, who were already subject to separate licensing statutes and who had qualified for licenses by meeting the conditions imposed thereby. Finally in 1962 the act in question, obviously a compromise measure (more of this later) was adopted with the acquiescence of the competing interests, as chapter 109 of the Laws of 1962.

The act provided that after July 10, 1962 no person could practice or offer to practice professional planning in this State unless he were licensed to do so under its provisions. The practice of professional planning is defined in most general terms in section 2 as "the administration, advising, consultation or performance of professional work in the development of master plans in accordance with the provisions of chapters 27 and 55 of Title 40 of the Revised Statutes, as amended and supplemented; and other professional planning services related thereto intended primarily to guide governmental policy for the assurance of the orderly and co-ordinated development of municipal, county, regional and metropolitan land areas, and the State or portions thereof." N.J.S.A. 45:14A-2.

Chapters 27 and 55 of Title 40 provide for the creation of county, regional and municipal planning boards to make and adopt master plans for the physical development of the political unit involved. * * *

In order to become licensed as a professional planner, a candidate must file an application under oath showing that he has the minimum educational qualifications. They are:

(a) A graduate degree in professional planning from an accredited college or university in a curriculum in recognized planning subjects as shall be approved by the State Board of Professional Planners, plus a minimum of three years experience in the full-time practice of professional planning; or (b) an undergraduate degree from an accredited college or university in a curriculum offering a major or option comprising a minimum of 21 credit hours in such recognized planning subjects as shall be approved by the board, with a minimum of four years experience in the full-time practice of professional planning; or (c) graduation from a secondary school and at least 12 years of professional planning experience acceptable to the board; or, (d) for a period of eight years only subsequent to July 1, 1963, a degree in a *closely related course of study such as architecture, landscape architecture, engineering,* law, sociology, geography, public administration, political science or economics, with a minimum of 18 credit hours in recognized planning subjects included as part of or in addition to such courses of study in an accredited college or university, plus a minimum of five years experience in the full-time practice of professional planning. (Emphasis ours) In addition the applicant must obtain a passing grade as determined by the board upon a qualifying examination to be prepared by the board or by experts chosen by it, and given annually. * * *

When the statute was adopted by the Legislature it contained section 11 consisting of five paragraphs dealing generally with the license-qualifying examinations. The fourth paragraph provides:

The board upon application therefor and the payment of the application and license fees fixed by this act shall issue a certificate of license as a professional planner to any duly licensed professional engineer, licensed land surveyor or registered architect of New Jersey.

This paragraph was not included in the bill, A 546, as introduced in 1961 under the sponsorship of the New Jersey Chapter of the American Institute of Planners. It was inserted however, (along with section 3, N.J.S.A. 45:14A–3, and part of section 17, N.J.S.A. 45:14A–17, to be more specifically referred to hereafter in connection with the discussion of severability of section 11), in order to exempt the described engineers, land surveyors and architects from the obligation of satisfying the qualifications required of other aspiring planners and from the burden of taking and passing the licensing examination.

Plaintiffs challenge the validity of the fourth paragraph, saying it denies them equal protection of the law contrary to the guaranties of the Federal Constitution and the New Jersey Constitution. More specifically they say that by requiring all persons except licensed professional engineers, licensed land surveyors and registered architects of this State to possess certain educational qualifications and experience in the field of planning, and to take and pass an examination on subjects related to that field in order to be licensed as a practitioner of planning, the legislation violates the cited constitutional strictures against discrimination.

* * *

In this instance we are satisfied from the legislative history and from an examination of the statute as a whole that the Legislature would not have adopted it without the exemption provision contained in the fourth paragraph of section 11.

The first proposed planners' licensing act * * * did not contain an exemption for engineers, land surveyors and architects. There is no doubt it encountered opposition from those groups, particularly from the New Jersey Society of Professional Engineers. It was not adopted. Thereafter futile attempts were made in 1959 and 1960 to procure passage of such legislation. Then in 1961 two bills were introduced, one sponsored by the Society of Professional Engineers (A 483), and the other by the Institute of Planners. (A 546). The bills continued the conflict between the professions. The engineers' bill provided for the registration and licensing of professional planners, and created an administrative and examining board to carry out its provisions. The board was to consist of five engineers, one of whom would also be a licensed land surveyor, and one a licensed professional planner. The planners' bill called for establishment of a separate board of licensed professional planners. The statement originally attached said among other things:

"Planning is a distinct, separate profession, which requires specialized training. It is not a branch of engineering, architecture, or any other profession. Thirty leading colleges and universities award degrees in planning, and more than 400 New Jersey municipalities and 15 counties have planning boards."

As we were advised at oral argument, it became apparent that neither bill could pass to the exclusion of the other. The engineers, land surveyors and architects seemed to feel there was no need at all to regard planning as a distinct profession and to require licenses for planners as such. But if the Legislature disagreed and found justification for such regulation, then they felt that persons in their professions who took and passed the examinations for licenses to practice in their respective fields, as already required by separate statutes, ought to receive automatic licensure under the planners' act. In 1962 an obvious compromise in the form of the present statute was submittted and adopted. It became chapter 109, L.1962.

* * *

The history of the act and its evolution into the form which made it acceptable legislatively demonstrate plainly that the establishment of prerequisites for licensing planners, and the provisions for exemption therefrom of licensed engineers, land surveyors and registered architects were intended to be interdependent and to exist as a whole or not at all. * * * We are satisfied that if the exemption provision were invalid, it would be usurpation of the legislative province for a court to allow the remainder of the enactment to stand without it. Washington National Ins. Co. v. Board of Review, 1 N.J. 545, 556, 64 A.2d 443 (1949). Therefore whether the entire act here shall stand or fall depends upon our determination of the constitutionality of the fourth paragraph of section 11, to which we now turn.

* * *

The more specific issue vigorously argued by plaintiffs is that by exempting licensed professional engineers, land surveyors and registered architects from the educational requirements and examination for a planner's license, while requiring all other persons, particularly those educated for and trained in planning to satisfy the requirements, the statute transgresses the constitutional mandate for equal protection of the law. They urge that all persons have a common right to aspire to and qualify for the practice of a profession or occupation, and are entitled to be treated equally with respect to State-imposed tests for license to do so. And they contend that creation of the exempt separate class of engineers, land surveyors and architects, and authorizing automatic licensure for such persons violates the basic charter right of all other persons not to be treated in discriminatory fashion.

* * *

There is no substantial dispute in the testimony of the expert witnesses who appeared on both sides of the case that there is a definite interrelationship among the disciplines of engineering, architecture, landscape architecture, land surveying and planning. * * *

Plaintiffs' experts concede that historically city planning had its origin and its early development "with architects, engineers and landscape architects. That is where we got our original planners"; "they were really planners"; they "came out of" architecture, engineering and landscape architecture. * * *

The text writers support the view that city planning had and has its roots in the three professions recognized by our Legislature. For example, McQuillin, in 1 Municipal Corporations 432 (1949) says:

> "The first instance of a comprehensive city plan was that of Christopher Wren for London following the destructive fire of 1666, but it was never adopted. In 1682 a plan for Philadelphia was drafted by civil engineers and surveyors appointed by William Penn. The plan adopted for the national capital was prepared by Major Pierre Charles L'Enfant, a French army engineer employed by Washington, who presented a scheme at once comprehensive and attractive, and the observance of which in the main has enabled the national capital to develop as one among the beautiful cities of the world."

Further:

> "As knowing how to do a thing before it is attempted is needed, it is plain that satisfactory city planning and zoning must be the result of the united efforts of the applied talents working in harmony of the various professions, arts and sciences, particularly that of the civil engineer, the architect, the landscape architect, or designer, the economist and the lawyer." Id., at pp. 434–435.

See also, James, Land Planning in the United States for the City, State and Nation (1926), where it is pointed out in chapter 3 that the concept of city planning in the modern sense was first introduced at the Chicago World's Fair in 1893, and that the exposition was the joint effort of architects, landscape architects and engineers.

Plaintiffs' witnesses assert that the modern "new breed" planner is one step removed from the engineers, architects and land surveyors. His claimed separate expertise in the preparation of master plans, they say, comes from knowledge of and training in community studies, which include preparation of base maps, land use surveys, housing conditions, review of business uses, environmental studies in neighborhoods, community facilities, population and economic surveys. This expertise is applied to the conditions and circumstances of a particular community, and a master plan for its physical development is evolved. Thus, plaintiffs say, planners operate on the top-most echelon of the process which in the ultimate produces the comprehensive master plan; at that level they apply their understanding of the operation of socio-economic forces to the component data prepared or compiled by the other professional groups such as engineers, architects and land surveyors, as well as lawyers, financial experts, and experienced men of public affairs, in order to fashion what they believe is the appropriate master plan.

There is no doubt that in more recent years community planning has drawn into its creative work social and economic considerations to a greater extent than in its formative period. And it may be that in the course of time the Legislature will conclude that such a high degree of specialized expertise has come into being in planning that the practice ought to be treated as uniquely separate from and independent of all other professional disciplines. * * * In this connection, however, the evidence is uncontradicted that at present there is a shortage of persons engaging in planning, whatever may be their professional, educational or experiential background. According to the Executive Director of the American Society of Planning Officials, the Society advertised about 1300 professional planning jobs during 1965, and at the end of the year about 400 of them were open and unfilled. That number was higher than at the end of 1964, which in turn was higher than in 1963. It may well be that the Legislature felt the need could be alleviated by admitting to the practice of planning without examination those persons who had already qualified for licenses in the related professional fields of engineering, land surveying and architecture. Under all of the circumstances it cannot be said reasonably that planning did not have its gestative stirrings and its early and continued practice in the three exempted disciplines, particularly in engineering and architecture. Nor can it be said on the record before us that it was wholly arbitrary and without reasonable basis for the Legislature to regard licensed members of the three professions as possessing sufficient minimal qualifications for planning to warrant treatment as a distinct class and to grant them exemption from the licensing requirements of the professional planners act, if they wish to practice in that field.

The notion that the lawmakers felt the desirability of some control of the developing practice of community planning must be accepted. It is reasonable also to conclude from the record that an awareness existed of the present shortage of persons engaged in the practice. Further, the evidence submitted warrants the inference that the legislators were aware of the historical part played by the engineers, land surveyors and architects in the development of community planning, and the continuing practice of such planning as an incident of their professional work. All of these circumstances suggest the view that the Legislature felt the current need in the field of community planning was for regulation of those persons who wished to engage in the practice but who had not demonstrated to any public agency that they had sufficient qualifications to do so. The circumstances suggest also satisfaction on the part of the lawmakers that achievement of licensure in one of the three named professions demonstrates possession of sufficient minimal competence to engage in planning to warrant treating such license holders as a separate class and exempting them from the requirements imposed upon those who have no license of any kind to practice planning. Under the principles of law laid down for the control of judicial review, we cannot say that the exempt class created by the fourth paragraph of section 11 is purely arbitrary and without any rational relation to the statutory objective of regulation of the planning profession.

Accordingly the challenged portions of the professional planners act cannot be declared violative of the constitutional mandate for equal protection of the laws. The judgment of the trial court is reversed, and the restraint imposed upon the New Jersey State Board of Professional Planners respecting the issuance of planners' licenses to those licensed in the exempt professions is vacated.

[A partial dissent is omitted.]

Note

In addition to the problem of the principal case, defining the "planner," the type of work done by the planner, whoever he may be, can raise serious questions. Planners frequently participate in the drafting of land use ordinances, and may also appear before some governmental agency as an advocate. Do these activities constitute unauthorized practice of law? Consider the following excerpts from an article, Care, The City Planner and the Unauthorized Practice of Law, 2 Land Use Controls Q. No. 4, pp. 23–30 (1968):

A zoning ordinance is a complicated, highly technical, legal instrument which is, or should be, related in some way to a comprehensive plan. Few attorneys are capable of preparing a zoning ordinance. Probably even fewer members of the planning profession have the experience and legal knowledge for such work despite the fact that many planners do prepare zoning ordinances as well as amendments to ordinances. In the past, planners have tended to utilize a "cut and paste" technique, with the almost verbatim transfer of language or standards from other zoning ordinances to their own. As a result, many communities are now saddled with zoning ordinances that are outmoded and inappropriate and which, in general, reflect the concepts and personal prejudices of the person or persons who prepared the original text. * * *

Although it is sometimes difficult to establish a line of demarcation between the functions of the planner and those of the municipal attorney during the preparation of a zoning ordinance, guidelines have been established by the professional legal and planning organizations. The American Institute of Planners has adopted a statement of principles of responsibility relating to the preparation of land-use control and other planning regulations which attempts to delineate the area of responsibility of both the planner and the attorney. This statement acknowledges the contribution of the legal profession to the planning process in these words:

Attorneys contribute significantly to the substantive portion of planning and to the application of planning concepts. They assist in developing and clarifying the relationship of planning to government, and to the means of applying planning processes and proposals to public policy and private activity * * *.[5]

This statement of principles also admits that "a planner, unless he is also an attorney and member of the Bar, *does not have the professional competence to put the technical provisions of an ordinance into suitable final legal form.*" (Emphasis added.) There are perhaps no more than a dozen planners in this country who can satisfy this requirement. There are a great many more practicing attorneys with some expertise in zoning enactments and litigation, but few of them have any practical experience in the technical phases of plan preparation. (There is a need for individuals with such dual competence within both professions.) It is apparent that the planners' professional organization is aware of the need for coordination of the activities of both the planner and the municipal attorney during the preparation of a zoning enactment. It is clear, also, that this organization realizes that the professional planner is not competent to relate the concepts of due process, private property rights, and other constitutional guarantees to planning proposals and land-use control regulations. It is unfortunate that many practicing planners recognize neither this limitation on their part nor the importance of preserving the constitutional guarantees with respect to the rights of individual property owners.

* * *

There is literally no case law relating to this subject, although in 1964 the Illinois State Bar filed suit against Evert Kinkaid and Associates, Inc., a planning consulting firm located in Chicago, alleging that the firm was in the business of drafting zoning ordinances for various municipalities in Illinois and that such activity constituted the unauthorized practice of law. The Circuit Court of Madison County, Illinois, entered a consent decree which enjoined the defendant from drafting zoning ordinances and which read in part as follows:

> "That the Defendant shall not prepare or purport to prepare any legal documents in a form which may be adopted as an ordinance or resolution by the legislative body of the County of Madison. That the Defendant and its agents and employees shall in connection with providing professional planning consultant services to the County of Madison restrict themselves solely and completely to the preparation and recommendation of technical planning standards which may be embodied in a subsequent draft of a zoning ordinance, it being understood that the preparation of the draft of such zoning ordinance shall be the responsibility of a member of the Bar of the State of Illinois to be designated by the Board of Supervisors of Madison County."[6]

It has been well established in the majority of states that representation before state agencies conducting adversary administrative proceedings constitutes the practice of law and that laymen may not appear in such proceedings in a representative capacity nor may they do the necessary

---

5. American Institute of Planners, A Statement of Principles of responsibility in the Preparation of Regulations for City Planning and Land Use Controls (The Institute, 1962).

6. Illinois State Bar Ass'n et al. v. Kinkaid and Associates, Inc. Circuit Court, Madison County, Illinois (1964).

preparatory work.[7] The practice of law has been broadly defined as including not only proceedings where trial work is involved but also "the preparation of legal documents, their interpretation, the giving of legal advice, or the *application of legal principles to problems of any complexity * * *.*"[8]

* * *

There is only one case of record which examines the nature of lay practice before either body. In Liebtag v. Dilworth[9] the Philadelphia Zoning Board of Adjustment had adopted a rule which prohibited non-lawyers from practicing before that body. The plaintiff, a planner, filed a mandamus suit, complaining that he had been unlawfully and improperly deprived of his right to earn a livelihood. The court not only held the rule to be valid and enforceable, but that such practice constituted the practice of law and that those sections of the city's zoning ordinance which related to the operation of the Zoning Board of Adjustment were invalid, null, and void to the extent that they purported to authorize any lay person to engage in the practice of law before that body. Thus the court indicated in no uncertain terms that the representation of an applicant before an administrative body of this nature by a non-lawyer—even a planner who may have specialized training in a related field—constitutes the unauthorized practice of law.[10]

Liebtag relates only to lay practice before a board of appeals, at least that was the only body directly involved in the case. It is suggested here that because of differences between the nature of the activities of a planning commission and a board of appeals, representation before a commission is not necessarily the practice of law although practice before a board may well be so.

* * *

It would appear, then, that whereas practice before a board of appeals may very well constitute the practice of law as defined by the court in Liebtag v. Dilworth, practice before a planning commission may not necessarily be considered as such. The legal elements of a proceeding before a board of appeals are obvious and inescapable, while proceedings before a planning commission may be entirely without legal significance. A final determination as to whether the practice of law is involved depends to a large extent upon the nature of the proceedings before the planning commission and the type of presentation made by the individual involved. If the

7. West Virginia State Bar v. Earley, 144 W.Va. 504, 109 S.E.2d 420 (1959).

8. Von Baur, Administrative Agencies and the Unauthorized Practice of Law, 48 ABA Journal 715 (1962). (Emphasis added.)

9. Court of Common Pleas, 1st Dist., Philadelphia, Pa. (1961).

10. Admittedly, numerous individuals in the planning profession have considerable knowledge with respect to the law as it relates to their work and have acquired an "expertise" in zoning. The court in *Liebtag* recognized not only the existence of such persons but also the limitations of their "expertise":

Such limited "expertise" would clearly not qualify the plaintiff to present cases before the Zoning Board. Competence in the practice of law requires many skills and in many interrelated fields. Experience in one limited field cannot be assumed to give the layman the ability to represent other parties * * * Ibid.

Also the code of professional ethics which governs the activities of the planner is neither as comprehensive as the legal canons nor oriented toward the same ethical problems. In addition, the professional sanctions which may be imposed upon planners are far less severe.

proceedings before a planning commission require the application of case law and legal principles, or an understanding of the rules of evidence and the historical development of property rights, the practice of law is involved, and it would be improper for a planner to appear in any capacity other than as an expert witness.

Thus far we have considered only the status of the planning consultant or privately employed planner practicing before a board of appeals and, under certain conditions, before a planning commission. A more complex, and perhaps more important, problem is raised by planners employed by public agencies. * * *

It is customary for planners employed by a planning commission or board of appeals to prepare a written analysis of each application considered by that agency. Such reports are frequently legally oriented and may recommend denial of a specific application because it constitutes a "spot zone" or a "strip zone," both of which are terms that require legal interpretation, or because the applicant is unable to satisfy certain legal criteria established by the courts or by enabling statutes. These comments may then be reiterated or even amplified during a verbal presentation of the staff recommendation, so that the planner is, in effect, using conclusions of law to influence the decision of an administrative agency. Such a situation is particularly unfair and inappropriate in view of the fact that, once a request for an ordinance amendment or a variance has been denied, there is a presumption that the legislative or administrative body involved has acted properly, and the courts will generally be loath to overturn such a decision.

The question, then, appears to be whether the public, and, more particularly, an applicant appearing before a planning commission or board of appeals, is being deprived of the proper determination of substantial rights in an instance where a publicly employed planner, acting in an advisory capacity, is able to convince such body that the applicant cannot legally substantiate his request. Is such an individual qualified to interpret the law, to quote legal precedent, and to relate precedent to the application under consideration? Under the circumstances, it is logical to conclude that this individual is performing much the same type of service that the court considered the practice of law in Liebtag v. Dilworth, the only distinction being that he is a public employee and his "client" is the administrative body rather than an individual appearing before the body.

Even more significant is the fact that many city planners, dissatisfied with "Euclidean" zoning because it does not provide either the amount of flexibility or the control felt necessary to achieve certain planning goals, are experimenting with new methods of land-use control—frequently without professional counsel and sometimes without the actual knowledge of the administrative agency involved. This is often accomplished by establishing requirements for the submission of so-called development plans, which may or may not contain restrictive covenants or be required to be filed of record. This is, however, only one of the methods being used to overcome the shortcomings of "Euclidean" zoning. Another method is to prepare and recommend the adoption of bylaws or rules of procedure that substantially affect the rights of the public, or suggest the use of restrictive methods of processing applications.

The most unfortunate aspect of this effort on the part of the planner is that, in most cases, he has little or no appreciation of the legal significance of some of the procedures and requirements that he has helped to establish. His concern is not with the property rights of individuals but with how to overcome such rights—rights he sometimes considers to be an impediment to the public welfare—in order to achieve the above-mentioned "goals." This is not to say that there is no need for an improvement in the existing land-use control system, but only that we should move in that direction only with the advice and assistance of legal counsel and only after the administrative body involved and the general public have been apprised of the rights they may be surrendering in the process.

SECTION 3.   THE CONTENT AND EFFECT OF THE MASTER PLAN

UNITED STATES DEPARTMENT OF COMMERCE, A STANDARD CITY PLANNING ENABLING ACT

(1928).

Sec. 6. General Powers and Duties—It shall be the function and duty of the commission to make and adopt a master plan for the physical development of the municipality, including any areas outside of its boundaries which, in the commission's judgment, bear relation to the planning of such municipality. Such plan, with the accompanying maps, plats, charts, and descriptive matter, shall show the commission's recommendations for the development of said territory, including, among other things, the general location, character, and extent of streets, viaducts, subways, bridges, waterways, water fronts, boulevards, parkways, playgrounds, squares, parks, aviation fields, and other public ways, grounds and open spaces, the general location of public buildings and other public property, and the general location and extent of public utilities and terminals, whether publicly or privately owned or operated, for water, light, sanitation, transportation, communication, power, and other purposes; also the removal, relocation, widening, narrowing, vacating, abandonment, change of use or extension of any of the foregoing ways, grounds, open spaces, buildings, property, utilities, or terminals; as well as a zoning plan for the control of the height, area, bulk, location, and use of buildings and premises. As the work of making the whole master plan progresses, the commission may from time to time adopt and publish a part or parts thereof, any such part to cover one or more major sections or divisions of the municipality or one or more of the aforesaid or other functional matters to be included in the plan. The commission may from time to time amend, extend, or add to the plan.

Sec. 7. Purposes in View—In the preparation of such plan the commission shall make careful and comprehensive surveys and studies of present conditions and future growth of the municipality and with due regard to its relation to neighboring territory. The plan shall be made with the general purpose of guiding and accomplishing a coordinated, adjusted, and harmonious development of the municipality and its environs which will, in accordance with present and future needs, best promote health, safety, morals, order, convenience, prosperity, and general welfare, as well as efficiency and economy in the process of development; including, among other things, adequate provision for traffic, the promotion of safety from fire and other dangers, adequate provision for light and air, the promotion of the healthful and convenient distribution of population, the promotion of good civic design and arrangement, wise and efficient expenditure of public funds, and the adequate provision of public utilities and other public requirements.

———

See Knack, Meck and Stollman, The Real Story Behind the Standard Planning and Zoning Acts of the 1920s, Land Use Law (Feb. 1996) p. 3. The Model Land Development Code[11] provides model enabling legislation for planning which differs considerably from the Standard Act. Some excerpts from Article 3 and the commentary follow:

* * *

Two key issues need to be resolved in regard to the content of the plan: First, to what extent should the plan concentrate on physical development? Second, should the plan emphasize long term goals or continuing processes?

1. *The Role of Physical Planning*

Traditional urban planning based on the SPEA has concentrated on (a) the proper location and intensity of activities which use land, and (b) the type, design, and location of physical structures and facilities that serve these activities. The planner has examined the present physical setting, made long range projections of population and employment, and forecasted land and facility demands to be generated. Then, applying professional judgments as to desired future conditions, he has prepared a plan locating activities and specified facilities.

This planning process has a number of objectives. (See, e.g., Mocine, Urban Physical Planning and the "New Planning," 32 J.A.I.P. 234 (July 1966).) One is to maximize economic efficiency by predicting physical facility needs and coordinating the size and location of such facilities with activity locations. Thus, for example, the process should lead to acquiring land and building schools near planned residential locations, constructing sewer lines large enough to serve adjacent activities, and locating expressways to connect places of residence and employment. This objective recognizes the long lead time required for major public improvements and the

---

11. This material from the code is based primarily on the work of Professor Ira Michael Heyman which appeared in Tentative Draft No. 1 of the Model Land Development Code. The Model Code has not been adopted in any state; however, portions of the Code have been utilized, principally for state regulation of critical areas in Colorado, Florida, Minnesota, Nevada, and Wyoming.

desirability of employing these improvements efficiently over their lifetimes to justify the original expense.

A second objective is to maximize desired relationships between different land use activities and their attendant physical structures. For example, a plan may call for areas exclusively developed for single family residences, but with provision for nearby shopping centers. Or it may seek to stimulate mixed residential densities and certain commercial activities. This objective assumes that the market is deficient in creating desired mixes of uses. It also assumes that without governmental intervention individual landowners will create external costs, and environments of maximum desirability will be largely unobtainable.

A third objective is to allocate land (a scarce resource in a locational sense) to desired activities. For instance, the city may decide that it wants to encourage only single family houses, but the market unhindered would result in numerous multiple dwellings. Or, the city may desire to encourage industrial investment and seek to preserve adequate space for new factories. This objective, like the second, assumes an imperfect market and the necessity of governmental intervention to stimulate private investment towards desired goals.

A fourth objective is to provide a general urban design which is pleasing. For instance, a plan might call for the preservation of open space for recreation and appearance, require tree planting and setbacks, attempt to order the three-dimensional design of areas, or group leisure activities in specified locations.

A growing number of planners reject this traditional approach. They argue that planning for physical development is based on insufficient information, has too limited a focus, and is unrelated to desirable economic and social goals. In addition, as explored below, they believe that long-range (end-state) planning is not effective; rather the planner should concentrate his efforts on short term programs to realize specific objectives.

* * *

The Code can take any of four major positions: (1) A plan should deal only with physical development without consideration of economic and social data and consequences. (This basically is the approach of the SPEA.) (2) The plan should have a physical development nucleus but should require that specified economic and social data be taken into consideration in its preparation and consideration. (This is the approach adopted.) (3) The plan should have a development focus and speak primarily in terms of economic and social objectives and means for their attainment including physical development. (This path is largely uncharted.) (4) There should be no section on planning because there is no solid urban planning theory at present.

Alternative (2) has been chosen for several reasons. First, the Model Land Development Code encompasses a variety of laws relating to the physical development of land but does not attempt direct regulation of social and economic affairs outside the sphere of land development. It is appropriate, therefore, that the planning powers authorized by the Code be limited to those that parallel its other Articles. Second, we have existing institutions of land planning which need a framework. The present statutory framework, built on the SPEA, is inadequate in a number of respects. We are beginning to appreciate better than before that we cannot realistically determine patterns and characteristics of physical development mainly on the basis of design and appearance. Rather, how and where development takes place relates more importantly to social and economic values and objectives. Therefore, we should require explicit analysis and disclosure to the greatest extent possible of a variety of social and economic consequences of planned physical development. Otherwise we hide such policy judgments, make them implicitly rather than explicitly, or, as often occurs, design a plan which will never be carried out because the implementing decisions will be politically unfeasible.

* * *

Most master plans have been of the long-range (end-state) type. They have sought to present a "picture" of what the planning area should look like some twenty or twenty-five years in the future. In the view of many planners, however, few of these plans have had a demonstrable impact on development. (See, e.g., Meyerson, Building the Middle–Range Bridge for Comprehensive Planning, 22 J.A.I.P. 58 (1956); Webber, Prospects for Policies Planning, in Duhl (ed.) The Urban Condition (1963), 319; Robinson, Beyond the Middle–Range Planning Bridge, 31 J.A.I.P. 304 (Nov. 1965); Mitchell, The New Frontier in Metropolitan Planning, 27 J.A.I.P. 169 (Aug. 1961).)

* * *

This Article provides for long-term goal setting. The goals, however, are to be put in terms of nature and rate of change rather than in static form. Further, the goals are primarily important as a framework for the short-term programming required by Section 3–105 and they are expected to change. In addition, the Code makes numerous references to the identification and treatment of major problems of physical development. These are the basic departure points for the programming. Thus the Article provides for a broad framework of objectives, but is concerned mainly with the preparation and evaluation of specific programs of public action.

* * *

The relationship between planning and regulation has been the subject of discussion for many years. Two articles debating the subject are Sullivan and Kressel, Twenty Years After—Renewed Significance of the Comprehensive Plan Requirement, 9 Urban Law Ann. 33 (1975) and Tarlock, Consistency with Adopted Land Use Plans as a Standard of Review: The Case Against, 9 Urban Law Ann. 69 (1975).

CREATIVE DISPLAYS, INC. v. CITY OF FLORENCE

Supreme Court of Kentucky, 1980.
602 S.W.2d 682.

STEPHENS, JUSTICE.

The issue before the court is whether Boone County and Florence, Kentucky, have properly enacted planning and zoning ordinances, pursuant to KRS chapter 100 (1966).

* * *

Until 1966, the City of Florence and Boone County fiscal court were separate planning bodies. The record shows that Florence adopted its zoning ordinance in December of 1962, and Boone County adopted its in February of 1966. In September of 1966, a county-wide planning unit was formed, encompassing Florence, Walton, Hopeful Heights, and Boone County, and known as the Boone County Planning and Zoning Commission. This entity was created in response to House Bill 390, which passed the Kentucky Legislature and became effective on June 16, 1966, and is presently contained in KRS chapter 100.

In October, 1966, the Boone County Planning and Zoning Commission adopted its "comprehensive plan," pursuant to KRS 100.183. This plan consisted solely of the already existing plans of Florence and Boone County. The statute provides that the minimum requirements for the plan include a statement of goals and objectives, a land use plan, a transportation plan, and a community facilities plan. KRS 100.187. It is not argued that the comprehensive plan adopted by the Commission did not contain these elements. On the contrary, it is admitted that the individual plans of Florence and Boone County comply in every respect with the substantive requirements of chapter 100. Yet, Creative Designs still challenges the plan adopted by the Commission as invalid under the statute, and we agree.

* * *

The actions of the Boone County Planning and Zoning Commission in *pro forma* adopting the pre-existing plans of Florence and Boone County do not constitute the "preparation" of a comprehensive plan for the newly created unit.

Further, although the plan adopted by the Commission contains all the elements listed in KRS 100.187, that section requires "a statement of goals and objectives, principles, policies, and standards, which shall serve as a guide for the physical development and economic and social well-being *of the planning unit.*" (emphasis added). In this instance the planning unit includes Florence, Walton, Hopeful Heights, and Boone County. The goals and objectives expressed by Florence and Boone County in their individual plans in no way address the question of the proper goals for the new, county-wide planning unit. The same is true of the specialized research, analysis, and projections which are required to support the elements of the comprehensive plan. KRS 100.191. Research into population distribution, economic and business activity, and transportation and community facility needs, done in advance of the local plans, will not suffice as the basis for the county-wide plan.

Finally, and probably most significantly, the statutory scheme set out in KRS 100.197 requires the planning commission to hold a public hearing before adoption of the comprehensive plan. Florence and Boone County admit that no hearing was held to consider the county-wide plan. They argue that the prior hearings held with regard to the individual plans of Florence and Boone County are sufficient to satisfy the mandates of the statute. We disagree. The citizens of Florence, the largest population center in the county, have never had the opportunity to express their opinions about the future planning and zoning of the rest of Boone County. Residents of Hopeful Heights, Walton, and rural areas of the county have not been able to voice their concerns about the same issues in Florence. And none of the people of Boone County have been allowed to speak their minds with regard to the comprehensive plan for the county-wide planning unit in which they now live. For this reason, we hold that the comprehensive plan adopted by the Boone County Planning and Zoning Commission does not comply with the requirements of KRS 100.183, et seq.

KRS 100.367 provides that all plans in existence on the effective date of KRS chapter 100 (June 16, 1966), may continue in effect until they are superseded by new plans or until five years have passed. Thus, all plans which did not conform to the new law on June 16, 1971, ceased to exist on that date. Regrettably, the comprehensive plan in the case at bar falls into that category. The comprehensive plan of the Boone County Planning and Zoning Commission, and any zoning ordinances adopted pursuant thereto, are void.

* * *

The decision of the Court of Appeals is reversed and the case is remanded to the trial court for entry of a judgment consistent with this opinion.

* * *

Notes

1. Compare with the principal case Lazy Mountain Land Club v. Matanuska–Susitna Borough Bd. of Adjustment and Appeals, 904 P.2d 373 (Alaska 1995) where the court rejected a developer's argument that piece-

meal adoption of various planning documents and incorporation by reference of a previous document evidenced the lack of a comprehensive plan.

2.   Courts have had very little concern with the question of adequacy of the plan. The enabling legislation for planning rarely makes provision for judicial (or any other) review of the finished product. One notable exception to this state of affairs is found in the State of Oregon. In 1973, Oregon amended its planning enabling statute to make land use planning mandatory for local government units, and created a state level administrative agency, the Land Conservation and Development Commission (LCDC), which has power to establish statewide planning "goals" and to review local plans for consistency with the established "goals." Since 1975, when the 14 statewide "goals" were promulgated, several hundred contested disputes concerning the consistency of local land use decisions with the "goals" have been adjudicated by LCDC. For three divergent views on the efficacy of this approach, see Comprehensive Plans and the Law: The Oregon Experience, 32 Land Use Law & Zoning Digest 6 (Sept. 1980). Also see Rajneesh Medical Corp. v. Wasco County, 300 Or. 107, 706 P.2d 948 (1985).

3.   The Creative Displays case is one of the few which looks at the process of adopting and evaluating the comprehensive plan. In many states the enabling legislation for zoning, subdivision regulations and other land use regulations specifies that these regulations may be adopted or enacted only after the adoption of a comprehensive plan. In Chapter VII the question of the validity of regulations where the comprehensive planning process was insufficient will be taken up in greater detail. In Wolf v. City of Ely, 493 N.W.2d 846 (Iowa 1992) the court held a zoning ordinance invalid because the town had not adopted a comprehensive plan; the court acknowledged that "A majority of courts in states where zoning must be 'in accordance with a comprehensive plan' hold a plan external to the zoning ordinance is not required." However, the court stated that the trend of decisions is in the other direction and aligned Iowa with the trend.

ELYSIAN HEIGHTS RESIDENTS ASSOCIATION, INC. v. CITY OF LOS ANGELES

California Court of Appeal, Second District, 1986.
182 Cal.App.3d 21, 227 Cal.Rptr. 226.

COMPTON, ACTING PRESIDING JUSTICE.

Elysian Heights Residents Association, Inc., et al., hereinafter appellants, appeal from a judgment of the superior court denying their petition for administrative mandamus. (See Code Civ.Proc., § 1094.5.) By way of this petition, appellants sought the revocation of a building permit issued by respondents City of Los Angeles, et al. to Morton Park Associates [Morton] for the construction of a three story, 45–unit apartment complex. Pursuant to appellants' request, and in order to preserve the status quo, we stayed further development of the project pending the outcome of this appeal. We now affirm the judgment and vacate the stay order.

* * *

In December 1984, while the administrative appeal was still pending, the Department of Building and Safety, pursuant to the terms of an ordinance imposing a moratorium on all projects which exceeded the zoning and height requirements of the District Plan, ordered Morton to immediately cease all construction work. At approximately the same time various homeowner associations filed an action in superior court, entitled *Federation of Hillside Canyon Associations, Inc. et al. v. City of Los Angeles* (Los Angeles Sup.Ct. No. 526,616), to prevent the City from issuing building permits for development of property inconsistent with the General Plan. * * *

[The court found that the existing plan would have permitted a 12–unit apartment building.]

In January 1985, the superior court, in ruling on the *Federation* case, issued a writ of mandate requiring the City to bring its zoning ordinances into conformity with the General Plan, but denied the petitioners' request for an injunction against the issuance of building permits for inconsistent development. * * *

We first consider appellants' contention that the disputed building permit was issued in violation of state statute and was thus void *ab initio* and must be revoked. The major thrust of appellants' argument in this regard is that building permits, to be validly issued, must be consistent with a municipality's general plan. It is, therefore, necessary to determine whether Government Code section 65860 mandates such conformity.

* * *

[W]e first note that in recent years the Legislature has enacted a number of statutes as part of the State Planning & Zoning Law (Gov. Code, § 65000, et seq.), the combined effect of which is to require that cities and counties adopt a general plan for the future development, configuration, and character of a city and county and require that future land use decisions be made in harmony with that general plan. (*City of Los Angeles v. State of California* (1982) 138 Cal.App.3d 526, 530, 187 Cal.Rptr. 893; *Bounds v. City of Glendale* (1980) 113 Cal.App.3d 875, 880, 170 Cal.Rptr. 342.) These requirements, forming what is generally referred to as the consistency doctrine, promote a particular nexus between land-use plans and government regulation of land use, such as zoning and subdivision map approval.

The doctrine has its roots in the language of the Standard Zoning Enabling Act (U.S. Dept. of Commerce, The Standard State Zoning Enabling Act, 1922 [rev. ed., 1926.]), which provides that zoning shall be done "in accordance with" a comprehensive plan. (See DiMento, *Improving Development Control through Planning: The Consistency Doctrine* (1978) 5 Colum.J.Envt'l L. 1.) Under this historical antecedent of the consistency doctrine, violations of the "in accordance with" language were found when (1) only selected areas within a municipality were regulated by zoning; (2) zoning was done by means of an interim ordinance that was enacted by legally questionable government practices; or (3) the zoning ordinance failed to control one or more of the factors it was intended to regulate. (See DiMento, *Developing the Consistency Doctrine: The Contribution of the California Courts* (1980) 20 Santa Clara L.Rev. 285, 286.)

California's state planning laws took what some may consider a giant step forward when the Legislature, in 1973, mandated that zoning changes and subdivision approvals be consistent with the local general plan, and that the plan itself be internally consistent. (Lefcoe, *California's Land Planning Requirements: The Case for Deregulation* (1981) 54 So.Cal.L.Rev. 447, 488.) Although the Planning and Zoning Law establishes the authority of most local government entities to regulate the use of land (*Topanga Assn. for the Scenic Community v. County of Los Angeles* (1974) 11 Cal.3d 506, 518–519, fn. 18, 113 Cal.Rptr. 836, 522 P.2d 12), it commands municipalities to adopt "a comprehensive, long-term general plan for the physical development of the county or city.... " (Gov.Code, § 65300.) The plan itself must include, inter alia, a statement of policies, and nine specified elements: land use, circulation, housing, conservation, open-space, seismic safety, noise, scenic highway, and safety. (Gov.Code, § 65302.) Section 65566 requires that acquisition, regulation, and any other actions of the local government related to open space conform to the local open-space plan. Under section 65567, building permits, subdivision maps, and zoning ordinances affecting *open space* must be consistent with the *open space* plan. Section 65803 exempts charter cities from the consistency statutes unless they adopt these requirements or fall within the provisions of section 65860. And, sections 66473 and 66474 set forth various requirements for attaining subdivision consistency with general and specific plans.

Most relevant here, of course, is section 65860, which generally requires that county or city zoning ordinances be consistent with the general plan of the county or city, and allows private citizens to bring suit to enforce consistency of zoning with the general plan. Subdivision (d) specifically makes the statute applicable to Los Angeles and establishes a time table for bringing the City's zoning ordinances into conformity with the general plan.

As can be seen, neither the language of section 65860 nor the statutory scheme in general mandates that building permits be scrutinized for plan consistency. Indeed, had the Legislature intended to fashion such a requirement, it clearly had the power to do so. In this regard, the State Planning and Zoning Law specifically prohibits the adoption or issuance of permits, subdivision maps, or zoning ordinances that are inconsistent with *open space* plans; requires that tentative subdivision tract maps be drawn in conformity with the general plan (Gov.Code, § 66474.61, subd. (a)); and allows a court to enjoin issuance of all permits where a *general plan* is found to be inadequate. (Gov.Code, § 65755.) There is, however, nothing in the legislative history of section 65860 to suggest that the Legislature intended to prohibit the issuance of building permits for projects consistent with the zoning of a particular community but not the general plan. Moreover, there is no mention of any remedies available to halt construction of projects which are not in conformity with the general plan, and no sanctions are provided for noncompliance with section 65860, subdivision (d).

* * *

Generally, the enumeration of acts or things as coming within the operation of a statute precludes the inclusion by implication of other acts or things not listed. (*Western Pioneer Insurance Co. v. Estate of Taira* (1982) 136 Cal.App.3d 174, 181, 185 Cal.Rptr. 887.) Applying this rule to the instant case, we think it clear that the Legislature has purposefully failed to prohibit the issuance of building permits while the consistency process is being implemented. In the absence of any such provision it would ill-behoove any court to indirectly mandate the withholding of permits that are not in conformity with a municipality's general plan. If the Legislature desires such consistency, it should specifically say so.

Recognizing that amending zoning ordinances to make them consistent with a general plan would take time, the Legislature added subdivision (c) to section 65860 which states: "In the event that a zoning ordinance becomes inconsistent with a general plan by reason of amendment to such plan, or to any element of such plan, such zoning ordinance *shall be amended within a reasonable time* so that it is consistent with the general plan as amended." (Emphasis added.) The trial court had before it evidence that in 1982 the City had approximately 200,000 lots which had zoning inconsistent with the applicable General Plan. If appellants' contentions were correct, no new building permits could be issued until all inconsistently-zoned lots were made to conform to the provisions of the General Plan. This would bring new construction in the City to a grinding halt and cause economic havoc. As one commentator has aptly observed, "Halting construction for the years it takes to adopt a general plan [or amend zoning ordinances] works great hardship. During those years of delay, some projects that were once economically feasible will become impracticable. Even those projects that survive the de facto moratorium will be costly to consumers if developers are able to recoup their increased land holding, construction, and borrowing costs through higher prices. For buyers priced out of the market by these delays, the loss may be irretrievable; anyone who doubts it should talk to a renter who could have afforded a house some years ago, but who had been left behind by rising prices. Neither the courts nor the Legislature seem to have understood who really pays the price when zone changes, building permits, and subdivision approvals are withheld pending the adoption of a general plan." (Lefcoe, *California's Land Planning Requirements: The Case for Deregulation, supra,* 54 So.Cal.L.Rev. 447, 489.)

* * *

The City's Interim Ordinance, which does require permit/plan consistency, was given only prospective application and thus did not affect the validity of Morton's permit. After balancing competing interests, the City Council properly determined that projects which had been approved prior to the ordinance's effective date, and did not vary from their originally approved plans, were entitled to go forward. As found by the trial court in the *Federation* case, the enactment of the Interim Ordinance represented a good faith effort by the City to bring its regulations into substantial compliance with state law. Zoning ordinances are, of course, presumed to be a valid exercise of the police power with every intendment in favor of their validity. "The wisdom of the prohibitions and restrictions is a matter for legislative determination, and even though a court may not agree with that determination it will not substitute its judgment for that of the zoning authorities if there is any reasonable justification for their action." (*Lockard v. City of Los Angeles* (1949) 33 Cal.2d 453, 461, 202 P.2d 38.) We agree with respondents that for this court to now say that the issuance of Morton's building permit constituted an abuse of discretion would seriously undermine the City Council's authority to enact land-use regulations and invite a further, unending spiral of litigation. It must be remembered that the Plan which appellants view as sacrosanct was itself a creature of the City and presumptively can be changed by the City.

Having concluded that the State Planning and Zoning Law does not preclude issuance of permits which may be inconsistent with a community's general plan, and that Morton's building permit was issued in compliance with City ordinances, we need not discuss appellants' remaining contentions.

The judgment is affirmed and the stay order is vacated.

[Dissenting opinion omitted.][12]

Notes

1.   Assuming that the plan is valid, how should a court view a land use regulation which is not consistent with the plan? See DiMento, The Consistency Doctrine: Continuing Controversy, 4 Zoning and Planning Law Report No. 1 (Jan. 1981). The author points out that only a few states have accepted the principle that a regulation must either be consistent with the plan or valid despite the plan because of changed circumstances. The majority of jurisdictions still view the plan as advisory to local officials. See, e.g., Barrie v. Kitsap County, 93 Wash.2d 843, 613 P.2d 1148 (1980), holding that a land use decision was not invalid because of inconsistency with the plan, and City of Sanibel v. Goode, 372 So.2d 181 (Fla.App.1979), holding a decision invalid despite its consistency with the plan.

2.   In Haines v. City of Phoenix, 151 Ariz. 286, 727 P.2d 339 (1986), the appellate court held that the city council could rationally have found consistency with the general plan in allowing a 500 foot building to be constructed, despite the plan's 250 foot height limit!

12. The dissenting judge appended the neighbor's reply brief to his opinion, a brief which is worth reading as a plea for recognizing the supremacy of the plan.

3. Some other California cases which explore the consistency doctrine at length are Lesher Communications, Inc. v. City of Walnut Creek, 262 Cal.Rptr. 337 (Cal.App.1989), reversed 52 Cal.3d 531, 277 Cal.Rptr. 1, 802 P.2d 317 (1990), and Mira Development Corp. v. City of San Diego, 205 Cal.App.3d 1201, 252 Cal.Rptr. 825 (1988).

4. If regulatory decisions are not readily subject to attack by way of the consistency doctrine, can citizens attack the plan itself prior to the issuance of building permits or the rendering of zoning decisions? Consider the following materials.

Cram, Master Planning Creates Clouds on Titles, 35 Mich.S.B.J. 9, 10 (April 1956):

Section 6 authorizes the adoption of a "master plan for the physical development of the municipality." The plan by maps, and other descriptive means, shall show the plan commission's recommendation for such development, including location of "parkways, playgrounds and open spaces."

Our case involved a "park," spread out on the master plan map over our property, without so much as a "by your leave" and certainly without benefit of condemnation or compensation nor even any thought in that direction. Nobody offered us any payment because nobody anticipated any present condemnation; one member of the plan commission conceded that our area might not be wanted for park purposes for 25 years. Who was going to pay taxes on the property during that time seemed nobody's concern. All we were left was a "green spot on the map," green being considered emblematic, map-wise, to represent a future park.

COCHRAN v. PLANNING BD. OF CITY OF SUMMIT

Superior Court of New Jersey, Law Division, 1965.
87 N.J.Super. 526, 210 A.2d 99.

FELLER, J.S.C. This is an action * * * challenging the adoption of a master plan by the Planning Board of the City of Summit and seeking to enjoin the city and its agencies, boards, and officials from implementing the master plan in any way. In particular, plaintiffs object to that part of the plan which would permit an expansion of the Ciba Corporation's parking area and research and office space into the residential area which adjoins the rear of plaintiffs' property.

Plaintiffs are citizens, taxpayers and owners of lands located at 249 Kent Place Boulevard in Summit. Their property is adjacent and contiguous to property owned by the Ciba Corporation (hereinafter Ciba). Plaintiffs' premises and that portion of the Ciba tract in question are presently in the A–15 zoning district, which is limited to one-family residences with a minimum lot area of 15,000 square feet. Prior to 1958 the Ciba tract was in an A–10 zone, which was limited to one-family residences with a minimum lot area of 10,000 square feet. The tract is bordered on three sides by one-family residences and is presently subject to enforceable deed restrictions which limit the use of the tract to the erection of one-family residences until 1975.

On December 9, 1963 defendant planning board adopted a master plan for the city, which provided in part that the Ciba tract, namely, 63½ acres in the A–15 zone, should be rezoned for parking areas and research and office building use. This rezoning is for the purpose of providing for the eventual expansion therein of Ciba's existing operations. The plan requires a 125–foot buffer zone, which would separate the rear line of plaintiffs' property from the proposed Ciba construction. This zone would contain trees, shrubs and a screen, all of them calculated to preserve the existing residential atmosphere of the area.

Plaintiffs claim that the adoption of the master plan is arbitrary, discriminatory, capricious, unreasonable and an abuse of the planning board's discretion; * * * that it was procedurally defective because it was adopted on improper notice, ten days' notice not having been given of the December 9, 1963 hearing at which the plan was adopted, as required by the act, and that the planning board was illegally constituted. Plaintiffs further contend that the master plan was an abuse of discretion in that it was contrary to the expressed wishes of the citizens of the city made known at the hearings thereon and prior thereto; was contrary to the purpose of the plan to preserve the already established pattern of the better single-family areas of Summit; was contrary to the general welfare and health of the citizens; was *ultra vires* the planning board's power, and did not conform to the character of the neighborhood.

Plaintiffs also contend that the * * * action of the board was allegedly based on insufficient and incompetent facts and findings and on insufficient surveys and studies, in violation of N.J.S.A. 40:55–1.12.

* * *

Defendants contend that the master plan was properly adopted at a meeting held on December 9, 1963; insist there was proper notice of the meeting, and that the meeting was a continuance of a previous one held on November 26, 1963. * * *

Defendants further contend that the plan was the result of a comprehensive study by the planning board which commenced in January 1962 and terminated on December 9, 1963, after an average of a meeting every two weeks with interested persons and citizens. They say that all the work and the final plan are in accordance with the requirements of N.J.S.A. 40:55–1.1 et seq.

A review of the evidence indicates that the following questions should be resolved: whether the planning board had the authority or power to adopt a master plan under the ordinance setting up the board; whether the plaintiffs' property has been harmed or damaged by the adoption of the plan or whether their suit is premature; whether the plan is arbitrary, capricious, unreasonable, or an abuse of discretion * * *.

I

Initially, plaintiffs contend that the ordinance of March 16, 1954, which created the Planning Board of the City of Summit, did not give the board the power to prepare and adopt a master plan; furthermore, they contend that since no other ordinance granted this power to the board, the provisions of N.J.S.A. 40:55–1.3 have been violated by such preparation and adoption, and that the master plan should be set aside as *ultra vires* the power of the planning board. N.J.S.A. 40:55–1.3 provides in relevant part that:

> "The governing body may by ordinance grant any of the powers exercisable by a planning board to a planning board continued by section twenty-seven of this act or to be created under section four of this act, *but no particular power may be exercised until expressly granted by ordinance* and until compliance is made with the conditions, standards, procedures and regulations enumerated in the sections describing such power." (Emphasis added).

The defendants rely in part on the passage of an ordinance by the Summit governing body on December 19, 1961, which made an appropriation for the engagement of special consultants for the preparation of a master plan. It is argued that this ordinance is sufficient to satisfy the demands of N.J.S.A. 40:55–1.3. The ordinance provided:

Section 1. That pursuant to Chapter 48, P.L.1956, the sum of $24,000 is hereby appropriated for the engagement of special consultants for the preparation and the preparation, of a master plan or plans, when required in order to conform to the planning laws of the State, and shall be deemed an emergency appropriation as defined and provide [sic] for in R.S. 40:50–12.

Such appropriation and/or the 'special emergency notes' authorized to finance the appropriation shall be provided for in succeeding annual budgets by the inclusion of at least ⅕ of the amount authorized pursuant to this act.

Section 2. This ordinance shall take effect immediately after final passage and publication as provided by law.

If the above ordinance does not by implication grant the planning board power to prepare and adopt a master plan, then the other sections of the Planning Act do. * * *

For the above reasons, and specifically because of the legislative expression in N.J.S.A. 40:55–1.10, this court is of the opinion that the Summit Planning Board had the power to enact a master plan and that such action by the board was not *ultra vires*.

II

The second question is whether plaintiffs' property has been harmed or damaged by the adoption of the master plan and whether their suit is premature. If the action is premature, they have sustained no damage or harm to their property, and a determination of the procedural inadequacies and conflicts of interest alleged by plaintiffs would be unnecessary.

Plaintiffs request the court to declare the master plan null and void because it represents a taking of private property for public use without just compensation. * * *

Defendants contend that plaintiffs' failure to allege and prove injury to their property rights results in the presentation of legal questions which are premature and which do not present justiciable controversies. This court agrees that such allegations and proof of injury to private property rights are necessary before the requested relief may be considered and granted by this court. Plaintiffs have not demonstrated that degree of injury which would entitle them to relief.

* * *

If plaintiffs cannot demonstrate injury, then they may not obtain relief; if their claims are based upon assumed potential invasions of rights, then these are not enough to warrant judicial intervention. See Ashwander v. T.V.A., 297 U.S. 288, 56 S.Ct. 466, 80 L.Ed. 688 (1936).

The crux of this problem is clear when it is remembered that a master plan is of no force and effect until it is adopted by the governing body of the municipality. Thus, the master plan under consideration in the City of Summit is of no effect until it is adopted by the municipal governing body.

The master plan represents at a given time the best judgment of the planning agency as to the proper course of action to be followed. In this stage the plan for community development remains flexible and is not binding, either on government or individual. See Webster, Urban Planning & Municipal Policy 265 (1958). A master plan is not a straitjacket delimiting the discretion of the legislative body, but only a guide for the city, Rhyne, Municipal Law, sec. 32–59, p. 977 (1957); furthermore, a master plan is nothing more than the easily changed instrumentality which will show a commission from day to day the progress it has made. Haar, Land Use Planning 693 (1959).

The mere adoption and recording of a master plan has no legal consequence. The plan is merely a declaration of policy and a disclosure of an intention which must thereafter be implemented by the adoption of various ordinances. Horack & Nolan, Land Use Controls 36 (1955).

In New Jersey the fact that a master plan adopted by a planning board has no legal consequences is substantiated, not only by the absence of statutory language to that effect, but also by the necessity of a municipality's adoption of the master plan by the governing body before the plan takes effect. See N.J.S.A. 40:55–1.13; Wollen v. Fort Lee, 27 N.J. 408, 424, 142 A.2d 881, 890 (1958), where the court said that "the master plan is not conclusive on the governing body." Moreover, it is not mandatory for a township to create a planning board, and a governing body could assume directly the duties of a planning board. Jones v.

Zoning Bd. of Adjustment of Long Beach Tp., 32 N.J.Super. 397, 406, 108 A.2d 498 (App.Div.1954).

* * *

It is clear that a master plan is only a plan, and that it requires legislative implementation before its proposals have binding effect and legal consequences. If the necessary legislative implementation is taken—and, of course, such implementation must be taken according to the applicable statutes—then a zoning ordinance and not a master plan would be before the court. Until appropriate municipal legislative action is taken, however, the municipality has only a dormant plan which differs from proposals that may be under consideration by any municipal board or citizen of the municipality in that it is comprehensive and has been reduced to printed form. Indeed, a master plan is not even a statutory prerequisite to zoning action. Kozesnik v. Montgomery Township, 24 N.J. 154, 165, 131 A.2d 1 (1957).

The issue here is whether a plan for municipal development, not yet implemented by the necessary legislative action, may be legally considered to deprive one of the enjoyment of his property, contrary to the United States and New Jersey Constitutions. The statutes providing for the adoption of a master plan were upheld as constitutional in Mansfield & Swett, Inc. v. West Orange, 120 N.J.L. 145, 198 A. 225 (Sup.Ct.1938). The court, in the course of its opinion, said that the State possesses the inherent authority to resort, in the building and expansion of its community life, to such measures as may be necessary to secure the essential common material and moral needs. The public welfare is of prime importance, and the correlative restrictions upon individual rights, either of person or of property, are considered a negligible loss compared with the resultant advantages to the community as a whole. Municipal planning confined to the common need is inherent in the authority to create the municipality itself. It is as old as government itself; it is of the very essence of civilized society. A comprehensive scheme of physical development is requisite to community efficiency and progress.

* * * The principle is firmly established in our federal jurisprudence that injury to private property ensuing from governmental action in a proper sphere, reasonably taken for the public good, and for no other purpose, is not necessarily classable as a "taking" of such property within the intendment of the constitutional guaranties against the deprivation of property without due process of law, or the taking of private property for public use without compensation.

* * *

Attention is also called to the following cases: Headley v. City of Rochester, 272 N.Y. 197, 5 N.E.2d 198 (Ct.App.1936); Reopening of Philadelphia Parkway Between Twentieth and Twenty-Second Street, 295 Pa. 538, 145 A. 600, 64 A.L.R. 542 (Sup.Ct.1929); Windsor v. Whitney, 95 Conn. 357, 111 A. 354, 12 A.L.R. 669 (Sup.Ct.Err.1920); Harrison v. City of Philadelphia, 217 F. 107 (E.D.Pa.1914); Bauman v.

Ross, 167 U.S. 548, 17 S.Ct. 966, 42 L.Ed. 270, 64 A.L.R. 542 (1897). These authorities indicate that the power of a municipality to plan for the future is part of the police power. The adoption of maps and/or reports, commonly called a "master plan," does not result in a "taking" of property in violation of our Federal and State Constitutions.

The plaintiffs have alleged that the adoption of the master plan destroys property values. To support this thesis they called as witnesses George Goldstein, who is a real estate appraiser and a consultant for the Federal Government and many public agencies, as well as for many of the largest industrial companies in the country, and Norman Lemcke, who is a retired vice-president of the Prudential Mortgage Loan Department. Goldstein testified that the adoption of the master plan had diminished adjacent property values up to 25%, as in the case of plaintiffs' home. Lemcke testified that before the plan he would have granted a 66% mortgage on the plaintiffs' house, but after its adoption he would only grant a 50% mortgage. He further testified that for financing purposes lending institutions take into account whether there is a master plan affecting the property, and the manner in which it is affected. Plaintiffs also rely upon N.J.S.A. 40:55–1.12, which requires, among other things, that a master plan be made with the general purpose of the maintenance of property values previously established. * * *

The contentions of plaintiffs' two experts are disputed by several witnesses for the defense; but without considering the relative merits of the contentions raised by the conflicting views, this court feels that the testimony, taken in the light most favorable to plaintiffs, is at best mere conjecture. There has been no attempted sale by plaintiffs of their property, and the damages which they claim they will sustain if and when they do try to sell their property, is at this point a matter of speculation. * * *

It is the opinion of this court that plaintiffs' suit is premature. Not until their property is actually taken or damaged will they be in a position to establish that its value will be destroyed or diminished.

III

Plaintiffs question the soundness of the master plan on the ground that it is arbitrary, capricious and unreasonable. In view of the position taken by this court that plaintiffs are premature in their suit, it is not necessary to discuss this issue. However, the court feels that even if the reasonableness of the master plan were properly before it, the result would be the same. The action of a planning board is only an initial step; it is not even required by law, Kozesnik v. Montgomery Township, supra; it is only the manifestation of an advisory step in connection with *quasi*-judicial action the board may take in the future. As stated by Horack and Nolan, Land Use Controls 36 (1955):

[The master plan] is merely a declaration of policy and a disclosure of an intention which must thereafter be implemented.

Since this master plan may never be adopted by the governing body of Summit, there is at present no justiciable controversy before the court. There may be such a controversy if and when the proposed plan is adopted by the governing body. Until implementation of the proposal is attempted, there can be no purpose in an adjudication by this court at this time.

If the court, for example, declared the master plan or any portion thereof arbitrary, capricious, and/or unreasonable, would a property owner be permitted to make use of his property other than in a manner now permitted or other than in a manner that would be permitted if the plan were sustained? Would the governing body be limited in the adoption of land use ordinances other than as they are at the moment if the plan were stricken by this court? The answers to these questions appear obvious.

This suit to test the reasonableness of the master plan is premature, and the issues involved are clearly not ready for judicial determination. Furthermore, should the plaintiffs follow the normal administrative pattern of going first to the planning board and then, if necessary, to the governing body, they may very well be able to persuade these bodies to compromise their differences in connection with the master plan, in which case they would be able to avoid further litigation.

* * *

Complaint dismissed and judgment for defendants.

BONE v. CITY OF LEWISTON

Supreme Court of Idaho, 1984.
107 Idaho 844, 693 P.2d 1046.

BISTLINE, JUSTICE.

HISTORY

On February 9, 1982, Mr. John Bone filed an application with the City of Lewiston Planning and Zoning Commission requesting that his land be rezoned from a low-density residential use to a limited commercial use. The City's land use plan map shows Mr. Bone's land as being zoned for commercial use.

The Commission recommended to the City Council that Mr. Bone's request be denied for the following reasons: (1) The uses allowed in the zoning classification Mr. Bone seeks would not be compatible with the established low-density residential uses of the various properties bordering Mr. Bone's land; and (2) Lewiston has an over-abundance of unused commercial properties. No need presently exists for further classification of property for commercial use. The City Council, without adopting any findings of fact and conclusions of law, agreed with the Commission's recommendation and denied Mr. Bone's application.

Mr. Bone subsequently filed suit in district court against the City, requesting declaratory relief and a writ of mandamus forcing the City to enact a zoning ordinance in conformity with its comprehensive plan pursuant to I.C. § 67–6511. * * *

[The Court first disposes of a procedural issue and then moves to discuss the question of conformity with the comprehensive plan.]

Mr. Bone argues that he is entitled to have his property zoned in conformance with the City's land use map. He cites I.C. § 67–6511 as support for his position. That section states that zoning ordinances shall be "in accordance with" a comprehensive plan. For Mr. Bone, § 67–6511's terminology "in accordance with" means as a matter of law that a zoning applicant is entitled to have his or her property zoned exactly as the City's land use map shows it to be zoned. We do not agree with such a proposition for two reasons.

First, construing § 67–6511 as Mr. Bone would have us read it results in an interpretation of the section that contradicts itself. Subsections 67–6511(a) and (b) discuss the amendment process of zoning districts. In subsection (b) it states that if a rezone request is in accordance with the applicable comprehensive plan, the planning and zoning commission *"may* recommend and the governing board *may* adopt or reject the [zoning] amendment [request]" as proposed. (Emphasis added.)

Requiring all rezone applications to be granted when they agree with the land use map's designation of the property ignores the permissive language used in subsection (b). Had the legislature intended the result Mr. Bone proposes, they would have used the word "shall" instead of "may" and not used the words "or reject."

* * *

Second, adopting Mr. Bone's interpretation would elevate the comprehensive plan and land use map to the status of a zoning ordinance. This result finds no basis in law or reason, for the three—the comprehensive plan, the land use map, and the zoning ordinances—serve different purposes. The City of Lewiston's land use map, as § 67–6508(c) indicates, is a map displaying *"suitable projected* land uses for the jurisdiction." (Emphasis added.) It is not a map of how the City should presently be zoned, but a map of projected uses in the year 2000. In fact, the City's comprehensive plan describes the City's land use map as depicting "the projected structure and land use interrelationships for the City in the year 2000." It goes on further to say, "This map is not an attempt to show precise boundaries or locations, but is a general representation of the relative extent and patterns of *projected land uses."* (Emphasis added.) Thus, the land use map, in essence, is a goal or forecast of future development in the City. This is contrasted with zoning ordinances, which represent the present uses allowable for the various pieces of property in the City.

It is illogical to say that what has been projected as a pattern of projected land use is what a property owner is entitled to have zoned today. The land use map is not intended to be a map of present zoning uses, nor even a map which indicates what uses are presently appropriate. Its only purpose is that which I.C. § 67–6508(c) mandates—to indicate "suitable projected land uses." Therefore, we hold that a city's land use map does not require a particular piece of property, as a matter of law, to be zoned exactly as it appears on the land use map.

Our holding is supported by a large body of case law which states that comprehensive plans do not themselves operate as legally controlling zoning law, but rather serve to guide and advise the various governing bodies responsible for making zoning decisions. *See Theobald v. Board of County Commissioners, Summit County,* 644 P.2d 942, 949 (Colo.1982); *Barrie v. Kitsap County,* 613 P.2d 1148, 1152 (Wash.1980); *Holmgren v. City of Lincoln,* 199 Neb. 178, 256 N.W.2d 686, 690 (1977); 82 Am.Jur.2d, Zoning and Planning, § 69; 3 Anderson, *American Law of Zoning* 609.

Our holding that "in accordance with" does not require that governing bodies, as a matter of law, zone their land as it appears on their land use maps does not mean that such bodies can ignore their comprehensive plans when adopting or amending zoning ordinances. Section 67–6511 requires governing bodies to zone in accordance with their comprehensive plan. We hold that "in accordance with" is a question of fact. What a governing body charged to zone "in accordance with" under § 67–6511 must do is make a factual inquiry into whether the requested zoning ordinance or amendment reflects the goals of, and takes into account those factors in, the comprehensive plan in light of the present factual circumstances surrounding the request.

Here, the district court found that Mr. Bone's rezone application was in accordance with the City's comprehensive plan without having before it the record of either the planning and zoning commission or the City Council. The district court furthermore refused to allow the City to submit evidence of whether Mr. Bone's rezone application was factually in accordance with its comprehensive plan and the present circumstances surrounding the application. Thus, the district court erred in reaching its conclusion by failing to have before it the necessary information upon which to decide the case.

For the foregoing reasons we reverse and remand this case to the district court with directions for that court to remand to the City Council for the adoption of findings of fact and conclusions of law.

* * *

DONALDSON, C.J., and SHEPARD, BAKES and HUNTLEY, JJ., concur.

Notes

1. In Selby Realty Co. v. City of San Buenaventura, 10 Cal.3d 110, 109 Cal.Rptr. 799, 514 P.2d 111 (1973), the court held that adoption of a comprehensive plan which showed proposed streets crossing the landowner's property did not amount to a taking of the property. The court said: "The fact that some of the proposed streets, if ultimately constructed, will cross

plaintiff's property gives this plaintiff no greater right to secure a declaration as to the validity of the plan or its effect upon his land than that available to any other citizen whose property is included within the plan. The plan is by its very nature merely tentative and subject to change. Whether eventually any part of plaintiff's land will be taken for a street depends upon unpredictable future events." Also see Biske v. City of Troy, 381 Mich. 611, 166 N.W.2d 453 (1969); Rancho La Costa v. County of San Diego, 111 Cal.App.3d 54, 168 Cal.Rptr. 491 (1980); Zanin v. Iacono, 198 N.J.Super. 490, 487 A.2d 780 (1984); Woodcrest Investments Corp. v. County of Skagit, 39 Wash.App. 622, 694 P.2d 705 (1985); Callies, Land Use: Herein of Vested Rights, Plans, and the Relationship of Planning and Controls, 2 U.Hawaii L.Rev. 167, 182–92 (1979).

2.   In Citizens Growth Management Coalition of West Palm Beach, Inc. v. City of West Palm Beach, 450 So.2d 204 (Fla.1984), the court held that a citizen association lacked standing to challenge the validity of a downtown large-scale redevelopment. And, in State ex rel. Chiavola v. Village of Oakwood, 886 S.W.2d 74 (Mo.App.1994) the court held that a zoning ordinance satisfied the statutory requirement despite the lack of a separate comprehensive plan, given the comprehensive scope of the ordinance and the nature of the village as a small suburb of a large city. Accord: State ex rel. Westside Development Co., Inc. v. Weatherby Lake, 935 S.W.2d 634 (Mo. App.1996).

3.   The most acute everyday problem in assessing the legal effect of the plan is the usual lack of public interest or participation in the adoption of the plan, especially in the undeveloped parts of the community. Some years after the adoption of the plan a developer may seek a zoning change or development approval on a vacant parcel which is designated as, say, multifamily. Nearby neighbors living in recently developed single-family subdivisions will be vociferous objectors to the implementation of the plan. Of course they were not participants in the adoption of the plan and probably never knew of its existence. Is there a solution to this problem? One possibility is suggested by the case of Dennis v. Mayor and City Council of Rockville, 286 Md. 184, 406 A.2d 284 (1979), where the city had enacted an ordinance requiring all sellers of property to either provide purchasers with a copy of the master plan or to escort them to a place where the plan could be inspected. Violation of the duty imposed on sellers gives the purchaser a right to terminate the sales agreement prior to conveyance. The Court of Appeals of Maryland upheld the ordinance against arguments that it works a forfeiture of property and interferes with contractual rights. Do you think the Rockville ordinance is a more effective means of promulgating the plan than the typical public hearings held by a planning commission attended by a handful of developers and real estate brokers?

Also see Nev. Rev. Stat. § 113.070 requiring sellers of residences to provide the buyer with a written document disclosing "the zoning designations and the designations in the master plan regarding land use * * * for the adjoining parcels of land."

Somewhat related is the problem of whether purchasers of homes in subdivisions must be given notice of off-site environmental hazards. See, in this regard, Strawn v. Canuso, 140 N.J. 43, 657 A.2d 420 (1995) where the court stated that a broker-developer of residential real estate may be liable for nondisclosure of off-site physical conditions known to it and unknown and not readily observable by the purchaser, if those conditions may affect the habitability, use, or enjoyment of the property; in this case the off-site condition was a closed toxic landfill near a residential development.

SECTION 4. STATE AND REGIONAL PLANNING

A. FEDERAL LAND USE LEGISLATION

The history of land use controls in the United States has primarily been one of delegation of the power to plan to local governments along with the power to implement the plans at that level of government. One major effect of localizing land use controls has been the fostering of parochialism and the avoidance of a rational basis for dealing with regional problems. Beginning in the late 1960's and accelerating in the 1970's, states and to some degree the federal government began to demonstrate greater interest in intervening in the local planning process. This was likely spurred in part by the increasing emphasis on environmental controls, in part by federal transportation, housing and urban redevelopment programs, and in part by a concern over the problems created by "urban sprawl" and the proliferation of local, largely uncoordinated controls over a widespread metropolitan area encompassing a multiplicity of municipalities. The energy crisis of the late 1970's has also been a factor. The movement toward state and regional planning has been in three directions:

(1) Federal land use legislation which would spur state level planning;

(2) Removal of some planning decisions from local to regional or state political jurisdiction;

(3) Interstate compacts.

Federal impact on land use planning has been evident for several years. The millions of acres still in the public domain have required, in addition to management, some thought devoted to planning for the future. Also, some of the massive federal spending programs that have land use impacts have led to requirements of planning by state agencies charged with operations. In addition to urban redevelopment, typical in this respect is the federal highway program (see, e.g., the Highway Act of 1962, 76 Stat. 1145). Much federal money has gone into education about planning as well as research and public dissemination of planning materials. In other words, there has been and continues to be pervasive federal influence on land use planning, albeit in a non-coordinated fashion. The influences just described, however, have been of low visibility.

Since 1972 an intense public debate has emerged, centered around a bill passed by the Senate (S. 632, 92d Cong.), known colloquially as the Jackson bill, and officially as the Land–Use Policy and Planning Assistance Act of 1972. That bill never passed the House, nor did any of the similar bills introduced in the House. A federal land use bill has, however, been an idea still raised in congressional sessions since. Strong forces have been aligned on both sides of the debate about the propriety and wisdom of a federal land use bill. So far, the forces of opposition to such legislation have prevailed. See John R. Nolon, National Land Use Planning: Revisiting Senator Jackson's 1970 Policy Act, Land Use Law, May, 1996, p. 3.

The proponents of federal intervention into the land use planning process base their case mainly on the failure of widespread planning on the state and regional levels, which is blamed for much of the preventable environmental damage occurring daily; also, leaving planning to local initiative is seen as no solution to regional problems. The opponents see federal support of state land use planning as the first step in a process that would lead next to federal demands for such planning and eventually to federal takeover of planning and even worse, federal implementation of plans through controls administered by a federal agency.

B. STATE PLANNING

Even apart from any handwriting on the federal wall, some states have already taken steps to provide for state agencies not only to engage in land use planning, but to regulate the development of land under the auspices of a state plan. The two leading states are Vermont and Hawaii. Consider the utility of these models in states with greater geographical area than Hawaii or Vermont.

In Vermont, Act 250 removed from local control certain large-scale developments. A state level agency was created to issue permits for developments within the definitions of the Act. A good description of Act 250 can be found in a federal case brought by a developer who was denied a permit to develop near a ski resort because the state agency found that a large part of the proposed development contained a deer-yard (winter habitat for white-tailed deer). In Southview Associates, Ltd. v. Bongartz, 980 F.2d 84 (2d Cir.1992) Chief Judge Oakes wrote:

> Act 250 has been a major feature of the Vermont legal landscape for over twenty years. Its enactment represented the culmination of an effort to create a process that would subject subdivisions and other large developments in Vermont to administrative review so as to ensure economic growth without environmental catastrophe. See Governor's Commission on Environmental Control, Reports to Governor 2 (January 1970; May 1970). A brief discussion of the backdrop to the statute's enactment underscores its purpose.
>
> Beginning in the mid–1960s, Vermont experienced a massive increase in second-home construction and other recreational development, particularly in the southern portion of the state and around ski areas. Robert K. Reis, *Vermont's Act 250: Reflections on the First Decade and Recommendations for the Second* 9 (1980); David G. Heeter, *Almost Getting it Together in Vermont, in Environmental*

and Land Controls Legislation 323, 326 (David R. Mandelker ed. 1976); Fred Bosselman & David Callies, *The Quiet Revolution in Land Use Control* 54 (1971) (prepared for the Executive Office of the President, Council on Environmental Quality); Erickson, *The Vermont Environmental Protection Act of 1970, in Environmental Protection* 678, 679 (Louis L. Jaffe & Laurence H. Tribe, eds. 1971). These developments shifted economic activity away from agriculture and forestry—the traditional mainstays of the region. Erickson, supra, at 679. The Town of Dover, located in Southern Vermont, provides an example. As one writer explained, in Dover, in 1969, developers were completing, building or planning 19 vacation home subdivisions. According to a regional planner, if all the planned lots had been improved and occupied, the town's population would have increased from 370 to 16,000 within a few years. Id.

This spate of development was fueled by several factors, including the construction of interstate highways, the increased popularity of skiing and other outdoor activities, and what might be termed America's fascination with "the country life." See Reis, supra, at 9. Although the development yielded considerable tax revenue and increased property values, at times it threatened to destroy the very base of its existence: Vermont's relatively unspoiled environment. Poorly planned vacation home subdivisions in mountainous areas—typified by steep slopes and thin soil cover—caused soil erosion, water pollution from sewage systems, and a decline in the aesthetic quality of the land. Erickson, supra, at 680; Bosselman & Callies, supra, at 54–55; Heeter, supra, at 327. Public concern over the side-effects of this new and rapid growth reached the high water mark when, in the summer of 1968, the International Paper Company proposed to construct a huge recreational and vacation home development on 20,000 acres of wilderness in the towns of Stratton and Winhall. Governor's Commission on Environmental Control, supra, at 3; Bosselman & Callies, supra, at 54; Heeter, supra, at 328.

In May of 1969, then Governor Dean C. Davis responded by creating the Governor's Commission on Environmental Control. Governor Davis charged the Commission with determining how economic growth could be attained without environmental destruction. Heeter, supra, at 329 (quoting opening remarks by Governor Deane C. Davis, *Proceedings of the Governor's Conference on Natural Resources* 1 (May 14, 1969)). The Commission's recommendations included the enactment of a land use law that would require large developments, including subdivisions, to undergo administrative review prior to construction. Governor's Commission on Environmental Control, supra, at 3–4. This proposal formed the basis of Act 250, enacted by the Legislature in 1970.

Not all development projects are subject to Act 250 review. Essentially, an Act 250 permit is required if a person wishes to construct (1) improvements on a parcel or parcels involving more than ten acres located within a radius of five miles; (2) housing projects with 10 or more units located on land owned or controlled by that person within a radius of 5 miles; (3) a subdivision partitioned for resale into ten or more lots within a radius of 5 miles; and (4) improvements above the elevation of 2500 feet. No permit is necessary for construction required for farming, logging or forestry purposes below the elevation of 2500 feet. 10 V.S.A. §§ 6001, 6081(a) (1984 & Supp.1991).

A person whose project is subject to Act 250 jurisdiction must file an application with the regional three-person district commission. 10 V.S.A. §§ 6026, 6083 (1984 & Supp.1991). The district commission evaluates the project according to ten criteria relating to: (1) water and air pollution that will result; (2) availability of water to meet the project's needs; (3) the project's burden on the existing water supply; (4) soil erosion that will result; (5) the project's effect on congestion and safety of transportation routes; (6) the burden the project will place on municipal and local government provision of educational and other services; (7) whether the project will have an undue adverse effect on "the scenic or natural beauty of the area, aesthetics, historic sites or rare and irreplaceable natural areas"; and (8) whether the project conforms with various state, regional and local development plans. 10 V.S.A. § 6086 (1984 & Supp.1991). If the district commission grants the application for a permit, it may attach conditions to it to assure compliance with the criteria for permit issuance. 10 V.S.A. § 6086(c) (1984).

A permit applicant may appeal the decision of the district commission to the nine-member Vermont Environmental Board. 10 V.S.A. §§ 6021(a), 6089(a) (1984 & Supp.1991). The Board reviews challenged findings de novo. 10 V.S.A. § 6089(a) (Supp.1991). The permit applicant may, in turn, appeal the Board's decision to the Supreme Court of Vermont, 10 V.S.A. § 6089(b) (Supp.1991), which will uphold the Board's findings of fact "if supported by substantial evidence in the record as a whole." 10 V.S.A. § 6089(c) (Supp.1991); see In re Southview Associates, 153 Vt. 171, 177, 569 A.2d 501, 504 (1989).

The Vermont Legislature accompanied the enactment of Act 250 with a statement of legislative intent, which provides, in part:

[T]he unplanned, uncoordinated and uncontrolled use of the lands and the environment of the state of Vermont has resulted in usages of the lands and the environment which may be destructive to the environment and which are not suitable to the demands and needs of the people of the state of Vermont . . . . .

. . . .

. . . it is necessary to regulate and control the utilization and usages of lands and the environment to ensure that, hereafter, the only usages which will be permitted are not unduly detrimental to the environment, [and] will promote the general welfare through orderly growth and development. . . .

Findings and declaration of intent, 1969, No. 250 (Adj.Sess.), § 1, in 10 V.S.A. annotations following § 6001 (1984).

Subsequently, in 1973, the legislature further clarified the purpose of the act by adopting a "Capability and Development Plan" to guide the implementation of Act 250. 1973 Capability and development plan; statement of intent and findings, 1973 No. 85, § 7, in 10 V.S.A. annotations following § 6042 (1984). See Norman Williams & Tammara Van Ryn–Lincoln, *The Aesthetic Criterion in Vermont's Environmental Law*, 3 Hofstra Prop.L.J. 89, 94–95 (1990). The plan states, in relevant part:

(2) Utilization of Natural Resources [C]onservation of the recreational opportunity afforded by the state's hills, forests, streams and lakes ... are matters of public good. Uses which threaten or significantly inhibit these resources should be permitted only when the public interest is clearly benefited thereby.

. . . .

(6) General Policies for Economic Development In order to achieve a strong economy ... economic development should be pursued selectively so as to provide maximum economic development with minimal environmental impact.

. . . .

(10) Recreational Resources The use and development of land and waters should occur in such a way as not to significantly diminish the value and availability of outdoor recreational activities to the people of Vermont, including hunting. . . .

. . . .

(11) Special Areas Lands that include or are adjacent to sites or areas of historical, cultural, scientific, architectural, or archeological value ... should only be developed in a manner that will not significantly reduce that value of the site or area.

Thus, the Legislature intended Act 250 to protect Vermont's environmental resources with an eye towards maintaining, among other things, existing recreational uses of the land—such as hunting, for example—and preserving lands, when possible, that have special values to the public. In recognition of the importance of economic growth, however, the focus of the Act is not on barring development but on molding it to minimize its environmental impact. And in practice, one commentator has stated that "[t]he statute has ... been administered not as a 'no-growth' law, but as a law designed to improve the quality of growth." Williams & Van Ryn–Lincoln, supra, at 94. We now turn to the dispute before us.

IN RE JUSTER ASSOCIATES

Supreme Court of Vermont, 1978.
136 Vt. 577, 396 A.2d 1382.

[Juster Associates had previously received a permit from the Vermont Environmental Conservation Board for a 31 acre shopping center in the Town of Rutland. After construction was completed and the center was in operation, the septic tank sewage disposal system failed. Several alternatives also failed and Juster Associates returned to the Board seeking an amendment of its original permit to allow installation of a new system on a 4 acre site near, but not abutting the shopping center. The Board granted the new permit and an appeal was taken by the city and downstream riparian owners.]

DALEY, JUSTICE.

* * *

No one questions the applicability of our so-called Act 250, found in 10 V.S.A. chapter 151. The project in question is to be located on more than one acre of land within a municipality which has not adopted permanent zoning and subdivision bylaws * * * and therefore comes within the scope of the statute. The initial issue * * * is whether the Board had jurisdiction over Juster's application for a permit to develop the four acre tract as a sewage disposal facility. * * *

The purpose of Act 250 is to protect and conserve the environment of the state and to insure that lands slated for development are devoted to uses which are not detrimental to the public welfare and interest. 1969 No. 250 (Adj.Sess.), § 1; In re Great Eastern Building Co., 132 Vt. 610, 614, 326 A.2d 152, 154 (1974). These ends are served by a system of land use permits established by the Legislature. Where the Act applies, property may not be developed without a permit. 10 V.S.A. § 6081. An application for a permit must be made to a District Commissioner. 10 V.S.A. § 6083. The District Commission must provide general notice, by newspaper publication, and notice to certain persons designated by statute and by Board rule. 10 V.S.A. § 6084. After hearing, the District Commission may approve the application and issue a permit. 10 V.S.A. § 6086. Within this framework, the Board acts as a quasi-judicial appellate body, to hear appeals from commission decisions. Environmental Board Regulations, Rule 1(C)(1).

Notwithstanding the statutory procedure of hearings at the District Commission level with appeals to the Board, the Board seeks, by granting an amendment to an outstanding permit, to allow a four acre tract of land to be developed without proceedings before the District Commission. It contends that its power to do so lies in its jurisdiction to enforce the permits that it issues. The Board argues that it has jurisdiction because the land is to be used to fulfill a condition attached to an existing permit. We cannot agree.

We do not dispute the Board's authority to police its permits. It may, under the statute, revoke a permit if the conditions attached to the permit are violated. 10 V.S.A. § 6090. But we cannot allow it, under the guise of permit enforcement, to subvert the protective scheme ordained by the Legislature. The statute is intended, by a system of notice and hearings, to assure full consideration of land use proposals for all parcels of land. In bypassing the District Commission, the Board precluded a complete discussion of the issues involved in constructing a waste disposal facility on new acreage. This land was not considered in the previous hearings. When the original permit was issued, the matters now under discussion were not even contemplated. Development of the four acre plot may affect persons other than those who participated in the hearings that were conducted on the shopping center. However, the public was not notified that the land was to be developed, thus circumventing its participation.

* * * To accept the Board's rationale is to diminish the scrutiny given to land use under the statutory framework, because it allows for approval of a development without the discussion provided for by the statute.

Our review of the record convinces us that the Board lacked authority to entertain the application filed by Juster. Initial consideration of a land use proposal is a function assigned by the Legislature to the District Commission. The Board is not vested with concurrent jurisdiction to hear and decide the same matters.

* * *

Notes

1. This case gives some illustration of how the Vermont system operates. Also see In re Wildlife Wonderland, Inc., 133 Vt. 507, 346 A.2d 645 (1975), where the court upheld the environmental board's denial of a permit to construct and operate a game farm where some 300 wild and domestic animals could be viewed by the paying public.

The Juster case has been one long saga illustrating a dispute between developer and city. The latest round in that dispute is Juster Associates v. City of Rutland, 901 F.2d 266 (2d Cir.1990), which involves an antitrust challenge against the city. This case is taken up in a later chapter, in the Section on Zoning and Antitrust Law.

2. In 1988 the Vermont legislature adopted Act 200, which has been referred to as a growth control law. The statute is designed to encourage towns to adopt comprehensive growth control regulations by offering state funds to pay for the planning; towns which do not elect to participate are disabled from participating in regional planning. Act 200 has fostered a bitter fight in Vermont. At least 51 towns rejected the Act in 1990 town meeting elections. Also, some towns returned money to the state and backed out of the program. The opposition to Act 200 appears to focus on the loss of

local control of land use regulation and a perceived threat to property rights. The future of the program is in some doubt.

In Hawaii the state has preempted a sizeable amount of what would normally be considered local zoning authority. The Hawaii statutory framework is set forth here:

Hawaii Revised Statutes (1968):

§ 205–1 Establishment of the commission. There shall be a state land use commission, hereinafter called the commission. The commission shall consist of nine members who shall hold no other public office and shall be appointed in the manner and serve for the term set forth * * *

§ 205–2 Districting and classification of lands. (a) There shall be four major land use districts in which all lands in the State shall be placed: urban, rural, agricultural, and conservation. The land use commission shall group contiguous land areas suitable for inclusion in one of these four major districts. The commission shall set standards for determining the boundaries of each district, provided that:

(1) In the establishment of boundaries of urban districts those lands that are now in urban use and a sufficient reserve area for foreseeable urban growth shall be included;

(2) In the establishment of boundaries for rural districts, areas of land composed primarily of small farms mixed with very low density residential lots, which may be shown by a minimum density of not more than one house per one-half acre and a minimum lot size of not less than one-half acre shall be included, except as herein provided;

(3) In the establishment of the boundaries of agricultural districts the greatest possible protection shall be given to those lands with a high capacity for intensive cultivation; and

(4) In the establishment of the boundaries of conservation districts, the "forest and water reserve zones" provided in Act 234, section 2, Session Laws of Hawaii 1957, are renamed "conservation districts" and, effective as of July 11, 1961, the boundaries of the forest and water reserve zones theretofore established pursuant to Act 234, section 2, Session Laws of Hawaii 1957, shall constitute the boundaries of the conservation districts; provided that thereafter the power to determine the boundaries of the conservation districts shall be in the commission.

In establishing the boundaries of the districts in each county, the commission shall give consideration to the master plan or general plan of the county.

(b) Urban districts shall include activities or uses as provided by ordinances or regulations of the county within which the urban district is situated.

(c) Rural districts shall include activities or uses as characterized by low density residential lots of not more than one dwelling house per one-half acre, except as provided by county ordinance pursuant to section 46–4(c), in areas where "city-like" concentration of people, structures, streets, and urban level of services are absent, and where small farms are intermixed with low density residential lots except that within a subdivision, as defined in section 484–1, the commission for good cause may allow one lot of less than one-half acre, but not less than 18,500 square feet, or an equivalent residential density, within a rural subdivision and permit the construction of one dwelling on such lot, provided that all other dwellings in the subdivision shall have a minimum lot size of one-half acre or 21,780 square feet. Such petition for variance may be processed under the special permit procedure. These districts may include contiguous areas which are not suited to low density residential lots or small farms by reason of topography, soils, and other related characteristics.

(d) Agricultural districts shall include activities or uses as characterized by the cultivation of crops, orchards, forage, and forestry; farming activities or uses related to animal husbandry, aquaculture, game and fish propagation; aquaculture, which means the production of aquatic plant and animal life for food and fiber within ponds and other bodies of water; wind generated energy production for public, private and commercial use; bona fide agricultural services and uses which support the agricultural activities of the fee or leasehold owner of the property and accessory to any of the above activities, whether or not conducted on the same premises as the agricultural activities to which they are accessory, including but not limited to farm dwellings as defined in section 205–4.5(a)(4), employee housing, farm buildings, mills, storage facilities, processing facilities, vehicle and equipment storage areas, and roadside stands for the sale of products grown on the premises; wind machines and wind farms; small-scale meteorological, air quality, noise and other scientific and environmental data collection and monitoring facilities occupying less than one-half acre of land, provided that such facilities shall not be used as or equipped for use as living quarters or dwellings; agricultural parks; and open area recreational facilities, including golf courses and golf driving ranges, provided that they are not located within agricultural district lands with soil classified by the land study bureau's detailed land classification as overall (master) productivity rating class A or B.

These districts may include areas which are not used for, or which are not suited to, agricultural and ancillary activities by reason of topography, soils, and other related characteristics.

(e) Conservation districts shall include areas necessary for protecting watersheds and water sources; preserving scenic and historic areas;

providing park lands, wilderness, and beach reserves; conserving indigenous or endemic plants, fish, and wildlife, including those which are threatened or endangered; preventing floods and soil erosion; forestry; open space areas whose existing openness, natural condition, or present state of use, if retained, would enhance the present or potential value of abutting or surrounding communities, or would maintain or enhance the conservation of natural or scenic resources; areas of value for recreational purposes; other related activities; and other permitted uses not detrimental to a multiple use conservation concept.

§ 205–3.1 **Amendments to district boundaries.** (a) District boundary amendments involving land areas greater than fifteen acres shall be processed by the land use commission pursuant to section 205–4.

(b) Any department or agency of the State, and department or agency of the county in which the land is situated, or any person with a property interest in the land sought to be reclassified may petition the appropriate county land use decision-making authority of the county in which the land is situated for a change in the boundary of a district involving lands less than fifteen acres presently in the agricultural, rural, and urban districts.

(c) District boundary amendments involving land areas of fifteen acres or less, except in conservation districts, shall be determined by the appropriate county land use decision-making authority for said district and shall not require consideration by the land use commission pursuant to section 205–4. District boundary amendments involving land areas of fifteen acres or less in conservation districts shall be processed by the land use commission pursuant to section 205–4. The appropriate county land use decision-making authority may consolidate proceedings to amend state land use district boundaries pursuant to this subsection, with county proceedings to amend the general plan, development plan, zoning of the affected land or such other proceedings. Appropriate ordinances and rules to allow consolidation of such proceedings may be developed by the county land use decision-making authority.

(d) The county land use decision-making authority shall serve a copy of the application for a district boundary amendment to the land use commission and the department of business, economic development and tourism and shall notify the commission and the department of the time and place of the hearing and the proposed amendments scheduled to be heard at the hearing. A change in the state land use district boundaries pursuant to this subsection shall become effective on the day designated by the county land use decision-making authority in its decision. Within sixty days of the effective date of any decision to amend state land use district boundaries by the county land use decision-making authority, the decision and the description and map of the affected property shall be transmitted to the land use commission and the department of planning and economic development, and tourism by the county planning director. [L 1985, c 230, § 3]

§ 205–4 Amendments to district boundaries involving land areas greater than fifteen acres. (a) Any department or agency of the State, any department or agency of the county in which the land is situated, or any person with a property interest in the land sought to be reclassified, may petition the land use commission for a change in the boundary of a district. This section applies to all petitions for changes in district boundaries of lands within conservation districts and all petitions for changes in district boundaries involving lands greater than fifteen acres in the agricultural, rural, and urban districts, except as provided in section 201E–210. * * *

(e) * * *

(2) All departments and agencies of the State and of the county in which the land is situated shall be admitted as parties upon timely application for intervention.

(3) All persons who have some property interest in the land, who lawfully reside on the land, or who otherwise can demonstrate that they will be so directly and immediately affected by the proposed change that their interest in the proceeding is clearly distinguishable from that of the general public shall be admitted as parties upon timely application for intervention.

(4) All other persons may apply to the commission for leave to intervene as parties. Leave to intervene shall be freely granted, provided that the commission or its hearing officer if one is appointed may deny an application to intervene when in the commission's or hearing officer's sound discretion it appears that: (A) the position of the applicant for intervention concerning the proposed change is substantially the same as the position of a party already admitted to the proceeding; and (B) the admission of additional parties will render the proceedings inefficient and unmanageable. A person whose application to intervene is denied may appeal such denial to the circuit court pursuant to section 91–14. * * *

§ 205–6 Special permit. The county planning commission may permit certain unusual and reasonable uses within agricultural and rural districts other than those for which the district is classified. Any person who desires to use his land within an agricultural or rural district other than for an agricultural or rural use, as the case may be, may petition the planning commission of the county within which his land is located for permission to use his land in the manner desired. Each county may establish the appropriate fee for processing the special permit petition.

The planning commission, upon consultation with the central coordinating agency, except in counties where the planning commission is advisory only in which case the central coordinating agency, shall establish by rule or regulation, the time within which the hearing and action on petition for special permit shall occur. The county planning commission shall notify the land use commission and such persons and agencies that may have an interest in the subject matter of the time and place of the hearing.

The county planning commission may under such protective restrictions as may be deemed necessary, permit the desired use, but only when the use would promote the effectiveness and objectives of this chapter. A decision in favor of the applicant shall require a majority vote of the total membership of the county planning commission.

Special permits for land the area of which is greater than fifteen acres shall be subject to approval by the land use commission. The land use commission may impose additional restrictions as may be necessary or appropriate in granting such approval, including the adherence to representations made by the applicant.

A copy of the decision together with the complete record of the proceeding before the county planning commission on all special permit requests involving a land area greater than fifteen acres shall be transmitted to the land use commission within sixty days after the decision is rendered. Within forty-five days after receipt of the complete record from the county planning commission, the land use commission shall act to approve, approve with modification, or deny the petition. A denial either by the county planning commission or by the land use commission, or a modification by the land use commission, as the case may be, of the desired use shall be appealable to the circuit court of the circuit in which the land is situated and shall be made pursuant to the Hawaii Rules of Civil Procedure.

* * *

§ 205–18 Periodic review of districts. The office of state planning shall undertake a review of the classification and districting of all lands in the State, within five years from December 31, 1985, and every fifth year thereafter. The office, in its five-year boundary review, shall focus its efforts on reviewing the Hawaii state plan, county general plans, and county development and community plans. Upon completion of the five-year boundary review, the office shall submit a report of the findings to the commission. The office may initiate state land use boundary amendments which it deems appropriate to conform to these plans. The office may seek assistance of appropriate state and county agencies and may employ consultants and undertake studies in making this review.

One notable feature of the Hawaii statute is the provision for a review of district boundaries and regulations each five years after the adoption of the first district boundaries (which occurred in 1964). The second review was completed in 1974, and published in February, 1975. See Report to the People (Hawaii Land Use Commission, 1975). The report indicates that during the 1969–1974 period proposals were made to change the district classification of 133,438 acres of land. Approved changes in that period totaled 66,670 acres. Id., at p. 25. Out of the approved changes, a total of 5,438 acres were placed in the urban district while 4,056 acres were removed from the urban district. Ibid. See, generally, P. Myers, Zoning Hawaii: An Analysis of the Passage and Implementation of Hawaii's Land Classification Law (1975) and Mandelker & Kolis, Whither Hawaii: Land Use Management in an Island State, 1 U.Hawaii L.Rev. 48 (1979). In 1978, Hawaii adopted a new state planning act, Hawaii Rev.Stat. § 226–1 et seq.

For a case interpreting the Hawaiian classifications in relation to the special permit procedures, see Neighborhood Bd. No. 24 (Waianae Coast) v. State Land Use Comm'n, 64 Hawaii 265, 639 P.2d 1097 (1982). A developer sought and received a special permit to construct an amusement park on a 103–acre parcel of land in the agricultural district. The court held that the special permit was improper and that the developer should have sought a district boundary amendment; use of the special permit procedure would, in this type of large scale development, allow ad hoc infusion of major urban uses into agricultural districts. Compare Maha'ulepu v. Land Use Comm'n, 71 Hawaii 332, 790 P.2d 906 (1990) where the court held that the commission could issue special permits for golf courses on prime agricultural land. (In 1985 the legislature amended the definition of permitted uses in agricultural districts (Section 205–2, supra) to include golf courses.) See Comment, *Maha'ulepu v. Land Use Commission*: A Symbol of Change; Hawaii's Land Use Law Allows Golf Course Development on Prime Agricultural Land by Special Use Permit, 13 Haw. L. Rev. 205 (1991).

C. REGIONAL PLANNING

The political culture in most states automatically rejects any notion of "regional" government; the rules governing life are either local or at the state level. Even at the local level, in many states cities view county government with suspicion and vice versa. One state that has a history of regional approaches to problem solving is Minnesota. Statutes in that state seek to promote regional land use problem solving. Some excerpts from Minnesota Statutes Annotated (1963):

462.383

The legislature finds that problems of growth and development in urban and rural regions of the state so transcend the boundary lines of local government units that no single unit can plan for their solution without affecting other units in the region; that various multi-county planning activities conducted under various laws of the United States are presently being conducted in an uncoordinated manner; that intergovernmental cooperation on a regional basis is an effective means of pooling the resources of local government to approach common problems; and that the assistance of the state is needed to make the most effective use of local, state, federal, and private programs in serving the citizens of such urban and rural regions.

It is the purpose of sections 462.381 to 462.398 to facilitate intergovernmental cooperation and to insure the orderly and harmonious coordination of state, federal, and local comprehensive planning and development programs for the solution of economic, social, physical, and governmental problems of the state and its citizens by providing for the creation of regional development commissions.

Laws 1969, c. 1122, § 3, eff. June 1, 1969.

* * *

462.387

Any combination of counties or municipalities representing a majority of the population of the region for which a commission is proposed may petition the commissioner by formal resolution setting forth its desire to establish, and the need for, the establishment of a regional development commission. For purposes of this section the population of a county does not include the population of a municipality within the county.

462.39

The commission shall prepare and adopt, after appropriate study and such public hearings as may be necessary, a comprehensive development plan for the region. The plan shall consist of a compilation of policy statements, goals, standards, programs, and maps prescribing guides for an orderly and economic development, public and private, of the region. The comprehensive development plan shall recognize and encompass physical, social, or economic needs of the region, and those future developments which will have an impact on the entire region including but not limited to such matters as land use, parks and open space land needs, access to direct sunlight for solar energy systems, the necessity for and location of airports, highways, transit facilities, public hospitals, libraries, schools, public and private housing, and other public buildings. In preparing the development plan the commission shall use to the maximum extent feasible the resources, studies and data available from other planning agencies within the region, including counties, municipalities, special districts, and subregional planning agencies, and it shall utilize the resources of the director to the same purpose. No development plan or portion thereof for the region shall be adopted by the commission until it has been submitted to the director for review and comment and a period of 60 days has elapsed after such submission. When a development plan has been adopted, the commission shall distribute it to all local government units within the region.

462.391 * * *

The commission may participate as a party in any proceedings originating before the Minnesota municipal board under chapter 414, if the proceedings involve the change in a boundary of a governmental unit in the region.

Notes

1. What major differences do you see between the Vermont approach, the Hawaii approach, and the Minnesota approach? Which model do you think affords the best accommodation between regional concerns and the

"rights" of local property owners? Are there practical considerations which commend one approach over the other?

2.   The approaches described above were hailed in the early 1970's as the "wave of the future." See Bosselman and Callies, The Quiet Revolution in Land Use Control (Council on Environmental Quality 1971). Statewide planning control as in Vermont and Hawaii did not spread to other states and regional planning has been utilized only in special circumstances. See, e.g., Booth, Developing Institutions for Regional Land Use Planning and Control—The Adirondack Experience, 28 Buffalo L.Rev. 645 (1979). See generally, Callies, The Quiet Revolution Revisited, American Planning Association J. 135 (Apr. 1980). Also see Marie L. York, Regions: Blind Isolation or Shared Vision?, Land Use Law, April, 1995, p. 3.

3.   Several states have adopted planning enabling legislation which is somewhere in between state level control and local autonomy. In Florida, for example, areas which have been designated as of "critical environmental concern" are subject to planning and regulation at the state level; this approach can be viewed as a partial preemption of the traditional planning function. Some states have opted for mandatory local planning with the state (either by statute or administrative regulation) mandating particular elements of the plans. See, e.g., Cal.Govt.Code § 65101; Or.Rev.Stat. § 215.505 et seq.; Rev.Code Wash.Ann. § 36.70.010. Many states have preempted local planning and regulation of particular types of activities which have a widespread impact, such as power plant sitings.[13] See, e.g., Town of Preston v. Connecticut Siting Council, 20 Conn.App. 474, 568 A.2d 799 (1990). Industrial pollution has also engendered preemption of local control. See, e.g., Niro, Illinois Environmental Law—State Preemption of Local Governmental Regulation of Pollution Related Activities, 67 Ill.Bar J. 118 (1978).

D.   INTERSTATE COMPACTS

PEOPLE EX REL. YOUNGER v. COUNTY OF EL DORADO

Supreme Court of California, In Bank, 1971.
5 Cal.3d 480, 96 Cal.Rptr. 553, 487 P.2d 1193.

SULLIVAN, JUSTICE. The Attorney General, on behalf of the People of the State of California, seeks a writ of mandate commanding the Counties of El Dorado and Placer to pay to the Tahoe Regional Planning Agency (Agency) the amounts of money respectively allotted to them by the Agency as being necessary to support its activities. We issued an alternative writ of mandate to which respondents have made return by answer. The issues thus presented to us are of great concern to California, to its neighbors and, indeed, to the entire country.

The controversy which we are required to review focuses upon the Lake Tahoe Basin—an area of unique and unsurpassed beauty situated

13.   For an overview of this area, see Development and the Environment: Legal Reforms to Facilitate Industrial Site Selection (Final Report by the Special Committee on Environmental Law, ABA 1974).

high in the Sierras along the California–Nevada border. Mark Twain, an early visitor to the region, viewed the lake as "a noble sheet of blue water lifted six thousand three hundred feet above the level of the sea * * * with the shadows of the mountains brilliantly photographed upon its still surface * * * the fairest picture the whole earth affords." Year after year the lake and its surrounding mountains have attracted and captivated countless visitors from all over the world.

However, there is good reason to fear that the region's natural wealth contains the virus of its ultimate impoverishment. A staggering increase in population, a greater mobility of people, an affluent society and an incessant urge to invest, to develop, to acquire and merely to spend—all have combined to pose a severe threat to the Tahoe region. Only recently has the public become aware of the delicate balance of the ecology, and of the complex interrelated natural processes which keep the lake's waters clear and fresh, preserve the mountains from unsightly erosion, and maintain all forms of wildlife at appropriate levels. Today, and for the foreseeable future, the ecology of Lake Tahoe stands in grave danger before a mounting wave of population and development.

In an imaginative and commendable effort to avert this imminent threat, California and Nevada, with the approval of Congress (Pub.Law 91–148, 83 Stat. 360), entered into the Tahoe Regional Planning Compact (Compact) the provisions of which are found in Government Code section 66801. The basic concept of the Compact is a simple one—to provide for the region as a whole the planning, conservation and resource development essential to accommodate a growing population within the region's relatively small area without destroying the environment.

To achieve this purpose, the Compact establishes the Tahoe Regional Planning Agency with jurisdiction over the entire region. (§ 66801, art. III, subd. (a).) The Agency has been given broad powers to make and enforce a regional plan of an unusually comprehensive scope. This plan, to be adopted on or before September 1, 1971, must include, as correlated elements, plans for land-use, transportation, conservation, recreation, and public services and facilities. (§ 66801, art. V, subd. (b).) The Compact emphasizes that in formulating and maintaining this regional plan, the Agency "shall take account of and shall seek to harmonize the needs of the region as a whole * * *." (Id.)

The Agency is given the power to "adopt all necessary ordinances, rules, regulations and policies to effectuate the adopted regional * * * "plan. (§ 66801, art. VI, subd. (a).) While ordinances so enacted establish minimum standards applicable throughout the region, local political subdivisions may enact and enforce equal or higher standards. "The regulations shall contain general, regional standards including but not limited to the following: water purity and clarity; subdivision; zoning; tree removal; solid waste disposal; sewage disposal; land fills, excavations, cuts and grading; piers, harbors, breakwaters; or channels and other shoreline developments; waste disposal in shoreline areas;

waste disposal from boats; mobile-home parks; house relocation; outdoor advertising; flood plain protection; soil and sedimentation control; air pollution; and watershed protection. Whenever possible without diminishing the effectiveness of the * * * general plan, the ordinances, rules, regulations and policies shall be confined to matters which are general and regional in application, leaving to the jurisdiction of the respective states, counties and cities the enactment of specific and local ordinances, rules, regulations and policies which conform to the * * * general plan." (Id.) The Compact also provides that "[v]iolation of any ordinance of the [A]gency is a misdemeanor." (§ 66801, art. VI, subd. (f).) Finally, it states that "all public works projects shall be reviewed prior to construction and [except for certain state public works projects] approved by the [A]gency as to the project's compliance with the adopted regional general plan." (§ 66801, art. VI, subd. (c).) * * *

The Compact permits the Agency to receive fees for its services, gifts, grants and other financial aids. It also provides for Agency financing as follows: "Except as provided in subdivision (e), on or before December 30 of each calendar year the agency shall establish the amount of money necessary to support its activities for the next succeeding fiscal year commencing July 1 of the following year. The agency shall apportion not more than $150,000 of this amount among the counties within the region on the same ratio to the total sum required as the full cash valuation of taxable property within the region in each county bears to the total full cash valuation of taxable property within the region. Each county in California shall pay the sum allotted to it by the agency from any funds available therefor and may levy a tax on any taxable property within its boundaries sufficient to pay the amount so allocated to it. Each county in Nevada shall pay such sum from its general fund or from any other moneys available therefor." (§ 66801, art. VII, subd. (a).)

After ratification of the Compact by Congress and upon proclamation of the Governors of California and Nevada, the Agency came into existence on March 19, 1970. It adopted a budget, pursuant to section 66801, article V, subdivisions (a) and (e), for the fourth quarter of the fiscal year 1969–1970—that is, for the months April through June 1970. Of the total budget of $81,770.85, $22,344.68 was allotted to El Dorado County, and $10,322.98 to Placer County. However, no specific demand was made upon the counties to pay the amounts apportioned to them, and they have consistently refused to do so.

The Agency has also adopted a budget of $180,000 for the fiscal year 1970–1971. Of this sum, the amount apportioned to El Dorado County is $60,150 and that allotted to Placer County is $33,600. No demand was made upon either county for such sums until December 29, 1970. The counties have refused to pay the above sums or any part of them.

For the fiscal year 1971–1972, the Agency has adopted a budget of $222,400, of which El Dorado County's share is $54,450, and Placer County's share is $40,350. The Attorney General asserts that, absent an order of this court, the counties will refuse to pay these sums.

The positions of the parties before us may be summarized as follows: the Attorney General contends that the respondent counties have a clear duty, imposed by the Compact, to pay their share of the funds necessary to support the activities of the Agency and that we should compel the performance of this duty by a writ of mandate. The counties contend first, that they are not required to make any payments to the Agency because the Compact is unconstitutional and void and, secondly, that the remedy here sought is inappropriate because the People have a plain, speedy and adequate remedy at law.[14] * * *

We turn to the merits. The counties first contend that the Compact violates former sections 11, 12 and 13 of article XI of the California Constitution * * * Generally speaking, these sections confer upon specified local governmental bodies broad powers over purely local affairs. But, as we shall point out, the Compact is unaffected by any of the above provisions since its subject matter is of regional, rather than local, concern.

The regional nature of the Compact is manifest from the express language of the legislation. Article I of the Compact which sets forth legislative findings and declarations of policy, provides in relevant part: "It is found and declared that the waters of Lake Tahoe and other resources of the Lake Tahoe region are threatened with deterioration or degeneration. [Par.] It is further declared that by virtue of the special conditions and circumstances of the natural ecology, developmental pattern, population distribution and human needs in the Lake Tahoe region, the region is experiencing problems of resources use and deficiencies of environmental control." The same article further declares the "need to maintain an equilibrium between the region's natural endowment and its manmade environment," and specifically recognizes "that for the purpose of enhancing the efficiency and governmental effective-

14. On March 19, 1971, the Counties of El Dorado and Placer brought an action for declaratory relief in El Dorado County against the Agency seeking a decree declaring that the Compact violates provisions of the United States and California Constitutions. The Agency filed an answer and cross-complaint on April 5, 1971. No further action has been taken in that suit.

Prior to Congressional approval of the Compact, California established the California Tahoe Regional Planning Agency. (See Gov.Code, § 67000 et seq.) The purpose of that agency is explained in the following portion of Senate Report 91–510, supra: "Because of the urgency of the regional planning needs the Nevada Legislature adopted interim legislation in February of 1969 creating the Nevada Tahoe Regional Planning Agency to work with a counterpart California agency that had been operating since 1967. This provided immediate authority for the States to prepare a regional plan and for the exercise of individual

controls pending congressional ratification of the bistate compact. Although the States cannot work together officially until the compact is ratified, the State agencies did undertake the employment of a joint staff to insure coordinated efforts. The Nevada agency, with the concurrence of the California agency, was prepared by the summer of 1969 to retain a planning consultant for the purpose of drawing up the Nevada portion of the regional plan." Although the Compact has since been approved, the California Tahoe Regional Planning Agency continues to exist. (See Note, supra, 22 Hastings L.J. 705, 713–715).

On October 30, 1970, the Counties of El Dorado and Placer brought an action for declaratory relief against that agency alleging that it, too, violated state and federal constitutional provisions. The Attorney General advises us that the trial court has ruled against the counties in that suit, but that the counties have indicated they will appeal.

ness of the region, it is imperative that there be established an areawide planning agency with power to adopt and enforce a regional plan of resource conservation and orderly development, to exercise effective environmental controls and to perform other essential functions * * *."[15] Of course, such findings and declarations of policy are entitled to great weight. (Bishop v. City of San Jose (1969) 1 Cal.3d 56, 63, 81 Cal.Rptr. 465, 460 P.2d 137; Housing Authority v. Dockweiler (1939) 14 Cal.2d 437, 449–450, 94 P.2d 794; Wilson, Consideration of Facts in Constitutional Cases (1944) 17 So.Cal.L.Rev. 335.)

Even without such explicit findings we could hardly avoid a conclusion that the purpose of the Compact is to conserve the natural resources and control the environment of the Tahoe Basin as a whole through area-wide planning. Lake Tahoe itself is an interstate body of water; the surrounding region, defined by the Compact, is also interstate, since it includes not only the lake but the adjacent parts of three counties of Nevada and two counties of California. (§ 66801, art. III, subd. (a).) The water that the Agency is to purify cannot be confined within one county or state; it circulates freely throughout Lake Tahoe. The air which the Agency must preserve from pollution knows no political boundaries. The wildlife which the Agency should protect ranges freely from one local jurisdiction to another. Nor can the population and explosive development which threaten the region be contained by any of the local authorities which govern parts of the Tahoe Basin.[16] Only an agency transcending local boundaries can devise, adopt and put into operation solutions for the problems besetting the region as a whole. Indeed, the fact that the Compact is the product of the cooperative efforts and mutual agreement of two states is impressive proof that its subject matter and objectives are of regional rather than local concern. * * *

15. "The Lake Tahoe Basin, shared by the States of California and Nevada, has five county political subdivisions, two municipalities, more than 10 general improvement districts, three public utility districts, several sewer and sanitation districts, and innumerable public entities for schools, fire protection, soil conservation, and varied public services. In addition, the Federal Government owns and manages nearly half the total basin land area. The threat to Lake Tahoe's environment has been obvious and efforts to contain development and control the dangers of irreparable damage have been genuine and determined. However, the political fragmentation in the basin has prevented a unified and organized approach to the mounting problems." (S.Rep. 91–510, supra.) The failure of local governmental bodies to cope with Lake Tahoe's problems is graphically detailed in Comment, Lake Tahoe: The Future of a National Asset—Land Use, Water, and Pollution (1964) 52 Cal.L.Rev. 563, 565–572.

16. "In the area of land use regulation, the present county zoning ordinances and their enforcement have proved inadequate to insure an orderly and ecologically sound pattern of development. The unwillingness of the five counties to subordinate sectarian economic interests in rapid growth and development of the lake basin to the national interest in preserving the lake as a natural resource has been manifested not only in deficiencies of the present zoning laws, but also in frequent departures from existing controls. Responsibility for inadequacies in approach lies partly with local government operating in county seats geographically and economically removed from the Lake Tahoe basin and partly with the permanent residents. Neither group has recognized that Tahoe must be protected with restrictions on private enterprise in the interest of conservation." (Comment, supra, 52 Cal. L.Rev. 563, 618–619.)

Furthermore, problems which exhibit exclusively local characteristics at certain times in the life of a community, acquire larger dimensions and changed characteristics at others. "It is * * * settled that the constitutional concept of municipal affairs is not a fixed or static quantity. It changes with the changing conditions upon which it is to operate." (Pac. Tel. & Tel. Co. v. City & County of S.F. (1959) 51 Cal.2d 766, 771, 336 P.2d 514, 517.) When the effects of change are felt beyond the point of its immediate impact, it is fatuous to expect that controlling such change remains a local problem to be solved by local methods.[17] Old attitudes confer no irrevocable license to continue looking with unseeing eyes. The Compact gives the Agency power to adopt regional planning and regional zoning ordinances to solve regional problems of resource management; it does not delegate to the Agency the same powers granted to the counties.

In short, since the powers conferred upon the Agency are for regional purposes, not local purposes, and since no power to enact penal legislation has been delegated to the Agency, former section 11 is not violated.

* * *

The Counties of El Dorado and Placer also contend that the Compact is void because it denies their residents equal protection of the laws in violation of sections 11 and 21 of article I of the California Constitution and of the Fourteenth Amendment to the United States Constitution. Such violation of equal protection is asserted on two separate grounds: (1) That the Compact by failing to provide therefor denies to the citizens of the Tahoe Basin their right of initiative, referendum and recall; and (2) that the method of selecting the governing body of the Agency violates the "one person, one vote" rule.

The counties' first argument is essentially this: Since the Legislature has provided for initiative, referendum and recall for counties but has made no such provision for the Agency, there is an unreasonable and arbitrary classification "[d]enying the citizens of the Tahoe Basin such basic rights * * *." The point seems to be that although the citizens of El Dorado and Placer Counties do have such rights in respect to their counties, they are constitutionally entitled to an additional bundle of

---

17. Indeed, it has been generally recognized that land-use planning and environmental control often present problems of regional (Stevens, Air Pollution and the Federal System (1971) 22 Hastings L.J. 661, 662; Comment, Preserving Rural Land Resources (1971) 1 Ecology L.Q. 330, 367–371), statewide (Richard M. Nixon, First Annual Report to Congress on the State of the Nation's Environment (1971) U.S. Code Cong. and Admin.News, pp. 51, 59–60; S. 912 and H.R. 4332, 92d Cong., 1st Sess. (1971)), national (42 U.S.C.A. § 4331) or even world-wide concern (Kennan, To Prevent a World Wasteland (1971) 1 Environmental Affairs 191). The inability of local governments to deal with environmental problems stems not only from the obvious fact that the ecology is a seamless web not tailored to fit local political boundaries, but also from the economic impact of large-scale development; such as the placement of airports (Berger, Nobody Loves an Airport (1970) 43 So.Cal.L.Rev. 631) or freeway interchanges (Gov.Code, § 66400 et seq.).

similar rights in respect to the Agency. We can discern no merit in this line of argument.

As we recently said, the concept of equal protection of the laws means simply "that persons similarly situated with respect to the legitimate purpose of the law receive like treatment." (Purdy & Fitzpatrick v. State of California (1969) 71 Cal.2d 566, 578, 79 Cal.Rptr. 77, 85, 456 P.2d 645, 653.) So far as the procedures of the initiative, referendum and recall are concerned, the Agency is treated no differently than other districts in California. All districts, including regional agencies such as the present one, are excluded from the initiative, referendum and recall provisions of the Elections Code where, as here, the district has been "formed under a law which does not provide a procedure for elections * * *." (Elec.Code, § 5150.) Since the residents of the Tahoe Basin are thus treated in the same way as those of other districts created under similar laws, they have suffered no denial of equal protection.

Nor can we discern any constitutional infirmity in the appointment, rather than the election of the governing body of the Agency. (See § 66801, art. III, subd. (a).) Certainly such a scheme of organization is not without precedent. (See, for example, the San Francisco Bay Conservation and Development Commission; Gov.Code, § 66620; see also Gov. Code, § 66400 et seq.; § 65063 et seq.; § 66500 et seq.) Indeed, in the instant case, the selection of the governing body by appointment would appear to be a necessary consequence of the interstate nature of the Agency. * * *

The counties' "one person, one vote" argument is also lacking in merit. They urge that the Agency exercises "general governmental powers" and that, therefore, under Avery v. Midland County (1968) 390 U.S. 474, 88 S.Ct. 1114, 20 L.Ed.2d 45 and its progeny, the governing board of the Agency must be apportioned in a manner which conforms with the "one person, one vote" requirement of the Fourteenth Amendment.

Clearly the members of the governing board of the Agency do not represent equal numbers of residents of the region. The United States census for 1970 gives the following populations for the counties here involved: Placer, 76,218; El Dorado, 41,704; Washoe, 119,965; Ormsby, 15,264; and Douglas, 6,046. Since one member of the Agency's governing board represents each of these counties some members of the board represent far more residents than do others. Furthermore, the 11,998 residents of the City of South Lake Tahoe are, in a sense, represented twice, since both that city and El Dorado County within which it is located have a member on the Agency. Finally, the *ex officio* members and the members appointed by the governors do not represent residents at all, but rather "the public at large." If the Agency's governing board must be selected on a "one person, one vote" basis, it obviously fails the test. (See Calderon v. City of Los Angeles (1971) 4 Cal.3d 251, 93 Cal.Rptr. 361, 481 P.2d 489.)

However, the members of the Agency's governing board are appointed, not elected. In Sailors v. Board of Education (1967) 387 U.S. 105, 87 S.Ct. 1549, 18 L.Ed.2d 650, the United States Supreme Court upheld a similar system of appointing members of a county school board over the objection that it violated the "one person, one vote" principle. There, the residents of each local school board district elected a local school board. Each of these boards, in turn, selected a delegate to a biennial meeting at which the delegates elected a five-member county board.

The court stated: "Viable local governments may need many innovations, numerous combinations of old and new devices, great flexibility in municipal arrangements to meet changing urban conditions. We see nothing in the Constitution to prevent experimentation. At least as respects nonlegislative officers, a State can appoint local officials or elect them or combine the elective and appointive systems as was done here. * * * Since the choice of members of the county school board did not involve an election and since none was required for these nonlegislative offices, the principle of 'one man, one vote' has no relevancy." (387 U.S. at pp. 110–111, 87 S.Ct. at p. 1553.)

* * *

The members of the Agency's governing board are appointed; consequently, the fact that they do not "represent" equal numbers of people does not deny those who are "underrepresented" equal protection of the laws.

Furthermore, we perceive significant state interests which justify the Compact's provisions for appointment of the Agency's governing board. In the first place, the Agency presents unique problems because of its interstate nature. If the board were apportioned on the basis of population within the region, Nevada would be accorded more votes than California, since the population of Washoe, Ormsby and Douglas Counties is 141,275 whereas the population of El Dorado and Placer Counties is 117,922. California, whose concurrence was essential to the formation of the Agency, would be less interested in the Agency if its vote were less than equal to Nevada's. Secondly, persons not residing within the Tahoe Basin have a very real and direct interest in the actions of the Agency. Aside from the general interest of the people of this state, including its vacationers, in the preservation of Lake Tahoe, it is common knowledge that many nonresidents own vacation homes and other property within the region. They will, of course, be directly affected by any planning or zoning by the Agency. Finally, the Compact represents an innovative attempt to deal with a problem directly affecting nonresidents of the Tahoe Basin, as well as residents. The Compact gives to the residents of the region a clear majority of the representation on the governing board, since such residents are the persons most intimately involved with the Agency. Yet, as we have seen, the general population of the state has a very substantial, if lesser, interest in the Agency. The public at large is represented by the two members sitting *ex officio* and by the two members appointed by the governors.

* * *

We, therefore, reach these final conclusions: Section 66801 of the Government Code, which constitutes the enactment by the California Legislature of the Tahoe Regional Planning Compact, is constitutional. The Compact imposes on respondent counties a clear and present duty to pay to the Tahoe Regional Planning Agency the sums heretofore and hereafter allotted to them by the Agency as representing their respective shares of the amount of money necessary to support the Agency's activities. Respondents have consistently failed and refused to perform their duty enjoined on them by said law. The performance of respondents' duty properly can and should be compelled by issuance of a peremptory writ of mandate.

* * *

Let a peremptory writ of mandate issue as prayed.

Notes

1. The Supreme Court of Nevada also ordered a county to pay its share of the expenses of the agency. State ex rel. List v. County of Douglas, 90 Nev. 272, 524 P.2d 1271 (1974). The exact governmental nature of the Tahoe agency has inspired a considerable amount of litigation. See, e.g., Lake Country Estates, Inc. v. Tahoe Regional Planning Agency, 440 U.S. 391, 99 S.Ct. 1171, 59 L.Ed.2d 401 (1979); California Tahoe Regional Planning Agency v. Jennings, 594 F.2d 181 (9th Cir.1979).

2. In the Lake Country Estates case, supra, the Supreme Court was asked to decide whether the Tahoe Agency was protected by sovereign immunity under the Eleventh Amendment. The agency argued that any agency that is so important that it could not even be created by the States without a special act of Congress should receive the same immunity that is accorded to the States themselves. The majority rejected the argument finding that the tenor of the interstate compact and the understanding of both states all indicated that the agency was a "political subdivision" like a county or municipality, and not an "arm of the State."

3. In People, California Dept. of Transportation v. City of South Lake Tahoe, 466 F.Supp. 527 (E.D.Cal.1978), the court held that the interstate agency could be held to the higher environmental standards of either state agency. The California Tahoe Regional Planning Agency had adopted a transportation plan which did not show a "loop road" extending from the City of South Lake Tahoe, California to an existing casino area in Nevada. The Tahoe Regional Planning Agency had adopted a plan showing such a road and authorized construction without submitting its plan or proposal to the California Tahoe Regional Planning Agency. Although the court held that both the city and the Tahoe Regional Planning Agency were bound to comply with the California requirements, an injunction against construction was denied because the project only involved a few thousand dollars and if it was ultimately disapproved by the California agency, the road could be blocked off.

Chapter V

PROPERTY RIGHTS, THE POLICE POWER, AND TAKINGS

SECTION 1. INTRODUCTION

At this point, you should recall the introductory material to Chapter I. Our society thrived, in part, on the inherited English notion of absolute property rights. We know that no such concept really existed because government has always regulated the use of property to some extent. Nevertheless, the concept was an important element in judicial formulation of the concept of the police power, which was regarded as justification for public intervention with property to the extent that governmental action stayed within certain bounds and did not cross that invisible line representing a "taking" of private property for public use. Defining that line has been the central problem in defining the limits of land use regulation.

Blackstone, Commentaries on the Law of England * 138:

III.   The third absolute right, inherent in every Englishman, is that of property: which consists in the free use, enjoyment, and disposal of all his acquisitions, without any control or diminution, save only by the laws of the land. * * *

So great moreover is the regard of the law for private property, that it will not authorize the least violation of it; no, not even for the general good of the whole community. If a new road, for instance, were to be made through the grounds of a private person, it might perhaps be extensively beneficial to the public; but the law permits no man, or set of men to do this without consent of the owner of the land. In vain may it be urged, that the good of the individual ought to yield to that of the community; for it would be dangerous to allow any private man, or even any public tribunal, to be the judge of this common good, and to decide whether it be expedient or no. Besides the public good is in nothing more essentially interested, than in the protection of every individual's private rights, as modelled by the municipal law. In this and similar cases the legislature alone can, and indeed frequently does interpose, and compel the individual to acquiesce. But how does it interpose and compel? Not by absolutely stripping the subject of his property in an arbitrary manner; but by giving him a full indemnification and equivalent for the injury thereby sustained. The public is now considered as an individual, treating with an individual for an exchange. All that the legislature does is to oblige the owner to alienate his possessions for a reasonable price; and even this is an exertion of power, which the legislature indulges with caution, and which nothing but the legislature can perform.

In Charles River Bridge v. Proprietors of Warren Bridge, 36 U.S. (11 Pet.) 420, 9 L.Ed. 773 (1837), Chief Justice Taney identified and recognized the concept of the police power. In this foundation case, the Charles River Bridge had been chartered by the state to operate a toll bridge; subsequently, the state authorized another company to construct and operate a free bridge over the Charles River in close proximity to the plaintiff's bridge. Although the plaintiff's charter did not contain an exclusive grant, it was argued that the state had impaired the charter. Taney, in denying the claim, stated:

"[T]he legislature in the very law extending the charter, asserts its rights to authorize improvements over Charles river which would take off a portion of the travel from this bridge and diminish its profits; and the Bridge Company accept the renewal thus given, and thus carefully connected with this assertion of the right on the part of the state. Can they, when holding their corporate existence under this law, and deriving their franchises altogether from it; add to the privileges expressed in their charter an implied agreement, which is in direct conflict with a portion of the law from which they derive their corporate existence? Can the legislature be presumed to have taken upon themselves an implied obligation, contrary to its own acts and declarations contained in the same law? It would be difficult to find a case justifying such an implication, even between individuals; still less will it be found where sovereign rights are concerned, and where the interests of a whole community would be deeply affected by such an implication. It would, indeed, be a strong exertion of judicial power, acting upon its own views of what justice required, and the parties ought to have done; to raise, by a sort of judicial coercion, an implied contract, and infer it from the nature of the very instrument in which the legislature appear to have taken pains to use words which disavow and repudiate any intention, on the part of the state, to make such a contract.

"Indeed, the practice and usage of almost every state in the Union, old enough to have commenced the work of internal improvement, is opposed to the doctrine contended for on the part of the plaintiffs in error. Turnpike roads have been made in succession, on the same line of travel; the later ones interfering materially with the profits of the first. These corporations have, in some instances, been utterly ruined by the introduction of newer and better modes of transportation, and travelling. In some cases, rail roads have rendered the turnpike roads on the same line of travel so entirely useless, that the franchise of the turnpike corporation is not worth preserving. Yet in none of these cases have the corporations supposed that their privileges were invaded, or any contract violated on the part of the state. Amid the multitude of cases which have occurred, and have been daily occurring for the last forty or fifty years, this is the first instance in which such an implied contract has been contended for, and this Court called upon to infer it from an ordinary act of incorporation, containing nothing more than the usual stipulations and provisions to be found in every such law. The absence of any such controversy, when there must have been so many occasions to give rise to it, proves that neither states, nor individuals, nor corporations, ever imagined that such a contract could be implied from such charters. It shows that the men who voted for these laws, never imagined that they were forming such a contract; and if we maintain that they have made it, we must create it by a legal fiction, in opposition to the truth of the fact, and the obvious intention of the party. We cannot deal thus with the rights reserved to the states; and by legal intendments and mere technical reasoning, take away from them any portion of that power over their own internal police and improvement, which is so necessary to their well being and prosperity."

For a discussion of the Charles River Bridge case, see Stanley I. Kutler, Privilege and Creative Destruction: The Charles River Bridge Case (New York: J. B. Lippincott Co., 1971; paperback reprint, Baltimore: Johns Hopkins Press, 1990). Also see, Wright, The Relation of Law in America to Socio–Economic Change, 28 Ark.L.Rev. 440, 471–474 (1975), and Munn v. Illinois, 94 U.S. (4 Otto) 113, 24 L.Ed. 77 (1876).

Ely, Property and Contract in their Relation to the Distribution of Wealth, pp. 218–221 (1914):

As in the United States all property is held subject to regulations, restrictions, and burdens under the police power, it is appropriate to quote from opinions of the United States Supreme Court giving the views of that high tribunal in noteworthy cases. In the celebrated Slaughter House Cases (1872) we find the following said of the police power:

The power is, and must be from its very nature, incapable of any very exact definition or limitation. Upon it depends the security of the social order, the life and health of the citizen, the comfort of an existence in a thickly populated community, the enjoyment of private and social life, and the beneficial use of property. As says another eminent judge, "* * * Persons and property are subjected to all kinds of restraints and burdens in order to secure the general comfort, health, and prosperity of the State. Of the perfect right of the legislature to do this, no question ever was, or *upon acknowledged general principles, ever can be made,* so far as natural persons are concerned." (Thorpe v. Rutland & Burlington R.R. Co., 27 Vt. 139, 1854).

This is clearly stated by Chief Justice Lemuel Shaw: "All property is acquired and held under the tacit condition that it shall not be used so as to injure the equal rights of others, or to destroy or greatly impair the public rights and interest of the community; under the maxim of the common law, *Sic utere tuo ut alienum non laedas.*"[1]

* * *

Still more noteworthy is the opinion of the court as expressed by Mr. Justice Holmes in Noble State Bank v. Haskell.

The police power extends to all the great public needs. It may be put forth in aid of what is sanctioned by usage, *or held by the prevailing morality or the strong and preponderant opinion to be greatly and immediately necessary to the public welfare.*[2]

Now there is more in this police power than regulation of property relations and contractual relations. But there is no difficulty except where property and economic relations are concerned. No one objects to general benevolence—to doing good without cost—so when we consider police power, its essence is the interpretation of property, and when we consider the real essence of the police power as found in the leading American decisions we find that it is consistent with this concept. *It is that power of the courts committed to them by American Constitutions whereby they must shape property and contract to existing social conditions by settling the question of how far social regulations may, without compensation, impose burdens on property.* It seeks to preserve the satisfactory development of the individual and social sides of private property and thus to maintain a satisfactory equilibrium between them. And it is noteworthy that compensation may be given when property is destroyed under the police power. Tuberculous cows are killed in Wisconsin, but a limited compensation is granted to the owner in pursuance of sound public policy, for it lessens the temptation to conceal disease and it diffuses the loss.

Regulation depends on the past—on what was done in England when the Constitution was framed, that is, precedent but likewise on present conditions and sentiments as seen in the quotation given from Mr. Justice Holmes.

The relationship between the police power of the state, which is the power to regulate for the health, safety, morals and general welfare of the public, and the constitutional prohibition against "taking" private

1. Commonwealth v. Tewksbury, 11 Metcalf (Mass.), 55 (1846), at p. 57.

2. Noble State Bank v. Haskell, 219 U.S. 104, 31 S.Ct. 186, 188, 62 L.Ed. 1006 (1911), p. 111.

property for public purposes without just compensation, presents the primary problem in understanding the limits of governmental power to regulate the use of land.

The entire scope of eminent domain law as it relates to the regulation of land use is beyond the reach of this course. Some of the more important articles that may be rewarding are: Berger, A Policy Analysis of the Taking Problem, 49 N.Y.U.L.Rev. 165 (1974); Costonis, "Fair" Compensation and the Accommodation Power: Antidotes for the Taking Impasse in Land Use Controversies, 75 Columbia L.Rev. 1021 (1975); Michelman, Property, Utility, and Fairness: Comments on the Ethical Foundations of "Just Compensation" Law, 80 Harv.L.Rev. 1165 (1967); Sax, Takings and the Police Power, 74 Yale L.J. 36 (1963); Van Alstyne, Taking or Damaging by Police Power: The Search for Inverse Condemnation Criteria, 44 So.Cal.L.Rev. 1 (1970). Lengthier treatments which are valuable include, Ackerman, Private Property and the Constitution (1977) and Hagman & Misczynski, Windfalls for Wipeouts: Land Value Capture and Compensation (1978), along with the book from which the following excerpt is taken:

Bosselman, Callies, and Banta, The Taking Issue, pp. 318–322 (1973):

The founding fathers placed in the Constitution the following words:

* * * nor shall private property be taken for public use without just compensation.

The application of this "taking clause" to land use regulation is the subject of this book.

Why do these twelve words deserve so much study? Because any system of land use regulation will work only if it satisfies each and every link in a chain of interconnected tests. It must be politically feasible; it must make sense economically; * * * and it must hold up in court. The taking issue is an important link in that chain, because if the courts find the system of regulation so severe that it constitutes a taking, the whole system collapses.

* * *

How did a constitutional clause concerned with the *taking* of land become applicable to the *regulation* of land anyway? Originally it wasn't. The "taking" clause derived from the English nobles' fear of the King's seizures of land for his own use, a fear that was reflected in the Magna Carta:

No free man shall be deprived * * * of his freehold * * * unless by the lawful judgment of his peers and by the law of the land.

But the use of land was being regulated—often very severely regulated—throughout English and early American history. Only around the turn of the Twentieth Century did judges and legal scholars popularize the notion that if regulation of the use of land became excessive, it could amount to the equivalent of a taking.

* * *

An examination and analysis of colonial regulations shows that the prevailing pattern of land use regulation was quite similar to that in England. Compensation was generally provided for physical takings of developed property, but literally hundreds of regulations of the use of land were enforced without any compensation to the landowner.

Nor was the issue of compensation for land use regulation raised either during the revolutionary period or in the drafting of the Constitution or Bill of Rights. Rather the draftsmen of the taking clause seem to have carried over the historic British concern over arbitrary seizure of land by the King,—perhaps as reflected in seizures during the then recent revolutionary war—and to have applied that concern to actions of the new Federal Government.

The courts have insisted that the taking clause be strictly observed. Whenever the government has needed land for some public purpose it has either purchased the land on the open market or exercised the power of condemnation, paying the owner the fair market value of his land.

Court decisions during the entire first half of the Nineteenth Century * * * find courts construing the taking clause strictly. To paraphrase a well-known commentator of the period writing in 1857, in order for an owner to be entitled to protection under the taking clause his property must have been actually taken in the physical sense of the word. No indirect or consequential damage, no matter how serious, warranted compensation.

The last half of the Nineteenth Century led to a certain ambivalence on the part of the courts, as the country's tremendous economic expansion inevitably produced conflicts with vested interests. Nonetheless, late in the Nineteenth Century the Supreme Court handed down cases such as Powell v. Pennsylvania and Mugler v. Kansas which denied compensation to the owners of business properties that became virtually valueless because of state regulatory statutes. These statutes were held to be valid police regulations, not takings of property within the meaning of the constitutional prohibition.

But Justice Holmes was soon to change the Court's direction * * * Only two years after Mugler v. Kansas, Holmes wrote from the bench of the Massachusetts Supreme Court in Rideout v. Knox[3] that the power of eminent domain (the power to acquire land) and the police power (the power to regulate land) differed only in degree and no clear line could be drawn between them. He continued to develop this philosophy in subsequent decisions and influenced a number of leading scholars of the period.

3.   148 Mass. 368, 19 N.E. 390 (1889).

Then, in December of 1922, in the now famous case of Pennsylvania Coal Co. v. Mahon, Holmes announced his famous rule:

The general rule at least is, that while property may be regulated to a certain extent, if regulation goes too far it will be recognized as a taking.

When a diminution of property values reaches a certain magnitude, he said, a taking occurs. Thus, Holmes declared Pennsylvania's Kohler Act, passed to prevent coal mine subsidence from destroying whole towns, unconstitutional as an undue regulation of the property of the coal company.[4]

SECTION 2.   WHAT IS A TAKING OF PROPERTY?

A.   THE BASIC CONSTITUTIONAL CONSIDERATIONS

MUGLER v. KANSAS

Supreme Court of the United States, 1887.
123 U.S. 623, 8 S.Ct. 273, 31 L.Ed. 205.

[The state had enacted legislation banning the sale and manufacture of spirituous beverages. Petitioner was owner of a brewery located in the state.]

Mr. Justice Harlan:

* * *

Upon this ground—if we do not misapprehend the position of defendants—it is contended that, as the primary and principal use of beer is as a beverage; as their respective breweries were erected when it was lawful to engage in the manufacture of beer for every purpose; as such establishments will become of no value as property, or, at least, will be materially diminished in value, if not employed in the manufacture of beer for every purpose; the prohibition upon their being so employed is, in effect, a taking of property for public use without compensation, and depriving the citizen of his property without due process of law. In other words, although the State, in the exercise of her police powers, may lawfully prohibit the manufacture and sale, within her limits, of intoxicating liquors to be used as a beverage, legislation having that object in view cannot be enforced against those who, at the time, happen to own property, the chief value of which consists in its fitness for such

---

4. Eminent domain law, or the law of expropriation, is not limited to the United States. For some comparative law material, see Raymond Cocks, The Expropriation of Rights *in rem* under English Law, (monograph published by the Jean Bodin Society for the Comparative History of Institutions, Antwerp, Belgium, 1996); Pia Letto–Vana- mo and Ditlev Tamm, The History of Expropriation in the Nordic Countries (monograph published by the Jean Bodin Society for the Comparative History of Institutions, Antwerp, Belgium, 1996). (Several other papers on the same topic from different nations were also published, but most of them are not in English.)

manufacturing purposes, unless compensation is first made for the diminution in the value of their property, resulting from such prohibitory enactments.

This interpretation of the Fourteenth Amendment is inadmissible. It cannot be supposed that the States intended, by adopting that Amendment, to impose restraints upon the exercise of their powers for the protection of the safety, health, or morals of the community.

* * *

It is supposed by the defendants that the doctrine for which they contend is sustained by Pumpelly v. Green Bay Co., 13 Wall. 168. But in that view we do not concur. That was an action for the recovery of damages for the overflowing of the plaintiff's land by water, resulting from the construction of a dam across a river. The defence was that the dam constituted a part of the system adopted by the State for improving the navigation of Fox and Wisconsin rivers; and it was contended that as the damages of which the plaintiff complained were only the result of the improvement, under legislative sanction, of a navigable stream, he was not entitled to compensation from the State or its agents. The case, therefore, involved the question whether the overflowing of the plaintiff's land, to such an extent that it became practically unfit to be used, was a taking of property, within the meaning of the constitution of Wisconsin, providing that "the property of no person shall be taken for public use without just compensation therefor." This court said it would be a very curious and unsatisfactory result, were it held that, "if the government refrains from the absolute conversion of real property to the uses of the public, it can destroy its value entirely, can inflict irreparable and permanent injury to any extent, can, in effect, subject it to total destruction, without making any compensation, because, in the narrowest sense of that word, it is not *taken* for the public use. Such a construction would pervert the constitutional provision into a restriction upon the rights of the citizen, as those rights stood at the common law, instead of the government, and make it an authority for the invasion of private right under the pretext of the public good, which had no warrant in the laws or practices of our ancestors." pp. 177, 178.

These principles have no application to the case under consideration. The question in Pumpelly v. Green Bay Company arose under the State's power of eminent domain; while the question now before us arises under what are, strictly, the police powers of the State, exerted for the protection of the health, morals, and safety of the people. That case, as this court said in Transportation Co. v. Chicago, 99 U.S. 635, 642, was an extreme qualification of the doctrine, universally held, that "acts done in the proper exercise of governmental powers, and not directly encroaching upon private property, though these consequences may impair its use," do not constitute a taking within the meaning of the constitutional provision, or entitle the owner of such property to compensation from the State or its agents, or give him any right of action. It was a case in which there was a "permanent flooding of private property," a "physical invasion of the real estate of the private owner, and a practical ouster of his possession." His property was, in effect, required to be devoted to the use of the public, and, consequently, he was entitled to compensation.

As already stated, the present case must be governed by principles that do not involve the power of eminent domain, in the exercise of which property may not be taken for public use without compensation. A prohibition simply upon the use of property for purposes that are declared, by valid legislation, to be injurious to the health, morals, or safety of the community, cannot, in any just sense be deemed a taking or an appropriation of property for the public benefit. Such legislation does not disturb the owner in the control or use of his property for lawful purposes, nor restrict his right to dispose of it, but is only a declaration by the State that its use by any one, for certain forbidden purposes, is prejudicial to the public interests. Nor can legislation of that character come within the Fourteenth Amendment, in any case, unless it is apparent that its real object is not to protect the community, or to promote the general well-being, but, under the guise of police regulation, to deprive the owner of his liberty and property, without due process of law. The power which the States have of prohibiting such use by individuals of their property as will be prejudicial to the health, the morals, or the safety of the public, is not—and, consistently with the existence and safety of organized society, cannot be—burdened with the condition that the State must compensate such individual owners for pecuniary losses they may sustain, by reason of their not being permitted, by a noxious use of their property, to inflict injury upon the community. The exercise of the police power by the destruction of property which is itself a public nuisance, or the prohibition of its use in a particular way, whereby its value becomes depreciated, is very different from taking property for public use, or from depriving a person of his property without due process of law. In the one case, a nuisance only is abated; in the other, unoffending property is taken away from an innocent owner.

* * *

HADACHECK v. SEBASTIAN

Supreme Court of the United States, 1915.
239 U.S. 394, 36 S.Ct. 143, 60 L.Ed. 348.

MR. JUSTICE McKENNA delivered the opinion of the court.

Habeas corpus prosecuted in the Supreme Court of the State of California for the discharge of plaintiff in error from the custody of defendant in error, Chief of Police of the City of Los Angeles.

Plaintiff in error, to whom we shall refer as petitioner, was convicted of a misdemeanor for the violation of an ordinance of the City of Los Angeles which makes it unlawful for any person to establish or operate a brickyard or brick kiln, or any establishment, factory or place for the manufacture or burning of brick within described limits in the city. Sentence was pronounced against him and he was committed to the custody of defendant in error as Chief of Police of the City of Los Angeles.

Being so in custody he filed a petition in the Supreme Court of the State for a writ of habeas corpus. The writ was issued. Subsequently defendant in error made a return thereto supported by affidavits, to which petitioner made sworn reply. The court rendered judgment discharging the writ and remanding petitioner to custody. The Chief Justice of the court then granted this writ of error.

* * *

How the Supreme Court dealt with the allegations, denials and affidavits we can gather from its opinion. The court said, through Mr. Justice Sloss, 165 California, p. 416:

> "The district to which the prohibition was applied contains about three square miles. The petitioner is the owner of a tract of land containing eight acres, more or less, within the district described in the ordinance. He acquired his land in 1902, before the territory to which the ordinance was directed had been annexed to the city of Los Angeles. His land contains valuable deposits of clay suitable for the manufacture of brick, and he has, during the entire period of his ownership, used the land for brickmaking, and has erected thereon kilns, machinery and buildings necessary for such manufacture. The land, as he alleges, is far more valuable for brickmaking than for any other purpose."

The court considered the business one which could be regulated and that regulation was not precluded by the fact "that the value of investments made in the business prior to any legislative action will be greatly diminished," and that no complaint could be based upon the fact that petitioner had been carrying on the trade in that locality for a long period.

And, considering the allegations of the petition, the denials of the return and the evidence of the affidavits, the court said that the latter tended to show that the district created had become primarily a residential section and that the occupants of the neighboring dwellings are seriously incommoded by the operations of petitioner; and that such evidence, "when taken in connection with the presumptions in favor of the propriety of the legislative determination, overcame the contention that the prohibition of the ordinance was a mere arbitrary invasion of private right, not supported by any tenable belief that the continuance of the business was so detrimental to the interests of others as to require suppression."

The court, on the evidence, rejected the contention that the ordinance was not in good faith enacted as a police measure and that it was intended to discriminate against petitioner or that it was actuated by any motive of injuring him as an individual.

The charge of discrimination between localities was not sustained. The court expressed the view that the determination of prohibition was for the legislature and that the court, without regard to the fact shown in the return that there was not another district in which brickmaking was prohibited, could not sustain the claim that the ordinance was not enacted in good faith but was designed to discriminate against petitioner and the other brick yard in the district. "The facts before us," the court finally said "would certainly not justify the conclusion that the ordinance here in question was designed, in either its adoption or its enforcement, to be anything but what it purported to be, viz., a legitimate regulation, operating alike upon all who came within its terms."

We think the conclusion of the court is justified by the evidence and makes it unnecessary to review the many cases cited by petitioner in which it is decided that the police power of a state cannot be arbitrarily exercised. The principle is familiar, but in any given case it must plainly appear to apply. It is to be remembered that we are dealing with one of the most essential powers of government, one that is the least limitable. It may, indeed, seem harsh in its exercise, usually is on some individual, but the imperative necessity for its existence precludes any limitation upon it when not exerted arbitrarily. A vested interest cannot be asserted against it because of conditions once obtaining. Chicago & Alton R.R. v. Tranbarger, 238 U.S. 67, 78, 35 S.Ct. 678, 59 L.Ed. 204. To so hold would preclude development and fix a city forever in its primitive conditions. There must be progress, and if in its march private interests are in the way they must yield to the good of the community. The logical result of petitioner's contention would seem to be that a city could not be formed or enlarged against the resistance of an occupant of the ground and that if it grows at all it can only grow as the environment of the occupations that are usually banished to the purlieus.

The police power and to what extent it may be exerted we have recently illustrated in Reinman v. Little Rock, 237 U.S. 171, 35 S.Ct. 511, 59 L.Ed. 900. The circumstances of the case were very much like those of the case at bar and give reply to the contentions of petitioner, especially that which asserts that a necessary and lawful occupation that is not a nuisance per se cannot be made so by legislative declaration. There was a like investment in property, encouraged by the then conditions; a like reduction of value and deprivation of property was asserted against the validity of the ordinance there considered; a like assertion of an arbitrary exercise of the power of prohibition. Against all of these contentions, and causing the rejection of them all, was adduced the police power. There was a prohibition of a business, lawful in itself, there as here. It was a livery stable there, a brick yard here. They differ in particulars, but they are alike in that which cause and justify prohibition in defined localities—that is, the effect upon the health and comfort of the community.

The ordinance passed upon prohibited the conduct of the business within a certain defined area in Little Rock, Arkansas. This court said of it: granting that the business was not a nuisance per se, it was clearly within the police power of the State to regulate it, "and to that end to declare that in particular circumstances and in particular localities a livery stable shall be deemed a nuisance in fact and in law." And the only limitation upon the power was stated to be that the power could not be exerted arbitrarily or with unjust discrimination. There was a citation of cases. We think the present case is within the ruling thus declared.

There is a distinction between Reinman v. Little Rock and the case at bar. There, a particular business was prohibited which was not affixed to or dependent upon its locality; it could be conducted elsewhere. Here, it is contended, the latter condition does not exist, and it is alleged that the manufacture of brick must necessarily be carried on where suitable clay is found and that the clay on petitioner's property cannot be transported to some other locality. This is not urged as a physical impossibility but only, counsel say, that such transportation and the transportation of the bricks to places where they could be used in construction work would be prohibitive "from a financial standpoint." But upon the evidence the Supreme Court considered the case, as we understand its opinion, from the standpoint of the offensive effects of the operation of a brick yard, and not from the deprivation of the deposits of clay, and distinguished Ex parte Kelso, 147 Cal. 609, 2 L.R.A. (N.S.) 796, 109 Am.St.Rep. 178, 82 Pac. 241, wherein the court declared invalid an ordinance absolutely prohibiting the maintenance or operation of a rock or stone quarry within a certain portion of the city and county of San Francisco. The court there said that the effect of the ordinance was "to absolutely deprive the owners of real property within such limits of a valuable right incident to their ownership,—viz., the right to extract therefrom such rock and stone as they might find it to their advantage to dispose of." The court expressed the view that the removal could be regulated but that "an absolute prohibition of such removal under the circumstances," could not be upheld.

In the present case, there is no prohibition of the removal of the brick clay; only a prohibition within the designated locality of its manufacture into bricks. And to this feature of the ordinance our opinion is addressed. Whether other questions would arise if the ordinance were broader, and opinion on such questions, we reserve.

Petitioner invokes the equal protection clause of the Constitution and charges that it is violated in that the ordinance (1) "prohibits him from manufacturing brick upon his property while his competitors are permitted, without regulation of any kind, to manufacture brick upon property situated in all respects similarly to that of plaintiff in error"; and (2) that it "prohibits the conduct of his business while it permits the maintenance within the same district of any other kind of business, no matter how objectionable the same may be, either in its nature or in the manner in which it is conducted."

If we should grant that the first specification shows a violation of classification, that is, a distinction between businesses which was not within the legislative power, petitioner's contention encounters the objection that it depends upon an inquiry of fact which the record does not enable us to determine. It is alleged in the return to the petition that brickmaking is prohibited in one other district and an ordinance is referred to regulating business in other districts. To this plaintiff in error replied that the ordinance attempts to prohibit the operation of certain businesses having mechanical power and does not prohibit the maintenance of any business or the operation of any machine that is operated by animal power. In other words, petitioner makes his contention depend upon disputable considerations of classification and upon a comparison of conditions of which there is no means of judicial determination and upon which nevertheless we are expected to reverse legislative action exercised upon matters of which the city has control.

To a certain extent the latter comment may be applied to other contentions, and, besides, there is no allegation or proof of other objectionable businesses being permitted within the district, and a speculation of their establishment or conduct at some future time is too remote.

In his petition and argument something is made of the ordinance as fostering a monopoly and suppressing his competition with other brickmakers. The charge and argument are too illusive. It is part of the charge that the ordinance was directed against him. The charge, we have seen, was rejected by the Supreme Court, and we find nothing to justify it.

It may be that brick yards in other localities within the city where the same conditions exist are not regulated or prohibited, but it does not follow that they will not be. That petitioner's business was first in time to be prohibited, does not make its prohibition unlawful. And it may be, as said by the Supreme Court of the State, that the conditions justify a distinction. However, the inquiries thus suggested are outside of our province.

There are other and subsidiary contentions which, we think do not require discussion. They are disposed of by what we have said. It may be that something else than prohibition would have satisfied the conditions. Of this, however, we have no means of determining, and besides we cannot declare invalid the exertion of a power which the city undoubtedly has because of a charge that it does not exactly accommodate the conditions or that some other exercise would have been better or less harsh. We must accord good faith to the city in the absence of a clear showing to the contrary and an honest exercise of judgment upon the circumstances which induced its action.

We do not notice the contention that the ordinance is not within the city's charter powers nor that it is in violation of the state constitution, such contentions raising only a local question which must be deemed to have been decided adversely to petitioner by the Supreme Court of the State.

Judgment affirmed.

Notes

1. Hadacheck v. Sebastian refers to and was decided in the same year as Reinman v. City of Little Rock, 237 U.S. 171, 35 S.Ct. 511, 59 L.Ed. 900 (1915). In Reinman, a livery stable was eliminated from the downtown area as a result of the ordinance. Other police power ordinances which predated comprehensive zoning were predicated upon nuisance-like situations and drew upon that analogy. Ordinances were upheld which regulated prostitution (L'Hote v. City of New Orleans, 177 U.S. 587, 20 S.Ct. 788, 44 L.Ed. 899 (1900)), Chinese laundries (Soon Hing v. Crowley, 113 U.S. 703, 5 S.Ct. 730, 28 L.Ed. 1145 (1885), but cf. Yick Wo v. Hopkins, 118 U.S. 356, 6 S.Ct. 1064, 30 L.Ed. 220 (1886)), heavy industrial smoke emissions (Northwestern Laundry v. City of Des Moines, 239 U.S. 486, 36 S.Ct. 206, 60 L.Ed. 396 (1916)), gasoline storage facilities (Pierce Oil Corp. v. City of Hope, 248 U.S. 498, 39 S.Ct. 172, 63 L.Ed. 381 (1919)) and fertilizer operations (Northwestern Fertilizing Co. v. Hyde Park, 97 U.S. (7 Otto) 659, 24 L.Ed. 1036 (1878)). These and the preceding cases provided, along with some others, the foundation for the suggestion that prohibiting nuisances or activities with nuisance characteristics did not constitute a taking of property even if the property owner was severely limited or even "wiped out." This distinction remains to be of continuing importance. See, e.g., Kuban v. McGimsey, 96 Nev. 105, 605 P.2d 623 (1980), which upheld a county ordinance prohibiting brothels after they had been legally permitted for seven years. The Nevada Court did not view this as resulting in a taking of the property of the owners of "Judy's Ranch" and "Sheri's Ranch."

2. What if a landowner complains that a nearby public land use so devalues his property that a nuisance-like taking has occurred? This, of course, is the other side of the coin, so to speak. For a case in which the property owner claimed that construction of a county jail and work release center on adjacent property amounted to a taking, see Florida East Coast Properties, Inc. v. Metropolitan Dade County, 572 F.2d 1108 (5th Cir.1978). Also see Hills Development Co. v. Township of Bernards, 229 N.J.Super. 318, 551 A.2d 547 (1988), where the court held that rezoning for construction of low and moderate income housing did not deprive adjoining landowners of all or most of their interest in their property and did not constitute a taking. What if the government's alleged nuisance results in a trespass? In Peterman v. State, Dept. of Natural Resources, 446 Mich. 177, 521 N.W.2d 499 (1994), the state agency constructed a poorly designed boat launch on its lakefront property that resulted in destruction of a nearby property owner's beach due to sand filtration, and consequent erosion of fast land. The court held that the property owner was entitled to damages for a taking.

3. If the owner's use of his property could not conveniently be labeled as a nuisance or as an activity possessing nuisance-like attributes, would a prohibition for the public good be considered a taking? The next step in the development of the question of what does or does not amount to a regulatory taking is represented by the following case, which forms the basis for the judicial approach currently employed in the United States.

PENNSYLVANIA COAL CO. v. MAHON

Supreme Court of the United States, 1922.
260 U.S. 393, 43 S.Ct. 158, 67 L.Ed. 322.

MR. JUSTICE HOLMES delivered the opinion of the Court.

* * *

The statute forbids the mining of anthracite coal in such way as to cause the subsidence of, among other things, any structure used as a human habitation, with certain exceptions, including among them land where the surface is owned by the owner of the underlying coal and is distant more than one hundred and fifty feet from any improved property belonging to any other person. As applied to this case the statute is admitted to destroy previously existing rights of property and contract. The question is whether the police power can be stretched so far.

Government hardly could go on if to some extent values incident to property could not be diminished without paying for every such change in the general law. As long recognized, some values are enjoyed under an implied limitation and must yield to the police power. But obviously the implied limitation must have its limits, or the contract and due process clauses are gone. One fact for consideration in determining such limits is the extent of the diminution. When it reaches a certain magnitude, in most if not in all cases there must be an exercise of eminent domain and compensation to sustain the act. So the question depends upon the particular facts. The greatest weight is given to the judgment of the legislature, but it always is open to interested parties to contend that the legislature has gone beyond its constitutional power.

This is the case of a single private house. No doubt there is a public interest even in this, as there is in every purchase and sale and in all that happens within the commonwealth. Some existing rights may be modified even in such a case. Rideout v. Knox, 148 Mass. 368. But usually in ordinary private affairs the public interest does not warrant much of this kind of interference. A source of damage to such a house is not a public nuisance even if similar damage is inflicted on others in different places. The damage is not common or public. Wesson v. Washburn Iron Co., 13 Allen, 95, 103. The extent of the public interest is shown by the statute to be limited, since the statute ordinarily does not apply to land when the surface is owned by the owner of the coal. Furthermore, it is not justified as a protection of personal safety. That could be provided for by notice. Indeed the very foundation of this bill is that the defendant gave timely notice of its intent to mine under the house. On the other hand the extent of the taking is great. It purports to abolish what is recognized in Pennsylvania as an estate in land—a very valuable estate—and what is declared by the Court below to be a contract hitherto binding the plaintiffs. If we were called upon to deal with the plaintiffs' position alone, we should think it clear that the statute does not disclose a public interest sufficient to warrant so extensive a destruction of the defendant's constitutionally protected rights.

But the case has been treated as one in which the general validity of the act should be discussed. The Attorney General of the State, the City of Scranton, and the representatives of other extensive interests were allowed to take part in the argument below and have submitted their contentions here. It seems, therefore, to be our duty to go farther in the statement of our opinion, in order that it may be known at once, and that further suits should not be brought in vain.

It is our opinion that the act cannot be sustained as an exercise of the police power, so far as it affects the mining of coal under streets or cities in places where the right to mine such coal has been reserved. As said in a Pennsylvania case, "For practical purposes, the right to coal consists in the right to mine it." Commonwealth v. Clearview Coal Co., 256 Pa.St. 328, 331. What makes the right to mine coal valuable is that it can be exercised with profit. To make it commercially impracticable to mine certain coal has very nearly the same effect for constitutional purposes as appropriating or destroying it. This we think that we are warranted in assuming that the statute does.

* * *

The rights of the public in a street purchased or laid out by eminent domain are those that it has paid for. If in any case its representatives have been so short sighted as to acquire only surface rights without the right of support, we see no more authority for supplying the latter without compensation than there was for taking the right of way in the first place and refusing to pay for it because the public wanted it very much. The protection of private property in the Fifth Amendment presupposes that it is wanted for public use, but provides that it shall not be taken for such use without compensation. A similar assumption is made in the decisions upon the Fourteenth Amendment. * * * When this seemingly absolute protection is found to be qualified by the police power, the natural tendency of human nature is to extend the qualification more and more until at last private property disappears. But that cannot be accomplished in this way under the Constitution of the United States.

The general rule at least is, that while property may be regulated to a certain extent, if regulation goes too far it will be recognized as a taking. It may be doubted how far exceptional cases, like the blowing up of a house to stop a conflagration, go—and if they go beyond the general rule, whether they do not stand as much upon tradition as upon principle. * * * In general it is not plain that a man's misfortunes or necessities will justify his shifting the damages to his neighbor's shoulders. * * * We are in danger of forgetting that a strong public desire to improve the public condition is not enough to warrant achieving the desire by a shorter cut than the constitutional way of paying for the change. As we already have said, this is a question of degree—and therefore cannot be disposed of by general propositions. But we regard this as going beyond any of the cases decided by this Court. * * *

We assume, of course, that the statute was passed upon the conviction that an exigency existed that would warrant it, and we assume that an exigency exists that would warrant the exercise of eminent domain. But the question at bottom is upon whom the loss of the changes desired should fall. So far as private persons or communities have seen fit to take the risk of acquiring only surface rights, we cannot see that the fact that their risk has become a danger warrants the giving to them greater rights than they bought.

Decree reversed.

MR. JUSTICE BRANDEIS, dissenting.

The Kohler Act prohibits, under certain conditions, the mining of anthracite coal within the limits of a city in such a manner or to such an extent "as to cause the * * * subsidence of any dwelling or other structure used as a human habitation, or any factory, store, or other industrial or mercantile establishment in which human labor is employed." Coal in place is land; and the right of the owner to use his land is not absolute. He may not so use it as to create a public nuisance; and uses, once harmless, may, owing to changed conditions, seriously threaten the public welfare. Whenever they do, the legislature has power to prohibit such uses without paying compensation; and the power to prohibit extends alike to the manner, the character and the purpose of the use. Are we justified in declaring that the Legislature of Pennsylvania has, in restricting the right to mine anthracite, exercised this power so arbitrarily as to violate the Fourteenth Amendment?

Every restriction upon the use of property imposed in the exercise of the police power deprives the owner of some right theretofore enjoyed, and is, in that sense, an abridgement by the State of rights in property without making compensation. But restriction imposed to protect the public health, safety or morals from dangers threatened is not a taking. The restriction here in question is merely the prohibition of a noxious use. The property so restricted remains in the possession of its owner. The State does not appropriate it or make any use of it. The State merely prevents the owner from making a use which interferes with paramount rights of the public. Whenever the use prohibited ceases to be noxious,—as it may because of further change in local or social conditions,—the restriction will have to be removed and the owner will gain be free to enjoy his property as heretofore.

The restriction upon the use of this property cannot, of course, be lawfully imposed, unless its purpose is to protect the public. But the purpose of a restriction does not cease to be public, because incidentally some private persons may thereby receive gratuitously valuable special benefits. Thus, owners of low buildings may obtain through statutory restrictions upon the height of neighboring structures, benefits equivalent to an easement of light and air. * * * Furthermore, a restriction, though imposed for a public purpose, will not be lawful, unless the restriction is an appropriate means to the public end. But to keep coal in place is surely an appropriate means of preventing subsidence of the surface; and ordinarily it is the only available means. Restriction upon use does not become inappropriate as a means, merely because it deprives the owner of the only use to which the property can then be profitably put. The liquor and the oleomargarine cases settled that. Mugler v. Kansas, 123 U.S. 623, 668, 669, 8 S.Ct. 273, 31 L.Ed. 205; Powell v. Pennsylvania, 127 U.S. 678, 682, 8 S.Ct. 992, 1257, 32 L.Ed. 253. See also Hadacheck v. Sebastian, 239 U.S. 394, 36 S.Ct. 143, 60 L.Ed. 348; Pierce Oil Corporation v. City of Hope, 248 U.S. 498, 39 S.Ct. 172, 63 L.Ed. 381. Nor is a restriction imposed through exercise of the police power inappropriate as a means, merely because the same end might be effected through exercise of the power of eminent domain, or otherwise at public expense. Every restriction upon the height of buildings might be secured through acquiring by eminent domain the right of each owner to build above the limiting height; but it is settled that the State need not resort to that power. Compare Laurel Hill Cemetery v. San Francisco, 216 U.S. 358, 30 S.Ct. 301, 54 L.Ed. 515; Missouri Pacific Ry. Co. v. Omaha, 235 U.S. 121, 35 S.Ct. 82, 59 L.Ed. 157. If by mining anthracite coal the owner would necessarily unloose poisonous gasses, I suppose no one would doubt the power of the State to prevent the mining, without buying his coal fields. And why may not the State, likewise, without paying compensation, prohibit one from digging so deep or excavating so near the surface, as to expose the community to like dangers? In the latter case, as in the former, carrying on the business would be a public nuisance.

It is said that one fact for consideration in determining whether the limits of the police power have been exceeded is the extent of the resulting diminution in value; and that here the restriction destroys existing rights of property and contract. But values are relative. If we are to consider the value of the coal kept in place by the restriction, we should compare it with the value of all other parts of the land. That is, with the value not of the coal alone, but with the value of the whole property. The rights of an owner as against the public are not increased by dividing the interests in his property into surface and subsoil. The sum of the rights in the parts cannot be greater than the rights in the whole. The estate of an owner in land is grandiloquently described as extending *ab orco usque ad coelum*. But I suppose no one would contend that by selling his interest above one hundred feet from the surface he could prevent the State from limiting, by the police power, the height of structures in a city. And why should a sale of underground rights bar the State's power? For aught that appears the value of the coal kept in place by the restriction may be negligible as compared with the value of the whole property, or even as compared with that part of it which is represented by the coal remaining in place and which may be extracted despite the statute. * * *

* * *

A prohibition of mining which causes subsidence of such structures and facilities is obviously enacted for a public purpose; and it seems, likewise, clear that mere notice of intention to mine would not in this connection secure the public safety. Yet it is said that these provisions of the act cannot be sustained as an exercise of the police power where the right to mine such coal has been reserved. The conclusion seems to rest upon the assumption that in order to justify such exercise of the police power there must be "an average reciprocity of advantage" as between the owner of the property restricted and the rest of the community; and that here such reciprocity is absent. Reciprocity of advantage is an important consideration, and may even be an essential, where the State's power is exercised for the purpose of conferring benefits upon the property of a neighborhood, as in drainage projects, Wurts v. Hoagland, 114 U.S. 606, 5 S.Ct. 1086, 29 L.Ed. 229; Fallbrook Irrigation District v. Bradley, 164 U.S. 112, 17 S.Ct. 56, 41 L.Ed. 369; or upon adjoining owners, as by party wall provisions, Jackman v. Rosenbaum Co., ante, 22. But where the police power is exercised, not to confer benefits upon property owners, but to protect the public from detriment and danger, there is, in my opinion, no room for considering reciprocity of advantage. There was no reciprocal advantage to the owner prohibited from using his oil tanks in 248 U.S. 498; his brickyard, in 239 U.S. 394, 36 S.Ct. 143, 60 L.Ed. 348; his livery stable, in 237 U.S. 171, 35 S.Ct. 511, 59 L.Ed. 900; his billiard hall, in 225 U.S. 623, 32 S.Ct. 697, 56 L.Ed. 1229; his oleomargarine factory, in 127 U.S. 678, 8 S.Ct. 992, 1257, 32 L.Ed. 253; his brewery, in 123 U.S. 623, 8 S.Ct. 273, 31 L.Ed. 205; unless it be the advantage of living and doing business in a civilized community. That reciprocal advantage is given by the act to the coal operators.

Notes

1. Pennsylvania Coal gave birth to the concept of a regulatory taking or police power taking, that is, a taking without physical occupation of the owner's land. The concept, however, has been troublesome both for the Supreme Court and the state courts. Soon after Pennsylvania Coal, the Supreme Court was faced with the question of the validity of comprehensive zoning ordinances which dictated the permissible land uses in zoning districts. In Village of Euclid v. Ambler Realty Co., 272 U.S. 365, 47 S.Ct. 114, 71 L.Ed. 303 (1926), a unanimous Court upheld comprehensive zoning, despite the owner's argument that placing some of its land in a residential district devalued it quite heavily as potential industrial land. Mr. Justice Sutherland, speaking for the Court, warned that " * * * where the equitable remedy of injunction is sought, as it is here, not upon the ground of a present infringement or denial of a specific right, or of a particular injury in process of actual execution, but upon the broad ground that the mere existence and threatened enforcement of the ordinance, by materially and adversely affecting values and curtailing the opportunities of the market, constitute a present and irreparable injury, the court will not scrutinize its provisions, sentence by sentence, to ascertain by a process of piecemeal dissection whether there may be, here and there, provisions of a minor character, or relating to matters of administration, or not shown to contrib-

ute to the injury complained of, which, if attacked separately, might not withstand the test of constitutionality." After the Euclid case, the Court, again in a unanimous opinion by Mr. Justice Sutherland, reversed a judgment denying an injunction against the enforcement of a zoning ordinance as to a particular piece of property. In Nectow v. Cambridge, 277 U.S. 183, 48 S.Ct. 447, 72 L.Ed. 842 (1928), the property had been placed in a residential zone, and after reviewing the facts, Mr. Justice Sutherland noted: "It is made pretty clear that because of the industrial and railroad purposes to which the immediately adjoining lands to the south and east have been devoted and for which they are zoned, the locus is of comparatively little value for the limited uses permitted by the ordinance." The Nectow case lay the basis for what has become the customary manner of attacking zoning— that as the ordinance is applied to a particular tract of land, it is arbitrary and unreasonable and amounts to confiscation as a result.

2. In Keystone Bituminous Coal Ass'n v. DeBenedictis, 480 U.S. 470, 107 S.Ct. 1232, 94 L.Ed.2d 472 (1987), the Court upheld the Pennsylvania Bituminous Mine Subsidence and Land Conservation Act, distinguishing Pennsylvania Coal in its opinion. Justice Steven's opinion for the Court stated that the 1922 decision did not implicitly overrule cases like Mugler, Hadacheck, and Reinman, and that the Subsidence Act was a valid exercise of the police power:

> We reject petitioners' implicit assertion that *Pennsylvania Coal* overruled these cases which focused so heavily on the nature of the state's interest in the regulation. Just five years after the *Pennsylvania Coal* decision, Justice Holmes joined the Court's unanimous decision in Miller v. Schoene, 276 U.S. 272, 48 S.Ct. 246, 72 L.Ed. 568 (1928), holding that the Takings Clause did not require the State of Virginia to compensate the owners of cedar trees for the value of the trees that the State had ordered destroyed. The trees needed to be destroyed to prevent a disease from spreading to nearby apple orchards, which represented a far more valuable resource. In upholding the state action, the Court did not consider it necessary to "weigh with nicety the question whether the infected cedars constitute a nuisance according to common law; or whether they may be so declared by statute." Id., at 280, 48 S.Ct., at 247. Rather, it was clear that the State's exercise of its police power to prevent the impending danger was justified, and did not require compensation. See also Euclid v. Ambler Realty Co., 272 U.S. 365, 47 S.Ct. 114, 71 L.Ed. 303 (1926); Omnia Commercial Co. v. United States, 261 U.S. 502, 509, 43 S.Ct. 437, 438, 67 L.Ed. 773 (1923). Other subsequent cases reaffirm the important role that the nature of the state action plays in our takings analysis.

* * *

> The second factor that distinguishes this case from *Pennsylvania Coal* is the finding in that case that the Kohler Act made mining of "certain coal" commercially impracticable. In this case, by contrast, petitioners have not shown any deprivation significant enough to satisfy the heavy burden placed upon one alleging a regulatory taking. For this reason, their takings claim must fail. * * *

Petitioners thus face an uphill battle in making a facial attack on the Act as a taking.

The hill is made especially steep because petitioners have not claimed, at this stage, that the Act makes it commercially impracticable for them to continue mining their bituminous coal interests in western Pennsylvania. Indeed, petitioners have not even pointed to a single mine that can no longer be mined for profit. * * *

Because our test for regulatory taking requires us to compare the value that has been taken from the property with the value that remains in the property, one of the critical questions is determining how to define the unit of property "whose value is to furnish the denominator of the fraction." Michelman, Property, Utility, and Fairness: Comments on the Ethical Foundations of "Just Compensation" Law, 80 Harv. L.Rev. 1165, 1192 (1967). * * *

The parties have stipulated that enforcement of the DER's 50% rule will require petitioners to leave approximately 27 million tons of coal in place. Because they own that coal but cannot mine it, they contend that Pennsylvania has appropriated it for the public purposes described in the Subsidence Act.

This argument fails for the reason explained in *Penn Central* and *Andrus*. The 27 million tons of coal do not constitute a separate segment of property for takings law purposes. Many zoning ordinances place limits on the property owner's right to make profitable use of some segments of his property. A requirement that a building occupy no more than a specified percentage of the lot on which it is located could be characterized as a taking of the vacant area as readily as the requirement that coal pillars be left in place. Similarly, under petitioners' theory one could always argue that a set-back ordinance requiring that no structure be built within a certain distance from the property line constitutes a taking because the footage represents a distinct segment of property for takings law purposes. Cf. Gorieb v. Fox, 274 U.S. 603, 47 S.Ct. 675, 71 L.Ed. 1228 (1927) (upholding validity of set-back ordinance) (per Holmes, J.). There is no basis for treating the less than 2% of petitioners' coal as a separate parcel of property. * * *

Pennsylvania property law is apparently unique in regarding the support estate as a separate interest in land that can be conveyed apart from either the mineral estate or the surface estate. Petitioners therefore argue that even if comparable legislation in another State would not constitute a taking, the Subsidence Act has that consequence because it entirely destroys the value of their unique support estate. It is clear, however, that our takings jurisprudence forecloses reliance on such legalistic distinctions within a bundle of property rights. * * *

Thus, in practical terms, the support estate has value only insofar as it protects or enhances the value of the estate with which it is associated. Its value is merely a part of the entire bundle of rights possessed by the owner of either the coal or the surface. Because petitioners retain the right to mine virtually all of the coal in their mineral estates, the burden the Act places on the support estate does not constitute a taking. Petitioners may continue to mine coal profitably even if they may not destroy or damage surface structures at will in the process.

But even if we were to accept petitioners' invitation to view the support estate as a distinct segment of property for "takings" purposes, they have not satisfied their heavy burden of sustaining a facial challenge to the Act. Petitioners have acquired or retained the support estate for a great deal of land, only part of which is protected under the Subsidence Act, which, of course, deals with subsidence in the immediate vicinity of certain structures, bodies of water, and cemeteries. See n. 6, supra. The record is devoid of any evidence on what percentage of the purchased support estates, either in the aggregate or with respect to any individual estate, has been affected by the Act. Under these circumstances, petitioners' facial attack under the takings clause must surely fail.

Justice Rehnquist's dissent (joined by Justices Powell, O'Connor and Scalia) stated that " * * * petitioner's interests in particular coal deposits have been completely destroyed. By requiring that defined seams of coal remain in the ground * * * the Subsidence Act has extinguished any interest one might want to acquire in this property. * * * Application of the nuisance exception in these circumstances would allow the State not merely to forbid one 'particular use' of property with many uses but to extinguish all beneficial uses of petitioners' property." Also see M & J Coal Co. v. United States, 47 F.3d 1148 (Fed.Cir.1995) where the court held the company did not suffer a taking when the Department of Interior, Office of Surface Mining Reclamation and Enforcement (OSM) issued an order prohibiting further mining in an area where there was considerable surface subsidence; even though many of the affected residents had conveyed away their right to support, the court held that the agency's actions were necessary to protect the public health and safety and that the mining company's actions posed a threat to the public in general: "That certain individuals or their predecessors may have unwisely deeded away their rights to surface support cannot estop OSM from exercising its authority to abate an imminent danger to the public health or safety. * * * Justice and fairness do not require that the community at large bear the 'burden' of M & J's inability to mine in a manner that is safe to the public."

GOLDBLATT v. TOWN OF HEMPSTEAD, N.Y.

Supreme Court of the United States, 1962.
369 U.S. 590, 82 S.Ct. 987, 8 L.Ed.2d 130.

MR. JUSTICE CLARK delivered the opinion of the Court.

The Town of Hempstead has enacted an ordinance regulating dredging and pit excavating on property within its limits. Appellants, who engaged in such operations prior to the enactment of the ordinance, claim that it in effect prevents them from continuing their business and therefore takes their property without due process of law in violation of the Fourteenth Amendment. * * *

Appellant Goldblatt owns a 38–acre tract within the Town of Hempstead. At the time of the present litigation appellant Builders Sand and

Gravel Corporation was mining sand and gravel on this lot, a use to which the lot had been put continuously since 1927. Before the end of the first year the excavation had reached the water table leaving a water-filled crater which has been widened and deepened to the point that it is now a 20–acre lake with an average depth of 25 feet. The town has expanded around this excavation, and today within a radius of 3,500 feet there are more than 2,200 homes and four public schools with a combined enrollment of 4,500 pupils.

The present action is but one of a series of steps undertaken by the town in an effort to regulate mining excavations within its limits. A 1945 ordinance, No. 16, provided that such pits must be enclosed by a wire fence and comply with certain berm and slope requirements. Although appellants complied with this ordinance, the town sought an injunction against further excavation as being violative of a zoning ordinance. This failed because appellants were found to be "conducting a prior non-conforming use on the premises. * * * " 135 N.Y.L.J., issue 52, p. 12 (1956). The town did not appeal.

In 1958 the town amended Ordinance No. 16 to prohibit any excavating below the water table[5] and to impose an affirmative duty to refill any excavation presently below that level. The new amendment also made the berm, slope, and fence requirements more onerous.

In 1959 the town brought the present action to enjoin further mining by the appellants on the grounds that they had not complied with the ordinance, as amended, nor acquired a mining permit as required by it.[6] Appellants contended, inter alia, that the ordinance was unconstitutional because (1) it was not regulatory of their business but completely prohibitory and confiscated their property without compensation, (2) it deprived them of the benefit of the favorable judgment arising from the previous zoning litigation, and (3) it constituted ex post facto legislation. However, the trial court did not agree, and the appellants were enjoined from conducting further operations on the lot until they had obtained a permit and had complied with the new provisions of Ordinance No. 16.

Concededly the ordinance completely prohibits a beneficial use to which the property has previously been devoted. However, such a characterization does not tell us whether or not the ordinance is unconstitutional. It is an oft-repeated truism that every regulation necessarily speaks as a prohibition. If this ordinance is otherwise a valid exercise of the town's police powers, the fact that it deprives the property of its most beneficial use does not render it unconstitutional. * * * Nor is it of controlling significance that the "use" prohibited here is of the soil itself as opposed to a "use" upon the soil, cf. United States v. Central Eureka Mining Co., 357 U.S. 155, 78 S.Ct. 1097, 2 L.Ed.2d 1228 (1958), or that

---

5. Specifically the ordinance provides that "[n]o excavation shall be made below two feet above the maximum ground water level at the site."

6. Under the ordinance the town may deny a permit if the proposed excavation will violate any of the provisions of the ordinance.

the use prohibited is arguably not a common-law nuisance, e.g., Reinman v. Little Rock, supra.

This is not to say, however, that governmental action in the form of regulation cannot be so onerous as to constitute a taking which constitutionally requires compensation. Pennsylvania Coal Co. v. Mahon, 260 U.S. 393, 43 S.Ct. 158, 67 L.Ed. 322 (1922); see United States v. Central Eureka Mining Co., supra. There is no set formula to determine where regulation ends and taking begins. Although a comparison of values before and after is relevant, see Pennsylvania Coal Co. v. Mahon, supra, it is by no means conclusive, see Hadacheck v. Sebastian, supra, where a diminution in value from $800,000 to $60,000 was upheld. How far regulation may go before it becomes a taking we need not now decide, for there is no evidence in the present record which even remotely suggests that prohibition of further mining will reduce the value of the lot in question.[7] Indulging in the usual presumption of constitutionality, * * * we find no indication that the prohibitory effect of Ordinance No. 16 is sufficient to render it an unconstitutional taking if it is otherwise a valid police regulation.

The question, therefore, narrows to whether the prohibition of further excavation below the water table is a valid exercise of the town's police power. The term "police power" connotes the time-tested conceptional limit of public encroachment upon private interests. Except for the substitution of the familiar standard of "reasonableness," this Court has generally refrained from announcing any specific criteria. The classic statement of the rule in Lawton v. Steele, 152 U.S. 133, 137, 14 S.Ct. 499, 38 L.Ed. 385 (1894), is still valid today:

> "To justify the State in * * * interposing its authority in behalf of the public, it must appear, first, that the interests of the public * * * require such interference; and, second, that the means are reasonably necessary for the accomplishment of the purpose, and not unduly oppressive upon individuals."

Even this rule is not applied with strict precision, for this Court has often said that "debatable questions as to reasonableness are not for the courts but for the legislature. * * *" E.g., Sproles v. Binford, 286 U.S. 374, 388, 52 S.Ct. 581, 76 L.Ed. 1167 (1932).

The ordinance in question was passed as a safety measure, and the town is attempting to uphold it on that basis. To evaluate its reasonableness we therefore need to know such things as the nature of the menace against which it will protect, the availability and effectiveness of other less drastic protective steps, and the loss which appellants will suffer from the imposition of the ordinance.

A careful examination of the record reveals a dearth of relevant evidence on these points. One fair inference arising from the evidence is that since a few holes had been burrowed under the fence surrounding

---

7. There is a similar scarcity of evidence relative to the value of the processing machinery in the event mining operations were shut down.

the lake it might be attractive and dangerous to children. But there was no indication whether the lake as it stood was an actual danger to the public or whether deepening the lake would increase the danger. In terms of dollars or some other objective standard, there was no showing how much, if anything, the imposition of the ordinance would cost the appellants. In short, the evidence produced is clearly indecisive on the reasonableness of prohibiting further excavation below the water table.

Although one could imagine that preventing further deepening of a pond already 25 feet deep would have a de minimis effect on public safety, we cannot say that such a conclusion is compelled by facts of which we can take notice. Even if we could draw such a conclusion, we would be unable to say the ordinance is unreasonable; for all we know, the ordinance may have a de minimis effect on appellants. Our past cases leave no doubt that appellants had the burden on "reasonableness." * * * This burden not having been met, the prohibition of excavation on the 20–acre–lake tract must stand as a valid police regulation.

We now turn our attention to the remainder of the lot, the 18 acres surrounding the present pit which have not yet been mined or excavated. Appellants themselves contend that this area cannot be mined. They say that this surface space is necessary for the processing operations incident to mining and that no other space is obtainable. This was urged as an important factor in their contention that upholding the depth limitation of the ordinance would confiscate the entire mining utility of their property. However, we have upheld the validity of the prohibition even on that supposition. If the depth limitation in relation to deepening the existing pit is valid, it follows a fortiori that the limitation is constitutionally permissible as applied to prevent the creation of new pits. We also note that even if appellants were able to obtain suitable processing space the geology of the 18–acre tract would prevent any excavation. The water table, appellants admit, is too close to the ground surface to permit commercial mining in the face of the depth restrictions of the ordinance. The impossibility of further mining makes it unnecessary for us to decide to what extent the berm and slope of such excavation could be limited by the ordinance.

Affirmed.

PENN CENTRAL TRANSP. CO. v. NEW YORK CITY

Supreme Court of the United States, 1978.
438 U.S. 104, 98 S.Ct. 2646, 57 L.Ed.2d 631.

[Under New York City's Landmarks Preservation Law, Grand Central Terminal, owned by Petitioner, was designated as a landmark. After the agency charged with enforcing the law denied permission to build a multi-story office building over the existing structure (on grounds that the proposed tower would impair the aesthetic quality of the terminal's existing facade), Petitioner brought suit claiming that the application of the law constituted a taking of its property.]

Mr. Justice Brennan delivered the opinion of the Court.

* * *

Before considering appellants' specific contentions, it will be useful to review the factors that have shaped the jurisprudence of the Fifth Amendment injunction "nor shall private property be taken for public use, without just compensation." The question of what constitutes a "taking" for purposes of the Fifth Amendment has proved to be a problem of considerable difficulty. While this Court has recognized that the "Fifth Amendment's guarantee [is] designed to bar Government from forcing some people alone to bear public burdens which, in all fairness and justice, should be borne by the public as a whole," Armstrong v. United States, 364 U.S. 40, 49, 80 S.Ct. 1563, 1569, 4 L.Ed.2d 1554 (1960), this Court, quite simply, has been unable to develop any "set formula" for determining when "justice and fairness" require that economic injuries caused by public action be compensated by the Government, rather than remain disproportionately concentrated on a few persons. See Goldblatt v. Hempstead, 369 U.S. 590, 594, 82 S.Ct. 987, 990, 8 L.Ed.2d 130 (1962). Indeed, we have frequently observed that whether a particular restriction will be rendered invalid by the Government's failure to pay for any losses proximately caused by it depends largely "upon the particular circumstances [in that] case." United States v. Central Eureka Mining Co., 357 U.S. 155, 168, 78 S.Ct. 1097, 1104, 2 L.Ed.2d 1228 (1958); see United States v. Caltex, Inc., 344 U.S. 149, 156, 73 S.Ct. 200, 203, 97 L.Ed. 157 (1952).

In engaging in these essentially ad hoc, factual inquiries, the Court's decisions have identified several factors that have particular significance. The economic impact of the regulation on the claimant and, particularly, the extent to which the regulation has interfered with distinct investment backed expectations are of course relevant considerations. See Goldblatt v. Hempstead, supra, 369 U.S., at 594, 82 S.Ct., at 990. So too is the character of the governmental action. A "taking" may more readily be found when the interference with property can be characterized as a physical invasion by Government, see, e.g., United States v. Causby, 328 U.S. 256, 66 S.Ct. 1062, 90 L.Ed. 1206 (1946), than when interference arises from some public program adjusting the benefits and burdens of economic life to promote the common good.

"Government could hardly go on if to some extent values incident to property could not be diminished without paying for every such change in the general law," Pennsylvania Coal Co. v. Mahon, 260 U.S. 393, 413, 43 S.Ct. 158, 159, 67 L.Ed. 322 (1922), and this Court has accordingly recognized, in a wide variety of contexts, that Government may execute laws or programs that adversely affect recognized economic values. Exercises of the taxing power are one obvious example. A second are the decisions in which this Court has dismissed "taking" challenges on the ground that, while the challenged Government action caused economic harm, it did not interfere with interests that were sufficiently bound up with the reasonable expectations of the claimant to constitute "property" for Fifth Amendment purposes. * * *

More importantly for the present case, in instances in which a state tribunal reasonably concluded that "the health, safety, morals or general welfare" would be promoted by prohibiting particular contemplated uses of land, this Court has upheld land use regulations that destroyed or adversely affected recognized real property interests. See Nectow v. City of Cambridge, 277 U.S. 183, 188, 48 S.Ct. 447, 448, 72 L.Ed. 842 (1928). Zoning laws are of course the classic example, see Euclid v. Ambler Realty Co., 272 U.S. 365, 47 S.Ct. 114, 71 L.Ed. 303 (1926) (prohibition of industrial use); Gorieb v. Fox, 274 U.S. 603, 608, 47 S.Ct. 675, 677, 71 L.Ed. 1228 (1927) (requirement that portions of parcels be left unbuilt); Welch v. Swasey, 214 U.S. 91, 29 S.Ct. 567, 53 L.Ed. 923 (1909) (height restriction), which have been viewed as permissible governmental action even when prohibiting the most beneficial use of the property. * * *

Zoning laws generally do not affect existing uses of real property, but taking challenges have also been held to be without merit in a wide variety of situations when the challenged governmental actions prohibited a beneficial use to which individual parcels had previously been devoted and thus caused substantial individualized harm.

[At this point, Mr. Justice Brennan discusses Miller v. Schoene, Hadacheck v. Sebastian, Goldblatt v. Hempstead, Pennsylvania Coal Co. v. Mahon, and United States v. Causby.]

* * *

In contending that the New York City law has "taken" their property in violation of the Fifth and Fourteenth Amendments, appellants make a series of arguments, which, while tailored to the facts of this case, essentially urge that any substantial restriction imposed pursuant to a landmark law must be accompanied by just compensation if it is to be constitutional. Before considering these, we emphasize what is not in dispute. Because this Court has recognized, in a number of settings, that States and cities may enact land use restrictions or controls to enhance the quality of life by preserving the character and desirable aesthetic features of a city, see City of New Orleans v. Dukes, 427 U.S. 297, 96 S.Ct. 2513, 49 L.Ed.2d 511 (1976); Young v. American Mini Theatres, Inc., 427 U.S. 50, 96 S.Ct. 2440, 49 L.Ed.2d 310 (1976); Village of Belle Terre v. Boraas, 416 U.S. 1, 9–10, 94 S.Ct. 1536, 39 L.Ed.2d 797 (1974); Berman v. Parker, 348 U.S. 26, 33, 75 S.Ct. 98, 102, 99 L.Ed. 27 (1954); Welch v. Swasey, supra, 214 U.S., at 108, 29 S.Ct., at 571, appellants do not contest that New York City's objective of preserving structures and areas with special historic, architectural, or cultural significance is an entirely permissible governmental goal. They also do not dispute that the restrictions imposed on its parcel are appropriate means of securing the purposes of the New York City law. Finally, appellants do not challenge any of the specific factual premises of the decision below. They accept for present purposes both that the parcel of land occupied by Grand Central Terminal must, in its present state, be regarded as capable of earning a reasonable return, and that the transferable development rights afforded appellants by virtue of the Terminal's designation as a landmark are valuable, even if not as valuable as the rights to construct above the Terminal. In appellants' view none of these factors derogate from their claim that New York City's law has effected a "taking."

* * *

Stated baldly, appellants' position appears to be that the only means of ensuring that selected owners are not singled out to endure financial hardship for no reason is to hold that any restriction imposed on individual landmarks pursuant to the New York scheme is a "taking" requiring the payment of "just compensation." Agreement with this argument would of course invalidate not just New York City's law, but all comparable landmark legislation in the Nation. We find no merit in it.

It is true, as appellants emphasize, that both historic district legislation and zoning laws regulate all properties within given physical communities whereas landmark laws apply only to selected parcels. But, contrary to appellants' suggestions, landmark laws are not like discriminatory, or "reverse spot," zoning: that is, a land use decision which arbitrarily singles out a particular parcel for different, less favorable treatment than the neighboring ones. See 2 Rathkopf, The Law of Zoning and Planning 26–4 and 26–4–26–5, n. 6 (2d Ed.1977). In contrast to discriminatory zoning, which is the antithesis of land use control as part of some comprehensive plan, the New York City law embodies a comprehensive plan to preserve structures of historic or aesthetic interest wherever they might be found in the city, and as noted, over 400 landmarks and 31 historic districts have been designated pursuant to this plan.

Equally without merit is the related argument that the decision to designate a structure as a landmark "is inevitably arbitrary or at least subjective because it basically is a matter of taste" * * *. [A]ppellants not only did not seek judicial review of either the designation or of the denials of the certificates of appropriateness and of no exterior effect, but do not even now suggest that the Commission's decisions concerning the Terminal were in any sense arbitrary or unprincipled. But, in any event, * * * there is no basis whatsoever for a conclusion that courts will have any greater difficulty identifying arbitrary or discriminatory action in the context of landmark regulation than in the context of classic zoning or indeed in any other context.

Next, appellants observe that New York City's law differs from zoning laws and historic district ordinances in that the Landmarks Law does not impose identical or similar restrictions on all structures located in particular physical communities. It follows, they argue, that New York City's law is inherently incapable of producing the fair and equitable distribution of benefits and burdens of governmental action which is characteristic of zoning laws and historic district legislation and which they maintain is a constitutional requirement if "just compensation" is not to be afforded. It is of course true that the Landmarks Law has a more severe impact on some landowners than on others, but that in itself does not mean that the law effects a "taking." Legislation designed to promote the general welfare commonly burdens some more than others. The owners of the brickyard in *Hadacheck,* of the cedar trees in Miller v. Schoene, and of the gravel and sand mine in Goldblatt v. Hempstead, were uniquely burdened by the legislation sustained in those cases. Similarly, zoning laws often impact more severely on some property owners than others but have not been held to be invalid on that account. For example, the property owner in *Euclid* who wished to use his property for industrial purposes was affected far more severely by the ordinance than his neighbors who wished to use their land for residences.

In any event, appellants' repeated suggestions that they are solely burdened and unbenefited is factually inaccurate. This contention overlooks the fact that the New York City law applies to vast numbers of structures in the city in addition to the Terminal—all the structures contained in the 31 historic districts and over 400 individual landmarks, many of which are close to the Terminal. Unless we are to reject the judgment of the New York City Council that the preservation of landmarks benefit all New York citizens and all structures, both economically and by improving the quality of life in the city as a whole—which we are unwilling to do—we cannot conclude that the owners of the Terminal have in no sense been benefited by the Landmarks Law. Doubtless appellants believe they are more burdened than benefited by the law, but that must have been true too of the property owners in *Miller, Hadacheck, Euclid,* and *Goldblatt.*

Appellants' final broad-based attack would have us treat the law as an instance, like that in United States v. Causby, supra, in which Government, acting in an enterprise capacity, has appropriated part of their property for some strictly governmental purpose. Apart from the fact that *Causby* was a case of invasion of airspace that destroyed the use of the farm beneath and this New York City law has in no wise impaired the present use of the Terminal, the Landmarks Law neither exploits appellants' parcel for city purposes nor facilitates nor arises from any entrepreneurial operations of the city. The situation is not remotely like that in *Causby* when the airspace above the Terminal was in the flight pattern for military aircraft. The Landmarks Law's effect is simply to prohibit appellants or anyone else from occupying portions of the airspace above the Terminal, while permitting appellants to use the remainder of the parcel in a gainful fashion. * * *

Rejection of appellants' broad arguments is not however the end of our inquiry, for all we thus far have established is that the New York law is not rendered invalid by its failure to provide "just compensation" whenever a landmark owner is restricted in the exploitation of property interests, such as air rights, to a greater extent than provided for under applicable zoning laws. We now must consider whether the interference with appellants' property is of such a magnitude that "there must be an exercise of eminent domain and compensation to sustain [it]." Pennsylvania Coal Co. v. Mahon, 260 U.S., at 413, 43 S.Ct., at 159. That inquiry may be narrowed to the question of the severity of the impact of the law on appellants' parcel, and its resolution in turn requires a careful assessment of the impact of the regulation on the Terminal site.

Unlike the governmental acts in *Goldblatt, Miller, Causby, Griggs,* and *Hadacheck,* the New York City law does not interfere in any way with the present uses of the Terminal. Its designation as a landmark not only permits but contemplates that appellants may continue to use the property precisely as it has for the past 65 years: as a railroad terminal containing office space and concessions. So the law does not interfere with what must be regarded as Penn Central's primary expectation concerning the use of the parcel. More importantly, on this record, we must regard the New York City law as permitting Penn Central not only to profit from the Terminal but to obtain a "reasonable return" on its investment.

Appellants, moreover, exaggerate the effect of the Act on its ability to make use of the air rights above the Terminal in two respects. First, it simply cannot be maintained, on this record, that appellants have been prohibited from occupying any portion of the airspace above the Terminal. While the Commission's actions in denying applications to construct an office building in excess of 50 stories above the Terminal may indicate that it will refuse to issue a certificate of appropriateness for any comparably sized structure, nothing the Commission has said or done suggests an intention to prohibit any construction above the Terminal. The Commission's report emphasized that whether any construction would be allowed depended upon whether the proposed addition "would harmonize in scale, material, and character with [the Terminal]." * * * Since appellants have not sought approval for the construction of a smaller structure, we do not know that appellants will be denied any use of any portion of the airspace above the Terminal.

Second, to the extent appellants have been denied the right to build above the Terminal, it is not literally accurate to say that they have been denied all use of even those pre-existing air rights. Their ability to use these rights has not been abrogated; they are made transferable to at least eight parcels in the vicinity of the Terminal, one or two of which have been found suitable for the construction of new office buildings. Although appellants and others have argued that New York City's transferable development rights program is far from ideal, the New York courts here supportably found that, at least in the case of the Terminal, the rights afforded are valuable. While these rights may well not have constituted "just compensation" if a "taking" had occurred, the rights nevertheless undoubtedly mitigate whatever financial burdens the law has imposed on appellants and, for that reason, are to be taken into account in considering the impact of regulation. Cf. Goldblatt v. Hempstead, supra, 369 U.S., at 594 n. 3, 82 S.Ct., at 990 n. 3.

On this record we conclude that the application of New York City's Landmarks Preservation Law has not effected a "taking" of appellants' property. The restrictions imposed are substantially related to the promotion of the general welfare and not only permit reasonable beneficial use of the landmark site but afford appellants opportunities further to enhance not only the Terminal site proper but also other properties.

Affirmed.

MR. JUSTICE REHNQUIST, with whom THE CHIEF JUSTICE and MR. JUSTICE STEVENS join, dissenting.

* * *

A

Appellees do not dispute that valuable property rights have been destroyed. And the Court has frequently emphasized that the term "property" as used in the Taking Clause includes the entire "group of rights inhering in the citizen's [ownership]." United States v. General Motors Corp., 323 U.S. 373, 65 S.Ct. 357, 89 L.Ed. 311 (1945). The term is not used in the

> vulgar and untechnical sense of the physical thing with respect to which the citizen exercises rights recognized by law. [Instead, it] denotes the *group of rights* inhering in the citizen's relation to the physical thing, *as the right to possess, use and dispose of it.* * * * The constitutional provision is addressed to *every sort of interest* the citizen may possess. Id., at 377–378, 65 S.Ct., at 359 (emphasis added).

While neighboring landowners are free to use their land and "air rights" in any way consistent with the broad boundaries of New York zoning, Penn Central, absent the permission of appellees, must forever maintain its property in its present state. The property has been thus subjected to a nonconsensual servitude not borne by any neighboring or similar properties.

B

Appellees have thus destroyed—in a literal sense, "taken"—substantial property rights of Penn Central. While the term "taken" might have been narrowly interpreted to include only physical seizures of property rights, the construction of the phrase has not been so narrow. * * * Because "not every destruction or injury to property by governmental action has been held to be a 'taking' in the constitutional sense," Armstrong v. United States, 364 U.S. 40, 48, 80 S.Ct. 1563, 1568, 4 L.Ed.2d 1554 (1960), however, this does not end our inquiry. But an examination of the two exceptions where the destruction of property does *not* constitute a taking demonstrates that a compensable taking has occurred here.

1

As early as 1887, the Court recognized that the government can prevent a property owner from using his property to injure others without having to compensate the owner for the value of the forbidden use.

"A prohibition simply upon the use of property for purposes that are declared, by valid legislation, to be *injurious to the health, morals, or safety of the community,* cannot in any just sense, be deemed a taking or an appropriation of property for the public benefit. Such legislation does not disturb the owner in the control or use of his property for lawful purposes, nor restrict his right to dispose of it, but is only a declaration by the State that its use by any one, for certain forbidden purposes, is prejudicial to the public interests. * * * The power which the States have of prohibiting such use by individuals of their property as will be prejudicial to the health, the morals, or the safety of the public, is not—and, consistently with the existence and safety of organized society, cannot be—burdened with the condition that the State must compensate such individual owners for pecuniary losses they may sustain, *by reason of their not being permitted, by a noxious use of their property, to inflict injury upon the community.*" Mugler v. Kansas, 123 U.S. 623, 668–669, 8 S.Ct. 273, 301, 31 L.Ed. 205 (1887).

Thus, there is no "taking" where a city prohibits the operation of a brickyard within a residential city, see Hadacheck v. Sebastian, 239 U.S. 394, 36 S.Ct. 143, 60 L.Ed. 348 (1915), or forbids excavation for sand and gravel below the water line, see Goldblatt v. Town of Hempstead, 369 U.S. 590, 82 S.Ct. 987, 8 L.Ed.2d 130 (1962). Nor is it relevant, where the government is merely prohibiting a noxious use of property, that the government would seem to be singling out a particular property owner. Hadacheck, 239 U.S., at 413, 36 S.Ct., at 146.

* * *

Appellees are not prohibiting a nuisance. The record is clear that the proposed addition to the Grand Central Terminal would be in full compliance with zoning, height limitations, and other health and safety requirements. Instead, appellees are seeking to preserve what they believe to be an outstanding example of Beaux Arts architecture. Penn Central is prevented from further developing its property basically because it did *too good* of a job in designing and building it. The city of New York, because of its unadorned admiration for the design, has decided that the owners of the building must preserve it unchanged for the benefit of sightseeing New Yorkers and tourists.

Unlike in the case of land use regulations, appellees are not *prohibiting* Penn Central from using its property in a narrow set of noxious ways. Instead, appellees have placed an *affirmative* duty on Penn Central to maintain the Terminal in its present state and in "good repair." Appellants are not free to use their property as they see fit within broad outer boundaries but must strictly adhere to their past use except where appellees conclude that alternative uses would not detract from the Landmark. While Penn Central may continue to use the Terminal as it is presently designed, appellees otherwise "exercise complete dominion and control over the surface of the land," United States v. Causby, 328 U.S. 256, 262, 66 S.Ct. 1062, 1066, 90 L.Ed. 1206 (1946), and must compensate the owner for his loss. Ibid. "Property is taken in the constitutional sense when inroads are made upon an owner's use of it to an extent that, as between private parties, a servitude has been acquired." United States v. Dickinson, 331 U.S. 745, 748, 67 S.Ct. 1382, 1385, 91 L.Ed. 1789 (1947). See also Dugan v. Rank, 372 U.S. 609, 625, 83 S.Ct. 999, 1009, 10 L.Ed.2d 15 (1963).

2

Even where the government prohibits a noninjurious use, the Court has ruled that a taking does not take place if the prohibition applies over a broad cross section of land and thereby "secure[s] an average reciprocity of advantage." Pennsylvania Coal Co. v. Mahon, 260 U.S. 393, 415, 43 S.Ct. 158, 160, 67 L.Ed. 322 (1922). It is for this reason that zoning does not constitute a "taking." While zoning at times reduces *individual* property values, the burden is shared relatively evenly and it is reasonable to conclude that on the whole an individual who is harmed by one aspect of the zoning will be benefited by another.

Here, however, a multimillion dollar loss has been imposed on appellants; it is uniquely felt and is not offset by any benefits flowing from the preservation of some 500 other "Landmarks" in New York. Appellees have imposed a substantial cost on less than one one-tenth of one percent of the buildings in New York for the general benefit of all its people. It is exactly this imposition of general costs on a few individuals at which the "taking" protection is directed. * * *

As Justice Holmes pointed out in Pennsylvania Coal Co. v. Mahon, "the question at bottom" in an eminent domain case "is upon whom the loss of the changes desired should fall." 260 U.S., at 416, 43 S.Ct., at 160. The benefits that appellees believe will flow from preservation of the Grand Central Terminal will accrue to all the citizens of New York. There is no reason to believe that appellants will enjoy a substantially greater share of these benefits. If the cost of preserving Grand Central Terminal were spread evenly across the entire population of the city of New York, the burden per person would be in cents per year—a minor cost appellees would surely concede for the benefit accrued. Instead, however, appellees would impose the entire cost of several million dollars per year on Penn Central. But it is precisely this sort of discrimination that the Fifth Amendment prohibits.

Appellees in response would argue that a taking only occurs where a property owner is denied *all* reasonable value of his property. The Court has frequently held that, even where a destruction of property rights would not *otherwise* constitute a taking, the inability of the owner to make a reasonable return on his property requires compensation under the Fifth Amendment. See, e.g., United States v. Lynah, 188 U.S. 445, 470, 23 S.Ct. 349, 357, 47 L.Ed. 539 (1903). But the converse is not true. A taking does not become a noncompensable exercise of police power simply because the government in its grace allows the owner to make some "reasonable" use of his property. "[I]t is the character of the invasion, not the amount of damage resulting from it, so long as the damage is substantial, that determines the question whether it is a taking." * * *

Notes

1.   Does the Penn Central case provide any guidance in discerning the line between a permissible regulation and an invalid taking? Does Justice Brennan's observation that the cases have been "essentially ad hoc, factual inquiries" mean that the line can never be drawn with the degree of certainty that would satisfy an attorney seeking to advise a client?

2.   If proof of no reasonable economic use is one way to demonstrate a taking, how can such proof be made? While this is really a question for students of evidence, some suggestions of value might be gleaned from the case of Schwartz v. City of Flint, 92 Mich.App. 495, 285 N.W.2d 344 (1979), reversed 426 Mich. 295, 395 N.W.2d 678 (1986), since extensive portions of the record in that case are reproduced in the opinion.

3.   The cases are clear in distinguishing proof of no reasonable permitted use from mere loss of value due to the regulation. State courts have followed the lead of the Supreme Court in Hadacheck and Goldblatt in holding that loss of value is not alone indicative of a taking. See, e.g., Pennington v. Rockdale County, 244 Ga. 743, 262 S.E.2d 59 (1979). An excellent presentation of this view is also found in William C. Haas & Co., Inc. v. City and County of San Francisco, 605 F.2d 1117 (9th Cir.1979).

4.   Sometimes a regulation can be characterized as a physical occupation of property. For example, in Seawall Associates v. City of New York, 74 N.Y.2d 92, 544 N.Y.S.2d 542, 542 N.E.2d 1059 (1989) the court held that a city ordinance establishing a five-year moratorium on conversion, alteration, or demolition of single-room occupancy housing and requiring restoration of such units to habitable condition and requiring them to be leased at controlled rents, constituted a physical occupation and was a per se compensable taking. The ordinance was aimed at curbing the rampant conversion of "welfare hotels" into other types of housing.

5.   Can the public counter an alleged taking by showing alternate possible uses of the land, even though such uses might be beyond the resources of the property owner? See the interesting case of Friedman v. City of Fairfax, 81 Cal.App.3d 667, 146 Cal.Rptr. 687 (1978), where the court noted that the rezoning of the property resulted in a designation which would allow successful operation of private tennis club, "a currently popular recreational use." (The appellate court reversed a trial court judgment for $1,200,000 damages and $115,000 attorney fees.)

LUCAS v. SOUTH CAROLINA COASTAL COUNCIL
Supreme Court of the United States, 1992.
505 U.S. 1003, 112 S.Ct. 2886, 120 L.Ed.2d 798.

JUSTICE SCALIA delivered the opinion of the Court.

In 1986, petitioner David H. Lucas paid $975,000 for two residential lots on the Isle of Palms in Charleston County, South Carolina, on which he intended to build single-family homes. In 1988, however, the South Carolina Legislature enacted the Beachfront Management Act, S.C.Code § 48–39–250 et seq. (Supp.1990) (Act), which had the direct effect of barring petitioner from erecting any permanent habitable structures on his two parcels. See § 48–39–290(A). A state trial court found that this prohibition rendered Lucas's parcels "valueless." This case requires us to decide whether the Act's dramatic effect on the economic value of Lucas's lots accomplished a taking of private property under the Fifth and Fourteenth Amendments requiring the payment of "just compensation." U.S. Const., Amdt. 5.

I

A

South Carolina's expressed interest in intensively managing development activities in the so-called "coastal zone" dates from 1977 when, in the aftermath of Congress's passage of the federal Coastal Zone Management Act of 1972, 86 Stat. 1280, as amended, 16 U.S.C.A. § 1451 et seq., the legislature enacted a Coastal Zone Management Act of its own. See S.C.Code § 48–39–10 et seq. (1987). In its original form, the South Carolina Act required owners of coastal zone land that qualified as a "critical area" (defined in the legislation to include beaches and immediately adjacent sand dunes, § 48–39–10(J)) to obtain a permit from the newly created South Carolina Coastal Council (respondent here) prior to committing the land to a "use other than the use the critical area was devoted to on [September 28, 1977]." § 48–39–130(A).

In the late 1970's, Lucas and others began extensive residential development of the Isle of Palms, a barrier island situated eastward of the City of Charleston. Toward the close of the development cycle for one residential subdivision known as "Beachwood East," Lucas in 1986 purchased the two lots at issue in this litigation for his own account. No portion of the lots, which were located approximately 300 feet from the beach, qualified as a "critical area" under the 1977 Act; accordingly, at the time Lucas acquired these parcels, he was not legally obliged to obtain a permit from the Council in advance of any development activity. His intention with respect to the lots was to do what the owners of the immediately adjacent parcels had already done: erect single-family residences. He commissioned architectural drawings for this purpose.

The Beachfront Management Act brought Lucas's plans to an abrupt end. Under that 1988 legislation, the Council was directed to establish a "baseline" connecting the landward-most "point[s] of erosion . . . during the past forty years" in the region of the Isle of Palms that includes Lucas's lots. § 48–39–280(A)(2) (Supp.1988). In action not challenged here, the Council fixed this baseline landward of Lucas's parcels. That was significant, for under the Act construction of occupiable improvements was flatly prohibited seaward of a line drawn 20 feet landward of, and parallel to, the baseline, § 48–39–290(A) (Supp.1988). The Act provided no exceptions.

B

Lucas promptly filed suit in the South Carolina Court of Common Pleas, contending that the Beachfront Management Act's construction bar effected a taking of his property without just compensation. Lucas did not take issue with the validity of the Act as a lawful exercise of South Carolina's police power, but contended that the Act's complete extinguishment of his property's value entitled him to compensation regardless of whether the legislature had acted in furtherance of legitimate police power objectives. Following a bench trial, the court agreed. Among its factual determinations was the finding that "at the time Lucas purchased the two lots, both were zoned for single-family residential construction and ... there were no restrictions imposed upon such use of the property by either the State of South Carolina, the County of Charleston, or the Town of the Isle of Palms." The trial court further found that the Beachfront Management Act decreed a permanent ban on construction insofar as Lucas's lots were concerned, and that this prohibition "deprive[d] Lucas of any reasonable economic use of the lots, ... eliminated the unrestricted right of use, and render[ed] them valueless." The court thus concluded that Lucas's properties had been "taken" by operation of the Act, and it ordered respondent to pay "just compensation" in the amount of $1,232,387.50.

The Supreme Court of South Carolina reversed. It found dispositive what it described as Lucas's concession "that the Beachfront Management Act [was] properly and validly designed to preserve ... South Carolina's beaches." 304 S.C. 376, 379, 404 S.E.2d 895, 896 (1991). Failing an attack on the validity of the statute as such, the court believed itself bound to accept the "uncontested ... findings" of the South Carolina legislature that new construction in the coastal zone— such as petitioner intended—threatened this public resource. Id., at 383, 404 S.E.2d, at 898. The Court ruled that when a regulation respecting the use of property is designed "to prevent serious public harm," id., at 383, 404 S.E.2d, at 899 (citing, inter alia, Mugler v. Kansas, 123 U.S. 623, 8 S.Ct. 273, 31 L.Ed. 205 (1887)), no compensation is owing under the Takings Clause regardless of the regulation's effect on the property's value.

Two justices dissented. They acknowledged that our Mugler line of cases recognizes governmental power to prohibit "noxious" uses of property—i.e., uses of property akin to "public nuisances"—without having to pay compensation. But they would not have characterized the Beachfront Management Act's *primary* purpose [as] the prevention of a nuisance." 304 S.C., at 395, 404 S.E.2d, at 906 (Harwell, J., dissenting). To the dissenters, the chief purposes of the legislation, among them the promotion of tourism and the creation of a "habitat for indigenous flora and fauna," could not fairly be compared to nuisance abatement. Id., at 396, 404 S.E.2d, at 906. As a consequence, they would have affirmed the trial court's conclusion that the Act's obliteration of the value of petitioner's lots accomplished a taking.

* * *

III

A

Prior to Justice Holmes' exposition in Pennsylvania Coal Co. v. Mahon, 260 U.S. 393, 43 S.Ct. 158, 67 L.Ed. 322 (1922), it was generally thought that the Takings Clause reached only a "direct appropriation" of property, Legal Tender Cases, 12 Wall. 457, 551, 20 L.Ed. 287 (1871), or the functional equivalent of a "practical ouster of [the owner's] possession." Transportation Co. v. Chicago, 99 U.S. 635, 642, 25 L.Ed. 336 (1879). See also Gibson v. United States, 166 U.S. 269, 275–276, 17 S.Ct. 578, 580, 41 L.Ed. 996 (1897). Justice Holmes recognized in Mahon, however, that if the protection against physical appropriations of private property was to be meaningfully enforced, the government's power to redefine the range of interests included in the ownership of property was necessarily constrained by constitutional limits. 260 U.S., at 414–415, 43 S.Ct., at 160. If, instead, the uses of private property were subject to unbridled, uncompensated qualification under the police power, "the natural tendency of human nature [would be] to extend the qualification more and more until at last private property disappear[ed]." Id., at 415, 43 S.Ct., at 160. These considerations gave birth in that case to the oft-cited maxim that, "while property may be regulated to a certain extent, if regulation goes too far it will be recognized as a taking." Ibid.

Nevertheless, our decision in Mahon offered little insight into when, and under what circumstances, a given regulation would be seen as going "too far" for purposes of the Fifth Amendment. In 70–odd years of succeeding "regulatory takings" jurisprudence, we have generally eschewed any " 'set formula' " for determining how far is too far, preferring to "engag[e] in ... essentially ad hoc, factual inquiries," Penn Central Transportation Co. v. New York City, 438 U.S. 104, 124, 98 S.Ct. 2646, 2659, 57 L.Ed.2d 631 (1978) (quoting Goldblatt v. Hempstead, 369 U.S. 590, 594, 82 S.Ct. 987, 990, 8 L.Ed.2d 130 (1962)). See Epstein, Takings: Descent and Resurrection, 1987 Sup.Ct. Rev. 1, 4. We have, however, described at least two discrete categories of regulatory action as compensable without case-specific inquiry into the public interest advanced in support of the restraint. The first encompasses regulations that compel the property owner to suffer a physical "invasion" of his property. In general (at least with regard to permanent invasions), no matter how minute the intrusion, and no matter how weighty the public purpose behind it, we have required compensation. For example, in Loretto v. Teleprompter Manhattan CATV Corp., 458 U.S. 419, 102 S.Ct. 3164, 73 L.Ed.2d 868 (1982), we determined that New York's law requiring landlords to allow television cable companies to emplace cable facilities in their apartment buildings constituted a taking, id., at 435–440, 102 S.Ct., at 3175–3178, even though the facilities occupied at most only 1 1/2 cubic feet of the landlords' property, see id., at 438, n. 16, 102 S.Ct., at 3177. See also United States v. Causby, 328 U.S. 256, 265, and n. 10, 66 S.Ct. 1062, 1067, and n. 10, 90 L.Ed. 1206 (1946) (physical invasions of airspace); cf. Kaiser Aetna v. United States, 444 U.S. 164,

100 S.Ct. 383, 62 L.Ed.2d 332 (1979) (imposition of navigational servitude upon private marina).

The second situation in which we have found categorical treatment appropriate is where regulation denies all economically beneficial or productive use of land. See Agins, 447 U.S., at 260, 100 S.Ct., at 2141; see also Nollan v. California Coastal Comm'n, 483 U.S. 825, 834, 107 S.Ct. 3141, 3147, 97 L.Ed.2d 677 (1987); Keystone Bituminous Coal Assn. v. DeBenedictis, 480 U.S. 470, 495, 107 S.Ct. 1232, 1247, 94 L.Ed.2d 472 (1987); Hodel v. Virginia Surface Mining & Reclamation Assn., Inc., 452 U.S. 264, 295–296, 101 S.Ct. 2352, 2370, 69 L.Ed.2d 1 (1981). As we have said on numerous occasions, the Fifth Amendment is violated when land-use regulation "does not substantially advance legitimate state interests *or denies an owner economically viable use of his land.*" Agins, supra, 447 U.S., at 260, 100 S.Ct., at 2141 (citations omitted) (emphasis added).

We have never set forth the justification for this rule. Perhaps it is simply, as Justice Brennan suggested, that total deprivation of beneficial use is, from the landowner's point of view, the equivalent of a physical appropriation. See San Diego Gas & Electric Co. v. San Diego, 450 U.S., at 652, 101 S.Ct., at 1304 (Brennan, J., dissenting). "[F]or what is the land but the profits thereof[?]" 1 E. Coke, Institutes ch. 1, § 1 (1st Am. ed. 1812). Surely, at least, in the extraordinary circumstance when no productive or economically beneficial use of land is permitted, it is less realistic to indulge our usual assumption that the legislature is simply "adjusting the benefits and burdens of economic life," Penn Central Transportation Co., 438 U.S., at 124, 98 S.Ct., at 2659, in a manner that secures an "average reciprocity of advantage" to everyone concerned. Pennsylvania Coal Co. v. Mahon, 260 U.S., at 415, 43 S.Ct., at 160. And the *functional* basis for permitting the government, by regulation, to affect property values without compensation—that "Government hardly could go on if to some extent values incident to property could not be diminished without paying for every such change in the general law," id., at 413, 43 S.Ct., at 159—does not apply to the relatively rare situations where the government has deprived a landowner of all economically beneficial uses.

On the other side of the balance, affirmatively supporting a compensation requirement, is the fact that regulations that leave the owner of land without economically beneficial or productive options for its use—typically, as here, by requiring land to be left substantially in its natural state—carry with them a heightened risk that private property is being pressed into some form of public service under the guise of mitigating serious public harm. See, e.g., Annicelli v. South Kingstown, 463 A.2d 133, 140–141 (R.I.1983) (prohibition on construction adjacent to beach justified on twin grounds of safety and "conservation of open space"); Morris County Land Improvement Co. v. Parsippany–Troy Hills Township, 40 N.J. 539, 552–553, 193 A.2d 232, 240 (1963) (prohibition on filling marshlands imposed in order to preserve region as water detention basin and create wildlife refuge). As Justice Brennan explained:

"From the government's point of view, the benefits flowing to the public from preservation of open space through regulation may be equally great as from creating a wildlife refuge through formal condemnation or increasing electricity production through a dam project that floods private property." San Diego Gas & Elec. Co., supra, 450 U.S., at 652, 101 S.Ct., at 1304 (Brennan, J., dissenting). The many statutes on the books, both state and federal, that provide for the use of eminent domain to impose servitudes on private scenic lands preventing developmental uses, or to acquire such lands altogether, suggest the practical equivalence in this setting of negative regulation and appropriation. See, e.g., 16 U.S.C.A. § 410ff–1(a) (authorizing acquisition of "lands, waters, or interests [within Channel Islands National Park] (including but not limited to scenic easements)"); § 460aa–2(a) (authorizing acquisition of "any lands, or lesser interests therein, including mineral interests and scenic easements" within Sawtooth National Recreation Area); §§ 3921–3923 (authorizing acquisition of wetlands); N.C. Gen.Stat. § 113A–38 (1990) (authorizing acquisition of, inter alia, " 'scenic easements' " within the North Carolina natural and scenic rivers system); Tenn.Code Ann. §§ 11–15–101—11–15–108 (1987) (authorizing acquisition of "protective easements" and other rights in real property adjacent to State's historic, architectural, archaeological, or cultural resources).

We think, in short, that there are good reasons for our frequently expressed belief that when the owner of real property has been called upon to sacrifice *all* economically beneficial uses in the name of the common good, that is, to leave his property economically idle, he has suffered a taking.

B

The trial court found Lucas's two beachfront lots to have been rendered valueless by respondent's enforcement of the coastal-zone construction ban. Under Lucas's theory of the case, which rested upon our "no economically viable use" statements, that finding entitled him to compensation. Lucas believed it unnecessary to take issue with either the purposes behind the Beachfront Management Act, or the means chosen by the South Carolina Legislature to effectuate those purposes. The South Carolina Supreme Court, however, thought otherwise. In its view, the Beachfront Management Act was no ordinary enactment, but involved an exercise of South Carolina's "police powers" to mitigate the harm to the public interest that petitioner's use of his land might occasion. 304 S.C., at 384, 404 S.E.2d, at 899. By neglecting to dispute the findings enumerated in the Act or otherwise to challenge the legislature's purposes, petitioner "concede[d] that the beach/dune area of South Carolina's shores is an extremely valuable public resource; that the erection of new construction, inter alia, contributes to the erosion and destruction of this public resource; and that discouraging new construction in close proximity to the beach/dune area is necessary to prevent a great public harm." Id., at 382–383, 404 S.E.2d, at 898. In the court's view, these concessions brought petitioner's challenge within a long line of this Court's cases sustaining against Due Process and

Takings Clause challenges the State's use of its "police powers" to enjoin a property owner from activities akin to public nuisances. See Mugler v. Kansas, 123 U.S. 623, 8 S.Ct. 273, 31 L.Ed. 205 (1887) (law prohibiting manufacture of alcoholic beverages); Hadacheck v. Sebastian, 239 U.S. 394, 36 S.Ct. 143, 60 L.Ed. 348 (1915) (law barring operation of brick mill in residential area); Miller v. Schoene, 276 U.S. 272, 48 S.Ct. 246, 72 L.Ed. 568 (1928) (order to destroy diseased cedar trees to prevent infection of nearby orchards); Goldblatt v. Hempstead, 369 U.S. 590, 82 S.Ct. 987, 8 L.Ed.2d 130 (1962) (law effectively preventing continued operation of quarry in residential area).

It is correct that many of our prior opinions have suggested that "harmful or noxious uses" of property may be proscribed by government regulation without the requirement of compensation. For a number of reasons, however, we think the South Carolina Supreme Court was too quick to conclude that that principle decides the present case. The "harmful or noxious uses" principle was the Court's early attempt to describe in theoretical terms why government may, consistent with the Takings Clause, affect property values by regulation without incurring an obligation to compensate—a reality we nowadays acknowledge explicitly with respect to the full scope of the State's police power. * * *

The transition from our early focus on control of "noxious" uses to our contemporary understanding of the broad realm within which government may regulate without compensation was an easy one, since the distinction between "harm-preventing" and "benefit-conferring" regulation is often in the eye of the beholder. It is quite possible, for example, to describe in *either* fashion the ecological, economic, and aesthetic concerns that inspired the South Carolina legislature in the present case. One could say that imposing a servitude on Lucas's land is necessary in order to prevent his use of it from "harming" South Carolina's ecological resources; or, instead, in order to achieve the "benefits" of an ecological preserve. Compare, e.g., Claridge v. New Hampshire Wetlands Board, 125 N.H. 745, 752, 485 A.2d 287, 292 (1984) (owner may, without compensation, be barred from filling wetlands because landfilling would deprive adjacent coastal habitats and marine fisheries of ecological support), with, e.g., Bartlett v. Zoning Comm'n of Old Lyme, 161 Conn. 24, 30, 282 A.2d 907, 910 (1971) (owner barred from filling tidal marshland must be compensated, despite municipality's "laudable" goal of "preserv[ing] marshlands from encroachment or destruction"). Whether one or the other of the competing characterizations will come to one's lips in a particular case depends primarily upon one's evaluation of the worth of competing uses of real estate. See Restatement (Second) of Torts § 822, Comment g, p. 112 (1979) ("[p]ractically all human activities unless carried on in a wilderness interfere to some extent with others or involve some risk of interference"). A given restraint will be seen as mitigating "harm" to the adjacent parcels or securing a "benefit" for them, depending upon the observer's evaluation of the relative importance of the use that the restraint favors. See Sax, Takings and the Police Power, 74 Yale L.J. 36, 49 (1964) ("[T]he problem [in this area] is not one of noxiousness or harm-creating activity at all; rather it is a problem of inconsistency between perfectly innocent and independently desirable uses"). Whether Lucas's construction of single-family residences on his parcels should be described as bringing "harm" to South Carolina's adjacent ecological resources thus depends principally upon whether the describer believes that the State's use interest in nurturing those resources is so important that *any* competing adjacent use must yield.

When it is understood that "prevention of harmful use" was merely our early formulation of the police power justification necessary to sustain (without compensation) *any* regulatory diminution in value; and that the distinction between regulation that "prevents harmful use" and that which "confers benefits" is difficult, if not impossible, to discern on an objective, value-free basis; it becomes self-evident that noxious-use logic cannot serve as a touchstone to distinguish regulatory "takings"—which require compensation—from regulatory deprivations that do not require compensation. *A fortiori* the legislature's recitation of a noxious-use justification cannot be the basis for departing from our categorical rule that total regulatory takings must be compensated. If it were, departure would virtually always be allowed. The South Carolina Supreme Court's approach would essentially nullify Mahon's affirmation of limits to the noncompensable exercise of the police power. * * *

Where the State seeks to sustain regulation that deprives land of all economically beneficial use, we think it may resist compensation only if the logically antecedent inquiry into the nature of the owner's estate shows that the proscribed use interests were not part of his title to begin with. This accords, we think, with our "takings" jurisprudence, which has traditionally been guided by the understandings of our citizens regarding the content of, and the State's power over, the "bundle of rights" that they acquire when they obtain title to property. It seems to us that the property owner necessarily expects the uses of his property to be restricted, from time to time, by various measures newly enacted by the State in legitimate exercise of its police powers; "[a]s long recognized, some values are enjoyed under an implied limitation and must yield to the police power." Pennsylvania Coal Co. v. Mahon, 260 U.S., at 413, 43 S.Ct., at 159. And in the case of personal property, by reason of the State's traditionally high degree of control over commercial dealings, he ought to be aware of the possibility that new regulation might even render his property economically worthless (at least if the property's only economically productive use is sale or manufacture for sale), see Andrus v. Allard, 444 U.S. 51, 66–67, 100 S.Ct. 318, 327, 62 L.Ed.2d 210 (1979) (prohibition on sale of eagle feathers). In the case of land, however, we think the notion pressed by the Council that title is somehow held subject to the "implied limitation" that the State may subsequently eliminate all economically valuable use is inconsistent with the historical compact recorded in the Takings Clause that has become part of our constitutional culture.

Where "permanent physical occupation" of land is concerned, we have refused to allow the government to decree it anew (without compensation), no matter how weighty the asserted "public interests" involved, Loretto v. Teleprompter Manhattan CATV Corp., 458 U.S., at 426, 102 S.Ct., at 3171—though we assuredly would permit the government to assert a permanent easement that was a pre-existing limitation upon the landowner's title. Compare Scranton v. Wheeler, 179 U.S. 141, 163, 21 S.Ct. 48, 57, 45 L.Ed. 126 (1900) (interests of "riparian owner in the submerged lands ... bordering on a public navigable water" held subject to Government's navigational servitude), with Kaiser Aetna v. United States, 444 U.S., at 178–180, 100 S.Ct., at 392–393 (imposition of navigational servitude on marina created and rendered navigable at private expense held to constitute a taking). We believe similar treatment must be accorded confiscatory regulations, i.e., regulations that prohibit all economically beneficial use of land: Any limitation so severe cannot be newly legislated or decreed (without compensation), but must inhere in the title itself, in the restrictions that background principles of the State's law of property and nuisance already place upon land ownership. A law or decree with such an effect must, in other words, do no more than duplicate the result that could have been achieved in the courts—by adjacent landowners (or other uniquely affected persons) under the State's law of private nuisance, or by the State under its complementary power to abate nuisances that affect the public generally, or otherwise.

On this analysis, the owner of a lake bed, for example, would not be entitled to compensation when he is denied the requisite permit to engage in a landfilling operation that would have the effect of flooding others' land. Nor the corporate owner of a nuclear generating plant, when it is directed to remove all improvements from its land upon discovery that the plant sits astride an earthquake fault. Such regulatory action may well have the effect of eliminating the land's only economically productive use, but it does not proscribe a productive use that was previously permissible under relevant property and nuisance principles. The use of these properties for what are now expressly prohibited purposes was *always* unlawful, and (subject to other constitutional limitations) it was open to the State at any point to make the implication of those background principles of nuisance and property law explicit. See Michelman, Property, Utility, and Fairness, Comments on the Ethical Foundations of "Just Compensation" Law, 80 Harv.L.Rev. 1165, 1239–1241 (1967). In light of our traditional resort to "existing rules or understandings that stem from an independent source such as state law" to define the range of interests that qualify for protection as "property" under the Fifth (and Fourteenth) amendments, * * * this recognition that the Takings Clause does not require compensation when an owner is barred from putting land to a use that is proscribed by those "existing rules or understandings" is surely unexceptional. When, however, a regulation that declares "off-limits" all economically productive or beneficial uses of land goes beyond what the relevant background principles would dictate, compensation must be paid to sustain it.

The "total taking" inquiry we require today will ordinarily entail (as the application of state nuisance law ordinarily entails) analysis of, among other things, the degree of harm to public lands and resources, or adjacent private property, posed by the claimant's proposed activities, see, e.g., Restatement (Second) of Torts §§ 826, 827, the social value of the claimant's activities and their suitability to the locality in question, see, e.g., id., §§ 828(a) and (b), 831, and the relative ease with which the alleged harm can be avoided through measures taken by the claimant and the government (or adjacent private landowners) alike, see, e.g., id., §§ 827(e), 828(c), 830. The fact that a particular use has long been engaged in by similarly situated owners ordinarily imports a lack of any common-law prohibition (though changed circumstances or new knowledge may make what was previously permissible no longer so), see Restatement (Second) of Torts, supra, § 827, comment *g*. So also does the fact that other landowners, similarly situated, are permitted to continue the use denied to the claimant.

It seems unlikely that common-law principles would have prevented the erection of any habitable or productive improvements on petitioner's land; they rarely support prohibition of the "essential use" of land, Curtin v. Benson, 222 U.S. 78, 86, 32 S.Ct. 31, 33, 56 L.Ed. 102 (1911). The question, however, is one of state law to be dealt with on remand. We emphasize that to win its case South Carolina must do more than proffer the legislature's declaration that the uses Lucas desires are inconsistent with the public interest, or the conclusory assertion that they violate a common-law maxim such as *sic utere tuo ut alienum non laedas*. As we have said, a "State, by *ipse dixit*, may not transform private property into public property without compensation.... " Webb's Fabulous Pharmacies, Inc. v. Beckwith, 449 U.S. 155, 164, 101 S.Ct. 446, 452, 66 L.Ed.2d 358 (1980). Instead, as it would be required to do if it sought to restrain Lucas in a common-law action for public nuisance, South Carolina must identify background principles of nuisance and property law that prohibit the uses he now intends in the circumstances in which the property is presently found. Only on this showing can the State fairly claim that, in proscribing all such beneficial uses, the Beachfront Management Act is taking nothing.

* * *

The judgment is reversed and the cause remanded for proceedings not inconsistent with this opinion.

JUSTICE KENNEDY, concurring in the judgment.

* * *

The finding of no value must be considered under the Takings Clause by reference to the owner's reasonable, investment-backed expectations. * * * The Takings Clause, while conferring substantial protection on property owners, does not eliminate the police power of the State to enact limitations on the use of their property. Mugler v. Kansas, 123 U.S. 623, 669, 8 S.Ct. 273, 301, 31 L.Ed. 205 (1887). The rights conferred by the Takings Clause and the police power of the State may coexist without conflict. Property is bought and sold, investments are made, subject to the State's power to regulate. Where a taking is alleged from regulations which deprive the property of all value, the test must be whether the deprivation is contrary to reasonable, investment-backed expectations.

There is an inherent tendency towards circularity in this synthesis, of course; for if the owner's reasonable expectations are shaped by what courts allow as a proper exercise of governmental authority, property tends to become what courts say it is. Some circularity must be tolerated in these matters, however, as it is in other spheres. * * * The definition, moreover, is not circular in its entirety. The expectations protected by the Constitution are based on objective rules and customs that can be understood as reasonable by all parties involved.

In my view, reasonable expectations must be understood in light of the whole of our legal tradition. The common law of nuisance is too narrow a confine for the exercise of regulatory power in a complex and interdependent society. Goldblatt v. Hempstead, 369 U.S. 590, 593, 82 S.Ct. 987, 989, 8 L.Ed.2d 130 (1962). The State should not be prevented from enacting new regulatory initiatives in response to changing conditions, and courts must consider all reasonable expectations whatever their source. The Takings Clause does not require a static body of state property law; it protects private expectations to ensure private investment. I agree with the Court that nuisance prevention accords with the most common expectations of property owners who face regulation, but I do not believe this can be the sole source of state authority to impose severe restrictions. Coastal property may present such unique concerns for a fragile land system that the State can go further in regulating its development and use than the common law of nuisance might otherwise permit.

The Supreme Court of South Carolina erred, in my view, by reciting the general purposes for which the state regulations were enacted without a determination that they were in accord with the owner's reasonable expectations and therefore sufficient to support a severe restriction on specific parcels of property. See 304 S.C. 376, 383, 404 S.E.2d 895, 899 (1991). The promotion of tourism, for instance, ought not to suffice to deprive specific property of all value without a corresponding duty to compensate. Furthermore, the means as well as the ends of regulation must accord with the owner's reasonable expectations. Here, the State did not act until after the property had been zoned for individual lot development and most other parcels had been improved, throwing the whole burden of the regulation on the remaining lots. This too must be measured in the balance. See Pennsylvania Coal Co. v. Mahon, 260 U.S. 393, 416, 43 S.Ct. 158, 160, 67 L.Ed. 322 (1922).

With these observations, I concur in the judgment of the Court.

JUSTICE BLACKMUN, dissenting.

Today the Court launches a missile to kill a mouse.

The State of South Carolina prohibited petitioner Lucas from building a permanent structure on his property from 1988 to 1990. Relying on an unreviewed (and implausible) state trial court finding that this restriction left Lucas' property valueless, this Court granted review to determine whether compensation must be paid in cases where the State prohibits all economic use of real estate. According to the Court, such an occasion never has arisen in any of our prior cases, and the Court imagines that it will arise "relatively rarely" or only in "extraordinary circumstances." Almost certainly it did not happen in this case.

Nonetheless, the Court presses on to decide the issue, and as it does, it ignores its jurisdictional limits, remakes its traditional rules of review, and creates simultaneously a new categorical rule and an exception (neither of which is rooted in our prior case law, common law, or common sense). I protest not only the Court's decision, but each step taken to reach it. More fundamentally, I question the Court's wisdom in issuing sweeping new rules to decide such a narrow case. Surely, as Justice KENNEDY demonstrates, the Court could have reached the result it wanted without inflicting this damage upon our Takings Clause jurisprudence.

My fear is that the Court's new policies will spread beyond the narrow confines of the present case. For that reason, I, like the Court, will give far greater attention to this case than its narrow scope suggests—not because I can intercept the Court's missile, or save the targeted mouse, but because I hope perhaps to limit the collateral damage.

* * *

The South Carolina Supreme Court found that the Beachfront Management Act did not take petitioner's property without compensation. The decision rested on two premises that until today were unassailable—that the State has the power to prevent any use of property it finds to be harmful to its citizens, and that a state statute is entitled to a presumption of constitutionality.

The Beachfront Management Act includes a finding by the South Carolina General Assembly that the beach/dune system serves the purpose of "protect[ing] life and property by serving as a storm barrier which dissipates wave energy and contributes to shoreline stability in an economical and effective manner." § 48–39–250(1)(a). The General Assembly also found that "development unwisely has been sited too close to the [beach/dune] system. This type of development has jeopardized the stability of the beach/dune system, accelerated erosion, and endangered adjacent property." § 48–39–250(4); see also § 48–39–250(6) (discussing the need to "afford the beach/dune system space to accrete and erode").

If the state legislature is correct that the prohibition on building in front of the setback line prevents serious harm, then, under this Court's prior cases, the Act is constitutional. "Long ago it was recognized that all property in this country is held under the implied obligation that the owner's use of it shall not be injurious to the community, and the Takings Clause did not transform that principle to one that requires compensation whenever the State asserts its power to enforce it." Keystone Bituminous Coal Assn. v. DeBenedictis, 480 U.S. 470, 491–492, 107 S.Ct. 1232, 1245, 94 L.Ed.2d 472 (1987) (internal quotations omitted); see also *id.*, at 488–489, and n. 18, 107 S.Ct., at 1244, n. 18. The Court consistently has upheld regulations imposed to arrest a significant threat to the common welfare, whatever their economic effect on the owner. * * *

* * *

Even if I agreed with the Court that there were no jurisdictional barriers to deciding this case, I still would not try to decide it. The Court creates its new taking jurisprudence based on the trial court's finding that the property had lost all economic value. This finding is almost certainly erroneous. Petitioner still can enjoy other attributes of ownership, such as the right to exclude others, "one of the most essential sticks in the bundle of rights that are commonly characterized as property." Kaiser Aetna v. United States, 444 U.S. 164, 176, 100 S.Ct. 383, 391, 62 L.Ed.2d 332 (1979). Petitioner can picnic, swim, camp in a tent, or live on the property in a movable trailer. State courts frequently have recognized that land has economic value where the only residual economic uses are recreation or camping. See, e.g., Turnpike Realty Co. v. Dedham, 362 Mass. 221, 284 N.E.2d 891 (1972) cert. denied, 409 U.S. 1108, 93 S.Ct. 908, 34 L.Ed.2d 689 (1973); Turner v. County of Del Norte, 24 Cal.App.3d 311, 101 Cal.Rptr. 93 (1972); Hall v. Board of Environmental Protection, 528 A.2d 453 (Me.1987). Petitioner also retains the right to alienate the land, which would have value for neighbors and for those prepared to enjoy proximity to the ocean without a house.

Yet the trial court, apparently believing that "less value" and "valueless" could be used interchangeably, found the property "valueless." The court accepted no evidence from the State on the property's value without a home, and petitioner's appraiser testified that he never had considered what the value would be absent a residence. Tr. 54–55. The appraiser's value was based on the fact that the "highest and best use of these lots . . . [is] luxury single family detached dwellings." Id., at 48. The trial court appeared to believe that the property could be considered "valueless" if it was not available for its most profitable use. Absent that erroneous assumption, see Goldblatt, 369 U.S., at 592, 82 S.Ct., at 989, I find no evidence in the record supporting the trial court's conclusion that the damage to the lots by virtue of the restrictions was "total." Record 128 (findings of fact). I agree with the Court, that it has the power to decide a case that turns on an erroneous finding, but I question the wisdom of deciding an issue based on a factual premise that does not exist in this case, and in the judgment of the Court will exist in the future only in "extraordinary circumstance[s]."

* * *

IV

* * *

This Court repeatedly has recognized the ability of government, in certain circumstances, to regulate property without compensation no matter how adverse the financial effect on the owner may be. More than a century ago, the Court explicitly upheld the right of States to prohibit uses of property injurious to public health, safety, or welfare without paying compensation: "A prohibition simply upon the use of property for purposes that are declared, by valid legislation, to be injurious to the health, morals, or safety of the community, cannot, in any just sense, be deemed a taking or an appropriation of property." Mugler v. Kansas, 123 U.S. 623, 668–669, 8 S.Ct. 273, 301, 31 L.Ed. 205 (1887). On this basis, the Court upheld an ordinance effectively prohibiting operation of a previously lawful brewery, although the "establishments will become of no value as property." * * *

Mugler was only the beginning in a long line of cases. In Powell v. Pennsylvania, 127 U.S. 678, 8 S.Ct. 992, 32 L.Ed. 253 (1888), the Court upheld legislation prohibiting the manufacture of oleomargarine, despite the owner's allegation that "if prevented from continuing it, the value of his property employed therein would be entirely lost and he be deprived of the means of livelihood." Id., at 682, 8 S.Ct., at 994. In Hadacheck v. Sebastian, 239 U.S. 394, 36 S.Ct. 143, 60 L.Ed. 348 (1915), the Court upheld an ordinance prohibiting a brickyard, although the owner had made excavations on the land that prevented it from being utilized for any purpose but a brickyard. Id., at 405, 36 S.Ct., at 143. In Miller v. Schoene, 276 U.S. 272, 48 S.Ct. 246, 72 L.Ed. 568 (1928), the Court held that the Fifth Amendment did not require Virginia to pay compensation to the owner of cedar trees ordered destroyed to prevent a disease from spreading to nearby apple orchards. The "preferment of [the public interest] over the property interest of the individual, to the extent even of its destruction, is one of the distinguishing characteristics of every exercise of the police power which affects property." Id., at 280, 48 S.Ct., at 247. Again, in Omnia Commercial Co. v. United States, 261 U.S. 502, 43 S.Ct. 437, 67 L.Ed. 773 (1923), the Court stated that "destruction of, or injury to, property is frequently accomplished without a 'taking' in the constitutional sense." Id., at 508, 43 S.Ct., at 437.

More recently, in Goldblatt, the Court upheld a town regulation that barred continued operation of an existing sand and gravel operation in order to protect public safety. 369 U.S., at 596, 82 S.Ct., at 991. "Although a comparison of values before and after is relevant," the Court stated, "it is by no means conclusive." Id., at 594, 82 S.Ct., at 990. In 1978, the Court declared that "in instances in which a state tribunal reasonably concluded that 'the health, safety, morals, or general welfare' would be promoted by prohibiting particular contemplated uses of land, this Court has upheld land-use regulation that destroyed ... recognized real property interests." Penn Central Transp. Co., 438 U.S., at 125, 98 S.Ct., at 2659. * * *

The Court recognizes that "our prior opinions have suggested that 'harmful or noxious uses' of property may be proscribed by government regulation without the requirement of compensation," but seeks to reconcile them with its categorical rule by claiming that the Court never has upheld a regulation when the owner alleged the loss of all economic value. Even if the Court's factual premise were correct, its understanding of the Court's cases is distorted. In none of the cases did the Court suggest that the right of a State to prohibit certain activities without paying compensation turned on the availability of some residual valuable use. Instead, the cases depended on whether the government interest was sufficient to prohibit the activity, given the significant private cost.

These cases rest on the principle that the State has full power to prohibit an owner's use of property if it is harmful to the public. "[S]ince no individual has a right to use his property so as to create a nuisance or otherwise harm others, the State has not 'taken' anything when it asserts its power to enjoin the nuisance-like activity." Keystone Bituminous Coal, 480 U.S., at 491, n. 20, 107 S.Ct., at 1245, n. 20. It would make no sense under this theory to suggest that an owner has a constitutionally protected right to harm others, if only he makes the proper showing of economic loss.

* * *

C

Finally, the Court justifies its new rule that the legislature may not deprive a property owner of the only economically valuable use of his land, even if the legislature finds it to be a harmful use, because such action is not part of the "long recognized" "understandings of our citizens." These "understandings" permit such regulation only if the use is a nuisance under the common law. Any other course is "inconsistent with the historical compact recorded in the Takings Clause." It is not clear from the Court's opinion where our "historical compact" or "citizens' understanding" comes from, but it does not appear to be history.

The principle that the State should compensate individuals for property taken for public use was not widely established in America at the time of the Revolution.

> "The colonists ... inherited ... a concept of property which permitted extensive regulation of the use of that property for the public benefit—regulation that could even go so far as to deny all productive use of the property to the owner if, as Coke himself stated, the regulation 'extends to the public benefit ... for this is for the public, and every one hath benefit by it.'" F. Bosselman, D. Callies & J. Banta, The Taking Issue 80–81 (1973), quoting *The Case of the*

King's Prerogative in Saltpetre, 12 Co.Rep. 12–13 (1606) (hereinafter Bosselman). See also Treanor, The Origins and Original Significance of the Just Compensation Clause of the Fifth Amendment, 94 Yale L.J. 694, 697, n. 9 (1985).

Even into the 19th century, state governments often felt free to take property for roads and other public projects without paying compensation to the owners. See M. Horwitz, The Transformation of American Law, 1780–1860, pp. 63–64 (1977) (hereinafter Horwitz); Treanor, 94 Yale L.J., at 695. As one court declared in 1802, citizens "were bound to contribute as much of [land], as by the laws of the country, were deemed necessary for the public convenience." McClenachan v. Curwin, 3 Yeates 362, 373 (Pa.1802). There was an obvious movement toward establishing the just compensation principle during the 19th century, but "there continued to be a strong current in American legal thought that regarded compensation simply as a 'bounty given ... by the State' out of 'kindness' and not out of justice." Horwitz 65 (quoting Commonwealth v. Fisher, 1 Pen. & W. 462, 465 (Pa.1830)). See also State v. Dawson, 3 Hill 100, 103 (S.C.1836).

Although, prior to the adoption of the Bill of Rights, America was replete with land use regulations describing which activities were considered noxious and forbidden, see Bender, The Takings Clause: Principles or Politics?, 34 Buffalo L.Rev. 735, 751 (1985); L. Friedman, A History of American Law 66–68 (1973), the Fifth Amendment's Takings Clause originally did not extend to regulations of property, whatever the effect. Most state courts agreed with this narrow interpretation of a taking. "Until the end of the nineteenth century ... jurists held that the constitution protected possession only, and not value." Siegel, Understanding the Nineteenth Century Contract Clause: The Role of the Property–Privilege Distinction and "Takings" Clause Jurisprudence, 60 S.Cal.L.Rev. 1, 76 (1986); Bosselman 106. Even indirect and consequential injuries to property resulting from regulations were excluded from the definition of a taking. See Bosselman 106; Callender v. Marsh, 1 Pick. 418, 430 (Mass.1823).

Even when courts began to consider that regulation in some situations could constitute a taking, they continued to uphold bans on particular uses without paying compensation, notwithstanding the economic impact, under the rationale that no one can obtain a vested right to injure or endanger the public. In the Coates cases, for example, the Supreme Court of New York found no taking in New York's ban on the interment of the dead within the city, although "no other use can be made of these lands." Coates v. City of New York, 7 Cow. 585, 592 (N.Y.1827). See also Brick Presbyterian Church v. City of New York, 5 Cow. 538 (N.Y.1826); Commonwealth v. Alger, 7 Cush. 53, 59, 104 (Mass.1851); St. Louis Gunning Advertisement Co. v. St. Louis, 235 Mo. 99, 145–146, 137 S.W. 929, 942 (1911), appeal dism'd, 231 U.S. 761, 34 S.Ct. 325, 58 L.Ed. 470 (1913). More recent cases reach the same result. See Consolidated Rock Products Co. v. Los Angeles, 57 Cal.2d 515, 20 Cal.Rptr. 638, 370 P.2d 342, appeal dism'd, 371 U.S. 36, 83 S.Ct. 145, 9

L.Ed.2d 112 (1962); Nassr v. Commonwealth, 394 Mass. 767, 477 N.E.2d 987 (1985); Eno v. Burlington, 125 Vt. 8, 209 A.2d 499 (1965); Turner v. County of Del Norte, 24 Cal.App.3d 311, 101 Cal.Rptr. 93 (1972).

In addition, state courts historically have been less likely to find that a government action constitutes a taking when the affected land is undeveloped. According to the South Carolina court, the power of the legislature to take unimproved land without providing compensation was sanctioned by "ancient rights and principles." Lindsay v. Commissioners, 2 S.C.L. 38, 57 (1796). "Except for Massachusetts, no colony appears to have paid compensation when it built a state-owned road across unimproved land. Legislatures provided compensation only for enclosed or improved land." Treanor, 94 Yale L.J., at 695 (footnotes omitted). This rule was followed by some States into the 1800s. See Horwitz 63–65.

With similar result, the common agrarian conception of property limited owners to "natural" uses of their land prior to and during much of the 18th century. See id., at 32. Thus, for example, the owner could build nothing on his land that would alter the natural flow of water. See id., at 44; see also, e.g., Merritt v. Parker, 1 Coxe 460, 463 (N.J.1795). Some more recent state courts still follow this reasoning. See, e.g., Just v. Marinette County, 56 Wis.2d 7, 201 N.W.2d 761, 768 (1972).

Nor does history indicate any common-law limit on the State's power to regulate harmful uses even to the point of destroying all economic value. Nothing in the discussions in Congress concerning the Takings Clause indicates that the Clause was limited by the common-law nuisance doctrine. Common law courts themselves rejected such an understanding. They regularly recognized that it is "for the legislature to interpose, and by positive enactment to prohibit a use of property which would be injurious to the public." Tewksbury, 11 Metc., at 57. Chief Justice Shaw explained in upholding a regulation prohibiting construction of wharves, the existence of a taking did not depend on "whether a certain erection in tide water is a nuisance at common law or not." Alger, 7 Cush., at 104; see also State v. Paul, 5 R.I. 185, 193 (1858); Commonwealth v. Parks, 155 Mass. 531, 532, 30 N.E. 174 (1892) (Holmes, J.) ("[T]he legislature may change the common law as to nuisances, and may move the line either way, so as to make things nuisances which were not so, or to make things lawful which were nuisances").

In short, I find no clear and accepted "historical compact" or "understanding of our citizens" justifying the Court's new taking doctrine. Instead, the Court seems to treat history as a grab-bag of principles, to be adopted where they support the Court's theory, and ignored where they do not. If the Court decided that the early common law provides the background principles for interpreting the Taking Clause, then regulation, as opposed to physical confiscation, would not be compensable. If the Court decided that the law of a later period provides the background principles, then regulation might be compensable, but the

Court would have to confront the fact that legislatures regularly determined which uses were prohibited, independent of the common law, and independent of whether the uses were lawful when the owner purchased. What makes the Court's analysis unworkable is its attempt to package the law of two incompatible eras and peddle it as historical fact.

V

The Court makes sweeping and, in my view, misguided and unsupported changes in our taking doctrine. While it limits these changes to the most narrow subset of government regulation—those that eliminate all economic value from land—these changes go far beyond what is necessary to secure petitioner Lucas' private benefit. One hopes they do not go beyond the narrow confines the Court assigns them to today.

I dissent.

JUSTICE STEVENS, dissenting. [Dissent omitted.]

[Separate statement by Justice SOUTER omitted.]

Notes

1. After remand the South Carolina court held that the Coastal Council did not have the ability under the common law to prohibit Lucas from constructing houses on his land. Lucas v. South Carolina Coastal Council, 309 S.C. 424, 424 S.E.2d 484 (1992). Reportedly, the state paid Lucas about $1 million for the temporary taking, and subsequently sold the land to another developer, recouping most of what it had paid.

2. Does the Lucas decision mean Penn Central is no longer valid? Most courts, since the Lucas decision, have utilized an analytical approach that asks, first, whether the regulation at issue is a "categorical taking" as described by Justice Scalia in Lucas. If the answer is "no" because the property owner still has viable economic uses (though not the "highest and best" uses), as happens in most cases, then the court will usually revert to the Penn Central factors in determining a regulatory taking. See, e.g., Taub v. Deer Park, 882 S.W.2d 824 (Tex. 1994).

3. What if the landowner has no viable economic use after the regulation, but when he purchased the property he knew or should have known of the impending regulation? If Lucas applies in this situation, one can see the implications as people make property investments—not for the purpose of development—but for the possibility of obtaining compensation for a taking. See, in this regard, Avenal v. United States, 100 F.3d 933 (Fed.Cir.1996) where a lessee of oyster beds in Louisiana was denied compensation after a Corps of Engineers freshwater diversion project wiped out the oysters. The court found that at the time of the lease, the claimant had full knowledge of the possibility of the diversion project. The court said:

> Though as entrepreneurs they are entitled to capitalize on the opportunities afforded by government action, they cannot here insist on a guarantee of non-interference by government when they well knew or should have known that, in response to widely-shared public concerns, including concerns of the oystering industry itself, government actions

were being planned and executed that would directly affect their new economic investments. * * * Assuming, as we must, that these plaintiffs did not invest in their leases until the 1970's, these plaintiffs, in the words of Penn Central, cannot have had reasonable investment-backed expectations that their oyster leases would give them rights protected from the planned freshwater diversion projects of the state and federal governments.

Also see Alegria v. Keeney, 687 A.2d 1249 (R.I.1997), a Rhode Island supreme court decision holding that the denial of an application to develop wetlands was not a regulatory taking because at the time he purchased the property, the owner knew that the property contained wetlands subject to regulation under the Freshwater Wetlands Act. The court found the owner did not have reasonable investment-backed expectations. Accord: Leonard v. Brimfield, 423 Mass. 152, 666 N.E.2d 1300 (1996); Gazza v. New York State Dept. of Environmental Conservation, 89 N.Y.2d 603, ___ N.Y.S.2d ___, ___ N.E.2d ___, 1997 WL 68590 (N.Y.1997).

4. How should courts interpret the language in Lucas that permits restrictions on property that "inhere in the title itself," (restrictions that background principles of the State's law of property and nuisance already place upon land ownership in terms of the state law that defines title)?

Consider the case of Hunziker v. State, 519 N.W.2d 367 (Iowa 1994), cert. denied ___ U.S. ___, 115 S.Ct. 1313, 131 L.Ed.2d 195 (1995). A developer sold a lot in his subdivision to a buyer who planned to build a home. Before construction could begin, the state archaeologist discovered a Native American burial mound on the property, and pursuant to a state statute, prohibited disinterment of the mound and required a buffer zone around the mound for protection. The developer refunded the price of the lot and took it back; he then brought an action for compensation for a regulatory taking. The court ruled against the developer, holding that, under Lucas, "the 'bundle of rights' the plaintiffs acquired by their fee simple title did not include the right to use the land contrary to the provisions [of the statutes denying permission to disinter human remains determined to have state and national significance from an historical or scientific standpoint]. * * * The plaintiffs took title to the land in question subject to the provisions of these sections. These sections and their resulting prohibitions concerning the use of the land ran—so to speak—with the land." In a dissenting opinion the dissenter said: "In this case, a dead bones doctrine has risen from the soil, like a phoenix, to consume the live marrow of land ownership. The history surrounding these ancient bones should be preserved by granting compensation for its resurrection."

Also see Kim v. New York City, ___ N.Y.2d ___, ___ N.Y.S.2d ___, ___ N.E.2d ___, 1997 WL 68593 (N.Y.1997) where the court held that a property owner's duty to maintain lateral support for roads that abut his property was a prevailing rule of property law inhering in his title, so that placement of fill by the city on the private property was not a taking. The dissenting opinion declared that the placement of fill was a physical taking for a public use—to shore up a roadway.

B. PUBLIC HEALTH AND SAFETY AND NECESSITY AS DEFENSES

UNITED STATES v. CALTEX

Supreme Court of the United States, 1952.
344 U.S. 149, 73 S.Ct. 200, 97 L.Ed. 157.

MR. CHIEF JUSTICE VINSON delivered the opinion of the Court.

Each of the respondent oil companies owned terminal facilities in the Pandacan district of Manila at the time of the Japanese attack upon Pearl Harbor. These were used to receive, handle and store petroleum products from incoming ships and to release them for further distribution throughout the Philippine Islands. Wharves, rail and automotive equipment, pumps, pipe lines, storage tanks, and warehouses were included in the property on hand at the outbreak of the war, as well as a normal supply of petroleum products.

* * *

The military situation in the Philippines grew worse. In the face of the Japanese advance, the Commanding General on December 23, 1941, ordered the withdrawal of all troops on Luzon to the Bataan Peninsula. On December 25, 1941, he declared Manila to be an open city. On that same day, the Chief Engineer on the staff of the Commanding General addressed to each of the oil companies letters stating that the Pandacan oil depots "are requisitioned by the U.S. Army." The letters further stated: "Any action deemed necessary for the destruction of this property will be handled by the U.S. Army." An engineer in the employ of one of the companies was commissioned a first lieutenant in the Army Corps of Engineers to facilitate this design.

On December 26, he received orders to prepare the facilities for demolition. On December 27, 1941, while enemy planes were bombing the area, this officer met with representatives of the companies. The orders of the Chief Engineer had been transmitted to the companies. Letters from the Deputy Chief of Staff, by command of General MacArthur, also had been sent to each of the oil companies, directing the destruction of all remaining petroleum products and the vital parts of the plants. Plans were laid to carry out these instructions, to expedite the removal of products which might still be of use to the troops in the field, and to lay a demolition network about the terminals. The representatives of Caltex were given, at their insistence, a penciled receipt for all the terminal facilities and stocks of Caltex.

At 5:40 p.m., December 31, 1941, while Japanese troops were entering Manila, Army personnel completed a successful demolition. All unused petroleum products were destroyed, and the facilities were rendered useless to the enemy. The enemy was deprived of a valuable logistic weapon.

After the war, respondents demanded compensation for all of the property which had been used or destroyed by the Army. The Government paid for the petroleum stocks and transportation equipment which were either used or destroyed by the Army, but it refused to compensate respondents for the destruction of the Pandacan terminal facilities. Claiming a constitutional right under the Fifth Amendment to just compensation for these terminal facilities, respondents sued in the Court of Claims. Recovery was allowed. We granted certiorari to review this judgment. * * * In United States v. Pacific R. Co., 1887, 120 U.S. 227, 7 S.Ct. 490, 30 L.Ed. 634, Justice Field, speaking for a unanimous Court, discussed the question at length. That case involved bridges which had been destroyed during the war between the states by a retreating Northern Army to impede the advance of the Confederate Army. Though the point was not directly involved, the Court raised the question of whether this act constituted a compensable taking by the United States and answered it in the negative:

"The destruction or injury of private property in battle, or in the bombardment of cities and towns, and in many other ways in the war, had to be borne by the sufferers alone, as one of its consequences. Whatever would embarrass or impede the advance of the enemy, as the breaking up of roads, or the burning of bridges, or would cripple and defeat him, as destroying his means of subsistence, were lawfully ordered by the commanding general. Indeed, it was his imperative duty to direct their destruction. The necessities of the war called for and justified this. The safety of the state in such cases overrides all considerations of private loss."

* * *

It may be true that this language also went beyond the precise questions at issue. But the principles expressed were neither novel nor startling, for the common law had long recognized that in times of imminent peril—such as when fire threatened a whole community—the sovereign could, with immunity, destroy the property of a few that the property of many and the lives of many more could be saved. * * * The short of the matter is that this property, due to the fortunes of war, had become a potential weapon of great significance to the invader. It was destroyed, not appropriated for subsequent use. It was destroyed that the United States might better and sooner destroy the enemy.

The terse language of the Fifth Amendment is no comprehensive promise that the United States will make whole all who suffer from every ravage and burden of war. This Court has long recognized that in wartime many losses must be attributed solely to the fortunes of war, and not to the sovereign. No rigid rules can be laid down to distinguish compensable losses from noncompensable losses. Each case must be judged on its own facts. But the general principles laid down in the Pacific Railroad case seem especially applicable here. Viewed realistically, then, the destruction of respondents' terminals by a trained team of engineers in the face of their impending seizure by the enemy was no different than the destruction of the bridges in the Pacific Railroad case. Adhering to the principles of that case, we conclude that the court below erred in holding that respondents have a constitutional right to compensation on the claims presented to this Court.

Reversed.

[Dissenting opinion omitted.]

NATIONAL BOARD OF Y.M.C.A. v. UNITED STATES

Supreme Court of the United States, 1969.
395 U.S. 85, 89 S.Ct. 1511, 23 L.Ed.2d 117.

MR. JUSTICE BRENNAN delivered the opinion of the Court.

Petitioners brought this suit against the United States in the Court of Claims seeking just compensation under the Fifth Amendment for damages done by rioters to buildings occupied by United States troops during the riots in Panama in January 1964. The Court of Claims held that the actions of the Army did not constitute a "taking" within the meaning of the Fifth Amendment and entered summary judgment for the United States. We affirm.

Petitioners' buildings, the YMCA Building and the Masonic Temple, are situated next to each other on the Atlantic side of the Canal Zone at its boundary with the Republic of Panama. Rioting began in this part of the Zone at 8 p.m. on January 9, 1964. Between 9:15 and 9:30 p.m., an unruly mob of 1,500 persons marched to the Panama Canal Administration Building at the center of the Atlantic segment of the Zone and there raised a Panamanian flag. Many members of the mob then proceeded to petitioners' buildings—and to the adjacent Panama Canal Company Office and Storage Building. They entered these buildings, began looting and wrecking the interiors, and started a fire in the YMCA Building.

At 9:50 p.m. Colonel Sachse, the commander of the 4th Battalion, 10th Infantry, of the United States Army, was ordered to move his troops to the Atlantic segment of the Zone with the mission of clearing the rioters from the Zone and sealing the border from further encroachment. The troops entered the three buildings, ejected the rioters, and then were deployed outside of the buildings. The mob began to assault the soldiers with rocks, bricks, plate glass, Molotov cocktails, and intermittent sniper fire. * * *

The buildings remained under siege throughout the night. On the morning of January 10, the YMCA Building was the subject of a concentrated barrage of Molotov cocktails. The building was set afire, and in the early afternoon the troops were forced to evacuate it and take up positions in the building's parking lot which had been sandbagged during the night. Following the evacuation, the YMCA Building continued to be a target for Molotov cocktails. The troops also withdrew from the Masonic Temple on the afternoon of January 10, except that a small observation post on the top floor of the building was maintained. The Temple, like the YMCA Building continued to be under heavy attack following withdrawal of the troops, the greatest damage being suffered on January 12 as a result of extensive fire-bomb activity. The third building under heavy attack in the area—the Panama Canal Company Office and Storage Building—was totally destroyed on January 11 by a fire started by Molotov cocktails.

On January 13, the mob dispersed, and all hostile action in the area ceased. The auditorium-gymnasium in the YMCA Building had been destroyed, and the rest of the building was badly damaged. The Masonic Temple suffered considerably less damage because of its predominantly concrete and brick construction. Other buildings in the Atlantic segment of the Canal Zone were also damaged or destroyed. These buildings were all located along the boundary between the Zone and the Republic of Panama, and none, except the Office and Storage Building, had been occupied by troops during the riot.

Petitioners' suit in the Court of Claims sought compensation for the damage done to their buildings by the rioters after the troops had entered the buildings. The basic facts were stipulated, and all parties moved for summary judgment.

* * *

The Just Compensation Clause was "designed to bar Government from forcing some people alone to bear public burdens which, in all fairness and justice, should be borne by the public as a whole." * * * Petitioners argue that the troops entered their buildings not for the purpose of protecting those buildings but as part of a general defense of the Zone as a whole. Therefore, petitioners contend, they alone should not be made to bear the cost of the damage to their buildings inflicted by the rioters while the troops were inside. The stipulated record, however, does not support petitioners' factual premise; rather, it demonstrates that the troops were acting primarily in defense of petitioners' buildings.

The military had made no advance plans to use petitioners' buildings as fortresses in case of a riot. Nor was the deployment of the troops in the area of petitioners' buildings strategic to a defense of the Zone as a whole. The simple fact is that the troops were sent to that area because that is where the rioters were. * * * [T]here can be no doubt that the United States Army troops were attempting to defend petitioners' buildings. Of course, any protection of private property also serves a broader public purpose. But where, as here, the private party is the particular intended beneficiary of the governmental activity, "fairness and justice" do not require that losses which may result from that activity "be borne by the public as a whole," even though the activity may also be intended incidentally to benefit the public. * * * Were it otherwise, governmental bodies would be liable under the Just Compensation Clause to property owners every time policemen break down the doors of buildings to foil burglars thought to be inside.

Petitioners' claim must fail for yet another reason. On oral argument, petitioners conceded that they would have had no claim had the troops remained outside the buildings, even if such presence would have incited the rioters to do greater damage to the buildings. We agree. But we do not see that petitioners' legal position is improved by the fact that the troops actually did occupy the buildings. Ordinarily, of course, governmental occupation of private property deprives the private owner of his use of the property, and it is this deprivation for which the Constitution requires compensation. There are, however, unusual circumstances in which governmental occupation does not deprive the private owner of any use of his property. For example, the entry by firemen upon burning premises cannot be said to deprive the private owners of any use of the premises. In the instant case, the physical occupation by the troops did not deprive petitioners of any use of their buildings. At the time the troops entered, the riot was already well under way, and petitioners' buildings were already under heavy attack. Throughout the period of occupation, the buildings could not have been used by petitioners in any way. Thus, petitioners could only claim compensation for the increased damage by rioters resulting from the presence of the troops. But such a claim would not seem to depend on whether the troops were positioned in the buildings. Troops standing just outside a building could as well cause increased damage by rioters to that building as troops positioned inside. In either case—and in any case where government action is causally related to private misconduct which leads to property damage—a determination must be made whether the government involvement in the deprivation of private property is sufficiently direct and substantial to require compensation under the Fifth Amendment. The Constitution does not require compensation every time violence aimed against government officers damages private property. Certainly, the Just Compensation Clause could not successfully be invoked in a situation where a rock hurled at a policeman walking his beat happens to damage private property. Similarly, in the instant case, we conclude that the temporary, unplanned occupation of petitioners' buildings in the course of battle does not constitute direct and substantial enough government involvement to warrant compensation under the Fifth Amendment. We have no occasion to decide whether compensation might be required where the Government in some fashion not present here makes private property a particular target for destruction by private parties.

Affirmed.

* * *

MR. JUSTICE HARLAN, concurring in the result.

* * *

I.

I start from the premise that, generally speaking, the Government's complete failure to provide police protection to a particular property owner on a single occasion does not amount to a "taking" within the meaning of the Fifth Amendment. Every man who is robbed on the street cannot demand compensation from the Government on the ground that the Fifth Amendment requires fully effective police protection at all times. The petitioners do not, of course, argue otherwise. Yet surely the Government may not be required to guarantee fully effective protection during serious civil disturbances when it is apparent that the police and the military are unable to defend all the property which is threatened by the mob. If the owners of *unprotected* property remain uncompensated, however, there seems little justice in compensating petitioners, who merely contend that the military occupation of their buildings provided them with *inadequate* protection.

* * *

II.

While I agree with the Court that no compensation is constitutionally available under the facts of this case, I have thought it appropriate to state my own views on this matter since the precise meaning of the rules the majority announces remains obscure at certain critical points. Moreover, in deciding this particular case we should spare no effort to search for principles that seem best calculated to fit others that may arise before American democracy once again regains its equilibrium.

The Court sets out two tests to govern the application of the Just Compensation Clause in riot situations. It first denies petitioners' recovery on the ground that each was the "particular intended beneficiary" of the Government's military operations. I do not disagree with this formula if it means that the Fifth Amendment does not apply whenever the policing power reasonably believes that its actions will not increase the risk of riot damage beyond that borne by the owners of unprotected buildings. But the language the Court has chosen leaves a good deal of ambiguity as to its scope. If, for example, the military deliberately destroyed a building so as to prevent rioters from looting its contents and burning it to the ground, it would be difficult indeed to call the building's owner the "particular intended beneficiary" of the Government's action. Nevertheless, if the military reasonably believed that the rioters would have burned the building anyway, recovery should be denied for the same reasons it is properly denied in the case before us. Cf. United States v. Caltex, Inc., 344 U.S. 149, 73 S.Ct. 200, 97 L.Ed. 157 (1952).

Moreover, the Court's formula might be taken to indicate that if the military's subjective intention was to protect the building, the courts need not consider whether this subjective belief was a reasonable one. While the widest leeway must, of course, be given to good-faith military judgment, I am not prepared to subscribe to judicial abnegation to this extent. If a court concludes, upon convincing evidence, that the military had good reason to know that its actions would significantly increase the risk of riot damage to a particular property, compensation should be awarded regardless of governmental good faith.

While I accept the Court's "intended beneficiary" test with these caveats, I cannot subscribe to the second ground the majority advances to deny recovery in the present case. The majority analogizes this case to one in which the military simply posted a guard in front of petitioners' properties. It is said that if the rioters had damaged the buildings as a part of their attack on the troops standing in front of them, the property damage caused would be too "indirect" a consequence of the military's action to warrant awarding Fifth Amendment compensation. It follows, says the Court, that even if the military's occupation of the buildings increased the risk of harm far beyond any alternative military strategy, the Army's action is nevertheless too "indirect" a cause of the resulting damage.

This argument, however, ignores a salient difference between the case the Court hypothesizes and the one which we confront. If the troops had remained on the street, they would not have obtained any special benefit from the use of petitioners' buildings. In contrast, the military did in this instance receive a benefit not enjoyed by members of the general public when the troops were ordered to occupy the YMCA and the Masonic Temple. As the Court's statement of the facts makes clear, the troops retreated into the buildings to protect themselves from sniper fire. Ordinarily, the Government pays for private property used to shelter its officials, and I would see no reason to make an exception here if the military had reason to know that the buildings would have been exposed to a lesser risk of harm if they had been left entirely unprotected.

On the premises set forth in this opinion, I concur in the judgment of the Court.

[Other opinions omitted.]

Notes

1. A number of state courts have faced inverse condemnation cases based on destruction of property by local law enforcement officials in the course of apprehending criminals. In two jurisdictions state supreme courts upheld eminent domain damages for property destroyed or seriously damaged by the use of tear gas or explosive grenades to flush out fleeing suspects who took refuge in the homes of innocent persons. Steele v. City of Houston, 603 S.W.2d 786 (Tex.1980); Wegner v. Milwaukee Mut. Ins. Co., 479 N.W.2d 38 (Minn.1991). However, most other courts considering the problem have held that such harms are not takings—even in states where the constitution provides that property shall not be taken or damaged without compensation. A very thorough review of the issue, with concurring and dissenting opinions, can be found in Customer Co. v. City of Sacramento, 10 Cal.4th 368, 41 Cal.Rptr.2d 658, 895 P.2d 900 (1995), cert. denied ___ U.S. ___, 116 S.Ct. 920, 133 L.Ed.2d 849 (1996). In this case the California Supreme Court held that eminent domain theory could not be raised in a case where police had cornered a fugitive in a convenience store and fired nearly a dozen tear gas canisters into the premises, causing severe damage to the building and destroying the stock; adding to the property owner's distress was the

estimate of $150,000 to dispose of the hazardous residue from the gas in an environmentally sound manner.

2. Although the preceding cases seem far afield from the typical land use regulation situation, the theory that some losses to property owners are beyond the concept of a taking because those losses are the inevitable consequences of wars, riots or other misfortunes common to all, will aid in understanding the more recent Court decisions involving public safety regulations which are alleged to be a taking.

FIRST ENGLISH EVANGELICAL LUTHERAN CHURCH v. LOS ANGELES COUNTY

Supreme Court of the United States, 1987.
482 U.S. 304, 107 S.Ct. 2378, 96 L.Ed.2d 250.

CHIEF JUSTICE REHNQUIST delivered the opinion of the Court.

In this case the California Court of Appeal held that a landowner who claims that his property has been "taken" by a land-use regulation may not recover damages for the time before it is finally determined that the regulation constitutes a "taking" of his property. We disagree, and conclude that in these circumstances the Fifth and Fourteenth Amendments to the United States Constitution would require compensation for that period.

In 1957, appellant First English Evangelical Lutheran Church purchased a 21–acre parcel of land in a canyon along the banks of the Middle Fork of Mill Creek in the Angeles National Forest. The Middle Fork is the natural drainage channel for a watershed area owned by the National Forest Service. Twelve of the acres owned by the church are flat land, and contained a dining hall, two bunkhouses, a caretaker's lodge, an outdoor chapel, and a footbridge across the creek. The church operated on the site a campground, known as "Lutherglen," as a retreat center and a recreational area for handicapped children.

In July 1977, a forest fire denuded the hills upstream from Lutherglen, destroying approximately 3,860 acres of the watershed area and creating a serious flood hazard. Such flooding occurred on February 9 and 10, 1978, when a storm dropped 11 inches of rain in the watershed. The runoff from the storm overflowed the banks of the Mill Creek, flooding Lutherglen and destroying its buildings.

In response to the flooding of the canyon, appellee County of Los Angeles adopted Interim Ordinance No. 11,855 in January 1979. The ordinance provided that "[a] person shall not construct, reconstruct, place or enlarge any building or structure, any portion of which is, or will be, located within the outer boundary lines of the interim flood protection area located in Mill Creek Canyon * * *." The ordinance was effective immediately because the county determined that it was "required for the immediate preservation of the public health and safety * * *." The interim flood protection area described by the ordinance included the flat areas on either side of Mill Creek on which Lutherglen had stood.

The church filed a complaint in the Superior Court of California a little more than a month after the ordinance was adopted. As subsequently amended, the complaint alleged two claims against the county and the Los Angeles County Flood Control District. The first alleged that the defendants were liable under Cal.Gov't Code Ann. § 835 (West 1980) for dangerous conditions on their upstream properties that contributed to the flooding of Lutherglen. As a part of this claim, appellant also alleged that "Ordinance No. 11,855 denies [appellant] all use of Lutherglen." The second claim sought to recover from the Flood District in inverse condemnation and in tort for engaging in cloud seeding during the storm that flooded Lutherglen. Appellant sought damages under each count for loss of use of Lutherglen. * * *

[The majority opinion determines that a property owner who has suffered a taking, even a temporary taking, has a cause of action in inverse condemnation. This portion of the opinion is taken up in Section 5 of this Chapter.]

Here we must assume that the Los Angeles County ordinances have denied appellant all use of its property for a considerable period of years, and we hold that invalidation of the ordinance without payment of fair value for the use of the property during this period of time would be a constitutionally insufficient remedy. The judgment of the California Court of Appeals is therefore reversed, and the case is remanded for further proceedings not inconsistent with this opinion.

It is so ordered.

JUSTICE STEVENS, with whom JUSTICE BLACKMUN and JUSTICE O'CONNOR join as to Parts I and III, dissenting.

One thing is certain. The Court's decision today will generate a great deal of litigation. Most of it, I believe, will be unproductive. But the mere duty to defend the actions that today's decision will spawn will undoubtedly have a significant adverse impact on the land-use regulatory process. The Court has reached out to address an issue not actually presented in this case, and has then answered that self-imposed question in a superficial and, I believe, dangerous way.

Four flaws in the Court's analysis merit special comment. First, the Court unnecessarily and imprudently assumes that appellant's complaint alleges an unconstitutional taking of Lutherglen. Second, the Court distorts our precedents in the area of regulatory takings when it concludes that all ordinances which would constitute takings if allowed to remain in effect permanently, necessarily also constitute takings if they are in effect for only a limited period of time. Third, the Court incorrectly assumes that the California Supreme Court has already decided that it will never allow a state court to grant monetary relief for a temporary regulatory taking, and then uses that conclusion to reverse a judgment which is correct under the Court's own theories. Finally, the Court errs in concluding that it is the Takings Clause, rather than the Due Process Clause, which is the primary constraint on the use of unfair and dilatory procedures in the land-use area.

* * *

This Court clearly has the authority to decide this case by ruling that the complaint did not allege a taking under the Federal Constitution, and therefore to avoid the novel constitutional issue that it addresses. Even though I believe the Court's lack of self-restraint is imprudent, it is imperative to stress that the Court does not hold that appellant is entitled to compensation as a result of the flood protection regulation that the County enacted. No matter whether the regulation is treated as one that deprives appellant of its property on a permanent or temporary basis, this Court's precedents demonstrate that the type of regulatory program at issue here cannot constitute a taking.

"Long ago it was recognized that 'all property in this country is held under the implied obligation that the owner's use of it shall not be injurious to the community.' " *Keystone Bituminous Coal Assn. v. De-Benedictis,* 480 U.S. 470, ___, 107 S.Ct. 1232, 1245, 94 L.Ed.2d 472 (1987), quoting *Mugler v. Kansas,* 123 U.S. 623, 665, 8 S.Ct. 273, 299, 31 L.Ed. 205 (1887). Thus, in order to protect the health and safety of the community, government may condemn unsafe structures, may close unlawful business operations, may destroy infected trees, and surely may restrict access to hazardous areas—for example, land on which radioactive materials have been discharged, land in the path of a lava flow from an erupting volcano, or land in the path of a potentially life-threatening flood. When a governmental entity imposes these types of health and safety regulations, it may not be "burdened with the condition that [it] must compensate such individual owners for pecuniary losses they may sustain, by reason of their not being permitted, by a noxious use of their property, to inflict injury upon the community." *Mugler, supra,* 123 U.S., at 668–669, 8 S.Ct. at 300–301.

In this case, the legitimacy of the County's interest in the enactment of Ordinance No. 11,855 is apparent from the face of the ordinance and has never been challenged. It was enacted as an "interim" measure "temporarily prohibiting" certain construction in a specified area because the County Board believed the prohibition was "urgently required for the immediate preservation of the public health and safety." Even if that were not true, the strong presumption of constitutionality that applies to legislative enactments certainly requires one challenging the constitutionality of an ordinance of this kind to allege some sort of improper purpose or insufficient justification in order to state a colorable federal claim for relief. A presumption of validity is particularly appropriate in this case because the complaint did not even allege that the ordinance is invalid, or pray for a declaration of invalidity or an injunction against its enforcement. Nor did it allege any facts indicating how the ordinance interfered with any future use of the property contemplated or planned by appellant. In light of the tragic flood and the loss of life that precipitated the safety regulations here, it is hard to understand how appellant ever expected to rebuild on Lutherglen.

Thus, although the Court uses the allegations of this complaint as a springboard for its discussion of a discrete legal issue, it does not, and could not under our precedents, hold that the allegations sufficiently alleged a taking or that the County's effort to preserve life and property could ever constitute a taking. As far as the United States Constitution is concerned, the claim that the ordinance was a taking of Lutherglen should be summarily rejected on its merits.

* * *

IV

There is, of course, a possibility that land-use planning, like other forms of regulation, will unfairly deprive a citizen of the right to develop his property at the time and in the manner that will best serve his economic interests. The "regulatory taking" doctrine announced in *Pennsylvania Coal* places a limit on the permissible scope of land-use restrictions. In my opinion, however, it is the Due Process Clause rather than that doctrine that protects the property owner from improperly motivated, unfairly conducted, or unnecessarily protracted governmental decisionmaking. Violation of the procedural safeguards mandated by the Due Process Clause will give rise to actions for damages under 42 U.S.C.A. § 1983, but I am not persuaded that delays in the development of property that are occasioned by fairly conducted administrative or judicial proceedings are compensable, except perhaps in the most unusual circumstances. On the contrary, I am convinced that the public interest in having important governmental decisions made in an orderly, fully informed way amply justifies the temporary burden on the citizen that is the inevitable by-product of democratic government. * * *

The policy implications of today's decision are obvious and, I fear, far reaching. Cautious local officials and land-use planners may avoid taking any action that might later be challenged and thus give rise to a damage action. Much important regulation will never be enacted, even perhaps in the health and safety area. Were this result mandated by the Constitution, these serious implications would have to be ignored. But the loose cannon the Court fires today is not only unattached to the Constitution, but it also takes aim at a long line of precedents in the regulatory takings area. It would be the better part of valor simply to decide the case at hand instead of igniting the kind of litigation explosion that this decision will undoubtedly touch off.

I respectfully dissent.

FIRST ENGLISH EVANGELICAL, LUTHERAN CHURCH OF GLENDALE v. COUNTY OF LOS ANGELES

California Ct. of Appeal, Second Dist., 1989.
210 Cal.App.3d 1353, 258 Cal.Rptr. 893, certiorari denied 493
U.S. 1056, 110 S.Ct. 866, 107 L.Ed.2d 950 (1990).

JOHNSON, ASSOCIATE JUSTICE.

In this opinion we consider an issue on remand from the United States Supreme Court. The high court held a landowner is entitled to compensation—not merely injunctive relief—when a court finds there has been an unconstitutional regulatory taking. But the Supreme Court expressly reserved the question whether respondent's regulatory action in this case amounted to an unconstitutional taking. We decide appellant failed to state a cause of action for two independent and sufficient reasons: (1) The interim ordinance in question substantially advanced the preeminent state interest in public safety and did not deny appellant all use of its property. (2) The interim ordinance only imposed a reasonable moratorium for a reasonable period of time while the respondent conducted a study and determined what uses, if any, were compatible with public safety.

* * *

The United States Supreme Court in *First English* made it abundantly clear the Court was deciding the remedies issue—and only that issue. The majority specifically held it was not deciding appellant had stated a cause of action.

* * *

This brings us to the question whether the substantive allegations of the "regulatory taking" claim state a valid cause of action. The answer to this question, in turn, depends upon whether the public is justified in placing the burden of these restrictions on this private landowner rather than compensating the landowner for the uses it is required to give up. Commentators have noted the law is not well-settled in this area. (See, e.g., Siemon and Larson, *The Taking Issue Trilogy: The Beginning of the End?, supra,* 33 Wash.Univ.J. of Urban & Contemporary L. 169.) Nevertheless, there are enough guideposts to resolve the instant case. It simply does not pose a close issue under any formulation the Supreme Court has suggested as the appropriate test for judging when compensation is required.

I. THE "PUBLIC SAFETY EXCEPTION" AND OTHER GOVERNMENTAL RESTRICTIONS ON THE USE OF PRIVATE PROPERTY

* * *

Erecting a dam which permanently submerges a property owner's land under a lake is one thing, a law limiting his use of that land quite another. As the *Mugler* court ruled: "A prohibition simply upon the use of property for purposes that are declared by valid legislation, to be injurious to the health, morals, or safety of the community, cannot, in any just sense, be deemed a taking or an appropriation of property for the public benefit. Such legislation does not disturb the owner in the control or use of his property for lawful purposes, nor restrict his right to dispose of it, but is only a declaration by the state that its use by anyone, for certain forbidden purposes, is prejudicial to the public interest. Nor can legislation of that character come within the 14th Amendment, * * * unless it is apparent that its real object is not to protect the community, or to promote the general well being, but, under the guise of police regulation to deprive the owner of his liberty and property, without due process of law. *The power which the states prohibiting such use by individuals of their property as will be prejudicial to the health, the morals, or the safety of the public, is not—and, consistently with the existence and safety of organized society, cannot be—burdened with the condition that the state must compensate such individual owners for pecuniary losses they may sustain by reason of their not being permitted * * * to inflict injury upon the community.*" (123 U.S. at pp. 668–669, 8 S.Ct. at pp. 300–301, italics added.)

We recognize a brewery is a far cry from a Bible camp. But here the threat to public health and safety emanates not from what is produced on the property but from the presence of any substantial structures on that property. The principles enunciated in *Mugler* have been applied by the Court to uphold prohibitions against a broad range of other uses of one's property—e.g., an ordinance prohibiting the manufacture of bricks inside the city limits of Los Angeles (*Hadacheck v. Sebastian* (1915) 239 U.S. 394, 36 S.Ct. 143, 60 L.Ed. 348); a requirement property owners cut down red cedars which were infected with a communicable plant disease fatal to neighboring apple orchards (*Miller v. Schoene* (1928) 276 U.S. 272, 48 S.Ct. 246, 72 L.Ed. 568); and a prohibition against excavating below the water table in order to extract gravel (*Goldblatt v. Town of Hempstead* (1962) 369 U.S. 590, 82 S.Ct. 987, 8 L.Ed.2d 130).

Sometimes government exercises its police powers through the enactment of zoning ordinances and other forms of land use regulation. Whether a specific regulation represents an unconstitutional "taking" involves the same considerations as suggested in *Mugler* and its progeny.

Recently, in *Agins v. Tiburon* (1980) 447 U.S. 255, 100 S.Ct. 2138, 65 L.Ed.2d 106, Justice Powell writing for a unanimous court gathered the strands of earlier cases and articulated the test which the high court now invokes in zoning cases. "The application of a general zoning law to particular property effects a taking if the ordinance does not substantially advance legitimate state interests (citation omitted) or denies an owner economically viable use of his land (citation omitted). The determination that governmental action constitutes a taking is, in essence, a determination that the public at large, rather than a single owner, must bear the burden of an exercise of state power in the public interest. Although no precise rule determines when property has been taken (citation omitted) the question necessarily requires a weighing of private and public interest. * * * Appellants [in the *Agins* case] * * * will share with other owners the benefit and burdens of the city's exercise of its police power. Assessing the fairness of the zoning ordinances, these benefits must be considered along with any diminution in market value that appellants may suffer." (447 U.S. at pp. 260–262, 100 S.Ct. at pp. 2141–2142.)

In *Agins,* the Supreme Court was called upon to apply this test to a zoning ordinance which limited landowners to one residence on each acre of land. The court found the prevention of premature urbanization was a "legitimate state interest" and a limitation of one dwelling per acre "substantially advanced" this interest. It further found the landowner shared in these public benefits which helped offset any diminution of market value he might suffer. Accordingly, the regulation imposing the limitation was not an unconstitutional "taking" of the landowner's property and the landowner was not entitled to compensation.

* * *

II. First English Is Not Entitled to Compensation Because the Interim Ordinance Did Not Deprive it of "All Uses" of Lutherglen and Whatever Uses Were Denied Were Properly Denied to Preserve Public Safety

One pair of commentators suggests the Supreme Court has held a private landowner is entitled to compensation when a land use regulation *either* does not substantially advance a legitimate public purpose *or* deprives the landowner of "all uses" of the property. (Falik and Shimko, *The Takings Nexus: The Supreme Court Forges a New Direction in Land-Use Jurisprudence, supra,* 23 Real Property, Probate & Trust J. 1.) To put it another way, they construe the Supreme Court's decision in *Agins v. City of Tiburon, supra,* to mean landowners are entitled to compensation if the land use regulation deprives them of "all uses" of the property even if the regulation involved substantially advances a legitimate public purpose. They admit there is conflict between this "either/or" test and some of the crucial language in Justice Rehnquist's majority opinion *First English.* There, as will be recalled, the Supreme Court majority clearly stated the land use regulation involved in this case—Interim Ordinance 11,855—would *not* constitute a compensable "taking" if the regulation did not deprive *First English* of "all use" of its property *or* even assuming it prohibited "all uses" if that deprivation of "all uses" promoted public safety. Under this formulation *First English* would not be entitled to compensation even if Interim Ordinance 11,855 deprived it of "all uses" of Lutherglen if that prohibition substantially advances the interest in public health and safety.

* * *

We need not choose between the *Agins* and *First English* formulations of the test, however. Interim Ordinance 11,855 survives under either formulation. It did not deny First English "all use" of the property and the uses it did deny could be constitutionally prohibited under the County's power to protect public safety.

* * *

On November 8, 1980—22 months after the interim ordinance went into effect and 21 months after First English filed its lawsuit—the Los Angeles County Regional Planning Commission issued a report on a proposed permanent Flood Protection District encompassing the Mill Creek area.

* * *

Among other things, the permanent ordinance prohibits construction or reconstruction of most buildings within the district. The exceptions, however, do permit "accessory buildings structures that will not substantially impede the flow of water, including sewer, gas, electrical, and water systems approved by the county engineer * * * [a]utomobile parking facilities incidental to a lawfully established use * * * [and] [f]lood control structures * * *." (§ 22.44.220.) Another provision instructs the county engineer to "enforce, as a minimum, the current Federal flood plan management regulations" when considering whether to issue building permits for buildings or other structures in this flood control zone.

If there is a hierarchy of interests the police power serves—and both logic and prior cases suggest there is—then the preservation of life must rank at the top. Zoning restrictions seldom serve public interests so far up on the scale. More often these laws guard against things like "premature urbanization" (*Agins v. Tiburon, supra,* 447 U.S. 255, 100 S.Ct. 2138, 65 L.Ed.2d 106), or "preserve open spaces" (*Morse v. County of San Luis Obispo* (1967) 247 Cal.App.2d 600, 55 Cal.Rptr. 710), or contribute to orderly development and the mitigation of environmental impacts (see, e.g., *Euclid v. Ambler Realty Co., supra,* 272 U.S. 365, 47 S.Ct. 114, 71 L.Ed. 303; *Friends of Westwood v. City of Los Angeles* (1987) 191 Cal.App.3d 259, 235 Cal.Rptr. 788). When land use regulations seek to advance what are deemed lesser interests such as aesthetic values of the community they frequently are outweighed by constitutional property rights (see, e.g., *Desert Outdoor Advertising v. County of San Bernardino* (1967) 255 Cal.App.2d 765, 63 Cal.Rptr. 543). Nonetheless, it should be noted even these lesser public interests have been deemed sufficient to justify zoning which diminishes—without compensation—the value of individual properties. (Van Alstyne, *Taking or Damaging by Police Power: The Search for Inverse Condemnation Criteria,* (1971) 44 So.Cal.L.Rev. 1, and cases cited therein.)

The zoning regulation challenged in the instant case involves this highest of public interests—the prevention of death and injury. Its enactment was prompted by the loss of life in an earlier flood. And its avowed purpose is to prevent the loss of lives in future floods. Moreover, the lives it seeks to save and the injuries it strives to prevent are not only those on other properties but on appellant's property as well.

We need not address the ultimate question—is the public interest at stake in this case so paramount that it would justify a law which prohibited *any* future occupancy or use of appellant's land. Certainly, the owners of red cedar trees were not entitled to any public compensation when the state required them to destroy those trees in order to save the "lives" of apple trees in *Miller v. Schoene, supra.* But the zoning limitation in the instant case is nowhere near as Draconian. Zoning for this property allowed several uses of Lutherglen throughout the term of the interim ordinance First English challenges. During that period and after enactment of the permanent ordinance, as well, this property could be used for "agricultural, and recreational uses." And under the permanent ordinance First English appellants are specifically allowed to build swimming pools, parking lots, and accessory buildings within the flood zone portion of its property. (Since First English does not allege it has been denied permits to build any alleged "accessory buildings" we cannot know the scope of this exception.) What First English can no longer do is rebuild the bunkhouses and similar permanent living structures which might house the potential victims of a future flood or if carried away by that flood cause death, injury and property damage to other properties further downstream.

We have no problem concluding these zoning restrictions represent a valid exercise of the police power and not an unconstitutional "taking without compensation." On balance, the public benefits this regulation confers far exceed the private costs it imposes on the individual property owner (especially after factoring in the public benefits this property owner shares). These are the considerations the Supreme Court deemed to control the decision whether government should be compelled to award compensation when its regulations drastically limit the uses of private property. On one side of the scale the zoning restriction "substantially advances" the highest possible public interest—the prevention of death and injury both on and off appellant's property. On the other side of the scale, appellants and their future campers not only share in this public benefit but are still left with some permissible uses of the property. The fact the zoning restrictions necessary to the preservation of life and health may cause a diminution in the use and economic value of this property does not create a legal entitlement to compensation for that loss of use and value.

This case presents a dramatic illustration of the principle of "reciprocity of advantage." Lutherglen is one of several properties running along this riverbed. Those who use Lutherglen are endangered by any structures that may be built on these other properties, just as those using the other properties are endangered by structures First English might erect on Lutherglen. First English enjoys the safety benefits accompanying the prohibition of construction on the other properties along the riverbed in return for the "reciprocal" safety benefits that flow to the other landowners because First English is subject to a similar ban.

The instant complaint contains no allegations controverting the legislative history nor does it present other facts we are entitled to judicially notice casting doubt on the avowed intent and effect of the interim ordinance. Indeed, after reciting the terms of the now-superseded ordinance the sole allegation is that "Ordinance No. 11,855 denies First Church all use of Lutherglen." The complaint does not allege the limitations imposed on First English's use of the property were motivated by a desire to acquire Lutherglen at a lower price or that it was unreasonable for the County to conclude these limitations would contribute substantially to the public safety.

* * *

The judgment dismissing the cause of action for inverse condemnation based on enactment of Ordinance 11,855 is affirmed for the reasons recited in this opinion. In all other respects the opinion this court filed on June 25, 1985, and in which remittitur issued on November 4, 1985, remains in full force and effect. Accordingly, the case is remanded for further proceedings consistent with that opinion as to the cause of action for inverse condemnation based on cloud seeding.

LILLIE, P.J., and FRED WOODS, J., concur.

Note

The closing down of a public nuisance is, of course, not a taking. The Lucas case put that doctrine on sound constitutional grounds. However, defining what is a public nuisance for takings analysis is not always easy. The cases that are so evident in these times involve real property used as "drug" houses or "crack" houses. Compare City of St. Petersburg v. Bowen, 675 So.2d 626 (Fla.App.1996) with Zeman v. City of Minneapolis, 540 N.W.2d 532 (Minn.App.1995). In the Florida case the court held that a city's order that completely closed an apartment complex for one year to curtail drug use by tenants and others was a compensable taking; the court stated that the Lucas language about the nuisance exception to takings was applicable only where the government can show that the property owner had no reasonable expectation of the proposed use when the property was acquired. In the Minnesota case the court held that Lucas was inapplicable because the owner's rental dwelling license was reinstated, and Lucas only applies to permanent takings. As for damages for a temporary taking during the period the owner's property was not permitted to be rented, the court remanded for a determination of damages.

SECTION 3.   WHAT IS PROPERTY?

Government regulations which take property may require compensation for the taking. Over the years courts have had to decide if what was taken amounts to "property." The cases run a wide gamut, from such takings as prospective profits from a contract frustrated by governmental regulation, or uncompensated appointment of attorneys to represent indigent defendants in federal courts, or loss of real estate sales commissions to a broker where the listed property is condemned, to more traditional situations involving diminution of access or airspace easements. In this Section we look only at the law involving regulation of land use as a deprivation of property.

A. INGRESS AND EGRESS

BACICH v. BOARD OF CONTROL OF CALIFORNIA

California Supreme Court, In Bank, 1943.
23 Cal.2d 343, 144 P.2d 818.

CARTER, JUSTICE.

* * *

Plaintiff alleges that he is the owner of an improved lot situated on the west side of Sterling Street between the intersection of that street with Bryant Street and Harrison Street in the City and County of San Francisco, the two latter streets being parallel; that before the construction of the improvement hereinafter mentioned Harrison Street was level with Sterling Street and he had access from his lot to Harrison Street by footpaths and street railway; that a street railway extending along Sterling Street served his property; that the area around his property was formerly used for residential purposes; that the construction of the approaches to the San Francisco Bay Bridge by defendants resulted in the lowering of Harrison Street fifty feet, leaving as the only access thereto an almost perpendicular flight of steps, the destruction of the residence property in the area, the removal of the street railway, and the erection of an elevated highway between his lot and Bryant Street which he must pass under to reach the latter street; that by reason of the foregoing his property has been damaged in the sum of $14,000; and that he filed a claim for those damages with defendant Board of Control which was rejected.

* * *

The instant action is predicated upon the constitutional provision that private property may not be taken or damaged for a public purpose without the payment of just compensation. Cal.Const. art. I, sec. 14. That clause of the Constitution is self-executing and hence neither consent to sue the State nor the creation of a remedy by legislative enactment is necessary to obtain relief thereunder. Rose v. State of California, 19 Cal.2d 713, 123 P.2d 505.

* * *

The major issue presented in this case is whether or not plaintiff may recover compensation under the constitutional provision (Cal.Const. art. I, sec. 14) in the light of the facts stated by him. He is entitled thereto under the wording of that provision if his property has been taken or damaged for a public use. The solution of that question depends largely upon the character and extent of his property right. If he has a property right and it has been impaired or damaged, he may recover. The test frequently mentioned by the authorities, that he may recover if he has suffered a damage peculiar to himself and different in kind, as differentiated from degree, from that suffered by the public generally, is of no assistance in the solution of the problem. If he has a property right and it has been impaired, the damage is necessarily peculiar to himself and is different in kind from that suffered by him as a member of the public or by the public generally, for his particular property right as a property owner and not as a member of the public has been damaged. See Rose v. State of California, supra.

In the instant case we are concerned with a property right known as the right of access which an owner has in the street upon which his property abuts and which is appurtenant to such abutting property. The function of the court is to determine and define the character and extent of that right. The right of access, being by its terms general in nature, requires definition and clarification as to its extent and character. This is especially true where we are concerned with the constitutional provision which requires that compensation be paid where property is taken or damaged. The property right of access generally is firmly established.

It has long been recognized in this state and elsewhere that an owner of property abutting upon a public street has a property right in the nature of an easement in the street which is appurtenant to his abutting property and which is his private right, as distinguished from his right as a member of the public. That right has been described as an easement of ingress and egress to and from his property or, generally, the right of access over the street to and from his property, and compensation must be given for an impairment thereof. We are not now inclined to question or disturb that rule. * * * The precise origin of that property right is somewhat obscure but it may be said generally to have arisen by court decisions declaring that such right existed and recognizing it. See 18 Am.Jur., Eminent Domain, sec. 181; 41 Yale Law Journal 221. For that reason, in the determination of the extent and character of that right most of the cases rely, without discussion, upon precedents which fit or are analogous to the circumstances present in the case before the court. If the question is one of first impression its answer depends chiefly upon matters of policy, a factor the nature of which, although at times discussed by the courts, is usually left undisclosed. It may be suggested that on the one hand the policy underlying the eminent domain provision in the Constitution is to distribute throughout the community the loss inflicted upon the individual by the making of public improvements. See 41 Yale Law Journal, 221–224; 52 Harv.L.Rev. 1176, 1177; 3 Harv.L.Rev. 189–205. Manifestly, the addition to the eminent domain clause in constitutions in most states, including California, of "or damaged" to the word "taken" indicates an intent to extend that policy to embrace additional situations. On the other hand, fears have been expressed that compensation allowed too liberally will seriously impede, if not stop, beneficial public improvements because of the greatly increased cost. See Davis v. County Com'rs, 153 Mass. 218, 26 N.E. 848, 850, 11 L.R.A. 750; 13 Va.L.Rev. 334–337. However, it is said that in spite of that so-called policy "the courts cannot ignore sound and settled principles of law safeguarding the rights and property of individuals. This [improvement] may be of great convenience to the public generally, but the properties of abutting owners ought not be sacrificed in order to secure it"; and, quoting from Sedgwick on Constitutional Law: "The tendency under our system is too often to sacrifice the individual to the community; and it seems very difficult in reason to show why the State should not pay for property which it destroys or impairs the value, as well as for what it physically takes. * * * " Liddick v. City of Council Bluffs, Iowa, 5 N.W.2d 361, 372, 382.

In some degree those opposed policies are manifested in the conflict between the constitutional mandate that compensation be paid when private property is taken or damaged for a public purpose and the exercise of police power where compensation need not be paid. The line between those two concepts is far from clearly marked. It will be recalled that in the instant case it is alleged that by reason of the lowering of Harrison Street fifty feet below the level of Sterling Street the access that plaintiff formerly had to Harrison Street from Sterling Street has now been lost except for an almost perpendicular flight of stairs. The condition resulted from the construction of a public improvement, namely, approaches to a bridge spanning San Francisco Bay. It does not appear that any compelling emergency or public necessity required its construction without the payment of compensation for property damaged. Therefore, the State may not escape the payment of compensation under the police power.

The ultimate effect of lowering Harrison Street was to place plaintiff's property in a cul-de-sac. Whereas, before he had access to Harrison Street, the next intersecting street from his property on Sterling Street, he now has access in one direction only, that is, to Bryant Street, the next intersecting street in the opposite direction. The existence of access in one direction to the general system of streets has been impaired to the extent that there is now left only the stairway. Plaintiff alleged that formerly Sterling Street was level with Harrison Street, which may be interpreted to mean that general access was available. He does state that formerly he had access by a streetcar line and footpaths. That being true his access by those modes has been lost except to the extent that the stairway is a substitute for pedestrian access. In that respect his property has been placed in a cul-de-sac. Moreover, his request for leave to amend may be construed to embrace a showing that formerly there was access to Harrison Street for vehicular traffic, or at least that there was a right of way or public street, improved or unimproved, joining Sterling Street with Harrison Street. Furthermore, it is apparently conceded by defendants that a cul-de-sac has been created. That plaintiff's property has been damaged by the impairment cannot be here questioned. The allegation in his complaint that it has been must be taken as true.

Whether or not such impairment is compensable must depend upon the character and extent of his easement of access. Does it extend to a right to pass to the next intersecting streets? Nothing more need be decided in this case; we are not concerned with the correct rule in a case where the obstruction occurs beyond the next intersecting street nor with what the rule may be for rural property. Practically all authorities hold, and we believe correctly, that no recovery may be had where the obstruction is beyond the next intersecting street. See cases cited: 4 McQuillin, Municipal Corporations, 2d Ed., 279–280, sec. 1527; 1 Lewis on Eminent Domain, 3d Ed., 350, 383, secs. 191, 203; 25 Am.Jur., Highways, sec. 318; In re Hull, 163 Minn. 439, 204 N.W. 534, 205 N.W. 613, 49 A.L.R. 330; New York, C. & St. L.R. Co. v. Bucsi, 128 Ohio St. 134, 190 N.E. 562, 93 A.L.R. 639. The extent of the easement of access may be said to be that which is reasonably required giving consideration to all the purposes to which the property is adapted. It is obvious that in the instant case the damage suffered is greater and different than if the obstruction had been beyond the next intersecting street. Where formerly plaintiff had an outlet from his property at both ends of Sterling Street, he now has access at only one end, which definitely affects ingress to and egress from his property. It would seem clear that the reasonable modes of egress and ingress would embrace access to the next intersecting street in both directions. It should be noted that the right is more extensive than the mere opportunity to go on to the street immediately in front of the property. Rose v. State of California, supra. We are not confronted with the necessity of balancing the conflicting policies heretofore referred to without the aid of persuasive precedent. Many authorities and writers have either declared or intimated that the creation of a cul-de-sac, that is, the blocking of access to the next intersecting street in one direction is compensable, although the access still exists in the opposite direction to an intersecting street. In other words, the easement is of that extent.

* * *

Defendants contend that the creation of the cul-de-sac causes nothing more than mere circuity of travel which is not compensable, citing Wolff v. City of Los Angeles, supra. The inapplicability of that case has heretofore been discussed. In any event, the phrase "circuity of travel" has varied meanings and is frequently misused by the courts.

There is more than merely a diversion of traffic when a cul-de-sac is created. The ability to travel to and from the property to the general system of streets in one direction is lost. One might imagine many circumstances, as has been shown by defendants, in which recovery should not be permitted or where the reasons for recovery in the cul-de-sac cases might not be logically applied, but we are here concerned with the particular facts of this case and do not purport to declare the law for all cases under all circumstances.

* * *

The judgment is reversed, and the court below is directed to permit the plaintiff to amend his complaint if he be so advised in conformity with the views herein expressed.

GIBSON, C.J., and SHENK and SCHAUER, JJ., concurred.

EDMONDS, JUSTICE (concurring).

I concur in the conclusion that the judgment against the property owner should be reversed, but for reasons different from those stated by my associates. And as the decision vitally affects the public interest in that it may largely determine whether highway improvements essential for modern transportation can be made without incurring liability for damages beyond the capacity of the state or a municipality reasonably to pay, I deem it appropriate to state the grounds upon which I believe the determination should rest.

* * *

[A] distinction must be made between a diminution in value because of an act of a private individual and the decrease in value resulting from a public highway improvement. Obviously, the courts will be more ready to protect even the less important interests connected with the use of land against interference by private individuals whose acts have no public utility, than when the governmental power is exercised in behalf of a public improvement for the general welfare. Therefore, the fact that a particular interest has been protected against impairment by a private person does not necessarily mean that it is of sufficient importance, as against the state, to be included in the term "private property" within the meaning of the eminent domain clause of the Constitution. * * * The factors to be considered are, on the one hand, the magnitude of the damage to the owner of the land, and, on the other, the desirability and necessity for the particular type of improvement and the danger that the granting of compensation will tend to retard or prevent it. * * * In addition, before compensation may be denied, the court must find that the particular improvement be not unreasonably more drastic or injurious than necessary to achieve the public objective. * * * Thus, if, in balancing these factors, the court decides that the interest affected by the improvement which results in a diminution in the value of the land is of sufficient importance to require the payment of compensation under the eminent domain clause of the Constitution, it is not necessary to consider the improvement as a "damaging" of the land; since the interest is recognized as entitled to the protection of the law, it becomes a property right included in the term "private property" within the meaning of article I, section 14 of the State Constitution. In the event, however, that the interest is deemed of insufficient magnitude to warrant the payment of compensation under the eminent domain provision, it obviously is not "private property" within the scope of that clause, and the diminution in value of the land attributable to it, when affected by public improvement, falls within the area of uncompensated loss occasioned by the exercise of essential governmental power.

* * *

The question whether a property owner is entitled to compensation under the eminent domain clause of the California Constitution (art. I, sec. 14) when his property is placed in a cul-de-sac by the obstruction or vacation of one end of a street upon which the property abuts, but where the obstruction is not directly in front of the property, is one of first impression in California. Although an interference with the abutting owner's right of access in one direction only, but leaving a less convenient means of egress in another direction, has been held not to be a taking of private property within the prohibition of the due process clause of the Fourteenth Amendment to the federal Constitution (Meyer v. City of Richmond, 172 U.S. 82, 19 S.Ct. 106, 43 L.Ed. 374), a majority of the courts which have considered the right of a property owner to damages, under the eminent domain clause of the jurisdiction, for being placed in a cul-de-sac have allowed recovery to those in the block where the obstruction occurs, even though one entrance to the block is left open. * * * But by the great weight of authority, as a matter of law, no compensation may be obtained because of an obstruction to or the vacation of a street in another block, even though the value of the complainant's property is substantially reduced thereby, and this regardless of whether the particular state Constitution requires compensation solely for property "taken" or "taken or damaged."

* * *

But the traveling of additional distances occasioned by modern traffic engineering to make travel more safe and to adapt the highway system to the adequate disposal of the increasingly heavy burden of automobile traffic—as, for example, by the construction of divided highways for various types of traffic, or the re-routing of traffic by one-way regulations or the prohibition of left-hand turns—is an element of damage for which the property owner may not complain in the absence of arbitrary action. City of San Mateo v. Railroad Comm., 9 Cal.2d 1, 9, 10, 68 P.2d 713; see note 100 A.L.R. 487, 491–493. It is therefore not surprising that so many courts have refused compensation in cul-de-sac cases because of the similarity in problems so far as the question of circuity is concerned. And therefore, in testing the merits of the majority rule, mere "circuity of travel," in the sense that it refers to the additional distance required to be traversed because of a proper highway construction, should not be used to justify the allowance of compensation to the owner abutting upon the street in the block where the obstruction exists.

There is a material difference, however, between the situation of the property owner in the block where one end of the street is obstructed and that of the persons whose lots abut on the same street beyond the first intersection. Whereas formerly he had an outlet at both ends of the street on which his lot fronts, after the obstruction, he has but one. This is obviously not true of the landowners beyond the first intersection, for they still have access in either direction.

But, it may be asked, of what practical significance is this distinction, so far as damage to the property owner is concerned? If, for example, the land is used for business or industrial purposes, the fact that it is in a block where the street terminates may seriously affect the easement of access, in considering the full and beneficial use of the property. All vehicles entering the block must either turn around or back out in order to leave it, to this extent impairing the right of egress. In the case of trucks or other large vehicles, such a requirement may substantially interfere with the highest and best use of the property. See Cartmell v. City of Maysville, 231 Ky. 666, 22 S.W.2d 102, 104. And the owner of a lot so located is more adversely affected than is one whose property abuts upon a street restricted to one-way traffic, for in the latter case free ingress and egress is possible.

* * *

TRAYNOR, JUSTICE (dissenting).

I dissent.

The majority opinion declares that the allowance of recovery to the owner in this case "depends largely upon the character and extent of his property right." It seeks such a right in the right of ingress and egress which, it declares, "being by its terms general in nature requires definition and clarification as to its extent and character." What follows is a definition amplifying that right to make it a basis for recovery in the present case in terms of the invasion of property rights. As there is no invasion of traditional rights, a new right is created by the simple process of redefinition. The frontiers of the right of ingress and egress are thus freely advanced to make the very recovery in question a foregone conclusion.

* * *

Whether the majority opinion allows recovery on the ground that there has been an impairment of a property right inhering in the right of ingress and egress or on the ground that such a right should now be judicially created, I cannot subscribe to it.

The basic question in this appeal is whether the property that plaintiff alleged was taken or damaged existed at all. If the abutting owner has an easement in the street longitudinally to the next intersection in each direction, compensation must be paid for the impairment of that easement. If he does not have such an easement he can have no recovery even though the value of the abutting property may be diminished as a result of the improvement. * * *

There is nothing in the history of the right of ingress and egress to indicate that it embraces any such easement. The right of ingress and egress is a creation of judicial decision. * * *

The trust that arises from the appropriation of land for public thoroughfares is for the benefit of the public at large and only incidentally for the benefit of abutting owners. The extension of the abutting owner's rights in the present case makes the primary consideration the benefit of abutting owners rather than the benefit of the public. Hitherto no California case has ever defined the right of ingress or egress as inclusive of an easement to the next intersecting street. The rule has been that the right of ingress and egress is limited to adequate and reasonable access to the property from the street, that it does not extend to the full width of the street, or to the full length thereof, or even to all points upon the street in front of the abutting property. It is sufficient if there is access to a street that in turn connects with the general street system. Any improvement that does not materially interfere with such access does no compensable damage. The California Vehicle Code, St.1935 p. 93, and city traffic ordinances abound with regulations that limit a property owner's freedom of movement upon the street on which his property abuts. Thus "U" turns or the making of left turns upon emerging from a building or private driveway are frequently prohibited, and the diversion of traffic into one-way streets is common. Frequently traffic moving in opposite directions is separated by some physical barrier such as a raised curbing. These restrictions have the same effect whether they ensue from traffic regulations or physical obstructions and there is no more reason to allow compensation because of the resulting diminution in property values or the inconvenience of circuity of travel in the one case than in the other.

The newly created property right in this case is inconsistent not only with the trust from which the right of ingress and egress is derived, but with the established rule in this state and others that street improvements give rise to no compensable damage if there is no injury to the abutting owner different in kind from that suffered by other property owners and the general public. This rule is repudiated in the majority opinion: "If he has a property right and it has been impaired, the damage is necessarily peculiar to himself and is different in kind than that suffered by him as a member of the public generally for his particular right as a property owner and not as a member of the public has been damaged." This statement draws its conclusion from an assumption of the very thing to be proved. The question is whether or not the owner has a property right that has been impaired, and it cannot be assumed that he has without drawing a line between his property and all the other property in the community. When the majority opinion draws the line at the next intersection it arbitrarily attaches a right to abutting property in one block on the street, but not to abutting property on the same street in the next block or to property abutting on neighboring streets even though they may likewise be diminished in value as a result of the improvement and the owners may be similarly inconvenienced by circuity of travel. Recovery therefore depends upon the accident of location.

* * *

Under the majority opinion new private property rights representing millions of dollars have been carved out of public streets and highways, at the expense not alone of the public treasury but of the public safety. Of recent years the growth of traffic has necessitated the construction of highways with fewer intersecting streets to expedite the flow of traffic and reduce the rate of motor vehicle accidents. Such highways have been constructed through the City of San Rafael, and the Arroyo Seco Parkway from Los Angeles to Pasadena, and the construction of many more is contemplated. In such cases it will be necessary either to close the cross streets or to carry them under or over the freeway, both costly projects. The plans contemplate overhead or subway crossings every few blocks over the freeway, necessarily creating cul-de-sacs of the remaining streets. Similar improvements are involved in the separation of grades of railroads and highways, for it is usually necessary to make a dead end of one or more streets as a highway is raised or lowered to cross the railroad tracks. In the present case the cul-de-sac on Sterling Street was an integral part of the rearrangement of the streets of the City of San Francisco made necessary by the construction of the San Francisco–Oakland Bay Bridge.

The cost of making such improvements may be prohibitive now that new rights are created for owners of property abutting on streets that would be at right angles to the improvements, for these rights must be condemned or ways constructed over or under the improvements. The construction of improvements is bound to be discouraged by the multitude of claims that would arise, the costs of negotiation with claimants or of litigation, and the amounts that claimants might recover. Such claims could only be met by public revenues that would otherwise be expended on the further development and improvement of streets and highways.

It must be remembered that the question is not whether existing easements should be taken without compensation, but whether private rights should be created for an arbitrarily chosen group of private persons, necessitating tribute from the public if it exercises public rights of long standing in the interest of safe and expeditious travel on public thoroughfares.

Notes

1. The principal case, coming at the dawn of the post-war explosion of modern, high-volume traffic development, clearly presents the policy issue of public improvements versus private property rights. Do you think the dire predictions in Justice Traynor's dissent have come to pass? See Perrin v. Los Angeles County Transportation Comm'n, 42 Cal.App.4th 1807, 50 Cal. Rptr.2d 488 (1996). If not, how were the myriad of easements in street access dealt with? Can you see a "bright line" distinction between diminution in value of property due to diminished access and mere annoyance because of circuity of travel? See, e.g., Matter of County of Rockland (Kohl Industrial Park Co.), 147 A.D.2d 478, 537 N.Y.S.2d 309 (1989); County of Anoka v. Esmailzadeh, 498 N.W.2d 58 (Minn.App.1993). Also see James P. Flannery, Jr., The Property Owner's Right of Access to Abutting Roadways, 79 Ill. Bar J. 148 (1991); Annotation, Abutting Owner's Right to Damages for Limitation of Access Caused by Traffic Regulation, 15 A.L.R.5th 821.

What about diminution in property value due to the construction of a highway improvement that substantially increases the noise levels on the property? In Felts v. Harris County, 915 S.W.2d 482 (Tex.1996) the court held that landowners were not entitled to compensation for increased noise on the theory that the impact of increased noise is community damage, not individual damage. Similarly, the rebuilding of two highways by the state that resulted in less visibility and traffic for plaintiff's shopping center did not result in a taking in Forty Mill Realty Venture v. State ex rel. Missouri Hwy. & Transportation Dept., 872 S.W.2d 528 (1994). The court held that the owners had no property right in existing traffic passing by the shopping center or in public access to or visibility of the property.

2. In Garrett v. City of Topeka, 259 Kan. 896, 916 P.2d 21 (1996), the court held that a reduction in direct commercial access to plaintiff's property (although residential access was not diminished) constituted a regulatory taking. The city had contemplated a commercial ring road in the neighborhood but later abandoned the concept after constructing a portion that provided access to plaintiff's property in a circuitous manner. Regulatory taking damages of $190,000 was affirmed. There were two dissenting judges, and the dissenting opinion charged that the majority was confusing access cases with regulatory taking cases. Also see State ex rel. OTR v. City of Columbus, 76 Ohio St.3d 203, 667 N.E.2d 8 (1996)

3. The problem of diminution of access to the landowner's property can have many dimensions. In Bydlon v. United States, 146 Ct.Cl. 764, 175 F.Supp. 891 (1959), the issue was whether an Executive Order barring air travel lower than 4,000 feet over the Superior National Forest wilderness areas was a taking of access in respect to owners of lodges and fishing camps within the forest. Another, perhaps more common, problem involves the conversion of streets in downtown areas of cities into pedestrian malls. Does termination of vehicular access constitute a taking? See City of Orlando v. Cullom, 400 So.2d 513 (Fla.App.1981). Other modern restrictions of access involve erection of medians on busy streets which limit the ability of vehicles to make left turns onto commercial properties, e.g., Division of Administration v. Capital Plaza, 397 So.2d 682 (Fla.1981); elimination of parking on certain streets, e.g., City of Phoenix v. Wade, 5 Ariz.App. 505, 428 P.2d 450 (1967); prohibition of heavy vehicles on certain streets, e.g., House v. City of Texarkana, 225 Ark. 162, 279 S.W.2d 831 (1955).

4. Recognizing that property owners adjacent to a street may have an easement in access is one side of a coin; the other side is the situation where owners of private property are required to allow access to members of the public. In Liberty v. California Coastal Commission, 113 Cal.App.3d 491, 170 Cal.Rptr. 247 (1980), the court held that conditioning a permit for construction of a restaurant in the coastal zone on the owner providing a parking lot which would have to be opened to the public until 5:00 p.m. daily (while the restaurant would be closed) was a disguised taking of private property. Also consider the implications of the following case.

KAISER AETNA v. UNITED STATES
Supreme Court of the United States, 1979.
444 U.S. 164, 100 S.Ct. 383, 62 L.Ed.2d 332.

MR. JUSTICE REHNQUIST delivered the opinion of the Court.

The Hawaii Kai Marina was developed by the dredging and filling of Kuapa Pond, which was a shallow lagoon separated from Maunalua Bay and the Pacific Ocean by a barrier beach. Although under Hawaii law Kuapa Pond was private property, the Court of Appeals for the Ninth Circuit held that when petitioners converted the pond into a marina and thereby connected it to the bay, it became subject to the "navigational servitude" of the Federal Government. Thus, the public acquired a right of access to what was once petitioners' private pond. * * *

The Government contends that petitioners may not exclude members of the public from the Hawaii Kai Marina because "[t]he public enjoys a federally protected right of navigation over the navigable waters of the United States." Brief for United States 13. It claims the issue in dispute is whether Kuapa Pond is presently a "navigable water of the United States." *Ibid.* When petitioners dredged and improved Kuapa Pond, the Government continues, the pond—although it may once have qualified as fast land—became navigable water of the United States. The public thereby acquired a right to use Kuapa Pond as a continuous highway for navigation, and the Corps of Engineers may consequently obtain an injunction to prevent petitioners from attempting to reserve the waterway to themselves.

* * *

Here, the Government's attempt to create a public right of access to the improved pond goes so far beyond ordinary regulation or improvement for navigation as to amount to a taking under the logic of *Pennsylvania Coal Co. v. Mahon,* 260 U.S. 393, 43 S.Ct. 158, 67 L.Ed. 322 (1922). More than one factor contributes to this result. It is clear that prior to its improvement, Kuapa Pond was incapable of being used as a continuous highway for the purpose of navigation in interstate commerce. Its maximum depth at high tide was a mere two feet, it was separated from the adjacent bay and ocean by a natural barrier beach, and its principal commercial value was limited to fishing. It consequently is not the sort of "great navigable stream" that this Court has previously recognized as being "[incapable] of private ownership." See, *e.g., United States v. Chandler–Dunbar Co.,* 229 U.S., at 69, 33 S.Ct., at 674; *United States v. Twin City Power Co., supra,* at 228, 76 S.Ct., at 262. And, as previously noted, Kuapa Pond has always been considered to be private property under Hawaiian law. Thus, the interest of petitioners in the now dredged marina is strikingly similar to that of owners of fast land adjacent to navigable water.

We have not the slightest doubt that the Government could have refused to allow such dredging on the ground that it would have impaired navigation in the bay, or could have conditioned its approval of the dredging on petitioners' agreement to comply with various measures that it deemed appropriate for the promotion of navigation. But what petitioners now have is a body of water that was private property under Hawaiian law, linked to navigable water by a channel dredged by them with the consent of the Government. While the consent of individual officials representing the United States cannot "estop" the United States, see *Montana v. Kennedy,* 366 U.S. 308, 314–315, 81 S.Ct. 1336,

1340–1341, 6 L.Ed.2d 313 (1961); *INS v. Hibi,* 414 U.S. 5, 94 S.Ct. 19, 38 L.Ed.2d 7 (1973), it can lead to the fruition of a number of expectancies embodied in the concept of "property"—expectancies that, if sufficiently important, the Government must condemn and pay for before it takes over the management of the landowner's property. In this case, we hold that the "right to exclude," so universally held to be a fundamental element of the property right, falls within this category of interests that the Government cannot take without compensation. This is not a case in which the Government is exercising its regulatory power in a manner that will cause an insubstantial devaluation of petitioners' private property; rather, the imposition of the navigational servitude in this context will result in an actual physical invasion of the privately owned marina. Compare *Andrus v. Allard,* 444 U.S. 51 at 65–66, 100 S.Ct. 318, at 326–327, 62 L.Ed.2d 210, with the traditional taking of fee interests in *United States ex rel. TVA v. Powelson,* 319 U.S. 266, 63 S.Ct. 1047, 87 L.Ed. 1390 (1943), and in *United States v. Miller,* 317 U.S. 369, 63 S.Ct. 276, 87 L.Ed. 336 (1943). And even if the Government physically invades only an easement in property, it must nonetheless pay just compensation. See *United States v. Causby,* 328 U.S. 256, 265, 66 S.Ct. 1062, 1067, 90 L.Ed. 1206 (1946); *Portsmouth Co. v. United States,* 260 U.S. 327, 43 S.Ct. 135, 67 L.Ed. 287 (1922). Thus, if the Government wishes to make what was formerly Kuapa Pond into a public aquatic park after petitioners have proceeded as far as they have here, it may not, without invoking its eminent domain power and paying just compensation, require them to allow free access to the dredged pond while petitioners' agreement with their customers calls for an annual $72 regular fee.

Accordingly the judgment of the Court of Appeals is

Reversed.

Mr. Justice Blackmun, with whom Mr. Justice Brennan and Mr. Justice Marshall join, dissenting.

* * *

Ordinarily, "[w]hen the Government exercises [the navigational] servitude, it is exercising its paramount power in the interest of navigation, rather than taking the private property of anyone." *United States v. Kansas City Ins. Co.,* 339 U.S. 799, 808, 70 S.Ct. 885, 890, 94 L.Ed. 1277 (1950). See also *United States v. Willow River Co.,* 324 U.S. 499, 509–510, 65 S.Ct. 761, 767, 89 L.Ed. 1101 (1945); *Lewis Blue Point Oyster Co. v. Briggs,* 229 U.S. 82, 87–88, 33 S.Ct. 679, 680–681, 57 L.Ed. 1083 (1913); *Gibson v. United States,* 166 U.S. 269, 276, 17 S.Ct. 578, 580, 41 L.Ed. 996 (1897). The Court's prior cases usually have involved riparian owners along navigable rivers who claim losses resulting from the raising or lowering of water levels in the navigable stream, or from the construction of artificial aids to navigation, such as dams or locks. In these cases the Court has held that no compensation is required for loss in water power due to impairment of the navigable water's flow, *e.g., United States v. Twin City Power Co.,* 350 U.S., at 226–227, 76 S.Ct., at 261–262; *United States v. Chandler–Dunbar Co.,* 229 U.S., at 65–66, 33 S.Ct., at 672–673; for loss in "head" resulting from raising the stream, *United States v. Willow River Co.,* 324 U.S., at 507–511, 65 S.Ct., at 766–768; for damage to structures erected between low-and high-water marks, *United States v. Chicago, M., St. P. & P.R. Co.,* 312 U.S. 592, 595–597, 61 S.Ct. 772, 774–776, 85 L.Ed. 1064 (1941); for loss of access to navigable water caused by necessary improvements, *United States v. Commodore Park, Inc.,* 324 U.S. 386, 390–391, 65 S.Ct. 803, 805–806, 89 L.Ed. 1017 (1945); *Scranton v. Wheeler,* 179 U.S., at 163, 21 S.Ct., at 57; or for loss of value to adjoining land based on potential use in navigational commerce, *United States v. Rands,* 389 U.S. 121, 124–125, 88 S.Ct. 265, 267–268, 19 L.Ed.2d 329 (1967). The Court also has held that no compensation is required when "obstructions," such as bridges or wharves, are removed or altered to improve navigation, despite their obvious commercial value to those who erected them, and despite the Federal Government's original willingness to have them built. See, *e.g., Greenleaf Lumber Co. v. Garrison,* 237 U.S. 251, 256, 258–264, 35 S.Ct. 551, 552, 553–556, 59 L.Ed. 939 (1915); *Union Bridge Co. v. United States,* 204 U.S. 364, 400, 27 S.Ct. 367, 380, 51 L.Ed. 523 (1907).

These cases establish a key principle that points the way for decision in the present context. In most of them, the noncompensable loss was related, either directly or indirectly, to the riparian owner's "access to, and use of, navigable waters." *United States v. Rands,* 389 U.S., at 124–125, 88 S.Ct., at 268. However that access or use may have been turned to account for personal gain, and no matter how much the riparian owner had invested to enhance the value, the Court held that these rights were shared with the public at large. Actions taken to improve their value for the many caused no reimbursable damage to the few who, by the accident of owning contiguous "fast land," previously enjoyed the blessings of the common right in greater measure. See, *e.g., United States v. Commodore Park, Inc.,* 324 U.S., at 390–391, 88 S.Ct., at 805–806. The Court recognized that encroachment on rights inhering separately in the adjoining "fast land," *United States v. Virginia Electric Co.,* 365 U.S. 624, 628, 81 S.Ct. 784, 788, 5 L.Ed.2d 838 (1961), or resulting from access to *nonnavigable* tributaries, see *United States v. Cress,* 243 U.S. 316, 37 S.Ct. 380, 61 L.Ed. 746 (1917), might form the basis for a valid compensation claim. But the principal distinction was that these compensable values had nothing to do with use of the navigable water.

Application of this principle to the present case should lead to the conclusion that the developers of Kuapa Pond have acted at their own risk and are not entitled to compensation for the public access the Government now asserts.

Note

Also see GTE Northwest, Inc. v. Public Utility Comm'n of Oregon, 321 Or. 458, 900 P.2d 495 (1995). In this case the state PUC created a regulatory framework for telecommunications, known as the Open Network Architecture. One feature of the regulations was a requirement that local exchange carriers under some circumstances allow enhanced service providers to place some equipment on the local exchange property. In particular, this dispute arose because GTE the local telephone carrier was concerned that a rival, MCI, would be able to place equipment on GTE property. The court held that such a regulation amounted to a taking and that PUC did not have eminent domain power in its enabling legislation. Therefore the challenged regulation was invalid.

B. THE PHYSICAL LIMITS OF PROPERTY

UNITED STATES v. CAUSBY

Supreme Court of the United States, 1946.
328 U.S. 256, 66 S.Ct. 1062, 90 L.Ed. 1206.

Mr. Justice Douglas delivered the opinion of the Court.

This is a case of first impression. The problem presented is whether respondents' property was taken within the meaning of the Fifth Amendment by frequent and regular flights of army and navy aircraft over respondents' land at low altitudes. The Court of Claims held that there was a taking and entered judgment for respondent, one judge dissenting. 60 F.Supp. 751. The case is here on a petition for a writ of certiorari which we granted because of the importance of the question presented. * * *

Various aircraft of the United States use this airport—bombers, transports and fighters. The direction of the prevailing wind determines when a particular runway is used. The north-west-southeast runway in question is used about four per cent of the time in taking off and about seven per cent of the time in landing. Since the United States began operations in May, 1942, its four-motored heavy bombers, other planes of the heavier type, and its fighter planes have frequently passed over respondents' land and buildings in considerable numbers and rather close together. They come close enough at times to appear barely to miss the tops of the trees and at times so close to the tops of the trees as to blow the old leaves off. The noise is startling. And at night the glare from the planes brightly lights up the place. As a result of the noise, respondents had to give up their chicken business. As many as six to ten of their chickens were killed in one day by flying into the walls from fright. The total chickens lost in that manner was about 150. Production also fell off. The result was the destruction of the use of the property as a commercial chicken farm. Respondents are frequently deprived of their sleep and the family has become nervous and frightened. Although there have been no airplane accidents on respondents' property, there have been several accidents near the airport and close to respondents' place. These are the essential facts found by the Court of Claims. On the basis of these facts, it found that respondents' property had depreciated in value. It held that the United States had taken an easement over the property on June 1, 1942, and that the value of the property destroyed and the easement taken was $2,000.

* * *

The United States concludes that when flights are made within the navigable airspace without any physical invasion of the property of the landowners, there has been no taking of property. It says that at most there was merely incidental damage occurring as a consequence of authorized air navigation. It also argues that the landowner does not own superadjacent airspace which he has not subjected to possession by the erection of structures or other occupancy. Moreover, it is argued that even if the United States took airspace owned by respondents, no compensable damage was shown. Any damages are said to be merely consequential for which no compensation may be obtained under the Fifth Amendment.

It is ancient doctrine that at common law ownership of the land extended to the periphery of the universe—*Cujus est solum ejus est usque ad coelum.* But that doctrine has no place in the modern world. The air is a public highway, as Congress has declared. Were that not true, every transcontinental flight would subject the operator to countless trespass suits. Common sense revolts at the idea. To recognize such private claims to the airspace would clog these highways, seriously interfere with their control and development in the public interest, and transfer into private ownership that to which only the public has a just claim.

But that general principle does not control the present case. For the United States conceded on oral argument that if the flights over respondents' property rendered it uninhabitable, there would be a taking compensable under the Fifth Amendment. It is the owner's loss, not the taker's gain, which is the measure of the value of the property taken. United States v. Miller, 317 U.S. 369, 63 S.Ct. 276, 87 L.Ed. 336, 147 A.L.R. 55. Market value fairly determined is the normal measure of the recovery. Id. And that value may reflect the use of which the land could readily be converted, as well as the existing use. United States v. Powelson, 319 U.S. 266, 275, 63 S.Ct. 1047, 1053, 87 L.Ed. 1390, and cases cited. If, by reason of the frequency and altitude of the flights, respondents could not use this land for any purpose, their loss would be complete. It would be as complete as if the United States had entered upon the surface of the land and taken exclusive possession of it.

* * *

We have said that the airspace is a public highway. Yet it is obvious that if the landowner is to have full enjoyment of the land, he must have exclusive control of the immediate reaches of the enveloping atmosphere. Otherwise buildings could not be erected, trees could not be planted, and even fences could not be run. The principle is recognized when the law gives a remedy in case overhanging structures are erected on adjoining land. The landowner owns at least as much of the space above the ground as he can occupy or use in connection with the land. The fact that he does not occupy it in a physical sense—by the erection of buildings and the like—is not material. As we have said, the flight of airplanes, which skim the surface but do not touch it, is as much an appropriation of the use of the land as a more conventional entry upon it. We would not doubt that if the United States erected an elevated railway over respondents' land at the precise altitude where its planes now fly, there would be a partial taking, even though none of the supports of the structure rested on the land. The reason is that there would be an intrusion so immediate and direct as to subtract from the owner's full enjoyment of the property and to limit his exploitation of it. While the owner does not in any physical manner occupy that stratum of airspace or make use of it in the conventional sense, he does use it in somewhat the same sense that space left between buildings for the purpose of light and air is used. The superadjacent airspace at this low altitude is so close to the land that continuous invasions of it affect the use of the surface of the land itself. We think that the landowner, as an incident to his ownership, has a claim to it and that invasions of it are in the same category as invasions of the surface.

* * *

The airplane is part of the modern environment of life, and the inconveniences which it causes are normally not compensable under the Fifth Amendment. The airspace, apart from the immediate reaches above the land, is part of the public domain. We need not determine at this time what those precise limits are. Flights over private land are not a taking, unless they are so low and so frequent as to be a direct and immediate interference with the enjoyment and use of the land. We need not speculate on that phase of the present case. For the findings of the Court of Claims plainly establish that there was a diminution in value of the property and that the frequent, low-level flights were the direct and immediate cause. We agree with the Court of Claims that a servitude has been imposed upon the land.

* * *

Since on this record it is not clear whether the easement taken is a permanent or a temporary one, it would be premature for us to consider whether the amount of the award made by the Court of Claims was proper.

The judgment is reversed and the cause is remanded to the Court of Claims so that it may make the necessary findings in conformity with this opinion.

Reversed.

MR. JUSTICE JACKSON took no part in the consideration or decision of this case.

MR. JUSTICE BLACK, dissenting.

[Dissenting opinion omitted.]

Notes

1. Also see Griggs v. County of Allegheny, Pennsylvania, 369 U.S. 84, 82 S.Ct. 531, 7 L.Ed.2d 585 (1962). Compare Batten v. United States, 306

F.2d 580 (10th Cir.1962) where the court held that in the absence of a physical intrusion into the landowners' airspace by flights, no taking could be shown where the property (next to an air base) was damaged by the noise, smoke and vibrations of jet engines. Also see Eyherabide v. United States, 345 F.2d 565 (Ct.Cl.1965), where the court found a taking in an unusual factual setting—the landowner's sheep ranch was surrounded on three sides by a gunnery range and shells were constantly whizzing through his airspace.

For a case in which the landowner successfully brought an inverse condemnation case upon allegations that noise, vibrations, and pollution from a new airport runway extension took his property, even though no overflights occurred, see Jackson v. Metropolitan Knoxville Airport Authority, 922 S.W.2d 860 (Tenn.1996). See, generally, annotations in 79 A.L.R.3d 253 (overflights as nuisances) and 22 A.L.R.4th 863 (overflights as takings). In Fitzgarrald v. City of Iowa City, 492 N.W.2d 659 (Iowa 1992) the court held that a landowner in the path of a runway extension did not suffer a regulatory taking because he still had a range of viable economic uses remaining after the adoption of a "Clear Overlay Zone" regulating uses near the runway project.

2. In Brown v. United States, 73 F.3d 1100 (Fed.Cir.1996) the owners of a recreational cattle ranch in Texas sought compensation for a physical taking due to low and frequent overflights from a nearby Air Force base. The trial court dismissed the action on the ground that although Brown met part of the Causby test—direct overflights, and frequent, low flights—the third element—interference with use and enjoyment of the property—was not shown. The government successfully argued in the trial court that unlike Causby's chickens, Brown's cows were not disturbed by the noise of the planes. The court of appeals reversed and remanded for a new trial:

> Under the Government's view, the Government would be able to make uncompensated use of private property if that use did not immediately interfere with the landowner's current use. Thus, overflights could not give rise to compensable takings on land held for investment purposes or for future development. The Government effectively could preclude future, lawful uses of the property—uses which have been recognized and valued by the market before the overflights—without compensation to the owner, simply by making such uses undesirable or unprofitable. The Fifth Amendment does not permit the Government to destroy individual rights in that manner.

CONSOLIDATED ROCK PRODUCTS CO. v. CITY OF LOS ANGELES

Supreme Court of California, 1962.
57 Cal.2d 515, 20 Cal.Rptr. 638, 370 P.2d 342, appeal dismissed
371 U.S. 36, 83 S.Ct. 145, 9 L.Ed.2d 112 (1962).

[Plaintiff's land was found by the lower court to have no appreciable economic value for any purpose other than excavation of rock, sand and gravel. Nevertheless, denial of an excavation permit under a zoning ordinance which restricted the land to agricultural and residential uses was upheld. There are nearby communities which are havens for those suffering from respiratory ailments. Only a very short part of a long opinion is presented here.]

DOOLING, JUSTICE. * * *

Too many cases have been decided upholding the constitutionality of comprehensive zoning ordinances prohibiting the removal of natural products from lands in certain zones for us now to accept at full value the suggestion that there is such an inherent difference in natural products of the property that in a case where reasonable minds may differ as to the necessity of such prohibition the same power to prohibit the extraction of natural products does not inhere in the legislative body as it has to prohibit uses of other sorts. Friel v. County of Los Angeles, 172 Cal.App.2d 142, 342 P.2d 374 [oil and gas]; In re Angelus, supra, 65 Cal.App.2d 441, 150 P.2d 908 [sand and gravel]; Marblehead Land Co. v. City of Los Angeles, supra, 9 Cir., 47 F.2d 528, certiorari denied 284 U.S. 634, 52 S.Ct. 18, 76 L.Ed. 540 [oil and gas]; West Bros. Brick Co. v. City of Alexandria, supra, 169 Va. 271, 192 S.E. 881, appeal dismissed 302 U.S. 658, 58 S.Ct. 369, 82 L.Ed. 508 [brick clay]; County Commissioners of Howard County v. Merryman, 222 Md. 314, 159 A.2d 854 [sand and gravel]; Township of Bloomfield v. Beardslee, 349 Mich. 296, 84 N.W.2d 537 [gravel]; Moore v. Memphis Stone & Gravel Co., 47 Tenn.App. 461, 339 S.W.2d 29 [gravel]; Raimondo v. Board of Appeals of Bedford, 331 Mass. 228, 118 N.E.2d 67 [sand and gravel]; Town of Seekonk v. John J. McHale & Sons, 325 Mass. 271, 90 N.E.2d 325 [gravel]; Fred v. Mayor and Council of Borough of Old Tappan, 10 N.J. 515, 92 A.2d 473 [topsoil]; Town of Burlington v. Dunn, supra, 318 Mass. 216, 61 N.E.2d 243, 168 A.L.R. 1181, certiorari denied 326 U.S. 739, 66 S.Ct. 51, 90 L.Ed. 441 [topsoil]; Miesz v. Village of Mayfield Heights, 92 Ohio App. 471, 111 N.E.2d 20 [topsoil]; People v. Gerus, 19 Misc.2d 389, 69 N.Y.S.2d 283 [sand and gravel]; Krantz v. Town of Amherst, 192 Misc. 912, 80 N.Y.S.2d 812 [topsoil]; K. & L. Oil Co. v. Oklahoma City, D.C.Okl., 14 F.Supp. 492 [oil]; and see Beverly Oil Co. v. Los Angeles, 40 Cal.2d 552, 254 P.2d 865; Pacific Palisades Ass'n v. City of Huntington Beach, 196 Cal. 211, 237 P. 538, 40 A.L.R. 782.

Plaintiffs rely heavily upon the finding of the trial court "that the subject property has no appreciable economic value for any of the uses permitted in the A1, A2 or RA zones, or for any other use except for the purpose of excavating, crushing and processing rock, sand and gravel and activities related or incidental thereto, and if such use is prohibited, it will destroy the economic value thereof." There was testimony before the legislative body that the property could be successfully devoted to certain other uses, i.e., for stabling horses, cattle feeding and grazing, chicken raising, dog kennels, fish hatcheries, golf courses, certain types of horticulture, and recreation. It must be conceded that in relation to its value for the extraction of rock, sand and gravel the value of the property for any of the described uses is relatively small if not minimal, and that as to a considerable part of it seasonal flooding might prevent its continuous use for any purpose. "However, the very essence of the police power as differentiated from the power of eminent domain is that the deprivation of individual rights and property cannot prevent its operation, once it is shown that its exercise is proper and that the method of its exercise is reasonably within the meaning of due process of law. * * * And it is recognized that oil production is a business which must operate, if at all, where the resources are found. Nevertheless city zoning ordinances prohibiting the production of oil in designated areas have been held valid." Beverly Oil Co. v. City of Los Angeles, supra, 40 Cal.2d 552, 557–558, 254 P.2d 865, 867.

In Beverly at page 557, 254 P.2d at page 867 this court quoted from Hadacheck v. Sebastian, 239 U.S. 394, 410, 36 S.Ct. 143, 60 L.Ed. 348: "It is to be remembered that we are dealing with one of the most essential powers of the government—one that is the least limitable. It may, indeed, seem harsh in its exercise, usually is on some individual but the imperative necessity for its existence precludes any limitation upon it when not exerted arbitrarily. A vested interest cannot be asserted against it because of conditions once obtaining. [Citation.] To so hold would preclude development and fix a city forever in its primitive conditions. There must be progress, and if in its march private interests are in the way, they must yield to the good of the community."

More than one court has pointed out, as was done by Judge Wilbur, in the passage quoted above from the Marblehead Land Co. case, 47 F.2d at page 532, that "there does not seem to be any distinction in principle between depriving an owner of the right to develop such inherent qualities of the land and a regulation which prohibits an owner from erecting upon his land structures which he believes will, and which in fact will, enhance the value of the property."

In Town of Seekonk v. John J. McHale & Sons, supra, 90 N.E.2d at page 327, the Supreme Judicial Court of Massachusetts put it this way: "The appealing defendant further contends that the zoning bylaw is unconstitutional if it prevents the owner from removing a natural product from his land. But all zoning restricts an owner in the uses he could otherwise make of his property. There seems to us to be no difference in principle whether the restriction takes the form of preventing the owner from building a factory or from establishing a gravel business."

The Supreme Court of Michigan in Township of Bloomfield v. Beardslee, supra, 84 N.W.2d at page 540, said:

"It is urged to us that the ordinance prohibits the removal of a natural resource. This, the owner insists is invalid. 'There exists', we are told, 'a legal right to exploit natural resources where they may be found.' * * * that the 'extraction of natural resources * * * must be undertaken at that spot or not at all.'

"Attractive though the argument may seem upon its first reading, it must be obvious that a logical application of its principle would be destructive of all zoning. For in each case the particular parcel has, it is always asserted, some peculiar utility: it is an ideal spot for a motel, or a factory, or a junk yard, or what not. It has that contiguity to traffic, that peculiar topographical structure, that supply of water or shade, which makes it unique. Yet, just as the surface user desired by the owner must give way, at times, to the public good, so must the sub-surface exploitation."

Finally on this point we quote from the West Bros. Brick Co. case, supra, 192 S.E. at page 890: "The enactment of zoning ordinances and cases which test them are all within the recollection of most of us. General rules applicable thereto are now well settled. They must not be wholly unreasonable, but they are presumed to be valid and to have been promulgated by those familiar with local conditions. Vested interests will not defeat them, and of course constitutional rights are not to be measured in terms of money. That, however, is a consideration to be remembered. Great financial losses should not be inflicted where benefits to others are negligible, but public welfare and public convenience do control and are in themselves terms constantly adjusted to meet new conditions. Upon those who would set aside such ordinances rests a heavy burden of proof. They stand when their validity is debatable."

It is our conclusion that, having found on substantial evidence that the necessity and propriety of the legislative action in this case is one upon which reasonable minds may differ, the trial court properly found in favor of the ordinance's constitutionality. * * *

SECTION 4. WHAT IS PUBLIC USE OR PUBLIC PURPOSE?

BERMAN v. PARKER

Supreme Court of the United States, 1954.
348 U.S. 26, 75 S.Ct. 98, 99 L.Ed. 27.

MR. JUSTICE DOUGLAS delivered the opinion of the Court.

This is an appeal, 28 U.S.C.A. sec. 1253, 28 U.S.C.A. sec. 1253, from the judgment of a three-judge District Court which dismissed a complaint seeking to enjoin the condemnation of appellants' property under the District of Columbia Redevelopment Act of 1945, 60 Stat. 790, D.C.Code 1951, §§ 5–701 to 5–719. The challenge was to the constitutionality of the Act, particularly as applied to the taking of appellants' property. The District Court sustained the constitutionality of the Act. 117 F.Supp. 705.

By § 2 of the Act Congress made a "legislative determination" that "owing to technological and sociological changes, obsolete layout, and other factors, conditions existing in the District of Columbia with respect to substandard housing and blighted areas, including the use of buildings in alleys as dwellings for human habitation, are injurious to the public health, safety, morals, and welfare, and it is hereby declared to be the policy of the United States to protect and promote the welfare of the inhabitants of the seat of the Government by eliminating all such injurious conditions by employing all means necessary and appropriate for the purpose."[8]

Section 2 goes on to declare that acquisition of property is necessary to eliminate these housing conditions.

Congress further finds in § 2 that these ends cannot be attained "by the ordinary operations of private enterprise alone without public participation"; that "the sound replanning and redevelopment of an obsolescent or obsolescing portion" of the District "cannot be accomplished unless it be done in the light of comprehensive and coordinated planning of the whole of the territory of the District of Columbia and its environs"; and that "the acquisition and the assembly of real property and the leasing or sale thereof for redevelopment pursuant to a project area redevelopment plan * * * is hereby declared to be a public use."

Section 4 creates the District of Columbia Redevelopment Land Agency (hereinafter called the Agency), composed of five members, which is granted power by § 5(a) to acquire and assemble by eminent domain and otherwise real property for "the redevelopment of blighted territory in the District of Columbia and the prevention, reduction, or elimination of blighting factors or causes of blight."

Section 6(a) of the Act directs the National Capital Planning Commission (hereinafter called the Planning Commission) to make and develop "a comprehensive or general plan" of the District, including "a land-use plan" which designates land for use for "housing, business, industry, recreation, education, public buildings, public reservations, and other general categories of public and private uses of the land." Section 6(b) authorizes the Planning Commission to adopt redevelopment plans for specific project areas. These plans are subject to the approval of the District Commissioners after a public hearing; and they prescribe the various public and private land uses for the respective areas, the "standards of population density and building intensity", and "the amount or character or class of any low-rent housing." § 6(b).

Once the Planning Commission adopts a plan and that plan is approved by the Commissioners, the Planning Commission certifies it to the Agency. § 6(d). At that point, the Agency is authorized to acquire and assemble the real property in the area. Id.

After the real estate has been assembled, the Agency is authorized to transfer to public agencies the land to be devoted to such public purposes as streets, utilities, recreational facilities, and schools, § 7(a) and to lease or sell the remainder as an entirety or in parts to a redevelopment company, individual, or partnership. § 7(b), (f). The leases or sales must provide that the lessees or purchasers will carry out

---

8. The Act does not define either "slums" or "blighted areas." Section 3(r), however states: " 'Substandard housing conditions' means the conditions obtaining in connection with the existence of any dwelling, or dwellings, or housing accommodations for human beings, which because of lack of sanitary facilities, ventilation, or light, or because of dilapidation, overcrowding, faulty interior arrangement, or any combination of these factors, is in the opinion of the Commissioners detrimental to the safety, health, morals, or welfare of the inhabitants of the District of Columbia."

the redevelopment plan and that "no use shall be made of any land or real property included in the lease or sale nor any building or structure erected thereon" which does not conform to the plan. §§ 7(d), 11. Preference is to be given to private enterprise over public agencies in executing the redevelopment plan. § 7(g).

The first project undertaken under the Act relates to Project Area B in Southwest Washington, D.C. In 1950 the Planning Commission prepared and published a comprehensive plan for the District. Surveys revealed that in Area B, 64.3% of the dwellings were beyond repair, 18.4% needed major repairs, only 17.3% were satisfactory; 57.8% of the dwellings had outside toilets, 60.3% had no baths, 29.3% lacked electricity, 82.2% had no wash basins or laundry tubs, 83.8% lacked central heating. In the judgment of the District's Director of Health it was necessary to redevelop Area B in the interests of public health. The population of Area B amounted to 5,012 persons, of whom 97.5% were Negroes.

The plan for Area B specifies the boundaries and allocates the use of the land for various purposes. It makes detailed provisions for types of dwelling units and provides that at least one-third of them are to be low-rent housing with a maximum rental of $17 per room per month.

After a public hearing the Commissioners approved the plan and the Planning Commission certified it to the Agency for execution. The Agency undertook the preliminary steps for redevelopment of the area when this suit was brought.

Appellants own property in Area B at 712 Fourth Street, S.W. It is not used as a dwelling or place of habitation. A department store is located on it. Appellants object to the appropriation of this property for the purposes of the project. They claim that their property may not be taken constitutionally for this project. It is commercial, not residential property; it is not slum housing; it will be put into the project under the management of a private, not a public, agency and redeveloped for private, not public use. That is the argument; and the contention is that appellants' private property is being taken contrary to two mandates of the Fifth Amendment—(1) "no person shall * * * be deprived of * * * property, without due process of law"; (2) "nor shall private property be taken for public use, without just compensation." To take for the purpose of ridding the area of slums is one thing; it is quite another, the argument goes, to take a man's property merely to develop a better balanced, more attractive community. The District Court, while agreeing in general with that argument, saved the Act by construing it to mean that the Agency could condemn property only for the reasonable necessities of slum clearance and prevention, its concept of "slum" being the existence of conditions "injurious to the public health, safety, morals and welfare." 117 F.Supp. 705, 724–725.

The power of Congress over the District of Columbia includes all the legislative powers which a state may exercise over its affairs. See District of Columbia v. Thompson Co., 346 U.S. 100, 108, 73 S.Ct. 1007, 1011, 97

L.Ed. 1480. We deal, in other words, with what traditionally has been known as the police power. An attempt to define its reach or trace its outer limits is fruitless, for each case must turn on its own facts. The definition is essentially the product of legislative determinations addressed to the purposes of government, purposes neither abstractly nor historically capable of complete definition. Subject to specific constitutional limitations, when the legislature has spoken, the public interest has been declared in terms well-nigh conclusive. In such cases the legislature, not the judiciary, is the main guardian of the public needs to be served by social legislation, whether it be Congress legislating concerning the District of Columbia (see Block v. Hirsh, 256 U.S. 135, 41 S.Ct. 458, 65 L.Ed. 865, 16 A.L.R. 165) or the States legislating concerning local affairs. See Olsen v. State of Nebraska ex rel. Western Reference & Bond Ass'n, 313 U.S. 236, 61 S.Ct. 862, 85 L.Ed. 1305, 133 A.L.R. 1500; Lincoln Federal Labor Union No. 19129, A.F. of L. v. Northwestern Co., 335 U.S. 525, 69 S.Ct. 251, 93 L.Ed. 212, 6 A.L.R.2d 473; California State Association v. Maloney, 341 U.S. 105, 71 S.Ct. 601, 95 L.Ed. 788. This principle admits of no exception merely because the power of eminent domain is involved. The role of the judiciary in determining whether that power is being exercised for a public purpose is an extremely narrow one. See Old Dominion Land Co. v. United States, 269 U.S. 55, 66, 46 S.Ct. 39, 40, 70 L.Ed. 162; United States ex rel. Tennessee Valley Authority v. Welch, 327 U.S. 546, 552, 66 S.Ct. 715, 718, 90 L.Ed. 843.

Public safety, public health, morality, peace and quiet, law and order—these are some of the more conspicuous examples of the traditional application of the police power to municipal affairs. Yet they merely illustrate the scope of the power and do not delimit it. See Noble State Bank v. Haskell, 219 U.S. 104, 111, 31 S.Ct. 186, 188, 55 L.Ed. 112. Miserable and disreputable housing conditions may do more than spread disease and crime and immorality. They may also suffocate the spirit by reducing the people who live there to the status of cattle. They may indeed make living an almost insufferable burden. They may also be an ugly sore, a blight on the community which robs it of charm, which makes it a place from which men turn. The misery of housing may despoil a community as an open sewer may ruin a river.

We do not sit to determine whether a particular housing project is or is not desirable. The concept of the public welfare is broad and inclusive. See Day–Brite Lighting, Inc. v. State of Missouri, 342 U.S. 421, 424, 72 S.Ct. 405, 407, 96 L.Ed. 469. The values it represents are spiritual as well as physical, aesthetic as well as monetary. It is within the power of the legislature to determine that the community should be beautiful as well as healthy, spacious as well as clean, well-balanced as well as carefully patrolled. In the present case the Congress and its authorized agencies have made determinations that take into account a wide variety of values. It is not for us to reappraise them. If those who govern the District of Columbia decide that the Nation's capital should be beautiful as well as sanitary, there is nothing in the Fifth Amendment that stands in the way.

Once the object is within the authority of Congress, the right to realize it through the exercise of eminent domain is clear. For the power of eminent domain is merely the means to the end. See Luxton v. North River Bridge Co., 153 U.S. 525, 529–530, 14 S.Ct. 891, 892, 38 L.Ed. 808; United States v. Gettysburg Electric R. Co., 160 U.S. 668, 679, 16 S.Ct. 427, 429, 40 L.Ed. 576. Once the object is within the authority of Congress, the means by which it will be attained is also for Congress to determine. Here one of the means chosen is the use of private enterprise for redevelopment of the area. Appellants argue that this makes the project a taking from one businessman for the benefit of another businessman. But the means of executing the project are for Congress and Congress alone to determine, once the public purpose has been established. See Luxton v. North River Bridge Co., supra; cf. Highland v. Russell Car & Snowplow Co., 279 U.S. 253, 49 S.Ct. 314, 73 L.Ed. 688. The public end may be as well or better served through an agency of private enterprise than through a department of government—or so the Congress might conclude. We cannot say that public ownership is the sole method of promoting the public purposes of community redevelopment projects. What we have said also disposes of any contention concerning the fact that certain property owners in the area may be permitted to repurchase their properties for redevelopment in harmony with the overall plan. That, too, is a legitimate means which Congress and its agencies may adopt, if they choose.

In the present case, Congress and its authorized agencies attack the problem of the blighted parts of the community on an area rather than on a structure-by-structure basis. That, too, is opposed by appellants. They maintain that since their building does not imperil health or safety nor contribute to the making of a slum or a blighted area, it cannot be swept into a redevelopment plan by the mere dictum of the Planning Commission or the Commissioners. The particular uses to be made of the land in the project were determined with regard to the needs of the particular community. The experts concluded that if the community were to be healthy, if it were not to revert again to a blighted or slum area, as though possessed by a congenital disease, the area must be planned as a whole. It was not enough, they believed, to remove existing buildings that were insanitary or unsightly. It was important to redesign the whole area so as to eliminate the conditions that cause slums—the overcrowding of dwellings, the lack of parks, the lack of adequate streets and alleys, the absence of recreational areas, the lack of light and air, the presence of outmoded street patterns. It was believed that the piecemeal approach, the removal of individual structures that were offensive, would be only a palliative. The entire area needed redesigning so that a balanced, integrated plan could be developed for the region, including not only new homes but also schools, churches, parks, streets, and shopping centers. In this way it was hoped that the cycle of decay of the area could be controlled and the birth of future slums prevented. Cf.

Gohld Realty Co. v. City of Hartford, 141 Conn. 135, 141–144, 104 A.2d 365, 368–370; Hunter v. Norfolk Redevelopment Authority, 195 Va. 326, 338–339, 78 S.E.2d 893, 900–901. Such diversification in future use is plainly relevant to the maintenance of the desired housing standards and therefore within congressional power.

The District Court below suggested that, if such a broad scope were intended for the statute, the standards contained in the Act would not be sufficiently definite to sustain the delegation of authority. 117 F.Supp. 705, 721. We do not agree. We think the standards prescribed were adequate for executing the plan to eliminate not only slums as narrowly defined by the District Court but also the blighted areas that tend to produce slums. Property may of course be taken for this redevelopment which, standing by itself, is innocuous and unoffending. But we have said enough to indicate that it is the need of the area as a whole which Congress and its agencies are evaluating. If owner after owner were permitted to resist these redevelopment programs on the ground that his particular property was not being used against the public interest, integrated plans for redevelopment would suffer greatly. The argument pressed on us is, indeed, a plea to substitute the landowner's standard of the public need for the standard prescribed by Congress. But as we have already stated, community redevelopment programs need not, by force of the Constitution, be on a piecemeal basis—lot by lot, building by building.

It is not for the courts to oversee the choice of the boundary line nor to sit in review on the size of a particular project area. Once the question of the public purpose has been decided, the amount and character of land to be taken for the project and the need for a particular tract to complete the integrated plan rests in the discretion of the legislative branch. See Shoemaker v. United States, 147 U.S. 282, 298, 13 S.Ct. 361, 390, 37 L.Ed. 170; United States ex rel. Tennessee Valley Authority v. Welch, supra, 327 U.S. at page 554, 66 S.Ct. at page 718, 90 L.Ed. 843; United States v. Carmack, 329 U.S. 230, 247, 67 S.Ct. 252, 260, 91 L.Ed. 209.

The District Court indicated grave doubts concerning the Agency's right to take full title to the land as distinguished from the objectionable buildings located on it. 117 F.Supp. 705, 715–719. We do not share those doubts. If the Agency considers it necessary in carrying out the redevelopment project to take full title to the real property involved, it may do so. It is not for the courts to determine whether it is necessary for successful consummation of the project that unsafe, unsightly, or insanitary buildings alone be taken or whether title to the land be included, any more than it is the function of the courts to sort and choose among the various parcels selected for condemnation.

The rights of these property owners are satisfied when they receive that just compensation which the Fifth Amendment exacts as the price of the taking.

The judgment of the District Court, as modified by this opinion, is affirmed.

Note

On this subject of "public use" and "public purpose," see Mandelker, Public Purpose in Urban Redevelopment, 28 Tul.L.Rev. 96 (1953); Note, Public Use as a Limitation on Eminent Domain in Urban Renewal, 68 Harv.L.Rev. 1422 (1955); and 22 Ark.L.Rev. 211 (1968). In City of Little Rock v. Raines, 241 Ark. 1071, 411 S.W.2d 486 (1967), the Arkansas court declined to depart from its "public use" position and embrace the "public purpose" concept. The case involved the condemnation of land for construction of port facilities, an industrial park and related uses. The court held the port facility to be a public use, but the sale of the property to private interests for industrial use was not considered a valid exercise of the power of eminent domain. The opinion said: "We prefer the result reached in Hogue v. Port of Seattle, 54 Wash.2d 799, 341 P.2d 171. There it was held that the Port of Seattle could not constitutionally acquire well-developed agricultural and residential lands for industrial development purposes by eminent domain as the use was private, not public. It was further held that before the power of eminent domain could properly be exercised, the courts must find that the proposed use of the property is a really public one. The condemning authority in that case had contended that the taking of this land was incidental to the reclamation of certain marginal lands in the proposed industrial district, just as appellant contends that this industrial park is incidental to the establishment of a Port."

HAWAII HOUSING AUTHORITY v. MIDKIFF

Supreme Court of the United States, 1984.
467 U.S. 229, 104 S.Ct. 2321, 81 L.Ed.2d 186.

JUSTICE O'CONNOR delivered the opinion of the Court.

The Fifth Amendment of the United States Constitution provides, in pertinent part, that "private property [shall not] be taken for public use, without just compensation." These cases present the question whether the Public Use Clause of that Amendment, made applicable to the States through the Fourteenth Amendment, prohibits the State of Hawaii from taking, with just compensation, title in real property from lessors and transferring it to lessees in order to reduce the concentration of ownership of fees simple in the State. We conclude that it does not.

I

A

The Hawaiian Islands were originally settled by Polynesian immigrants from the western Pacific. These settlers developed an economy around a feudal land tenure system in which one island high chief, the ali'i nui, controlled the land and assigned it for development to certain subchiefs. The subchiefs would then reassign the land to other lower ranking chiefs, who would administer the land and govern the farmers and other tenants working it. All land was held at the will of the ali'i nui and eventually had to be returned to his trust. There was no private ownership of land.

Beginning in the early 1800's, Hawaiian leaders and American settlers repeatedly attempted to divide the lands of the kingdom among the crown, the chiefs, and the common people. These efforts proved largely unsuccessful, however, and the land remained in the hands of a few. In the mid–1960's, after extensive hearings, the Hawaii Legislature discovered that, while the State and Federal Governments owned almost 49% of the State's land, another 47% was in the hands of only 72 private landowners. The legislature further found that 18 landholders, with tracts of 21,000 acres or more, owned more than 40% of this land and that on Oahu, the most urbanized of the islands, 22 landowners owned 72.5% of the fee simple titles. The legislature concluded that concentrated land ownership was responsible for skewing the State's residential fee simple market, inflating land prices, and injuring the public tranquility and welfare.

To redress these problems, the legislature decided to compel the large landowners to break up their estates. The legislature considered requiring large landowners to sell lands which they were leasing to homeowners. However, the landowners strongly resisted this scheme, pointing out the significant federal tax liabilities they would incur. Indeed, the landowners claimed that the federal tax laws were the primary reason they previously had chosen to lease, and not sell, their lands. Therefore, to accommodate the needs of both lessors and lessees, the Hawaii Legislature enacted the Land Reform Act of 1967 (Act), Haw.Rev.Stat., ch. 516, which created a mechanism for condemning residential tracts and for transferring ownership of the condemned fees simple to existing lessees. By condemning the land in question, the Hawaii Legislature intended to make the land sales involuntary, thereby making the federal tax consequences less severe while still facilitating the redistribution of fees simple.

Under the Act's condemnation scheme, tenants living on single-family residential lots within developmental tracts at least five acres in size are entitled to ask the Hawaii Housing Authority (HHA) to condemn the property on which they live. Haw.Rev.Stat. §§ 516–1(2), (11), 516–22 (1977). When 25 eligible tenants, or tenants on half the lots in the tract, whichever is less, file appropriate applications, the Act authorizes HHA to hold a public hearing to determine whether acquisition by the State of all or part of the tract will "effectuate the public purposes" of the Act. § 516–22. If HHA finds that these public purposes will be served, it is authorized to designate some or all of the lots in the tract for acquisition. It then acquires, at prices set either by condemnation trial or by negotiation between lessors and lessees, the former fee owners' full "right, title, and interest" in the land. § 516–25.

After compensation has been set, HHA may sell the land titles to tenants who have applied for fee simple ownership. HHA is authorized to lend these tenants up to 90% of the purchase price, and it may condition final transfer on a right of first refusal for the first 10 years following sale. §§ 516–30, 516–34, 516–35. If HHA does not sell the lot to the tenant residing there, it may lease the lot or sell it to someone else, provided that public notice has been given. § 516–28. However, HHA may not sell to any one purchaser, or lease to any one tenant, more than one lot, and it may not operate for profit. §§ 516–28, 516–32. In practice, funds to satisfy the condemnation awards have been supplied entirely by lessees. While the Act authorizes HHA to issue bonds and appropriate funds for acquisition, no bonds have issued and HHA has not supplied any funds for condemned lots.

* * *

III

The majority of the Court of Appeals next determined that the Act violates the "public use" requirement of the Fifth and Fourteenth Amendments. On this argument, however, we find ourselves in agreement with the dissenting judge in the Court of Appeals.

A

The starting point for our analysis of the Act's constitutionality is the Court's decision in *Berman v. Parker,* 348 U.S. 26 (1954). In *Berman,* the Court held constitutional the District of Columbia Redevelopment Act of 1945. * * *

There is, of course, a role for courts to play in reviewing a legislature's judgment of what constitutes a public use, even when the eminent domain power is equated with the police power. But the Court in *Berman* made clear that it is "an extremely narrow" one. *Id.,* at 32. The Court in *Berman* cited with approval the Court's decision in *Old Dominion Co. v. United States,* 269 U.S. 55, 66 (1925), which held that deference to the legislature's "public use" determination is required "until it is shown to involve an impossibility." The *Berman* Court also cited to *United States ex rel. TVA v. Welch,* 327 U.S. 546, 552 (1946), which emphasized that "[a]ny departure from this judicial restraint would result in courts deciding on what is and is not a governmental function and in their invalidating legislation on the basis of their view on that question at the moment of decision, a practice which has proved impracticable in other fields." In short, the Court has made clear that it will not substitute its judgment for a legislature's judgment as to what constitutes a public use "unless the use be palpably without reasonable foundation." *United States v. Gettysburg Electric R. Co.,* 160 U.S. 668, 680 (1896).

To be sure, the Court's cases have repeatedly stated that "one person's property may not be taken for the benefit of another private person without a justifying public purpose, even though compensation be paid." *Thompson v. Consolidated Gas Corp.,* 300 U.S. 55, 80 (1937). See, *e.g., Cincinnati v. Vester,* 281 U.S. 439, 447 (1930); *Madisonville Traction Co. v. St. Bernard Mining Co.,* 196 U.S. 239, 251–252 (1905); *Fallbrook Irrigation District v. Bradley,* 164 U.S. 112, 159 (1896). Thus, in *Missouri Pacific R. Co. v. Nebraska,* 164 U.S. 403 (1896), where the "order in question was not, *and was not claimed to be,* * * * a taking of private property for a public use under the right of eminent domain," *id.,* at 416 (emphasis added), the Court invalidated a compensated taking of property for lack of a justifying public purpose. But where the exercise of the eminent domain power is rationally related to a conceivable public purpose, the Court has never held a compensated taking to be proscribed by the Public Use Clause. See *Berman v. Parker, supra; Rindge Co. v. Los Angeles,* 262 U.S. 700 (1923); *Block v. Hirsh,* 256 U.S. 135 (1921); cf. *Thompson v. Consolidated Gas Corp., supra* (invalidating an *uncompensated* taking)'.

On this basis, we have no trouble concluding that the Hawaii Act is constitutional. The people of Hawaii have attempted, much as the settlers of the original 13 Colonies did,[9] to reduce the perceived social and economic evils of a land oligopoly traceable to their monarchs. The land oligopoly has, according to the Hawaii Legislature, created artificial deterrents to the normal functioning of the State's residential land market and forced thousands of individual homeowners to lease, rather than buy, the land underneath their homes. Regulating oligopoly and the evils associated with it is a classic exercise of a State's police powers. See *Exxon Corp. v. Governor of Maryland,* 437 U.S. 117 (1978); *Block v. Hirsh, supra;* see also *People of Puerto Rico v. Eastern Sugar Associates,* 156 F.2d 316 (CA1), cert. denied, 329 U.S. 772 (1946). We cannot disapprove of Hawaii's exercise of this power.

Nor can we condemn as irrational the Act's approach to correcting the land oligopoly problem. The Act presumes that when a sufficiently large number of persons declare that they are willing but unable to buy lots at fair prices the land market is malfunctioning. When such a malfunction is signalled, the Act authorizes HHA to condemn lots in the relevant tract. The Act limits the number of lots any one tenant can purchase and authorizes HHA to use public funds to ensure that the market dilution goals will be achieved. This is a comprehensive and rational approach to identifying and correcting market failure.

* * *

B

The Court of Appeals read our cases to stand for a much narrower proposition. First, it read our "public use" cases, especially *Berman,* as requiring that government possess and use property at some point during a taking. Since Hawaiian lessees retain possession of the property for private use throughout the condemnation process, the court found that the Act exacted takings for private use. 702 F.2d, at 796–797. Second, it determined that these cases involved only "the review of * * * *congressional* determination[s] that there was a public use, *not* the

---

9. After the American Revolution, the colonists in several States took steps to eradicate the feudal incidents with which large proprietors had encumbered land in the Colonies. See, *e.g.,* Act of May 1779, 10 Henning's Statutes At Large 64, ch. 13, § 6 (1822) (Virginia statute); Divesting Act of 1779, 1775–1781 Pa.Acts 258, ch. 139 (1782) (Pennsylvania statute). Courts have never doubted that such statutes served a public purpose. See, *e.g., Wilson v. Iseminger,* 185 U.S. 55, 60–61 (1902); *Stewart v. Gorter,* 70 Md. 242, 244–245, 16 A. 644, 645 (1889).

review of * * * state legislative determination[s]." *Id.*, at 798 (emphasis in original). Because state legislative determinations are involved in the instant cases, the Court of Appeals decided that more rigorous judicial scrutiny of the public use determinations was appropriate. The court concluded that the Hawaii Legislature's professed purposes were mere "statutory rationalizations." *Ibid.* We disagree with the Court of Appeals' analysis.

The mere fact that property taken outright by eminent domain is transferred in the first instance to private beneficiaries does not condemn that taking as having only a private purpose. The Court long ago rejected any literal requirement that condemned property be put into use for the general public. "It is not essential that the entire community, nor even any considerable portion, * * * directly enjoy or participate in any improvement in order [for it] to constitute a public use." *Rindge Co. v. Los Angeles,* 262 U.S., at 707. "[W]hat in its immediate aspect [is] only a private transaction may * * * be raised by its class or character to a public affair." *Block v. Hirsh,* 256 U.S., at 155. As the unique way titles were held in Hawaii skewed the land market, exercise of the power of eminent domain was justified. The Act advances its purposes without the State's taking actual possession of the land. In such cases, government does not itself have to use property to legitimate the taking; it is only the taking's purpose, and not its mechanics, that must pass scrutiny under the Public Use Clause.

Similarly, the fact that a state legislature, and not the Congress, made the public use determination does not mean that judicial deference is less appropriate. Judicial deference is required because, in our system of government, legislatures are better able to assess what public purposes should be advanced by an exercise of the taking power. State legislatures are as capable as Congress of making such determinations within their respective spheres of authority. See *Berman v. Parker,* 348 U.S., at 32. Thus, if a legislature, state or federal, determines there are substantial reasons for an exercise of the taking power, courts must defer to its determination that the taking will serve a public use.

IV

The State of Hawaii has never denied that the Constitution forbids even a compensated taking of property when executed for no reason other than to confer a private benefit on a particular private party. A purely private taking could not withstand the scrutiny of the public use requirement; it would serve no legitimate purpose of government and would thus be void. But no purely private taking is involved in these cases. The Hawaii Legislature enacted its Land Reform Act not to benefit a particular class of identifiable individuals but to attack certain perceived evils of concentrated property ownership in Hawaii—a legitimate public purpose. Use of the condemnation power to achieve this purpose is not irrational. Since we assume for purposes of these appeals that the weighty demand of just compensation has been met, the requirements of the Fifth and Fourteenth Amendments have been satisfied. Accordingly, we reverse the judgment of the Court of Appeals, and remand these cases for further proceedings in conformity with this opinion.

Note

In 1991 the city of Honolulu enacted an ordinance that allowed the city to condemn leaseholds in condominium structures and resell them to the lessees. The federal district court relying heavily on the Midkiff case held the ordinance constitutional. Small Landowners of Oahu v. City and County of Honolulu, 832 F.Supp. 1404 (D.Haw.1993).

CITY OF CENTER LINE v. CHMELKO

Court of Appeals of Michigan, 1987.
164 Mich.App. 251, 416 N.W.2d 401.

SHEPHERD, PRESIDING JUDGE.

Plaintiff city instituted condemnation proceedings in an attempt to acquire two parcels of property upon which were located a print shop, a party store, several apartments, a newspaper distribution center and vacant store space. Pursuant to M.C.L. § 213.56(1); M.S.A. § 8.265(6)(1) defendants, the owners and tenants of the properties, filed a motion in Macomb Circuit Court challenging the necessity for the taking. Judge Frank E. Jeannette of the Macomb Circuit Court ruled that the proposed taking was for a private purpose and thus contrary to Const.1963, art. 10, § 2 and dismissed the condemnation action. We affirm because it seems clear that at the hearing on the necessity for the condemnation the reasons given by the city for the condemnation were revealed to be a complete fiction. The record reveals that the city acted as an agent for a private interest, a local car dealership, Rinke Toyota.

The city's purported reasons for seeking the condemnation were set forth in the city resolution attached to its condemnation complaint:

"(1). For the acquisition, demolition and removal of a use of land that is nonconforming under provisions of the City of Center Line's Zoning Ordinance, which specify certain requirements for off-street parking and loading space not met by the present use; (2) for the acquisition, demolition and removal of a structure which, because of age, physical disrepair, deterioration, physical obsolescence, inadequate facilities and other conditions is a blighted structure, and a factor in and a cause of blight in the immediate vicinity thereof; (3) for the prevention of the deterioration of commercial property in the City to improve and stabilize the commercial business district and the tax base of the City; (4) for the demolition and removal of the structures and improvements on the land, and the conveyance of the land to a private developer for use and development for commercial purposes in a manner that will improve the economic viability of the existing commercial district of the City, and that will improve and stabilize property values in the area and the tax base of the City, all of which purposes are hereby found, determined and deemed to be public purposes necessary for the public use and benefit of the citizens of the City of Center Line."

Ronald D. Reiterman, Assistant City Manager, Community Development Director and City Assessor, testified that in June, 1984, a representative from Rinke Toyota had approached the city about the acquisition of these two parcels of property. Rinke Toyota is located adjacent to the property in question. Representatives of Rinke Toyota explained to the city that it was extremely interested in acquiring the property so that it could expand its space for the storage of new cars. Reiterman indicated that Rinke Toyota representatives told the city that, without the ability to expand, it might have to relocate somewhere else, a move which Reiterman concluded would have a serious economic impact on the city. Rinke's legal counsel indicated to the city that it had tried unsuccessfully to purchase the property privately, and this testimony was corroborated by Sabah Hermiz, land contract purchaser of one of the parcels. Reiterman also disclosed that the city planned to turn the property over to Rinke Toyota and had accepted its offer to financially underwrite all of the expenses incurred in acquiring the property, including court costs, attorney fees, appraisal and survey costs. The city contended that the private funding of the condemnation did not alter the significant public purpose behind the taking.

The city presented the proposed taking in the instant case as just one more logical step in its continuing and long-term efforts to address the parking shortage and other urban problems it was experiencing. Testimony at the hearing indicated that the city initiated a renewal program in 1962 to redevelop a blighted area near Van Dyke and Ten Mile Road. In 1979, to prevent further deterioration of the city's business district, the city created the Downtown Development Authority (DDA). The DDA hired a consultant who identified a series of parking shortages in the city.

The city planner testified that neither parcel conformed to the off-street parking requirements of the city zoning ordinance. Thus the properties constituted nonconforming uses under the zoning ordinance. The city planner testified that the proposed taking would alleviate the parking shortage by eliminating the buildings causing the deficiency.

Defendants' testimony rebutted the city's parking shortage claim. John Chmelko, owner of the print shop, testified that a nearby parking lot was sufficient for his needs. He testified that he and his family lived close by and did not need a space. He testified that the three spots next to his shop were adequate since he rarely had more than one customer at a time.

Mikhael Sitto, owner and operator of a party store, testified that the nine off-street parking spaces next to his building were more than adequate. Hermiz testified that neither of the two renters owned a car. He testified that the users of the newspaper distribution center used the alley to drop papers. Delivery people picked up the papers relatively quickly and were generally on bicycles. Chmelko, Sitto and Hermiz all testified that they had never received a complaint from other businesses or city authorities about a parking problem.

Reiterman conceded that the alleged parking deficiency involved more of a shortage on paper than in fact. In regard to these two buildings, Reiterman acknowledged that, despite the inadequacy of off-street parking as specified in the zoning ordinance, no actual parking shortage existed now or in the past at this location. Reiterman admitted that no critical parking problems had been observed and no complaints about any parking problems had been received from any city official or from other businesses. Reiterman suggested that the taking of the two properties would eliminate the parking deficiency but he conceded that Rinke's redevelopment plans meant no new public parking places would be created.

City officials also testified that the structures were blighted. The buildings date back to the early 1900's, but Reiterman conceded that the buildings were well-maintained. The consultant hired by the DDA focused his criticism on the newspaper distribution center. Chmelko testified to a variety of improvements to his business and Hermiz testified to the structural soundness of his building.

The real rationale behind the condemnation was explained by the DDA consultant, Gerald Luedtke. He testified to the necessity of preventing the deterioration of the tax base and improving the economic viability of the city's commercial district. He indicated that Rinke Toyota was one of the "economic anchors" of the city and a "magnet" for consumers. "If that dealership were not there, this portion of downtown would be economically dead."

The trial court was unconvinced "that the taking of these properties advances clear and significant public interests."

I

The city first argues that the trial court changed the burden of proof by initially concluding, in a pretrial motion, that defendant property owners had the burden of proof to show a lack of necessity, either by fraud, error of law or abuse of discretion. M.C.L. § 213.56(2); M.S.A. § 8.265(6)(2). That section of the statute provides:

> "(2) With respect to an acquisition by a public agency, the determination of public necessity by that agency shall be binding on the court in the absence of a showing of fraud, error of law, or abuse of discretion."

Plaintiff then argues that in its final ruling the trial court held against the city by applying a burden of proof other than that which the court originally stated and by holding that it could not find a clear and significant public interest in the taking, after applying the "heightened scrutiny" test of Poletown Neighborhood Council v. Detroit, 410 Mich. 616, 304 N.W.2d 455 (1981).

We can find no merit in plaintiff's argument. This is not a case where the city presented only its resolution and left it to defendants to prove their case. In fact, plaintiff presented two top city officials and a consultant intimately familiar with the city's condemnation action. Plaintiff does not argue that it did not put forward evidence in reliance on the prehearing ruling regarding the burden of proof. Plaintiff does not proffer other evidence which would weigh in its favor. We believe plaintiff received a full and fair hearing and was not, in fact, unfairly prejudiced by the court's ruling.

In Poletown our Supreme Court ruled:

"Where, as here, the condemnation power is exercised in a way that benefits specific and identifiable private interests, a court inspects with heightened scrutiny the claim that the public interest is the predominant interest being advanced. Such public benefit cannot be speculative or marginal but must be clear and significant if it is to be within the legitimate purpose as stated by the Legislature." Poletown at 634–635, 304 N.W.2d 455.

In ruling, the trial court applied this standard to the facts here presented. The nonconforming use argument was a fiction. Proofs at the hearing indicated that parking was more than adequate. This case is distinct from one in which a nonconforming use presents a real hazard. Moreover, the city's "blight" argument also lacked factual substance. We believe that the proofs at the hearing indicate that the city's determination was either fraudulent or an abuse of discretion, especially under the heightened scrutiny test of Poletown. We therefore find no error in the trial court's ruling. Plaintiff can show no prejudice to its position by the trial court's ultimate holding which changed neither the law nor the burden of proof.

* * *

Plaintiff relies on language in Poletown, supra, in support of its proposition that the city resolution of public purpose should be conclusive on the courts. We now turn in greater detail to the Poletown decision.

Poletown arose out of the economic crisis which faced Detroit and its most significant economic buttress, the automobile industry, in the 1970s and early 1980s. In 1981, unemployment in the City of Detroit reached eighteen percent. Poletown, 410 Mich. at 647, 304 N.W.2d 455 (Ryan, J., dissenting). In 1980 General Motors entered discussions with the city to build a "new generation facility" in Detroit if a suitable site could be found to replace its aging Cadillac and Fisher Body facilities. Underlying the discussions was the threat that if no such site could be found, taken and made available to General Motors, it would close its plant, take the six thousand jobs those plants represented and go elsewhere.

Reacting to the dismal economic climate and the steady loss of manufacturing facilities in Michigan, the Michigan Legislature had previously passed the Economic Development Corporations Act, 1974 P.A. 338, M.C.L. § 125.1601 et seq.; M.S.A. § 5.3520(1) et seq. The act provided that in order to "alleviate and prevent conditions of unemployment" municipalities were granted the power to assist "industrial and commercial enterprises" to revitalize their facilities. M.C.L. § 125.1602; M.S.A. § 5.3520(2). To further this objective, the Legislature authorized municipalities to acquire property by condemnation in order to provide industrial and commercial sites and the means of transfer from the municipality to private users. M.C.L. § 125.1622; M.S.A. § 5.3520(22).

The narrow question presented in Poletown was whether the statute authorizing the taking was constitutional. The Supreme Court deferred to the legislative determination of public purpose, and concluded that the benefit to the city was "clear and significant" and therefore sufficient to satisfy the Court that this "project was an intended and a legitimate object of the Legislature" even though "a private party will also * * * receive a benefit as an incident thereto." Poletown at 634, 304 N.W.2d 455.

We read the factual context of Poletown as extremely significant to the holding in that case. We do not take Poletown to be a complete refutation of the judiciary's ultimate power to review a city council's determination of public purpose. Rather, we believe the decision illuminates the deference which must be accorded the state Legislature in the context of the Economic Development Corporations Act.

* * *

Our ruling here is further confirmed by a recent decision of the Delaware Supreme Court. In Wilmington Parking Authority v. Land With Improvements, 521 A.2d 227 (Del., 1986), the Wilmington Parking Authority brought a condemnation action against property in the downtown area of Wilmington adjacent to the News–Journal Company's principal facility. The authority alleged that the property was necessary for a public parking facility. The condemnation plan, however, provided for the transfer of a substantial portion of the property to the News–Journal for construction of an addition to its facility. The trial court found that the "paramount benefit" of the project was to the News–Journal and dismissed the condemnation action.

The Delaware Supreme Court affirmed. Initially the supreme court noted the Poletown "heightened scrutiny" test and determined that the question of public purpose was ultimately a judicial one, citing Cincinnati, supra. Determining that a decision on public versus private primary purpose required an examination of the "consequences and effects" of a particular project, the court concluded that review of the "underlying purpose" was appropriate. In affirming, the supreme court concluded that the lower court had committed no legal error in its determination of the primary purpose of the project.

We approve the reasoning in that decision. Any benefit to the public is purely derivative of the primary purpose: the city's continued good relations with Rinke Toyota. While it may be true that the public would derive some benefit from the expansion plans of Rinke Toyota, that would be true of any business. That the automobile dealer is a substantial factor in the business life of the city does not permit it to use city government to eliminate small businesses in order to facilitate its growth. We do not interpret Poletown to mean that whenever a substantial corporate enterprise needs room to expand it can threaten to move and then use that threat, even if real, as leverage to induce the local government to destroy smaller interests. Before that can be allowed to occur, the courts as protectors of the interests of all must look at the purpose of the taking with great vigilance. That is precisely what Judge Jeannette did. He reached the correct result.

Notes

1. In Michigan, the use of the eminent domain power to condemn private property and turn it over to another private entity has been a subject of controversy since the General Motors case, Poletown Neighborhood Council v. City of Detroit, 410 Mich. 616, 304 N.W.2d 455 (1981). In City of Detroit v. Vavro, 177 Mich.App. 682, 442 N.W.2d 730 (1989), the Court of Appeals upheld a similar condemnation for the benefit of Chrysler Corp.; the court, however, stated:

> In sum, we believe that plaintiff is permitted to take the defendants' property and turn it over to Chrysler Corporation in light of the decision in Poletown, supra, and that the procedures employed in doing so met the minimum legal requirements. However, we do agree with defendants that the Poletown decision was incorrect and we urge the Supreme Court to take this matter up and overrule Poletown and restore the constitutional protections of private property.

This type of controversy also comes up in connection with the use of eminent domain and taxing powers to involve public government in joint redevelopment efforts with the private sector. See the concluding section of Chapter VI.

2. Some other cases that raise the issue of Poletown are Day v. Development Authority of City of Adel, 248 Ga. 488, 284 S.E.2d 275 (1981) (public development of facility to be used as a retail grocery store by a private corporation); Mayor v. Thomas, 645 So.2d 940 (Miss.1994) (city could not condemn riverfront property for purpose of private development of riverboat gaming enterprise); High Ridge Ass'n, Inc. v. County Comm'rs of Carroll County, 105 Md.App. 423, 660 A.2d 951 (1995) (city could not condemn a 50 foot strip of land so as to make it easier for an adjacent property owner to develop his land).

The other side of the coin is represented by Borough of Essex Fells v. Kessler Institute for Rehabilitation, Inc., 289 N.J.Super. 329, 673 A.2d 856 (1995) where the local government stated it was taking property for a park, but the court found that was a cover for the real purpose which was to prevent the private corporation from building a rehabilitation facility. The court said: "[W]here a condemnation is commenced for an apparently valid, stated purpose but the real purpose is to prevent a proposed development which is considered undesirable, the condemnation may be set aside."

3. In City of Bozeman, Dept. of Transportation of State of Montana v. Vaniman, 271 Mont. 514, 898 P.2d 1208 (1995) the court held that plans for a highway interchange complex improperly included a provision for a private Chamber of Commerce to occupy 40 percent of the proposed offices; however, excluding the chamber from the plan was a sufficient remedy and the remainder of the proposal met the public purpose test.

Pennsylvania has a private road act dating back to 1836, whereby landowners who do not have access to a public road may petition for public viewers to lay out a private road across private property; the act requires the private road beneficiary to pay for the easement. See T.L.C. Services, Inc. v. Kamin, 162 Pa.Cmwlth. 547, 639 A.2d 926 (1994), appeal denied 538 Pa. 679, 649 A.2d 679, cert. denied __ U.S. __, 115 S.Ct. 1314, 131 L.Ed.2d 195 (1995).

4. Closely related to the question of whether a proposed condemnation is for a public purpose or public use is the question of whether a public entity can use its eminent domain powers to enter into an activity which is normally regarded as being in the private sector. The following cases illustrate this question.

COURTESY SANDWICH SHOP, INC. v. PORT OF NEW YORK AUTHORITY

Court of Appeals of New York, 1963.
12 N.Y.2d 379, 240 N.Y.S.2d 1, 190 N.E.2d 402, appeal dismissed
375 U.S. 78, 84 S.Ct. 194, 11 L.Ed.2d 141 (1963).

BURKE, JUDGE.

Chapter 209 of the Laws of New York, 1962, McK.Unconsol.Laws, § 6601 et seq., together with concurrent New Jersey legislation (Laws of N.J., 1962, ch. 8, N.J.S.A. 32:1–35.50 et seq.), authorizes the Port of New York Authority, through the appellant subsidiary, to effectuate a single port development project to consist of the present Hudson & Manhattan Railroad system and a new development to be known as the "World Trade Center", all on a site in lower Manhattan, part of which is now occupied by the existing Hudson & Manhattan Terminal. Appellant is authorized to condemn property to achieve this purpose and under this power, instituted the condemnation proceeding here challenged by respondents, who have an interest in the subject property. Respondents argue that chapter 209 violates section 7 of article I of the New York Constitution and the United States Constitution * * * in that it authorizes the taking of private property by eminent domain for other than a public use.

The proposed World Trade Center is defined by statute as that part of the unified project that is "a facility of commerce * * * for the centralized accommodation of functions, activities and services for or incidental to the transportation of persons, the exchange, buying, selling and transportation of commodities * * * in world trade and commerce [and] governmental services". It also states that as far as structures are concerned the World Trade Center also includes any such structure not devoted to railroad functions (thus preserving the distinction between the Hudson & Manhattan part of the project and the World Trade Center functions) even though portions of such structures are not functionally related to the project's purpose and are used solely for "the production of incidental revenue * * * for the expenses of all or part of the port development project" (ch. 209, § 2).

All of the Appellate Division Justices are agreed that the World Trade Center concept represents a public purpose. The majority found, however, the statute was on its face unconstitutional, in that the act granted a power to condemn property to be used for no other purpose than the raising of revenue for the expenses of the project, and for a class of tenants with a remote relationship with world trade. * * *

The prime issue, then, is whether the language of the act must be interpreted so as to authorize condemnation for the production of revenue without subordination to any primary purpose. If that is so the act goes beyond what the cases authorize * * * and beyond what can be constitutionally permitted. We think that the statute is valid.

* * * No further demonstration is required that improvement of the Port of New York by facilitating the flow of commerce and centralizing all activity incident thereto is a public purpose supporting the condemnation of property for any activity functionally related to that purpose. Nor can it be said that the use of property to produce revenue to help finance the operation of those activities that tend to achieve the purpose of the project does not itself perform such a function, provided, of course, that there are in fact such other activities to be supported by incidental revenue production * * *. The crux of the problem here, however, is that the statute has been read by the Appellate Division as allowing unfettered erection of structures that are solely revenue producing. As the dissent below maintains, this misreads the statute. The act was construed so as to raise rather than settle a constitutional question. We have said that where there are two possible interpretations the court will accept that which avoids constitutional doubts. * * * The act may properly be read to authorize only incidental extensions of a site required for a public use. * * *

* * *

The orders appealed from should be reversed, the orders of Special Term in the condemnation proceeding reinstated, a judgment rendered that chapter 209 of the Laws of 1962 is constitutional, and the certified question answered in the negative.

VAN VOORHIS, JUDGE (dissenting).

This statute (L.1962, ch. 209), as drafted, includes a great deal more than the sponsors of a World Trade Center were talking about, and renders it in my opinion subject to the constitutional defects which the Appellate Division has found. These provisions, as analyzed and criticized by the Appellate Division, appear to have been due to no inadvertence; they bear every indication of having been consciously and deliberately inserted so as to grant to the Port Authority extensive and uncontrolled governmental power to condemn and manage private real property for private purposes as a major object of the act.

The cases upholding the constitutionality of public ownership and maintenance of piers in the Hudson River (Matter of Mayor of City of N.Y., 135 N.Y. 253, 263, 31 N.E. 1043, 1045) or public markets or world's fairs or airports (Matter of Cooper, 28 Hun. 515, app. dsmd. 93 N.Y. 507; Hesse v. Rath, 249 N.Y. 436, 164 N.E. 342; John Kennedy & Co. v. New York World's Fair, 288 N.Y. 494, 41 N.E.2d 789) are wide of the mark. This statute puts the Port Authority in the real estate business, by making it a potential landlord, as it says itself at page 6 of its own brief, of "a community of firms engaged in direct import-export activities and it is hoped that they will establish quarters in the World Trade Center and use the Port of New York for increasing volumes of cargo. These include some share of the 200 combination export managers, 2000 general exporters, 4200 general importers and in addition, 2900 United States manufacturers responsible for seventy-six per cent of current United States exports." These are in addition, the Port Authority's brief says, to "over 100 banking organizations financing world trade."

All of these and many more private activities, the Authority contends on this appeal, become public purposes if only they are "centralized" in some nebulous manner in the 13 blocks on the west side of lower Manhattan within which the Hudson & Manhattan terminal is located. This selected area was transferred from the east side, where it had been located by chapter 312 of the Laws of 1961, including the New York Stock Exchange, which apparently is no longer deemed to be one of the financial organs of world trade that needs to be "centralized."

* * *

The courts of other States have had occasion to rule upon the constitutionality of legislation of this character, holding it to be invalid (Matter of Opinion of Justices, 332 Mass. 769, 126 N.E.2d 795 [1955]; Hogue v. Port of Seattle, 54 Wash.2d 799, 341 P.2d 171 [1959]; Opinion of Justices, 152 Me. 440, 131 A.2d 904 [1957]; Opinion to Governor, 76 R.I. 365, 70 A.2d 817).

State v. Inter–American Center Auth. (84 So.2d [Fla., 1955]; 143 So.2d 1 [Fla., 1962]) is not to the contrary, inasmuch as the Authority which was there involved was limited to educational and scientific purposes in strengthening cultural relations among the countries of the western hemisphere. If the New York Port Authority had been content with powers like that, this litigation would not have arisen.

* * *

This is not all a matter of policy for the Legislature. It is the function of courts to give effect to the Constitutions, State and Federal. It is the solemn duty of courts to enforce the constitutional limitation against taking private property by eminent domain except for public purposes. It is idle to suggest that respondents and others in like position are protected by condemnation procedures against taking for nonpublic purposes, inasmuch as the effect of the majority decision is to characterize the condemnation of any real estate in this 13-block area as being for a public purpose. What constitutes private property or public purposes changes from time to time, but the basic concept of private property does not change. If powers such as these be upheld to condemn property in good condition which is not potentially slum (cf. Cannata v. City of New York, 11 N.Y.2d 210, 227 N.Y.S.2d 903, 182 N.E.2d 395), without even paying for the good will, what may appear to be for the advantage of the New York City Chamber of Commerce or the Downtown Lower Manhattan Association or the New Jersey State Chamber of Commerce, or the Chambers of Commerce of Jersey City or Newark today may be turned against them tomorrow, as their counterparts learned in other countries to their sorrow and dismay after they had surrendered to the collectivist state. This ever-growing ascendency of government over private property and over free enterprise is no respecter of persons and cannot long be harnessed by those who expect to use it for private ends. As governmental ascendency is increasingly sanctioned by the constitutional law of our State, private capital is less likely to be invested to develop the Port of New York and more likely to fold its tents and silently move toward other States where government competition and expropriation are more restricted. As the cases show that have been previously cited, the power of government in these respects has been curbed by the courts of other States.

Disregard of the constitutional protection of private property and stigmatization of the small or not so small entrepreneur as standing in the way of progress has everywhere characterized the advance of collectivism. To hold a purpose to be public merely for the reason that it is invoked by a public body to serve its ideas of the public good, it seems to me, can be done only on the assumption that we have passed the point of no return, that the trade, commerce and manufacture of our principal cities can be conducted by private enterprise only on a diminishing scale and that private capital should progressively be displaced by public capital which should increasingly take over. The economic and geographical advantages of the City of New York have withstood a great deal of attrition and can probably withstand more, but there is a limit beyond which socialization cannot be carried without destruction of the constitutional bases of private ownership and enterprise. It seems to me to be the part of courts to enforce the constitutional rights of property which are involved here.

* * *

* * * Injecting the Port Authority into a huge project to compete with private enterprise in the real estate field, for the supposed purpose of maintaining the ascendency of New York over eastern coastal seaports in other States, is outside of the original compact between New York and New Jersey.

PRINCE GEORGE'S COUNTY v. COLLINGTON
CROSSROADS, INC.

Court of Appeals of Maryland, 1975.
275 Md. 171, 339 A.2d 278.

[The county sought to condemn defendant's property as part of a plan to assemble land for a 1700–acre industrial park. Defendant challenged the validity of such a taking under the "public use" provision of the state constitution.]

ELDRIDGE, JUDGE.

* * *

On May 23, 1974, the circuit court rendered its opinion, stating that the purpose of the condemnation in this case was for private use, not public use. The court based its ruling on the fact that the commercial land "will be owned by private entities" when the park is fully developed. The court dismissed the County's amended petition for condemnation, and the County filed the present appeal.

We have concluded, upon consideration of the facts of this case, that the use proposed by the County for the land sought to be condemned is a public use rather than a private use and that, therefore, the condemnation is constitutionally permissible.

Two factors relating to the condemnation sought in this case should be emphasized.

First, the County Council for Prince George's County and the County Executive, in adopting the task force's comprehensive plan, made the finding that the type of industrial park which it considered necessary for the economic well-being of the County would be too costly for private developers to carry out. The planned industrial park was meant to attract "research and development and other 'clean' industrial types" which the County had had difficulty attracting. Appellee did not present any evidence to dispute the County Council's and the County Executive's findings in this case. At oral argument, one of its contentions seemed to be that the County had an unfair advantage because of its exemption from taxes and power of condemnation, and thus should not be allowed to compete with private developers. Whatever merit this contention might have is lost in this case since the record indicates that the County will not be in direct competition with private entrepreneurs. Here the County plans a type of project which the private developers were apparently unable or unwilling to undertake.

Second, the County will maintain significant control over the industrial park after the commercial land therein is sold to private owners. The County will subject land conveyed to private parties to certain "development covenants." The comprehensive plan provides that "[t]hese covenants will deal with management of natural features, maintenance of health, safety and welfare, control of hazards and nuisances, and guidelines for assuring a high quality physical environment." The entire industrial park will be placed in an EIA (Comprehensive Design for Employment and Institutional Areas) zoning classification. As the comprehensive plan states, the classification "will offer Prince George's County the opportunity to control the detailed development of this 1700 acre area through the use of a three phase process of review and approval of detailed plans." Finally, the comprehensive plan provides that over 20% of the industrial park site will be preserved as permanent public or private open space. The public open space will include the "Collington Branch floodplain * * * [which] will receive open space improvements pursuant to the Maryland–National Capital Park and Planning Commission guidelines for stream valley parks." Private open space will include a golf course.

The above factors, failure of private developers to provide the necessary industrial park facilities and the continuing control the County will exert over the development of this facility, must be kept in mind in applying the cases which have dealt with the issue of what constitutes a public use.

* * *

However, the courts have had some difficulty in their efforts to define "public use." No satisfactory single clear-cut rule regarding what is a public use, which can decide all cases, has yet been formulated. Moreover, even if it were possible to formulate such a rule, it would probably not be prudent to do so. * * *

See Nichols, Eminent Domain § 7.2 (1974); 26 Am.Jur.2d Eminent Domain § 27 (1966).

This Court has made clear that "public use" does not mean that in all cases the public must literally or physically be permitted to use the property taken by eminent domain. Nor is it necessary that title to the condemned property be in the government.

* * *

Marchant v. Baltimore, 146 Md. 513, 126 A. 884 (1924) involved Baltimore City's condemnation of property situated on the shore of the Patapsco River for use in carrying out a comprehensive plan of harbor development. The plan provided for the construction of wharves, piers, docks, warehouses, and buildings and for the rental of these facilities to private users. In holding that the contemplated use was public, the Court * * * looked to the economic benefit to be realized by the public. The Court also pointed out that the public use limitation to the eminent domain power does not literally mean in all cases "use of the public." * * *

* * *

As previously pointed out, the cases discussed above demonstrate that the constitutional term "public use" is not synonymous with physical use or access by the general public. * * * Furthermore, these cases * * * show that merely because private businesses or private persons will also receive benefit from the condemnation does not destroy the public character of the action. Moreover, as the Court * * * made clear, the fact that the government may be getting involved in an area which was formerly the domain of private enterprise does not require a conclusion that the taking is not for a public use. Finally, with respect to the principal factor apparently relied on by the court below, the public character of a condemnation is not necessarily changed because a private entity will own the property. * * *

* * *

None of the cases in this Court applying Art. III, § 40, of the Maryland Constitution, have involved condemnations of land for industrial or commercial purposes in contexts other than those associated with railroads, public utilities, or port development. However, governmental acquisition of land at the intersection of two major highways, to create a type of industrial development which was desired but not present in the County, for the purpose of providing employment and general economic benefit to the County, does not seem very different from the condemnation of land upheld in *New Central Coal Co., Pitznogle* and *Marchant.* Moreover, in several cases we have held that the governmental issuance of bonds to provide funds for the financing of private industrial and commercial development is a "public purpose." See, e.g., Wilson v. Board of Co. Comm'rs, 273 Md. 30, 327 A.2d 488 (1974) (issuance of county bonds to finance the installation of antipollution devices by a private industry located in the county); Lerch v. Maryland Port Authority, 240 Md. 438, 214 A.2d 761 (1965) (issuance of revenue bonds by a state agency for the construction of an International Trade Center in which office space was to be leased to private businesses); Frostburg v. Jenkins, 215 Md. 9, 136 A.2d 852 (1957) (City of Frostburg revenue bonds to purchase facilities for a private manufacturing company which had agreed to locate in the city).

In light of the prior decisions by this Court, we conclude that the circuit court erred in holding that the condemnation here was not for a "public use." There has been no suggestion in this case that the purpose of the County's action is to benefit any particular private businesses or persons, * * * Instead, the purpose is to provide for a type of industrial development believed by the County's elected officials to be needed in the County, which the private sector of the economy had failed to provide. The industrial park will, in the judgment of the State Legislature and the County officials, provide employment opportunities as well as general economic benefit for the residents of Prince George's County. To say that Prince George's County may not accomplish these purposes by condemning land for the establishment of certain desired types of private businesses in an industrial park along its major highways, whereas the City of Baltimore can accomplish the same purposes by condemning land for private businesses along its waterway * * * would be wholly illogical. Under our cases, projects reasonably designed to benefit the general public, by significantly enhancing the economic growth of the State or its subdivisions, are public uses, at least where the exercise of the power of condemnation provides an impetus which private enterprise cannot provide.

Judgment of the Circuit Court for Prince George's County reversed, case remanded for further proceedings consistent with this opinion. Costs to be paid by the appellee.

Notes

1. The leading case for the view that condemnation for an industrial park is not for a valid public use is Hogue v. Port of Seattle, 54 Wash.2d 799, 341 P.2d 171 (1959). Virtually all of the recent cases, however, uphold condemnation for ultimate redevelopment in industrial or commercial uses.

2. Note that the court in the Maryland case stressed the fact that the industrial park would in no way compete with private enterprise because the private sector was unable to undertake such a large scale project. Do you think such a finding is necessary to uphold condemnation? In light of the Courtesy Sandwich Shop case, could a public agency, using its tax exempt status and condemnation power, build office and commercial buildings in direct competition with private developers? Would the private developers have standing to challenge such takings if the condemnee declines to litigate? Could a local government agency use such power to generate revenue for the purpose of underwriting future acquisitions and redevelopments? Is that the fear expressed by Judge Van Voorhis in his dissent?

3. Compare In re United Nations Development Dist., 72 Misc.2d 535, 339 N.Y.S.2d 292 (Sup., N.Y.County 1972) where the court upheld condemnation by a public agency, the United Nations Development Corporation, in the face of attacks that the corporation intruded the state into foreign affairs, that the United Nations already owned vacant land for future building, and that private uses would be allowed in the buildings to be constructed.

4. As the preceding cases illustrate, courts sometimes view public purpose as a broader term than public use and may uphold many condemnations which do not involve any semblance of public ownership, development or use. In several states, however, courts may take a stricter view, either by way of a "heightened scrutiny" approach, as in Michigan, or by assessing a proposed condemnation in light of whether the overall project is predominately public or predominately private. An example of the latter approach is Petition of City of Seattle, 96 Wash.2d 616, 638 P.2d 549 (1981); in this case a portion of the redevelopment project was for a public square, park, museum, and off-street parking, but the court found that the dominant purpose was to promote retail shopping and forestall core city decay.

5. What if the city wants to lease or convey land which has always been in public use to private parties? At common law, private encroachment on public property was called a purpresture. See, e.g., City of Nampa v. Swayne, 97 Idaho 530, 547 P.2d 1135 (1976). Most of the cases in the United States in the 20th century involve such matters as theater marquees built over public sidewalks, or private vending on public sidewalks. Another aspect of this

problem involves selling off all or portions of public parks or buildings. For a case challenging a public decision to lease riverfront property which had been used as a "common" to private interests, see Historic Licking Riverside Civic Ass'n v. City of Covington, 774 S.W.2d 436 (Ky.1989). And see Hinton v. City of St. Joseph, Mo., 889 S.W.2d 854 (Mo.App.1994) where neighbors brought an action to stop trustees and the city from selling land that had been devised to acquire public parks for the city; the land was to be sold for a Wal–Mart store and the funds used to develop parks elsewhere in the city. The court held that the neighbors did not have standing (lack of special injury) and as taxpayers they did not have standing either. In England a controversy erupted when water authorities were privatized and they began to sell off land set aside many years earlier for watershed protection. See William E. Schmidt, Privatizing of Land in England Sets Off Battle, N.Y. Times, Sept. 8, 1991 p. 16.

6. Smaller cities have, for many years, sought to use the mechanism of public investment in facilities which would attract industries seeking to relocate. State constitutional provisions adopted in the late 1800's which were designed to prohibit public investment in private enterprise constituted obstacles to the technique of leasing public land in industrial parks, or building factories with money raised by city bond issues and leasing to private industry. Many states, particularly in the South, amended their constitutions in the 1940's and 1950's to accommodate such industry-luring devices. An excellent review of this area may be found in Pinsky, State Constitutional Limitations on Public Industrial Financing: An Historical and Economic Approach, 111 U.Pa.L.Rev. 265 (1963). For a typical, modern statutory framework for the enabling of municipal industrial development, see Smith–Hurd Ill.Ann.Stat. ch. 24, § 11–74–1 et seq. and § 11–74.2–1 et seq. Also see Tierney v. Planned Industrial Expansion Auth. of Kansas City, 742 S.W.2d 146 (Mo.banc 1987); Annotation, Industrial Park as Public Use, 62 A.L.R.4th 1183 (1988).

SECTION 5.   INVERSE CONDEMNATION

HFH, LTD. v. SUPERIOR COURT OF LOS ANGELES COUNTY

Supreme Court of California, In Bank, 1975.
15 Cal.3d 508, 125 Cal.Rptr. 365, 542 P.2d 237.

TOBRINER, JUSTICE.

We face in these mandate proceedings the narrow issue of whether a complaint alleging that a zoning action taken by a city council reduced the market value of petitioners' (hereafter plaintiffs) land states a cause of action in inverse condemnation; we conclude that it does not. We also face numerous amici, some of whom urge on us significant changes in the law of liability and compensation in public land use regulation; we have concluded that neither the state and federal Constitutions nor public policy compel or counsel these changes.

* * *

* * * In one of the seminal zoning cases coming before us, in considering and rejecting a contention that a zoning ordinance forbidding the establishment of a non-conforming use in a residential area unconstitutionally deprived the landowners of their property, we quoted with approval the following language of the Wisconsin Supreme Court: " 'It is thoroughly established in this country that the rights preserved to the individual by these constitutional provisions are held in subordination to the rights of society. Although one owns property, he may not do with it as he pleases any more than he may act in accordance with his personal desires. * * * [I]ncidental damages to property resulting from governmental activities, or laws passed in the promotion of the public welfare are not considered a taking of the property for which compensation must be made.' (Carter v. Harper [1923] 182 Wis. 148[, 153], 196 N.W. 451. * * *)" (Miller v. Board of Public Works, supra, 195 Cal. 477, 488, 234 P. 381, 385.)

In an attempt to escape the clear import of such rulings plaintiffs emphasize that their complaint sounds in inverse condemnation, and that they therefore need only show some diminution in value rather than the arbitrary or confiscatory action imposed by the line of cases they seek to avoid. Several appellate courts in California have considered and rejected precisely this contention.

The Court of Appeal in Morse v. County of San Luis Obispo, supra, 247 Cal.App.2d 600, 55 Cal.Rptr. 710, spoke as follows in affirming a judgment of dismissal following the sustaining of a demurrer to a complaint seeking damages in inverse condemnation for the down-zoning of property: "Plaintiffs are apparently attempting to recover profits they might have earned if they had been successful in getting their land rezoned to permit subdivision into small residential lots, but *landowners have no vested right in existing or anticipated zoning ordinances.* (Anderson v. City Council [1964] 229 Cal.App.2d 79, 88–90, 40 Cal.Rptr. 41.) A purchaser of land merely acquires a right to continue a *use* instituted before the enactment of a more restrictive zoning. Public entities are not bound to reimburse individuals for losses due to changes in zoning, for within the limits of the police power 'some uncompensated hardships must be borne by individuals as the price of living in a modern enlightened and progressive community.' (Metro Realty v. County of El Dorado [1963] 222 Cal.App.2d 508, 518, 35 Cal.Rptr. 480, 486. * * *)" (247 Cal.App.2d at pp. 602–603, 55 Cal.Rptr. at p. 712; emphasis added.)

* * *

Numerous amici who have entered this case on behalf of the plaintiffs urge that the constitutional values of "fairness" protected by the compensation clauses of the state and federal Constitutions require us to hold that inverse condemnation lies for any zoning action which substantially reduces the market value of any tract of land. Without attempting a detailed discussion of the many points raised by amici or a review of the still more voluminous secondary literature on the taking issue, we shall briefly indicate the grounds for our declining to do so.

In this case, as in most instances, zoning is not an arbitrary action depriving someone of property for the purpose of its use by the public or transfer to another; rather it involves reciprocal benefits and burdens which the circumstances of this case well illustrate. The shopping center which plaintiffs seem at various times to have contemplated erecting, would derive its value from the existence of residential housing in the surrounding area. That residential character of the neighborhood, we may assume, results in part from the residential zoning of the area around the tract in question. Plaintiffs in this case therefore find themselves in a somewhat uncomfortable position: they wish to reap the benefit in the form of higher market values of their land, of the restrictive zoning on other properties, but do not wish to bear the reciprocal burden of such zoning when it applies to their property. They thus would avoid the enforcement of residential zoning on their property while benefiting from its enforceability as to other property.

The long settled state of zoning law renders the possibility of change in zoning clearly foreseeable to land speculators and other purchasers of property, who discount their estimate of its value by the probability of such change. The real possibility of zoning changes for the tract in question finds ample demonstration in plaintiffs' insistence that their grantor procure such a change before conveying the land to them. Having obtained the benefits of such rezoning, but having failed to take advantage of it by building, they now assert that the termination of such rezoning rendered the city liable in damages. A distinguished commentator has thus described plaintiffs' situation: "[They] bought land which [they] knew might be subjected to restrictions; and the price [they] paid should have been discounted by the possibility that restrictions would be imposed. Since [they] got exactly what [they] meant to buy, it can perhaps be said that society has effected no redistribution so far as [they are] concerned, any more than it does when it refuses to refund the price of [their] losing sweepstakes ticket." (Michelman, Property, Utility, and Fairness: Comments on the Ethical Foundations of "Just Compensation" Law (1967) 80 Harv.L.Rev. 1165, 1238; see also Berger, A Policy Analysis of the Taking Problem (1974) 49 N.Y.U.L.Rev. 165, 195–196.)

* * *

Plaintiffs in this case desire a change in longstanding principles of the law of just compensation; they ask that we hold municipal zoning bodies liable for full compensation for any fall in market price due to zoning actions. Yet plaintiffs can cite no case and little by way of other considerations to support their claim of entitlement to compensation by reason of a change in zoning. Hoping to build a shopping center, they purchased a tract previously zoned as agricultural land. For reasons which do not appear in the record, they did not build for five years, although no zoning impediments are alleged to have existed. Now they desire to sell that land at a profit to yet another developer and complain that the city has in the meantime concluded that its interests would best be served by residential rather than commercial development of the tract in question. Unable to make the desired profit from the sale of their land, they now seek to recoup it from the city; in so doing they mistake the law.

* * *

The alternative writs are discharged, and the peremptory writs denied.

WRIGHT, C.J., and McComb, Mosk, Sullivan and Richardson, JJ., concur.

Clark, Justice (dissenting).

I dissent.

* * *

The 80 percent decrease in fair market value of the subject property clearly constitutes damage to plaintiffs. The issue then is whether plaintiffs' damage is compensable under the California Constitution.

* * *

The point at which an injury becomes compensable is determined by balancing two fundamental—yet inconsistent—policy considerations. (Bacich v. Board of Control, supra, 23 Cal.2d 343, 144 P.2d 818.) "[O]n the one hand the policy underlying the eminent domain provision in the Constitution is to distribute throughout the community the loss inflicted upon the individual by the making of public improvements. * * * On the other hand, fears have been expressed that compensation allowed too liberally will seriously impede, if not stop, beneficial public improvements because of the greatly increased cost." (Id. at p. 350, 144 P.2d at p. 823.)

* * *

As this court has recently recognized in viewing these conflicting policies, the ultimate test whether compensation is constitutionally required, resolves itself into one of fairness. * * *

* * *

Not all governmental downzoning must be compensated. However, the compensatory "or damaged" provision of the California Constitution should apply when by public action land has (1) suffered substantial decrease in value, (2) the decrease is of long or potentially infinite duration and (3) the owner would incur more than his fair share of the financial burden.

Applying this fairness test to the instant factual situation, plaintiffs have stated a valid cause of action in inverse condemnation. The 80 percent decrease in value of plaintiffs' property—from a market value of $400,000 to $75,000—is obviously substantial. Because the action is taken pursuant to Government Code section 65300, this decrease clearly is of long duration. Of the four quadrants of the subject intersection, three are zoned for commercial use and only plaintiffs' quadrant has been rezoned to "low-density single family residential." Plaintiffs therefore are being forced to shoulder a burden that surrounding landowners have not been made to share.

Applying the tripartite test of fairness to downzoning should not impose an undue burden on governmental agencies. Once the landowner establishes his cause of action for damage, the condemning agency has several alternatives including: (1) compensating the landowner for the decrease in value; (2) paying total value for the land and acquiring title; (3) rescinding the downzoning, in which case the agency would be abandoning a condemnation, becoming liable to the landowner for interim damage, costs and attorney's fees. * * * The first two alternatives assume the validity of the zoning ordinance and therefore are inapplicable when the ordinance itself is invalid. In the case of an invalid ordinance, the court in issuing mandate should follow the third alternative, awarding interim damage, costs and attorney's fees.

* * *

FRED F. FRENCH INVESTING CO., INC. v. CITY OF NEW YORK

Court of Appeals of New York, 1976.
39 N.Y.2d 587, 385 N.Y.S.2d 5, 350 N.E.2d 381.

BREITEL, CHIEF JUDGE.

Plaintiff Fred F. French Investing Co., purchase money mortgagee of Tudor City, a Manhattan residential complex, brought this action to declare unconstitutional a 1972 amendment to the New York City Zoning Resolution and seeks compensation as for "inverse" taking by eminent domain. The amendment purported to create a "Special Park District", and rezoned two private parks in the Tudor City complex exclusively as parks open to the public. It further provided for the granting to the defendant property owners of transferable development (air) rights usable elsewhere. It created the transferable rights by severing the above-surface development rights from the surface development rights, a device of recent invention.

* * *

Tudor City is a four-acre residential complex built on an elevated level above East 42nd Street, across First Avenue from the United Nations in mid-town Manhattan. Planned and developed as a residential community, Tudor City consists of 10 large apartment buildings housing approximately 8,000 people, a hotel, four brownstone buildings, and two 15,000 square-foot private parks. The parks, covering about 18½% of the area of the complex, are elevated from grade and located on the north and south sides of East 42nd Street, with a connecting viaduct.

* * *

Soon after acquiring the Tudor City property, the new owner announced plans to erect a building, said to be a 50–story tower, over East 42nd Street between First and Second Avenues. This plan would have required New York City Planning Commission approval of a shifting of development rights from the parks to the proposed adjoining site and a corresponding zoning change. Alternatively, the owner proposed to erect on each of the Tudor City park sites a building of maximum size permitted by the existing zoning regulations.

There was immediately an adverse public reaction to the owner's proposals, especially from Tudor City residents. After public hearings, the City Planning Commission recommended, over the dissent of one commissioner, and on December 7, 1972 the Board of Estimate approved, an amendment to the zoning resolution establishing Special Park District "P". By contemporaneous amendment to the zoning map, the two Tudor City parks were included within Special Park District "P".

Under the zoning amendment, "only passive recreational uses are permitted" in the Special Park District and improvements are limited to "structures incidental to passive recreational use". When the Special Park District would be mapped, the parks are required to be open daily to the public between 6:00 a.m. and 10:00 p.m.

The zoning amendment permits the transfer of development rights from a privately owned lot zoned as a Special Park District, denominated a "granting lot," to other areas in midtown Manhattan, bounded by 60th Street, Third Avenue, 38th Street and Eighth Avenue, denominated "receiving lots." Lots eligible to be receiving lots are those with a minimum lot size of 30,000 square feet and zoned to permit development at the maximum commercial density. The owner of a granting lot would be permitted to transfer part of his development rights to any eligible receiving lot, thereby increasing its maximum floor area up to 10%. Further increase in the receiving lot's floor area, limited to 20% of the maximum commercial density, is contingent upon a public hearing and approval by the City Planning Commission and the Board of Estimate. Development rights may be transferred by the owner directly to a receiving lot or to an individual or organization for later disposition to a receiving lot. Before development rights may be transferred, however, the Chairman of the City Planning Commission must certify the suitability of a plan for the continuing maintenance, at the owner's expense, of the granting lot as a park open to the public.

It is notable that the private parks become open to the public upon mapping of the Special Park District, and the opening does not depend upon the relocation and effective utilization of the transferable development rights. Indeed, the mapping occurred on December 7, 1972, and the development rights have never been marketed or used.

Plaintiff contends that the rezoning of the parks constitutes a compensable "taking" within the meaning of constitutional limitations.

* * *

As noted above, when the State "takes", that is appropriates, private property for public use, just compensation must be paid. In contrast, when there is only regulation of the uses of private property, no compensation need be paid. Of course, and this is often the beginning of confusion, a purported "regulation" may impose so onerous a burden on the property regulated that it has, in effect, deprived the owner of the reasonable income productive or other private use of his property and thus has destroyed its economic value. In all but exceptional cases, nevertheless, such a regulation does not constitute a "taking," and is therefore not compensable, but amounts to a deprivation or frustration of property rights without due process of law and is therefore invalid.

True, many cases have equated an invalid exercise of the regulating zoning power, perhaps only metaphorically, with a "taking" or a "confiscation" of property, terminology appropriate to the eminent domain power and the concomitant right to compensation when it is exercised.
* * *

The metaphor should not be confused with the reality. Close examination of the cases reveals that in none of them, anymore than in the *Pennsylvania Coal* case (supra), was there an actual "taking" under the eminent domain power, despite the use of the terms "taking" or "confiscatory." Instead, in each the gravamen of the constitutional challenge to the regulatory measure was that it was an invalid exercise of the police power under the due process clause, and the cases were decided under that rubric * * *.

In the present case, while there was a significant diminution in the value of the property, there was no actual appropriation or taking of the parks by title or governmental occupation. The amendment was declared void at Special Term a little over a year after its adoption. There was no physical invasion of the owner's property; nor was there an assumption by the city of the control or management of the parks. Indeed, the parks served the same function as before the amendment, except that they were now also open to the public. Absent factors of governmental displacement of private ownership, occupation or management, there was no "taking" within the meaning of constitutional limitations (see City of Buffalo v. Clement Co., 28 N.Y.2d 241, 255–257, 321 N.Y.S.2d 345, 357–359, 269 N.E.2d 895, 903–905). There was, therefore, no right to compensation as for a taking in eminent domain.

Since there was no taking within the meaning of constitutional limitations, plaintiff's remedy, at this stage of the litigation, would be a declaration of the amendment's invalidity, if that be the case. Thus, it is necessary to determine whether the zoning amendment was a valid exercise of the police power under the due process clauses of the State and Federal Constitutions.

* * *

A zoning ordinance is unreasonable, under traditional police power and due process analysis, if it encroaches on the exercise of private property rights without substantial relation to a legitimate governmental purpose. A legitimate governmental purpose is, of course, one which furthers the public health, safety, morals or general welfare. * * * Moreover, a zoning ordinance, on similar police power analysis, is unreasonable if it is arbitrary, that is, if there is no reasonable relation between the end sought to be achieved by the regulation and the means used to achieve that end * * *.

Finally, and it is at this point that the confusion between the police power and the exercise of eminent domain most often occurs, a zoning ordinance is unreasonable if it frustrates the owner in the use of his property, that is, if it renders the property unsuitable for any reasonable income productive or other private use for which it is adapted and thus destroys its economic value, or all but a bare residue of its value * * *.

The ultimate evil of a deprivation of property, or better, a frustration of property rights, under the guise of an exercise of the police power is that it forces the owner to assume the cost of providing a benefit to the public without recoupment. There is no attempt to share the cost of the benefit among those benefitted, that is, society at large. Instead, the accident of ownership determines who shall bear the cost initially. Of course, as further consequence, the ultimate economic cost of providing the benefit is hidden from those who in a democratic society are given the power of deciding whether or not they wish to obtain the benefit despite the ultimate economic cost, however initially distributed (Dunham, Legal and Economic Basis for Planning, 58 Col.L.Rev. 650, 665). In other words, the removal from productive use of private property has an ultimate social cost more easily concealed by imposing the cost on the owner alone. When successfully concealed, the public is not likely to have any objection to the "cost-free" benefit.

In this case, the zoning amendment is unreasonable and, therefore, unconstitutional because, without due process of law, it deprives the owner of all his property rights, except the bare title and a dubious future reversion of full use. The amendment renders the park property unsuitable for any reasonable income productive or other private use for which it is adapted and thus destroys its economic value and deprives plaintiff of its security for its mortgages. * * *

It is recognized that the "value" of property is not a concrete or tangible attribute but an abstraction derived from the economic uses to which the property may be put. Thus, the development rights are an essential component of the value of the underlying property because they constitute some of the economic uses to which the property may be put. As such, they are a potentially valuable and even a transferable commodity and may not be disregarded in determining whether the ordinance has destroyed the economic value of the underlying property * * *.

Of course, the development rights of the parks were not nullified by the city's action. In an attempt to preserve the rights they were severed from the real property and made transferable to another section of mid-Manhattan in the city, but not to any particular parcel or place. There was thus created floating development rights, utterly unusable until they could be attached to some accommodating real property, available by happenstance of prior ownership, or by grant, purchase, or devise, and subject to the contingent approvals of administrative agencies. In such case, the development rights, disembodied abstractions of man's ingenuity, float in a limbo until restored to reality by reattachment to tangible real property. Put another way, it is a tolerable abstraction to consider development rights apart from the solid land from which as a matter of zoning law they derive. But severed, the development rights are a double abstraction until they are actually attached to a receiving parcel, yet to be identified, acquired, and subject to the contingent future approvals of administrative agencies, events which may never happen because of the exigencies of the market and the contingencies and exigencies of administrative action. The acceptance of this contingency-ridden arrangement, however, was mandatory under the amendment.

The problem with this arrangement, as Mr. Justice Waltemade so wisely observed at Special Term, is that it fails to assure preservation of the very real economic value of the development rights as they existed when still attached to the underlying property (77 Misc.2d 199, 201, 352 N.Y.S.2d 762, 764). By compelling the owner to enter an unpredictable real estate market to find a suitable receiving lot for the rights, or a purchaser who would then share the same interest in using additional development rights, the amendment renders uncertain and thus severely impairs the value of the development rights before they were severed (see Note, The Unconstitutionality of Transferable Development Rights, 84 Yale L.J. 1101, 1110–1111). Hence, when viewed in relation to both the value of the private parks after the amendment, and the value of the development rights detached from the private parks, the amendment destroyed the economic value of the property. It thus constituted a deprivation of property without due process of law.

* * *

Accordingly, the order of the Appellate Division should be affirmed, without costs, and the certified question answered in the affirmative.

* * *

Notes

1. The battle between the residents of Tudor City and the owner continued for several years. Ownership of the complex changed several times; in 1985, after sale of half the complex to a pair of developers, a settlement began to emerge. The new developers were interested in converting about 2,500 of the apartments into cooperatives. The settlement, achieved in 1987, had at its core, an agreement by the tenants' association not to block conversions, in exchange for transfer of the parks to the Trust for Public Land with permanent protection. Also, the developers agreed to donate $820,840 for an endowment to upgrade and maintain the park and $50,000 for a reserve to cover legal expenses in protecting the conservation

easement. See Gross, Fight for 2 Parks Won by Tudor City 'Kingpin', N.Y. Times, May 4, 1987, p. B 3.

2.   A number of state courts have reached the same conclusion as California did in HFH, Ltd., and New York did in Fred F. French. Some other leading cases are Davis v. Pima County, 121 Ariz. 343, 590 P.2d 459 (App.1978); Gold Run, Ltd. v. Board of County Comm'rs, 38 Colo.App. 44, 554 P.2d 317 (1976); Eck v. City of Bismarck, 283 N.W.2d 193 (N.D.1979); and Pamel Corp. v. Puerto Rico Highway Auth., 621 F.2d 33 (1st Cir.1980). All four cases held that the proper remedy for excessive land use regulation is invalidation of the regulation rather than damages by way of a suit in inverse condemnation. The North Dakota court in the Eck case did indicate in dictum that inverse condemnation in cases of excessive regulation might be available in special circumstances, but it acknowledged that such a case would be rare. Also see Minch v. City of Fargo, 297 N.W.2d 785 (N.D.1980).

3.   California extended the holding in HFH, Ltd. to a case where the complaint alleged more than a reduction in market value. In Agins v. City of Tiburon, 24 Cal.3d 266, 157 Cal.Rptr. 372, 598 P.2d 25 (1979), affirmed 447 U.S. 255, 100 S.Ct. 2138, 65 L.Ed.2d 106 (1980), the plaintiff in an inverse condemnation action alleged that a zoning regulation forbade substantially all use of the land and was a taking. The California Supreme Court again held the inverse condemnation remedy inappropriate in that such a remedy would hamper flexibility in land use planning, and would have a chilling effect on local regulation because of judicial control of expenditure of public funds which is basically a legislative responsibility. The California Supreme Court dealt with the issue of the application of the Pennsylvania Coal case by noting:

> In balancing the constitutional rights of the landowner against the legitimate needs of government we do not ignore well established precedent. In Pennsylvania Coal Co. v. Mahon, 260 U.S. 393, 43 S.Ct. 158, 67 L.Ed. 322 (1922), an injunction was sought to prevent a coal company from causing subsidence of property due to the company's underground mining activities. This Supreme Court opinion has generated some confusion and has even been cited erroneously for the proposition that inverse condemnation is readily available as a remedy in zoning cases because of Justice Holmes' statement that "The general rule at least is, that while property may be regulated to a certain extent, if regulation goes too far it will be recognized as a taking." (Mahon, supra, at p. 415, 43 S.Ct., at p. 160.) It is clear both from context and from the disposition in Mahon, however, that the term 'taking' was used solely to indicate the limit by which the acknowledged social goal of land control could be achieved by regulation rather than by eminent domain. The high court set aside the injunctive relief which had been granted by the Pennsylvania courts and declared void the exercise of police power which had limited the company's right to mine its land. The court did not attempt, however, to transmute the illegal governmental infringement into an exercise of eminent domain and the possibility of compensation was not even considered.

The court also held that the plaintiff failed to establish a case for invalidation of the ordinance as depriving him of substantially all use of the property because he could still, under the terms of the ordinance, build one to five dwellings on his five acre parcel. On appeal, the United States Supreme Court used the latter holding to avoid the issue of whether plaintiff could be denied the remedy of inverse condemnation, stating that since there was no taking, the question of the proper remedy did not have to be decided.

In San Diego Gas & Electric Co. v. City of San Diego, 450 U.S. 621, 101 S.Ct. 1287, 67 L.Ed.2d 551 (1981), the Supreme Court again skirted the issue of the inverse condemnation remedy for regulatory takings by dismissing the appeal on the ground that the California Supreme Court judgment denying damages was not a final judgment. In a dissenting opinion by Justice Brennan, joined by three other Justices, and approvingly referred to in Justice Rehnquist's concurring opinion, five Justices indicated that invalidation of a land use regulation so oppressive as to amount to a taking is an inadequate remedy and that a landowner in such a situation might be entitled to monetary relief for a "temporary taking" with damages to be measured from the time of the adoption of the oppressive regulation to the time of invalidation. Justice Brennan cited for support of this idea, Hagman & Misczynski, Windfalls for Wipeouts 296–297 (1978) and Bosselman, The Third Alternative in Zoning Litigation, 17 Zoning Dig. 113, 114–119 (1965). Also see Duerksen & Mantell, Interim Damages: A Remedy in Land Use Cases?, 33 Land Use Law & Zoning Dig. 6 (April 1981).

The distinction between a takings claim and a denial of substantive due process claim has several dimensions; most important are the differences between the two theories in terms of ripeness and exhaustion of administrative remedies and the differing measures of damages, if damages are appropriate. The distinction has tempted lawyers to combine the causes of action, thus shifting to the courts the difficulty of determining an analytical framework for the case. See Thomas E. Roberts, Karen Edginton Milner and Robert I. McMurry, Land Use Litigation: Doctrinal Confusion Under the Fifth and Fourteenth Amendments, 28 The Urban Lawyer 765 (1996). Consider the following cases:

PRESBYTERY OF SEATTLE v. KING COUNTY

Supreme Court of Washington, 1990.
114 Wash.2d 320, 787 P.2d 907, certiorari denied 498
U.S. 911, 111 S.Ct. 284, 112 L.Ed.2d 238.

ANDERSEN, JUSTICE.

* * *

In 1978 the Presbytery of Seattle purchased a single family home located on approximately 4.5 acres of land in Federal Way for $60,000. The financing documents indicate the property was purchased for the construction of a church.

In 1979 the Presbytery informed the Federal Way Planning and Development Commission that in 1980 it intended to begin construction of a church. However, for financial reasons, that building plan fell through. The Presbytery continued to rent out the existing home located on the property and has never filed an application for a development permit for the property.

Part of the Presbytery's property contains a "wetland". * * * The record before us indicates that in 1981 King County conducted an inventory of wetlands and concluded that the wetlands involved in this case, Hylebos Wetland No. 18, was a "class 1" wetland. The County provided affidavits to show that this wetland is in excess of 12,000 years old, is one of the last major wetlands in the Federal Way area and is of major environmental significance to King County. It also contains one of the few old growth cedar bogs still in existence in the Pacific Northwest. For purposes of this appeal, the parties concur that Wetland No. 18 comprises approximately one-third of the Presbytery's property.

In 1986 the County enacted ordinance 7746 (hereafter the 1986 Wetland Ordinance). The ordinance includes prohibitions on creation of new construction within the wetland boundaries and creates a buffer zone around the wetland (which may be increased if endangered species exist within the buffer) and a native growth protection easement. It is the Presbytery's argument that the ordinance prohibits the development of a substantial portion of its property and thereby effects a taking of property without just compensation. The Presbytery's inverse condemnation action alleges that the County's wetland regulations prevent it from using its land for a church or for any other economically reasonable or profitable use.

* * *

The trial court granted the County's motion to dismiss based on the landowner's failure to exhaust its administrative remedies. The Court of Appeals affirmed in an unpublished opinion. We herein consider the two issues we have determined to be dispositive and affirm both the Superior Court and the Court of Appeals.

* * *

A land use regulation which prohibits development of one portion of an undivided parcel of property does not necessarily constitute a "taking" of the portion which must remain undeveloped. Mere regulation on the use of land has never constituted a "taking" or a violation of due process under federal or state law. The problem in any given case is to determine when such a regulation exceeds constitutional bounds. In order to determine whether such a regulation would be unconstitutional either as a "taking" or as a violation of substantive due process, it is necessary to follow the proper tests for inverse condemnation and for substantive due process violations due to excessive land use regulation.

* * *

The "tests" for over-regulation have until recently proved somewhat of a quagmire of constitutional theory vacillating between substantive due process and "takings" theory. Both this court and the United States

Supreme Court have in the past struggled with the difficult determination of where a mere regulation ends and a "taking" commences.

* * *

In this state, a land use regulation which too drastically curtails owners' use of their property can cause a constitutional "taking" or can constitute a denial of substantive due process. These two constitutional theories are alternatives in cases where overly severe land use regulations are alleged. It is critical that these two grounds be separately considered and independently analyzed because the remedies for each of these types of constitutional violation are different.

To determine which of these two constitutional tests to utilize, the threshold inquiry a court must make is whether the challenged regulation safeguards the public interest in health, safety, the environment or the fiscal integrity of an area. A regulation which does that is to be contrasted with one that goes beyond preventing a public harm and actually enhances a publicly owned right in property. Secondly, the court should ask whether the regulation destroys one or more of the fundamental attributes of ownership—the right to possess, to exclude others and to dispose of property. If a regulation does not infringe upon a fundamental attribute of ownership, and if it protects the public from one of the foregoing listed harms, then no constitutional "taking" requiring just compensation exists.

However, even if the regulation protects the public from harm, and does not deny the owners a fundamental attribute of ownership (and is thus insulated from a "takings" challenge), it still must withstand the due process test of reasonableness. The inquiry here must be whether the police power (rather than the eminent domain power) has exceeded its constitutional limits. To determine whether the regulation violates due process, the court should engage in the classic 3–prong due process test and ask: (1) whether the regulation is aimed at achieving a legitimate public purpose; (2) whether it uses means that are reasonably necessary to achieve that purpose; and (3) whether it is unduly oppressive on the land owner. * * *

The "unduly oppressive" inquiry lodges wide discretion in the court and implies a balancing of the public's interest against those of the regulated landowner. We have suggested several factors for the court to consider to assist it in determining whether a regulation is overly oppressive, namely: the nature of the harm sought to be avoided; the availability and effectiveness of less drastic protective measures; and the economic loss suffered by the property owner. Another well regarded commentator in this area of the law, Professor William B. Stoebuck of the University of Washington Law School, has suggested a helpful set of nonexclusive factors to aid the court in effecting this balancing. On the public's side, the seriousness of the public problem, the extent to which the owner's land contributes to it, the degree to which the proposed regulation solves it and the feasibility of less oppressive solutions would all be relevant. On the owner's side, the amount and percentage of value loss, the extent of remaining uses, past, present and future uses, temporary or permanent nature of the regulation, the extent to which the owner should have anticipated such regulation and how feasible it is for the owner to alter present or currently planned uses. Stoebuck, San Diego Gas: Problems, Pitfalls and a Better Way, 25 J.Urb. & Contemp.L. 3, 33 (1983). Use of these factors can materially assist the court in determining whether or not the regulation on use is unduly oppressive to the landowner.

If the regulation is not aimed at a legitimate public purpose, or uses a means which does not tend to achieve it, or if it unduly oppresses the landowner, then the ordinance will be struck down as violative of due process and the remedy is invalidation of the regulation. No compensation (which properly belongs with a "taking" analysis) is warranted in the face of a due process violation.

Invalidation of the ordinance (instead of compensation) also avoids intimidating the legislative body, a situation about which we have previously expressed concern. For example, as commentators have observed in this connection,

> if local governments in the past had thought that enactment of a land use regulation might result in monetary awards, then "very likely no one would have proposed the planned unit development, the cluster zone, or the floating zone and even if those efforts had received the prior blessing of developers, it is highly unlikely that environmental concerns or regulation of coastal and inland waterways would ever have been risked."

Sallet, Regulatory "Takings" and Just Compensation: The Supreme Court's Search for a Solution Continues, 18 Urb.Law. 635, 636 (1986) (quoting Wright, Exclusionary Land Use Controls and the Taking Issue, 8 Hastings Const. L.Q. 545, 583 (1981)). Accordingly, many challenges to land use regulations will most appropriately be analyzed under a due process formula rather than under a "taking" formula. This is not to say, however, that a certain class of cases will not have to face a "taking" challenge.

* * *

The "taking" analysis requires that the court first ask whether the regulation substantially advances legitimate state interests. If it does not, then it constitutes a "taking". If it does substantially advance a legitimate state interest, then it becomes necessary to look further and see if the challenge to the regulation is a facial challenge or one involving application of the regulation to specific property. It would not be necessary for the challengers to exhaust administrative remedies in a facial challenge because the allegation would be that application of the regulation to any property would constitute a "taking". If the case is a facial challenge, then the landowner must show that the regulation denies all economically viable use of any parcel of regulated property in order to constitute a taking.

* * *

Returning to our "taking" analysis, if the challenge to the regulation is a facial one, and if the landowner succeeds in showing that a regulation denies all economically viable use of any parcel of regulated property, then a constitutional taking has occurred. Practically, however, this should prove to be a relatively rare occurrence.

If the challenge involves an application of the regulation to specific property, then the court should consider: (1) the economic impact of the regulation on the property; (2) the extent of the regulation's interference with investment-backed expectations; and (3) the character of the government action.

If the court determines a "taking" has, in fact, occurred, then just compensation is mandated by the Fifth and Fourteenth Amendments and by Const. art. 1, § 16. If the taking was due to an overly severe land use regulation, and was temporary and reversible, the governmental unit involved has the option of curing the taking or maintaining the status quo by exercising its eminent domain power. Whichever it chooses, just compensation must be paid for the period during which the taking is effective.

As previously noted, exhaustion would be unnecessary if the landowner was engaging in a facial challenge to the ordinance. However, the record presented in this case demonstrates that the landowner has not carried the burden of showing that the regulation denies it all economically viable use of any parcel of regulated property. Therefore, we consider the landowner's exhaustion argument in the context of an "as applied" challenge.

Applying the analysis discussed above to the present case, we could arguably conclude that the challenged regulation seeks to safeguard the public interest in the environment and does not appear to enhance a publicly owned right in other property. However, it would be premature at this time to decide whether the regulation denies an essential attribute of ownership. Assuming without deciding, that the regulation should be scrutinized under the 3–prong due process analysis, we simply do not have all of the required facts needed in order for this court to apply that formula.

Although it might be possible to determine that the regulation was aimed at achieving a legitimate public purpose and that it used means to achieve that purpose, on the limited record here presented it is not possible to determine whether the regulation was unduly oppressive to this landowner. Without knowledge of the uses to which this property can legally be put, it is not feasible to consider the factors which help to determine "undue oppressiveness". Exhaustion of administrative remedies is, therefore, necessary in order for a court to have before it the facts necessary to make such a determination.

Although the landowners argue that exhaustion would be futile in this particular case, we disagree. Exhaustion of administrative remedies is generally required before resort to the courts, although exhaustion is excused if a resort to administrative procedures would be futile.

* * *

Our recent decision in Estate of Friedman v. Pierce Cy., 112 Wash.2d 68, 768 P.2d 462 (1989) involved a challenge to a planned unit development (PUD) map which required that a substantial amount of land in the PUD remain "open space". The present case is similar in that some portion (perhaps one-third) of the owner's land will have to remain "open space" to protect the Hylebos wetland under present regulations. Estate of Friedman made clear that it will be the uncommon case where a landowner can show a constitutional violation without first exhausting available procedures in an attempt to secure a permit for possible use. As noted earlier herein, King County argues that resort to administrative channels would not have been futile because the Sensitive Area Ordinance does allow development of wetlands if application of the wetland ordinance "would deny all reasonable uses of a property". As also noted, the County further argues that it is entirely possible that the landowner may be permitted to build a church on its land under existing regulations.

Because the landowner has not as yet sought any development permits, it is not possible to know what effect SEPA and other applicable regulations might have on the property in question. The Court of Appeals appropriately observed that without engaging in the application process, there is no way to know what beneficial use may be made of Presbytery's property, nor any way to know what deprivation of beneficial use was proximately caused by the Hylebos Wetland Ordinance.

Affirmed.

BURROWS v. CITY OF KEENE

Supreme Court of New Hampshire, 1981.
121 N.H. 590, 432 A.2d 15.

GRIMES, CHIEF JUSTICE.

The issue in this case is whether an amendment to the Keene zoning ordinance, which had the effect of including a substantial part of the plaintiffs' land in a conservation district, resulted in a taking of the plaintiffs' property entitling them to damages for inverse condemnation. We hold that it did.

On October 15, 1973, the plaintiffs, John P. Burrows and George Whitham, purchased approximately 124 acres of undeveloped woodland on the southern side of Goose Pond Road in Keene for $45,000. Plaintiff Burrows is, and has been for many years, a real estate developer, and the property was purchased for the purpose of subdivision development, which was a permitted use in the rural zone in which it was located.

Because of its proximity to the city, a golf course, and Goose Pond, the plaintiffs thought that the property was very desirable for development.

In January 1975, the plaintiffs went to the Keene Planning Board and presented three plans for subdividing the property. The planning board indicated that the prospects of subdivision approval were not favorable because the city was trying to preserve as open space the area in which the plaintiffs' land was located. Accordingly, the board advised the plaintiffs to consult the city conservation commission concerning the possibility of selling the land to the conservation commission as an alternative to development. The conservation commission expressed a desire to purchase the property and requested a delay so that it could obtain federal funding to make the purchase. The plaintiffs agreed.

In August 1975, the city had the property appraised for $27,000, which was much less than either the purchase price of $45,000 or the city's assessment for tax purposes of $41,406. It appears that the appraiser improperly underassessed the value of the land based on the city's intended noncommercial use of the land. Nevertheless, the city offered the plaintiffs only $27,900 for the land.

Because the parties could not reach agreement on price, the plaintiffs went forward with their subdivision plans. * * *

After various studies and meetings, a public hearing was held on September 27, 1976, following which the board denied the plaintiffs' application for subdivision approval and adopted a resolution favoring acquisition of the plaintiffs' land.

The plaintiffs did not appeal from the planning board's denial of their subdivision plan but instead brought this action for equitable relief in the superior court. In December 1977, the city amended its zoning ordinance. The effect of this amendment was to include 109 acres of the plaintiffs' land in a conservation zone and the balance in a rural zone. Thereafter, the plaintiffs amended their petition in the superior court to include a claim that the amendment to the zoning ordinance had deprived them of all reasonable use of that portion of their property which was included in the conservation zone and, in effect, sought damages for inverse condemnation.

* * *

The Trial Court dismissed the plaintiffs' claim regarding the denial of subdivision approval because of their failure to appeal the planning board decision. The court also found that there were valid reasons for the board's denial of the plaintiffs' application for subdivision approval. However, the court considered the claim based on inverse condemnation, ruled that the inclusion of the land in the conservation zone did constitute inverse condemnation and ordered that damages be determined by a jury if no appeal was taken from its ruling. The city appealed.

* * *

The substantive issue raised in this case involves a principle that lies at the very foundation of civilized society as we know it. The principle that no man's property may be taken from him without just compensation reaches at least as far back as 1215, when on "the meadow which is called Runnymede" the Barons of England exacted from King John the Magna Carta, which contains at least three references to this fundamental truth. Magna Carta, arts. 28, 30 & 31, *reprinted in* 1 Mass.Gen.Laws Ann. (West); *see Ferguson v. Keene,* 108 N.H. 409, 415, 238 A.2d 1, 5 (1968) (Grimes, J., dissenting). Our own constitution provides that "no part of a man's property shall be taken from him, or applied to public uses, without his consent * * *." N.H.Const. pt. I, art. 12. Early on, this clause was held to require just compensation. *Piscataqua Bridge v. N.H. Bridge,* 7 N.H. 35, 66–70 (1834); *Eaton v. B.C. & M.R.R.,* 51 N.H. 504, 510–11 (1872). The same principle was embodied in the Fifth Amendment to the Constitution of the United States at the insistence of a majority of the states, including New Hampshire, in ratifying the Constitution. It has now been made binding on the states through the Fourteenth Amendment. *Webb's Fab. Pharmacies, Inc. v. Beckwith,* 449 U.S. ___, ___, 101 S.Ct. 446, 450, 66 L.Ed.2d 358 (1980).

It should be noted that the New Hampshire Constitution makes explicit what is implicit in the Fifth Amendment to the Federal Constitution, namely, that "no *part* of a man's property shall be taken from him . . . without his consent * * *." N.H.Const. pt. I, art. 12. (Emphasis added.) Furthermore, our New Hampshire Bill of Rights provides that among the "natural, essential and inherent rights" of all men is the right of "acquiring, possessing, and protecting property; and, in a word, of seeking and obtaining happiness." N.H.Const. pt. I, art. 2. This fundamental right is recognized in the same article which recognizes the right of "enjoying and defending life and liberty." *Id. Gazzola v. Clements,* 120 N.H. 25, 411 A.2d 147 (1980).

The rights mentioned in N.H.Const. pt. I, art. 2 are not bestowed by that constitutional provision but rather are recognized to be among the natural and inherent rights of all humankind. This provision of our Bill of Rights "has been held to be so specific that it 'necessarily limits all subsequent grants of power to deal adversely with it.'" *Metzger v. Town of Brentwood,* 117 N.H. 497, 502, 374 A.2d 954, 957 (1977) (quoting *Woolf v. Fuller,* 87 N.H. 64, 68, 174 A. 193, 196 (1934)). Because it limits all subsequent express grants of power, it necessarily limits the so-called police power, which is only an implied power. "The right to just compensation is [likewise] a constitutional restriction on the police power and is therefore superior to it." *Robbins Auto Parts, Inc. v. City of Laconia,* 117 N.H. 235, 237, 371 A.2d 1167, 1169 (1977). Indeed, we have specifically stated that both N.H.Const. pt. I, art. 2 and N.H.Const. pt. I, art. 12 "are limitations on the so-called police power of the State and subdivisions thereof * * *." *L. Grossman & Sons, Inc. v. Town of Gilford,* 118 N.H. 480, 482, 387 A.2d 1178, 1180 (1978).

Because the constitution prohibits any taking of private property by whatever means without compensation, the just compensation requirement applies whenever the exercise of the so-called police power results in a "taking of property." The government may not do under an implied power that which it cannot do under an express power. In other words, it cannot do indirectly that which it cannot do directly. *Eaton v. B.C. & M.R.R.,* 51 N.H. at 510; *cf. Girard v. Town of Allenstown,* 428 A.2d 488, 490 (1981).

The question in the case before us is whether the action of the city constituted a taking of the plaintiffs' property. "Property," in the constitutional sense, is not the physical thing itself but is rather the group of rights which the owner of the thing has with respect to it. *United States v. General Motors Corp.,* 323 U.S. 373, 377–78, 65 S.Ct. 357, 359, 89 L.Ed. 311 (1945); *Eaton v. B.C. & M.R.R., supra* at 511. The term refers to a person's right to "possess, use, enjoy and dispose of a thing and is not limited to the thing itself." *Metzger v. Town of Brentwood,* 117 N.H. at 502, 374 A.2d at 957; *see United States v. General Motors Corp., supra.* The property owner's rights of "indefinite user (or of using indefinitely) * * * necessarily includes the right * * * "to exclude others from using the property, whether it be land or anything else. *Eaton v. B.C. & M.R.R., supra* at 511. "From the very nature of these rights of user and of exclusion, it is evident that they cannot be materially abridged without, *ipso facto,* taking the owner's 'property.' " *Id.* "The principle must be the same whether the owner is wholly deprived of the use of his land, or only partially deprived of it * * *." *Id.* at 512.

Although the interference with the property rights in *Eaton* involved a physical invasion of the land, the just compensation principle likewise applies if the abridgement of the rights is accomplished by a governmental regulation restricting the exercise of these rights. *Metzger v. Town of Brentwood,* 117 N.H. at 502, 374 A.2d at 957; *see San Diego Gas & Elec. v. City of San Diego,* 450 U.S. 621, 101 S.Ct. 1287, 1302–08, 67 L.Ed.2d 551 (1981) (Brennan, J., dissenting); *Pennsylvania Coal Co. v. Mahon,* 260 U.S. 393, 415, 43 S.Ct. 158, 160, 67 L.Ed. 322 (1922). Even though the United States Supreme Court found no taking in *Agins v. Tiburon,* 447 U.S. 255, 261–63, 100 S.Ct. 2138, 2141–43, 65 L.Ed.2d 106 (1980) and *Penn Central Transp. Co. v. New York City,* 438 U.S. 104, 123–38, 98 S.Ct. 2646, 2659–66, 57 L.Ed.2d 631 (1978), it recognized in both cases that the application of a zoning regulation to particular property effects a taking if it "denies an owner economically viable use of his land * * *." 447 U.S. at 260, 100 S.Ct. at 2138; *see* 438 U.S. at 138 n. 36, 98 S.Ct. at 2666 n. 36.

"Police power regulations such as zoning ordinances and other land-use restrictions can destroy the use and enjoyment of property in order to promote the public good just as effectively as formal condemnation or physical invasion of property." *San Diego Gas & Elec. v. City of San Diego,* 101 S.Ct. at 1304 (Brennan, J., dissenting). It matters not to the owner whether the use of his land is taken from him by actual physical invasion or condemnation or whether he is prevented from using it by regulation. *Id.* On the other hand, the benefits resulting to the public from the taking may be equally great whether the taking is accomplished by regulation or actual condemnation. *Id.*

This is not to say that every regulation of private property through the police power constitutes a taking. Reasonable regulations that prevent an owner from using his land in such a way that it causes injury to others or deprives them of the reasonable use of their land may not require compensation. *See Penn Central Transp. Co. v. New York City,* 438 U.S. at 144–45, 98 S.Ct. at 2669–70 (Rehnquist, J., dissenting) (quoting *Mugler v. Kansas,* 123 U.S. 623, 668–69, 8 S.Ct. 273, 300–01, 31 L.Ed. 205 (1887)); *Sibson v. State,* 115 N.H. 124 at 128, 336 A.2d 239 at 242. Nor do reasonable zoning regulations which restrict economic uses of property to different zones and which do not substantially destroy the value of an individual piece of property effect a taking requiring compensation. But arbitrary or unreasonable restrictions which substantially deprive the owner of the "economically viable use of his land" in order to benefit the public in some way constitute a taking within the meaning of our New Hampshire Constitution requiring the payment of just compensation. *See Sundell v. Town of New London,* 119 N.H. at 845, 409 A.2d at 1318; *Metzger v. Town of Brentwood,* 117 N.H. at 503, 374 A.2d at 958. It is a matter of degree. *Pennsylvania Coal Co. v. Mahon,* 260 U.S. at 416, 43 S.Ct. at 160. The owner need not be deprived of all valuable use of his property. If the denial of use is substantial and is especially onerous, a taking occurs. There can be no set test to determine when regulation goes too far and becomes a taking. Each case must be determined under its own circumstances. The purpose of the regulation is an element to be considered. *See Agins v. Tiburon,* 447 U.S. at 260–62, 100 S.Ct. 2138, 2141–42, 65 L.Ed.2d 106. It will only be the cases which lie close to the line of constitutionality which will cause difficulty. The case before us, however, does not lie anywhere near the line.

We are aware of cases such as *Agins v. Tiburon,* 24 Cal.3d 266, 157 Cal.Rptr. 372, 598 P.2d 25 (1979), *aff'd on other grounds* 447 U.S. 255, 100 S.Ct. 2138, 65 L.Ed.2d 106 (1980), which hold that a landowner who is the victim of an excessive use of the police power may not recover damages for inverse condemnation but must be satisfied with the remedies of mandamus or declaratory judgment to invalidate the regulation.

We reject this approach out of hand. It is contrary to our well-established law, which goes back at least as far as *Eaton v. B.C. & M.R.R.,* 51 N.H. 504 (1872). It is also, we believe, in violation of the Constitution of the United States. *See San Diego Gas & Elec. Co. v. City of San Diego,* 101 S.Ct. at 1294, 1301–08 (Brennan, J., dissenting and Rehnquist, J., concurring). We agree with Justice Brennan that it is always open to the governmental entity involved to rescind or repeal the offending regulation and thus avoid payment of damages for inverse condemnation from that point on. *Id.* at 1304–07. Until that is done, however, the owner's property has been taken during the interim period and he is entitled to compensation for that taking. *Id.* Limiting the landowner to actions which only invalidate the offending regulation will encourage municipal planners and other public officials to attempt to throw the burdens accompanying "progress" upon individual landowners rather than on the public at large. The allowance of damages for inverse condemnation during the period of the taking, however, should encourage such officials to stay well on the constitutional side of the line, *San Diego Gas & Elec. Co. v. City of San Diego, supra* at 1308 n. 26 (Brennan, J., dissenting), and should also discourage harassment of property owners by repeated amendments of zoning regulations and the enactment of new ones. *See id.* at 1305–06 n. 22.

Planners and other officials should be aware of possible personal liability for bad faith violations of a landowner's constitutional rights which may go beyond the damages recoverable for inverse condemnation. Cities and towns should also be aware of possible 42 U.S.C.A. § 1983 actions for damages and for violations of the constitutional rights of citizens to be compensated for injuries suffered. *Owen v. City of Independence,* 445 U.S. 622, 100 S.Ct. 1398, 63 L.Ed.2d 673 (1980); *Monell v. New York City Dept. of Social Services,* 436 U.S. 658, 98 S.Ct. 2018, 56 L.Ed.2d 611 (1978).

As we have said before, public officials have a duty to obey the constitution, and they have no right or legitimate reason to attempt to spare the public the cost of improving the public condition by thrusting that expense upon an individual. *See J.E.D. Associates, Inc. v. Town of Atkinson,* 121 N.H. at ___, 432 A.2d at 15; *Robbins Auto Parts, Inc. v. City of Laconia,* 117 N.H. at 237, 371 A.2d at 1169. The greater the cost of accomplishing something which is considered to be in the public interest, the greater the reason why a single individual should not be required to bear that burden. *See Armstrong v. United States,* 364 U.S. 40, 49, 80 S.Ct. 1563, 1569, 4 L.Ed.2d 1554 (1960); *Monongahela Navigat'n Co. v. United States,* 148 U.S. 312, 325, 13 S.Ct. 622, 626, 37 L.Ed. 463 (1893). Almost 110 years ago, Justice Jeremiah Smith of this court stated that the prospect of a great public benefit "may afford an excellent reason for taking the plaintiff's land in the constitutional manner, but not for taking it without compensation." *Eaton v. B.C. & M.R.R.,* 51 N.H. at 518; *see Ferguson v. Keene,* 108 N.H. at 415, 238 A.2d at 5 (Grimes, J., dissenting). Justice Holmes used similar language fifty years later in *Pennsylvania Coal Co. v. Mahon,* 260 U.S. at 416, 43 S.Ct. at 160.

Turning now to the zoning amendment involved in this case, we have already stated that it does not come anywhere near the line dividing constitutional and unconstitutional regulation.

From the outset, it was plain that the city wished that the plaintiffs' land be devoted to open space. The city's comprehensive plan sets out a goal of having fifty per cent of the city remain as open space, and the Goose Pond area is one of those designated for preservation. The planning board and the conservation commission both took positions opposed to subdivision and in favor of acquisition of the plaintiffs' land by the city. The city, however, would not pay a reasonable price for the property, electing instead to offer to purchase the property for a sum representing the land's value based on the city's intended use of the land rather than the price to which the plaintiffs were entitled, which was one reflecting the land's highest and best use. In denying the plaintiffs' application, the planning board stated that the land should be protected as a wilderness area and passed a resolution favoring acquisition of the land by the city.

Instead of acquiring the plaintiffs' land by paying just compensation as required by our constitution, however, the city, when it found that it was unable to acquire it for little more than half its value, elected to accomplish its purpose by regulating the use of the property so as to prohibit all "normal private development." It is plain that the city and its officials were attempting to obtain for the public the benefit of having this land remain undeveloped as open space without paying for that benefit in the constitutional manner. The city sought to enjoy that public benefit by forcing the plaintiffs to devote their land to a particular purpose and prohibiting all other economically feasible uses of the land, thus placing the entire burden of preserving the land as open space upon the plaintiffs. The trial court found, in a well-considered opinion, that the uses permitted were "so restrictive as to be economically impracticable, resulting in a substantial reduction in the value of the land" and that they prevented a private owner from enjoying "any worthwhile rights or benefits in the land."

The court also found that the interference with the plaintiffs' right to use that portion of their land falling within the conservation district was "sufficiently direct, sufficiently peculiar and of sufficient magnitude as to compel the court to conclude that fairness and justice require that the burden be borne by the city and not by the plaintiffs." These findings are amply supported by the evidence.

The purpose of the regulation is clearly to give the public the benefit of preserving the plaintiffs' land as open space. Its purpose is not to restrain an injurious use of the property. Although there may undoubtedly be some uses of the land which are sufficiently injurious to others that their use may be prohibited, the normal development of the land for residential purposes is not one of them.

* * *

We hold that the creation of the "conservation district" in Keene constituted a taking with respect to all of the plaintiffs' land which falls within it, entitling the plaintiffs to compensation for inverse condemnation in an amount equal to the diminution in the value of the plaintiffs' land resulting from the taking. Although cases of the United States Supreme Court have been cited, we decide this case solely on the basis of the New Hampshire Constitution.

Because a citizen should not be compelled to bear the financial burden of protecting himself from unconstitutional abuses of power, we hold that the plaintiffs are entitled to reasonable counsel fees and double costs incurred in this appeal. *See* RSA 490:14–a (Supp.1979); Supreme

Court Rule 23. The matter is remanded for a determination of damages and for assessment of additional reasonable counsel fees and costs at the trial level. *See Harkeem v. Adams,* 117 N.H. 687, 691, 377 A.2d 617, 619 (1977).

Appeal dismissed; remanded.

All concurred.

Notes

1.   Which case makes more sense, the one from Washington or the one from New Hampshire? Does the exhaustion of administrative remedies doctrine itself place an inordinate burden on a property owner to expend large sums on preparation of plans and dealings with the local government in order to determine just what development will be allowed? Is this process of planning and presentation itself a "temporary taking"? On the application of a statute of limitations to an inverse condemnation claim, see McCuskey v. Canyon County Commissioners, 128 Idaho 213, 912 P.2d 100 (1996).

2.   See also Zinn v. State, 112 Wis.2d 417, 334 N.W.2d 67 (1983), in which a ruling of a state agency regarding the high-water mark of a public navigable lake had the effect of converting 200 acres of land around the lake to public land was held to be a regulatory taking even though the ruling was subsequently rescinded. The Wisconsin Court stated in part:

> Governmental action which merely causes damage to private property is not the basis for compensation under this provision of the state constitution. DeBruin v. Green County, 72 Wis.2d 464, 470, 241 N.W.2d 167 (1976). Rather, in order to trigger the "just compensation" clause there must be a "taking" of private property for public use. Id. A "taking" in the constitutional sense occurs when the government restriction placed on the property " 'practically or substantially renders the property useless for all reasonable purposes.' " Howell Plaza, Inc. v. State Highway Comm., 92 Wis.2d 74, 85, 284 N.W.2d 887 (1979), quoting *Buhler v. Racine County,* 33 Wis.2d 137, 143, 146 N.W.2d 403 (1966). A taking can occur short of actual occupation by the government if the restriction "deprives the owner of all, or substantially all, of the beneficial use of his property." Howell Plaza, Inc. v. State Highway Comm., 66 Wis.2d 720, 726, 226 N.W.2d 185 (1975). However, "[a] taking can occur absent physical invasion only where there is a legally imposed restriction upon the property's use." *Howell Plaza,* 92 Wis.2d at 88, 284 N.W.2d 887.

> Thus, the threshold question is whether the plaintiff's property was "taken." This involves the difficult determination of whether an erroneous ch. 227 administrative decision by the DNR can result in the "taking" of private property thus triggering the just compensation clause.

> * * *

> Because the DNR's ruling, which was within its statutory authority to make, converted Zinn's private property by operation of law into public lands, there can be no dispute that there was a "taking" within the meaning of Art. I, sec. 13. Contrary to the holding of the court of

appeals, we find that this ruling which transferred title to Zinn's land to the state constituted a legally imposed restriction on Zinn's property under this court's decision in *Howell Plaza* (1979). It is difficult to conceive of a greater restriction on the property, in the absence of actual physical occupancy, than the loss of title to private land. We find that the allegations of the complaint, which demonstrate that the plaintiff temporarily lost title to her land to the state, are sufficient without more to allege a constitutionally compensable taking. The court of appeal's concern with the absence of allegations in the complaint as to the actual restriction on the *use* of Zinn's land as a result of the ruling is a matter of the proof as to the amount of damages suffered by Zinn and is not relevant in the context of a motion to dismiss.

We also disagree with the court of appeal's holding that a taking can not occur when the governmental restraint on the property is only temporary. Because the original ruling of the DNR was later rescinded by the DNR, it is clear that the alleged "taking" was only temporary. However, it would violate the constitutional mandate of the just compensation clauses of the Wisconsin and United States Constitutions to hold that a temporary taking is not compensable.

The Court then quoted from Justice Brennan's dissent in *San Diego Gas and Electric Company* with which it agreed.

FIRST ENGLISH EVANGELICAL LUTHERAN CHURCH v. LOS ANGELES COUNTY

Supreme Court of the United States, 1987.
482 U.S. 304, 107 S.Ct. 2378, 96 L.Ed.2d 250.

[The facts of this case appear earlier in this chapter.]

* * * Appellant asks us to hold that the Supreme Court of California erred in Agins v. Tiburon in determining that the Fifth Amendment, as made applicable to the States through the Fourteenth Amendment, does not require compensation as a remedy for "temporary" regulatory takings—those regulatory takings which are ultimately invalidated by the courts. Four times this decade, we have considered similar claims and have found ourselves for one reason or another unable to consider the merits of the Agins rule. See MacDonald, Sommer & Frates v. Yolo County, 477 U.S. 340 (1986); Williamson County Regional Planning Comm'n v. Hamilton Bank, 473 U.S. 172 (1985); San Diego Gas & Electric Co., supra; Agins v. Tiburon, supra. For the reasons explained below, however, we find the constitutional claim properly presented in this case, and hold that on these facts the California courts have decided the compensation question inconsistently with the requirements of the Fifth Amendment.

* * *

Consideration of the compensation question must begin with direct reference to the language of the Fifth Amendment, which provides in relevant part that "private property [shall not] be taken for public use, without just compensation." As its language indicates, and as the Court has frequently noted, this provision does not prohibit the taking of private property, but instead places a condition on the exercise of that power. See Williamson County, 473 U.S., at 194; Hodel v. Virginia Surface Mining & Reclamation Assn., Inc., 452 U.S. 264, 297, n. 40 (1981); Hurley v. Kincaid, 285 U.S. 95, 104 (1932); Monongahela Navigation Co. v. United States, 148 U.S. 312, 336 (1893); United States v. Jones, 109 U.S. 513, 518 (1883). This basic understanding of the Amendment makes clear that it is designed not to limit the governmental interference with property rights per se, but rather to secure compensation in the event of otherwise proper interference amounting to a taking. Thus, government action that works a taking of property rights necessarily implicates the "constitutional obligation to pay just compensation." Armstrong v. United States, 364 U.S. 40, 49 (1960).

We have recognized that a landowner is entitled to bring an action in inverse condemnation as a result of " 'the self-executing character of the constitutional provision with respect to compensation * * *.' " United States v. Clarke, 445 U.S. 253, 257 (1980), quoting 6 P. Nichols, Eminent Domain § 25.41 (3d rev. ed. 1972). As noted in JUSTICE BRENNAN's dissent in San Diego Gas & Electric Co., 450 U.S., at 654–655, it has been established at least since Jacobs v. United States, 290 U.S. 13 (1933), that claims for just compensation are grounded in the Constitution itself:

> "The suits were based on the right to recover just compensation for property taken by the United States for public use in the exercise of its power of eminent domain. That right was guaranteed by the Constitution. The fact that condemnation proceedings were not instituted and that the right was asserted in suits by the owners did not change the essential nature of the claim. The form of the remedy did not qualify the right. It rested upon the Fifth Amendment. Statutory recognition was not necessary. A promise to pay was not necessary. Such a promise was implied because of the duty to pay imposed by the Amendment. The suits were thus founded upon the Constitution of the United States." Id., at 16. (Emphasis added.)

Jacobs, moreover, does not stand alone, for the Court has frequently repeated the view that, in the event of a taking, the compensation remedy is required by the Constitution. See, e.g., Kirby Forest Industries, Inc. v. United States, 467 U.S. 1, 5 (1984); United States v. Causby, 328 U.S. 256, 267 (1946); Seaboard Air Line R. Co. v. United States, 261 U.S. 299, 304–306 (1923); Monongahela Navigation, supra, at 327.

* * *

While the Supreme Court of California may not have actually disavowed this general rule in Agins, we believe that it has truncated the rule by disallowing damages that occurred prior to the ultimate invalidation of the challenged regulation. The Supreme Court of California justified its conclusion at length in the Agins opinion, concluding that:

"In combination, the need for preserving a degree of freedom in the land-use planning function, and the inhibiting financial force which inheres in the inverse condemnation remedy, persuade us that on balance mandamus or declaratory relief rather than inverse condemnation is the appropriate relief under the circumstances." Agins v. Tiburon, 24 Cal.3d, at 276–277, 598 P.2d, at 31.

We, of course, are not unmindful of these considerations, but they must be evaluated in the light of the command of the Just Compensation Clause of the Fifth Amendment. The Court has recognized in more than one case that the government may elect to abandon its intrusion or discontinue regulations. See, e.g., Kirby Forest Industries, Inc. v. United States, supra; United States v. Dow, 357 U.S. 17, 26 (1958). Similarly, a governmental body may acquiesce in a judicial declaration that one of its ordinances has effected an unconstitutional taking of property; the landowner has no right under the Just Compensation Clause to insist that a "temporary" taking be deemed a permanent taking. But we have not resolved whether abandonment by the government requires payment of compensation for the period of time during which regulations deny a landowner all use of his land.

* * *

These cases reflect the fact that "temporary" takings which, as here, deny a landowner all use of his property, are not different in kind from permanent takings, for which the Constitution clearly requires compensation. Cf. San Diego Gas & Electric Co., 450 U.S., at 657 (BRENNAN, J., dissenting) ("Nothing in the Just Compensation Clause suggests that 'takings' must be permanent and irrevocable"). It is axiomatic that the Fifth Amendment's just compensation provision is "designed to bar Government from forcing some people alone to bear public burdens which, in all fairness and justice, should be borne by the public as a whole." Armstrong v. United States, 364 U.S., at 49. See also Penn Central Transportation Co. v. New York City, 438 U.S., at 123–125; Monongahela Navigation Co. v. United States, 148 U.S., at 325. In the present case the interim ordinance was adopted by the County of Los Angeles in January 1979, and became effective immediately. Appellant filed suit within a month after the effective date of the ordinance and yet when the Supreme Court of California denied a hearing in the case on October 17, 1985, the merits of appellant's claim had yet to be determined. The United States has been required to pay compensation for leasehold interests of shorter duration than this. The value of a leasehold interest in property for a period of years may be substantial, and the burden on the property owner in extinguishing such an interest for a period of years may be great indeed. See, e.g., United States v. General Motors, supra. Where this burden results from governmental action that amounted to a taking, the Just Compensation Clause of the Fifth Amendment requires that the government pay the landowner for the value of the use of the land during this period. Cf. United States v. Causby, 328 U.S., at 261 ("It is the owner's loss, not the taker's gain, which is the measure of the value of the property taken"). Invalidation of the ordinance or its successor ordinance after this period of time, though converting the taking into a "temporary" one, is not a sufficient remedy to meet the demands of the Just Compensation Clause.

* * *

Nothing we say today is intended to abrogate the principle that the decision to exercise the power of eminent domain is a legislative function " 'for Congress and Congress alone to determine.' " Hawaii Housing Authority v. Midkiff, 467 U.S. 229, 240 (1984), quoting Berman v. Parker, 348 U.S. 26, 33 (1954). Once a court determines that a taking has occurred, the government retains the whole range of options already available—amendment of the regulation, withdrawal of the invalidated regulation, or exercise of eminent domain. Thus we do not, as the Solicitor General suggests, "permit a court, at the behest of a private person, to require the * * * Government to exercise the power of eminent domain * * *." Brief for United States as Amicus Curiae 22. We merely hold that where the government's activities have already worked a taking of all use of property, no subsequent action by the government can relieve it of the duty to provide compensation for the period during which the taking was effective.

We also point out that the allegation of the complaint which we treat as true for purposes of our decision was that the ordinance in question denied appellant all use of its property. We limit our holding to the facts presented, and of course do not deal with the quite different questions that would arise in the case of normal delays in obtaining building permits, changes in zoning ordinances, variances, and the like which are not before us. We realize that even our present holding will undoubtedly lessen to some extent the freedom and flexibility of land-use planners and governing bodies of municipal corporations when enacting land-use regulations. But such consequences necessarily flow from any decision upholding a claim of constitutional right; many of the provisions of the Constitution are designed to limit the flexibility and freedom of governmental authorities, and the Just Compensation Clause of the Fifth Amendment is one of them. As Justice Holmes aptly noted more than 50 years ago, "a strong public desire to improve the public condition is not enough to warrant achieving the desire by a shorter cut than the constitutional way of paying for the change." Pennsylvania Coal Co. v. Mahon, 260 U.S., at 416.

Here we must assume that the Los Angeles County ordinance has denied appellant all use of its property for a considerable period of years, and we hold that invalidation of the ordinance without payment of fair value for the use of the property during this period of time would be a constitutionally insufficient remedy. The judgment of the California Court of Appeal is therefore reversed, and the case is remanded for further proceedings not inconsistent with this opinion.

Notes

1.   On remand the California Court of Appeal, supra, found that the church's property had not been taken. Does this mean that the case has become moot? If further appeals continue to find no taking, what precedential value does First English have?

2.   Between the time of the San Diego Gas & Electric case and First English, other courts at the state level found that a cause of action in inverse condemnation would lie for a temporary taking. In addition to the New Hampshire decision, see Rippley v. City of Lincoln, 330 N.W.2d 505 (N.D. 1983); Suess Builders Co. v. City of Beaverton, 294 Or. 254, 656 P.2d 306 (1982); Corrigan v. City of Scottsdale, 149 Ariz. 538, 720 P.2d 513 (1986), cert. denied 479 U.S. 986, 107 S.Ct. 577, 93 L.Ed.2d 580. Also see A.A. Profiles, Inc. v. City of Ft. Lauderdale, 850 F.2d 1483 (11th Cir.1988).

3.   In Meighan v. U.S. Sprint Communications Co., 924 S.W.2d 632 (Tenn.1996) the court held that under the Tennessee statutory framework for inverse condemnation suits a landowner could alternatively sue the alleged taker on a trespass theory and seek punitive as well as compensatory damages. In this case, the telecommunications company struck a deal with a railroad to run fiber optic cable along the right-of-way across plaintiffs' lands. The plaintiffs brought a class action against U.S. Sprint alleging a taking of property and trespass; defendant moved to dismiss the trespass and punitive damages claim.

4.   In Del Oro Hills v. City of Oceanside, 31 Cal.App.4th 1060, 37 Cal.Rptr.2d 677 (1995) the court held that a developer who sought taking damages from a city after the city's growth control ordinance was found invalid, could not simply allege an invalid regulation and claim per se damages. The court found that the developer had sold all of his development, albeit not at the highest price he might have obtained (according to the developer's allegations) and that his land had enjoyed viable economic uses during the period the invalid ordinance was in effect. And, in Ellison v. County of Ventura, 217 Cal.App.3d 455, 265 Cal.Rptr. 795 (1990) the court found that amendments to a zoning ordinance could not be a taking because the value of the property had doubled despite the more restrictive zoning provisions adopted after the owner had purchased the property. See Donald L. Elliott, Givings and Takings, Land Use Law (Jan. 1996) p. 3, for a proposal that courts look to the values added to property by governmental actions as a factor in measuring governmental takings.

5.   How to measure the compensation damages for a temporary taking is left to the lower courts. Since the First English case, federal courts have struggled with the problem. Two cases are illustrative:

(a).   In Joseph Wheeler v. City of Pleasant Grove, 896 F.2d 1347 (11th Cir.1990) the court found that the developer had suffered a temporary taking by virtue of a city ordinance that prohibited the construction of new apartment buildings. The trial court refused to award damages on a theory of qualified immunity. The court of appeals reversed and remanded; the district court again refused to award damages stating that the ordinance was not responsible for plaintiff's loss. Again the court of appeals reversed for a calculation of damages. This time, the district court concluded that the developer had shown some $206,000 in increased construction costs, but they still retained the property and could have sold it and the property had appreciated in value throughout the period of the temporary taking. Once more the appeals court reversed and specifically instructed the district court to award the market rate return computed over the period of the temporary taking on the difference between the property's fair market value with and without the regulation. The district court held a hearing and concluded that the fair market value of the land was not diminished by the ordinance and again awarded no damages. Finally, the appeals court calculated damages by finding that the fair market value of the proposed apartment complex was $2.3 million in 1978. After the city's prohibition, the owners only had the land, appraised at $200,000. In 1978 the loan-to-value ratio was 75 percent of the value of the project, meaning that the expected return was 25 percent, or $575,000. After the city withdrew the permit, the owner had 25 percent equity in the land, or $50,000. The loss in fair market value was $525,000 and the period of temporary taking was 14 months and 3 days; the market rate of return for that period was 9.77 percent which equalled damages of $59,841.23. That amount was awarded to the owners.

(b).   Corn v. City of Lauderdale Lakes, 771 F.Supp. 1557 (S.D.Fla.1991) involved a rezoning of the plaintiff's land to prohibit the construction of mini-warehouses. After a state court held the rezoning to be arbitrary, the property owner sought damages for a temporary taking. The federal district court applied the same formula as the Wheeler court and found temporary taking damages of $291,622.59 and after calculating interest, awarded the property owner $727,875.02. In a lengthy appendix to the opinion the court sets forth its worksheet of calculations illustrating the application of the fair market value/rate of return formula described by the Eleventh Circuit in Wheeler. The court of appeals reversed the award in 997 F.2d 1369 and remanded the case to the district court which then ruled that there was no taking. Another appeal followed, 95 F.3d 1066. The appellate court held that Corn failed to show "no viable economic uses" remaining, but remanded once again to the district court for further findings on the validity of a city moratorium that delayed the property owner's plans for a significant time, so that his competitors occupied the market for mini-warehouses.

6.   A very unusual compensation problem was presented in Bd. of County Supervisors of Prince William County, Virginia v. United States, 48 F.3d 520 (Fed.Cir.1995). A real estate developer proposed to develop 550 acres of land adjacent to Manassas Battlefield Park, a historic Civil War site. As a part of the rezoning process the developer presented the local government with a proffer of amenities he would provide, including storm drains, a community trail system, a community center and swimming pool, tennis courts, a ballfield, and a commitment to contribute a sum of money to the county for school purposes, plus five acres for a fire station and commuter parking lot; in addition to the proffer, the developer deeded several acres of his land to the county for road improvements. After a public outcry about the potential harm to the battlefield site, Congress enacted a statute to take the 550 acres as an addition to the Manassas Battlefield National Park, and to pay just compensation to the owners of any property taken pursuant to the Act. The United States paid the developer, but the county sued in the Court of Claims demanding compensation for the value of the proffers accepted by the county, and for the 16 acres of land the developer had

conveyed for road improvements in connection with the proposed development (the road improvements were no longer necessary due to the federal taking). The appellate court held that the proffers made to the county were not "property" for the purposes of the taking clause, but that the county was entitled to compensation for the land that the developer had previously conveyed to the county for road improvements, reasoning that even though the land was in reality dedicated for public roads that now would never be built, there was some residual value in the land; the case was remanded for determination of that value.

SECTION 6. OTHER REMEDIES

LITTLEFIELD v. CITY OF AFTON

United States Court of Appeals, Eighth Circuit, 1986.
785 F.2d 596.

McMILLIAN, CIRCUIT JUDGE.

James W. Littlefield and Bonnie J. Littlefield appeal from a final order entered in the District Court for the District of Minnesota granting summary judgment in favor of the City of Afton, members of the Afton City Council, and Helen H. Baker (the City) and dismissing their 42 U.S.C.A. § 1983 (1982) action without prejudice.

* * *

On August 26, 1983, appellants acquired by warranty deed a 19.3 acre parcel of land located in Afton, Minnesota. This parcel of land is bordered on the south by South Indian Trail, a Washington County public road. On September 9, 1983, appellee Helen H. Baker, the zoning administrator of the City of Afton, advised appellants that they could not obtain a building permit to erect a residence on their land because the conveyance constituted a subdivision of their seller's property which had not been approved by the City of Afton as required by ordinance. Helen H. Baker and her husband and Robert Fritz and his wife jointly own a parcel of land to the north of but not adjoining appellants' property. The Baker–Fritz property has never had access to South Indian Trail.

* * *

The planning commission held a public hearing on October 11, 1983, and subsequently recommended to the city council that the subdivision be approved subject to the earlier stated conditions. The City in its brief asserts that one of the conditions was the dedication of a public right of way across appellants' property to provide access to a landlocked parcel of land. The City Council adopted the recommendation.

The City of Afton in a letter dated July 10, 1984, advised appellants that "the city now stands willing and ready to grant you a building permit once you have conveyed to Mr. and Mrs. Baker and Mr. and Mrs. Fritz the additional public right of way."

In November 1983 appellants filed suit in federal court. Appellants sought injunctive relief and damages for deprivation of their fourteenth amendment rights. The complaint, construed liberally in accordance with Fed.R.Civ.P. 8(f), alleges a denial of procedural and substantive due process and a taking without just compensation and for a non-public purpose.

The district court, relying on *Parratt v. Taylor,* 451 U.S. 527, 535, 101 S.Ct. 1908, 1912–13, 68 L.Ed.2d 420 (1981) (Parratt), and *Collier v. City of Springdale,* 733 F.2d 1311, 1314–15, 1317 (8th Cir.1984) (Collier), granted summary judgment in favor of the City. On December 14, 1984, the district court granted appellants' motion to alter the judgment and entered an order dismissing the complaint without prejudice. The district court viewed appellants' complaint as alleging a procedural due process claim and a taking claim. Appellants' claims based on arbitrary action and taking for a non-public purpose were not considered by the district court as separate substantive due process claims but rather as part of the procedural due process and taking claims. The district court held that plaintiffs did not have a protected property interest in a building permit and that denial of a building permit, even if in violation of state law, is reviewable only in state court. The district court similarly held that appellants' taking claim could not be brought in federal court because state remedies, *e.g.,* an inverse condemnation action and a writ of mandamus, were available.

* * *

PROCEDURAL DUE PROCESS

Appellants initially argue that the district court erred in holding that they did not have a protected property interest in the building permit. Appellants argue that under Minnesota law the issuance of a building permit is not discretionary and that a building permit must be issued if the applicant has met all the qualifications for the permit. Appellants further argue that they have complied with all the applicable provisions of the Afton ordinances related to land use and building permits.

* * *

* * * [I]n analyzing a claim that the deprivation of property violates procedural due process, a court must first consider if the plaintiff has a constitutionally protected property interest. If there is a protected property interest, the court then considers whether the plaintiff has a right to a predeprivation hearing for the violation. A plaintiff has a right to a predeprivation hearing unless the action is random and unauthorized or the state cannot possibly provide a predeprivation hearing or the circumstances are those which the Supreme Court has recognized as excusing a predeprivation hearing. *E.g., North American Cold Storage Co. v. City of Chicago,* 211 U.S. 306, 320, 29 S.Ct. 101, 106, 53 L.Ed. 195 (1908) (seizure of contaminated food). If the plaintiff has the right to a predeprivation hearing, then the inquiry proceeds to what type of predeprivation hearing is required. If a predeprivation hearing is not required, the inquiry is whether state post-deprivation remedies are adequate. State post-deprivation remedies cannot satisfy due process if a predeprivation hearing is required.

* * *

To establish a claim under § 1983, plaintiffs must show that they have been deprived of a federally protected right, privilege or immunity as a result of action taken by persons acting under color of state law. *E.g., Parratt,* 451 U.S. at 535, 101 S.Ct. at 1912–13. Property interests are created and their dimensions defined by existing rules or understandings that stem from an independent source, such as state law, rules or understandings that support claims of entitlement to certain benefits. *Id.,* at 529, 101 S.Ct. at 1910; *Ervin v. Blackwell,* 733 F.2d 1282, 1285 (8th Cir.1984). A legitimate claim of entitlement can arise from procedures established in statutes or regulations adopted by states or political subdivisions. *Parks v. Watson,* 716 F.2d 646, 656–57 (9th Cir.1983) (*Parks*); *Wilson v. Robinson,* 668 F.2d 380, 382–83 (8th Cir.1981).

* * *

The Fourth Circuit, in *Scott v. Greenville County,* 716 F.2d 1409, 1418–1419 (4th Cir.1983), held that an applicant for a building permit had a protected property interest in the permit "upon presentation of an application and plans showing a use expressly permitted under the then-current zoning ordinance." *Id.* at 1418; *see Niggel v. City of Columbia,* 173 S.E.2d 136, 137–38 (S.C.1970). The interest in the building permit was a "cognizable property interest, rooted in state law, to which federal due process protection extended." *Scott v. Greenville County,* 716 F.2d at 1418–19 (footnote omitted).

Under Minnesota law, an applicant is likewise entitled to a building permit upon compliance with applicable laws and codes. *Alexander v. City of Minneapolis,* 267 Minn. 155, 125 N.W.2d 583, 585 (1963); *see Arcadia Development Corporation v. City of Bloomington,* 267 Minn. 221, 125 N.W.2d 846, 849 (1964). If the landowner complies with the laws and codes, the municipality lacks discretion and must issue a building permit.

* * *

Because Minnesota state law and the ordinance of the City of Afton require that the City of Afton issue a permit upon appellants' compliance with the ordinance, the City's decision-making power is significantly and substantially restricted. Thus, an applicant for a building permit has a constitutionally protected property interest in the permit, which is conditioned only by compliance with the ordinances. *See Parks,* 716 F.2d at 657.

We hold that appellants have a property interest in the building permit because they complied with all the *legal* requirements contained in the ordinances of the City of Afton. Appellants need not comply with illegal conditions in order to have a property interest in the permit. The City had no authority under the dedication statute to require that appellants convey a right of way to private parties. Minn.Stat. § 462.358 (1984); *Collis v. City of Bloomington,* 310 Minn. 5, 246 N.W.2d 19, 21, 26 (1976).

* * *

Appellants allege in their complaint that they were not provided a hearing. The City states in its brief that a public hearing on the minor subdivision of appellants' property was held and also that appellant attended a city council meeting where the subdivision of appellants' land was discussed. The district court in its opinion states: "In their quest for a building permit, plaintiffs [appellants] had to attend a series of meetings. The final meeting plaintiffs attended was the Oct. 18, 1983, Afton City Council Meeting." At this October 18, 1983, meeting the City Council approved the subdivision subject to certain conditions. We hold that appellants were provided procedural due process because they were afforded actual notice of the meetings and they were given an opportunity to be heard at these meetings.

<h3 style="text-align:center">SUBSTANTIVE DUE PROCESS</h3>

Appellants next argue that their due process rights were violated because appellees acted arbitrarily and capriciously in denying the building permit. Appellants also argue that their constitutional rights were violated by the City's conditioning of the issuance of a building permit upon the conveyance of land to private parties for a nonpublic use.[10] The City does not address this contention but argues that the building permit was denied because of appellants' noncompliance with the land use ordinances.[11] The district court considered this argument as part of

---

10. The State of Minnesota authorizes a municipality to acquire land for public use by two methods. Minn.Stat. § 117.011 *et seq* (1984) authorizes a municipality to acquire land by eminent domain. The land must be for a public use and compensation must be paid. Minn. Const. art. 1, § 13. The second method is set out in Minn.Stat. § 462.358 (1984), which permits a municipality to require dedication of land for public use. "The regulation [of the municipality] may require that a reasonable portion of any proposed subdivision be dedicated to the public use or preserved for public use as streets, roads, sewers, * * * and similar utilities and improvements." *Id.* The Minnesota Supreme Court has held that municipalities may only require land developers to dedicate an amount of land which reasonably relates to the increased public needs caused by the subdivision. *Collis v. City of Bloomington,* 310 Minn. 5, 246 N.W.2d 19, 21, 26 (1976).

It is unclear from the City's briefs and oral arguments whether the City relies on either or both of these statutory provisions as authority to require appellants to make a conveyance of a portion of their land. In a July 1984 letter to appellants, the City indicated that appellants must convey to "Mr. and Mrs. Baker and Mr. and Mrs. Fritz the additional public right of way." At oral argument the City indicated that the conveyance was to be to the City. The City also stated at oral argument that appellants will receive compensation from Baker and Fritz and that the amount of the compensation will be "negotiated" by appellants and Baker and Fritz. These latter statements are inconsistent with either eminent domain or dedication. Eminent domain requires that the taking be for a public purpose and that the governmental entity pay compensation for the land. Dedication likewise requires a public use for the land but compensation is not required.

11. The City has not clearly and consistently stated the reason for not granting a building permit to appellants. The City's

appellants' taking claim and did not address the argument directly. The district court, relying on *Collier v. City of Springdale,* held that appellants must seek a remedy in state court.

This circuit has not previously considered whether an arbitrary, capricious or illegal denial of a building permit states a substantive due process claim under § 1983. A number of other circuits have considered this question and all but the First Circuit generally recognize such claims.

The First Circuit has consistently held that a § 1983 claim may not be based on a denial of a permit, even if the denial was malicious, in bad faith, and for invalid and illegal reasons. *Chiplin Enterprises, Inc. v. City of Lebanon,* 712 F.2d 1524, 1526–28 (1st Cir.1983) (damages sought for five-year delay between initial application and grant of building permit); *see Alton Land v. Town of Alton,* 745 F.2d 730, 732 (1st Cir.1984); *Roy v. City of Augusta,* 712 F.2d 1517, 1522 (1st Cir.1983). In an earlier case, *Creative Environments, Inc. v. Estabrook,* 680 F.2d 822, 833 (1st Cir. 1982), involving the rejection of a corporation's definitive subdivision plan, the First Circuit held

> [T]he conventional planning dispute—at least when not tainted with fundamental procedural irregularity, racial animus, or the like * * * is a matter primarily of concern to the state and does not implicate the Constitution. This would be true even were planning officials to clearly violate, much less distort the state scheme under which they operate. A federal court, after all, should not * * * sit as a zoning board of appeals.

Id. at 833 (citation omitted) (emphasis added).

* * *

Other circuits have been more liberal than the First Circuit in recognizing a § 1983 claim based on a denial of a land use permit. The

letter of July 10, 1984, to appellants states that "the city now stands willing and ready to grant you a building permit once you have conveyed to Mr. and Mrs. Baker and Mr. and Mrs. Fritz the additional public right of way."

On October 5, 1984, the City stated to the district court: "Regarding the platting question, I don't believe we state * * * in our brief, that it's necessary the land has to be platted at this time. I think that was in a general discussion of the area." The City in its brief on appeal argues that appellants failed to comply with the subdivision ordinances but does not specify the particular requirement which is not met. The City, however, cites numerous cases upholding the platting requirement as a precondition to the granting of a building permit. The inference which is drawn from the City's brief is that appellants have failed to comply with the platting requirement.

On oral argument, the City concedes however that platting is not required. The City further concedes that appellants' land complies with the ordinance but argues that conveyances have resulted in an illegal subdivision. The City contends that approval of the subdivision, a prerequisite to the issuance of a building permit, was denied because the conveyance resulted in the Baker–Fritz property being landlocked.

Appellants argue that the Baker–Fritz property is not landlocked because it has access to another road and that the conveyance of their land did not change the access of the Baker–Fritz property to the roads. Appellants further argue that the City may not require dedication of their property because no additional public needs arise as a result of their proposed use of their land.

Fifth Circuit in *Shelton v. City of College Station,* held that the arbitrary deprivation of a zoning variance, a property right under Texas Law, "implicates the invasion of Fourteenth Amendment due process rights." 754 F.2d at 1256–57. The plaintiff in *Shelton* sought a variance from the city's off-street parking requirements. The city denied the variance although "almost all other businesses in the area including * * * the successor to the plaintiff's interest in the identical property" were granted variances. *Id.* at 1255. The Fifth Circuit reversed the summary judgment and remanded to the district court for a determination whether "the action of the zoning commission is arbitrary and capricious, having no substantial relation to the general welfare." *Id., citing South Gwinnett Venture v. Pruitt,* 491 F.2d 5, 7 (5th Cir.) (en banc) (zoning reclassification, normally not subject to federal court scrutiny, may violate due process where "the action of the zoning commission is arbitrary and capricious"), *cert. denied,* 416 U.S. 901, 94 S.Ct. 1625, 40 L.Ed.2d 119 (1974).

The Seventh Circuit has likewise recognized that an arbitrary denial of a building permit may be the basis for a § 1983 action. *Scudder v. Town of Greendale,* 704 F.2d 999, 1002 (7th Cir.1983) (decision on the merits; denial of building permit was not arbitrary or capricious). In *Albery v. Redding,* the Seventh Circuit, stated: "To prevail on this theory [substantive due process], plaintiff must allege and prove that the Zoning Ordinance or the Uniform Building Code * * * is arbitrary and unreasonable or that its application bears no substantial relation to the public health, safety, or morals." 718 F.2d 245, 251 (7th Cir.1983). On the merits, the Seventh Circuit held that the decision denying a variance to allow the completion of a 21 foot garage instead of a 15 foot garage was not arbitrary or unreasonable. *Id.*

The Third, Fourth, Sixth, Ninth, and Eleventh Circuits have similarly held that a substantive due process claim may be based on the denial of a land use permit. The Fourth Circuit, in *Scott v. Greenville County,* 716 F.2d at 1418–21, held that a fourteenth amendment claim is properly stated where "there is fairly alleged a basis for finding either 'abuse of discretion [or] caprice in [a] zoning administrator's refusal to issue' a building permit * * *." *Id.* at 1419, *citing United Land Corporation v. Clarke,* 613 F.2d 497 (4th Cir.1980). The county council's moratorium on building permits directed exclusively at plaintiff was held to be "extraordinary, extralegal, and in derogation of its regular practice of non-involvement in permit issuance." *Scott v. Greenville County,* 716 F.2d at 1421. The court further stated that the county council by so doing directly contravened an express section of its own zoning ordinance. *Id.* at 1419.

The Sixth Circuit has held that the denial of a license because of bias and the desire to avoid competition violates a property owner's substantive due process rights. *Wilkerson v. Johnson,* 699 F.2d 325, 328 (6th Cir.1983). The Sixth Circuit held that the defendants impermissibly imposed conditions not required by the statute and that the defendants had denied plaintiff's request for a license to operate a barbershop because of their direct pecuniary interest in avoiding competition.

The Eleventh Circuit has also held that imposition of requirements, not included in the ordinance, upon an applicant for a permit violates substantive due process. *Southern Cooperative Development Fund v. Driggers,* 696 F.2d 1347, 1356 (11th Cir.), *cert. denied,* 463 U.S. 1208, 103 S.Ct. 3539, 77 L.Ed.2d 1389 (1983). The defendants had an administrative duty to approve the proposed plat upon the property owner's compliance with the applicable regulations. *Id.*

The Third Circuit in *Rogin v. Bensalem Township,* 616 F.2d 680, 689–90 (3d Cir.1980), *cert. denied,* 450 U.S. 1029, 101 S.Ct. 1737, 68 L.Ed.2d 223 (1981) held that a substantive due process claim may be based on a permit denial. The court concluded on the basis of the facts before it that the denial of the remaining permits was not arbitrary and capricious and therefore did not violate substantive due process.

The Ninth Circuit, in a case factually similar in many respects to the present case, held that a city may not require an applicant for a permit under land use ordinances to dedicate its property in exchange for the issuance of a permit. *Parks v. Watson,* 716 F.2d at 646. In *Watson* a development company requested the vacation of certain public streets. The development company was willing to pay $1.00 for each square foot of street that was vacated and to convey to the city an easement for a 20 foot strip of property. However, the city wanted dedication of the property in order that the city would gain rights to the geothermal wells on the property. The development company based its claim on the doctrine of unconstitutional conditions.[12] The court concluded that a condition requiring an applicant for a governmental benefit to forego a constitutional right is unlawful if the condition is not rationally related to the benefit conferred. The court held that it was a violation of the fifth amendment for the city to condition the vacation of certain platted city streets on the relinquishment of the right to just compensation for the taking of the geothermal wells.

This circuit addresses the issue of a § 1983 substantive due process claim based on a denial of a building permit for the first time in this case. We are concerned that federal courts not sit as zoning boards of appeals "when presented with claims which, although couched in constitutional language, at bottom amount only to 'the run of the mill dispute between a developer and a town planning agency.' " *Scott v. Greenville County,* 716 F.2d at 1419, *citing Creative Environments,* 680 F.2d at 833.

---

12. [E]ven though a person has no "right" to a valuable government benefit and even though the government may deny him the benefit for any number of reasons, there are some reasons upon which the government may not rely. It may not deny a benefit to a person on a basis that infringes his constitutionally protected interests.... Such interference with constitutional rights is impermissible.

Perry v. Sindermann, 408 U.S. 593, 597, 92 S.Ct. 2694, 2697, 33 L.Ed.2d 570 (1972); *see Bynum v. Schiro,* 219 F.Supp. 204, 210 (E.D.La.1963), (NAACP's license to use City auditorium unconstitutionally conditioned on comments compatible with segregation), *aff'd,* 375 U.S. 395, 84 S.Ct. 452, 11 L.Ed.2d 412 (1964).

[It is] primarily the province of the municipal body to determine the use and purpose to which property within its boundaries may be devoted, and it is neither the province nor the duty of a federal court to interfere with the discretion with which such bodies are vested, unless the legislative action of the municipality is shown to significantly invade the * * * constitutional rights of the complaining party.

Sternaman v. County of McHenry, 454 F.Supp. 240, 242 (N.D.Ill.1978). "The only question which federal district courts may consider is whether the action of the zoning commission is arbitrary and capricious, having no substantial relation to the general welfare." *South Gwinnett Venture v. Pruitt,* 491 F.2d at 7.

We are persuaded by the almost unanimous decisions of our sister circuits that the denial of a building permit under some circumstances may give rise to a substantive due process claim. We hold therefore that appellants stated a substantive due process claim when they alleged that the City acted capriciously and arbitrarily and imposed an unconstitutional condition on the granting of the permit. The district court did not decide this claim; we therefore remand for a determination whether the city acted arbitrarily or capriciously or imposed an unconstitutional condition. We express no opinion on the merits of this claim.

The City argues that even if appellants state a claim, the claim may not be brought in federal court because adequate state remedies are available. The City cites *Parratt* as authority for their position. This reliance on *Parratt* is misplaced. By its express terms, *Parratt* applies only to procedural due process claims and bars the claim only if the plaintiff has no right to a predeprivation hearing.

The applicability of *Parratt* to claims of deprivation of property rights in violation of substantive due process is not clear.

* * *

We agree with the Fifth Circuit that *Parratt* does not bar a claim based on a violation of a substantive constitutional right. Claims based on substantive due process, as distinguished from some procedural due process claims, may be brought in federal court.

TAKING

Appellants next argue that the City's denial of the building permit is in violation of their fifth amendment rights because the City has denied them the beneficial use of their land without compensation. Appellants also argue that the City's action is a taking because the action is beyond the scope of the City's police powers and was for a private rather than a public purpose. The City does not directly address this issue but does assert that the City in accordance with its ordinances denied the permit because of appellants' non-compliance with the requirements of the ordinances.

The district court, relying on this court's decision in *Collier v. Springdale,* 733 F.2d at 1317, held that appellant could not bring this taking claim in federal court because of the availability of state remedies. The district court concluded that appellants must seek their redress in state court, although "the City appear[s] to have treated [appellants] poorly." *Littlefield v. City of Afton,* No. 4–83–1003, slip op. at 7 (D.Minn. Nov. 13, 1984).

The United States Supreme Court in a very recent case has considered when a taking claim may be brought in federal court. *Williamson County Regional Planning Commission v. Hamilton Bank,* 473 U.S. 172, 105 S.Ct. 3108, 87 L.Ed.2d 126 (1985) * * *

Appellants' claim in the present case is also premature for the reasons stated in *Williamson.* In the instant case, appellants did not request a variance pursuant to § 909.01 of the ordinances of the City of Afton. Although there is no requirement that a plaintiff exhaust administrative remedies before bringing a § 1983 action, the decision of the administrative agency must be final. *Id.* at 3120. In this case, the decision is not final because appellants have not sought and been denied a variance.

Appellants also did not seek compensation from the state. Appellants argue that the decision of the Minnesota Supreme Court in *McShane v. City of Faribault,* 292 N.W.2d 253 (Minn.1980) (*McShane*) bars an inverse condemnation action. The *McShane* court stated that "every regulation challenged as a taking [does not give] rise to an action for inverse condemnation. Only where the taking or damage is irreversible would an injunction against enforcement not provide an adequate remedy". *Id.* at 259. The Minnesota Supreme Court limits "the use of inverse condemnation to cases where an injunction would not restore plaintiffs to their original status." *Id.* at 260 n. 6. Our review of the court's holding in *McShane* convinces us that an inverse condemnation action may be available to appellants. Until the Minnesota courts have ruled that an inverse condemnation action may not be brought or denies damages in such an action, appellants' claim of taking without just compensation is not ripe for decision by a federal court. *Id.* at 3121–22.

We hold therefore that appellants' claim for a taking is premature because the decision of the planning commission is not final because a variance has not been sought and denied. Further the claim is premature because a constitutional violation has not occurred until compensation has been denied by the state.

* * *

Accordingly, the judgment of the district court is affirmed in part and this case is remanded for further proceedings consistent with this opinion.

AMENDED ORDER

Appellees' petition for rehearing has been considered by the court and is hereby denied.

The main thrust of the City's argument in support of its petition for rehearing is that this court misapprehended the underlying facts and decided issues which should not have been decided. The City argues that the Littlefields were denied a building permit because they failed to dedicate a portion of their land for a public right of way. The City for the first time asserts that the July 1984 letter, wherein the City required the Littlefields to convey land to adjacent landowners, was sent pursuant to earlier negotiations between the parties.

The factual allegations made by the City do not affect our holding in this case. The Littlefields, under Minnesota law, have a property interest in a building permit. Thus they must be afforded procedural due process before their application is denied. Because we determined that the Littlefields were afforded procedural due process, we need not decide whether they complied with the dedication requirement.

Concerning the substantive due process claim, we held only that the Littlefields had stated a claim. We remanded to the district court because the district court had not previously considered the substantive due process claim. The district court will determine what condition was imposed on the Littlefields and whether the condition was arbitrary and capricious or a constitutionally impermissible condition.

Notes

1. As noted in the principal case, the federal courts have, for the most part, recognized the theory of a Section 1983 action where land use decisions amount to a denial of procedural or substantive due process or constitute a "taking." A successful 1983 suit could produce compensatory damages, punitive damages in cases which warrant such damages, costs and attorney's fees. Although numerous cases recognize the cause of action, precious few examples of actual award of damages can be found in the reports, although a definite increase the number can be detected since the mid–1990's. The hurdles of ripeness, exhaustion of remedies, and the issue of whether a development permit is a property right are frequently impediments. The ripeness doctrine, in particular, can be a severe impediment. See, e.g., Long Beach Equities, Inc. v. County of Ventura, 231 Cal.App.3d 1016, 282 Cal. Rptr. 877 (1991); Town of Sunnyvale v. Mayhew, 905 S.W.2d 234 (Tex.App. 1994). Also see Gregory M. Stein, Regulatory Takings and Ripeness in the Federal Courts, 48 Vand. L Rev. 1 (1995); Michael K. Whitman, The Ripeness Doctrine in the Land–Use Context: The Municipality's Ally and the Landowner's Nemesis, 29 The Urban Lawyer 13 (1997). The courts also closely examine allegations of disparate treatment of the plaintiff developer, that is, if a regulation seems to be neutral and applicable to all developers, the claim of a denial of constitutional rights is weaker. Nevertheless, the potential damages in such cases generate many Section 1983 suits in federal and state courts. Compare the following cases:

(a) Resolution Trust Corp. v. Town of Highland Beach, 18 F.3d 1536 (11th Cir.1994). The developer, in 1974, received permission to develop his 24.8 acres as a Planned Unit Development for 846 units. Under local rules at the time of the rezoning in 1975, approval of the PUD required that work begin within one year and that the project be completed in ten years. The local rules were interpreted to mean that the ten year completion period began to run at the time the first building permit was issued in 1980. The developer asked for and received a letter from the mayor stating that the PUD approval expired on August 8, 1990. Shortly thereafter, there was a turnover in local officials and a change in attitude toward dense condo development. Rejecting the advice of the city attorney who sought to educate the planning commission about estoppel, the new commission took the position that the developer's time period began in 1975 and an ordinance was passed to terminate the PUD on July 1, 1985. In 1985, the town notified the developer that the PUD project was "dead" and in 1987 the land was downzoned to permit eight units per acre. In 1990, the land was further downzoned to allow six units per acre. The developer filed suit in state court and the town removed the case to federal court. The district judge ruled as a matter of law that the developer possessed a vested property right to the PUD zoning until 1990 based on the mayor's letter. A jury assessed damages of $16,150,000 for a temporary taking, and $15,000,000 for a permanent taking; the district judge also awarded nearly $1.8 million in attorney's fees. The court of appeals affirmed the judgment, holding that developer's acts of reliance on the 1990 expiration date "created a reasonable expectation rising to the level of a property right." The court also held that ripeness defense was inapplicable because it was clear that the town's actions in 1985 and 1987 were final. On substantive due process, the court stated:

> Deprivation of a property interest rises to the level of a substantive due process violation if done for improper motives and achieved through means that are arbitrary and capricious, and lacking any rational basis. * * * The question before us then is whether the Town acted in an arbitrary and capricious manner when it reinterpreted Ordinance 282. We conclude that it did.

> The record demonstrates that the Commission knew that the joint venture was relying upon the mutual understanding with the Town, and committed substantial funds to develop the RPUD. In fact, on several occasions, the Town's own attorney warned the Commission about the repercussions of its unilateral actions. Specifically, the attorney and other public officials informed the Town that the joint venture was relying upon the Mayor's letter declaring the completion date as 1990. The town attorney further cautioned that changing the existing interpretation of Ordinance 282 would create an "estoppel." Likewise, the Town ignored the mayor's warning that the Town led the joint venture down the "primrose path" to rely upon the 1990 completion date. Additionally, after the RPUD lapsed, causing the property designation to revert to "no zoning," the Town took an extended period of time to rezone the site, denying the joint venture use of the property. Finally, the Town refused to accept applications for the reissuance of previous permits, even though it previously had promised such permits were forthcoming. This evidence supports the jury's finding that the Town acted in an arbitrary and capricious manner without respect to the joint venture's rights.

A similar case, although one that was remanded for a new trial, is Blanche Road Corp. v. Bensalem Twp., 57 F.3d 253 (3d Cir.1995). Also see Del Monte Dunes at Monterey, Ltd. v. City of Monterey, 95 F.3d 1422 (9th

Cir.1996) where the court upheld a $1,450,000 jury verdict in a § 1983 suit for a regulatory taking.

(b) Stubblefield Construction Co. v. City of San Bernardino, 32 Cal. App.4th 687, 38 Cal.Rptr.2d 413 (1995). The developer owned 600 acres of land in the hills outside the city. In the early 1960's he began to develop a residential community and built several homes from 1964 to 1968. In 1968 the developer consented to the annexation of his property and the mayor agreed that the city would zone the property in accord with the developer's plan. The city did zone the land, including a portion zoned R–3 for multi-family housing. In 1983 the developer began to plan his apartment project. By this time, a number of residents in the area were opposed to apartments and enlisted the aid of the city councilman who represented the area. The councilman apparently took steps to block the necessary permits for the construction of the apartments. The city refused all requests by the developer to honor the annexation promises, and also refused to grandfather the developer's apartment project under new rules promulgated by the city (only two-story buildings, while developer all along planned three-story buildings). The developer sued in state court under Section 1983, and a jury awarded damages of $11 million. On appeal, the court reversed, holding:

> The City's first argument is that plaintiffs had no vested rights to develop their property. Although the proposed use was in accordance with the existing zoning of the property, the City argues that plaintiffs had no right to a particular zoning or to a building permit. * * *

The City thus frames the issue as to whether plaintiffs had a right to build apartments on their property under state law. It argues that no such right arose under California law. It cites Avco Community Developers, Inc. v. South Coast Regional Com. (1976) 17 Cal.3d 785, 132 Cal.Rptr. 386, 553 P.2d 546. In that case, our Supreme Court considered whether a developer had vested rights under California law. The court said: "It has long been the rule in this state and in other jurisdictions that if a property owner has performed substantial work and incurred substantial liabilities in good faith reliance upon a permit issued by the government, he acquires a vested right to complete construction in accordance with the terms of the permit. [Citations.] Once a landowner has secured a vested right the government may not, by virtue of a change in the zoning laws, prohibit construction authorized by the permit upon which he relied." (Id., at p. 791, 132 Cal.Rptr. 386, 553 P.2d 546.) After discussing vested rights at common law, the court found that applicable precedent "stand[s] for the proposition that neither the existence of a particular zoning nor work undertaken pursuant to governmental approvals preparatory to construction of buildings can form the basis of a vested right to build a structure which does not comply with the laws applicable at the time a building permit is issued. By zoning the property or issuing approvals for work preliminary to construction the government makes no representation to a landowner that he will be exempt from the zoning laws in effect at the subsequent time he applies for a building permit or that he may construct particular structures on the property, and thus the government cannot be estopped to enforce the laws in effect when the permit is issued." (Id., at p. 793, 132 Cal.Rptr. 386, 553 P.2d 546.) The court also suggested that other permits, such as a conditional use permit, might create a vested right if they gave substantially the same specificity and definition to a project as a building permit.* * *

We find Avco persuasive and thus conclude that Stubblefield had no vested right to build any particular apartment buildings because it had not applied for or received a building permit for its project. We also agree that, under Avco, plaintiffs here had no vested right to develop their property in accordance with the zoning in existence at the time they submitted their review of plans application.

Also see Freeman v. Planning Board of West Boylston, 419 Mass. 548, 646 N.E.2d 139 (1995) where the Massachusetts Supreme Court held that a developer whose proposed subdivision was unduly delayed by repeated demands of the town planning board could not receive monetary relief under 42 U.S.C.A. § 1983 or under a state civil rights act except in a "truly horrendous situation." The opinion sets forth the trial court's jury instructions which are worthy of note.

2.   In Anastasio v. Planning Board, 197 N.J.Super. 457, 484 A.2d 1358 (1984) a developer submitted a site plan for a townhouse development in May of 1979, the planning board delayed action for several months and finally denied the plan. The developer sued and won a favorable judgment in October, 1982; in November, 1982, the board approved the plan but delayed signing off on it until December, 1983. By then the developer had lost so much money, he was forced to sell the property. A section 1983 suit resulted in compensatory damages of over $66,000 plus interest, punitive damages of $5,000 against each of the three planning board members, and attorney's fees. On appeal of the punitive damage claim, the individual defendants were held to be immune. 209 N.J.Super. 499, 507 A.2d 1194 (1986), cert. denied 107 N.J. 46, 526 A.2d 136. Also see DeBlasio v. Zoning Bd. of Adjustment for the Twp. of West Amwell, 53 F.3d 592 (3d Cir.1995) where the court reversed a summary judgment and remanded the case for a trial on a property owner's claim that he was denied a variance because the secretary of the board of adjustment had a personal financial interest in the resolution of the owner's zoning problems.

3.   Cases which allege selective application of land use regulations, harassment of the property owner, or discrimination are fairly common. See, for example, Cutting v. Muzzey, 724 F.2d 259 (1st Cir.1984) (alleging racial animus against the developer's purchasers, all of whom had Italian surnames); Sylvia Development Corp. v. Calvert County, Maryland, 48 F.3d 810 (4th Cir.1995) (alleging discrimination against developer because he was born in Czechoslovokia, or, in the alternative, that he was from outside the county); Rodrigues v. Village of Larchmont, New York, 608 F.Supp. 467 (S.D.N.Y.1985) (harassment of nurseryman by denying him access to village dump and arbitrary denial of variance); Shelton v. City of College Station, 754 F.2d 1251 (5th Cir.1985) (denial of a variance to a businessman where every other applicant in similar situation received a variance). On the other hand, the courts rarely uphold Section 1983 suits which appear to be nothing more than an attempt to seek judicial review of an unfavorable land use decision. The best known example is Hernandez v. City of Lafayette, 699 F.2d 734 (5th Cir.1983) where a landowner who was denied a rezoning of his

16 acre parcel from residential to commercial, sued in state and federal court alleging a denial of due process and a taking. The Fifth Circuit Court of Appeals in the first appeal held that the pleadings stated a cause of action under Section 1983 and remanded the case, 643 F.2d 1188 (5th Cir.1981). Shortly thereafter, the state court held the city decision was proper, Hernandez v. City of Lafayette, 399 So.2d 1179 (La.App.1981) cert. denied 401 So.2d 1192 (La.), appeal dismissed 455 U.S. 901, 102 S.Ct. 1242, 71 L.Ed.2d 440 (1982). After remand, the federal district court granted a summary judgment in the city's favor, which was affirmed by the Fifth Circuit Court of Appeals.

4. Section 1983 can, in a proper case, provide a remedy. In Bodor v. East Coventry Twp., 325 F.Supp. 1102 (E.D.Pa.1971), plaintiff successfully sued to restrain the township officials from preventing him from establishing a seventy foot by twelve foot mobile home as a permanent residence on a four acre tract of land. "Plaintiffs' complaint raises the substantial constitutional issues of due process of law and equal protection under the law in that in order for Plaintiffs to avail themselves of the administrative remedies provided in the township's zoning ordinance and building code ordinance, Plaintiffs would allegedly have to pay a $750.00 filing fee. * * * Plaintiffs have alleged facts which, if proved, establish a concerted effort by the Board of Supervisors of East Coventry Township to preclude the review of their Zoning and Building Code Ordinances through the establishment of a prohibitive filing fee. Such an allegation sets forth a claim upon which relief can be granted." In Minshew v. Smith, 380 F.Supp. 918 (N.D.Miss.1974), several homeowners sued the owner of a motel and city officials for compensatory and punitive damages on the theory that the defendants conspired to achieve an illegal amendment of the zoning ordinance to allow the motel to expand into the adjacent residential zone. The court found for the plaintiffs and awarded compensatory damages of $6,000 for diminution in value of the plaintiffs' property, costs and attorney's fees, but refused to award punitive damages.

5. One should not overlook the possibility of state court damage actions for improper activities of government officials in zoning cases. For an illustrative example, see River Park, Inc. v. City of Highland Park, 281 Ill.App.3d 154, 217 Ill.Dec. 410, 667 N.E.2d 499 (1996) where a developer whose zoning petition was not considered by the city successfully established a cause of action for tortious interference with a business expectancy and breach of contract (an implied contract to consider a petition where all fees were properly paid). The city's immunity argument was rejected because the plaintiff sufficiently alleged corruption, malice, or bad faith (a statutory exception to the state immunity statutes). The court remanded the case for further proceedings.

6. A number of law review articles deal with the question of damages in land use litigation. See, e.g., Pearlman, Section 1983 and the Liability of Local Officials for Land Use Decisions, 23 Urban Law Ann. 57 (1982); Rockwell, Constitutional Violations in Zoning: The Emerging Section 1983 Damage Remedy, 33 U.Fla.L.Rev. 168 (1981); Wright, Damages or Compensation for Unconstitutional Land Use Regulation, 37 Ark.L.Rev. 612 (1983).

A Note on "Property Rights" Legislation

In March, 1988, the President signed Executive Order 12,630, 53 Fed. Reg. 8859, known as the Federal Takings Executive Order; implementing guidelines were issued by the Attorney General on June 30, 1988 (see Env.L.Rptr.Admin.Materials, p. 35172 (1988)). These federal regulations are discussed in Pollot, The Effect of the Federal Takings Executive Order, Land Use Law, May 1989, p. 3. Also see, Hill, Reflections, Refractions, and Regulations: Variations on the Takings Theme, American Bar Ass'n, Urban, State and Local Law Newsletter, Vol. 12, No. 3 (1989). The thrust of the Executive Order was to require federal agencies to consider the impact of regulations on private property rights. The Executive Order is regarded as the beginning of a movement to provide some sort of statutory protection for property owners against excessive governmental regulation. By 1996, some sort of statutory property rights protection had been introduced in nearly every state and in Congress.

In 1991 one state enacted takings legislation. In 1992 and 1993 two states in each year enacted takings legislation. In 1994 six states enacted legislation although thirty-one states considered about seventy bills. In 1995 thirty-nine states considered takings bills (about ninety separate bills) and eleven states enacted legislation. Only two states, Ohio and Connecticut have not considered takings legislation. Much of the legislation introduced in 1995 is still pending.

The House of Representatives passed a takings bill in connection with the "Contract for America" movement in 1994–95. That bill has languished in the Senate along with a Senate bill that is quite different. The House bill only applies to a select group of federal environmental regulations, while the Senate bill applies to all federal regulations that devalue property. The Senate Bill provides in S. 605, Title V, Section 508 (1995), that property owners are entitled to compensation for reductions of more than one third in market value of land (entirety or a portion) as a consequence of use restrictions imposed under the Endangered Species Act or Section 404 of the Federal Water Pollution Control Act (the wetlands provision). Title II of S. 605 goes even further in providing compensation for reductions of one third or more due to any federal statute and also defines property to include all property to which the Fifth Amendment under any circumstances might apply. In May of 1996 a letter was sent to the U.S. Senate, signed by 380 law professors at 125 law schools voicing strong disagreement with S. 605 and urging its defeat.

The state legislation that has been enacted falls into two major categories: (1) statutes that require some sort of review of regulations to ascertain the impact on private property, and (2) statutes that require compensation for regulations that devalue private property by a specified amount. A number of variations in these two major categories can be found:

1. In the "assessment" type of legislation, there are variations in the agency that is required to assess. Some acts require the state attorney general to review proposed regulations for impact on property, e.g. West's Ann. Indiana Code § 4–22–2–32, or require the attorney general to promulgate a checklist for agencies to follow, e.g. Idaho Code Ann. § 67–8003, some require the enacting agency to conduct the assessment, e.g. Utah Code Ann.

§ 63–90–4, and some create a special review agency under legislative auspices, e.g. Mo. Rev. Stat. ch. 536.017. Also, there is variation in what happens after the assessment. Most of the statutes are silent on post-assessment practice; some require reconsideration or modification of regulations that have an effect on private property value.

2. In the "compensation" statutes there is considerable variation on the points of (a) whether the devaluation is measured by the property owner's holdings in their entirety versus segmentation, (b) whether the statute applies to urban zoning regulations, (c) whether compensation can be avoided by "rolling back" the regulation, (d) whether alternative dispute proceedings are required or encouraged.

Five states have enacted "compensation" statutes as of January, 1996. A brief description of those statutes follows:

1. Mississippi passed the first compensation statute in 1994. 1994 Miss. Laws Ch. 647. It provides for compensation whenever timber harvesting regulations devalue private property by 40% or more. In 1995 the statute was amended to include agricultural regulations. It does not apply to urban zoning.

2. Louisiana passed a compensation statute in 1995 that gives property owners a cause of action for compensation in cases of reduction in value of 20% or more. It applies only to agricultural and timber lands and gives agencies the option of avoiding compensation by rescission of the regulations. La. Rev. Stat. § 3:3608.

3. Oregon passed a compensation statute applying to "ecotakes" that result in a reduction of 10% or more of property value. Ecotake regulations are defined as those seeking to preserve scenic areas, natural areas, open space, historical/archeological/cultural properties of significance. Compensation is not in cash, but in credits against personal or corporate income taxes. 1995 Or. Laws S.B. 600. The statute was vetoed by the governor, and the veto sustained. The statute has been re-introduced in the 1997 legislative session.

4. Texas provides for compensation for 25% or more reductions in value of all or part of land or water rights, whether temporary or permanent. It applies to urban regulations. Compensation is not awarded if the agency rescinds or rolls back the challenged regulation. There are many statutory exceptions. 1995 Tex. Sess. Law Serv. Ch. 517.

5. Florida provides a compensation remedy for those whose real property has been "inordinately burdened" by government action and also provides for a mediation process to resolve disputes. Fl. Stat. § 70.001 et seq. "Inordinate burden" is carefully defined in the statute to track the idea of "investment backed expectations" and "vested property rights."

The Florida statute provides: "When a specific action of a governmental entity has inordinately burdened an existing use of real property or a vested right to a specific use of real property, the property owner of that real property is entitled to relief, which may include compensation for the actual loss to the fair market value of the real property caused by the action of government." The statute also defines inordinate burden, as follows:

The terms "inordinate burden" or "inordinately burdened" mean that an action of one or more governmental entities has directly restricted or limited the use of real property such that the property owner is permanently unable to attain the reasonable, investment-backed expectation for the existing use of the real property or a vested right to a specific use of the real property with respect to the real property as a whole, or that the property owner is left with existing or vested uses that are unreasonable such that the property owner bears permanently a disproportionate share of a burden imposed for the good of the public, which in fairness should be borne by the public at large. The terms "inordinate burden" or "inordinately burdened" do not include temporary impacts to real property; impacts to real property occasioned by governmental abatement, prohibition, prevention, or remediation of a public nuisance at common law or a noxious use of private property; or impacts to real property caused by an action of a governmental entity taken to grant relief to a property owner under this section.

The statute requires landowners who are making a claim to do so within six months after the governmental action and the claim must be accompanied by a written bona fide appraisal that demonstrates the loss in fair market value; after the claim is filed notice must be given to all contiguous property owners and a settlement period begins to run. If no settlement is reached, the property owner may go to circuit court and have a jury trial.

The Texas statute, effective Sept. 1, 1995, defines a "taking" to include (in addition to the traditional constitutional law definitions) a governmental action that:

(i) affects an owner's private real property that is the subject of the governmental action, in whole or in part or temporarily or permanently, in a manner that restricts or limits the owner's right to the property that would otherwise exist in the absence of the governmental action; and

(ii) is the producing cause of a reduction of at least 25 percent in the market value of the affected private property, determined by comparing the market value of the property as if the governmental action is not in effect and the market value of the property determined as if the governmental action is in effect.

The question of whether a governmental action is a taking under the Texas statute is determined by a lawsuit filed by the property owner in district court. If the court finds that a taking has occurred, the remedy is an order to rescind the regulation; if the regulation is not rescinded then the governmental entity must pay the landowner. The Texas statute also has some significant exceptions, including:

(11) an action taken by a political subdivision:

(A) to regulate construction in an area designated under law as floodplain;

(B) to regulate on-site sewage facilities;

(C) under the political subdivisions statutory authority to prevent waste or protect rights of owners of interest in groundwater, or

(D) to prevent subsidence;

* * *

(13) an action that:

(A) is taken in response to a real and substantial threat to public health and safety;

(B) is designed to significantly advance the health and safety purpose; and

(C) does not impose a greater burden than is necessary to achieve the health and safety purpose;

None of the compensation type statutes have been court-tested yet and most of them have just gone into effect in the last quarter of 1995. Anecdotal evidence indicates that in some of the above states the existence of the statute has had a "chilling effect" on pending regulations. In the state of Washington a far-reaching compensation statute was subjected to a ballot referendum and defeated by 60% to 40% in November, 1995. See Carol M. Rose, A Dozen Propositions on Private Property, Public Rights, and the New Takings Legislation, 53 Wash. & Lee L. Rev. 265 (1996).

None of the statutes has been in effect long enough to ascertain the fiscal impact of providing compensation to landowners who have been subject to regulations allegedly reducing the fair market value of their land, but short of a constitutional taking. See, generally, Robert Meltz, "Property Rights" Laws in the United States, Congressional Research Service, Library of Congress (Dec. 2, 1996).

CAN THE TAKING PROBLEM BE SOLVED?

The concept and problem of the regulatory taking spawned in Pennsylvania Coal has bedeviled commentators and scholars for years. As might be expected, proposed solutions to the problem abound. One group, sometimes called the police power enthusiasts, would say that any regulation for a valid public purpose short of an actual physical appropriation should go uncompensated. Some leading advocates of this approach are Bosselman, Callies & Banta, The Taking Issue (U.S.Govt.Printing Off.1973), and Sax, Takings, Private Property and Public Rights, 81 Yale L.J. 149 (1971). The logical development of this approach, if it could legally be implemented, would necessarily result in a redefinition of property rights as well as a redefinition of taking, as perhaps illustrated by the following excerpt:

Reilly (ed.), The Use of Land: A Citizens' Policy Guide to Urban Growth, pp. 140–143 (1973):[13]

Density transfer, or any measure that separates ownership of land from the rights to build on it, raises a question with far-reaching implications: Where do development rights come from in the first place?

---

13. A Task Force Report Sponsored by the Rockefeller Brothers Fund, Copyright 1973. Reprinted with permission of Thomas Y. Crowell Co., publisher.

Historically, Americans have thought of these rights as coming from the land itself, "up from the bottom" like minerals or crops. As a result, land-use regulations have been viewed as restrictions on each landowner's pre-existing rights rather than as grants of rights he did not have before. If a regulation permits construction of one dwelling unit for each 50 acres of land area, the owner of a 500–acre tract thinks, not that he has been granted a right to build 10 units, but that he has been deprived of a right to build more than 10.

But land planning must look not only "up from the bottom," from the vantage point of each land parcel, but also "down from the top," from the vantage point of the region or community as a whole. From this second perspective, a quantity of needed development is agreed upon and then spread, unevenly, over the community or region.

American land-use regulations, starting with bottom-up assumptions, have had great difficulty in applying top-down limits. The cluster principle, however, even in its routine application to set aside open space within a single project, starts with a top-down limit. Take the 100–acre tract on which 100 dwelling units are permitted. Where did that 100–unit limit come from? Just because all 100 units are built on 80 acres, why should more units not later be built on the 20 acres reserved as open space? The limit did not come from an inherent inability of the tract to hold more than 100 units. If it had, clustering would presumably be impossible. Rather, the 100–unit limit represents a decision that 100 units are that tract's share of the total quantity of development planned for the community (or region or block).

Clustering, which is being used to obtain open space in "planned unit developments" all across the country, illustrates the usefulness of changing—in whole or in part—to a different way of thinking about where urbanization rights come from. With such a change, land planning and regulations would come to be seen as giving out rights created by society rather than as restricting or taking away rights that come from the land itself. Present land-use regulations would then be seen as parceling out rights unevenly, with land in some zones getting a bigger share than land in other zones, and with many exceptions made for individual parcels within each zone (an invitation to corruption). The present allocation of shares would be seen as a give-away by society (with no cost to the landowner) of rights that often virtually determine property value.

Density transfer, from this standpoint, would appear as a helpful mechanism to smooth out differences in land values caused by the uneven allocations of development shares. Its result would be a more nearly uniform distribution of rights among landowners, with the owners of historic buildings and open spaces receiving some of the cash benefits of development by transferring their unused development rights to others.

If a workable system of density transfer can be devised, it may eventually be considered preferable to tax incentives and less-than-fee acquisition, since those incentives would be seen as arrangements to pay for recovering rights that the government had previously given away.

Yet density transfer may be only a halfway measure, more equitable than the present approach to land-use regulation but still less equitable than one in which development rights are sold by government. Density transfer would allocate development rights more evenly among landowners but still would not allocate them among those members of society who did not happen to own land. Some might compare it to dividing up the whole pool of rights to operate television stations only among those people who happened to own transmitting equipment, with those who actually got broadcasting franchises paying some compensation to those who lost out.

We think it highly likely that in forthcoming decades Americans will gradually abandon the traditional assumption that urbanization rights arise from the land itself. Development potential, on any land and in any community, results largely from the actions of society (especially the construction of public facilities). Other free societies, notably Great Britain, have abandoned the old assumption in their legal systems and now treat development rights as created and allocated to the land by society.

For now, when we need incentives to back protective regulations for open spaces and historic preservation, the old assumption remains very much in force. Today's incentives must be fashioned to be workable with today's attitudes. Noneconomic incentives can do some of the job. Density transfer may prove workable enough to do part, as well. Tax and other economic incentives, despite their cost and possible inequity, may be useful in some circumstances.

None of these incentives, though, is likely to be sufficient to protect the amounts of open space or the numbers of historic sites that would be ideally desirable. What is needed is a changed attitude toward land, not simply a growing awareness of the importance of stewardship, but a separation of commodity rights in the land from urbanization rights.

Do you think it is "highly likely" that there will be a redefinition of "urbanization rights"? Is this suggested by cases or other developments in the law since the foregoing was written?

At the opposite end of the spectrum from the police power enthusiasts are those who suggest that any substantial deprivation of market value by governmental action should be compensated. The most extreme advocates of this position actually go to the point of suggesting that government should get out of the land use regulation field entirely. See, Richard Epstein, Takings: Private Property and the Power of Eminent Domain (Cambridge: Harvard Univ. Press, 1985); Bernard H. Siegan, Economic Liberties and the Constitution (Chicago: Univ. of Chicago Press, 1980); Ellickson, Alternatives to Zoning: Covenants, Nuisance Rules and Fines as Land Use Controls, 40 U.Chi.L.Rev. 681, 781 (1973).

A useful short, analysis of the taking problem by an attorney who frequently argues takings cases is Michael M. Berger, They Found the Quark—Why Not a Takings Formula?, Land Use Law (May 1995) p. 3.

As might be expected, between the two extremes, a whole range of solutions can be found. Two of the most intriguing are Hagman & Misczynski, Windfalls for Wipeouts: Land Value Capture and Compensation (1978), which advocates capturing land value gains attributable to governmental action by taxation of such windfalls and using those funds to compensate land owners who are harmed by land use regulations, and Costonis, "Fair" Compensation and the Accommodation Power: Antidotes for the Taking Impasse in Land Use Controversies, 75 Colum.L.Rev. 1021 (1975), which advocates "fair" (not "just") compensation where the landowner is bearing a burden of regulation which is unduly heavy. (The latter may be viewed as a variant on the device of "zoning with compensation," a rarely used concept. See 5 Williams, American Land Planning Law Chap. 159 (1986).)

Another solution which has received much attention is the widespread utilization of development rights as a form of compensation instead of money. The Fred F. French case held that such transferable development rights would not be "adequate compensation" under the New York City scheme, although this must be viewed in the light of the Penn Central case which treated the development rights as valuable. "TDR" schemes still are advanced and are being utilized. The following discussion provides some additional information on "TDR" and its problems:

In the mid-1970's, a new technique of land use control came on the scene, Transfer of Development Rights (TDR). Although many variations of the idea have been utilized or proposed, the basic idea can be simply stated— the right to develop property can be separated from the bundle of rights and be sold or otherwise transferred, leaving the original owner with all the other sticks in the bundle. The technique has been advanced as a solution for particular problems such as landmark preservation (Costonis, Space Adrift (1974)), or open space preservation (Rose, A Proposal for the Separation and Marketability of Development Rights As a Technique to Preserve Open Space, 2 Real Estate L.J. 635 (1974)) and as a replacement for zoning as the primary instrument of land use control (Carmichael, Transferable Development Rights As a Basis for Land Use Control, 2 Fla.State U.L.Rev. 35 (1974)). The entire subject is explored in Rose (ed.), The Transfer of Development Rights: A New Technique of Land Use Regulation (1975).

The Rose book, supra, at pp. 295–297 discusses the problem of fitting the TDR concept into the proper category. TDR schemes are not quite like subdivision and zoning controls on land development, nor are they quite like eminent domain:

> One of the legal problems of the TDR concept is that it does not fit precisely into either category. It combines the characteristics of both. To use legal phraseology, it is *sui generis;* it is in a class by itself.

* * *

The issue is further complicated by the debatable significance of the issuance of certificates of development rights to the owners of property restricted to open space use. Does the receipt of such certificates remove the harshness of the deprivation of use of the land by the owner to make the proposal a valid exercise of the police power? Or, does the acceptance of the certificates constitute a "payment" to fulfill the just compensation requirements of the *exercise of the eminent domain power?*

See Dennis J. McEleney, Using Transferable Development Rights to Preserve Vanishing Landscapes and Landmarks, 83 Ill. Bar. J. 634 (1995).

WEST MONTGOMERY COUNTY CITIZENS ASSOCIATION v. MARYLAND–NATIONAL CAPITAL PARK AND PLANNING COMMISSION

Court of Appeals of Maryland, 1987.
309 Md. 183, 522 A.2d 1328.

McAULIFFE, JUDGE.

We shall here invalidate a Montgomery County zoning decision concerning density of residential development because that decision was made by the District Council through the planning process, rather than through the zoning process mandated by State law.

* * *

In October, 1980, the Functional Master Plan for the Preservation of Agriculture and Rural Open Space in Montgomery County ("Agricultural Preservation Plan") was approved and adopted. This plan recommended broad and innovative changes in the zoning text of Montgomery County, to be followed by dramatic zoning map changes that would directly affect one-fourth of the land in the County. The principal purpose of the plan was to preserve open space and agricultural land in the upper part of the County by restricting development of the land. An important adjunct of the plan was the recommendation that Montgomery County adopt and implement a system of transferable development rights ("TDRs"), to provide a form of compensation to owners whose rights to develop their properties would be significantly impaired by down-zoning, and to help ensure long term preservation of the agricultural use of the land.

The concept of TDRs is simple and straightforward. Ownership of land carries with it a bundle of rights, including the right to construct improvements on the land. These rights are subject to governmental regulation where reasonably required to accommodate public health, safety, or general welfare, and ordinarily these limitations of use may be imposed without the necessity of paying compensation to the landowner. There may arise situations, however, where the limitation of use imposed for the public good inflicts an economic impact on the landowner that, while not confiscatory, is so substantial as to prompt the government to provide some type of compensation. Cases involving the preservation of scenic easements and historic or architecturally valuable landmarks, preserving as they do benefits to the public that are largely cultural or aesthetic, yet concentrating the burden upon relatively few, have moved government officials to find ways to compensate the affected property owners. Maryland, recognizing the importance of agricultural land, and the efficacy of restricting the right to develop land as a means of accomplishing that objective, has developed a system for purchasing agricultural land preservation easements. See Md.Code (1974, 1985 Repl.Vol.) Agriculture Article, §§ 2–501 thru 2–515. Purchasing development rights with public funds is not the exclusive method of providing compensation, however. Other jurisdictions have accomplished the desired objective by permitting the transfer of development rights from the burdened property to certain other properties in the political subdivision, and have given value to this right by permitting a greater than normal intensity of development of the transferee or "receiving" property. *See, e.g. Penn Central Transp. Co. v. City of New York,* 438 U.S. 104, 98 S.Ct. 2646, 57 L.Ed.2d 631 (1978); *Fred F. French Investing Co., Inc. v. City of New York,* 39 N.Y.2d 587, 385 N.Y.S.2d 5, 350 N.E.2d 381 (1976).

Montgomery County chose the latter course—the creation of a system of transferable development rights. In accordance with the recommendations of the Agricultural Preservation Plan, the District Council amended various provisions of the zoning text to provide for a new Rural Density Transfer zone ("RDT zone") having a base density of one single family dwelling unit for each 25 acres, and to create TDRs in favor of the owners of property placed in that classification. Montgomery County Code, 1984, §§ 59–C–11.2 thru 59–C–11.5. The owners of property down-zoned to the RDT zone are granted one TDR for each five acres, less one TDR for each existing dwelling unit. Other amendments to the zoning text provide that if the owners execute a covenant not to develop their land at its base density, the TDRs can be transferred to any property within a properly designated receiving zone, and under certain circumstances can be used to increase by one dwelling unit per TDR the density of development of the receiving property. The text provides that any property in six designated single family residential zones is eligible for designation as a receiving area for TDRs. The actual designation of the properties that would constitute the "receiving zone," *i.e.* those designated as available for more intense development through the use of TDRs, is to be made through the planning, rather than the zoning process. * * *

* * *

In addition to making the zoning text changes recommended by the Agricultural Preservation Plan, the District Council adopted a sectional map amendment, down-zoning 88,000 acres of land to the RDT zone, and thereby creating nearly 17,000 TDRs. It is the attempt by Appellees to utilize some of these TDRs to achieve increased density development of their property that has generated this controversy.

* * *

The principal questions presented by this appeal involve the validity of the process legislated by the District Council for the classification of properties within the TDR receiving zone and the determination of the density limitation that shall apply to each property within the zone. Appellants also present two questions relating to alleged procedural irregularities in the granting of the preliminary plan of subdivision and the approval of the site plan. In view of the conclusion we reach concerning the substantive questions, we do not reach the procedural matters.

Although important subsidiary questions are involved, Appellants' principal contentions are that the zoning authority was not validly exercised, either by the District Council itself or by any proper delegation of its authority, and that there is a lack of required uniformity within the zones designated as potential TDR receiving areas. In our view, the questions are interrelated. If there has been a valid exercise of the zoning power, there is no lack of uniformity because the effect of what has been done has been to create subclassifications of zones that afford equal treatment to all properties within them. On the other hand, if the District Council did not properly exercise or delegate its zoning authority, then the necessary zoning action is incomplete and there does in fact exist a lack of uniformity.

* * *

We conclude, however, that this chartered county is precluded, by the express and unequivocal language of the statute that granted it zoning power, from exercising that power in any manner other than that specifically authorized—namely, by the zoning map and zoning text amendment procedures. Art. 28, § 8–101(b) provides in pertinent part that:

> Each district council, respectively, in accordance with the conditions and procedures specified in this article, may by ordinance adopt and amend the text of the zoning ordinance and may by resolution or ordinance adopt and amend the map or maps accompanying the zoning ordinance text to regulate, in the portion of the regional district lying within its county * * *; (iv) the density and distribution of population; * * *.

The authority "to regulate * * * the density and distribution of population" is expressly to be accomplished by adoption and amendment of "the text of the zoning ordinance" and adoption and amendment of "the map or maps accompanying the zoning ordinance text." Thus, where the District Council purports to act in the exercise of its zoning authority, it must do so by adopting or changing the zoning text or zoning map.

* * *

Applying the established criteria to the facts of this case, we find the delegation of authority impermissible. No legislative determination was made to limit or define the optional densities that could or should be assigned to any property in the vast area involved. Nor did the Legislature establish precise standards by which the Planning Board might determine which properties should be placed in the TDR receiving zone, or what TDR density should be assigned to each. By contrast, the

Planning Board in this case was given unlimited authority to select from a vast pool of residentially zoned property spread over the entire lower portion of the County, and to assign increased density potential to those properties without limitation. Although *Coffey* and *Gaster* are analogous cases in that density is ultimately controlled by the Master Plan, we see a vast difference between on the one hand permitting a Master Plan and subdivision regulations to reduce density where necessary for the orderly development of subdivisions, and on the other hand permitting an unlimited increase in density beyond that established by the legislative body.

In this case we note the absence of any effective zoning action by the District Council to generally classify properties within the TDR receiving zone. Virtually all of the single family residential properties in three-fourths of the County were declared eligible for that classification, but the ultimate decision of classification was left to the Planning Board. Additionally, there was no valid legislative action to assign different density classifications to properties within the receiving area, nor was there any ceiling on density established so as to leave the Planning Board with but limited authority to fix reduced densities. What appears to have been contemplated by the District Council in its attempts to implement the receiving area prong of the TDR concept is the creation of zoning subclassifications within the designated single family zones. These subclassifications would contain the properties approved as TDR receiving areas, grouped according to the density level assigned. This concept was accurately reflected in this case by the use of the TDR–1 thru TDR–6 classifications assigned by the Planning Board. Proper implementation of that structure would result in uniformity of zones, and informative identification of the precise classification of the property on the zoning map. By way of example, every property that is zoned R–200 and approved as a TDR receiving property with an optional density value of TDR–2 would be in the same zone, and each would be identified on the zoning map as R–200 TDR–2. This is the practical effect of the implementation attempted by the Planning Board—an attempt that failed because the Board lacked the requisite zoning authority. We do not suggest that this is the only method by which the desired end might be attained. Rather, we outline the structure that was employed to identify its flaws.

The major deficiency in this entire process is the absence of the final step in the planning and zoning process—the amendment of the zoning map, and where necessary the zoning text, to implement the changes recommended by the Master Plan. Certainly comprehensive planning should form an integral part of the process of identifying TDR receiving areas and assigning density classifications. Once the planning has been accomplished and the recommendations made, however, it becomes the duty of the legislative authority to make any necessary changes in the zoning law. Ordinarily, these changes are accomplished through a sectional map amendment, which once proposed enjoys a strong presumption of validity and correctness, and requires no showing of change or mistake.

These deficiencies, although perhaps easily remedied by appropriate changes in the zoning text, are fatal to the designation and classification of TDR receiving areas in this case.

JUDGMENT OF THE CIRCUIT COURT FOR MONTGOMERY COUNTY REVERSED. CASE REMANDED TO THAT COURT WITH INSTRUCTIONS TO REVERSE SO MUCH OF THE DECISION OF THE MONTGOMERY COUNTY PLANNING BOARD AS PERTAINS TO THE CLASSIFICATION AND DETERMINATION OF DENSITY LEVELS OF PROPERTY WITHIN THE TRANSFERABLE DEVELOPMENT RIGHTS RECEIVING ZONE. COSTS TO BE PAID BY APPELLEES.

Notes

1. Compare Barancik v. County of Marin, 872 F.2d 834 (9th Cir.1988) cert. denied 493 U.S. 894, 110 S.Ct. 242, 107 L.Ed.2d 193 (1989) where the court upheld a countywide plan which recommended a zoning density of one residence per 60 acres in areas designated for agricultural use and permitted transfer of development rights. The suit was brought by a rancher who sought to develop 28 residences and was willing to pay up to $8,000 per development right; his neighbors, however, wanted about $30,000 per development right which the rancher refused to pay. In the opinion, the court answered the plaintiff's claim that the TDR scheme was the sale of zoning dispensations by stating that a developer buying development rights is not paying for a dispensation because the TDR does not increase the total amount of development allowed and the government is indifferent as to who does the development.

2. In some parts of the country TDR schemes work rather well, while in other places they are roundly condemned. One lawyer in Florida complains that the the TDR system does not work in the Florida Keys because of severe density restrictions tied to the TDR scheme; owners are not willing to sell their development rights for what amounts, in practice, to 10% or so of the fair market value of their property and the developers who need the TDRs are unwilling to buy all the excess land necessary to meet rigorous density restrictions. On the other hand, a lawyer from California reports that a TDR scheme in the Santa Monica mountains works well because the land that is restricted to create the TDRs does not have to be developable and thus the costs of a TDR are less than the costs of buildable land, so the market in TDRs is active; the result is that of encouraging clustering, leaving extensive areas as open space, and avoiding excessive grading and building on cliff edges.

3. In Suitum v. Tahoe Regional Planning Agency, 80 F.3d 359 (9th Cir.1996) the owner of a parcel that had been placed in its entirety in a Stream Environmental Zone was awarded a TDR. Suitum's parcel is only 18,300 square feet in size, and under the TDR scheme her TDR is 183 square feet in size. In her lawsuit to receive damages for an uncompensated regulatory taking, the agency successfully argued that the case was not ripe for adjudication because the owner had taken no steps to seek allocation and

potential sale of the TDR. Until she did apply for a transfer of the allocation the agency could not consider the impact on the property. The owner claimed that further proceedings before the agency would be futile and the case was indeed ripe. The Supreme Court decided on May 27, 1997, ___ U.S. ___, 117 S.Ct. 1659, ___ L.Ed.2d ___, that it would not consider whether the TDRs "may be considered in deciding the issue of whether there has been a taking in this case, as opposed to the issue of whether just compensation has been afforded for such a taking." The Court's opinion is confined to the ripeness issue and the opinion finds sufficient finality in the agency's decision that placed all of Suitum's land in the stream environment zone. The Court held that Suitum did not have to sell or attempt to sell the TDR in order for the case to be ripe for judicial review. Justice Scalia's concurring opinion (Justices Thomas and O'Connor joining), however, spoke to the issue of whether TDRs are properly part of the equation of determining whether a taking has occurred (his view is they are not) or rather are only relevant to determine whether just compensation has been awarded. Scalia says that if you look at TDRs as a way of allocating residual value to the property that cannot be developed, the government can do an "end run" around regulatory takings jurisprudence and avoid *Lucas*. One provocative statement made in the concurring opinion is that TDRs might be considered partial or even full compensation for a taking. Supreme Court decisions going back nearly a hundred years are consistent in holding that compensation for a taking must be in cash.

Chapter VI

PUBLIC REGULATION OF LAND DEVELOPMENT

SECTION 1. PREVENTION OF DEVELOPMENT

The complex relationship between the police power and the takings clauses of state and federal constitutions suggests that a regulation which precludes all development of property must be supported by a very strong public interest. The Anglo–American legal tradition of defining property in terms of a "bundle of rights" accords very high priority to the right of economic development. Although early English common law placed great stress on the "right to exclude" as the most important right in the bundle—one of the most stressful problems in the 12th and 13th centuries in England was the development and enforcement of the laws of the forest—, the Roman law idea of *jus utendi,* the right to use property, became a part of the common law conception of property. In the modern capitalist society the *jus utendi* was transmuted from viewing property in the static sense of possession and *rentier* interests to a dynamic view which values property for its economic utility. The United States in the 19th century moved clearly toward a dynamic view of property. (Refer back to the Charles River Bridge case in the preceding chapter.) Toward the end of the 20th century, an ongoing debate on whether the dynamic view must give way to societal concerns about the environment and the quality of social life is reflected in controversial legal problems of preventing all economic development of certain lands. The cases in this section reflect that debate.

A. ENVIRONMENTAL CONCERNS

MORRIS COUNTY LAND IMPROVEMENT CO. v. TOWNSHIP OF PARSIPPANY–TROY HILLS

Supreme Court of New Jersey, 1963.
40 N.J. 539, 193 A.2d 232.

HALL, J. The fundamental question in this case is the constitutional validity of provisions of defendant township's zoning ordinance which greatly restrict the use of swampland and have for their prime object the retention of the land substantially in its natural state, essentially for public purposes. The provisions not only control land uses in the district, but also strictly regulate any reclamation or improvement of land therein. The Law Division sustained the provisions in a prerogative writ action brought by the plaintiff, a land owner within the area. We certified its appeal on our own motion before it was heard in the Appellate Division.

Parsippany–Troy Hills is a large, sprawling township in Morris County, with a great quantity of vacant land, which has in late years undergone very considerable development activity, accompanied by concomitant increase in population, with the usually resultant problems of planning and zoning. * * *

The particular area here involved is a large swamp of 1500 or more acres known as Troy Meadows. It is located mostly in the southeasterly corner of the township extending to some extent easterly into East Hanover Township and to a slight degree southerly across the boundary of Hanover Township. It and other similar formations in nearby municipalities represent the remaining parts of what was once Lake Passaic, a huge body of water formed eons ago by action of the last glacier in blocking the original channel of the Passaic River. Now, Troy Meadows slowly drains, by means of small streams and man-made ditches running through it, into tributaries of the present Passaic River and forms a portion of that river's basin.

As might be expected, the elevation of the area is low in relation to the surrounding land and considerably below the grade of the roads encircling or running through it. The terrain is typical swampland, with a high water table and marsh grass and cattail vegetation. The surface soil is black or dark brown muck and peat, two to six feet deep, wet and very unstable. The second stratum, from two to four feet in thickness, consists of clay and silt materials which drain poorly and are highly compressible in nature. The bottom layer is composed of sand and gravel, found, on the average, seven or eight feet beneath the surface. The testimony in the case is uncontradicted that the two top layers will not bear structures, are unsuitable for fill and would have to be removed and the land filled with proper material before it could be used for any active purpose, except possibly the raising of fish or the growing of aquatic plants.

At the present time, there are practically no active land uses in the Parsippany–Troy Hills portion of the area. About 75% of it is owned by Wildlife Preserves, Inc. (Wildlife), a private noncommercial, but taxpaying corporation, interested in conservation and preservation of the natural state of the area as a public or quasi-public wildlife sanctuary and nature study refuge. This organization has been energetic and apparently quite influential in urging the local authorities to restrict use of all of the land accordingly. It has even opposed filling of any of the land on the basis that the effect of the fill on the water would be biologically adverse to the conservation of wildlife.

There is no doubt that the area in its present state, acting essentially as a sponge, constitutes a natural detention basin for flood waters in times of very heavy rainfall, which would otherwise run off more quickly and aggravate damaging flood conditions occurring with some frequency in municipalities farther down the Passaic River valley. During such periods, Troy Meadows itself is flooded to some extent, but apparently with little, if any, effect on surrounding higher land.

Plaintiff's property consists of 66 acres in the lower corner of the meadows, fronting several hundred feet on Perrine (or Troy) Road, a dirt highway which is the boundary line in this section with Hanover Township. This acreage is part of a large tract, the balance of which is located across the road in Hanover. The entire parcel was acquired in 1952. The Hanover portion consisted mostly of high land, with a small amount of swamp near the road. At the time of acquisition and since, it has been zoned for industrial use. Plaintiff operates a sand and gravel business at the location in Hanover and has filled in the swampy portion of its property in that township with overburden and other unusable material from the sand and gravel pit.

At the time of acquisition, plaintiff's 66 acres in Parsippany–Troy Hills, along with the rest of Troy Meadows, was zoned, like the high land to the west, in the most restrictive residential classification under the township's original zoning ordinance adopted in 1945. The validity of the inclusion of the swamp in such a zone is indeed most doubtful, but apparently it was never attacked and, since no one would build an expensive home in a marsh, it served the practical purpose of precluding all development.

In 1954 an amendment to the zoning ordinance established "The Indeterminate Zone Classification * * * to cover such parts of the Township as Troy Meadows, where the nature of the land is such that its most appropriate future use is dependent on decisions by others than the government of the Township, such as with respect to flood control, and any change of present use and condition should be subject to special and individual consideration." The amendment forbade any new use, or change in existing use except for agricultural purposes or the growing of fish, water fowl and water plants, and also forbade any dumping or other disposal of material or any change in the natural or existing grade of the land, without the obtaining of a special permit from the Township Committee. From the evidence in the instant case, it is apparent that these almost "freezing" regulations were enacted as a stopgap or interim measure with the expectation or hope that higher governmental authority might well acquire the area as part of a large and much discussed flood control project to benefit the entire Passaic Valley—a project which has not yet come to pass.

Plaintiff attempted no utilization whatever of its Parsippany–Troy Hills land from 1952 until June 1959 when it commenced to fill along the edge of the road with overburden and excess material from the gravel pit operation, without obtaining any permit. Wildlife made a complaint against it in the Municipal Court for violation of the indeterminate zone regulations. While the complaint was pending, plaintiff unsuccessfully applied to the governing body to rezone its property for industrial use. Thereafter, in January 1960, plaintiff was granted a limited permission by the Township Committee to place fill to a depth of 300 feet from Perrine Road at its own risk, since the matter of the revision of land uses in the area was then under study by the township. This permission was conditioned upon submission to, and approval by, the Township Engineer of a sketch showing grades. Plaintiff resumed filling, but did not submit the sketch.

In March 1960, after an extended consideration of the meadows area by planning consultants and township officials, the indeterminate zone provisions were repealed and a new zoning classification created for the area under the title "Meadows Development Zone." The first paragraph of the new regulations set forth the purpose:

> "The Meadows Development Zone classification is established to be applied to areas of the Township with a high water table. These areas can perform a function for the Township of Parsippany–Troy Hills, if they are properly regulated in their uses. Therefore, the following special regulations become necessary to provide for the most appropriate uses of land in the district which will permit development in harmony with its character and the regional requirements for the area."

The new regulations permitted the following uses as of right: agricultural uses; raising of woody or herbaceous plants; commercial greenhouses; raising of aquatic plants, fish and fish food (with a one-family dwelling as an adjunct to any of these uses, provided its lowest floor was a specified distance above flood level); outdoor recreational uses operated by a governmental division or agency; conservation uses "including drainage control, forestry, wildlife sanctuaries and facilities for making same available and useful to the public"; hunting and fishing preserves; public utility transmission lines and substations; radio or television transmitting stations, and antenna towers; and township sewage treatment plants and water supply facilities.

The section went on to provide for what were designated as "uses which may be permitted as special exceptions by the Board of Adjustment under R.S. 40:55–39(b)," with the following preamble:

> " * * * In determining whether a special exception shall be granted, the Board shall apply the standards set forth for each particular use and, in addition, shall determine that in its development and operation the proposed use will conform to the general purposes for which the district is established, and will not impair present or potential use of adjacent properties, as may be permitted under the terms of this section."

These so-called permitted uses amounted, for the most part, to strict regulation of land reclamation in aid of uses allowed as of right. Thus, a special exception, with particular conditions, was required for any permitted use which involved a change in any drainage ditch, for the removal of earth products, such as gravel, sand, fill-dirt and peat, and for the diking, damming or filling of any land within the zone with an existing elevation of less than 175 feet above sea level (apparently this limitation would encompass practically all the land in the zone). The standards and conditions for exceptions to permit removal of earth products and filling included intricate site plan approval by the Planning Board together with studies and reports by other township officials and agencies before favorable action could be taken by the Board of Adjustment. Moreover, no filling was allowed except by the use of material taken from land within the zone. In addition, approval was required of ponds and lakes which would inevitably be created by a filling operation (since the fill had to come from within the zone and the only suitable material was the sand and gravel found below the first two strata of soil).

The removal of earth products from the zone, as a use in itself, previously permitted, became prohibited by an amendment of these provisions in June 1960. This forbade such removal on a commercial or profit basis and completely banned taking earth products beyond the boundaries of the zone.

Plaintiff continued to fill its lands after the adoption of the Meadows Development Zone provisions, without municipal authorization, until further complaints made by Wildlife put an end to the work. By that time the fill extended 1000 feet or more along the road to a depth of 150 feet or greater. It then applied to the Board of Adjustment in August 1960 for a special exception, allegedly in accordance with the ordinance, to fill its lands further as shown on a map submitted, to excavate for an 18–acre reservoir of unspecified depth, to use the material taken therefrom to supply the fill and to sell the excess to defray the cost of the operation. Since the application sought leave to do things forbidden by the ordinance, it amounted also to a request for variance. The application was ultimately denied in January 1961. This suit against the Township and the Board of Adjustment followed.

[The court first ruled adversely to the plaintiff on claims (1) that the board of adjustment abused its discretion; (2) the court erred in making a visit to the land unaccompanied by counsel; and (3) the plaintiff had established a nonconforming use. The court then continued:]

This brings us to the important and decisive question in the case— the matter of the validity of the 1960 Meadows Development Zone provisions. Plaintiff's attack is full-scale and is not confined to unconstitutional effect of the regulations as applied to its property.

* * *

There cannot be the slightest doubt from the evidence that the prime object of the zone regulations is to retain the land substantially in its natural state. As we have already said, the testimony is uncontradicted that the character of the surface soil is such that it is unsuited for any of the permitted active uses, except possibly the raising of fish and aquatic plants. The first two layers would have to be removed and replaced with proper fill which would support structures where the use involved the construction of buildings, and with appropriate top soil where agriculture and similar soil uses were contemplated. And land reclamation along these lines is, for all practical purposes, rendered impossible. Apart from the matter of having to obtain permission subject to exceedingly difficult conditions, the regulations absolutely prohibit not only the removal of the unusable top two layers of earth from the zone (and, indeed, even from the particular premises within the zone under the amendment to the soil removal ordinance), but also forbid the importation from outside the zone of suitable fill material or soil. As a practical matter, the only available method seems to be to dredge fill material from the bottom stratum of sand and gravel in some other portion of the premises (which, however, does not have the qualities of fertile top soil) and to fill the excavation as far as possible with the unusable upper layers from the area being excavated and filled. Even then it appears that a pond or lake would probably result in the unfilled portion of the excavation because of the high water table. And the regulations also require approval of such a formation. Moreover, the regulations further provide that earth removal will be permitted only if it "will not impair the present and potential use of adjacent properties." This might well become another block to any land reclamation since, it will be recalled, Wildlife has objected to any filling on the ground of an adverse biological effect on the water and the swamp creatures in its sanctuary.

In addition, it will be noted that many of the previously listed permitted uses in the zone are public or *quasi*-public in nature, rather than of the type available to the ordinary private landowner as a reasonable means of obtaining a return from his property, i.e., outdoor recreational uses to be operated only by some governmental unit, conservation uses and activities, township sewage treatment plants and water facilities and public utility transmission lines, substations and radio and television transmitting stations and towers. All in all, about the only practical use which can be made of property in the zone is a hunting or fishing preserve or a wildlife sanctuary, none of which can be considered productive.

One has to conclude that the uses to which a private landowner may put his property in the zone under the 1960 regulations are little more favorable to him than the almost "freezing" provisions which controlled the area when subject to the stop-gap Indeterminate Zone regulations. One also has the strong feeling that the ordinance changes made in 1960 were adopted essentially, not to benefit the landowner or to permit practical change in the natural state of the area, but rather because it was considered, and quite properly so, that the indeterminate zone provisions were or had become invalid for any number of reasons.

It is equally obvious from the proofs, and legally of the highest significance, that the main purpose of enacting regulations with the practical effect of retaining the meadows in their natural state was for a public benefit. This benefit is twofold, with somewhat interrelated aspects: first, use of the area as a water detention basin in aid of flood control in the lower reaches of the Passaic Valley far beyond this municipality; and second, preservation of the land as open space for the benefits which would accrue to the local public from an undeveloped use such as that of a nature refuge by Wildlife (which paid taxes on it).

This prime public, rather than private, utilization can be clearly implied from the purpose sections of the zone regulations previously quoted. And it is established beyond any question by the testimony of the township's own witnesses. * * * It is fair to conclude from the proofs that any other factors which were taken into consideration in arriving at the detailed regulations were clearly subordinate to these two public purposes.

Private property may not, of course, be taken for public use without just compensation. N.J. Const., Art. I, par. 20. The measures here adopted to accomplish public benefits do not amount to a direct or outright taking, as were those struck down in Grosso v. Board of Adjustment of Millburn Township, 137 N.J.L. 630, 61 A.2d 167 (Sup.Ct. 1948), where use of the plaintiff's property was precluded by placing the lot in the bed of a proposed street on the official map; in Hager v. Louisville & Jefferson County Planning & Zoning Commission, 261 S.W.2d 619 (Ky.Ct.App.1953), where the plaintiff's land was rendered useless by zoning it as ponding areas for temporary storage basins in accordance with a flood control plan; and in Miller v. City of Beaver Falls, 368 Pa. 189, 82 A.2d 34 (Sup.Ct.1951), where private utilization of the tract was inhibited for a period of years, pursuant to a statute, by its inclusion in a territory encompassed by an ordinance adopting a general plan for present and future parks.

* * *

While the issue of regulation as against taking is always a matter of degree, there can be no question but that the line has been crossed where the purpose and practical effect of the regulation is to appropriate private property for a flood water detention basin or open space. These are laudable public purposes and we do not doubt the high-mindedness of their motivation. But such factors cannot cure basic unconstitutionality. Nor is the situation saved because the owner of most of the land in the zone, justifiably desirous of preserving an appropriate area in its natural state as a wetland wildlife sanctuary, supports the regulations. Both public uses are necessarily so all-encompassing as practically to prevent the exercise by a private owner of any worthwhile rights or benefits in the land. So public acquisition rather than regulation is required. See Dunham, "Flood Control Via the Police Power", 107

U.Pa.L.Rev. 1098 (1959); Krasnowiecki and Paul, "The Preservation of Open Space in Metropolitan Areas", 110 U.Pa.L.Rev. 179, 184–189 (1961); Note, "Techniques for Preserving Open Spaces", 75 Harv.L.Rev. 1622 (1962); and, generally, Dunham, "A Legal and Economic Basis for City Planning", 58 Colum.L.Rev. 650, 658–670 (1958). Cf. Alford v. Finch, 155 So.2d 790 (Fla.Sup.Ct.1963). Our statutes empower the State and its subdivisions to purchase or condemn property needed for flood control, see e.g., N.J.S.A. 58:16A–1 et seq., and N.J.S.A. 40:69–4.1 et seq., and that found desirable for open-space, park, playground, conservation and recreation purposes, see e.g., R.S. 40:61–1, N.J.S.A. and N.J.S.A. 13:8A–1 et seq. (New Jersey Green Acres Land Acquisition Act of 1961). And the federal government has provided for grants to states in aid of open space programs. 42 U.S.C.A. §§ 1500–1500e.

We cannot agree with the trial court's thesis that, despite the prime public purpose of the zone regulations, they are valid because they represent a reasonable local exercise of the police power in view of the nature of the area and because the presumption of validity was not overcome. In our opinion the provisions are clearly far too restrictive and as such are constitutionally unreasonable and confiscatory. * * *

The judgment of the Law Division is reversed and the cause remanded for the entry of a judgment consistent with this opinion.

JUST v. MARINETTE COUNTY

Supreme Court of Wisconsin, 1972.
56 Wis.2d 7, 201 N.W.2d 761.

HALLOWS, CHIEF JUSTICE. Marinette county's Shoreland Zoning Ordinance Number 24 was adopted September 19, 1967, became effective October 9, 1967, and follows a model ordinance published by the Wisconsin Department of Resource Development in July of 1967. See Kusler, Water Quality Protection For Inland Lakes in Wisconsin: A Comprehensive Approach to Water Pollution, 1970 Wis.L.Rev. 35, 62–63. The ordinance was designed to meet standards and criteria for shoreland regulation which the legislature required to be promulgated by the department of natural resources under sec. 144.26, Stats. These standards are found in 6 Wis.Adm.Code, sec. NR 115.03, May, 1971, Register No. 185. The legislation, secs. 59.971 and 144.26, Stats., authorizing the ordinance was enacted as a part of the Water Quality Act of 1965 by ch. 614, Laws of 1965.

Shorelands for the purpose of ordinances are defined in sec. 59.971(1), Stats., as lands within 1,000 feet of the normal high-water elevation of navigable lakes, ponds, or flowages and 300 feet from a navigable river or stream or to the landward side of the flood plain, whichever distance is greater. The state shoreland program is unique. All county shoreland zoning ordinances must be approved by the department of natural resources prior to their becoming effective. 6 Wis.Adm. Code, sec. NR 115.04, May, 1971, Register No. 185. If a county does not enact a shoreland zoning ordinance which complies with the state's standards, the department of natural resources may enact such an ordinance for the county. Sec. 59.971(6), Stats.

There can be no disagreement over the public purpose sought to be obtained by the ordinance. Its basic purpose is to protect navigable waters and the public rights therein from the degradation and deterioration which results from uncontrolled use and development of shorelands. In the Navigable Waters Protection Act, sec. 144.26, the purpose of the state's shoreland regulation program is stated as being to "aid in the fulfillment of the state's role as trustee of its navigable waters and to promote public health, safety, convenience and general welfare." In sec. 59.971(1), which grants authority for shoreland zoning to counties, the same purposes are reaffirmed. The Marinette county shoreland zoning ordinance in secs. 1.2 and 1.3 states the uncontrolled use of shorelands and pollution of navigable waters of Marinette county adversely affect public health, safety, convenience, and general welfare and impair the tax base.

The shoreland zoning ordinance divides the shorelands of Marinette county into general purpose districts, general recreation districts, and conservancy districts. A "conservancy" district is required by the statutory minimum standards and is defined in sec. 3.4 of the ordinance to include "all shorelands designated as swamps or marshes on the United States Geological Survey maps which have been designated as the Shoreland Zoning Map of Marinette County, Wisconsin or on the detailed Insert Shoreland Zoning Maps." The ordinance provides for permitted uses[1] and conditional uses.[2] One of the conditional uses requiring a permit under sec. 3.42(4) is the filling, drainage or dredging of wetlands according to the provisions of sec. 5 of the ordinance. "Wetlands" are defined in sec. 2.29 as "(a)reas where ground water is at or near the surface much of the year or where any segment of plant cover is

---

1. "3.41 Permitted Uses.

(1) Harvesting of any wild crop such as marsh hay, ferns, moss, wild rice, berries, tree fruits and tree seeds.

(2) Sustained yield forestry subject to the provisions of Section 5.0 relating to removal of shore cover.

(3) Utilities such as, but not restricted to, telephone, telegraph and power transmission lines.

(4) Hunting, fishing, preservation of scenic, historic and scientific areas and wildlife preserves.

(5) Non-resident buildings used solely in conjunction with raising water fowl, minnows, and other similar lowland animals, fowl or fish.

(6) Hiking trails and bridle paths.

(7) Accessory uses.

(8) Signs, subject to the restriction of Section 2.0."

2. "3.42 Conditional Uses. The following uses are permitted upon issuance of a Conditional Use Permit as provided in Section 9.0 and issuance of a Department of Resource Development permit where required by Sections 30.11, 30.12, 30.19, 30.195 and 31.05 of the Wisconsin Statutes.

(1) General farming provided farm animals shall be kept one hundred feet from any non-farm residence.

(2) Dams, power plants, flowages and ponds.

(3) Relocation of any water course.

(4) Filling, drainage or dredging of wetlands according to the provisions of Section 5.0 of this ordinance.

(5) Removal of top soil or peat.

(6) Cranberry bogs.

(7) Piers, docks, boathouses."

deemed an aquatic according to N.C. Fassett's 'Manual of Aquatic Plants.' " Section 5.42(2) of the ordinance requires a conditional-use permit for any filling or grading "Of any area which is within three hundred feet horizontal distance of a navigable water and which has surface drainage toward the water and on which there is: (a) Filling of more than five hundred square feet of any wetland which is contiguous to the water * * * (d) Filling or grading of more than 2,000 square feet on slopes of twelve per cent or less."

In April of 1961, several years prior to the passage of this ordinance, the Justs purchased 36.4 acres of land in the town of Lake along the south shore of Lake Noquebay, a navigable lake in Marinette county. This land had a frontage of 1,266.7 feet on the lake and was purchased partially for personal use and partially for resale. During the years 1964, 1966, and 1967, the Justs made five sales of parcels having frontage and extending back from the lake some 600 feet, leaving the property involved in these suits. This property has a frontage of 366.7 feet and the south one half contains a stand of cedar, pine, various hard woods, birch and red maple. The north one half, closer to the lake, is barren of trees except immediately along the shore. The south three fourths of this north one half is populated with various plant grasses and vegetation including some plants which N.C. Fassett in his manual of aquatic plants has classified as "aquatic." There are also non-aquatic plants which grow upon the land. Along the shoreline there is a belt of trees. The shoreline is from one foot to 3.2 feet higher than the lake level and there is a narrow belt of higher land along the shore known as a "pressure ridge" or "ice heave," varying in width from one to three feet. South of this point, the natural level of the land ranges one to two feet above lake level. The land slopes generally toward the lake but has a slope less than twelve per cent. No water flows onto the land from the lake, but there is some surface water which collects on land and stands in pools.

The land owned by the Justs is designated as swamps or marshes on the United States Geological Survey Map and is located within 1,000 feet of the normal high-water elevation of the lake. Thus, the property is included in a conservancy district and, by sec. 2.29 of the ordinance, classified as "wetlands." Consequently, in order to place more than 500 square feet of fill on this property, the Justs were required to obtain a conditional-use permit from the zoning administrator of the county and pay a fee of $20 or incur a forfeiture of $10 to $200 for each day of violation.

In February and March of 1968, six months after the ordinance became effective, Ronald Just, without securing a conditional-use permit, hauled 1,040 square yards of sand onto this property and filled an area approximately 20–feet wide commencing at the southwest corner and extending almost 600 feet north to the northwest corner near the shoreline, then easterly along the shoreline almost to the lot line. He stayed back from the pressure ridge about 20 feet. More than 500 square feet of this fill was upon wetlands located contiguous to the water and which had surface drainage toward the lake. The fill within 300 feet of the lake also was more than 2,000 square feet on a slope less than 12 percent. It is not seriously contended that the Justs did not violate the ordinance and the trial court correctly found a violation.

The real issue is whether the conservancy district provisions and the wetlands-filing restrictions are unconstitutional because they amount to a constructive taking of the Justs' land without compensation. Marinette county and the state of Wisconsin argue the restrictions of the conservancy district and wetlands provisions constitute a proper exercise of the police power of the state and do not so severely limit the use or depreciate the value of the land as to constitute a taking without compensation.

To state the issue in more meaningful terms, it is a conflict between the public interest in stopping the despoliation of natural resources, which our citizens until recently have taken as inevitable and for granted, and an owner's asserted right to use his property as he wishes. The protection of public rights may be accomplished by the exercise of the police power unless the damage to the property owner is too great and amounts to a confiscation. The securing or taking of a benefit not presently enjoyed by the public for its use is obtained by the government through its power of eminent domain. The distinction between the exercise of the police power and condemnation has been said to be a matter of degree of damage to the property owner. In the valid exercise of the police power reasonably restricting the use of property, the damage suffered by the owner is said to be incidental. However, where the restriction is so great the landowner ought not to bear such a burden for the public good, the restriction has been held to be a constructive taking even though the actual use or forbidden use has not been transferred to the government so as to be a taking in the traditional sense. Stefan Auto Body v. State Highway Comm. (1963), 21 Wis.2d 363, 124 N.W.2d 319; Buhler v. Racine County (1966), 33 Wis.2d 137, 146 N.W.2d 403; Nick v. State Highway Comm. (1961), 13 Wis.2d 511, 109 N.W.2d 71, 111 N.W.2d 95; State v. Becker (1934), 215 Wis. 564, 255 N.W. 144. Whether a taking has occurred depends upon whether "the restriction practically or substantially renders the land useless for all reasonable purposes." Buhler v. Racine County, supra. The loss caused the individual must be weighed to determine if it is more than he should bear. As this court stated in *Stefan,* at pp. 369–370, 124 N.W.2d 319, p. 323, " * * * if the damage is such as to be suffered by many similarly situated and is in the nature of a restriction on the use to which land may be put and ought to be borne by the individual as a member of society for the good of the public safety, health or general welfare, it is said to be a reasonable exercise of the police power, but if the damage is so great to the individual that he ought not to bear it under contemporary standards, then courts are inclined to treat it as a 'taking' of the property or an unreasonable exercise of the police power."

Many years ago, Professor Freund stated in his work on The Police Power, sec. 511, at 546–547, "It may be said that the state takes property by eminent domain because it is useful to the public, and under the police power because it is harmful * * * From this results the difference between the power of eminent domain and the police power, that the former recognises a right to compensation, while the latter on principle does not." Thus the necessity for monetary compensation for loss suffered to an owner by police power restriction arises when restrictions are placed on property in order to create a public benefit rather than to prevent a public harm. Rathkopf, The Law of Zoning and Planning, Vol. 1, ch. 6, pp. 6–7.

This case causes us to reexamine the concepts of public benefit in contrast to public harm and the scope of an owner's right to use of his property. In the instant case we have a restriction on the use of a citizen's property, not to secure a benefit for the public, but to prevent a harm from the change in the natural character of the citizen's property. We start with the premise that lakes and rivers in their natural state are unpolluted and the pollution which now exists is man made. The state of Wisconsin under the trust doctrine has a duty to eradicate the present pollution and to prevent further pollution in its navigable waters. This is not, in a legal sense, a gain or a securing of a benefit by the maintaining of the natural *status quo* of the environment. What makes this case different from most condemnation or police power zoning cases is the interrelationship of the wetlands, the swamps and the natural environment of shorelands to the purity of the water and to such natural resources as navigation, fishing, and scenic beauty. Swamps and wetlands were once considered wasteland, undesirable, and not picturesque. But as the people became more sophisticated, an appreciation was acquired that swamps and wetlands serve a vital role in nature, are part of the balance of nature and are essential to the purity of the water in our lakes and streams. Swamps and wetlands are a necessary part of the ecological creation and now, even to the uninitiated, possess their own beauty in nature.

Is the ownership of a parcel of land so absolute that man can change its nature to suit any of his purposes? The great forests of our state were stripped on the theory man's ownership was unlimited. But in forestry, the land at least was used naturally, only the natural fruit of the land (the trees) were taken. The despoilage was in the failure to look to the future and provide for the reforestation of the land. An owner of land has no absolute and unlimited right to change the essential natural character of his land so as to use it for a purpose for which it was unsuited in its natural state and which injures the rights of others. The exercise of the police power in zoning must be reasonable and we think it is not an unreasonable exercise of that power to prevent harm to public rights by limiting the use of private property to its natural uses.

This is not a case where an owner is prevented from using his land for natural and indigenous uses. The uses consistent with the nature of the land are allowed and other uses recognized and still others permitted by special permit. The shoreland zoning ordinance prevents to some extent the changing of the natural character of the land within 1,000 feet of a navigable lake and 300 feet of a navigable river because of such land's interrelation to the contiguous water. The changing of wetlands and swamps to the damage of the general public by upsetting the natural environment and the natural relationship is not a reasonable use of that land which is protected from police power regulation. Changes and filling to some extent are permitted because the extent of such changes and fillings does not cause harm. We realize no case in Wisconsin has yet dealt with shoreland regulations and there are several cases in other states which seem to hold such regulations unconstitutional; but nothing in this court has said or held in prior cases indicates that destroying the natural character of a swamp or a wetland so as to make that location available for human habitation is a reasonable use of that land when the new use, although of a more economical value to the owner, causes a harm to the general public.

* * *

The Justs rely on several cases from other jurisdictions which have held zoning regulations involving flood plain districts, flood basins and wetlands to be so confiscatory as to amount to a taking because the owners of the land were prevented from improving such property for residential or commercial purposes. While some of these cases may be distinguished on their facts, it is doubtful whether these differences go to the basic rationale which permeates the decision that an owner has a right to use his property in any way and for any purpose he sees fit. In Dooley v. Town Plan & Zon. Com. of Town of Fairfield (1964), 151 Conn. 304, 197 A.2d 770, the court held the restriction on land located in a flood plain district prevented its being used for residential or business purposes and thus the restriction destroyed the economic value to the owner. The court recognized the land was needed for a public purpose as it was part of the area in which the tidal stream overflowed when abnormally high tides existed, but the property was half a mile from the ocean and therefore could not be used for marina or boathouse purposes. In Morris County Land I. Co. v. Parsippany–Troy Hills Tp. (1963), 40 N.J. 539, 193 A.2d 232, a flood basin zoning ordinance was involved which required the controversial land to be retained in its natural state. The plaintiff owned 66 acres of a 1,500–acre swamp which was part of a river basin and acted as a natural detention basin for flood waters in times of very heavy rainfall. There was an extraneous issue that the freezing regulations were intended as a stop-gap until such time as the government would buy the property under a flood-control project. However, the court took the view the zoning had an effect of preserving the land as an open space as a water-detention basin and only the government or the public would be benefited, to the complete damage of the owner.

In State v. Johnson (1970), Me., 265 A.2d 711, the Wetlands Act restricted the alteration and use of certain wetlands without permission. The act was a conservation measure enacted under the police power to protect the ecology of areas bordering the coastal waters. The plaintiff owned a small tract of a salt-water marsh which was flooded at high tide.

By filling, the land would be adapted for building purposes. The court held the restrictions against filling constituted a deprivation of a reasonable use of the owner's property and, thus, an unreasonable exercise of the police power. In MacGibbon v. Board of Appeals of Duxbury (1970), 356 Mass. 635, 255 N.E.2d 347, the plaintiff owned seven acres of land which were under water about twice a month in a shoreland area. He was denied a permit to excavate and fill part of his property. The purpose of the ordinance was to preserve from despoilage natural features and resources such as salt marshes, wetlands, and ponds. The court took the view the preservation of privately owned land in its natural, unspoiled state for the enjoyment and benefit of the public by preventing the owner from using it for any practical purpose was not within the limit and scope of the police power and the ordinance was not saved by the use of special permits.

It seems to us that filling a swamp not otherwise commercially usable is not in and of itself an existing use, which is prevented, but rather is the preparation for some future use which is not indigenous to a swamp. Too much stress is laid on the right of an owner to change commercially valueless land when that change does damage to the rights of the public. It is observed that a use of special permits is a means of control and accomplishing the purpose of the zoning ordinance as distinguished from the old concept of providing for variances. The special permit technique is now common practice and has met with judicial approval, and we think it is of some significance in considering whether or not a particular zoning ordinance is reasonable.

A recent case sustaining the validity of a zoning ordinance establishing a flood plain district is Turnpike Realty Co. v. Town of Dedham (June, 1972), 362 Mass. 221, 284 N.E.2d 891. The court held the validity of the ordinance was supported by valid considerations of public welfare, the conservation of "natural conditions, wildlife and open spaces." The ordinance provided that lands which were subject to seasonal or periodic flooding could not be used for residences or other purposes in such a manner as to endanger the health, safety or occupancy thereof and prohibited the erection of structures or buildings which required land to be filled. This case is analogous to the instant facts. The ordinance had a public purpose to preserve the natural condition of the area. No change was allowed which would injure the purposes sought to be preserved and through the special-permit technique, particular land within the zoning district could be excepted from the restrictions.

The Justs argue their property has been severely depreciated in value. But this depreciation of value is not based on the use of the land in its natural state but on what the land would be worth if it could be filled and used for the location of a dwelling. While loss of value is to be considered in determining whether a restriction is a constructive taking, value based upon changing the character of the land at the expense of harm to public rights is not an essential factor or controlling.

We are not unmindful of the warning in Pennsylvania Coal Co. v. Mahon (1922), 260 U.S. 393, 416, 43 S.Ct. 158, 160, 67 L.Ed. 322:

> * * * We are in danger of forgetting that a strong public desire to improve the public condition is not enough to warrant achieving the desire by a shorter cut than the constitutional way of paying for the change.

This observation refers to the improvement of the public condition, the securing of a benefit not presently enjoyed and to which the public is not entitled. The shoreland zoning ordinance preserves nature, the environment, and natural resources as they were created and to which the people have a present right. The ordinance does not create or improve the public condition but only preserves nature from the despoilage and harm resulting from the unrestricted activities of humans.

* * *

The Judgment in case number 106, dismissing the Justs' action, is modified to set forth the declaratory adjudication that the shoreland zoning ordinance of respondent Marinette County is constitutional; that the Justs' property constitutes wetlands and that particularly the prohibition in the ordinance against the filling of wetlands is constitutional; and the judgment, as so modified, is affirmed. * * *

Note

Other cases which "look in the same direction" as the Just case are, Candlestick Properties, Inc. v. San Francisco Bay Conservation and Development Comm'n, 11 Cal.App.3d 557, 89 Cal.Rptr. 897 (1970) (denial of a permit to place fill in the bay was upheld); Potomac Sand and Gravel Co. v. Governor of Maryland, 266 Md. 358, 293 A.2d 241 (1972), certiorari denied 409 U.S. 1040, 93 S.Ct. 525, 34 L.Ed.2d 490 (1972) (upholding wetlands legislation which forbade dredging on plaintiff's property); In re Loveladies Harbor, Inc., 176 N.J.Super. 69, 422 A.2d 107 (1980) (upholding denial of permit for filling and dredging 51 acres for development of 108 homes); Chokecherry Hills Estates, Inc. v. Deuel County, 294 N.W.2d 654 (S.D.1980) (upholding a Natural Resources District which prevented development of homesites on a lake); State, Dept. of Ecology v. Pacesetter Constr. Co., Inc., 89 Wash.2d 203, 571 P.2d 196 (1977) (upholding an injunction against construction of two lakefront houses which would significantly block the view of other homeowners near the lake).

In Security Management Corp. v. Baltimore County, 104 Md.App. 234, 655 A.2d 1326 (1995) the court upheld placement of the developer's 215 acre tract into an RC–4 zone (resource conservation, which allowed one house for every five acres). Other uses permitted by right were farms, public schools, and transit facilities; uses permitted by special exception were antique shops, camps, community buildings, churches, restaurants, and offices. Also see Zerbetz v. Municipality of Anchorage, 856 P.2d 777 (Alaska 1993) where the developer's land was placed in a conservation wetlands zone, limiting development to some residences. Also see A. Dan Tarlock, Local Government Protection of Biodiversity: What Is Its Niche?, 60 U. Chi. L. Rev. 555 (1993).

MOSKOW v. COMMISSIONER OF THE DEPARTMENT OF ENVIRONMENTAL MANAGEMENT

Supreme Judicial Court of Massachusetts, Suffolk, 1981.
384 Mass. 530, 427 N.E.2d 750.

ABRAMS, JUSTICE.

The Commissioner of the Department of Environmental Management (Commissioner) appeals from a judgment which held that a restrictive order issued pursuant to G.L. c. 131, § 40A (Inland Wetlands Act), was the "equivalent of a taking." We granted the Commissioner's application for direct appellate review. We reverse.

We summarize the judge's findings of fact. The plaintiff owns approximately 297,000 square feet of undeveloped land in Newton (parcel). The judge found that approximately 55% of the parcel (area 17) is inland wetland, because its vegetation and muck soil are typical of that found in such areas. The dominance of vegetation characteristic of wetlands "indicates that the ground water is at or near the surface of the ground during the majority of the year. The ground beneath area 17 is composed of between 3.5 and 5.5 feet of muck soil, which has a high organic content and contains silt and fine sand."

On April 7, 1977, the Commissioner placed a restrictive order on area 17. Under this order, the plaintiff may not dredge, fill, or alter the wetland. The judge found that "[p]arcel 17's low, flat topography, muck soils and dense vegetation retain peak flows during periods of flooding and release this water slowly and evenly over extended periods of time. This moderates extremes in water level and velocity, and reduces flood damages in downstream areas of the Charles River Watershed. The parcel's profuse vegetation and muck soil functions as a natural filter system, removing sediments, salt, petroleum products, and other pollutants from the water. In addition, area 17 helps to maintain base flows in downstream areas during periods of low flow, thereby diluting concentration of water pollutants during these periods." The judge therefore found that area 17 plays an important role in preventing floods and reducing pollution in the Charles River Watershed.

Under the Commissioner's order, the judge found that the plaintiff could still use area 17 for certain limited purposes. These uses include: "a. The construction and maintenance of catwalks, wharves, boathouses, boat shelters, fences[,] duckblinds, wildlife management shelters, foot bridges, observation decks and shelters; b. The construction and maintenance of a roadway or driveway of minimum and practical width where reasonable alternative means of access from a public way to unrestricted land of the same owner is unavailable; c. The installation and maintenance of underground or overhead utilities; d. Commercial and noncommercial outdoor recreation activities including hiking, boating[,] trapping[,] hunting; e. Other works which are designed to enhance the appearance and attractiveness of open space of recreational areas without altering their use as such; and f. The use or improvement of land or water for agricultural purposes."

The judge correctly concluded that the Commonwealth can reasonably regulate private property in the public interest. See *Lovequist v. Conservation Comm'n of Dennis,* 379 Mass. 7, ___, 393 N.E.2d 858; *Turnpike Realty Co. v. Dedham,* 362 Mass. 221, 227–229, 284 N.E.2d 891 (1972), cert. denied, 409 U.S. 1108, 93 S.Ct. 908, 34 L.Ed.2d 689 (1973); *Penn Cent. Transp. Co. v. New York City,* 438 U.S. 104, 125, 98 S.Ct. 2646, 2659, 57 L.Ed.2d 631 (1978). "Controlling and restricting the filling of wetlands is clearly within the scope of the police power of the State." *Sibson v. State,* 115 N.H. 124, 126, 336 A.2d 239 (1975). * * * The judge also correctly concluded that the "crucial issue is whether, notwithstanding the meritorious character of the regulation, there has been such a deprivation of the practical uses of a landowner's property as to be the equivalent of a taking."

* * *

The judge then determined that the order was the "equivalent of a taking" for two reasons. "First, any and all profitable use of [area] 17 has been prohibited; the ban is permanent. The owner is to be denied effectively the use of more than half of his parcel. Second, unlike zoning and historical district types of cases, there is no reciprocity of benefit."

The findings of the judge do not support his conclusion. He found that after the restrictive order the plaintiff could build a single family residence on his land. A single family house is a sufficient practical use to prevent the wetland restrictions from constituting a taking. * * *

" 'Taking' jurisprudence does not divide a single parcel into discrete segments and attempt to determine whether rights in a particular segment have been entirely abrogated. In deciding whether a particular governmental action has effected a taking, this Court focuses rather both on the character of the action and on the nature and extent of the interference with rights in the parcel as a whole * * *." *Penn Cent. Transp. Co. v. New York City,* 438 U.S. at 130–131, 98 S.Ct. at 2662. Since the plaintiff may still use his property for a dwelling or dwellings, there has not been such an extensive interference with the parcel as a whole that it constitutes a taking.[3]

3. The construction of a single family house may not be the only practical use. At trial, there was evidence that the plaintiff could subdivide his parcel into four lots without violating the restrictions. In addition, there was evidence that twenty years earlier the plaintiff had planned to subdivide his parcel into eight lots. The judge found that the plan as proposed did not comply with Newton's existing zoning ordinance. He also found that, even without the department's restrictions, the plaintiff could subdivide his parcel into eight lots. We need not determine whether there is any inconsistency in these findings, for even if an eight lot subdivision were permissible in the absence of restrictions, the Commissioner's order would still not be a taking. A reduction in the number of houses that an owner may build is a diminution in value and not a taking. "There is no set formula to determine where regulation ends and taking begins. Although a comparison of values before and after is relevant * * * it is by no means conclusive * * *." *Turnpike*

Although the judge realized that he should look at the effect of the restriction on the plaintiff's entire parcel, not just area 17, nevertheless he did not do so. Rather, the judge focused solely on area 17 and the limitations on its use. Consequently, the judge erred in concluding that the restrictive order was a taking.

The judge also determined that the restrictions were the "equivalent of a taking," because the plaintiff received "no reciprocity of benefit" from the restrictions. He found that "the area receiving the benefit is an area downstream and far removed from the locus." Since the plaintiff received no direct benefit from the restrictions, the judge determined that he was unconstitutionally deprived of his property without compensation. Even if we were to assume that the plaintiff received no benefit, however, the restrictions did not constitute a taking. The fact that the Inland Wetlands Act "has a more severe impact on some landowners than on others * * * does not mean that the law effects a 'taking.' Legislation designed to promote the general welfare commonly burdens some more than others." *Penn Cent. Transp. Co. v. New York City,* 438 U.S. 104, 133, 98 S.Ct. 2646, 2663, 57 L.Ed.2d 631 (1978). See *Hadacheck v. Sebastian,* 239 U.S. 394, 36 S.Ct. 143, 60 L.Ed. 348 (1915). As long as "the restrictions [are] reasonably related to the implementation of a policy * * * expected to produce a widespread public benefit and applicable to all similarly situated property," they need not produce a reciprocal benefit. *Penn Cent. Transp. Co. v. New York City,* 438 U.S. 104, 134 n. 30, 98 S.Ct. 2646, 2664, 57 L.Ed.2d 631 (1978). Since the Inland Wetlands Act is reasonably related to the goals of flood and pollution control, its application to the plaintiff is not unconstitutional.

The judgment is reversed, and the case is remanded to the Superior Court for the entry of a judgment that the Commissioner's restrictive order is not the "equivalent of a taking" and that the restrictive order for the city of Newton, as it applies to area 17, is valid and enforceable.

So ordered.

Notes

1. Compare with the Moskow case K & K Construction, Inc. v. Department of Natural Resources, 217 Mich.App. 56, 551 N.W.2d 413 (1996). Plaintiffs owned four adjacent tracts of land totaling 82 acres; they sought to develop a restaurant on Parcel 1, fifty-five acres. A permit was denied by defendant on the ground that about twenty-eight acres of Parcel 1 was protected wetlands. The state court of claims held there was a taking and awarded compensation of more than $3 million, plus $1.5 million in interest, and $450,000 for a temporary taking. The intermediate appellate court affirmed on the basis of the Lucas decision, rejecting, inter alia, the agency argument that a fundamental principle of Michigan property law subor-

Realty Co. v. Dedham, 362 Mass. 221, 236, 284 N.E.2d 891 (1972), cert. denied, 409 U.S. 1108, 93 S.Ct. 908, 34 L.Ed.2d 689 (1973), quoting from *Goldblatt v. Hempstead,* 369 U.S. 590, 594, 82 S.Ct. 987, 990, 8 L.Ed.2d 130 (1962). The plaintiff offered no evidence which showed that he suffered an actual financial loss as a result of the restrictions. Thus, there is no factual support for his claim of confiscation.

dinates property rights to environmental protection. The court also held that the measure of compensation should be applied only to the totality of Parcel 1 which was rendered commercially valueless because the irregular twenty-eight acre wetland rendered any development of the fifty-five acre parcel for commercial uses impossible; Parcel 1 was the only part of plaintiffs' tract that was zoned commercial, and thus should not be lumped with Parcels 2, 3, and 4 for purposes of determining whether a taking had occurred. This case presents unusual facts; in the more common situation of designating a portion of the owner's property as wetlands, the Michigan courts will look at the property as a whole to determine whether a taking has occurred. Volkema v. Dept. of Natural Resources, 214 Mich.App. 66, 542 N.W.2d 282 (1995).

Bergen County Associates v. Borough of East Rutherford, 265 N.J.Super. 1, 625 A.2d 524 (1993) was not a wetlands taking case, but rather a tax assessment dispute. The taxpayer was successful in obtaining a reduction of the assessment of his wetlands property from $19,978,100 to $976,500. The reduction was upheld after the borough appealed.

For a case where the landowner's parcel was partly in a wetland and partly in a sand dune area and he was denied a permit to build on top of the sand dune under the state's Sand Dune Protection and Management Act, see Oceco Land Co. v. Dept. of Natural Resources, 216 Mich.App. 310, 548 N.W.2d 702 (1996).

2.   The issue of looking at a regulatory taking by examining the parcel as a whole, rather than discrete segments, is especially acute in wetlands cases where a part of the owner's property is designated wetland. Most of the courts considering the issue have decided to look to the parcel as a whole. See, e.g., Zealy v. City of Waukesha, 201 Wis.2d 365, 548 N.W.2d 528 (1996); State Dept. of Environmental Regulation v. Schindler, 604 So.2d 565 (Fla.App.1992). This approach works relatively well when a wetlands designation is imposed on undeveloped property, but what if the developer has completed most of a development and the wetlands designation comes near the end of the project? In this situation consider the following case:

LOVELADIES HARBOR v. UNITED STATES

United States Court of Appeals, Federal Circuit, 1994.
28 F.3d 1171.

PLAGER, CIRCUIT JUDGE.

* * *

The property at issue in this dispute is a 12.5 acre parcel (the parcel) consisting of 11.5 acres of wetlands and one acre of filled land, located on Long Beach Island, Ocean County, New Jersey.* * * The 12.5 acres is part of a 51 acre parcel owned by Loveladies, which in turn is part of an original 250 acre tract which Loveladies had acquired in 1958. The balance of the 250 acres—199 acres—had been developed before 1972 and the enactment of § 404 of the Clean Water Act.

In order to develop the remaining 51 acre parcel for residential use, Loveladies needed to fill 50 acres, the one acre having been previously filled, and that in turn required Loveladies to obtain permission from both the New Jersey Department of Environmental Protection (NJDEP) and the Corps. That process proved to be lengthy and contentious, marked by several years of negotiation (with Loveladies submitting progressively less ambitious and less environmentally objectionable proposals), a 1977 permit denial, appeal of that denial to the Commissioner of NJDEP, and judicial review in state court.

During the course of the proceedings, NJDEP offered, as a compromise, permission for Loveladies to develop 12.5 of the 51 acres. Loveladies initially declined that offer. Eventually Loveladies acquiesced to the 12.5 acre limitation, the dispute was resolved, and the permit, on September 9, 1981, issued. See In re Loveladies Harbor, Inc., 422 A.2d 107 (N.J.Super.Ct.App.Div.1980), certif. denied 427 A.2d 588 (N.J.1981). The permit granted permission to fill and develop 11.5 acres in addition to the one acre which had been filled previously—this is the 12.5 acre parcel at issue—and to construct 35 single family homes thereon. * * *

The Corps rejected Loveladies' § 404 permit application on May 5, 1982. Loveladies again resorted to the courts. As previously noted, the § 404 permit denial was challenged in Federal District Court under § 554 of the APA, and that challenge was unsuccessful. Loveladies Harbor, Inc. and Loveladies Harbor, Unit D, Inc., v. Baldwin, supra. Between the time the District court made its decision and the appeal was decided, Loveladies filed a claim in the Court of Federal Claims for just compensation under the Fifth Amendment. That case proceeded to trial following issuance of the Third Circuit's affirmance of the district court's rejection of Loveladies' APA claims. * * *

Following a full hearing, those factual issues were resolved in favor of Loveladies. Loveladies 2, 21 Cl.Ct. at 153. The court found that the fair market value of the parcel prior to the permit denial was $2,658,000 whereas the value after the permit denial was $12,500. This greater than 99% diminution of value, "coupled with the court's earlier determination of a lack of a countervailing substantial legitimate state interest," led the court to conclude that there had been a taking. Loveladies 2, 21 Cl.Ct. at 160 (referring to Loveladies 1, 15 Cl.Ct. at 388–90). The Government appeals the judgment of the Court of Federal Claims. * * *

* * *

In sum, then, to restate the law of regulatory taking as currently applicable to the case before us:

a) A property owner who can establish that a regulatory taking of property has occurred is entitled to a monetary recovery for the value of the interest taken, measured by what is just compensation.

b) With regard to the interest alleged to be taken, there has been a regulatory taking if (1) there was a denial of economically viable use of the property as a result of the regulatory imposition; (2) the property owner had distinct investment-backed expectations; and (3) it was an interest vested in the owner, as a matter of state property law, and not within the power of the state to regulate under common law nuisance doctrine.

The effect, then, of Lucas was to dramatically change the third criterion, from one in which courts, including federal courts, were called upon to make ad hoc balancing decisions, balancing private property rights against state regulatory policy, to one in which state property law, incorporating common law nuisance doctrine, controls. This sea change removed from regulatory takings the vagaries of the balancing process, so dependent on judicial perceptions with little effective guidance in law. It substituted instead a referent familiar to property lawyers everywhere, and one which will have substantial (though varying from state to state) likelihood of predictability for both property owners and regulators.

With regard to the second criterion—investment-backed expectations—it is not disputed that Loveladies purchased the land involved with the reasonable expectation and intention of developing it over time for sale to purchasers of the improved lots; that the regulation constitutes an interference with their investment-backed expectations cannot be denied. There is, however, less agreement between the parties with regard to the first and third criteria. We will address each in turn.

A. DENIAL OF ECONOMICALLY VIABLE USE AND THE DENOMINATOR PROBLEM

In Lucas, the Court discussed but was not called upon to decide the question of whether a regulatory taking requires that there be a denial of essentially all remaining economic use, or whether loss of a substantial part, but not all, of the economic use may constitute a compensable partial taking. The earlier cases sometimes use language that suggests that was so, and sometimes did not. Lucas, itself contains a discussion that acknowledges both viewpoints. Lucas, 112 S.Ct. at 2895 n. 8.

In Florida Rock Industries, Inc. v. United States, 18 F.3d 1560 (Fed.Cir.1994), we concluded that, depending on the legal import of the final fair market value before and after the regulatory imposition on the particular property involved, a partial taking may have occurred. We explained that in making that determination there was "the difficult task of resolving when a partial loss of economic use of the property has crossed the line from a noncompensable 'mere diminution' to a compensable 'partial taking.' " Florida Rock, 18 F.3d at 1570. The reference to 'mere diminution' is to those decreases in property value resulting from shared economic impacts which are the consequence of certain types of land use controls, those in which the property owner has in a sense been compensated by the public program "adjusting the benefits and burdens of economic life to promote the common good." Penn Central, 438 U.S. at 124. The Court in Lucas described it as: "adjusting the benefits and burdens of economic life ... in a manner that secures an 'average reciprocity of advantage' to everyone concerned." Lucas, 112 S.Ct. at 2894 (internal citations omitted).

On the facts of the case before us, the question of whether there has been a partial or total loss of economic use depends on what is the specific property that was affected by the permit denial. If the tract of land that is the measure of the economic value after the regulatory imposition is defined as only that land for which the use permit is denied, that provides the easiest case for those arguing that a categorical taking occurred. On the other hand, if the tract of land is defined as some larger piece, one with substantial residuary value independent of the wetlands regulation, then either a partial or no taking occurred, depending on the test as described in Florida Rock, 18 F.3d at 1567 et seq. This is the denominator problem.

In this case, the Government assumes that virtually all economic use must be taken (that is, destroyed by the regulatory imposition) in order to have a compensable regulatory taking. Under that assumption, the key question is, when comparing the value of the property before and after the imposition, what is the property whose value is compared. On the facts here, is the test the effect of the imposition on the value of just the 12.5 acres, or is it the effect of the imposition on the total value of, say, the original 250 acres, or on some other size unit.

The Government argues that the proper denominator is the original 250 acre parcel or, at the least, the total acreage remaining unsold in 1982, when the permit was denied. In 1982, as we have noted, Loveladies owned 51 undeveloped acres; the other 199 had been developed and all but 6.4 of those acres had been sold. Under their agreement with New Jersey in settlement of its lawsuit, Loveladies could develop only the 12.5 acres of the 51; the development rights in the remaining 38.5 acres were to be dedicated to the state in return for the NJDEP permit. Of the 12.5 acres, one acre was already filled; there remained 11.5 acres of wetlands for which Loveladies sought the § 404 permit. This array of possible denominators bears out the Lucas Court's observation that "the rhetorical force of [the] 'deprivation of all economically feasible use' rule is greater than its precision." Lucas, 112 S.Ct. at 2894 n. 7.

Loveladies and the amici urge this court to adopt a brightline rule that the denominator of the takings fraction is that parcel for which the owner seeks a permit. The Government, on the other hand, argues that such bright-line rules would encourage strategic behavior on the part of developers—"conveying away the non-wetlands portions of their parcels prior to applying to the Corps for a permit to fill the remaining wetlands."

Our precedent displays a flexible approach, designed to account for factual nuances. In Deltona Corp. v. United States, 657 F.2d 1184 (Ct.Cl.1981), cert. denied, 455 U.S. 1017 (1982), the court was concerned with whether there remained substantial economically viable uses for plaintiff's property after the regulatory imposition. In determining this, the court took into account the facts that while plaintiffs were blocked from developing two of the three projects for which they sought permits, they were granted a permit for the third; and that within the two that were denied, they had 111 acres of uplands which could be developed, and whose value exceeded by twice the original price paid for the two tracts. There was no taking.

In Whitney Benefits, Inc. v. United States, 926 F.2d 1169 (Fed.Cir. 1991), cert. denied, 112 S.Ct. 406 (1991), this court concluded that the regulatory enactment, the Surface Mining Control and Reclamation Act of 1977, had its intended effect, precluding the surface mining of plaintiff's coal field because of the overlying alluvial valley floor. This was based on extensive fact finding by the trial court regarding the purpose of the imposition, the nature of the property, its alternative uses, and the extent to which all or only a portion of plaintiff's property was so limited. "That finding [that the imposition deprived the plaintiff of all economically viable use of its property and destroyed its value] is not only correct and fully supported by the evidence, it is entitled to respect and may be upset only if it is shown to have been clearly erroneous." Whitney Benefits, 926 F.2d at 1172–73. The Claims Court judgment of compensable taking was affirmed.

These factual nuances include consideration of the timing of transfers in light of the developing regulatory environment. New Jersey apparently made no effort to impose restrictions on the development of this wetland area until after the initial project had been approved for development, and until 199 acres had been developed. This development occurred over a substantial period of years beginning in 1958, and involved many kinds of government permits. The trial court concluded that land developed or sold before the regulatory environment existed should not be included in the denominator. The Government has failed to convince us that the trial court clearly erred in this conclusion.

With regard to the land remaining after the regulatory fabric was in place, the trial court excluded from consideration the 38.5 acres which for all practical purposes had been promised to New Jersey in exchange for the NJDEP permit. This is only logical since whatever substantial value that land had now belongs to the state and not to Loveladies. It would seem ungrateful in the extreme to require Loveladies to convey to the public the rights in the 38.5 acres in exchange for the right to develop 12.5 acres, and then to include the value of the grant as a charge against the givers.

This leaves the conclusion that the relevant property for the takings analysis is the 12.5 acres, for which the trial court found the remaining value to be de minimis. This is not, then, a case of a partial taking, involving linedrawing between noncompensable "mere diminution" and compensable partial taking. See Florida Rock Industries, Inc. v. United States, 18 F.3d 1560 (1994). Rather, this is a case in which the owner of the relevant parcel was deprived of all economically feasible use. The trial court's conclusion that the permit denial was effectively a total taking of the property owner's interest in these acres is fully supported in the record; there is no clear error in that conclusion.

Affirmed.

Note

See Marc R. Lisker, Regulatory Takings and the Denominator Problem, 27 Rutgers L. J. 663 (1996).

Would Loveladies apply to a case where someone purchases property for development and subsequently a wetlands protection scheme is instituted, and the purchaser wants to stop payments on his purchase agreement? In Felt v. McCarthy, 78 Wash.App. 362, 898 P.2d 315 (1995) the vendor sued to recover the amount owing on the purchase agreement and the purchaser counterclaimed to be discharged of the obligation pursuant to the doctrine of supervening frustration. The court held the doctrine did not apply to discharge the purchaser, even though he agreed to pay $310,000 for nine acres of vacant land solely on the expectation that the land could be developed commercially, an expectation frustrated by subsequent wetlands legislation; the purchaser's development goals were not the basic assumption upon which the vendor entered into the contract.

GLISSON v. ALACHUA COUNTY

District Court of Appeal of Florida, First District, 1990.
558 So.2d 1030.

JOANOS, JUDGE.

This appeal concerns land use regulations adopted by the Alachua County Board of County Commissioners which will impact on appellants' future use of their property.

* * *

Pursuant to the provisions of its comprehensive plan, Alachua County designated the Cross Creek region as a special study area. The Cross Creek Special Study Area includes 3,100 acres lying on either side of Cross Creek, between Orange Lake and Lake Lochloosa in southeast Alachua County. The area contains the site of the Marjorie Kinnan Rawlings house (a State of Florida Historic Site). There is little development in the area, and it is surrounded by the Lochloosa Wildlife Management Area and the two lakes. The two lakes and the Cross Creek body of water have been designated as Outstanding Florida Waters. *See* § 403.061(27)(a), Fla.Stat. (1987).

Appellants are eighteen landowners in the Cross Creek Special Study Area. Their holdings range from less than one acre to 522 acres, held by Mr. Ernest Southward, as trustee for several investors in the property. Appellants Southward and Brown purchased property in the Cross Creek area for development purposes. Other appellants are long-term residents or property owners in or near Cross Creek.

On August 13, 1985, the Alachua County Board of County Commissioners adopted CPA–5–85 as an amendment to the Alachua County Comprehensive Plan. The amendment established specific development guidelines for the Cross Creek area, and was the culmination of the special study of the Cross Creek area. The study contained three general sets of guidelines or policies for the Village Center development area and the Village periphery development area, four resource protection areas, and general development guidelines. The resource protection areas are the wetlands, exceptional upland habitat, hammock zones, and active use zones.

The wetland areas are restricted from all construction activity, except minor accessory uses. Under the regulations, permitted density could be transferred at a rate of one unit per five acres, where there was appropriate contiguous property under the same ownership. Areas designated as exceptional upland habitat are considered conservation areas, where only one dwelling unit per five acres is permitted. Lot sizes are reduced to one acre and the remaining four acres of the area are to be protected in their natural state. Removal of the existing indigenous vegetation is discouraged, except for bona fide agricultural practices on existing farm lands. The hammock zones are designated as areas which will serve as wildlife habitats of secondary value and generally act as transitional zones to buffer the conservation areas. In the Village periphery, one dwelling unit per five acres is permitted on lot sizes of one acre, clustered so as to preserve the most sensitive or unique areas. The active use zones are designated as areas having comparatively little ecological value, and will be the focus of future development. No active use is permitted within a radius of 750 feet of an eagle nest. Within an additional 750 feet, all residential density has to be transferred to appropriate contiguous property under the same ownership.

CPA–5–85 existed without change or amplification until December 22, 1987, when the Commission adopted Ordinance 87–25. Ordinance 87–25 modified CPA–5–85 by adding provisions for variance applications and created a system for transfer of development rights (TDR's) within the study area to qualifying property within an urban cluster. Under CPA–5–85, if TDR's were issued, they could only be used outside the Cross Creek area, because no urban cluster is located in Cross Creek. With the passage of Ordinance 87–25 two years later, a property owner could transfer density in a restricted use zone to appropriate contiguous property under the same ownership, or to appropriate adjoining property not under the same ownership if all the affected properties were presented for development as a planned unit development (PUD).

Evidence adduced at trial indicated that the areas designated as exceptional upland habitat and hammock are found throughout Alachua County, and are not unique to the Cross Creek area. In addition, there was evidence that many of these areas had been disturbed, either by timbering or by agricultural activities, and that only six of the forty-five active eagles' nests in Alachua County are located in the Cross Creek area. Expert testimony indicated that farming, and cattle grazing are not economically feasible in the Cross Creek area. According to the expert witness, the restrictions imposed under Ordinance 87–25 and CPA–5–85 make it unlikely that a prospective buyer would consider purchasing the property for agricultural purposes. In addition, testimony from a land planner and developer indicated that the value of the individual parcels of property in Cross Creek had been seriously reduced as a result of

Ordinance 87–25, and that individual property owners had been denied beneficial uses of their property. The record reflects that appellants Southward, Glisson, and Brown expended varying sums of money prior to passage of CPA–5–85 to prepare their land for residential development. Although Mr. Glisson's plan had received conceptual approval, after passage of CPA–5–85, he was advised by the County Attorney's office that conceptual approval did not entitle a property owner to obtain a permit of any kind. Due to the advice he received from the county attorney, and his personal knowledge of the unsuccessful development approval efforts of Mr. Southward and Mr. Brown, Mr. Glisson considered that any further expenditures for obtaining development permits would be futile.

The county agrees that appellants' property located in the special study area would be more valuable if appellants were free to develop it for use as recreational vehicle and mobile home parks, condominiums, or at suburban intensities. On the other hand, the record reflects that only one appellant has applied for development approval since the adoption of CPA–5–85, and that his application was approved, and the subdivided lots were sold for a substantial sum.

* * *

The first issue concerns appellants' contention that the land use regulations promulgated by the county constitute an attempt to exercise the power of eminent domain, disguised as an exercise of the police power. In support of this contention, appellants assert that the language of the comprehensive plan amendments and zoning ordinance 87–25, together with trial testimony concerning specific details of the regulations and their impact on appellants' property, demonstrate that the Cross Creek plan constitutes the creation of a "public benefit." Appellants further assert that the evidence demonstrates that the boundaries for application of the Cross Creek plan were drawn on the assumption that the state would buy and preserve the surrounding area, and restrictions were accordingly imposed in the Cross Creek area to conform land uses in the area to those uses in the surrounding areas which are under state ownership. In essence, appellants contend that as owners of property in the Cross Creek area, they are entitled to compensation because the regulations require them to maintain the status quo with regard to present uses of their property, in order to preserve an area as a benefit to be enjoyed by the public at large.

At the outset, it is well settled that the state may, by regulation or condemnation, restrict the use of private property. The fifth amendment was not designed "to limit the governmental interference with property rights per se, but rather to secure compensation in the event of otherwise proper interference amounting to a taking." *First English Evangelical Lutheran Church of Glendale v. County of Los Angeles, Cal.,* 482 U.S. 304, 107 S.Ct. 2378, 2386, 96 L.Ed.2d 250 (1987). *See also Department of Agriculture v. Mid–Florida Growers, Inc.,* 521 So.2d 101, 103 (Fla.), *cert. denied,* 488 U.S. 870, 109 S.Ct. 180, 102 L.Ed.2d 149 (1988). There is no set formula or test for determining where legitimate government regulation ends and taking begins, in the sense that the regulation has gone too far. *MacDonald, Sommer & Frates v. Yolo County,* 477 U.S. 340, 106 S.Ct. 2561, 2566, 91 L.Ed.2d 285 (1986); *Penn Central Transportation Co. v. New York City,* 438 U.S. 104, 124, 98 S.Ct. 2646, 2659, 57 L.Ed.2d 631 (1978); *Goldblatt v. Hempstead,* 369 U.S. 590, 594, 82 S.Ct. 987, 990, 8 L.Ed.2d 130 (1962); *Graham v. Estuary Properties, Inc.,* 399 So.2d 1374, 1380 (Fla.), *cert. denied, sub nom., Taylor v. Graham,* 454 U.S. 1083, 102 S.Ct. 640, 70 L.Ed.2d 618 (1981). Not surprisingly, the difficulty has always been in defining "too far," i.e., in distinguishing "the point at which regulation becomes so onerous that it has the same effect as an appropriation of the property through eminent domain or physical possession." *MacDonald, Sommer & Frates v. Yolo County,* 106 S.Ct. at 2566. "The general rule * * * is that while property may be regulated to a certain extent, if regulation goes too far it will be recognized as a taking." *Pennsylvania Coal Co. v. Mahon,* 260 U.S. 393, 43 S.Ct. 158, 160, 67 L.Ed. 322 (1922).

The propriety of a land use regulation which requires a property owner to maintain the status quo with respect to land use was decided adversely to appellants' position in *Graham v. Estuary Properties, Inc.* In *Graham,* the court reaffirmed the rule that the "exercise of the state's police power must relate to health, safety, and welfare of the public and may not be arbitrarily and capriciously applied." 399 So.2d at 1379. *See also Sarasota County v. Barg,* 302 So.2d 737, 741 (Fla.1974); *Davis v. Sails,* 318 So.2d 214, 217 (Fla. 1st DCA 1975); *City of Sunrise v. D.C.A. Homes, Inc.,* 421 So.2d 1084, 1085 (Fla. 4th DCA 1982); *Moviematic Industries Corp. v. Board of County Commissioners of Metropolitan Dade County,* 349 So.2d 667, 669 (Fla. 3d DCA 1977). The issue in *Graham* was whether the denial of an application for approval of a development of regional impact (DRI) constituted a taking. The permit was denied primarily to prevent the destruction of a large mangrove forest as called for by the development plan. The court reviewed the question primarily on the basis of a harm-benefit test involving the following factors:

(1) whether there has been a physical invasion of the property;

(2) the diminution in value of the property, i.e., whether the regulation precludes all economically reasonable use of the property;

(3) whether the regulation confers a public benefit or prevents a public harm;

(4) whether the regulation promotes the health, safety, welfare, or morals of the public;

(5) whether the regulation was applied arbitrarily and capriciously; and

(6) the extent to which the regulation has curtailed investment-backed expectations.

Graham, 399 So.2d at 1380–1381.

In *Graham*, the court held that the restrictions on development constituted a valid exercise of the police power. The court concluded that denial of a DRI permit prevented a public harm in that the proposed development would pollute the surrounding bays. While recognizing the public would be benefited because the bays would remain clean, the benefit was not deemed compensable because it was "in the form of maintaining the status quo." *Graham*, 399 So.2d at 1382.

The interests purportedly protected by the regulations at issue in this case are appropriate subjects for exercise of the police power. For example, among the interests deemed legitimate for exercise of the state's police power are such matters as: (1) protection of aesthetic interests, *City of Sunrise v. D.C.A. Homes*, 421 So.2d at 1085, *Moviematic v. County Commissioners*, 349 So.2d at 669; (2) preservation of residential or historical character of a neighborhood, *Moviematic*, 349 So.2d at 669; and (3) protection of environmentally sensitive areas and pollution control, *Graham v. Estuary Properties*, 399 So.2d at 1381; *Moviematic*, 349 So.2d at 669. Under certain circumstances, a regulation may meet the standards necessary for exercise of the police power, but still result in a taking which requires compensation. *See Department of Agriculture v. Mid–Florida Growers*, 521 So.2d at 103; *Dade County v. National Bulk Carriers, Inc.*, 450 So.2d 213, 215 (Fla.1984); *Joint Ventures v. Department of Transportation*, 519 So.2d 1069, 1070 (Fla. 1st DCA 1988).

To succeed in a regulatory taking claim, a property owner must demonstrate (1) that a regulation is unreasonable or arbitrary, or (2) that it denies a substantial portion of the beneficial use of the property. *Joint Ventures v. Department of Transportation*, 519 So.2d at 1070. *See also Nollan v. California Coastal Commission*, 483 U.S. 825, 107 S.Ct. 3141, 97 L.Ed.2d 677 (1987); *First English Evangelical Lutheran Church v. Los Angeles County*, 107 S.Ct. at 2386; *MacDonald, Sommer & Frates v. Yolo County*, 106 S.Ct. at 2566; *Herrington v. Sonoma County*, 834 F.2d 1488, 1497 (9th Cir.1987), *cert. denied*, 489 U.S. 1090, 109 S.Ct. 1557, 103 L.Ed.2d 860 (1989). A police power regulation is not invalid simply because it denies the highest and best use of the property, *Penn Central Transportation Co. v. New York City*, 438 U.S. 104, 125, 98 S.Ct. 2646, 2659–2660, 57 L.Ed.2d 631 (1978); *Goldblatt v. Town of Hempstead*, 369 U.S. 590, 82 S.Ct. 987, 8 L.Ed.2d 130 (1962); *Graham v. Estuary Properties*, 399 So.2d at 1382, or because it dramatically diminishes the value of the property. *Hadacheck v. Sebastian*, 239 U.S. 394, 36 S.Ct. 143, 60 L.Ed. 348 (1915); *Graham v. Estuary Properties*, 399 So.2d at 1382. Rather, "[i]f the regulation is a valid exercise of the police power, it is not a taking if a reasonable use of the property remains." *Agins v. City of Tiburon*, 447 U.S. 255, 100 S.Ct. 2138, 2141, 65 L.Ed.2d 106 (1980); *American Savings & Loan Association v. Marin County*, 653 F.2d 364, 368 (9th Cir.1981).

Courts considering the police power/taking dichotomy have held that a taking issue is not ripe for determination until such time as the property owner has received a final determination from the government as to the permissible uses of the property. *Joint Ventures v. Department of Transportation,* 519 So.2d at 1073–1074, J. Ervin, specially concurring; *Moviematic,* 349 So.2d at 671. *See also MacDonald, Sommer & Frates v. Yolo County,* 106 S.Ct. at 2566. In other words, "an essential prerequisite to a taking claim is a final decision by the government as to what use of the property will be allowed." *MacDonald, Sommer & Frates,* 106 S.Ct. at 2566; *Unity Ventures v. Lake County,* 841 F.2d 770, 774 (7th Cir.1988). A final decision may be shown by (1) a rejected development plan, and (2) a denial of a variance. *Unity Ventures,* 841 F.2d 770, 774 (7th Cir.1988); *Kinzli v. City of Santa Cruz,* 818 F.2d 1449 (9th Cir.1987), *cert. denied,* 484 U.S. 1043, 108 S.Ct. 775, 98 L.Ed.2d 861 (1988). Although the final decision prerequisite also may be satisfied by proof that attempts to comply would be futile, futility is not established until at least one meaningful application has been filed. *Unity Ventures,* 841 F.2d at 775; *Kinzli,* 818 F.2d at 1454.

Where, as in the instant case, a taking claim arises in the context of a facial challenge rather than in the context of a concrete controversy concerning the effect of a regulation on a specific parcel of land, the only issue is whether the mere enactment of the regulation constitutes a taking. *Keystone Bituminous Coal Association v. DeBenedictis,* 480 U.S. 470, 107 S.Ct. 1232, 1247, 94 L.Ed.2d 472 (1987); *Agins v. City of Tiburon,* 100 S.Ct. at 2141. The test to be applied in considering a facial challenge is relatively straightforward, i.e., "[a] statute regulating the uses that can be made of property effects a taking if it 'denies an owner economically viable use of his land. * * *'" *Keystone Bituminous Coal Association v. DeBenedictis,* 107 S.Ct. at 1247, quoting *Hodel v. Virginia Surface Mining and Reclamation Assn., Inc.,* 452 U.S. 264, 101 S.Ct. 2352, 69 L.Ed.2d 1 (1981). In determining whether a development restriction denies a landowner economically viable use of his property, the focus is on the existence of permissible uses. *Hodel v. Virginia Surface Mining and Reclamation Act; Agins v. City of Tiburon; Lake Nacimiento Ranch Co. v. San Luis Obispo County,* 830 F.2d 977, 982 (9th Cir.1987). To prevail, the landowner must show that there is no available beneficial use of his property under the land use ordinance. *Nacimiento,* 830 F.2d at 982. *See also Penn Central,* 98 S.Ct. at 2662.

* * * Application of the test for determining the facial validity of a regulation demonstrates that in this case, the contested regulations substantially advance legitimate state interests, in that the regulations are directed to protection of the environment and preservation of historic areas. Furthermore, because the regulations permit most existing uses of the property, and provide a mechanism whereby individual landowners may obtain a variance or a transfer of development rights, the regulations on their face do not deny individual landowners all economically viable uses of their property. The county concedes that the regulations have diminished the value of appellants' property by restricting some of the more economically rewarding uses to which the property may be put. However, diminution in value of the property is not the test. Rather, it is incumbent upon appellants to demonstrate that they have

been denied all or a substantial portion of the beneficial uses of their property, and this they have failed to do.

Furthermore, we note that the "status quo" test set forth in *Graham v. Estuary Properties* imposes a more stringent test for recovery than the traditional balancing test. *See,* generally, *Keystone Bituminous Coal Association v. DeBenedictis; City of Miami Beach v. Ocean & Inland Co.,* 147 Fla. 480, 3 So.2d 364 (1941). In *Graham,* the court determined that reducing the amount of the property to be developed by one-half, did not so diminish the value of the property or the owner's investment-backed expectations as to render the exercise of the police power unreasonable. On the basis of the record before us, even if a proposed development plan had been pursued to a final determination, it is arguable whether under *Graham,* appellants could show a sufficient diminution in value or loss of investment-backed expectations, to warrant a finding that the contested land use regulations are unreasonable, hence invalid.

* * *

In summary, we conclude that the challenged amendments and regulations are not facially unconstitutional, and that the amendments and regulations properly address conservation concerns, as mandated by section 163.3177(6)(d), Florida Statutes (1987). Furthermore, the new restrictions on their face do not constitute a taking. However, since the restrictions have not been applied to a specific land use proposal, the taking issue cannot be determined as a factual matter. Accordingly, the amended final judgment is affirmed in all respects.

ERVIN and BARFIELD, JJ., concur.

Note

Also see Gardner v. New Jersey Pinelands Comm'n, 125 N.J. 193, 593 A.2d 251 (1991). In this case the court upheld a restriction placing most of an existing agricultural operation in a district restricting uses to agricultural with limited possibilities to develop the land. The court rejected the takings claim, finding a lack of investment-backed expectations, and in the course of the opinion, disapproved of much of the language in the Morris County case:

Plaintiff also cites Morris County Land Improvement Co. v. Parsippany–Troy Hills Township, 40 N.J. 539, 193 A.2d 232 (1963) (Morris County Land), to support his contention that preservation zoning can constitute a taking if it interferes too greatly with the landowner's use of its property. Morris County Land held that a zoning ordinance that maintained an entire swamp area in its natural state, permitting use only for raising fish and aquatic plants and as a flood water detention basin, constituted a taking because the landowner had been deprived of "any worthwhile rights or benefits in the land." Id. at 555–56, 193 A.2d 232. We find Morris County Land inapposite. Plaintiff does not deny that the uses allowed under the Act and the CMP are "worthwhile rights or benefits in the land." In contrast to the permitted uses in Morris County Land, agriculture in the pinelands region is an existing, indeed a longstanding, endeavor that is economically supported locally and nationally. Moreover, the vitality of Morris County Land has declined with the emerging priority accorded to the ecological integrity of the environment. The decision, now nearly thirty years old, arose in a time before the environmental and social harms of indiscriminate and excessive development were widely understood or acknowledged. That the same facts would occasion the same result today is by no means certain. See AMG Assocs. v. Township of Springfield, 65 N.J. 101, 112 n. 4, 319 A.2d 705 (1974). Indeed, many more recent decisions have overtly or tacitly failed to follow Morris County Land in environmental contexts. E.g., Loveladies Harbor, Inc., supra, 176 N.J.Super. 69, 422 A.2d 107; Usdin, supra, 173 N.J.Super. 311, 414 A.2d 280; New Jersey Builders Ass'n, supra, 169 N.J.Super. 76, 404 A.2d 320; Toms River Affiliates, supra, 140 N.J.Super. 135, 355 A.2d 679; Sands Point Harbor, Inc., supra, 136 N.J.Super. 436, 346 A.2d 612. For example, in American Dredging Co. v. State, 161 N.J.Super. 504, 391 A.2d 1265 (Ch.Div.1978), aff'd, 169 N.J.Super. 18, 404 A.2d 42 (App.Div.1979), the Department of Environmental Protection, acting pursuant to the Wetlands Act of 1970, N.J.S.A. 13:9A–1 to–10, issued an order prohibiting the plaintiff from placing dredged material on a portion of its land. The court distinguished Morris County Land by explaining, "Where the effect of the governmental prohibition against use is not in furtherance of a governmental activity, such as flood control or preservation of land for a park or recreational area, but rather to preserve the land for ecological reasons in its natural environment without change, the consideration of the reasonableness of the exercise of the police power must be redetermined." Id. 161 N.J.Super. at 509, 391 A.2d 1265.

A Note on the Endangered Species Act

The issues arising from application of the Endangered Species Act, 16 U.S.C.A. §§ 1531–1544, to land development are beginning to appear in the courts. In particular, Section 9 of the Act prohibits anyone from "taking" a threatened or endangered species. In 16 U.S.C.A. § 1532 (19) the word "take" is defined to include "to harass, harm, pursue, wound, or kill." For land developers, the question is whether that prohibition precludes habitat modification (development); in other words, is land clearing in areas that may not be presently occupied by an endangered species prohibited because that habitat is suitable for the species in question. In an early case, Palila v. Hawaii Dept. of Land and Natural Resources, 639 F.2d 495 (9th Cir.1981), the court held that habitat modification could constitute an unlawful taking of a species. In 1994 the District of Columbia Circuit Court of Appeals held the opposite, Sweet Home Communities Chapter for a Greater Oregon v. Babbitt, 17 F.3d 1463 (D.C.Cir.1994). The majority in this case reasoned that the word "harm" in the act should be interpreted by the canon of *nositur a sociis* (known by the company it keeps); thus, the words around harm, "wound," "kill" require "harm" to be interpreted narrowly to cover only the application of direct force.

The Supreme Court reversed the D.C. Circuit in Babbitt v. Sweet Home, ___ U.S. ___, 115 S.Ct. 2407, 132 L.Ed.2d 597 (1995). The majority opinion, per Justice Stevens, rejected the *nositur a sociis* theory of the appeals court and held that the "ordinary meaning" canon of statutory interpretation should apply. The ordinary meaning of the word "harm" includes indirect as well as direct injury; moreover, the majority opinion held that this broad interpretation was consistent with Congressional intent and the Court's earlier decision in the "snail darter case," Tennessee Valley Authority v. Hill, 437 U.S. 153, 98 S.Ct. 2279, 57 L.Ed.2d 117 (1978). The opinion pointed out that the Act, as amended by Congress in 1982, provided a variance procedure to allow permits to be issued for "incidental takes."

Opponents of the Endangered Species Act in its entirety and those who are concerned about the broad implications of the Supreme Court approval of a broad interpretation of takes have shifted their attention to seeking Congressional modification of the Act. In the meantime, a clash between the implications of the Sweet Home case and the Lucas case, supra, seems inevitable. In Bennett v. Spear, ___ U.S. ___, 117 S.Ct. 1154, ___ L.Ed.2d ___ (1997) the Supreme Court, in a unanimous opinion, held that property owners whose interests may be affected by the application of the Endangered Species Act, have standing to seek judicial review of rulings or official opinions under the Act's provision that "any person may commence a civil suit." The Court of Appeals for the Ninth Circuit had rejected standing under the theory that the Act's standing provision was meant to enable citizens interested in the protection of endangered species to challenge rulings detrimental to species protection, rather than affected property owners protecting their development rights.

The implication of this decision on the takings issue is clear. If a court finds that habitat protection for an endangered species results in a deprivation of all reasonable economic use of land by the landowner, then the court might well declare that the constitutionally guaranteed protection against the "taking" of property is superior to the congressionally ordained guarantee that an endangered species not be subjected to a "take." This would not lead to the invalidation of the Act presumably, but to the conclusion, as in zoning, that as applied in that particular circumstance the regulatory result amounts to inverse condemnation.

A good, short discussion of these problems can be found in A. Dan Tarlock, Greater Protection for Endangered Species: The Sweet Home Case, Land Use Law (Aug. 1996), p. 3. Also see Harvey M. Jacobs, The Anti–Environmental "Wise Use" Movement in America, Land Use Law (Feb. 1995), p. 3, and Stephen P. Foley, Does Preventing "Take" Constitute an Unconstitutional "Taking"? An Analysis of Possible Defenses to Fifth Amendment Taking Claims Based on the Endangered Species Act, 14 UCLA J. Env. L. & Policy 327 (1996).

As the Glisson case illustrates, state law may also take endangered species into account. In that case the concern was eagle nests. In Department of Community Affairs v. Moorman, 664 So.2d 930 (Fla.1995) the Florida court addressed the protection of the Florida Key Deer. The court described the issue:

> This case involves the validity of a land-use ordinance enacted to protect an endangered species, the miniature Florida Key deer. The regulation affects Big Pine Key where the deer now are largely concentrated. Human development on the Key has put the deer perilously close

to extinction, and their numbers are estimated to be only 350 to 400 animals. The minimum number needed to sustain a viable species is considered 100 to 250 animals. The animals are further endangered by human attempts to feed them, by pet dogs that may kill them, and by automobiles.

The ordinance in question prohibits the erection of fencing in portions of Big Pine Key, where the respondents own property. It was enacted because, in a natural environment, Key deer must roam freely over slash pinelands and wetlands in search of food and water. This necessarily means the deer also must roam over some privately owned lands.

The court upheld the revocation of the landowner's permit to erect a six-foot high, 400–foot long fence on his property, holding that the state's police power included protection of the environment and that "environmental degradation threatens not merely aesthetic concerns vital to the State's economy but also the health, welfare, and safety of substantial numbers of Floridians." Residents of the Florida Keys are sharply divided over whether the species is really declining and whether further development of property on the Keys should be severely restricted. See Mireya Navarro, Striking a Balance Between Deer and Residents in the Florida Keys, N.Y. Times, Mar. 18, 1997, p. A 12.

In Moerman v. State, 17 Cal.App.4th 452, 21 Cal.Rptr.2d 329 (1993) the court denied a landowner compensation for damage to his property after the state relocated endangered tule elk to an area near his land; the animals destroyed Moerman's fences and ate forage intended for his livestock. The court reasoned that there was no physical taking of Moerman's property because the tule elk were neither controlled by the state nor instrumentalities of the state; as for a regulatory taking, the court found that argument had not been preserved for appeal.

In Southview Associates, Ltd. v. Bongartz, 980 F.2d 84 (2d Cir.1992) a developer purchased an 88–acre parcel of land near a ski resort in Vermont with the intent of developing 78 vacation homes. The Vermont Conservation Commission found that the proposed development was situated within a 280 acre deeryard, i.e., a winter habitat for white-tailed deer; this deeryard is the sole remaining, active deeryard within a 10.7 square mile area. The Commission denied the development permit and on appeal to the state Environmental Board, the decision was affirmed on the ground that the development, if allowed to proceed, would "destroy and significantly imperil wildlife habitat." Even though white-tailed deer are not endangered (and the Endangered Species Act was not implicated in the case), the court held that the developer had not suffered a physical taking and that the question of a regulatory taking was not ripe for review. Judge Oakes, in the opinion, said that his colleagues ended their inquiry after finding a lack of ripeness, but he went on to indicate that, even if the case was ripe for review, he would uphold the denial of the permit and find no regulatory taking.

IN RE SPRING VALLEY DEVELOPMENT

Supreme Judicial Court of Maine, 1973.
300 A.2d 736.

WEATHERBEE, JUSTICE. Raymond Pond is located in the town of Raymond and is slightly more than one mile in length. Lakesites, Inc. is the owner of a large tract of land containing about 92 acres located on one side of the Pond. Lakesites' development of this land into a residential subdivision has been interrupted by an order of the Environmental Improvement Commission directing it to cease the operation of this development until Lakesites has applied for and received the Commission's approval of its development.

The Commission claims to have derived its authority for this order from 38 M.R.S.A. §§ 481–488, Site Location of Development Law, hereinafter referred to as the Site Location Law. Lakesites' appeal attacks both the Commission's interpretation of the Act as including residential subdivisions and the Act's constitutionality. We conclude that the authority of the Commission does extend to residential subdivisions and that the statute represents a valid exercise of the police power. We deny the appeal.

The agreed statement of facts and the testimony presented at hearing before the Commission reveal that Lakesites' property extends along the shore of the Pond at least 3400 feet. Lakesites has subdivided this tract into 90 lots ranging in size from 20,000 square feet to 53,000 square feet with several other areas reserved from sale. It refers to this property as its Spring Valley Development.

Lakesites has cleared and graded portions of this land, has built a road for ingress and egress and has surveyed the property, marking off the boundaries of the individual lots. While it contemplates that purchasers will build year-round or part-time homes on their lots it does not intend to construct or participate in the construction of the buildings or to control the use of the lots "except insofar as there are any required deed restrictions". No action has been taken with respect to providing services for any of the lots.

Lakesites proposes that the selling of these lots be a profitable venture and it has placed their sale in the hands of licensed real estate brokers.

Lakesites submitted its subdivision plan to the Raymond Planning Board which, after some changes had been made, approved it as satisfying the only subdivision requirement then existing in the town ordinance—that of lot size. The subdivision plan was then recorded in the Cumberland County Registry of Deeds.

There was in effect at this time the Site Location Law the constitutionality of which is under attack. This law required persons intending to construct or operate a development which may substantially affect local environment to notify, before commencing the construction or operation, the Environmental Improvement Commission of their intent and the nature and location of the development. If the Commission determines it to be necessary, a hearing shall be held at which the developer has the burden of satisfying the Commission that the development will not substantially adversely affect the environment or pose a threat to the public's health, safety or general welfare. 38 M.R.S.A. §§ 483, 484.

The Legislature defined developments which may substantially affect environment as meaning

> " * * * [1] any commercial or industrial development which requires a license from the Environmental Improvement Commission, [2] or which occupies a land area in excess of 20 acres, [3] or which contemplates drilling for or excavating natural resources, excluding borrow pits for sand, fill or gravel, regulated by the State Highway Commission and pits of less than 5 acres, [4] or which occupies on a single parcel a structure or structures in excess of a ground area of 60,000 square feet." 38 M.R.S.A. § 482(2).

Although Lakesites' development did occupy a land area in excess of 20 acres, it did not notify the Commission of its intentions. However, the Commission eventually learned of Lakesites' plans and proceeded at once to schedule and conduct a hearing as it is authorized to do by section 485. Notice of the hearing was given Lakesites.

Lakesites was represented at the hearing by its attorney who challenged the Commission's jurisdiction to regulate Lakesites' activity contending that the mere subdivision of land does not constitute a "commercial or industrial development" within the scope of the Site Location Law. The attorney made a formal objection to all testimony other than that relating to jurisdiction. He elected to waive his right to contest as to the merits of the case although he was offered full opportunity to do so, choosing not to offer evidence or to cross-examine witnesses who testified regarding the proposed development.

These witnesses testified at length as to various aspects of the environment which they said would be substantially adversely affected by the proposed development. Later, after consideration of the matter, the Commission made findings of fact[4] and held that Lakesites had failed

---

4. "1. Lakesites, Inc. is the owner of a lot or parcel of land located in Raymond, Maine, on or near Raymond Pond, exceeding 20 acres in size, to wit, 92 acres more or less.

2. Lakesites, Inc. has divided said 92 acres more or less, into approximately 90 lots ranging in size from 20,000 to 53,000 square feet.

3. Lakesites, Inc. has sold, is selling or is planning to sell or otherwise transfer interests in and to said lots to purchasers as a commercial venture, such lots to be used

for year round or seasonal residential and/or recreational purposes.

4. Lakesites, Inc. has been and is operating a commercial development within the meaning of Title 38 M.R.S.A. § 482(2).

5. Lakesites, Inc. has made no application to nor submitted any evidence at the hearing held by the E.I.C. for approval pursuant to the Site Location of Development Law, although it was given ample opportunity to do so.

6. The record indicated that most of the soil in the area being developed by Lakes-

in its burden to prove that its proposed development meets the standards for approval established by the Legislature in section 484[5] and had failed to demonstrate that it had plans that would adequately protect the public's health, safety and general welfare. It issued an order denying Lakesites the right to proceed with its development until such time as it has made a proper application to the Environmental Improvement Commission and has received the Commission's approval.

From this decision of the Commission, Lakesites has appealed to the Supreme Judicial Court sitting as the Law Court, [38 M.R.S.A. § 487] raising specifically the issue as to whether the offering for sale of subdivided lots of the type owned by Lakesites is either a commercial or an industrial development subject to the provisions of 38 M.R.S.A. §§ 481–488 and, secondarily, if the Site Location Law is applied to this developer, are there constitutional violations of Equal Protection and Due Process.

* * *

The Legislature's concise statement of its Findings and Purpose makes clear to us the basis for its conclusion that state action was essential to insure that commercial and industrial developments, which *because of their nature or their size,* will impose unusually heavy demands upon the natural environment, shall not be located in areas where the environment does not have the capacity to withstand the impact of the development. But did the Legislature intend to bring *residential* developments within the application of the law? If so, did it intend to include mere subdivisions?

* * *

ites, Inc. is of a steep slope and has a high seasonable water table.

7. The record indicated that most of the soil in the area is unsuitable for septic tank disposal of domestic sewage.

8. The development has been subdivided in such a fashion so that it will support housing for 90 families, all of whom must dispose of domestic sewage in some manner.

9. Since the developer, Lakesites, Inc., has not indicated that it has made any provision for collection, treatment or disposal of such sewage, and no municipal treatment and disposal system exists in the vicinity of the development, the only alternative is underground disposal of such sewage by means of a septic tank or related system.

10. The installation of up to 90 septic tank disposal systems in and upon the said development could degrade the quality of ground water in and around the said development, such ground water possibly being used for a drinking water supply, and degrade the waters of Raymond Pond."

5. "The commission shall approve a development proposal whenever it finds that:

1. Financial capacity. The proposed development has the financial capacity and technical ability to meet state air and water pollution control standards, has made adequate provision for solid waste disposal, the control of offensive odors, and the securing and maintenance of sufficient and healthful water supplies.

2. Traffic movement. The proposed development has made adequate provision for loading, parking and traffic movement from the development area onto public roads.

3. No adverse effect on natural environment. The proposed development has made adequate provision for fitting itself harmoniously into the existing natural environment and will not adversely affect existing uses, scenic character, natural resources or property values in the municipality or in adjoining municipalities.

4. Soil types. The proposed development will be built on soil types which are suitable to the nature of the undertaking."

We think that the use of the word "commercial" was intended to describe the *motivation* for the development and not the type of activity to be performed on the property after it is developed. We consider that the Legislature chose to distinguish between commercial and non-commercial developments for a sound reason—it doubtless concluded that a greater need for supervision exists in the case of a commercially motivated development where the dominant factor is the hope for profit than in a non-commercial development where land is being prepared for public enjoyment or divided for family distribution or for some other purpose than profit. In other words, commercial residential developments have a propensity for being big, concentrated and exhausting to the resources of the environment.

It seems to us that the business of subdividing large tracts of land and selling the lots must be considered a commercial venture. The Legislature doubtless so viewed it. Certainly, this construction best accords with the purpose of the statute. Strout v. Burgess, 144 Me. 263, 275, 68 A.2d 241, 250 (1949).

This interpretation finds support in the history of the legislation we are examining.

* * *

We find it significant in our assessment of legislative intent that the 105th Legislature, aware that the Commission was interpreting the Act to include residential subdivisions, took no affirmative action to indicate a contrary intent, rejected two attempts to remove *some* residential subdivisions from the operation of the Act and finally acted to add the specific words "including subdivisions."

In our opinion the 104th Legislature intended to include commercial residential developments among those developments which may substantially affect environment. But did the Legislature intend the Act to affect commercial residential developments where the developer merely plots the tract, subdivides it into lots by plan and offers the lots for sale to the public?

* * *

The Appellant argues to us that it was the Legislature's intention to prevent acts being done to the land which would harm the land and that, therefore, the law is directed to the person who will do the act—such as the builder—and not to the person who merely subdivides and sells the land. With this we cannot agree. The Legislature intended the Commission to scrutinize the proposals *before* the harmful act could be done. The Act is a preventive measure and the injury sought to be avoided can best be prevented as soon as plans for development reveal the harm which will occur upon its completion. We would hardly expect that the Legislature intended to postpone the determination of suitability of an area for a residential development until the lots had been sold to purchasers who will, upon starting construction, discover that they are participants in— as well as victims of—a local environmental disaster.

Furthermore, if a subdivider has sold the lots to numerous individual purchasers each of whom, among other things, is to construct his own building, grade his own land, build his own driveway to the street, and provide for his own sanitary sewage disposal, there would be no one "intending to construct or operate a development" who could be held responsible under the statute. We do not ascribe to the Legislature an intention that legislation so important to the public welfare would suffer from such inherent futility.

We consider that both the legislative intent and the statutory language of the Act encompass residential developments in which the developer merely subdivides the land into lots and offers the lots for sale without any intention to construct buildings or to provide additional improvements or services on the lots. We do not find that the Act as so interpreted and applied is constitutionally impermissible. The subdividing is the initial step in such a development.

The Commission correctly ruled as fact that this particular residential development is a commercial development which may substantially affect environment requiring compliance with the provisions of the Site Location Law.

* * *

CONSTITUTIONALITY OF APPLICATION OF THE ACT TO ONE WHO ONLY SUBDIVIDES

Lakesites does not deny the power of the State to act properly under the police power to protect the environment but urges us that the application of the Act to one who merely subdivides is constitutionally forbidden. It argues that a remedial Act must be designed and applied rationally and reasonably to achieve the purposes for which the Act was devised. The evil to be avoided, the appellant contends, is the damaging impact of the development upon the environment and the impact occurs and the damage is sustained only with the construction and occupation of the premises—not when the land is only subdivided on plans and the lots are sold. Until such activity creating the impact occurs on the land, the appellant argues, there is no burden or impact which can affect the environment and so the application of the Act to a mere subdivider as a prerequisite to his selling his land is not directly related to the Act's purpose.

It is true that the Act and its application under the police power must have a clear, real and substantial relation to the purpose of the Act.
* * *

In our opinion such a connection between the purpose of the Act and its application to the subdivider is clear and reasonable. We have concluded earlier in this opinion that the Legislature intended to empower the Commission to prevent ecological damage before it occurs rather than to permit the occurrence of harm which can then be cured only at great public expense—if at all. It is not unreasonable to place upon the subdivider who plans the number, size and location of the lots to be offered for sale the responsibility for avoiding an inevitable large scale ecological calamity. The subdividing for sale is the first step in a commercial residential development and the Legislature reasonably concluded that the public welfare requires that control be exercised through the subdivider rather than attempting it through (in this case) 90 different purchasers whose properties can perhaps never at that later point—because of sheer weight and concentration of numbers—avoid environmental misadventure.

* * *

Lakesites protests that as it is only a subdivider it cannot accurately foresee the activity to be performed on the lots it sells and so cannot control the future adequacy of provisions relating to pollution control and maintenance of healthful water supplies. To be sure, the Act imposes upon the developer—including the mere subdivider—responsibilities which he has not had in the past. The Legislature has determined that an owner of a large tract of undeveloped land may no longer subdivide it, sell the lots and then walk away from the transaction indifferent to the local catastrophe that may result when construction and occupancy reveal the incapacity of the environment to withstand the impact of the development. It may be that this responsibility can more *easily* be met by a subdivider who is also a constructor of the buildings but it is equally the responsibility of the subdivider who chooses only to sell the bare lots. The duty is no doubt more burdensome as the land is less suitable and it may be impossible of compliance if the environment is of a type incapable of sustaining the proposed development. In the latter situation the public welfare demands that the land be used for another purpose or that the impact of the same use be diminished. In many situations the subdivider may be able to meet his burden of affirmatively demonstrating to the Commission that he has met the criteria through satisfactory conditions in his instruments of sale. We do not consider the burden to be unreasonable in view of the overriding public interest.

* * *

Does the Act Deny the Developer Equal Protection of the Law?

Finally, Lakesites argues that the Act denies a developer—and especially it—equal protection under the law. It argues that the subdivider of over 20 acres must receive the Commission's approval while the subdivider of under 20 acres faces no such requirements, and so it contends it is denied equal protection because size, it says, has no rational or reasonable correlation to the environmental impact. A 21 acre subdivision, it argues, may contain 5 residences while one of 19 acres may contain 19 residences. It is elementary that the Legislature may in its judgment create classifications so long as they are not arbitrary and are based upon actual differences in classes which differences bear a substantial rational relation to the public purpose sought to be accomplished by the statute. In re Milo Water Company, 128 Me. 531, 149 A. 299 (1930).

The purpose, as we have said, was to control the locations of those commercial and industrial developments which could substantially adversely affect the environment. The Legislature evidently concluded that the size of a development has a distinct relationship to the amount of its potential adverse impact upon the environment and concluded that at this time the public interest could best be served by applying the admittedly severe restrictions of the new law to large developments. The justification of the distinction as to size seems most clear in such legislation as this. For example, in an area with no municipal sewage disposal system, such as in Spring Valley Development, and where much of the soil has a high seasonal water table and is unsuitable for septic tank disposal of domestic sewage, the potential danger to the environment from the discharge of sewage from 90 residences must be greater than the discharge from 2 or from 19. Drawing the line at 20 acres is not a denial of equal protection.

* * *

We see no irrational or arbitrary discrimination in the application of the Act to the large mere-subdivider. It is his act of subdividing that initially indicates the volume of the impact likely to fall upon the environment.

The distinction made by the Legislature does not appear to be unreasonable.

* * *

We find that the application of the Act to Lakesites does not offend the provisions of either the state or federal constitutions.

Notes

1. Compare with the principal case Thoma v. Planning and Zoning Comm'n of Town of Canterbury, 31 Conn.App. 643, 626 A.2d 809 (1993) where the court held that a town zoning regulation prohibiting the planning commission from approving an application for the subdivision of land containing inland wetlands without approval by the town's "inland wetland agency" was an invalid delegation of authority contrary to a state statute.

2. The preceding cases all involve a landowner or developer who is frustrated in his development plans by a state or local regulation which purports to utilize the police power to protect certain aspects of the environment. A more dramatic and highly visible problem pits citizens or neighbors against a land use which may be permitted by the government. This of course is the NIMBY problem (not in my back yard) which may occur at the highest governmental levels (states taking action to preclude nuclear waste sites) or at the local level (citizens seeking to enjoin a landfill). Frequently, nuisance law is invoked as the basis for litigation. Sometimes, preventive legislation is involved (such as a statute to prevent importation of solid waste from any other state). The NIMBY disputes are generally covered in courses in Environmental Law.

B. PUBLIC HEALTH AND SAFETY

APRIL v. CITY OF BROKEN ARROW

Supreme Court of Oklahoma, 1989.
775 P.2d 1347.

DOOLIN, JUSTICE.

The question presented is whether the adoption of two municipal land-use ordinances on their face substantially interfered with landowner's use and enjoyment of his property so as to constitute a permanent "taking" of property without just compensation in violation of the United States and Oklahoma Constitutions. Put another way, the question is, does a taking result if the limitations on the use of owner's property do "not substantially advance legitimate state interests, or denies an owner economical, viable use of his land, [citations omitted]."

I.

Appellee Paul April, M.D., ("Owner"), purchased 40 acres of undeveloped agricultural land, for investment purposes, in the City of Broken Arrow, Tulsa County, Oklahoma ("City"). City is a suburban residential area south of the city of Tulsa. Owner's real property, used as pasture land, is located within an existing 100–year flood plain of Haikey Creek and its tributaries ("Haikey"). Haikey is a "natural water drainage system" in and around City.

Property adjacent to Haikey, including Owner's land which is transversed by three pre-existing wet-weather creeks converging in the flood plain, is naturally subject to flooding following periods of heavy rainfall. Haikey drains over "one square mile" of Owner's property, because the elevation of Owner's property is lower than the elevation of the periodic hundred year flood. City has not made any physical intrusions or entered upon Owner's property. Nor has City diverted any additional water into Haikey's drainage system, or erected any facilities upstream from Owner's property, or granted any building permits altering the natural water flow throughout the topography of the 100–year flood plain.

Owner, intending to sell his land to a developer, requested and was granted R–2 residential single family zoning for his property in 1975, after his previous request for R–6 high density multifamily apartment zoning was denied by City. When R–2 zoning was approved, allowing three family dwellings per acre (theoretically 120 homes), City's planning commission and planning commission staff informed Owner:

> the majority of (your) property is within the 100–year frequency flood and is also within the adopted Flood Hazard Area * * *, (therefore) the developer will be required to build all house pads at least one foot above the 100–year frequency flood elevation * * *.

This was City's only regulatory requirement for development of land within the flood plain. In October 1977, Owner requested his property be rezoned from 40 acres of R–2, residential single family to 20 acres of R–

4, duplex and 20 acres of R–5, apartments. Owner's request was denied by City's planning commission and staff.

In January 1978, Owner made another application to the City's planning commission, requesting his property be re-zoned from R–2 single family to R–4, Duplex. City's planning commission and staff again denied Owner's petition for re-zoning, and Owner, for the first time, appealed to the City Council. "[I]n anticipation of the 'floodplain' ordinance being adopted * * *, (Owner) sought relief in the form of a 'waiver' or variance from the * * * City Council on March 13, 1978 which was, * * *, denied. * * * "(Emphasis added.)

On March 20, 1978, the city council enacted "The Flood Damage Protection Ordinance, No. 735",[6] regulating the development of land in Haikey's flood plain, and "The Earth Change Resolution Ordinance No. 736",[7] controlling all excavations and earth modifications throughout the municipality (both hereinafter, "Land–Use Ordinances"). Both land-use ordinances became effective immediately. On May 1, 1978, the city council denied Owner's appeal for rezoning.

Owner initiated the present inverse condemnation suit in December of 1978, alleging, inter alia, City's "overt actions;" that is, adoption of its land-use ordinances, limiting his property to "Flood Tolerant Land Uses," and city's approval of building permits to other developers in the flood plain has resulted in the appropriation of Owner's property for "general public use" as "a detention pond as part of a municipal stormwater drainage system." Owner further alleges City's action prohibits construction on Owner's land by restricting its use to "public or semi-public purposes," that it effectively limits Owner's use of his land

---

6. City's flood plain ordinance, administered and enforced by the city manager, limits development within the one hundred year flood plain by requiring a building permit, which is also issued by the city manager. The general provisions covering the basis for establishing areas of special flood hazards [§ 3(B)(3)], provides that:

The floodplain, at locations where the point in question has a drainage area of over one square mile shall be reserved for flood tolerant uses.

Section 5(D), "Flood Tolerant Land Uses," provides that the:

Flood plain may be utilized for, but not limited to, the following uses: (1) Recreational Parks; (2) Linear Park or Tree belt; (3) School Playground; (4) Common Area or Open Spaces; (5) Golf Course or Driving Range; (6) Nature Areas; (7) Backyards; (8) Parking Lots; (9) Drive-in Theaters; (10) Agriculture or Stables; (11) Landscape Nursery or Nursery Stock Production; (12) Other uses consistent with terms of the ordinance. (Emphasis added).

City's flood plain appeal board hears request for variances or modifications from the requirements of the floodplain ordinance, and any aggrieved landowner may appeal to the city council.

7. City enacted this ordinance to protect "the general health, safety, and welfare of (its) citizens from the hazards and dangers of flooding or improper drainage by imposing standards and conditions upon the excavating, grading, regrading, landfilling, berming, and diking of land within the city." Any major earth changes on any tract of land in City over five acres in size must be approved by the city manager, who then issues a permit. This ordinance also has a variance system, and allows aggrieved landowners to appeal to city's flood plain appeal board and to the city council. Any landowner with property in the flood plain would be required to obtain an earth change permit to raise land out of the flood plain. Once land is out of the flood plain, the landowner's use of his property is no longer restricted to the flood tolerant land uses; however, a building permit must be granted to develop the land.

as a "horse pasture," and finally that it denies Owner beneficial use of his property by destroying his reasonable "investment-backed expectations." After various motions and pleadings, Owner dismissed three other causes of action.

At trial, Owner asserted his "property lies in the path of (City's) future plans for a public park, Haikey Creek detention reservoir, levee pump station and channel improvements." (Emphasis added.) Owner argued City's land-use ordinance "goes too far," because his property is "economically worthless, as evidenced by the Report of Commissioners," appointed by the trial court. The commissioners' report found the value of Owner's property "taken and damaged," resulting from City's enactment of the land-use ordinances, amounted to $240,000.00.

Before and during trial, City insistently argued two propositions to support its contention that there was no basis in either fact or law for the trial court to determine the constitutionality of the ordinances as applied to Owner's property. One, City's mere enactment of its ordinance regulating the general use of land within the flood plain does not, as a matter of law, constitute substantial interference with nor amount to an overt action exercising dominion and control over Owner's property, because Owner's property floods as a result of a natural phenomenon beyond City's exercise of its police power. Two, Owner has never applied for or been denied a building permit, or a variance under the land-use ordinances, thus, Owner has an adequate remedy at law to determine the beneficial use of his property.

City urged dismissal of Owner's action because the trial court lacked a justiciable issue. However, the jury rendered a verdict in favor of Owner and against City for $240,000.00. Thereafter, the trial court awarded attorney fees, appraisers fees, city engineering-planning fees, and trial cost against City pursuant to 27 O.S.1981 § 12. Owner retains possession of the land in question.

II.

In resolving this appeal we are confronted, as we were in *Mattoon v. City of Norman*,[8] with the following contentions: One, whether a municipality's adoption of a flood plain ordinance constitutes a taking of property without just compensation for which a landowner may seek damages under an action in inverse condemnation. Two, whether the doctrine requiring exhaustion of administrative remedies is applicable to preclude judicial review of the action.

City and its amici argue that opinion does not control the instant case, because *Mattoon* is significantly distinguishable. Owner argues *Mattoon* provides the applicable rule to govern the results of this appeal. Therefore, we deem it important to reiterate, and go further into the statement of our opinion and reasons for our *Mattoon* decision, because due to the procedural posture of that appeal, we found ourselves unable to address the merits of the "taking" question.

---

8. 617 P.2d 1347 (Okl.1980).

In *Mattoon,* city enacted a flood plain ordinance, reserving landowner's (and approximately 500 other similarly situated landowners') property for flood drainage purposes. Landowner filed a class action for inverse condemnation, alleging city adopted its flood plain ordinance unreasonably, neglected and refused to properly maintain its drainage system, and had diverted surface waters into tributaries which crossed and flooded landowner's property. The trial court sustained city's demurrer to landowner's petition by merely finding the ordinance was a valid exercise of city's police power.

We recognized "a valid enactment of a flood plain ordinance is not per se a taking," because "acts done in the proper exercise of the police power which merely impair the use (or value) of property do not constitute a 'taking.' " We held "the test of whether there can be a recovery in inverse condemnation is whether there is a sufficient interference with the landowner's use and enjoyment to constitute a taking." More importantly, we acknowledged governmental land-use regulations may amount to an actual or de facto taking—"(i)f there is an overt act by the governmental agency resulting in an assertion of dominion and control over property." (Emphasis added.)

Two components were implicit in the taking claim advanced by landowner's petition in *Mattoon.* First, landowner had alleged city's unreasonable adoption of its flood plain ordinance had "taken" his property, that is, the ordinance "goes too far," and any proffered compensation was not "just." Thus, landowner's factual contentions adequately alleged a "regulatory taking" claim, by contending city's ordinance was an extreme regulation destroying a major portion of landowner's property value. Second, landowner alleged a "physical taking" of property, that is, city also *overtly* acted to flood landowner's property by unreasonably diverting surface water, and improperly maintaining its drainage channels.[9]

Accordingly, we reversed and remanded the trial court's judgment with directions to reinstate landowner's action, because first, merely finding an ordinance was validly enacted within city's lawful exercise of its police power, without considering the general principles of due process, does not "absolutely preclude compensation for property taken or damaged by such exercise." (Emphasis added.) Second, landowner's petition alleged a question of fact, the reasonableness of city's diversion of surface water over landowner's property, and such challenge was sufficient to withstand city's demurrer.

* * *

III.

In cases such as this, the nature of the government's action and the type of taking alleged are critical factors in our analysis. Without

---

9. Flooding is an easily identifiable physical invasion which destroys all uses of property and is virtually always deemed to constitute a "taking." See e.g., *Pumpelly v.* *G.B. & M. Canal Co.,* 80 U.S. (13 Wall.) 166, 20 L.Ed. 557 (1871); *City of Wewoka v. Mainard,* 155 Okl. 156, 8 P.2d 676 (1932).

undertaking to survey the historical intricacies of regulatory zoning ordinances it is fair to say—any local government seeking to participate in the National Flood Insurance Program is required by federal law and authorized by state law to enact land use and regulatory control measures.[10] Other provisions enforcing such measures, (including a building permit and appeal system), are also required in mitigating flood hazards. City's legitimate exercise of its police power, asserted for the public welfare, controls owner's use of his property.

In balancing the private and public interests herein, Owner's potential use of all property, under our system of government, is subordinate to the right of City's reasonable regulations, ordinances, and all similar laws that are clearly necessary and bear a rational relation to preserving the health, safety, and general welfare of the residents of Broken Arrow.

* * *

While asserted with great vigor, Owner's argument that City has appropriated his property for general public use as a detention reservoir, is quite simply untenable under the particular facts of this case. We find no evidence, or persuasive testimony, indicating City has adopted any recommendations with respect to appropriating Owner's land as a detention pond. City has acquired no property interest in Owner's land, has not physically invaded Owner's property, nor has his land been set aside for a public use.

Indeed, Owner stipulated City has not proposed or approved the building of any facilities or taken any action increasing the natural flow of water over Owner's property or flooding his land. We note that as a result of Pre Trial Conference, Sec. 9 thereof, the owner declared and admitted;

"9. (1) That the City of Broken Arrow has not constructed or caused to be constructed any facilities upstream from plaintiff's property which has increased the waterflow over plaintiff's property." (Emphasis added.) Unlike the extreme factual circumstances found in *Mattoon,* in the instant case, Owner's property floods following periods of heavy rainfall, and such a natural phenomenon is definitely beyond City's ordinary exercise of its police power.

Furthermore, even if Owner's allegations were substantiated by the record, City's future plans for inclusion of his property for "potential" public use in a flood control plan would not give rise to a cause of action for inverse condemnation. For as Justice Stewart wrote in his concurring opinion in *Hughes v. Washington:* "[T]he Constitution measures a taking of property not by what a state says, or what it intends, but by what it does."

Accepting as we must the general proposition that local public officials must be afforded reasonable "elasticity" in planning and implementing legitimate land-use interests, and given the "particular facts" of

---

10. National Flood Insurance Act of 1968, 42 U.S.C.A. § 4001, et seq.; Oklahoma Floodplain Management Act, 82 O.S. 1981 § 1601, et seq.

this case; we hold such limitations substantially advance City's legitimate goals of; one, reducing risks of loss of life and property; two, protecting the public's interest in health; three, preserving the aesthetic environment and fiscal integrity of Haikey's flood prone areas; four, enabling landowners to develop their property located within the flood plain, as well as allowing landowners to purchase federally-sponsored flood hazard insurance to protect their investments.

Our conclusion that City's land-use ordinances are lawful and valid exercises of its police power does not conclude this matter; for as we explicitly held in *Mattoon,* such a mere finding does not "absolutely preclude compensation for property taken or damaged by such exercises." In this connection, we proceed then to a consideration of whether Owner has been denied economical viable use of his land.

IV.

It is relevant at this juncture to recognize Owner merely alleges a "regulatory taking" of property. Given the absence of any administrative decision regarding the application of City's land-use ordinances to Owner's property, City and its amici challenge our appellate jurisdiction and the trial court's adjudicatory authority, arguing Owner's "regulatory taking" claim is premature, because "an essential prerequisite to its assertion is a final and authoritative determination of the type and intensity of development legally permitted on the subject property." We agree.

Owner is completely incorrect when he asserts he has no "adequate" remedy at law. Owner alleged the development of 120 homesites "was permitted by existing zoning" prior to City's adoption of its land-use ordinances. Owner asserts such development "is not consistent with the terms of the ordinance (and) if permitted would seriously undermine the purpose of the ordinances." Owner contends he requested a waiver or variance from the city council by agreeing to reduce the number of dwelling units from 120 to 88. Owner further asserts he asked City to repeal the effect of the ordinance as it pertains to his property. This argument is misleading, and inaccurate.

Owner has never submitted a plan or subdivision plat to use or improve his real property. Nor did he properly seek and receive any concrete and definitive statement from City as to how many single family dwelling units he could build on his land, if the floor of such dwelling units were built one foot above the existing 100–year flood elevation.

Regardless of how many homesites are erected, City's land-use ordinances neither prevent the present and presumably most beneficial use of Owner's property, "nor extinguish a fundamental attribute of ownership." The disputed property, as earlier requested by Owner, is still zoned for single residential family dwellings.

Furthermore, and most significant, Owner has never applied for a building permit to develop his property, or an earth change permit to raise his land out of the flood plain, nor has he ever properly requested a hardship variance under the "established" administrative procedures of the land-use ordinances. In summary, the record indicates Owner failed to submit a plan for development of his property prior to or subsequent to the City's adoption of its land-use ordinances.

* * *

We conclude the trial court was presented with no justiciable issue to hear Owner's regulatory taking claim, because Owner has never applied for a building or earth change permit, has failed to exhaust his administrative remedies, and has presented no competent evidence showing the pursuit of such remedies would be futile or inadequate. We hold there is as yet no concrete controversy regarding the application of City's land-use ordinances to Owner's property, because even though City has denied Owner's increased zoning intensity applications, there are other economically viable uses available to Owner.

Lastly, it is important to note that Owner purchased flood-prone property in Haikey Creek and its tributaries. Even if City had taken no action with regards to flood-damage prevention, Owner's property would continue to flood following periods of heavy rainfall.

The judgment of the trial court is REVERSED, and the cause is REMANDED to the district court WITH DIRECTIONS TO DISMISS Owner's complaint—for want of a justiciable issue.

Notes

1. In New City Office Park v. Planning Bd., Town of Clarkstown, 144 A.D.2d 348, 533 N.Y.S.2d 786 (1988), the court upheld denial of final site approval for an office park development located within the 100–year flood plain. The specific basis for the denial was that the project would have required a considerable amount of fill to elevate his buildings above the flood plain and the developer was unable to provide sufficient land for compensatory storage of floodwaters in the event of a 100–year flood. Also see Leonard v. Town of Brimfield, 423 Mass. 152, 666 N.E.2d 1300 (1996), where the court held that flood plain restrictions were not a taking; the case takes a hard look at the issue of investment-backed expectations.

2. The National Flood Insurance Act of 1968, 42 U.S.C.A. § 1601 et seq. requires local governments to enact flood plain regulations prior to making flood insurance available to residents of the community. This act has had a widespread effect in spurring flood plain regulations. See Dinkins, The Federal Zoning Program: Regulation of Flood Plain Use Under the National Flood Insurance Act, ABA Law Notes, Spring 1978, Vol. 14, No. 2. An excellent overview of the Act can be found in Weinstein, Revisiting the National Flood Insurance Program, 48 Land Use Law No. 10 (Oct. 1996), pp. 3–8.

3. The general trend of decisions is to uphold restrictions which prohibit building structures in the flood plain. See Dunham, Flood Control Via the Police Power, 107 U.Pa.L.Rev. 1098 (1959); U.S. Water Resources Council, Regulation of Flood Hazard Areas (1971); American Society of

Planning Officials, Regulations for Flood Plains, Planning Advisory Service Report No. 277 (1972). Also see Vartelas v. Water Resources Comm'n, 146 Conn. 650, 153 A.2d 822 (1959), upholding the setting of encroachment lines along a stream and a regulation forbidding the placing of buildings within the lines; Turner v. County of Del Norte, 24 Cal.App.3d 311, 101 Cal.Rptr. 93 (1972), upholding an absolute prohibition of structures in a flood plain along the Klamath River; Turnpike Realty Co. v. Town of Dedham, 362 Mass. 221, 284 N.E.2d 891 (1972), upholding flood plain restrictions in a swampy area; Dur–Bar Realty Co. v. City of Utica, 57 A.D.2d 51, 394 N.Y.S.2d 913 (1977), affirmed 44 N.Y.2d 1002, 408 N.Y.S.2d 502, 380 N.E.2d 328 (1978), upholding a "Land Conservation District" which limited uses to farming, marinas, recreational uses, and landfill operations. See generally, Comment, Various Aspects of Flood Plain Zoning, 55 N.Dak.L.Rev. 429 (1980).

4. A typical state enabling statute authorizing flood plain regulation is Ariz.Rev.Stat. § 48–3601 et seq. (Flood Plain Act of 1973). One possible weakness in such enabling acts is that flood plain regulation is not mandatory for local governments. In some states control of flood plain construction is vested in a state level agency. Typical of this approach is Wisconsin. See State v. Trudeau, 139 Wis.2d 91, 408 N.W.2d 337 (1987), cert. denied 484 U.S. 1007, 108 S.Ct. 701, 98 L.Ed.2d 652 (1988), where the state sued the developer and the local government for granting a flood plain variance. Also see City of La Crosse v. Wisconsin Dept. of Natural Resources, 120 Wis.2d 168, 353 N.W.2d 68 (1984).

5. In Karches v. City of Cincinnati, 38 Ohio St.3d 12, 526 N.E.2d 1350 (1988), the court held a zoning ordinance invalid as applied to property in a flood plain which had been downzoned to Riverfront District, RF–1; the court found that none of the RF–1 uses were economically feasible.

SELLON v. CITY OF MANITOU SPRINGS

Supreme Court of Colorado, En Banc, 1987.
745 P.2d 229.

KIRSHBAUM, JUSTICE.

Landowners David R. Sellon, Kris J. Kovalik and Crystal Hills Development Co., plaintiffs-appellants, appeal an order of the El Paso County District Court upholding the constitutionality of a zoning ordinance (hereinafter referred to as the hillside ordinance) adopted by the City of Manitou Springs (the City) and its City Council, defendants-appellees. The landowners assert that the hillside ordinance is unconstitutional on its face and as applied to them, and also argue that the City Council acted arbitrarily and capriciously and abused its discretion in adopting the hillside ordinance. We affirm.

I

In July of 1973, the City adopted a master plan for a parcel of property, referred to as "Crystal Hills," located adjacent to the City. That plan provided that 194 home sites could be developed on the property. On September 1, 1981, the City annexed Crystal Hills. The landowners purchased the property in March 1982.

The City contains many areas characterized by hills of varying degrees of slope. Consequently, problems of erosion, drainage and access are of particular concern to property owners, residents and city planners. On May 4, 1982, after much debate and discussion, the City Council adopted the hillside ordinance in an effort to deal in a meaningful fashion with some of these concerns. The ordinance created a special hillside low density residential zone and established an equation for calculating the minimal lot sizes necessary for development of property placed in that zone.[11] When applied to steeply graded property, the equation requires in general that development plans be based on larger lot sizes than those required for properties not so steeply sloped. The equation also distinguishes between "platted" and "unplatted" land and requires larger lots for development of areas which are designated "unplatted" land at the time the property is zoned or rezoned hillside residential than in areas which are designated "platted" land.

On September 23, 1983, the City Council adopted a resolution placing Crystal Hills in a low density residential zone and authorizing the development of 108 residential units on the property. Many citizens disapproved of this decision, however, and the City Council decided to place the question of the rezoning of Crystal Hills before the voters of the City. In November of 1983, a majority of the City's voting electorate indicated approval for the rezoning of Crystal Hills as hillside low density residential property.

* * *

II

The landowners assert that the hillside ordinance is insufficiently related to public health, safety and welfare objectives of the City and that its terms are impermissibly vague. They suggest that because of these alleged deficiencies the hillside ordinance violates the due process clauses of the United States and Colorado Constitutions. We disagree.

A

The principles applicable to a determination of whether a particular municipal legislative enactment violates constitutional due process standards are well settled. A presumption of validity attaches to zoning decisions of municipal zoning authorities. * * * Thus, a party challeng-

---

11. That segment of the ordinance reads:

(3) Development Requirements

  (a) Minimum Lot Size—Allowable lot size shall be based on the average percent of slope, defined as follows:

    Average Percent of Slope shall mean the percent of slope as computed by the following formula—

$$S = \frac{100IL}{A}$$

Where S = average percent of slope
      I = contour interval in feet
      L = summation of length of all contour lines in feet
     A = area in square feet of parcel being considered

ing a zoning ordinance on constitutional grounds assumes the burden of proving the asserted invalidity beyond a reasonable doubt. * * *

For purposes of the United States Constitution, an ordinance containing provisions that bear a rational relationship to legitimate state concerns satisfies due process requirements. * * * The due process clause of article II, section 25, of Colorado's Constitution requires a reasonable relation between an ordinance and a valid interest, such as public health, safety, morals or general welfare. * * * The hillside ordinance must be evaluated pursuant to these standards.

The record reflects that prior to the adoption of the hillside ordinance great attention had been directed by the City Council to problems that had developed after improvements were made to property containing relatively steep slopes. For example, the city manager testified that the development of single-family units on steeply graded plots of land continually forced the City to deal with erosion, drainage, maintenance and emergency access issues. The record also contains evidence that residents of various areas of the City historically had experienced significant difficulties with some or all of these problems. The adoption of the hillside ordinance reflected a considered effort by the City Council to deal with these very real problems. Viewed in light of these facts, the ordinance addresses significant issues directly affecting the health and welfare of the City's residents.

At the review hearing conducted by the district court the landowners introduced evidence to the effect that the hillside ordinance was not the best means available to address problems of erosion, drainage or emergency access associated with development of residential housing units in steep slope areas of the City. However, the question is not whether other solutions to a governmental problem are feasible or superior to the program actually adopted; the question is whether the decision made is itself reasonably and rationally related to the problem being addressed. * * * In this case, it is abundantly clear that the provisions of the hillside ordinance are rationally and reasonably related to problems of erosion, drainage, maintenance and emergency access occurring on sloping terrain that affect the health and safety of the City's residents.

* * *

III

The landowners next contend that the hillside ordinance is confiscatory and therefore unconstitutional as applied to them because it, in effect, precludes the use of the Crystal Hills property for any reasonable purpose. It is true that a zoning ordinance that prohibits the use of property for any reasonable purpose will be deemed confiscatory and therefore violative of just compensation and due process protections afforded by Colorado's Constitution. * * * However, our decisions have consistently emphasized the principle that a landowner is not entitled to obtain maximum profits from the use of property, and that so long as the zoning ordinance leaves some reasonable use for the property, the ordinance does not violate state constitutional standards. * * *

The evidence establishes that the hillside ordinance does not render the Crystal Hills property devoid of any reasonable use, and that the landowners may still build a minimum of sixty residential units on the land. They are not entitled to obtain maximum profits from the use of their land or to obtain the highest and best use for the property. * * * The landowners failed to establish that as the result of the hillside ordinance they could not put their property to any reasonable use. They therefore failed to satisfy their burden of demonstrating beyond a reasonable doubt that the ordinance was confiscatory.

* * *

V

Finally, the landowners argue that the City Council's decision to rezone Crystal Hills was arbitrary, capricious and an abuse of discretion in violation of C.R.C.P. 106(a)(4). A trial court reviewing a quasi-judicial action pursuant to C.R.C.P. 106(a)(4) must uphold that decision unless there is no competent evidence in the record to support it. * * * The record in this case reflects that the City Council adopted the hillside ordinance because of long-standing concern over problems of erosion, drainage, maintenance and emergency access affecting hilly property. The decision to place Crystal Hills in the zone established by the hillside ordinance was entirely consistent with prior actions of the City seeking to address these problems. The record also establishes that the sharply contrasting geographical configurations of Crystal Hills make it well-suited for the zoning requirements established in the hillside ordinance. The City Council's action represents a reasonable and responsible effort to reconcile the interests of property owners and residents in the context of the geographical realities of the City. It was not arbitrary and capricious.

VI

For the foregoing reasons, the judgment of the district court is affirmed.

CORRIGAN v. CITY OF SCOTTSDALE

Supreme Court of Arizona, En Banc, 1986.
149 Ariz. 538, 720 P.2d 513, cert. denied 479 U.S.
986, 107 S.Ct. 577, 93 L.Ed.2d 580 (1986).

CAMERON, JUSTICE.

This is a petition for review of an opinion of the court of appeals, which reversed the trial court judgment in favor of the City of Scottsdale and declared its zoning ordinance void as an unconstitutional taking of Ms. Corrigan's property without just compensation. Corrigan v. City of Scottsdale, 149 Ariz. 553, 720 P.2d 528 [App.1985]. We have jurisdiction pursuant to art. 6 § 5(3) of the Arizona Constitution, A.R.S. § 12–120.24 and Rule 23, Ariz.R.Civ.App.Proc., 17A A.R.S.

The only issue to be decided on review is whether a landowner is entitled to money damages for a temporary taking of property by reason of an invalid zoning ordinance.

The facts follow. Ms. Corrigan owns 5,738 acres of undeveloped land, which is made up of three contiguous parcels. The largest parcel of land is approximately 4,800 acres; a smaller parcel of 608 acres adjoins the large parcel in a single point, at its northwest corner. A third parcel of approximately 330 acres connects with the large parcel, at the large parcel's southwest corner. All of this property is a part of, or close to, the McDowell Mountains. This land previously had been part of the DC Ranch, owned by Corrigan's father and E.E. Brown. Ms. Corrigan obtained her part of the property by purchase for two million dollars from Brown's children.

In 1963, the City of Scottsdale (city) annexed the southern part of the DC Ranch, including the land involved herein. The McDowell Mountains thus became the only hilly or mountainous terrain within the city limits. The land was zoned by the city as R–1–35 which allows one single family residence on a lot of at least 35,000 square feet.

Later in 1977, the city, in accordance with its earlier general use plans, added sections 6.800 through 6.807 to its zoning ordinance thus creating the Hillside District. This ordinance established two areas, the Hillside Conservation Area and the Hillside Development Area. The two areas are divided by a "no development" line. This line is located wherever one of the following conditions is first encountered: unstable slopes subject to rolling rocks or landslides; bedrock areas; slopes of 15 percent or more; or shallow, rocky mountain soils subject to severe erosion. This line under certain conditions may be adjusted to where two of the enumerated conditions are present. The Conservation Area, which is all land above the "no development" line, is to be used solely for the conservation of open space with the land legally secured for such conservation by easement or dedication. The Development Area may be developed with some limitations, such as retaining a fixed minimum percentage of the land in its natural state. Finally, the ordinance provided density credits for the land in the Conservation Area which may be transferred to contiguous land in the Development Area.[12]

The Hillside District ordinance did not affect Ms. Corrigan's two smaller parcels of land; however, 3,836 acres or 80 percent of her 4,800 acre parcel is in the Conservation Area. Assuming that all possible adjustments in the "no development" line were made, 3,523 acres or 74 percent of this land would still remain in the Conservation Area.

---

12. Density credits are also known as transferable development rights. An ordinance, such as the one in this case, "provides that development which is prohibited on one parcel of land may instead be applied to other parcels, allowing these other parcels to be developed to a greater extent than zoning normally would allow." Note, The Transferability of Development Rights, 53 U.Colo.L.Rev. 165, 165 (1981). Thus, Ms. Corrigan may now build in the Development Area alone the same number of housing units that she could previously build before the ordinance in the Conservation and Development Areas combined. We express no opinion as to the legality or constitutionality of this scheme.

Ms. Corrigan filed suit seeking a declaration that the ordinance was unconstitutional and further claiming money damages for the temporary taking of her property. Ms. Corrigan did not submit a development plan to the city either prior to or after filing the suit. The trial court entered findings of fact and conclusions of law that the ordinance was constitutional and that no taking of Ms. Corrigan's property had occurred. Accordingly, it dismissed the claim for damages.

The court of appeals reversed, stating that an unconstitutional taking without just compensation of Ms. Corrigan's land had occurred under both the United States and Arizona Constitutions. *Corrigan v. City of Scottsdale,* at 565, 720 P.2d at 540. Further, the appeals court held that the transfer of density credits could not constitute just compensation under the Arizona Constitution, as the Arizona Constitution requires payment of a judicially determined amount of money as compensation for such a taking. *Id.* Nevertheless, the appeals court upheld the dismissal by the trial court of the damages claim based on *Davis v. Pima County,* 121 Ariz. 343, 590 P.2d 459 (App.1978), *cert. denied,* 442 U.S. 942, 99 S.Ct. 2885, 61 L.Ed.2d 312 (1979), which held that the sole remedy for confiscatory zoning is invalidation of the ordinance and not money damages. Corrigan, supra, 149 Ariz. at 565, n. 14, 720 P.2d at 540, n. 14. This court granted Ms. Corrigan's petition for review to determine whether the remedy for a temporary unconstitutional taking of a person's property by virtue of a confiscatory zoning ordinance should be so limited.

* * *

In *Davis,* the court of appeals stated:

> When a zoning ordinance is confiscatory it results in a "taking of the property and is, in effect, the exercise of the power of eminent domain."

* * *

> However, *though appellants established a "taking" if the board's action were not undone,* this does not mean they are entitled to money damages. * * * The proper remedy when zoning is confiscatory is either to seek by declaratory judgment to invalidate the general zoning ordinance or to challenge the particular rezoning determination by means of a special action.

121 Ariz. at 345, 590 P.2d at 461. (emphasis added) (citations omitted). We do not agree. * * *

We are not alone in holding that a landowner may recover damages for a temporary taking by zoning. In a case where the plaintiff-landowner's Waterway Development Permit application was denied because the city "sought to impose a servitude upon the property to preserve 'the natural and traditional character of the land and waterway' ", the Texas Supreme Court stated, "[t]here was no suggestion that government may take or hold another's property without paying for it, just because the land is pretty. Our conclusion is that the City of Austin was liable in damages to the plaintiffs." *City of Austin v. Teague,* 570 S.W.2d 389, 394 (Tex.1978).

In New Jersey, it has been flatly held that "[t]emporary takings are compensable." *Sheerr v. Township of Evesham,* 184 N.J.Super. 11, 445 A.2d 46, 73 (1982).

In a case where the City of Lincoln zoned the plaintiff's land for public use and clearly intended to use the land for a school and other government buildings, the North Dakota Supreme Court stated:

> We believe [the compensation remedy proposed by Justice Brennan] for cases involving a regulatory taking constitutes not only a legally correct analysis of the "taking" involved but also provides a practical and fair solution for all parties. If a landowner proves that governmental regulation has deprived him of all reasonable use of his property, he is entitled to receive just compensation.

Rippley v. City of Lincoln, 330 N.W.2d 505, 511 (N.D.1983).

More significantly, in a case very similar to the one before us the New Hampshire Supreme Court not only allowed damages for a temporary taking but also reasonable attorneys fees and double costs. *Burrows v. City of Keene,* 121 N.H. at 601–602, 432 A.2d at 22. * * * [See the Burrows case in Chapter V, supra.]

* * *

We note that the reasons generally given for denying damages are that: (1) it usurps a legislative function; (2) it threatens substantial fiscal liability on local governments; and (3) it would inhibit governmental land planning. Note, *Just Compensation or Just Invalidation: The Availability of a Damages Remedy in Challenging Land Use Regulations,* 29 UCLA L.Rev. 711, 725 (1982). *See also* Wright, *Damages or Compensation for Unconstitutional Land Use Regulations,* 37 Ark.L.Rev. 612, 643–644 (1983). We believe these reasons do not justify such a rule.

First, since zoning is an exercise of the police power, it is often deemed a legislative function. *Davis v. Pima County,* 121 Ariz. at 345, 590 P.2d at 461; Note, *supra* at 725. Thus some argue that the awarding of damages deprives the legislative body of being the one to decide whether the regulation is appropriate in light of the fact that compensation will be paid. Such an argument misses the point. No legislative prerogative is usurped by awarding damages for the time the property was temporarily taken under an invalid zoning ordinance. The regulating body can still weigh all the relevant considerations and determine for itself how best to effectuate its policy in the future. The same alternatives are open to them after a remedy of invalidation plus temporary damages as exist after invalidation alone. The legislative body may pay to acquire the land outright, agree to pay the landowner a certain amount in order to continue the regulation, or simply abandon the regulation altogether. All that is added by an award of temporary damages is that the landowner is compensated for losses that he has already suffered by virtue of the unconstitutional taking. *See San Diego Gas & Elec. v. City of San Diego,* 450 U.S. at 656–657, 101 S.Ct. at 1306; Note, *supra* at 725–729.

Second, fears of fiscal liability did not stop courts from limiting or abolishing municipal sovereign immunity and likewise should not bar a person's constitutionally guaranteed compensation for the impermissible taking of his property. *Id.* at 726–727. Further, fiscal liability may be an incentive for responsible public planning. In this we note that a local government will not be liable for any substantial liability unless it irresponsibly imposed staggering losses onto a private citizen by its land regulation. D. Hagman, *Temporary Or Interim Damages Awards In Land Use Control Cases,* in *1982 Zoning and Planning Law Handbook* 201 (F. Strom. ed. 1982) (also found in Zoning & Plan.L.Rep. v. 4, n. 6 (June 1981)).

Finally, we do not believe that advocating responsible governmental planning is the same thing as inhibiting governmental planning. Public officials should consider their actions before enacting them. Mere invalidation does not provide any incentive for public planners not to experiment at an individual property owner's expense. Neither does invalidation provide any deterrent impact; instead the city can and often does enact another similarly restrictive regulation and force the landowner to undergo another costly litigation battle. Without a damages remedy, invalidation alone is a toothless tiger "capable of great roars about constitutional property rights but ineffectual in guarding against even obvious excesses resulting from multiple regulation." Note, *supra* at 734.

The policy reasons in favor of denying damages are not persuasive. Governmental entities should be as mindful of a person's constitutional rights as anyone else. Therefore, under our constitutional provision requiring a payment of money for an unconstitutional taking of a person's property, we hold that invalidation is not the sole remedy, and the landowner is entitled to money damages from the time the regulation was protested or challenged. Statements in Davis which prohibit any recovery of money damages for a regulatory taking, by a confiscatory zoning ordinance, are overruled.

The Proper Measure of Damages

Having determined that money damages are recoverable for a temporary taking by reason of an invalid zoning ordinance under art. 2 § 17 of the Arizona Constitution, we must now determine how those damages should properly be measured.

There has been extensive legal writing on the subject of how damages should be measured for a temporary taking. See generally D. Hagman & D. Miscznski, Windfalls for Wipeouts (1978); Johnson, Compensation for Invalid Land–Use Regulations, 15 Ga.L.Rev. 559 (1981); D. Hagman, Temporary Or Interim Damages Awards In Land Use Control Cases, supra; Wright, Damages or Compensation for Unconstitutional Land Use Regulations, supra. *From these and many other writings have emerged "five basic rules for measuring damages: rental return, option price, interest on lost profit, before-after valuation (two alternatives), and benefit to the government." D. Hagman, Temporary or Interim Damages Awards in Land Use Control Cases in 1982 Zoning & Planning Law Handbook at 218–227.*

Each of these damage measures works well in some "taking" cases and inequitably, if at all, in others. This is because no one rule adequately fits each of the many factual situations that may be present in a particular case. Such problems as: whether the losses are speculative; when the taking actually occurred; whether it caused any damage; and whether it was an acquisitory or nonacquisitory setting combine to make each measure of damages, in some cases, a "guessing game" between too little compensation on the one hand and providing a windfall on the other.

Recognizing this problem, we feel the best approach is not to require the application of any particular damage rule to all temporary taking cases. Instead we hold that the proper measure of damages in a particular case is an issue to be decided on the facts of each individual case. It is our intent to compensate a person for the losses he has actually suffered by virtue of the taking. Either the parties may agree to an appropriate damage measure or each may present evidence as to the actual damages in the case and its correct method of determination. The damages awarded and the way to measure those damages thus may be adapted to compensate the party whose land has been taken for his actual losses.

We emphasize, however, that no matter what measure of damages is appropriate in a given case, the award must only be for actual damages. Such actual damages must be provable to a reasonable certainty similar to common law tort damages. See Carey v. Piphus, 435 U.S. 247, 98 S.Ct. 1042, 55 L.Ed.2d 252 (1978). This approach will compensate for losses actually suffered while avoiding the threat of windfalls to plaintiffs at the expense of substantial government liability. Wright, *Damages or Compensation for Unconstitutional Land Use Regulations,* 37 Ark.L.Rev. at 637–39; *City of Austin v. Teague,* 570 S.W.2d at 395. In adopting this approach we agree with Professor Wright that:

> Most of the policy arguments in opposition to compensation or damages for regulatory takings are premised on the fear that Draconian liability on local governments will result. However, limiting recovery to a landowner's actual losses where the regulatory taking is temporary should help eliminate the threat of such burdensome liability. This approach adequately balances the public interest against private interests by requiring compensation for regulatory takings while limiting that compensation to actual losses for temporary takings. Such a balance between public and private interests will not be achieved by the extreme approach of denying all compensation for regulatory takings and limiting landowners to injunctive and declaratory relief.

Wright, *Damages or Compensation for Unconstitutional Land Use Regulations,* 37 Ark.L.Rev. at 645.

Applying this principle of compensation for actual loss caused by a temporary taking to the present case reveals an insufficient record on the damages issue. The evidence of damages presented to the trial court was not focused on what actual losses, if any, were suffered by Ms. Corrigan. *See Id.* at 638, (an owner with no plans for undeveloped property at the time of the regulatory taking may have difficulty proving actual damages). However, we cannot fault counsel for their failure to predict our ruling on this issue. We, therefore, remand this matter to the trial court for a determination as to the proper measure of damages in accordance with this opinion.

Notes

1. Do you agree with the conclusion of the Arizona court that prohibition of development on the steep hillsides amounted to an invalid taking of property rights? If you do agree, then how can you reconcile the decision in Corrigan with the flood plain cases?

2. Another case involving restrictions on hillside development is City of San Marcos v. R.W. McDonald Development Corp., 700 S.W.2d 674 (Tex.App. 3 Dist.1985). The court assumed the validity of the ordinance which restricted development of land "located on hillsides or in areas with soil subject to erosion," but the decision turns on whether the developer made serious misrepresentations to the city (the city initially approved developer's subdivision but sued when it learned of the misrepresentations). Also see Hensler v. City of Glendale, 8 Cal.4th 1, 32 Cal.Rptr.2d 244, 876 P.2d 1043 (1994), cert. denied ___ U.S. ___, 115 S.Ct. 1176, 130 L.Ed.2d 1129 (1995) where the court dismissed a developer's inverse condemnation action for failure to exhaust administrative remedies; the developer was challenging a city ordinance that precluded the building of houses on ridge lines, and the developer claimed that 40% of his land was taken by the regulation. And, in Lake Shore Estates, Inc. v. Denville Twp. Planning Bd., 127 N.J. 394, 605 A.2d 1073 (1992) the court upheld the retroactive application of a steep slope ordinance that frustrated a developer's subdivision plan. In Anello v. Zoning Bd. of Appeals of Dobbs Ferry, 1997 WL 68232 (N.Y.1997) the court held that denial of a variance to build a single-family dwelling under the city's steep slope ordinance was not a taking because the owner acquired her property after the enactment of the ordinance; thus, she was not deprived of any property interest under the rationale of the Lucas case (see previous chapter).

3. An explanation of the rationale and planning considerations for hillside development can be found in Robert B. Olshansky, Planning for Hillside Development, in Environment & Development (American Planning Ass'n, Sept./Oct. 1995).

4. One can easily see the public health and safety aspects of the police power in the flood plain and hillside cases, but can the concept of public safety include traffic problems? Consider the balancing of interests and implications of the following case.

GRANT'S FARM ASSOCIATES, INC.
v. TOWN OF KITTERY

Supreme Judicial Court of Maine, 1989.
554 A.2d 799.

McKUSICK, CHIEF JUSTICE.

In this action under M.R.Civ.P. 80B, Grant's Farm Associates, Inc. and its two principal shareholder-officers ("the developers") seek reversal of the Kittery Planning Board's denial of preliminary subdivision approval for their proposed condominium development, to be called Shepard's Cove. The developers argued before the Superior Court, and argue again before us on appeal, that the Board's denial was not supported by the record before it. We do not agree, and we therefore affirm the judgment of the Superior Court (York County; Brennan, J.) upholding the Planning Board's action.

The Shepard's Cove proposal calls for some 200 condominium units developed in clusters, with more than 90% of the site left as open space. The site, measuring almost 100 acres, is adjacent to the town hall complex near the Kittery traffic circle. It appears to be the largest tract of undeveloped land in the area between the most densely populated section of Kittery and the commercial strip along U.S. Route One. The site falls within the "Urban Residence" zone, and a portion of the site is subject to two additional zoning regimes because the site is bounded on two sides by the tidal estuaries of Spruce Creek and Gerry Cove. A 250–foot–wide strip along the shoreline is subject to shoreland restrictions. Of that, a 100–foot strip is further subject to resource protection restrictions.

The Shepard's Cove proposal attracted considerable public attention in Kittery, with active citizen participation on both sides at the public hearings. Circulators of a petition against the project claimed to have collected signatures in a number surpassing a quarter of the total votes cast in the preceding municipal election. After an extensive period of study and negotiation, almost two years after the developers submitted their first sketch plan to the Planning Board and almost a year after the initial public hearing on the proposal, they submitted the final version of their preliminary subdivision plan to the Board at a public meeting on December 11, 1986. That same evening, the Board voted to deny preliminary subdivision approval and to meet in an open workshop session on December 17 to prepare detailed written findings of fact.

After receiving the Board's findings, the developers commenced a multi-count action against the Board and the Town. Only the count seeking direct review under rule 80B of the Board's decision is the subject of this appeal: that count was heard first under a bifurcation order, and the Superior Court entered final judgment in favor of the Town pursuant to M.R.Civ.P. 54(b).

* * *

Here the only contention made by the developers is an evidentiary one; namely, that the record before the Board does not support its denial of subdivision approval. We do not agree. The developers had the burden of proof before the Board. * * * The Board, however, did not rest its denial merely on a ruling that the developers had failed to carry their burden of proof; rather it found as fact on the record before it that the proposed project would have specific adverse consequences in violation of the criteria for subdivision approval prescribed by law. In this situation, to prevail on appeal the developers must show not only that those Board findings of adverse consequences are unsupported by record evidence, but also that the record compels contrary findings. * * *

Under the Town's subdivision ordinance, "[p]reliminary approval * * * [is] an expression of approval of the design submitted on the preliminary plan as a guide to the preparation of the final plan." Kittery, Me., Subdivision Standards, § 6.1.7 (May 31, 1973). In its three-page "Decision and Findings of Fact," the Board set forth in detail its conclusion that the project design would violate five distinct criteria prescribed by the subdivision ordinance. Because the applicant must demonstrate that the proposed subdivision will satisfy every requirement of the state statute and the town ordinance, the Board's five grounds for denial are alternative and independent of one another. Finding substantial evidence supporting at least two of the Board's grounds for denial, namely, traffic conditions and shoreline impact, we need not address the other three. Since on each of those grounds the record amply supports the Board's finding of fact adverse to the developers, the record *a fortiori* did not compel the Board to find that the developers had carried their burden of proof.

One criterion the proposed subdivision had to satisfy is that it "not cause unreasonable highway or public road congestion or unsafe conditions with respect to use of the highways or public roads existing or proposed." 30 M.R.S.A. § 4956(3)(E) (Pamph.1988); Kittery Subdivision Standards § 1.1(E). The Board found that "sight factors, slope, sight distance, road width and anticipated traffic volumes despite proposed mitigating measures" would all contribute to unsafe conditions at the entrance to Shepard's Cove from State Highway 236. It also found that existing problems at the Kittery traffic circle would be aggravated by prolonging the rush hour and increasing overall traffic volume by 10%.

Rotary traffic during the Portsmouth Naval Shipyard rush hour is already characterized as "unacceptable" by the State Department of Transportation. The developers argue that the obligation not to *"cause* unreasonable * * * congestion or unsafe conditions" must be read narrowly so that exacerbation of preexisting traffic hazards cannot be grounds for denial of a permit. That argument belies common sense. Whether exacerbation of an existing problem is merely part of the background effect of inevitable growth, or can properly be said to "cause" a further traffic hazard, must be determined by the balancing analysis inherent in the "reasonableness" standard of the statute and ordinance.

In any event, the primary focus of the Planning Board's traffic hazard findings was not the congestion at the rotary. The Board also found that the intersection between Route 236 and the proposed access road for the project "would create unsafe conditions despite proposed mitigating measures," especially in winter driving conditions. As it passes the proposed entrance, the highway slopes toward the rotary, some 450 feet away, with a 5.8% downgrade, which the developers downplay as "slightly greater (by eight tenths of one percent) than would be recommended for a new road." The existing condition is more accurately characterized as *sixteen* percent higher than the acceptable slope. We cannot say it was unreasonable for the Board to find that the proposed entrance location would create a substantial traffic hazard on the artery connecting the Naval Shipyard with all points north.

A second criterion the proposed subdivision had to satisfy is that "[w]henever situated, in whole or part, within two hundred and fifty (250) feet of any pond, lake, river or tidal waters, [it] will not adversely affect the quality of such body of water or unreasonably affect the shoreline of such body of water." 30 M.R.S.A. § 4956(3)(L); Kittery Subdivision Standards § 1.1(L). In its review of the Shepard's Cove proposal, the Planning Board found that untreated surface water, possibly polluted, would run into Spruce Creek; that construction would change drainage patterns for the worse; that nesting and brooding areas for waterfowl and salt water wetland birds would be eliminated; and that the "critical edge" wildlife habitat along the shoreline would be damaged.

The developers respond that the Board is applying an unduly stringent standard of review for a site that is in the urban residence zone. We do not agree. Although the urban residence zoning of the area to the east of Route One arguably embodies a legislative preference for competing human needs that would be met by the Shepard's Cove proposal, that argument has little force within the 250–foot shoreland zone which encompasses most of the so-called critical edge. Chapter II, section I(I)(1) of the Kittery Zoning Ordinance expressly provides: "Such areas intentionally embrace and overlay parts of other Kittery Zoning Districts in order that the purposes of the Shoreland Control Law [38 M.R.S.A. §§ 435–447 (Pamph.1988)] can best be served." It is simply not true that all parts of the urban residence zone must be regarded as equally well suited to high-density development.

* * *

This case turns on factual issues. The developers had the burden of proof, and they have not shown that a factfinder would rationally be compelled to find that their project factually met each and every one of the requirements prescribed by law for subdivision approval. The presence in the record of substantial evidence supporting the Board's findings to the contrary establishes *a fortiori* the developers' failure to carry their burden of proof.

The entry is: Judgment affirmed.

Note

Also see Babcock Co. v. Florida, 558 So.2d 76 (Fla.App.1990) where a permit was withheld for a 62–acre development on an island in Tampa Bay, accessible by a causeway. The regional planning council recommended denial after a traffic study showed that the causeway could not handle any more traffic. The court held that the burden was on the developer to show that his proffered overpass to alleviate traffic flow would actually remedy the adverse impacts, and that the burden was not met.

C. PRESERVATION OF OPEN SPACE

There has been much discussion about the need for preserving open space in and near populous areas. The objectives may be (1) aesthetic, (2) prevention of development of physically unsuitable or uneconomic locations, (3) prevention of congestion or creation of cohesive communities using open spaces (green belts) as dividers, (4) protection of agricultural production, (5) provision for recreation areas, (6) the preservation of elements of beauty, spaciousness or what the British call "amenities" in our environment, or (7) a mixture of two or more of these objectives. To what degree can the police power be used to achieve such objectives? When will it be necessary to turn to public purchase programs? Can regulation and purchase be combined to achieve these goals and if so how? William H. Whyte vigorously urged programs for the purchase of development easements. See Whyte, Open Space Action (Outdoor Recreation Review Commission Study Rep. 15, 1962). This approach was criticized by a Comment, Control of Urban Sprawl or Securing Open Space: Regulation by Condemnation or by Ordinance, 50 Calif.L.Rev. 483 (1962). Krasnowiecki & Paul, The Preservation of Open Space in Metropolitan Areas, 110 U.Pa.L.Rev. 179 (1961), urged a combined police power, public purchase program. In general see Jordahl, Conservation and Scenic Easements: An Experience Resume, 39 Land Econ. 343 (1963); Siegel, The Law of Open Space (N.Y. Regional Plan Ass'n, Inc., 1960); and Proceedings, Conservation Easements and Open Space Conference. (Wis.Dep't Resource Development, Dec. 13–14, 1961); 5 Williams, American Land Planning Law, Chap. 159 (1988). For an unusual perspective on the open space problem, see Platt, Feudal Origins of Open Space Law, 4 Land Use Controls Q. 27 (No. 4, 1970). Also see Williams, Scenic Protection as a Legitimate Goal of Public Regulation, 38 Wash.U.J.Urb. & Contemp.L. 3 (1990).

ROSS v. CITY OF ROLLING HILLS ESTATES

California Court of Appeal, Second District, 1987.
192 Cal.App.3d 370, 238 Cal.Rptr. 561, appeal dismissed
484 U.S. 983, 108 S.Ct. 497, 98 L.Ed.2d 496 (1987).

COLE, ASSOCIATE JUSTICE.

Appellants W. Kenneth Ross and Carole A. Ross appeal from a judgment entered in favor of respondents, the City of Rolling Hills Estates (the City), the Planning Commission of the City of Rolling Hills

Estates (the Commission), and the City Council of the City of Rolling Hills Estates (the Council) denying appellants' petition for writ of mandate. The mandate was sought to compel respondents to approve plans presented by appellants to expand and alter their home, located in the City. The writ also sought to compel the issuance of a variance to zoning ordinances concerning lot requirements. Principally at issue is a view protection ordinance of the City. We reject appellants' contentions that the ordinance is unconstitutionally vague and that the City abused its discretion in denying them a building permit and a variance. Accordingly, we affirm.

Background

On December 21, 1984, appellants filed an application for a variance to permit a two-story addition to their home which would encroach into a code-required 15–foot street-side yard setback and to allow the proposed lot coverage to exceed the code permitted 30 percent limit. The Commission denied the zone variance request on May 20, 1985. No appeal was taken from this decision.

On June 6, 1985, appellants submitted revised plans for the addition to their residence. The revised plans eliminated the zoning violations and the need for any variance. Because the views of other property owners would be impaired to some degree, those owners were notified by the City of their right to file objections and to appear before the Commission. They filed objections to clearance of the revised plans. The Commission conducted a public hearing on August 19, 1985. It found that the proposed addition did not conform to the objectives of the view protection ordinance and denied approval of the plans.

Appellants appealed the Commission's decision to the Council. The Council held a public hearing on October 10, 1985, and affirmed the decision of the Commission.

The View Protection Ordinance

Appellants' challenge to the ordinance asserts that due process is denied them because the ordinance language is unconstitutionally vague. This argument is without merit. Appellants base the argument on semantic challenges to the ordinance's stated purposes and guidelines. The full text of the ordinance is set forth in the margin.[13] Thus, they

---

13. 1950. PURPOSES. The hillsides of the City constitute a limited natural resource in their scenic value to all residents of and visitors to the City and their potential for vista points and view lots. It is found that the public health, safety and welfare require prevention of needless destruction and impairment of views and promotion of the optimum utilization and discouragement of the blockage and misuse of such sites and view lots. The purpose of this ordinance is to promote the health, safety and general welfare of the public through:

"(a) The protection, enhancement, perpetuation and use of sites and view lots that offer views to the residents because of the unique topographical features which the Palos Verdes Peninsula offers, or which provide unique and irreplaceable assets to the City and its neighboring communities or which provide for this and future generations examples of the unique physical surroundings which are characteristic of the City.

"(b) The maintenance of settings which provide the amenity of a view.

argue that words such as "needless," "discourage," "view," "impairment" and "significantly obstructed," appearing in various portions of the text, do not provide sufficient guidance and are "unintelligible concepts."

The tests which apply when a statute or ordinance is challenged for vagueness are set forth in *Hand v. Board of Examiners* (1977) 66

"(c) The establishment of a process of design review by which the City may render its assistance toward the objective that views enjoyed by residents of the City will not be significantly obstructed.

"1951. EVALUATION AND REVIEW. To protect the visual quality of highly scenic areas and maintain the rural character of the City, new development should not degrade highly scenic natural historical or open areas and shall be visually subordinate to the scenic quality of these areas.

"New development within the various view sheds contained in the City that would have a significant visual impact to those living adjacent to the development, shall be subject to design review. This review shall ensure that development and its cumulative impact is consistent with the previously mentioned standards.

"The design procedures and standards employed in new developments, alterations and additions to existing structures and lots should include appropriate measures that are consistent with appearance and design goals of the View Protection Ordinance. Development proposals should be coordinated in order to:

"(a) Maximize open space preservation.

"(b) Protect view corridors, natural vegetation, land forms, and other features.

"(c) Minimize the appearance of visually intrusive structures.

"(d) Prevent the obstruction of property owners' views by requiring appropriate construction of new structures or additions to existing buildings or adjacent parcels.

"(e) Assess the potential view loss from public areas of any proposed major structures as well as alterations and additions to existing structures.

"(f) Determine whether other suitable design options are available to the property owner in order that view obstructions may be eliminated or lessened in severity.

"1952. CLEARANCE PROCEDURES. Should it appear that a potential view

impairment may result from a proposed development, addition or alteration, the site shall be subjected to a View Preservation Site inspection. A fee shall be charged for such inspection as the City Council shall fix by resolution.

"1953. INSPECTION. Upon such inspection, should the City zone clearance official determine that the proposed development addition or alteration will impair a view site, the matter shall be referred for hearing and review by the Planning Commission pursuant to Sections 1954 and 1955 below.

"1954. ADMINISTRATION AND REVIEW. It shall be the duty of the Planning Commission to administer the provisions of the View Protection Ordinance. Review of any site for such purposes shall be initiated by the City pursuant to a View Preservation Site Inspection or otherwise, or by any person aggrieved.

"1955. POWERS AND DUTIES OF PLANNING COMMISSION. The Planning Commission shall hold a public meeting when complaint opposed to any pending development addition or alteration has been filed by a person aggrieved or referred by the City zone clearance official. In connection with the foregoing, the Planning Commission:

"(a) Shall hear and review such complaints or referrals regarding the proposed construction, alteration, or additions.

"(b) May request, following a public meeting, that proposed action on a particular site or plans to make any additions to existing structures or new accessory structures on the lot in question will meet the mitigation measures of the View Protection Ordinance as outlined by the Planning Commission.

"(c) Coordinate and conciliate to the maximum extent possible the resolution of disputes among property owners concerning view obstructions.

"1956. APPEAL. Any person aggrieved may appeal the Planning Commission decision to the City Council within twenty (20) days after determination of required view protection mitigation measures."

Cal.App.3d 605, 620–621, 136 Cal.Rptr. 187: "In *McMurtry v. State Board of Medical Examiners* (1960) 180 Cal.App.2d 760, 766–767 [4 Cal.Rptr. 910], the court stated various tests for vagueness: 'It is well settled that "a statute which either forbids or requires the doing of an act in terms so vague that men of common intelligence must necessarily guess at its meaning and differ as to its application violates the first essential of due process of law." [Citations.] This principle applies not only to statutes of a penal nature but also to those prescribing a standard of conduct which is the subject of administrative regulation. [Citations.] *The language used in such legislation "must be definite enough to provide a standard of conduct" for those whose activities are prescribed as well as a standard by which the agencies called upon to apply it can ascertain compliance therewith.* [Citation.] Approved rules by which to judge the sufficiency of a statute in the premises have been applied in numerous decisions, i.e., the words used in the statute should be "well enough known to enable those persons within its purview to understand and correctly apply them." [Citation]; words of long usage, or which have an established or ascertainable meaning in the profession or industry involved, or those which have been given a definite and restrictive interpretation by the courts, or the meaning of which may be determined from a fund of human knowledge and experience, will meet the test of certainty. [Citations]; if the words used may be made reasonably certain by reference to the common law, to the legislative history of the statute involved, or to the purpose of that statute, the legislation will be sustained [citations]; and a standard fixed by language which is reasonably certain, judged by the foregoing rules, meets the test of due process "notwithstanding an element of degree in the definition as to which estimates might differ. [Citations.]" (Italics added.)

Applying these tests we do not find the ordinance to be too vague. A reasonably certain standard in light of the need for view protection can be determined. Indeed, we find it ironic that appellants, arguing in their reply brief that their house is located in a highly built-up residential area and not an untouched scenic wilderness, choose to argue that this case involves only "a normal residential addition in an area where there is a scenic view already *significantly obstructed* * * *." (Emphasis added.) That very underlined phrase, readily understood, is one they themselves challenge as too vague to be enforced.

* * *

The Commission found that the proposal would have an adverse impact on existing views and that appellants had failed to provide design alterations to minimize the view impact of their proposal. Those findings are sufficient to apprise the parties and the court of the basis for the City Council's action.

The trial court apparently determined, as we have done, that the Council in effect adopted the Commission's findings regarding impact on existing views and failure to mitigate that impact.

* * *

The record discloses that the Council had before it appellants' proposal, a staff recommendation that mitigating factors be incorporated into the design from the City's planning director, graphs and photographs indicating the view of city lights from the impacted properties and the extent that the proposal would affect the view, and the testimony of Stan Crawford and Margaret Larson, who testified that their views from their residences would be affected by the proposed addition. That evidence supports findings of significant view impairment and of failure to mitigate the impact on existing views.

DENIAL OF VARIANCE

We do not consider the merits of appellants' contention that the City abused its discretion in denying them a variance, because the issue is not properly preserved.

* * *

The judgment is affirmed. Respondents to recover their costs on appeal.

Notes

1. If the Rolling Hills Estates ordinance were to be applied to a developer who desired to build a tall office building on a parcel, and the city restricted the developer to a one or two story building, do you think a taking argument would be successful?

2. In Batchelder v.City of Seattle, 77 Wash.App. 154, 890 P.2d 25 (1995) the court reversed the trial court's order rejecting a developer's plan to subdivide his waterfront parcel into four lots, rehabilitate an existing house and build three new houses. A neighbor challenged the proposed plat on the ground that the plan would diminish his view. Seattle has a Shoreline Substantial Development Permit procedure and the court cited with approval a regulation promulgated to protect views of Portgage Bay; however, the court found that the impact of the proposed development on the neighbor's view was relatively minor, and after construction he would retain 80 percent of his view. The court remanded the case with instructions to reinstate the developer's permit.

3. A very interesting open space case is Kinzli v. City of Santa Cruz, 620 F.Supp. 609 (N.D.Cal.1985), reversed and vacated 818 F.2d 1449 (9th Cir.1987), cert. denied 484 U.S. 1043, 108 S.Ct. 775, 98 L.Ed.2d 861 (1988). In that case the Kinzli property which had been purchased in 1925 and used over the years as a dairy farm was placed in a greenbelt under an initiated ordinance. The greenbelt provisions allowed only eight uses within the greenbelt, all of which prohibited intense development; under the previous comprehensive plan the Kinzli property was slated for intense development. Two attempts to sell the property to developers were frustrated by the adoption of the greenbelt measure. The federal district court concluded that the Kinzli's property was not taken by the greenbelt restrictions, primarily because the Kinzlis could not show any investment-backed expectations; the court concluded that from 1925, when the property was purchased until 1980, when the greenbelt measure went into effect, the economic returns on

the property were sufficient to establish that the owners had lost "nothing" when the greenbelt provisions restricted development. On appeal, the decision was reversed because the case was not ripe for adjudication.

4. In Arastra Ltd. Partnership v. City of Palo Alto, 401 F.Supp. 962 (N.D.Cal.1975), vacated 417 F.Supp. 1125 (N.D.Cal.1976) the court found, in an inverse condemnation action, that the city's open space zoning amendment was the final step in a plan to acquire the plaintiff's 500 acres of unimproved foothill property without compensation. Refer back to the Fred F. French case in the previous Chapter and note the court's attitude toward the regulation which permitted only "passive recreational" uses for the Tudor parks. Also see Barbaccia v. County of Santa Clara, 451 F.Supp. 260 (N.D.Cal.1978), Oceanic California, Inc. v. City of San Jose, 497 F.Supp. 962 (N.D.Cal.1980) and Horizon Adirondack Corp. v. State of New York, 88 Misc.2d 619, 388 N.Y.S.2d 235 (1976).

5. The uncertainty of using the police power to preserve significant amounts of open space has led to increased emphasis on tax incentives to encourage donation or self limitation of development as a technique of open space preservation. See, e.g., Browne, The Impact of Existing and Proposed Federal Income, Estate and Gift Taxes on Open Space, in Tax Policies to Achieve Land–Use Goals 65 (Lincoln Inst. monograph 1978). If a landowner acquires property burdened with a conservation restriction to preserve open space in its natural condition, and the restriction prohibits the erection of structures, could the owner put an in-ground swimming pool on the land? An appellate court said "no" in Goldmuntz v. Town of Chilmark, 38 Mass.App.Ct. 696, 651 N.E.2d 864 (1995).

D. HISTORICAL AND LANDMARK PRESERVATION

(1) Historic Districts

OPINION OF THE JUSTICES TO THE SENATE

Supreme Judicial Court of Massachusetts, 1955.
333 Mass. 773, 128 N.E.2d 557.

On July 7, 1955, the Justices submitted the following answers to questions propounded to them by the Senate:

To the Honorable the Senate of the Commonwealth of Massachusetts:

The Justices of the Supreme Judicial Court respectfully submit these answers to questions set forth in an order of the Senate dated June 14, 1955, and transmitted to us on June 21.

The questions relate to a proposed act known as House No. 775, now pending before the Senate, entitled "An Act establishing an historic districts commission for the town of Nantucket and defining its powers and duties, and establishing historic districts in the town of Nantucket."

The purpose of the act is stated to be to promote the general welfare of the inhabitants of the town "through the preservation and protection of historic buildings, places and districts of historic interest; through the development of an appropriate setting for these buildings, places and districts; and through the benefits resulting to the economy of Nantucket in developing and maintaining its vacation-travel industry through the promotion of these historic associations." § 1.

The act establishes a historic districts commission of five members, who shall be resident taxpayers of the town, to be appointed by the selectmen. § 2. It establishes by definite boundaries two districts in the town to be known as (1) Old and Historic Nantucket District, and (2) Old and Historic Siasconset District. § 3. It contains provisions applicable in those districts that "No building or structure shall hereafter be erected, reconstructed, altered or restored" until an application for a building permit "shall have been approved as to exterior architectural features which are subject to public view from a public street, way or place," and evidence of such approval shall be "a certificate of appropriateness" issued by the commission (§ 4); that no building or structure shall be raised (razed?) without a permit approved by the commission, which may be refused for any building or structure "the removal of which in the opinion of said commission would be detrimental to the public interest" of the town or the village of Siasconset (§ 5); that occupational or other signs exceeding two feet in length and six inches in width, or the erection or display of more than one such sign, irrespective of size, on any lot, building or structure must be approved and certified by the commission (§ 6); and that the commission may hold public or private hearings as it may deem advisable (§ 7). It shall be the function and duty of the commission "to pass upon the appropriateness of exterior architectural features of buildings and structures hereafter to be erected, reconstructed, altered or restored * * * wherever such exterior features are subject to public view from a public street or way" and also to pass upon the removal of buildings and the erection or display of signs according to §§ 5 and 6 (§ 8[a]). It is provided that the commission "in passing upon appropriateness of exterior architectural features in any case, shall keep in mind the purposes set forth" in § 1, and "shall consider among other things the general design, arrangement, texture, material and color of the building or structure in question, and the relation of such factors to similar features of buildings and structures in the immediate surroundings" (§ 8[b]). It is expressly provided that the commission shall not consider detailed designs, relative size of buildings, interior arrangement or building features not subject to public view, and shall make no recommendations or requirements except for the purpose of preventing developments obviously incongruous to the historic aspects of the surroundings and the Old and Historic Districts (§ 8[c]). Upon approval of plans the commission shall cause a certificate of appropriateness to be issued (§ 8[e]). There are provisions for a penalty for violations of the act and for appeal to the selectmen and ultimately to the Superior Court. §§ 9–11. Appeal to the Superior Court with "rights of appeal and exception as in other equity cases" is to be the final exclusive remedy. § 11. The provision for appeal to the court is in terms similar to those employed in statutes providing for appeal to the court from decisions of zoning boards of appeals, which in Pendergast v. Board of Appeals of Barnstable, 331 Mass. 555, 120 N.E.2d 916, were held to carry up questions of law. The act is to take effect upon acceptance by the voters of the town. § 14.

The act contains no provision for compensation as for property taken. The commission is to be "unpaid." § 2. But under § 7 it "may incur expenses necessary to the carrying on of its work within the amount of its annual appropriation."

* * *

If the proposed act is to be construed as a taking of the property of owners affected by it, manifestly it is unconstitutional, since no provision is made for compensation as required by art. 10 of the Declaration of Rights. On the other hand, there may be many regulations and restrictions upon the use of private property under the so called police power which do not amount to a taking of the property and which rest upon the general power to legislate for the public safety, health, morals, and welfare. We are of opinion that the proposed act is not a taking. There is no provision for a formal taking, and title will remain in the owner as will also the possession and usufruct for nearly all purposes, even though restricted in ways that conceivably may in occasional instances bear down heavily. See American Unitarian Association v. Commonwealth, 193 Mass. 470, 476–477, 79 N.E. 878.

The question then arises whether the proposed act can be supported without a taking and the paying of compensation as a police regulation in the interest of public safety, health, morals, or welfare. There are many regulations belonging in these categories too numerous and too familiar to require specific reference here. Those which in many respects most nearly resemble the proposed act are the zoning laws the constitutionality of which is in general thoroughly established. * * * Many zoning regulations are as severe in their operation upon landowners as any of the provisions of the proposed act would be likely to be.

But the zoning regulations are in general directly related to the public safety and health, and less directly to the public morals. The proposed act can hardly be said in any ordinary sense to relate to the public safety, health, or morals. Can it rest upon the less definite and more inclusive ground that it serves the public welfare? The term public welfare has never been and cannot be precisely defined. Sometimes it has been said to include public convenience, comfort, peace and order, prosperity, and similar concepts, but not to include "mere expediency." Opinion of the Justices, 234 Mass. 597, 603, 127 N.E. 525. And it has been held or stated that aesthetic considerations alone are not enough, but that they may be taken into account, if the primary objects of the regulation are sufficient to justify it. * * * There is reason to think that more weight might now be given to aesthetic considerations than was given to them a half century ago.

* * *

The definition of the purpose of the proposed act as set forth in § 1 is along these same lines and includes "the preservation and protection of historic buildings, places and districts of historic interest; through the development of an appropriate setting for these buildings, places and districts; and through the benefits resulting to the economy of Nantucket in developing and maintaining its vacation-travel industry through the promotion of these historic associations." In the case of City of New Bedford v. New Bedford, Woods Hole, Martha's Vineyard & Nantucket Steamship Authority, 330 Mass. 422, 114 N.E.2d 553, this court took judicial notice of the general characteristics of the island of Nantucket and of its great interest in the entertainment of summer visitors. We may also take judicial notice that Nantucket is one of the very old towns of the Commonwealth; that for perhaps a century it was a famous seat of the whaling industry and accumulated wealth and culture which made itself manifest in some fine examples of early American architecture; and that the sedate and quaint appearance of the old island town has to a large extent still remained unspoiled and in all probability constitutes a substantial part of the appeal which has enabled it to build up its summer vacation business to take the place of its former means of livelihood. In a general way much the same can be said of the village of Siasconset, which is a part of the town of Nantucket. There has been substantial recognition by the courts of the public interest in the preservation of historic buildings, places, and districts. Opinion of the Justices, 297 Mass. 567, 8 N.E.2d 753. General Outdoor Advertising Co., Inc. v. Department of Public Works, 289 Mass. 149, 187–189, 197–198, 200–201, 193 N.E. 799. United States v. Gettysburg Electric Railway, 160 U.S. 668, 16 S.Ct. 427, 40 L.Ed. 576. State v. Kemp, 124 Kan. 716, 261 P. 556. Flaccomio v. Mayor & City Council of Baltimore, 194 Md. 275, 71 A.2d 12. See art. 51 of the Amendments to the Constitution of this Commonwealth.

It is not difficult to imagine how the erection of a few wholly incongruous structures might destroy one of the principal assets of the town, and we assume that the boundaries of the districts are so drawn as to include only areas of special value to the public because of possession of those characteristics which it is the purpose of the act to preserve.

We think the requirements of the proposed act are not too indefinite or lacking in sufficient standards. The act does not require anything to be done to existing structures with the possible exception of signs (§ 6). With the same possible exception, it applies only to exterior architectural features subject to public view from a public place (§ 4). It does not apply to details of design or sizes of buildings or interior arrangement of building features not subject to public view, and requirements by the commission must be limited to the preventing of developments "obviously incongruous to the historic aspects of the surroundings" (§ 8[c]). This last provision is apparently intended to prevent decisions based upon peculiar individual tastes. All provisions must be interpreted with reference to the main purposes of the act. See § 8(b). In at least two very recent cases regulations based in part upon standards of architecture intended to comport with the established surroundings have been sustained. City of New Orleans v. Levy, 223 La. 14, 64 So.2d 798. State ex rel. Saveland Park Holding Corp. v. Wieland, 269 Wis. 262, 69 N.W.2d 217. See 64 U.S.Sts. at Large, p. 903, c. 984, relating to "Old Georgetown."

We are of opinion that in a general sense the proposed act would be an act for the promotion of the public welfare and would be constitutional, and we answer the questions on that basis. * * *

Notes

1. On the same day as the decision in the principal case, the justices rendered an opinion that a similar historic district to preserve Beacon Hill in Boston would be constitutional. See Opinion of the Justices to the Senate, 333 Mass. 783, 128 N.E.2d 563 (1955). The court stated:

> In addition to the facts appearing from the proposed act itself there are other facts of common knowledge in relation to Beacon Hill. The area was closely built up for the homes of persons of taste and culture in the architectural style of urban residences prevailing a century or more ago. There is general uniformity in design and structure. Although the area is not far from the business center of Boston, commercial development has proceeded in other directions, and the Beacon Hill section, with some exceptions, has remained to this day rather surprisingly free from inharmonious intrusions. Its general appearance is substantially what it was several generations ago. The Bulfinch front, so called, of the State House, completed before the year 1800, is at the highest point of the hill. The famous Boston Common is located on the side of Beacon Street opposite the southerly boundary of the proposed district. The area has contained the homes of many persons of distinction in the life of the State and Nation. That it is a locality of historic significance can hardly be doubted.

> The announced purpose of the act is to preserve this historic section for the educational, cultural, and economic advantage of the public. If the General Court believes that this object would be attained by the restrictions which the act would place upon the introduction into the district of inappropriate forms of construction that would destroy its unique value and associations, a court can hardly take the view that such legislative determination is so arbitrary or unreasonable that it cannot be comprehended within the public welfare.

> In our answers to recent questions of the Senate pertaining to proposed historic districts in Nantucket we have discussed at some length the constitutional aspects of restrictions upon the character of building in areas set apart as such districts, whether or not there is involved any element of aesthetic considerations, and we cited authorities revealed by our research into the subject. We beg to refer to what we there said without repeating it here. In that instance the districts of historic interest intended to be preserved were in ancient villages that had survived into our day. In this instance it is an ancient section of the capital city of the Commonwealth. But the principles are the same. There are some other differences between the two proposed acts, but we

think none is sufficient to render what we said in our discussion in the former instance inapplicable in this later instance.

2. In Gumley v. Board of Selectmen of Nantucket, 371 Mass. 718, 358 N.E.2d 1011 (1977), the court held that a decision of the Nantucket Historic District Commission denying a certificate of appropriateness to a developer was improper to the extent that it was based on incongruence with the open space aspect of Nantucket. The court said: "That decision did not relate to 'exterior architectural features.' It went beyond the statutory purpose of 'preventing developments obviously incongruous to the historic aspects of the surroundings' and the district. It therefore exceeded the authority of the commission * * *."

3. See also, City of Santa Fe v. Gamble–Skogmo, 73 N.M. 410, 389 P.2d 13 (1964), upholding zoning seeking to preserve "Old Santa Fe Style" architecture. Similar to the Santa Fe situation were the earlier efforts of New Orleans to preserve the distinctive character of the French Quarter. This effort was embodied in the "Vieux Carre Ordinance," discussed in 2 Anderson, American Law of Zoning § 8.54 (1986) and 3 Williams, American Land Planning Law §§ 71.05–71.10 (1988). The ordinance sought to exercise control over the architecture in the French Quarter, but was based on specific authorization by the Louisiana Constitution (Art. 14, § 22A). Construed on several occasions, it was held that the ordinance adopted by the city pursuant to the constitutional provision, which would result in preserving the Quarter, was not just "sentimental" but also for the purpose of preserving the commercial value of the Vieux Carre and thus was a valid exercise of the police power. See City of New Orleans v. Pergament, 198 La. 852, 5 So.2d 129 (1941), which stated that it was not a denial of equal protection to require a gasoline station owner to obtain a permit from the commission to erect or maintain an advertising sign. See also, City of New Orleans v. Levy, 223 La. 14, 64 So.2d 798 (1953); and City of New Orleans v. Impastato, 198 La. 206, 3 So.2d 559 (1941). Although the New Orleans cases were based on an ordinance adopted and a commission created pursuant to specific constitutional authority, they helped lay the groundwork for acceptance of the idea that municipalities (as in the Santa Fe case) could rely upon a general delegation of authority to sustain zoning for preservation purposes. In Williamsburg, Virginia, the zoning power was employed to protect a *restored* area, rather than to preserve an historic area in its existing state. See Agnor, Beauty Begins a Comeback: Aesthetic Considerations in Zoning, 11 J.Pub.L. 260, 274 (1962); and Note, Zoning: Aesthetics: The Chameleon of Zoning, 4 Tulsa L.J. 48, 56 (1967).

SOUTH OF SECOND ASSOCIATES
v. GEORGETOWN

Supreme Court of Colorado, En Banc, 1978.
196 Colo. 89, 580 P.2d 807.

ERICKSON, JUSTICE.

Georgetown is a municipal corporation created by the Colorado territorial legislature in 1868. The town and surrounding area are rich in the culture and history of early Colorado. In 1966, the National Park

Service of the U.S. Department of the Interior designated the Georgetown/Silver Plume area as a registered National Historic Landmark District.

On May 18, 1970, the Board of Selectmen of Georgetown enacted Ordinance No. 205. The ordinance amended Georgetown's existing zoning ordinance by creating a Historic Preservation District (District) and a seven-member Historic Preservation Commission (Commission). The District boundaries encompassed all real property within the municipal limits of Georgetown. * * *

South of Second Associates, one of the plaintiffs, owns approximately five acres of undeveloped real property in Georgetown located on Leavenworth Mountain south of the developed portion of the municipality. The property, at all times relevant to this proceeding, was zoned for multi-family use. On December 18, 1972, the plaintiffs submitted an application for a certificate of appropriateness to construct 57 townhouses which would occupy approximately 30% of their property on Leavenworth Mountain. The Commission reviewed the application and unanimously decided not to issue the requested certificate. The Georgetown Board of Selectmen voted four to two not to overrule the Commission's decision.

* * *

The pertinent provisions of Ordinance No. 205 provide:

"Section VII.   'HP—Historic Preservation District'

"A) GENERAL DESCRIPTION

This District is intended to promote the educational, cultural, economic, and general welfare of the public through the protection, enhancement, and use of structures and areas of historical and/or architectural significance. In order to maintain the character and beauty of such structures, and areas, restrictive requirements governing both the use of land and the erection, moving, demolition, reconstruction, restoration, or alteration of structures thereon are provided.

* * *

"B) DEFINITIONS FOR THE HISTORICAL PRESERVATION DISTRICT

* * *

4.   Historical and/or Architectural Significance. That which has a special historical or aesthetic interest or value as part of the development, heritage, or cultural character of the city, region, state, or nation.

5.   Area. Any land or buildings having notable character qualities of historical and/or architectural significance as determined by the Historical Preservation Commission. An area may include structures or other physical improvements on, above, or below the surface of the earth.

* * *

"C) Role of Historical Preservation Commission

* * *

"In determining the recommendation to be made concerning the issuance of a certificate of appropriateness, the Commission shall consider the following criteria:

(1) The effect of the proposed change upon the general historical and/or architectural character of the structure or area."

* * *

The trial court concluded that the ordinances were unconstitutionally vague:

"After reviewing the ordinances and after hearing the testimony of numerous witnesses concerned with their enforcement (each of whom seemed to have a different opinion as to the meaning of the term 'historical and architectural significance') the Court is convinced that the ordinances do not contain sufficient standards to advise ordinary and reasonable men as to the conduct which they attempt to proscribe or direct."

The trial court seems to have based its decision upon a finding that the "historical and/or architectural significance" language of the ordinance was vague. We find such language sufficiently definite, but hold the ordinances unconstitutionally vague in failing to delineate the differently classified areas within the District.

* * *

Courts in other jurisdictions have found similar enactments, although somewhat uncertain in the abstract, to be sufficiently definite in the context of actual application. In Town of Deering v. Tibbetts, 105 N.H. 481, 202 A.2d 232 (1964), the Court declared:

"While determination of what is compatible with the 'atmosphere' of the town may on first impression be thought to be a matter of arbitrary and subjective judgment, under consideration it proves not to be. As stated in Anderson, 'Architectural Controls,' 12 Syracuse L.Rev. 26, 45, the language 'takes clear meaning from the observable character of the district to which it applies.' See also, 1 Rathkopf, The Law of Zoning and Planning (3d ed. 1969) 11–29."

Our conclusion that the "historical and/or architectural" language in the Georgetown ordinance is sufficiently definite reflects the consensus of those courts which have considered similar provisions designed to preserve historical areas through the enactment of reasonable regulations. Figarsky v. Historic District Commission of the City of Norwich, 171 Conn. 198, 368 A.2d 163 (1976); Trustees of Sailors' Snug Harbor v. Platt, 29 A.D.2d 376, 288 N.Y.S.2d 314 (1968); Town of Deering v. Tibbetts, supra; City of Santa Fe v. Gamble–Skogmo, Inc., 73 N.M. 410, 389 P.2d 13 (1964); Opinion of the Justices to the Senate, 333 Mass. 773, 128 N.E.2d 557 (1955); City of New Orleans v. Levy, 223 La. 14, 64 So.2d

798 (1953); See also 1 Rathkopf § 15.01, The Law of Zoning and Planning (4th ed.).

We conclude that the "historical and/or architectural character" language of the ordinance, when considered in conjunction with the objective factors contained in the ordinance, and in the context of the public purposes to be achieved, is sufficiently definite to pass constitutional muster. The ordinance contains sufficient standards to advise ordinary and reasonable men as to the type of construction permitted, permits reasonable application by the Commission, and limits the Commission's discretionary powers.

* * *

Georgetown's historical preservation ordinance designates all property within the municipal limits as a historical preservation district. Most municipalities which have established similar historical preservation districts, however, specifically delineate those areas which possess such a unique character as to be entitled to preservation. See Figarsky v. Historical District Commission of the City of Norwich, supra; Maher v. City of New Orleans, 516 F.2d 1051 (5th Cir.1975); Rebman v. City of Springfield, 111 Ill.App.2d 430, 250 N.E.2d 282 (1969); Opinion of the Justices to the Senate, supra; Opinion of the Justices to the Senate, 333 Mass. 783, 128 N.E.2d 563 (1955); see also section 24–65.1–201(1)(c), C.R.S.1973 (1977 Supp.).

Although the ordinance contains standards sufficient to give substance to the "historical and/or architectural character" language of the ordinance by reference to the area in which the proposed construction or structural alteration is to occur, nowhere in the ordinance is a delineation of the relevant areas to be found. The ordinances' definition of area * * * fails to set forth sufficient criteria to enable the potential applicant to reasonably ascertain in which area his property is situated.

The record indicates that the Commission members divide Georgetown into two or three distinct areas. Several members testified that Georgetown was divided into northern and southern areas. Still others, while agreeing that the northern and southern areas exist, felt that a transitional or buffer area exists between the two larger areas. The Commission's unpublished and indefinite delineation of the areas is legally insufficient.

We conclude that Ordinance Nos. 205 and 206 vested unreviewable discretion in the Commission. Under the ordinances a property owner cannot reasonably ascertain which architectural designs would entitle him to a certificate of appropriateness. Areas entitled to protection must be clearly delineated in the ordinance. The ordinances, therefore, are void for vagueness.

* * *

The judgment is affirmed.

Notes

1. After the decision in this case the plaintiffs were denied a building permit and sought a declaratory judgment that they were entitled to immediate issuance of a permit and damages for the delay in issuing a permit. The supreme court held that the plaintiffs were entitled to declaratory relief and remanded the case for a hearing on the damages issue. South of Second Associates v. Georgetown, 199 Colo. 394, 609 P.2d 125 (1980). In Unruh v. City of Asheville, 97 N.C.App. 287, 388 S.E.2d 235, rev. denied 326 N.C. 487, 391 S.E.2d 813 (1990) the court held that the city's historic district ordinance was invalid because the city did not follow the prescribed adoption procedures in the state enabling legislation.

2. Can historic districts be empowered to control development outside the district which might have a deleterious effect upon the district? In Rebman v. City of Springfield, 111 Ill.App.2d 430, 250 N.E.2d 282 (1969), the court upheld denial of a rezoning to permit a restaurant on a commercial street adjacent to a four block historic district containing one historical structure, the Abraham Lincoln home. Also see, Hall County Historical Soc., Inc. v. Georgia Dept. of Transp., 447 F.Supp. 741 (N.D.Ga.1978), where the county historical society sought to protect an established district from a highway widening project close to the district boundaries. After finding that the society had standing based on the allegation that several members resided in or owned property in the historical district, the court held that (1) the plaintiffs failed to meet their burden of proof that the defendants' decision not to file an environmental impact statement was unreasonable under the National Environmental Policy Act; (2) defendants had not violated Section 4(f) of the Transportation Act (23 U.S.C.A. § 138) mandating that the Secretary of Transportation not approve any project which requires the use of land from an historic site if there is a feasible alternative; (3) the Department of Transportation did violate the National Historic Preservation Act (16 U.S.C.A. § 470f) which requires the federal agency to take into account the effect of a project on historic sites, by merely "rubber stamping" the conclusions of the state highway department that the project would not affect the district. An injunction against completion of the project was granted. In Bellevue Shopping Center Associates v. Chase, 574 A.2d 760 (R.I.1990) the court upheld denial of a proposal to add a new building to an existing shopping center because the design of the building would seriously impair the historic or architectural value of the surrounding historic district.

3. In Globe Newspaper Co. v. Beacon Hill Architectural Comm'n, 847 F.Supp. 178 (D.Mass.1994) the court held that the architectural commission for the Beacon Hill historic district did not have power to regulate the placement of newsracks, and that the guidelines promulgated by the commission violated the First Amendment as being too broad and not content neutral.

(2) Preserving Landmark Structures

KENT COUNTY COUNCIL FOR HISTORIC
PRESERVATION v. ROMNEY

United States District Court, Western District, Michigan, 1969.
304 F.Supp. 885.

THORNTON, DISTRICT JUDGE. "This is a case of first impression insofar as the National Historic Sites Act of 1966, 16 U.S.C.A. § 470 et seq. is concerned, certainly in its application to the urban renewal process. Plaintiff is unaware of any reported decisions construing this Act. Potentially, it is a landmark case. For as it is true of the Act itself, the issue at hand is the capacity of the American people to prevent improvidence in matters relating to the conservation of our natural and man-made heritage."

Thus reads plaintiff's brief in support of its motions for preliminary injunction in the two cases before the Court (now consolidated for trial purposes). The defendants include George W. Romney, Secretary of the Department of Housing and Urban Development, the Mayor of the City of Grand Rapids and numerous City administration officials, and the Union Bank and Trust Company. The Court set down plaintiff's preliminary injunction motions for early hearing because of the imminence of the demolition (Old Grand Rapids City Hall), which plaintiff seeks to at least forestall, if not prevent entirely. Prior to the commencement of the hearing there were filed motions to dismiss by all defendants, lack of jurisdiction being a basis common to all. Also advanced are contentions of non-retroactivity of the applicable legislative enactments and lack of standing. The preliminary injunction hearing, therefore, was held in abeyance so as to give precedence to a hearing on and determination of the various motions to dismiss.

* * *

It should be clear from the above that the Old Grand Rapids City Hall is on a parcel which is only a small segment of a substantial renewal plan area, that the plan was adopted by the City on April 4, 1961 and that execution of the plan has been proceeding since that time. The Act which plaintiff seeks to take advantage of came into existence October 15, 1966. The section of said Act relied upon by plaintiff is as follows:

"16 U.S.C.A. § 470f. Effect of Federal undertakings upon property listed in the National Register; comment by Advisory Council on Historic Preservation.

"The head of any Federal agency having direct or indirect jurisdiction over a proposed Federal or federally assisted undertaking in any State and the head of any Federal department or independent agency having authority to license any undertaking shall, prior to the approval of the expenditure of any Federal funds on the undertaking or prior to the issuance of any license, as the case may be, take into account the effect of the undertaking on any district, site, building, structure, or object that is included in the National Register. The head of any such Federal agency shall afford the Advisory Council on Historic Preservation established under sections 470i–470m of this title a reasonable opportunity to comment with regard to such undertaking. Pub.L. 89–665, Title I, § 106, Oct. 15, 1966, 80 Stat. 917.''

* * *

[W]e are concerned with a statute, 16 U.S.C.A. § 470f whose function is to provide the Advisory Council on Historic Preservation a reasonable opportunity to comment with regard to an undertaking and its effect on any district, site, building, structure or object that is included in the National Register, and further to provide that the undertaking conform to other requirements of the statute. The National Historic Preservation Act provides in part as follows:

"(a) The Secretary of the Interior is authorized—

"(1) to expand and maintain a national register of districts, sites, buildings, structures, and objects significant in American history, architecture, archeology, and culture, hereinafter referred to as the National Register, and to grant funds to States for the purpose of preparing comprehensive statewide historic surveys and plans, in accordance with criteria established by the Secretary, for the preservation, acquisition, and development of such properties;" 16 U.S.C.A. § 470a.

Thus we are concerned with a statute that has application to federal agencies, heads of federal departments or individual agencies and the Advisory Council on Historic Preservation, with the duties of each clearly spelled out. [The Advisory Council on Historic Preservation, composed of seventeen members (not to be confused with Kent County Council for Historic Preservation), is not a party to this suit, either as a plaintiff or a defendant.] We are concerned with inanimate objects such as districts, sites, buildings, structures, or objects that are included in the National Register, rather than with individuals, organizations or corporations. * * *

Plaintiff has failed to establish by proof, argument or citation that it has any interest that would give it the right to bring this action. Accordingly, it lacks standing to sue.

The motions to dismiss heretofore filed herein should be granted. The moving parties may submit orders in accordance with this Memorandum, for consideration by the Court, incorporating therein such proposed supplemental comments as they may find desirable.

Notes

1. Federal involvement in historic preservation has increased significantly since the adoption of the National Historic Preservation Act of 1966[14]

14. 80 Stat. 915, 16 U.S.C.A. § 470 et seq.

which establishes the National Register of historic sites and defines historic preservation to include "the protection, rehabilitation, restoration, and reconstruction of districts, sites, buildings, structures, and objects significant in American history, architecture, archeology, or culture." The act is primarily directed at federal agencies and imposes no duties on state or local government.[15] The effect of having a building or site listed on the National Register is limited; preservation is not guaranteed.[16] The act does not even afford full protection from federally-financed demolition, merely requiring the agency to "take into account the effect of the undertaking" on any site in the National Register. A 1980 amendment to the act allows the private owner of an historic property to object to and block its listing on the Register. Also, a majority of the owners within a district may block listing of the district.

2. Compare with the principal case, Edwards v. First Bank of Dundee, 393 F.Supp. 680 (N.D.Ill.1975), which allowed residents standing to challenge demolition of a building on the National Register on the theory that the structure was a bank and relocation of a bank is subject to approval by the Federal Deposit Insurance Corporation which has responsibilities under both the National Environmental Policy Act and the National Historical Preservation Act. (The court did not reach the merits.) Also see Hart v. Denver Urban Renewal Auth., 551 F.2d 1178 (10th Cir.1977).

3. Although the National Historic Preservation Act imposes no duties other than consideration of the impact of federally funded projects on registered sites, Executive Order 11593 (May 13, 1971) provides in part that federal agencies shall institute procedures to assure that projects contribute to the preservation of historically and archeologically significant sites. Regulations promulgated pursuant to the Executive Order may be found at 36 C.F.R. Part 800. At least one court has held that the order and regulations may be enforced by a private right of action. Aluli v. Brown, 437 F.Supp. 602 (D.Haw.1977), reversed on other grounds 602 F.2d 876 (9th Cir.1979).

4. The Aluli case, cited in the previous note, and Romero–Barcelo v. Brown, 478 F.Supp. 646 (D.Puerto Rico 1979), modified 643 F.2d 835 (1st Cir.1981), both involve attempts to enjoin the United States Navy from using archeologically and environmentally significant areas for bombing, shelling and other training operations. Although both courts found violations of NEPA and the National Historic Preservation Act, the district court in Barcelo refused to enjoin the Navy for reasons of national defense and the Ninth Circuit in Aluli reversed an injunction requiring the Navy to file annual environmental impact statements.

PENN CENTRAL TRANSP. CO. v. CITY OF NEW YORK

Court of Appeals of New York, 1977.
42 N.Y.2d 324, 397 N.Y.S.2d 914, 366 N.E.2d 1271, affirmed
438 U.S. 104, 98 S.Ct. 2646, 57 L.Ed.2d 631 (1978).

[The Supreme Court opinion in this case, which appears in Chapter V, deals primarily with the "taking" issue.]

---

15. Ely v. Velde, 451 F.2d 1130 (4th Cir.1971), reversed on other grounds 497 F.2d 252 (4th Cir.1974).

16. South Hill Neighborhood Ass'n v. Romney, 421 F.2d 454 (6th Cir.1969), certiorari denied 397 U.S. 1025, 90 S.Ct. 1261, 25 L.Ed.2d 534 (1970).

BREITEL, CHIEF JUDGE.

In broad terms, the problem in this case is determining the scope of governmental power, within the Constitution, to preserve, without resorting to eminent domain, irreplaceable landmarks deemed to be of inestimable social or cultural significance. In controversy is the constitutionality of regulation which would prohibit appellants, owner and proposed developer of the air rights above Grand Central Terminal, from constructing an office building atop the terminal.

* * *

Plaintiffs, Penn Central Transportation Company and its affiliates, who have a fee interest in Grand Central Terminal, and UGP Properties, Inc., lessee of the development rights over the terminal, seek a declaration that the landmark preservation provisions of the Administrative Code of the City of New York, as applied to the terminal property, are unconstitutional. They also seek to enjoin defendants, the City of New York and the City Landmarks Preservation Commission, from enforcing those provisions against the subject property. Trial Term granted the requested relief, but a divided Appellate Division reversed and granted judgment to defendants. Plaintiffs appeal.

The order of the Appellate Division should be affirmed. Although government regulation is invalid if it denies a property owner all reasonable return, there is no constitutional imperative that the return embrace all attributes, incidental influences, or contributing external factors derived from the social complex in which the property rests. So many of these attributes are not the result of private effort or investment but of opportunities for the utilization or exploitation which an organized society offers to any private enterprise, especially to a public utility, favored by government and the public. These, too, constitute a background of massive social and governmental investment in the organized community without which the private enterprise could neither exist nor prosper. It is enough, for the limited purposes of a landmarking statute, albeit it is also essential, that the privately created ingredient of property receive a reasonable return. It is that privately created and privately managed ingredient which is the property on which the reasonable return is to be based. All else is society's contribution by the sweat of its brow and the expenditure of its funds. To that extent society is also entitled to its due.

Moreover, in this case, the challenged regulation provides Penn Central with transferable above-the-surface development rights which, because they may be attached to specific parcels of property, some already owned by Penn Central or its affiliates, may be considered as part of the owner's return on the terminal property.

Thus, the regulation does not deprive plaintiffs of property without due process of law, and should be upheld as a valid exercise of the police power.

* * *

This is not a zoning case. In many ways, the restrictions imposed on the use of the property are similar to zoning restrictions, but the purposes are different, and in determining whether regulation is reasonable, the purposes behind the regulation assume considerable significance * * *. Zoning restrictions operate to advance a comprehensive community plan for the common good. Each property owner in the zone is both benefited and restricted from exploitation, presumably without discrimination, except for permitted continuing nonconforming uses. The restrictions may be designed to maintain the general character of the area, or to assure orderly development, objectives inuring to the benefit of all, which property owners acting individually would find difficult or impossible to achieve * * *.

Nor does this case involve landmark regulation of a historic district. Historic district regulation, like zoning regulation, may be designed to maintain the character, both economic and esthetic or cultural, of an area (see Maher v. City of New Orleans, 5 Cir., 516 F.2d 1051, esp. p. 1060, cert. den. 426 U.S. 905, 96 S.Ct. 2225, 48 L.Ed.2d 830; Opinion of the Justices to the Senate, 333 Mass. 773, 778–780, 128 N.E.2d 557). The difference, generally, is that zoning does this largely by regulating construction of new buildings, while historic district regulation concentrates instead on preventing alteration or demolition of existing structures. In each case, owners although burdened by the restrictions also benefit, to some extent, from the furtherance of a general community plan.

Nor does this case partake of the principles applicable to a taking in eminent domain. As noted earlier, there is no taking for which just compensation must be paid. And it is the concept of just compensation which is so integrally related to value based on return. Instead, landmark regulation is a limitation on exploitation of property, an attribute shared with the classifications of zoning and historic districting. Yet landmark regulation is different because the burden of limitation is borne by a single owner. He may or may not benefit from that limitation but his neighbors most likely will. In contrast both an owner and his neighbors benefit to some degree and in some manner from zoning and historic districting.

Restrictions on alteration of individual landmarks are not designed to further a general community plan. Landmark restrictions are designed to prevent alteration or demolition of a single piece of property. To this extent, such restrictions, resemble "discriminatory" zoning restrictions, properly condemned, affecting properties singled out in a zoning district for more restrictive or more liberal zoning limitations * * * There is, however, a significant difference. Discriminatory zoning is condemned because there is no acceptable reason for singling out one particular parcel for different and less favorable treatment. When land-mark regulation is involved, there is such a reason: the cultural, archi-tectural, historical, or social significance attached to the affected parcel. Even when regulation is designed to achieve such an acceptable purpose, however, the landowner must be allowed a reasonable return or equiva-lent private use of his property * * * That is, in the case of commercial property, the owner must be assured of a continued reasonable return on the property.

* * *

Grand Central Terminal is no ordinary landmark. It may be true that no property has economic value in the absence of the society around it, but how much more true it is of a railroad terminal, set amid a metropolitan population, and entirely dependent on a heavy traffic of travelers to make it an economically feasible operation. Without people Grand Central would never have been a successful railroad terminal, and without the terminal, a major transportation center, the proposed build-ing site would be much less desirable for an office building.

Of course it may be argued that had Grand Central Terminal never been built, the area would not have developed as it has. Thus, the argument runs, construction of the terminal triggered growth of the area, and created much of the terminal property's current value. Indeed, the argument has some validity. But, in reality, it is of little moment which comes first, the terminal or the travelers. For it is the interaction of economic influences in the greatest megalopolis of the western hemi-sphere—the terminal initially drawing people to the area, and the society developing the area with shops, hotels, office buildings, and unmatched civil services—that has made the property so valuable. Neither factor alone accounts for the increase in the property's value; both, in tandem, have contributed to the increase.

* * *

To put the matter another way, the massive and indistinguishable public, governmental, and private contributions to a landmark like the Grand Central Terminal are inseparably joint, and for most of its existence, made both the terminal and the railroads of which it was an integral part, a great financial success for generations of stockholders and bondholders. Their investment has long been eliminated or impaired by the recent vicissitudes of the Penn Central complex. It is exceedingly difficult but imperative, nevertheless, to sort out the merged ingredients and to assess the rights and responsibilities of owner and society. A fair return is to be accorded the owner, but society is to receive its due for its share in the making of a once great railroad. The historical, cultural, and architectural resource that remains was neither created solely by the private owner nor solely by the society in which it was permitted to evolve.

* * *

The discussion thus far is in accord with the teachings of Lutheran Church in Amer. v. City of New York, 35 N.Y.2d 121, 359 N.Y.S.2d 7, 316 N.E.2d 305, supra. The Lutheran Church, owner of the landmark site, established, as plaintiffs here have not, that economic considerations did not permit maintenance of the landmark building in its existing form (id., p. 132, 359 N.Y.S.2d p. 16, 316 N.E.2d p. 312). Moreover, the Lutheran Church was a charitable institution which, over the years, did not and could not reap the same pecuniary benefits of massive governmental investment enjoyed by the railroads and Grand Central Terminal. Yet, the regulatory provisions prohibited replacement of the landmark building without any new ameliorative provisions, other than the pre-existing tax exemption to which it had always been entitled, to assure that the property remained capable of usefulness on a reasonable economic basis. The same problem was reached and discussed in Matter of Trustees of Sailors' Snug Harbor v. Platt, 29 A.D.2d 376, esp. p. 378, 288 N.Y.S.2d 314, 316. In recognizing the invalidity of the landmark regulation as applied to *Lutheran Church,* however, this court as had the court in the *Sailors' Snug Harbor* case, supra, declined to strike down the landmarks preservation provisions of the city administrative code * * *. In this case, by contrast, there has been no showing that the property, owned not by a charitable enterprise but by an entity existing to make a profit, is incapable in its economic context of producing a reasonable return, even if its development is limited.

Moreover, plaintiffs have not been wholly deprived of the development rights above the terminal. Those rights have been made transferable to other parcels of land in the vicinity, at least eight of them owned by Penn Central, including the sites of the Biltmore, Commodore, Barclay, and Roosevelt Hotels.

The many defects in New York City's program for development rights transfers have been detailed elsewhere (Costonis, The Chicago Plan: Incentive Zoning and the Preservation of Urban Landmarks, 85 Harv.L.Rev. 574, 585–589). The area to which transfer is permitted is severely limited, complex procedures are required to obtain a transfer permit, and the program, it has been said, has the unfortunate consequence of encouraging large, bulky buildings around landmarks which are dwarfed by comparison. But the possibility that a better program could have been devised does not preclude analysis and justification of the existing one in this particular application.

* * *

* * * Plaintiffs in this case have failed to meet that burden. In none of their analyses do they include the benefits provided to Penn Central's varied real estate holdings by the terminal's operation. These real, albeit indirect, benefits alone might suffice to provide Penn Central with a reasonable return. But there is more. The development rights above Grand Central Terminal have been made transferable, and could be transferred to several sites owned by Penn Central and suitable for office building construction. These substitute rights are valuable, and provide

significant, perhaps "fair", compensation for the loss of rights above the terminal itself. Hence, no constitutional violation has been established.

In times of easy affluence, preservation of historic landmarks through use of the eminent domain power might be desirable, or even required. But when a less expensive alternative is available, especially when a city is in financial distress, it should not be forced to choose between witnessing the demolition of its glorious past and mortgaging its hopes for the future. The landmark preservation provisions of the Administrative Code represent an effort to take a middle way (Marcus, Mandatory Development Rights Transfer and the Taking Clause: The Case of Manhattan's Tudor City Parks, 24 Buff.L.Rev. 77, 78, 107–110). The statute needs improvement. In some cases it protects property owners inadequately * * *. But, in its generality and as applied to Grand Central Terminal, the statute does not deprive plaintiffs of due process of law.

* * *

Accordingly, the order of the Appellate Division should be affirmed, with costs.

Notes

1. As noted by Judge Breitel in the principal case, the court had, in 1974, found the landmarks ordinance unconstitutional as applied to the Lutheran Church in America insofar as the commission had refused a permit for demolition of the J.P. Morgan house owned by the church and used as its national headquarters. Judge Breitel was one of the two dissenters in the Lutheran Church case. Note that in Penn Central the court distinguished the Lutheran Church case by drawing a distinction between a charitable property owner which had not received the accumulated economic benefits enjoyed by commercial ventures through surrounding property development. Is that a sufficient distinction to demarcate a valid regulation from a taking? After the Supreme Court affirmed Penn Central, a New York Court upheld the landmark designation of a charitable corporation in a fact situation much like that in Lutheran Church. See Society for Ethical Culture v. Spatt, 68 A.D.2d 112, 416 N.Y.S.2d 246 (1979), affirmed 51 N.Y.2d 449, 434 N.Y.S.2d 932, 415 N.E.2d 922 (1980).

2. Some years after the Penn Central decision the developer of a building site a few blocks from Grand Central Terminal sought a permit for a 74–story office building utilizing TDRs from the railroad. Public opposition to the proposal was strong and the commission denied the TDR transfer on the ground that the developer's parcel was not adjacent to the landmarked terminal. In 383 Madison Associates v. City of New York, 193 A.D.2d 518, 598 N.Y.S.2d 180 (1993), appeal dismissed 82 N.Y.2d 748, 602 N.Y.S.2d 806, 622 N.E.2d 307, cert. denied 511 U.S. 1081, 114 S.Ct. 1830, 128 L.Ed.2d 459 (1994) the court sided in part with the commission, rejecting the commission's finding that the proposed building would have a disproportionate impact on the neighborhood, but upholding the finding that even though a pattern of common ownership once joined the parcel with the terminal, because of intervening sales of the parcel in question and also sales of

intervening lots by Penn Central, the requisite "adjacency" was broken. The developer had argued that despite the sales of surface lots, underground tracks still connected the parcels.

3.   The question of landmark designation for religious structures has been especially controversial. A controversy in New York City over granting air rights development permission to St. Bartholomew's Church on Park Avenue raged for several years with a number of celebrity residents taking sides. A federal district court upheld the landmark designation of the church and the denial of the permit in Rector, Wardens, and Members of the Vestry of St. Bartholomew's Church v. City of New York, 728 F.Supp. 958 (S.D.N.Y. 1989) affirmed 914 F.2d 348 (2d Cir.1990), cert. denied 499 U.S. 905, 111 S.Ct. 1103, 113 L.Ed.2d 214 (1991). In 1987 Chicago amended its landmark ordinance to give owners of religious property the right to veto landmarking of property used for religious worship.

4.   The Religious Freedom Restoration Act required that government regulations affecting religion be justified by a compelling governmental interest.   Federal courts divided on the constitutionality of the act in cases requiring preservation of religious structures under landmark ordinances. In Flores v. City of Boerne, 73 F.3d 1352 (5th Cir.1996), the court upheld the validity of RFRA in a case challenging the inclusion of portions of a Roman Catholic Cathedral in the city's historic district. The Supreme Court granted certiorari in the case late in 1996 and on June 25, 1997, the Court held the act unconstitutional as exceeding the power of Congress (1997 WL 345322). Although RFRA is no longer a factor in deciding how courts should approach the application of local ordinances to historic or landmark religious buildings, under existing First Amendment free exercise of religion theory, churches can raise the free exercise argument. For example, in Keeler v. Mayor & City Council of Cumberland, 940 F.Supp. 879 (D.Md.1996) Cardinal Keeler sued to challenge the city's refusal to allow demolition of a monastery in the historic district, despite the church argument that maintenance of the building was financially ruinous. The district court held that RFRA was unconstitutional, but that the refusal to allow the demolition permit violated the church's freedom of religion and was a taking; the court also ordered that the church could proceed to try and establish damages for the taking.

5.   A Pennsylvania court upheld landmark designation for the interior as well as the exterior of an art deco movie house in Sameric Corp. of Chestnut St., Inc. v. City of Philadelphia, 125 Pa.Cmwlth. 520, 558 A.2d 155 (1989). When the case got to the Pennsylvania supreme court, an opinion was rendered that rejected the landmark ordinance, United Artists Theater Circuit, Inc. v. City of Philadelphia, 528 Pa. 12, 595 A.2d 6 (1991). Shortly thereafter, and after much public criticism, the court granted a reargument in the case. After reargument, the court partially reversed itself and held that the designation of the theater as a historical landmark without the consent of the owners did not constitute a taking; however, the court also held that the Philadelphia ordinance did not authorize designation of the interior of the building as historical. 535 Pa. 370, 635 A.2d 612 (1993). Compare Teachers Insurance and Annuity Ass'n of America v. City of New York, 82 N.Y.2d 35, 603 N.Y.S.2d 399, 623 N.E.2d 526 (1993) (decided one month earlier than the Pennsylvania case) where the court held that designation of the Four Seasons Restaurant inside the Seagram Building as a landmark was within the powers of the Landmark Preservation Commis-

sion. The owners argued, without success, that the interior of a restaurant is not the same sort of public space as the interior of a railroad station, which is habitually and customarily open to the public at large, the standard prescribed by the ordinance.

FGL & L PROPERTY CORP. v. CITY OF RYE

Court of Appeals of New York, 1985.
66 N.Y.2d 111, 495 N.Y.S.2d 321, 485 N.E.2d 986.

MEYER, JUDGE.

* * *

I

Plaintiff is the owner in fee of a parcel of land situated in the City of Rye (City) of approximately 22 acres on which are located the Jay Mansion, built in 1838 by Peter Jay, son of John Jay, the first Chief Justice of the United States Supreme Court, and another building known as the Carriage House, built around 1912 in the Colonial Revival style. There is some dispute between the parties concerning the historic or landmark significance of the Carriage House, but for purposes of this opinion we assume that both buildings have such significance. * * *

* * * In June 1983, the City Council adopted Local Law No. 5–1983, which added a new section 197–13.2 to the City Code creating the Alansten Landmarks Preservation District (LPD–A). As the revised zoning map demonstrates, and defendants do not deny, the only property zoned LPD–A was plaintiff's 22 acres. Plaintiff then began the present action, which in seven causes of action sought an injunction against enforcement of the section, a declaration that it is invalid as ultra vires, unconstitutional, site specific, spot zoning and not in accordance with a well-considered zoning plan, and money damages under 42 U.S.C.A. § 1983. * * *

II

The section as enacted declares that in order to provide for flexibility in the City's zoning "so that the significant historic buildings, the Jay Mansion and the Carriage House, and site features which characterize this site * * * are preserved for the future and that new construction be undertaken with care and consideration for these features and the environment", the new district is adopted. Subdivision B establishes standards for the new district, which include that "[t]he lot as approved shall have a minimum area of twenty-two (22) acres and shall be and remain in single ownership"; that "[t]he exterior of the Jay Mansion and Carriage House shall be rehabilitated and the interiors converted to residential use", for the Jay Mansion not to exceed three units and for the Carriage House not to exceed six; that there be a trapezoidal view way 90 feet in width at the rear of the Jay Mansion and 300 feet in width at the southerly property line; that the new dwelling units may not be occupied until the exteriors of the Jay Mansion and the Carriage House have been restored and the interiors converted to residential use and available for occupancy and that a bond be posted to assure such rehabilitation and conversion; and that the application for site plan approval be accompanied by, among other things, a draft condominium offering statement together with a draft of an easement and/or agreement for perpetual maintenance of the exteriors of the Jay Mansion and the Carriage House. Neither the statutes authorizing enactment of zoning provisions nor those dealing with historic landmarks empower the City Council to adopt a local law with such provisions, nor does anything in the Landmarks Preservation chapter of the City Code support its so doing.

* * *

B

Authority to enact section 197–13.2 of the Code of the City of Rye does not exist, therefore, unless it can be found in the historical preservation provisions contained in section 96–a and article 5–K of the General Municipal Law or the Landmarks Preservation provision of the Rye City Code (ch. 117).

Section 96–a of the General Municipal Law reads as follows: "In addition to any power or authority of a municipal corporation to regulate by planning or zoning laws and regulations or by local laws and regulations, the governing board or local legislative body of any county, city, town or village is empowered to provide by regulations, special conditions and restrictions for the protection, enhancement, perpetuation and use of places, districts, sites, buildings, structures, works of art, and other objects having a special character of special historical or aesthetic interest or value. Such regulations, special conditions and restrictions may include appropriate and reasonable control of the use or appearance of neighboring private property within public view, or both. In any such instance such measures, if adopted in the exercise of the police power, shall be reasonable and appropriate to the purpose, or if constituting a taking of private property shall provide for due compensation, which may include the limitation or remission of taxes." Article 5–K is broader in scope, covering historic preservation not only by regulation but by governmental acquisition as well. Section 119–bb(4) defines "historic preservation" to mean "for the purposes of this article and notwithstanding any other provision of law, the study, designation, protection, restoration, rehabilitation and use of buildings, structures, districts, areas, sites or objects significant in the history, architecture, archeology or culture of this state, its communities, or the nation." The operative provisions of the article are contained in section 119–dd, which is set forth in full in the margin.[17]

---

17. The section, entitled "Local historic preservation programs," reads as follows:

"In addition to existing powers and authorities for local historic preservation programs including existing powers and authorities to regulate by planning or zoning laws and regulations or by local laws and regulations for preservation of historic landmarks and districts and use of techniques including transfer of development rights, the legislative body of any county, city, town or village is hereby empowered to:

"1. Provide by regulations, special conditions and restrictions for the pro-

Of importance to the present issue is the fact that the regulation, special condition or restriction by which section 119–dd(1) authorizes control of private property is "for the protection, enhancement, perpetuation and use of places, districts, sites, buildings, structures". Nothing in the subdivision speaks to regulation of ownership. Noteworthy also is the fact that though section 119–bb(4) refers to "restoration" and "rehabilitation", those words are not to be found in section 119–dd(1), presumably because it was intended to permit a municipality acting under section 119–dd(3) after acquisition of a fee or lesser interest to restore and rehabilitate historic buildings and sites, but not to permit the municipality to impose an obligation to restore or rehabilitate such buildings or sites as remain in private ownership. Here the Code sections creating the Alansten Landmarks Preservation District not only mandate that the entire 22–acre district remain in single ownership but also impose upon the developer the duty of rehabilitating the exteriors of the Jay Mansion and the Carriage House, proscribe the use of any new dwelling unit until that has been done, thus effectively requiring that the cost of rehabilitation be shared by owners in the district of units other than the Jay Mansion and the Carriage House, and by dictating condominium ownership of the entire district impose the cost of maintenance of the exteriors of the Mansion and the Carriage House upon owners of such units as well.

The right to impose reasonable controls on the use and appearance of neighboring private property within public view, given by General Municipal Law §§ 96–a and 119–dd(1), cannot be stretched to cover payment of restoration and maintenance costs, for such a construction, which would impose those costs upon every unit in the district, not just

tection, enhancement, perpetuation and use of places, districts, sites, buildings, structures, works of art and other objects having a special character or special historical, cultural or aesthetic interest or value. Such regulations, special conditions and restrictions may include appropriate and reasonable control of the use or appearance of neighboring private property within the public view, or both.

"2. Establish a landmark or historical preservation board of commission with such powers as are necessary to carry out all or any of the authority possessed by the municipality for a historic preservation program, as the local legislative body deems appropriate.

"3. After due notice and public hearing, by purchase, gift, grant, bequest, devise, lease or otherwise, acquire the fee or any lesser interest, development right, easement, covenant or other contractual right necessary to achieve the purposes of this article, to historical or cultural property within its jurisdiction. After acquisition of any such interest pursuant to this subdivision, the effect of the acquisition on the valuation placed on any remaining private interest in such property for purposes of real estate taxation shall be taken into account.

"4. Designate, purchase, restore, operate, lease and sell historic buildings or structures. Sales of such buildings and structures shall be upon such terms and conditions as the local legislative body deems appropriate to insure the maintenance of the historic quality of the buildings and structures, after public notice is appropriately given at least thirty days prior to the anticipated date of availability and shall be for fair and adequate consideration of such buildings and structures which in no event shall be less than the expenses incurred by the municipality with respect to such buildings and structures for acquisition, restoration, improvement and interest charges.

"5. Provide for transfer of development rights for purposes consistent with the purposes of this article."

those "within public view," would render meaningless the limitation intended by those words which appear in both sections. Yet there is no question that such was the Council's intention, for its findings with respect to the final environmental impact statement flatly stated that "[o]nly under [condominium] ownership can the cost of maintaining the exteriors of the historic buildings be shared by all the homeowners", and that theme is repeatedly emphasized in the City's brief to this court. While that may be true, clearer authorization to enact such provisions than are contained in the General Municipal Law sections referred to is essential before section 197–13.2 can be upheld against the argument that it was beyond the City's power to enact.

Noteworthy also, in view of the requirement that the Mansion and Carriage House be completely restored before any other unit can be occupied is the absence from the General Municipal Law sections of authority to require restoration, as distinct from maintenance. Landmark and historic preservation laws normally prevent alteration or demolition of existing structures unless the owner can demonstrate hardship (*Penn Cent. Transp. Co. v. City of New York*, 42 N.Y.2d 324, 330, 397 N.Y.S.2d 914, 366 N.E.2d 1271, *affd.* 438 U.S. 104, 98 S.Ct. 2646, 57 L.Ed.2d 631), but if they place an undue and uncompensated burden on the individual owner may be held unconstitutional (*Lutheran Church in Am. v. City of New York*, 35 N.Y.2d 121, 129, 359 N.Y.S.2d 7, 316 N.E.2d 305) because "it forces the owner to assume the cost of providing a benefit to the public without recoupment" (*French Investing Co. v. City of New York*, 39 N.Y.2d 587, 596, 385 N.Y.S.2d 5, 350 N.E.2d 381; *see,* Dunham, *A Legal and Economic Basis For City Planning*, 58 Colum.L.Rev. 650, 665). Here, society at large bears no part of the cost of restoration, it is rather to be borne initially by plaintiff and ultimately by the purchasers of dwelling units within the district. Yet the City's expert appraiser agreed that restoration costs of approximately $627,000 for the Jay Mansion and $588,000 for the Carriage House would be required.

We do not hold that the General Municipal Law sections could not be drafted to impose restoration costs on an owner without violating the Constitution, nor need we reach the question whether as applied to plaintiff's property section 197–13.2 is constitutional. We hold rather that in light of the well-recognized rule that statutes are to be construed so as to avoid constitutional issues if such a construction is fairly possible * * * the General Municipal Law sections under consideration as presently written should be construed not to authorize imposition of restoration costs solely upon plaintiff and purchasers from plaintiff or maintenance costs upon purchasers of properties other than those to be preserved.

* * *

For the foregoing reasons, the order of the Appellate Division declaring Rye City Code § 197–13.2 invalid is affirmed, with costs.

WACHTLER, C.J., and JASEN, SIMONS, KAYE, ALEXANDER AND TITONE, JJ., concur.

Order affirmed, with costs.

Notes

1. After the decision in this case the county board of legislators voted to take the property by eminent domain, and the developer entered into negotiations to sell the property to the county. Although the developer purchased the Jay house and land for $1.1 million in 1983, she set a price of $13.6 million on the property. The county had appraised the property at $6.9 million in 1989 and did not want to pay much more than the appraisal. The county also figured that the cost to rehabilitate the buildings would range from $2 million to $2.5 million and annual maintenance would run about $185,000.

2. The use of the police power to designate individual buildings as landmarks has proven to be much more controversial than the designation of areas as historic districts. One obvious reason for the disparate treatment is the view that creation of an historic district usually enhances the value of all the property in the district while the designation of a single building as a landmark usually imposes uncompensated burdens on the property owner. The validity of landmark ordinances has been questioned in several states. The Texas courts have used the constitutional principles of vagueness and unlawful delegation of legislative powers to strike down landmark designation efforts at both the state and local levels. See Texas Antiquities Committee v. Dallas County Community College Dist., 554 S.W.2d 924 (Tex.1977) and Southern Nat'l Bank of Houston v. City of Austin, 582 S.W.2d 229 (Tex.Civ.App.1979). Other cases showing some hostility to landmark preservation (although they do not involve particular ordinances) are Galich v. Catholic Bishop of Chicago, 75 Ill.App.3d 538, 31 Ill.Dec. 370, 394 N.E.2d 572 (1979) and Hoboken Environment Committee, Inc. v. German Seaman's Mission of New York, 161 N.J.Super. 256, 391 A.2d 577 (1978). An intermediate appellate court upheld denial of a demolition permit for a church building in First Presbyterian Church of York v. City Council of City of York, 25 Pa.Cmwlth. 154, 360 A.2d 257 (1976), but a concurring opinion in the case made the following observation:

> * * * [T]he legislatures and courts are adding a new dimension which may do violence to constitutional private property rights, for now we hold that a private property owner must make his property available without compensation for public view. In effect, he must dedicate his property without compensation for public historical, aesthetic, educational, and museum purposes, which in reality are public uses. Under the provisions of the ordinance in question, the Church can permit the interior or rear portions of its property to rot or deteriorate in a burned condition in any manner it sees fit, but it can't touch that portion of its property viewable from the street without permission of the local governing body, which uses vague standards founded on aesthetics and historical values, two concepts upon which reasonable men can disagree.

There are no state health or safety standards involved whatsoever, rather the standards are based solely upon the feelings or observations of people interested in protecting neighboring properties in the historical district in the name of public welfare. I am concerned that we have reached a constitutional precipice and that an advancement of even a fraction of an inch will result in excessive governmental encroachment upon private property rights.

I want to make it clear that I agree with and applaud the scheme to protect, restore, and maintain places of historical value, but if the public wants to use, take, or apply a private property for that public purpose, then the public should pay for that laudatory purpose through constitutional means, e.g., eminent domain. In the past we have accomplished these purposes through parks and museums provided by public funds or the benevolence of private donors. Today we change that trend by our holding and instead provide for the establishment of public museums through restrictions on private property owners' rights. The very thought that the next step may be a governmental regulation that all buildings in York's historical district must be painted colonial blue is to me repugnant to the Constitution, and if anything like that should develop, perhaps that will be the place to draw the line.

Also see Lafayette Park Baptist Church v. Board of Adjustment of City of St. Louis, 599 S.W.2d 61 (Mo.App.1980), which involved a church seeking a demolition permit for a run-down structure it had purchased in order to expand parking facilities. Although the case deals with an historic district rather than a landmark designation, the opinion discusses the just compensation issue and the economics of preservation in a useful manner. Compare: Committee to Save the Bishop's House, Inc. v. Medical Center Hosp. of Vermont, Inc., 137 Vt. 142, 400 A.2d 1015 (1979). Another interesting case is Shubert Organization, Inc. v. Landmarks Preservation Comm'n of the City of New York, 166 A.D.2d 115, 570 N.Y.S.2d 504, appeal denied 79 N.Y.2d 751, 579 N.Y.S.2d 651, 587 N.E.2d 289, cert. denied 504 U.S. 946, 112 S.Ct. 2289, 119 L.Ed.2d 213 (1992). In this case the commission designated 45 theaters in central Manhattan as landmarks. The plaintiffs challenged the designation on the ground that the mass designation had nothing to do with the individual architectural worth of the theater buildings but was, instead, a back-door effort to create a theater district and to preserve the industry rather than buildings. The court ruled in favor of the designations.

In Prentiss v. City of South Pasadena, 15 Cal.App.4th 85, 18 Cal.Rptr.2d 641 (1993) the court sided with a homeowner whose application for a permit to build an addition was denied because the city concluded the existing house was a "qualified historic structure" and that the city had discretion to require that alterations to the home be done in a manner best preserving the historical character of the architecture. The court agreed that the issuance of a building permit where the application showed compliance with all building codes was a ministerial act, negating any discretionary power to impose conditions on the permit.

SECTION 2. DELAY AND LIMITATIONS ON THE RATE OF DEVELOPMENT

A. REGULATION OF URBAN GROWTH

GOLDEN v. PLANNING BD. OF TOWN OF RAMAPO

Court of Appeals of New York, 1972.
30 N.Y.2d 359, 334 N.Y.S.2d 138, 285 N.E.2d 291, appeal dismissed 409
U.S. 1003, 93 S.Ct. 436, 34 L.Ed.2d 294 and 93 S.Ct. 440 (1972).

SCILEPPI, JUDGE. Both cases arise out of the 1969 amendments to the Town of Ramapo's Zoning Ordinance. * * *

Experiencing the pressures of an increase in population and the ancillary problem of providing municipal facilities and services, the Town of Ramapo, as early as 1964, made application for grant under section 801 of the Housing Act of 1964 (78 U.S.Stat. 769) to develop a master plan. The plan's preparation included a four-volume study of the existing land uses, public facilities, transportation, industry and commerce, housing needs and projected population trends. The proposals appearing in the studies were subsequently adopted pursuant to section 272–a of the Town Law, Consol.Laws, c. 62, in July, 1966 and implemented by way of a master plan. The master plan was followed by the adoption of a comprehensive zoning ordinance. Additional sewage district and drainage studies were undertaken which culminated in the adoption of a capital budget, providing for the development of the improvements specified in the master plan within the next six years. Pursuant to section 271 of the Town Law, authorizing comprehensive planning, and as a supplement to the capital budget, the Town Board adopted a capital program which provides for the location and sequence of additional capital improvements for the 12 years following the life of the capital budget. The two plans, covering a period of 18 years, detail the capital improvements projected for maximum development and conform to the specifications set forth in the master plan, the official map and drainage plan.

Based upon these criteria, the Town subsequently adopted the subject amendments for the alleged purpose of eliminating premature subdivision and urban sprawl. Residential development is to proceed according to the provision of adequate municipal facilities and services, with the assurance that any concomitant restraint upon property use is to be of a "temporary" nature and that other private uses, including the construction of individual housing, are authorized.

The amendments did not rezone or reclassify any land into different residential or use districts, but, for the purposes of implementing the proposals appearing in the comprehensive plan, consist, in the main, of additions to the definitional sections of the ordinance, section 46–3, and the adoption of a new class of "Special Permit Uses", designated

"Residential Development Use." "Residential Development Use" is defined as "The erection or construction of dwellings on any vacant plots, lots or parcels of land" (§ 46–3, as amd.); and, any person who acts so as to come within that definition, "shall be deemed to be engaged in residential development which shall be a separate use classification under this ordinance and subject to the requirement of obtaining a special permit from the Town Board" (§ 46–3, as amd.).

The standards for the issuance of special permits are framed in terms of the availability to the proposed subdivision plat of five essential facilities or services: specifically (1) public sanitary sewers or approved substitutes; (2) drainage facilities; (3) improved public parks or recreation facilities, including public schools; (4) State, county or town roads—major, secondary or collector; and, (5) firehouses. No special permit shall issue unless the proposed residential development has accumulated 15 development points, to be computed on a sliding scale of values assigned to the specified improvements under the statute. Subdivision is thus a function of immediate availability to the proposed plat of certain municipal improvements; the avowed purpose of the amendments being to phase residential development to the Town's ability to provide the above facilities or services.

Certain savings and remedial provisions are designed to relieve of potentially unreasonable restrictions. Thus, the board may issue special permits vesting a present right to proceed with residential development in such year as the development meets the required point minimum, but in no event later than the final year of the 18–year capital plan. The approved special use permit is fully assignable, and improvements scheduled for completion within one year from the date of an application are to be credited as though existing on the date of the application. A prospective developer may advance the date of subdivision approval by agreeing to provide those improvements which will bring the proposed plat within the number of development points required by the amendments. And applications are authorized to the "Development Easement Acquisition Commission" for a reduction of the assessed valuation. Finally, upon application to the Town Board, the development point requirements may be varied should the board determine that such a variance or modification is consistent with the on-going development plan.

The undisputed effect of these integrated efforts in land use planning and development is to provide an over-all program of orderly growth and adequate facilities through a sequential development policy commensurate with progressing availability and capacity of public facilities. While its goals are clear and its purposes undisputably laudatory, serious questions are raised as to the manner in which these ends are to be effected, not the least of which relates to their legal viability under present zoning enabling legislation, particularly sections 261 and 263 of the Town Law. The owners of the subject premises argue, and the Appellate Division has sustained the proposition, that the primary purpose of the amending ordinance is to control or regulate population growth within the Town and as such is not within the authorized objectives of the zoning enabling legislation. We disagree.

In enacting the challenged amendments, the Town Board has sought to control subdivision in all residential districts, pending the provision (public or private) at some future date of various services and facilities. A reading of the relevant statutory provisions reveals that there is no specific authorization for the "sequential" and "timing" controls adopted here. That, of course, cannot be said to end the matter, for the additional inquiry remains as to whether the challenged amendments find their basis within the perimeters of the devices authorized and purposes sanctioned under current enabling legislation. Our concern is, as it should be, with the effects of the statutory scheme taken as a whole and its role in the propagation of a viable policy of land use and planning.

* * *

Of course, zoning historically has assumed the development of individual plats and has proven characteristically ineffective in treating with the problems attending subdivision and development of larger parcels, involving as it invariably does, the provision of adequate public services and facilities. To this end, subdivision control (Town Law, §§ 276, 277) purports to guide community development in the directions outlined here, while at the same time encouraging the provision of adequate facilities for the housing, distribution, comfort and convenience of local residents (Village of Lynbrook v. Cadoo, 252 N.Y. 308, 314, 169 N.E. 394, 396). It reflects in essence, a legislative judgment that the development of unimproved areas be accompanied by provision of essential facilities (Matter of Brous v. Smith, 304 N.Y. 164, 106 N.E.2d 503; see, also, 3 Rathkopf, The Law of Zoning and Planning [3d ed.], pp. 71–1 to 71–7; Cutler, Legal and Illegal Methods for Controlling Community Growth on the Urban Fringe, 1961 Wis.L.Rev. 370). And though it may not, in a definitional or conceptual sense be identified with the power to zone, it is designed to complement other land use restrictions, which, taken together, seek to implement a broader, comprehensive plan for community development (see Haar, The Master Plan: An Impermanent Constitution, 20 Law & Contemp.Probs. 353).

It is argued, nevertheless, that the timing controls currently in issue are not legislatively authorized since their effect is to prohibit subdivision absent precedent or concurrent action of the Town, and hence constitutes an unauthorized blanket interdiction against subdivision.

It is, indeed, true that the Planning Board is not in an absolute sense statutorily authorized to deny the right to subdivide. That is not, however, what is sought to be accomplished here. The Planning Board has the right to refuse approval of subdivision plats in the absence of those improvements specified in section 277, and the fact that it is the Town and not the subdividing owner or land developer who is required to make those improvements before the plat will be approved cannot be said to transform the scheme into an absolute prohibition any more than it would be so where it was the developer who refused to provide the facilities required for plat approval.[18] Denial of subdivision plat approval, invariably amounts to a prohibition against subdivision, albeit a conditional one (Real Property Law, Consol.Laws, c. 50, §§ 334–a, 335; see, also, 3 Rathkopf, Law of Zoning and Planning [3d ed.], pp. 71–122, supra); and to say that the Planning Board lacks the authority to deny subdivision rights is to mistake the nature of our inquiry which is essentially whether development may be conditioned pending the provision by the municipality of specified services and facilities. Whether it is the municipality or the developer who is to provide the improvements, the objective is the same—to provide adequate facilities, off-site and on-site; and in either case subdivision rights are conditioned, not denied.

* * *

Recognition of communal and regional interdependence, in turn, has resulted in proposals for schemes of regional and State-wide planning, in the hope that decisions would then correspond roughly to their level of impact (see, e.g., Proposed Land Use and Development Planning Law, §§ 2–101, 4–101, 4–102; ALI, A Model Land Development Code, art. 7). Yet, as salutary as such proposals may be, the power to zone under current law is vested in local municipalities, and we are constrained to resolve the issues accordingly. What does become more apparent in treating with the problem, however, is that though the issues are framed in terms of the developer's due process rights, those rights cannot, realistically speaking, be viewed separately and apart from the rights of others " 'in search of a [more] comfortable place to live.' " (Concord Twp. Appeal, 439 Pa. 466, 474, n. 6, 268 A.2d 765, 768, supra; National

---

18. The difference between the ordinary situation and the situation said to subsist here resides in the fact that where plat approval is denied for want of various improvements, the developer is free to provide those improvements at his own expense. In the ordinary case where the proposed improvements will not be completed before the plat is filed the developer's obligation is secured by a performance bond (Town Law, § 277; see, also, Control of Land Subdivision, Office of Planning Coordination [1968 ed.], p. 32). On the other hand, in the present case, plat approval is conditioned upon the Town's obligation to undertake improvements in roads, sewers and recreational facilities. As the Town may not be held to its program, practices do vary from year to year "and fiscal needs cannot be frozen beyond review and recall" (concurring opn. Hopkins, J., 37 A.D.2d 244, 324 N.Y.S.2d 187), the "patient owner" who relied on the capital program for qualification then is said to face the prospect that the improvements will be delayed and the impediments established by the ordinance further extended by the Town's failure to adhere to its own schedule.

The reasoning, as far as it goes, cannot be challenged. Yet, in passing of the validity of the ordinance on its face, we must assume not only the Town's good faith, but its assiduous adherence to the program's scheduled implementation. We cannot, it is true, adjudicate in a vacuum and we would be remiss not to consider the substantial risk that the Town may eventually default in its obligations. Yet, those are future events, the staple of a clairvoyant, not of a court in its deliberations. The threat of default is not so imminent or likely that it would warrant our prognosticating and striking down these amendments as invalid on their face. When and if the danger should materialize, the aggrieved landowner can seek relief by way of an article 78 proceeding, declaring the ordinance unconstitutional as applied to his property. Alternatively should it arise at some future point in time that the Town must fail in its enterprise, an action for a declaratory judgment will indeed prove the most effective vehicle for relieving property owners of what would constitute absolute prohibitions.

Land & Inv. Co. v. Easttown Twp. Bd. of Adj., 419 Pa. 504, 527–528, 215 A.2d 597, supra; see, generally, Sager, Tight Little Islands: Exclusionary Zoning, Equal Protection and the Indigent, 21 Stan.L.Rev. 767; Roberts, Demise of Property Law, 57 Cornell L.Rev. 1).

There is, then, something inherently suspect in a scheme which, apart from its professed purposes, effects a restriction upon the free mobility of a people until sometime in the future when projected facilities are available to meet increased demands. Although zoning must include schemes designed to allow municipalities to more effectively contend with the increased demands of evolving and growing communities, under its guise, townships have been wont to try their hand at an array of exclusionary devices in the hope of avoiding the very burden which growth must inevitably bring (see National Land & Inv. Co. v. Easttown Twp. Bd. of Adj., 419 Pa. 504, 532, 215 A.2d 597, supra; Girsh Appeal, 437 Pa. 237, 263 A.2d 395; Concord Twp. Appeal, 439 Pa. 466, 268 A.2d 765, supra; see, also, Roberts, Demise of Property Law, 57 Cornell L.Rev. 1, 5). Though the conflict engendered by such tactics is certainly real, and its implications vast, accumulated evidence, scientific and social, points circumspectly at the hazards of undirected growth and the naive, somewhat nostalgic imperative that egalitarianism is a function of growth. (See, generally, Lewis, Ecology and Politics: II, New York Times, March 6, 1972, p. 33, cols. 1, 2).

Of course, these problems cannot be solved by Ramapo or any single municipality, but depend upon the accommodation of widely disparate interests for their ultimate resolution. To that end, Statewide or regional control of planning would insure that interests broader than that of the municipality underlie various land use policies. Nevertheless, that should not be the only context in which growth devices such as these, aimed at population assimilation, not exclusion, will be sustained; especially where, as here, we would have no alternative but to strike the provision down in the wistful hope that the efforts of the State Office of Planning Coordination and the American Law Institute will soon bear fruit.

Hence, unless we are to ignore the plain meaning of the statutory delegation, this much is clear: phased growth is well within the ambit of existing enabling legislation. And, of course, it is no answer to point to emergent problems to buttress the conclusion that such innovative schemes are beyond the perimeters of statutory authorization. These considerations, admittedly real, to the extent which they are relevant, bear solely upon the continued viability of "localism" in land use regulation; obviously, they can neither add nor detract from the initial grant of authority, obsolescent though it may be. The answer which Ramapo has posed can by no means be termed definitive; it is, however, a first practical step toward controlled growth achieved without forsaking broader social purposes.

* * *

The subject ordinance is said to advance legitimate zoning purposes as it assures that each new home built in the township will have at least a minimum of public services in the categories regulated by the ordinance. The Town argues that various public facilities are presently being constructed but that for want of time and money it has been unable to provide such services and facilities at a pace commensurate with increased public need. It is urged that although the zoning power includes reasonable restrictions upon the private use of property, exacted in the hope of development according to well-laid plans, calculated to advance the public welfare of the community in the future (Arverne Bay Constr. Co. v. Thatcher, 278 N.Y. 222, 229, 15 N.E.2d 587, 590; Hesse v. Rath, 249 N.Y. 436, 438, 164 N.E. 342), the subject regulations go further and seek to avoid the increased responsibilities and economic burdens which time and growth must ultimately bring (see National Land & Inv. Co. v. Easttown Twp. Bd. of Adj., 419 Pa. 504, 532, 215 A.2d 597, supra; Girsh Appeal, 437 Pa. 237, 263 A.2d 395, supra; Concord Twp. Appeal, 439 Pa. 466, 268 A.2d 765, supra).

* * *

What we will not countenance, then, under any guise, is community efforts at immunization or exclusion. But, far from being exclusionary, the present amendments merely seek, by the implementation of sequential development and timed growth, to provide a balanced cohesive community dedicated to the efficient utilization of land. The restrictions conform to the community's considered land use policies as expressed in its comprehensive plan and represent a bona fide effort to maximize population density consistent with orderly growth. True other alternatives, such as requiring off-site improvements as a prerequisite to subdivision, may be available, but the choice as how best to proceed, in view of the difficulties attending such exactions (see Heyman & Gilhool, The Constitutionality of Imposing Increased Community Costs on New Suburban Residents through Subdivision Exactions, 73 Yale L.J. 1119; see, also, ALI, A Model Land Development Code, § 3–104, subd. [6]), cannot be faulted.

Perhaps even more importantly, timed growth, unlike the minimum lot requirements recently struck down by the Pennsylvania Supreme Court as exclusionary, does not impose permanent restrictions upon land use (see National Land & Inv. Co. v. Easttown Twp. Bd. of Adj., 419 Pa. 504, 215 A.2d 597, supra; Concord Twp. Appeal, 439 Pa. 466, 268 A.2d 765, supra). Its obvious purpose is to prevent premature subdivision absent essential municipal facilities and to insure continuous development commensurate with the Town's obligation to provide such facilities. They seek, not to freeze population at present levels but to maximize growth by the efficient use of land, and in so doing testify to this community's continuing role in population assimilation. In sum, Ramapo asks not that it be left alone, but only that it be allowed to prevent the kind of deterioration that has transformed well-ordered and thriving residential communities into blighted ghettos with attendant hazards to health, security and social stability—a danger not without substantial basis in fact.

* * *

The proposed amendments have the effect of restricting development for onwards to 18 years in certain areas. Whether the subject parcels will be so restricted for the full term is not clear, for it is equally probable that the proposed facilities will be brought into these areas well before that time. Assuming, however, that the restrictions will remain outstanding for the life of the program, they still fall short of a confiscation within the meaning of the Constitution.

An ordinance which seeks to permanently restrict the use of property so that it may not be used for any reasonable purpose must be recognized as a taking: The only difference between the restriction and an outright taking in such a case "is that the restriction leaves the owner subject to the burden of payment of taxation, while outright confiscation would relieve him of that burden" (Arverne Bay Constr. Co. v. Thatcher, 278 N.Y. 222, 232, 15 N.E.2d 587, 592, supra). An appreciably different situation obtains where the restriction constitutes a *temporary* restriction, promising that the property may be put to a profitable use within a reasonable time. The hardship of holding unproductive property for some time might be compensated for by the ultimate benefit inuring to the individual owner in the form of a substantial increase in valuation; or, for that matter, the landowner might be compelled to chafe under the temporary restriction, without the benefit of such compensation, when that burden serves to promote the public good (cf. Arverne Bay Constr. Co. v. Thatcher, 278 N.Y. 222, 232, 15 N.E.2d 587, 592, supra).

We are reminded, however, that these restrictions threaten to burden individual parcels for as long as a full generation and that such a restriction cannot, in any context, be viewed as a temporary expedient. The Town, on the other hand, contends that the landowner is not deprived of either the best use of his land or of numerous other appropriate uses, still permitted within various residential districts, including the construction of a single-family residence, and consequently, it cannot be deemed confiscatory. Although no proof has been submitted on reduction of value, the landowners point to obvious disparity between the value of the property, if limited in use by the subject amendments and its value for residential development purposes and argue that the diminution is so considerable that for all intents and purposes the land cannot presently or in the near future be put to profitable or beneficial use, without violation of the restrictions.

* * *

Without a doubt restrictions upon the property in the present case are substantial in nature and duration. They are not, however, absolute. The amendments contemplate a definite term, as the development points are designed to operate for a maximum period of 18 years and during that period, the Town is committed to the construction and installation of capital improvements. The net result of the on-going development provision is that individual parcels may be committed to a residential development use prior to the expiration of the maximum period. Similarly, property owners under the terms of the amendments may elect to accelerate the date of development by installing, at their own expense, the necessary public services to bring the parcel within the required number of development points. While even the best of plans may not always be realized, in the absence of proof to the contrary, we must assume the Town will put its best effort forward in implementing the physical and fiscal timetable outlined under the plan. Should subsequent events prove this assumption unwarranted, or should the Town because of some unforeseen event fail in its primary obligation to these landowners, there will be ample opportunity to undo the restrictions upon default. For the present, at least, we are constrained to proceed upon the assumption that the program will be fully and timely implemented (n. 7, p. 373, 334 N.Y.S.2d p. 148, 285 N.E.2d p. 298, supra).

* * *

In sum, where it is clear that the existing physical and financial resources of the community are inadequate to furnish the essential services and facilities which a substantial increase in population requires, there is a rational basis for "phased growth" and hence, the challenged ordinance is not violative of the Federal and State Constitutions. Accordingly, the order appealed from should be reversed and the actions remitted to Special Term for entry of a judgment declaring section 46–13.1 of the Town Ordinance constitutional.

BREITEL, JUDGE (dissenting). The limited powers of district zoning and subdivision regulation delegated to a municipality do not include the power to impose a moratorium on land development. Such conclusion is dictated by settled doctrine that a municipality has only those powers, and especially land use powers, delegated or necessarily implied.

But there is more involved in these cases than the arrogation of undelegated powers. Raised are vital constitutional issues, and, most important, policy issues trenching on grave domestic problems of our time, without the benefit of a legislative determination which would reflect the interests of the entire State. The policy issues relate to needed housing, planned land development under government control, and the exclusion in effect or by motive, of walled-in urban populations of the middle class and the poor. The issues are raised by a town ordinance, which, as one of the Appellate Division Justices noted below, reflect a parochial stance without regard to its impact on the region or the State, especially if it becomes a valid model for many other towns similarly situated.

* * *

It is important to note how radically the Ramapo scheme differs from those used and adopted under existing enabling acts. The zoning acts, starting from 50 years ago, based on national models, provided simply for district zoning to control population density and some planning to protect preferred uses of land, such as single-family dwellings, from other uses considered less desirable or even harmful to residential living or environmental balance. Since the beginning, in this State and elsewhere, by amendment to the enabling acts by the Legislature, provision has been made for subdivision planning and, in some instances, planned unit development, to prevent large-scale developers from dumping homes wholesale in raw land areas without private and, to some extent, public facilities essential to the use of the homes. In more recent years, since World War II, the need for a much enlarged kind of land planning has become critical. The evils of uncontrolled urban sprawl on the one hand, and the suburban and exurban pressure to exclude urban population on the other hand, have created a massive conflict, with social and economic implications of the gravest character. Throughout the nation the conflict has risen or threatened and solutions are being sought in careful intensive examination of the problem affecting those within and those without the localities to be regulated.

* * *

Decisive of the present appeals, however, is the absence in the town of legislative authorization to postpone growth, let alone to establish unilaterally phased population levels, through the expedient of barring residential development for scheduled periods of up to 18 years. It has always been the rule that a municipality has only those land use powers delegated or necessarily implied (1 Anderson, American Law of Zoning, § 3.10). Existing enabling legislation does not grant the power upon which the Ramapo ordinance rests. And for policy reasons, one should not strain the reading of the enabling acts, even if straining would avail, to distort them, beyond any meaning ever attributed to them, except by the ingenious draftsmen of the Ramapo ordinance.

* * *

Going beyond district zoning, the statute provides for subdivision platting (§ 276 et seq.). It does not provide support for the procedures essayed in the Ramapo ordinance. But what is important is that even intensive subdivision regulation was required to be authorized by statute before towns could control subdivision developers. Statutory authorization was all the more important because the then drastic regulation required the developers to provide private and public facilities for the wholesale distribution of homes and to provide moneys and bonds to make sure that they performed as promised. Notably, no developer is forbidden to develop for a period of years.

The urgent need to control the tempo and sequence of land development has been recognized by courts, government commissions, and commentators (see Cutler, Legal and Illegal Methods of Controlling Community Growth, 1961 Wis.L.Rev. 370; Fagin, Regulating the Timing of Urban Development, 20 Law & Contemp.Prob. 298; Report of National Commission on Urban Problems, pp. 245, 251; New York State, Office of Planning Coordination, Planning Law Revision Study, Draft Outline, pp. 13, 17). Techniques to control the rate, nature and sequence of community development are plentiful although not all are presently authorized or comport with constitutional limitations. Thus, in Albrecht Realty Co. v. Town of New Castle, 8 Misc.2d 255, 167 N.Y.S.2d 843, the Town of New Castle in Westchester County sought to control growth by placing a moratorium on the issuance of building permits for unspecified periods and with no apparent object other than controlling growth. The measure was voided because the enabling act did not authorize "a direct regulation of the rate of growth" (at p. 256, 167 N.Y.S.2d at p. 844). For another technique, in California the purchase of "development rights" or a time-limited easement by the local government reportedly has been employed. The community is saved the expense of purchasing the fee simple of the owner. It obtains flexibility by the power to release land for development while landowners are compensated. The method is also said to justify assessing or taxing the owner at a lower rate (see Cutler, op. cit., supra, at p. 394). A similar approach is followed in England and has been recently recommended by the President's National Commission on Urban Problems (Report, at p. 251; Mandelker, Notes from the English: Compensation in Town and County Planning, 49 Cal.L.Rev. 699; see, also, Ann., Zoning—With Compensation, 41 ALR3d 636).

* * *

The exclusionary effect of local efforts to preserve the country's Edens has been largely noted. Professor Roberts, in an important essay, explores the conditions bedevilling places like Ramapo but also assesses the calamitous effects of ill-advised parochial devices (E.F. Roberts, The Demise of Property Law, 57 Cornell L.Rev. 1). The problems of development of the larger community run so deep, he suggests that: " 'Snob zoning,' of course, may best be 'solved' by the legislature. This really is the lesson contained in *Girsh* which seems, moderately enough, to suggest that a regional planning mechanism should be devised to create a pluralist suburbia in which each class could find its proper place. More interest, however, is being generated by the notion of statewide land-use planning which presumably would allow each class its niche outside center city. Whether this interest in formulating state planning derives from a concern for the lower orders or reflects instead an irritation at the lack of order when a multitude of tiny hamlets makes any planning impossible, is difficult to tell." (at p. 37). To leave vital decisions controlling the mix and timing of development to the unfettered discretion of the local community invites disaster.

* * *

A glance at history suggests that Ramapo's plan to have public services installed in advance of development is unrealistic. Richard Babcock, the distinguished practitioner in land development law, some years ago addressed himself to the natural desire of communities to stay development while they caught up with the inexorable thrust of population growth and movement. He observed eloquently that this country was built and is still being built by people who moved about, innovated, pioneered, and created industry and employment, and thereby provided both the need and the means for the public services and facilities that followed (Babcock, The Zoning Game, at pp. 149–150). Thus, the movement has not been in the other direction, first the provision of public and utility services and then the building of homes, farms, and businesses. This court has said as much, in effect, in Westwood Forest Estates v. Village of South Nyack, 23 N.Y.2d 424, 297 N.Y.S.2d 129, 244 N.E.2d 700, supra, unanimously and in reliance on commonplace authority and precedent.

As said earlier, when the problem arose outside the State the judicial response has been the same, frustrating communities, intent on walling themselves from the mainstream of development, namely, that the effort was invalid under existing enabling acts or unconstitutional (National Land & Inv. Co. v. Easttown Twp. Bd. of Adj., 419 Pa. 504, 215 A.2d 597, supra; Girsh Appeal, 437 Pa. 237, 263 A.2d 395, supra; Bristow v. City of Woodhaven, 35 Mich.App. 205, 192 N.W.2d 322, supra; Lakeland Bluff v. County of Will, 114 Ill.App.2d 267, 252 N.E.2d 765, supra; Concord Twp. Appeal, 439 Pa. 466, 268 A.2d 765, supra; Oakwood at Madison v. Township of Madison, 117 N.J.Super. 11, 283 A.2d 353 supra). The response may not be charged to judicial conservatism or self-restraint. In short, it has not been illiberal. It has indeed reflected the larger understanding that American society is at a critical crossroads in the accommodation of urbanization and suburban living, with effects that are no longer confined, bad as they are, to ethnic exclusion or "snob" zoning (see Roberts, op. cit., supra, at pp. 36–49). Ramapo would preserve its nature, delightful as that may be, but the supervening question is whether it alone may decide this or whether it must be decided by the larger community represented by the Legislature. Legally, politically, economically, and sociologically, the base for determination must be larger than that provided by the town fathers.

Accordingly, I dissent and vote to affirm the orders in both cases.

FULD, C.J., and BURKE, BERGAN and GIBSON, JJ., concur with SCILEPPI, J.

BREITEL, J., dissents and votes to affirm in a separate opinion in which JASEN, J., concurs.

Notes

1. The Ramapo case has spawned a great deal of literature. Some of the more interesting articles on the case and its implications are Bosselman, Can the Town of Ramapo Pass a Law to Bind the Rights of the Whole World? 1 Fla.St.U.L.Rev. 234 (1973) and O'Keefe, Time Controls on Land Use: Prophylactic Law for Planners, 57 Cornell L.Rev. 827 (1972). Also see Freilich and Greis, Timing and Sequencing Development: Controlling Growth, in Burchell and Listokin (ed.), Future Land Use, p. 59 (1975). A

comprehensive treatment of the problem is found in Management & Control of Growth (Urban Land Institute 1975).

2. Is the Ramapo case really as significant as the court and the literature seem to suggest? For a view that Ramapo is no more than a variation on traditional subdivision control, see Hagman, Commentary—Land Use Controls: Emerging and Proposed Reforms, in Burchell and Listokin, supra, p. 126. On the other hand, consider: (a) the legitimacy of a plan which was designed to exclude or greatly limit growth as opposed to one which sought orderly growth in keeping with a reasonable program of expansion; and (b) the effect, if any, under the Constitution of limitations which impinge upon the right to travel and move freely from town to town and from state to state.

CONSTRUCTION INDUSTRY ASS'N OF SONOMA COUNTY v. CITY OF PETALUMA

United States Court of Appeals, Ninth Circuit, 1975.
522 F.2d 897, certiorari denied 424 U.S. 934,
96 S.Ct. 1148, 47 L.Ed.2d 342 (1976).

CHOY, CIRCUIT JUDGE: The City of Petaluma (the City) appeals from a district court decision voiding as unconstitutional certain aspects of its five-year housing and zoning plan. We reverse.

STATEMENT OF FACTS

The City is located in southern Sonoma County, about 40 miles north of San Francisco. In the 1950's and 1960's, Petaluma was a relatively self-sufficient town. It experienced a steady population growth from 10,315 in 1950 to 24,870 in 1970. Eventually, the City was drawn into the Bay Area metropolitan housing market as people working in San Francisco and San Rafael became willing to commute longer distances to secure relatively inexpensive housing available there. By November 1972, according to unofficial figures, Petaluma's population was at 30,500, a dramatic increase of almost 25 per cent in little over two years.

The increase in the City's population, not surprisingly, is reflected in the increase in the number of its housing units. From 1964 to 1971, the following number of residential housing units were completed:

1964	270	1968	379
1965	440	1969	358
1966	321	1970	591
1967	234	1971	891

In 1970 and 1971, the years of the most rapid growth, demand for housing in the City was even greater than above indicated. Taking 1970 and 1971 together, builders won approval of a total of 2000 permits although only 1482 were actually completed by the end of 1971.

Alarmed by the accelerated rate of growth in 1970 and 1971, the demand for even more housing, and the sprawl of the City eastward, the City adopted a temporary freeze on development in early 1971. The construction and zoning change moratorium was intended to give the City Council and the City planners an opportunity to study the housing and zoning situation and to develop short and long range plans. The Council made specific findings with respect to housing patterns and availability in Petaluma, including the following: That from 1960–1970 housing had been in almost unvarying 6000 square-foot lots laid out in regular grid patterns; that there was a density of approximately 4.5 housing units per acre in the single-family home areas; that during 1960–1970, 88 per cent of housing permits issued were for single-family detached homes; that in 1970, 83 per cent of Petaluma's housing was single-family dwellings; that the bulk of recent development (largely single-family homes) occurred in the eastern portion of the City, causing a large deficiency in moderately priced multi-family and apartment units on the east side.

To correct the imbalance between single-family and multi-family dwellings, curb the sprawl of the City on the east, and retard the accelerating growth of the City, the Council in 1972 adopted several resolutions, which collectively are called the "Petaluma Plan" (the Plan).

The Plan, on its face limited to a five-year period (1972–1977),[19] fixes a housing development growth rate not to exceed 500 dwelling units per year.[20] Each dwelling unit represents approximately three people. The 500–unit figure is somewhat misleading, however, because it applies only to housing units (hereinafter referred to as "development-units") that are part of projects involving five units or more. Thus, the 500–unit figure does not reflect any housing and population growth due to construction of single-family homes or even four-unit apartment buildings not part of any larger project.

The Plan also positions a 200 foot wide "greenbelt" around the City,[21] to serve as a boundary for urban expansion for at least five years, and with respect to the east and north sides of the City, for perhaps ten to fifteen years. One of the most innovative features of the Plan is the Residential Development Control System which provides procedures and criteria for the award of the annual 500 development-unit permits. At the heart of the allocation procedure is an intricate point system, whereby a builder accumulates points for conformity by his projects with the City's general plan and environmental design plans, for good archi-

---

19. The district court found that although the Plan is ostensibly limited to a five-year period, official attempts have been made to perpetuate the Plan beyond 1977. Such attempts include the urban extension line (see text infra) and the agreement to purchase from the Sonoma County Water Agency only 9.8 million gallons of water per day through the year 1990. This flow is sufficient to support a population of 55,000. If the City were to grow at a rate of about 500 housing units per year (approximately three persons per unit), the City would reach a population of 55,000 about the year 1990. The 55,000 figure was mentioned by City officials as the projected optimal (and maximum) size of Petaluma. See, e.g., R.T. at 135–43, 145–46.

20. The allotment for each year is not an inflexible limitation. The Plan does provide for a 10 percent variance (50 units) below or above the 500 unit annual figure, but the expectation of the Council is that not more than 2500 units will be constructed during the five-year period.

21. At some points this urban extension line is about one-quarter of a mile beyond the present City limits.

tectural design, and for providing low and moderate income dwelling units and various recreational facilities. The Plan further directs that allocations of building permits are to be divided as evenly as feasible between the west and east sections of the City and between single-family dwellings and multiple residential units (including rental units),[22] that the sections of the City closest to the center are to be developed first in order to cause "infilling" of vacant area, and that 8 to 12 per cent of the housing units approved be for low and moderate income persons.

In a provision of the Plan, intended to maintain the close-in rural space outside and surrounding Petaluma, the City solicited Sonoma County to establish stringent subdivision and appropriate acreage parcel controls for the areas outside the urban extension line of the City and to limit severely further residential infilling.

PURPOSE OF THE PLAN

The purpose of the Plan is much disputed in this case. According to general statements in the Plan itself, the Plan was devised to ensure that "development in the next five years will take place in a reasonable, orderly, attractive manner, rather than in a completely haphazard and unattractive manner." The controversial 500–unit limitation on residential development-units was adopted by the City "[i]n order to protect its small town character and surrounding open space."[23] The other features of the Plan were designed to encourage an east-west balance in development, to provide for variety in densities and building types and wide ranges in prices and rents, to ensure infilling of close-in vacant areas, and to prevent the sprawl of the City to the east and north. The Construction Industry Association of Sonoma County (the Association) argues and the district court found, however, that the Plan was primarily enacted "to limit Petaluma's demographic and market growth rate in housing and in the immigration of new residents." Construction Industry Ass'n v. City of Petaluma, 375 F.Supp. 574, 576 (N.D.Cal.1974).

MARKET DEMAND AND EFFECT OF THE PLAN

In 1970 and 1971, housing permits were allotted at the rate of 1000 annually, and there was no indication that without some governmental control on growth consumer demand would subside or even remain at the 1000–unit per year level. Thus, if Petaluma had imposed a flat 500–unit limitation on *all* residential housing, the effect of the Plan would clearly be to retard to a substantial degree the natural growth rate of the City. Petaluma, however, did not apply the 500–unit limitation across

---

22. By providing for the increase of multi-family dwellings (including townhouses as well as rental apartments), the Plan allows increased density. Whereas, during the years just preceding the Plan, housing density was about 4.5 units per acre, under the Plan single-family housing will consist of not only low (4.5 units per acre) but also medium density (4.5 to 10 units per acre). And multi-family housing, to comprise about half of the housing under the Plan,

will be built at a density of 10 or more units per acre.

23. After the appellees initiated this suit, the City attempted to show that the Plan was implemented to prevent the overtaxing of available water and sewage facilities. We find it unnecessary, however, to consider the claim that sewage and water problems justified implementation of the Plan.

the board, but instead exempted all projects of four units or less. Because appellees failed to introduce any evidence whatsoever as to the number of exempt units expected to be built during the five-year period, the effect of the 500 *development-unit* limitation on the natural growth in housing is uncertain. For purposes of this decision, however, we will assume that the 500 development-unit growth rate is in fact below the reasonably anticipated market demand for such units and that absent the Petaluma Plan, the City would grow at a faster rate.

According to undisputed expert testimony at trial, if the Plan (limiting housing starts to approximately 6 per cent of existing housing stock each year) were to be adopted by municipalities throughout the region, the impact on the housing market would be substantial. For the decade 1970 to 1980, the shortfall in needed housing in the region would be about 105,000 units (or 25 per cent of the units needed). Further, the aggregate effect of a proliferation of the Plan throughout the San Francisco region would be a decline in regional housing stock quality, a loss of the mobility of current and prospective residents and a deterioration in the quality and choice of housing available to income earners with real incomes of $14,000 per year or less. If, however, the Plan were considered by itself and with respect to Petaluma only, there is no evidence to suggest that there would be a deterioration in the quality and choice of housing available there to persons in the lower and middle income brackets. Actually, the Plan increases the availability of multi-family units (owner-occupied and rental units) and low-income units which were rarely constructed in the pre-Plan days.

COURT PROCEEDINGS

Two landowners (the Landowners) and the Association instituted this suit under 28 U.S.C.A. §§ 1331, 1343 and 42 U.S.C.A. § 1983 against the City and its officers and council members, claiming that the Petaluma Plan was unconstitutional. The district court ruled that certain aspects of the Plan unconstitutionally denied the right to travel insofar as they tended "to limit the natural population growth of the area." 375 F.Supp., at 588. The court enjoined the City and its agents from implementing the unconstitutional elements of the Plan, but the order was stayed by Justice Douglas pending this appeal.

* * *

Appellees claim that the Plan is arbitrary and unreasonable and, thus, violative of the due process clause of the Fourteenth Amendment. According to appellees, the Plan is nothing more than an exclusionary zoning device,[24] designed solely to insulate Petaluma from the urban

---

24. "Exclusionary zoning" is a phrase popularly used to describe suburban zoning regulations which have the effect, if not also the purpose, of preventing the migration of low and middle-income persons. Since a large percentage of racial minorities fall within the low and middle income brackets, exclusionary zoning regulations may also effectively wall out racial minorities. See generally Aloi, Goldberg & White, Racial and Economic Segregation by Zoning: Death Knell for Home Rule?, 1969 U.Tol.L.Rev. 65 (1969); Bigham & Bostick, Exclusionary Zoning Practices: An Exami-

complex in which it finds itself. The Association and the Landowners reject, as falling outside the scope of any legitimate governmental interest, the City's avowed purposes in implementing the Plan—the preservation of Petaluma's small town character and the avoidance of the social and environmental problems caused by an uncontrolled growth rate.

In attacking the validity of the Plan, appellees rely heavily on the district court's finding that the express purpose and the actual effect of the Plan is to exclude substantial numbers of people who would otherwise elect to move to the City. 375 F.Supp. at 581. The existence of an exclusionary purpose and effect reflects, however, only *one* side of the zoning regulation. Practically all zoning restrictions have as a purpose and effect the *exclusion* of some activity or type of structure or a certain density of inhabitants. And in reviewing the reasonableness of a zoning ordinance, our inquiry does not terminate with a finding that it is for an exclusionary purpose. We must determine further whether the *exclusion* bears any rational relationship to a *legitimate state interest.* If it does not, then the zoning regulation is invalid. If, on the other hand, a legitimate state interest is furthered by the zoning regulation, we must defer to the legislative act. Being neither a super legislature nor a zoning board of appeal, a federal court is without authority to weigh and reappraise the factors considered or ignored by the legislative body in passing the challenged zoning regulation.[25] The reasonableness, not the wisdom, of the Petaluma Plan is at issue in this suit.

In determining whether the City's interest in preserving its small town character and in avoiding uncontrolled and rapid growth falls within the broad concept of "public welfare," we are considerably assisted by two recent cases. *Belle Terre,* supra, and Ybarra v. Town of Los Altos Hills, 503 F.2d 250 (9th Cir.1974) each of which upheld as not unreasonable a zoning regulation much more restrictive than the Petaluma Plan, are dispositive of the due process issue in this case.

In *Belle Terre* the Supreme Court rejected numerous challenges to a village's restricting land use to one-family dwellings excluding lodging houses, boarding houses, fraternity houses or multiple-dwelling houses. By absolutely prohibiting the construction of or conversion of a building to other than single-family dwelling, the village ensured that it would never grow, if at all, much larger than its population of 700 living in 220

nation of the Current Controversy, 25 Vand.L.Rev. 1111 (1972); Davidoff & Davidoff, Opening the Suburbs: Toward Inclusionary Land Use Controls, 22 Syracuse L.Rev. 509 (1971); Note, Exclusionary Zoning and Equal Protection, 84 Harv.L.Rev. 1645 (1971).

Most court challenges to and comment upon so-called exclusionary zoning focus on such traditional zoning devices as height limitations, minimum square footage and minimum lot size requirements, and the prohibition of multi-family dwellings or mobile homes. The Petaluma Plan is unique in

that although it assertedly slows the growth rate it replaces the past pattern of single-family detached homes with an assortment of housing units, varying in price and design.

25. Appellees' brief is unnecessarily oversize (125 pages) mainly because it is rife with quotations from writers on regional planning, economic regulation and sociological policies and themes. These types of considerations are more appropriate for legislative bodies than for courts.

residences. Nonetheless, the Court found that the prohibition of boarding houses and other multi-family dwellings was reasonable and within the public welfare because such dwellings present urban problems, such as the occupation of a given space by more people, the increase in traffic and parked cars and the noise that comes with increased crowds. According to the Court,

> "A quiet place where yards are wide, people few, and motor vehicles restricted are legitimate guidelines in a land-use project addressed to family needs. This goal is a permissible one within Berman v. Parker, supra. The police power is not confined to elimination of filth, stench, and unhealthy places. It is ample to lay out zones where family values, youth values, and the blessings of quiet seclusion, and clean air make the area a sanctuary for people."

416 U.S. at 9, 94 S.Ct. at 1541. While dissenting from the majority opinion in *Belle Terre* on the ground that the regulation unreasonably burdened the exercise of First Amendment associational rights, Mr. Justice Marshall concurred in the Court's express holding that a local entity's zoning power is extremely broad:

> "[L]ocal zoning authorities may properly act in furtherance of the objectives asserted to be served by the ordinance at issue here: *restricting uncontrolled growth,* solving traffic problems, keeping rental costs at a reasonable level, and making the community attractive to families. The police power which provides the justification for zoning is not narrowly confined. And, it is appropriate that we afford zoning authorities *considerable latitude in choosing the means by which to implement such purposes.*"

416 U.S. at 13–14, 94 S.Ct. at 1543 (Marshall, J., dissenting) (emphasis added) (citations omitted).

Following the *Belle Terre* decision, this court in *Los Altos Hills* had an opportunity to review a zoning ordinance providing that a housing lot shall contain not less than one acre and that no lot shall be occupied by more than one primary dwelling unit. The ordinance as a practical matter prevented poor people from living in Los Altos Hills and restricted the density, and thus the population, of the town. This court, nonetheless, found that the ordinance was rationally related to a legitimate governmental interest—*the preservation of the town's rural environment*—and, thus, did not violate the equal protection clause of the Fourteenth Amendment. 503 F.2d at 254.

Both the Belle Terre ordinance and the Los Altos Hills regulation had the purpose and effect of permanently restricting growth; nonetheless, the court in each case upheld the particular law before it on the ground that the regulation served a legitimate governmental interest falling within the concept of the public welfare: the preservation of quiet family neighborhoods (Belle Terre) and the preservation of a rural environment (Los Altos Hills). Even less restrictive or exclusionary than the above zoning ordinances in the Petaluma Plan which, unlike those ordinances, does not freeze the population at present or near-present levels.[26] Further, unlike the Los Altos Hills ordinance and the various zoning regulations struck down by state courts in recent years, the Petaluma Plan does not have the undesirable effect of walling out any particular income class nor any racial minority group.[27]

Although we assume that some persons desirous of living in Petaluma will be excluded under the housing permit limitation and that, thus, the Plan may frustrate some legitimate regional housing needs, the Plan is not arbitrary or unreasonable. We agree with appellees that unlike the situation in the past most municipalities today are neither isolated nor wholly independent from neighboring municipalities and that, consequently, unilateral land use decisions by one local entity affect the needs and resources of an entire region. See, e.g., Golden v. Planning Board of Town of Ramapo, 30 N.Y.2d 359, 334 N.Y.S.2d 138, 285 N.E.2d 291, appeal dismissed, 409 U.S. 1003, 93 S.Ct. 436, 34 L.Ed.2d 294 (1972); National Land & Investment Co. v. Kohn, 419 Pa. 504, 215 A.2d 597 (1965); Note, Phased Zoning: Regulation of the Tempo and Sequence of Land Development, 26 Stan.L.Rev. 585, 605 (1974). It does not necessarily follow, however, that the *due process* rights of builders and landowners are violated merely because a local entity exercises in its own self-interest the police power lawfully delegated to it by the state. See *Belle Terre,* supra; *Los Altos Hills,* supra. If the present system of delegated zoning power does not effectively serve the state interest in furthering the general welfare of the region or entire state, it is the state legislature's and not the federal courts' role to intervene and adjust the system. As stated supra, the federal court is not a super zoning board

---

26. Under the Petaluma Plan, the population is expected to increase at the rate of about 1500 persons annually. This rate approximates the rate of growth in the 1960's and represents about a 6 per cent increase per year over the present population.

27. Although appellees have attempted to align their business interests in attacking the Plan with legitimate housing needs of the urban poor and racial minorities, the Association has not alleged nor can it allege, based on the record in this case, that the Plan has the purpose and effect of excluding poor persons and racial minorities. Cf. Board of County Supervisors of Fairfax County v. Carper, 200 Va. 653, 107 S.E.2d 390 (1959). Contrary to the picture painted by appellees, the Petaluma Plan is "inclusionary" to the extent that it offers new opportunities, previously unavailable, to minorities and low and moderate-income persons. Under the pre-Plan system single family, middle-income housing dominated the Petaluma market, and as a result low and moderate income persons were unable to secure housing in the area. The Plan radically changes the previous building pattern and requires that housing permits be evenly divided between single-family and multi-family units and that approximately eight to twelve per cent of the units be constructed specifically for low and moderate income persons.

In stark contrast, each of the exclusionary zoning regulations invalidated by state courts in recent years impeded the ability of low and moderate income persons to purchase or rent housing in the locality. See, e.g., Southern Burlington County NAACP v. Township of Mount Laurel, 67 N.J. 151, 336 A.2d 713 (Mar. 24, 1975) (zoned exclusively for single-family detached dwellings and multi-family dwellings designed for middle and upper income persons); Oakwood at Madison, Inc. v. Township of Madison, 117 N.J.Super. 11, 283 A.2d 353 (1971) (minimum one or two acre requirement and severe limitation on multi-family units); Appeal of Kit–Mar Builders, Inc., 439 Pa. 466, 268 A.2d 765 (1970) (two to three acre minimum lot size); Appeal of Girsh, 437 Pa. 237, 263 A.2d 395 (1970) (prohibition of apartment buildings); National Land & Investment Co. v. Kohn, 419 Pa. 504, 215 A.2d 597 (1965) (four acre minimum lot); Board of County Supervisors of Fairfax County v. Carper, 200 Va. 653, 107 S.E.2d 390 (1959) (rezoning to minimum two acre lots with the effect of keeping poor in another section of municipality).

and should not be called on to mark the point at which legitimate local interests in promoting the welfare of the community are outweighed by legitimate regional interests. See Note, supra, at 608–11.

We conclude therefore that under *Belle Terre* and *Los Altos Hills* the concept of the public welfare is sufficiently broad to uphold Petaluma's desire to preserve its small town character, its open spaces and low density of population, and to grow at an orderly and deliberate pace.[28]

COMMERCE CLAUSE

The district court found that housing in Petaluma and the surrounding areas is produced substantially through goods and services in interstate commerce and that curtailment of residential growth in Petaluma will cause serious dislocation to commerce. 375 F.Supp. at 577, 579. Our ruling today, however, that the Petaluma Plan represents a reasonable and legitimate exercise of the police power obviates the necessity of remanding the case for consideration of appellees' claim that the Plan unreasonably burdens interstate commerce.

It is well settled that a state regulation validly based on the police power does not impermissibly burden interstate commerce where the regulation neither discriminates against interstate commerce nor operates to disrupt its required uniformity. Huron Cement Co. v. Detroit, 362 U.S. 440, 448, 80 S.Ct. 813, 4 L.Ed.2d 852 (1960). * * *

Consequently, since the local regulation here is rationally related to the social and environmental welfare of the community and does not discriminate against interstate commerce or operate to disrupt its required uniformity, appellees' claim that the Plan unreasonably burdens commerce must fail.[29]

Reversed.

28. Our decision upholding the Plan as not in violation of the appellees' due process rights should not be read as a permanent endorsement of the Plan. In a few years the City itself for good reason may abandon the Plan or the state may decide to alter its laws delegating its zoning power to the local authorities; or to meet legitimate regional needs, regional zoning authorities may be established. See, e.g., Cal.Gov.Code §§ 66600 et seq. (San Francisco Bay Conservation and Development Commission); Cal.Gov.Code §§ 66801, 67000 et seq. (Tahoe Regional Planning Agency); Public Resources Code §§ 27000 et seq. (California Coastal Zone Conservation Commission). To be sure, housing needs in metropolitan areas like the San Francisco Bay Area are pressing and the needs are not being met by present methods of supplying housing. However, the federal court is not the proper forum for resolving these problems. The controversy stirred up by the present litigation, as indicated by the number and variety of amici on each side, and the complex economic, political and social factors involved in this case are compelling evidence that resolution of the important housing and environmental issues raised here is exclusively the domain of the legislature.

29. Our decision today conforms with others which have upheld reasonable state environmental legislation despite some burden incidentally placed on interstate commerce. See, e.g., Huron Cement Co. v. Detroit, supra (air pollution statute); Procter & Gamble Co. v. City of Chicago, 509 F.2d 69 (7th Cir.), certiorari denied, 421 U.S. 978, 95 S.Ct. 1980, 44 L.Ed.2d 470 (1975) (ban on phosphate detergents); American Can Co. v. Oregon Liquor Control Commission, 15 Or.App. 618, 517 P.2d 691 (1973) (ban on non-returnable beverage containers).

Notes

1. The courts, in growth regulation cases, frequently refer to the exclusionary effects of certain zoning practices as being part of the issue of growth regulation. See, e.g., Begin v. Inhabitants of Sabattus, 409 A.2d 1269 (Me.1979). This particular aspect of the problem is taken up in a subsequent chapter in some detail. For our purposes at this point, it is sufficient to point out that zoning usually deals with the permitted uses on a parcel of land or within a geographic district, and that although zoning regulations may have a very real impact on population densities and housing types, the problem of regulating growth is more closely tied to land subdivision regulations, provision of municipal facilities, and rationing of building permits.

2. The Ramapo and Petaluma cases sparked nationwide interest in techniques of growth control. Despite the concerns expressed in the dissenting opinion in Ramapo and the district court opinion in Petaluma about local parochialism and the need for addressing the problem on a regional or statewide basis, most of the development in the area has continued to focus on individual communities and local plans. As you read the next principal case, determine whether the majority adequately deals with the issue of local parochialism in the context of regional housing needs and regional welfare.

ASSOCIATED HOME BUILDERS OF THE GREATER EASTBAY, INC. v. CITY OF LIVERMORE

Supreme Court of California, In Bank, 1976.
18 Cal.3d 582, 135 Cal.Rptr. 41, 557 P.2d 473.

TOBRINER, JUSTICE.

We face today the question of the validity of an initiative ordinance enacted by the voters of the City of Livermore which prohibits issuance of further residential building permits until local educational, sewage disposal, and water supply facilities comply with specified standards. Plaintiff, an association of contractors, subdividers, and other persons interested in residential construction in Livermore, brought this suit to enjoin enforcement of the ordinance. The superior court issued a permanent injunction, and the city appealed.

* * *

[At this point the court reversed the trial court in holding that notice and hearing requirements in the zoning enabling legislation also applied to initiatives. These were held to be inapplicable to enactments by the voters. The court also reversed a trial court finding that the ordinance was unconstitutionally vague.]

Finally, we reject plaintiff's suggestion that we sustain the trial court's injunction on the ground that the ordinance unconstitutionally attempts to bar immigration to Livermore. Plaintiff's contention symbolizes the growing conflict between the efforts of suburban communities to check disorderly development, with its concomitant problems of air and water pollution and inadequate public facilities, and the increasing public need for adequate housing opportunities. We take this opportunity, therefore, to reaffirm and clarify the principles which govern validity of land use ordinances which substantially limit immigration into a community; we hold that such ordinances need not be sustained by a compelling state interest, but are constitutional if they are reasonably related to the welfare of the region affected by the ordinance. Since on the limited record before us plaintiff has not demonstrated that the Livermore ordinance lacks a reasonable relationship to the regional welfare, we cannot hold the ordinance unconstitutional under this standard.

1. SUMMARY OF PROCEEDINGS

The initiative ordinance in question was enacted by a majority of the voters at the Livermore municipal election of April 11, 1972, and became effective on April 28, 1972. The ordinance, set out in full in the margin,[30] states that it was enacted to further the health, safety, and welfare of the citizens of Livermore and to contribute to the solution of air pollution. Finding that excessive issuance of residential building permits has caused school overcrowding, sewage pollution, and water rationing, the ordinance prohibits issuance of further permits until three standards are met: "1. EDUCATIONAL FACILITIES—No double sessions in the schools nor overcrowded classrooms as determined by the California Education Code. 2. SEWAGE—The sewage treatment facilities and capacities meet the standards set by the Regional Water Quality Control Board. 3. WATER SUPPLY—No rationing of water with respect to human consumption or irrigation and adequate water reserves for fire protection exist."

Plaintiff association filed suit to enjoin enforcement of the ordinance and for declaratory relief. After the city filed its answer, all parties

---

30. The initiative provides as follows: "INITIATIVE ORDINANCE RE BUILDING PERMITS

"An ordinance to control residential building permits in the City of Livermore:

"A. The people of the City of Livermore hereby find and declare that it is in the best interest of the City in order to protect the health, safety, and general welfare of the citizens of the city, to control residential building permits in the said city. Residential building permits include single-family residential, multiple residential, and trailer court building permits within the meaning of the City Code of Livermore and the General Plan of Livermore. Additionally, it is the purpose of this initiative measure to contribute to the solution of air pollution in the City of Livermore.

"B. The specific reasons for the proposed position are that the undersigned believe that the resulting impact from issuing residential building permits at the current rate results in the following prob-

lems mentioned below. Therefore no further residential permits are to be issued by the said city until satisfactory solutions, as determined in the standards set forth, exist to all the following problems:

"1. EDUCATIONAL FACILITIES—No double sessions in the schools nor overcrowded classrooms as determined by the California Education Code.

"2. SEWAGE—The sewage treatment facilities and capacities meet the standards set by the Regional Water Quality Control Board.

"3. WATER SUPPLY—No rationing of water with respect to human consumption or irrigation and adequate water reserves for fire protection exist.

"C. This ordinance may only be amended or repealed by the voters at a regular municipal election.

"D. If any portion of this ordinance is declared invalid the remaining portions are to be considered valid."

moved for judgment on the pleadings and stipulated that the court, upon the pleadings and other documents submitted, could determine the merits of the cause. On the basis of that stipulation the court rendered findings and entered judgment for plaintiff. The city appeals from that judgment.

* * *

[The portion of the decision dealing with the conflict between the notice and hearing provisions of the zoning enabling act and the initiative procedures act is omitted.]

3.   THE LIVERMORE ORDINANCE IS NOT VOID FOR VAGUENESS

The trial court found the ordinance unconstitutionally vague on two grounds: (1) that the ordinance did not contain sufficiently specific standards for the issuance or denial of building permits, and (2) that it did not specify what person or agency was empowered to determine if the ordinance's standards have been met. We disagree with both rationales and find the ordinance sufficiently specific to fulfill constitutional requirements.

The controversy concerning the specificity of the ordinance centers upon the standard as to education. The ordinance prohibits issuance of residential building permits until a "satisfactory solution" has been evolved to the problem of "Educational Facilities"; it defines a satisfactory solution as one characterized by "No double sessions in the schools nor overcrowded classrooms as determined by the California Education Code."

The term "double sessions" is sufficiently specific; as stated by Professor Deutsch, it "can be defined by reference to common practice, since the term is frequently used to refer to a situation where different groups of students in the same grade are attending the same school at different times of the day because of a lack of space." (Deutsch, op. cit., supra, pp. 22–23.) The phrase "overcrowded classrooms as determined by the California Education Code," however, is less clear, since nowhere in the Education Code does there appear a definition of "overcrowded classrooms."

The City of Livermore, however, points out that the ordinance does not refer to a definition of "overcrowded classrooms" contained in the Education Code, but to a determination of that subject. The language, it contends—and plaintiff does not dispute the contention—was intended to refer to resolution 3220, adopted by the board of the Livermore Valley Joint School District on January 18, 1972, in which that board, pursuant to authority granted it by Education Code section 1052, established clear and specific standards for determining whether schools are overcrowded.[31]

31. Board Resolution 3220 provides as follows:

"ADEQUACY OF SCHOOLS

"1.   Sufficient instructional space shall be determined to exist when:

a.   For elementary schools:

Rather than interpret the ordinance in a manner which would expose it to the charge of unconstitutional vagueness, we adopt the suggestion of the city and construe the ordinance's standard on education to incorporate the specific guidelines established in board resolution 3220. In so doing we conform to the rule that enactments should be interpreted when possible to uphold their validity * * * and the corollary principle that courts should construe enactments to give specific content to terms that might otherwise be unconstitutionally vague. * * *

* * *

The ordinance's standards relating to sewage and water supply present no constitutional difficulties. The sewage provision incorporates the "standards set by the Regional Water Quality Control Board"; that agency has in fact established specific and detailed standards of water purification and sewage disposal. The water supply provision describes a "satisfactory solution" as one in which water is not rationed, and "adequate water reserves for fire protection exist." The existence of rationing is an objective fact which can be ascertained by inquiry to the agencies having authority to ration. Although individuals may differ as to the adequacy of reserves for fire protection, the considered judgment of the agencies responsible for fire protection would provide a reliable guide.

Although we have determined that the ordinance's standards meet constitutional requirements of certainty, plaintiff argues, and the trial court held, that the ordinance is void because it fails to designate what agency or person determines whether these standards have been achieved. We question plaintiff's underlying assumption that an ordinance or statute is void if it does not specify on its face the agency that is to adjudge disputes concerning its application; by such a test most of the civil and criminal laws of this state would be invalidated. In any event, we believe that the Livermore ordinance, read in the light of the

(1) All students can be housed in single session classes in affected schools.

(2) At least 900 square feet of functional instructional area are available for each classroom or teaching station.

(3) Class sizes average 30 students or less throughout the District.

b. For secondary schools:

(1) All students can be housed within the capacity of existing schools on regular day session. Capacity will be determined by applying State Department of Education criteria in keeping with maximum class size.

"2. Minimum support services exist when:

a. Sufficient shelf and cabinet space is provided to accommodate books and equipment normally associated with a classroom.

b. A faculty workroom exists.

c. Off-street parking for 1½ cars per teaching station is provided.

d. Sufficient playground area and playground equipment is provided to support outdoor play activity.

e. Sufficient furniture and equipment for each classroom to accommodate all students and teachers.

f. A library is established equivalent to at least one classroom for each 600 students.

"3. School construction and outfitting, in terms of classroom space, architectural layout, space relationship, outdoor facilities, utilities, grounds development, and furniture and equipment, shall meet or exceed State Bureau of Education standards."

structure of Livermore's city government and the applicable judicial decisions, does indicate the method by which disagreements concerning the ordinance's standards are resolved.

The Livermore ordinance establishes standards to govern the issuance or denial of residential building permits. These standards must be directed in the first instance to the city building inspector, the official charged with the duty of issuing or denying such permits. Since the duties of this official are ministerial in character, his decisions can be reviewed by writ of mandamus. * * * Thus the ultimate decision as to compliance with the standards will be rendered by the courts. * * *

4. ON THE LIMITED RECORD BEFORE US, PLAINTIFF CANNOT DEMONSTRATE THAT THE LIVERMORE ORDINANCE IS NOT A CONSTITUTIONAL EXERCISE OF THE CITY'S POLICE POWER

Plaintiff urges that we affirm the trial court's injunction on a ground which it raised below, but upon which the trial court did not rely. Plaintiff contends that the ordinance proposes, and will cause, the prevention of nonresidents from migrating to Livermore, and that the ordinance therefore attempts an unconstitutional exercise of the police power, both because no compelling state interest justifies its infringement upon the migrant's constitutionally protected right to travel, and because it exceeds the police power of the municipality.[32]

The ordinance on its face imposes no absolute prohibition or limitation upon population growth or residential construction. It does provide that no building permits will issue unless standards for educational facilities, water supply and sewage disposal have been met, but plaintiff presented no evidence to show that the ordinance's standards were unreasonable or unrelated to their apparent objectives of protecting the public health and welfare. Thus, we do not here confront the question of the constitutionality of an ordinance which limits or bars population growth either directly in express language or indirectly by the imposition of prohibitory standards; we adjudicate only the validity of an ordinance limiting building permits in accord with standards that reasonably measure the adequacy of public services.

* * * [T]he limited record here prevents us from resolving that constitutional issue. We deal here with a case in which a land use ordinance is challenged solely on the ground that it assertedly exceeds the municipality's authority under the police power; the challenger eschews any claim that the ordinance discriminates on a basis of race or wealth. Under such circumstances, we view the past decisions of this court and the federal courts as establishing the following standard: the

32. Plaintiff does not contend that the ordinance constitutes an inverse condemnation of property (compare Associated Home Builders, etc., Inc. v. City of Walnut Creek (1971) 4 Cal.3d 633, 94 Cal.Rptr. 630, 484 P.2d 606), that it unreasonably burdens interstate commerce (compare Construction Ind. Assn., Sonoma Cty. v. City of Petaluma (9th Cir.1975) 522 F.2d 897, 909) or that it denies the equal protection of the laws either to landowners (compare Town of Los Altos Hills v. Adobe Creek Properties, Inc. (1973) 32 Cal.App.3d 488, 108 Cal.Rptr. 271) or to migrants (compare Ybarra v. Town of Los Altos Hills (9th Cir.1974) 503 F.2d 250).

land use restriction withstands constitutional attack if it is fairly debatable that the restriction in fact bears a reasonable relation to the general welfare. For the guidance of the trial court we point out that if a restriction significantly affects residents of surrounding communities, the constitutionality of the restriction must be measured by its impact not only upon the welfare of the enacting community, but upon the welfare of the surrounding region. We explain the process by which the court can determine whether or not such a restriction reasonably relates to the regional welfare. Since the record in the present case is limited to the pleadings and stipulations, and is devoid of evidence concerning the probable impact and duration of the ordinance's restrictions, we conclude that we cannot now adjudicate the constitutionality of the ordinance. Thus we cannot sustain the trial court judgment on the ground that the ordinance exceeds the city's authority under the police power; that issue can be resolved only after trial.

* * *

We therefore reaffirm the established constitutional principle that a local land use ordinance falls within the authority of the police power if it is reasonably related to the public welfare. Most previous decisions applying this test, however, have involved ordinances without substantial effect beyond the municipal boundaries. The present ordinance, in contrast, significantly affects the interests of nonresidents who are not represented in the city legislative body and cannot vote on a city initiative. We therefore believe it desirable for the guidance of the trial court to clarify the application of the traditional police power test to an ordinance which significantly affects nonresidents of the municipality.

When we inquire whether an ordinance reasonably relates to the public welfare, inquiry should begin by asking *whose* welfare must the ordinance serve. In past cases, when discussing ordinances without significant effect beyond the municipal boundaries, we have been content to assume that the ordinance need only reasonably relate to the welfare of the enacting municipality and its residents. But municipalities are not isolated islands remote from the needs and problems of the area in which they are located; thus an ordinance, superficially reasonable from the limited viewpoint of the municipality may be disclosed as unreasonable when viewed from a larger perspective.

These considerations impel us to the conclusion that the proper constitutional test is one which inquires whether the ordinance reasonably relates to the welfare of those whom it significantly affects. If its impact is limited to the city boundaries, the inquiry may be limited accordingly; if, as alleged here, the ordinance may strongly influence the supply and distribution of housing for an entire metropolitan region, judicial inquiry must consider the welfare of that region.

* * *

We explain the process by which a trial court may determine whether a challenged restriction reasonably relates to the regional welfare. The first step in that analysis is to forecast the probable effect and duration of the restriction. In the instant case the Livermore ordinance posits a total ban on residential construction, but one which terminates as soon as public facilities reach specified standards. Thus to evaluate the impact of the restriction, the court must ascertain the extent to which public facilities currently fall short of the specified standards, must inquire whether the city or appropriate regional agencies have undertaken to construct needed improvements, and must determine when the improvements are likely to be completed.

The second step is to identify the competing interests affected by the restriction. We touch in this area deep social antagonisms. We allude to the conflict between the environmental protectionists and the egalitarian humanists; a collision between the forces that would save the benefits of nature and those that would preserve the opportunity of people in general to settle. Suburban residents who seek to overcome problems of inadequate schools and public facilities to secure "the blessing of quiet seclusion and clean air" and to "make the area a sanctuary for people" (Village of Belle Terre v. Boraas, supra, 416 U.S. 1, 9, 94 S.Ct. 1536, 1541, 39 L.Ed.2d 797) may assert a vital interest in limiting immigration to their community. Outsiders searching for a place to live in the face of a growing shortage of adequate housing, and hoping to share in the perceived benefits of suburban life, may present a countervailing interest opposing barriers to immigration.

Having identified and weighed the competing interests, the final step is to determine whether the ordinance, in light of its probable impact, represents a reasonable accommodation of the competing interests. We do not hold that a court in inquiring whether an ordinance reasonably relates to the regional welfare, cannot defer to the judgment of the municipality's legislative body. But judicial deference is not judicial abdication. The ordinance must have a *real and substantial* relation to the public welfare. (Miller v. Board of Public Works, supra, 195 Cal. 477, 490, 234 P. 381.) There must be a reasonable basis in fact, not in fancy, to support the legislative determination. (Consolidated Rock Products Co. v. City of Los Angeles (1962) 57 Cal.2d 515, 522, 20 Cal.Rptr. 638, 370 P.2d 342.) Although in many cases it will be "fairly debatable" (Euclid v. Ambler Co., supra, 272 U.S. 365, 388, 47 S.Ct. 114, 71 L.Ed. 303) that the ordinance reasonably relates to the regional welfare, it cannot be assumed that a land use ordinance can *never* be invalidated as an enactment in excess of the police power.

The burden rests with the party challenging the constitutionality of an ordinance to present the evidence and documentation which the court will require in undertaking this constitutional analysis. Plaintiff in the present case has not yet attempted to shoulder that burden. Although plaintiff obtained a stipulation that as of the date of trial the ordinance's goals had not been fulfilled, it presented no evidence to show the likely duration or effect of the ordinance's restriction upon building permits. We must presume that the City of Livermore and appropriate regional agencies will attempt in good faith to provide that community with adequate schools, sewage disposal facilities, and a sufficient water supply; plaintiff, however, has not presented evidence to show whether the city and such agencies have undertaken to construct the needed improvements or when such improvements will be completed. Consequently we cannot determine the impact upon either Livermore or the surrounding region of the ordinance's restriction on the issuance of building permits pending achievement of its goals.

With respect to the competing interests, plaintiff asserts the existence of an acute housing shortage in the San Francisco Bay Area, but presents no evidence to document that shortage or to relate it to the probable effect of the Livermore ordinance. Defendants maintain that Livermore has severe problems of air pollution and inadequate public facilities which make it reasonable to divert new housing, at least temporarily, to other communities but offer no evidence to support that claim. Without an evidentiary record to demonstrate the validity and significance of the asserted interests, we cannot determine whether the instant ordinance attempts a reasonable accommodation of those interests.

In short, we cannot determine on the pleadings and stipulations alone whether this ordinance reasonably relates to the general welfare of the region it affects. The ordinance carries the presumption of constitutionality; plaintiff cannot overcome that presumption on the limited record before us. Thus the judgment rendered on this limited record cannot be sustained on the ground that the initiative ordinance falls beyond the proper scope of the police power.

* * *

The judgment of the superior court is reversed, and the cause remanded for further proceedings consistent with the views expressed herein.

WRIGHT, C.J. and McCOMB, SULLIVAN and RICHARDSON, JJ., concur.

* * *

[A dissenting opinion by JUSTICE CLARK is omitted.]

MOSK, JUSTICE (dissenting).

I dissent.

Limitations on growth may be justified in resort communities, beach and lake and mountain sites, and other rural and recreational areas; such restrictions are generally designed to preserve nature's environment for the benefit of all mankind. They fulfill our fiduciary obligation to posterity. As Thomas Jefferson wrote, the earth belongs to the living, but in usufruct.

But there is a vast qualitative difference when a suburban community invokes an elitist concept to construct a mythical moat around its perimeter, not for the benefit of mankind but to exclude all but its fortunate current residents.

* * * Where I part company with the majority is in its substantive holding that a total exclusion of new residents can be constitutionally accomplished under a city's police power.

The majority, somewhat desultorily, deny that the ordinance imposes an absolute prohibition upon population growth or residential construction. It is true that the measure prohibits the issuance of building permits for single-family residential, multiple residential and trailer residential units until designated public services meet specified standards. But to see such restriction in practicality as something short of total prohibition is to employ ostrich vision.

First of all, the ordinance provides no timetable or dates by which the public services are to be made adequate. Thus the moratorium on permits is likely to continue for decades, or at least until attrition ultimately reduces the present population. Second, it is obvious that no inducement exists for *present* residents to expend their resources to render facilities adequate for the purpose of accommodating *future* residents. It would seem more rational, if improved services are really contemplated for any time in the foreseeable future, to admit the new residents and compel them to make their proportionate contribution to the cost of the educational, sewage and water services. Thus it cannot seriously be argued that Livermore maintains anything other than total exclusion.

The trial court found, inter alia, that the ordinance prohibited the issuance of building permits for residential purposes until certain conditions are met, but the measure does not provide that any person or agency is required to expend or commence any efforts on behalf of the city to meet the requirements. Nor is the city itself obliged to act within any specified time to cure its own deficiencies. Thus, in these circumstances procrastination produces its own reward: continued exclusion of new residents.

The significant omissions, when noted in relation to the ordinance preamble, reveal that the underlying purpose of the measure is "to control residential building permits in the City of Livermore"—translation: to keep newcomers out of the city—and not to solve the purported inadequacies in municipal educational, sewage and water services. Livermore concedes no building permits are now being issued and it relates no current or prospective schedule designed to correct its defective municipal services.

A municipal policy of preventing acquisition and development of property by nonresidents clearly violates article I, sections 1 and 7, subdivisions (a) and (b), of the Constitution of California.

Exclusion of unwanted outsiders, while a more frequent phenomenon recently, is not entirely innovative. The State of California made an abortive effort toward exclusivity back in the 1930s as part of a scheme to stem the influx of poor migrants from the dust bowl states of the southwest. The additional burden these indigent new residents placed on California services and facilities was severely aggravated by the great depression of that period. In Edwards v. California (1941) 314 U.S. 160, 62 S.Ct. 164, 86 L.Ed. 119, the Supreme Court held, however, that the nature of the union established by the Constitution did not permit any one state to "isolate itself from the difficulties common to all of them by restraining the transportation of persons and property across its borders." The sanction against immigration of indigents was invalidated.

If California could not protect itself from the growth problems of that era, may Livermore build a Chinese Wall to insulate itself from growth problems today? And if Livermore may do so, why not every municipality in Alameda County and in all other counties in Northern California? With a patchwork of enclaves the inevitable result will be creation of an aristocracy housed in exclusive suburbs while modest wage earners will be confined to declining neighborhoods, crowded into sterile, monotonous, multifamily projects, or assigned to pockets of marginal housing on the urban fringe. The overriding objective should be to minimize rather than exacerbate social and economic disparities, to lower barriers rather than raise them, to emphasize heterogeneity rather than homogeneity, to increase choice rather than limit it.

* * *

One thing emerges with clarity from the foregoing and from numerous related cases: access to housing is regarded by the Supreme Court as a matter of serious social and constitutional concern. While this interest has generally been manifest in the context of racial discrimination, there is no valid reason for not invoking the principle when persons of all races and of all economic groups are involved. There are no invariable racial or economic characteristics of the goodly numbers of families which seek social mobility, the opportunities for the good life available in a suburban atmosphere, and access to types of housing, education and employment differing from those indigenous to crowded urban centers.

There is a plethora of commentary on efforts, in a variety of contexts, of local communities to discourage the influx of outsiders. In virtually every instance, however, the cities limited availability of housing; until now it has never been seriously contemplated that a community would attempt total exclusion by refusing all building permits. * * *

* * *

In sum, I realize the easiest course is for this court to defer to the political judgment of the townspeople of Livermore, on a they-know-what's-best-for-them theory (Eastlake v. Forest City Enterprises, Inc. (1976) 426 U.S. 668, 96 S.Ct. 2358, 49 L.Ed.2d 132; James v. Valtierra (1971) 402 U.S. 137, 91 S.Ct. 1331, 28 L.Ed.2d 678). But conceptually, when a locality adopts a comprehensive, articulated program to prevent any population growth over the foreseeable future, it places its public policy intentions visibly on the table for judicial scrutiny and constitutional analysis.

Communities adopt growth limits from a variety of motives. There may be conservationists genuinely motivated to preserve general or specific environments. There may be others whose motivation is social exclusionism, racial exclusion, racial discrimination, income segregation, fiscal protection, or just fear of any future change; each of these purposes is well served by growth prevention.

Whatever the motivation, total exclusion of people from a community is both immoral and illegal. (Cal. Const. art. I, §§ 1, 7, subds. (a) & (b).) Courts have a duty to prevent such practices, while at the same time recognizing the validity of genuine conservationist efforts.

The problem is not insoluble, nor does it necessarily provoke extreme results. Indeed, the solution can be relatively simple if municipal agencies would consider the aspirations of society as a whole, rather than merely the effect upon their narrow constituency. (See, e.g., A.L.I. Model Land Development Code, art. 7.) Accommodation between environmental preservation and satisfaction of housing needs can be reached through rational guidelines for land-use decision-making. Ours, of course, is not the legislative function. But two legal inhibitions must be the benchmark of any such guidelines. First, any absolute prohibition on housing development is presumptively invalid. And second, local regulations, based on parochialism, that limit population densities in growing suburban areas may be found invalid unless the community is absorbing a reasonable share of the region's population pressures.

Under the foregoing test, the Livermore ordinance is fatally flawed. I would affirm the judgment of the trial court.

Notes

1. In light of the decision in the principal case, how do you think a court would respond to a local referendum or initiated ordinance expressing either an absolute cap on population or a specific limit on the number of building permits to be issued? In City of Boca Raton v. Boca Villas Corp., 371 So.2d 154 (Fla.App.1979), certiorari denied 449 U.S. 824, 101 S.Ct. 86, 66 L.Ed.2d 27 (1980), the court affirmed a trial court judgment holding invalid an initiated ordinance adopted by the citizens of Boca Raton establishing a limit of 40,000 dwelling units in the city. The court stated that a determination that the ordinance was confiscatory was not necessary in that the trial court found that the ordinance bore no rational relationship to the general welfare. The court stated:

> Our study of the briefs and record convinces us that there is substantial competent evidence to support the finding of an absence of a rational relationship regarding the charter amendment and zoning ordinance. That being the case, we need not reach the question of confiscation vel non because the finding that there is no compelling need justifying an exercise of the police power burdening private property is sufficient to warrant striking down the legislative act. * * * That is not to say there must be an absolute necessity requiring the enactment of certain zoning restrictions before they can be tolerated as a proper exercise of the police power. But, as here, an excessive restriction on the

use of private property which does not contribute substantially to the public health, morals, safety and welfare is arbitrary and unreasonable and thus unconstitutional. * * * The trial court found, and the record supports such finding, that the charter amendment and implementing ordinances bore no such rational relationship to the requisite purposes.

We would concede that most of the cases where judicial invalidation of zoning laws has been upheld have in some measure involved the issue of confiscation. Those cases hold that as applied to the property involved the zoning ordinance was unreasonable because it deprived a property owner of the beneficial use of his property. We suggest the reason that the confiscation issue is so pervasive in the case law on this subject is because someone's ox is getting gored. Who is going to institute litigation but the person who feels his property rights infringed upon by excessive restrictions upon the use thereof?

There are cases, however, which support the principle that zoning which unnecessarily restricts property, zoning which bears no rational relationship to the public health, safety, morals and welfare is unconstitutional without raising the confiscation issue.

* * *

In view of our conclusion that an otherwise valid attack may be made upon the charter amendment and implementing ordinances, we need not consider the trial judge's findings that the cap and implementing ordinances are so drastic and restrictive as to be confiscatory as applied to appellees' property.

2.   In 1971, in Boulder, Colorado, local citizens led by the Zero Population Growth group, placed a 100,000 resident population cap measure on the ballot; the measure was defeated, but an alternative measure sponsored by the city council directed toward studying means of limiting growth, passed handily. See, Godschalk, Brower, McBennett, Vestal & Herr, Constitutional Issues of Growth Management 255–66 (1979).

3.   After the decision in the Livermore case, several California cities and towns experienced initiated growth limitation ordinances. In 1987, the California Evidence Code section 669.5 was amended to provide that, in cases involving an ordinance which numerically limits residential construction permits, the city "shall bear the burden of proof that the ordinance is necessary for the protection of the public health, safety, or welfare of the population * * * " This provision is discussed in Building Industry Ass'n of San Diego v. Superior Court, 211 Cal.App.3d 277, 259 Cal.Rptr. 325 (1989). Also see Lesher Communications, Inc. v. City of Walnut Creek, 52 Cal.3d 531, 277 Cal.Rptr. 1, 802 P.2d 317 (1990) where the court struck an initiated growth control ordinance challenged as inconsistent with the existing general plan, finding that the ordinance was not labeled as, or intended to be viewed as, an amendment to the plan.

STEEL HILL DEVELOPMENT, INC.
v. TOWN OF SANBORNTON

United States Court of Appeals, First Circuit, 1972.
469 F.2d 956.

COFFIN, CHIEF JUDGE. Located in the rolling hills of Belknap County, New Hampshire is the tiny town of Sanbornton with a year-round population of approximately 1,000 persons living in some 330 regular homes. Long popular as a major recreational and resort area, Belknap County commenced to share its rural beauty with visitors in considerably greater degree with the opening in the 1960's of Interstate Highway 93 which funneled droves of touring urbanites from the Boston area, one hundred miles away, into towns like Sanbornton. Since Sanbornton borders Lake Winnisquam, is within easy reach of Lake Winnipesaukee and affords simple access to most New Hampshire ski areas, it is no surprise that its summer population is about 2,000 persons, that it has around 400 seasonal homes, and now is afforded the unique opportunity to serve as a seasonal second home paradise for persons who would buy the proposed 500 to 515 family units planned by appellant Steel Hill Development, Inc. In short, as the district court stated, "this case reflects the current clash between those interested in opening up new and hitherto undeveloped land for sale and profit and those wishing to preserve the rural character of Northern New England and shield it from the relentless pressure of an affluent segment of our society seeking new areas for rest, recreation and year round living." Steel Hill Development, Inc. v. Town of Sanbornton, 338 F.Supp. 301, 302 (D.N.H. 1972).

Steel Hill acquired its 510 acres in December 1969 and immediately began surveying the land, mapping the topography and creating plans for conventional and "cluster" development. At that time, and until March 9, 1971 the entire Steel Hill tract was zoned as General Residence and Agricultural, requiring a minimum lot size of 35,000 square feet, or about three-fourths of an acre. Desirous of effectuating the "cluster" plan which appellant knew would require amending the zoning ordinance, appellant engaged in extensive and cordial negotiations with the town planning board during 1970. In order to permit some development while the "cluster" concept was under consideration, the board accepted a plan for 50 conventional lots meeting the 35,000 square feet requirement and scheduled, according to usual practice, a public hearing on the matter. About one hundred townsfolk attending the meeting on November 13, 1970 expressed opposition to any development by Steel Hill. Nevertheless, the planning board later approved the subdivision plan for thirty-seven lots, in the face of a petition, presented by about thirty town residents, for zoning the entire town as six acre minimum lots. Because public interest had been heightened in preserving Sanbornton's "charm as a New England small town", the planning board then proposed amendments to the zoning ordinance designed to enlarge the Forest

Conservation areas, and to establish separate General Residential Districts and Agricultural Districts, with increased minimum acreage requirements in these districts and in the Historical Preservation and the Recreational Districts. These were passed.

As a result of the re-zoning, approximately 70 per cent of appellant's land is in the Forest Conservation District and 30 per cent in the Agricultural District. Clearly, its plans for "cluster" or conventional development are inconsistent with the new zoning ordinance. Appellant filed suit in the district court alleging that the three and six acre minimum lot size requirements are unconstitutional because they bear no rational relationship to the health, safety, morals or general welfare of the community and are therefore violative of N.H. R.S.A. 31:60 and the due process clause of the Fourteenth Amendment; that the rezoning greatly reduced the value of its land so as to constitute a taking without compensation; and that the classification of its land was violative of the equal protection clause of the Fourteenth Amendment because it was arbitrary and discriminatory in the restrictions imposed on development. The district court found adversely to appellant on all counts.

* * *

New Hampshire, like most states, has granted authority to localities to zone in order to promote public health, safety, morals and general welfare. N.H. R.S.A. 31:60. A zoning ordinance under such a statute may not be declared unconstitutional unless its "provisions are clearly arbitrary and unreasonable, having no substantial relation to the public health, safety, morals, or general welfare." Village of Euclid v. Ambler Realty Co., 272 U.S. 365, 47 S.Ct. 114, 71 L.Ed. 303 (1926); Gorieb v. Fox, 274 U.S. 603, 47 S.Ct. 675, 71 L.Ed. 1228 (1927). Thus a court does not sit as a super zoning board with power to act *de novo,* but rather has, in the absence of alleged racial or economic discrimination, a limited role of review.

The district court found that, as the Sanbornton Planning Board had itself determined, topography and soil conditions posed severe problems of pollution, improper sewage disposal, poor drainage and erosion to large-scale development of the Steel Hill Tract, justifying imposition of the three-acre minimum lot size requirement in accordance with the public health. We have carefully read the conflicting trial testimony of the various experts who expressed an opinion on these matters and cannot say that the court's finding is clearly erroneous. In any event, appellant does not seem to challenge that ruling, but rather directs its argument to the unreasonableness of the six acre lot requirement.

The district court stated that it could not find the six acre requirement reasonable if only health and safety were considered, but that such requirement was reasonably related to the promotion of the general welfare of the community. N.H. R.S.A. 31:60. The court considered the pollution of Lake Winnisquam, possible interference with smelt spawning in Black Brook, increased traffic problems inherent in large-scale development, and increased air pollution. Testimony of planning board members and citizens opposed to Steel Hill's plans additionally reveals a desire to discourage density of population, and most importantly, a fear of premature development which was manifested in this effort to provide for orderly growth of the unspoiled areas of the town in a logical way. Several witnesses testified that not only would the town's rural character be destroyed by Steel Hill's massive plans, which would, in effect, double the town's population, but that there could be immeasurable ecological harm.

* * * [A]ppellant here does not seek to satisfy an already existing demand for suburban expansion, but rather seeks to create a demand in Sanbornton on behalf of wealthy residents of Megalopolis who might be willing to invest heavily in time and money to gain their own haven in bucolic surroundings. Note, 57 Iowa L.Rev. 126, 127 (1972). These different problems of suburban and rural expansion, their scientific and legal analyses, and their appropriate solutions cannot so easily be equated.

More appropriate to appellant's argument, and not cited to us, is Kavanewsky v. Zoning Board of Appeals of Town of Warren, 160 Conn. 397, 279 A.2d 567 (1971), where the town, when threatened with rapid development, increased minimum lot size requirements from one to two acres, an increase which the court found motivated by a "demand of the people to keep Warren a rural community with open spaces and keep undesirable businesses out", id. at 570, a goal not within the general welfare. In contrast, perhaps, is Confederacion de la Raza Unida v. City of Morgan Hill, 324 F.Supp. 895 (N.D.Cal.1971), which permitted a restriction, imposed by a zoning ordinance, on the development of a charming mountainous area of a city because of esthetic and environmental concerns. Yet even *Kavanewsky,* so far as appears, was dealing with an effort to keep out permanent residents and businesses, not to damp down a promoter's goal of doubling the housing in a small town by its large-scale second home plans. If, however, appellant has failed to present us with any controlling authority, neither have appellees. *Morgan Hill* involved a more detailed ordinance regulating density which resulted in a minimum lot size of only one half acre on the average. County Commissioners of Queen Anne's County v. Miles, 246 Md. 355, 228 A.2d 450 (1967), involved the upholding of a five acre minimum lot size requirement. The affected land comprised only 6.7 per cent of the county and the zoning was done pursuant to a long-range plan to preserve an unusually beautiful country estate section of a river. While we note that it is not within judicial competence to say that the forests in Sanbornton are any less worth preserving than country river estates, we do find it significant that the six acre requirement extends to approximately 50 per cent of the town, including the only area currently under any sort of development.

In short, no precedent compels its application to the case before us. We are faced with "a local legislative determination that the general welfare will be promoted by exclusion of an unwanted use from a non-metropolitan community [which exclusion] is not likely to conflict with a regional need for local space for that use." 57 Iowa L.Rev. at 140. We recognize, as within the general welfare, concerns relating to the construction and integration of hundreds of new homes which would have an irreversible effect on the area's ecological balance, destroy scenic values, decrease open space, significantly change the rural character of this small town, pose substantial financial burdens on the town for police, fire, sewer, and road service, and open the way for the tides of weekend "visitors" who would own second homes. If the federal government itself has thought these concerns to be within the general welfare, see, e.g., 42 U.S.C.A. § 4321, et seq., we cannot say that Sanbornton cannot similarly consider such values and reflect them in its zoning ordinance. Though some courts may have rejected them within the suburban zoning context, as in *Kohn,* and its progeny, or where permanent first homes are involved, as in *Kavanewsky,* but cf. *Morgan Hill,* we think they are persuasive in the case before us. "Many environmental and social values are involved in a determination of how land would best be used in the public interest. The choice of the voters of [the city] is not lacking in support in this regard." Southern Alameda Spanish Speaking Organization v. City of Union City, 424 F.2d 291 (9th Cir.1970).

Yet, though it may be proper for Sanbornton to consider the foregoing factors, we think the town has done so in a most crude manner. We are disturbed by the admission here that there was never any professional or scientific study made as to why six, rather than four or eight, acres was reasonable to protect the values cherished by the people of Sanbornton. On reviewing the record, we have serious worries whether the basic motivation of the town meeting was not simply to keep outsiders, provided they wished to come in quantity, out of the town. We cannot think that expansion of population, even a very substantial one, seasonal or permanent, is by itself a legitimate basis for permissible objection. Were we to adjudicate this as a restriction for all time, and were the evidence of pressure from land-deprived and land-seeking outsiders more real, we might well come to a different conclusion. Where there is natural population growth it has to go somewhere, unwelcome as it may be, and in that case we do not think it should be channelled by the happenstance of what town gets its veto in first. But, at this time of uncertainty as to the right balance between ecological and population pressures, we cannot help but feel that the town's ordinance, which severely restricts development, may properly stand for the present as a legitimate stop-gap measure.

In effect, the town has bought time for its citizens not unlike the action taken in referendum by the City of Boulder, Colorado to restrict growth on an emergency basis until an adequate study can be made of future needs. 60 Georgetown L.J. 1363 (1972). See also Golden v. Planning Board of Town of Ramapo, 30 N.Y.2d 359, 334 N.Y.S.2d 138, 285 N.E.2d 291 (1972), appeal dismissed 409 U.S. 1003, 93 S.Ct. 440, 34 L.Ed.2d 294 (1972). It was evident to the zoning board, and the district court, that haphazard and uncontrolled development of the town's hill areas would be inimical to present and future Sanbornton residents, see

Candlestick Properties, Inc. v. San Francisco Bay Conservation & Development Comm., 11 Cal.App.3d 557, 89 Cal.Rptr. 897 (1970), and that if the zoning laws do become "permanent barriers", then as the district court said, resort to the courts is always possible. *Steel Hill Development,* supra, 338 F.Supp. at 307. The zoning ordinance here in question has been in existence less than two years. Hopefully, Sanbornton has begun or soon will begin to plan with more precision for the future taking advantage of numerous federal or state grants for which it might qualify. Additionally, the New Hampshire legislature, to the extent it expects small towns like Sanbornton to cope with environmental problems posed by private developments, might adopt legislation similar to the federal National Environmental Policy Act, 42 U.S.C.A. § 4321 et seq. and thereby require developers to submit detailed environmental statements, if such power does not already reside within the town's arsenal of laws. Thus, while we affirm the district court's determination at the present time, we recognize that this is a very special case which cannot be read as evidencing a general approval of six-acre zoning, and that this requirement may well not indefinitely stand without more homework by the concerned parties.

Lastly, we find little merit to appellant's contentions that the zoning ordinance has resulted in a taking of appellant's property without just compensation or that it is discriminatory. As the district court found, appellant still has the land and buildings for which it paid $290,000. The estimated worth, had Steel Hill's original plans been approved, is irrelevant. Though the value of the tract has been decreased considerably, it is not worthless or useless so as to constitute a taking. Hadacheck v. Sebastian, 239 U.S. 394, 36 S.Ct. 143, 60 L.Ed. 348 (1915); Sibson v. State, N.H., 282 A.2d 664 (1971). Cf. State v. Johnson, 265 A.2d 711 (Me.1970); Bartlett v. Zoning Comm. of Town of Old Lyme, 161 Conn. 24, 282 A.2d 907 (1971). As to appellant's claim of discrimination, we note that its land, like all other land zoned six acres, is essentially virgin forest. It is adjacent to, and its March 1971 re-zoning represented an extension of, the Forest Conservation District created in 1970. Thus the ordinance cannot be said to discriminate unreasonably against Steel Hill, be it the only developer in the town.

Affirmed.

Notes

1. For the subsequent history of the Steel Hill case, see Steel Hill Development, Inc. v. Town of Sanbornton, 392 F.Supp. 1134, and 392 F.Supp. 1144 (D.N.H.1974).

2. Do you think that a rural community far from the expanding metropolis is in a better legal position to preserve its "way of life" by preventing virtually all large developments than a rural community right in the path of the growing urban area? See Ybarra v. Town of Los Altos Hills, 503 F.2d 250 (9th Cir.1974) and Sturges v. Town of Chilmark, 380 Mass. 246, 402 N.E.2d 1346 (1980).

3. In New Hampshire, the courts have held that growth control ordinances must comply with the zoning enabling statutes. See Beck v. Town of Raymond, 118 N.H. 793, 394 A.2d 847 (1978) and Stoney–Brook Development Corp. v. Town of Pembroke, 118 N.H. 791, 394 A.2d 853 (1978). After these decisions the legislature passed enabling legislation authorizing towns and cities to enact growth control ordinances. See N.H.Rev.Stat.Ann. 31:62–a and 31:62–b.

In Stoney–Brook Development Corp. v. Town of Fremont, 124 N.H. 583, 474 A.2d 561 (1984), the town had set a three percent growth rate which was challenged by the developer (who had received only three of the four building permits it sought). The court ruled for the developer holding that growth controls must be the product of careful study and must be constantly reviewed with a general view of relaxing the controls. Under this test, the court found the town's three percent figure to be arbitrary and artificial.

B. DENIAL OF ACCESS TO THE INFRASTRUCTURE

DATELINE BUILDERS, INC. v. CITY OF SANTA ROSA

California Court of Appeal, First District, 1983.
146 Cal.App.3d 520, 194 Cal.Rptr. 258.

WHITE, PRESIDING JUSTICE.

On this appeal by Dateline Builders, Inc. (Builders) from a judgment in favor of the City of Santa Rosa (City), the major question is whether the City was required to connect its existing sewer trunk line to Builders' proposed "leap frog" housing development beyond the City's boundaries. For the reasons set forth below we have concluded that the City reasonably exercised its police power because Builders' proposed housing development was not consistent with the City's compact land use and development policy as set forth in the City and County's previously adopted General Plan.

The pertinent facts substantially as found below and revealed by the record are as follows: Builders, a California corporation, held an option on a parcel of real property located beyond the limits of the city boundary, on Todd Road in an undeveloped rural area known as the Santa Rosa Plain. The City is a charter city located in Sonoma County (County).

The County Board of Supervisors determined that: 1) there was a need for development of sewer facilities in the Santa Rosa Plain; 2) it was in the public interest to avoid the proliferation of small and scattered un-unified sewer treatment facilities by a cooperative effort with the City to create a single regional facility to be owned and operated by the City. On October 17, 1964 the City and County entered into the "Plains Agreement," a mutual expression of policy and intent to exercise their police powers cooperatively for the orderly development of the Santa Rosa Plain, and to prevent a proliferation of fragment sewer districts and systems.

Paragraph 10 of the Plains Agreement provided that both the City and County would adopt a policy that the areas in the Santa Rosa Plain adaptable to urban type development, would be developed consistent with the City and County's General Plan and with the development standards of the City. To implement this policy the City and County agreed to enact subdivision, building, zoning and other property development regulations "to prevent haphazard or substandard property development." Paragraph 10 further provided that any development proposal in the Santa Rosa Plain be accompanied by proof that the proposed development was consistent with the City and County's joint General Plan and consistent with the City's development standards and regulations.

To implement one of the policies of the Plains Agreement the City Council adopted a procedure that required the proponent of a development to apply for and receive a certificate of compliance (certificate) prior to the extension of new service outside the city; the certificate then served as proof of compliance with the city's development standards.

* * *

Builders' application for a certificate was reviewed by the City for consistency with its plan, and development policies and standards. The City determined that Builders' proposed development in an agricultural area well beyond the city boundaries represented "leap-frog" development inconsistent with the city's plans, policies and standards. On December 9, 1971, the City denied the request without prejudice; Builders never submitted a subsequent or renewed application for a certificate. Builders appealed the determination to the City Council. On January 4, 1972 the City Council heard the appeal and refused to issue the certificate, on the same grounds, i.e., inconsistent with the City's General Plan and standards for compact development.

* * *

Builders rely on and urge us to follow, *Robinson v. City of Boulder* (1976) 190 Colo. 357, 547 P.2d 228 and *Delmarva Enterprises, Inc. v. Mayor and Council of the City of Dover* (Del.1971) 282 A.2d 601. In both *Robinson* and *Delmarva, supra,* the owners of property outside of the city limits successfully argued that each city had unlawfully discriminated against them by refusing to hook up their properties to the city's exclusive water and sewer services. Both the Delaware and Colorado courts reasoned that: 1) as the exclusive supplier of these services, each city acting in a proprietary capacity as a public utility, was held to the same standards as a private utility, and therefore could refuse to do so only for utility-based reasons, such as insufficient capacity; and 2) each city was bound by the rule that a municipality is without jurisdiction over territory beyond its limits in the absence of legislation. In *Boulder, supra,* 547 P.2d at 230–231, however, the court did not reach the City's argument that the rules applicable to private utilities should not apply to a governmental utility authorized to implement governmental objectives such as the adoption of a Master-plan. The City of Boulder and the county in which it was located had jointly developed and adopted a Boulder Valley comprehensive plan to provide for discretionary land use decisions. The court specifically noted that the proposed Boulder development complied with the county zoning regulations and that the county, rather than the city, had the ultimate responsibility for the approval of the proposed development.

Builders argue that the *Boulder* case, *supra,* is on all fours with the facts of the instant case. Builders, however, ignore the fact that its Todd Road project had the tentative approval of the county conditioned, inter alia, upon a change in zoning and other conditions with which Builders admittedly did not attempt to comply. However, we do not base our holding only on this factual distinction. By failing to seek rezoning from the County or meet the other 23 conditions imposed by the County in its tentative approval of the subdivision map, and then pursuing this action against the City, Builders was trying to play off against each other, the City and County who had agreed to cooperative planning. Basically, Builders argues that because a City cannot exercise its police power beyond its boundaries, the City was prevented from using the denial of the sewer hookup as a planning tool.

Builders ignores the joint policy of the City and County as expressed in the Plains Agreement, for orderly growth in conformance with the guidelines of the jointly adopted General Plan. Agreements such as that here in issue that lead to joint planning by cities and counties should and have been encouraged by the Legislature. The complex economic, political and social factors involved in land use planning are compelling evidence that resolution of the important housing and environmental issues raised here, is the domain of the Legislature. (Cf. *Construction Ind. Ass'n, Sonoma Co. v. City of Petaluma, supra,* 522 F.2d fn. 17 at 909.) Unfortunately, the experience of many communities in this state has been that when planning is left to developers, the result is urban sprawl. The City's express and reiterated reason for denying the certificate was that Builders' proposed development violated its policy of orderly compact development from the urban core, and would result in a "leap-frog" development and "urban sprawl." A municipality cannot be forced to take a stake in the developer's success in the area. (Cf. *Reid Dev. Corp. v. Parsippany–Troy Hills Tp.* (1954) 31 N.J.Super. 459, 107 A.2d 20, at 23.) Neither common law nor constitutional law inhibits the broad grant of power to local government officials to refuse to extend utility service so long as they do not act for personal gain nor in a wholly arbitrary or discriminatory manner. (See authorities cited in *Control of the Timing and Location of Government Utility Extensions* (1974) 26 Stanford L.Rev. 945–963.)

Builders rely on the line of California authorities holding that where a municipality provides a public utility service "[g]enerally it is true that where the scope of a project transcends the boundaries of a municipality it ceases to be for a municipal purpose." (*Santa Barbara etc. Agency v. All Persons* (1957) 47 Cal.2d 699, 710, 306 P.2d 875, revd. on other grounds (1958) 357 U.S. 275, 78 S.Ct. 1174, 2 L.Ed.2d 1313, dealing with a county water agency.) The California Supreme Court in upholding the right of a charter city to issue notices of sale for revenue bonds for sewerage improvements applied the above principle to sewer systems: " * * * sewer projects may transcend the boundaries of one or several municipalities * * *. In such circumstances the project 'ceases to be a municipal affair and comes within the proper domain and regulation of the general laws of the state.' (*Wilson v. City of San Bernadino* (1960) 186 Cal.App.2d 603, 604, 611 [9 Cal.Rptr. 431] * * *)" (*City of Santa Clara v. Von Raesfeld* (1970) 3 Cal.3d 239, 246, 90 Cal.Rptr. 8, 474 P.2d 976; see also *Pixley v. Saunders* (1914) 168 Cal. 152, 160, 141 P. 815.) These authorities, of course, predate *Associated Home Builders etc., Inc. v. City of Livermore, supra,* 18 Cal.3d 582, 601, 135 Cal.Rptr. 41, 557 P.2d 473. We agree with the City that unlike the situation in the past, most municipalities today are neither isolated nor wholly independent from neighboring entities, and consequently, land use decisions by one local unit affect the needs and resources of the entire region. The Plains Agreement and the General Plan demonstrate that the City and County were aware of these realities.

Builders recognize that in this state, as elsewhere, publicly owned municipal utilities are not regulated by the Public Utilities Commission (PUC) or any other supervisory agency in the absence of a legislative grant of authority while privately owned utilities are. (*American Microsystems Inc. v. City of Santa Clara* (1982) 137 Cal.App.3d 1037, 1042–1043, 187 Cal.Rptr. 550.) It has long been the rule in this state that when operating a municipal utility, a city retains its character as a municipal corporation. Reasons must be found for holding it liable to the same extent as a private utility corporation. (*Pasadena v. R.R. Com.* (1920) 183 Cal. 526, 530, 192 P. 25.) Builders here argue that there were sufficient reasons here because the City was the only supplier, could not act beyond its boundaries and could not use sewer hookup as a planning device. We do not agree.

In *Associated Home Builders, etc., Inc. v. City of Livermore, supra,* 18 Cal.3d 582, 601, 135 Cal.Rptr. 41, 557 P.2d 473, our Supreme Court intimated that in California a city may enact restrictions that are effective beyond its boundaries. *Associated Home Builders* also reiterated the desirability of regional planning. As to a city's alleged inability to act beyond its boundaries, we note that Government Code section 65859 set forth below, a part of the same enactment as Government Code section 65300 and 65302 (discussed above at footnote 9 on page 14) expressly provides otherwise.

Builders' contention that denial of the certificate could not be used as a planning device overlooks a fundamental distinction between such a decision as an improper initial use of the police power, and as here, a necessary and proper exercise of the power once the planning decision had been made. Here, of course, the adoption of the General Plan with its policy of orderly and compact growth to avoid urban sprawl was made in 1967. The policy was a proper exercise of the police power for the general welfare (*Associated Home Builders, supra,* 18 Cal.3d 601, 135 Cal.Rptr. 41, 557 P.2d 473; cf. *Wilson v. Hidden Valley Mun. Water Dist.* (1967) 256 Cal.App.2d 271, 288, 63 Cal.Rptr. 889) previously adopted by the City Council and the County. (Cf. *Golden v. Ramapo* (1972) 30 N.Y.2d 359, 334 N.Y.S.2d 138, 285 N.E.2d 291, app. dism. 409 U.S. 1003, 93 S.Ct. 440, 34 L.Ed.2d 294.) Builders' argument that only zoning may be used for planning sits poorly in its mouth as they never sought to rezone the property or meet any of the County's other conditions.

The judgment is affirmed.

Notes

1. The Robinson v. City of Boulder case discussed in the principal case was overruled in 1986. Board of County Commissioners v. Denver Board of Water Commissioners, 718 P.2d 235 (Colo.1986). For discussion of the problems of regulating growth by controlling access to water service see Kelly, Piping Growth: The Law, Economics, and Equity of Sewer and Water Connection Policies, Land Use Law (July 1984) p. 3; Biggs, No Drip, No Flush, No Growth: How Cities Can Control Growth Beyond Their Boundaries by Refusing to Extend Utility Services, 22 Urban Lawyer 285 (1990). Also see City of Little Rock v. Chartwell Valley Ltd., 299 Ark. 542, 772 S.W.2d 616 (1989).

2. In Front Royal and Warren County Industrial Park Corp. v. Town of Front Royal, 922 F.Supp. 1131 (W.D.Va.1996), the developer of a proposed industrial park petitioned for annexation to the town so that he could obtain water and sewer services. Subsequent to the annexation, the town decided to develop its own industrial park across a state highway from the developer's land, and refused to extend water and sewer service to the developer. After protracted proceedings in federal court, including a period of abstention, the district court held that the developer had been subjected to a regulatory taking by denial of water and sewer, and was entitled to compensatory damages for the period of temporary taking.

CHARLES v. DIAMOND

Court of Appeals of New York, 1977.
41 N.Y.2d 318, 392 N.Y.S.2d 594, 360 N.E.2d 1295.

JASEN, JUDGE.

Petitioner, a landowner in the Village of Camillus, planned to construct three apartment buildings, totaling 36 units, on his property. Village law required that such buildings had to be connected to the village sewage system. On May 9, 1972, the village board authorized issuance of a building permit. However, on May 22, 1972, the State Department of Environmental Conservation informed petitioner that he could not connect into the village sewage system until "the Village undertakes a program to correct the deficiencies of their sewage system". The State likewise directed the Onondaga County Health Department not to authorize the petitioner to connect into the existing system until the present deficiencies were corrected. Thereafter, in June, 1972, petitioner commenced this article 78 proceeding against the State Commissioner of Environmental Conservation, the Deputy Commissioner, Onondaga County Department of Health, and the Village of Camillus, contending that the actions of the State, county and village were arbitrary and capricious, resulting in an unconstitutional appropriation of his property without compensation. Petitioner sought a judgment directing the respondents to approve the village connection to his property, requiring the village to take appropriate steps so that the State and county would allow petitioner to use the village sewer system and awarding damages in the amount of $50,000 for damages already sustained. Alternatively, petitioner sought damages in the amount of $100,-000 for the appropriation of his property in the event "that sewers are not approved * * * and he is not allowed to build the apartments on his property".

* * *

At the threshold, we note that this case does not involve the potentially troublesome issue of whether mere failure to provide municipal services can result in an inverse condemnation for which the municipality must pay compensation. Much more is involved here than merely an asserted failure to provide a service due equally to all members of the community. It is, of course, old law that a municipality is under no obligation to furnish sewers to particular property owners. Municipal corporations have ample opportunity to provide sewers "but it is not their duty to make every sewer or drain which may be desired by individuals, or which a jury might even find to be necessary and proper." Although municipal sewage disposal obligations have been discussed at great length in the tort realm, and little mentioned elsewhere, it is virtually beyond question that an individual property owner has no right to insist that the municipality provide him with a system, at least where the problem is unique to his land and can be remedied at his expense. Article 14 of the Village Law provides for the optional construction of sewers in a village, with the cost to be borne entirely by the village, entirely by the owners of the property benefited or by the village and the property owners jointly, at the option of the village. It is also old law that once a municipality has acted to provide a sewer and its improvement causes damage, the municipality is liable to compensate for the injuries sustained.

In this case, it is undisputed that the village provided a sewage disposal system and that local law requires that if a sewer is provided, it must be used. Moreover, the local law requires sewer-connected toilet facilities if the property is intended for any human use. The vice of the situation is that the municipality requires the use of public sewers if the property is to be developed for human use and yet has not provided an adequate system for meeting the requirement imposed by the ordinance. Hence, the claim is more than an undifferentiated demand for municipal service due to all citizens equally. The contention, stripped to its essence, is that the sewer ordinance is being applied unconstitutionally to petitioner's property, thereby frustrating nearly all reasonable development.

* * *

A police power regulation to be reasonable must be kept within the limits of necessity. In *Matter of Belle Harbor Realty Corp. v. Kerr,* 35 N.Y.2d 507, 364 N.Y.S.2d 160, 323 N.E.2d 697, we established a three-pronged test for measuring whether necessity limits have been exceeded. "To justify interference with the beneficial enjoyment of property the municipality must establish that it has acted in response to a dire necessity, that its action is reasonably calculated to alleviate or prevent the crisis condition, and that it is presently taking steps to rectify the problem." In that case, the municipality revoked a building permit on the ground that evidence uncovered since the issuance of the permit revealed that sewers were "grossly inadequate" for present use and new sewer connections were not advisable. The builder contended that the city had not acted because of sewer inadequacy but in response to community opposition to the planned development. We authorized the commencement of a proceeding to determine whether the revocation was a necessary health measure or was, in fact, motivated by political considerations. However, there was no contention that the developer would be entitled to money damages for any delay, whether justified by health requirements or not.

Similarly, in [*Westwood Forest Estates v. Village of South Nyack,* 23 N.Y.2d 424, 297 N.Y.S.2d 129, 244 N.E.2d 700 (1969)], we struck down a village zoning ordinance that prohibited all apartment house construction. The ordinance was purportedly justified by the fact that the village had inadequate sewage treatment facilities and new multiple dwellings would increase pollution of the Hudson River. Yet the sewage problem was not caused by the nature of the plaintiff's land but was general to the community. It was, we concluded, impermissible to single out one landowner to bear a heavy financial burden caused by a general community condition. We were careful to note that the village, while it could not blanketly prohibit development, could impose moratoriums or other temporary measures in order to deal with the problem. Indeed, we have sustained development restrictions, pursuant to a general community plan, for periods as long as 18 years. (See *Matter of Golden v. Planning Bd. of Town of Ramapo,* 30 N.Y.2d 359, 334 N.Y.S.2d 138, 285 N.E.2d 291, app. dsmd., 409 U.S. 1003, 93 S.Ct. 436, 34 L.Ed.2d 294.) However, the crucial factor, perhaps even the decisive one, is whether the ultimate economic cost of the benefit is being shared by the members of the community at large, or, rather, is being hidden from the public by the placement of the entire burden upon particular property owners. (See *French Investing Co. v. City of New York,* 39 N.Y.2d 587, 596–597, 385 N.Y.S.2d 5, 10–11, 350 N.E.2d 381, 386–387, *supra.*)

* * *

In this case, the delay, as measured from the time the difficulty first surfaced, has been substantial. Petitioner has been through a tortured course of litigation and appeal. Yet the reasons, if any, for apparent municipal inactivity in the face of sewage difficulties have never been explained. The present record, even after two appeals to the Appellate Division, is woefully silent. While it is true that the municipality has not submitted any justification for the delay, we also note that the property owner has not submitted any proof, apart from his conclusory allegations, that the municipal delay has exposed him to, or has caused him, significant economic injury of some sort. It is, of course, the property owner that must come forward with such proof in support of the claim that the zoning ordinance is being applied to the property unconstitutionally, in order to put the municipality to the task of justifying its action. On this inadequate record, it would be inappropriate for us to determine the constitutionality of the municipal action. Both parties have not submitted the proof necessary for an intelligent and conclusive judicial evaluation of their respective claims. Since the parties should be given an opportunity, which neither has yet had, to submit their proof on trial, any temporary relief, short of a final declaration on the constitutionality of the village action, would be an idle gesture.

* * *

Assuming that the landowner has been prejudiced by an unreasonable delay on the part of the municipality, the question of proper constitutional remedy is reached. Of course, in the event that unreasonable delay is established, the landowner is entitled to a declaration that the ordinance, insofar as it requires the use of public sewers, may not be constitutionally applied to him. Thus, this petitioner would be constitutionally free from the requirement that his property be tied into the public sewer system. The property could be developed by the use of private sewer disposal systems, provided compliance is made with pertinent provisions of local law. He should have that option.

A permit for the construction of a private sewage disposal system may be obtained by the owner. Of course, the proposed facility must comply with all relevant State health and sanitary requirements and is subject to village inspection. In addition, the property owner would be required to operate and maintain the facility in a sanitary manner at all times.

* * *

The order of the Appellate Division should be modified and, as modified, affirmed, without costs.

Order modified, without costs, and the matter remitted to Supreme Court, Onondaga County, for further proceedings in accordance with the opinion herein and, as so modified, affirmed.

BREITEL, C.J., and GABRIELLI, JONES, WACHTLER, FUCHSBERG and COOKE, JJ., concur.

Note

Also see Walz v. Town of Smithtown, 46 F.3d 162 (2d Cir.1995) where homeowners brought a successful civil rights action against the town and the town's superintendent of highways for denial of a permit to connect their home to the public water system after the failure of their well. The court upheld a jury verdict of $102,000 in compensatory damages against the town, $9,500 in punitive damages against the superintendent, and over $48,000 in attorney's fees.

C. DEVELOPMENT MORATORIA

MARYLAND–NAT'L CAPITAL PARK AND PLANNING COMM'N v. CHADWICK

Court of Appeals of Maryland, 1979.
286 Md. 1, 405 A.2d 241.

MURPHY, CHIEF JUDGE.

The central issue in this case is whether the appellant, Maryland–National Capital Park and Planning Commission (the Commission), by placing the appellees' land in public "reservation" without their consent for a period not to exceed three years, as authorized by * * * the Montgomery County Code * * *, unconstitutionally deprived the landowners of the use of their property without payment of just compensation.

* * *

Under § 7–115(a), the Commission's approval is required before any subdivision plat within the regional district may be recorded in the land records of Montgomery or Prince George's Counties. The Commission is empowered under § 7–116(a)(4) to prepare subdivision regulations which may provide for

> "the reservation of lands for schools and other public buildings and for parks, playgrounds, and other public purposes, provided no reservation of land for traffic, recreation or any other public purposes as herein provided shall continue for longer than three years without the written approval of all persons holding or otherwise owning any legal or equitable interest in the property; and provided further that the properties reserved for public use shall be exempt from all State, county, and local taxes during the period."

Pursuant to the state enabling legislation, Montgomery County adopted an ordinance authorizing the placement of land in public reservation. Under the provisions of the ordinance * * * the Commission's Planning Board for Montgomery County, which is authorized to administer subdivision regulations in that jurisdiction, is required to "refer all preliminary subdivision plans to the general plan or parts thereof, adopted or proposed or studies related thereto, or shall otherwise determine the need for reserving for public use any of the land included in the preliminary subdivision plan." The ordinance specifies that reservations "for a period of three years may be required for road or street rights of way, public school and building sites, parks, playgrounds or other recreational areas or other public purposes." The ordinance also provides that placement of land in public reservation shall be by resolution of the Commission, which shall state the time, not over three years, that the reservation will be effective.

Under the provisions of the ordinance, property in reservation is exempt from all state, county and local taxes * * *. It is also subject to restrictions on its use, as detailed in § 50–31(a)(5):

> "(5) PRESERVATION. During the reservation period, no building or structure shall be erected upon the land so reserved. No trees, topsoil or cover shall be removed or destroyed; no grading shall be done; no storm drainage structure shall be so built as to discharge water on the reservation except for storm drainage construction in accordance with a storm drainage plan approved by the department of public works or the Washington Suburban Sanitary Commission; *nor shall any land so reserved be put to any use whatsoever, except upon written approval of the board.* Nothing in this section shall be construed as prohibiting the owner from removing weeds or trash from property so reserved, nor from selling when approved by the board such parts of the land as may be necessary for water, sewer or road right of way for public agencies." (Emphasis added.)

Nothing in the state enabling act, or in Montgomery County's implementing ordinance, obligates the Commission to acquire property placed by it in reservation, either during or at the expiration of the reservation period. No provision is made for payment of compensation to the property owner for the time that his property is held in reservation, whether or not it is ultimately acquired by the Commission.

* * *

On April 25, 1978, the Chadwicks filed suit in the Circuit Court for Montgomery County, seeking the issuance of a writ of mandamus directing the Commission to approve their preliminary subdivision plan, and requesting a declaratory judgment that the reservation of their property and any statute requiring such reservation were unconstitutional as a taking of property without payment of just compensation. The court (McAuliffe, J.) held that the Commission's resolution placing the Chadwicks' property in public reservation under § 50–31 of the County Code was unconstitutional and it ordered the Commission to approve the preliminary subdivision plan. * * *

* * * Our cases have recognized and applied the distinction between a compensable taking under the eminent domain power and a noncompensable regulation under the police power. * * * We have consistently upheld regulations which may have, as an incidental effect, the diminution of value of property, so long as those regulations have been shown to be fair exercises of the police power. * * * A regulation which prohibits a beneficial use of private property constitutes a fair exercise of

the police power if the public interest generally requires it and the regulation is reasonably necessary to achieve the public goal without being unduly oppressive upon individuals. * * * However, we have recognized that a governmental action, while not rising to the status of a compensable "taking" of property, may amount to an invalid deprivation of property rights without due process of law, either because the purpose of the action was improper, see, e.g., Hoyert v. Bd. of County Comm'rs, 262 Md. 667, 278 A.2d 588 (1971) (attempt to depress value of property in anticipation of subsequent condemnation); Carl M. Freeman, Inc. v. St. Rds. Comm'n, 252 Md. 319, 250 A.2d 250 (1969) (sole purpose of ordinance is to freeze land values) or because the means chosen were too burdensome on the individual property owner. See, e.g., Spaid v. Board of Co. Comm'rs, 259 Md. 369, 269 A.2d 797 (1970) ("buffer zoning" to establish a border of vacant property around a residential neighborhood). * * *

* * *

The present case does not involve a valid exercise of the police power regulating, in the public interest, a mere beneficial use of private property for which compensation need not be paid to the affected landowner. On the contrary, we think the Commission's resolution placing appellees' land in reservation for a period up to three years stripped the landowners, for that extended period of time, of all reasonable use of their property and was tantamount to a "taking" without compensation as the lower court declared. In so concluding, we recognize the commendable governmental objective sought to be achieved by placing the land in reservation but, as was said in Pennsylvania Coal Co. v. Mahon, supra (260 U.S. at 416, 43 S.Ct. at 160), "a strong public desire to improve the public condition is not enough to warrant achieving the desire by a shorter cut than the constitutional way of paying for the change."

We construe the ordinance under which the Commission acted as not permitting the landowner to make, as a matter of right, any use of the property placed in reservation (other than to remove trash and weeds). We further construe the ordinance as not authorizing the planning board to permit, upon the landowner's application, any use of the reserved property which conflicts with the flat prohibition contained in the ordinance against grading the land, erecting any structures thereon, or removing trees, top soil or other cover. Restrictions of such totality upon the use of property placed in reservation *for a three-year period* bring this case within the principle, so well illustrated in *Pennsylvania Coal,* that a governmental restriction imposed on the use of land may be so onerous as to constitute a taking which constitutionally requires the payment of just compensation.

* * *

Considered together, *Pennsylvania Coal* and *Penn Central* provide ample guidance for determining whether a governmental restriction on the use of land, sought to be imposed under the police power, is of such magnitude as to constitute a taking in the constitutional sense. As we have indicated, the Commission's resolution placing appellees' land in reservation for a period of up to three years, with no reasonable uses permitted, amounts to a virtual "freeze" on the use of the property in its entirety. The resolution does not merely circumscribe a beneficial use of the property; it inhibits all beneficial use for up to three years, without any guarantee that the property will be acquired in the future. That the Commission's resolution is tantamount to a taking is, we think, clearly buttressed by cases in other jurisdictions.

In Miller v. Beaver Falls, 368 Pa. 189, 82 A.2d 34 (1951), Pennsylvania's Supreme Court invalidated a state law and implementing city ordinance which allowed a municipality to designate private property as parklands for up to three years, but which imposed no duty upon the municipality to acquire the designated property. The enactments provided that no compensation for improvements located on the property after notice was given of its placement in reservation would be paid if the property was subsequently acquired for public use. While the court conceded the desirability of the purpose to be achieved (establishment of parks for public use), it said that the city's action "in plotting [the] ground for a park or playground and freezing it for three years is, in reality, a taking of property by possibility, contingency, blockade and subterfuge, in violation of the clear mandate of our Constitution that property cannot be taken * * * without just compensation having been first made and secured." 82 A.2d at 37.

* * *

* * * See also Gordon v. City of Warren Plan. & Urb. Renew. Comm'n, 388 Mich. 82, 199 N.W.2d 465 (1972); Peacock v. County of Sacramento, 271 Cal.App.2d 845, 77 Cal.Rptr. 391 (1969). Compare Washington Sub. San. Comm'n v. Nash, 284 Md. 376, 396 A.2d 538 (1979); Hoyert v. Bd. of County Comm'rs, 262 Md. 667, 278 A.2d 588 (1971); Carl M. Freeman, Inc. v. St. Rds. Comm'n, 252 Md. 319, 250 A.2d 250 (1969).

The Commission, supported by a well-prepared amicus curiae brief filed by the Attorney General, urges that we apply the rationale of cases like Headley v. City of Rochester, 272 N.Y. 197, 5 N.E.2d 198 (1936), and State v. Manders, 2 Wis.2d 365, 86 N.W.2d 469 (1957), sustaining the constitutionality of so-called official map laws—statutes which establish the location of existing and planned streets and place restrictions on the issuance of permits to build structures in the bed of proposed roadways. These statutes restricting development in the bed of mapped streets contained provisions for variances to assure the landowner of a reasonable return on affected property, including the granting of a building permit to prevent substantial damage accruing to the owner where that course of action is required by justice and equity. Maryland's statute controlling development in mapped streets is similar to those involved in *Headley* and *Manders*. * * *

The facts of the present case clearly distinguish it from the cited cases involving the reservation of street locations. As in those cases, we recognize the need to promote intelligent planning by placing reasonable restrictions on the improvement of land scheduled to be acquired for public use. We do not, therefore, condemn as beyond the police power the enactment of reservation statutes which are reasonable in their application both as to duration and severity. Our holding today is a narrow one, limited to the facts before us. We conclude only that the Commission's resolution passed pursuant to * * * the County Code, placing appellees' land in reservation for up to three years, without any reasonable uses permitted as of right, was tantamount to a "taking" in the constitutional sense. Because the Commission's resolution did not provide for the payment of just compensation, it was unconstitutional as applied to the appellees' property and was thus of no effect. Consequently, the trial judge correctly ruled, in accordance with the requested prayer for relief, that the Commission's resolution was a nullity and that the Commission was required to forthwith approve appellees' preliminary subdivision plan.

Judgment affirmed, with costs.

Notes

1.   Regulations which have the effect of preventing any development of land so as to make future acquisition by condemnation less costly are almost invariably held to be takings. One example is Ventures in Property I v. City of Wichita, 225 Kan. 698, 594 P.2d 671 (1979), where the city denied the property owner permission to plat his property preparatory to development because a future highway was scheduled to be built on a portion of the land. Also see Joint Ventures, Inc. v. Department of Transportation, 563 So.2d 622 (Fla.1990).

2.   Many land use enabling statutes have provisions similar to the one litigated in the principal case. However, most such statutes provide for a shorter period of time for the public to decide whether or not to condemn. The typical time period is one year. Would such a provision have saved the Maryland scheme? The court in Chadwick acknowledged a distinction between temporary restrictions on development (valid regulation) and tying up land for a long period (taking), but relied in part on a New Jersey case invalidating a one year reservation scheme. Perhaps one reason for judicial mistrust of reservation schemes is that the way they typically work in practice is that just when the landowner is ready to develop, his land is put into limbo while the public decides whether it can afford to buy him out.

3.   Reservation schemes should be distinguished from situations where public discussion about the acquisition of land takes place or bond elections for such purposes fail to pass. A good discussion of this distinction may be found in Toso v. City of Santa Barbara, 101 Cal.App.3d 934, 162 Cal.Rptr. 210 (1980).

4.   Closely related to reservation schemes and efforts to keep land undeveloped so that it may be condemned at lower cost are situations where the public, through the condemning agency, engages in improper behavior.

Consider the following: A farmer is approached by state highway commission employees seeking right of way for a road across the farmer's land. The farmer, a benevolent person and good citizen, says he will give the land for the road if the highway commission will in turn pave another road leading into a nearby town. The highway commission makes such a verbal promise but fails to perform. Does the farmer have any remedy? See, Arkansas State Highway Comm'n v. Cunningham, 239 Ark. 890, 395 S.W.2d 13 (1965).

NEW JERSEY SHORE BUILDERS ASSOCIATION v. MAYOR AND TOWNSHIP COMMITTEE OF TOWNSHIP OF MIDDLETOWN

Superior Court of New Jersey, Law Division, 1989.
234 N.J.Super. 619, 561 A.2d 319.

PESKOE, J.S.C.

In this action in lieu of prerogative writs, plaintiff attacks the validity of the Middletown Township moratorium ordinance adopted pursuant to *N.J.S.A.* 40:55D–90b. For reasons set forth below, this court concludes that the ordinance is invalid because it was based on a health officer's opinion that lacked the factual basis to demonstrate the existence of a "clear imminent danger to the health of the inhabitants." No published opinion has yet addressed what constitutes the statutorily required demonstration that a municipality must consider. I hold that a moratorium ordinance is not tested by the usual standard applied to a municipal land use ordinance. Rather, the statute requires that municipal action have clear and specific factual support.

* * *

The Municipal Land Use Law (MLUL) governs land use in this State. It delegates to each municipality significant and specific powers to control the use of land within its boundaries. *N.J.S.A.* 40:55D–1 *et seq.* Among these is the power to impose a moratorium on all development. *N.J.S.A.* 40:55D–90b, effective March 21, 1986, sets forth the applicable standards. Prior to the passage of this MLUL amendment, courts had disagreed about a municipality's power to enact moratoriums and, if there was such power, under what circumstances it could be exercised. *N.J. Shore Builders Ass'n v. Dover Tp. Committee,* 191 *N.J.Super.* 627, 468 A.2d 742 (Law Div.1983). There is no longer any doubt about the power or the legislative intent strictly to limit the use of that power.

The power to impose any moratorium may be exercised only upon the determination that there exists "a clear imminent danger to the health of the inhabitants" and the moratorium may endure only for a maximum of six months. In exercising the moratorium power, the municipality is held to a strict necessity test that contrasts strikingly with the general judicial respect accorded municipal land use legislation.
* * *

* * *

Middletown enacted a moratorium applicable only to major site plan and subdivision applications on October 17, 1988. Applications for other development were not affected in any way. The moratorium ordinance was introduced and had a first reading on July 25, 1988. At that time no qualified health officer had submitted a written (or any other) opinion that there existed a clear imminent danger to the inhabitants' health. Earlier that month some residents of Middletown had experienced low water pressure and at its July 18 meeting the township committee discussed the possibility of a building moratorium to alleviate water problems.

* * *

The moratorium ordinance restricts planning board consideration of major subdivisions for six months. It expires in March 1989. The municipal governing body had been considering the moratorium since at least July 25, 1988 and had heard many statements from those attending the hearings prior to adoption of the ordinance. The information provided by the representatives of the water companies was to be considered, as was all other information bearing on the committee's concern, whether given under oath or not. The water company speakers explained in detail the utility's planned augmentation of the pumping system. They explained carefully the status of the raw water supply and the irrelevance of the reservoir level at that time to the problems experienced in Middletown. The relevant concern, in order to increase the water supply, was the pumping and treatment capacity of the system. They pointed out that the failure to approve requests to build pumping stations and water towers had led to the inadequacy of water pressure during peak demand periods in certain locations and from time to time otherwise. There was no raw water shortage in view of the rate by which the reservoirs are naturally replenished. * * *

* * *

The evidence provided by the water company officers was overwhelming that the emergency, if any, was not caused by a shortage of raw water but by an inadequate distribution system. The utility's capacity to pump water was shown to be sufficient to meet the usual level of demand and to meet increased seasonal demand on a short-term basis. If improvements underway were completed on schedule the capacity would soon be adequate for all purposes.

No evidence was presented to the Middletown governing body by fire protection experts or others qualified to evaluate the existence of dangers from inadequate fire protection. The complaints regarding low pressure in particular areas of the township were recurring and were not new, nor were they related to the level of raw water in reservoirs. Those complaints concerned mainly the areas long known to the water company as requiring water towers or similar means to improve the condition.

There was no indication that businesses requiring abundant water were unable to operate. Voluntary conservation measures urged by the water company had apparently resulted in some thirsty lawns but no particular hazard otherwise. Those measures caused the water demand to drop sufficiently so that the water distribution system was no longer overburdened. No witness showed any facts from which the township committee reasonably could find that an imminent health hazard threatened Middletown Township.

The statute requires "a written opinion by a qualified health professional that a clear imminent danger to the health of the inhabitants of the municipality exists." It must be inferred that the Legislature intended that the opinion on which the municipality is to rely has an adequate and fully disclosed factual basis.

The statute requires the municipality to *demonstrate* on the basis of a health expert's opinion that a hazard exists. "Demonstrate" is not defined in the statute. *The Random House Dictionary of the English Language* (1967), unabridged, defines it as "to make evident or establish by arguments or reasoning; prove; to describe, explain or illustrate by examples, specimens, experiments or the like." No such demonstration occurred so as to warrant Middletown's moratorium. The recitation of findings incorporated in ordinance #2061 refers to an exploration of less restrictive measures, but does not enumerate them. No evidence of such exploration was set forth at the hearings. The six findings of fact set forth are not supported by the record.

* * *

Clearly the Legislature did not regard a moratorium as a device to be utilized casually. There are only two provisions in the MLUL dealing with moratoriums. One forbids a municipality's utilization of a moratorium for the purpose of developing and adopting a master plan. The other permits a moratorium solely where the municipality demonstrates a clear imminent danger to the community and requires a health expert's written opinion as a basis for the demonstration.

The Legislature used the word "clear" as to the imminence of danger to be found by the municipality. The word does not appear anywhere else in the MLUL as a basis for decision. Although I am reluctant to enunciate a standard by which to measure the municipality's duty to weigh facts in relation to a legislative act in terms ordinarily relevant to a decision between adversaries, it appears that the Legislature intended that a clear and convincing need for a moratorium be shown before one is enacted.

It is evident that the Legislature intended to set a high standard for the showing that would justify a moratorium. This court infers that had the Legislature specifically addressed the issue, it would have required, at least, that the expert explain in full the reasons for the opinion and that the municipal governing body weigh available credible evidence and consider the adequacy of the reasons in light of all the circumstances. Had the municipality adhered to such a standard, it could not rationally and reasonably have enacted the moratorium ordinance on October 17, 1988.

* * *

* * * Although it is not necessary that I reach this issue, I deem it helpful to state that I conclude further, even if the moratorium had had an adequate statutory basis, its terms were not rationally designed to meet the hazard as defined.

Notes

1. Most situations involving moratoria on development because of water or sewer system emergencies pit developers against a state level agency, usually an environmental agency. This type of moratorium is not litigated frequently because the state's police power interest in public health and safety is easily defended. See, e.g., Ungar v. State, 63 Md.App. 472, 492 A.2d 1336 (1985); Friel v. Triangle Oil Co., 76 Md.App. 96, 543 A.2d 863 (1988). In Estate of Scott v. Victoria County, 778 S.W.2d 585 (Tex.App.1989) the property owner sought compensation for a taking due to a sewer moratorium. The court held that a property owner has no property right in sewer extensions, merely an expectancy of service. In Foster v. Board of Comm'rs of Warrick County, 647 N.E.2d 1147 (Ind.App.1995) the court upheld a moratorium on further building permits in a previously approved subdivision because earlier construction by the developer caused severe drainage problems affecting nearby residents; the county board imposed the moratorium until the inadequate drainage system previously installed by the developer was corrected. And in McNaughton Co. v. Witmer, 149 Pa.Cmwlth. 307, 613 A.2d 104 (1992) the court held that a developer could not recover damages for delay in his project for the period while a validly enacted sewer connection moratorium was in effect.

The New York Times reported on November 20, 1989 (page B 6) a two-year old moratorium on all new sewer mains from Mt. Kisco to Yonkers, New York: "Much of the county's new construction has come to a halt. Although individual home builders can still hook up to existing sewer mains, dozens of developers, who must extend the mains before erecting homes now own land they can neither build on nor sell." Also see Kawaoka v. City of Arroyo Grande, 17 F.3d 1227 (9th Cir.1994) where the court upheld a city's temporary water moratorium against charges of spot zoning, differential treatment, and racial bias against persons of Japanese ancestry; Gilbert v. State, 218 Cal.App.3d 234, 266 Cal.Rptr. 891 (1990), upholding a moratorium on new water connections.

Sometimes a moratorium is enacted specifying one particular land use. In Duncanson v. Board of Supervisors of Danville Twp., 551 N.W.2d 248 (Minn.App.1996) the court upheld a moratorium on feedlots despite the fact that the plaintiff's proposed feedlot was the only project known to be affected by the moratorium. And in First Bet Joint Venture v. City of Central City, 818 F.Supp. 1409 (D.Colo.1993) a moratorium on zoning permits for future gaming facilities was upheld (the plaintiff's taking claim was held not ripe).

See Wendy U. Larsen and Marcella Larsen, Moratoria as Takings Under *Lucas*, Land Use Law (June 1994), p. 3.

2.   Another type of moratorium is one which halts development for a temporary period of time pending adoption of a new comprehensive plan or new zoning ordinance. The validity of this type of moratorium depends upon interpretation of the state's enabling statutes which may or may not expressly grant such power to municipalities. See, e.g., Noghrey v. Acampora, 152 A.D.2d 660, 543 N.Y.S.2d 530 (1989), and Section 2 in the next chapter.

SECTION 3.   REGULATION OF THE SUBDIVISION OF LAND

A.   THE ESSENTIAL REASONS FOR AND NATURE OF SUBDIVISION REGULATION

POMEROY, PREFACE TO THE SUBDIVISION OF LAND IN SAN MATEO COUNTY, CALIFORNIA 11
(1932).

A subdivision is not merely a means of marketing land; it is far more, a process of community building. All the flurry of subdivision sales, all the financial considerations involved at the time, all the huge importance of immediate details—these are infinitesimal factors in the ultimate result, which is the addition of an integral part of the community, a part, which, once established in the comparatively short flash of time involved, is fixed as to its physical framework and permanently marked in its character. The fleeting economic effect of the act of subdividing gives way to the permanent, inexorable economic and social effect of the subdivision as a part of the form and life of the community. No subdivision is too small to have character. It may be no more than a particular curve to a street, or the placing of the lots, or the skillful use of setbacks, or the planting plan; but it may give to a mere linear design the impulse of life and set it throbbing with vitality.

MELLI, SUBDIVISION CONTROL IN WISCONSIN
1953 Wis.L.Rev. 389.

Subdivision control, the regulation of the division of raw land into building lots, is a vital component of land-use control. It has become particularly important in the post World War II period as communities have sprung up in previously rural areas. Its importance is not limited to urban communities and their immediate environs. The trend to country living has turned whole sections some distance from large cities into semi-urban areas. The tremendous expansion of recreational areas has created numerous communities along the shores of lakes and rivers. Fortunately, after the ill-fated experience with uncontrolled subdivision in the 1920's, control of that process has become recognized as an integral part of any land-use planning scheme and the statutes of all states, except one, make some sort of provisions for it.

Subdivision control is, of course, only one of the instruments used by a community to regulate the use of privately owned land in the public interest. It is closely related to zoning control in that both are preventive measures intended to avert community blight and deterioration by requiring that new development proceed in defined ways and according to prescribed standards. Zoning relates to the type of building development which can take place on the land; subdivision control relates to the way in which the land is divided and made ready for building development. The two are mutually dependent because the layout of an area is inseparable from the character of the use to be made of the land. * * *

I.   WHY HAVE SUBDIVISION CONTROLS?

One of the basic problems involved in any type of governmental control is the justification for that control. Just why, many people ask, should a land owner be compelled to obtain the approval of a governmental agency when he is going to divide a parcel of his land into lots for sale. The answer to this question is not simple because the subdividers are not the only group involved. The home buyer, the mortgage lender and, more importantly, the community as a whole are vitally concerned in the process of subdivision. It is only by understanding the relationship of all of these groups to subdivision control that its validity can be determined.

(1) *The Community.* The most important reason for having subdivision control is to provide an effective instrument for land-use control by the community. The community has a legitimate interest in any new subdivision for a number of reasons.

Permanence of development. The original layout of an area will determine its character for an indefinite period of time. Even though another plan may be clearly more desirable, the cost of changing it once the area has been built up is almost prohibitive. Therefore, whether he realizes it or not the subdivider is setting the pattern for the future community. Many of the perplexing problems facing communities today—traffic congestion, high maintenance costs, cramped school areas, slums—are directly traceable to the manner in which they were originally laid out. Obviously the most practical and economical way of meeting these problems is to provide some method by which the original subdivision of raw land can be suited to the needs of the developing community. The alternative to governmental supervision of the private subdivider is municipal ownership and development of outlying areas. This method has been used successfully by a number of European cities and is sometimes advocated as the solution to the problems of American communities. Whether or not it would be an effective solution is difficult to determine in the absence of experience, but traditionally Americans have preferred the first alternative.

Future services. As society becomes more complex the community is called upon to furnish more services to its residents. Because such services will have to be furnished to any new area the community should have an opportunity to consider each new subdivision in relation to the services it is expected to provide. For example, the community will have to furnish schools and recreational facilities to the area, and it should have notice of where an increase in population is expected so that it can plan accordingly.

Safety considerations. The community will have to provide police and fire protection to the new area. It should have an opportunity to make sure that the streets are wide enough to get fire-fighting apparatus in and that the lots are of sufficient size for safety from fire hazards. It will want to check the layout of the area for traffic control and parking problems. The streets must be adequate for modern traffic. The main thoroughfares should be wide and should link with existing main thoroughfares; there should not be too many streets at an intersection and they should intersect at right angles, particularly on main thoroughfares; the street grades and curves should be safe for modern traffic; adequate off-street parking should be provided for commercial and industrial areas. From the safety angle the community will also want to check the subdivision to be sure that there are adequate places for children to play so that they will not have to play in the streets.

Health considerations. Health is another community consideration. The governing unit will want to be sure that the area is one which will be safe for people to live in. For example, the drainage should be checked to be sure that basements will not flood; an investigation should be made to determine whether the sewage disposal plant of the community is adequate to take care of the new area and, if the area is one which cannot be served by public sewer and water, the community will want to be sure that the lots are of a sufficient size so that private disposal of waste will not create a health problem.

Fiscal considerations. In addition to the services which it is called upon to furnish, the community must always keep in mind the pocketbooks of its citizens and must consider each new development in relation to tax revenues. From this standpoint the community is vitally interested in making sure that new subdivisions will not become blighted areas. Blighted areas from which the tax return is low are one of the biggest problems facing communities today because such areas are unable to pay their way. The cost of services furnished by the community—fire and police protection, schools, recreation facilities, sewage disposal, street repairs—exceeds the revenues obtained from them, and the cost of their services must be borne by higher tax rates which bear heavily on those in the more desirable areas. It is generally agreed that the best means of dealing with blighted areas is to prevent them from developing in the first place by insisting on a desirable layout. Areas with narrow streets and lots and inadequate play space for children deteriorate much more rapidly than others.

Just as important, from a fiscal viewpoint, as the layout of the subdivision is the question of whether it should ever have been subdivided in the first place. The scattering of subdivisions too far from community services such as water and sewer, fire protection, public transportation and schools should be prevented if possible. Subdivisions which are not within reasonable reach of all these services will not only be less desirable places for people to live, but will also tax the resources of the community in attempting to furnish the services. For example, the necessity of extending sewer and water mains a great distance may make the lots so expensive that they will not sell and the community—the taxpayers—will have to shoulder the cost of useless improvements.

Another important question in the determination of whether an area should be subdivided is the problem of whether there are too many lots already available for the demand. An excess of subdivided lots may mean not only that whole areas will end up as dead-land, undeveloped but useless as agricultural land because of divided ownerships, confused titles and high tax assessments, but also that areas will be left only partially developed. This means that in order to furnish the necessary services to the developed lots the community will have to extend sewers, water mains and streets past many vacant lots. Of course, it may be both undesirable and unconstitutional to give a community absolute power to prohibit subdivision only because it may create an excess of subdivided lots. For one thing, the basis for such prohibition is not too sound. Predictions about population trends and economic prosperity have been known to err sadly. But the approving authorities should point out the disadvantages to the subdivider in situations like this.

Accurate records. There is one other reason clearly behind many statutory provisions controlling the subdivision of land. This is the necessity of having a clear and accurate description of the subdivided lots. When land is divided into such small parcels, the awkward and frequently inaccurate metes and bounds description is undesirable. Very early in the history of many states a survey and plat of new subdivisions was required. For example, in Wisconsin the original statutes of 1849 made such a requirement. This means that for purposes of transfer and taxes the parcels can be referred to by block and lot in the subdivision.

(2) *The Home Buyer and Mortgage Lender*

In addition to protecting the community interests subdivision control protects the lot purchaser or home buyer and his mortgage lender. Actually much of his protection arises as an incident of the community supervision because any scheme for orderly land-use development will benefit individuals who have invested in the subdivided lots. For example, subdivisions located too far from fire protection, public transportation and schools are a poor investment for the average home owner. Areas so far from public water and sewer that the cost of extending those services is prohibitive should also be avoided. This is true of subdivisions which, because of an excess of subdivided lots, may never be fully built up. In discouraging the subdivision of these areas the community is protecting the potential buyer.

The purchase of a home is a major investment for the average citizen which he usually amortizes over many years. By requiring that the original layout be of a type that will maintain its character for a long period of years, the community is protecting his investment. Aesthetic considerations, such as the orientation of the subdivision away from near-by areas which are undesirable and the requirement of a certain percentage of curved streets and of planting strips along major traffic ways, are of vital importance here. Any study of real estate values will show that these requirements are not for aesthetic purposes only. They prevent deterioration of the area and preserve property values. They are probably the best protection the home owner has for his investment.

In protecting the investment of the home owner, the mortgage lender and the seller under a land contract are also protected. The great interest shown by the FHA in the original planning of subdivisions in which it may be insuring the mortgages is ample evidence of the fact that the original layout of the subdivision affects the investment of the mortgage lender.

Besides protecting his investment from early obsolescence, community control of subdivision also benefits the home owner in other ways. By requiring a survey and plat of the planned area for official scrutiny, the community provides the buyer with accurate boundary lines thus eliminating costly boundary disputes. In addition when the buyer is purchasing in an undeveloped area the plat gives him an idea of what the area will be like when it is fully developed. For example, the plat shows him what the subdivider's plans are as to street layout, location of commercial and recreational areas, if any, and size of other lots. To a certain extent it also protects him from changes in that development plan. The majority rule is that the sale of lots by reference to a plat showing certain streets and public places estops the subdivider from later changing those streets and public places. There is a possibility that the sale of lots by reference to a plat may also estop the subdivider from later lowering the size of the lots shown on the plat although the majority rule is contra.

(3) *The Subdivider*

Subdivision control by the community also benefits the subdividers themselves. Excessive subdivision and the platting of areas which are too far from community services or which are not good for development frequently spell financial ruin for the subdivider. In discouraging this type of subdivision, the community is therefore protecting his interests as well as those of the public and of potential buyers.

By requiring that the subdivider comply with certain standards, the subdivision control law protects the honest subdivider from the fly-by-night operator. The subdivider who invests the money and time necessary to comply with these requirements is not a speculator who is out to make a quick profit and move on to greener fields. Furthermore, while one subdivider may lay out a very desirable subdivision without any community control, he is being protected from subdividers who without such supervision might surround his development with very undesirable areas which would decrease the value of his subdivision.

This does not mean to say that the subdivider receives only benefit from governmental supervision of subdivision. There are many areas where his interests conflict with the other interests involved. While recognizing that there is legitimate need for control of his business, the fact that certain types of requirements may bear too heavily on him cannot be overlooked. Because the subdivider is so important to the development of the community and because it is so necessary that he be encouraged to develop his land in compliance with the platting laws, a complete discussion of the subdivider and his problems is included in this report. * * *

B. GOVERNMENTAL POWER TO REGULATE SUBDIVISIONS

RIDGEFIELD LAND CO. v. DETROIT

Supreme Court of Michigan, 1928.
241 Mich. 468, 217 N.W. 58.

McDONALD, J. The plaintiff has brought certiorari to review the action of the Wayne circuit court in denying a writ of mandamus to compel the defendants to approve a plat. The proposed plat, known as Ridgefield subdivision No. 1, contains 80 acres of land, and is bounded on the north by Pembroke avenue and on the east by Livernois avenue. To conform to the general plan for streets adopted by the city of Detroit, Pembroke avenue ought to be 86 feet wide and Livernois avenue 120 feet wide. In respect to the width of these two streets, the plat did not conform to the general plan. It was submitted to the city plan commission on several occasions, and finally was conditionally approved as follows:

"In order that Mr. Fry may be able to file a plat on the property in question and have his property assessed by lot numbers, the commission agrees to make certain concessions and to approve the plat providing the following changes are made:

1. A 10 foot building line is to be established on Pembroke avenue to conform with property platted to the west.

2. Seventeen feet is to be dedicated for Livernois avenue in addition to the regular 33–foot dedication."

The plaintiff refused to accept the changes, and began this proceeding to compel the approval of the plat as offered.

It is first contended that there is no statute or ordinance authorizing the city plan commission or the city council to require the dedication of an additional 17 feet on Livernois avenue and the establishment of a 10 foot building line on Pembroke avenue as conditions precedent to the approval of this plat.

Under authority of Act No. 279, Pub.Act 1909, as amended (1 Comp.Laws 1915, sec. 3304 et seq.), the city of Detroit provided in its charter for the appointment of a city plan commission of nine members with "power to pass upon the acceptance of all plats of land within and for a distance of three miles beyond the limits of the city."

The authority of the common council with reference to the approval of plats is derived from Act No. 360, Pub.Acts 1925, the applicable portion of which reads as follows:

"The governing body shall determine as to whether such lands are suitable for platting purposes and shall have the right to require that all streets and private roads shall be graveled or cindered and properly drained, and bridges and culverts installed where necessary, and where lots are platted of a width of 60 feet or less, may require that concrete or gravel walks shall be built and that all highways, streets and alleys conform to the general plan that may have been adopted by the governing body of the municipality for the width and location of highways, streets and alleys; * * * The governing body shall reject said plat if the same does not conform to the provisions of this act."

It thus appears that the common council, which is the governing body referred to in the statute, has power to adopt a general plan for the width of streets and to refuse to approve any plan which does not conform thereto. It adopted such a plan. This plan called the "master plan" was prepared by the city plan commission and rapid transit commission in collaboration with the road commissions of Wayne, Oakland, and Macomb counties and the authorities of the included municipalities. It was adopted by resolution of the common council of the city of Detroit on April 14, 1925. As to width and location, it classifies streets as super-highways, major highways, and secondary thoroughfares. Super-highways are required to be 204 feet wide, major highways are section line roads 120 feet in width, and secondary thoroughfares are quarter section lines 86 feet wide. Livernois avenue is a section line road and Pembroke avenue is a quarter section line road. The proposed plat gives these two streets a width of 66 feet each. The plaintiff concedes that in this respect its plat does not conform to the general street plan but it contends that it does conform to the width of Pembroke and Livernois avenues as dedicated in other plats; that the statute gives the city no power to require a greater width as a condition to the approval of the plat and that if it can be interpreted as conferring such power, it is an infringement on the constitutional rights of the plaintiff in that it compels the dedication of private property for public use without compensation therefor. There is no merit to this contention. The other plats referred to were approved and recorded before the present general street plan was adopted; so it cannot be said that it was not made applicable alike to all persons.

The streets in the city of Detroit, as elsewhere, were originally laid out for the horse and buggy age. They are too narrow for the present traffic conditions. It has become necessary for the general convenience and the public safety to widen them and to prevent others of the same

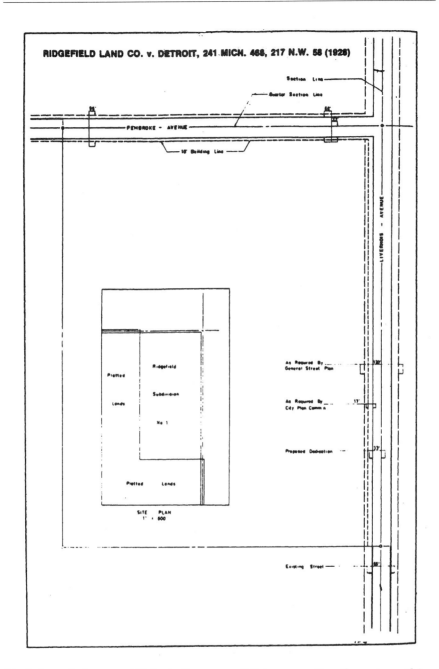

RIDGEFIELD LAND CO. v. DETROIT, 241 MICH. 468, 217 N.W. 58 (1928)

kind from being established. Because of this necessity, there is nothing unreasonable in the demand of the city that the streets designated in the plaintiff's plat shall be of such a width as to conform to the general street plan. It has been determined that streets of a certain width are necessary to accommodate the traffic. They are necessary for the public safety and therefore the right to provide for them is within the police power of the city.

The error in plaintiff's position is the assumption that in requiring an additional dedication and the establishment of a building line to conform to its general plan, the city is exercising power of eminent domain. Its argument would have merit and the authorities cited would have application if this were a case where the plat had been recorded and the city were undertaking to widen the streets or to establish a building line. But this is not such a case. Here the city is not trying to compel a dedication. It cannot compel the plaintiff to subdivide its property or to dedicate any part of it for streets. It can, however, impose any reasonable condition which must be complied with before the subdivision is accepted for record. In theory, at least, the owner of a subdivision voluntarily dedicates sufficient land for streets in return for the advantage and privilege of having his plat recorded. Unless he does so, the law gives him no right to have it recorded. In Ross v. Goodfellow, 7 App.Cas.D.C. 1, 10, 11, it is said:

It must be remembered that each owner has the undoubted right to lay off his land in any manner that he pleases, or not to subdivide it at all. He cannot be made to dedicate streets and avenues to the public. If public necessity demands parts of his lands for highways, it can be taken only by condemnation and payment of its value. But he has no corresponding right to have his plat of subdivision so made admitted to the records.

In providing for public record, congress can accompany the privilege with conditions and limitations applicable alike to all persons. In providing for such record in the act of 1888, congress sought to conserve the public interest and convenience by requiring practical conformity in all subdivisions of land into squares, streets, and avenues, with the general plan of the city as originally established, and this, regardless of the fact that it might in instances practically coerce the dedication of streets to public use which would otherwise have to be paid for.

In the instant case, the defendants have imposed two conditions with which the plaintiff is required to comply for the privilege of having its plat recorded. They are reasonable and necessary for the public welfare. In the exercise of its power under the statute and its charter, the city had a right to impose them. They do not constitute the taking of private property for public use, and are not an infringement on plaintiff's constitutional rights. The circuit judge was right in holding that the statute conferred power upon the city of Detroit to adopt its present general street plan and to refuse to approve and record all plats that did not conform thereto.

The order is affirmed, with costs to the defendants. * * *

Notes

1. The Ridgefield case has been cited in many jurisdictions over the years for the proposition that subdivision regulation is a fair exchange for the privilege of recording the plat and enabling the subdivider to sell lots by

number rather than legal description. Other rationales for subdivision regulation can be found in earlier materials:

A. Consider the following description of the District of Columbia program which ties regulation to public acceptance for maintenance of streets which the subdivider delineates on the proposed plat and offers to dedicate to the public:

Tooke, Methods of Protecting the City Plan in Outlying Districts, 15 Geo.L.J. 127, 137 (1927):

> * * * This third method of protecting the city plan is by a control of the privilege of the owner to dedicate streets and highways in making a subdivision for residential or business purposes. * * * The Act of August 27, 1888, "to regulate the subdivision of land within the District of Columbia" authorized the Commissioners to promulgate general orders regulating the platting and subdividing of all lands within the District and provided that such plats must be approved by them before being admitted to record. Section 5 of the Act laid down that "no future subdivision of land in the District of Columbia, without the limits of the cities of Washington and Georgetown, shall be recorded in the Surveyor's office of the said District, unless made in conformity with the general plan of the city of Washington." In 1893, in order to carry out more completely the same object, Congress passed a supplemental Act providing for a plan for the extension of a permanent system of highways throughout that part of the District lying outside of Washington and Georgetown, which system was to be made as nearly in conformity with the street plan of the city of Washington as the Commissioners should deem advisable and practicable.

> The provisions of the second * * * section were as follows:

> "Sec. 2. And after any such map shall have been so recorded, no further subdivision of any land included therein shall be admitted to record in the office of the surveyor of said district, or in the office of the recorder of deeds thereof, unless the same be first approved by the Commissioners, and be in conformity to such map. Nor shall it be lawful, when any such map shall have been so recorded, for the Commissioners of the District of Columbia, or any other officer or person representing the United States or the District of Columbia, to thereafter improve, repair or assume any responsibility in regard to any abandoned highway within the area covered by such map, or to accept, improve, repair or assume any responsibility in regard to any highway that any owner of land in such area shall thereafter attempt to lay out or establish, unless such landowner shall first have submitted to the Commissioners a plat of such proposed highway, and the Commissioners shall have found the same to be in conformity to such map, and shall have approved such plat, and caused it to be recorded in the office of said surveyor."

* * *

The constitutionality of this Act came before the Supreme Court of the United States in 1896 in the case of Bauman v. Ross, 167 U.S. 548, 17 S.Ct. 966, 42 L.Ed. 270, and was unanimously upheld by the Court.

The opinion of Gray, J., reviewed not only the history of the legislation on the condemnation of lands for public purposes in the District, but also the adjudications of the Courts of the several States upon similar statutory provisions for the taking of lands by eminent domain. As to section 2, the Court said:

"The recording of the map under section 2 does not constitute a taking of any land, nor in any way interfere with the owner's use and enjoyment thereof. The provision of that section that after the map has been recorded, no further subdivision, not in conformity with the map, shall be admitted to record, goes no further than the earlier acts of Congress of January 12, 1809, c. 8, and August 27, 1888, c. 916, cited at the beginning of this opinion; and is clearly within the authority of Congress to prevent anything being placed upon the public records, which may tend to defeat its object of securing uniformity in the entire system of highways in the District. The provision of section 3, giving to any deed or will, duly recorded, which refers to the subdivision made by the map, the same effect as if such subdivision had been made and recorded by the grantor or testator, tends to promote the same object and benefits rather than injures owners of lands. The provision of section 2, forbidding the Commissioners of the District of Columbia and all other public officers or agents to accept, improve, repair, or assume any responsibility in regard to highways not in conformity with the map, does not touch the rights of owners of lands; but was evidently intended to prevent the District of Columbia from being held responsible to travelers upon such highways, under the law prevailing in the District, as declared by this Court, and suffered to remain unchanged by Congress. The object of the recording of the map is to give notice to all persons of the system of highways proposed to be established by subsequent proceedings of condemnation. It does not restrict in any way the use or improvement of lands by their owners before the commencement of proceedings for condemnation of lands for such highways; nor does it limit the damages to be awarded in such proceedings. The recording of the map, therefore, did not of itself entitle the owners of lands to any compensation or damages."

B.   In Trawalter v. Schaefer, 142 Tex. 521, 179 S.W.2d 765 (1944), The Texas Supreme Court upheld the requirement of approval of proposed subdivisions on the theory that such approval was necessary to enable tax assessors to properly locate the newly created lots. Also see Merton v. Dolphin, 28 Wis. 456 (1871).

C.   In many jurisdictions the rationale for subdivision regulation is founded on an expansive and general view of the police power. One of the most sweeping statements can be found in Mansfield & Swett, Inc. v. West Orange, 120 N.J.L. 145, 198 A. 225 (1938):

The state possesses the inherent authority—it antedates the constitution—to resort, in the building and expansion of its community life, to such measures as may be necessary to secure the essential common material and moral needs. The public welfare is of prime importance; and the correlative restrictions upon individual rights—either of person or of property—are incidents of the social order, considered a negligible loss compared with the resultant advantages to the community as a whole. Planning confined to the common need is inherent in the authority to create the municipality itself. It is as old as government itself; it is of the very essence of civilized society. A comprehensive scheme of physical development is requisite to community efficiency and progress.

To particularize, the public health, safety, order and prosperity are dependent upon the proper regulation of municipal life. The free flow of traffic with a minimum of hazard of necessity depends upon the number, location and width of streets, and their relation to one another, and the location of building lines; and these considerations likewise enter into the growth of trade, commerce and industry. Housing, always a problem in congested areas affecting the moral and material life of the people, is necessarily involved in both municipal planning and zoning. And it is essential to adequate planning that there be provision for future community needs reasonably to be anticipated. We are surrounded with the problems of planless growth. The baneful consequences of haphazard development are everywhere apparent. There are evils affecting the health, safety and prosperity of our citizens that are well-nigh insurmountable because of the prohibitive corrective cost. To challenge the power to give proper direction to community growth and development in the particulars mentioned is to deny the vitality of a principle that has brought men together in organized society for their mutual advantage. A sound economy to advance the collective interest in local affairs is the primary aim of municipal government.

The police power of the state may be delegated to the state's municipal subdivisions created for the administration of local self-government, to be exerted whenever necessary for the general good and welfare. It reaches to all the great public needs; and the right of property yields to the exercise of this reserve element of sovereignty. The authority is of the essence of the social compact. The genius of organized government is the subordination of individual personal and property rights to the collective interest. In Commonwealth v. Alger, 61 Mass. (7 Cush.) 53, 84, Chief Justice Shaw spoke thus: "We think it is a settled principle, growing out of the nature of well-ordered civil society, that every holder of property, however absolute and unqualified may be his title, holds it under the implied liability that his use of it may be so regulated, that it shall not be injurious to the equal enjoyment of others having an equal right to the enjoyment of their property, not injurious to the rights of the community. All property in this commonwealth is * * * held subject to those general regulations which are necessary to the common good and general welfare. Rights of property, like all other social and conventional rights, are subject to such reasonable limitations in their enjoyment, as shall prevent them from being injurious, and to such reasonable restraints and regulations established by law, as the legislature, under the governing and controlling power vested in them by the constitution, may think necessary and expedient. This is very different from the right of eminent domain, the right of a government to take and appropriate private property to public use, whenever the public exigency requires it; which can be done only on condition of providing a

reasonable compensation therefor. The power we allude to is rather the police power, the power vested in the legislature by the constitution, to make, ordain and establish all manner of wholesome and reasonable laws, statutes and ordinances, either with penalties or without, not repugnant to the constitution, as they shall judge to be for the good and welfare of the commonwealth, and of the subjects of the same. It is much easier to perceive and realize the existence and sources of this power, than to mark its boundaries, or prescribe limits to its exercise."
* * *

D.   Just as "blue sky" laws regulate sales of securities, so, also to guard against fraud and sharp practices, it is legitimate to regulate land subdivision. This justification for regulation is articulated in Matter of Robert R. Sidebotham, 12 Cal.2d 434, 85 P.2d 453, 122 A.L.R. 496 (1938), cert. denied 307 U.S. 634, 59 S.Ct. 1031, 83 L.Ed. 1516 (1939).

2.   In connection with the "blue sky" theory just mentioned, attention should be given at this point to an important area of federal regulation that has a great impact on land subdivision. The Interstate Land Sales Full Disclosure Act, 15 U.S.C.A. §§ 1701–1720, basically requires developers of residential subdivisions of fifty or more lots to register the subdivision with the Department of Housing and Urban Development, prepare a detailed "property report" which must be provided to every would-be purchaser of a lot, and refrain from certain advertising practices. A cause of action for damages for misrepresentation or omission in the property report is given to the purchaser (§ 1709), and a limited right to revoke a purchase agreement is provided (§ 1703(b)). Among other information required in the property report, is

> "(5) a statement of the present condition of access to the subdivision, the existence of any unusual conditions relating to noise or safety which affect the subdivision and are known to the developer, the availability of sewage disposal facilities and other public utilities (including water, electricity, gas, and telephone facilities) in the subdivision, the proximity in miles of the subdivision to nearby municipalities, and the nature of any improvements to be installed by the developer and his estimated schedule for completion."

The coverage provisions of the act, § 1702, exempt many of the typical urban and suburban subdivisions of more than 50 lots; however, the coverage of the act is still widespread. An indication of the importance and implications of the act can be gathered from the letter which was widely circulated in 1973 by the Office of Interstate Land Sales Registration of the U.S. Department of Housing and Urban Development (HUD):

Re: Interstate Land Sales Full Disclosure Act

Dear Member:

The purpose of this letter is to alert you to consequences which may ensue from your failure to understand fully the Interstate Land Sales Full Disclosure Act and its implementing regulations.

The 1968 Interstate Land Sales Full Disclosure Act became effective April 28, 1969, and has now been operative for nearly four years. Although the

Office of Interstate Land Sales Registration (OILSR) has processed thousands of registrations on both domestic and foreign subdivisions, it is nevertheless likely that an even larger number of subdivisions covered by this Act are still unregistered.

Unless exempt, any developer having 50 or more lots or parcels of subdivided land who sells these lots by using the U.S. mails or any other instruments of interstate commerce, without first registering with OILSR and providing the purchaser in advance of sale with an approved property report, is in violation of the law and may be sentenced to a jail term of 5 years or a $5,000 fine, or both.

In addition, all such contracts are voidable at the absolute and unconditional election of the purchaser. Besides refunding the purchase price of the lot, the developer may be required to pay the reasonable costs of all improvements on the lot or lots. Once an unregistered developer is faced with the wholesale repurchasing of properties previously sold, many of which have already been improved, his bankruptcy is more than a remote possibility. All developers should be forewarned to reassess their positions on the need for registration before it is too late. Attorneys who have developers as clients have a professional responsibility to familiarize themselves with the provisions of the Interstate Land Sales Full Disclosure Act and its implementing regulations, and to advise their clients accordingly.

In addition to the direct penalties that the developer may face, there may be serious derivative consequences for the accountants, bankers and title companies, and even the real estate brokers of unregistered developers under certain circumstances.

We urge you to read and study the Interstate Land Sales Full Disclosure Act and the OILSR Regulations. We are ready at all times to answer any questions from concerned parties.

> Sincerely,
> George K. Bernstein
> Interstate Land Sales Administrator

The Interstate Land Sales Full Disclosure Act has been held to apply to condominium developments. See Winter v. Hollingsworth Properties, Inc., 777 F.2d 1444 (11th Cir.1985) and Schatz v. Jockey Club Phase III, Ltd., 604 F.Supp. 537 (S.D.Fla.1985).

3. The preceding materials all deal with the question of the validity and scope of enabling legislation authorizing municipal regulation of the subdivision of land. In the absence of enabling legislation, could a city regulate subdivisions? See Bella Vista Ranches, Inc. v. City of Sierra Vista, 126 Ariz. 142, 613 P.2d 302 (App.1980) where the court held that a 1966 subdivision ordinance was invalid because the state did not enact enabling legislation until 1974.

DAWE v. CITY OF SCOTTSDALE

Supreme Court of Arizona, In Banc, 1978.
119 Ariz. 486, 581 P.2d 1136.

STRUCKMEYER, VICE CHIEF JUSTICE.

This is an action by appellants to have the recorded plat of the Palo Verde Terrace declared a legally existing subdivision, for a declaration that the City of Scottsdale's annexation of the property covered by the plat and its ordinance adopted after the plat was recorded did not affect the validity of the subdivision plan or the owners' right to develop the property, and to compel Scottsdale to issue certain construction permits. The Superior Court entered a judgment in favor of Scottsdale, declaring Scottsdale's zoning applicable to the Palo Verde Terrace and denying appellants' construction permits. The Court of Appeals reversed, 119 Ariz. 493, 581 P.2d 1143 (App.1978). We accepted review. Opinion of the Court of Appeals vacated. Judgment of the Superior Court affirmed.

* * *

* * * During the time when the county was without any zoning, appellants' predecessors in interest, in order to avoid the 35,000 square-foot minimum lot size requirements of the prior zoning ordinance and the ordinance adopted on February 27, 1960, recorded the Palo Verde Terrace subdivision plat. This plat provided for 120 lots of a maximum 10,000 square feet each. No attempt was made to improve the property and it has remained vacant and unimproved from the date the subdivision was recorded in 1960 through the date of the filing of this action, January 17, 1975. In the year 1963, Scottsdale annexed an area which included the Palo Verde Terrace. Scottsdale's zoning permitted a minimum size of 35,000 square feet per lot in the annexed area.

The principal question at issue is whether the appellants have had since 1963 a vested right to develop substandard lots within the City of Scottsdale because of the recording of their plat. We think not.

It has been repeatedly held that subdivision ordinances apply to lots on prior recorded maps which were unsold at the time of the ordinance's enactment. Ziman v. Village of Glencoe, 1 Ill.App.3d 912, 275 N.E.2d 168 (1971); Sherman–Colonial Realty Corp. v. Goldsmith, 155 Conn. 175, 230 A.2d 568 (1967); Blevens v. City of Manchester, 103 N.H. 284, 170 A.2d 121 (1961); State ex rel. Mar–Well, Inc. v. Dodge, 113 Ohio App. 118, 177 N.E.2d 515 (1960); Caruthers v. Board of Adjustment, 290 S.W.2d 340 (Tex.Civ.App.1956).

* * *

Appellants, however, argue that the case of Robinson v. Lintz, 101 Ariz. 448, 420 P.2d 923 (1966), holds that a subdivision lot becomes legally established as to size and description when it is properly recorded and that it is unaffected by subsequent zoning enactments or amendments. Robinson v. Lintz is authority for the proposition that a subdivision lot becomes legally established as to size and description when a plat containing it is recorded. But it does not hold that such a lot is unaffected by subsequent zoning enactments.

* * *

* * * *Robinson* did not concern itself with the problem we must decide here; namely, whether the filing of a plat immunizes a parcel of real estate from subsequent zoning regardless of how urgent the need for regulation might be.

A. Rathkopf, in The Law of Zoning and Planning, Ch. 71, § 11, page 93 (4th ed. 1978), states:

> " * * * whether the subdivider has the right to continue the development of his subdivision as planned in the face of changed rules and regulations of the planning board, or an amendment to the zoning ordinance which changes the permitted uses or the nonuse restrictions of land covered by the plat, is in great measure governed by the same considerations which determine vested rights under a building permit."

We have held that where the amount of work which was done toward the construction of a service station was of small consequence, the permittee acquired no vested right to complete the construction of the building if the board of supervisors exercised its power to rezone the property and revoked the building permit. Verner v. Redman, 77 Ariz. 310, 271 P.2d 468 (1954).

* * *

Judgment of the Superior Court affirmed.

Notes

1. Does this case indicate that any new subdivision requirement may be applied retroactively to the development of land which was platted at an earlier time? The problem of retroactive subdivision regulation is not unusual, but the case law is sparse. See Brous v. Smith, 304 N.Y. 164, 106 N.E.2d 503 (1952); Town of Seabrook v. Tra–Sea Corp., 119 N.H. 937, 410 A.2d 240 (1979); Lampton v. Pinaire, 610 S.W.2d 915 (Ky.App.1980); Williamson Pointe Venture v. City of Austin, 912 S.W.2d 340 (Tex.App.1995); State ex rel. Dreher v. Fuller, 257 Mont. 445, 849 P.2d 1045 (1993).

Presumably, if the new requirements are within the police power, the community may impose them through the building permit or similar administrative process as well as by way of subdivision plat approval. However, if the landowner has changed his position in reliance on old requirements or the absence of requirements, some courts might approach the problem by finding a vested right in the landowner to proceed without meeting the new conditions. Some cases which shed light on the vested right theory are Gruber v. Mayor and Twp. Committee of Raritan Twp., 39 N.J. 1, 186 A.2d 489 (1962); Spindler Realty Corp. v. Monning, 243 Cal.App.2d 255, 53 Cal.Rptr. 7 (1966), certiorari denied 385 U.S. 975, 87 S.Ct. 515, 17 L.Ed.2d 437 (1966) and Western Land Equities, Inc. v. City of Logan, 617 P.2d 388

(Utah 1980).[33] In Town of Orangetown v. Magee, 88 N.Y.2d 41, 643 N.Y.S.2d 21, 665 N.E.2d 1061 (1996) the court upheld a $5 million dollar verdict for a developer whose building permit was wrongfully revoked in mid-project. The trial court found that the developer had spent over $4 million on preparation and land clearing before work was halted by the town. A similar case is Reserve, Ltd. v. Town of Longboat Key, 17 F.3d 1374 (11th Cir.1994) where after spending $6 million the developer's permit was revoked under an ordinance provision providing for revocation of a permit if, after construction was commenced, no substantial work was accomplished in any 30–day period.

2. In Prince George's County v. Sunrise Development Limited Partnership, 330 Md. 297, 623 A.2d 1296 (1993) the court set out the following factual situation:

> In this case the developer of a proposed twelve-story apartment building contends that the project was sufficiently advanced on May 1, 1990, to prevent downzoning. The developer's vested rights argument ultimately rests on a single footing, one that was placed in the ground during the preceding December for a proposed column at a proposed outside corner of a proposed portico.

> * * *

> [The court accepted the Maryland rule as embodying a two-prong test, (1) a manifest commencement of labor on the ground which everyone can readily see and recognize as the commencement of a building, and (2) the work must have been begun with the intention to continue the work until completion of the building.]

> Turning from semantics to the merits of this controversy, the question is whether the Board acted arbitrarily, capriciously or without substantial evidence in concluding that the footing in the middle of the 9.9591 acre site was not readily visible or recognizable on May 1, 1990, as the commencement of a highrise apartment building. The footing's dimensions, as reflected by the Board, result in an area of four square feet. A four square foot footing occupies 9/1,000,000 of the R–10 zone, considered in two dimensions. The footing occupies none of the air space of the R–10 zone, if it is considered in three dimensions. The Board did not err in declining to conclude that this swatch of cement would alert persons who came on the property that construction of a building had begun under the R–10 use.

Also see Lake Bluff Housing Partners v. South Milwaukee,197 Wis.2d 157, 540 N.W.2d 189 (1995) holding that a change in zoning during the developer's activities did not upset the developer's vested rights. The state bar association is apparently drafting legislation to provide for development

33. In California, where judicial rulings have consistently rejected the vested right argument, the legislature, in 1979, enacted a provision authorizing cities and developers to enter into development agreements. Cal.Govt.Code § 65864 et seq. For analysis of this legislation, see Hagman, Development Agreements, 3 Zoning and Planning Law Report Nos. 9 and 10 (Oct., Nov.1980). In the Utah case the court held that a developer's rights should vest at the time of application for a building permit; the court discusses several alternative theories in the opinion.

agreements in Wisconsin in order to overcome the uncertainties created by the case.

3.   With the principal case, compare Selby Realty Co. v. City of San Buenaventura, 10 Cal.3d 110, 109 Cal.Rptr. 799, 514 P.2d 111 (1973). Also see State ex rel. Craven v. City of Tacoma, 63 Wash.2d 23, 385 P.2d 372 (1963).

4.   Does the reasoning in the principal case suggest that compulsory subdivision is within the police power? If so, what becomes of the theory that subdivision is a privilege which can be conditioned on the dedication of land for streets and other amenities? Should the classic theory be modified to one which allows any kind of land development to be subjected to conditions and permits? Consider the following case and the notes thereafter.

CITY OF CORPUS CHRISTI v. UNITARIAN CHURCH OF CORPUS CHRISTI

Court of Civil Appeals of Texas, 1968.
436 S.W.2d 923, refused n.r.e.

NYE, JUSTICE. The Unitarian Church of Corpus Christi as the owner of certain property, applied to the City of Corpus Christi for a building permit to improve its property for church purposes. The church was told by a city department employee that the church property would have to be platted prior to the issuance of the permit. The church prepared a plat of the property, outlining the boundaries of its lot, designating utility easements and submitted it to the City Planning Commission for approval. After a hearing on the church's application, the Commission conditionally approved the church's plat. Approval was subject to the church dedicating a strip of their land, 25 feet by 630 feet for the purpose of widening an easement so that an existing street could be extended. The church was dissatisfied and appealed this decision to the City Council seeking approval of their plat without the requirement of street dedication. After a hearing, the City Council denied the relief sought by the church. The church then filed suit in the district court seeking a declaratory judgment: that the City had no authority under the applicable statutes, charters, and ordinances to require the church to file a map or plat of its property as a condition to granting the building permit. The church sought additionally, the issuance of a writ of manda-mus to compel the City to approve their submitted plat. The trial was had before the court without a jury, resulting in a judgment granting the writ of mandamus against the City and ordering approval of the plat as submitted by the church. * * *

The church's lot faces a major dedicated city street (Carroll Lane) on the southeast side. The lot was and is presently served with public utilities. Adjoining the church's property on the northeast side is a tract of land (also 2½ acres) called the Hancock Tract which has heretofore been platted. The owners of the Hancock Tract had dedicated to the City a strip of land 25 feet by 630 feet, being one half of the proposed extension of Kay Street. The City by its present action would require the church to dedicate the other half of the Kay Street extension as a condition to the approval of the plat and the subsequent granting of a building permit. See the following diagram.

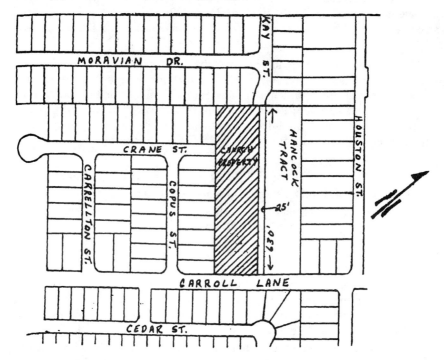

The church is the owner of the property within the City that is not now platted into lots and blocks. The charter of the City of Corpus Christi provides that the City " * * * shall never grant any permit to construct or repair any house or structure within such area (unplatted property) until such map shall be so approved and filed * * *." It follows as we discuss this point in more detail later, that it would be necessary that as a condition precedent to the granting of a building permit by the City, that the church must file a plat of its unplatted property. It is likewise proper for a city to require a property owner to obtain a building permit prior to the erection of a building. This requirement is a valid exercise of a municipality's police power. * * *

This is a limited type law suit involving a single lot owner whose unplatted property was annexed into the City. The property owner wishes to obtain a building permit to build in connection with the entire lot, understanding that such lot would not now or ever, under its proposed plat, be subdivided into two or more lots.

If the statutes, charter provisions or ordinances pertaining to the City of Corpus Christi do not impose upon the church a legal obligation to dedicate a portion of its land for street purposes under these facts, or if such statutes, charter provisions or ordinances do not authorize the City to require a property owner to make such dedication, then the issuance of a mandamus will be proper. Where the church has done all that the statutes and law demands, the authorized granting of a building permit becomes a mere ministerial duty, the performance of which may be compelled by mandamus. Thus where the City itself or by and through its planning commission, in its construction of the law, deprives a citizen of an unquestionable legal right and there is no other adequate remedy, the court having power to issue mandamus may review the matter. Commissioners' Court v. Frank Jester Development Co., 199 S.W.2d 1004 (Tex.Civ.App.—Dallas 1947, n.r.e.)

* * * Article V, Section 6 of the charter of the City of Corpus Christi provides in part as follows:

> "Any property within the City * * * *not now platted into blocks and lots,* shall be platted * * * to conform to the requirements of * * * (the) * * * Department of Public Works and Zoning and Planning Commission. Its owners, before such property is laid off and *subdivided* shall file * * * a correct map thereof. The City shall never pay for the property used for streets * * * within any such subdivision, * * * "(emphasis supplied)

> " * * * After approval such map shall be filed in the office of the County Clerk in the manner provided by law. The head of the engineering * * * (Department) * * * shall never grant any permit to construct or repair any house or structure within such area until such map shall be so approved and filed * * *."

The City, by ordinance adopted in part the rules and regulations governing the platting of land into subdivisions as provided in Art. 974a, Vernon's Ann.Civ.St. Section 1 of such article provides in part as follows:

> "Hereafter every owner of any tract of land situated within the corporate limits * * * who may hereafter *divide* the same in two or more parts *for the purpose of laying out any subdivision* of any tract of land or any addition to any * * * city, or for laying out suburban lots or building lots, * * * shall cause a plat to be made thereof * * *." (emphasis supplied).

The City's ordinance above referred to a defined a subdivision as follows:

> "C. *SUBDIVISION.* A subdivision *is the division* of any lot, tract or parcel of land *into two or more parts,* lots or sites, *for the purpose,* whether immediate or future *of sale or division of ownership.* This definition also includes the resubdivision of land or lots which are a part of a previously recorded subdivision * * *." (emphasis supplied).

> "D. *SUBDIVIDER AND/OR DEVELOPER.* The terms 'subdivider' and 'developer' are synonymous and used interchangeably, and shall include any person, * * * who does, or participates in the *doing of, any act toward the subdivision of land* within the intent, scope, and purview of this ordinance. The singular shall include the plural, and the plural shall include the singular." (emphasis supplied).

The language of Section 1 of Art. 974 is plural and relates to a division of property into parts. The same is true of the City charter and the applicable provisions of its ordinances. It contemplates subdivision for subdivision development purposes. The City's argument that the singular and plural include each other is not applicable to the provisions. A municipal charter is to be read as a whole and every word, phrase, and expression must be considered and interpreted as if deliberately chosen and used for a purpose. 39 Tex.Jur.2d, § 45, Municipal Corporations, p. 397. The church does not propose to divide its property into two or more parts or to lay out a subdivision as stated in Art. 974a and the City's charter.

We believe that the applicability of the language in Art. 974a is controlled by the word "divide". The statute states that "every owner of any tract of land * * * who may hereafter *divide* the same in two or more parts * * * "controls the disposition of those who are affected thereby.

The City relies upon the case of Ayres v. City Council of Los Angeles, 34 Cal.2d 31, 207 P.2d 1, 11 A.L.R.2d 503 (1949) and Southern Pacific Company v. City of Los Angeles, 242 Cal.App.2d 38, 51 Cal.Rptr. 197 (1966). However, in each of these cases an ordinance or statute gave the authority required of them.

It is urged upon us that since the City's platting ordinance provides that whenever a half street has already been provided for, adjacent to a tract *"to be subdivided,"* the other remaining half street shall be platted in such *subdivision* in accordance with Section VI–A of the ordinance. (emphasis supplied). This platting ordinance refers to subdivisions and the emphasis is on "subdivide". The City summarizes the record and contends that the overwhelming evidence shows that the trial court erred and abused its discretion in ordering a writ of mandamus to issue against the City to approve the church's plat in the face of the statutes, charter and ordinance which govern the approval of such plats. This is not a discretionary matter. There is no statute, charter or ordinance which would require the church as a single lot owner to dedicate a portion of its property for streets in order to get approval of its plat to obtain a building permit, where the church does not propose to subdivide the lot into smaller lots or otherwise divide it into a subdivision.

We have no quarrel with the trial court's judgment that the various articles and ordinances make the reasonable requirement that the church must file a plat of its unplatted lot. However, the withholding of a building permit upon the condition that a portion (amounting to 15%) of the church's property be dedicated to public use as a condition for the approval of such plat, is not by law authorized in this case.

* * *

We have considered all of appellant's points of error and they are overruled.

The judgment of the trial court is affirmed.

Notes

1.   Is the problem in the principal case that the city had geared all of its required exactions to the concept of "subdivision" and failed to anticipate the problem of "development" of a large parcel without dividing it into two or more lots? Is the cure for the problem to define the city's power in a way which would include more than just the division of land? Some enabling statutes do just that. The Arkansas statute, for example, provides in Ark. Code Ann. § 14–56–417: "Following adoption and filing of a master street plan, the planning commission may prepare and shall administer, after approval of the legislative body, regulations controlling the development of land. The development of land includes, but is not limited to the provision of access to lots and parcels, the extension or provision of utilities, the subdividing of land into lots and blocks, and the parceling of land resulting in the need for access and utilities." Compare with the principal case Bethlehem Evangelical Lutheran Church v. City of Lakewood, 626 P.2d 668 (Colo.1981).

In Village of Lake Bluff v. Jacobson, 118 Ill.App.3d 102, 73 Ill.Dec. 637, 454 N.E.2d 734 (1983), the court held that a village could enforce its subdivision ordinance to enjoin construction of an apartment building on non-subdivided property outside the city limits but within the statutory planning jurisdiction.

Two Texas decisions in 1985 held that development of mobile home parks, with spaces leased to individual mobile home owners, constituted subdivisions. See Cowboy Country Estates v. Ellis County, 692 S.W.2d 882 (Tex.App.1985) and City of Weslaco v. Carpenter, 694 S.W.2d 601 (Tex.App. 1985).

2.   In those states where the enabling legislation is tied to the subdivision plat as the triggering event for regulation or exactions, the problem of how to deal with avoidance of regulation through metes and bounds sales arises. By not subdividing into lots and blocks, can the developer avoid all regulation?

The metes and bounds problem plagues land planners almost everywhere. By selling off individual parcels without benefit of recorded plat, the subdivider avoids meeting the conditions which he knows would be imposed if he presented a formal plat for approval. If a great many metes and bounds parcels are created, attempts at public planning of land development are frustrated, and prospective subdividers become less and less willing to subject themselves to regulations which so many neighbors have escaped. One approach to the problem is that of a statute which would refuse a building permit to the metes and bounds owner, unless reasonable planning conditions (like construction of a road) are met. Of course this may penalize the innocent purchaser instead of the fellow who schemed to avoid the law. What about providing by law for a right to avoid the sale?

Another approach is to define "subdivision" as including 2 or more lots. Then every land division (a division always produces at least two parcels) means a survey, a plat, and plat approval. The expense and delay for the man who has only a few lots to dispose of make this difficult to sell to local municipal governing bodies or to state legislatures. And even if sold it must be carefully policed, by inadequately manned staffs.

A further approach is not to require a formal survey or plat, for divisions into just a few lots, but to insist nevertheless on planning commission approval on the deeds of transfer. This approach is evidenced by the following Oklahoma statute:[34]

" * * * [W]hoever, being the owner or agent of the owner of any parcel of ground, transfers, or sells, or agrees to sell, or negotiates to sell any tract of land of two and one half (2½) acres or less where such tract was not shown of record in the office of the County Clerk as separately owned at the effective date of the regulations hereinafter provided for and not located within a subdivision approved according to law and filed of record in the office of the County Clerk, or if so located, not comprising at least one (1) entire lot as recorded, without first obtaining the written approval of the Commission by its endorsement on the instrument of transfer, shall be subject to the penalties of this Act provided; and such transaction shall be unlawful and the deed or other instrument of transfer shall not be valid, and if recorded, shall not import notice; and the description of 'such lot or parcel by metes and bounds, in the instrument of transfer or other document used in the process of selling or transferring, shall not exempt the transaction or the parties from such penalties or from the remedies in this Act provided.

"In its consideration of such transfers, referred to as 'lot-splits', the Commission shall apply the same regulations as are applied to subdivisions in order to accomplish the purposes of planning as herein provided."[35]

Compare with this approach the case of State ex rel. Anaya v. Select Western Lands, Inc., 94 N.M. 555, 613 P.2d 425 (App.1979).

Another approach to the metes and bounds problem is through a blue sky type of statute requiring real estate sales contracts to state that the land fronts on a private street, or on no street at all, and that the municipality has no liability to install improvements or utilities. See Cornick, Problems Created by Premature Subdivision of Urban Lands in Selected Metropolitan Districts 316 (N.Y.Ex.Dept., Div. State Planning 1938).

A 1953 attempt in Wisconsin to get at the metes and bounds problem is worth recounting largely because of caveats implicit in it for those who would presume to draft land use legislation. The State's Director of Regional Planning prepared a so-called metes and bounds bill for the 1953 session of the legislature. With the backing of the State League of Municipalities, the bill passed both houses of the legislature without any difficulty, and was signed by the Governor. This bill, later known as Chapter 351 of the Laws of 1953, applied only to lands located within cities and villages and to lands within their respective platting "jurisdictions"—a mile and a half out from the boundaries of villages and fourth class cities and three miles out for all other cities. No conveyance of a parcel within such areas creating a new metes and bounds description was to be valid or recordable unless: (1) The parcel was surveyed and monumented in accordance with requirements just a shade less rigorous than those for "subdivisions" of 5 or more lots; (2) A

34. Okl.Stat. Tit. 19, § 863.10 (1962).

35. Little seems to be known about the actual operation of this statute. See 19 Okl. Bar J. 933 (1948).

map was prepared as specified; (3) Access to a public road or street was provided, certain lot size minima were met, and, for land adjoining lakes and streams, regulations of the state board of health were met; (4) The governing body of the village or city certified compliance with the requirements on the map; and (5) The certified map accompanied the instrument of conveyance when it was offered for recordation.

After a copy of the act had been circulated by the state bar association, loud cries of mortification were heard from the conveyancers, bankers, and realtors. The act was particularly offensive to the bar in that it required the title examiner to check to see whether or not all the terms of the act had been complied with, because without that the conveyance was void and title under it unmarketable. Besides, the minimum area and highway access requirements made no provision for the transfer of a narrow strip of land by one neighbor to another for driveway or garage building purposes. And it was thought that the act threw an undue burden of administrative responsibility upon the register of deeds. In addition a great deal was made of the fact that the act attempted to regulate even the transfer of a single parcel. In any event at an adjourned session of the legislature in October 1953, the law was quickly wiped off the books.

3. Can a testamentary devise establish a subdivision? See In re Estate of Sayewich, 120 N.H. 237, 413 A.2d 581 (1980). How about a judicial partition of land? See Mount Laurel Twp. v. Barbieri, 151 N.J.Super. 27, 376 A.2d 541 (1977). A Minnesota statute enables counties with subdivision regulations to require review of all real estate transfer agreements for compliance with subdivision regulations. 1977 Minn.Laws Ch. 189. Is this a workable solution to the metes and bounds problem? In Hyler v. Town of Blue Hill, 570 A.2d 316 (Me.1990) the court found that execution of seven deeds dividing a parcel of land among family members, after the grantor had failed to get a subdivision approved, was an attempt to evade the subdivision ordinance. (Maine has a statute exempting gifts to family members from subdivision regulation).

4. In Town of Tuftonboro v. Lakeside Colony, Inc., 119 N.H. 445, 403 A.2d 410 (1979), the court held that conversion of an existing colony of rental cottages to a condominium development constituted a subdivision requiring the developer to comply with the subdivision ordinance.

Compare Ivy Club Investors v. City of Kennewick, 40 Wash.App. 524, 699 P.2d 782 (1985), where the court held that the city could not condition approval of a conversion of apartments to condominiums upon the payment of park fees as prescribed in the subdivision ordinance.

C. SUBDIVISION EXACTIONS AND OTHER REGULATION IS-SUES

Can a local unit require as a condition to subdivision plat approval:

a. Installation of public improvements such as street grading, street surfacing, sanitary and storm sewers, water mains, curb and gutter, sidewalks, street trees and street signs; or

b. Dedication of subdivision streets and widening strips along existing boundary streets; or

    c. Imposition of restrictive covenants dictated by the local unit but promised by the developer; or

    d. Dedication of land (or first rights of purchase) for park, playground, school, police or fire station, sites; or

    e. Payment of fees in lieu of such dedication; or

    f. Written findings by the local school board that school facilities will be adequate to take care of the children from the proposed subdivision; or

    g. A "contract" by the developer to contribute a substantial sum for school construction, a water or sewerage or other public facility?

These pose issues faced by developers on the growth fringes of many of America's urban areas. Obviously, answers to many if not most of the questions may turn on factual variables, not stated. How wide a widening strip? What restrictive covenants? Is the fee for a neighborhood park or one that is city-wide? Clearly also, in analyzing such issues in particular cases, a first step is to ascertain whether the applicable enabling statute authorizes the action taken. Here, admittedly, the attitude a court brings to the task of construing the statute may make a major difference. But also, the action may be ultra vires and void even on the most liberal construction. Thus, to get to issues of constitutionality, we must assume sufficient enabling delegation. Notice that we talk about what would happen if the particular action were reviewed in a court. Actually, dozens of conditions of doubtful validity imposed on developers are as a practical fact accepted by them and not contested in court. The developer is after all a businessman anxiously awaiting the day when he can begin realizing on his substantial investment by selling lots or lots and houses. A court review may delay that day for a long time. In addition, he may be quite anxious not to arouse the antagonism of the very local officials before whom he may again be shortly reappearing and asking approval for another subdivision. Finally, he may be able to pass the additional cost of the imposed condition on to his customer. In fact, the developer may even be able to charge a profit on the additional cost.

An undeniable fact stands out. The subdivider is in a business which places costs (externalities) onto the community at large. How do we measure these costs? And once measured can they be charged back, regardless of the manner of charge? And can the charging back be premised on rough and ready estimates or must there be precise cost-benefit analyses? What if any role does municipal past practice play? Police stations have always been paid for out of general taxes; small parks are sometimes paid for through special assessments. Are such facts significant?

(1) Traditional Exactions

PETTERSON v. CITY OF NAPERVILLE

Supreme Court of Illinois, 1956.
9 Ill.2d 233, 137 N.E.2d 371.

[The plaintiff obtained a declaratory judgment from the trial court declaring the city of Naperville's subdivision control ordinance void. The case is up on direct appeal from this judgment. Plaintiff's land is located in Du Page County outside Naperville but within its 1½ mile extraterritorial plat approval jurisdiction. Du Page County approved the plat under its subdivision control ordinance requiring bituminous streets only 20 feet wide, without curbs and gutters. On its review the Naperville city planning commission under the city's ordinance required bituminous streets 25 feet wide and plaintiffs agreed to provide these. But the planning commission also required curbs and gutters and suitable storm water drainage facilities. These it was estimated, would cost $19,000 more than the county approved scheme, and the plaintiff refused to provide them. The planning commission then refused to approve the plat. Plaintiff claims the commission's action is (1) ultra vires as to the enabling statutes and (2) arbitrary and unreasonable and therefore unconstitutional.]

Mr. Justice Davis [after reviewing the facts and analyzing the applicable Illinois statutes]:

* * * A consideration of the above statutes and their amendatory provisions reveals the clear intention of our legislature to grant to municipalities adopting an official plan exclusive control and jurisdiction over the subdivision of lands located not more than one and one-half miles beyond the corporate limits of the municipality. Cities ordinarily have no jurisdiction beyond their corporate limits, and municipal ordinances are confined in their application to the territory of the municipality adopting them. Dean Milk Co. v. City of Elgin, 405 Ill. 204, 90 N.E.2d 112; City of Rockford v. Hey, 366 Ill. 526, 9 N.E.2d 317. But the legislature may, if it sees fit, confer special extraterritorial powers on municipalities, and when it does so the courts recognize and give effect to them. City of West Frankfort v. Fullop, 6 Ill.2d 609, 129 N.E.2d 682; Chicago Packing and Provision Co. v. City of Chicago, 88 Ill. 221. The exercise of such extraterritorial powers by a municipality is, of course, always subject to the requirement that the ordinance passed pursuant to legislative authority constitutes a valid exercise of the police power, and bears a reasonable and substantial relation to the public health, safety or general welfare. City of Park Ridge v. American Nat. Bank and Trust Co., 4 Ill.2d 144, 122 N.E.2d 265, 50 A.L.R.2d 900. It is true that the legislature has given to counties certain powers relative to maps, plats and subdivisions. This power was first conferred in 1915 (Laws of 1915, p. 334–335) and enlarged in 1949. (Ill.Rev.Stat.1949, ch. 34, par. 25.09.) However, there is nothing in these legislative provisions relative to the powers of counties which indicates that it was not the intention of the

legislature to give exclusive control in those areas within one and one-half miles outside the territorial limits of a municipality to municipalities which have an official plan in effect in such territory. Thus, even though the county of Du Page adopted a resolution regulating subdivisions in the county, the lands in question here, being within the limits prescribed by the City Plan Commission Act and the subdivision control ordinance, are subject to the exclusive control and jurisdiction of the city of Naperville so far as the subdivision of lands and the approval of maps and plats of such subdivisions are concerned.

Plaintiffs contend that the ordinance as drawn is void as an exercise of power by the defendant beyond the grant of the statute; that the statute by granting the right to include "reasonable requirements with reference to streets, alleys, and public grounds," does not contemplate that a city may include such requirements as curbs and gutters or the other improvements prescribed by the ordinance. In this connection the plaintiffs rely on those cases which hold that the legislative powers of cities are strictly construed, and if there is any reasonable doubt as to the existence of the power, the doubt must be resolved against the municipality. But the primary object of statutory construction is to ascertain and give effect to legislative intent. In ascertaining legislative intent, the courts should consider the reason or necessity for the enactment and the meaning of the words, enlarged or restricted, according to their real intent. Likewise the court will always have regard to existing circumstances, contemporaneous conditions, and the object sought to be obtained by the statute. People ex rel. Holvey v. Kapp, 355 Ill. 596, 189 N.E. 920; Chicago Packing and Provision Co. v. City of Chicago, 88 Ill. 221.

Subsection 2 of section 2 of the City Plan Commission Act (Ill.Rev. Stat.1953, ch. 24, par. 53–2(2)) in force at the time of the adoption of the subdivision control ordinance, grants to planning commissions in municipalities of more than 500,000 inhabitants, or in municipalities lying wholly or partly within a radius of thirty miles from the corporate limits of municipalities of more than 500,000 inhabitants, the power to recommend to the corporate authorities a plan or plans for the development and redevelopment of the municipality and contiguous unincorporated territory not more than one and one-half miles beyond the corporate limits of the municipality, and further empowers the commission "To provide for the health, safety, comfort and convenience of the inhabitants of the municipality and contiguous territory, such plan or plans may establish reasonable standards of design for subdivisions and for resubdivisions of unimproved land and of areas subject to redevelopment, including reasonable requirements for public streets, alleys, ways for public service facilities, parks, playgrounds, school grounds, and other public grounds." We believe that the power to prescribe reasonable requirements for public streets in the interest of the health and safety of the inhabitants of the city and contiguous territory includes more than a mere designation of the location and width of streets as plaintiffs seem to contend. The legislature undoubtedly had in mind the complex problems connected with the development of territory contiguous to cities as bearing on the health and safety of all inhabitants within and without the municipality; that in such territory, in the interest of uniformity, continuity, and of public health and safety, the streets should be constructed in such a way as to afford reasonably safe passage to the traveling public and provide reasonable drainage in the interests of health. Plaintiffs made no objection to the paving requirements set forth in the ordinance and agreed to comply with those provisions, apparently considering them to be within the powers granted. Considering the expressed object and purpose of the legislation, it is our conclusion that the provisions of the ordinance requiring curbs and gutters and proper drainage are within the powers conferred by the statute.

The trial court found that the ordinance, as applied to plaintiffs and their property, was arbitrary, unreasonable and discriminatory and had no reasonable relation to the public health, safety or general welfare, and that it was therefore unconstitutional and void. The only proof offered to sustain this finding was evidence which compared the cost of complying with the county regulations and the cost of complying with the requirements of the subdivision control ordinance, together with some testimony that the surface waters drained westward to the river and not toward the city. The fact alone that the cost of curbs and gutters and the drainage facilities prescribed by the subdivision control ordinance would be greater than the cost of open ditches and culverts forms no basis for the finding that the ordinance is arbitrary, unreasonable or discriminatory. There is no proof whatever to show that the ordinance affects plaintiffs' property any differently than other property within the area in question or that it imposes unreasonable or excessive burdens upon the plaintiffs. One who challenges the validity of an ordinance as arbitrary and unreasonable must prove by clear and affirmative evidence that the ordinance constitutes arbitrary, capricious and unreasonable municipal action; that there is no permissible interpretation which justified its adoption, or that it will not promote the safety and general welfare of the public. First Nat. Bank of Lake Forest v. County of Lake, 7 Ill.2d 213, 130 N.E.2d 267. The fact alone that the ordinance may operate to impose burdens or restrictions on the property which would not have existed without the enactment of the ordinance is never determinative of the question of validity. Miller Brothers Lumber Co. v. City of Chicago, 414 Ill. 162, 111 N.E.2d 149. The privilege of the individual to use his property as he pleases is subject always to a legitimate exercise of the police power under which new burdens may be imposed upon property and new restrictions placed upon its use when the public welfare demands. 2700 Irving Park Bldg. Corp. v. City of Chicago, 395 Ill. 138, 69 N.E.2d 827. Plaintiffs offered no convincing proof to support their contention that the ordinance bears no reasonable relation to the public health, safety or general welfare. Such proof as was adduced on this question was introduced by defendant and supports the opposite conclusion. The trial court erred in holding the ordinance unconstitutional on the ground that it was arbitrary, unreasonable and confiscatory and without proper relation to the legitimate objects of the police powers.

* * *

Plaintiffs further urge that the subdivision control ordinance is unconstitutional because it amounts to either taxation without the consent of the taxpayers, or to an exercise of the power of eminent domain without providing compensation to the property owner for the property taken for public use; that if the statute is construed as providing for a form of taxation or special assessment for local improvements, it is void as violating the constitutional provision for uniformity of taxation; and that if the power exercised thereunder is a power of eminent domain, it violates the constitutional requirement that private property shall not be taken for public use without just compensation. This argument ignores the fact that this is not a proceeding initiated by the city for the construction of a local improvement, or to take property under the law of eminent domain. It is a lawsuit in which the plaintiffs seek approval of a proposed plat of a subdivision under an ordinance which exacts compliance with certain requirements as a condition precedent to approval. They cite in support of this contention the case of City of Chicago v. Larned, 34 Ill. 203, followed in 34 Ill. 283, which involved an assessment for improvements made by the city council on the basis of the frontage of the lots upon the street to be improved. There the court held that under the provisions of the constitution of 1848, then in effect, all taxes were subject to the principles of equality and uniformity, and since this special assessment violated these constitutional provisions, it was not a tax, but an exercise of the power of eminent domain for which just compensation must be made; that though compensation could be made by benefits, when these were exhausted it then became a question of taxation, and the principles of equality and uniformity must apply; that the assessment of injuries and benefits is a judicial proceeding not to be made by a city council and that the purported assessment was void. Since the adoption of our present constitution, however, the power to levy and collect special assessments is regarded as a branch of the taxing power and the assessment is regarded as a species of taxation. Chicago and Alton Railroad Co. v. City of Joliet, 153 Ill. 649, 654, 39 N.E. 1077. The case at bar does not involve the imposition of a tax by the municipal authorities, but rather involves the imposition of regulatory provisions by way of the exercise of the police power through an ordinance requiring certain conditions precedent to the subdivision of lands and the approval of plats thereof. The validity of the ordinance is to be tested, neither by the principle of uniformity of taxation nor by the law of eminent domain, but rather by the settled rules of law applicable to cases involving the exercise of police powers. The fact that the exercise of such powers imposes certain burdens, or prevents the most profitable use of the property in private hands, does not of itself render the legislation invalid as a taking of the property without just compensation. City of West Frankfort v. Fullop, 6 Ill.2d 609, 129 N.E.2d 682. The imposition of reasonable regulations as a condition precedent to the subdivision of lands and the recording of plats thereof is not a violation of the constitutional requirement of uniformity of taxation or tantamount to the taking of private property for public use without just compensation.

We find that the judgment of the circuit court of Du Page County was erroneous and it must be reversed.

Notes

1.   See Melli and DeVoy, Extraterritorial Planning and Urban Growth, 1959 Wis.L.Rev. 55.

2.   With the principal case compare, Ayres v. City Council of City of Los Angeles, 34 Cal.2d 31, 207 P.2d 1, 11 A.L.R.2d 503 (1949). The court upheld as valid conditions to the approval of a 13 acre subdivision:

>   (1) Dedication of a 10 foot strip, 1500 feet along an important traffic artery;
>
>   (2) Reservation of an additional 10 foot strip along the same street for trees and shrubs to assure non-access to the artery;
>
>   (3) Dedication of an 80 foot, rather than a proffered 60 foot, width for a new street across the subdivision; and,
>
>   (4) Dedication of a triangular shaped parcel 12½ _ 75 feet to eliminate a traffic hazard.

(With regard to the first two conditions, similar dedications and reservations had been required of earlier subdivisions along the artery.)

The state legislature had given the city of Los Angeles subdivision control powers in its city charter and had by the so-called "Map Act" also empowered cities generally to control subdividing. The city had enacted a subdivision ordinance, but the subdivider contended the conditions, particularly the one requiring dedication of land along an existing street, were not expressly provided for either in the state legislation or in the local ordinance. Said the California court (two judges dissenting):

> The status of an autonomous city, Const. Art. XI, sec. 6; West Coast Advertising Co. v. San Francisco, 14 Cal.2d 516, 95 P.2d 138 (1939); City of Oakland v. Williams, 15 Cal.2d 542, 103 P.2d 168 (1940), is recognized by express references to city ordinances in the Subdivision Map Act. Where as here no specific restriction or limitation on the city's power is contained in the Charter, and none forbidding the particular conditions is included either in the Subdivision Map Act, or the city ordinances, it is proper to conclude that conditions are lawful which are not inconsistent with the Map Act and the ordinances and are reasonably required by the subdivision type and use as related to the character of local and neighborhood planning and traffic conditions.

Compare Rohn v. City of Visalia, 214 Cal.App.3d 1463, 263 Cal.Rptr. 319 (1989) where the court held that a required dedication of 14 per cent of the land to correct a street alignment was an invalid taking.

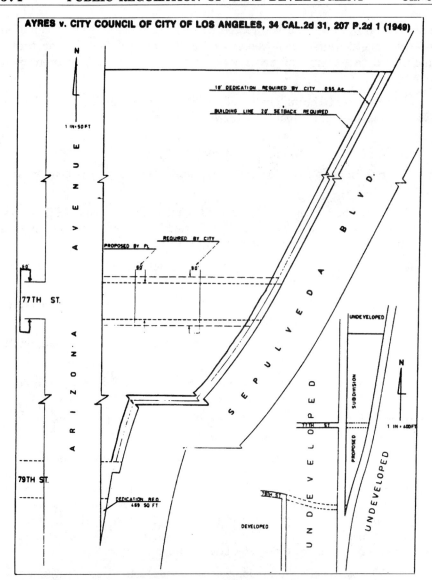

AYRES v. CITY COUNCIL OF CITY OF LOS ANGELES, 34 CAL.2d 31, 207 P.2d 1 (1949)

3. The Ayres case involves a "home rule" municipality in a state with a strong tradition of municipal home rule. In states where the powers of municipal corporations are strictly construed, the question of whether the requirements imposed on subdivision approval are *ultra vires* with regard to the enabling legislation is frequently litigated. For example, in State ex rel. Strother v. Chase, 42 Mo.App. 343 (1890), the court held that the city could not require the subdivider to plat an alley extension through his adjacent unplatted land as a condition of subdivision approval. For other cases strictly limiting the approving body to the standards or conditions specified in the enabling legislation, see Tuxedo Homes v. Green, 258 Ala. 494, 63 So.2d 812 (1953) (City engineer in absence of statutory authorization could not require installation of a lift pump for sewage, but the city might later refuse street dedications); People ex rel. Jackson & Morris, Inc. v. Smuczynski, 345 Ill. 63,

102 N.E.2d 168 (1951) (Village, having failed to adopt a subdivision ordinance for its guidance as required by statutes, must approve plat as a "ministerial" act); State ex rel. Lewis v. City Council of Minneapolis, 140 Minn. 433, 168 N.W. 188 (1918) (Could not require grading under a statute referring only to direction and width of streets); Rahway v. Raritan Homes Inc., 21 N.J.Super. 541, 91 A.2d 409 (1952) (No power to regulate subdividing until city complied with state statute requiring appointment of planning board and adoption of local ordinance); Magnolia Development Co. v. Coles, 10 N.J. 223, 89 A.2d 664 (1952) (No power to require sidewalks, curbs, gutters and gravel roadway in absence of enabling authority); In re Lake Secor Development Co., 141 Misc. 913, 252 N.Y.S. 809 (1931) (Could not force installation of water system under statute referring only to streets, light and air); Eyde Const. Co. v. Charter Twp. of Meridian, 149 Mich.App. 802, 386 N.W.2d 687 (1986) (Township lacked authority to condition plat approval on provision of recreational facilities). See also Annot., Validity and Construction of Regulations as to Subdivision Maps or Plats, 11 A.L.R.2d 524, 535 (1950).

4. Assuming a carefully worded enabling act, and a local subdivision ordinance based on it, there is little doubt that "reasonable" improvements can be required. Mefford v. City of Tulare, 102 Cal.App.2d 919, 228 P.2d 847 (1951) upheld as valid requirements that a profile map be furnished and sewer and water installed. Allen v. Stockwell, 210 Mich. 488, 178 N.W. 27 (1920) upheld ordinance provisions requiring grading and graveling of streets; sidewalks; installation of surface drains and sanitary sewers, apparently under general home rule delegations. Also see Colborne v. Village of Corrales, 106 N.M. 103, 739 P.2d 972 (1987). In Three Guys Real Estate v. Harnett County, 122 N.C.App. 362, 469 S.E.2d 578 (1996) the court held that the county was entitled to deny approval of a subdivision plat because the proposed development did not show any public roads, only private easements along logging trails.

Bolstering the position these courts have taken are (1) widespread use of requirements for installation of improvements or submission of a bond for their installation and (2) the findings of many of the studies of free and easy subdividing in the roaring 20's when to "develop" a subdivision one drove a few stakes, mounted some flags, and perhaps erected a pair of grotesque gate posts.[36]

36. Reference may be had, in this regard, to the following:

Adams, VII Regional Survey of New York and Environs (1929);

Cornick, Premature Subdivision and Its Consequences (1938)—Also published by N.Y. Division of State Planning under title "Problems created by premature Subdivision of Urban Lands in Selected Metropolitan Districts";

Fisher, Real Estate Subdividing Activity and Population Growth in Nine Urban Areas (1928)—Deals with Detroit, Cleveland, Milwaukee, Toledo, Birmingham, Grand Rapids, Flint and Ann Arbor areas;

Monchow, Seventy Years of Real Estate Subdividing in the Region of Chicago (1939);

Smith and Fisher, Land Subdividing and the Rate of Utilization (1932)—Intensive study of Grand Rapids area making use of techniques learned in previous study; Whitten, A Research into the Economics of Land Subdivision (1927); New Jersey State Planning Board, Land Subdivision in New Jersey (1938); and,

New Jersey State Planning Board, Premature Land Subdivision a Luxury (1941)—Tax Delinquency, Municipal Debt and Premature Subdivision in New Jersey.

Usually the developer is offered the following alternatives:

(1) Install the improvements before the final plat approval—(usually here he will be relying on approval of his preliminary plat); or,

(2) Furnish escrow money to cover the cost of the improvements; i.e., the plat is approved, and the escrow money is released in installments as the improvements are put in; or,

(3) Furnish a surety bond guaranteeing installation of improvements.

Small developers complain about the additional capital required to be risked where improvements must be installed. Large developers know that improvements make lots and houses more saleable and are quite willing to install them, particularly in the typical modern development which involves mass production of houses on the subdivided land. Their complaint is that often the municipal requirements are unreasonable in that the streets required are too wide, the pavement too thick, the sewer too big, etc. See Urban Land Institute, The Community Builders Handbook 39–40 (1954 ed.). We have little or no case law on such questions as these:

(1) Considering the subdivision alone a 10 inch sewer would be adequate, but considering probable development on other lands further out, the developer is required to install and pay for a 15 inch sewer. Is this a valid requirement? See Wright Development, Inc. v. City of Wellsville, 608 P.2d 232 (Utah 1980).

(2) How wide should the roadway of a minor residential street be? The developer says 26 feet, the city says 33 feet?

(3) Is a sidewalk on one side of the street enough?

Improvement requirements should vary with density, topography, soil and whether or not the subdivision is a quiet backwater or is in the mainstream of development. In addition as we cease to be exclusively concerned with residential subdivisions and begin to regulate subdivisions for commercial and industrial uses, we recognize that improvement requirements must differ. In California, for example, exactions for major thoroughfares is a problem. See Committee of Seven Thousand v. Superior Court, 45 Cal.3d 491, 247 Cal.Rptr. 362, 754 P.2d 708 (1988).

5. The question of what is a "reasonable" improvement, especially in regard to expensive utility or drainage installations, is sometimes litigated. In Texas, for example, subdividers may be required to pay the entire cost of installing water mains which must subsequently be donated to the city water and sewer authority. See Crownhill Homes, Inc. v. City of San Antonio, 433 S.W.2d 448 (Tex.Civ.App.1968) and Johnson v. Benbrook Water and Sewer Auth., 410 S.W.2d 644 (Tex.Civ.App.1966). Compare Reid Development Corp. v. Parsippany–Troy Hills Twp., 10 N.J. 229, 89 A.2d 667 (1952); Reid Development Corp. v. Parsippany–Troy Hills Twp., 31 N.J.Super. 459, 107 A.2d 20 (1954); Lake Intervale Homes, Inc. v. Parsippany–Troy Hills, 28 N.J. 423, 147 A.2d 28 (1958).

6. If the developer pays his fair share of fees for the water and sewer system and then is forced to abandon his project because of financial

difficulties, can the developer get a refund? In McNair v. City of Cedar Park, Texas, 993 F.2d 1217 (5th Cir.1993) the city determined that a major capital expansion of its water system was necessary to accommodate any new development. It imposed a community impact fee of $2,400 per living unit, payable by developers at the time of obtaining subdivision approval. The city, in turn, obligated itself to provide water and sewer services to all new developments. McNair had 100 acres of land, purchased for $1.65 million; he planned an upscale trailer park for 1,600 new residents. After some negotiation with the city, McNair paid the city $1.3 million based on the $2,400 fee for 542 units. Subsequently, McNair abandoned his project and sought a refund of the water fee, plus accrued interest, but by that time, Cedar Park was well into a five-year plan to construct a new system, having already spent $2 million and committed an additional $8 million. The city refused the refund and McNair sued the city alleging unjust enrichment and assumpsit; the case was removed to federal court after McNair added federal law claims. The court held for the city: "The City's retention of the fee is fundamentally fair when one considers that McNair received exactly what he bargained for. He has paid his share of the systemic water and sewer expansion costs and cannot be asked to pay same again. His tract of land is entitled to those city services. At the same time, the City has incurred a substantial expense and obligation. Equity and the controlling law demand that the agreement between the City and McNair be honored. Nothing more; nothing less."

7. What if the developer fails to install the improvements? In Vale Dean Canyon Homeowners Ass'n v. Dean, 100 Or.App. 158, 785 P.2d 772 (1990) the court held that lot owners were third-party beneficiaries of the contract to install roadway improvements made between the developer and the county, and could bring a breach of contract action against the developer.

8. Expensive water and sewer facilities may, however, give rise to a challenge that the city is using the exaction for revenue raising purposes or that the fees are not based on an equitable formula. In Lafferty v. Payson City, 642 P.2d 376 (Utah 1982), the court held that a $1,000 impact fee imposed on a single family dwelling was out of line with the actual costs and was really a revenue raising device. Also consider the following case:

SOUTHERN NEVADA HOMEBUILDERS ASS'N, INC. v. LAS VEGAS VALLEY WATER DISTRICT

Supreme Court of Nevada, 1985.
101 Nev. 99, 693 P.2d 1255.

Per Curiam:

This is an appeal from a judgment entered for respondent, the Las Vegas Valley Water District, denying appellant's request for declaratory, injunctive, and other relief. The appellants, principally the Southern Nevada Homebuilders Association, Inc., a trade organization, challenged the ruling of the district court that certain sections of the Water District's 1975 service rules imposing connection fees as a pre-condition of obtaining new or expanded water service are legal. Because we agree with the Association's contention that the Water District exceeded its statutory authority by imposing a fee on new customers in order to pay for expansion within the existing system, we reverse the decision of the district court.

* * *

Two groups are affected by the Water District's policies on rates and charges: the customers, or water users, and the applicants, a group consisting mainly of property developers. Various mixes of rates and charges have been used by the Water District in an attempt to balance the burden imposed by each group. In general, the customers are charged a flat rate plus an amount based on the water used. * * *

The group referred to as the applicants has been required to contribute to the costs of providing new services. Since 1955 the developers have been required to build off-site main extensions from the development to the existing system (defined in the Water District rules as a "feeder main"). When the developer has been required to install an oversized main, if requested to do so by the Water District, the developer pays only for that cost of the main capacity necessary to serve his development. Since 1960, the Water District has collected a connection fee from those tying into a Water District-constructed main. Subsequent developers have been charged a fee for connecting to a main constructed by others. The developers are required to build at their own expense whatever water mains are necessary within their development's boundaries.

Because of the rapidly increasing population in the area served by the Water District, the Act has been amended numerous times, which has been followed by corresponding changes within the rules and regulations. In 1975, the legislature amended § 16d to provide specifically that the Water District be authorized to charge a connection fee. After this enactment, the Water District implemented its new service rules imposing a "feeder main connection charge" on all new applicants to the system. The new rules attempted to equalize the burden on developers by providing that the initial developer installing the feeder main from the development to the existing system receive a credit for the amount paid for the main against the feeder main connection charge imposed on the development. The developer then pays the difference, if the connection charge is greater. If the cost of the main exceeds the connection charge, the developer is entitled to reimbursement from subsequent applicants connecting to that main. The feeder main connection charge is imposed on all new applicants regardless of whether the development connects directly to the existing system or utilizes a newly installed feeder main.

The money collected from this charge is not segregated but it is placed within the general fund. The money has been used, in part, to reimburse developers for their costs of installing the feeder mains. In addition the money has been spent on oversizing mains being built by developers so that anticipated growth in an area could be accommodated by the system quickly. The money has also been utilized, however, for bolstering or reinforcing water mains within the existing system in order to provide for increased demand and capacity for the new growth.

THE FEEDER MAIN CHARGE

The Association suggests that the feeder main connection charge is illegal for various reasons. Because we find it exceeds the authority granted to the Board by the legislature, only this issue need be discussed.

* * *

The Board is given extensive authority * * * to impose rates and charges. This authority, however, is limited by the requirement that such rates and charges be "an equitable allocation and recovery of costs of providing facilities and delivery of water service."

We do not believe that imposing a feeder main connection charge to aid in funding the major construction projects of the Water District is such an equitable allocation. Instead, we conclude that the Board is limited to charging a connection fee only if it is used to recover costs identifiable with the properties charged. Thus the costs of building a "feeder main" would be proper, as would the initial costs of oversizing the lines to prepare for anticipated growth. Financing the bolstering or enlarging of lines already part of the existing system, however, is outside the scope of power given in § 16d.

We believe that to conclude otherwise allows the Water District to recover the costs of the same facilities twice. The Water District is empowered by § 16d to charge water rates to recover the costs of delivery of service and to issue bonds to provide for the major construction projects, with the interest and principal being paid from the revenues of the Water District. The evidence produced at trial showed that the water rates collected were ample to pay for the costs of system expansion and replacement of obsolete or worn parts in the system. To allow the Water District to charge water rates to its customers, issue bonds, and then also to charge a connection fee to pay for some of the major construction projects, permits the Water District to expand its surplus revenue after the costs of providing the service have already been recovered. Such is not the intent of the legislature.

Finally, it is not equitable that the new applicants for service be forced to pay a connection fee which is spent on a facility which may not benefit them or which benefits all members of the system. Although it may be necessary for some purposes for the Water District to divide the people affected by its rules into two groups—the customers and the applicants—it is not equitable to impose a charge on only one of the groups when the funds produced are used to pay for facilities benefiting both groups. The Water District can impose its water rates and issue bonds to recover the costs of providing facilities and delivery of service benefiting both groups; it can only impose a separate fee on the new applicants fairly if it recovers the costs directly identifiable with the applicants' properties.

* * *

In summary, we conclude that the Board is limited to imposing a feeder main connection charge only if it is used to recover costs identifiable with the properties charged. Any other charge does not represent "an equitable allocation and recovery of costs of providing facilities and delivery of water service" as required by § 16d of the Act and is outside the power granted to the Board by the legislature.

We therefore order this judgment reversed and the case remanded for further proceedings consistent with this opinion.

Note

Also see Southern Nevada Homebuilders Ass'n v. City of North Las Vegas, 112 Nev. 297, 913 P.2d 1276 (1996) where the court held that imposition of money exactions for expansion of fire and emergency medical services was ultra vires. The enabling statute permitted exactions only for capital improvements or facility expansion necessitated by and attributable to new development.

181 INC. v. SALEM COUNTY PLANNING BD.

Superior Court of New Jersey, Law Division, 1975.
133 N.J.Super. 350, 336 A.2d 501, modified on appeal
140 N.J.Super. 247, 356 A.2d 34 (1976).

MILLER, J.C.C., Temporarily Assigned.

Plaintiff challenges, as unconstitutional, actions of the Salem County Planning Board compelling it to dedicate to the county a portion of land, owned by it, bordering upon a county road, as a condition precedent to approval by the county of a site plan submitted for the construction of a law office. * * *

Plaintiff is the owner of a tract of land in Woodstown, Salem County. The tract abuts on Elm Street (County Road 40) and on U.S. 40 and is irregular in shape. Following its purchase in December 1971 plaintiff applied to the Salem County Planning Board for site plan approval. The site plan review committee recommended approval subject, among other things, to the dedication of 8.25_ along its border on Elm Street, to be used for a proposed widening of Elm Street from 49.5_ to 66_ pursuant to the official map. The time of such widening is indefinite.

* * *

The original site plan review resolution was adopted January 21, 1970 by the board of freeholders pursuant to N.J.S.A. 40:27–6.6. It provided in § 8 that, "As a condition to the approval of a site plan, the planning board *shall* require the dedication of additional right of way

* * * " (emphasis supplied). It was this mandatory feature to which plaintiff objected. * * *

* * *

The vice in the county's resolution is that it sets up a blanket policy of taking frontage along every county road without regard to present need, imminency of proposed use or, indeed, of any standard whatsoever. To then expect a landowner to prove himself outside the perimeter of so nebulously defined an area makes it impossible for him to meet his burden. A perusal of the record in this case and an analysis of the testimony which was necessarily adduced by the plaintiff illustrates the predicament of the landowner.

In order, therefore, for the county to place upon the landowner the burden of proof * * * the county must first make its position clear. This must be done, not in generalities, but in specifics applicable to the land sought to be obtained. While obviously there should be the adoption of an official map and a master plan, this is not enough. There should be, at the bare minimum, a proposal for the imminent use of the land, not a mere "banking" for unscheduled future use. While it is true that road appropriations are made on an annual basis it is also true that plans for road work involve "lead time." If the county does not intend to use the land proposed to be taken within such "lead time," to take it without compensation merely because opportunity presents itself runs afoul of the Constitution.

The planning board felt that there was a sufficient rational *nexus* between the proposed use and the widening *in futuro* of Elm Street to justify the requirement of a compulsory dedication. This finding constitutes error.

* * *

In Brazer v. Mountainside, 55 N.J. 456, 465–466, 262 A.2d 857 (1970), the court said that statutory and ordinance provisions for a compulsory dedication could only be valid where the proposed street bears a realistic relation to or is reasonably made necessary by the subdivision. See also Princeton Res. Lands v. Princeton Tp., 112 N.J.Super. 467, 474, 475, 271 A.2d 719 (App.Div.1970), holding that a developer may not be compelled to donate land to increase the width of an existing abutting street.

The constitutional basis of the nexus requirement is neither strange nor novel. It appears in the earlier zoning cases, for instance, Grosso v. Millburn Tp. Adjustment Bd., 137 N.J.L. 630, 633, 61 A.2d 167 (Sup.Ct. 1948), which held that "lands may not be taken for highway use, presently or in futuro, without just compensation." Grosso, supra at 633, 61 A.2d at 169. See also Lomarch Corp. v. Mayor of Englewood, 51 N.J. 108, 237 A.2d 881 (1968). And Battaglia v. Wayne Tp. Planning Board, 98 N.J.Super. 194, 236 A.2d 608 (App.Div.1967), is particularly apposite since, like the instant case, it involved a site plan approval:

Unlike the case of a land subdivision, no new streets are necessitated by the plaintiff's planned use; there are no purchasers to whom the cost of the improvements can be passed, and plaintiff's land receives no discernible benefit from compliance with the imposed conditions. [at 200, 236 A.2d at 611]

Had Battaglia not applied for official action, Wayne Township could not have imposed upon him the obligations sought to be imposed. The same logic is inescapable here.

* * *

Since the case must go back, the board of freeholders should revise the site plan (and subdivision) standards, eliminating automatic dedication and limiting compulsory taking to those occasions when it meets the rational nexus test and the county's proposed use is specific and imminent. For example, most (although certainly not all) minor subdivisions will probably be found not to meet the rational nexus test as defined herein.

The actions of the planning board are reversed. The case is remanded to the planning board * * *. Jurisdiction is retained. No costs.

Notes

1. Compare with the principal case Sparks v. Douglas County, 127 Wash.2d 901, 904 P.2d 738 (1995). In this case the developer sought approval for four separate small plats in an "in-fill" situation. The county planning commission found that the existing road abutting the proposed developments was substandard and would, after the developer's building, require widening and structural rebuilding; the county asked for dedication of right-of-way for the future widening of the streets. The developer appealed and ultimately the Supreme Court of Washington held that the facts established a sufficient nexus between the developer's activity and the need for road improvements; even though the maximum possible development proposed would be sixteen houses or thirty-two duplex units, that amount of development would nearly double the amount of traffic on the road and would accelerate the need for widening and rebuilding. Also see Pengilly v. Multnomah County, 810 F.Supp. 1111 (D.Or.1992) where the court upheld a county requirement that home builders dedicate several feet of additional right-of-way as a condition of receiving a building permit on the ground that the requirement promoted aesthetics and traffic efficiency.

2. Similar to the principal case are Simpson v. City of North Platte, 206 Neb. 240, 292 N.W.2d 297 (1980); Howard County v. JJM, Inc., 301 Md. 256, 482 A.2d 908 (1984); Lee County v. New Testament Baptist Church, 507 So.2d 626 (Fla.App. 2 Dist.1987); Middlemist v. City of Plymouth, 387 N.W.2d 190 (Minn.App.1986); Unlimited v. Kitsap County, 50 Wash.App. 723, 750 P.2d 651 (1988); Board Of Supervisors of West Marlborough Twp. v. Fiechter, 129 Pa.Cmwlth. 537, 566 A.2d 370 (1989).

3. In addition to holding that compulsory dedications of portions of the landowner's property for future widening is invalid, courts have utilized the same reasoning when the governing entity seeks to require the landowner to

improve an existing road which abuts his property. See Hylton Enterprises v. Board of Supervisors, 220 Va. 435, 258 S.E.2d 577 (1979); Charter Twp. of Harrison v. Calisi, 121 Mich.App. 777, 329 N.W.2d 488 (1982). In Luxembourg Group, Inc. v. Snohomish County, 76 Wash.App. 502, 887 P.2d 446 (1995) the court held that requiring a landowner to dedicate an access road not necessary for his development in order to provide access to a neighbor's landlocked parcel was a taking without compensation.

4. Several right-of-way dedication cases involve the conversion of existing gasoline service stations into the ubiquitous and fast-spreading combination convenience store/gasoline station type of business. In Amoco Oil Co. v. Village of Schaumburg, 277 Ill.App.3d 926, 214 Ill.Dec. 526, 661 N.E.2d 380 (1995), app. denied 167 Ill.2d 549, 217 Ill.Dec. 662, 667 N.E.2d 1055, cert. denied ___ U.S. ___, 117 S.Ct. 413, 136 L.Ed.2d 325 (1996) the court held that a demanded dedication of a 40 by 40 foot triangular section of the landowner's property to rebuild and improve traffic safety at a busy intersection constituted a taking. The dedication would have amounted to about twenty percent of the owner's property and the current defects in the intersection were due to poor original design, not the gas station's activities. Also see William J. (Jack) Jones Insurance Trust v. City of Fort Smith, 731 F.Supp. 912 (W.D.Ark.1990).

(2) Off–Site Improvements

DIVAN BUILDERS, INC. v. PLANNING BD. OF TWP. OF WAYNE

Supreme Court of New Jersey, 1975.
66 N.J. 582, 334 A.2d 30.

PASHMAN, J.

* * *

* * * Divan's proposal contemplated the construction of 31 single family dwellings in a residential zone of the Township. Because a substantial portion of the building site was covered by a pond, the developer's plan called for its draining and the construction of a conduit which would pipe the water from its upstream source through the development and into an existing drainage facility on the downstream border of the site.

* * *

On June 21, 1972, the Wayne governing body amended its subdivision ordinance by adopting Ordinance No. 69–1972. The ordinance establishes procedures to be followed when off-site improvements are deemed necessary to service a subdivision. The ordinance provides in part that:

"Prior to the granting of final approval of all subdivisions hereafter submitted to the Planning Board, and prior to the issuance of any building permits for any land use, including land uses which require site plan approval * * * and any residence or other use of property on an unimproved street or where any off-site improvements have not then been installed, the subdivider or other named type of applicant * * * shall have installed, posted a performance bond, or made cash payments, in the manner provided in Section 5 below, with respect to the immediate or ultimate installation of any required off-site improvements."

Off-site improvements include the installation of new, or the extension or modification of existing improvements made necessary in whole or in part by the subdivision which will be benefited by the improvement. The ordinance also provides that the cost of off-site improvements shall be allocated between the applicant, other property owners, or any one or more of them. The cost allocation is based upon such factors as the benefit conferred upon the subdivision, the cost of the improvement, and the extent to which the improvement is necessary to protect neighboring property under the proposed plan.

On June 26, 1972, the Planning Board recommended final approval of plaintiff's remaining 26 lots subject to certain conditions, including the following:

[T]hat the applicant contribute to the Township of Wayne a sum of $20,000 as their share of improving the downstream conditions of the stream which carries the drainage from the subdivision.

In July 1972 plaintiff received final approval for the remaining portion of its subdivision on the condition that it pay the Township $20,000. This sum represented approximately 8% of the estimated $250,000 cost of the off-site improvement deemed necessary to serve the entire drainage basin. Only one other developer, however, was required to contribute a similar sum pursuant to the ordinance.

* * *

It is clear * * * that a municipality may condition subdivision approval upon the developer's installation of those improvements which the local governing body finds necessary for the protection of the public interest. The problem, of course, is that the statutory scheme makes no specific reference to off-site improvements in this context.

In our view, however, this omission does not preclude a determination that the Planning Act authorizes municipalities to adopt both on-site and off-site improvement ordinances. * * * In our judgment, the constitutional and legislative direction to resolve questions of municipal authority broadly in favor of the local unit, compels the conclusion that, by necessary implication, N.J.S.A. 40:55–1.21 empowers a planning agency to require both on-site and off-site improvements of the physical character and type referred to in N.J.S.A. 40:55–1.20 and N.J.S.A. 40:55–1.21, including off-site improvements made necessary by reason of the subdivision's effect on lands other than the subdivision property, provided that the agency acts pursuant to a valid local ordinance containing suitable standards governing construction and installation of improvements. See Deerfield Estates v. Twp. of East Brunswick, 60 N.J. 115, 286 A.2d 498 (1972).

* * *

We have heretofore recognized that a municipality may utilize three principal ways to finance an off-site improvement. In *Deerfield Estates,* supra, the defendant municipality refused to install water mains to serve plaintiff's lots. As a threshold question, the Court held that a municipality which had created a planning board and adopted an adequate subdivision ordinance could validly condition subdivision approval upon installation of necessary water mains. 60 N.J. 122, 286 A.2d 498.

Proceeding to the question of financing the water main extension, Justice Mountain set forth three principal ways in which the municipality could defray the cost of the improvements:

> "First, it may be undertaken entirely at municipal cost and expense. * * * In the second place the municipality may undertake the project as a local improvement and assess the cost against the owners of the properties benefited pursuant to the procedure outlined in N.J.S.A. 40:56–1, et seq.

> "The third course is to require that the work be done at the expense of the developer either with or without a formula providing for partial or total reimbursement. Recourse to this third alternative, as to which there has hitherto existed some question, may be had only where appropriate local legislation permits the imposition and when it is fair and equitable that this be done." [60 N.J. at 131, 286 A.2d at 507; footnote omitted].

* * *

Because the need for the off-site improvement was so created, the municipality in recognition of that fact may, in any event, fairly and properly call upon the subdivider to pay the difference between the cost of the improvement and the total amount by which all properties served thereby, including the subdivision, have been specially benefited by the improvement.

Further, but only if the off-site improvement is to be constructed as a "local improvement," * * * with all properties specially benefited thereby to be assessed for the amount of special benefits accruing to each—the subdivider may be called upon to pay in addition to the amount above set forth the amount by which the subdivision property was specially benefited by the improvement.

If the off-site improvement is to be constructed by the municipality as a general improvement—no part of the cost of which may be specially assessed on properties specially benefited thereby—or if the off-site improvement is to be constructed by the subdivider with a provision for later reimbursement by the municipality, then the subdivider may not be charged with the amount by which the subdivision property was specially benefited. To do so would result in patent discrimination in the treatment afforded the subdivision property as contrasted with the other properties specially benefited by the improvement. * * *

We pass now from the question of cost allocation to a consideration of how provision therefor may be made at the time subdivision approval is granted, a date antecedent to the actual construction of the improvement.

It is at once apparent that before the stated conditions are actually imposed on the applicant for subdivision approval, the governing body must decide whether the off-site improvement is to be constructed (1) by the municipality as a general improvement or (2) as a local improvement or (3) whether it is to be done by the developer with a formula providing for partial reimbursement if the improvement specially benefits properties other than the subdivision.

Once that decision has been made, the planning agency should be required to estimate, with the aid of the municipal engineer and such other persons having pertinent information or expertise (a) the cost of the improvement and (b) the amount by which all properties to be serviced thereby, including the subdivision property, will be specially benefited therefrom.

When that has been determined, the subdivider may be required to provide, as a condition for approval of his subdivision application, a bond (or a cash deposit, in lieu thereof) to insure payment to the municipality of one of the following amounts:

(a) If the improvement is to be constructed by the municipality as a general improvement, an amount equal to the difference between the estimated cost of the improvement and the estimated total amount by which all properties to be serviced thereby, including the subdivision property, will be specially benefited by the improvement;

(b) If the improvement is to be constructed by the municipality as a local improvement, then in addition to the amount referred to in (a) the estimated amount by which the subdivision property will be specially benefited by the improvement; or

(c) If the improvement is to be constructed by the subdivider, an amount equal to the estimated cost of the improvement.

If the subdivider should deem that any of the amounts so estimated by the planning agency are unreasonable, it may challenge them and seek to have them revised in appropriate proceedings brought to compel subdivision approval.

Further, since the amounts are only estimated amounts, they should be redetermined once the improvement is completed to the end that the subdivider will be required to pay his appropriate and only his appropriate share of the cost thereof. If the municipality and the subdivider cannot agree with respect thereto, the dispute will have to be decided in a judicial proceeding or proceedings. * * *

It is evident that neither Ordinance 69–1972 nor the action taken by the municipality here conformed to the controlling principles herein set forth. Further, it *prima facie* appears—although defendants deny it—that there has been a disregard of the fundamental principle prohibiting discrimination in cost apportionment in requiring plaintiff to pay $20,-000 and allocating no part of the cost to the other properties allegedly specially benefited by [the] improvement, which was constructed as a general improvement.

* * *

To that end, since the improvement was constructed by the municipality as a general improvement, the judgment is reversed and the cause remanded to the trial court for a determination at a trial, following appropriate discovery proceedings and a pretrial conference, of the difference between the cost of the improvement and the total amount by which all properties served thereby were specially benefited therefrom. That difference is fairly chargeable, under the circumstances indicated by the record, in equal shares to plaintiff and the other developer who made a $20,000 payment since their subdivisions created the need for the off-site improvement. Plaintiff will then be entitled to recover from the municipality only that portion, if any of the $20,000 it paid which exceeds the amount fairly chargeable to it.

Reversed and remanded.

Notes

1. The rational nexus test has been utilized by most jurisdictions facing the problem of imposing on developers the requirement of dedicating land outside the proposed subdivision for future improvements or the actual construction of improvements outside the boundaries of the subdivision. As in the principal case, courts are suspicious of schemes which require a developer to pay the total cost of an off-site improvement. See Baltica Construction Co., Inc. v. Planning Board of Franklin Twp., 222 N.J.Super. 428, 537 A.2d 319 (1988); Longridge Builders, Inc. v. Planning Board of Princeton Twp., 52 N.J. 348, 245 A.2d 336 (1968); Kode Harbor Dev. Assoc. v. County of Atlantic, 230 N.J.Super. 430, 553 A.2d 858 (1989); Christopher Lake Development Co. v. St. Louis County, 35 F.3d 1269 (8th Cir.1994)

2. Even where developers are asked only to pay a pro rata share of necessary off-site improvements, the rational nexus test must be carefully applied. In New Jersey Builders Association v. Mayor and Twp. Committee of Bernards Twp., 108 N.J. 223, 528 A.2d 555 (1987), the court held requiring new developments to pay a pro rata share of the township's long-range $20 million road improvement plan was ultra vires. Also see Albany Area Builders Association v. Town of Guilderland, 74 N.Y.2d 372, 547 N.Y.S.2d 627, 546 N.E.2d 920 (1989), where a town's Transportation Impact Fee Law was held to have been preempted by the state statutes dealing with road improvements and financing. In Land/Vest Properties, Inc. v. Town of Plainfield, 117 N.H. 817, 379 A.2d 200 (1977), the court upheld the theory of off-site road improvements, but struck down the proposed exaction for

failure to establish the rational nexus. Compare KBW, Inc. v. Town of Bennington, 115 N.H. 392, 342 A.2d 653 (1975).

3.   In Arrowhead Development Co. v. Livingston County Road Commission, 413 Mich. 505, 322 N.W.2d 702 (1982), the court found that a requirement that the developer regrade an existing county road to eliminate a dangerous condition which would be exacerbated by the development exceeded the commission's statutory powers.

4.   In Northwest Land and Investment, Inc. v. City of Bellingham, 31 Wash.App. 742, 644 P.2d 740 (1982), the developer brought a tort action against the city for unlawfully requiring him to install off-site improvements; the court denied relief because the developer did not pursue a challenge to the requirement, and thus, the proximate cause of his loss was his compliance.

Village Square No. 1, Inc. v. Crow–Frederick, 77 Md.App. 552, 551 A.2d 471 (1989) was a case involving a "recapture agreement," a common device used in off-site or in oversized on-site improvements that will, in the future, benefit subsequent developers. The usual agreement provides for the city to calculate how much of the improvement installed by a developer will benefit future nearby developments, a provision that the city will charge the future development(s) that portion of previously installed improvement that benefits the new development, and a promise to reimburse the original developer that amount. As you might expect, a lot of guesswork goes into this process, and there is no guarantee that the original developer will ever see any money. In addition to the Maryland case, where the original developer lost, see Beneficial Development Corp. v. City of Highland Park, 239 Ill.App.3d 414, 179 Ill.Dec. 1005, 606 N.E.2d 837 (1992). In this case, the court upheld the recapture agreement, but the amount obtained by the developer was minimal. Also see Fischer v. Dover, 131 N.H. 469, 554 A.2d 1293 (1989), cert. denied 502 U.S. 899, 112 S.Ct. 276, 116 L.Ed.2d 228, where a developer who had installed a road with a recapture agreement received $8,000 10 years later when another developer came along. The installing developer argued, without success, that he should receive an additional sum to represent the inflation in road costs over the 10 year period.

(3) Non-traditional Exactions

PIONEER TRUST & SAV. BANK v. VILLAGE OF MOUNT PROSPECT

Supreme Court of Illinois, 1961.
22 Ill.2d 375, 176 N.E.2d 799.

MR. JUSTICE HERSHEY delivered the opinion of the court:

Plaintiffs brought a mandamus proceeding in the circuit court of Cook County to compel the corporate authorities of the village of Mount Prospect to approve a plat of subdivision which complied with all the provisions of the official plan of the municipality except that requiring a dedication of land for public use. The case was submitted to the court on an agreed statement of facts. The court entered an order finding the land dedication requirements of the village's official plan invalid and directed the issuance of a writ of mandamus commanding the corporate authorities to approve the plat. The trial court has certified that the validity of a municipal ordinance is involved and that the public interest requires a direct appeal.

Article 53 of the Revised Cities and Villages Act authorizes municipalities to establish plan commissions with authority to recommend to the corporate authorities the adoption of an official plan. Section 53–2 (Ill.Rev.Stat.1959, c. 24, par. 53–2) provides that the plan may "establish reasonable standards of design for subdivisions and for resubdivisions of unimproved land and of areas subject to redevelopment, including reasonable requirements for public streets, alleys, ways for public service facilities, parks, playgrounds, school grounds, and other public grounds." Section 53–3 provides that no plat of subdivision "shall be entitled to record or shall be valid unless the subdivision shown thereon provides for streets, alleys, * * * and public grounds in conformity with the applicable requirements of the official plan."

The village of Mount Prospect has established a plan commission and has adopted by ordinance an official plan as recommended by the commission. Section 6 of article II of that plan contains a requirement for the dedication of public grounds as follows:

> "Dedication of Lands for Public Use: The plat shall have lettered upon it a statement of dedications properly conveying all usable lands dedicated for such public uses as streets, public schools, parks or any other public use, and there shall be attached to the plat a certificate of title certifying the ownership of all such lands to be so dedicated by said plat. Public grounds, other than streets, alleys and parking areas, shall be dedicated in appropriate locations by the plat (a) at the rate of at least one (1) acre for each sixty (60) residential building sites or family living units, which may be accommodated under the restrictions applying to the land; or (b) at the rate of at least one-tenth ($\frac{1}{10}$) acre for each one (1) acre of business or industrial building sites which may be accommodated under the restrictions applying to the land."

Plaintiff Salvatore Dimucci is engaged in the business of subdividing real estate for residential purposes and caused a plat of the subdivision to be submitted to the plan commission for approval which complied in all respects with the aforesaid ordinance except as to the dedication of some 6.7 acres of land which would be required under the language of section 6 of article II quoted above. The plaintiffs have refused to dedicate land, and, in view of that refusal, the village board has refused to approve the plat of the subdivision. It is established in the record that the 6.7 acres of land sought to be required to be dedicated or donated would be for the use of an elementary school and for the use of the Mount Prospect Park District as an elementary school site and a secondary use as a playground. The proposed subdivision shows some 250 residential units.

The issue here presented for determination is the validity of the quoted section of the ordinance, and no provision of the ordinance other than that requiring the dedication is under attack by the plaintiffs in this proceeding.

The statute from which the village derives its authority has been before us on two previous occasions. Petterson v. City of Naperville, 9 Ill.2d 233, 137 N.E.2d 371; Rosen v. Village of Downers Grove, 19 Ill.2d 448, 167 N.E.2d 230. In each of these cases the issue presented for decision was narrowly circumscribed, and in neither case did we pass upon the precise point that is involved here. The Petterson case did not involve any question of required dedication of land, but rather concerned the reasonableness of a requirement that the subdivider provide curbs and gutters for the streets of the subdivision. We sustained the validity of such a requirement, stating that "the power to prescribe reasonable requirements for public streets in the interest of the health and safety of the inhabitants of the city and contiguous territory includes more than a mere designation of the location and width of streets." The Rosen case involved a portion of an ordinance of the village of Downers Grove which required subdividers to dedicate land for educational facilities but also provided that if the plan commission should deem that the dedication of such land would not of itself meet the reasonable requirements of providing educational facilities for the proposed subdivision, then the plan commission might require any additional means for providing reasonable facilities. Acting under this ordinance, the municipality attempted to require subdividers to pay a certain sum per lot for educational purposes. We held this attempt invalid because the specific technique employed was not authorized by the statute, and also because the term "educational purposes" was broader than the language of the statute. The Downers Grove ordinance did contain a paragraph, similar to that involved in the instant case, requiring the dedication for public grounds of at least one acre of land for each 75 family living units; but this particular provision was not directly involved in the litigation and we refused to pass on its validity.

Our opinion in the Rosen case thus specifically left undecided the question that is now presented for decision. It did, however, suggest some basic principles for distinguishing between permissible and forbidden requirements. We stated in the Rosen case that the statutory provisions with respect to reasonable requirements for streets and public grounds were based upon the theory that "the developer of a subdivision may be required to assume those costs which are specifically and uniquely attributable to his activity and which would otherwise be cast upon the public." We further observed: "But because the requirement that a plat of subdivision be approved affords an appropriate point of control with respect to costs made necessary by the subdivision, it does not follow that communities may use this point of control to solve all of the problems which they can foresee. The distinction between permissible and forbidden requirements is suggested in Ayres v. The City Council of Los Angeles, 34 Cal.2d 31, 207 P.2d 1, 11 A.L.R.2d 503, which indicates that the municipality may require the developer to provide the streets which are required by the activity within the subdivision but can not require him to provide a major thoroughfare, the need for which stems from the total activity of the community." It is in the light of these basic principles that the reasonableness of the requirement sought to be imposed by the defendant village must be determined. If the requirement is within the statutory grant of power to the municipality and if the burden cast upon the subdivider is specifically and uniquely attributable to his activity, then the requirement is permissible; if not, it is forbidden and amounts to a confiscation of private property in contravention of the constitutional prohibitions rather than reasonable regulation under the police power.

* * *

There can be no controversy about the obvious fact that the orderly development of a municipality must necessarily include a consideration of the present and future need for school and public recreational facilities. Neither the plaintiffs nor the defendants in this case take the negative side of the question as to the desirability either of education or recreation. The question is not one of the desirability of education or recreation, nor of the desirability to improve the public condition, but, rather, the question presented here is one of determining who shall pay for such improvements. Is it reasonable that a subdivider should be required under the guise of a police power regulation to dedicate a portion of his property to public use; or does this amount to a veiled exercise of the power of eminent domain and a confiscation of private property behind the defense of police regulations?

That the addition by this subdivision of some 250 residential units to the municipality would of course aggravate the existing need for additional school and recreational facilities is admitted by the parties to this cause. No complaint is made by the plaintiff in this cause that the land required to be dedicated for such purposes by subdivision control ordinance is unnecessary. The sole question thus presented here is whether the state of law is such that a mandatory dedication of the land without cost to the public may be sustained in the regulation of proposed subdivision when it is admitted that such land may well be needed.

However, this record does not establish that the need for recreational and educational facilities in the event that said subdivision plat is permitted to be filed, is one that is specifically and uniquely attributable to the addition of the subdivision and which should be cast upon the subdivider as his sole financial burden. The agreed statement of facts shows that the present school facilities of Mount Prospect are near capacity. This is the result of the total development of the community. If this whole community had not developed to such an extent or if the existing school facilities were greater, the purported need supposedly would not be present. Therefore, on the record in this case the school problem which allegedly exists here is one which the subdivider should not be obliged to pay the total cost of remedying, and to so construe the statute would amount to an exercise of the power of eminent domain without compensation. Sanitary District of Chicago v. Chicago and Alton R. Co., 267 Ill. 252, 108 N.E. 312, and cases there cited; Ridgemont Develop. Co. v. City of East Detroit, 358 Mich. 387, 100 N.W.2d 301.

Section 6 of article II of the defendant village ordinance imposes an unreasonable condition precedent for the approval of a plat of a subdivision and purports to take private property for public use without compensation. The circuit court of Cook County was correct in so holding, and the judgment of that court is affirmed.

JORDAN v. VILLAGE OF MENOMONEE FALLS

Supreme Court of Wisconsin, 1965.
28 Wis.2d 608, 137 N.W.2d 442, appeal dismissed
385 U.S. 4, 87 S.Ct. 36, 17 L.Ed.2d 3 (1966).

Action by plaintiffs Martin A. Jordan and James F. McMicken and their wives against defendant village to recover $5,000 paid by plaintiffs as an equalization fee in lieu of dedicating land as required by defendant's ordinance governing the subdivision of lands within the village.

In October, 1959, Jordan and McMicken (hereinafter "plaintiffs") commenced negotiations for the purchase of a 7.85 acre tract of land in defendant village for the purpose of subdividing it into lots and selling the lots. While negotiating, plaintiffs became aware that defendant had enacted an ordinance in March, 1959, which required subdividers to either dedicate a portion of their land or pay a fee in lieu thereof. Pertinent sections of the ordinance are:

> "In order that adequate open spaces and sites for public uses may be properly located and preserved as the community develops; and in order that the cost of providing the public school, park, and recreation sites and facilities necessary to serve the additional families brought into the community by subdivision development may be most equitably apportioned on the basis of the additional need created by the individual subdivision development, the following provisions are established:

> "8.01.   Reservation of Potential Sites.

> "(1) In the design of the plat, consideration shall be given to the adequate provision of and correlation with such public sites or open areas.

> "(2) Where it is determined by the plan commission that a portion of the plat is required for such public sites or open spaces, the subdivider may be required to reserve such area for a period not to exceed three years, after which the Village shall either acquire the property or release the reservation.

> "8.02.   Dedication of Sites.

"(1)   Within the corporate limits of the Village, where feasible and compatible with the comprehensive plan for development of the community, the subdivider shall provide and dedicate to the public adequate land to provide for the school, park and recreation needs of the subdivision.

"(2)   The amount of land to be provided shall be determined on the basis of an amount equal in value to $200.00 per residential lot created by the subdivision. Such value shall be determined by the Village assessor on the basis of full and fair market value of the land. If the owner is not satisfied with such appraisal, he may appeal such determination, in which case an appraisal board consisting of one appraiser selected by the Village at its own expense, one selected by the property owner at his own expense and a third selected by the two other appraisers at Village expense, shall determine the value.

"8.03.   Proportionate Payment in Lieu of Dedication.

"(1)   Where such dedication is not feasible or compatible with the comprehensive plan, the subdivider shall in lieu thereof pay to the Village a fee equivalent to the value of the required dedication. Such fee shall be distributed as follows:

'A. $120.00 per residential lot created by the subdivision to be held in a non-lapsing fund for the benefit of the school district or districts in which the plat lies, on the basis of proper apportionment between districts where the plat is in more than one district, and to be made available to the appropriate district or districts upon their request.

'B. $80.00 per residential lot created by the subdivision to be placed in a non-lapsing fund to be used for park and recreation area development.'

"(2)   Such fees shall be used exclusively for immediate or future site acquisition or capital improvement. * * *

"8.05.   Determination of Feasibility.

"The determination as to the feasibility of dedication shall be made by the Village Plan Commission. The subdivider shall however have the option of choosing to make payment in lieu of dedication."

With full knowledge of the ordinance, plaintiffs purchased the property for $22,000. Plaintiff Jordan did once voice an informal objection to Gottlieb, village commissioner, stating that he thought the ordinance was unconstitutional. Because of the small area and the particular layout of the subdivision planned, it did not occur to plaintiffs to dedicate any land for school or park sites. They proceeded on the assumption that they would pay the $5,000 equalization fee in lieu of land dedication, which fee they paid by check September 12, 1960, and typed "paid under protest" on the check. Plaintiffs then proceeded to complete the subdivision at a total cost of $73,896.98, including the $5,000 platting fee. All 25 lots were sold between September, 1961, and April, 1963, for a total sum of $100,000.

On October 26, 1962, plaintiffs served on defendant a formal demand and claim for return of the payment, which was denied by defendant.

Plaintiffs alleged that the payment was a tax which the village could not levy because (1) it did not have authorization from the legislature and (2) it was an unconstitutional taking of property without just compensation. Trial was to the court and judgment was entered February 12, 1965, for plaintiffs, requiring defendants to repay to plaintiffs the $5,000 plus interest from September 12, 1960.

Defendant has appealed.

* * *

CURRIE, CHIEF JUSTICE.

The issue on this appeal is the constitutionality of the ordinance pursuant to which the $5,000 equalization fee was paid. Defendant asserts that the ordinance is a valid exercise of its police power in controlling subdivision development to assure its burgeoning population adequate parks and schools. Plaintiffs contend that section 8.03 of the ordinance levies a tax which is not authorized by the legislature and unconstitutional.

* * *

Preliminary to considering the constitutionality of the equalization fee provisions of the ordinance, we deem it advisable to pass on the requirement that the subdivider, where practicable, be required to dedicate a portion of the subdivision for sites for school, park and recreational needs of a value of $200 per residential lot. If this provision of the ordinance is unconstitutional, then of course the provision for payment of a cash fee in lieu of dedicating land for school, park and recreational sites would of necessity also be unconstitutional.

No claim has been asserted in this litigation that the $200 per lot value of land required to be dedicated by the subdivision owner is unreasonable in amount. Nelson, defendant's municipal planning expert, testified that the experience of municipal planners throughout the country has shown that for a good environment for human habitation, for each family in the area, there must be a minimum of 3,000 square feet of land devoted to park and school purposes. After some study of average land values in the village, the village planning commission and the village board determined that land valued at $200 would by and large provide the added park and school lands required for each family brought into the village by creation of the subdivision.

The grounds of the attack upon the land dedication requirement is that it is not authorized by statute and is an unconstitutional taking of private property for public use without just compensation.

Upon careful analysis of sec. 236.45, Stats., we conclude that it does authorize the land dedication requirement of the instant ordinance. Sub. (1) of this statute declares that the purposes of the statute include facilitating "adequate provision for transportation, water, sewerage, schools, parks, playgrounds and other public requirements." The common practice of providing for transportation in a subdivision is for municipal platting ordinances to require dedication of land for streets by the subdivider. Likewise the accepted way to provide water and sewerage facilities for a proposed subdivision is to require the subdivider to provide the same as a condition to the municipality approving the proposed plat. In Zastrow v. Village of Brown Deer[37] this court stated:

> "The Village could require as a condition of its approval of a plat that the subdivider make and install any public improvements reasonably necessary, including a water system, and it could require as a condition for accepting the dedication that the designated facilities previously constructed and provided be without cost to the Village, and that such facilities be according to the Village's specifications and under its inspection, including water mains and laterals."

Similarly it would seem to follow that the way to facilitate provision for schools, parks, and playgrounds to serve the subdivision would be to require the subdivider to dedicate a portion of the subdivision for such purposes. Sec. 236.13(2)(a) and (b), Stats.,[38] which apply statewide to all municipalities, irrespective of whether they have planning commissions, grants to municipalities the right to require the subdivider to pay for such public improvements as water and sewer mains, and to dedicate land for public streets, as a condition to the municipality approving the proposed subdivision plat. Sec. 236.45 was intended by the legislature to vest additional authority in those municipalities which had created planning commissions to impose further requirements upon the subdivider. In addition to the aforequoted language spelling out legislative purpose in sub. (1) of this statute, the first sentence of sub. (2)(a), of sec. 236.45, makes clear this intent. The third sentence of this subsection reads, "Such ordinances may make applicable to such divisions any of the provisions of this chapter, or may provide other surveying, monumenting, mapping and approving requirements for such division." Standing alone the statutory words "other * * * approving requirements" would normally be confined to requirements of the same general nature as the antecedent enumerated specific words "surveying, monumenting, mapping." We reject such a restrictive interpretation in favor

37. 9 Wis.2d 100, 100 N.W.2d 359 (1960).

38. These subsections provide: "(a) As a further condition of approval, the governing body of the town or municipality within which the subdivision lies may require that the subdivider make and install any public improvements reasonably necessary or that he execute a surety bond to insure that he will make those improvements within a reasonable time.

"(b) Any city or village may require as a condition for accepting the dedication of public streets, alleys or other ways, * * * that designated facilities shall have been previously provided without cost to the municipality, * * *"

of the broader one which will encompass the objectives stated in sub. (1). We are further motivated in favor of such a broad interpretation by the direction of sub. (2)(b) requiring a liberal construction of sec. 236.45.

Having concluded that sec. 236.45, Stats., does authorize the land dedication provisions of the instant ordinance, we turn now to the question of whether they constitute an unconstitutional taking of private property for a public purpose. The Illinois supreme court in Pioneer Trust & Sav. Bank v. Village of Mt. Prospect laid down this test of the constitutionality of a requirement placed upon a subdivider, as a condition for approval of the subdivision plat:

> "If the requirement is within the statutory grant of power to the municipality and if the burden cast upon the subdivider is specifically and uniquely attributable to his activity, then the requirement is permissible; if not, it is forbidden and amounts to a confiscation of private property in contravention of the constitutional prohibitions rather than reasonable regulation under the police power."

We deem this to be an acceptable statement of the yardstick to be applied, provided the words "specifically and uniquely attributable to his activity" are not so restrictively applied as to cast an unreasonable burden of proof upon the municipality which has enacted the ordinance under attack. In most instances it would be impossible for the municipality to prove that the land required to be dedicated for a park or a school site was to meet a need solely attributable to the anticipated influx of people into the community to occupy this particular subdivision. On the other hand, the municipality might well be able to establish that a group of subdivisions approved over a period of several years had been responsible for bringing into the community a considerable number of people making it necessary that the land dedications required of the subdividers be utilized for school, park and recreational purposes for the benefit of such influx. In the absence of contravening evidence this would establish a reasonable basis for finding that the need for the acquisition was occasioned by the activity of the subdivider. Possible contravening evidence would be a showing that the municipality prior to the opening up of the subdivisions, acquired sufficient lands for school, park and recreational purposes to provide for future anticipated needs including such influx, or that the normal growth of the municipality would have made necessary the acquisition irrespective of the influx caused by opening up of subdivisions.

There also may be situations, unlike the instant one, where there is no substantial influx from the outside and the proposed subdivision only fulfills a purely local need within the community. In those situations it may be more difficult to adduce proof sufficient to sustain a land dedication requirement.

We conclude that a required dedication of land for school, park or recreational sites as a condition for approval of the subdivision plat should be upheld as a valid exercise of police power if the evidence reasonably establishes that the municipality will be required to provide more land for schools, parks and playgrounds as a result of approval of the subdivision.

We deem that the evidence in this case does establish such reasonable connection. There is the testimony of planning expert Nelson that for a good environment for human habitation for each family in the area there should be a minimum of 3,000 square feet of land devoted to park and school purposes. Because of its close proximity to Milwaukee, Menomonee Falls has felt the tremendous impact of urban development in recent years. Between July 23, 1959, and March 15, 1963, 41 plats containing 638 lots were approved pursuant to the instant ordinance. There were five dedications of land by the subdividers, four utilized for parks and one for building an addition to a public school. During this period the village also purchased additional park sites. The increase in school population by school years has been as follows:

Year	Increase
1958–59	342
1959–60	512
1960–61	773
1961–62	531
1962–63	685

The village population increased from 6,262 in 1950 to 18,276 in 1960, and to an estimated 25,000 in 1964. Part of the increase in population between 1950 and 1960 was due to the entire town of Menomonee Falls being annexed to the village in 1958.

We do not consider the fact that other residents of the village as well as residents of the subdivision may make use of a public site required to be dedicated by subdivider for school, park or recreational purposes is particularly material to the constitutional issue. This is also true of land required to be dedicated for public street purposes.

The test of reasonableness is always applicable to any attempt to exercise the police power. The basis for upholding a compulsory land dedication requirement in a platting ordinance in the nature of the instant ordinance is this: The municipality by approval of a proposed subdivision plat enables the subdivider to profit financially by selling the subdivision lots as home building sites and thus realizing a greater price than could have been obtained if he had sold his property as unplatted lands. In return for this benefit the municipality may require him to dedicate part of his platted land to meet a demand to which the municipality would not have been put but for the influx of people into the community to occupy the subdivision lots.

For the reasons stated we determine that the provision of the ordinance requiring dedication of land when practicable for school, park and recreational sites is constitutional as a proper exercise of police power.

We turn now to the issue of the constitutionality of the equalization fee provision contained in section 8.03 of the ordinance whereby the subdivider is required to pay a total of $200 per lot in lieu of dedicating land of that value for school, park or recreational needs where the village planning commission finds dedication of land for such purposes is not feasible. In respect to this provision, the question which poses the greater difficulty is not whether there is an attempted illegal taking which cannot be justified as a reasonable exercise of the police power, but whether the legislature has authorized such a provision.

The reason why we consider that the exercise of police power aspect of the equalization fee question, as distinguished from a requirement that land be dedicated for school, park or recreational purposes, is not troublesome, is because the same reasons which under the facts of this case prompt us to hold that the land dedication requirement constitutes a reasonable exercise of the police power apply with equal force to the equalization fee requirement. The evidence reasonably supports the conclusions that: (1) the approval of the instant and other subdivision plats during the four-year period following the enactment of the ordinance has required defendant village and the encompassing school districts to expend large sums for acquisition of park and school lands and construction of additional school facilities; (2) these expenditures were made necessary by the influx of people into these subdivisions; and (3) these expenditures are greater than the amount which has been exacted from the subdividers by way of land dedication and equalization fees paid in lieu of land dedication. For example, in 1962 a 13 room addition to the Shady Lane School, which is located in the vicinity of plaintiffs' subdivision, was completed at a cost of $28,000 per room or $364,000. During the four-year period following enactment of the ordinance, the total value of all land dedications made and equalization fees collected amounted to only $127,000.

However, even though the equalization fee requirement provision can be sustained as a reasonable exercise of the police power, it is unconstitutional unless authorized by the legislature. The provision possesses sufficient attributes of a tax so that it cannot be grounded upon the home-rule amendment, sec. 3, art. XI of the Wisconsin constitution. While under this amendment, and the implementing statutes, secs. 61.34 and 63.04, Stats., villages and cities have wide powers to tax for the general welfare, they can only resort to the types of taxes that the legislature has authorized them to use.

Is the equalization fee such a concomitant of the land dedication provision of the ordinance that its authorization can be found in the language of subs. (1) and (2) of sec. 236.45 hereinbefore relied upon to sustain the land dedication requirement of the ordinance? We conclude that it is.

Where a comparatively small tract of land is subdivided, as in the instant situation, and there is no adjoining land already devoted to school park, or playground purposes to which a portion of the proposed subdivision might be attached, it usually would be impracticable to require dedication of any land of the subdivision. The two alternatives are either to relieve the subdivider from any obligation whatever in this direction, or to require payment of an equalization fee of the nature of that here imposed. The latter is in keeping with the stated purpose of the statute.

While section 8.03(2) of the ordinance permits use of the proceeds of the equalization fee for capital improvement of schools, parks and recreation areas in addition to site acquisition, nevertheless the making of these capital improvements is encompassed by the words of sub. (1) of sec. 236.45 which declare that the purposes of the statute include facilitating "adequate provision for * * * schools, parks, playgrounds and other public requirements."

The equalization fee exacted pursuant to the ordinance is not a property tax. It is not imposed upon the land in the subdivision as such but is imposed on the transaction of obtaining approval of the plat. Thus, if a tax, it partakes of the nature of an excise tax and does not violate the uniformity clause found in sec. 1, art. VIII of the Wisconsin constitution.

While plaintiffs do not openly contend that the equalization fee is in the nature of a special assessment, they employ arguments that tend in that direction. Thus they point to the fact that the ordinance does not require that park and school sites purchased with funds paid in lieu of dedication bear any relationship to the subdivision providing the funds. This argument would be pertinent if the equalization fee's validity were dependent on justifying it as a special assessment. The argument, however, does have some pertinency on the previously considered issue of unconstitutional taking of private property for a public purpose as opposed to a reasonable exercise of police power.

To conclude, we determine that the imposition of the instant $5,000 equalization fee is not invalid as unconstitutional. In so holding we are cognizant that this result is contra to the conclusions reached by the Illinois and Kansas courts in the well considered cases of Rosen v. Village of Downers Grove[39] and Coronado Development Co. v. City of McPherson[40] with respect to the issue of the validity of the attempted exercise of the police power. While we have great respect for these courts, we believe that there is a reasonable basis for upholding the exercise of the police power voiced in the instant ordinance.

Judgment reversed and cause remanded with directions to dismiss the complaint.

HALLOWS, JUSTICE (dissenting).

I must disagree with the interpretation that sec. 236.45, Stats., authorizes the land-dedication requirement found in secs. 8.02 and 8.03 of the village ordinance. I can find no such grant of power in the language "other surveying, monumenting, mapping and approving re-

39. 19 Ill.2d 448, 167 N.E.2d 230 (1960).   **40.** 189 Kan. 174, 368 P.2d 51 (1962).

quirements for such division." A liberal construction required by sec. 236.45(2)(b) does not justify the disregarding of a fundamental rule of construction. The conferring of such an important power as a police power whose exercise curtails the rights of individuals should be expressed in nothing less than clear and concise language. Consequently, the power to require land to be given for school and park purposes as a condition of the approval by a municipality of a plat of a subdivision should be granted in more definite language than the terms "approving requirements" and "to facilitate adequate provision for * * * schools, parks, playgrounds." Specific language authorizing the requirements for dedication of land for school and park purposes could have been used as it has been used in reference to roads, waters and sewers in sec. 236.13(2)(a) and (b).

Assuming sec. 236.45, Stats., authorizes the land-dedication provisions of the village ordinance, the provisions, especially the requirement of the payment of $200 in lieu of land dedication, constitute an unconstitutional taking of private property for public purposes. The majority opinion reasons these provisions may be justified on the ground a subdivider receives some benefit by the approval of the plat and in return the municipality may require him to dedicate part of his land to meet a demand of the municipality because of the influx of people to the community who occupied the subdivided lots. That may be a justification if there is a reasonable relationship between the amount of land taken and the need of the proposed plat for parks and schools. The majority opinion seems to indicate prior need for public land caused by other subdividers who have not so contributed justifies the exaction of land from a subsequent subdivider.

By analogy, any dedication of land for parks and school purposes or money in lieu thereof should be governed by the same rules which apply to public roads and sewer and water in the subdivision. When land is dedicated for public streets or for the furnishing of water mains and sewers, their location insures some definite benefit to the rest of the land in the plat. While these are of special benefit to the lots, they are, of course, incidentally of benefit to the community at large.

In respect to the alternative provision for the payment of money in lieu of land for school and park purposes, I find no authority for the municipality to enact such an alternative and no restriction or requirement that the money be used for parks and schools in the vicinity of the subdivision. The money may be used anywhere in the municipality and is not restricted for the direct benefit of the subdivision. Consequently, this requirement of the payment of a fee which a municipality has the option to demand in lieu of land is nothing more than a revenue-raising device for the general welfare of the municipality and as such is in the nature of a tax and cannot be justified as an exercise of the police power. City of Milwaukee v. Milwaukee & S.T. Corp., 6 Wis.2d 299, 94 N.W.2d 584 (1959); 51 Am.Jur., Taxation, p. 35, sec. 3, and p. 46, sec. 12. I think the trial court was correct in finding the requirement to be in the nature of a tax and the village had no power and was not authorized by the legislature to impose it. Whitney v. Department of Taxation, 16 Wis.2d 274, 114 N.W.2d 445 (1962). There is no implementing authorization conferring the power to impose such a tax nor does the Home–Rule Amendment (sec. 3, Art. XI, Wis. Const.) authorize it since a tax is not a local matter. City of Plymouth v. Elsner, 28 Wis.2d 102, 135 N.W.2d 799 (1965). Being in the nature of a tax it makes no difference whether the tax is a property tax bound by the uniformity requirement or an excise tax not so restricted.

It is quite apparent the so-called equalizing fee bears no reasonable relationship to the subdivision since it is not restricted to its benefit. The placing of such payments in the general treasury of the municipality cannot be justified on the theory that parks and schools will eventually be built or have been built in the subdivision area out of the general fund. Such a view ignores the vital distinction between the taxing power and the police power.

The unconstitutionality of the provisions requiring subdividers to pay such fees has been held in Coronado Development Co. v. City of McPherson, 189 Kan. 174, 368 P.2d 51 (1962); Haugen v. Gleason, 226 Or. 99, 359 P.2d 108 (1961); Rosen v. Village of Downers Grove, 19 Ill.2d 448, 167 N.E.2d 230 (1960). Under slightly more narrow enabling statutes the requirement of payment of fees for approval of subdivision plats was found unauthorized in Kelber v. City of Upland, 155 Cal. App.2d 631, 318 P.2d 561 (1957), and Santa Clara County Contractors & Homebuilders Ass'n v. City of Santa Clara, 232 Cal.App.2d 564, 43 Cal.Rptr. 86 (1965). A town ordinance which requires the dedication of land or payment in lieu thereof for a neighborhood park playground for recreational purposes was held unconstitutional so far as it provided for the payment of money in lieu of a dedication because the payment exacted could be spent on any recreational area in the city and not necessarily for the benefit of the subdivision. Gulest Associates, Inc. v. Town of Newburgh, 25 Misc.2d 1004, 209 N.Y.S.2d 729 (1960); see also Jenad, Inc. v. Village of Scarsdale, 23 A.D.2d 784, 258 N.Y.S.2d 777 (1965), which held a village code was unconstitutional in so far as it provided for payment in lieu of dedication of land where the statute authorizing a land requirement was silent as to the alternative payment.

I would affirm.

Notes

1. For cases holding park or school site dedications or fees in lieu of dedications invalid because unauthorized by enabling statutes see: Rosen v. Village of Downers Grove, 19 Ill.2d 448, 167 N.E.2d 230 (1960); Coronado Development Co. v. City of McPherson, 189 Kan. 174, 368 P.2d 51 (1962); and Haugen v. Gleason, 226 Or. 99, 359 P.2d 108 (1961), all of which are cited in support of the dissent in the Jordan case. Other cases striking down such exactions include City of Montgomery v. Crossroads Land Co., Inc., 355 So.2d 363 (Ala.1978); Admiral Development Corp. v. City of Maitland, 267 So.2d 860 (Fla.App.1972); Sanchez v. City of Santa Fe, 82 N.M. 322, 481 P.2d 401 (1971); Frank Ansuini, Inc. v. City of Cranston, 107 R.I. 63, 264

A.2d 910 (1970); Berg Development Co. v. City of Missouri City, 603 S.W.2d
273 (Tex.Civ.App.1980); J.E.D. Associates, Inc. v. Town of Atkinson, 121
N.H. 581, 432 A.2d 12 (1981); Kamhi v. Planning Bd. of Yorktown, 59
N.Y.2d 385, 465 N.Y.S.2d 865, 452 N.E.2d 1193 (1983); City of Fayetteville v.
IBI, Inc., 280 Ark. 484, 659 S.W.2d 505 (1983); and Town of Longboat Key v.
Lands End, Ltd., 433 So.2d 574 (Fla.App.1983). Compare Gulest Associates
v. Town of Newburgh, 25 Misc.2d 1004, 209 N.Y.S.2d 729 (1960) and
Midtown Properties v. Township of Madison, 68 N.J.Super. 197, 172 A.2d 40,
47 (1961), affirmed 78 N.J.Super. 471, 189 A.2d 226 (1963). See also Reps
and Smith, Control of Urban Land Subdivision, 14 Syracuse L.Rev. 405, 411
(1963), and Comment, Requiring Dedication of Park Land, 1961 Wis.L.Rev.
310.

In Haugen v. Gleason, supra, the court reversed the lower court and
invalidated a $37.50 per lot fee for park purposes. It treated the fee as a tax
upon subdividers for public purposes and held that such a tax was not
authorized by any enabling legislation.

In Gulest, supra, the enabling act expressly authorized fees in an
amount to be determined by the town board, "which amount shall be
available for use by the town for neighborhood park, playground or recreation purposes including the acquisition of property." Nevertheless, the
Supreme Court of Orange County, New York annulled a $50.00 per lot fee
because (1) the fee could be used in any section of the town and thus was for
the benefit, not of subdivision residents, but of the town as a whole, and (2)
the statute failed to set out standards or tests.

On the basis of the Gulest case, the developer in Jenad, Inc. v. Village of
Scarsdale, 38 Misc.2d 658, 238 N.Y.S.2d 156 (1963) tried unsuccessfully to
recover fees he had paid voluntarily in lieu of land dedications. "Plaintiff had
a preliminary remedy had it felt aggrieved * * * and no facts have been
presented to the court to indicate that plaintiff would have been deprived of
the reasonable use of its lands during the pendency of a lawsuit to attack the
legality or constitutionality of the Scarsdale regulation before it paid the
money in question. Everything before the court points to a business arrangement entered into between plaintiff and the village, and concluded in an
amicable fashion resulting in plaintiff thanking the Village Attorney for his
'cooperation' in the matter." Also see Joseph v. Yorktown Planning Bd., 140
A.D.2d 670, 529 N.Y.S.2d 17 (1988). In Video Aid Corp. v.Town of Wallkill,
85 N.Y.2d 663, 628 N.Y.S.2d 18, 651 N.E.2d 886 (1995), a developer paid a
$27,000 sewer and water connection fee only after the town indicated it
would not grant a building permit unless the fee was paid; the developer
then contested the fee as an unconstitutional exaction and sought reimbursement. The New York Court of Appeals held, in a four to three decision
that even though the exaction was unconstitutional, the developer could not
claim coercion and obtain a refund. The majority concluded that the developer had not even taken the simple step of making a notation on the check that
the payment was under protest, and that some indication of protest is
necessary when making such payments in order to permit public agencies to
operate on a sound fiscal basis and that such agencies need to made aware
when collected funds may have to be refunded. The majority also indicated
that an exception to the rule would be recognized in cases where payments
are made under duress, but that exception would be applied very narrowly.

The message of this case is that in every case where a developer may think that an exaction is excessive, exaction payments should be made under protest; such a practice might also be wise in jurisdictions other than New York.

On the other hand, several cases have followed the holding in the Jordan case and have upheld equalization assessments or dedications for park purposes. See Aunt Hack Ridge Estates, Inc. v. Planning Comm'n of the City of Danbury, 160 Conn. 109, 273 A.2d 880 (1970); Associated Home Builders of Greater East Bay, Inc. v. City of Walnut Creek, 4 Cal.3d 633, 94 Cal.Rptr. 630, 484 P.2d 606 (1971), appeal dismissed 404 U.S. 878, 92 S.Ct. 202, 30 L.Ed.2d 159 (1971); Cimarron Corp. v. Board of County Comm'rs, 193 Colo. 164, 563 P.2d 946 (1977); Collis v. City of Bloomington, 310 Minn. 5, 246 N.W.2d 19 (1976); Home Builders Ass'n of Greater Kansas City v. City of Kansas City, 555 S.W.2d 832 (Mo.1977); Call v. City of West Jordan, 614 P.2d 1257 (Utah 1980); Town of Auburn v. McEvoy, 131 N.H. 383, 553 A.2d 317 (1988) (overruling the J.E.D. Associates case, supra); Messer v. Town of Chapel Hill, 59 N.C.App. 692, 297 S.E.2d 632 (1982), appeal dismissed 307 N.C. 697, 301 S.E.2d 390 (1983); City of College Station v. Turtle Rock Corp., 680 S.W.2d 802 (Tex.1984); and Bayswater Realty and Capital Corp. v. Planning Bd., 76 N.Y.2d 460, 560 N.Y.S.2d 623, 560 N.E.2d 1300 (1990). Also see the annotation in 43 A.L.R.3d 862. In the Walnut Creek case, the court rejected arguments that: (1) the exaction discriminated in favor of apartment builders (the court said that apartment development does not diminish the available supply of open land to the same extent as the activity of subdividers); (2) the exaction amounted to double taxation, once in the higher cost to the lot purchaser, and again in subsequent property taxes to maintain the parks.

Two cases from Florida, both intermediate appellate court decisions, reached opposite conclusions on the validity of money exactions. Compare Broward County v. Janis Development Corp., 311 So.2d 371 (Fla.App.1975) with City of Dunedin v. Contractors and Builders Ass'n of Pinellas County, 312 So.2d 763 (Fla.App.1975) quashed 329 So.2d 314 (1976). See Rhodes, Impact Fees: The Cost–Benefit Dilemma in Florida, 27 Land Use Law & Zoning Dig. 7 (No. 10, 1975). Also see City of Key West v. R.L.J.S. Corp., 537 So.2d 641 (Fla.App.1989), review denied 545 So.2d 1367 (1989) where the court upheld retroactive sewer impact fees for units already sold by a condominium developer (the city had held back occupancy permits for newly-sold units until the fees were paid for units previously sold).

In Riegert Apartments Corp. v. Planning Bd., 105 Misc.2d 298, 432 N.Y.S.2d 43 (1979), a trial court upheld a money exaction in addition to a compulsory land dedication for flood control purposes. The Court of Appeals reversed. 57 N.Y.2d 206, 455 N.Y.S.2d 558, 441 N.E.2d 1076 (1982). Compare Hillis Homes, Inc. v. Snohomish County, 97 Wash.2d 804, 650 P.2d 193 (1982).

2. For a comprehensive discussion of the rationale of exactions see, Heyman and Gilhool, The Constitutionality of Imposing Increased Community Costs on New Suburban Residents Through Subdivision Exactions, 73 Yale L.J. 1119 (1964) and Johnston, Constitutionality of Subdivision Control Exactions: The Quest for a Rationale, 52 Cornell L.Q. 871 (1967). For a

practical overview, see Delaney and Smith, Development Exactions: Winners and Losers, Land Use Law, Nov. 1989, p. 3. A review of state enabling legislation regarding impact fees is found in Morgan, State Impact Fee Legislation: Guidelines for Analysis, Land Use Law, Mar. 1990, p. 3 (Part I) and Apr. 1990, p. 3 (Part II). Also see Eastern Diversified Properties, Inc. v. Montgomery County, 319 Md. 45, 570 A.2d 850 (1990); Blaesser & Kentopp, Impact Fees: The "Second Generation," 38 Wash.U.J.Urb. & Contemp.L. 55 (1990). For interesting examples of impact fee enabling legislation, see Va.Code Ann. § 15.1–498.1 et seq. (effective July 1, 1990); N. Mex. St. § 5–8–1 et seq. (1993); Idaho Rev. Stat. §§ 67–8201 to 67–8216 (1992). In Idaho Bldg. Contractors Ass'n v. Coeur d'Alene, 126 Idaho 740, 890 P.2d 326 (1995) the court struck down an ordinance imposing a development impact fee on all new construction, holding that the act was inapplicable and the city was really using the fee as a revenue raising device. Also see, Arthur C. Nelson, Development Impact Fees: The Next Generation, 26 The Urban Lawyer 541 (1994).

3. Compare Miller v. City of Beaver Falls, 368 Pa. 189, 82 A.2d 34 (1951) with In re Lake Secor Development Co., 141 Misc. 913, 252 N.Y.S. 809 (1931). In Miller an attempt to require the subdivider in effect to grant the city a three year first right of purchase of park land was declared invalid. The city did not pass the contested ordinance until after the council knew of the intention to subdivide, and the ordinance applied to 4½ acres of the subdivider's total of 16 acres. Construction of 12 houses had been commenced prior to the ordinance on part of the 16 acres, but not on the 4½ acre portion. Said Justice Bell for the Pennsylvania Court:

"The city is not without remedy, but cannot eat its cake and have its penny too. If it desires plaintiff's land for a park or playground which it considers desirable or necessary for its future progress, it can readily and lawfully obtain this land in accordance with the Constitution which, we repeat, is the Supreme Law of the land * * * All that is required is that just compensation be paid therefor."

In the Secor case the planning board denied approval of a 138–acre (2000 lot) subdivision for several reasons, among them "insufficient park area." There is no indication how large a dedication the planning board demanded. The court, after first holding that the planning board had exceeded its enabling authority by insisting on a water system, said at page 812:

"The demand of the planning board for additional park area is reasonable. The argument that 'all Putnam County is a park' advanced by the petitioner is without merit. The apparent purpose of the petitioner is to establish a summer colony. It must dedicate to public use sufficient area to provide for the ultimate use to be made of this plat. It argues that the residents there can trespass upon other lands for recreational purposes. The mere statement of the proposition is its answer."

4. In connection with park and school site dedication problems recall that it is constitutional under appropriate legislation to require the subdivider to dedicate, free of charge, all land needed for new streets of ordinary width within the subdivision. (Recall the cross street in the Ayres case,

supra.) And the requirement seems universal even though the land may amount to 20 or 25% of the total area, where a gridiron street pattern is used.

As was seen from the Ridgefield case and the Ayres case, supra, there is also authority sustaining required dedications of strips for the purpose of widening existing streets abutting in the subdivision. See also Newton v. American Sec. Co., 201 Ark. 943, 148 S.W.2d 311 (1941).

5.   Consider Board of Educ. of Community Consol. Sch. Dist. No. 59 v. E.A. Herzog Constr. Co., 29 Ill.App.2d 138, 172 N.E.2d 645 (1961). Herzog on May 9, 1957 in writing agreed to pay $95,000 toward the cost of a school and the board of education agreed to hold a special referendum to approve the school and to begin construction no later than July 15, 1958. Next day, on May 10, 1957, the county commissioner rezoned Herzog's land and authorized his project. On August 27, 1958, the original agreement was amended with the board of education acknowledging that its delay in commencing construction had undoubtedly affected Herzog's sales and consequently his revenues. Herzog's commitment to pay the $95,000 was restated but the time for payment was postponed until completion of the school. The school was completed. Herzog refused to pay and the board sued. Herzog claimed the agreements void as against public policy as contracts "for the purchase of influence upon the action of public officers." He also charged the board of education conspired with members of the county board to withhold rezoning until Herzog agreed to contribute to the cost of the school. The court took judicial notice that the school district has no control over the actions of the county board, brushed aside "these wild and irresponsible charges" and affirmed judgment against Herzog. Said the court:

> "The defendant voluntarily agreed to pay the $95,000 toward construction of the building, as it realized that the proposed school building was essential to its sales program. Having accepted the benefits of the agreement, it is now attempting to renege on its voluntary agreement to contribute money to the school board. It will not be permitted to do so."

Compare Midtown Properties v. Township of Madison, 68 N.J.Super. 197, 172 A.2d 40 (1961), affirmed 78 N.J.Super. 471, 189 A.2d 226 (1963) where a detailed contract between subdivider and a local unit was set aside as an attempt to do by contract what can only be done by following statutory procedures.

6.   In Quirk v. Town of New Boston, 140 N.H. 124, 663 A.2d 1328 (1995) the court upheld a requirement that campground developments provide a 200 foot buffer zone around the perimeter of the property. The owner of an existing campground who had invested considerably in installation of oversized septic systems was denied a permit for a new recreation hall that would have encroached on the buffer zone. The court found that the regulation was akin to a setback requirement, that it was not arbitrary, and that the campground owner had not suffered a taking.

NOLLAN v. CALIFORNIA COASTAL COMMISSION

Supreme Court of the United States, 1987.
483 U.S. 825, 107 S.Ct. 3141, 97 L.Ed.2d 677.

JUSTICE SCALIA delivered the opinion of the Court.

I

The Nollans own a beachfront lot in Ventura County, California. A quarter-mile north of their property is Faria County Park, an oceanside public park with a public beach and recreation area. Another public beach area, known locally as "the Cove," lies 1,800 feet south of their lot. A concrete seawall approximately eight feet high separates the beach portion of the Nollans' property from the rest of the lot. The historic mean high tide line determines the lot's oceanside boundary.

The Nollans originally leased their property with an option to buy. The building on the lot was a small bungalow, totaling 504 square feet, which for a time they rented to summer vacationers. After years of rental use, however, the building had fallen into disrepair, and could no longer be rented out.

The Nollans' option to purchase was conditioned on their promise to demolish the bungalow and replace it. In order to do so, under California Public Resources Code §§ 30106, 30212, and 30600 (West 1986), they were required to obtain a coastal development permit from the California Coastal Commission. On February 25, 1982, they submitted a permit application to the Commission in which they proposed to demolish the existing structure and replace it with a three-bedroom house in keeping with the rest of the neighborhood.

The Nollans were informed that their application had been placed on the administrative calendar, and that the Commission staff had recommended that the permit be granted subject to the condition that they allow the public an easement to pass across a portion of their property bounded by the mean high tide line on one side, and their seawall on the other side. This would make it easier for the public to get to Faria County Park and the Cove. The Nollans protested imposition of the condition, but the Commission overruled their objections and granted the permit subject to their recordation of a deed restriction granting the easement.

On June 3, 1982, the Nollans filed a petition for writ of administrative mandamus asking the Ventura County Superior Court to invalidate the access condition. They argued that the condition could not be imposed absent evidence that their proposed development would have a direct adverse impact on public access to the beach. The court agreed, and remanded the case to the Commission for a full evidentiary hearing on that issue.

On remand, the Commission held a public hearing, after which it made further factual findings and reaffirmed its imposition of the condition. It found that the new house would increase blockage of the view of the ocean, thus contributing to the development of "a 'wall' of residential structures" that would prevent the public "psychologically * * * from realizing a stretch of coastline exists nearby that they have every right to visit." The new house would also increase private use of the shorefront. These effects of construction of the house, along with other area development, would cumulatively "burden the public's ability to traverse to and along the shorefront." Therefore the Commission could properly require the Nollans to offset that burden by providing additional lateral access to the public beaches in the form of an easement across their property. The Commission also noted that it had similarly conditioned 43 out of 60 coastal development permits along the same tract of land, and that of the 17 not so conditioned, 14 had been approved when the Commission did not have administrative regulations in place allowing imposition of the condition, and the remaining 3 had not involved shorefront property.

The Nollans filed a supplemental petition for a writ of administrative mandamus with the Superior Court, in which they argued that imposition of the access condition violated the Takings Clause of the Fifth Amendment, as incorporated against the States by the Fourteenth Amendment. The Superior Court ruled in their favor on statutory grounds, finding, in part to avoid "issues of constitutionality," that the California Coastal Act of 1976, Cal.Pub.Res.Code Ann. § 30000 et seq., authorized the Commission to impose public access conditions on coastal development permits for the replacement of an existing single-family home with a new one only where the proposed development would have an adverse impact on public access to the sea. In the Court's view, the administrative record did not provide an adequate factual basis for concluding that replacement of the bungalow with the house would create a direct or cumulative burden on public access to the sea. Accordingly, the Superior Court granted the writ of mandamus and directed that the permit condition be struck.

The Commission appealed to the California Court of Appeal. * * *

The Court of Appeal reversed the Superior Court. 177 Cal.App.3d 719, 223 Cal.Rptr. 28 (1986). It disagreed with the Superior Court's interpretation of the Coastal Act, finding that it required that a coastal permit for the construction of a new house whose floor area, height or bulk was more than 10% larger than that of the house it was replacing be conditioned on a grant of access. Id., at 723–724, 223 Cal.Rptr., at 31; see Cal.Pub.Res.Code § 30212. It also ruled that the requirement did not violate the Constitution under the reasoning of an earlier case of the Court of Appeal, Grupe v. California Coastal Comm'n, 166 Cal.App.3d 148, 212 Cal.Rptr. 578 (1985). In that case, the court had found that so long as a project contributed to the need for public access, even if the project standing alone had not created the need for access, and even if there was only an indirect relationship between the access exacted and the need to which the project contributed, imposition of an access condition on a development permit was sufficiently related to burdens created by the project to be constitutional. * * * The Court of Appeal ruled that the record established that that was the situation with respect to the Nollans' house. * * * It ruled that the Nollans' taking claim also failed because, although the condition diminished the value of the Nollans' lot, it did not deprive them of all reasonable use of their property. * * * Since, in the Court of Appeal's view, there was no statutory or constitutional obstacle to imposition of the access condition, the Superior Court erred in granting the writ of mandamus. The Nollans appealed to this Court, raising only the constitutional question.

II

Had California simply required the Nollans to make an easement across their beachfront available to the public on a permanent basis in order to increase public access to the beach, rather than conditioning their permit to rebuild their house on their agreeing to do so, we have no doubt there would have been a taking. To say that the appropriation of a public easement across a landowner's premises does not constitute the taking of a property interest but rather, (as Justice Brennan contends) "a mere restriction on its use," is to use words in a manner that deprives them of all their ordinary meaning. Indeed, one of the principal uses of the eminent domain power is to assure that the government be able to require conveyance of just such interests, so long as it pays for them. Perhaps because the point is so obvious, we have never been confronted with a controversy that required us to rule upon it, but our cases' analysis of the effect of other governmental action leads to the same conclusion. We have repeatedly held that, as to property reserved by its owner for private use, "the right to exclude [others is] 'one of the most essential sticks in the bundle of rights that are commonly characterized as property.' " *Loretto v. Teleprompter Manhattan CATV Corp.,* 458 U.S. 419, 433, 102 S.Ct. 3164, 3175, 73 L.Ed.2d 868 (1982), quoting *Kaiser Aetna v. United States,* 444 U.S. 164, 176, 100 S.Ct. 383, 391, 62 L.Ed.2d 332 (1979). In *Loretto* we observed that where governmental action results in "[a] permanent physical occupation" of the property, by the government itself or by others, "our cases uniformly have found a taking to the extent of the occupation, without regard to whether the action achieves an important public benefit or has only minimal economic impact on the owner." We think a "permanent physical occupation" has occurred, for purposes of that rule, where individuals are given a permanent and continuous right to pass to and fro, so that the real property may continuously be traversed, even though no particular individual is permitted to station himself permanently upon the premises.[41]

* * *

41. The holding of *PruneYard Shopping Center v. Robins,* 447 U.S. 74, 100 S.Ct. 2035, 64 L.Ed.2d 741 (1980), is not inconsistent with this analysis, since there the owner had already opened his property to the general public, and in addition permanent access was not required. The analysis of *Kaiser Aetna v. United States,* 444 U.S. 164, 100 S.Ct. 383, 62 L.Ed.2d 332 (1979), is not inconsistent because it was affected

Given, then, that requiring uncompensated conveyance of the easement outright would violate the Fourteenth Amendment, the question becomes whether requiring it to be conveyed as a condition for issuing a land use permit alters the outcome. We have long recognized that land use regulation does not effect a taking if it "substantially advance[s] legitimate state interests" and does not "den[y] an owner economically viable use of his land," *Agins v. Tiburon,* 447 U.S. 255, 260, 100 S.Ct. 2138, 2141, 65 L.Ed.2d 106 (1980). See also *Penn Central Transportation Co. v. New York City,* 438 U.S. 104, 127, 98 S.Ct. 2646, 2660, 57 L.Ed.2d 631 (1978) ("a use restriction may constitute a 'taking' if not reasonably necessary to the effectuation of a substantial government purpose"). Our cases have not elaborated on the standards for determining what constitutes a "legitimate state interest" or what type of connection between the regulation and the state interest satisfies the requirement that the former "substantially advance" the latter. They have made clear, however, that a broad range of governmental purposes and regulations satisfies these requirements. * * * The Commission argues that among these permissible purposes are protecting the public's ability to see the beach, assisting the public in overcoming the "psychological barrier" to using the beach created by a developed shorefront, and preventing congestion on the public beaches. We assume, without deciding, that this is so—in which case the Commission unquestionably would be able to deny the Nollans their permit outright if their new house (alone, or by reason of the cumulative impact produced in conjunction with other construction) would substantially impede these purposes, unless the denial would interfere so drastically with the Nollans' use of their property as to constitute a taking.

The Commission argues that a permit condition that serves the same legitimate police-power purpose as a refusal to issue the permit should not be found to be a taking if the refusal to issue the permit would not constitute a taking. We agree. Thus, if the Commission attached to the permit some condition that would have protected the public's ability to see the beach notwithstanding construction of the new house—for example, a height limitation, a width restriction, or a ban on fences—so long as the Commission could have exercised its police power (as we have assumed it could) to forbid construction of the house altogether, imposition of the condition would also be constitutional. Moreover (and here we come closer to the facts of the present case), the condition would be constitutional even if it consisted of the requirement that the Nollans provide a viewing spot on their property for passersby with whose sighting of the ocean their new house would interfere. Although such a requirement, constituting a permanent grant of continuous access to the property, would have to be considered a taking if it were not attached to a development permit, the Commission's assumed power to forbid construction of the house in order to protect the public's view of the beach must surely include the power to condition construc-

by traditional doctrines regarding navigational servitudes. Of course neither of those cases involved, as this one does, a classic right-of-way easement.

tion upon some concession by the owner, even a concession of property rights, that serves the same end. If a prohibition designed to accomplish that purpose would be a legitimate exercise of the police power rather than a taking, it would be strange to conclude that providing the owner an alternative to that prohibition which accomplishes the same purpose is not.

The evident constitutional propriety disappears, however, if the condition substituted for the prohibition utterly fails to further the end advanced as the justification for the prohibition. When that essential nexus is eliminated, the situation becomes the same as if California law forbade shouting fire in a crowded theater, but granted dispensations to those willing to contribute $100 to the state treasury. While a ban on shouting fire can be a core exercise of the State's police power to protect the public safety, and can thus meet even our stringent standards for regulation of speech, adding the unrelated condition alters the purpose to one which, while it may be legitimate, is inadequate to sustain the ban. Therefore, even though, in a sense, requiring a $100 tax contribution in order to shout fire is a lesser restriction on speech than an outright ban, it would not pass constitutional muster. Similarly here, the lack of nexus between the condition and the original purpose of the building restriction converts that purpose to something other than what it was. The purpose then becomes, quite simply, the obtaining of an easement to serve some valid governmental purpose, but without payment of compensation. Whatever may be the outer limits of "legitimate state interests" in the takings and land use context, this is not one of them. In short, unless the permit condition serves the same governmental purpose as the development ban, the building restriction is not a valid regulation of land use but "an out-and-out plan of extortion." *J.E.D. Associates, Inc. v. Atkinson,* 121 N.H. 581, 584, 432 A.2d 12, 14–15 (1981); * * *

III

The Commission claims that it concedes as much, and that we may sustain the condition at issue here by finding that it is reasonably related to the public need or burden that the Nollans' new house creates or to which it contributes. We can accept, for purposes of discussion, the Commission's proposed test as to how close a "fit" between the condition and the burden is required, because we find that this case does not meet even the most untailored standards. The Commission's principal contention to the contrary essentially turns on a play on the word "access." The Nollans' new house, the Commission found, will interfere with "visual access" to the beach. That in turn (along with other shorefront development) will interfere with the desire of people who drive past the Nollans' house to use the beach, thus creating a "psychological barrier" to "access." The Nollans' new house will also, by a process not altogether clear from the Commission's opinion but presumably potent enough to more than offset the effects of the psychological barrier, increase the use of the public beaches, thus creating the need for more "access." These burdens on "access" would be alleviated by a requirement that the Nollans provide "lateral access" to the beach.

Rewriting the argument to eliminate the play on words makes clear that there is nothing to it. It is quite impossible to understand how a requirement that people already on the public beaches be able to walk across the Nollans' property reduces any obstacles to viewing the beach created by the new house. It is also impossible to understand how it lowers any "psychological barrier" to using the public beaches, or how it helps to remedy any additional congestion on them caused by construction of the Nollans' new house. We therefore find that the Commission's imposition of the permit condition cannot be treated as an exercise of its land use power for any of these purposes. Our conclusion on this point is consistent with the approach taken by every other court that has considered the question, with the exception of the California state courts. See *Parks v. Watson,* 716 F.2d 646, 651–653 (C.A.9 1983); *Bethlehem Evangelical Lutheran Church v. Lakewood,* 626 P.2d 668, 671–674 (Colo.1981); *Aunt Hack Ridge Estates, Inc. v. Planning Comm'n,* 160 Conn. 109, 117–120, 273 A.2d 880, 885 (1970); *Longboat Key v. Lands End, Ltd.,* 433 So.2d 574 (Fla.App.1983); *Pioneer Trust & Saving Bank v. Mount Prospect,* 22 Ill.2d 375, 380, 176 N.E.2d 799, 802 (1961); *Lampton v. Pinaire,* 610 S.W.2d 915, 918–919 (Ky.App.1980); *Schwing v. Baton Rouge,* 249 So.2d 304 (La.App.), application denied, 259 La. 770, 252 So.2d 667 (1971); *Howard County v. JJM, Inc.,* 301 Md. 256, 280–282, 482 A.2d 908, 920–921 (1984); *Collis v. Bloomington,* 310 Minn. 5, 246 N.W.2d 19 (1976); *State ex rel. Noland v. St. Louis County,* 478 S.W.2d 363 (Mo.1972); *Billings Properties, Inc. v. Yellowstone County,* 144 Mont. 25, 33–36, 394 P.2d 182, 187–188 (1964); *Simpson v. North Platte,* 206 Neb. 240, 292 N.W.2d 297 (1980); *Briar West, Inc. v. Lincoln,* 206 Neb. 172, 291 N.W.2d 730 (1980); *J.E.D. Associates v. Atkinson, supra; Longridge Builders, Inc. v. Planning Bd. of Princeton,* 52 N.J. 348, 350–351, 245 A.2d 336, 337–338 (1968); *Jenad, Inc. v. Scarsdale,* 18 N.Y.2d 78, 271 N.Y.S.2d 955, 218 N.E.2d 673 (1966); *In re Mackall v. White,* 85 App.Div.2d 696, 445 N.Y.S.2d 486 (1981), appeal denied, 56 N.Y.2d 503, 450 N.Y.S.2d 1025, 435 N.E.2d 1100 (1982); *Frank Ansuini, Inc. v. Cranston,* 107 R.I. 63, 68–69, 71, 264 A.2d 910, 913, 914 (1970); *College Station v. Turtle Rock Corp.,* 680 S.W.2d 802, 807 (Tex.1984); *Call v. West Jordan,* 614 P.2d 1257, 1258–1259 (Utah 1980); *Board of Supervisors of James City County v. Rowe,* 216 Va. 128, 136–139, 216 S.E.2d 199, 207–209 (1975); *Jordan v. Menomonee Falls,* 28 Wis.2d 608, 617–618, 137 N.W.2d 442, 447–449 (1965), appeal dismissed, 385 U.S. 4, 87 S.Ct. 36, 17 L.Ed.2d 3 (1966). See also *Littlefield v. Afton,* 785 F.2d 596, 607 (C.A.8 1986); * * * We view the Fifth Amendment's property clause to be more than a pleading requirement, and compliance with it to be more than an exercise in cleverness and imagination. As indicated earlier, our cases describe the condition for abridgement of property rights through the police power as a *"substantial* advanc[ing]" of a legitimate State interest. We are inclined to be particularly careful about the adjective where the actual conveyance of property is made a condition to the lifting of a land use restriction, since in that context there is heightened risk that the purpose is avoidance of the compensation requirement, rather than the stated police power objective.

We are left, then, with the Commission's justification for the access requirement unrelated to land use regulation:

"Finally, the Commission notes that there are several existing provisions of pass and repass lateral access benefits already given by past Faria Beach Tract applicants as a result of prior coastal permit decisions. The access required as a condition of this permit is part of a comprehensive program to provide continuous public access along Faria Beach as the lots undergo development or redevelopment." App. 68.

That is simply an expression of the Commission's belief that the public interest will be served by a continuous strip of publicly accessible beach along the coast. The Commission may well be right that it is a good idea, but that does not establish that the Nollans (and other coastal residents) alone can be compelled to contribute to its realization. Rather, California is free to advance its "comprehensive program," if it wishes, by using its power of eminent domain for this "public purpose," see U.S. Const., Amdt. V; but if it wants an easement across the Nollans' property, it must pay for it.

Reversed.

[Dissenting opinions omitted.]

Notes

1. Is the "nexus" test articulated by Justice Scalia in the Nollan case the same as the "rational nexus" test used in the off-site improvement cases? How does or will the Nollan case impact on traditional exactions? See, generally, Lemon, Feinland & Deihl, The First Applications of the Nollan Nexus Test: Observations and Comments, 13 Harv.Env.L.Rev. 585 (1989); Comment, The Future of Municipal Parks in a Post–Nollan World: A Survey of Takings Tests as Applied to Subdivision Exactions, 8 Va.Nat.Resources L. 141 (1988). Also see, Sterk, Nollan, Henry George, and Exactions, 88 Colum.L.Rev. 1731 (1988); Karlin, Back to the Future: From Nollan to Lochner, 17 Southwest. U.L.Rev. 627 (1988).

2. Does the "heightened scrutiny" rule of Nollan apply to non-possessory exactions, such as impact fees? The California Court of Appeal said "no" in Blue Jeans Equities West v. City and County of San Francisco, 3 Cal.App.4th 164, 4 Cal.Rptr.2d 114, cert. denied 506 U.S. 866, 113 S.Ct. 191, 121 L.Ed.2d 135 (1992), a case involving a traffic impact fee imposed on developers of office buildings in downtown San Francisco. Even if "heightened scrutiny" should be given to money exactions, does the rationale in Nollan doom any impact fee which is not earmarked for an improvement which would specifically benefit the proposed development? In Holmdel Builders Association v. Township of Holmdel, 232 N.J.Super. 182, 556 A.2d 1236 (1989), the court held that a mandatory development fee imposed for the purpose of aiding the municipality to provide realistic opportunities for

affordable housing was invalid as nothing more than a revenue raising device and illegal tax. The court, however, also said that if developers were given something in return, such as an opportunity to build at higher densities if they paid the fee, such a fee might be valid. The New jersey Supreme Court partially reversed (see the opinion in the next chapter). Also consider, in light of Nollan, a measure adopted by the voters of San Francisco which imposes an impact fee on developers of office towers in the downtown district for the purpose of providing housing and day care opportunities. A case similar to Nollan, but without constitutional issues is Clinton v. Summers, 144 A.D.2d 145, 534 N.Y.S.2d 473 (1988).

DOLAN v. CITY OF TIGARD

Supreme Court of the United States, 1994.
512 U.S. 374, 114 S.Ct. 2309, 129 L.Ed.2d 304.

CHIEF JUSTICE REHNQUIST delivered the opinion of the Court.

Petitioner challenges the decision of the Oregon Supreme Court which held that the city of Tigard could condition the approval of her building permit on the dedication of a portion of her property for flood control and traffic improvements. 317 Ore. 110, 854 P. 2d 437 (1993). We granted certiorari to resolve a question left open by our decision in Nollan v. California Coastal Comm'n, 483 U. S. 825 (1987), of what is the required degree of connection between the exactions imposed by the city and the projected impacts of the proposed development.

I

The State of Oregon enacted a comprehensive land use management program in 1973. Ore. Rev. Stat. §§ 197.005–197.860 (1991). The program required all Oregon cities and counties to adopt new comprehensive land use plans that were consistent with the statewide planning goals. §§ 197.175(1), 197.250. The plans are implemented by land use regulations which are part of an integrated hierarchy of legally binding goals, plans, and regulations. §§ 197.175, 197.175(2)(b). Pursuant to the State's requirements, the city of Tigard, a community of some 30,000 residents on the southwest edge of Portland, developed a comprehensive plan and codified it in its Community Development Code (CDC). The CDC requires property owners in the area zoned Central Business District to comply with a 15% open space and landscaping requirement, which limits total site coverage, including all structures and paved parking, to 85% of the parcel. CDC, ch. 18.66, App. to Pet. for Cert. G16–G17. After the completion of a transportation study that identified congestion in the Central Business District as a particular problem, the city adopted a plan for a pedestrian/bicycle pathway intended to encourage alternatives to automobile transportation for short trips. The CDC requires that new development facilitate this plan by dedicating land for pedestrian pathways where provided for in the pedestrian/bicycle pathway plan.

The city also adopted a Master Drainage Plan (Drainage Plan). The Drainage Plan noted that flooding occurred in several areas along Fanno

Creek, including areas near petitioner's property. The Drainage Plan also established that the increase in impervious surfaces associated with continued urbanization would exacerbate these flooding problems. To combat these risks, the Drainage Plan suggested a series of improvements to the Fanno Creek Basin, including channel excavation in the area next to petitioner's property. Other recommendations included ensuring that the floodplain remains free of structures and that it be preserved as greenways to minimize flood damage to structures. The Drainage Plan concluded that the cost of these improvements should be shared based on both direct and indirect benefits, with property owners along the waterways paying more due to the direct benefit that they would receive. * * *

Petitioner Florence Dolan owns a plumbing and electric supply store located on Main Street in the Central Business District of the city. The store covers approximately 9,700 square feet on the eastern side of a 1.67–acre parcel, which includes a gravel parking lot. Fanno Creek flows through the southwestern corner of the lot and along its western boundary. The year-round flow of the creek renders the area within the creek's 100–year floodplain virtually unusable for commercial development. The city's comprehensive plan includes the Fanno Creek floodplain as part of the city's greenway system.

Petitioner applied to the city for a permit to redevelop the site. Her proposed plans called for nearly doubling the size of the store to 17,600 square feet, and paving a 39–space parking lot. The existing store, located on the opposite side of the parcel, would be razed in sections as construction progressed on the new building. In the second phase of the project, petitioner proposed to build an additional structure on the northeast side of the site for complementary businesses, and to provide more parking. The proposed expansion and intensified use are consistent with the city's zoning scheme in the Central Business District.

The City Planning Commission granted petitioner's permit application subject to conditions imposed by the city's CDC. The CDC establishes the following standard for site development review approval:

"Where landfill and/or development is allowed within and adjacent to the 100–year floodplain, the city shall require the dedication of sufficient open land area for greenway adjoining and within the floodplain. This area shall include portions at a suitable elevation for the construction of a pedestrian/bicycle pathway within the floodplain in accordance with the adopted pedestrian/bicycle plan."

Thus, the Commission required that petitioner dedicate the portion of her property lying within the 100–year floodplain for improvement of a storm drainage system along Fanno Creek and that she dedicate an additional 15–foot strip of land adjacent to the floodplain as a pedestrian/bicycle pathway. The dedication required by that condition encompasses approximately 7,000 square feet, or roughly 10% of the property. In accordance with city practice, petitioner could rely on the dedicated property to meet the 15% open space and landscaping requirement mandated by the city's zoning scheme. The city would bear the cost of maintaining a landscaped buffer between the dedicated area and the new store.

Petitioner requested variances from the CDC standards. Variances are granted only where it can be shown that, owing to special circumstances related to a specific piece of the land, the literal interpretation of the applicable zoning provisions would cause "an undue or unnecessary hardship" unless the variance is granted. Rather than posing alternative mitigating measures to offset the expected impacts of her proposed development, as allowed under the CDC, petitioner simply argued that her proposed development would not conflict with the policies of the comprehensive plan. The Commission denied the request.

The Commission made a series of findings concerning the relationship between the dedicated conditions and the projected impacts of petitioner's project. First, the Commission noted that "[i]t is reasonable to assume that customers and employees of the future uses of this site could utilize a pedestrian/bicycle pathway adjacent to this development for their transportation and recreational needs." The Commission noted that the site plan has provided for bicycle parking in a rack in front of the proposed building and "[i]t is reasonable to expect that some of the users of the bicycle parking provided for by the site plan will use the pathway adjacent to Fanno Creek if it is constructed." In addition, the Commission found that creation of a convenient, safe pedestrian/ bicycle pathway system as an alternative means of transportation "could offset some of the traffic demand on [nearby] streets and lessen the increase in traffic congestion."

The Commission went on to note that the required floodplain dedication would be reasonably related to petitioner's request to intensify the use of the site given the increase in the impervious surface. The Commission stated that the "anticipated increased storm water flow from the subject property to an already strained creek and drainage basin can only add to the public need to manage the stream channel and floodplain for drainage purposes." Based on this anticipated increased storm water flow, the Commission concluded that "the requirement of dedication of the floodplain area on the site is related to the applicant's plan to intensify development on the site." The Tigard City Council approved the Commission's final order, subject to one minor modification; the City Council reassigned the responsibility for surveying and marking the floodplain area from petitioner to the city's engineering department.

Petitioner appealed to the Land Use Board of Appeals (LUBA) on the ground that the city's dedication requirements were not related to the proposed development, and, therefore, those requirements constituted an uncompensated taking of their property under the Fifth Amendment. In evaluating the federal taking claim, LUBA assumed that the city's findings about the impacts of the proposed development were supported by substantial evidence. * * * Given the undisputed fact that the proposed larger building and paved parking area would increase the amount of impervious surfaces and the runoff into Fanno Creek, LUBA concluded that "there is a 'reasonable relationship' between the proposed development and the requirement to dedicate land along Fanno Creek for a greenway." With respect to the pedestrian/bicycle pathway, LUBA noted the Commission's finding that a significantly larger retail sales building and parking lot would attract larger numbers of customers and employees and their vehicles. It again found a "reasonable relationship" between alleviating the impacts of increased traffic from the development and facilitating the provision of a pedestrian/bicycle pathway as an alternative means of transportation.

The Oregon Court of Appeals affirmed, rejecting petitioner's contention that in Nollan v. California Coastal Comm'n, 483 U. S. 825 (1987), we had abandoned the "reasonable relationship" test in favor of a stricter "essential nexus" test. 113 Ore. App. 162, 832 P. 2d 853 (1992). The Oregon Supreme Court affirmed. 317 Ore. 110, 854 P. 2d 437 (1993). The court also disagreed with petitioner's contention that the *Nollan* Court abandoned the "reasonably related" test. Id., at 118, 854 P. 2d, at 442. Instead, the court read *Nollan* to mean that an "exaction is reasonably related to an impact if the exaction serves the same purpose that a denial of the permit would serve." Id., at 120, 854 P. 2d, at 443. The court decided that both the pedestrian/bicycle pathway condition and the storm drainage dedication had an essential nexus to the development of the proposed site. Id., at 121, 854 P. 2d, at 443. Therefore, the court found the conditions to be reasonably related to the impact of the expansion of petitioner's business. * * *

II

* * *

Petitioner contends that the city has forced her to choose between the building permit and her right under the Fifth Amendment to just compensation for the public easements. Petitioner does not quarrel with the city's authority to exact some forms of dedication as a condition for the grant of a building permit, but challenges the showing made by the city to justify these exactions. She argues that the city has identified "no special benefits" conferred on her, and has not identified any "special quantifiable burdens" created by her new store that would justify the particular dedications required from her which are not required from the public at large.

III

In evaluating petitioner's claim, we must first determine whether the "essential nexus" exists between the "legitimate state interest" and the permit condition exacted by the city. *Nollan*, 483 U. S., at 837. If we find that a nexus exists, we must then decide the required degree of connection between the exactions and the projected impact of the proposed development. We were not required to reach this question in *Nollan*, because we concluded that the connection did not meet even the loosest standard. 483 U. S., at 838. Here, however, we must decide this question.

A

We addressed the essential nexus question in *Nollan.* * * * We resolved, however, that the Coastal Commission's regulatory authority was set completely adrift from its constitutional moorings when it claimed that a nexus existed between visual access to the ocean and a permit condition requiring lateral public access along the Nollan's beach-front lot. How enhancing the public's ability to "traverse to and along the shorefront" served the same governmental purpose of "visual access to the ocean" from the roadway was beyond our ability to countenance. The absence of a nexus left the Coastal Commission in the position of simply trying to obtain an easement through gimmickry, which converted a valid regulation of land use into "an out-and-out plan of extortion."

No such gimmicks are associated with the permit conditions imposed by the city in this case. Undoubtedly, the prevention of flooding along Fanno Creek and the reduction of traffic congestion in the Central Business District qualify as the type of legitimate public purposes we have upheld. It seems equally obvious that a nexus exists between preventing flooding along Fanno Creek and limiting development within the creek's 100–year floodplain. Petitioner proposes to double the size of her retail store and to pave her now-gravel parking lot, thereby expanding the impervious surface on the property and increasing the amount of stormwater run-off into Fanno Creek.

The same may be said for the city's attempt to reduce traffic congestion by providing for alternative means of transportation. In theory, a pedestrian/bicycle pathway provides a useful alternative means of transportation for workers and shoppers: "Pedestrians and bicyclists occupying dedicated spaces for walking and/or bicycling ... remove potential vehicles from streets, resulting in an overall improvement in total transportation system flow." A. Nelson, Public Provision of Pedestrian and Bicycle Access Ways: Public Policy Rationale and the Nature of Private Benefits 11, Center for Planning Development, Georgia Institute of Technology, Working Paper Series (Jan. 1994). See also, Intermodal Surface Transportation Efficiency Act of 1991, Pub. L. 102–240, 105 Stat. 1914; (recognizing pedestrian and bicycle facilities as necessary components of any strategy to reduce traffic congestion).

B

The second part of our analysis requires us to determine whether the degree of the exactions demanded by the city's permit conditions bear the required relationship to the projected impact of petitioner's proposed development. * * *

The city required that petitioner dedicate "to the city as Greenway all portions of the site that fall within the existing 100–year floodplain [of Fanno Creek] ... and all property 15 feet above [the floodplain] boundary." In addition, the city demanded that the retail store be designed so as not to intrude into the greenway area. The city relies on the Commission's rather tentative findings that increased stormwater flow from petitioner's property "can only add to the public need to manage the [floodplain] for drainage purposes" to support its conclusion that the "requirement of dedication of the floodplain area on the site is related to the applicant's plan to intensify development on the site."

The city made the following specific findings relevant to the pedestrian/bicycle pathway:

"In addition, the proposed expanded use of this site is anticipated to generate additional vehicular traffic thereby increasing congestion on nearby collector and arterial streets. Creation of a convenient, safe pedestrian/bicycle pathway system as an alternative means of transportation could offset some of the traffic demand on these nearby streets and lessen the increase in traffic congestion."

The question for us is whether these findings are constitutionally sufficient to justify the conditions imposed by the city on petitioner's building permit. Since state courts have been dealing with this question a good deal longer than we have, we turn to representative decisions made by them.

In some States, very generalized statements as to the necessary connection between the required dedication and the proposed development seem to suffice. See, e.g., Billings Properties, Inc. v. Yellowstone County, 144 Mont. 25, 394 P. 2d 182 (1964); Jenad, Inc. v. Scarsdale, 18 N. Y. 2d 78, 218 N. E. 2d 673 (1966). We think this standard is too lax to adequately protect petitioner's right to just compensation if her property is taken for a public purpose.

Other state courts require a very exacting correspondence, described as the "specifi[c] and uniquely attributable" test. The Supreme Court of Illinois first developed this test in Pioneer Trust & Savings Bank v. Mount Prospect, 22 Ill. 2d 375, 380, 176 N. E. 2d 799, 802 (1961). Under this standard, if the local government cannot demonstrate that its exaction is directly proportional to the specifically created need, the exaction becomes "a veiled exercise of the power of eminent domain and a confiscation of private property behind the defense of police regulations." Id., at 381, 176 N.E. 2d, at 802. We do not think the Federal Constitution requires such exacting scrutiny, given the nature of the interests involved.

A number of state courts have taken an intermediate position, requiring the municipality to show a "reasonable relationship" between the required dedication and the impact of the proposed development. Typical is the Supreme Court of Nebraska's opinion in Simpson v. North Platte, 206 Neb. 240, 245, 292 N. W. 2d 297, 301 (1980), where that court stated:

"The distinction, therefore, which must be made between an appropriate exercise of the police power and an improper exercise of eminent domain is whether the requirement has some reasonable relationship or nexus to the use to which the property is being made or is merely being used as an excuse for taking property simply because at that particular moment the landowner is asking the city for some license or permit."

Thus, the court held that a city may not require a property owner to dedicate private property for some future public use as a condition of obtaining a building permit when such future use is not "occasioned by the construction sought to be permitted." Id., at 248, 292 N. W. 2d, at 302.

Some form of the reasonable relationship test has been adopted in many other jurisdictions. See, e.g., Jordan v. Menomonee Falls, 28 Wis. 2d 608, 137 N. W. 2d 442 (1965); Collis v. Bloomington, 310 Minn. 5, 246 N. W. 2d 19 (1976) (requiring a showing of a reasonable relationship between the planned subdivision and the municipality's need for land); College Station v. Turtle Rock Corp., 680 S. W. 2d 802, 807 (Tex.1984); Call v. West Jordan, 606 P. 2d 217, 220 (Utah 1979) (affirming use of the reasonable relation test). Despite any semantical differences, general agreement exists among the courts "that the dedication should have some reasonable relationship to the needs created by the [development]." Ibid. See generally, Morosoff, Take My Beach Please!: Nollan v. California Coastal Commission and a Rational–Nexus Constitutional Analysis of Development Exactions, 69 B. U. L. Rev. 823 (1989); see also Parks v. Watson, 716 F. 2d 646, 651–653 (C.A.9 1983).

We think the "reasonable relationship" test adopted by a majority of the state courts is closer to the federal constitutional norm than either of those previously discussed. But we do not adopt it as such, partly because the term "reasonable relationship" seems confusingly similar to the term "rational basis" which describes the minimal level of scrutiny under the Equal Protection Clause of the Fourteenth Amendment. We think a term such as "rough proportionality" best encapsulates what we hold to be the requirement of the Fifth Amendment. No precise mathematical calculation is required, but the city must make some sort of individualized determination that the required dedication is related both in nature and extent to the impact of the proposed development.

* * *

We turn now to analysis of whether the findings relied upon by the city here, first with respect to the floodplain easement, and second with respect to the pedestrian/bicycle path, satisfied these requirements.

It is axiomatic that increasing the amount of impervious surface will increase the quantity and rate of storm-water flow from petitioner's property. Therefore, keeping the floodplain open and free from development would likely confine the pressures on Fanno Creek created by petitioner's development. In fact, because petitioner's property lies within the Central Business District, the Community Development Code already required that petitioner leave 15% of it as open space and the undeveloped floodplain would have nearly satisfied that requirement.

But the city demanded more—it not only wanted petitioner not to build in the floodplain, but it also wanted petitioner's property along Fanno Creek for its Greenway system. The city has never said why a public greenway, as opposed to a private one, was required in the interest of flood control.

The difference to petitioner, of course, is the loss of her ability to exclude others. As we have noted, this right to exclude others is "one of the most essential sticks in the bundle of rights that are commonly characterized as property." Kaiser Aetna, 444 U. S., at 176. It is difficult to see why recreational visitors trampling along petitioner's floodplain easement are sufficiently related to the city's legitimate interest in reducing flooding problems along Fanno Creek, and the city has not attempted to make any individualized determination to support this part of its request.

The city contends that recreational easement along the Greenway is only ancillary to the city's chief purpose in controlling flood hazards. It further asserts that unlike the residential property at issue in *Nollan*, petitioner's property is commercial in character and therefore, her right to exclude others is compromised. * * *

Admittedly, petitioner wants to build a bigger store to attract members of the public to her property. She also wants, however, to be able to control the time and manner in which they enter. The recreational easement on the Greenway is different in character from the exercise of state-protected rights of free expression and petition that we permitted in *PruneYard*. In *PruneYard*, we held that a major private shopping center that attracted more than 25,000 daily patrons had to provide access to persons exercising their state constitutional rights to distribute pamphlets and ask passersby to sign their petitions. We based our decision, in part, on the fact that the shopping center "may restrict expressive activity by adopting time, place, and manner regulations that will minimize any interference with its commercial functions." By contrast, the city wants to impose a permanent recreational easement upon petitioner's property that borders Fanno Creek. Petitioner would lose all rights to regulate the time in which the public entered onto the Greenway, regardless of any interference it might pose with her retail store. Her right to exclude would not be regulated, it would be eviscerated.

If petitioner's proposed development had somehow encroached on existing greenway space in the city, it would have been reasonable to require petitioner to provide some alternative greenway space for the public either on her property or elsewhere. * * * But that is not the case here. We conclude that the findings upon which the city relies do not show the required reasonable relationship between the floodplain easement and the petitioner's proposed new building.

With respect to the pedestrian/bicycle pathway, we have no doubt that the city was correct in finding that the larger retail sales facility proposed by petitioner will increase traffic on the streets of the Central Business District. The city estimates that the proposed development would generate roughly 435 additional trips per day. Dedications for streets, sidewalks, and other public ways are generally reasonable exactions to avoid excessive congestion from a proposed property use. But on the record before us, the city has not met its burden of demonstrating that the additional number of vehicle and bicycle trips generated by the petitioner's development reasonably relate to the city's requirement for a dedication of the pedestrian/bicycle pathway easement. The city simply found that the creation of the pathway "could offset some of the traffic demand . . . and lessen the increase in traffic congestion."

As Justice Peterson of the Supreme Court of Oregon explained in his dissenting opinion, however, "[t]he findings of fact that the bicycle pathway system *'could* offset some of the traffic demand' is a far cry from a finding that the bicycle pathway system *will*, or is *likely to*, offset some of the traffic demand." 317 Ore., at 127, 854 P. 2d, at 447 (emphasis in original). No precise mathematical calculation is required, but the city must make some effort to quantify its findings in support of the dedication for the pedestrian/bicycle pathway beyond the conclusory statement that it could offset some of the traffic demand generated.

IV

Cities have long engaged in the commendable task of land use planning, made necessary by increasing urbanization particularly in metropolitan areas such as Portland. The city's goals of reducing flooding hazards and traffic congestion, and providing for public greenways, are laudable, but there are outer limits to how this may be done. "A strong public desire to improve the public condition [will not] warrant achieving the desire by a shorter cut than the constitutional way of paying for the change." *Pennsylvania Coal*, 260 U. S., at 416.

The judgment of the Supreme Court of Oregon is reversed, and the case is remanded for further proceedings consistent with this opinion.

JUSTICE STEVENS, with whom JUSTICE BLACKMUN and JUSTICE GINSBURG join, dissenting.

The record does not tell us the dollar value of petitioner Florence Dolan's interest in excluding the public from the greenway adjacent to her hardware business. The mountain of briefs that the case has generated nevertheless makes it obvious that the pecuniary value of her victory is far less important than the rule of law that this case has been used to establish. It is unquestionably an important case.

* * *

I

Candidly acknowledging the lack of federal precedent for its exercise in rulemaking, the Court purports to find guidance in 12 "representative" state court decisions. To do so is certainly appropriate. The state cases the Court consults, however, either fail to support or decidedly undermine the Court's conclusions in key respects.

First, although discussion of the state cases permeates the Court's analysis of the appropriate test to apply in this case, the test on which the Court settles is not naturally derived from those courts' decisions. The Court recognizes as an initial matter that the city's conditions satisfy the "essential nexus" requirement announced in Nollan v. California Coastal Comm'n, 483 U. S. 825 (1987), because they serve the legitimate interests in minimizing floods and traffic congestions. The Court goes on, however, to erect a new constitutional hurdle in the path of these conditions. In addition to showing a rational nexus to a public purpose that would justify an outright denial of the permit, the city must also demonstrate "rough proportionality" between the harm caused by the new land use and the benefit obtained by the condition. The Court also decides for the first time that the city has the burden of establishing the constitutionality of its conditions by making an "individualized determination" that the condition in question satisfies the proportionality requirement.

Not one of the state cases cited by the Court announces anything akin to a "rough proportionality" requirement. For the most part, moreover, those cases that invalidated municipal ordinances did so on state law or unspecified grounds roughly equivalent to Nollan' s "essential nexus" requirement. See, e.g., Simpson v. North Platte, 206 Neb. 240, 245–248, 292 N. W. 2d 297, 301–302 (1980) (ordinance lacking "reasonable relationship" or "rational nexus" to property's use violated Nebraska constitution); J. E. D. Associates, Inc. v. Town of Atkinson, 121 N. H. 581, 583–585, 432 A. 2d 12, 14–15 (1981) (state constitutional grounds). One case purporting to apply the strict "specifically and uniquely attributable" test established by Pioneer Trust & Savings Bank v. Mount Prospect, 22 Ill. 2d 375, 176 N. E. 2d 799 (1961), nevertheless found that test was satisfied because the legislature had decided that the subdivision at issue created the need for a park or parks. Billings Properties, Inc. v. Yellowstone County, 144 Mont. 25, 33–36, 394 P. 2d 182, 187–188 (1964). In only one of the seven cases upholding a land use regulation did the losing property owner petition this Court for certiorari. See Jordan v. Village of Menomonee Falls, 28 Wis. 2d 608, 137 N. W. 2d 442 (1965), appeal dism'd, 385 U. S. 4 (1966) (want of substantial federal question). Although 4 of the 12 opinions mention the Federal Constitution—two of those only in passing—it is quite obvious that neither the courts nor the litigants imagined they might be participating in the development of a new rule of federal law. Thus, although these state cases do lend support to the Court's reaffirmance of Nollan's reasonable nexus requirement, the role the Court accords them in the announcement of its newly minted second phase of the constitutional inquiry is remarkably inventive.

In addition, the Court ignores the state courts' willingness to consider what the property owner gains from the exchange in question. The Supreme Court of Wisconsin, for example, found it significant that the village's approval of a proposed subdivision plat "enables the subdivider to profit financially by selling the subdivision lots as home-building sites and thus realizing a greater price than could have been obtained if he had sold his property as unplatted lands." Jordan v. Village of Menomonee Falls, 28 Wis. 2d 608, 619–620; 137 N. W. 2d 442, 448 (1965). The required dedication as a condition of that approval was permissible "[i]n return for this benefit." Ibid. See also Collis v. Bloomington, 310 Minn. 5, 11–13, 246 N. W. 2d 19, 23–24 (1976) (citing Jordan); College Station v. Turtle Rock Corp., 680 S. W. 2d 802, 806 (Tex.1984) (dedication requirement only triggered when developer chooses to develop land). In this case, moreover, Dolan's acceptance of the permit, with its attached conditions, would provide her with benefits that may well go beyond any advantage she gets from expanding her business. As the United States pointed out at oral argument, the improvement that the city's drainage plan contemplates would widen the channel and reinforce the slopes to increase the carrying capacity during serious floods, "confer[ring] considerable benefits on the property owners immediately adjacent to the creek."

The state court decisions also are enlightening in the extent to which they required that the entire parcel be given controlling importance. All but one of the cases involve challenges to provisions in municipal ordinances requiring developers to dedicate either a percentage of the entire parcel (usually 7 or 10 percent of the platted subdivision) or an equivalent value in cash (usually a certain dollar amount per lot) to help finance the construction of roads, utilities, schools, parks and playgrounds. In assessing the legality of the conditions, the courts gave no indication that the transfer of an interest in realty was any more objectionable than a cash payment. See, e.g., Jenad, Inc. v. Scarsdale, 18 N. Y. 2d 78, 218 N. E. 2d 673 (1966); Jordan, supra; Collis, supra. None of the decisions identified the surrender of the fee owner's "power to exclude" as having any special significance. Instead, the courts uniformly examined the character of the entire economic transaction.

II

It is not merely state cases, but our own cases as well, that require the analysis to focus on the impact of the city's action on the entire parcel of private property. In Penn Central Transportation Co. v. New York City, 438 U. S. 104 (1978), we stated that takings jurisprudence "does not divide a single parcel into discrete segments and attempt to determine whether rights in a particular segment have been entirely abrogated." Id., at 130–131. Instead, this Court focuses "both on the character of the action and on the nature and extent of the interference with rights in the parcel as a whole." Ibid. Andrus v. Allard, 444 U. S. 51 (1979), reaffirmed the nondivisibility principle outlined in Penn Central, stating that "[a]t least where an owner possesses a full 'bundle' of property rights, the destruction of one 'strand' of the bundle is not a taking, because the aggregate must be viewed in its entirety." Id., at 65–66. As recently as last Term, we approved the principle again. See Concrete Pipe & Products, Inc. v. Construction Laborers Pension Trust, 508 U. S. , (1993) (slip op., at 42) (explaining that "a claimant's parcel of property [cannot] first be divided into what was taken and what was left" to demonstrate a compensable taking). Although limitation of the right to exclude others undoubtedly constitutes a significant infringement upon property ownership, Kaiser Aetna v. United States, 444 U. S. 164, 179–180 (1979), restrictions on that right do not alone constitute a taking, and do not do so in any event unless they "unreasonably impair the value or use" of the property. PruneYard Shopping Center v. Robins, 447 U. S. 74, 82–84 (1980).

The Court's narrow focus on one strand in the property owner's bundle of rights is particularly misguided in a case involving the development of commercial property. As Professor Johnston has noted:

"The subdivider is a manufacturer, processer, and marketer of a product; land is but one of his raw materials. In subdivision control disputes, the developer is not defending hearth and home against the king's intrusion, but simply attempting to maximize his profits from the sale of a finished product. As applied to him, subdivision control exactions are actually business regulations." Johnston, Constitutionality of Subdivision Control Exactions: The Quest for A Rationale, 52 Cornell L. Q. 871, 923 (1967).

The exactions associated with the development of a retail business are likewise a species of business regulation that heretofore warranted a strong presumption of constitutional validity.

In Johnston's view, "if the municipality can demonstrate that its assessment of financial burdens against subdividers is rational, impartial, and conducive to fulfillment of authorized planning objectives, its action need be invalidated only in those extreme and presumably rare cases where the burden of compliance is sufficiently great to deter the owner from proceeding with his planned development." Id., at 917. The city of Tigard has demonstrated that its plan is rational and impartial and that the conditions at issue are "conducive to fulfillment of authorized planning objectives." Dolan, on the other hand, has offered no evidence that her burden of compliance has any impact at all on the value or profitability of her planned development. Following the teaching of the cases on which it purports to rely, the Court should not isolate the burden associated with the loss of the power to exclude from an evaluation of the benefit to be derived from the permit to enlarge the store and the parking lot.

The Court's assurances that its "rough proportionality" test leaves ample room for cities to pursue the "commendable task of land use planning,"—even twice avowing that "[n]o precise mathematical calculation is required,"—are wanting given the result that test compels here. Under the Court's approach, a city must not only "quantify its findings," and make "individualized determination[s]" with respect to the nature and the extent of the relationship between the conditions and the impact, but also demonstrate "proportionality." The correct inquiry should instead concentrate on whether the required nexus is present and venture beyond considerations of a condition's nature or germaneness only if the developer establishes that a concededly germane condition is so grossly disproportionate to the proposed development's adverse effects that it manifests motives other than land use regulation on the part of the city. The heightened requirement the Court imposes on cities is even more unjustified when all the tools needed to resolve the questions presented by this case can be garnered from our existing case law.

III

Applying its new standard, the Court finds two defects in the city's case. First, while the record would adequately support a requirement that Dolan maintain the portion of the floodplain on her property as undeveloped open space, it does not support the additional requirement that the floodplain be dedicated to the city. Second, while the city adequately established the traffic increase that the proposed development would generate, it failed to quantify the offsetting decrease in automobile traffic that the bike path will produce. Even under the Court's new rule, both defects are, at most, nothing more than harmless error.

In her objections to the floodplain condition, Dolan made no effort to demonstrate that the dedication of that portion of her property would be any more onerous than a simple prohibition against any development on that portion of her property. Given the commercial character of both the existing and the proposed use of the property as a retail store, it seems likely that potential customers "trampling along petitioner's floodplain," are more valuable than a useless parcel of vacant land. Moreover, the duty to pay taxes and the responsibility for potential tort liability may well make ownership of the fee interest in useless land a liability rather than an asset. That may explain why Dolan never conceded that she could be prevented from building on the floodplain. The City Attorney also pointed out that absent a dedication, property owners would be required to "build on their own land" and "with their own money" a storage facility for the water runoff. Dolan apparently "did have that option," but chose not to seek it. If Dolan might have been entitled to a variance confining the city's condition in a manner this Court would accept, her failure to seek that narrower form of relief at any stage of the state administrative and judicial proceedings clearly should preclude that relief in this Court now.

The Court's rejection of the bike path condition amounts to nothing more than a play on words. Everyone agrees that the bike path "could" offset some of the increased traffic flow that the larger store will generate, but the findings do not unequivocally state that it will do so, or tell us just how many cyclists will replace motorists. Predictions on such matters are inherently nothing more than estimates. Certainly the assumption that there will be an offsetting benefit here is entirely reasonable and should suffice whether it amounts to 100 percent, 35 percent, or only 5 percent of the increase in automobile traffic that would otherwise occur. If the Court proposes to have the federal judiciary micromanage state decisions of this kind, it is indeed extending its welcome mat to a significant new class of litigants. Although there is no reason to believe that state courts have failed to rise to the task, property owners have surely found a new friend today.

IV

The Court has made a serious error by abandoning the traditional presumption of constitutionality and imposing a novel burden of proof on a city implementing an admittedly valid comprehensive land use plan. Even more consequential than its incorrect disposition of this case, however, is the Court's resurrection of a species of substantive due process analysis that it firmly rejected decades ago.

* * *

This case inaugurates an even more recent judicial innovation than the regulatory takings doctrine: the application of the "unconstitutional conditions" label to a mutually beneficial transaction between a property owner and a city. The Court tells us that the city's refusal to grant Dolan a discretionary benefit infringes her right to receive just compensation for the property interests that she has refused to dedicate to the city "where the property sought has little or no relationship to the benefit." Although it is well settled that a government cannot deny a benefit on a basis that infringes constitutionally protected interests"—especially [one's] interest in freedom of speech," Perry v. Sindermann, 408 U. S. 593, 597 (1972)—the "unconstitutional conditions" doctrine provides an inadequate framework in which to analyze this case. Dolan has no right to be compensated for a taking unless the city acquires the property interests that she has refused to surrender. Since no taking has yet occurred, there has not been any infringement of her constitutional right to compensation. * * *

Even if Dolan should accept the city's conditions in exchange for the benefit that she seeks, it would not necessarily follow that she had been denied "just compensation" since it would be appropriate to consider the receipt of that benefit in any calculation of "just compensation." See Pennsylvania Coal Co. v. Mahon, 260 U. S. 393, 415 (1922) (noting that an "average reciprocity of advantage" was deemed to justify many laws); Hodel v. Irving, 481 U. S. 704, 715 (1987) (such " 'reciprocity of advantage' "weighed in favor of a statute's constitutionality). Particularly in the absence of any evidence on the point, we should not presume that the discretionary benefit the city has offered is less valuable than the property interests that Dolan can retain or surrender at her option. But even if that discretionary benefit were so trifling that it could not be considered just compensation when it has "little or no relationship" to the property, the Court fails to explain why the same value would suffice when the required nexus is present. In this respect, the Court's reliance on the "unconstitutional conditions" doctrine is assuredly novel, and arguably incoherent. The city's conditions are by no means immune from constitutional scrutiny. The level of scrutiny, however, does not approximate the kind of review that would apply if the city had insisted on a surrender of Dolan's First Amendment rights in exchange for a building permit. * * *

In our changing world one thing is certain: uncertainty will characterize predictions about the impact of new urban developments on the risks of floods, earthquakes, traffic congestion, or environmental harms. When there is doubt concerning the magnitude of those impacts, the public interest in averting them must outweigh the private interest of the commercial entrepreneur. If the government can demonstrate that the conditions it has imposed in a land-use permit are rational, impartial and conducive to fulfilling the aims of a valid land-use plan, a strong presumption of validity should attach to those conditions. The burden of demonstrating that those conditions have unreasonably impaired the economic value of the proposed improvement belongs squarely on the shoulders of the party challenging the state action's constitutionality. That allocation of burdens has served us well in the past. The Court has stumbled badly today by reversing it.

I respectfully dissent.

JUSTICE SOUTER, dissenting. [Dissenting opinion omitted.]

Notes

1. Does the Dolan case really change the burden of proof in exaction cases, requiring the city to justify its subdivision demands? If so, what impact would this decision have on traditional exactions? Could a developer protest that the subdivision requirement of thirty-foot-wide streets is a taking because the number of houses he intends to build does not justify a street wider than, say, twenty feet? Consider the case, Lexington–Fayette Urban County Government v. Schneider, 849 S.W.2d 557 (Ky.App.1992), where a developer who had built 200 homes in a subdivision sought a rezoning in order to develop an additional 33 lots on an 18–acre tract at the southern end of his property. The planning commission conditioned approval upon the construction of a bridge over the creek that ran through the existing subdivision to connect two portions of a boulevard that had not been in existence when the developer began his subdivision. Arguing that the boulevard was not needed to provide access or regular traffic to the proposed 33 new homes, developer refused to bear the cost of the bridge (between $125,000 and $250,000). The Court of Appeals held that the bridge was an unreasonable burden on the developer when viewed in relation to the development of 33 lots. Also see Art Piculell Group v. Clackamas County, 142 Or.App. 327, 922 P.2d 1227 (1996) where the court discussed how to determine rough proportionality in a case where a subdivider was asked to construct a road to collector standards at the edge of his subdivision; to the east and west of the proposed subdivision the collector road already was built. The subdivider argued that his subdivision would contribute a small percentage of future traffic on the road and that, under Dolan, he should not have to pay more than his fair share for an improvement that would benefit the public at large and his subdivision at small.

2. One result of the Dolan case was to require a closer look at just what are exactions. In Clark v. City of Albany, 137 Or.App. 293, 904 P.2d 185 (1995), rev. denied 322 Or. 644, 912 P.2d 375 (1996) the court reviewed seven separate conditions imposed on a developer's plan for a fast food restaurant. The court held that a condition requiring the developer to design

and construct off-site street improvements was an exaction, and that a condition requiring a sidewalk was an exaction; however, conditions that the developer designate an on-site area as traffic-free and that he provide a storm drainage plan and construct a storm drain were not exactions. The court remanded for a determination of rough proportionality of those conditions found to be exactions.

3. Another issue left open by the Dolan decision is whether the analysis applies to exactions other than land dedications. Does Dolan apply to money exactions? The California Supreme Court has held that it does apply in money exaction cases. In Ehrlich v. City of Culver City, 12 Cal.4th 854, 50 Cal.Rptr.2d 242, 911 P.2d 429 (1996), the court, applying Dolan, held that a $280,000 fee imposed on a developer to mitigate the loss of community recreational facilities (the proposed development would replace a failed private tennis club with luxury condominiums), was not shown by the city to be roughly proportional to the impact of the proposed development; on the other hand, a requirement that the developer provide for art reasonably accessible to the public in connection with a generally applicable exaction requirement was upheld in the case. The court said:

> [I]t is not at all clear that the rationale (and the heightened standard of scrutiny) of Nollan and Dolan applies to cases in which the exaction takes the form of a generally applicable development fee or assessment ... But when a local government imposes special, discretionary permit conditions on development by individual property owners—as in the case of the recreational fee at issue in this case—Nollan and Dolan require that such conditions, whether they consist of possessory dedications or monetary exactions, be scrutinized under the heightened standard.

Compare with the California case, Home Builders Ass'n of Central Arizona v. City of Scottsdale, 233 Ariz. Adv. Rep. 23, 930 P.2d 993 (1997) where the plaintiffs challenged a water resources development fee imposed by the city in order to obtain new water in the future. The court considered the Dolan case and found it inapplicable because under the Arizona enabling act a reasonable relationship between the fee and the public burden is required and that standard was met in this case. Also, the court said that a money exaction is a considerably more benign form of regulation than a demand that land be ceded to the city. In Northern Illinois Home Builders Ass'n, Inc. v. County of DuPage, 165 Ill.2d 25, 208 Ill.Dec. 328, 649 N.E.2d 384 (1995) the court upheld one of two state enabling statutes that authorized counties to create schedules of exactions for transportation impacts. The court found that Dolan was no impediment to the imposition of transportation impact fees because of the state police power concern over traffic congestion and the continued adherence of Illinois to the "specifically and uniquely attributable" test for exactions.

4. On the federalism aspects of Dolan see Matthew J. Cholewa and Helen L. Edmonds, Federalism and Land Use After Dolan: Has the Supreme Court Taken Takings from the States?, 28 The Urban Lawyer 401 (1996).

Subdivision Exactions and Energy Conservation

The energy crisis of the late 1970's and early 1980's had an effect on land use regulation at all levels of government. At one point the federal government considered the possibility of mandating energy consumption standards for new commercial and residential buildings. The proposal went by the acronym of BEPS—Building Energy Performance Standards. The standards would have set performance goals expressed in BTUs per square foot per year. The proposed standards, promulgated in a series of public hearings in early 1980, did not engender much public enthusiasm. Most of the criticism centered around the envisioned bureaucratic nightmare of monitoring and inspecting thousands of buildings for "energy leaks."

At the state level most of the legislative activity has been in the area of providing legislative protection for solar access easements and encouraging local governments to make energy conservation a part of the comprehensive planning process. The doctrine of ancient lights is currently being revived by statute in a majority of the states, changing the common law rule that a landowner is not entitled to light from across adjacent property. See Fontainebleau Hotel Corp. v. Forty–Five Twenty–Five, Inc., 114 So.2d 357 (Fla.App.1959); Palomeque v. Prudhomme, 664 So.2d 88 (La.1995) (owner of condominium did not have a servitude of light so as to prevent Chef Prudhomme from putting a second story on his adjacent Paul K's restaurant building and bricking over windows). See generally, Thomas, Miller and Robbins, Overcoming Legal Uncertainties About Use of Solar Energy Systems (American Bar Foundation Monograph 1978).

At the local level, the subdivision approval process is seen as the likely place to institute energy conservation goals. Also, building codes can be used to require developers to provide proper insulation and glazing to conserve energy, and can even require solar water heating systems.[42] In U.S. Dept. of Housing and Urban Development, Protecting Solar Access for Residential Development: A Guidebook for Planning Officials (1979), the use of exactions for solar access is treated at page 93:

Subdivision Exactions and Solar Access

Subdivision exactions include requirements for open space and the dedication of easements for public utilities and roads. Both types of exactions may be required by a community. Subdivision requirements for dedication of open space in new developments can be used to protect solar access. Open space, free of buildings, can be used to provide buffering from shadows cast by some buildings towards

---

42. In 1979, San Diego County, California adopted an ordinance requiring installation of solar water heating devices in all dwellings constructed after Oct. 1, 1979, in all areas served only by electricity. The ordinance was amended to include areas served by natural gas as of Oct. 1, 1980. Sacramento County and Santa Clara County, both in California, have adopted similar ordinances, as has the city of Soldiers Grove, Wisconsin.

others. Some shading problems can be avoided by the strategic location of dedicated open space.

Open Space Dedication

This technique involves setting guidelines for (1) the location of dedicated open space for access protection, and/or (2) increasing the amount of dedicated open space for greater buffering. This approach may be particularly useful in developments that abut high-rise districts or PUDs that include tall buildings.

Most subdivision regulations have only general locational guidelines and leave the location of parks and open space to the developer, because regulations only specify the *amount* of land to be dedicated. Modifying for solar access protection means that somewhat more specific locational guidelines be included.

———

The entire publication provides a great deal of useful information for drafting and implementing local ordinances to protect solar access.

Some cities have utilized their subdivision regulation powers to require construction techniques and orientation of buildings so as to maximize energy conservation. The city of Davis, California, is noted for its energy conservation land use ordinances. See, e.g., Davis, Calif.Ord. No. 784 (Oct. 15, 1975), "An Ordinance Establishing Energy Conservation Performance Standards for Residential Construction Within the City of Davis."

Apart from solar access and conservation of energy through construction techniques, some observers have noted that the greatest energy savings can be realized in the elimination of urban sprawl and promoting compact cities. This "big picture" approach to energy conservation is outlined in "Compact Cities: Energy Saving Strategies for the Eighties" (Subcommittee on the City, House Committee on Banking, Finance and Urban Affairs, 96th Cong., 2d Sess.1980).

The problems of urban sprawl involve more than energy conservation; as you will see at the end of the next chapter, the development of shopping centers and other commercial and office complexes at the edge of a city has a tremendous effect on the continuing vitality of downtown areas. In many small towns and cities around the country the concern over sprawl has been manifested in land use battles when the nation's largest retailer, Wal–Mart, undertakes to build a store. That company eschews downtown locations, preferring to build at the edges of a community. Citizens who oppose these projects often refer to the "enemy" as "Sprawl–Mart." For years, despite all its efforts, Wal–Mart was excluded from Vermont by stringent application of state and local land use regulations. In 1996 Wal–Mart finally entered into a compromise agreement allowing it to build its first store in Vermont, but in a downtown location. See, e.g., Nancie L. Katz, "Sprawl–Mart" vs. the green mountain state, Houston Chronicle, Aug. 22, 1993, p. 6 E, for a description of the battle in its mid-stages. Also see Jonathan Walters, National "Sprawl Buster" Coalition Emerges, Historic Preservation News (Dec., 1994/Jan. 1995) p. 10.

(4) Denial of Subdivision Approval

COFFEY v. MARYLAND–NATIONAL CAPITAL PARK AND PLANNING COMMISSION

Court of Appeals of Maryland, 1982.
293 Md. 24, 441 A.2d 1041.

SMITH, JUDGE.

* * *

Appellant, Wade S. Coffey, owns 15.85 acres of land on Riverdale Road in Prince George's County, located approximately 1,800 feet east of that road's intersection with the Baltimore–Washington Parkway. The land is zoned R–T (Townhouse Development). This permits a maximum development density of 8.0 to 11.9 units per acre. The master plan for that area, approved in December 1980 by the District Council for Prince George's County, restricts density to 2.7 to 3.5 dwelling units per acre. Almost immediately after adoption of the plan, in January 1981, Coffey submitted an application for approval of a preliminary plan of subdivision. The planning for the subdivision had been in progress for some time. He proposed 117 townhouse units on the tract, a density of 7.38 dwelling units per acre.

Prince George's County Code § 24–103(a)(1) requires subdivision plats to conform to the master plan. Relying upon our decision in *Board of County Comm'rs v. Gaster*, 285 Md. 233, 401 A.2d 666 (1979), the Prince George's County Planning Board of the Maryland–National Capital Park and Planning Commission (the Commission) rejected the proposed subdivision because of noncompliance with the master plan. The Circuit Court for Prince George's County affirmed. Coffey then appealed to the Court of Special Appeals. Because we have not previously addressed such an issue under Art. 66D, we issued the writ of certiorari ex mero motu prior to consideration of the appeal by the intermediate appellate court.

* * *

Coffey's argument runs that prior to *Gaster* planning boards regarded master plans as only a set of recommendations, that *Gaster* was the first case where noncompliance with a master plan caused rejection of a proposed subdivision, and that noncompliance with the master plan constituted insufficient grounds for disapproval of a proposed subdivision. Cases making statements relative to master plans being guides have arisen in the context of an attempted piecemeal change in zoning. For instance, in *Chapman v. Montgomery County*, 259 Md. 641, 643, 271

A.2d 156 (1970), Judge Finan said for the Court, "A 'Master Plan' is not to be confused as a substitute for a comprehensive zoning or rezoning map, nor may it be equated with it in legal significance." No opinion of this Court has made a statement relative to master plans acting only as guides in the context of the facts here involved.

At oral argument, counsel for the Commission said that its past practice had been to treat the master plan as a guide in zoning matters. Counsel further stated, however, that the Commission regarded the master plan as binding in subdivision matters subsequent to the enactment of the regulation requiring proposed subdivisions to conform to the master plan.

* * *

As the author points out in 4 R. Anderson, *American Law of Zoning 2d* § 23.20, at 89 (1977), "Subdivision controls are imposed for the purpose of implementing a comprehensive plan for community development. To achieve this end, plats submitted to a planning commission for approval must be examined in relation to the official map and the master plan." Moreover, as the court observed in *Popular Refreshments, Inc. v. Fuller's Milk Bar, etc.,* 85 N.J.Super. 528, 537, 205 A.2d 445 (1964), petition for certification denied, 44 N.J. 409, 209 A.2d 143 (1965), "If planning boards had no alternative but to rubber-stamp their approval on every subdivision plat which conformed with the zoning ordinance, there would be little or no reason for their existence. While planning and zoning complement each other and serve certain common objectives, each represents a separate municipal function and neither is a mere rubber-stamp for the other," citing *Levin v. Livingston Tp.,* 35 N.J. 500, 506, 173 A.2d 391 (1961).

In this regard, the language used by the court in *Shoptaugh v. County Comm.,* 37 Colo.App. 39, 543 P.2d 524 (1975), *cert. denied* (1976), is significant here. The court there said:

> "Here, the landowner argues that since the proposed use of the land was a use of right under the zoning laws, the Board had no alternative but to either change the zoning or approve the plat. This argument fails to take into consideration that a subdivider must first meet the zoning regulations and then additionally must comply with the state and county subdivision regulations." 37 Colo.App. at 41–42, 543 P.2d 524.

The process of comprehensive zoning or rezoning is a time consuming one. It would be virtually impossible to adopt comprehensive rezoning changes calculated to impose the same density requirements as the master plan which would become effective simultaneously with the adoption of a new master plan that called for lower density development than the preceding plan.

Here we have a regulation duly enacted by the legislative body for Prince George's County which specifies that the planning board shall not approve a subdivision plat not in compliance with the master plan. This subdivision regulation is as much entitled to obedience as any other legislative enactment. The need for the regulation specifying that a subdivision plan must conform to the master plan can be illustrated by comparison to the putting of water in a teacup drop by drop. After a period of time there comes the drop which will cause the cup to overflow. By analogy, developing some of the lots in conformity with the existing zoning will not disrupt the master plan. Concentrated use and development, however, will disrupt it. The legislative body wished to avoid this when it specified that subdivisions must comply with the master plan. Accordingly, the Commission was justified in rejecting Coffey's proposed subdivision for his failure to conform that proposal with the master plan.

Judgment affirmed; Appellant to pay the costs.

MARYLAND–NAT'L CAPITAL PARK AND PLANNING COMM'N v. ROSENBERG

Court of Appeals of Maryland, 1973.
269 Md. 520, 307 A.2d 704.

McWILLIAMS, JUDGE. In this appeal, stemming from the confrontation of a landowner and the appellant (the Commission), we are asked to consider what is known in Prince George's County as the "Adequate Public Facilities Ordinance." * * * As we see this case the single issue is whether the action of the Commission was arbitrary and capricious. We think it was. However, before we undertake to relate the facts, we shall set forth the pertinent parts of both the enabling act (Code of Public Local Laws of Prince George's County, § 59–76 (1963)), and the ordinance (Code of Ordinances and Resolutions of Prince George's County, § 3(a) 16 (1967)):

"* * * The regulations may provide for (1) the harmonious development of the district; (2) the coordination of roads within the subdivision with other existing, planned or platted roads or with other features of the district or with the commission's general plan or with any road plan adopted or approved by the commission as part of the commission's general plan; (3) adequate open spaces for traffic, recreation, light, and air by dedication or otherwise, and the dedication to public use or conveyance of areas designated for such dedication under the provisions of zoning regulations relating to average lot size or planned community subdivision and for the payment of a monetary fee in lieu of dedication, not to exceed five percent of the total assessed value of the land, to be used by the commission to purchase such open spaces for the use and benefit of the subdivision in cases where dedication would be impractical; (4) the reservation of lands for schools and other public buildings and for parks, playgrounds, and other public purposes, provided no reservation of land for traffic, recreation or any other public purposes as herein provided shall continue for longer than three (3) years without the written approval of all persons holding or otherwise owning any legal or equitable interest in said property; and provided further that such properties so reserved for public use as hereinbefore provided shall be exempt from all state, county and local taxes during such period; (5) the conservation of or production of adequate transportation, water, drainage and sanitary facilities; (6) the preservation of the location of and the volume and flow of water in and other characteristics of natural streams and other waterways; (7) the avoidance of population congestion; (8) the avoidance of such scattered or premature subdivision of land as would involve danger or injury to health, safety or welfare by reason of the lack of water supply, drainage, transportation or other public services or necessitate an excessive expenditure of public funds for the supply of such services; (9) conformity of resubdivided lots to the character of lots within the existing subdivision with respect to area, frontage and alignment to existing lots and streets; (10) control of subdivision or building (except for agricultural or recreational purposes) in flood plain areas or streams and drainage courses, and on unsafe land areas; (11) preservation of outstanding natural or cultural features and historic sites or structures; or (12) other benefits to the health, comfort, safety or welfare of the present and future population of the regional district."

"16. Before preliminary approval may be granted for any subdivision plat the Planning Board must find that: sufficient public facilities and services exist or are programmed for the area. It is the intent of this section that public facilities and services should be adequate to preclude danger or injury to the health, safety and welfare and excessive expenditure of public funds.

"i. The Planning Board shall give due weight to the potential of the proposed subdivision in relation to the surroundings, including the nature, extent and size of the proposed subdivision; the estimated increase in population; the anticipated timing of the development of the land proposed for subdivision; and the degree of urbanization or development within a reasonable distance of the subject property; and the following factors:

"The availability of existing or programmed sewerage or water mains.

"The potential effect of the proposed subdivision on the efficient and economic operation of existing or programmed public facilities.

"The distance of any necessary extension of sewerage and water facilities through unsubdivided lands which are indicated for eventual development on an approved plan.

"The location of the proposed subdivision in respect to the approved Ten Year Water and Sewerage Plan, or in any future plan which designated the timing of construction of facilities.

"The availability of access roads adequate to serve traffic which would be generated by the subdivision, or the presence of a proposal for such road(s) on an adopted Master Plan and in the current

Capital Improvement Program or the State Roads Commission program.

"The availability within a reasonable distance, and the adequacy of school, fire, police, utility, and park and recreation services."

The 31 acre tract of land (the property) with which we shall be concerned abuts the northwest side of the Pennsylvania Railroad which at that point serves also as one side of an equilateral triangle; the northeast side is the Capital Beltway (Interstate Rte 495); the south side is the John Hanson Highway (U.S. Rte 50). The property lies within the development known as West Lanham Hills which is about four miles northeast of the District line. Except for the land inside the triangle one can safely say the area surrounding the property is fully developed. Since 1964 the zoning classification of the property has been R–18 (Multiple Family, Medium Density, Residential), a classification with which the owner (appellee) seems content. It is said that a six acre strip has been or will be acquired to serve as the site for the Metro's Ardmore station.

In June 1971 the appellee submitted to the Commission for its approval, as required by the subdivision regulations, a preliminary plan for the subdivision of two parcels of the property. The Commission referred the application to its staff which, in turn, sent it to various county agencies for review and comment. The Board of Education was one of the agencies whose comment was solicited. It referred the matter to its Office of Population Analysis. On 16 June the Office of Population Analysis sent a memorandum to F. Harris Allen, Principal Development Coordinator of the Commission. The memorandum indicated a "Projected Pupil Yield" of 134 for the West Lanham Hills Elementary School, the capacity of which was 640 and which, at the time, had an actual enrollment of 657.

Several weeks later there came into existence an "adequate public facilities check sheet" apparently prepared by someone on the Commission's technical staff. Allen said he used this "in the course of the review of preliminary plans." This check sheet, dated 6 July 1971, indicates that the property had a "potential" of 651 units and that, fully developed and occupied, it would yield 175.8 pupils. The Office of Population Analysis, it will be recalled, developed a figure of 134. The September 1970 enrollment at the West Lanham Hills Elementary School was stated, in the check sheet, to be 668 pupils or 11 more than the enrollment reported by the Office of Population Analysis. There appears also, in the check sheet, the following notation:

There are no additions in the CIP [Capital Improvement Program] which would increase the capacity of this school *or any other elementary schools in the vicinity*. (Emphasis added.)

It is conceded that the technical staff of the Commission recommended approval of the appellee's application. It was considered by the Prince George's County Planning Board of the Commission on 9 August and disapproved the same day. A letter from Allen to the appellee, dated 13 August, states, in part:

"* * * West Lanham Hills Elementary School which would serve this property is currently operating over its listed capacity and there are no plans for any elementary schools in the Capital Improvements Program which would relieve this situation. The property, if developed in accordance with the allowable density, would generate approximately 134 elementary school children which would further overload the existing school.

"It was therefore the opinion of the Planning Board that since adequate public facilities are neither existing or programmed to serve the area the proposed subdivision should be denied."

* * *

Nothing in the record suggests the Board held any kind of a hearing and Allen's testimony makes it quite clear that the only evidence or information before the Board when it denied the appellee's application was the check sheet sent up from the technical staff. All the Board could have learned from the check sheet was that last year's (September 1970) enrollment at West Lanham Hills Elementary was 28 pupils in excess of its capacity and that the property could yield 651 dwelling units. * * * The Board could also have learned that an increase in the capacity of West Lanham Hills *"or any other elementary schools in the vicinity"* was not contemplated. What is meant by "vicinity" or which "other elementary schools" the staff had in mind is anyone's guess. We are not to be persuaded that the Board could have given "due weight * * * [to] [t]he availability within a reasonable distance, and the adequacy of school * * * services," in the light of such trivial and inaccurate evidence.

In Baltimore Planning Commission v. Victor Development Co., 261 Md. 387, 275 A.2d 478 (1971), we chose not to deal with the question whether the (Baltimore) Commission had "the power to formulate a rule dealing with the effect of subdivisions upon schools," although we hinted there might be some question about it. Here we choose not to deal with the question whether public schools are "public services" as that expression is used in the enabling act. The appellee urges that the principle of ejusdem generis should apply because of the juxtaposition of "public services" with "lack of water supply, drainage, transportation, or other public services," and it is, to be sure, not a wholly unattractive argument.

The subdivision regulation does not undertake to restrict pupils to the school within the boundaries of the service area in which they reside. The only limitation is that there must be an adequate school available "within a reasonable distance." Nor do the school authorities consider the boundaries of the service areas to be static and inflexible. Panor, it will be recalled, testified that they have "from year to year changed literally—practically all service areas of all existing schools." Reflecting upon Panor's testimony that the schools in the four contiguous areas have a capacity of 2,300 pupils and that the enrollment as of September 1972 was 251 less than capacity, one need not be especially perceptive to suppose that the area boundaries could readily be adjusted to take care of the 45 pupils said to be in excess of the capacity of West Lanham Hills Elementary School. One must, of course, assume the instant development and occupancy of the appellee's project, but one need not assume that it has been in the R–18 classification since 1964. That is a fact. The regulation does not define "reasonable distance" but we do not think the Board can be heard to say that a mile, or even a mile and one-half, is not a "reasonable distance."

Since we are fully persuaded that the Board's refusal to approve the appellee's preliminary plan was arbitrary and capricious the order of the trial court will be affirmed.

Order affirmed. Costs to be paid by the appellant.

Notes

1. In Corona–Norco Unified School Dist. v. City of Corona, 13 Cal. App.4th 1577, 17 Cal.Rptr.2d 236 (1993) the court held that a school district could not enjoin a city from giving subdivision approval for two projects on the ground of inadequate school facilities. The court based its decision on state statutes that allow school districts to impose exactions of developments for school purposes and concluded that the complex statutory scheme precluded denial of subdivision approval. Also see Grupe Development Co. v. Superior Court, 4 Cal.4th 911, 16 Cal.Rptr.2d 226, 844 P.2d 545 (1993).

In Cherokee Water & Sanitation Dist. v. El Paso County, 770 P.2d 1339 (Colo.App.1988), the court upheld a county regulation requiring all developers to demonstrate a 300 year water supply prior to subdivision approval. The case was a declaratory judgment action presenting a facial challenge to the regulation. The court said:

> Nor have the plaintiffs shown an unconstitutional taking of property. As the challenge is facial, plaintiffs must prove that the mere enactment deprived them of all reasonable use of their property. Landmark Land Co. v. City & County of Denver, 728 P.2d 1281 (Colo.1986), appeal dismissed sub nom., Harsh Investment Corp. v. City & County of Denver, 483 U.S. 1001, 107 S.Ct. 3222, 97 L.Ed.2d 729 (1987). Plaintiffs were unable to demonstrate that the regulation will prevent even residential development on their property, let alone any other reasonable use. Thus, no taking occurred by enactment of the regulation.

> Nor are we convinced that the regulation is arbitrary or capricious. Plaintiffs bore the burden of proving beyond a reasonable doubt that the regulations are not rationally and reasonably related to a valid governmental interest. Sellon v. City of Manitou Springs, 745 P.2d 229 (Colo. 1987). The evidence presented by the county demonstrates that the regulation is designed to insure that no development take place where there are not adequate water supplies for the future. Such an interest is valid, and the regulation is rationally and reasonably related thereto, thus satisfying both the federal and state constitutional requirements.

Also see Christianson v. Gasvoda, 242 Mont. 212, 789 P.2d 1234 (1990) where the court upheld denial of a subdivision because it would exacerbate drainage and flooding problems in flatlands below the developer's land. The same developer had previously developed three subdivisions in the uplands area, and the court said the problems created by previous development justified rejection of the proposed subdivision. A similar case from Connecticut involved a steep slope development. Krawski v. Planning and Zoning Comm'n of Town of South Windsor, 21 Conn.App. 667, 575 A.2d 1036 (1990).

In Beach v. Planning and Zoning Comm'n, 141 Conn. 79, 103 A.2d 814 (1954), the commission denied subdivision plat approval for a 145–lot subdivision for the following reasons: "(1) This land is adjacent to a new development which will contain 79 homes. (2) The Council has stated that the financial situation of the town is such that no schools could be built in this area for some time. (3) The additional Police and Fire protection which would be needed in this area cannot now be provided due to the financial situation of the town. (4) The report of the school superintendent shows that the new school in this area will be inadequate to provide for the children already living in this area soon after it opens." The court held that neither the enabling statute nor the subdivision ordinance authorized rejection of plat approval on those grounds and that the rejection was ultra vires. Compare Fallen Leaf Protection Ass'n v. South Tahoe Public Utility Dist., 46 Cal.App.3d 816, 120 Cal.Rptr. 538 (1975) which upheld an absolute prohibition of septic tanks and cesspools for waste disposal. Also compare Board of County Comm'rs of Cecil County v. Gaster, 285 Md. 233, 401 A.2d 666 (1979), where the court upheld denial of a subdivision because of traffic congestion in an area not programmed for new roads until 1990. And see Batch v. Town of Chapel Hill, 326 N.C. 1, 387 S.E.2d 655 (1990) where the court upheld denial of a subdivision plat for failure to coordinate with the town's transportation plan.

2. In Walls v. Planning and Zoning Comm'n, 176 Conn. 475, 408 A.2d 252 (1979), the court held that adjacent property owners had no standing to challenge the approval of a subdivision. In State ex rel. Menkhus v.City of Pevely, 865 S.W.2d 871 (Mo.App.1993) the court held a property owner whose subdivision plat met all the requirements of the ordinance could not be denied approval, and in Ex Parte Pine Brook Lakes, Inc., 617 So.2d 1014 (Ala.1992) the court held that the county board improperly denied subdivision approval by merely referring to some possible future road construction in the area.

3. Put yourself in the position of a planning commissioner or other local official of a unit on the growth fringe of an urban area. Yours is one of the toughest jobs in government. Your town or borough, or village, or satellite city is perhaps reasonably well-equipped with "paper" legal powers. But it is woefully weak in terms of revenue sources and technical competence to wrestle with the problems of urban growth that plague it. There are pressures on you to slow down development so it will not outstrip the community's ability to finance demanded services, especially schools. Other pressure from "old timers" push for preservation of neighborhood "amenities" and the character of the community, by which may be meant, "Keep the little houses with their swarms of kids out" or "Let's have big lots and big houses only and, for goodness sakes, no trailer camps." Other strong-minded citizens will be pushing hard for "getting some industry in to take some of the property tax load off us householders." And every citizen, even the one who has just moved in last week, will agree that in the future you

should make all newcomers "pay their own way." There will be little pressure on you to do what is best in terms of the needs of the metropolitan region; instead you will be asked to wear intellectual blinders and do what is "best" for your political entity and let neighboring units take the consequences.

You will soon realize that although subdivision controls are important to you in your unenviable plight, they are not the only available tools. This is graphically indicated by Richard Cutler in his article, Legal and Illegal Methods for Controlling Community Growth in the Urban Fringe, 1961 Wis.L.Rev. 370.

See also Fagin, Financing Municipal Services in a Metropolitan Region, 19 J.Am.Inst. of Planners 214 (1953); Nat'l Science Foundation, Municipal Service Pricing: Impact on Urban Development and Finance (1975); Council on Environmental Quality, The Growth Shapers: The Land Use Impacts of Infrastructure Investments (1976).

In the 1980's two developments made an impact on the conventional wisdom surrounding subdivision exactions. The twin forces of rapid inflation and the property tax revolt made more people aware of the fact that subdivision exactions have a powerful role in the cost of housing. In those states which have adopted limitations on the property tax, notably California through Proposition 13, one result was an increase in subdivision exactions and permit fees. Cities saw the loss of property tax revenues as reducing funding for municipal services which could be made up only by increasing revenues from other sources. Subdivision exactions, in this sense, would be a hidden tax imposed on new residents, reflected in the cost of housing. However, when coupled with rapid inflation, the increase in exactions became a more visible factor in housing costs. In some communities estimates were that exactions and other development regulations accounted for as much as twenty-five percent of the cost of a single-family dwelling. One result of this problem has been increased attention to ways in which the cost of housing can be lowered. See U.S. Dept. Housing and Urban Development, Reducing the Development Costs of Housing: Actions for State and Local Governments (1979); Ellickson, Suburban Growth Controls: An Economic and Legal Analysis, 66 Yale L.J. 385 (1977). In many communities, even in states without property tax revolt problems, inflationary forces have induced developers to seek reductions in exactions in order to keep the cost of housing down. Even traditional exactions have come under attack. Developers are questioning the necessity of sidewalks in residential subdivisions and the established street widths. They may ask for elimination of curb and gutter requirements, reduction of minimum lot sizes, and revision of building codes, all in the name of making housing affordable (and, incidentally, keeping them in business). In some cities developers are seeking permission to develop single-family and multi-family areas with private drives, rather than streets constructed to city standards and dedicated to the public. If a community resists the pressure for reduction of exactions, developers will frequently raise the spectre that they will pick up and move their operations to nearby cities where the regulatory costs are lower, leaving the community without a housing industry. No easy answers to the turmoil of the early 1980's are available. However, some questions may be posed. Should exactions be standardized at the state level, rather than delegated to local government as is the present practice? Presumably, exactions are a result of the police power, delegated in the enabling legislation. Does the health, safety, morals and general welfare of the public justify thirty-foot wide streets with curb and gutter in the residential subdivisions of City A and twenty-five foot wide streets without curb or gutter in City B? Would it be better and cheaper to have a standard set of exactions and codes for the entire state? Would such a change be politically feasible? Further, what is the relationship, if any, between growth controls, exactions, inflation and the cost of housing? See Patricia E. Salkin, Barriers to Affordable Housing: Are Land–Use Controls the Scapegoat?, Land Use Law (April 1993) p. 3. Also see Jerry Cheslow, Impact Fees Re-examined in California, N.Y. Times, Apr. 4, 1993, p. 31; this article discusses how impact fees can stunt growth in a financial recession.

SECTION 4.   THE OFFICIAL MAP
AND PUBLIC STREETS

In 1925, Philip Nichols and Frank B. Williams debated whether to use eminent domain or the police power to prevent building in officially mapped streets. See the 1925 Proceedings, National City Planning Conference 378 and following. Mr. Nichols argued for eminent domain pointing to the quaint Yankee custom of exactly off-setting damages for eminent domain taking with the special benefits to the rest of the land. Mr. Williams took the police power position urging a board of adjustment to take care of hardship cases. It was pointed out that William Penn laid out a system of checkerboard streets for Philadelphia and that the official map has been popular in Pennsylvania ever since. The Randall map for New York City was authorized in 1807, and an official map for Baltimore in 1817. Mr. Williams said (at 396):

> The age of Washington was the age of city planning. The street plan of New York City, [way out to 155th street] already referred to, was protected by a state law providing that a property owner, when the city was ready to lay out the street and took the land necessary for the purpose, could recover no damages for improvements which he had made in the bed of a mapped street; and there were similar laws in other states. For many years these laws remained unchallenged in our statute books and were generally regarded as valid. But, before our Civil War, in 1861, a change of attitude occurred, and today except in the State of Pennsylvania, all these laws are, under decisions of our highest state courts, held to be a taking of property rights without compensation contrary to our state constitutions.

Kucirek and Beuscher, Wisconsin's Official Map Law, 1957 Wis. L.Rev. 176, 177, state:

> In essence the official map is a simple device. It is one way, but not the only way, to fix building lines. The official map may plat future as well as existing streets. Where future streets are mapped, subdividers must conform to the mapped street lay-out, unless they can prevail upon the proper officials to amend the map. Public sewer

and water will be installed only in the bed of the mapped streets. Even more important, a landowner who builds in the bed of the mapped street may be refused compensation for his building when the street is ultimately opened and the mapped land taken. To guard against this drastic consequence, official map laws now customarily require the landowner to obtain a building permit before proceeding with construction.

The official map of future streets has obvious advantages in terms of the public coffers. It assures that land needed for future streets will be available at bare land prices. Mapping of future streets also gives direction and pattern to future growth of the community, though some feel that the map casts the mold too inflexibly, especially if minor as well as major streets are mapped.

Where existing streets have been officially mapped, the map will often set widening lines (set-backs) warning that new structures must be located in conformance with their lines, and these also have obvious advantages in cutting costs of street widening. Again, a building permit is usually used to assure compliance.

The official map is not the only means of establishing building lines. Other familiar methods are:

(1) Set-back provisions in zoning ordinances;

(2) Set-back ordinances as such—ordinances stating that for prescribed streets no buildings are to be built any closer to the street line than a specified distance;

(3) Set-backs established on plats as a condition to subdivision approval;

(4) Set-back provisions in privately established deed restrictions (restrictive covenants);

(5) The now virtually obsolete method of purchasing set-back easements through eminent domain proceedings.

(6) In the subdivision process, as we have already seen, subdividers may be required to honor the master street plan insofar as that plan indicates street locations; and, of course, the subdivider may be required to install the street at his expense and in compliance with published standards.

The name "official map" is not universal. In Pennsylvania and California for instance, the same planning device is there referred to as "confirmed map" and "precise map" respectively. The name "official map" seems to have originated with Edward M. Bassett and Frank B. Williams, who wrote New York's 1926 act and in 1935 published a model official map act. They distinguished the "official map" sharply from the "master plan":

> A master plan embraces many features not included in an official map. The master plan, therefore, does not usually show precise data founded in careful surveys, while the official map, upon

which the details of both public and private works must be based, should be capable of accurate interpretation. The master plan, therefore, may be characterized as plastic, the official map as rigid.

In other words under the Bassett–Williams scheme, the master plan is not binding upon landowners; the official map is. The master plan is the general formulation, often reflected by non-precise maps, of the results of planning studies—studies not only of the circulatory system, but also of land use districts, location of parks and recreation areas, sites for public buildings and facilities, location of public utilities and other matters. The official map is intended to reflect some aspects of the master plan in a precise, accurate and legally binding manner.

Nonetheless, it is easy to overemphasize in practical terms the differences to the landowner between the officially enacted map on one hand and the commission-approved "unofficial" street plan on the other. Knowledgeable landowners are not apt to build in the bed of an "unofficially" mapped street or other proposed public site. True, the owner may know that he is entitled to compensation for his building when the land is ultimately taken for the public purpose. But he knows of the vagaries of valuation juries and in any case, compensation or no compensation, he does not want to build a structure only to have it torn down, perhaps only a short time later. Consequently many cities successfully guide development along future streets through master street plans, not backed by any legal sanctions except subdivision plat approval. Such plans are less successful in achieving voluntary set-backs along existing streets. Here the legal sanctions of a set-back ordinance or a precise official map are needed to keep the uncooperative owner "in line."

Another point of comparison between a master plan and an official map needs to be made. Even though the master plan is not backed by legal sanctions, it may blight the market for mapped real estate quite as effectively as an official map. If a would-be buyer learns that the land has been marked with a "green spot" on the master plan for a park or has been "master planned" as the bed of a proposed street or thoroughway, he will be as reluctant to buy as if the land had been officially mapped. He does not want to buy and develop land for his private use when he knows that it is earmarked for public taking.

HEADLEY v. CITY OF ROCHESTER

Court of Appeals of New York, 1936.
272 N.Y. 197, 5 N.E.2d 198.

LEHMAN, J. The plaintiff since 1918 has been the owner of premises in the city of Rochester which are bounded on the south by East avenue and on the west by North Goodman street. East avenue and North Goodman street have been, for more than twenty years, public streets or highways. In 1931, pursuant to article 3 of the General City Law (Cons.Laws, ch. 21), the Council of the city of Rochester passed an ordinance which amended, changed and added to an official map or plan previously adopted by the Council "so as to correct and revise said established Official Map or Plan and to lay out new streets and highways and to widen existing highways." In that map or plan the southerly twenty-five feet of plaintiff's said premises are included in East avenue, as widened, and a strip of plaintiff's premises extending along its westerly edge is included in North Goodman street, as widened. The plaintiff has brought an action to obtain a judgment declaring "that the ordinance and map and plan adopted by the said City of Rochester as aforesaid is unconstitutional and void." At Special Term the complaint was dismissed. The Appellate Division reversed and granted judgment "declaring that the ordinance, map and plan herein involved, are void and ineffectual to create any limitations or restrictions upon the use or conveyance of plaintiff's property."

By chapter 690 of the Laws of 1926 the Legislature added article 3, entitled "Official Maps and Planning Boards," to the General City Law. That article empowers the legislative body of every city to establish an official map or plan of the city showing the streets, highways and parks theretofore laid out and established by law. (Sec. 26.) It empowers such legislative body "whenever and as often as it may deem it for the public interest, to change or add to the official map or plan of the city so as to lay out new streets, highways or parks, or to widen or close existing streets, highways or parks." (Sec. 29.) It further empowers the legislative body of the city to create a planning board of five members and it requires that before making any addition or change in an official map in accordance with section 29 "the matter shall be referred to the planning board for report thereon." The planning board is given "power and authority to make such investigations, maps and reports and recommendations in connection therewith relating to the planning and development of the city as to it seems desirable." (Sec. 31.)

The adoption or revision of a general map pursuant to the provisions of the General City Law does not have the effect of divesting the title of the owner of land in the bed of a street as shown on the map; it does not have the effect of placing upon the city a duty to begin, presently, condemnation proceedings to acquire such land. Article 3 of the statute provides the machinery for intelligent planning in advance for the needs of the city as the city is expected to grow in the future. Only time can prove whether the city has wisely gauged the future, and the city is under no compulsion to open any street shown on the map unless and until the legislative body of the city decides that it is actually needed.

The mere adoption of a general plan or map showing streets and parks to be laid out or widened in the future, without acquisition by the city of title to the land in the bed of the street, can be of little benefit to the public if the development of the land abutting upon and in the bed of the proposed streets proceeds in a haphazard way, without taking into account the general plan adopted and, especially, if permanent buildings are erected on the land in the bed of the proposed street which would hamper its acquisition or use for its intended purpose. So long as the owners of parcels of land which lie partly in the bed of streets shown on such a map are free to place permanent buildings in the bed of a proposed street and to provide private ways and approaches which have no relation to the proposed system of public streets, the integrity of the plan may be destroyed by the haphazard or even malicious development of one parcel or tract to the injury of other owners who may have developed their own tracts in a manner which conforms to the general map or plan.

A statutory requirement that a city must acquire title to the land in the bed of the streets shown on the general map or plan, and to provide compensation for the land taken, would create practical difficulties which would drastically limit, if, indeed, they did not render illusory, any power conferred upon the city to adopt a general map or plan which will make provision for streets which will be needed only if present anticipations of the future development of the city are realized. On the other hand, to leave the land in private ownership, and, without compensation to the owner, incumber it with restrictions upon its use which would result in diminution in its value might be inequitable and perhaps even beyond the power of the State. To meet the difficulty, the Legislature has provided in section 35 of the General City Law that "for the purpose of preserving the integrity of such official map or plan no permit shall hereafter be issued for any building in the bed of any street or highway shown or laid out on such map or plan, provided, however, that if the land within such mapped street or highway is not yielding a fair return on its value to the owner, the board of appeals or other similar board in any city which has established such a board having power to make variances or exception in zoning regulations shall have power in a specific case * * * to grant a permit for a building in such street or highway which will as little as practicable increase the cost of opening such street or highway, or tend to cause a change of such official map or plan, and such board may impose reasonable requirements as a condition of granting such permit, which requirements shall inure to the benefit of the city." The sole complaint of the plaintiff is that so long as that section remains in force the effect of the ordinance adopted by the city is to restrict the use to which the plaintiff may put his land in the bed of the street and to that extent constitutes a taking of his property, and that, since the city is not required to pay any compensation to him unless or until at some time in the indefinite future it may choose to take title to the land, the effect of the ordinance is to deprive him of his property without due process of law.

Not every restriction placed by authority of the State upon the use of property for the general welfare of the State, without payment of compensation, constitutes a deprivation of property without due process of law. This court has sustained a reasonable restriction upon the height of signs on roofs, saying: "Compensation for such interference with and restriction in the use of property is found in the share that the owner enjoys in the common benefit secured to all."

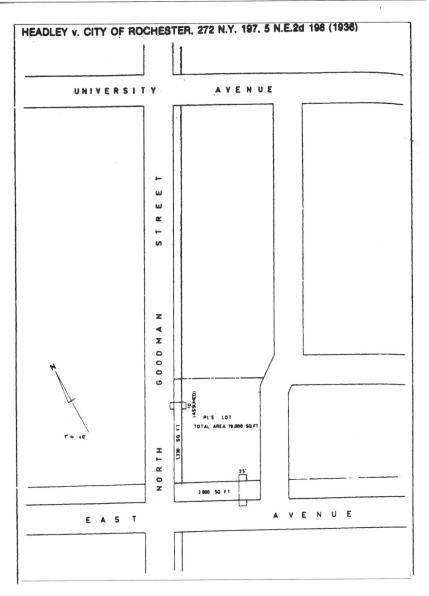

HEADLEY v. CITY OF ROCHESTER. 272 N.Y. 197. 5 N.E.2d 198 (1936)

People ex rel. M. Wineburgh Adv. Co. v. Murphy, 195 N.Y. 126, 131, 88 N.E. 17. Under the provisions of the General City Law the owner of land in the bed of the street shown in a map remains as free to alien the land or to use it as he sees fit as he was before the map was adopted, except in one respect. If he desires to improve the property by erecting a building for which a permit is required, the grant of such a permit is surrounded by drastic conditions or restrictions which will in many cases act as an obstacle to such use of the land.

* * *

* * * The complaint alleges only the conclusion of the pleader that by reason of the filing of the ordinance and map or plan "the plaintiff

has been, and is, deprived of his property without the payment of compensation therefor." The complaint is silent as to how the plaintiff is injured by the ordinance and the map. The stipulation of facts upon which the case was submitted for decision again fails to indicate in what manner the ordinance has caused damage to the plaintiff or interferes with any use to which the plaintiff desires to put the land. On the contrary, it appears from the stipulated facts that "the plaintiff has at present no plans for the use of said premises nor any particular desire as to the purposes for which he expects to use the same" and "that the plaintiff, because of the claim of the defendant under said ordinance and map, is undecided as to whether he shall endeavor to build upon said premises or endeavor to sell the same." It may be added, incidentally, that the stipulated facts fail to show that there is at present any actual controversy with the city as to the use to which the property may be put, and it appears "that the plaintiff has made no application to the Planning Board, Board of Appeals or Supervisor of Zoning of the City of Rochester for a permit to use those portions of his property included in said map as widened streets or to build thereon or to alter any existing structures therein."

Regardless of the form of action in which relief is sought, the courts will not declare a statute unconstitutional unless and until such relief is necessary for the protection of some right of the suitor guaranteed by the Constitution. * * *

The opinion of the Appellate Division leans heavily upon Forster v. Scott, 136 N.Y. 577, 32 N.E. 976, as authority for its decision. The analogy between the cases is quite illusory and the principles here involved are not touched by that case. There the city of New York, in accordance with the provisions of chapter 681 of the Laws of 1886, filed a map of a proposed street or avenue which as the court pointed out "covers the entire lot" of the plaintiff. The statute provided that "no compensation shall be allowed for any building, erection or construction which at any time, subsequent to the filing of the maps, plans, or profiles mentioned in section six hundred and seventy-two of the act, may be built, erected or placed in part or in whole upon or through any street, avenue, road, public square or place exhibited upon such maps, plans or profiles." (p. 582.) The plaintiff made a contract to sell his land to the defendant. He agreed to convey a good title to the land "in fee simple free from any lien or encumbrance." The defendant refused the title, claiming that the filing of the map created an incumbrance upon the property. The validity of the title was submitted to the court upon stipulated facts. It appeared from them that no building was erected on the plaintiff's land and "the same is a vacant lot which derives almost its entire value from the possibility of being used for building purposes. If the lot cannot now be built upon without the house being destroyed, without compensation in the event of the street being opened as prescribed by the statutes above set forth, the lot is not worth what defendant agreed to pay, whereas if it can be used for building purposes it is worth at least $5,000." In other words, the statute purported to give the city the right at some indefinite time in the future to appropriate the land of the plaintiff shown on the map without paying for it the value it would then have if, pending such appropriation, its owner chose to improve it for the only purpose for which it had substantial value.

The court there said: "An encumbrance is said to import every right to or interest in the land, which may subsist in another, to the diminution of the value of the land, but consistent with the power to pass the fee by a conveyance." (p. 582.) If the statute was valid the land "could not be used for building purposes, except at the risk to the owner of losing the cost of the building at some time in the future." (p. 583.) The value of the land was derived from its availability for building purposes and that value would be drastically reduced if the owner could not obtain compensation for the improvements put upon the land. Since these facts were stipulated it could hardly be doubted that the statute attempted to create a public right or interest in the land which diminished its value and would, therefore, constitute an incumbrance as defined by the court. Then in an action between vendor and vendee under a contract of sale, the court was bound to pass upon the validity of the statute.

Every element which led the court to find in that case that the filing of the map, in accordance with the statute there challenged, created, if the statute were valid, an incumbrance upon the property, is wanting in the case now under review. The statute here does not purport to give to the city the right to appropriate the plaintiff's land or any part of it for less than the full value of the lands with the improvements thereon erected at the time of such appropriation. The only restrictions upon the use of any part of the plaintiff's land while title thereto remains in the plaintiff result indirectly from the conditions which the statute attaches to the grant thereafter of a permit to erect a building upon the small portion of plaintiff's land which, as shown on the map, will lie in the bed of the street on which the plaintiff's land abuts, if or when at some time in the future the city may desire to carry out its intention to widen the street. Since it is affirmatively shown that the plaintiff has no plans at present for the use of the premises it seems plain that what this court said and decided in the case of Forster v. Scott (supra) cannot possibly be regarded as any precedent, for the grant of a judgment declaring the statute invalid, unless from the facts here presented the court as matter of law would be constrained to draw the inference that the conditions which the Legislature has sought to impose upon the grant of a permit for the use of a small part of plaintiff's land, creates a limitation upon its use "to the diminution of the value of the land."

No inference of law, indeed no inference of fact, that the attempted condition has affected or will affect the use to which the plaintiff's land will be put or has diminished the value of the land, may be drawn from the stipulated facts. There is no suggestion that a plot of nineteen thousand square feet cannot be suitably improved and put to the most profitable use by the erection of a building which does not encroach upon the small portions which may be used hereafter to widen the street. Sometimes land owners in a particular district assume mutual obligations to set back buildings some distance from the streets. Sometimes such obligations are imposed by zoning ordinance. Sometimes an owner does so voluntarily because he believes that such a setback is the best use for the land immediately abutting on the street. The plaintiff or any successor in title to the property could use the land within the bed of the widened street for such purpose even without a permit. It may be the best use to which that land could be put, even if no map had been adopted, and there were no probability that the city would in time widen the street. Certainly it cannot be said that owners of property do not receive any benefit from the adoption of general maps or plans for the development of city streets, if they can develop their land with some assurance that other owners will not be permitted to frustrate the plan, maliciously or unreasonably. Whether the State may impose conditions for the issuance of permits in order to protect the integrity of the plan of a city where it appears that such conditions interfere with a reasonable use to which the land would otherwise be put or diminishes the value of the land, should not now be decided. Without proof that the imposition of such conditions has deprived an owner of land of some benefit he would otherwise derive from the land, there can be no deprivation of property for which compensation should be made.

Solicitude for the protection of the rights of private property against encroachment by government for a supposed public benefit does not justify the courts in declaring invalid a public law which serves a public purpose, because ten years after it has been on the statute books a single owner, without proof, or even claim, of actual injury, asserts that he has been deprived of his property.

The judgment of the Appellate Division should be reversed and that of the Special Term affirmed, with costs in this court and in the Appellate Division.

NIGRO v. PLANNING BOARD OF BOROUGH OF SADDLE RIVER

Superior Court of New Jersey, Appellate Division, 1989.
237 N.J.Super. 305, 567 A.2d 1010.

PER CURIAM.

This is an appeal by a planning board from a final judgment of the Law Division reversing its denial of an application for preliminary subdivision approval as unreasonable, arbitrary and capricious. Defendant Saddle River Planning Board contends the street layout of the proposed subdivision did not conform to the officially adopted official map; that the official map was statutorily conclusive with respect to the street location; that it therefore could not lawfully approve a proposal that failed to conform to the official map; and that *ergo,* of necessity, its action could not have been unreasonable, arbitrary or capricious. We agree.

This litigation involves a 25.5 acre tract in Saddle River which is still devoted to farming. It is essentially surrounded by the rear lots of developed residential properties containing at least two acres. Importantly to this case, it is bounded to the north by lots facing Glenwood Drive and to the south by lots facing Twin Brooks Road.

Plaintiff James Nigro is the contract purchaser of some eight acres on the western side of the undeveloped tract. The present owners, the Demarests, are unwilling to sell the remaining 17.5 acres upon which they plan to continue their farming operation. Nigro applied to the Planning Board for preliminary approval of a major subdivision in which four new residential lots would be created in the western part of the Demarest tract. The lots in the proposed subdivision conform with the required areas and frontages but the proposed street access does not conform to that shown in the existing master plan and official map. Nigro proposes to provide access by the construction of a new street running north from Twin Brooks Road; the official map shows access to the Demarest tract will be provided by a proposed street running south from Glenwood Drive. * * *

The Planning Board denied the application upon findings, *inter alia,* that the proposed subdivision was inconsistent with the master plan and the official map. In its conclusions, it properly identified the basic issue.

> The basic problem arises in that the property owner wishes to develop the property in a manner different than that recognized in the Master Plan and Official Map of the municipality. Those documents provide for development of the tract from Glenwood Drive. The property owner has chosen to sell off the portion of the property in question which is located some distance from the roadway access to the property at Glenwood Drive. The applicant has been able to acquire property on Twin Brooks Road and provide an area of access by way of public street. The basic conflict arises in creating a public street in an area where single family residential homes exist where no street was ever contemplated, and in a location not conforming to the planning process of the municipality which clearly contemplated development from Glenwood Drive.

The trial judge considered the street locations as shown in the master plan and official map as proposed locations—merely tentative proposals for later discussion and consideration. They were, she concluded, nonbinding. In her view, the evidence showed good planning reasons for the development of the property from the south. She found the action of the Planning Board to be arbitrary and capricious and remanded the matter with directions to grant the requested subdivision approval.

We are satisfied that the trial judge's action in treating the official map as tentative—as merely showing a nonbinding proposed rights-of-way—was error. Such is not the law. The legislature has decreed to the contrary.

> The official map shall be deemed conclusive with respect to the location and width of streets and public drainage ways and the location and extent of flood control basins and public areas, whether

or not such streets, ways, basins or areas are improved or unimproved or are in actual physical existence.

[N.J.S.A. 40:55D–32]

The language is clear and unambiguous. We are not at liberty to construe it otherwise. *See Service Armament Co. v. Hyland,* 70 *N.J.* 550, 556, 362 *A.*2d 13 (1976); *Gangemi v. Berry,* 25 *N.J.* 1, 10, 134 *A.*2d 1 (1957).

Moreover, this clear meaning construction is supported by an examination of the nature of an official map. New Jersey early accepted the notion of planning the systematic physical development of a community. *See Kligman v. Lautman,* 53 *N.J.* 517, 534, 251 *A.*2d 745 (1969); Cunningham, *Control of Land Use in New Jersey,* 15 *Rut.L.Rev.* 1, 2–3 (1960). Municipal planning has been authorized since 1930. *Ibid.* And from the beginning New Jersey permitted the adoption, by ordinance, of an official map to be deemed conclusive with respect to the location and width of streets, parks and playgrounds; *Mansfield & Swett v. West Orange,* 120 *N.J.L.* 145, 149, 198 *A.* 225 (Sup.Ct.1938). This concept has been continued and is presently contained in Article 5 of the Municipal Land Use Law. *N.J.S.A.* 40:55D–32 to 34. Unlike other planning devices, the official map forecasts with precision the location of streets, drainage ways, parks and playgrounds so as to provide some continuity in the planning process. *See* 5 Williams, *American Planning Law* § 155 (1985) at 325–326. It not only provides a blueprint of the size and location of such existing and proposed public uses but protects proposed sites from other use and guides the development of land in accordance with the preconceived lines for sound and orderly growth. *See* 4 Anderson, *American Law of Zoning 2nd* § 24.02 (1977). It has been described as "a device for putting some teeth on the otherwise advisory effect of certain aspects of a master plan." *See Kligman v. Lautman, supra,* 53 *N.J.* at 535, n. 2, 251 *A.*2d 745. Unlike other planning devices, the official map represents solemn action by the governing body which adopts it by ordinance after public hearing. *See* Bernstein, *The Impact of the New Official Map on Municipalities,* New Jersey Municipalities (February 1955) 23. It can be fairly characterized as the skeletal framework upon which the community can develop and grow.

The integrity of this framework is a repeated theme. No structures can be built on the bed of a proposed street. *N.J.S.A.* 40:55D–34. In general, buildings must be on lots which abut streets appearing on the official map. *N.J.S.A.* 40:55D–35. *See also* Bernstein, *supra.* This is not to say that lots cannot be developed which do not abut such a street. Streets which appear on a planning board approved plat are sufficient, *ibid.,* but by implication such streets are intended to fill out the skeleton, not conflict with it. *See Levin v. Livingston Tp.,* 35 *N.J.* 500, 511, 173 *A.*2d 391 (1961). It is significant that the legislature provided hardship relief from the bar to construction in the bed of a proposed street. *N.J.S.A.* 40:55D–34, but made no similar provision for street alignment. In the case of construction in a proposed street bed, the relief must interfere with the planned street as little as practicable. *N.J.S.A.* 40:55D–34. Amendments, *i.e.,* a restructuring of the skeleton, are for the governing body. *N.J.S.A.* 40:55D–32. Whether the official map should be amended to provide access to the tract which plaintiff seeks to develop is a matter for the governing body.

In sum, we are satisfied that the Planning Board could not lawfully approve plaintiff's application because it conflicted with the official map. Its action was proper and must be sustained.

Reversed.

Notes

1. The Bartholomew street map for Rochester, N.Y., was involved in Vangellow v. City of Rochester, 190 Misc. 128, 71 N.Y.S.2d 672 (Sup.Ct. 1947). There, old buildings were built right up to the street line. The map required a 10 foot setback. Plaintiffs, who proposed to tear down and reconstruct the buildings, wanted to build showrooms right up to the street line. They brought this action for a declaratory judgment declaring the map invalid as applied to the plaintiffs. Held: The official map as applied to the plaintiffs is not totally void and the court has no jurisdiction until the plaintiffs have exhausted their administrative review remedy before the Rochester zoning board of appeals.

See also S.S. Kresge Co. v. City of New York, 194 Misc. 645, 87 N.Y.S.2d 313 (Sup.Ct.1949); Jensen v. City of New York, 42 N.Y.2d 1079, 399 N.Y.S.2d 645, 369 N.E.2d 1179 (1977); St. Luke's German Evangelical Lutheran Church v. City of Rochester, 115 Misc.2d 199, 453 N.Y.S.2d 1012 (1982).

In Ward v. Bennett, 79 N.Y.2d 394, 583 N.Y.S.2d 179, 592 N.E.2d 787 (1992) the New York Court of Appeals held that a landowner denied a building permit to construct a single-family house in the bed of a mapped but unopened street could bring a takings claim for compensation even though the city argued that the owner had not exhausted the available remedy of seeking to have the street de-mapped; the court said that the case was "ripe" for judicial review. This holding seems inconsistent with that in the Vangellow case, supra.

2. In Grosso v. Board of Adjustment, 137 N.J.L. 630, 61 A.2d 167 (1948) the official map as hastily amended after the plaintiff applied for a building permit placed plaintiff's entire property in the bed of a proposed street. The court had little difficulty holding that the map was invalid as applied to the plaintiff. Compare Barsel v. Woodbridge Twp. Zoning Bd. of Adjustment, 189 N.J.Super. 75, 458 A.2d 1303 (1983). Also see Barile v. City of Port Republic, 186 N.J.Super. 587, 453 A.2d 284 (1982).

3. What do you think about the following statement from 2 Nichols, Eminent Domain § 6.03 (Rev.3d ed. 1989):

> The mapping out of streets upon vacant land near large and growing cities has often been provided for, so that a systematic plan for the gradual enlargement of the city can be followed. A mere provision that after the recording of the map no streets shall be laid out which are not in accordance therewith is unobjectionable; but it is sometimes

enacted that if the owner builds upon the land marked out for a street, when the street is actually laid out he shall receive no compensation for his building. As the platting of a street under such a statute amounts substantially to a deprivation of the owner's use of the land within the limits of the projected street for any temporary purposes, it is generally held that such statutes are unconstitutional unless the owner is compensated for his loss or allowed to build in the bed of a mapped street if the land, as restricted, is not yielding its owner a fair return.

The land lying within the limits of such projected streets can only be considered "taken" within the meaning of the constitutional provision when the streets have been actually opened by governmental authority or where the statute authorizing the filing of the map provides that the appropriation shall be complete upon such filing.

See also Annots., 12 A.L.R. 679 (1921) and 62 A.L.R. 546 (1929).

4. In a report prepared for the U.S. Bureau of Public Roads, Professors Daniel Mandelker and Graham Waite summarize official map enabling acts for the 28 states which have such statutes. (Mandelker and Waite, A Study of Future Acquisition and Reservation of Highway Rights-of-Way (Mimeo prepared under Contract CPR 11–8006, 1963) Charts 2 and 3, Part I, Appendix). In general these statutes are built on one of three models: (1) the so-called Standard Act; (2) the Bettman model; and (3) the Bassett–Williams model.

The Standard Act calls for payment for the reserved rights-of-way from the time of reservation. As might be expected, little use has been made of this procedure in the four states that have enacted it into law.

Both the Bettman and Bassett–Williams acts authorize the mapping of future streets and widening lines through exercise of the police power. Both include provisions intended to take care of hardship cases, but hardship is defined differently in the two acts.

The Bettman act requires a showing (1) that a reasonable return cannot be earned from the property including the mapped part, or (2) that balancing the interests of the municipality against the interests of the owner, considerations of equity and justice dictate the grant of a permit.

The Bassett–Williams model requires not only a showing that the land in the bed of the mapped street is not yielding a fair return, but it also authorizes refusal of a building permit where the applicant will not be substantially damaged by placing his building outside the mapped street. See, for example, State ex rel. Miller v. Manders, 2 Wis.2d 365, 86 N.W.2d 469 (1957).

These hardship standards should be compared with the standards for zoning variances taken up in Chapter VII. It may be that a city is well advised to use its zoning power to establish set-back lines, rather than establish widening lines under the official map act. See Kucirek and Beuscher, Wisconsin's Official Map Act, 1957 Wis.L.Rev. 176, 196–197 and Phillips v. Board of Adjustment, 44 N.J.Super. 491, 130 A.2d 866 (1957).

Notice the hardship provisions of the Bettman and the Bassett–Williams acts are phrased in terms of *new* buildings. Nothing is said about alterations of buildings which were already in place when the land was mapped. See

Golden v. Aldell Realty Corp., 70 N.Y.S.2d 341 (Sup.Ct.Queens 1947); Agliata v. D'Agostino, 124 N.Y.S.2d 212 (Sup.Ct.Queens 1953); and Kucirek and Beuscher, Wisconsin's Official Map Law, 1957 Wis.L.Rev. 176, 208–210.

Though based generally on the Bassett–Williams or Bettman models the following states have enabling acts which do not classify neatly under one or the other: California, Connecticut, Kentucky (Jefferson County), Maine, Michigan, Minnesota, Missouri, North Carolina, Oklahoma, South Carolina, Texas and Washington. Other states' enabling acts can be grouped as follows:

Standard Act	Bettman	Bassett–Williams
Alabama	Alabama (for counties	Delaware
Colorado	over 400,000)	Massachusetts
Kentucky	Georgia	New Jersey
Maryland	New Hampshire	New York
	New Mexico	Pennsylvania (for 2nd
	Tennessee	class townships)
	Utah	Wisconsin
	Wyoming	

Instead of providing variance procedures for hardship cases, it is also possible to map future streets and widening lines and protect them by a "first right of refusal." Such statutes exist in at least 12 states and unlike hardship laws several of them apply to the mapping of major highways in the open country. Under right of refusal statutes, the governing unit has a specified period of time, 30, 60 or 90 days, for example, after the owner seeks a building permit or indicates an intention to sell within which to buy him out on a voluntary basis or bring condemnation. See Mandelker and Waite, "A Study of Future Acquisition and Reservation of Highway Rights-of-Way" (Mimeo, prepared under Contract CPA 11–8006, 1963) Chart 3, Appendix I. For an illustrative statute of this type, see Wis.Stat. § 84.295 (1961); and see Miller v. City of Beaver Falls, 368 Pa. 189, 82 A.2d 34 (1951).

5. Is a person suing for breach of covenants in a warranty deed charged with knowledge or notice of the official map? See Bibber v. Weber, 199 Misc. 906, 102 N.Y.S.2d 945 (1951), affirmed 278 App.Div. 973, 105 N.Y.S.2d 758 (1951).

SECTION 5. PUBLIC PARTICIPATION IN PRIVATE DEVELOPMENT

In the latter part of the 19th century state constitutions and statutes enforced a strict separation of public and private sectors. Cities were prohibited from investing or participating in private ventures. This separation prevailed until the Great Depression of the 1930's, when several states amended their constitutions to allow public entities to engage in encouraging growth and development to create jobs and rebuild the economies devastated by the depression. Gradually, beginning for the most part in the 1950's, public investment and tax subsidies to private development became commonplace in many jurisdictions—not, however, without controversy.

The availability of federal money through urban renewal programs in the 1950's began the large scale public involvement in redevelopment. In the 1980's and 1990's the decline of federal subsidies has shifted the focus to state programs such as "tax increment" financing and "enterprise zones." Some of the history and current status of the programs are presented here.

The renovation of our urban environment received its first great boost with the enactment of the National Housing Act of 1949,[43] which provided for the clearing of slum areas and their redevelopment for new purposes. In 1953, an advisory commission appointed by President Eisenhower recommended that the slum clearance program include the conservation and rehabilitation of neighborhoods.[44] The term, "urban renewal," was employed as descriptive of the aims and objectives of the program, and the federal statute was amended accordingly.[45]

The urban renewal program is said to be the first federal program to require comprehensive planning.[46] The program itself is carried on through local agencies which acquire deteriorated areas of the urban complex, demolish and remove the obsolete buildings and sell the land under a redevelopment plan for the area; or under which property owners rehabilitate the structures in an area, accompanied by the improvement of community facilities by the local government, resulting in urban conservation. Numerous slum clearance or urban renewal programs have resulted, and these programs have been described at some length in literature on the subject.[47] Not all of these programs, however, nor even the strict concept of urban redevelopment emanated from federal thinking or federal programs. An eminent scholar points out that the urban renewal concept was first conceived in the late twenties and early thirties by such leaders in the field as Harland Bartholomew.[48] Their work, however, did not receive either political or

43. Act of July 15, 1949, Pub.L. No. 81–171, 63 Stat. 413, which was approved July 15, 1949. See "Federal Laws, Urban Renewal," a pamphlet published by the Housing and Home Finance Agency. It is pointed out that the 1949 Act was the culmination of several years of effort to secure a comprehensive federal housing program. In 1946, the Senate passed the Wagner–Ellender–Taft bill, but it failed in the House, and later efforts were unsuccessful until 1949. See Johnstone, The Federal Urban Renewal Program, 25 U.Chi.L.Rev. 301, 311 (1958). See also, on these early efforts, Foard and Fefferman, Federal Urban Renewal Legislation, 25 Law & Contemp.Prob. 635, 636–648 (1960), in which it is pointed out that the 1949 legislation first began to take shape in proposals as early as 1941.

44. President's Advisory Comm. on Gov't Housing Policies and Programs, A Report to the President of the United States 115 (1953).

45. Mandelker, The Comprehensive Planning Requirement in Urban Renewal, 116 U.Pa.L.Rev. 25, n. 3 (1967).

46. Id. at 25.

47. Id. at 44–64, describes the Capitol Hill project in Nashville and the Mill Creek Valley project in St. Louis. See also Johnstone, supra note 43, at 319; the charts in the appendices to Foard and Fefferman, supra note 43, at 701–704; and Note, Citizen Participation in Urban Renewal, 66 Colum.L.Rev. 485, 500–521 (1966).

48. Mandelker, supra note 45, at 27.

financial support and their problems were compounded by the depression. Nonetheless, methods of redeveloping blighted areas were considered in New York and elsewhere during the depression period.[49] Moreover, even before the National Housing Act of 1949, a number of states adopted slum clearance legislation[50] based on model acts which had been prepared. However, it was the federal legislation, activity and financial support which gave the real impetus to urban renewal in the United States.

The 1950's and 1960's were a period during which the earlier housing policies were broadened and the programs expanded. The Housing Act of 1954 included federal assistance for the prevention of urban blight and the spread of slums through rehabilitation provisions and through provisions relating to the conservation of deteriorating areas. It resulted in large measure from the 1953 advisory commission report to the President which was mentioned above. This report sought to involve the private sector to a greater degree by encouraging rehabilitation of existing, deteriorating structures. The cities were to assume greater involvement and responsibility. It was hoped that private enterprise would be more involved also in the development of private residences giving emphasis to providing low-cost housing for displaced families. The thrust was toward prevention of slums and improvement of run-down areas of cities. This 1954 Act was broadened by the Housing Act of 1956 to provide relocation assistance to private citizens and businesses for moving expenses and loss of property due to displacement resulting from urban renewal. Federal funds could be expended for "general neighborhood renewal plans." A new alternative capital grant formula was provided in the Housing Act of 1957, and the Housing Act of 1959 again increased the authorization for federal assistance. There were new provisions for grants to "community renewal programs" intended to provide long-range plans for urban renewal needs in each metropolitan area. Federal grants were again increased in 1961, and the federal percentage of contribution was increased for smaller cities. Throughout the 1960's there was a steady broadening of the program and an increase in funding. Much attention was directed to relocation and rehabilitation. The 1964 Act provided in Title III for a new program of three percent rehabilitation loans for private persons and businessmen in urban renewal areas for improvement of property and provided additional benefits for displaced persons and businesses. The 1965 Act sought to diminish relocation difficulties, and it continued the three percent loan provision.

Extensive changes resulted from the Housing and Urban Development Act of 1968, including the Neighborhood Development Program and grants for open land urban renewal projects. It greatly increased the grant funds, extended the three percent rehabilitation loans to other areas, and authorized HUD to issue grants to aid in alleviating slum and blight in situations where immediate action was needed.

---

49. Id. at 29.   **50.** Johnstone, supra note 43, at 307.

Criticism of urban renewal produced several results. In the Housing and Urban Development Act of 1968, P.L. 90–448, 82 Stat. 476, the urban renewal programs directed toward high-income luxury housing were to be replaced with projects designed to produce low and moderate-income housing. Perhaps the most important result of criticisms, however, was the gradual reduction of availability of federal funds for urban renewal in favor of other programs of HUD. By 1974, urban development, insofar as federal programs are concerned, appears quite different than in 1949, when the first act went into effect.

The Housing and Community Development Act of 1974, P.L. 93–383 purports to consolidate urban renewal and several other community development programs into a new omnibus "block grant" approach designed to give local communities more control over meeting their redevelopment needs. The following summary is from the Senate Report, 1974, Cong. & Adm.News 4273:

"The Committee bill reported herewith is an omnibus bill of 8 chapters covering a broad range of Federal housing and urban development programs. Although the main thrust of the proposed legislation is to consolidate and simplify existing programs, it contains authority for the development of several new programs, the most important of which is a new and far-reaching block grant community development program.

"The consolidation provisions of the bill involve both housing and community development programs. The housing consolidation calls for a complete overhaul of legislation involving the FHA mortgage insurance programs and the low-rent public housing program. The former program goes back to 1934 when the National Housing Act authorized the Federal government insurance of mortgages, and the latter goes back to the United States Housing Act of 1937 which provided the authority for the low-rent public housing program.

"The consolidation of community development programs involved the urban renewal program which was authorized by the Housing Act of 1949 and rewritten by the Housing Act of 1954, also the Model Cities program authorized by the Housing Act of 1966 and several community facility programs authorized by the Housing Acts of 1954, 1955, 1961, and 1965.

"The most significant feature of the bill is the new block grant program to provide Federal assistance to localities for community development. This is brought about by consolidating and simplifying ten categorical urban development grant programs and replacing them with a single, more comprehensive, flexible and soundly financed community development block grant program. The new program finally approved by the Committee is basically the product of S. 1744, the Community Development Assistance Act of 1973 introduced by Senator Sparkman. Many features of the Administration's special revenue sharing Better Communities Act, S. 1743, were also incorporated. The Committee adopted the block grant approach primarily to insure that Federal funds would be used with a priority to eliminate slums and blight and to upgrade and make the Nation's cities more livable, attractive and viable places in which to live. One of the most important provisions of the Committee bill is the development of a 2–year Federal funding cycle at an assured and adequate level so that localities are always working with a known level of Federal grants for the next year as well as the current year subject only to the meeting of minimum Federal performance standards.

"In approving alternative provisions to the Administration-supported special revenue sharing proposals, the Committee followed the Administration's plan calling for an overhaul and consolidation of existing urban renewal and related programs, but disagreed with the proposed plan for distributing Federal funds automatically to the Nation's cities without proper regard to the use of such funds in carrying out national objectives specified in the Act. The Committee bill outlines specific objectives of the program and contains procedures to insure that the Federal funds are used to meet these objectives to the maximum extent feasible. This is done through four requirements.

"(1) a summary of a 4–year plan for meeting the community's development needs, including proposed programs to meet housing needs, to prevent and eliminate slums and blight, and to improve community services; (2) a description of proposed activities and expenditures; (3) a certification that the applicant has met certain requirements related to the objectives of the act, citizen participation, and the provision of housing; and (4) a performance report assessing activities carried out under the program in relation to the community's goals and the bill's objectives.

* * *

"The bill also contains a number of significant amendments to Title V of the Housing Act of 1949 on rural housing. For the most part, the new provisions would broaden or liberalize the provisions of existing law to cover deficiencies in existing law relative to the authority of the Farmers Home Administration to provide assistance for lower income rural families.

"In addition to the consolidation provisions, the development of a new community development program, a major overhaul of the comprehensive planning grant program and a new Federally assisted State housing program, the Committee bill contains an array of miscellaneous provisions that update and perfect existing HUD-administered statutes and related mortgage credit authorities. * * *"

In the early years of the Community Development Block Grant program most of the money, especially in the smaller cities was used for capital improvements in lower income neighborhoods (as measured by census tracts). Water, sewer and street projects for long-neglected areas were paid for with CD funds, and some critics of the program argued that cities were considering CD funds as the only monies that could be made available for improving the neighborhoods occupied by the poorest elements of the population, and thus regular tax revenues of the city would be used anywhere but the target neighborhoods receiving CD projects. By 1977, HUD began to increase monitoring of CD programs and in that year the emphasis began to shift from capital improvements to housing rehabilitation. This shift also meant increased opportunities for minority contractors, one of the goals of the program. Increased monitoring and auditing by HUD also eliminated most of the misapplication of CD funds which occurred in the first years of the program (e.g., use of CD funds to build tennis courts which would primarily benefit upper income neighborhoods).

Litigation involving CDBG programs has been most importantly concerned with the use, misuse or nonuse of CD funds to perpetuate housing discrimination. For example, in United States v. City of Parma, Ohio, 494 F.Supp. 1049 (N.D.Ohio 1980), the court found a racially discriminatory intent under the Fair Housing Act in part by the city's refusal to submit an adequate housing assistance plan in connection with its CDBG application. The court suggested that by rejecting CD funds (the result of its inadequate application) the city was determined to continue its status as an almost totally segregated community. In Angell v. Zinsser, 473 F.Supp. 488 (D.Conn.1979), citizens by the referendum process adopted an ordinance barring further participation in the CDBG program. The court enjoined the town government from withdrawing its application for continued participation in the CDBG program on the ground that the ordinance was designed to prevent the integration of the town, which was overwhelmingly white. The court also stated that withdrawal from the program would probably be a violation of the Fair Housing Act, relying on the Arlington Heights case (Chapter VIII, infra).

Notes

1. After the Supreme Court decision in Berman v. Parker, 348 U.S. 26, 75 S.Ct. 98, 99 L.Ed. 27 (1954), which is reproduced in the previous chapter, litigation over the validity of urban renewal programs was focused mostly in the state courts. One leading case, which exhaustively reviews the decisions in other jurisdictions, and which upheld the urban renewal scheme, is Davis v. City of Lubbock, 160 Tex. 38, 326 S.W.2d 699 (1959). Other cases and authorities favoring urban renewal are:

Redevelopment Agency v. Hayes, 122 Cal.App.2d 777, 266 P.2d 105 (1954), certiorari denied, Van Hoff v. Redevelopment Agency of City and County of San Francisco, 348 U.S. 897, 75 S.Ct. 214, 99 L.Ed. 705 (1954); Gohld Realty Co. v. City of Hartford, 141 Conn. 135, 104 A.2d 365 (1954); Land Clearance for Redevelopment Authority of City of St. Louis v. City of

St. Louis, 270 S.W.2d 58 (Mo.1954); Velishka v. City of Nashua, 99 N.H. 161, 106 A.2d 571, 44 A.L.R.2d 1406 (1954); Miller v. City of Tacoma, 61 Wash.2d 374, 378 P.2d 464 (1963); and David Jeffrey Co. v. City of Milwaukee, 267 Wis. 559, 66 N.W.2d 362 (1954). A list of citations up to the date of the material is provided in HHFA, State Enabling Legislation, Urban Redevelopment and Urban Renewal, List of Citations to Statutes, Constitutional Provisions, and Court Decisions (June 1, 1962). See also, Johnstone, The Federal Urban Renewal Program, 25 U.Chi.L.Rev. 301, 312 (1958); and Annot., Validity, Construction and Effect of Statutes Providing for Urban Redevelopment by Private Enterprise, 44 A.L.R.2d 1414 (1955). In addition to the South Carolina ruling, cases which have held urban renewal enabling legislation to be unconstitutional include Adams v. Housing Authority, 60 So.2d 663 (Fla.1952); Housing Authority of City of Atlanta v. Johnson, 209 Ga. 560, 74 S.E.2d 891 (1953), and State ex rel. Fatzer v. Redevelopment Authority, 176 Kan. 145, 269 P.2d 484 (1954). Also see Brady v. City of Dubuque, 495 N.W.2d 701 (Iowa 1993) where the court upheld a statutory exemption from urban renewal and economic development projects for "century farms." A century farm is defined as one that contains at least 40 acres that has remained in the same family for 100 or more years.

To the contrary, consider Edens v. City of Columbia, 228 S.C. 563, 91 S.E.2d 280 (1956), which was decided after Berman v. Parker, but which adopted a more restrictive interpretation. In the Edens case, the Housing Authority of the city had proceeded under the state's redevelopment law and had determined that an area was a blighted area, principally occupied by slum dwellings. They proposed to take the property, clear it and sell it partly to the University of South Carolina for expansion and partly (the larger part) to private parties for light industrial sites. There was no problem about the portion which was to go to the University, but the court refused to go along with the rest of the scheme because of the plan to ultimately place that part of the land in private hands. The South Carolina Constitution provided that private property could not be taken for *public use* without just compensation. Acknowledging that a "greater number of the decided cases sustain condemnation of private property for 'redevelopment' purposes," the court distinguished a "public use" from a "public purpose" stating: "Some of the decisions of other courts immediately in point that are contrary to our view, which are not distinguishable upon different constitutional provisions or former judicial interpretations, proceed upon the theory that a public use is accomplished by the seizure and destruction of slum or 'blighted' areas and the disposition of the land thereafter to private owners for private purposes is merely incidental. We think that this would be a strained view of the facts in the case sub judice, and we cannot follow it. The purpose here is not to provide better, low-cost housing to the present occupants of the area, or indeed any housing at all; but is to transform it from a predominantly low-class residential area to a commercial and industrial area. It seems to us to be a grandiose plan which cannot be dissected and the result of it reasonably said to be incidental. However desirable the object is from a municipal planning viewpoint, it cannot be attained by exercise of the power of eminent domain. Other contrary decisions hold that restrictions upon the future use of 'redeveloped' land is a public use; but that is in the nature of zoning, which derives from the police power." Also see Mayor and City Council of Baltimore v. Chertkof, 293 Md. 32, 441 A.2d 1044 (1982).

A redevelopment law provided for the clearance, reconstruction and rehabilitation of "substandard" and "insanitary" areas. This was held to contemplate elimination of "slums" and not to apply to vacant land even though covered with abandoned tires, barrels, rubbish and assorted debris. Beebe Imp. Corp. v. City of New York, 129 N.Y.S.2d 263 (Sup.Ct.1954). The court said:

> * * * The area involved in the case at bar is at best an eyesore, and I doubt if it would be seriously contended even by plaintiff that it is not a blight on the community and a detriment to the growing residential quality of the neighborhood. But this does not necessarily mean that it is a slum or insanitary or substandard within the purview of the statute. No persons live in the area. It consists entirely of vacant land—the sheds and shacks in no sense of the word constitute improvements; the only improvements are the gasoline stations and welding plant, and these do not themselves appear to be either substandard or insanitary. I cannot regard this as a condemnation of 'buildings or improvements not in themselves insanitary or substandard' because such taking is necessary for the redevelopment of a slum area, but rather deem it to be the inclusion of a modicum of such structures with an area of vacant land the acquisition of which is the primary purpose of the undertaking.

> I therefore conclude that it may be demonstrated on a trial that the city is here attempting to stretch the concept of 'area' in order to seize private property for a purpose which, laudable as some may consider it, is not within the powers conferred by the Constitution and statutes of the State. A trial of the issues is accordingly necessary to enable the Court to determine whether or not the governmental agencies involved have acted in a capricious and arbitrary manner and applied a statute to a situation to which it was never intended to have application. * * *

Also see Prestonia Area Neighborhood v. Abramson, 797 S.W.2d 708 (Ky. 1990).

3. Must the city pay for even the worst substandard structures or can it order the owner to tear them down at no cost to the city? Assuming an appropriate enabling statute and an appropriate local ordinance and an aggressive inspection and elimination program, the city can save substantial sums in this way. See Rhyne, "Demolition, Vacation or Repair of Substandard Buildings" (Rep. No. 111, NIMLO, 1945). Sometimes the owner will try to delay demolition until a full fledged slum clearance program is instituted largely with federal money. He hopes thereby to be paid for his building instead of having to tear it down at his own expense. Thus in Yen Eng v. Board of Building and Safety Commissioners, 184 Cal.App.2d 514, 7 Cal. Rptr. 564 (1960), officials of the City of Los Angeles ordered the demolition of a 50 year old, wooden, seven story apartment-hotel building, poorly constructed, a fire trap, standing on unsafe footings. The owners stalled. Said the court:

> * * * [I]t is not the province of this reviewing court in this case to consider the cautiously disclosed hope of appellants that with property in the Bunker Hill area being taken for an extensive community

redevelopment project that if they can keep their building from falling down or burning until condemnation proceedings are instituted, they might receive an award of money in payment for a structure which under the present judgment they must at their own expense demolish and remove. We find no comment by appellants on the danger to the lives, persons and property of their tenants and others in case of collapse or fire in the intervening time.

This case and Takata v. City of Los Angeles, 184 Cal.App.2d 154, 7 Cal.Rptr. 516 (1960), and cases cited by the courts in both opinions are evidence of an active inspection and demolition program in the "Downtown Rehabilitation District" of Los Angeles. On the difficulty of drawing the legal line between a building that can be ordered taken down under the police power and one that must be paid for through eminent domain see Guandolo, Housing Codes in Urban Renewal, 25 Geo.Wash.L.Rev. 1, 24 (1956).

Also see Hoeck v. City of Portland, 57 F.3d 781 (9th Cir.1995) where the court held that the city's action in demolishing an old, partially renovated 6–story hotel after the owner lost his financing for the project did not constitute either a physical or regulatory taking.

4.   For a stimulating exchange on the possibilities of encouraging urban renewal through income tax laws, see Sporn, Some Contributions of the Income Tax Law to the Growth and Prevalence of Slums, 59 Colum.L.Rev. 1026 (1959); Blum and Dunham, Income Tax Law and Slums: Some Further Reflections, 60 Colum.L.Rev. 447 (1960); and Sporn, Slums and the Income Tax: A Brief Rejoinder, 60 Colum.L.Rev. 454 (1960).

5.   It is one thing to acquire slums through eminent domain powers of a local public agency and to clear the land. It is another to enlist responsible and competent developers into the kind of private risk taking required for effective, imaginative redevelopment. See Ratcliff, "Private Investment in Urban Redevelopment" (U. of Calif., Real Estate Research Program Rep. No. 17, 1961); and Scheuer, Goldston and Sogg, Disposition of Urban Renewal Land—A Fundamental Problem in the Rebuilding of our Cities, 62 Colum.L.Rev. 989 (1962). The authors of the latter article conclude:

> The cities, in conducting their negotiations and competitive procedures, ought to be wary of competition based upon unreasonable and impractical undertakings by would-be redevelopers. Such misdirected competition can succeed only in bringing into play a Gresham's Law of urban renewal, wherein the irresponsible developers drive out the prudent. Many LPAs [Local Public Agencies] overlook the fact that legal controls and disposition contract covenants can not by themselves assure sound redevelopment.

This is not of course to say that use of covenants in connection with urban redevelopment should be abandoned. See Ascher, "Private Covenants in Urban Redevelopment," Urban Redevelopment: Problems and Practices (Woodbury ed. 1953).

As urban renewal gave way in the mid–1970's to community block grant programs, cities looked for alternative methods of financing redevelopment of run-down areas in the city. What has emerged is a new kind of urban renewal which relies on public sector and private sector cooperation.

R.E. SHORT CO. v. CITY OF MINNEAPOLIS
Supreme Court of Minnesota, 1978.
269 N.W.2d 331.

ROGOSHESKE, JUSTICE.

This is an appeal from a judgment of the district court permanently enjoining and restraining appellants from implementing the parking-facility agreement, the management agreement, and the option agreement contained in the contract entitled "Contract for the Lease and Development of Certain Land in Development District No. 51 (Loring Park)." * * *

In 1971, the legislature enacted L.1971, c. 677, which authorized the cities of Minneapolis and Robbinsdale to create development districts, to issue general obligation bonds to carry out development programs, and to utilize tax-increment financing to pay off the interest and principal on such bonds. In 1974, L.1971, c. 677, § 2, was amended to permit the city of Minneapolis to acquire land or easements by eminent domain. L.1974, c. 357, § 2.

During the same session the legislature also enacted L.1974, c. 485, codified as Minn.St. c. 472A, which authorized other municipalities to create development districts and to utilize tax-increment financing for urban redevelopment. * * *

The purpose of tax-increment financing of urban redevelopment is to create economically productive property where none presently exists by providing inducements to private commercial development. The municipality, either with or without the power of eminent domain, acquires all the property in an area in which the value of real estate is declining or there is a high proportion of underutilized or tax-delinquent land. Pursuant to a development plan for the area, the municipality then delineates a number of new disposition parcels which it markets to private developers. Inducements to such private development include promises to construct certain support facilities or various other types of incentives affording substantial savings to the developer. Once the land becomes productive, the increment over the prior tax revenues is utilized to pay off the interest and principal on the bonds issued to finance the redevelopment, and the municipality retains in its general treasury the amount equal to the former tax revenue from the area. After the bonds are paid off, the area is expected to remain economically productive, providing substantially increased tax revenues for municipal government.

This philosophy of development financing underlays the decision to create the Loring Park Development District just south of downtown Minneapolis. Acting pursuant to L.1971, c. 677, the city council established this district by a resolution dated June 9, 1972. At that time, there were 58 privately owned land parcels, many of which were economically unproductive. The goal of the Loring Park Development District was to renew the area by the private construction of additional residential units, convention and hotel facilities, and various other commercial enterprises. The city also planned to upgrade the public works and beautify the district by constructing the Loring Greenway. All of this development, the city council determined, would provide not only employment during the construction phase of the project but also additional permanent employment, increased tax revenues, and a more productive tax base for the district and the city. In April 1973, the city held the first of four bond sales, and in August it began acquisition of the land, first by purchase and, after April 1974, by eminent domain proceedings. The district was then replatted into 14 disposition parcels which were to be offered to developers willing to construct structures that would conform to the alternative land uses outlined in the development program.

* * *

In 1976, Convention Hotel Associates, the predecessor of appellant Mart Plaza Hotel, Inc., proposed to construct a hotel and trade mart on parcel 2D if the city would build a 750–car, public parking ramp on parcel 2E. In October 1976, the city council issued to it a letter of intent, which was renewed in July 1977. The proposal and the development contract were discussed in two city council committees in December 1977, and the contract was unanimously approved by the council on December 16, 1977. After Mayor Stenvig vetoed this resolution, all interested parties were permitted to present their positions on the proposal to the full city council. The council then weighed the testimony and overrode the veto on December 30, 1977.

Among its terms the contract provided that the city would construct a public parking facility, the lower level of which would be rented by the developer for use as a convention hall. The city also agreed to design the parking ramp to be compatible with the hotel and to ensure that tennis facilities for hotel guests could be erected by the developer on its roof. Another part of the contract contained a management agreement under which the developer was to manage the parking ramp for a term of 20 years, and the developer was granted a 50–year exclusive option to purchase the parking ramp and convention hall. The city, however, retained exclusive control over the ramp. The rates, hours, and methods of operation were to be set by the city, and the hotel, the trade mart, and their customers would receive no preferential treatment. All income from the ramp would go directly to the city, and the entire agreement could be canceled by the city if the developer did not perform in a satisfactory manner. Finally, the ramp and the land upon which it would be constructed were in no way made subordinate to the mortgage that the developer secured to finance the construction of the hotel.

* * *

The major issue presented in this appeal concerns the legality of the decision by the city council that a public purpose would be served by its erection of a public parking ramp to induce a private developer to construct a hotel and trade mart complex on the adjoining property. The trial court found that this expenditure was for a private purpose. We believe that the reason the trial judge erred in reaching this conclusion was because he focused solely on the decision to construct the parking ramp rather than looking at the public benefits that would flow from the development contract for the coordinated construction of a convention hotel *and* a public parking ramp.

The public purpose doctrine which permits the expenditure of public funds only in furtherance of a public purpose is well-settled law in Minnesota. * * * Thus, once the legislature authorizes tax-increment financing by a municipality, declares such financing to serve a public purpose, and enumerates the type of projects that may be so financed and that such projects will serve a public purpose, these declarations are given great weight by the courts. Furthermore, the city, in implementing the powers delegated to it by the legislature, is also vested with broad discretion in determining whether particular projects will serve a public purpose. While such decisions are reviewable, they can only be set aside if it is established that the city's action is manifestly arbitrary and capricious because the projects primarily serve a private interest.

Laws 1971, c. 677, § 1, sets out the public purpose to be served by tax-increment financing of redevelopment by the city of Minneapolis:

> "In mature cities such as Minneapolis * * *, it is found that there is a need for new development in areas of the city which are already built up. * * * This new development is crucial in providing employment opportunities for Minneapolis * * * citizens, in improving the tax base for the community, and in improving the general economy for the metropolitan area. Under this act, the cit[y] of Minneapolis * * * would be authorized to develop a program for improving a district of the city in such ways as * * * providing impetus for commercial development, providing increased employment, * * * providing off-street parking to serve the shoppers and employees of the district; providing open space relief within the district; and providing such other facilities as are outlined in the development program adopted by the governing body. It is hereby declared by the legislature of the state of Minnesota that the actions required to assist the implementation of such development programs are a public purpose and that the execution and financing of such programs are a public purpose."

This statement of public purpose is reiterated almost verbatim in Minn. St. 472A.01. Since the city council has determined that these purposes will be served by the developer's construction of a hotel and trade mart and that the city's construction of a public parking ramp is essential to the developer's decision to construct, under the restricted standard of review a court can only overturn the city's decision if it is found to be manifestly arbitrary and capricious.

There are numerous statutes that declare the construction of public parking ramps in Minneapolis to be in the public interest, L.1971, c. 677, § 1; Minn.St. 472A.01 and 459.14, and respondents do not challenge the construction of the ramp per se. Instead, respondents contend that because the city decided to induce private commercial development of a convention hotel by constructing a public parking ramp; by leasing the ramp to the developer; by leasing the space below the ramp and the air rights above the ramp for conversion into convention facilities and tennis courts, respectively; and by conforming the design of the ramp to the design of the hotel to which it is attached its expenditure of public funds to construct a parking ramp is primarily for the benefit of the hotel developer and thus serves a private, rather than a public, purpose.

Despite the trial court's decision that the city acted improperly in attempting to induce the developer to build the hotel, inducements are routinely permitted by the courts. The legal effect of the construction of a parking ramp is no different from such inducements to commercial redevelopment as the city's sale of the land to a developer at substantially less than its cost of acquisition or its market value or the city's installation, at no cost to the developer, of such utilities as sewer and water. We have gone so far as to approve the condemnation of land by a public authority and its later sale or lease to private developers, Housing & Redevelopment Authority of St. Paul v. Greenman, 255 Minn. 396, 96 N.W.2d 673, and the construction of buildings by the public authority to be leased to private persons, City of Pipestone v. Madsen, 287 Minn. 357, 178 N.W.2d 594; Port Authority of City of St. Paul v. Fisher, 275 Minn. 157, 145 N.W.2d 560; Visina v. Freeman, 252 Minn. 177, 89 N.W.2d 635; Erickson v. King, 218 Minn. 98, 15 N.W.2d 201, as permissible inducements to lure the private sector into the redevelopment plan.[51] Whether the form of inducement used by the city—namely, the construction of a public parking ramp—is an action "required to assist the implementation of * * * development programs," L.1971, c. 677, § 1, is a determination that rests largely with the municipality under the public purpose doctrine.

* * *

---

51. Respondents attempt to distinguish some of these cases on the ground that they involve a different form of financing which would not create general taxpayer liability. Just such a distinction, however, was rejected recently by the Illinois Supreme Court in People ex rel. City of Urbana v. Paley, 68 Ill.2d 62, 73, 11 Ill.Dec. 307, 312, 368 N.E.2d 915, 920 (1977): "We might note here the attempt of the mayor to characterize as critical the distinction between general obligation bonds and revenue bonds.

* * * We believe this contention to be illogical. * * * At issue in this case, * * * is not the existence of a pledge of credit, but rather the nature of the ultimate purpose for which money is spent or credit is pledged or extended. A public purpose insulates the bonds from constitutional attack, whether they be general obligation or revenue bonds." See, also, Richards v. City of Muscatine, 237 N.W.2d 48 (Iowa 1975), upholding tax-increment financing of urban renewal.

The trial court erroneously held that the construction of a public parking ramp served primarily a private, rather than a public, purpose because it was persuaded to view the parking ramp in a vacuum. When the ramp's financing is separated from the dominant purpose of the entire development contract between the city and the developer, the benefits to the developer would appear to outweigh the public benefits and permit the court to conclude that this was an illegal expenditure of public funds. When the development contract is viewed in its entirety, however, the parking ramp becomes a necessary adjunct of a project which, according to the city council, is crucial to the success of the entire development district. Under the proper standard of review, the trial court could only have disregarded the testimony of the city's expert regarding the public benefits to be derived from the construction of the hotel and ramp complex—a $26,000,000–hotel; $1,200,000 in taxes from land that at present generates no taxes; an increased tax base; 700 new jobs; increased liquor taxes and hotel taxes; the revitalization of Minneapolis as a convention and tourist attraction; and the assurance the Loring Park Development District would be successful—if the city's reliance on such evidence were completely unreasonable. Since respondents introduced no evidence that such was the case, the city's reliance on this evidence in approving the proposed uses for parcels 2D and 2E cannot be disregarded. These enumerated public benefits upon which the city council relied preclude a conclusion that its decision to accept the development contract was based on whim or caprice or was completely unsupported by the evidence.

* * *

Reversed.

Notes

1. In accord with the principal case is Richards v. Muscatine, 237 N.W.2d 48 (Iowa 1975) which upheld tax increment financing against an attack that alleged a disparate burden on taxpayers outside the redevelopment area for the duration of the project; the court also rejected an argument that the scheme violated a constitutional provision on uniformity of taxation, holding that the private developer pays taxes on his development at the same rate as all other taxpayers. Compare Miller v. Covington Development Auth., 539 S.W.2d 1 (Ky.1976) where the court held tax increment financing violative of the state constitution and struck down the statute with State v. Miami Beach Redevelopment Agency, 392 So.2d 875 (Fla.1980), upholding the Florida statute.

Most of the cases which present a broad constitutional attack on the tax increment financing programs have upheld the theory of the device. In addition to the principal case and those cited above, see Tax Increment Financing Comm'n of Kansas City v. J.E. Dunn Construction Co., Inc., 781 S.W.2d 70 (Mo.1989); Dennehy v. Department of Revenue, 308 Or. 423, 781 P.2d 346 (1989); In re Request for Advisory Opinion on Constitutionality of 1986 PA 281, 430 Mich. 93, 422 N.W.2d 186 (1988); City of El Paso v. El Paso Community College Dist., 729 S.W.2d 296 (Tex.1986); Wolper v. City

Council of City of Charleston, 287 S.C. 209, 336 S.E.2d 871 (1985); Meier-henry v. City of Huron, 354 N.W.2d 171 (S.D.1984); Kuehn, Tax Increment Financing, Land Use Law (May, 1985) p. 3.

2. Even in states which have upheld tax increment financing, courts may give close scrutiny to the specific projects proposed. See, e.g., Downey Cares v. Downey Community Development Comm'n, 196 Cal.App.3d 983, 242 Cal.Rptr. 272 (1987) (ordinance invalidated because one city council member owned property and a real estate business within the redevelopment area); Emmington v. Solano County Redevelopment Agency, 195 Cal.App.3d 491, 237 Cal.Rptr. 636 (1987) (occasional flooding and lack of infrastructure insufficient to support a finding that the area was blighted); East Grand County School Dist. No. 2 v. Town of Winter Park, 739 P.2d 862 (Colo.App. 1987) (failure to hold required public meetings not cured by submitting proposal to voters); Card v. Community Redevelopment Agency of South Pasadena, 61 Cal.App.3d 570, 131 Cal.Rptr. 153 (1976) (taxpayers successful-ly challenged a project which made no provision for relocation of displaced citizens); Regus v. City of Baldwin Park, 70 Cal.App.3d 968, 139 Cal.Rptr. 196 (1977) (evidence failed to show that the redevelopment area was blight-ed). Compare Smith v. Independence Tax Increment Finance Comm'n, 919 S.W.2d 292 (Mo.App.1996). The Regus case illustrates one of the frequently heard criticisms of tax increment financing, that the scheme provides more benefits for the private developer than for the public. Do you think the principal case provides a sufficient answer to that criticism? Another criti-cism of such redevelopment programs is that the city chooses redevelopment projects which are most likely to generate tax increments, e.g., shopping centers and office buildings, rather than housing projects for low-income or even moderate-income persons.[52] In Reed–Custer Community Unit School Dist. No. 255–U v. City of Wilmington, 253 Ill.App.3d 503, 192 Ill.Dec. 421, 625 N.E.2d 381 (1993) the court struck down a proposed TIF district. The plaintiffs, a local school district, a library district and a mosquito abatement district claimed that the defective TIF District would eat into their property tax revenues. The court found that a prerequisite for a TIF district under Illinois law was that the land be substantially vacant. Here the 600 acre proposed district, a former strip mine area, was occupied by a sales office, a beach house, maintenance and storage buildings, and twelve permanent homes. (Also, there were more than 100 recreational vehicles parked in the area, although the court could not clarify their status under the statute).

3. The "public purpose" doctrine delineated by the court in the princi-pal case was extended to include a sports stadium in Lifteau v. Metropolitan Sports Facilities Comm'n, 270 N.W.2d 749 (Minn.1978), and in City of Minneapolis v. Wurtele, 291 N.W.2d 386 (Minn.1980), the court upheld the eminent domain power of redevelopment districts. Also see CLEAN v. State, 130 Wash.2d 782, 928 P.2d 1054 (Wash. 1996) where the court found the state's stadium act consistent with the public purpose provision of the Washington constitution. The sports stadium problem is rather common in recent years. Should the public extend its credit to the development of an

---

52. In 1980, the California legislature amended its statutes to require that twenty percent of the revenues from some TIF projects be placed in a "Low and Moderate Income Housing Fund" to be used for hous-ing assistance. Cal.Health & Safety Code § 33487. See Craig v. City of Poway, 28 Cal.App.4th 319, 33 Cal.Rptr.2d 528 (1994).

expensive stadium either to satisfy a local sports franchise or to lure one? Is it a good deal for the public? See Ronald Smothers, Cities Warned the Odds Aren't Good in Sports Deals, N.Y. Times, Sept. 18, 1995, p. A 7.

4. In Cannata v. City of New York, 11 N.Y.2d 210, 227 N.Y.S.2d 903, 182 N.E.2d 395 (1962), sixty-eight home owners in a section of Brooklyn sought a declaratory judgment that an ordinance was unconstitutional on its face and as applied to them. The provision authorized cities to condemn for reclamation and redevelopment purposes predominantly vacant areas which are economically dead to the point that their existence impairs community growth and tends to promote slums. The ordinance listed various criteria for determining such areas. Of the area involved in the case, 75% was vacant. The trial court and appellate division held for the city. On appeal, the Court of Appeals affirmed, stating: "This complaint does not allege any failure to carry out any of the statutory procedures. It points out that the Planning Board in this case made findings not only as to the vacancy of a large part of the area but also of these statutory factors: that the land is subdivided into plots of such form, shape and insufficient size as to prevent effective economic development, that the streets are obsolete and of poorly designed patterns, and that the improvements are scattered and incompatible with appropriate development. The real basis of the complaint is its statement that there is in the area no such 'tangible physical blight' as to constitute the area a slum. Plaintiffs' argument, most simply put, is that this taking is not for a 'public use' because it is a taking of nonslum land for development into a so-called 'Industrial Park' or area set aside for new industrial development. We agree with the courts below that an area does not have to be a 'slum' to make its redevelopment a public use nor is public use negated by a plan to turn a predominantly vacant, poorly developed and organized area into a site for new industrial buildings." The court added that the condemnation of "substandard real estate by a municipality for redevelopment by private corporations has long been recognized as a species of public use." In his dissent, Justice Van Voorhis stated that this case was not one involving slum clearance "as the condemnation site was held to be in Kaskel v. Impellitteri, 306 N.Y. 73, 115 N.E.2d 659. The present exercise of the power of eminent domain transcends anything involved therein. * * * This proceeding is not instituted on the basis that this area is substandard or insanitary but that the city will be improved if real property in good condition is transferred to other private owners who, in the judgment of city planners, will use it for more progressive purposes deemed to be more in accord with development of the municipality. Such a practice may bear hard on the owner, * * * and in a world where politics is seldom absent from municipal administration, runs the risk of having his property taken from him to be transferred to more deserving owners."

5. Also see Opinion of the Justices, 332 Mass. 769, 126 N.E.2d 795 (1955). An act which concerned the development of an area in the Back Bay portion of Boston which had been abandoned or about to be abandoned was declared unconstitutional where it provided for the development of such area to prevent economic blight and a potential breeding place for crime; the court declaring, among other things, that the area was not presently a slum and that there was "only an apprehension lest it become one." In Sweetwater Valley Civic Ass'n v. National City, 18 Cal.3d 270, 133 Cal.Rptr. 859, 555

P.2d 1099 (1976), the court found a golf course could not be designated as blighted in order for a redevelopment agency to build a shopping center.

6. For an attack on urban blight through vigorous enforcement of "fix-up" ordinances requiring interior plastering, whitewashing, hot water equipment, minimum room temperatures, etc., see Newark v. Charles Realty Co., 9 N.J.Super. 442, 74 A.2d 630 (1950), and Newark v. Charlton Holding Co., 9 N.J.Super. 433, 74 A.2d 641 (1950). The ordinances were upheld. See Annot., Validity and Construction of Statute or Ordinance Providing for Repair or Destruction of Residential Building by Public Authorities at Owner's Expense, 43 A.L.R.3d 916 (1972).

7. Virtually every state has enacted legislation allowing communities to establish enterprise zones, and a majority of states have tax increment financing legislation. As the principal case illustrates, the two devices often go hand in hand. Although the statutes on enterprise zones differ, a typical preamble reads:

> The legislature of Alabama hereby finds and declares that the health, safety and welfare of the people of Class 1 cities are enhanced by the continual encouragement, development, growth and expansion of private enterprise within this state. That there are certain economically depressed areas in such cites that need particular attention to create new jobs, stimulate economic activity and attract private sector investment rather than government subsidy to improve the quality of life of their citizens. It is the purpose of this section to encourage new economic activity in these depressed areas of such Class 1 cities by means of reduced taxes and the removal of unnecessary governmental barriers to the production and earning of wages and profits and the creation of economic growth.

Alabama Code § 11–40–16.

The key to enterprise zones is tax reduction incentives to encourage private redevelopment; many of the statutes also provide for zoning incentives and relaxation of exactions. Public infrastructure improvements may be allowed. Challenges to designation of enterprise zones are rare, as are challenges to particular proposals.

8. Although dated, a good general reference to the problems of revival of cities through tax subsidy programs is Mandelker, Feder & Collins, "Reviving Cities with Tax Abatement," (Rutgers Univ. Ctr. for Urban Policy Research, 1980).

9. When state or local governments use the techniques of tax increment financing and enterprise zones in areas which are not truly blighted, the propriety of the action is clearly questionable. Consider the following report, Wilkerson, "What Illinois Gave to Keep Sears," New York Times, Aug. 27, 1989:

* * *

Amid reports that Sears was planning to move from the Chicago Loop to Texas or North Carolina, state officials suggested that there was a suitable site in the suburb of Hoffman Estates, 35 miles northwest of the city. The officials not only offered $61 million to prepare the location and build highways near it, but also pledged that the town would be designated an enterprise zone, making Sears eligible for a host of incentives normally used to attract businesses to depressed areas.

* * *

Hoffman Estates, a community where houses cost as much as $300,000 and unemployment is 3.2 percent, would not normally qualify as an enterprise zone. With Sears promising thousands of jobs, the State Legislature changed the law so that Hoffman Estates would qualify.

Meanwhile, vast stretches of Chicago's rundown West Side that were already designated as enterprise zones remained abandoned, and legislators from the area opposed the Hoffman Estates deal. But the critics were even angrier about the approval of a second measure allowing Sears to qualify for another incentive. The benefit, called tax increment financing, is essentially a giveaway program usually reserved for companies willing to locate in bleak neighborhoods. Extending this incentive to the Sears–Hoffman Estates deal—and to other potential arrangements in which 2,000 or more jobs are gained—means Sears will acquire an 800–acre site valued at $100 million in exchange for agreeing to pay property taxes on the land.

State officials argued that the arrangement would leave Hoffman Estates "less blighted."

The type of outrage described by the above article exists in other states as well. In 1995 the Colorado state auditor reported that the state's enterprise zone program had failed to help blighted communities, and he cited national research to the effect that tax incentives do not necessarily create jobs. The Denver Post, Dec. 26, 1995, p. 1. On the following day the newspaper continued its exposé with a front-page article describing how $12.5 million of enterprise zone funds since 1989 went to help all sorts of charities and non-profits rather than poor areas; some of the recipients named were the Potato Administrative Committee in Monte Vista, Colorado; the Southeast Game and Fish Club in Lamar, Colorado; the University of Southern Colorado Sports Complex. The Denver Post, Dec. 27, 1995 p. 1.

Chapter VII

THE BASICS OF ZONING

SECTION 1. HISTORY OF ZONING

Even by American standards, in which it seems that each decade differs from the one which came before and the one which is yet to come, zoning is a relatively recent phenomenon. One of America's great cities, Houston, has yet to enact a zoning ordinance, and it may be contended by some that Houston has gotten along about as well in its urban development as cities which have passed such ordinances. Houston may not have zoned, but neither has it thereafter participated in permitting the numerous variances or exceptions of cities which have zoning provisions, nor has it indulged itself in excessive "spot zoning" or the like. An immediate and initial question, therefore, which the student must ask himself and must carry with him throughout this chapter, is that of whether zoning is *in fact* an effective instrument for the controlled and orderly development of land use in such a way as to promote the community welfare. This latter concern is, after all, the underlying legal rationale (emanating from the police power) by which zoning is sustained and justified.

If you conclude, at least theoretically, that zoning *is* justified and that a rational basis exists to sustain the validity of the principle and the aim involved, then you should consider how effective zoning is or has been in the light of rulings by courts or administrative agencies. To what extent have such rulings impinged upon the theoretical validity, the philosophical underpinnings, and the legal rationale of zoning as an effective device to control the ordered development and use of land for the general benefit?

These are hard questions which are not intended to be hostile to the basic concept of zoning. But the student would do well at this point to divest himself of any view which he may have of zoning as a panacea for either the ills of the cities or for land-use planning within them. As lawyers, we are almost instinctively pragmatists in the Holmesian tradition. We face reality as we find it. And part of that reality is the recognition that the effectiveness of zoning will vary from community to community and from state to state. Houston's non-zoning may thus turn

771

out to be no less effective in some circumstances than the charade in which some zoned communities participate.

As inventive as we have been, we Americans are generally not credited with inventing zoning. One authority states that zoning for use first emanated from a decree by Napoleon in 1810.[1] He also points out that several decades later, the Prussian Code provided a more comprehensive development of the concept and that this was later followed and developed by the laws of the German empire.[2] Another authority refers to the beginnings of zoning in Germany in 1884, although he also makes reference to French activity in the laying out of Parisian boulevards in 1853.[3]

To the contrary, however, a bulletin for the United States Department of Agriculture states that zoning regulations have been in use in various and sporadic ways for several centuries, beginning in this country long before we were one nation in the settlement along the Atlantic seaboard.[4] These early precursors of modern zoning regulated gunpowder mills and storehouses; and later on, fire districts were established in some cities with wooden buildings being prohibited in certain areas.[5] It is stated that as early as 1692, Massachusetts' authorization of certain market towns to assign places for slaughterhouses and similar noxious businesses constituted zoning.[6] This same source points out that in 1889, a Wisconsin statute permitted municipalities to designate fire zones and control buildings erected therein.[7]

Be that as it may, it is generally agreed that the first zoning ordinance in the United States which possessed any comprehensive or well-rounded approach was that adopted in New York City in 1916, and subsequently sustained in a state court decision a few years later.[8] In 1923, Wisconsin extended zoning to land areas outside of the corporate limits of municipalities, and in 1929, it authorized rural zoning.[9] Clearly, then, despite such antecedents as we might look back upon, comprehensive zoning in America is a product of the last sixty years or so, and for most cities and towns, it is of even more recent vintage.

McGOLDRICK, ET AL., BUILDING REGULATIONS IN NEW YORK CITY
91–93 (1944).

* * * The increase in population, the construction of subways and elevated lines, and the erection of skyscrapers during the first years of the twentieth century, combined to create dense centers of residence and

1. Metzenbaum, Law of Zoning 12 (1955).

2. Id.

3. Yokley, Zoning Law and Practice 4 (1978). See also Gallion and Eisner, The Urban Pattern 79 (2d ed. 1963).

4. Solberg, "Rural Zoning in the United States" (Ag.Info.Bull. 59, U.S.D.A., 1952).

5. Id.

6. Id.

7. Id.

8. Lincoln Trust Co. v. The Williams Building Corp., 229 N.Y. 313, 128 N.E. 209 (1920).

9. Solberg, supra note 4.

business. But this development was unplanned and haphazard. The absence of effective legal controls on the use, height and area of buildings created a condition which verged on economic and social calamity. In various parts of the city there was a mushroom growth of office buildings and hotels which occupied every square inch of their plots and rose to formidable heights. Not only did the ordinary citizen suffer from the resulting darkened buildings and insufficient air, but throughout the city property owners themselves faced economic death through the destruction of existing realty values. Garages and gasoline selling stations nestled next door to costly homes. Factories sprawled over residence districts. Business areas were invaded by industrial buildings.

Out of this chaos came a demand for some orderly solution that would prevent the city from becoming a tangle of tall conglomerate buildings whose streets would be dark and airless canyons. It was also essential to protect established real estate values. The solution born of three years of painstaking research and investigation was forthcoming in 1916 when the Board of Estimate adopted the Building Zone Resolution. The principle of zoning had already found expression in certain isolated instances not only in New York itself but in other cities as well. Los Angeles had adopted an elementary zoning ordinance regulating only the building uses; Boston had made provision for height regulations, and numerous cities had established fire districts. But New York's 1916 zoning ordinance was epoch-making in that it was a complete and comprehensive system of building control. It established restrictions on the uses to be permitted for property within the city, the height of buildings and the proportion of the area which might be built upon. These regulations applied throughout the five boroughs of the city.

The resolution was aimed generally at the promotion of the general welfare, public health and public safety, and, more particularly safety from fire, adequate light and air and convenience of access. Its provisions were prospective and not retroactive in their effect. It did not attempt to cure past and existing evils by ordering the demolition of particular types of buildings or the removal of certain types of businesses to other areas. But it did prescribe a rational plan for future building in the city.

The resolution adopted what was then a sensible, but what is now an antiquated, arrangement. It provided for three separate classes of districts, each expressed in a separate set of maps. These classes of districts dealt with use, height and land coverage (i.e., area to be left vacant). Within each of these categories various distinctions were made. Thus, use districts were divided into residence districts, business districts and unrestricted districts. In the first, trade and industry of every kind were prohibited. In the second, various specified trades and industries were excluded. For the most part, the excluded trades and industries were nuisance types of manufacturing such as boiler making, ammonia manufacturing, paint manufacturing and the like. In the third, any kind of industrial business or residential use was permitted. * * *

STATEMENT OF JOHN FOX, NEW YORK CITY, 1925 PROCEEDINGS, NATIONAL CONFERENCE ON CITY PLANNING

499–500.

I first want to take this opportunity to express our gratitude to Germany for the introduction of zoning into this country. In 1907 Mr. Benjamin Marsh started the preaching of zoning but it wasn't until Mr. Frank B. Williams in 1916 brought back from Germany the details—the maps and ordinances—that we really had a clear understanding of its value.

TRANSLATED REMARKS OF DR. J. STÜBBEN, MÜNSTER, WESTPHALIA, GERMANY, IN REPLY

500–501.

Dr. Stübben wishes to thank the delegates for the gracious expression of indebtedness to Germany for the principles of zoning. The German zoning movement had the same difficulty with the courts in the early stages that we are having. Gradually the very necessity of civilized life under modern complex conditions gave zoning its opportunity, and its usefulness and its relationship to social welfare became so apparent that the courts were forced to recognize its legality. * * *

STATEMENT BY HARLAND BARTHOLOMEW, ST. LOUIS, 1925 PROCEEDINGS, NATIONAL CONFERENCE ON CITY PLANNING

501–502.

Most of the favorable decisions on zoning appear to me to be the result of a clear expression of ideas and the principles in the minds of city planners by competent lawyers. I should like to cite two illustrations. Two years ago the Ware case in Wichita, Kansas, was decided by the Supreme Court in favor of the constitutionality of zoning. More recently Mr. Ware brought a whole series of cases involving practically every phase of zoning. When these cases came before the court, the city was represented by an exceedingly able city attorney who presented to the courts the broader aspects of zoning and only ten days ago one of the most clean-cut and remarkable decisions in favor of zoning was handed down, sustaining, among other things, one-family districts and the principles of the nonconforming use.

* * *

Another case emphasized the importance of getting broad principles to the attention of the court. The Illinois Supreme Court some time ago handed down an adverse decision in the Aurora case, which seemed to nullify most of the zoning in Illinois. Lawyers seem to agree that the case was poorly handled from a legal standpoint. At about the same time in the same court there were argued two cases from Evanston on zoning. The court did not pass immediately on the case because questions of fact and principle were raised which caused them to think, with the result that the Aurora Case has been reopened. The lawyers interested in the Evanston and Chicago suburb cases have gotten the minds of the courts raised above mere minutiae, to the relationship of zoning to the social well being.

Although seventy-five years is a short span in the affairs of mankind, the pervasive growth of the institution of zoning in the large and small cities of the United States has generated a spate of books and articles dealing with the subject. For the student who wishes to understand zoning in the overall sense, as an institution, four books are highly recommended. In Toll, Zoned American (1969), the author presents a detailed and perceptive history of the 1916 New York zoning ordinance. This book by an author who is also an attorney is well-illustrated and highly readable; also, it presents a fine account of the litigation on zoning in the early years, especially the landmark Euclid case decided by the Supreme Court of the United States.

Babcock, The Zoning Game (1966), is an account of municipal zoning practices and policies as seen through the eyes of one of the nation's best known practitioners of planning law. Particularly useful is the author's discussion of zoning decision-making analyzed from the points-of-view of various participants in the process. The student who reads this book will also acquire some insight into the unwritten law of zoning, i.e., the decision-making process in the vast multitude of cases which never reach the courts. Also see the later works, Weaver & Babcock, City Zoning: The Once and Future Frontier (1979); Babcock & Siemon, The Zoning Game Revisited (1985).

A more theoretical approach to zoning will be found in Mandelker, The Zoning Dilemma (1971). Professor Mandelker presents an excellent account of the legal framework for zoning and then focuses on a typical type of difficult zoning problem, apartment housing in the suburbs.

Finally, in Siegan, Land Use Without Zoning (1972), the student will find an articulate, well-documented attack on the social utility of zoning. Among other things, the author presents a detailed comparison between Houston and comparable cities which are zoned. Mr. Siegan's basic conclusions are that zoning does not maintain or protect property values, nor does it aid in the implementation of planning.

As we move into the last decade of the twentieth century, the relationship between zoning (and other land use control devices) and environmental controls assumes greater importance. In the latest jargon, we must pay greater attention to the interface between zoning and environmental regulation. As attorneys we usually are concerned with process and procedure to a greater extent than the average person, and attorneys will be the first to struggle with the problem of resolving conflicts between independent institutions. The beginnings of this problem can be discerned in the following overview of zoning:

FIFTH ANNUAL REPORT OF THE COUNCIL ON ENVIRONMENTAL QUALITY

Pp. 51–54 (1974).

Zoning, the most common system of land use control, attempts to predesignate the purposes for which land can be used. In doing so, it serves to segregate uses into assigned geographic areas, keeping, for example, heavy industries apart from residences, or even single family housing apart from multifamily housing.

Zoning can have significant impact on land values, though the direction and significance of the impact depends on how well zoning is administered and on supply and demand situations in the land market. The character of a residential neighborhood, for example, is a major determinant of the value of its houses. Zoning assists in the creation and preservation of these characteristics by excluding conflicting land uses, such as industry and large-scale commerce. Zoning may also increase property values by restricting the amount of land available for particular uses. For example, if there is a large demand for multifamily housing but very little land zoned for that purpose, the small supply of land is likely to find a very high market price.

Zoning can also reduce property values. Land that is permanently zoned for less profitable uses, such as agriculture or large-lot single family homes, will bring a lower price than land zoned for higher density uses. The degree to which land can be restricted to less profitable uses is an issue of constitutional law * * *.

Zoning has certain inherent problems as a land use control. Inasmuch as it can change the price of land from its free market value, zoning may create economic incentives which work against the successful implementation of the desired development patterns. For example, if two parcels of land, alike in every other respect, are zoned for different purposes—e.g., one for multifamily and the other for single family housing—and if the land prices differ because multifamily development is more profitable, then a potential developer of multifamily units has an incentive to buy the cheaper land and use his influence in the locality to get the zoning changed. When this "spot zoning" occurs, it results in such land use aberrations as garden apartments surrounded by farms— not where proper land use planning would locate apartments nor even where they would be built were there a completely free market.

A second problem with zoning derives from its underlying assumption that different uses should be segregated. In terms of convenience, environmental effects, and energy consumption, there are often significant advantages to locating neighborhood facilities such as a grocery store or a pharmacy within a residential area. Traditional zoning, however, generally prohibits such an intermingling of uses. Recent trends in planning and zoning seek to remedy this deficiency by moving toward a more beneficial integration of different land uses at the proper scale.

An even more basic question in zoning is whether it is possible, or even desirable, for a community to establish firm criteria for land use that are expected to remain unchanged over a long period of time. Experience suggests that it is not. Commonly, zoning regulations are transformed. Amendments and variances which were originally intended as rarely used safety valves often become the rule. As a result, zoning provides neither stability of use nor a logical mechanism for definition of use. * * *

Aside from various inherent problems, the manner in which communities actually implement their zoning ordinances is often criticized. It is said that many communities have intentionally or unintentionally adopted zoning regulations which effectively bar low or even middle income housing from the community, primarily through regulation of lot size, frontage, living space, and setback.

It is generally, though not unanimously, accepted that zoning plays a part in the determination of housing costs. Because housing costs and lot size has a direct and positive relationship to municipal tax revenues, while public service costs per given household are relatively constant regardless of housing costs, municipalities have an incentive to engage in "fiscal" zoning—attempting to maximize the revenue provided by the land and improvements, while limiting the number of new families entering the community.

Many communities have adopted large-lot zoning in the belief that it will preserve open space and slow development. Under these ordinances, a house may be built only if it is on a lot of several acres. But large-lot zoning may increase environmental problems and create undesirable economic and social consequences. It is damaging to environmental quality in that it takes low density development farther and farther into the countryside. This requires more roads because of the greater distances and necessitates more travel by car, thereby increasing energy consumption and air pollution. As a result of the greater distances between houses, large-lot zoning forces communities to pay more per resident for sewer, electric, water, and other infrastructure systems, which in turn leads to increased property taxes and provides additional stimulus for "fiscal" zoning.

Fortunately, there are new zoning techniques available which deal more efficiently with some of the problems of traditional zoning. Two of the most important are the planned unit development (PUD) and the special purpose district.

The PUD technique is seeing increased use across the country, particularly in communities at the urban fringe. Usually embodied as part of the local zoning ordinance, it provides increased flexibility for the design and siting of residential development. Under the PUD technique, the builder is permitted to aggregate the total density permitted for his tract into clusters of higher density development. The specific plan is determined through negotiation between the developer and the planning board, working within broad legislative guidelines. For the developer, this results in savings in building costs. For the community, it preserves relatively large unbroken areas of open space (usually 10–20 percent of the total) and reduces many of the costs caused by typical sprawl development.

The PUD technique can apply equally well to luxury developments or moderate priced housing. Some of the most desirable housing in many communities is located in the PUD's where savings in housing costs are applied to better community facilities. Or the cost savings can be used to provide a greater diversity in housing to serve better the individual needs and economic capabilities of potential residents. Smaller units for elderly residents, for example, can be interspersed with larger residences.

The second innovative technique is the special purpose district. Like the PUD, the special district is typically a part of the local zoning ordinance, designed generally to give greater leeway in development and to break traditional zoning's inflexible focus on the single lot. Whereas the PUD is designed for new developments, the special purpose district generally is created to protect existing desirable uses in particular areas of social, cultural, or historical importance that are threatened by pressures for redevelopment. The special purpose district is subject to controls on design and use, and it provides various incentives and bonuses to complying developers.

The technique has been used most often in the preservation of historic districts, such as New York City's Greenwich Village. But it has found application as well in other areas of that city, where it has helped to revitalize the Broadway theatre district, to encourage the continued existence of luxury shops along Fifth Avenue, and to preserve low income housing.

Special purpose districts and PUD's attempt to come to terms with the problems and potentials of a specific area. Both techniques grow from a recognition that normal zoning ordinances are often too clumsy to deal with the delicate process of preserving and enhancing environmental quality.

GOLDMAN v. CROWTHER

Court of Appeals of Maryland, 1925.
147 Md. 282, 128 A. 50, 38 A.L.R. 1455.

[Only a small part of the lengthy opinion is given.]

OFFUTT, J. Daniel Goldman and his wife, as tenants by the entireties, own the property known as 1513 Park Avenue in a part of Baltimore City, which, under Ordinance No. 922 of the Mayor and City Council of

Baltimore City, known as the "zoning ordinance," is classified as a residence district. In May, 1923, Goldman undertook to use the basement of a four story dwelling on that property for repairing, by hand and an ordinary sewing machine, for hire, used clothing for such patrons as had occasions to require his services. The business which he thus carried on required no alteration or repair of the building, and in the opinion of Goldman no permit was necessary to use it for that purpose. He was however informed that by so using it without a permit he was violating certain ordinances of the Mayor and City Council of Baltimore and shortly thereafter he was arrested for such violation, and while that complaint against him was pending he applied to the inspector of buildings of Baltimore City for a permit to use the premises for the purposes referred to. The inspector of buildings refused to grant the permit, partly at least on the ground that he was compelled under the zoning law to disapprove applications for such a use of property in a residence district. Goldman then filed in the Superior Court of Baltimore City a petition in which he asked that a writ of mandamus be issued against the building inspector of Baltimore City and the mayor of said city, directing them to issue to him a permit for the use of his premises for the purposes referred to above. The defendants answered that petition, and in their answer they averred that the permit was refused not only upon the authority of the zoning ordinance, but as well, upon the authority of other ordinances of the City of Baltimore vesting a discretion in the building inspector as to the issuance of permits in such cases, and that in refusing the permit in this case the building inspector acted in the exercise of that discretion. In connection with such issues of fact as were presented by the petition and the answer thereto, an agreed statement of facts was filed, and from that statement and the admissions found in the pleadings it further appears that the real and substantial reason for refusing the permit was that Goldman's property is located in a residence district of Baltimore City, the outlines of which are fixed by the zoning ordinance referred to. The verdict of the trial court was in favor of the defendants and the writ of mandamus refused, and from the judgment on that verdict this appeal was taken.

The important and controlling, and indeed under the agreed statement of fact the only question presented by the appeal is whether the zoning ordinance of Baltimore City, known as Ordinance No. 922, in so far as it affects the right of the appellant to use his property in the manner we have described, is a valid and an enforceable enactment, and in dealing with that question it can be said that there is nothing in the record from which it can be inferred that such use is offensive to the eye, the ear, or the nose of a person of ordinary sensibilities, or that it imperils the public health, welfare or safety, any more than would the same character of work if done by Goldman for himself and his family, except that possibly more of it is done.

This question can be approached by either of two avenues: One legal; the other political and sociological. If approached by the former the validity of the restraints and prohibitions of the ordinance must depend upon whether they violate certain definite guaranties and assurances found in the Federal and State Constitutions and the law of the land. If approached by the latter, the question is to an extent freed from the embarrassment of harmonizing any apparently repugnant provisions of the act with those guaranties, since in such case the end to be accomplished and the benefit to be derived are the main factors to be considered, and the rights of mere individuals may be subordinated to the public convenience, upon the principle that such rights are always subject to the paramount authority of the State to subordinate them to what is conceived by those speaking for it to be for the benefit of the State, as representing all the citizens.

Which one of these two methods of approach should be used in this case is a question which goes to the root of our system of government, but without referring further to that, it is sufficient to say that in our opinion, we are not at liberty to examine the question from any other than a legal standpoint, and therefore we cannot be controlled in our consideration of the validity of this ordinance by its possible benefit to the public, if in point of fact that benefit is purchased by appropriating the rights and property of individuals to the public use without just compensation, and by the violation of the guaranties of the State and Federal Constitutions.

* * *

By this ordinance all the land in the city of Baltimore is subjected to restrictions which limit the number of families who may dwell on it, the use to which it may be put, the height of buildings which may be constructed on it, and the proportion of each lot of ground which a building may occupy, except that in the "industrial use district" the land or structures thereon may be used for any lawful purpose. Many of these restrictions relating to the use of property bear no apparent relation to the public health, safety or welfare, nor does the ordinance contain any definite or fixed standards by which the reasonableness or the necessity for the restrictions may be measured or determined, nor are they necessarily uniform or definite in their application. For after specifying with the most meticulous particularity the nature, extent and application of the restrictions, the board of zoning appeals is authorized in its discretion to disregard the "strict letter" of the ordinance, and to vary or modify any of the regulations or provisions contained in it relating to "the use, construction or alteration of buildings or structures or the use of land, so that the spirit of the ordinance shall be observed, public safety and welfare secured and substantial justice done." This sonorous but vague and cloudy formula is to say the least of it a poor and uncertain substitute for those guaranties of the State and Federal Constitutions which assure to every citizen the right to hold and enjoy and use his property in any manner he pleases so long as he does not thereby injuriously affect the health, security or welfare of his neighbor or the public, as the words health, security and welfare have hitherto been understood in this State. There may also be an appeal from the board of zoning appeals to the Baltimore City Court, but that remedy, if anything, increases rather than lessens the difficulty and hardship which the ordinance inflicts upon the landowner, for it only transfers the discretion from the board of zoning appeals, which would presumably have some special knowledge and training, to a jury which might have none and who, in the absence of any fixed or definite rules or standards to guide them, would naturally exercise that discretion varyingly in accordance with the views of different juries.

Before dealing with the constitutionality of the ordinance in whole or in part, we will refer briefly to the territory upon which it is to operate.

From a small village containing a few scattered houses on the shores of the Patapsco in 1729, Baltimore City has grown into a great maritime city, with a population currently estimated in round numbers at eight hundred thousand, occupying over eighty square miles. Within its confines are found an infinite variety of commercial and industrial enterprises and activities. Its commerce is borne over the world by great land and water transportation systems which serve its people. It includes within its boundaries property devoted to every variety of use, including residential, commercial, agricultural, industrial, maritime and recreational. It is constantly expanding and constantly with its growth and changing conditions the use of property in it changes, so that what was formerly residential property has become commercial property, and property which was at one time most useful for commercial or agricultural purposes is now most valuable for industrial purposes. Heretofore these changes have been in response to conditions created by the growth of the city, the increase of its population, the demands of new enterprises, changes in transportation facilities, changing markets, and various other factors which cannot be readily anticipated or controlled. This ordinance at a stroke arrests that process of natural evolution and growth, and substitutes for it an artificial and arbitrary plan of segregation, under which the landowner may only use his property for certain designated purposes, and under which he may be forbidden to use it for the only purpose for which it is adapted and most valuable.

* * *

There is a theory which has obtained some recognition, that the guaranties of written constitutions are not inflexible, and that the decisions construing them at one period of the state's history, under conditions existing then, ought not to bind the courts at some later period when conditions have changed, and when from economic, sociological or political considerations it is desirable that a different or more liberal construction be given. That theory is based upon the conception that any constitutional guaranty, no matter how plain and clear it may be, can be dissolved and avoided by the application of the police power of the state. That the police power is a real and essential element in the sovereignty of the state cannot be questioned or denied, and that written constitutions are presumed to have been made with conscious knowledge of that fact must be admitted. But it has never been supposed in this State that the police power is a universal solvent by which all constitutional guaranties and limitations can be loosed and set aside regardless of their clear and plain meaning, nor that it is a substitute for those guaranties, for far-reaching and powerful as it is, it has its limitations. Just what those limits are have not been, and in the nature of things, cannot be clearly and definitely marked, except that any exercise of the power which interferes with some right protected by the letter of the Constitution must bear some substantial relation to the public health, morals, safety, comfort or welfare. For while the existence of the police power may be invoked to determine what rights are guaranteed by the Constitution, it can never be invoked to justify an invasion of those rights once they have been ascertained. * * *

One of the most striking manifestations of this tendency [to encroach on individual rights] is the great volume of so-called zoning legislation which has in recent years been written into the laws of the several states, of which the ordinance before us is an apt illustration and which subject private property to an infinite variety and number of restrictions limiting its use, many of which rest for sanction upon no more definite or substantial foundation than that they are supposed to be in the interest of general prosperity or the public convenience. That the right to hold, enjoy and use property is not absolute but subject to the police power of the State is axiomatic (6 R.C.L. 194), and that that power may be affected by changing conditions is inevitable and unquestionable, for a use which at one time may be inoffensive and harmless may at another affect the security or the welfare of others with equal rights, and one of the sources of the police power is the maxim, "Sic utere tuo ut alienum non laedas." So, property in a populous urban community may be properly subjected to restrictions which would be unreasonable and arbitrary in a thinly settled rural community, so long as the restrictions bear some definite relation to the protection of the public health, morals, safety or comfort. These principles are self evident and are almost universally accepted. But the question before us goes much further than that. It is whether the power to hold, use and enjoy property can be restricted or taken away by the State under the guise of the police power for purely aesthetic reasons or for any such elastic and indeterminate object as the general prosperity without compensation.

* * *

From an examination of the maps which form a part of the ordinance, it appears that the residence zones or districts of Baltimore City comprise a number of separated areas varying in extent, irregular in outline, and located without apparent reference to any definite plan, but which nevertheless in the aggregate include a very large part of the total area of that city. And by reference to the ordinance it appears that in those districts no land or building can be used and no buildings erected except for one of fifteen specified uses, to which reference has already been made, unless specially authorized by the board of zoning appeals.

These restrictions are wholly arbitrary and have no logical relation to the public welfare, but rest solely upon aesthetic grounds. Under the provisions of sections 3 and 7d and 7g of article 3 of the ordinance, a neighborhood drug store might be forbidden, and a crematory permitted, a bakery forbidden and a sewage disposal plant permitted, an office building prohibited and a refuse dump permitted, a grocery store forbidden and an amusement park allowed. Nor is there any rule or standard prescribed to guide the discretion of those entrusted with the administration of the ordinance in deciding what shall be allowed or what forbidden any more definite than that, in any departure from the letter of the law, the spirit of the ordinance shall be preserved, public safety and welfare secured, and substantial justice done. But as the ordinance itself is based upon the theory that its prescriptions are in the interest of the public welfare, it is not clear how any departure from them can be justified on that ground, for if the restrictions are not necessary to the public welfare, there can be no justification for them at all, and in fact there is none. Their only apparent purpose was to prevent the encroachment of business establishments of any kind upon residential territory, regardless of whether they affected in any degree the public health, morals, safety, or welfare. In effecting that purpose they take from the property owner the right to use his property for any purpose not sanctioned by the letter of the ordinance or allowed by the practically unfettered discretion of the board of zoning appeals, and deprive him of privileges guaranteed by the twenty-third article of the Maryland Bill of Rights.

We have reached the conclusion, therefore, that so much of the ordinance as attempts to regulate and restrict the use of property in Baltimore City is void: first, because it deprives property owners of rights and privileges protected by the Constitution of the State; second, because such deprivation is not justified by any consideration for the public welfare, security, health, or morals apparent in the ordinance itself; and third, because it does not require that the restrictions shall in fact be based upon any such consideration. But in reaching this conclusion we do not hold that the use of property in Baltimore City may not be regulated or restricted where such regulation or restriction is based upon such consideration. * * *

STATE EX REL. CARTER v. HARPER

Supreme Court of Wisconsin, 1923.
182 Wis. 148, 196 N.W. 451, 33 A.L.R. 269.

Mandamus to compel the issuance of a building permit. The relator is in the wholesale and retail milk and dairy products business in the city of Milwaukee. In September, 1919, he purchased a lot and erected thereon a building which he is using as a dairy and milk pasteurizing plant. During the summer of 1921 he found that his business had outgrown the capacity of his plant to such an extent that it became impossible for him to conduct his business in said building in accordance with city and state health regulations. He made application to the inspector of buildings of the city of Milwaukee for a permit to erect an addition to the present building. The application was denied for the reason that the proposed addition to the building was in violation of the terms of the so-called zoning ordinance of the city of Milwaukee, adopted pursuant to authority conferred by sec. 62.23, Stats.

An alternative writ of mandamus issued out of the circuit court for Milwaukee county in the usual form, addressed to the inspector of buildings of the city of Milwaukee, to compel the issuance of said permit. The respondent made return setting forth the so-called zoning ordinance, to which return the relator demurred. The demurrer was overruled, and judgment ordered quashing the alternative writ and dismissing the petition. From the judgment thus entered this appeal is taken.

OWEN, J. The so-called zoning ordinance of the city of Milwaukee established within said city four classes of use districts designated: residence districts, local business districts, commercial and light manufacturing districts, and industrial districts. Relator's property is within a residence district. The ordinance then prescribes the uses to which property within the districts so created may be devoted. The present use of relator's property does not conform to the use permitted by the ordinance in residence districts. The ordinance further provides that no building within a residence district devoted to a non-conforming use shall be enlarged unless the use is changed to a conforming use.

This is a brief statement of the provisions of the ordinance upon which the building inspector relies as a justification for the denial of the permit. That the terms of the ordinance do furnish such justification, if the ordinance is a valid regulation, is not denied by the appellant. He claims, however, that the ordinance is unreasonable and oppressive, that it deprives him of the equal protection of the laws, and takes his property without due process of law and without just compensation.

The constitution of this state, sec. 13, art. I, provides that the property of no person shall be taken for public use without just compensation therefor, and the Fourteenth amendment of the federal constitution provides that no person shall be deprived of his property without due process of law. These provisions are intended to secure the enjoyment of most substantial and fundamental rights, and the allegation that one is being deprived of his property without just compensation or without due process of law calls for most serious consideration. It has long been settled, however, that these constitutional provisions interpose no barrier to the exercise of the police power of the state. Thus it was said in State ex rel. Kellogg v. Currans, 111 Wis. 431, 87 N.W. 561, at page 435, speaking of constitutional limitations upon legislative power:

"These limitations, however, according to all the authorities, state and federal, are to be read as not extending so far as to deprive the states of their power to so control the conduct of individuals as to protect the welfare of the community—a power commonly described as the 'police power.'"

Many declarations appear in our Reports, coming from the pen of Mr. Justice Marshall, tending to create the impression that there are constitutional limitations upon the exercise of this power. State ex rel. Milwaukee Med. Coll. v. Chittenden, 127 Wis. 468, 107 N.W. 500; Bonnett v. Vallier, 136 Wis. 193, 116 N.W. 885; Mehlos v. Milwaukee, 156 Wis. 591, 146 N.W. 882. A careful reading of these cases, however, will indicate that the constitutional limitations which were there in the mind of the court were either some express constitutional provision prohibiting certain specified legislation, or the line of reasonableness beyond which the legislature could not go. * * *

It is thoroughly established in this country that the rights preserved to the individual by these constitutional provisions are held in subordination to the rights of society. Although one owns property he may not do with it as he pleases, any more than he may act in accordance with his personal desires. As the interest of society justifies restraints upon individual conduct, so also does it justify restraints upon the use to which property may be devoted. It was not intended by these constitutional provisions to so far protect the individual in the use of his property as to enable him to use it to the detriment of society. By thus protecting individual rights, society did not part with the power to protect itself or to promote its general well-being. Where the interest of the individual conflicts with the interest of society, such individual interest is subordinated to the general welfare. If in the prosecution of governmental functions it becomes necessary to take private property, compensation must be made. But incidental damage to property resulting from governmental activities, or laws passed in the promotion of the public welfare, is not considered a taking of the property for which compensation must be made. * * *

The legislation authorizing so-called zoning ordinances is of comparatively recent origin, and it is not unnatural that those adversely affected shall regard them as an unjust and unwarranted interference with their property rights. The question of whether such ordinances fall legitimately within the realm of the police power has been considered by a few courts, presently to be noted, with conflicting results. The pioneer nature of the legislation requires that it have careful consideration, tested by the fundamental principles to which we have alluded. We are required to consider whether such ordinances have any reasonable tendency to promote the public morals, health, or safety or the public comfort, welfare, or prosperity.

The purpose of the law is to bring about an orderly development of our cities; to establish residence districts into which business, commercial, and industrial establishments shall not intrude; and to fix business districts and light industrial districts upon which heavy industrial concerns may not encroach. This is no new idea, although it has but recently taken the form of legislation. Everyone who has observed the haphazard development of cities, the deterioration in the desirability of certain residential sections by the encroachment of business and industrial establishments upon and into such sections, resulting in the consequent destruction of property values and in the ultimate abandonment of such sections for residential purposes, has appreciated the desirability of regulating the growth and development of our urban communities. The homeseeker shuns a section of a city devoted to industrialism and seeks a home at some distance from the business center. A common and natural instinct directs him to a section far removed from the commerce, trade, and industry of the community. He does this because the home instinct craves fresh air, sunshine, and well-kept lawns—home association beyond the noise of commercial marts and the dirt and smoke of industrial plants. Fresh air and sunshine add to the happiness of the home and have a direct effect upon the well-being of the occupants. It is not uncommon to witness efforts of promoters to preserve the residential character of their additions by placing covenants in their deeds restricting the use of the property to residential purposes and, in some instances, requiring the erection of a home according to specified standards. It cannot be denied that a city systematically developed offers greater attractiveness to the homeseeker than a city that is developed in a haphazard way. The one compares to the other about as a well-ordered department store compares to a junk-shop. If such regulations stabilize the value of property, promote the permanency of desirable home surroundings, and if they add to the happiness and comfort of the citizens, they thereby promote the general welfare.

When we reflect that one has always been required to so use his property as not to injure his neighbors, and that restrictions against the use of property in urban communities have increased with changing social standards, and that the luxuries of one decade become the necessities of another, can it be said that an effort to preserve various sections of a city from intrusion on the part of institutions that are offensive to and out of harmony with the use to which such sections are devoted is unreasonable? The present standards of society prompt a revolt against such unbecoming intrusions, and they constitute such a recognized interference with the rights of the residents of such sections as to justify regulation.

The benefits to be derived by cities adopting such regulations may be summarized as follows: They attract a desirable and assure a permanent citizenship; they foster pride in and attachment to the city; they promote happiness and contentment; they stabilize the use and value of property and promote the peace, tranquility, and good order of the city. We do not hesitate to say that the attainment of these objects affords a legitimate field for the exercise of the police power. He who owns property in such a district is not deprived of its use by such regulations. He may use it for the purposes to which the section in which it is located is dedicated. That he shall not be permitted to use it to the desecration of the community constitutes no unreasonable or permanent hardship and results in no unjust burden.

* * *

Issue #2

There remains a further question to be considered. Appellant claims that the ordinance is unreasonable in that it prohibits him from enlarging the business to which his property was devoted prior to the passage of the ordinance. The reasonableness of this feature of the ordinance, as well as its main purpose, is subject to judicial review. Where, however, a given situation is conceded to present a proper field for the exercise of the police power, the extent of the interference is a matter which lies very greatly in legislative discretion. Mehlos v. Milwaukee, 156 Wis. 591, 146 N.W. 882. If the appellant has acquired a vested right to enlarge his business, then every other person having an embryo business in a residential section must be accorded the same privilege, and an infant industry may grow to mammoth proportions, thereby to a very large extent defeating the purposes of the regulation.

In Hadachcck v. Scbastian, 239 U.S. 394, 36 S.Ct. 143, 60 L.Ed. 348, a brickyard of the value of $800,000, situated far outside the city limits when acquired, was suppressed after it had been included in the city limits. If property of that nature and of that value must yield to the supremacy of the police power, it is difficult to see how a regulation prohibiting appellant's enlargement of his business can be held unreasonable. Then, too, it may be remarked that an ordinance permitting those already engaged in business to enlarge the same while prohibiting all others from engaging therein, would not tend to make the ordinance less vulnerable. See People ex rel. Roos v. Kaul, 302 Ill. 317, 134 N.E. 740, and cases there cited.

It is further contended that the ordinance amounts to class legislation by reason of the provisions of sec. 26.46, Milwaukee Code, 1921 Supp., which provides that "A structure or premises may be erected or used in any location by a public-service corporation for any purpose which the railroad commission decides is reasonably necessary for the public convenience or welfare." When it is remembered that such buildings are erected to promote the comfort and convenience of the public and that it is within the power of the state to compel such erection, it would appear that this constitutes a reasonable and valid classification. It must be apparent that an ordinance enacted pursuant to state authority which prevents the erection of buildings or the conduct of business deemed inimical to public interest need not also prohibit the erection of buildings or the conduct of business which is essential to the comfort and convenience of the public and which the duly constituted authority of the state determines to be necessary for the public service which a public utility is required to render. A similar provision received the consideration of the court in Opinion of the Justices, 234 Mass. 597, 127 N.E. 525, concerning which it was said (p. 606) that the provision "is within settled principles touching legislative control over property devoted to that use."

It is our conclusion that the ordinance is, in the respects here considered, a reasonable, valid, and constitutional enactment. It is appreciated that there are other provisions of the ordinance the validity of which may be the subject of future challenge. It is to be understood that no opinion is expressed with reference to any features of the ordinance except such as are herein treated. So far as the ordinance affects the rights of appellant, it fully authorizes the denial of a building permit the issuance of which he seeks to coerce.

Judgment affirmed.

Note

For a review of pre-Euclid land use regulation cases in the United States Supreme Court, see Johnson, Constitutional Law and Community Planning, 20 Law & Contemp. Prob. 199, 200 (1955).

VILLAGE OF EUCLID v. AMBLER REALTY CO.

Supreme Court of the United States, 1926.
272 U.S. 365, 47 S.Ct. 114, 71 L.Ed. 303, 54 A.L.R. 1016.

MR. JUSTICE SUTHERLAND delivered the opinion of the court.

The village of Euclid is an Ohio municipal corporation. It adjoins and practically is a suburb of the city of Cleveland. Its estimated population is between 5,000 and 10,000, and its area from 12 to 14 square miles, the greater part of which is farm lands or unimproved acreage. It lies, roughly, in the form of a parallelogram measuring approximately 3½ miles each way. East and west it is traversed by three principal highways: Euclid avenue, through the southerly border, St. Clair avenue, through the central portion, and Lake Shore boulevard, through the northerly border, in close proximity to the shore of Lake Erie. The Nickel Plate Railroad lies from 1,500 to 1,800 feet north of Euclid avenue, and the Lake Shore Railroad 1,600 feet farther to the north. The three highways and the two railroads are substantially parallel.

Appellee is the owner of a tract of land containing 68 acres, situated in the westerly end of the village, abutting on Euclid avenue to the south and the Nickel Plate Railroad to the north. Adjoining this tract, both on the east and on the west, there have been laid out restricted residential plats upon which residences have been erected.

On November 13, 1922, an ordinance was adopted by the village council, establishing a comprehensive zoning plan for regulating and restricting the location of trades, industries, apartment houses, two-family houses, single family houses, etc., the lot area to be built upon, the size and height of buildings, etc.

The entire area of the village is divided by the ordinance into six classes of use districts, denominated U–1 to U–6, inclusive; three classes of height districts, denominated H–1 to H–3, inclusive; and four classes of area districts, denominated A–1 to A–4, inclusive. The use districts are classified in respect of the buildings which may be erected within their respective limits, as follows: U–1 is restricted to single family dwellings, public parks, water towers and reservoirs, suburban and interurban electric railway passenger stations and rights of way, and farming, noncommercial greenhouse nurseries and truck gardening; U–2 is extended to include two-family dwellings; U–3 is further extended to include apartment houses, hotels, churches, schools, public libraries, museums, private clubs, community center buildings, hospitals, sanitariums, public playgrounds and recreation buildings and a city hall and courthouse; U–4 is further extended to include banks, offices, studios, telephone exchanges, fire and police stations, restaurants, theaters, and moving picture shows, retail stores and shops, sales offices, sample rooms, wholesale stores for hardware, drugs and groceries, stations for gasoline and oil (not exceeding 1,000 gallons storage) and for ice delivery, skating rinks and dance halls, electric sub-stations, job and newspaper printing, public garages for motor vehicles, stables and wagon sheds (not exceeding five horses, wagons or motor trucks) and distributing stations for central store and commercial enterprises; U–5 is further extended to include billboards and advertising signs (if permitted), warehouses, ice and ice cream manufacturing and cold storage plants, bottling works, milk bottling and central distribution stations, laundries, carpet cleaning, dry cleaning and dyeing establishments, blacksmith, horseshoeing, wagon and motor vehicle repair shops, freight stations, streetcar barns, stables and wagon sheds (for more than five horses, wagons or motor trucks), and wholesale produce markets and salesrooms; U–6 is further extended to include plants for sewage disposal and for producing gas, garbage and refuse incineration, scrap iron, junk, scrap paper and rag storage, aviation fields, cemeteries, crematories, penal and correctional institutions, insane and feeble minded institutions, storage of oil and gasoline (not to exceed 25,000 gallons), and manufacturing and industrial operations of any kind other than, and any public utility not included in, a class U–1, U–2, U–3, U–4 or U–5 use. There is a seventh class of uses which is prohibited altogether.

Class U–1 is the only district in which buildings are restricted to those enumerated. In the other classes, the uses are cumulative; that is to say, uses in class U–2 include those enumerated in the preceding class, U–1; class U–3 includes uses enumerated in the preceding classes, U–2 and U–1; and so on. In addition to the enumerated uses, the ordinance provides for accessory uses, that is, for uses customarily incident to the principal use, such as private garages. Many regulations are provided in respect of such accessory uses.

The height districts are classified as follows: In class H–1, buildings are limited to a height of two and one-half stories or thirty-five feet; in class H–2, to four stories or fifty feet; in class H–3, to eighty feet. To all of these, certain exceptions are made, as in the case of church spires, water tanks, etc.

The classification of area districts is: In A–1 districts, dwellings or apartment houses to accommodate more than one family must have at least 5,000 square feet for interior lots and at least 4,000 square feet for corner lots; in A–2 districts, the area must be at least 2,500 square feet for interior lots, and 2,000 square feet for corner lots; in A–3 districts, the limits are 1,250 and 1,000 square feet, respectively; in A–4 districts, the limits are 900 and 700 square feet, respectively. The ordinance contains, in great variety and detail, provisions in respect of width of lots, front, side and rear yards, and other matters, including restrictions and regulations as to the use of billboards, sign boards and advertising signs.

A single family dwelling consists of a basement and not less than three rooms and a bathroom. A two-family dwelling consists of a basement and not less than four living rooms and a bathroom for each family; and is further described as a detached dwelling for the occupation of two families, one having its principal living rooms on the first floor and the other on the second floor.

Appellee's tract of land comes under U–2, U–3 and U–6. The first strip of 620 feet immediately north of Euclid avenue falls in class U–2, the next 130 feet to the north, in U–3, and the remainder in U–6. The uses of the first 620 feet, therefore, do not include apartment houses, hotels, churches, schools, or other public and semi-public buildings, or other uses enumerated in respect of U–3 to U–6, inclusive.

Annexed to the ordinance, and made a part of it, is a zone map, showing the location and limits of the various use, height and area districts, from which it appears that the three classes overlap one another; that is to say, for example, both U–5 and U–6 use districts are in A–4 area districts, but the former is in H–2 and the latter in H–3 height districts. The plan is a complicated one and can be better understood by an inspection of the map, though it does not seem necessary to reproduce it for present purposes.

The lands lying between the two railroads for the entire length of the village area and extending some distance on either side to the north and south, having an average width of about 1,600 feet, are left open, with slight exceptions, for industrial and all other uses. This includes the larger part of appellee's tract. Approximately one-sixth of the area of the entire village is included in U–5 and U–6 use districts. That part of the village lying south of Euclid avenue is principally in U–1 districts. The lands lying north of Euclid avenue and bordering on the long strip just described are included in U–1, U–2, U–3, and U–4 districts, principally in U–2.

The enforcement of the ordinance is entrusted to the inspector of buildings, under rules and regulations of the board of zoning appeals. Meetings of the board are public, and minutes of its proceedings are kept. It is authorized to adopt rules and regulations to carry into effect provisions of the ordinance. Decisions of the inspector of buildings may be appealed to the board by any person claiming to be adversely affected by any such decision.

The board is given power in specific cases of practical difficulty or unnecessary hardship to interpret the ordinance in harmony with its general purpose and intent, so that the public health, safety and general

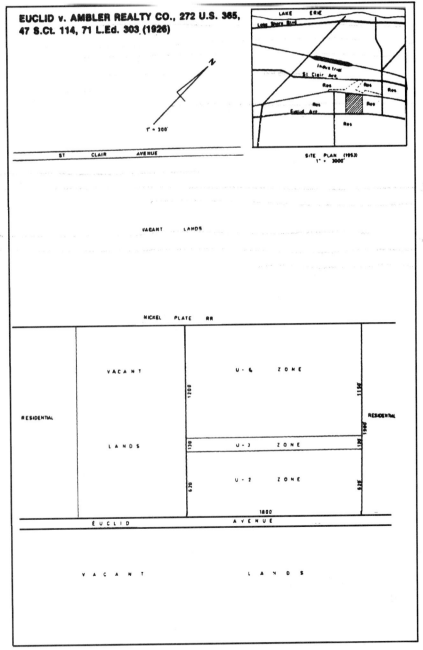

welfare may be secure and substantial justice done. Penalties are prescribed for violations, and it is provided that the various provisions are to be regarded as independent and the holding of any provision to be unconstitutional, void or ineffective shall not affect any of the others.

The ordinance is assailed on the grounds that it is in derogation of Sec. 1 of the 14th Amendment to the Federal Constitution in that it deprives appellee of liberty and property without due process of law and denies it the equal protection of the law, and that it offends against certain provisions of the Constitution of the state of Ohio. The prayer of the bill is for an injunction restraining the enforcement of the ordinance and all attempts to impose or maintain as to appellee's property any of the restrictions, limitations or conditions. The court below held the ordinance to be unconstitutional and void, and enjoined its enforcement. 297 F. 307.

Before proceeding to a consideration of the case, it is necessary to determine the scope of the inquiry. The bill alleges that the tract of land in question is vacant and has been held for years for the purpose of selling and developing it for industrial uses, for which it is especially adapted, being immediately in the path of progressive industrial development; that for such uses it has a market value of about $10,000 per acre, but if the use be limited to residential purposes the market value is not in excess of $2,500 per acre; that the first 200 feet of the parcel back from Euclid avenue, if unrestricted in respect of use, has a value of $150 per front foot, but if limited to residential uses, and ordinary mercantile business be excluded therefrom, its value is not in excess of $50 per front foot.

It is specifically averred that the ordinance attempts to restrict and control the lawful uses of appellee's land so as to confiscate and destroy a great part of its value; that it is being enforced in accordance with its terms; that prospective buyers of land for industrial, commercial and residential uses in the metropolitan district of Cleveland are deterred from buying any part of this land because of the existence of the ordinance and the necessity thereby entailed of conducting burdensome and expensive litigation in order to vindicate the right to use the land for lawful and legitimate purposes; that the ordinance constitutes a cloud upon the land, reduces and destroys its value, and has the effect of diverting the normal industrial, commercial and residential development thereof to other and less favorable locations.

The record goes no farther than to show, as the lower court found, that the normal, and reasonably to be expected, use and development of that part of appellee's land adjoining Euclid avenue is for general trade and commercial purposes, particularly retail stores and like establishments, and that the normal, and reasonably to be expected, use and development of the residue of the land is for industrial and trade purposes. Whatever injury is inflicted by the mere existence and threatened enforcement of the ordinance is due to restrictions in respect of these and similar uses; to which perhaps should be added—if not included in the foregoing—restrictions in respect to apartment houses. Specifically, there is nothing in the record to suggest that any damage results from the presence in the ordinance of those restrictions relating to churches, schools, libraries and other public and semi-public buildings. It is neither alleged nor proved that there is or may be a demand for any part of appellee's land for any of the last named uses; and we cannot assume the existence of facts which would justify an injunction upon this record in respect of this class of restrictions. For present purposes the provisions of the ordinance in respect of these uses may therefore be put aside as unnecessary to be considered. It is also unnecessary to consider the effect of the restrictions in respect of U–1 districts, since none of the appellee's land falls within that class.

* * *

Building zone laws are of modern origin. They began in this country about twenty-five years ago. Until recent years, urban life was comparatively simple; but with the great increase and concentration of population, problems have developed, and constantly are developing, which require, and will continue to require, additional restrictions in respect of the use and occupation of private lands in urban communities. Regulations, the wisdom, necessity and validity of which, as applied to existing conditions, are so apparent that they are now uniformly sustained, a century ago, or even half a century ago, probably would have been rejected as arbitrary and oppressive. Such regulations are sustained, under the complex conditions of our day, for reasons analogous to those which justify traffic regulations, which, before the advent of automobiles and rapid transit street railways, would have been condemned as fatally arbitrary and unreasonable. And in this there is no inconsistency, for while the meaning of constitutional guaranties never varies, the scope of their application must expand or contract to meet the new and different conditions which are constantly coming within the field of their operation. In a changing world, it is impossible that it should be otherwise. But although a degree of elasticity is thus imparted, not to the *meaning,* but to the *application* of constitutional principles, statutes and ordinances, which, after giving due weight to the new conditions, are found clearly not to conform to the Constitution, of course, must fall.

The ordinance now under review and all similar laws and regulations must find their justification in some aspect of the police power, asserted for the public welfare. The line which in this field separates the legitimate from the illegitimate assumption of power is not capable of precise delimitation. It varies with circumstances and conditions. A regulatory zoning ordinance, which would be clearly valid as applied to the great cities, might be clearly invalid as applied to rural communities. In solving doubts, the maxim "sic utere tuo ut alienum non laedas," which lies at the foundation of so much of the common law of nuisances, ordinarily will furnish a fairly helpful clew. And the law of nuisances, likewise, may be consulted, not for the purpose of controlling, but for the helpful aid of its analogies in the process of ascertaining the scope of, the power. Thus the question whether the power exists to forbid the erection of a building of a particular kind or for a particular use, like the question whether a particular thing is a nuisance, is to be determined, not by an abstract consideration of the building or of the thing considered apart, but by considering it in connection with the circumstances and the locality.

* * *

We find no difficulty in sustaining restrictions of the kind thus far reviewed. The serious question in the case arises over the provisions of the ordinance excluding from residential districts, apartment houses, business houses, retail stores and shops, and other like establishments. This question involves the validity of what is really the crux of the more recent zoning legislation, namely, the creation and maintenance of residential districts, from which business and trade of every sort, including hotels and apartment houses, are excluded. Upon that question this court has not thus far spoken. The decisions of the state courts are numerous and conflicting; but those which broadly sustain the power greatly outnumber those which deny it altogether or narrowly limit it; and it is very apparent that there is a constantly increasing tendency in the direction of the broader view. * * *

The matter of zoning has received much attention at the hands of commissions and experts, and the results of their investigations have been set forth in comprehensive reports. These reports, which bear every evidence of painstaking consideration, concur in the view that the segregation of residential, business and industrial buildings will make it easier to provide fire apparatus suitable for the character and intensity of the development in each section; that it will increase the safety and security of home life; greatly tend to prevent street accidents, especially to children, by reducing the traffic and resulting confusion in residential sections; decrease noise and other conditions which produce or intensify nervous disorders; preserve a more favorable environment in which to rear children, etc. With particular reference to apartment houses, it is pointed out that the development of detached house sections is greatly retarded by the coming of apartment houses, which has sometimes resulted in destroying the entire section for private house purposes; that in such sections very often the apartment house is a mere parasite, constructed in order to take advantage of the open spaces and attractive surroundings created by the residential character of the district. Moreover, the coming of one apartment house is followed by others, interfering by their height and bulk with the free circulation of air and monopolizing the rays of the sun which otherwise would fall upon the smaller homes, and bringing, as their necessary accompaniments, the disturbing noises incident to increased traffic and business, and the occupation, by means of moving and parked automobiles, of larger portions of the streets, thus detracting from their safety and depriving children of the privilege of quiet and open spaces for play, enjoyed by those in more favored localities,—until, finally, the residential character of the neighborhood and its desirability as a place of detached residences are utterly destroyed. Under these circumstances, apartment houses, which in a different environment would be not only entirely unobjectionable but highly desirable, come very near to being nuisances.

If these reasons, thus summarized, do not demonstrate the wisdom or sound policy in all respects of those restrictions which we have indicated as pertinent to the inquiry, at least, the reasons are sufficiently cogent to preclude us from saying, as it must be said before the ordinance can be declared unconstitutional, that such provisions are clearly arbitrary and unreasonable, having no substantial relation to the public health, safety, morals, or general welfare. * * *

It is true that when, if ever, the provisions set forth in the ordinance in tedious and minute detail, come to be concretely applied to particular premises, including those of the appellee, or to particular conditions, or to be considered in connection with specific complaints, some of them, or even many of them, may be found to be clearly arbitrary and unreasonable. But where the equitable remedy of injunction is sought, as it is here, not upon the ground of a present infringement or denial of a specific right, or of a particular injury in process of actual execution, but upon the broad ground that the mere existence and threatened enforcement of the ordinance, by materially and adversely affecting values and curtailing the opportunities of the market, constitute a present and irreparable injury, the court will not scrutinize its provisions, sentence by sentence, to ascertain by a process of piecemeal dissection whether there may be, here and there, provisions of a minor character, or relating to matters of administration, or not shown to contribute to the injury complained of, which, if attacked separately, might not withstand the test of constitutionality. In respect of such provisions, of which specific complaint is not made, it cannot be said that the landowner has suffered or is threatened with an injury which entitles him to challenge their constitutionality. * * *

Under these circumstances, therefore, it is enough for us to determine, as we do, that the ordinance in its general scope and dominant features, so far as its provisions are here involved, is a valid exercise of authority, leaving other provisions to be dealt with as cases arise directly involving them.

And this is in accordance with the traditional policy of this court. In the realm of constitutional law, especially, this court has perceived the embarrassment which is likely to result from an attempt to formulate rules or decide questions beyond the necessities of the immediate issue. It has preferred to follow the method of a gradual approach to the general by a systematically guarded application and extension of constitutional principles to particular cases as they arise, rather than by out of hand attempts to establish general rules to which future cases must be fitted. This process applies with peculiar force to the solution of questions arising under the due process clause of the Constitution as applied to the exercise of the flexible powers of police, with which we are here concerned.

Decree reversed.

Notes

1. A year and a half after the Euclid decision, the U.S. Supreme Court, again speaking through Mr. Justice Sutherland, summarily declared a zoning ordinance unreasonable and unconstitutional as applied to the plaintiff's particular tract of land. Nectow v. Cambridge, 277 U.S. 183, 48 S.Ct. 447, 72

L.Ed. 842 (1928). During the six terms, 1949–50 to 1954–55, appeals were dismissed or petitions for certiorari denied in twenty-one cases involving zoning and local planning. See Johnson, Constitutional Law and Community Planning, 20 Law & Contemp.Prob. 199, 208 (1955). See also Williams, Planning Law and the Supreme Court, Zoning Digest (March 1961).

2. Bassett in his classic on Zoning (Russell Sage Foundation, 1936) states at 46–47:

> Height and area regulations brought little or no criticism from the courts. It was not so, however with the regulation of use. Opposition was intense, especially in states along the Atlantic coast, from New Jersey to Texas. Gradually courts in all the states pronounced use-zoning regulations lawful if reasonable. The decision of the United States Supreme Court in the Euclid case had much to do with this change of attitude.

3. Although the Euclid case was hailed as a great legal victory for the concept of zoning, in recent years a more critical re-analysis of Euclid has emerged. Today, many are questioning the philosophy expressed that the essence of zoning is strict segregation of uses with protection of single-family dwellings as the highest purpose of zoning. For example, Jane Jacobs, the urban economist, in her book, The Death and Life of Great American Cities, points out that in an earlier era the mixture of apartments, stores and small industrial uses promoted safety and vitality, as well as a sense of neighborhood and community which is lacking in newer and redeveloped portions of our older cities. Some developers are harking back to that earlier era. See Maureen Milford, New Village With a 16th-Century Concept, N.Y. Times, Dec. 3, 1995, p. 31. The article describes a $30 million development in rural Pennsylvania, Stoudtburg Village, where the homeowners live over their shops

The Euclid rationale is the basic source of the philosophy of zoning as a protectionist device, a philosophy which is currently receiving a searching reexamination in cases dealing with the problem we now call "exclusionary zoning" dealt with in the next chapter. Also, compare with Euclid, Justice Douglas' opinion in the Belle Terre case, infra.

SECTION 2. ENABLING AUTHORITY TO ZONE

It is generally held that local units of government have no power to enact zoning ordinances in the absence of express enabling authority. This authority may be delegated by (1) a provision in the state's constitution (rare); (2) an enabling statute; or (3) a provision in the municipal charter. The usual broad grant of police power by a state legislature to local units in matters of health, safety and morals is thought not to be sufficiently specific to enable zoning. See 8 McQuillin on Municipal Corporations §§ 25.35, 25.37 (3d ed. 1983 rev. vol.). Frequently, then, you will find landowners claiming that a particular zoning provision is void not because it is unconstitutional but because it is "ultra vires" with respect to the enabling statute.

In the 1920's an advisory committee appointed by Herbert Hoover, then Secretary of Commerce of the United States, prepared a "Standard

Zoning Enabling Act." This standard act known variously as the "Department of Commerce Standard Enabling Act," the "Standard Enabling Act," the "Standard Zoning Act," or as just the "Standard Act" has been revised several times and is in force in many states, although usually today in a revised and sometimes substantially amended form. See Haar, The Master Plan: An Impermanent Constitution, 20 Law & Contemp.Prob. 353, 400 (1955).

At one time, all 50 states had adopted all or portions of the Standard Act, with some variations. According to Norman Williams, the Standard Act is still the basis for zoning in 47 states. See Williams, American Land Planning Law § 18.01 (1988).

Rarely is a zoning ordinance or zoning decision attacked as ultra vires with respect to the enabling act. Occasionally, however, a community either passes an interim zoning ordinance to freeze development while planning studies are done or the local government fails to undertake the preliminary studies prior to passing the ordinance.

The first situation is typified by cases like State ex rel. Kramer v. Schwartz, 336 Mo. 932, 82 S.W.2d 63 (1935), where the court held that an interim zoning ordinance was ultra vires because the state enabling act did not anywhere mention authority to enact interim zoning. Also see Annotation, Validity and Effect of "Interim" Zoning Ordinance, 30 A.L.R.3d 1196 (1970); Bryant Development Ass'n v. Dagel, 166 Mont. 252, 531 P.2d 1320 (1975); Bank of the Orient v. Town of Tiburon, 220 Cal.App.3d 992, 269 Cal.Rptr. 690 (1990).

The second situation, failure to follow the statutory procedure prescribed for zoning, is more common. See, e.g., City of Searcy v. Roberson, 224 Ark. 344, 273 S.W.2d 26 (1954), where the court held that the zoning ordinance was invalid in its entirety because the city had not done a comprehensive plan which the statute prescribed as a condition precedent to zoning. Not all states make planning a condition precedent, a state of affairs which has led to much debate in the law reviews. Consider the following exchange of views:

McBRIDE AND BABCOCK, THE MASTER PLAN— A STATUTORY PREREQUISITE TO A ZONING ORDINANCE?

Zoning Digest 353, 357–358 (Nov. 1960).

To say that a municipality cannot adopt a zoning ordinance unless it has a "master plan" is an invitation to prostitute the concept of planning by municipalities which, wishing a zoning ordinance, are unable or unwilling to expend the funds and energy necessary to do an adequate job of planning. If every community must have a plan before it can regulate, for example, lot sizes, location of commercial and residential uses and off-street parking, we will see (indeed, we have seen!) a degeneration of planning. Nor does it follow that a community cannot have a reasonably efficient and fair (and, therefore, constitutional) zoning ordinance unless it has a master plan, as a house can provide shelter and yet offend an elementary sense of good taste. Let us admit, without the fear of undercutting a good thing, that it is possible to have a zoning ordinance which will accomplish many useful things without a preexisting community plan. To make a plan (comprehensive, master, or general) mandatory not only encourages bastardization of planning, but also deprives the conscientious, if impecunious, municipality of the chance to have a zoning ordinance.

Our alternative may resolve this dilemma. The preamble to each zoning ordinance must state whether or not it is based upon a community plan, the optional elements of which are enumerated in the enabling act. If that statement is in the affirmative, the preamble must set forth precisely what is meant by that "plan." Such requirements indicate a legislative recognition of the significant relationship between zoning and planning. The community that adopts a zoning ordinance without a plan must make such an admission and, such admission being required by the legislature, it follows that this is a material fact in any judicial determination as to the reasonableness of that ordinance. On the other hand, if a plan is claimed, then the drafters of the zoning ordinance must disclose on the face of the zoning ordinance what they mean by that term. Being required to display their linen, they must be certain that it bears inspection. On this premise it is reasonable to assume they will exercise greater concern with genuine cleanliness than would be so if the statutory requirement were that no laundry shall be washed without the application of a bleach.

HAAR AND MYTELKA, PLANNING AND ZONING
Zoning Digest 33, 35–36 (Feb. 1961).

Now, observe the effects of * * * [the McBride–Babcock] proposal:

First, since a community may opt for zoning without planning, there is neither legal coercion to plan, nor moral impetus in that direction. The suggested statute would be like much planning enabling legislation today: hortatory at best. By contrast, requiring a master plan in the statute would make clear that the legislative policy is that zoning implement planning. Even without the legal sanction of invalidation of ordinances in the courts, municipal authorities would be under responsibility to carry out this policy.

Second, the proposal seems to positively discourage planning. A municipality confronted with the threat of attack on a proposed zoning ordinance would be unlikely to go through the long and expensive process of adopting a master plan since, if it did, the plan would become subject to judicial scrutiny and might cause invalidation. What would the municipality's attorney advise? Certainly, he would caution against giving the potential litigant another target, besides the zoning ordinance itself, to throw darts at.

Third, the standard set up by the proposal is so vague that it would not improve the present situation in most states. The courts will consider the lack of a master plan in evaluating the reasonableness of the zoning ordinance under attack. But surely they will not invalidate for this reason alone, since the legislature has not made the master plan mandatory. How then will the decisions go?

Court A will say that so long as the ordinance is within the police power and does not arbitrarily discriminate, it is valid. Court B will say that some planning is required; that is, that the zoners must consider the effect of their zoning on the community, though they need not map out or study other aspects of municipal development. Court C might require full scale planning just short of the adoption of a master plan. And other courts will shade their opinions a degree to one side or the other of these positions. * * *

Hence, the real issue—and one in which conscientious practitioners like McBride and Babcock could make a genuine contribution—is the dilemma of relating planning to the tools of implementation. Of what avail is a proposed solution by a hastily drafted enabling act that raises more difficulties than it resolves?

What, then, are some of the issues in reformulating planning enabling legislation on which light could be cast? A preliminary list would encompass at least the following:

1. What is the effect of requiring accordance with the plan upon existing zoning ordinances—especially those where no comprehensive plan is presently in existence?

2. What is the effect of subsequent amendments, either of the master plan or of the zoning ordinance?

3. Is there an idealized set of elements for the plan—in terms of details and specificity for its long-range, generalized effects; and for type-sizes and type-populations of communities?

4. How would these fit into a regional pattern of controls?

5. What is the effect of the master plan on marketability of titles?

6. Given this prominent role, what should be the procedures for promulgation, popularization, and adoption of the master plan?

No one can claim that the basing of land use regulations upon land planning will produce the millenium. The authors are right in rejecting unchallenged premises. But scoffing at the issue will not aid us in the refashioning of land objectives and means to ensure a more efficient and rational basis for community development.

————

For cases in which the Babcock and the Haar and Mytelka views came into contention, see E & M Investments v. Town of Dickson, 713 P.2d 1052 (Okl.App.1985). In that case the town (population 1,000) adopted a zoning ordinance without any preceding planning or creation of a planning commission. The entire town was zoned residential. When the ordinance was challenged, the town contended that it should not have to engage in the planning process because of the expense involved and the lack of funds. The court rejected the town's argument. Also see Bell v. City of Elkhorn, 122 Wis.2d 558, 364 N.W.2d 144 (1985) where the court held that the zoning ordinance also served as the general plan and thus satisfied the statute. And, in State ex rel. Chiavola v. Village of Oakwood, 886 S.W.2d 74 (Mo.App.1994) the court held that a zoning ordinance satisfied the statutory requirement despite the lack of a separate comprehensive plan, given the comprehensive scope of the ordinance and the nature of the village as a small suburb of a large city. Compare Wolf v. City of Ely, 493 N.W.2d 846 (Iowa 1992) where the court held a zoning ordinance invalid because the town had not adopted a comprehensive plan; the court acknowledged that a "majority of courts in states where zoning must be 'in accordance with a comprehensive plan' hold a plan external to the zoning ordinance is not required." However, the court stated that the trend of decisions is in the other direction and aligned Iowa with the trend.

SECTION 3.   THE RELATIONSHIP BETWEEN ZONING AND COMPREHENSIVE PLANNING

In the early years of zoning, the legislative process frequently began and ended with the production of a zoning map and written ordinance. Comprehensive planning studies, the subject matter of Chapter IV, as a condition precedent to zoning came on the scene in the late 1930's, and more commonly, after World War II. The early theory, reflected in the Euclid case opinion, was that zoning was an end in itself. Today, most enabling statutes reflect the theory that zoning is a means to an end, the implementation of the comprehensive land use plan or master plan.

Assuming that a community has both a land use plan and a zoning map, the question frequently arises as to what extent may the city change zoning district boundaries or the zoning classification of a particular piece of property when such change is inconsistent with the comprehensive plan? Refer back to Chapter IV and the material dealing with the effect of the plan; you will recall that most courts are reluctant to impose the consistency doctrine. One term which almost always is encountered in dealing with this question is the rubric, "spot zoning."

Although students and faculty alike will gnash their teeth in pain at the pun, it may be said in all candor that the problem of the courts in dealing with spot zoning is in spotting it. When is relief from the application of zoning provisions applied in such a way that it constitutes that demon of demons, spot zoning? When is the comprehensive plan sufficiently ravished that a court will say that the proposed change is such that it constitutes spot or piecemeal zoning? As a matter of fact, is there such a thing as spot zoning, or is it simply a ready brand to be employed by zoning boards or by courts when they feel the occasion calls for it? The fact that there are variations from jurisdiction to jurisdiction in case and statutory law, in the flexibility of action available to planners and developers, and in the approach to zoning and the attitude toward the comprehensive plan combine to make it difficult for students and lawyers alike to recognize and categorize spot zoning.

In a very broad sense, it might be said that spot zoning is any change which departs from the comprehensive plan. More specifically, it is the singling out by a zoning amendment of a small parcel of land and permitting the owner to use it in a manner inconsistent with the permissible uses in the area. (See generally, 3 Anderson, American Law of Zoning § 18.04 (3d ed. 1986); 1 Williams, American Land Planning Law §§ 27.01–27.08 (1988); and Annot., Spot Zoning, 51 A.L.R.2d 263 (1957).) Some courts, in discussing it, apply the terms "arbitrary," "capricious," "unreasonable" and similar adjectives. See, e.g., Cassel v. Mayor and City Council of Baltimore, 195 Md. 348, 73 A.2d 486 (1950); and Pierce v. King County, 62 Wash.2d 324, 382 P.2d 628 (1963). In the oft-cited Cassel case, the court stated:

> Spot zoning, the arbitrary and unreasonable devotion of a small area within a zoning district to a use which is inconsistent with the use to which the rest of the district is restricted, has appeared in many cities in America as a result of pressure put upon councilmen to pass amendments to zoning ordinances solely for the benefit of private interest. * * * It is, therefore, universally held that a 'spot zoning' ordinance, which singles out a parcel of land within the limits of a use district and marks it off with a separate district for the benefit of the owner, thereby permitting a use of that parcel inconsistent with the use permitted in the rest of the district, is invalid if not in accordance with the comprehensive plan and is merely for private gain. (195 Md. at 355, 73 A.2d at 488–489.)

Obviously, every departure from the plan which was originally instituted for a district does not constitute illicit spot zoning. Otherwise zoning would rigidify permissible land uses within the district to the point that no changes—not even variances or special permits—could be made without a general overhaul. As the A.L.R. annotation cited above points out, the term is often simply a convenient label for courts to apply to a conclusion at which they have arrived. Other courts use the term more descriptively, in the sense that whether the zoning of a "spot" is valid or not will depend on the circumstances involved. Thus, in Penning v. Owens, 340 Mich. 355, 65 N.W.2d 831 (1954), the court said that the inconsistent zoning of a small area must be carefully scrutinized and can be sustained only when the circumstances are such as to warrant the action taken. In Little v. Winborn, 518 N.W.2d 384 (Iowa 1994) the court held that rezoning of agricultural property from "agricultural protection district" to "agricultural" in order to allow the owner to use his property for a shooting range was invalid spot zoning.

Whatever courts may purport to be doing in the spot zoning cases, much of it comes back to the adjectives previously mentioned: Is the action taken arbitrary and unreasonable? Did the zoning ordinance or amendment which singled out this parcel make good sense in the light of the facts involved? As the Iowa court said in Keller v. City of Council Bluffs, 246 Iowa 202, 209–210, 213–214, 66 N.W.2d 113, 117–118, 120, 51 A.L.R.2d 251 (1954):

> The original zoning ordinance clearly relegated this property to a single purpose for which it was and continued to be unfit and therefore almost useless. It seems only reasonable the council should be able to reclassify those portions of the neighborhood under the statutory enactments. In fact, it may be important that such authority as well as duty exists in that body in order to make a zoning law constitutional. * * * Property cannot be confiscated under the guise of police power. Thus an ordinance may be valid in its general aspect and at the same time be clearly arbitrary and unreasonable as applied to a particular state of facts.

* * *

> The spirit of a zoning ordinance is not violated nor is it inconsistent with a comprehensive zoning ordinance to grant a just and reasonable exception by amendment based upon the character and use of property not similar to other property in the district, but [which] is now and was distinguishable before the adoption of the comprehensive zoning ordinance.

* * *

> "Spot zoning" when construed to mean reclassification of one or more *like tracts* or *similar lots* for a use prohibited by the original zoning ordinance and out of harmony therewith is illegal. When done under certain other conditions and circumstances in accordance with a comprehensive zoning plan, such action will not be declared void. It depends upon the circumstances of each case.

EVES v. ZONING BD. OF ADJUSTMENT OF LOWER GWYNEDD TWP.

Supreme Court of Pennsylvania, 1960.
401 Pa. 211, 164 A.2d 7.

COHEN, JUSTICE.

These appeals, involving specifically the validity of two ordinances which amend respectively the general zoning ordinance and the zoning map of Lower Gwynedd Township, present the problem of the validity of a method of zoning aptly termed by the appellants as "flexible selective zoning."

On April 28, 1958 the Board of Supervisors of Lower Gwynedd Township adopted Ordinance 28 which officially amended the General Zoning Ordinance of the township to provide for the new zoning district known as "F–1" Limited Industrial District. This ordinance sets forth in detail the requirements, conditions and restrictive uses for an "F-1" classification, including the requirements that any proposed development be constructed in accordance with an overall plan; that any plan shall be designed as a single architectural scheme with appropriate common landscaping and shall provide a minimum size of 25 acres; that adequate parking space shall be provided for all employees and visitor's vehicles; that parking, loading or service areas used by motor vehicles shall be located within the lot lines of the Limited Industrial District, and shall be physically separated from the public streets by a buffer strip; that no building or other permanent structure, nor parking lot, shall be located within 200 feet of a public street, right-of-way, or property line; and that the area of land occupied by the buildings shall not exceed 10% of each site within the Limited Industrial District. The ordinance reserves the right in the board of supervisors to prescribe particular requirements or any further reasonable conditions deemed appropriate with respect to the suitability of the Limited Industrial District in the neighborhood.

Ordinance 28, however, does not itself delineate the boundaries of those specific areas which are to be classified as "F-1" districts. Instead, the ordinance outlines a procedure whereby any one may submit to the board an application requesting that his land be rezoned to "F-1" limited industrial, together with plans showing the nature of the industry the applicant wishes to establish and the conformity of any proposed construction with the requirements of the district as enumerated in the ordinance. The supervisors must in turn refer the application and plans to the Planning Commission of Lower Gwynedd Township, which is to review them and then return them to the supervisors accompanied by its recommendations within 45 days. The board of supervisors must then hold public hearings and finally decide whether or not to reject or approve the application and accordingly amend the zoning map. The ordinance finally provides that should any successful applicant fail to undertake substantial construction of any proposed buildings within 18 months after the rezoning, or after the issuance of a permit for an area previously zoned "F-1" Limited Industrial District, the area is to revert to its former zoning classification.

Pursuant to the terms of Ordinance 28, on September 11, 1958, the Moore Construction Company, a Pennsylvania corporation desiring to construct an industrial plant and a sewage treatment plant in Lower Gwynedd Township, applied for a rezoning of a 103 acre tract of land known as the "Hardwick Tract" from "A" residential to "F-1" Limited Industrial. A public hearing was held by the supervisors to consider the rezoning on September 20, 1958, at which time a petition signed by 300 residents, all property owners, who opposed the change, was filed. On January 5, 1959, the supervisors adopted Ordinance 34 which rezoned the area in question to the requested "F-1" classification (although it reduced the area rezoned from 103 acres to 86 acres). On January 14, 1959, a certificate of conformity (building permit) was issued to the Moore Products Company. Schuyler Eves, a resident of the township, and the Sisters of Mercy appealed to the zoning board, challenging the validity of the two ordinances on the grounds that they were unconstitutional and that they failed to conform to the enabling legislation. Sustaining the validity of the ordinances, the board dismissed the appeal. The Court of Common Pleas of Montgomery County affirmed and these appeals followed.

* * *

"Zoning is the legislative division of a community into areas in each of which only certain designated uses of land are permitted so that the community may develop in an orderly manner in accordance with a comprehensive plan." Best v. Zoning Board of Adjustment, 1958, 393 Pa. 106, 110, 141 A.2d 606, 609. The zoning regulations of a second class township, by legislative edict, must be the implementation of such a comprehensive plan. Just what the precise attributes of a comprehensive plan must be, or the extent to which the plan must approach a development plan for the township formulated by a planning commission should one exist is not now before us. * * * For present purposes, it is only important to point out that the focus of any plan is land use, and the considerations in the formulation of a plan for the orderly development of a community must be made with regard thereto. * * *

The role of the township supervisors in the field of zoning, as contemplated by the enabling legislation, emerges quite clearly upon consideration of the powers granted the supervisors and the duties they are bound to perform. Their duty is to implement the comprehensive plan by enacting zoning regulations in accordance therewith. Section 2003, 53 P.S. § 67003. They are to shape the land uses "into districts of such number, shape and area as may be deemed best suited to carry out the purpose of this article * * *," Section 2002, 53 P.S. § 67002, which "purpose in view" is set out above in Section 2003. They may regulate or restrict "the erection, construction, reconstruction, alteration, repair or use of buildings, structures or land" within any district, and may regulate one district differently from the next, but all "such regulations shall be uniform for each class or kind of buildings throughout each district * * *." Section 2002, 53 P.S. § 67002. All such regulations are to be embodied initially in a general zoning ordinance for the township, which may be subsequently amended, supplemented or repealed by the supervisors as conditions require, Section 2004, 53 P.S. § 67004, although again such alterations must be "in accordance with a comprehensive plan."

* * *

The adoption of a procedure whereby it is decided which areas of land will eventually be zoned "F–1" Limited Industrial Districts on a case by case basis patently admits that at the point of enactment of Ordinance 28 there was no orderly plan of particular land use for the community. Final determination under such a scheme would expressly await solicitation by individual landowners, thus making the planned land use of the community dependent upon its development. In other words, the development itself would become the plan, which is manifestly the antithesis of zoning "in accordance with a comprehensive plan."

Several secondary evils of such a scheme are cogently advanced by counsel for the appellants. It would produce situations in which the personal predilections of the supervisors or the affluence or political power of the applicant would have a greater part in determining rezoning applications than the suitability of the land for a particular use from an overall community point of view. Further, while it may not be readily apparent with a minimum acreage requirement of 25 acres, "flexible selective zoning" carries evils akin to "spot zoning," for in theory it allows piecemeal placement of relatively small acreage areas in differently zoned districts. Finally, because of the absence of a simultaneous delineation of the boundaries of the new "F–1" district, no notice of the true nature of his vicinity or its limitations is afforded the property owner or the prospective property owner. While it is undoubtedly true that a property owner has no vested interest in an existing zoning map and, accordingly, is always subject to the possibility of a rezoning without notice, the zoning ordinance and its accompanying zoning maps should nevertheless at any given time reflect the current planned use of the community's land so as to afford as much notice as possible.

Appellees vigorously contend that a comprehensive plan does exist for the Township of Lower Gwynedd and is set forth in the record. Essentially, appellees argue, the plan contemplates a "greenbelt" township predominantly residential in character with a certain amount of compatible nonresidential occupancy consisting of shopping centers, research and engineering centers and limited industrial uses. It also contemplates that these non-residential uses shall be strictly controlled as to setback, building area, noise, smoke, sewage disposal, etc., and that the means of such control shall be vested in the supervisors through strict ordinances of general application such as Ordinance 28, supra, setting up the requirements and limitations on limited industrial uses. In turn, these tools of control and minimum standards are to be the polestars (along with other factors, such as the proximity of through highways, availability of adequate streams for effluent disposal, etc.), in any further consideration to be given by the planning commission and the supervisors to applications for specific locations or areas. By adopting this approach, the appellees have confused comprehensive planning with a comprehensive plan. The foregoing are certainly the rudiments and fundamentals which enter into the promulgation of a planned zoning scheme for the township. They are, however, only the most preliminary and basic considerations from which the ultimate decision of selective land uses are to be made. Until such time, no final formulation exists which satisfies the "comprehensive plan" requirement within the meaning of the enabling legislation.

As to the second objection, the township supervisors have gone beyond their function of implementing a comprehensive plan with zoning regulations: they are to analyze on a case by case basis for rezoning purposes individual applications and accompanying technical plans for structure and development to determine their suitability and compliance with the standards they themselves established in the ordinance.

* * *

Under the "flexible selective zoning" scheme here under attack, changes in the prevailing zoning regulations are to be made on a case by case basis, not, however, by a specialized body such as the zoning board of adjustment, but by the legislative body, without rigid statutory standards and without any scintilla of notice of potential change as in the case of special exceptions. The standard review by the courts, as indeed the appellees argue we should adopt herein, would be nothing more than to assure ourselves that each legislative act of amending the zoning map by the township supervisors was not "arbitrary, capricious, or unreasonable." If the legislature contemplated such a novel scheme of zoning, withdrawing as it does a close standard of court review in the very delicate area of protecting property rights, and shifting as it does the focus from planned land use to individual solicitation, we are convinced it would have said so in more clear and exact terms than are found anywhere in the enabling legislation.

Order reversed.

[Concurring opinion omitted.]

Notes

1.   The New York Court of Appeals in Rodgers v. Village of Tarrytown, 302 N.Y. 115, 96 N.E.2d 731 (1951), upheld a zoning provision creating a special zone for garden apartments without locating any such areas on the zoning map and inviting owners of land meeting the minimum requirements to submit requests for rezoning; the court found that the provision was in accord with a comprehensive plan and not illegal spot zoning. This case is reproduced in the subsequent section dealing with floating zones.

2.   Compare Case v. City of Los Angeles, 218 Cal.App.2d 36, 32 Cal. Rptr. 271 (Dist.Ct.App.1963). Applicants owned 47 acres in an R1 zone. They applied for a "conditional use permit" for a deluxe apartment complex. The zoning administrator issued the permit under an ordinance which permitted housing projects as conditional uses in the single family zone. Housing projects were defined: "A group of residential buildings, most of which contain more than one dwelling unit, located on a lot having an area of five acres or more and arranged in accordance with a plan of development for the entire project, with provision for adequate open spaces and conveniently located service facilities." The ordinance authorized the zoning administrator to issue a conditional use permit if he found the proposed location would be " * * * desirable to the public convenience and welfare and * * * in harmony with the various elements and objectives of the Master Plan."

On appeal, issuance of the permit was affirmed in turn by the planning commission, city council, trial court and intermediate appellate court. Neighbors contesting the permit urged that the conditional use provisions were unconstitutional because they provided for rezoning without an ordinance amending the master plan. The California appeals court rejected this, saying:

"The acts of the administrative agencies in approving the location of a conditional use is not a rezoning of the property. The agency in this case simply found that the legislatively imposed standards exist and thereby effectuated the legislative permission to construct a housing project in the R1 zone."

Also see Tilles Investment Co. v. Town of Huntington, 74 N.Y.2d 885, 547 N.Y.S.2d 835, 547 N.E.2d 90 (1989), where the owner of 52 acres zoned residential challenged the town's refusal to rezone his land for commercial (2 other parcels had been rezoned). The court held that the decision was in accord with the comprehensive plan, stating that the statute mandated comprehensive planning, not slavish servitude to any particular comprehensive plan.

3. In Giger v. City of Omaha, 232 Neb. 676, 442 N.W.2d 182 (1989), the city and a developer entered into a development agreement, the property was rezoned and building permits were issued. At that point neighbors sought to enjoin the rezoning and permits. The court upheld the development agreement as not invalid spot zoning.

4. In many jurisdictions voters can initiate ordinances (see the section of this chapter on citizen involvement, infra). What if voters initiate a zoning change that downzones an individual's property? Can the owner challenge the initiated ordinance as spot zoning? Compare Lum Yip Kee, Ltd. v. City and County of Honolulu, 70 Hawaii 179, 767 P.2d 815 (1989) where the court found that the initiated ordinance was not illegal spot zoning with Kaiser Hawaii Kai Development Co. v. City and County of Honolulu, 70 Hawaii 480, 777 P.2d 244 (1989) where the court held that the initiative procedure was improper to downzone one tract of land.

BARTRAM v. ZONING COMMISSION

Supreme Court of Errors of Connecticut, 1949.
136 Conn. 89, 68 A.2d 308.

MALTBIE, CHIEF JUSTICE. This is an appeal by the defendants from a judgment sustaining an appeal from a decision of the zoning commission of the city of Bridgeport taken in accordance with the provisions of sec. 845 of the General Statutes. The commission changed the classification of a Sylvan Avenue lot, with a frontage of 125 feet and a depth of 133 feet, from a residence zone to a business No. 3 zone.

With some corrections to which the defendants are entitled, the controlling facts found by the court are these: Zoning regulations became effective in Bridgeport on June 1, 1926. They provided for three classes of residence zones, two classes of business zones, and two classes of industrial zones. In 1937 the regulations were amended to establish business zones No. 3 and special regulations were adopted as to them. These regulations, as further amended, contain provisions as to the type of construction of buildings and require open yards about them, a setback of thirty feet from the street and parking facilities for cars on private property; the sale of liquors was originally restricted but this provision was amended to forbid sales of liquor under any permit for a tavern, restaurant or all-liquor package store. The territory surrounding the lot in question is contiguous to the northern boundary of the city and quite a distance from its shopping and business center. Previous to 1936, both sides of Sylvan Avenue to a depth of 100 feet had for a considerable distance been in a business No. 1 zone, but in that year the classification was changed to residence A; and since that date, as before, a considerable territory in the neighborhood of the premises in question has been in residential zones. When zoning was originally adopted, the area was sparsely built up and contained much farm land. Beginning before 1936, people desiring to get away from the noise and congestion of the center of the city began to build homes there; at present it is quite generally built up with residences, at least 40 per cent of which have been constructed since 1936. Most of the houses in the immediate vicinity of the premises in question are comparatively new; they are neat, one-family homes, with well-kept lawns and attractive plantings; and they give every indication that a self-respecting community of people of moderate means have moved to this outlying section of the city. In the vicinity of the premises in question there exist as nonconforming uses four stores, three selling groceries or meat and one a liquor package store. One of the former is a small store in a building almost opposite the premises in question, the second floor of which is occupied as a residence. There is no drug store in the vicinity. There is also, near the premises in question, a small church. Sylvan Avenue is a street sixty feet wide and it is a principal traffic artery to and from the section surrounding it.

The application for the change of zone was made by the defendant Rome. He presented to the commission at the hearing before it plans for a building he proposes to erect, which in all respects would comply with the regulations for a business No. 3 zone, which would contain provision for five places of business—a drug, a hardware and a grocery store, a bakeshop and a beauty parlor—and which would provide for the parking of cars in the rear of the building, and between it and the street line. Aside from Rome, no one appeared to support his application, but ten residents and property owners in the neighborhood opposed it. They gave various reasons for the position they took, among them these: They desired to have the residential character of the section preserved from business development; in many instances they had purchased or developed their properties in reliance upon the residence zoning of the area and in the expectation that this zoning status would remain unchanged; they were fearful that the business zoning of any portion of the area would be destructive of the peace and quiet they desired to have preserved; they believed that the business zoning of any part of it, however small and wherever located, would have a tendency to break down the residence zoning of the area by making further business zoning in it more likely; and there was no present need for further and more adequate shopping facilities in the neighborhood. A remonstrance against granting the application signed by more than seventy residents in the neighborhood was also filed with the commission; but only some forty-six different addresses of the signers appear on it; in a number of instances the signers were husband and wife or two or more residing in the same house; and many of them lived at a considerable distance from the premises in question. Within a radius no longer than the distance to the addresses given by some of the signers are more than 200 residences.

The commission gave the following reasons for its decision: 1. The location is on Sylvan Avenue, a sixty-foot street, and there is no shopping center within a mile of it. To the north of this tract there is a very large development but only small nonconforming grocery stores to serve the people. 2. There is practically only one house, adjacent to this tract on the north, which will be directly affected by this change of zone. 3. Business No. 3 regulations, with their thirty-foot setback and liquor restrictions, were designed to meet conditions like this and help alleviate the great congestion in the centralized shopping districts. The court also found that a member of the commission testified that it was its policy to encourage decentralization of business in order to relieve traffic congestion and that, as part of that policy, it was considered desirable to permit neighborhood stores in outlying districts; and nowhere in the record is there any suggestion that this testimony is not true.

The trial court concluded that the change was an instance of "spot zoning." A limitation upon the powers of zoning authorities which has been in effect ever since zoning statutes were made applicable generally to municipalities in the state is that the regulations they adopt must be made "in accordance with a comprehensive plan." Public Acts, 1925, c. 242, sec. 3 (Rev.1949, sec. 837). "A 'comprehensive plan' means 'a general plan to control and direct the use and development of property in a municipality or a large part of it by dividing it into districts according to the present and potential use of the properties.' " Bishop v. Board of Zoning Appeals, 133 Conn. 614, 618, 53 A.2d 659; State ex rel. Spiros v. Payne, 131 Conn. 647, 652, 41 A.2d 908. Action by a zoning authority which gives to a single lot or a small area privileges which are not extended to other land in the vicinity is in general against sound public policy and obnoxious to the law. It can be justified only when it is done in furtherance of a general plan properly adopted for and designed to serve the best interests of the community as a whole.

The vice of spot zoning lies in the fact that it singles out for special treatment a lot or a small area in a way that does not further such a plan. Where, however, in pursuance of it, a zoning commission takes such action, its decision can be assailed only on the ground that it abused the discretion vested in it by the law. To permit business in a small area within a residence zone may fall within the scope of such a plan, and to do so, unless it amounts to unreasonable or arbitrary action, is not unlawful. Bishop v. Board of Zoning Appeals, supra; see Parsons v. Wethersfield, 135 Conn. 24, 29, 60 A.2d 771. The zoning regulations of Bridgeport were adopted under the provisions of the General Statutes which gave the commission power to divide the municipality into districts and in each district to regulate the construction and use of buildings and land, and to change the regulations from time to time.

General Statutes, Rev.1930, secs. 424, 425, as amended (Rev.1949, secs. 837, 838); see De Palma v. Town Plan Commission of Greenwich, 123 Conn. 257, 265, 193 A. 868. The commission might be guilty of spot zoning either in the original regulations it made or in later amendments, but, if in one or the other it decides, on facts affording a sufficient basis and in the exercise of a proper discretion, that it would serve the best interests of the community as a whole to permit a use of a single lot or small area in a different way than was allowed in surrounding territory, it would not be guilty of spot zoning in any sense obnoxious to the law. That was the situation in this case, and we cannot sustain the conclusion of the trial court that the action of the commission was improper as an instance of spot zoning.

The trial court also concluded that the change in zoning was in violation of the declared objects of the zoning regulations of Bridgeport, as stated in their first section. That section states among the purposes to be served by them the promotion of the health, safety, morals and general welfare of the community and the lessening of congestion in streets. The reasons which led the commission to take the action it did, as we have stated them above, fall well within the scope of these purposes. The fact that the change was advocated only by Rome at the hearing and was opposed by numerous property owners and residents in the neighborhood did not, as the trial court concluded, deprive the commission of power to make it. It does not appear that there was anything like unanimous opposition to the change of property owners in the surrounding territory; but, even if there had been, it was the duty of the commission to look beyond the effect of the change upon them to the general welfare of the city. The reasons given before the commission by those who opposed the change were quite largely based on fear that other like changes might be made rather than upon the effect of the particular one in question. The property of no one was taken by the commission's decision; nor is there any finding or, indeed, evidence that property values would be affected; and no such situation is before us as was presented in Strain v. Mims, 123 Conn. 275, 193 A. 754, where, in speaking of a change in zoning from business to residence which practically affected only a single property, we said (p. 286): "However, where the value of property of an individual is seriously affected by a zoning regulation especially applicable to it, this fact imposes an obligation carefully to consider the question whether the regulation does in fact tend to serve the public welfare and the recognized purposes of zoning." Property owners in the neighborhood had no right to a continuation of the existing situation which could be effective against a decision by the commission reached legally and properly. The state, through the authority it vests in zoning authorities, "may regulate any business or the use of any property in the interest of the public health, safety or welfare, provided this be done reasonably. To that extent the public interest is supreme and the private interest must yield." Windsor v. Whitney, 95 Conn. 357, 366, 111 A. 354, 356, 12 A.L.R. 669; Strain v. Mims, supra.

The commission could not properly be held, upon the record in this case, to have acted in violation of law in making the change it did.

How best the purposes of zoning can be accomplished in any municipality is primarily in the discretion of its zoning authority; that description is a broad one; and unless it transcends the limitations set by law its decisions are subject to review in the courts only to the extent of determining whether or not it has acted in abuse of that discretion. First Nat. Bank & Trust Co. v. Zoning Board of Appeals, 126 Conn. 228, 237, 10 A.2d 691. A court is without authority to substitute its own judgment for that vested by the statutes in a zoning authority. Piccolo v. West Haven, 120 Conn. 449, 455, 181 A. 615; Mrowka v. Board of Zoning Appeals, 134 Conn. 149, 155, 55 A.2d 909. In view of the facts presented in this case, the trial court could not properly find that the policy which determined the decision of the commission would so clearly fail to serve the proper purposes of zoning in the city that the court might set aside that decision; nor do the facts show that it was unreasonable to apply that policy in the situation before us. This is illustrated by the fact that, had this lot been placed in a business No. 3 zone as an incident to the adoption of an original plan for zoning the city as a whole, that action could not on this record be held an unreasonable exercise by the commission of its powers.

There is error, the judgment is set aside and the case is remanded with direction to enter judgment dismissing the appeal. * * *

[Dissenting opinion omitted.]

Notes

1.   Although the Bartram case is rather old, the approach taken by the court in that case is still the prevailing approach in most jurisdictions. For another example, see Vella v. Town of Camden, 677 A.2d 1051 (Me.1996) where the owner of an inn sued to set aside zoning amendments that favored a competing innkeeper on grounds of spot zoning inconsistent with the comprehensive plan.

2.   Compare spot zoning which creates a small residential district in the heart of a commercial district, Geisenfeld v. Shorewood, 232 Wis. 410, 287 N.W. 683 (1939) and Rowland v. City of Racine, 223 Wis. 488, 271 N.W. 36 (1937), with spot zoning which creates a small business district in the heart of a residential district as in the principal case. See also Town of Marblehead v. Rosenthal, 316 Mass. 124, 55 N.E.2d 13 (1944); Wilkins v. San Bernardino, 29 Cal.2d 332, 175 P.2d 542 (1946); C.L. Associates v. Board of Supervisors of Montgomery Twp., 51 Pa.Cmwlth. 627, 415 A.2d 134 (1980); Mesolella v. City of Providence, 439 A.2d 1370 (R.I.1982). For further discussion of the principal case, see 1 Williams, American Land Planning Law § 26.05 (1988).

3.   Is a decision refusing to rezone a parcel to a classification called for by the comprehensive plan presumptively invalid? See City of Gainesville v. Hope, 377 So.2d 736 (Fla.App.1979), and Clinkscales v. City of Lake Oswego, 47 Or.App. 1117, 615 P.2d 1164 (1980).

SECTION 4. ZONING ADMINISTRATION
AND FLEXIBILITY

A. INTRODUCTION

Refresh your recollection about the relationship between the master plan and zoning. Then read the planning and zoning enabling legislation in your state, paying particular attention to the administrative machinery for zoning.

A common pattern set by the Standard Enabling Act includes: (1) a zoning or planning commission to make necessary studies, develop and prepare zoning ordinances or amendments and recommend them to the local governing body; (2) a zoning board of adjustment (sometimes called a board of review or board of appeals) to consider individual applications for zoning variances and exceptions and for the continuance of non-conforming uses; and (3) building inspectors or other officials to receive applications, to issue use or building permits, inspect the premises, issue stop orders and the like.

There has not been in the zoning field as much delegation of rule-making authority to administrative agencies as is present in other fields of regulation.

"Flexibility" in zoning is obtained in a variety of ways. First of all, a carefully drawn ordinance based on complete studies and hard work is apt to provide for a problem situation about which another less carefully done ordinance is silent. Other ways of putting play (sometimes too much play) into the joints of zoning are (1) construction or interpretation of the ordinance, (2) the zoning variance, (3) the exception, (4) the special use permit not quite classifiable as an exception, and (5) amendment of the ordinance.

For a case in which the court held that planners cannot have ad hoc flexibility, see Hardin County v. Jost, 897 S.W.2d 592 (Ky.App.1995). Here the entire county was placed in one zone and every land use, except agriculture, was designated as a conditional use. To determine if a conditional use permit would issue, a point system under a "growth guidance assessment" scheme was utilized. The court found the entire ordinance invalid in that sufficient standards were not set forth, and the ordinance left land use "to the subjective whim and caprice of the zoning authority."

GREEN, ARE "SPECIAL USE" PROCEDURES
IN TROUBLE?
12 Zoning Digest 73–75 (1960).

* * * Suppose we have a city whose zoning ordinance divides residential districts into two classifications: a single-family residence district and a multi-family residence district. And suppose that the city council, beseiged with requests to rezone individual lots in single-family districts so as to permit erection of apartment houses, decides to study

all possible ways in which it could handle this problem. It discovers the following possibilities.

Single amendment. First, the council might try a "once and for all" amendment to the zoning ordinance, in hopes that it would never have to face the problem again. This might take any of three forms:

(a) The "wide open" approach—amending the ordinance to permit apartments, without restraint, in any single-family residence district. This would amount to a reversal of the assumption embodied in the existing ordinance that apartment houses are usually detrimental to single-family neighborhoods.

(b) The "performance standards" approach—attempting to pick out and deal with the noxious features of apartment houses by direct regulation rather than merely barring all such houses from single-family districts. For example, the ordinance might permit apartment houses in such districts *provided* the house was situated on a proportionally larger lot then required for a single-family dwelling, had larger than usual yards, and furnished off-street parking space.

(c) The "eye to the future" approach—rezoning as multi-family districts the maximum amount of land which could conceivably be used for apartment houses in a 20–, 30–, or 40–year period. The effects could be disastrous, of course.

Periodic amendments. Second, the council might decide that the matter would be handled better by "slicing off a little bit of the dog's tail at a time;" i.e., by a series of amendments, usually made in response to applications from property owners but occasionally on the recommendation of the planning commission. This approach too might take several forms:

(a) The "spot zoning" approach—amending the ordinance without rhyme or reason, so as to rezone scattered single-family lots to multi-family. This, of course, is subject to legal difficulties.

(b) The "rezoning according to plan" approach—mapping the areas eventually to be devoted to multi-family use and then gradually rezoning these areas from single-family to multi-family.

(c) The "floating zone" approach—amending the ordinance to specify the circumstances under which an area will be rezoned to multi-family (or garden apartment, planned residential district, etc.) and then rezoning, on application, tracts that can meet these specifications.

(d) The "contract rezoning" approach—amending the ordinance on request, but only subject to a contract with the owner that he will develop the property in a given way or subject to the owner's placing appropriate deed restrictions on his property. The legal infirmities of this approach have been widely discussed, and we need not go into them here.

Administrative treatment. Third, the council might decide that the problem could best be handled as an administrative matter by the board of adjustment. It could once again follow two approaches:

(a) The "special exception" approach—amending the ordinance so as to authorize the board of adjustment to permit apartment houses in single-family districts in cases where the board makes findings specified in the ordinance and subject to such reasonable and appropriate conditions as the board might impose. This, of course, allows more detailed treatment of individual cases and the provision of safeguards for neighboring properties.

(b) The "variance" approach—not amending the ordinance at all, and forcing the applicant to seek a variance from the board of adjustment on the basis of his individual "practical difficulty or unnecessary hardship" (as those phrases have been defined and amplified by the courts). In most states by court decision, and under many ordinance or enabling act provisions, "use variances" are illegal, but this does not always stop boards from granting them.

"Special use" procedure. Fourth, the council might decide upon an approach somewhat between the "floating zone" amendment procedure and the "special exception" procedure. This we shall call the "special use" approach.[10]

The "special use" approach is designed to handle those uses whose side effects may be of neighborhood or citywide importance—such as unified housing developments (typically garden apartments) or unified commercial areas (the shopping center, neighborhood or regional) or uses with marked nuisance-like characteristics (such as fat rendering plants). Because of these effects, the location of this type of use is thought to raise planning considerations that the board of adjustment has neither the background nor the staff to handle properly. On the other hand, there is a desire to give such applications the detailed type of consideration and control that is possible under the board's "special exception" procedures, but which is not possible under amendment procedures due to legal limitations on "spot zoning" and "contract zoning." * * *

B. AMENDMENT OF ORDINANCE

(1) Single Amendment

DUGGAN v. COOK COUNTY

Supreme Court of Illinois, 1975.
60 Ill.2d 107, 324 N.E.2d 406.

[The landowner's 147–acre farm was zoned for single-family dwellings on 20,000 square foot lots. He requested that the ordinance be

---

10. Here our terminology differs somewhat from that of the New Jersey court, which regards "special use" as merely a more precise label for the "special exception." Tullo v. Township of Millburn, 54 N.J.Super. 483, 149 A.2d 620 (1959).

amended to rezone the property and sought a special use permit for development of a mobile home park, both of which were denied at the administrative level. The Illinois Appellate Court reversed and remanded and the county appealed to the supreme court. Only a small portion of the opinion is given.]

DAVIS, JUSTICE:

* * *

The defendants contend that the appellate court ignored the legal precedents which are applicable when the validity of a zoning ordinance is challenged, as applied to a particular piece of property, and that the appellate court, in effect, overruled the trial court judgment even though it was not contrary to the manifest weight of the evidence. We will consider and further comment on these contentions, but first we will consider the law applicable to this case.

The zoning ordinance of defendant Cook County is presumed valid, and plaintiffs carry the burden of establishing that the existing classification is unreasonable and oppressive as applied to their land. (Camboni's, Inc. v. County of Du Page (1962), 26 Ill.2d 427, 432, 187 N.E.2d 212.) The plaintiffs must establish by clear and convincing evidence that the existing ordinance, as applied to their property, is arbitrary and unreasonable and without substantial relation to the public health, safety, comfort, morals or general welfare. (Bennett v. City of Chicago (1962), 24 Ill.2d 270, 273–274, 181 N.E.2d 96.) Specifically, when plaintiffs have been denied the issuance of a special use permit, as sought in this case, they carry the burden of showing that such denial bears no real and substantial relation to the public health, safety, morals or general welfare. Pioneer Trust & Savings Bank v. McHenry County (1968), 41 Ill.2d 77, 84, 241 N.E.2d 454.

The general factors considered in arriving at this determination include the uses and zoning of nearby properties, the extent to which existing zoning diminishes the property's value and the proposed zoning enhances it, the suitability of the property for the purposes permitted under the existing zoning, and the relative gain to the public as compared to the hardship imposed upon the property owner by the existing and the proposed zoning uses. (Tillitson v. City of Urbana (1963), 29 Ill.2d 22, 27, 193 N.E.2d 1; La Salle National Bank of Chicago v. Cook County (1957), 12 Ill.2d 40, 47, 145 N.E.2d 65.) Ultimately if it clearly appears that the relative gain to the public is small when compared with the hardship imposed upon the property owner by the zoning restriction, there is then no valid basis for the exercise of the police power to so limit the owner's right to the use of his property. Pioneer Trust & Savings Bank v. McHenry County (1968), 41 Ill.2d 77, 85, 241 N.E.2d 454; Marquette National Bank v. Cook County (1962), 24 Ill.2d 497, 502, 182 N.E.2d 147.

* * *

It is a fair conclusion from all of the evidence that the land cannot reasonably be developed under its present R3 zoning. While some witnesses felt the highest and best use of the land was for development as a mobile-home park and others felt it was for industrial use, they readily concurred in the view that the present R3 single-family zoning would not permit economical residential development.

While the witnesses differed in their conclusions to some extent, we believe the appellate court correct in concluding that the proposed zoning would not unduly adversely affect surrounding properties. While much of the land is zoned R3 in the area, little is being developed. The manager of the adjoining manufacturing use testified that the proposed development would depreciate the value of its property. He also testified that they would not wish to locate their plant next to a school, a shopping center, or certain types of industrial developments. Other witnesses, plaintiffs' and defendants', testified that the proposed development would not have an adverse effect on the adjoining manufacturing property. The worst that could be said was that the proposed development might cause a "wait and see" attitude for the development of other lands located close by, lands which were not being developed anyway. Opinions customarily differ in a zoning case. This, however, does not necessarily mean that plaintiffs have failed in their burden of proof. Myers v. City of Elmhurst (1958), 12 Ill.2d 537, 544, 147 N.E.2d 300; La Salle National Bank of Chicago v. Cook County (1957), 12 Ill.2d 40, 47, 145 N.E.2d 65.

* * *

Affirmed in part and remanded, with directions.

Notes

1. In the Duggan case the court cites La Salle Nat'l Bank v. County of Cook, 12 Ill.2d 40, 145 N.E.2d 65 (1957). In an oft-cited portion of the opinion in the latter case, the court said:

> Even though the validity of each zoning ordinance must be determined on its own facts and circumstances * * * yet an examination of numerous cases discloses that among the facts which may be taken into consideration in determining validity of an ordinance are the following: (1) The existing uses and zoning of nearby property * * * (2) the extent to which property values are diminished by the particular zoning restrictions * * * (3) the extent to which the destruction of property values of plaintiff promotes the health, safety, morals or general welfare of the public * * * (4) the relative gain to the public as compared to the hardship imposed upon the individual property owner * * * (5) the suitability of the subject property for the zoned purposes * * * (6) the length of time the property has been vacant as zoned considered in the context of land development in the area in the vicinity of the subject property. * * *

> No one factor is controlling. It is not the mere loss in value alone that is significant, but the fact that the public welfare does not require

the restriction and resulting loss. When it is shown that no reasonable basis of public welfare requires the limitation or restriction and resulting loss, the ordinance fails and the presumption of validity is dissipated. * * * The law does not require that the subject property be totally unsuitable for the purpose classified but it is sufficient that a substantial decrease in value results from a classification bearing no substantial relation to the public welfare.

2. If the original zoning ordinance and map is a "legislative" act of the local government, then why should not the courts treat a zoning amendment as new "legislation" subject to a very narrow scope of judicial review? Few courts have taken the trouble to articulate a theory of review of zoning amendments. In some states, however, unusual theories have evolved. One of the more interesting theories is what has been called the Maryland rule to the effect that a zoning amendment can only be justified by a showing of mistake in the original ordinance or a sufficient change in the physical circumstances surrounding the property in question. See the interesting case, Finney v. Halle, 241 Md. 224, 216 A.2d 530 (1966). The Maryland view has been followed elsewhere. See, Davis v. City of Albuquerque, 98 N.M. 319, 648 P.2d 777 (1982); City of New Albany v. Ray, 417 So.2d 550 (Miss.1982). Also see Information Please, Inc. v. Board of County Comm'rs, 42 Colo.App. 392, 600 P.2d 86 (1979). In City of Virginia Beach v. Virginia Land Investment Ass'n No. 1, 239 Va. 412, 389 S.E.2d 312 (1990) the court held that the downzoning of some 400 acres of land from planned unit development to agricultural was invalid as piecemeal downzoning not justified by change in circumstances or prior mistake.

3. Various judicial approaches to reviewing local zoning decisions will be explored in more detail in the subsequent section, Judicial Review of Zoning.

4. When a zoning amendment has been adopted, usually the nearby neighbors are the parties who object and may seek judicial review of the amendment. Courts have rarely considered the question of standing to be a problem in such cases[11]; the problem is usually seen as what burden of proof the neighbors must meet. The burden is typically stated as the establishment of the city's rezoning as "arbitrary." On the other hand, when a zoning amendment is denied and the property owner seeking rezoning goes to court, should his burden be one of showing that the failure to amend the zoning ordinance amounts to a "taking" of his property? If the property

---

11. But see Palmer v. St. Louis County, 591 S.W.2d 39 (Mo.App.1979) where the court held homeowners within the zoning district had no standing to challenge a rezoning because they lived more than a mile from the proposed development and had neither "audio nor visual contact" with it; Nautilus of Exeter, Inc. v. Town of Exeter, 139 N.H. 450, 656 A.2d 407 (1995) (property owners from .8 miles to 6 miles from hospital's proposed exercise and rehabilitation facility held not to have standing); Cohen v. Zoning Bd. of Appeals of Plymouth, 35 Mass.App. 619, 624 N.E.2d 119 (1993) (next door business competitor denied standing to challenge shopping center rezoning); Macon–Bibb County Planning & Zoning Comm. v. Vineville Neighborhood Ass'n, 218 Ga.App. 668, 462 S.E.2d 764 (1995) where the court held neighborhood association lacked standing to challenge a rezoning for a shopping center. Also see Annotation, Standing of Owner of Property Adjacent to Zoned Property, but not within Territory of Zoning Authority, to Attack Zoning, 69 A.L.R.3d 805 (1976). A nonabutting property owner who was a business competitor was allowed standing in Weeks Restaurant Corp. v. City of Dover, 119 N.H. 541, 404 A.2d 294 (1979).

owner convinces the court that the existing zoning as applied to his property is confiscatory, what is the proper remedy? Declare the ordinance unconstitutional in whole? In part? Either way, is the result that the property in question is unzoned leaving the victorious owner free to do anything? Pennsylvania has adopted a procedure known as the "curative amendment" to deal in part with this problem. See Krasnowiecki, Zoning Litigation and the New Pennsylvania Procedures, 120 U.Pa.L.Rev. 1029 (1972). In the absence of a legislative solution to this problem, some courts have framed orders in zoning cases which are sensitive to the potential disaster if property is subject to no zoning restrictions whatsoever. See e.g., Union Oil Co. of California v. City of Worthington, 62 Ohio St.2d 263, 405 N.E.2d 277 (1980); Ed Zaagman, Inc. v. City of Kentwood, 406 Mich. 137, 277 N.W.2d 475 (1979). In the Michigan case the court identified five alternatives in situations where a city's denial of a rezoning is found to be arbitrary and confiscatory. These alternatives are: (1) Leave the parcel in issue unzoned until either a use is instituted by the owner or the parcel is rezoned; (2) enjoin the city from enforcing a zoning classification other than that urged by the owner and determined appropriate by the court; (3) enjoin the city from enforcing the zoning classification and affirmatively order the use proposed by the owner; (4) enjoin the city, but remand to the appropriate municipal authority to present for the trial court's consideration within 60 days an amendatory ordinance comporting with the dictates of equity and constitutional reasonableness as applied to owner's parcel; (5) remand to the appropriate municipal authority for an administrative hearing to determine an appropriate use for the parcel. The majority of the court adopted alternative (4) along with detailed instructions on the course to be followed by the lower court if the proposed amendatory ordinance is not satisfactory to either side. The court also made its finding retroactive to all zoning cases filed prior to the date of the opinion and still pending in trial and appellate courts. An extensive concurring opinion by Justice Levin argues for alternative (5) (remand for a full administrative hearing on the proper use for the parcel in dispute).

The Supreme Court of Michigan overruled the Ed Zaagman case in Schwartz v. City of Flint, 426 Mich. 295, 395 N.W.2d 678 (1986), holding that allowing a trial court to prescribe the proper zoning constitutes a judicial usurpation of a legislative function, violative of the separation of powers provisions of the state constitution. The court then opted for an approach which would leave the municipality free to rezone the property, but would allow the trial court to enjoin the municipality from interfering with a use the property owner shows to be reasonable by a preponderance of the evidence. Again, Justice Levin filed an extensive concurring opinion. After the remand in the Schwartz case, the city and the developer negotiated a zoning settlement; then, in 1989, the developer sought $7 million in compensation for the previous "taking" of his property. In a per curiam opinion, Schwartz v. City of Flint, 187 Mich.App. 191, 466 N.W.2d 357 (1991), the court held that the zoning settlement was res judicata and barred the suit for a money judgment.

5. What if a city refuses to rezone property in a case where the nearby neighbors do not object? Is any legal significance to be given to the nonobjec-

tions of neighbors? See Gitelman, The Role of the Neighbors in Zoning Cases, 28 Ark.L.Rev. 221 (1975).

6. Granted that neighbors are almost always given standing to challenge a zoning amendment, what about an unincorporated neighborhood association or civic group? In Douglaston Civic Ass'n, Inc. v. Galvin, 36 N.Y.2d 1, 364 N.Y.S.2d 830, 324 N.E.2d 317 (1974) the defendant challenged the standing of the civic association. The court awarded standing and in the course of the opinion discussed the provisions of the Model Land Development Code, §§ 2–304, 2–307, which specifically give standing to neighborhood associations. The note to § 2–307 of the Code offers a good discussion of the problem. Compare with the Galvin case, Friends of Pine Bush v. Planning Bd. of City of Albany, 71 A.D.2d 780, 419 N.Y.S.2d 295 (1979), appeal dismissed 49 N.Y.2d 860, 427 N.Y.S.2d 797, 404 N.E.2d 1338 (1980). Also see Citizens Growth Management Coalition of West Palm Beach, Inc. v. City of West Palm Beach, 450 So.2d 204 (Fla.1984) where the court rejected standing by a citizen association to challenge a downtown redevelopment project.

(2) Contract or Conditional Rezoning

SYLVANIA ELECTRIC PRODUCTS, INC. v. CITY OF NEWTON

Supreme Judicial Court of Massachusetts, 1962.
344 Mass. 428, 183 N.E.2d 118.

[Landowners challenge an amendment of Newton's zoning ordinance, which changed the classification of 153.6 acres of land owned by Sylvania from residence A to limited manufacturing. Other facts appear in the opinion. The trial judge held the rezoning valid and landowners appeal.]

WHITTEMORE, JUSTICE. * * * The principal issue is the effect of Sylvania's imposition of restrictions on the locus in connection with the enactment of the amending ordinance and of steps taken by the planning board, and others acting for the city, to cause Sylvania so to do.

In respect of this issue the judge found these facts: Sylvania on April 14, 1960, having an option to purchase a parcel containing 180 acres, inclusive of the rezoned locus, petitioned the board of aldermen (aldermen) to reclassify the parcel. On May 11, 1960, the planning board, after a public hearing held jointly with the aldermen's committee on claims and rules, reported that it had asked the city's planning consultant to review the petition and had decided to withhold action until he should report. On June 2, 1960, the board reported to the aldermen its vote to approve Sylvania's petition except that it recommended retaining in the residence A district a substantial frontage on Nahanton Street, including a parcel of about eighteen and one-half acres on the east side of the parcel adjacent to the property of the Charles River Country Club.

"Meanwhile, Sylvania in consultation with the planning consultant * * * and members of the planning board and the claims and rules committee * * *, had agreed to certain restrictions upon its use of * * * [the locus]." and had agreed to cede three acres, comprising the south-easterly tip of the parcel, to "Oak Hill Park Association" to be retained in the residence district. The restrictions, to be operative for thirty years from September 1, 1960, were set out in a draft of a deed attached to a proposed option agreement whereby Sylvania would give the city an option to purchase, within a thirty year period, for $300, a strip of land on the west and southwesterly side (the river side) of the parcel, adjacent to the land of the metropolitan district commission, containing thirty and one-half acres. By the option agreement Sylvania would agree to abide by the restrictions in the draft deed during the option term pending the city's exercise thereof. The intention would be to give the city a dominant estate capable of enforcing the restrictions. The deed was to convey the thirty and one-half acres subject to the restriction for the benefit of Sylvania's adjoining premises that for a period of fifty years no buildings or structures (other than fences) should be erected or maintained on the granted premises.

The proposed restrictions limited the floor area of all buildings to be constructed on the premises to 800,000 square feet; required that sixty per cent of the ground area, or seventy-three and nine-tenths acres, be maintained in open space not occupied by buildings, parking areas or roadways; set back the building line from forty to eighty feet; imposed a sliding scale of height restrictions; called for a buffer zone of comparable size to the three acres to be ceded to Oak Hill Park Association and adjacent thereto, on which no structures might be erected; restricted the number and type of signs and the type of lighting; limited the use of buildings to certain, but not all, of the uses permitted in a limited manufacturing district; and established a pattern for traffic in connection with construction on the premises.

On June 27, 1960, the aldermen's committee on claims and rules reported its approval of the petition as modified by the planning board in its formal vote of approval, except that the committee recommended that the strip of Nahanton Street reserved for the residence district be increased in depth from 140 to 180 feet. There was submitted to the June 27 meeting a memorandum by the planning consultant, addressed to the mayor and to the alderman who was chairman of the committee on claims and rules. This memorandum summarized "the acreage break-down on the Sylvania site, based upon the tentative deed restrictions as of June 23, 1960," and included a sketch map of the site delineating the areas and restrictions.

Thereafter, at the June 27 meeting, the aldermen enacted the ordinance which approved Sylvania's petition as modified in accordance with its committee's recommendation "and in connection therewith passed [the] order * * * authorizing the mayor to accept the proposed option agreement."

Sylvania took title to the Nahanton Street parcel on July 6, 1960, and thereafter on that day executed the option agreement with attached form of deed. Certified copies of the ordinance of June 27, 1960, which amended the zoning ordinance and of the order which authorized the mayor to accept the option bear the indorsement "Executive Department Approved July 7, 1960." The deed form and option agreement were recorded on July 8, 1960.

In several other jurisdictions votes to rezone on the express condition that the owner impose restrictions (sometimes called "contract zoning") have been held invalid. Hartnett v. Austin, 93 So.2d 86 (Fla.). Baylis v. City of Baltimore, 219 Md. 164, 148 A.2d 429; Rose v. Paape, 221 Md. 369, 157 A.2d 618; Carole Highlands Citizens Ass'n, Inc. v. Board of County Com'rs of Prince Georges County, 222 Md. 44, 158 A.2d 663; V.F. Zahodiakin Engr. Corp. v. Zoning Bd. of Adjustment of City of Summit, 8 N.J. 386, 86 A.2d 127. See Houston Petroleum Co. v. Automotive Prod. Credit Ass'n, 9 N.J. 122, 87 A.2d 319.

Rathkopf, The Law of Zoning and Planning (3d ed.) pp. 74–79, states that "The basis of such rule is that the rezoning of a particular parcel of land upon conditions not imposed by the zoning ordinance generally in the particular district into which the land has been rezoned is prima facie evidence of 'spot zoning' in its most maleficent aspect, is not in accordance with a comprehensive plan and is beyond the power of the municipality."

The only decision squarely to the contrary which has come to our attention is Church v. Town of Islip, 8 N.Y.2d 254, 259, 203 N.Y.S.2d 866, 869, 168 N.E.2d 680, 683, which the judge in the Land Court found persuasive. The change of zone, sustained in a majority opinion by Desmond, C.J., had been voted on condition that the owners agree that the building should not occupy more than twenty-five per cent of the area, that a six foot fence be erected five feet within the boundary line, and that shrubbery be planted and maintained at fence height. The court said: "Since the Town Board could have, presumably, zoned this * * * corner for business without any restrictions, we fail to see how reasonable conditions invalidate the legislation. * * * All legislation 'by contract' is invalid in the sense that a Legislature cannot bargain away or sell its powers. But we deal here with actualities, not phrases. To meet increasing needs of Suffolk County's own population explosion, and at the same time to make as gradual and as little of an annoyance as possible the change from residence to business on the main highways, the Town Board imposes conditions. There is nothing unconstitutional about it." See Pecora v. Zoning Comm. of Town of Trumbull, 145 Conn. 435, 441, 144 A.2d 48; Pressman v. Mayor & City Council of Baltimore, 222 Md. 330, 344–345, 160 A.2d 379.

We turn to an analysis of what was done in Newton and note that although no condition was imposed by the aldermen in their vote, the conclusion is inescapable that the option proposal was a significant inducement of the zoning amendment and the amendment induced the giving of the option.

It is said that there was a purported, invalid exercise of the zoning power, for the vote operated to subject the locus not only to the restrictions of a limited manufacturing district but also to the restrictions of the option and deed form. But that is not, precisely, what happened. The induced, voluntary action of Sylvania, not the vote of the council, imposed the option restrictions; the vote reclassified land which was being subjected to those restrictions. The zoning decision was that the locus, so restricted by its owner, should be made a limited manufacturing district. That, in form, was an appropriate and untainted exercise of the zoning power.

What was done involved no action contrary to the best interest of the city and hence offensive to general public policy. It involved no extraneous consideration (as, for example, a request to give land for a park elsewhere in the city) which could impeach the enacting vote as a decision solely in respect of rezoning the locus.

We discern no aspect of spot zoning, lack of uniformity, or failure to conform to the comprehensive zoning plan. Even if the restrictions had been made a part of the zoning ordinance, they would not have created spot zoning. The site was all the land in the neighborhood which was proposed for reclassification. The private restrictions in no way made the locus less appropriate for classification as a limited manufacturing district. It is inconsequential that other areas elsewhere in the city, in, or to be put in, such a zoning district, would not have those restrictions. Requirements of uniformity and conformity to a plan do not mean that there must be identity of every relevant aspect in areas given the same zoning classification.

It does not infringe zoning principles that, in connection with a zoning amendment, land use is regulated otherwise than by the amendment. Zoning regulations, as Sylvania points out, exist unaffected by, and do not affect, deed restrictions. Vorenberg v. Bunnell, 257 Mass. 399, 153 N.E. 884, 48 A.L.R. 1431; Snow v. Van Dam, 291 Mass. 477, 197 N.E. 224. The owner of the locus could have imposed restrictions on it prior to the original filing of the petition for rezoning without effect upon the subsequent rezoning vote.

Since the private regulation was, beyond dispute, harmonious, consistent, and beneficial, no hurtful effect requires that we look behind the form of what was done.

It is pointed out that proposals for zoning change can be adopted only after notice and a hearing. G.L. c. 40A, § 6. But the option restrictions did not make the locus a different subject for rezoning from what it was when the notice was given and the hearing held. The voluntary limitations imposed on the use of the land, although relevant in considering the proposal to rezone it, did not call for a new notice and hearing. They could have no adverse effect on anyone other than Sylvania. As noted, none of these restrictions was inconsistent with the requirements for the zoning district. It is far fetched to suggest that citizens opposed to any change might have stayed away from the original hearing in expectation that the proposal would be disapproved. The imposition of these restrictions, subsequent to the hearing, is no more significant than are changes in the zoning proposal itself which are within the scope of the original proposal. Such changes do not require further notice. Town of Burlington v. Dunn, 318 Mass. 216, 218–219, 61 N.E.2d 243, 168 A.L.R. 1181; Doliner v. Town Clerk of Millis, Mass., 175 N.E.2d 925.

It is objected that the council has not determined that the locus, unrestricted, is appropriate to be put in the limited manufacturing district. We agree that the zoning decision applied to the locus as affected by the option agreement. It was not, however, conditioned upon the validity of the option restrictions. The council made an appropriate zoning decision when it determined that the locus, subject to whatever limitations on its use the option effectively placed thereon, be put in the limited manufacturing district. Although not directly in issue, it may be noted that the restrictions appear to have been validly imposed by a sealed and recorded instrument. Sylvania is bound for thirty years even if the option is not exercised. Nothing now turns on an issue of the power of the mayor and council to pay for the dominant estate and take a deed.

The appellants urge that citizens should be able to look with confidence only to the zoning law to ascertain what are the zoning restrictions. The answer is that the option restrictions are not zoning restrictions, and all who have any interest in restriction in the chain of title may find them of record.

The final objection is that even though the officials acted with good intent, beneficially to the city, and consistently with zoning principles, they were nevertheless making an unauthorized use of the zoning power. Unquestionably the officials let it be known that favorable rezoning depended in great likelihood on the adoption of the option restrictions. The planning board acted as a board when it suggested that "the following conditions be obtained by agreement with the proper parties concerned"; the planning consultant was acting as an adviser in respect of zoning when he submitted to the aldermen and the mayor the memorandum which summarized the proposed restrictions; and the aldermen confirmed their participation as a board by the vote which authorized the mayor to accept the proposed option agreement. This was all extrastatutory but nevertheless, proper activity, precedent to the exercise of the zoning power, not the exercise thereof. Whether the city may have the benefit of the pressures of its officials on Sylvania without adoption of the restrictions into the zoning proposal turns on the effect of the restrictions thereon. Since, as stated, the zoning proposal was not essentially changed, it was not necessary to reinitiate the amending process.

The locus was a unique site which was about to go into a specialized use. It was appropriate and lawful to ask the prospective owner to take consistent action to ameliorate the effect of the pending drastic change of zoning classification.

It is, as other courts have noticed, anomalous for owners of nearby land who object to any change away from the residence district to object on the ground that, contemporaneously, ameliorating restrictions have been imposed. But, since they would be aggrieved by the purported change if it were illegal, we have considered the issue on its merits.

It is not necessary to consider Sylvania's appeal from the denial in the Land Court of its motion to dismiss the respondent landowners' appeal.

Decision affirmed.

KIRK, JUSTICE (dissenting).

I do not agree. The mutual advantages gained by Newton and Sylvania by their arrangement are not in issue. The motives of the participants are not questioned. The central thesis of this dissent is that the method used by Newton to impose restrictions on the use of land owned by Sylvania is invalid. * * *

There would seem to be no question (and it appears the majority agrees) that (1) each and every restriction imposed by the "option agreement" (contract) is one which the city is empowered to impose by ordinance under c. 40A, § 2; and (2) each and every restriction imposed by the contract was imposed in order to further the purposes stated in c. 40A, § 2 and § 3.

With equal certainty it should be clear that when a municipality elects to impose restrictions on the use of land for the purposes set out in c. 40A, §§ 2, 3, it must, under the express provisions of c. 40A, § 2, impose them "by a zoning ordinance or by-law." The attempt to impose them by contract is "beyond the authority conferred * * * [and] not in compliance with the terms and conditions governing its exercise" and therefore is invalid.

Moreover, c. 40A, § 6 (see also § 7), prescribes explicitly the procedural steps which must be taken prior to the adoption, amendment or repeal of ordinances or by-laws relating to land restrictions. Included among the steps is the requirement of public hearings before both the planning board and the city council after notice thereof has been given to the city's inhabitants so that "all interested persons shall be given an opportunity to be heard." There is no similar requirement for notice or hearing when restrictions are to be imposed by a city on a parcel of land, however large, by contract. What we have, then, is not only an invalid method for imposing restrictions but an invalid method which admits the added evil of circumvention of the declared legislative requirement that interested parties be fully informed of the particulars of proposed municipal land restriction and be given an opportunity to be heard on these particulars.

The majority, however, states, that the restrictions here imposed are not "zoning restrictions" and equates them with contract restrictions negotiated by private landowners for the benefit of adjoining land. I submit that this characterization will not withstand analysis. In the first place, the benefit of these contract restrictions does not run to or with any land now owned by Newton. Secondly, and more significantly, these restrictions were negotiated and agreed to by Newton and Sylvania in conjunction with, and as an integral part of, the enactment of the amendment to the Newton zoning ordinance. The amendment subjected the land to restrictions uniformly imposed on limited manufacturing districts; the contract subjected the land to additional restrictions in order, as the opinion recognizes, "to ameliorate the effect of the pending drastic change of zoning classification."

To my mind, the conclusion seems inescapable that, in truth and substance, the action of Newton was not the mere rezoning of a parcel of land which was already subject to privately negotiated contract restrictions but was, rather, one double-barrelled attempt to exercise the zoning power delegated to it by the Legislature under c. 40A, § 2. If the phrases "zoning restrictions" and "exercise of the zoning power" have any meaning, they must include the restrictions here imposed by contract. To say, as the majority in effect says, that they are not "zoning restrictions" or do not constitute "an exercise of the zoning power" because the city imposes them by contract and not by ordinance seems to me to be a play on words and to beg the question. The purpose and effect of their imposition is the same whether they are accomplished by ordinance or contract. It is the method of imposition which is the critical issue.

Whatever the action of Newton may or may not be called, it (1) in fact results in the imposition of restrictions by a city (Newton is the party that can and would enforce these restrictions) (2) for the purposes set out in c. 40A, §§ 2, 3, (3) upon the use of land by the owner (4) by the contract method (5) which method is prohibited by the Legislature (6) which alone can prescribe the method, and (7) hence is illegal.

Although the burden of the foregoing discussion is the invalidity of the contract restrictions, it is my opinion that the amendment to the zoning ordinance is itself also invalid. Newton's use of two methods in close and complementary co-ordination to accomplish a single purpose, namely the regulation of use of Sylvania's land is, in fact and in substance, a single act. All indications are that, unless Newton had first obtained the additional contract restrictions, it would not have effected the "drastic change of zoning classification" by enacting the amendment. As the opinion states, the amendment and the contract were mutually induced.

The elimination of the invalid contract restrictions, here used in combination with the ordinance restrictions resulting from the amendment to accomplish a single purpose, defeats the single purpose. It also reveals the essential oneness or interdependence of the methods used. Thus viewed as one, it would seem inevitably to follow that such ordinance restrictions fall with the contract restrictions as being in excess of the power conferred in c. 40A, § 2.

I would require compliance with the statute, and accordingly would reverse the decision.

MONTGOMERY COUNTY v. NATIONAL CAPITAL REALTY CORP.

Court of Appeals of Maryland, 1972.
267 Md. 364, 297 A.2d 675.

[The property owner sought rezoning from C–O, commercial office building, to C–2, general commercial. The planning staff recommended disapproval of the application, primarily on grounds of the height and ground coverage permissible in the C–2 zone. The Planning Board rejected the staff recommendation and approved the application after the applicant submitted a set of covenants, conditions and restrictions which would "become effective upon the approval" of the zoning application. The local legislative body reversed the Planning Board, relying on a memorandum from the County Attorney to the effect that conditional zoning was not allowed in Montgomery County. The trial court reversed and ordered approval of the application, and the county appealed.]

LEVINE, JUDGE.

* * *

Entirely apart from the "change" argument, we think resolution of the question whether the covenants constituted a form of impermissible conditional zoning is decisive of this case. For, as we have seen, by a determination of that point in appellant's favor, two of the main props to appellee's case would topple, i.e., the favorable recommendations of the Planning Board and Mr. Hussmann, respectively. This would then confront appellee with unfavorable positions of the staff and Hussmann and without any public agency support.

We think it clear that the covenants, coupled with the site plan attached thereto, if adopted as a basis for the requested reclassification, would have produced a form of conditional zoning. If recorded, the covenants would have bound appellee to compliance only on the condition that the C–2 classification first had been granted. Had the Council then granted the application on the strength of the covenants, as encouraged to do so by Mr. Hussmann and the Planning Board it would have committed what we believe would have been a classic illustration of conditional zoning. The invalidity of conditional zoning in Maryland is not seriously open to question. Citizens Ass'n v. Pr. Geo. County, 222 Md. 44, 158 A.2d 663 (1960); Rose v. Paape, 221 Md. 369, 376–377, 157 A.2d 618 (1960); Baylis v. City of Baltimore, 219 Md. 164, 169–170, 148 A.2d 429 (1959). It is interesting to note that in none of those cases was there cited a provision comparable to § 111–48(d) of the Montgomery County Zoning Ordinance also codified by that same designation in the Montgomery County Code, 1965, which provides:

"No application for a local or a sectional or District plan map amendment shall be approved conditionally for the erection on the land of a structure at a particular location, or within a particular time, or by a particular person, or of a particular type, or for the subdivision of the land in a particular manner, or on any other condition."

In 3 Rathkopf, Zoning and Planning 74–9, it is stated:

" * * * The general rule in these jurisdictions in which the validity of such covenants has been litigated is that they are illegal. The basis of such rule is that the rezoning of a particular parcel of land upon conditions not imposed by the zoning ordinance generally in the particular district into which the land has been rezoned is prima facie evidence of 'spot zoning' in its most maleficent aspect, is not in accordance with a comprehensive plan and is beyond the power of the municipality.

"Legislative bodies must rezone in accordance with a comprehensive plan, and in amending the ordinance so as to confer upon a particular parcel a particular district designation, it may not curtail or limit the uses and structures placed or to be placed upon the lands so rezoned differently from those permitted upon other lands in the same district. Consequently, where there has been a concatenated rezoning and filing of a 'declaration of restrictions' the general view (where the question has been litigated) is that both the zoning amendment and the restrictive covenant are invalid for the reasons expressed above."

Although the rule followed in Maryland has undergone erosion in some states we believe that it continues to be supported by the weight of authority.

Nor is appellee helped by our decisions in Funger v. Mayor of Somerset, 249 Md. 311, 328, 239 A.2d 748 (1968) and Greenbelt v. Bresler, 248 Md. 210, 215–216, 236 A.2d 1 (1967). What distinguishes those cases from those we have cited earlier is that in each, the municipality within which the subject land was located agreed to support the rezoning application before the respective county legislative body in exchange for certain commitments entered into by the applicant. Thus, since in both cases the legislative body was not a party to the agreement, neither the rezoning nor the agreement was invalidated. For the reasons we have stated, the Council was correct in refusing to grant the rezoning upon the conditions expressed in the Declaration of Covenants and the attached site plan.

Nothing we have said in distinguishing *Funger* and *Greenbelt* from the cases involving agreements entered into by legislative bodies supports enforceability of the covenants here by the Planning Board, since, as we have noted, the covenants were to become binding on appellee only if the Council granted the application. In short, we are concerned here merely with the fact that the Planning Board's favorable report was predicated solely on the existence of covenants which, in light of our holding, were worthless. Thus, they imparted the same value to the recommendation of the Board. What we have just said doubtlessly applies with greater force to Mr. Hussmann's recommendation, as he, being a county employee and in no respect a party to the covenants, gratuitously considered them in arriving at his favorable conclusion. Thus, we think the Council was correct in refusing to rely upon the covenants while deciding the zoning application, and the favorable recommendation of the Planning Board and Mr. Hussmann were entitled to no weight.

* * *

Order reversed.

Notes

1.   Also see Carlino v. Whitpain Investors, 499 Pa. 498, 453 A.2d 1385 (1982). Although dated, a good state-by-state survey of judicial attitudes to contract/conditional zoning can be found in Kramer, Contract Zoning—Old Myths and New Realities, Land Use Law (August 1982) p. 4.

2.   Conditional zoning, in the sense that certain conditions are "unilaterally" imposed on the premises by the city in order for rezoning to become effective, or in the sense that the land is rezoned conditionally and subject to revocation of the action if the conditions are not met, has been upheld in Wisconsin (State ex rel. Zupancic v. Schimenz, 46 Wis.2d 22, 174 N.W.2d 533 (1970)); Kansas (Arkenberg v. Topeka, 197 Kan. 731, 421 P.2d 213 (1966)); Nebraska (Bucholz v. Omaha, 174 Neb. 862, 120 N.W.2d 270 (1963)); Massachusetts (the Sylvania case, supra); New York (Church v. Islip, 8 N.Y.2d 254, 203 N.Y.S.2d 866, 168 N.E.2d 680 (1960)); North Carolina (Hall v. City of Durham, 323 N.C. 293, 372 S.E.2d 564 (1988)); and some other jurisdictions. But a number of jurisdictions, particularly in the South, have rejected conditional rezoning as being the same as contract rezoning or as amounting to spot zoning. A key issue is whether there is really a distinction and whether conditions are in fact imposed unilaterally by the city without there first having been a bargaining or negotiating process. A further question might be whether it should matter as to whether there is a discussion process which takes on the colorations of negotiation or bargaining. In any event, consider the following explanation of conditional rezoning excerpted from Stefaniak, The Status of Conditional Rezoning in Illinois—An Argument to Sustain a Flexible Zoning Tool, 63 Ill.Bar J. 132 (1974):

> The concept of conditional rezoning has been the subject of much confusion, and the terms "conditional rezoning" and "contract zoning" are often used interchangeably. The term "conditional rezoning" has been utilized here and it is utilized to denote a broad concept with express contractual agreements and the unilateral imposition of conditions being forms of the larger concept. Conditional rezoning occurs whenever a municipal authority reclassifies land with the reclassification being subject to special limitations on the use of the rezoned property not imposed upon other lands in the same classification or where the reclassification requires the landowner to perform some act such as making improvements on the rezoned property or paying money

to meet community expenses incurred as a result of the reclassification. The special limitations on use or the acts required can be brought about through either the unilateral imposition of conditions or an express agreement between the landowner and the municipality or rezoning authority. The unilateral imposition of conditions most commonly takes one of two forms:

"Where a landowner requests that his property be rezoned to allow a use not permitted under existing restrictions, he may be advised that his land will be reclassified if he first executes and files a covenant which limits the use of his parcel in specific ways not common to other property similarly classified. * * * [or] * * * Land may be reclassified subject to conditions not applicable to other property in the same or similar districts."

The form of conditional rezoning typically referred to as contract zoning occurs when the municipality and the landowner enter into an express agreement in which both undertake reciprocal obligations. Any distinction between the two forms is tenuous and of no real import because both bring about the same result. Conditional rezoning in either of its forms is intended to reclassify land to allow a more beneficial use while imposing conditions ameliorating any hardships that the reclassification may impose on adjoining property owners or the community as a whole. The same arguments are lodged against the validity of both forms of conditional rezoning, except that contract zoning is subject to the further criticism that it constitutes a bargaining away of the police power. Dealing with conditional rezoning as a broader concept encompassing two forms is more precise and does away with nebulous distinctions. * * *

3. Neither the Standard Zoning Enabling Act nor the enabling legislation of most states contemplated the problem of contract or conditional rezoning. In recent years, some state legislatures have sought to provide authority for this device in order to promote flexibility in rezoning. In 1973, for example, the Indiana legislature amended its enabling legislation (Public Law No. 185, April 23, 1973):

Section 1 IC 1971, 18–7–2–20 is amended to read as follows: Sec. 20. To effectuate the purposes of this chapter, the metropolitan plan commission shall have the power and duty to:

* * *

17. If deemed advisable by the commission, require or allow the owner of any parcel of property, in connection with any petition for amendment to the zoning ordinance changing the zoning classification of that parcel, to make written commitments relative to the use or development of that parcel of property. The commission shall have power to establish rules and regulations governing the creation, form, and recording of commitments and the designation of specially affected persons and categories of specially affected persons entitled to enforce commitments. Commitments shall be recorded in the office of the County Recorder and shall be effective upon adoption of the amendment to the zoning ordinance. Commitments, unless modified or terminated

by the commission as hereinafter provided, shall be binding on the owner, subsequent owners of the parcel of property and other persons acquiring an interest therein. Commitments may be modified or terminated by the decision of the commission made at a public hearing after notice as provided by the rules and regulations. The requiring or allowing of such commitments shall not obligate the commission to take any official action nor shall it limit the power of the commission to take any official action regarding the parcel of property. The provisions of this subsection shall not affect the validity of any covenant, easement, equitable servitude or other land use restriction which is presently in effect or may be created in accordance with law.

Compare Va.Code Ann. § 15.1–491.1 et seq. (1989).

4. What should happen if the city breaches its part of the agreement? In Sprenger, Grubb & Associates v. City of Hailey, 127 Idaho 576, 903 P.2d 741 (1995) a developer with a 654 acre parcel entered into a development agreement with the city that provided for a master residential-business plan and annexation into the city. After the annexation in 1973 the city zoned 12.6 acres of the land for business. From 1973 to 1993 the developer gradually built out the plan. The city, at the behest of the mayor and with a great deal of public support pushed for rezonings to protect the core downtown business area that resulted in downzoning the developer's 12.6 acre parcel from business to "limited business." (The mayor had wanted downzoning to residential, but settled for the limited business designation.) The developer sued alleging that the downzoning devalued the property by $800,000, that the city was estopped from rezoning in breach of the development agreement, and that the downzoning was a taking. The supreme court held for the city, noting that under some circumstances a city might be estopped from breaching a development agreement, but that in this case the downzoning was not a breach because the limited business designation was in substantial compliance with the agreement. The court also found that the devaluation was not a taking because the developer still had residual economic value in the land.

5. Another case with a cautionary message for developers is Metropolitan Dade County v. Fontainebleau Gas & Wash, Inc., 570 So.2d 1006 (Fla.App.1990). In 1975 a developer sought rezoning of a parcel from professional office to limited business and, in a letter accompanying the application indicated that the company would offer a written covenant restricting use of the property to a bank. The county granted the rezoning, expressing in the resolution that the use would be limited to a bank but the covenant was never recorded. The bank was never built and the property changed hands many times. Fifteen years after the rezoning the present owner received a building permit and built a gas station. Just before the station was finished the county discovered the old restriction and issued a stop work order. In a suit by the developer the court held for the county stating that owners are deemed to purchase property with constructive knowledge of applicable land use regulations, the county applies the zoning code by resolution, and the resolutions that are passed subsequent to public hearings can modify districts and restrict property use. "Anyone attempting to learn what, if any, use limitations apply to his property need only turn to the applicable resolution." The court went on to hold that the owner could

not claim detrimental reliance on the permit inadvertently issued by the county.

Despite the holding in this case, equitable estoppel and detrimental reliance might well be viewed as valid defenses by other courts.

C. ADMINISTRATIVE TREATMENT

Virtually all of the material that follows is concerned with the substance of flexibility devices under the zoning ordinance. Neither the enabling statutes nor the cases deal to any great extent with the problems of administrative procedure in local zoning agencies. One of the useful contributions of the Model Land Development Code is the careful attention which has been accorded to the problem of procedural due process in the work of zoning agencies. Article 2, Part 3, of the Code provides a framework of administrative procedure to govern agency rulemaking, administrative hearings, and legislative type hearings. Much of the material in this part of the Code would be familiar to the student taking Administrative Law and is beyond the scope of this course. However, reading the Code, §§ 2–301 to 2–312, and the notes to those sections will provide the student in this course with a useful overview of the procedural problems and the minimum requirements of due process with regard to the operations of local land use control agencies.

(1) Variance

So many cases involve variances that a casebook editor has a rather difficult time in attempting to select a few representative ones to be included. We have attempted to select some cases which are fairly representative of the problems encountered. In considering these and others you may notice the difficulty sometimes encountered by courts or administrative boards in distinguishing between the types of zoning devices with which they are dealing. Along the same line, it may be well to consider whether courts are operating on the same premise in the utilization of a particular approach.

LARSEN v. ZONING BOARD OF ADJUSTMENT OF CITY OF PITTSBURGH

Supreme Court of Pennsylvania, 1996.
543 Pa. 415, 672 A.2d 286.

CASTILLE, JUSTICE.

[The owners of a house with a very steep back yard sloping toward the Ohio River sought and received a variance to add a twenty-by-twenty foot deck off the rear of the house to provide their two-year-old child with an outside play area. A neighbor residing in a multi-unit condominium next door appealed the grant of a variance. The trial court ruled that the house owners had failed to satisfy the criteria needed to support a variance, and the house owners appeal.]

* * *

There are essentially four factors that appellants must prove to be entitled to a variance under the applicable statute and ordinance. The factors are:

(1) that an unnecessary hardship exists which is not created by the party seeking the variance and which is caused by unique physical circumstances of the property for which the variance is sought;

(2) that a variance is needed to enable the party's reasonable use of the property;

(3) that the variance will not alter the essential character of the district or neighborhood, or substantially or permanently impair the use or development of the adjacent property such that it is detrimental to the public's welfare; and

(4) that the variance will afford the least intrusive solution.

53 P.S. § 10910.2; § 909.05 of the Pittsburgh Code of Ordinance ("PCO"). * * * The failure of a zoning board to consider each requirement of a zoning ordinance prior to granting a variance is an error of law. * * * Here, the zoning board failed to consider each of these requirements. Furthermore, the record reveals that appellants failed to provide evidence that would satisfy even the first criteria. Accordingly, appellants' claim must fail.

1. HARDSHIP CAUSED BY UNIQUE PHYSICAL CHARACTERISTICS

(a) Unnecessary Hardship

In order to satisfy the first prong under both the statute and PCO, appellants must prove: (1) that the variance is needed to avoid an "unnecessary hardship;" (2) that the "unnecessary hardship" was not created by them; and (3) that the "unnecessary hardship" was caused by unique physical circumstances of the property for which the variance is sought. With respect to the first factor, in determining whether the denial of the variance would cause the level of hardship needed to warrant a variance, this Court held in Richman v. Zoning Board of Adjustment, 391 Pa. 254, 259–60, 137 A.2d 280, 283 (1958), that the hardship must truly be an "unnecessary" one, and not simply a " 'mere' hardship." Furthermore, the "unnecessary" hardship must be one that is "unique or peculiar" to the property. Id.

Here, the Board found that appellants would suffer an "unnecessary hardship" from a denial of the variance because they would be denied the reasonable use of their land if they could not provide a play area for their child. However, the mere desire to provide more room for a family member's enjoyment fails to constitute they type of "unnecessary hardship" required by the law of this Commonwealth.

In the matter of In re Kline Zoning Case, 395 Pa. 122, 124, 148 A.2d 915, 916 (1959), a property owner sought a variance from a thirty-foot setback requirement in order to enclose his front porch. The basis for his variance request was that his wife suffered from asthma and hay fever, and that his son suffered from a severe respiratory ailment as well as hay fever. The enclosure of the porch would have allowed his family to have additional room in which to habitate. This Court, applying the test set forth by Richman, supra, upheld the zoning board's denial of the variance finding that the owner's need for additional room for his family failed to establish an unnecessary hardship justifying the variance.

The circumstances of In re Kline Zoning case are analogous to the circumstances at hand. In both cases, the property owners sought variances to modify their homes to add a greater area for the family members to play in or to use. Thus, under In re Kline Zoning Case, we find that the Zoning Board erred as a matter of law in granting the variance based simply upon appellants' need to provide a greater play area for their child. Variances are meant to avoid "unnecessary" hardships; the granting of relief cannot be done simply to accommodate the changing needs of a growing family.

(b) Creation of Hardship

Notwithstanding appellants' failure to establish an unnecessary hardship, appellants further failed to establish that the physical circumstances allegedly causing the unnecessary hardship were not created by them. * * * Section 909.05(a)(1)(A) of the Pittsburgh Code of Ordinances expressly provides that parties are not entitled to a variance for circumstances which are the result of "any act of the appellant or his predecessors in title subsequent to the adoption of this Zoning Ordinance, whether in violation of the provisions hereof or not." See also, 53 P.S. § 10910.2(a)(3). To the extent that the hardship found by the zoning board was the result of the fact that appellants' first addition to their residence covered 75% of the property, thereby precluding any additional building absent a variance, appellants themselves created the complained of hardship. When appellants purchased the property, the house had a seventy-six foot setback from the rear property line. It was appellants themselves who built the forty-four foot deep addition which left them with insufficient space to erect an outside deck that would have complied with the ordinance at issue without the need for a variance. Therefore, appellants failed to prove that the "unnecessary hardship" was not caused by their own making.

(c) Unique Physical Circumstances

Appellants also failed to demonstrate that the "unique physical circumstances" of their property caused the hardship. In order to prove that the physical circumstances of a property justify a variance, the party seeking the variance must demonstrate that the circumstances are unique or peculiar to the property in question and not a condition common to the neighborhood or zoning district. * * * Here, the record establishes that the physical circumstances were in fact not unique to appellants' property and that most of the properties along Grandview Avenue had similar precipitously steep backyards. This Court has held that a condition which affects only a small portion of a district is not sufficiently unique to warrant a variance, but rather should be remedied by re-zoning. English v. Zoning Board of Adjustment of Norristown, 395

Pa. 118, 120–21, 148 A.2d 912, 914 (1959) (where zoning board grants a variance where neighborhood changes affect a small group of properties on one street, it is "virtually enacting zoning legislation instead of merely performing its function of administering the zoning law prescribed by the governing body of the municipality"). See also, Walter v. Zoning Board of Adjustment, 437 Pa. 277, 280, 263 A.2d 123, 126 (1970) (party seeking variance cannot complain of hardship existing at time the land was purchased). Thus, the condition which gave rise to appellants' alleged "unnecessary hardship" was not unique or peculiar to their property.

2. Variance Needed to Enable Reasonable Use of Property

Even if appellants had established the existence of an unnecessary hardship, they would be entitled to a variance only if they could establish that the variance was necessary for the reasonable use of the land. * * * At the outset, the Zoning Board's failure to address this issue is an error of law. Furthermore, in order to meet this requirement, appellants would have to show that a denial of the requested variance would make the property practically useless. Abe Oil Co. v. Zoning Hearing Board of Richmond Twp., 168 Pa.Commw. at 120, 125, 649 A.2d 182, 185 (1994) (variance for construction of gas station not justified where property was amenable to "any number" of uses) * * * Because appellants' property can be used as a residential dwelling absent the 400–square foot deck, they have failed to meet this requirement for a grant of a variance.

3. Variance's Impact Upon Neighborhood

Appellants also had to establish that the variance would "not alter the essential character of the neighborhood or district in which the property is located" or be contrary to the public interest. Although the zoning board found that the variance would not be contrary to the public interest, the only factual finding on which that conclusion was based was that the objections to the variance were related to "precedence and aesthetics."

Appellee stated in his appeal that the variance would permit the construction of a deck further out over the hillside than any other property in the neighborhood, thereby obstructing the view of the Ohio River from other properties along the street and substantially altering the character of the neighborhood. Appellee's concerns that the variance will set a precedent for the granting of future variances which will result in an obstruction of the view of the Ohio River afforded from the properties along Grandview Avenue is a concern that the "essential character" of the neighborhood will be altered as a result of the variance. The zoning board's failure to consider appellee's concerns or otherwise address the effect of the variance on the neighborhood was a failure to address a requirement of the statute. * * *

4. Variance Must Be the Least Intrusive Solution

Finally, once the zoning board determines that a variance is justified, the variance granted must be the minimum variance necessary to afford relief, resulting in the least modification of the regulation at issue. No testimony was heard by the zoning board as to the possibility of less drastic alternatives. * * *

Because the zoning board committed both a manifest abuse of discretion in determining that appellants had established an unnecessary hardship and numerous errors of law in failing to address the majority of the requirements under both the state and local zoning laws, the Commonwealth Court did not exceed its standard of review in reversing the order. * * *

For the foregoing reasons, the order of the Commonwealth Court is affirmed.

[Concurring opinion omitted.]

Notes

1. The universal standard for granting a variance from the literal terms of the zoning ordinance is hardship. As you might expect, defining that term has been anything but simple for the courts. Consider the following examples:

(a) R–N–R Associates v. Zoning Board of Review, 100 R.I. 7, 210 A.2d 653 (1965), mentioned in Bryden, Zoning: Rigid, Flexible or Fluid?, 44 J. Urban L. 287, 308 (1967), illustrates the showing which one court required to be made by an applicant for a variance in order to demonstrate sufficient hardship. How "hard" should the "hardship" be, however? This case involved an application for a variance to allow the operation of a laundromat in a C–1 district when the zoning provisions only permitted the operation of laundromats in C–2 districts. The court in affirming a denial of the variance, stated that "it is the purpose of the variance to immunize zoning legislation against attack on the ground that it may in some instances operate to effect a taking of property without just compensation." The court added: "It is important, in our opinion, that zoning boards of review be informed that the right of a landowner to a variance turns upon a showing of unnecessary hardship, that is, a showing that an ordinance restriction deprives him of all beneficial use of his land. When such is established, confiscation must be avoided by the grant of some alternate use by way of a variance. The provision of the statute that such use, when granted by way of variance, be not contrary to the public interest does not operate to negative a landowner's right to a variance in a proper case. It simply restricts the board as to the scope and character of the use that may be allowed by way of variance in order to relieve a landowner from the confiscatory effect of a literal enforcement of the pertinent provision of the ordinance." Does this statement go too far? Must there be the equivalent of a taking or confiscation of the property or its beneficial use before a variance may be granted? See similarly, Mount Pleasant Realty & Constr. Co. v. Zoning Bd. of Review, 100 R.I. 31, 210 A.2d 877 (1965), in which the Rhode Island court affirmed a denial of an application for an exception or variance to the zoning ordinance to allow petitioner to build a store building in a residential area, the court stating that there was no proof that "devoting the property to residential purposes would result in a loss of all beneficial use." Also see Rozes v. Smith, 120 R.I. 515, 388 A.2d 816 (1978).

(b) Consider the foregoing Rhode Island cases in the light of Williams v. Kuehnert, 243 Ark. 746, 421 S.W.2d 896 (1967). This case involved the expansion of a building which had to be enlarged or the kindergarten which it housed would have to be shut down. Obviously, there was substantial hardship which some courts might view as sufficient to constitute "unnecessary hardship." But the Arkansas court stated: "It is contended there is no evidence to show a hardship would have been imposed on Roper if the expansion had been denied. We cannot agree. In the first place no such showing is required under section 43–22 quoted previously. Moreover the testimony does show that the addition to the building was required by the Health Department in order for the kindergarten to continue in operation." Does this mean that unless the city zoning ordinance specifically requires a showing of unnecessary hardship, a variance in the form of the expansion of a nonconforming use is fully permissible if the board chooses to permit it? Compare City of West Helena v. Bockman, 221 Ark. 677, 256 S.W.2d 40 (1953), which the court found not to be controlling because the proposed expansion in that case would extend so close to the property line as to violate the city zoning ordinance. In 1 Anderson, American Law of Zoning 3d § 6.50 (1986) it is noted that variances permitting additions to nonconforming uses have generally been treated with less severity than those involving original construction of nonconforming buildings. But is the Arkansas statement that "no showing is required" under the city zoning ordinance overly cavalier in dealing with the problem? See Fortuna v. Zoning Bd. of Adjustment, 95 N.H. 211, 60 A.2d 133 (1948); Re Mack's Appeal, 384 Pa. 586, 122 A.2d 48 (1956). It may very well be that the problem of expanding a nonconforming use should be viewed largely separate and apart from that of the normal variance situation—i.e., the original establishment of a nonconforming use.

(c) Compare also with the Rhode Island cases cited previously, Brown v. Beuc, 384 S.W.2d 845 (Mo.App.1964), in which it was held that a lack of parking facilities was not a sufficient ground to prevent the enforcement of a provision requiring a front yard of not less than twenty-five feet in a multiple family dwelling district. The court stated that "the practical difficulty or undue hardship relied on as a ground for variance must be unusual or peculiar to the property involved and must be different from that suffered throughout the zone or neighborhood." The court added: "When we say inherent in the land and that the hardship must be due to conditions not personal to the owner, but rather to conditions affecting the land we mean such hardships as result from the peculiar topography or condition of the land which makes the land unsuitable for the use permitted in the zone in which it lies." Although the variance was denied, the test seems to be less stringent than that employed in Rhode Island. Of course, as the Missouri case indicates, an applicant must do more than establish economic or financial hardship; he must establish a hardship which is unique or peculiar to the property involved. See Dishler v. Zoning Bd. of Adjustment, 414 Pa. 244, 199 A.2d 418 (1964); and Appeal of McClure, 415 Pa. 285, 203 A.2d 534 (1964). In the McClure case, the land zoned for residential purposes was apparently no longer suitable for residential use, but the court held that this did not require that a variance be granted to permit the erection of a branch bank, since the answer lay in rezoning rather than in seeking a variance.

(d) One consideration which arises is illustrated by Booe v. Zoning Bd. of Appeals, 151 Conn. 681, 202 A.2d 245 (1964), in which the court stated: "We have repeatedly held that the hardship which justifies a board of appeals in granting a variance must be one which originates from the zoning ordinance. When the claimed hardship arises because of the actions of the applicant, the board is without power to grant a variance." In this case the landowner had created his own difficulty by conveying away a substantial amount of land, while retaining only a four-acre parcel, which he sought to use for a hotel in contravention of a five-acre requirement in the zoning ordinance. See also Appeal of McClure, supra; and Smith v. Zoning Bd. of Appeals, 347 Mass. 755, 200 N.E.2d 279 (1964).

(e) If the variance involved the construction of a swimming pool and related recreational facilities in an area zoned residential, could this be justified as being in keeping with the spirit and intent of the zoning ordinance and as enhancing rather than adversely affecting the character of the neighborhood? Or should the "unnecessary hardship" doctrine be applied? See City of Little Rock v. Leawood Property Owners' Ass'n, 242 Ark. 451, 413 S.W.2d 877 (1967).

If anything, the foregoing cases seem to suggest that policies relative to variances differ from state to state even when the same general "unnecessary hardship" principle is expressly followed in one way or another. Yet, facts and figures available suggest that a substantial majority of all applications for departures from zoning requirements are approved in locations which are widely separated geographically. (See Note, Administrative Discretion in Zoning, 82 Harv.L.Rev. 668, 673 (1969), which concludes that if the test of a system is the number of departures from it, zoning is a spectacular failure.)

2. In most jurisdictions the requirement for obtaining a variance also states that the problem causing the need comes from the property and not from any act of the owner. Not too many cases present this issue, but one interesting example can be found in Board of Zoning Appeals of Evansville and Vanderburgh County v. Kempf, 656 N.E.2d 1201 (Ind.App.1995). In this case the property owner had his development plat approved on condition that he install a ten-foot wide greenspace across the front of his property. After the property was developed the city discovered that the owner had paved over the ten-foot area where the green space was to have been installed. The owner then sought a variance on the ground that none of the other adjacent business had green space and that economic necessity established a hardship. The court held for the city, stating: "The Board concluded that Kempf was not entitled to the requested variance because he himself had created the need for the variance by paving over the area in question. We hold this requirement advances a legitimate governmental interest in preventing the type of 'end run' around the zoning ordinances and procedures employed in the present case."

SASSO v. OSGOOD

Court of Appeals of New York, 1995.
86 N.Y.2d 374, 633 N.Y.S.2d 259, 657 N.E.2d 254.

[The owner of a waterfront parcel of land containing a boathouse sought a variance to allow him to demolish the existing structure and build a larger boathouse. Neighbors objected to the application on the ground that the proposed boathouse would obstruct their access to light, air, and view, and that the foundations of their boathouses and septic systems would be damaged by construction and altered drainage patterns. The zoning board granted the variance and the neighbors appealed; the intermediate appellate court determined that the applicant had failed to show "practical difficulties sufficient to justify an area variance" primarily because he had not shown that strict enforcement of the ordinance would cause him a significant economic injury.]

* * *

Prior to July 1, 1992, the authority of town zoning boards of appeal to grant variances from local zoning ordinances was defined in former Town Law § 267. Zoning boards were authorized to grant variances "[w]here there are practical difficulties or unnecessary hardships in the way of carrying out the strict letter of [local] ordinances" provided that "the spirit of the ordinance shall be observed, public safety and welfare secured and substantial justice done" (former Town Law § 267[5]). Although the former statute did not distinguish between "use" and "area" variances or assign the specific tests to them, court decisions generally applied the "unnecessary hardship" test in use variance cases, while requiring a demonstration of "practical difficulties" in area variance cases (see, Matter of Village of Bronxville v. Francis, 1 A.D.2d 236, 238, affd 1 N.Y.2d 839; see also, Matter of Hoffman v. Harris, 17 N.Y.2d 138, 144; Dauernheim, Inc. v. Town Bd. of Town of Hempstead, 33 N.Y.2d 468, 471; Matter of Off Shore Rest. Corp. v. Linden, 30 N.Y.2d 160, 168).

A three-pronged test of "unnecessary hardship" was clearly articulated more than fifty years ago (see, Matter of Otto v. Steinhilber, 282 N.Y. 71, 76) and that test, now embodied in Town Law § 267–b(2), has been applied in use variance cases without substantial difficulty. * * * The definition and application of the "practical difficulties standard" has proven far more troublesome.

Lacking a statutory definition, we have recognized the existence of "practical difficulties" where the unusual topography of the subject parcel interfered with construction of a building (see, Matter of Wilcox v. Zoning Bd. of Appeals of City of Yonkers, 17 N.Y.2d 249, 255), and where area variances were required to build a house on an amply sized but oddly shaped parcel that did not meet frontage and side yard requirements (Conley v. Town of Brookhaven Zoning Bd. of Appeals, 40 N.Y.2d 309, 316). We have also suggested that an area variance could be granted upon a showing of "significant economic injury" (Matter of Fulling v. Palumbo, 21 N.Y.2d 30, 33; see also, Matter of Cowan v. Kern, 41 N.Y.2d 591, 596). In Matter of National Merritt v. Weist (41 N.Y.2d 438) we considered both unique topography and economic injury relevant to the application for an area variance. We have noted several times, however, that there is no precise definition of the term "practical difficulties" (Matter of Doyle v. Amster, 79 N.Y.2d 592, 595; Matter of Fuhst v. Foley, 45 N.Y.2d 441, 445), observing that "[t]he basic inquiry at all times is whether strict application of the ordinance in a given case will serve a valid public purpose which outweighs the injury to the property owner" (Matter of DeSena v. Board of Zoning Appeals of Inc. Vil. of Hempstead, 45 N.Y.2d 105, 108).

Without any legislative guidance defining the requirements for an area variance, the courts began to develop a list of criteria to be applied under former Town Law § 267 (see, Matter of Wachsberger v. Michalis, 19 Misc.2d 909, aff'd 18 A.D.2d 921; see also, Matter of Friendly Ice Cream Corp. v. Barrett, 106 A.D.2d 748; Matter of Human Dev. Servs. of Port Chester v. Zoning Bd. of Appeals of Vil. of Port Chester, 110 A.D.2d 135, aff'd 67 N.Y.2d 702). Although originally offered as guidance for determining whether "the spirit of the ordinance is observed, public safety and welfare secured and substantial justice done" (see, Wachsberger v. Michalis, supra, 19 Misc.2d, at 912 [Meyer, J.]), these criteria came to be known as the "practical difficulties" test (see, 2 Anderson, New York Zoning Law and Practice, § 23.34, at 208–209 [3d ed.]). These criteria notwithstanding, precise and concise definition of "practical difficulties" never emerged from the case law. In particular, it remained unclear whether a showing of "significant economic injury" was part of the "practical difficulties" test.* * *

Effective July 1, 1992, the Legislature repealed former Town Law § 267, and enacted comprehensive provisions governing zoning boards of appeals. Unlike former Town Law § 267, the new statute defines "use" and "area" variances, as well as the criteria to be evaluated in determining applications for each. Use variances may be granted upon an applicant's showing "that applicable zoning regulations and restrictions have caused unnecessary hardship," expressly incorporating that phrase as it existed in former Town Law § 267. The statute defines the elements of proof necessary to establish unnecessary hardship, essentially codifying the criteria originally set forth in Matter of Otto v. Steinhilber (282 N.Y. 71, 76, supra), with the added requirement that the applicant prove that "the alleged hardship has not been self-created" (Town Law § 267–b[2][b][4]).

The standard for area variances is governed by Town Law § 267–b(3) in a provision that does not expressly require the applicant to prove "practical difficulties". It states:

In making its determination [whether to grant an area variance], the zoning board of appeals shall take into consideration *the benefit to the applicant if the variance is granted, as weighed against the detriment to the health, safety and welfare of the neighborhood or community by such grant.* In making such determination the board shall also consider: (1) whether an undesirable change will be produced in the character of the neighborhood or a detriment to nearby properties will be created by the granting of the area variance; (2) whether the benefit sought by the applicant can be achieved by some other method, feasible for the applicant to pursue, other than an area variance; (3) whether the requested area variance is substantial; (4) whether the proposed variance will have an adverse effect or impact on the physical or environmental conditions in the neighborhood or district; and (5) whether the alleged difficulty was self-created, which consideration shall be relevant to the decision of the board of appeals, but shall not necessarily preclude the granting of the area variance. (Town Law § 267–b[3][b] [emphasis added]).

The five factors listed parallel the criteria previously used by the lower courts and identified by Professor Anderson as the "practical difficulties" test.* * *

The precise question posed on this appeal is whether by failing to include the phrase "practical difficulties" in the new statute, the Legislature has eliminated the requirement that the applicant for an area variance make that showing.

* * *

Reference to the bill jacket for chapter 692 of the Laws of 1991 supports intervenor's contention that an applicant for an area variance need not show "practical difficulties" as required under former Town Law § 267 and prior case law. The Legislature enacted the statute to clarify existing law by setting forth readily understandable guidelines for both zoning boards of appeal and applicants for variances and to eliminate the confusion that then surrounded applications for area variances. As one memorandum in the bill jacket states:

> The rules governing the granting of area variances that have been established by the courts are not nearly as clear as those governing use variances, and the result has been a great deal of confusion by boards of appeals, with a high degree of potential exposure to litigation. The new Town Law, section 267–b(3) and Village Law, section 7–712–b(3) resolve this problem by establishing a statutory test for the issuance of area variances which is flexible and which incorporates what we believe are the best features of the court decisions in order to protect the community (Bill Jacket, L 1991, ch 692, at 26, Memorandum of Executive Deputy Secretary of State James Baldwin).

The same intent may be found in several other memoranda and establish that the legislation was enacted to aid laypersons—both applicants and lay members of zoning boards of appeal—in understanding and implementing the existing case-law; it was intended to have "little impact on existing laws since the main thrust of the legislation is to clarify and establish, in statute, the powers of the Zoning Board as already defined by jurisprudence." * * *

We conclude Town Law § 267–b(3)(b) requires the Zoning Board to engage in a balancing test, weighing "the benefit to the applicant" against "the detriment to the health, safety and welfare of the neighborhood or community" if the area variance is granted, and that an applicant need not show "practical difficulties" as that test was formerly applied.

Applying the new statute we conclude that the action of the Henderson Zoning Board was rational and not arbitrary and capricious. * * * As required by Town Law § 267–b(3)(b), the Zoning Board addressed five specific criteria. First, it determined that no undesirable change would be produced in the character of the neighborhood, because Graham's Creek serves primarily as a site for boathouses and commercial marinas, and that the addition of intervenor's proposed three-slip boathouse will not result in a significant increase in boat traffic or noise. The Zoning Board's conclusion that the variance will have minimal impact on nearby properties is supported by evidence that intervenor's boathouse will comply with all setback and height restrictions imposed by local ordinances. In making this finding, the Board had before it and considered the conditions imposed on intervenor's construction by the Town Planning Board which mitigated concerns voiced by petitioners (see, Town Law § 267–b[3][b][1]).

Next, the Zoning Board concluded that no alternatives other than the grant of area variances existed, because intervenor's lot is of substandard size, and no improvement to the property could be made without the requested lot size and width variances. The Zoning Board then acknowledged that the variances sought were substantial, but that there was no available adjacent land for intervenor to purchase so that he could meet the zoning requirements, and granting the variances would merely permit intervenor to use his property for a permitted use equal to all other neighboring lots. The Zoning Board's conclusion under subdivision (4) that granting the variances would lead to no adverse effect or impact on the neighborhood other than the previously discussed effect on petitioners is also supported by the record.

The only determination of the Zoning Board not supported by the record is its conclusion that intervenor's difficulty was not self-created. The record reveals that the parcel was of substandard lot size when intervenor purchased it in 1989 and it is well established that, in such circumstances, the variance applicant's difficulty or hardship is self-created. Nevertheless, the statute expressly states that the fact that the applicant's difficulty was self-created does not necessarily preclude the granting of the area variance. Under all the circumstances presented, the Board did not act arbitrarily in granting a variance notwithstanding the applicant's self-created difficulty.

In sum, the Zoning Board weighed the benefit to intervenor—the opportunity to fully use his property for a permitted use—against any detriment to the health, safety and welfare of the neighborhood or community, and determined to grant the variance. Its conclusions find ample support from the photographs and other materials in the record, and its determination was not irrational, arbitrary or capricious. Thus, the Appellate Division erred in reversing the order of Supreme Court confirming the determination.

Accordingly, the order of the Appellate Division should be reversed, with costs to intervenor against petitioners, and the judgment of Supreme Court, Jefferson County reinstated.

Order reversed, with costs to intervenor against petitioners, and judgment of Supreme Court, Jefferson County, reinstated.

Notes

1.   Other jurisdictions have recognized a different standard of hardship for area variances as opposed to use variances. See, e.g., Board of Adjustment v. Kwik–Check Realty, Inc., 389 A.2d 1289 (Del.1978); Arens v. City of St. Louis, 872 S.W.2d 631 (Mo.App.1994). But see Ouimette v. City of Somersworth, 119 N.H. 292, 402 A.2d 159 (1979), where the court held that the standard of proof is the same for both area and use variances.

2.   In a jurisdiction applying the law of this case, would the result have differed if the facts were those of the Larsen case?

McMORROW v. BOARD OF ADJUSTMENT FOR CITY OF TOWN & COUNTRY

Missouri Court of Appeals, Eastern District, 1989.
765 S.W.2d 700.

SMITH, PRESIDING JUDGE.

Petitioners appeal from a judgment of the trial court which upheld the action of the Board of Adjustment of the City of Town and Country refusing to grant variances from the zoning ordinances to petitioners. We affirm.

Petitioners' lot is slightly over an acre in area. It is shaped, however, like an anteater's snout, with widths of 31.25 feet and 193.04 feet on the ends and lengths of 523.65 feet and 562.87 feet on the sides. Because of set back and building lines established by the Town and Country ordinances, the area on which structures are permitted on the lot is quite restricted. In fact the single family residence on the property is non-conforming because it infringes upon both set-back and building lines. The residence was built prior to annexation of the property by Town and Country. The area is zoned Suburban Estate which is single family residential with a one acre minimum lot size. The McMorrows desire to build an in-ground swimming pool on the lot. The only feasible location, because of the lot configuration and topography, would require substantial variance from the set-back and building line requirements of the ordinances. In addition, a variance would be required for expansion of what is already a non-conforming structure, the residence. The Board denied the variances requested on the basis that there was no showing of "practical difficulties or unnecessary hardships" requiring granting of the variances.

It is petitioners' position that by establishing that the configuration and topography of their lot makes construction of the pool impossible without the variances they have carried their burden for obtaining the variances. We disagree.

The authority to grant a variance should be exercised sparingly and only under exceptional circumstances. *Matthew v. Smith*, 707 S.W.2d 411 (Mo. banc 1986) l.c. 413. Otherwise continued viability of the zoning code is compromised. *Ogawa v. City of Des Peres*, 745 S.W.2d 238 (Mo.App. 1987) [8]. The statutory authorization for granting variances is found in Sec. 89.090(3) RSMo 1986, and occurs upon a finding of "practical difficulties or unnecessary hardship." The Town and Country ordinances parallel this statutory mandate. In *Matthew v. Smith, supra*, [2], the court indicated that "practical difficulties" was a slightly less rigorous test than "unnecessary hardship" and then stated:

> "To obtain a use variance, an applicant must demonstrate, *inter alia*, unnecessary hardship; and to obtain an area variance, an applicant must establish, *inter alia*, the existence of conditions *slightly* less rigorous than unnecessary hardship." (Emphasis in original).

Petitioners seek area variances. "Unnecessary hardship" has been considered in this state as involving circumstances where the refusal to grant the variance would amount to a denial of any permitted use under the ordinances. *Ogawa v. City of Des Peres, supra*, [13]; *Conner v. Herd*, 452 S.W.2d 272 (Mo.App.1970) [14]; *Brown v. Beuc*, 384 S.W.2d 845 (Mo.App.1964) [9]. Such denial may include not only the impossibility of use but unwarranted economic hardship in achieving a permitted use. *Conner v. Herd, supra* [10, 11]. It is clear from the cases that variances are to be granted only for severe interferences with the ability of the landowner to use his land and not for "mere inconvenience." *Volkman v. City of Kirkwood*, 624 S.W.2d 58 (Mo.App.1981) [5, 6].

The record does not establish that petitioners have carried their burden to justify the variances sought. The land is useable, and is being used, for the use permitted by the zoning ordinances as a single family residence. Petitioners want to add to that residential complex a swimming pool, a permitted structure in the district. They have failed to establish that a swimming pool is a necessity, that they will suffer undue financial burdens if one is not built, or that their satisfactory residential use of the property is impossible without a pool. Throughout the hearing the Board sought petitioners' explanation of why the absence of a pool constituted a "practical difficulty" or "unnecessary hardship." No explanation was advanced other than that the configuration and topography made construction of a pool impossible without the variances. That a structure permitted in the area cannot be built because of the zoning restrictions does not alone establish that a variance must be granted. Even under the "slightly less rigorous" test of area variances set forth in *Matthew v. Smith,* the record does not authorize the variances sought.

Judgment Affirmed.

Notes

1.   Also see City of Ladue v. Zwick, 904 S.W.2d 470 (Mo.App.1995) where the property owner was denied a variance to build a tennis court. The property owner argued that a tennis court must be located on a north/south axis and that such orientation was precluded by hilly topography and odd shape of his lot. The court said: "[N]ot every lot, even in Ladue, is a buildable lot. It is elementary that not every odd scrap of land in an unrestricted commercial district is suitable for a skyscraper, even though a skyscraper may be a 'permitted use.' Likewise, even though [the ordinance] permits tennis courts in residential districts, it is the proposed owner's burden to find a buildable lot. To take advantage of the City's permitted use, a tennis enthusiast must find a lot with less hills, larger acreage, or a more conventional shape."

2.   Many states, in their zoning enabling legislation, prohibit the granting of use variances. In these states the distinction between unnecessary hardship for use variances and practical difficulties for area variances is meaningless. Should hardship be construed strictly in states which do not allow use variances? See International Funeral Services v. DeKalb County, 244 Ga. 707, 261 S.E.2d 625 (1979). Also see Nucholls v. Board of Adjustment of City of Tulsa, 560 P.2d 556 (Okl.1976), where the court held that the city zoning ordinance was unconstitutional insofar as it prohibited the granting of use variances.

3.   Should a court be more or less ready to permit a variance where expansion of a non-conforming use is involved? See Grundlehner v. Dangler, 29 N.J. 256, 148 A.2d 806, 812 (1959). Compare Johnny Cake, Inc. v. Zoning Bd. of Appeals of Burlington, 180 Conn. 296, 429 A.2d 883 (1980) with In re Kenney, 374 N.W.2d 271 (Minn.1985). In the Connecticut case the court held that the zoning board had no authority to grant a variance extending a nonconforming use; the applicant, a seminary, wanted to convert an old fire watchtower to an FM radio transmitter. In the Minnesota case the court held that the board of adjustment had the authority to issue a variance which would expand a nonconforming boathouse, despite language in the enabling act stating that "no variance may be granted that would allow any use that is prohibited in the zoning district." Also see Burbridge v. Governing Body of the Twp. of Mine Hill, 117 N.J. 376, 568 A.2d 527 (1990) where the court held that a variance to expand a nonconforming use could be granted on the ground that the final result would be more aesthetic (the nonconforming use was an auto body repair shop).

4.   On the relationship between variances and special use permits, see Dallstream and Hunt, Variations, Exceptions and Special Uses, 1954 U.Ill. L.F. 213, and for a case illustration, see Waeckerle v. Board of Zoning Adjustment, 525 S.W.2d 351 (Mo.App.1975).

5. On the problem of notice in the variance procedure, see the exhaustive annotation, "Construction and Application of Statute or Ordinance Provisions Requiring Notice as Prerequisite to Granting Variance or Exception to Zoning Requirement," 38 A.L.R.3d 167 (1971).

6. Several interesting and instructive articles describe the results of empirical observation of particular zoning boards of adjustment in the handling of variance cases. See Dukeminier and Stapleton, The Zoning Board of Adjustment: A Case Study of Misrule, 50 Ky.L.J. 273 (1962); Note, Zoning Variances and Exceptions: The Philadelphia Experience, 103 U.Pa. L.Rev. 516 (1955); Comment, Zoning: Variance Administration in Alameda County, 50 Calif.L.Rev. 101 (1962). Dukeminier and Stapleton conclude that (1) the issues are not made clear; (2) the board frequently does not follow the law or find facts or state reasons, or have a correct view of its function; and (3) that Euclidean zoning after 50 years [now 65 or 70 years] has hardening of the arteries that even massive doses of Geritol might not cure. Newer land use control techniques, perfected in the twenty years since this article was written, have possibly aided somewhat in reducing the reliance on traditional administrative forms of relief. These techniques, such as cluster zoning, zero lot line development, or the planned unit development, however, are customarily applied to larger tracts of land and do not address themselves to the problem of abuses relating to one or two lots—which is where the abuses generally occur.

(2) Special Exceptions and Special or Conditional Use Permits

TULLO v. TOWNSHIP OF MILLBURN

Superior Court of New Jersey, Appellate Division, 1959.
54 N.J.Super. 483, 149 A.2d 620.

[In 1928, a club was granted a zoning exception for use of certain lands in a single family residence zone. Now it seeks a special use permit for the construction of a swimming pool. Nine neighbors oppose. The neighbors lost, both before the Township governing body and in the lower court.

Only one appeals. The special permit provision requires an application first to the board of adjustment which then recommends approval or disapproval to the township governing body. The enabling statute contemplated application to and action by the board of adjustment only. The provision of the ordinance which passed the power of ultimate decision to the governing body was nevertheless upheld by the court. Only part of the long opinion affirming the lower court is given.]

HALL, J. * * * In order that our subsequent discussion of the issues in this case may be viewed in their proper legal perspective, we interrupt the factual narrative to comment on the true nature of a "special exception" under our statute. The term might well be said to be a misnomer. "Special uses" or "special use permits" would be more accurate. The theory is that certain uses, considered by the local legislative body to be essential or desirable for the welfare of the community and its citizenry or substantial segments of it, are entirely appropriate and not essentially incompatible with the basic uses in any zone (or in certain particular zones), but not at every or any location therein or without restrictions or conditions being imposed by reason of special problems the use or its particular location in relation to neighboring properties presents from a zoning standpoint, such as traffic congestion, safety, health, noise, and the like. The enabling act therefore permits the local ordinance to require approval of the local administrative agency as to the location of such use within the zone. If the board finds compliance with the standards or requisites set forth in the ordinance, the right to the exception exists, subject to such specific safeguarding conditions as the agency may impose by reason of the nature, location and incidents of the particular use. Without intending here to be inclusive or to prescribe limits, the uses so treated are generally those serving considerable numbers of people, such as private schools, clubs, hospitals and even churches, as distinguished from governmental structures or activities on the one hand and strictly individual residences or businesses on the other. This method of zoning treatment is also frequently extended to certain unusual kinds of strictly private business or activity which, though desirable and compatible, may by their nature present peculiar zoning problems or have unduly unfavorable effect on their neighbors if not specially regulated. Gasoline stations (also treated as special exceptions in the business and industrial zones in the Millburn ordinance and the subject of the ordinance provision under review in the Schmidt case) are an example of this second category. The point is that such special uses are permissive in the particular zone under the ordinance and neither nonconforming nor akin to a variance. The latter must be especially clearly distinguished. In the sense here discussed it relates primarily to the allowance of a use of a particular property *prohibited* in the particular zone for "special reasons." R.S. 40:55–39(d), as amended, N.J.S.A. Moriarty v. Pozner, 21 N.J. 199, 210–211, 121 A.2d 527 (1956); Ranney v. Istituto Pontificio Delle Maestre Filippini, 20 N.J. 189, 198–199, 119 A.2d 142 (1955); Schmidt v. Board of Adjustment of the City of Newark, supra. Cf. Rockhill v. Township of Chesterfield, Burlington County, 23 N.J. 117, 128 A.2d 473 (1957); Borough of North Plainfield v. Perone, 54 N.J.Super. 1, 148 A.2d 50 (App.Div.1959). * * *

CITY OF COLORADO SPRINGS v. BLANCHE

Supreme Court of Colorado, En Banc, 1988.
761 P.2d 212.

ERICKSON, JUSTICE.

Richard Blanche (Blanche) and Faith Bible Fellowship International (Faith Bible), appellants, appeal the entry of a permanent injunction, and finding and penalty for contempt for violation of the injunction.

* * *

Faith Bible owned and operated a church in Colorado Springs that was sold in April 1985. Thereafter, Faith Bible purchased residential property at 2804 Country Club Circle in Colorado Springs. Subsequently, title was conveyed to Blanche and his wife. Faith Bible is a Colorado nonprofit corporation with 501(c)(3) tax exempt status from the Internal Revenue Service. Blanche and Faith Bible commenced, organized, and institutionalized religious activities within the residence knowing that the property was located in an R–1 6000 zone. In an R–1 6000 zone, religious institutions are not allowed as a permitted use, but may be allowed as a conditional use. In Colorado Springs, religious institutions are allowed as principal permitted uses in eight zones, and nine zones permit religious institutions as conditional uses. Neither of the appellants filed an application for permission to conduct religious activities as a conditional use.

Richard Blanche, who is the pastor for Faith Bible, and his family lived in the Country Club Circle home. The residence is a four bedroom home with a family room containing a piano and approximately 50 folding chairs set up in rows facing a podium. Blanche conducted religious services and other congregational activities at the home four times a week. These activities, which typically included sixty to seventy-five people, consisted of praying, singing, studying the bible, and teaching Sunday school.

* * *

On appeal to this court, appellants defend their use of the residence for religious purposes by contending that: (1) the zoning ordinance is unconstitutional because it violates due process and equal protection; (2) the trial court's grant of injunctive relief was an abuse of discretion; (3) the term "religious institution," as contained in the zoning ordinance, is unconstitutionally vague; and (4) the permanent injunction was issued by a trial court which had no jurisdiction to do so.

* * *

Blanche and Faith Bible claim that sections 14–3–504(2) and 14–1–109 of the Code of the City of Colorado Springs (1980) deny them due process and equal protection of the law by unconstitutionally abridging appellants' rights to freedom of speech, assembly, association, and religion. To support their claim, appellants rely upon *City of Englewood v. Apostolic Christian Church,* 146 Colo. 374, 362 P.2d 172 (1961).

The applicable zoning ordinance in *City of Englewood* provided that land located in single-and two-family districts could be used for religious purposes only if a conditional use permit was first obtained from the Englewood Board of Adjustment and Appeals. The Apostolic Church applied for a conditional use permit to build a church in a district zoned for single-and two-family housing. The Board of Adjustment and Appeals denied the church's application whereupon the church initiated an action against the Board in district court. The district court reversed the Board's order, finding that the zoning ordinance violated the first and fourteenth amendments to the United States Constitution and article II, section 25 of the Colorado Constitution. The court directed the City of

Englewood to issue a permit for the construction of the church building. On appeal, this court affirmed the district court's order.

A majority of the court concluded that the ordinance was a blanket exclusion of churches from single-and double-family residence districts, and held the ordinance to be unconstitutional. 146 Colo. at 380, 362 P.2d at 175. By way of contrast, the special concurrence of Justice McWilliams construed the Englewood ordinance as permissive and upheld the constitutionality of the ordinance. Regardless of how the Englewood ordinance should have been characterized, we have no doubt that the ordinance involved in this case is permissive. The analysis of Justice McWilliams in *City of Englewood* is persuasive and is applicable in this case.

> Zoning ordinances which purport to regulate and control the new construction of churches in a given zoned area are generally divided into three types: (1) those which expressly authorize the location of a church in a given zoned area; (2) those which purport to expressly exclude or ban churches from a given zoned area; and (3) those which are "permissive" as to the location of a church within a particular zoned area. The latter type permits a church to locate in a given zoned area only after obtaining a permit therefor as the result of favorable action by an administrative body designated to consider such requests. *The zoning ordinance of Englewood with which we are here concerned is of the latter or "permissive" type. In other words the zoned area where plaintiff church * * * seeks to locate is not one where the ordinance contains a blanket exclusion of all churches. Rather it is an area where the right of a church to locate therein is permissive rather than absolute.*

146 Colo. at 380, 362 P.2d at 175–76 (emphasis added) (McWilliams, J. concurring).

Here, as in *City of Englewood,* the zoning ordinance at issue is the "permissive" type. A majority of jurisdictions have held these types of ordinances to be constitutional. *See, e.g., Grosz v. City of Miami Beach,* 721 F.2d 729 (11th Cir.1983); *Lakewood, Ohio Congregation of Jehovah's Witnesses, Inc. v. City of Lakewood,* 699 F.2d 303 (6th Cir.1983); *West Hartford Methodist Church v. Zoning Bd. of Appeals,* 143 Conn. 263; 121 A.2d 640 (1956); *Rogers v. Mayor & Aldermen,* 110 Ga.App. 114, 137 S.E.2d 668 (1964); *Diocese of Rochester v. Planning Bd.,* 1 N.Y.2d 508, 154 N.Y.S.2d 849, 136 N.E.2d 827 (1956); *State ex rel. Anshe Chesed Congregation v. Bruggemeier,* 97 Ohio App. 67, 115 N.E.2d 65 (1953); *Milwaukie Co. of Jehovah's Witnesses v. Mullen,* 214 Or. 281, 330 P.2d 5 (1958); *State ex rel. Wenatchee Congregation of Jehovah's Witnesses v. City of Wenatchee,* 50 Wash.2d 378, 312 P.2d 195 (1957); Annotation, *Zoning Regulations as Affecting Churches,* 74 A.L.R.2d 377 (1960); 2 A. & D. Rathkopf, *The Law of Zoning and Planning* 20–9 to–10 (1987). We join the majority of jurisdictions that are consistent with the special concurrence in *City of Englewood.* To the extent that our decision in *City of Englewood* conflicts with our decision in this case, it is overruled.

An administrative board's refusal to issue a conditional use permit will be upheld only if there is substantial evidence to establish that denial of the permit is beneficial to the health, safety, morals or general welfare of the community. *See, e.g., State ex rel. Anshe Chesed Congregation v. Bruggemeier,* 97 Ohio App. 67, 115 N.E.2d 65 (1953); *Milwaukie Co. of Jehovah's Witnesses v. Mullen,* 214 Or. 281, 330 P.2d 5 (1958); *State ex rel. Wenatchee Congregation of Jehovah's Witnesses v. City of Wenatchee,* 50 Wash.2d 378, 312 P.2d 195 (1957).

However, because appellants never applied for a conditional use permit, we need only review whether the district court abused its discretion in imposing injunctive relief against appellants.

* * *

The appellants' remaining arguments are without merit. Accordingly, we affirm the district court's issuance of a permanent injunction and the orders, penalties, and fines imposed for contempt of court.

Notes

1. The "special permit" device is discussed in 3 Anderson, American Law of Zoning §§ 19.01–19.32 (3d ed. 1986). In his discussion, Anderson distinguishes variances, exceptions and amendments. He points out that devices which are designated as a "special exception" or "special permit" or "special use permit" are all in reality the same, as far as the result reached is concerned, even though different courts or different ordinances may employ one term in preference to the other. Essentially the same observation is made in an excellent Note, The Administration of Zoning Flexibility Devices: An Explanation for Recent Judicial Frustration, 49 Minn.L.Rev. 973, 997 (1965). In this subsection we have lumped together a case which uses the term "special exception" in connection with the extension of a nonconforming use and a case which views the term as "a misnomer" and prefers "special uses" or "special use permits." Obviously, there is a difference in the "special use permit" or "special exception" as compared to the variance. Variances allow a *prohibited* use, while "special exceptions" or "special use permits" are allowed under the terms of the zoning provisions. On this, see Stacy v. Montgomery County, 239 Md. 189, 210 A.2d 540 (1965).

2. The term, "special exception," is a particularly confusing one due to the existence also of *exceptions* in zoning ordinances which usually involve non-discretionary determinations of whether the property in question falls within the exceptions made for peculiarities in the land (such as substandard lots). See 3 Anderson, supra § 19.03. Recall that in the introductory material taken from Green, Are "Special Use" Procedures in Trouble?, 12 Zoning Digest 73 (1960), a differentiation is also made between the "special exception" and what he refers to as the " 'special use' procedure." The latter is distinguished as being a sort of super form of special exception, in which uses are permitted which are of more substantial importance than those normally dealt with through the special exception device. We have not attempted to make such a differentiation in the order in which the cases and materials are presented in this book on the thought that this might heighten the confusion.

3. In 2 Anderson, American Law of Zoning § 9.18 (3d ed. 1986), it is pointed out that there is a division of opinion among experts in the field on whether the "special permit" device is an appropriate technique or whether it results in limiting a landowner in the uses which he may establish as a matter of right. This raises the question as to who really benefits in such a situation from the requirement of special use permits—the landowner or his neighbors.

4. For a couple of cases in which special permits were denied, see Golden v. City of St. Louis Park, 266 Minn. 46, 122 N.W.2d 570 (1963), and Olsen v. City of Minneapolis, 263 Minn. 1, 115 N.W.2d 734 (1962). These cases are discussed in the Minnesota Law Review note cited in note 1 above. In these cases, the Minnesota commentator feels that insufficient attention was given to the device involved, its flexibility and method of use. The Minnesota Court overruled Golden in 1979. Northwestern College v. City of Arden Hills, 281 N.W.2d 865 (Minn.1979).

5. One constitutional principle which is particularly important in conditional use and special permit cases is the principle that the ordinance contain adequate standards for the issuance of the permit so that a reviewing court may ascertain whether the decision-maker stayed within the bounds of delegated authority. See, e.g., Alpha Portland Cement Co. v. Missouri Dept. of Natural Resources, 608 S.W.2d 451 (Mo.App.1980). The absence of standards would make the grant of a special permit or conditional use wholly discretionary with the agency.

6. A question which arises frequently is whether the planning commission or zoning board can impose special conditions or restrictions on the special permit or conditional use. In Montgomery County v. Mossburg, 228 Md. 555, 180 A.2d 851 (1962) the court upheld the authority of the county to condition a special exception allowing a night club on the applicant's agreement to observe closing hours more restrictive than allowable under the state alcoholic beverage license. The court indicated that the reason for the special exception device was to enable the local authority to protect nearby properties and to tailor the scope of permission so as to strike a reasonable balance. Also see Stevenson v. Palmer, 223 Tenn. 485, 448 S.W.2d 67 (1969) (upholding a condition requiring an apartment complex developer to construct a brick wall around three sides of the complex); Vlahos Realty Co. v. Little Boar's Head Dist., 101 N.H. 460, 146 A.2d 257 (1958) (upholding an 11:00 p.m. closing hour as a condition to a variance); Van Sciver v. Zoning Bd. of Adjustment, 396 Pa. 646, 152 A.2d 717 (1959) (overruling a restriction on the hours of operation of a laundromat on the grounds that the restriction was erroneous, arbitrary and unreasonable); and Lough v. Zoning Bd. of Review, 74 R.I. 366, 60 A.2d 839 (1948) (sustaining the zoning board in granting an exception allowing a gasoline station and garage to be constructed at an intersection, since the zoning board attached nine conditions for the protection of neighboring property owners). Generally, see Strine, The Use of Conditions in Land–Use Control, 67 Dick.L.Rev. 109 (1963).

7. In Pollard v. Palm Beach County, 560 So.2d 1358 (Fla.App.1990) the court held that an applicant for a special exception who met all the standards specified in the ordinance could not be denied the exception

because of neighbors' objections. (The exception was for an adult congregate living facility for the elderly.)

8.   In Wakelin v. Town of Yarmouth, 523 A.2d 575 (Me.1987) the court struck down an ordinance which specified that the zoning board should grant a special exception if the proposed use is "compatible with existing uses" defining compatible "with respect to size, visual impact, intensity of use, proximity to other structures, and density of development." The court held that the definition was unconstitutionally vague and constituted an unlawful delegation of authority.

(3) Floating Zone

RODGERS v. VILLAGE OF TARRYTOWN

Court of Appeals of New York, 1951.
302 N.Y. 115, 96 N.E.2d 731.

FULD, JUDGE. This appeal, here by our permission, involves the validity of two amendments to the General Zoning Ordinance of the Village of Tarrytown, a suburban area in the County of Westchester, within twenty-five miles of New York City.

Some years ago, Tarrytown enacted a General Zoning Ordinance dividing the village into seven districts or zones—Residence A for single-family dwellings, Residence B for two-family dwellings, Residence C for multiple dwellings and apartment houses, three business districts and an industrial zone. In 1947 and 1948, the board of trustees, the village's legislative body, passed the two amendatory ordinances here under attack.

The 1947 ordinance creates "A new district or class of zone * * * [to] be called 'Residence B–B' ", in which, besides one-and two-family dwellings, buildings for multiple occupancy of fifteen or fewer families were permitted. The boundaries of the new type district were not delineated in the ordinance but were to be "fixed by amendment of the official village building zone map, at such times in the future as such district or class of zone is applied, to properties in this village." The village planning board was empowered to approve such amendments and, in case such approval was withheld, the board of trustees was authorized to grant it by appropriate resolution. In addition, the ordinance erected exacting standards of size and physical layouts for Residence B–B zones: a minimum of ten acres of land and a maximum building height of three stories were mandated; setback and spacing requirements for structures were carefully prescribed; and no more than 15% of the ground area of the plot was to be occupied by buildings.

A year and a half after the 1947 amendment was enacted, defendant Elizabeth Rubin sought to have her property, consisting of almost ten and a half acres in the Residence A district, placed in a Residence B–B classification. After repeated modification of her plans to meet suggestions of the village planning board, that body gave its approval, and, several months later, in December of 1948, the board of trustees, also approving, passed the second ordinance here under attack. In essence, it provides that the Residence B–B district "is hereby applied to the [Rubin] property * * * and the district or zone of said property is hereby changed to 'Residence B–B' and the official building Zone Map of the Village of Tarrytown is hereby amended accordingly [by specification of the various parcels and plots involved]".

Plaintiff, who owns a residence on a six-acre plot about a hundred yards from Rubin's property, brought this action to have the two amendments declared invalid and to enjoin defendant Rubin from constructing multiple dwellings on her property. The courts below, adjudging the amendments valid and the action of the trustees proper, dismissed the complaint. We agree with their determination.

While stability and regularity are undoubtedly essential to the operation of zoning plans, zoning is by no means static. Changed or changing conditions call for changed plans, and persons who own property in a particular zone or use district enjoy no eternally vested right to that classification if the public interest demands otherwise. Accordingly, the power of a village to amend its basic zoning ordinance in such a way as reasonably to promote the general welfare cannot be questioned. * * *

The Tarrytown board of trustees was entitled to find that there was a real need for additional housing facilities; that the creation of Residence B–B districts for garden apartment developments would prevent young families, unable to find accommodations in the village, from moving elsewhere; would attract business to the community; would lighten the tax load of the small home owner, increasingly burdened by the shrinkage of tax revenues resulting from the depreciated value of large estates and the transfer of many such estates to tax-exempt institutions; and would develop otherwise unmarketable and decaying property.

The village's zoning aim being clear, the choice of methods to accomplish it lay with the board. Two such methods were at hand. (1) It could amend the General Zoning Ordinance so as to permit garden apartments on any plot of ten acres or more in Residence A and B zones (the zones more restricted) or (2) it could amend that Ordinance so as to invite owners of ten or more acres, who wished to build garden apartments on their properties, to apply for a Residence B–B classification. The board chose to adopt the latter procedure. That it called for separate legislative authorization for each project presents no obstacle or drawback—and so we have already held. See, e.g., Nappi v. La Guardia, 184 Misc. 775, 781, 55 N.Y.S.2d 80, 86 [per Froessel, J.], affirmed 269 App.Div. 693, affirmed 295 N.Y. 652; Matter of Green Point Sav. Bank v. Board of Zoning Appeals, 281 N.Y. 534, 539. Whether we would have made the same choice is not the issue; it is sufficient that the board's decision was neither arbitrary nor unreasonable.

As to the requirement that the applicant own a plot of at least ten acres, we find nothing therein unfair to plaintiff or other owners of smaller parcels. The board undoubtedly found, as it was privileged to find, that garden apartments would blend more attractively and harmoniously with the community setting, would impose less of a burden upon village facilities, if placed upon larger tracts of land rather than scattered about in smaller units. Obviously, some definite acreage had to be chosen, and, so far as the record before us reveals, the choice of ten acres as a minimum plot was well within the range of an unassailable legislative judgment. * * *

The charge of illegal "spot zoning"—levelled at the creation of a Residence B–B district and the reclassification of defendant's property—is without substance. Defined as the process of singling out a small parcel of land for a use classification totally different from that of the surrounding area, for the benefit of the owner of such property and to the detriment of other owners, see Harris v. City of Piedmont, 5 Cal.App.2d 146, 152, 42 P.2d 356; Cassel v. Mayor & City Council of Baltimore, 73 A.2d 486, 488–489 (Md.); Board of Co. Comrs. of Anne Arundel County v. Snyder, 186 Md. 342, 345–346, 46 A.2d 689; Leahy v. Inspector of Bldgs. of New Bedford, 308 Mass. 128, 134, 31 N.E.2d 436; Page v. City of Portland, 178 Or. 632, 641, 165 P.2d 280; Weaver v. Ham, 232 S.W.2d 704, 709 (Tex.); see, also, Yokley, Zoning Law and Practice (1948), sec. 85; cf. People v. Cohen, 272 N.Y. 319, 5 N.E.2d 835, "spot zoning" is the very antithesis of planned zoning. If, therefore, an ordinance is enacted in accordance with a comprehensive zoning plan, it is not "spot zoning," even though it (1) singles out and affects but one small plot, see, e.g., Shepard v. Village of Skaneateles, supra, 300 N.Y. 115, 89 N.E.2d 619 or (2) creates in the center of a large zone small areas or districts devoted to a different use. See Nappi v. La Guardia, supra, 295 N.Y. 652, 64 N.E.2d 716, affirming 269 App.Div. 693, 54 N.Y.S.2d 722, affirming 184 Misc. 775, 55 N.Y.S.2d 80—business area in residence zone; Marshall v. Salt Lake City, 105 Utah 111, 126–127, 141 P.2d 704, 149 A.L.R. 282—business district in residence zone; Higbee v. Chicago, B. & Q. R.R. Co., 235 Wis. 91, 98–99, 292 N.W. 320, 128 A.L.R. 734—railroad station in residence zone; see, also, Avery v. Village of La Grange, 381 Ill. 432, 442, 45 N.E.2d 647; Town of Marblehead v. Rosenthal, 316 Mass. 124, 126, 55 N.E.2d 13; Rathkopf, Law of Zoning and Planning (2d ed., 1949), p. 72 et seq. Thus, the relevant inquiry is not whether the particular zoning under attack consists of areas fixed within larger areas of different use, but whether it was accomplished for the benefit of individual owners rather than pursuant to a comprehensive plan for the general welfare of the community. Having already noted our conclusion that the ordinances were enacted to promote a comprehensive zoning plan, it is perhaps unnecessary to add that the record negates any claim that they were designed solely for the advantage of defendant or any other particular owner. Quite apart from the circumstance that defendant did not seek the benefit of the 1947 amendment until eighteen months after its passage, the all-significant fact is that that amendment applied to the entire territory of the village and accorded each and every owner of ten or more acres identical rights and privileges.

* * *

In point of fact, there would have been no question about the validity of what was done had the board simply amended the General Zoning Ordinance so as to permit property in Residence A and Residence B zones—or, for that matter, in the other districts throughout the village—to be used for garden apartments, provided that they were built on ten-acre plots and that the other carefully planned conditions and restrictions were met. It may be conceded that, under the method which the board did adopt, no one will know, from the 1947 ordinance itself, precisely where a Residence B–B district will ultimately be located. But since such a district is simply a garden apartment development, we find nothing unusual or improper in that circumstance. The same uncertainty—as to the location of the various types of structures—would be present if a zoning ordinance were to sanction garden apartments as well as one-family homes in a Residence A district—and yet there would be no doubt as to the propriety of that procedure. See Nappi v. La Guardia, supra, 295 N.Y. 652, 64 N.E.2d 716, affirming 269 App.Div. 693, 54 N.Y.S.2d 722, affirming 184 Misc. 775, 55 N.Y.S.2d 80. Consequently, to condemn the action taken by the board in effectuating a perfectly permissible zoning scheme and to strike down the ordinances designed to carry out that scheme merely because the board had employed two steps to accomplish what may be, and usually is, done in one, would be to exalt form over substance and sacrifice substance to form.

* * * Whether it is generally desirable that garden apartments be freely mingled among private residences under all circumstances, may be arguable. In view, however, of Tarrytown's changing scene and the other substantial reasons for the board's decision, we cannot say that its action was arbitrary or illegal. While hardships may be imposed on this or that owner, "cardinal is the principal that what is best for the body politic in the long run must prevail over the interests of particular individuals." Shepard v. Village of Skaneateles, supra, 300 N.Y. 115, 118, 89 N.E.2d 619.

The judgment of the Appellate Division should be affirmed, with costs.

[Dissenting opinion not given.]

Notes

1. Consider and compare McQuail v. Shell Oil Co., 40 Del.Ch. 396, 183 A.2d 572 (1962). The county zoning code explained:

While R–2 districts are designated as one of the R districts, they include large undeveloped areas for which the ultimate purpose cannot now be determined. * * * It is expected that, as the development of New Castle County takes place, portions of these R–2 districts will be required for other uses. * * * Requests for rezoning such portions will be studied and acted upon on their own merits, following the * * * [amendment procedure] of this code.

Later the county legislative body amended the R–2 district so as to change 2625 acres of land owned by Shell Oil from R–2 to M–3, industrial, so Shell could build a refinery. The Delaware Court upheld the zoning amendment. Assuming appropriate language in an enabling act, could so extensive a "delayed zoning" change be made administratively by variance or special use permit or floating zone? See Adams v. Zoning Bd. of Review, 86 R.I. 396, 135 A.2d 357 (1957), where the court said:

> The decision of the board to grant the exception sought here has the effect of establishing a multiple dwelling area entirely within an area restricted to a one-family use. The area in question here contains almost 160,000 square feet of land, which is equivalent to twenty-six house lots of the minimum size required by the ordinance in one-family zones. In our opinion it cannot be argued reasonably that this does not effect a substantial change in the lines of the zone. It is so extensive that it invades the power reserved to the council by § 2 of the enabling act.

See contra: Olson v. Zoning Bd. of Review, 96 R.I. 1, 188 A.2d 367 (1963) (where 408,000 square feet were involved, and where the council had just two months before denied a rezoning petition).

2. A good discussion of the concept and the potential uses of the floating zone is contained in a Comment, Zoning—The Floating Zone: A Potential Instrument of Versatile Zoning, 16 Cath.U.L.Rev. 85 (1966). The writer points out that the floating zone in theory floats above the landscape in anticipation of being brought down to earth by an amendment rezoning the area in question. It is a use classification which is not employed until needed nor pinned down to any area until the necessity arises. Obviously, where such a use or category of uses may reasonably be anticipated, the floating zone device offers the planner some substantial flexibility in dealing with the problem as it arises. Moreover, there may be new kinds of uses which will arise and cannot be anticipated but which the planner will have to provide for. The beauty of the floating zone is that it "descends to earth" at the time and place desired. It thus frees the hands of the planner from some of the limitations of Euclidean-type zoning. To the contrary, however, the "floating zone" may be said to float over the heads of landowners somewhat like a dark raincloud. Thus the argument against the floating zone is that it is unfair to property owners because the protection accruing to them as the result of the more traditional Euclidean zoning techniques has been substantially diminished. On this, see Comment, Zoning Change: Flexibility vs. Stability, 26 Md.L.Rev. 48, 60 (1966), as well as Haar and Hering, The Lower Gwynedd Township Case, 74 Harv.L.Rev. at 1573 (1961). The Maryland commentator points out that it has also been argued that a floating zone is simply another, perhaps more grandiose, form of spot zoning.

3. In Beall v. Montgomery County Council, 240 Md. 77, 212 A.2d 751 (1965), the Maryland Court of Appeals sustained the county council in rezoning 41.6 acres of land from single-family residential use to multiple-family, high rise residential use. Prior to the application for rezoning, the county council had created a new type of zone, known as the R–H zone. Its purpose was to provide suitable sites for high density residential develop-

ment and to allow numerous types of commercial, recreational and educational uses within the area. The court stated that no evidence of a mistake in the original zoning or of a substantial change in the character of the neighborhood was necessary or applicable "in view of the conclusion of the Technical Staff, adopted by the Planning Commission and the Council, that the applications complied with the purposes of the R–H zone, and of our decisions in Costello v. Sieling, 223 Md. 24, 161 A.2d 824 (1960) and in Huff v. Board of Zoning Appeals, 214 Md. 48, 133 A.2d 83 (1957)." Commenting further, the court said:

> The new R–H zone, created on February 13, 1962, is a residential zone compatible with existing residential zones. It has some of the qualities of the so-called "floating zone." Professor Reno of the University of Maryland School of Law describes the "floating zone" as an example of "Non–Euclidean" zoning, in his interesting and instructive article in 23 Md.Law Review, 105, entitled, "Non–Euclidean Zoning: The Use of the Floating Zone." He points out that the floating zone, which is implemented by legislative action in the nature of a special exception, is a new concept in zoning and frees the legislative body from the shackles of the conventional "Euclidean zone" fixed as to definite areas. The validity of this type of "zone" has been the subject of litigation with differing results. In Pennsylvania, for example, the Supreme Court of Pennsylvania, held that this type of zone was not within the purview of the State Zoning Enabling Act. See Eves v. Zoning Bd. of Adjustment of Lower Gwynedd Twp., 401 Pa. 211, 164 A.2d 7 (1960). On the other hand, the Court of Appeals of New York sustained a floating zone permitting garden type of apartments, with adequate provisions for set backs, spacing of buildings and for a minimum 10.5 acre lot, upon application of an individual property owner and the approval of the Board. See Rodgers v. Village of Tarrytown, 302 N.Y. 115, 96 N.E.2d 731 (1951). We have approved the New York rule and followed and applied the decision in the Rodgers case in Huff v. Board of Zoning Appeals, 214 Md. 48, 133 A.2d 83 (1957), supra. [This case upheld a 5 acre minimum floating zone for restricted manufacturing.]

* * *

We followed Huff and treated it as controlling in Costello by a unanimous court. In Costello, three zones called "Tourist Accommodation Districts" had been created. The T–1 district, among other uses, permitted "motels and tourist cabins and hotels." The T–2 district, among other uses, permitted a "trailer coach park." In the T–2 district a minimum lot area of 3 acres was required, a 50 foot set back for any trailer from a street or road, a 20 foot set back from any side line, and a 25 foot set back from a rear line. The lot coverage could not be more than 50% by trailer coaches or buildings. In 1959, the County Commissioners for Howard County upon the application of the contract purchaser of a 92 acre tract of land, zoned "R" (Residential) reclassified that tract to T–2. The tract in question was surrounded by properties devoted to residential and agricultural uses. The protestant owned an 878 acre farm, the principal improvements on which were located ½ mile from the southern end of the rezoned tract. In the proposal the applicants indicated that they would provide and maintain a water system, swimming pool, an auditorium and an administration building, with a fountain and a loggia for adornment. There was testimony that existing trailer parks were inadequate to meet the needs of the community but this was contradicted by the owners of two large trailer park areas. The expert testimony indicated, with one exception, that the establishment of the trailer park would not adversely affect surrounding properties. The Planning Commission of Howard County *recommended denial* of the application on the grounds that there would be an undue concentration of occupants in a small area, it would create a greater demand for community facilities than would be required for the normal half-acre residential development, there would be major sewerage and water supply problems and the original zoning was much more desirable on the tract. The County Commissioners *approved* the reclassification, noting that the use was closely related to residential use, there was a need for the new trailer park, the surrounding properties, save one, would not be adversely affected and there would be no undue demand for county facilities. The Circuit Court, on appeal *reversed* on the grounds 1) that the T–2 classification was not analogous to a special exception as in Huff and 2) there was no substantial evidence before the County Commissioners that there was either a mistake in the original zoning or of a substantial change in the character of the neighborhood. We reversed, holding that Huff controlled and that the "mistake-change in conditions" rule was not applicable.

* * *

It may be added that neither Huff nor Costello has been overruled or modified by our subsequent opinions. Both cases have been distinguished from the situation arising in Baltimore County in regard to action by the County Board of Appeals in reclassifying land from R–6 (residential, one or two family) to R–A (residential, apartment). See Shadynook Improvement Ass'n v. Molloy, 232 Md. 265, 192 A.2d 502 (1963), Levy v. Seven Slade, Inc., 234 Md. 145, 198 A.2d 267 (1964), and Rohde v. County Bd., 234 Md. 259, 199 A.2d 216 (1964).

* * *

[I]n the Baltimore County cases the R–A zone is not a floating zone like M–R and hence the holding in Huff was held to be inapplicable. In the case at bar, however, the local legislature has indicated that the new classification and the classification of neighboring property are compatible, hence the holdings in Costello and Huff do apply and control the decision in the case at bar.

4. Reps, Requiem for Zoning, ASPO Info.Rep. 56, 62 (1964), proposes:

First, I think it highly desirable to combine such zoning-type restrictions with other related public controls into a set of what might be called Development Regulations. From the standpoint of procedure we have already moved some distance in this direction. The use of floating zones, increased reliance on special exception or conditional use devices, and the requirements of site plan review as a condition of zoning permit approval, to name three among several methods that are currently employed, have all brought the procedure for securing permits under the zoning ordinance closer to that of subdivision control. I suggest that we pursue this approach much further and require most types of proposed development to be submitted to a local agency that would administer, through discretionary review, an ordinance combining at least zoning-type and subdivision regulations. This should simplify development control. Elimination of conflicting provisions and greater convenience for both administrative officials and land developers are but two of the advantages that would result.

Second, to guide administrative officials in reaching discretionary decisions, there should be a plan for community development and a comprehensive set of development objectives and standards. This plan should be made mandatory, it should be adopted by the legislative body, and review and readoption at fixed intervals should be required. Such plans should show generalized proposed future land uses, circulation systems, population density patterns, and community facilities.

* * *

Third, while I have referred to the discretionary administrative review body as local, I envisage this body ultimately as one with a geographical jurisdiction more extensive than the present city, town or borough boundaries. The new pessimists from the left-bank of the Charles River have lately been stating that multi-purpose metropolitan government is impossible to achieve and probably undesirable anyway. Perhaps they are correct, but as they point out, ad hoc metropolitan working agreements, authorities, special districts, and other single-purpose arrangements or agencies will be necessary as partial substitutes.

* * *

Fourth, the land use regulations themselves would need to differ substantially from those presently encompassed under zoning. Except as I will mention later, no district boundaries—no zoning map—would exist. The comprehensive plan, expressed in graphic form and in statements of development objectives, would be one guide to the discretionary administrative body, which might be called the Office of Development Review. While ultimately the plan itself might be regarded as a sufficient standard or rule of conduct to guide discretionary action, probably we shall need in addition rather detailed standards enacted by legislative bodies. These would be similar to those we now find in the better ordinances which authorize floating zones, conditional uses, and site plan approval permits. I suggest that these standards need to do more than merely specify the public good as a rule of conduct. In other words, the standards should be fairly specific and should relate to defined categories of land use. Such requirements should take the form of performance standards, rather than rigid specifications. Permissible ranges of height and bulk, for example, should be expressed in such measures as floor area ratios and angles of light obstruction. Emphasis should be placed on such performance criteria as noise, traffic generation, smoke emission and air pollution, odor production, vibration, and the like. Even so, some specification standards would doubtless be needed.

Within this rather general framework of plans, goals, and standards, the Office of Development Review would exercise broad discretionary power in granting or denying or modifying requests for development permission. Such permits would be for both tract development and single buildings on individual sites. As in most current floating zone procedures, approval would be for specific uses and building designs as shown on site plans, elevation drawings and as described in supplementary text material. This procedure, then, would not be at all like present zoning, the effect of which is blanket permission for any of a wide range of uses permitted in the zoning district. The discretionary powers would be broad; the development permit would be narrow in the development rights that would be conferred.

5. A recent trend, similar to the program outlined by Reps in the previous note, is receiving attention by many planners. The device, usually referred to as performance zoning, eliminates conventional zoning districts in favor of a few major distinctions and then proceeds to regulate in terms of the impact on the land and the need to preserve particular uses. See Kendig, Performance Zoning (American Planning Ass'n 1980). The prototypical ordinance presented in this publication contains eight zoning districts, Agricultural, Rural, Estate, Development, Urban Core, Neighborhood Conservation, Commercial Conservation, and Holding. Five general use categories are either permitted, denied or conditionally permitted in these districts (the five categories are agriculture, residential, institutional, commercial, and industrial). The heart of the ordinance is the performance standards provisions which provide minimum standards for open space, density, impervious surface coverage, and lot area. The publication contains detailed illustrations as well as a model ordinance with commentary. Also see Porter, Phillips & Lassar, Flexible Zoning: How It Works (Urban Land Inst.1988).

6. After studying the materials on Planned Unit Development, infra, consider whether the PUD is a device that meets the problems outlined by Reps. In this light, also, take account of the fact that the floating zone device has not spread appreciably since its first use, while PUD has literally swept the nation. Note, however, that the floating zone device has not disappeared and is still in use. See, e.g., Treme v. St. Louis County, 609 S.W.2d 706 (Mo.App.1980); Howard Research & Development Corp. v. Howard County, 46 Md.App. 498, 418 A.2d 1253 (1980).

(4) Planned Unit Development and Cluster Zoning

CHRINKO v. SOUTH BRUNSWICK
TWP. PLANNING BD.

Superior Court of New Jersey, Law Division, 1963.
77 N.J.Super. 594, 187 A.2d 221.

FURMAN, J.S.C. This prerogative writ action contests the validity of two ordinances of South Brunswick Township in Middlesex County permitting cluster or open space zoning. By their terms a subdivision developer may reduce minimum lot sizes by 20% or 30% and minimum frontages by 10% or 20% upon his concurrently deeding 20% or 30% of the subdivided tract for parks, school sites and other public purposes, with the approval of the planning board.

South Brunswick Township is in the western section of Middlesex County abutting Somerset and Mercer Counties. Its land area is over 41 square miles. The New Jersey Turnpike, three main arterial highways and the main line of the Pennsylvania Railroad bisect the township. Once predominantly agricultural, with settled communities at Kingston, Dayton, Monmouth Junction and Deans, South Brunswick has experienced an estimated doubling of its population in the three years between 1957 and 1960 and an onrush of new industry and commercial establishments, particularly along the highways.

Downtown New York and downtown Philadelphia are within a radius of 35 miles, drawn from South Brunswick Township. The urban sprawl from the New York metropolitan area reaches within a few miles of the township on the north and east. Residential developments for the wage earners of Philadelphia, Trenton and vicinity are pushing towards South Brunswick from the south and west. Kendall Park, which was developed recently for one-family housing on lots approximating 13,500 square feet, now holds about 40% of the population of South Brunswick Township in an area slightly over one square mile along the northern boundary.

A similar project, Brunswick Acres, is proposed for a 235–acre tract in the Residential 20 Zone in the northeast corner of the township. This development is intertwined with the legal and factual issues before the court. The plaintiffs contend that the cluster or open space ordinances were enacted for the special benefit of the owner, Yenom Corporation. The defendants' position is that they responded with reasonable legislation, general in effect, to the problem of large subdivision developments without land areas available for schools, recreation areas and green spaces.

Facing multiple housing developments and a population upsurge, the South Brunswick Planning Board authorized a master plan report from a firm of planning consultants in 1960. The master plan report, which recommended balanced growth, was submitted in late 1961. No master plan has been adopted. On the subject of cluster or open space zoning, the master plan report suggested an optional system parallel to that enacted in the zoning ordinances under attack here, but applicable only in zones with a minimum lot size of 45,000 square feet and allowing reductions of minimum lot sizes but not minimum frontages. The planning consultants label this recommended scheme "density zoning," stressing that no more homes can be built in a subdivision despite smaller size lots, because the land thus saved must be deeded to the municipality.

The need for preserving woods and parklands in a natural state, as well as lands adequate for other public purposes, is widely recognized.

The voters of this State approved by referendum in 1961 the expenditure of $60,000,000 for the acquisition of so-called "green acres" by the State or political subdivisions. L.1961, c. 45, N.J.S.A. 13:8A–1 et seq. Technical Bulletin 42 of the Urban Land Institute, published in 1961, endorses density zoning, which it designates as organic zoning for planned residential developments. Other discussions of the various governmental techniques for acquiring or maintaining recreation and park areas are found in Krasnowiecki & Paul, "Preservation of Open Space in Metropolitan Areas," 110 U.Pa.L.Rev. 179 (1961); Comment, "Techniques for Preserving Open Spaces," 75 Harv.L.Rev. 1622 (1962); Comment, "Control of Urban Sprawl or Securing Open Space: Regulation by Condemnation or by Ordinance?" 50 Cal.L.Rev. 483 (1962).

The cluster or open space zoning ordinance of South Brunswick Township was adopted as No. 19–62, an amendment to the zoning ordinance of 1958. Its main pertinent provisions are as follows:

"Section 2. The purpose of this subsection is to provide a method of development of residential land which will nevertheless preserve desirable open spaces, school sites, recreation and park areas and lands for other public purposes.

"Section 3. At the discretion of the Planning Board, a subdivider may be allowed to reduce the minimum lot size and dimension requirements in accordance with the provisions of this Ordinance, provided the following conditions are met:

(a) The resulting net lot density of the area to be subdivided shall be no greater than the net lot density of the said area without regard to the provisions of this Ordinance.

(b) All lands within the subdivision other than streets, building lots and private recreational areas shall be deeded to the Township for public purposes simultaneously with the granting of final subdivision approval.

(c) The lands to be deeded for public purposes shall be located, shaped and improved as required by the Planning Board, which shall consider the suitability, physical condition and location of the lands with regard to its proposed uses and to the needs of the Township, in reaching its determination. The Planning Board shall, prior to reaching its determination, cause at least one of its members to confer with the Board of Education, Recreation Commission, Shade Tree Commission, Municipal Utilities Authority, Engineer and other interested municipal agencies as to the potential uses and advisability of accepting the lands offered to be donated.

(d) A portion of the land to be donated for public purposes shall be at least a usable single five acre tract.

(e) With the exception of minimum lot sizes and lot dimension requirements, the subdivision must comply with all other provisions of the Zoning Ordinance, such as front, rear and side setbacks, size of buildings, etc.

(f) There must exist approved plans for public water and public sewer systems which shall be available to all lots in the subdivision prior to the issuance of any Certificates of Occupancy.

(g) A developer may apply to the Planning Board for permission to reduce lot sizes and donate lands to the Township in accordance with this Ordinance at any time prior to applying for final subdivision approval.

"Section 4. If the tract to be subdivided is located in a zone which requires a minimum lot size of 20,000 square feet or less, the developer must donate, exclusive of open drainage water courses, 20% of the tract to the Township; if the tract to be subdivided is located in a zone which requires a minimum lot size in excess of 20,000 square feet, the developer must donate, exclusive of open drainage water courses, 30% of the tract to the Township. The area of the tract shall be determined from a certified outline survey submitted by the subdivider.

"Section 5. If the minimum lot size requirement of the tract to be subdivided be 20,000 square feet or less, the minimum lot size requirement shall be reduced 20% and the minimum frontage requirement shall be reduced 10%. If the minimum lot size requirement of the tract to be subdivided be in excess of 20,000 square feet, the minimum lot size requirement shall be reduced 30% and the minimum frontage requirement shall be reduced 20%."

A companion zoning ordinance amendment, No. 20–62, also challenged in this litigation, amplifies previous requirements concerning performance guarantees by developers to cover specifically improvements to lands to be deeded to the township for public purposes.

* * *

Although the state zoning law does not in so many words empower municipalities to provide an option to developers for cluster or density zoning, such an ordinance reasonably advances the legislative purposes of securing open spaces, preventing overcrowding and undue concentration of population, and promoting the general welfare. Nor is it an objection that uniformity of regulation is required within a zoning district. N.J.S.A. 40:55–31. Such a legislative technique accomplishes uniformity because the option is open to all developers within a zoning district, and escapes the vice that it is compulsory. Midtown Properties, Inc. v. Madison Tp., 68 N.J.Super. 197, 210, 172 A.2d 40 (Law Div.1961).

Zoning ordinances in rapidly growing municipalities may be founded on an outmoded concept that houses will be built one at a time for individual owners in accordance with zoning regulations, with latitude for variances in hardship or other exceptional cases, and that the municipality can take steps whenever warranted to acquire school, park and other public sites. Such a gradual and controlled development is not practicable in many municipalities today. Confronted with a subdivision plan for several hundred homes in a tract meeting all water drainage, sanitation and other conditions, a municipality must anticipate school needs but without lands set aside for that purpose; it must anticipate a large population concentration without recreation areas, parks or green spaces, or lands for firehouses or other public purposes. Cluster or density zoning is an attempted solution, dependent, as set up in the South Brunswick zoning ordinance, upon the agreement of the large-scale developer whose specific monetary benefit may be only that he saves on street installation costs.

* * *

The broad charge that ordinances Nos. 19–62 and 20–62 were enacted to advance the special interest of Yenom Corporation is without support in the proof. Admittedly, the Brunswick Acres development was predominantly in the minds of Jack Stein, chairman of the planning board, and other municipal officials prior to the planning board resolutions and zoning ordinance amendments.

To avoid the consequences of a drastic expansion in population without green spaces or adequate school or other public sites, the municipality sought relief through legislation. The deadline of December 9, 1962 for final approval of the first Yenom Corporation plan was a significant consideration. Rebutting the contention that municipal officials acted in the interest of Yenom Corporation, not that of the municipality, are the statements of various officials on the witness stand that they voted for ordinances Nos. 19–62 and 20–62 because of projected growth, need for school sites, need for recreation sites and parklands and reduction of street maintenance costs.

The benefits to Yenom Corporation, other than a saving in street construction costs, are obscure. The same number of homes may be constructed, but on smaller lots. Lands acceptable to the planning board, including at least one five-acre parcel, must be deeded to the municipality. The paramount concern of the municipal officials, as one of them graphically described, was to avoid a "bad deal," the Brunswick Acres plan for 526 homes on 13,500–square–foot lots with only ten acres reserved for public use. Such an objective is valid, if enacted as ordinance No. 19–62 was enacted, as general, not special legislation.

* * *

The specific points raised by the plaintiffs, in support of the argument that the municipal officials favored Yenom Corporation, are that cluster or open space zoning deviates from the master plan report, that there are surface and subsurface drainage problems on the Brunswick Acres tract, that there are other lands available for public uses in the municipality, and that Yenom Corporation should have proceeded by application for zoning variance.

Deviations from a master plan report are not fatal. Professional advice supports the good faith of a municipal governing body in promulgating a zoning ordinance or master plan, S & L Associates, Inc. v. Washington Township, 61 N.J.Super. 312, 324, 160 A.2d 635 (App.Div. 1960), but it need not be followed to the letter. The legislative decision is the township's not the planning consultant's. Testimony here amply supported the modifications of the master plan report. South Brunswick Township officials considered that cluster or density zoning was more advantageous in zoning districts permitting smaller lot sizes, with intensified school and parkland needs, and that reduction of minimum frontage as well as minimum lot size requirements, by smaller percentages, was a practical adjustment.

The master plan report advocated industrial-research zoning for the northeast corner of the township, including the proposed Brunswick Acres site, but this was in fact part of the Residential 20 Zone for which there was a pending and valid preliminary approval for a large subdivision for residential development.

Various engineers and soil specialists testified at the trial on the limitations of Brunswick Acres tract for dwelling sites because of flooding and drainage problems. The consensus was that these could be overcome, but no advantage facilitating building is discernible because of the cluster or open space amendments.

Public ownership of other lands in the 41 square miles of South Brunswick Township is of little relevance. One 74–acre tract, inaccessible by any road and spongy in soil texture, is in the Sand Hills area between Kendall Park and Brunswick Acres. While it may be of future value for public use in the municipality, the existence of this tract is not support for the claim that the cluster or open space zoning ordinance was enacted in the private interests of Yenom Corporation and not for valid legislative purposes.

Ordinance No. 19–62 is applicable in 60 to 65% of the land area in South Brunswick Township. Proper procedure was followed in amending the zoning ordinance to accomplish such a broad scale revision. Judicial decisions striking down zoning ordinances because they constitute spot zoning and by-pass the board of adjustment deal with single parcels or limited areas. Conlon v. Bd. of Public Works, Paterson, 11 N.J. 363, 94 A.2d 660 (1953); cf. Kozesnik v. Montgomery Twp., 24 N.J. 154, 131 A.2d 1 (1957).

* * *

The proofs in this litigation establish adequate consideration of cluster or density zoning by the South Brunswick Township Planning Board, including four new members who took office on July 1, 1962; specific approval of the concept in the resolutions dated August 25 and September 11, 1962; and endorsement of the ordinances under attack on September 18, 1962, within two weeks of their final adoption.

* * *

For all the foregoing reasons decision is in favor of the defendants.
* * *

Notes

1. Compare with the principal case, Mountcrest Estates, Inc. v. Rockaway, 96 N.J.Super. 149, 232 A.2d 674 (1967), where another New Jersey court struck down an ordinance similar to that of South Brunswick on the ground that there was no limitation as to the nature of the public use to be made of the donated property (—the court said the land could be used for a dog pound, jail, or sewage disposal plant—) and on the ground that the planning board had unfettered discretion as to location and shape of donated land. Also see Creative Environments, Inc. v. Estabrook, 491 F.Supp. 547 (D.Mass.1980) where the court held that plaintiff had no constitutional right to construct a development utilizing the cluster concept; Croteau v. Planning Bd. of Hopkinton, 40 Mass.App.Ct. 922, 663 N.E.2d 583 (1996) where the court upheld denial of a cluster development plan because the open space would not be of public significance.

In 1965 a model act for Planned Unit Development was prepared by Babcock, Krasnowiecki and McBride. It was published in Legal Aspects of Planned Unit Residential Development, Technical Bulletin 52, Urban Land Institute. See Babcock, An Introduction to the Model Enabling Act for Planned Unit Residential Development, 114 U.Pa.L.Rev. 136 (1965). In 1967 New Jersey adopted a Municipal Planned Unit Development Act based on the model act. N.J.Stat.Ann. § 40:55–55, et seq.

2. The basic aim of the "cluster" plan is to make suburbia more attractive by eliminating row on row of blocks of similar houses, located on lots of similar size, each an equal distance from the street and approximately an equal distance from one another. This type of suburban planning creates something which has all the charm of a high-rent army camp. The "cluster" type of planning seeks to retain the attractiveness of country living in urban or semi-urban areas by eliminating conformity and standardization and by placing a high priority on diversity of lot sizes, house locations and by placing a premium on open spaces, trees and natural beauty. The next case differentiates between the PUD and the cluster development, although the terminology is sometimes used interchangeably and there is an obvious relationship.

ORINDA HOMEOWNERS COMMITTEE
v. BOARD OF SUPERVISORS

California Court of Appeals, 1970.
11 Cal.App.3d 768, 90 Cal.Rptr. 88.

DEVINE, PRESIDING JUSTICE. Appellants sought unsuccessfully to gain invalidation by the superior court of a rezoning ordinance of Contra Costa County, in the unincorporated Orinda area. Injunction and writ of mandate were denied and judgment was rendered against plaintiffs. Although a question of standing exists as to some of the plaintiffs, we have no doubt that three of the plaintiffs, homeowners, are qualified because Contra Costa County Ordinance No. 1975, section 2205.10, gives standing to appeal from decisions of the County Planning Commission to anyone whose property rights are adversely affected. It seems to have been taken for granted in the trial court, and understandably so, that the property rights of the homeowners would be adversely affected to a certain extent by the rezoning of the adjacent property, and the question whether rezoning conformed with the general plan was an issue in the case. There is no need, therefore, to make a problem of this matter, and when we refer to plaintiffs, or appellants, herein, we mean the three property owners. We take note, however, of the fact that the litigation is of personal interest to many others in the Orinda area.

Plaintiffs are homeowners upon lands adjacent to a parcel of 187 acres which is owned by real party in interest. The Board of Supervisors of Contra Costa County, on recommendation of the County Planning Commission, rezoned the 187–acre parcel from R–20 (single family residential) to P–1 (planned unit development). The plan called for development of "residential clusters" as well as single family residential lots. The maximum density of the clusters would be eight units per acre. Approximately 345 dwelling units would be constructed, of which about 236 would be located in clusters. The actual number of units is subject to change, but "in no case shall the total number of dwelling units exceed 368." The density of the entire property would not exceed two residential units per acre, which is within the density requirements of the master plan previously adopted by the county. The plan provided for approval by the County Director of Planning of the design of all clusters.

PLANNED UNIT DEVELOPMENT

In Hagman, Larson & Martin, California Zoning Practice (Cont.Ed. Bar) p. 236, it is said that a "planned unit development might be described as a tract of land absolved from conventional zoning to permit clustering of residential uses and perhaps compatible commercial and industrial uses, and permitting structures of differing heights." Although planned unit development (which in professional zoning circles has attained the dignity of alphabetical titles—PD or PUD) is often regarded as synonymous with cluster development, "It is more accurate to define cluster development as a device for grouping dwellings to increase dwelling densities on some portions of the development area in order to have other portions free of buildings." (Id., at p. 240.) Since the ordinance in the present case permits as well as regulates residential units only, the term "cluster development" probably fits the situation better than the broader term "planned unit development." But whatever title be given to the concept, the plan is to devise a better use of undeveloped property than that which results from proceeding on a lot-to-lot basis. Control of density in the area to be developed is an essential part of the plan. The reservation of green, or at least open, spaces in a manner differing from the conventional front or back yard is another ingredient. Conformity to good landscaping, as the planners devise it, is also an objective. We do not mean to give a treatise on the subject of planned unit development, however. An excellent description of this species of zoning and a compendium of the literature on the subject is to be found in 114 Pa.L.Rev. 3–170.

GOVERNMENT CODE, SECTION 65852

Appellants contend that the planned unit development or cluster development, as enacted by the ordinance, conflicts with Government Code, section 65852, which provides: "All such regulations shall be uniform for each class or kind of building or use of land throughout each zone, but the regulation in one type of zone may differ from those in other types of zones." It is remarked in Hagman, Larson & Martin, California Zoning Practice (Cont.Ed.Bar) p. 237, that no California court has passed on the validity of the planned unit development, although it was presumed to be valid in Millbrae Ass'n for Residential Survival v. City of Millbrae, 262 Cal.App.2d 222, 69 Cal.Rptr. 251, and the authors cite possible nonconformity with Government Code, section 65852.

We hold that a residential planned unit development (a cluster development) does not conflict with section 65852 merely by reason of the fact that the units are not uniform, that is, they are not all single family dwellings and perhaps the multi-family units differ among themselves. Section 65852 provides that the *regulations* shall be uniform for each class or kind of building or use of land through-out the zone. It does not state that the units must be alike even as to their character, whether single family or multi-family. In conventional zoning, where apartment houses are permitted in a particular zone, single family dwellings, being regarded (whether rightly or wrongly) as a "higher" use, are also allowed. This causes no conflict with section 65852.

We find nothing to indicate that the Legislature's policy, as expressed in the section, was to prevent county planning agencies and boards of supervisors from applying the concept of planned unit development for the use that is best and most harmonious for the area as the planners and the county legislators conceive it to be. In Cheney v. Village 2 at New Hope, Inc., 429 Pa. 626, 241 A.2d 81, a leading case sustaining planned unit development, it was observed that large scale residential developments, particularly in suburban areas, have resulted in more efficient and aesthetic use when there are not inflexible rules applying to individual lots.

In fact, section 65852 seems to have been discussed but once, in Scrutton v. County of Sacramento, 275 Cal.App.2d 412, 417, 79 Cal.Rptr. 872, 877. In that case, appellant contended that rezoning of her property from agricultural to multiple family residential use, upon condition that she pave an adjoining street at her own expense, violated the section. But the court rejected this, holding that section 65852 "aims at the general objective of uniform land use within each land zone," and that the conditional zoning which had been enacted did not conflict with the code section. In Desert Outdoor Advertising, Inc. v. County of San Bernardino, 255 Cal.App.2d 765, 63 Cal.Rptr. 543, an ordinance which prohibited billboards, except in certain areas and under certain conditions, was upheld because it was uniform in application wherever equal conditions existed. It had been contended by appellant in that case that former section 65802, the predecessor to present section 65852, of the Government Code had been violated. No other cases involving these sections (or their predecessor, Government Code, section 38697) have been found. These sections were derived from section 2 of the Standard State Zoning Enabling Act, and it is said in 1 Anderson, American Law of Zoning, § 5.17, p. 288, that the purpose of the section was mainly a political rather than a legal one, namely, to give notice to property owners that there shall be no improper discriminations. This was useful in the early days of zoning. Professor Anderson suggests that the fact that the section is an expression of policy may be the reason for the scarcity of judicial construction of the uniformity requirement.

* * *

Appellants complain that the ordinance leaves to the Planning Agency the matter of density within a zone. But the rezoning resolution provides, in paragraph 10, for the maximum number of dwelling units for the entire property. Although variations from the estimated number of dwelling units are permissible within the maximum, these are not to be made by the Planning Director solely, but only upon approval by the Planning Commission after a hearing. We discern no unlawful delegation of legislative power.

The case is different from that of People v. Perez, 214 Cal.App.2d Supp. 881, 882, 29 Cal.Rptr. 781, cited by appellants, in which a zone was created which nominally was for agricultural use, but which was made subject to varying types of residential use by special permit, no guides being given to the planning body save the most general (the identical standards given to the city council by the Government Code). In the case before us, a single use, residential, is projected.

* * *

The judgment is affirmed.

Notes

1. The principal case indicates that special enabling legislation may not be necessary to accommodate PUDs or cluster zoning techniques if a court is willing to interpret the zoning enabling act broadly. In Cetrulo v. City of Park Hills, 524 S.W.2d 628 (Ky.1975), the court held that PUD approval was basically a legislative act and not like a rezoning, which required an adjudicatory hearing. The PUD in this case was a seven-story condominium structure on an undivided 7½ acre tract.

2. A PUD has some attributes of subdivision and some attributes of zoning. In City of Urbana v. County of Champaign, 76 Ill.2d 63, 27 Ill.Dec. 777, 389 N.E.2d 1185 (1979) the court was faced with the problem of a proposed PUD outside the city limits of Urbana. The county had a zoning and subdivision ordinance as did the city; however, the city zoning ordinance

stopped at the city limits and the subdivision ordinance projected into the extraterritorial planning area. The court held that the developer was not required to comply with the city's subdivision ordinance because the PUD was to be developed as a unitary 50 acre parcel. The creation of a PUD was held, in Jurkiewicz v. Butler County Bd. of Elections, 85 Ohio App.3d 503, 620 N.E.2d 146 (1993), to be a legislative act and therefore subject to referendum.

3.   In City of Waukesha v. Town Board of Town of Waukesha, 198 Wis.2d 592, 543 N.W.2d 515 (1995) the court held the town's PUD ordinance invalid because it permitted the town to designate a PUD in any district as a conditional use. The town had approved a PUD for a strip commercial mall in an area zoned residential and limited industrial:

> In this case, the ordinance at issue allowed the Town Board, without any zoning district restrictions, to authorize a PUD through the grant of a conditional use permit. A conditional use must be consistent with the use classification of a particular zone. * * * By failing to require that an approved PUD be in harmony with the zoning restrictions of the underlying district, the ordinance allowed the Town Board to approve a PUD in any district. * * * Under the guise of a conditional use, the Town Board in essence rezoned without seeking the necessary approval of the county board.

4.   In Village of Los Ranchos de Albuquerque v. Shiveley, 110 N.M. 15, 791 P.2d 466 (1989) the court allowed the city to enforce the PUD covenant establishing common open space after the home owners undertook to sell some of the open space for additional development. The court rejected the argument that to allow the city to enforce the covenant amounted to a restraint on alienation. Also see River Birch Associates v. City of Raleigh, 326 N.C. 100, 388 S.E.2d 538 (1990) where the court addressed the relationship between the city and the homeowners association in enforcing PUD covenants.

5.   While the case law on PUDs is sparse, the literature is voluminous. In the legal journals the most useful work may be found in Goldston and Scheuer, Zoning of Planned Residential Developments, 73 Harv.L.Rev. 241 (1959) and Symposium: Planned Unit Development, 114 U.Pa.L.Rev. 3–170 (1965). A more general treatment has been published as a result of a conference on PUD sponsored by the Center for Urban Policy Research at Rutgers University, held in 1973, Burchell, (ed.), Frontiers of Planned Unit Development: A Synthesis of Expert Opinion (1973).

6.   In 1980, the National Conference of Commissioners on Uniform State Laws adopted the Uniform Planned Community Act. The Act does not deal with the land use aspects of PUDs, but it deals extensively with the rights of residents and developers in the common areas and with the property owners' associations which may be created in connection with PUDs and with the declarations and covenants used for PUDs.

SECTION 5.   JUDICIAL REVIEW OF ZONING

FRITTS v. CITY OF ASHLAND

Court of Appeals of Kentucky, 1961.
348 S.W.2d 712.

CULLEN, COMMISSIONER. The Board of Commissioners of the City of Ashland rezoned from R–2 Residential to I–1 Light Industrial a tract of four acres which was in single ownership. A group of neighboring property owners brought action attacking the rezoning ordinance on the ground that it was arbitrary, capricious and unreasonable. The circuit court entered judgment upholding the ordinance and the plaintiffs have appealed.

Ashland adopted a comprehensive zoning ordinance in 1955, following a study with the assistance of state experts that began in 1951. The city bounds on the Ohio River on the northeast and extends to the south and west. The area along the river was zoned for industrial and commercial uses. Aside from this area only two other districts were zoned for light industry, one in the northwest quarter of the city and the other near the west boundary. The rest of the city was zoned residential, except for appropriately located small commercial districts and for necessary educational, institutional and recreational areas. The tract here in question, which is called the Wilson tract, is located near the geographical center of the city in a neighborhood that is residential in character. The tract is two blocks from a grade school accommodating 350 children and three blocks from the presently being constructed senior high school which will have an enrollment of some 1200 students. The nearest industrially zoned property is one and one-half miles away.

* * *

The Wilson tract was rezoned in September 1960. It is clear from the record that the zoning change was made because the owners of a garment factory, which had outgrown its existing location in the city, desired to build a new factory on the Wilson tract, and threatened to leave the city unless this tract was made available. There is no pretense that the zoning change was a step in any coordinated plan for establishment of industrial districts.

The contention of the appellants is, of course, that this is a case of spot zoning.

There was no evidence of any change in the neighborhood since the enactment of the original zoning ordinance in 1955, nor was there proof that the Wilson tract was by its situation distinguishable in character from the surrounding or adjoining property. Therefore, under the decision in Byrn v. Beechwood Village, Ky., 253 S.W.2d 395, the zoning change on its face was arbitrary, capricious and unreasonable, and the burden was on the city authorities to justify the change.

The city authorities have attempted to justify their action on two grounds. One is that the "general welfare" of the city will be promoted by reason of employment being provided for some 400 citizens in the relocated garment factory. The other is that zoning in Ashland was still in a formative state and therefore the city should be entitled to great latitude in modifying the original plan.

The argument with respect to the first ground points up a common fallacy that seems to exist in the minds of zoning agencies. It is that the particular use that a particular owner says he intends to make of a particular tract of land is a controlling factor. Here the Wilson tract was rezoned because the Wilsons said they intended to convey it to the owners of the garment factory who said they intended to build a new garment factory there. However, the ordinance did not rezone the tract for use by the Ashland Crafts Garment Factory but for any appropriate light industry use. There was no guaranty that either the Wilsons or the garment factory people would not change their minds, resulting in the tract being occupied by some light industry that would not have the appealing features of the proposed garment factory. * * * The point is that in establishing a light industry zone the only proper consideration is whether in the light of a comprehensive, coordinated zoning plan the particular area should be set aside for general light industry uses. See Pierson Trapp Co. v. Peak, Ky., 340 S.W.2d 456.

Regardless of the foregoing considerations, the general welfare argument is not sound. The providing of employment opportunities is merely one element of general welfare as that term relates to the zoning field. Sociological factors, protection of property values, traffic and safety considerations, preservation of health, providing adequate light and air, all enter into the question of general welfare. See KRS 100.066, 100.520. If the appellees' argument were carried to its logical conclusion the mere fact that employment would be provided through a particular use of land would overcome all other factors, and a boiler factory could be put in the middle of a beautiful residential neighborhood.

The appellees argue that it is essential to the welfare of the city that the garment factory be retained, and that there are not suitable light industry sites in the city other than the Wilson tract. Our answer to that is that if the lack of suitable industrial sites is due to the restrictions of the present zoning ordinance a study and survey of the situation should be made, suitable areas for industrial development selected, and changes made in the zoning ordinance in accordance with systematic planning. On the other hand, if lack of suitable sites is due to other factors no real solution to the long range problem is reached by momentarily satisfying one particular industry.

The proposition that zoning in Ashland is in the formative state is based upon a statement in the report of the consultants who prepared the 1959 *master plan,* to the effect that the work on the master plan was of limited scope and therefore should be considered subject to modification when additional studies were made, and that the "Land Use Plan" and the "Major Street Plan" were designated as "preliminary". As hereinbefore mentioned, the master plan relates only to *public facilities,* such as streets, sewers, parks, public utilities, airports, etc., and does not establish private use restrictions or districts. Accordingly, the fact that the master plan may have been in a formative state does not mean that the zoning ordinance establishing private use restrictions and districts was in any way preliminary or conditional. Furthermore, even if the zoning ordinance should be considered in a formative state it would not follow that modifications could be made without regard to any coordinated plan.

The circuit court found as a fact that the zoning change was "in accord with an orderly plan of zoning development." The evidence does not support that finding but on the contrary shows that the change was made solely to meet a particular exigency.

The circuit court further found that there was no evidence to show that the plaintiffs or other property owners would be injured by the rezoning, and that there was substantial proof that the neighborhood would be improved. However, as pointed out in Byrn v. Beechwood Village, Ky., 253 S.W.2d 395, Shemwell v. Speck, Ky., 265 S.W.2d 468, and Pierson Trapp Co. v. Peak, Ky., 340 S.W.2d 456, the effect of a zoning change on the value of neighboring property is only one factor to be considered, and the purpose of zoning is not to protect the value of the property of particular individuals but rather to promote the welfare of the community as a whole. The entire community is damaged by haphazard zoning because it causes insecurity of property values throughout the city. So the mere fact that the particular complaining parties may not suffer a decrease in the value of their property will not redeem a zoning change that is not related to proper zoning objects.

In our opinion we have here a clear case of spot zoning and the ordinance making the zoning change must be held invalid.

We feel impelled to express briefly our view of the proper theory of zoning as relates to the making of changes in an original comprehensive ordinance. We think the theory is that after the enactment of the original ordinance there should be a continuous or periodic study of the development of property uses, the nature of population trends, and the commercial and industrial growth, both actual and prospective. On the basis of such study, changes may be made intelligently, systematically, and according to a coordinated plan designed to promote zoning objectives. An examination of the multitude of zoning cases that have reached this court leads us to the conclusion that the common practice of zoning agencies, after the adoption of an original ordinance, is simply to wait until some property owner finds an opportunity to acquire a financial advantage by devoting his property to a use other than that for which it is zoned, and then struggle with the question of whether some excuse can be found for complying with his request for a rezoning. The result has been that in most of the rezoning cases reaching the courts there actually has been spot zoning and the courts have upheld or invalidated the change according to how flagrant the violation of true zoning principles has been. It is to be hoped that in the future zoning authorities will give recognition to the fact that an essential feature of zoning is *planning*.

The judgment is reversed, with directions to enter judgment holding the rezoning ordinance invalid.

Notes

1. In addition to the principal case, see Landgrave v. Watson, 593 S.W.2d 875 (Ky.App.1979), where the local legislative authority refused to rezone property for use as a liquor store in an area where the factual setting prevented any realistic development for residential purposes. The trial court ordered the rezoning and the court of appeals reversed, stating: "The scope of the circuit court's inquiry in reviewing the action of a legislative body in a zoning case is limited. It can decide if the agency acted in excess of granted powers and if it afforded procedural due process to all parties * * *. Further, a de novo trial is impermissible." Also see State ex rel. Barber & Sons Tobacco Co., Inc. v. Jackson County, 869 S.W.2d 113 (Mo.App.1993) where the court affirmed the refusal to rezone a 12–acre parcel from residential to a zoning classification to permit construction of a concrete batch mixing plant despite the fact that the property was in the middle of a rock quarry, adjacent to an asphalt plant and rock crusher, and was used to store crushed rock and by-products.

2. The opinion in the Fritts case is an uncommon example of a court's attempt to articulate a theory of judicial review for zoning cases. One difficulty prominent in zoning cases is the uncertainty about whether to classify zoning decisions as legislative in character, which would dictate a narrow scope of review (arbitrary, irrational), or quasi-judicial, which would give the court more flexibility in considering the "reasonableness" of the zoning decision. Complicating the problem even more is the evident penchant of some courts to engage in what might be called "judicial zoning." For an analysis of the problem in one state, see Gitelman, Judicial Review of Zoning in Arkansas, 23 Ark.L.Rev. 22 (1969).

Consider the following expressions of judicial opinion:

a. Lowe v. City of Missoula, 165 Mont. 38, 525 P.2d 551 (1974):

The city argued that under Montana's section 11–2703, R.C.M.1947, it cannot be charged with an abuse of discretion if the record indicates the City Council and the district court had before them reasonable evidence or testimony upon which they could find that one or more of the purposes of the enabling statute had been accomplished. Further, that the matter was largely within the council's legislative authority and there is a presumption that it had investigated and found the conditions to be such that the legislation which it enacted was appropriate and that the courts must hold that the action of the legislative body (the City Council) is valid.

While neither the trial court nor this Court can substitute its discretion for that of the City Council, the judiciary does have the power to find whether or not there has been an abuse of discretion. Freeman v.

Board of Adjustment, 97 Mont. 342, 34 P.2d 534. There is under Montana statutes and case law a sound distinction between "zoning" and the act of "rezoning" or granting or refusing a variance. The former constitutes a legislative act while the latter is more of an administrative or quasi-judicial act in applying provisions of existing ordinance or law. In such application the exercise of sound discretion is limited by the provisions of the statute, including such standards as are set forth therein. Low v. Town of Madison, 135 Conn. 1, 60 A.2d 774. * * *

HASWELL, JUSTICE (specially concurring):

* * *

Rezoning by a city council is a legislative act. Bishop v. Town of Houghton, 69 Wash.2d 786, 420 P.2d 368; 1 Anderson, American Law of Zoning, § 4.28. The courts will not interfere unless the rezoning ordinance violates the enabling statutes or the Constitution. State v. Stark, 100 Mont. 365, 52 P.2d 890; Leischner v. Knight, 135 Mont. 109, 337 P.2d 359. The majority opinion here, while giving lip service to the enabling statute, has misapplied the applicable standards of review, grounding the opinion on standards of review of orders of administrative boards under special statutes. The standards of review of orders of the Public Serv. Comm'n in Fulmer v. Board of R.R. Comm'rs, 96 Mont. 22, 28 P.2d 849 and the standards of review of variances granted by Boards of Adjustments in Lambros v. Missoula, 153 Mont. 20, 452 P.2d 398 and Freeman v. Board of Adjustment, 97 Mont. 342, 34 P.2d 534 quoted in the majority opinion have no application to legislative acts of a city council in my opinion.

b.   City of Phoenix v. Beall, 22 Ariz.App. 141, 524 P.2d 1314 (1974):

The plaintiffs concede that the enactment of an overall zoning ordinance is legislative action. They contend that the City Council, in enacting or declining to enact a zoning amendment of the type which the plaintiffs request, is acting more nearly in a judicial than in a legislative capacity. This contention appears to relate to the quantum of proof necessary for a court decision overturning the refusal to rezone. We do not agree. The United States Supreme Court in Village of Belle Terre v. Boraas, 416 U.S. 1, 94 S.Ct. 1536, 39 L.Ed.2d 797 (1974), stated:

* * * But every line drawn by a legislature leaves some out that might well have been included. That exercise of discretion, however, is a legislative not a judicial function. [Footnote omitted.] 416 U.S. at 7, 94 S.Ct. at 1540, 39 L.Ed.2d at 803, 804.

The Arizona Legislature in empowering cities to zone specifies that zoning and zoning changes be "by ordinance." The Arizona cases recognize that zoning is legislative and that there is a presumption of the validity of zoning enactments. * * * Zoning will be upheld unless it is clearly arbitrary and unreasonable and without a substantial relation to public health, safety, morals or general welfare. * * *

If the evidence is fairly debatable the zoning or failure to change the zoning as requested will be upheld in the appellate courts. * * *

The test to be used by the trial court is that zoning will be upheld unless it is clearly arbitrary and unreasonable and without substantial relation to public health, safety, morals or general welfare. Zoning ordinances are presumed valid, and where the reasonableness of the ordinance is fairly debatable, the trial court must uphold its validity.

What is the applicable standard to be used by the appellate court in reviewing the trial court's decision to upset the zoning ordinance which in effect finds that the presumption of validity of zoning has been overcome? In one case, City of Phoenix v. Burke, 9 Ariz.App. 395, 452 P.2d 722 (1969), a case not presented to our Supreme Court for review, the majority of the Court used the usual standards of review in civil actions, namely, that the trial court will be upheld if there is evidence in support of its judgment. We hold that the test applied in Burke is not the law in Arizona. * * * The ruling of a trial court which upsets zoning will be upheld only if the zoning is clearly arbitrary and unreasonable and without substantial relation to the public health, safety, morals or general welfare. Furthermore, if in a review of the record, the appellate court finds that it is fairly debatable as to whether the zoning is clearly arbitrary and unreasonable and without a substantial relation to the above factors, then the zoning or the failure to amend the zoning will be upheld and the trial court will be reversed. The fact that the property would be more valuable if zoned for a different use is not controlling.

c.　Carter v. Adams, 928 S.W.2d 39 (Tenn.App.1996):

[Landowners sought a zoning change from A–1, Agriculture, Light Industry to M–2, Heavy Industry to operate a demolition landfill; the planning commission denied the request, but the county commission rezoned the land. The lower court held the zoning change to be unreasonable and arbitrary.] On appeal:

Zoning bodies are legislative in nature and the scope of judicial review for their actions is restricted. * * * Over time, the standards of "fairly debatable," "rational basis," and "arbitrary and capricious" have come to hold the same meaning. . . . Whichever term is applied, the level of scrutiny required of the court is to "refrain from substituting its judgment for that of a local governmental body . . . If any possible reason exists justifying the action, it will be upheld." [Citation omitted.]

d.　MacDonald v. Board of County Comm'rs, 238 Md. 549, 210 A.2d 325 (1965) (dissenting opinion):

The majority states, in effect, that rezoning can only be sustained when there is "strong evidence of mistake" in the original zoning or where there is "a substantial change in conditions" in the neighborhood. This "mistake-change in conditions" rule came into the Maryland law by way of dicta of our predecessors and in a rather oblique way. The "change in conditions" concept seems to be first stated, without any supporting authority, in Northwest Merchants Terminal v. O'Rourke, 191 Md. 171, 60 A.2d 743 (1948). It was repeated in a restricted form in Cassel v. Mayor and City Council of Baltimore, 195 Md. 348, 358, 73 A.2d 486, 488 (1950). This *dictum* was then expanded by additional *dicta* in Kracke v. Weinberg, 197 Md. 339, 79 A.2d 387, 391 (1951) which added "mistake in original zoning" to a "change in the character of the neighborhood"—and so the Maryland Rule of "mistake-change in conditions" was born. It was entirely judicially conceived and delivered. It had no legislative assistance. It has had a rapid and, to my mind, unhealthy growth in the Maryland law. The formulae have become talismanic phrases now applied with Draconian severity to the rezoning efforts of the local legislative bodies, with unfortunate results. In my opinion, the time to re-examine the entire doctrine and its premises is long overdue. As it is entirely "judge-made," a change in, or broadening of, the doctrine would operate only prospectively and would in no way impair vested rights, inasmuch as it is not a rule of property. Under these circumstances, the doctrine of *stare decisis* is not a substantial obstacle in effecting a much-needed change. If my Brethren are reluctant to overrule or modify the "mistake-change" doctrine, I suggest with great respect, that the Legislative Council and ultimately the General Assembly give serious thought to a change by appropriate legislation.

In Buckel v. Board of County Commissioners, 80 Md.App. 305, 562 A.2d 1297 (1989), cert. denied 318 Md. 96, 566 A.2d 1112 (1989) the court, applying the same principles decried by the dissenter in the MacDonald case, held that a small increase in population, construction of a shopping center and neighborhood rezonings did not constitute a substantial change. The planning staff and the board had both approved the rezoning of land zoned agricultural for the construction of a motel and the neighbors were the appellants.

NEUZIL v. CITY OF IOWA CITY

Supreme Court of Iowa, 1990.
451 N.W.2d 159.

LAVORATO, JUSTICE.

In this law action, the district court concluded a zoning amendment that downzoned undeveloped property was valid. The property owners appealed. We transferred the case to the court of appeals, which reversed. Because we think the district court was right, we vacate the decision of the court of appeals and affirm the judgment of the district court.

I. BACKGROUND FACTS AND PROCEEDINGS.

The Neuzil family owns an eight and one-half acre tract of land (tract) southwest of the University of Iowa Hospitals and Clinics in Iowa City. They have owned the tract since 1941. Mrs. Ella Neuzil and a son Gregory occupy houses on the tract. There also is a rental house there, but the remainder of the tract is undeveloped.

* * *

In 1962 Iowa City adopted a comprehensive zoning plan known as the Bartholomew Plan. Under the plan the tract was zoned R–3A. The R–3A zoning allowed multi-family dwellings and permitted up to forty-four units per acre.

In 1972 the tract was rezoned from R–3A to R–3. The R–3 zoning also allowed multi-family dwellings but limited the number of units per acre to fourteen.

In 1978 Iowa City adopted a new comprehensive plan. * * *

There was no new zoning concerning the tract pursuant to the 1978 Comprehensive Plan. However, this plan recommended that the tract be limited to residential development at a density of eight to sixteen dwellings per acre.

In 1983 Iowa City updated its comprehensive zoning plan. The tract was then zoned RM–12, a zoning that had the same limitations as the R–3 zoning. For all practical purposes the tract was under the same use restrictions as it was in 1972.

In 1985 after many requests from area residents, the tract was again downzoned, this time to RS–8. RS–8 zoning is for single-family or duplex dwellings and permits only eight units per acre.

The Neuzil family has consistently objected to the downzoning. Each time the family claimed that the proposed zoning would decrease the value of the tract. The family, however, had agreed not to sell or begin developing the tract for commercial purposes while Ella was still alive.

In the 1960s and 1970s much of the area surrounding the tract was highly developed. The tract borders University Heights on the north and west side. In fact, the only access to the tract is through streets from University Heights although the tract is in Iowa City. The land abutting the tract in University Heights is single-family residential. The land to the east and south of the tract consists of single-family dwellings. A ravine runs east and west on the tract and drains into Melrose Lake, which is on the land immediately east of the tract. The land * * * immediately east of the tract was also downzoned to RS–8 in 1985. But its owners did apply for, and received, a variance to permit multi-family occupancy.

Because the tract was undeveloped, the neighbors often used it for recreational purposes. In fact, residents in the area tried unsuccessfully to get University Heights and Iowa City to purchase the tract for a neighborhood park.

Shortly after the 1983 zoning ordinance was adopted, owners of the Smith land were making plans to develop their land as permitted under the then existing zoning ordinance. Residents from University Heights and Iowa City who lived close to the tract organized the Melrose Lake Association.

Because the association did not want more multi-family housing in the area, it petitioned the Iowa City Planning Commission to downzone the tract, as well as the Smith land to RS–8. When the commission refused, the association petitioned the city council of Iowa City to downzone the tract.

The city council held two public hearings on the petition in March and April 1985. Proponents and opponents of the proposed downzoning were heard. On June 4, 1985, the council voted to downzone the tract to RS–8.

The city council drafted its findings and reasons for approving the downzoning after the Neuzils filed the present lawsuit. The district court, however, found that the council had indeed relied on these reasons in downzoning the tract. These reasons included the following: 1. The Neuzil tract contains 8.5 acres of land, with direct access only into streets through residential neighborhoods. 2. The Neuzil tract is surrounded on three sides by single-family residential neighborhoods, those on the north and west being located in the Town of University Heights. On June 4, 1985, the property to the east of the Neuzil tract was also rezoned to RS–8. 3. The streets in the single-family neighborhood abutting the Neuzil tract were not designed to handle heavy amounts of traffic, and the other streets in the area are already heavily traveled. 4. Development of the Neuzil tract at the maximum density permitted in the RM–12 zone would allow construction of approximately 126 additional dwelling units raising the potential for generating approximately 1550 motor vehicle trips daily. 5. The allowable density on the Neuzil tract will reduce the potential increase to traffic congestion on the streets in the immediate area. 6. The area is shown on the City's Comprehensive Plan as being developed at 8 to 16 dwellings per acre, and the RS–8 zoning is consistent with that Plan. 7. Multi-family development of the tract, at the density permitted in the RM-12 zone, would have a negative impact on the value of property surrounding the tract. Development of the density permitted in the RS–8 zone should help maintain the value of neighboring properties. 8. The Neuzil tract contains a pond and two large, partially wooded ravines, and the property immediately to the east of the Neuzil tract contains Melrose Lake, an environmentally sensitive and important feature of the area. 9. Storm water runoff occasionally causes Melrose Lake to overflow, floods areas downstream, and contributes to pollution of the lake. 10. Development at a lower density will reduce the magnitude of the increase in Melrose Lake drainage, flooding and pollution problems, but will still permit development which is sensitive to the fragile environment.

Following the 1985 rezoning, the Neuzils brought this suit against Iowa City, seeking a declaratory judgment and damages. They wanted the 1985 downzoning declared void as unreasonable. They also sought damages based on claims of tortious interference with business opportunities, an unconstitutional taking without just compensation, and inverse condemnation. The suit was filed at law and tried to the court. On the day of trial, the Neuzils withdrew their inverse condemnation claim.

The district court found that the 1985 downzoning amendment was reasonable and that the Neuzils had not proven their claims of tortious interference or civil rights violation. The Neuzils appealed, raising one issue: Was the 1985 downzoning amendment valid under the circumstances?

The court of appeals, using a de novo review, reversed. We granted the city's petition for further review, and the case is now before us.

* * *

III. VALIDITY OF THE 1985 AMENDMENT DOWNZONING THE TRACT.

Zoning is an exercise of the police powers delegated by the State to municipalities. Iowa Code § 414.1 (1985). A zoning ordinance, including any amendments to it, carries a strong presumption of validity. This means that if the ordinance is facially valid and the reasonableness of the ordinance is fairly debatable, it must be allowed to stand. Anderson v. City of Cedar Rapids, 168 N.W.2d 739, 742 (Iowa 1969). Stated another way,

> [t]he validity of an ordinance is said to be fairly debatable when for any reason it is open to dispute or controversy on grounds that make sense or point to a logical deduction that in no way involves its constitutional validity, and validity is fairly debatable where reasonable minds may differ, or where the evidence provides a basis for a fair difference of opinion as to the constitutionality of the ordinance or its application to particular property. 1 Anderson, American Law of Zoning 3d, § 3.20, at 137 (1986) (citations omitted).

So "if there is some basis for the ordinance ... and there is room for two opinions, the challenged ordinance is valid." Id.

An ordinance is valid if it has any real, substantial relation to the public health, comfort, safety, and welfare, including the maintenance of property values. Anderson v. City of Cedar Rapids, 168 N.W.2d at 742; Iowa Code § 414.1. In applying this test, the court's prime consideration is the ordinance's general purpose and not the hardship of an individual case. Id.

Even though a challenged zoning ordinance adversely affects a property interest or prohibits the most beneficial use of the property, a court should not, for that reason alone, strike it down. Stone v. City of Wilton, 331 N.W.2d 398, 402 (Iowa 1983). This rule applies to the original zoning ordinance and amendments to it because we recognize that zoning is not static. Id. at 403.

Iowa law requires municipalities to pass all zoning ordinances in accordance with a comprehensive plan. Iowa Code § 414.3. Among other things, such ordinances should be designed to encourage efficient urban development patterns; to lessen congestion in the streets; to service the public from fire, flood, panic, and other dangers; to promote health and the general welfare; to provide adequate light and air; to prevent the overcrowding of land; and to avoid undue concentration of population. Id. In passing such ordinances a municipality is required by law to give reasonable consideration ... to the character of the [area in question] and the peculiar suitability of [the area] for particular uses, and with a view to conserving the value of buildings and encouraging the most appropriate use of land throughout [the] city. Id.

A change in conditions sometimes calls for a change in plans. For this reason, a property owner has no vested right to continuity of zoning of the general area in which the owner resides. Likewise, the owners of property adjacent to a district which is restricted to a particular use have no vested right in the continuation of that use when the public interest dictates otherwise. Anderson, § 4.26, at 286.

A municipality's power to amend zoning ordinances does have some restrictions. Generally, the municipality may not "amend a comprehensive zoning law to remove or impose more or less onerous restrictions upon a small tract or lot similar in character and use to the surrounding property." Hermann v. City of Des Moines, 250 Iowa 1281, 1286–87, 97 N.W.2d 893, 896 (1959). A zoning amendment reflecting such a discrepancy in similarly-situated property is discriminatory. Id. This type of regulation is called spot zoning and should be upheld only if there are "substantial and reasonable grounds or basis" for the discriminatory treatment. Id. 97 N.W.2d at 897.

Nor may the municipality downzone property to the point that the property cannot be improved with any development that would be economically feasible. Kempf v. City of Iowa City, 402 N.W.2d 393, 400 (Iowa 1987). In these circumstances the downzoning amounts to an unconstitutional taking. Id. at 400–01. Such a result is another way of saying that the ordinance, as applied to the particular property, is unreasonable.

The Neuzils did not contend in the district court that the 1985 downzoning amendment constituted spot zoning. Although the Neuzils did claim the amendment constituted inverse condemnation, they withdrew that claim on the day of trial.

In the district court the Neuzils tried the case on the theory that the 1985 rezoning amendment was unreasonable, arbitrary, and capricious. In support of their theory the Neuzils urged a number of reasons why the amendment was unreasonable. We restrict our review to that theory and to those reasons.

The district court noted that for the Neuzils to prevail the court would have to adopt the Maryland rule on rezoning. The district court properly refused to do so, recognizing that it was bound to follow our pronouncements on the subject.

Under the Maryland rule once land is zoned it can only be rezoned to correct an original error or because of a change in circumstances. Northwest Merchants Terminal v. O'Rourke, 191 Md. 171, 189–193, 60 A.2d 743, 752–53 (1948). Undergirding the rule is the presumption of reasonableness as to the original ordinance. Id. Moreover, if the question of correctness or change is fairly debatable, the court will not substitute its judgment for that of the zoning authority. Wakefield v. Kraft, 202 Md. 136, 147, 96 A.2d 27, 29 (1953). Such an approach gives the original zoning regulation a greater presumption of correctness than the amendment.

After surveying cases concerning the Maryland rule, one writer observed that the greatest drawback in using the rule is that it completely thwarts the efforts of legislative or zoning authorities in the absence of satisfaction of [the "mistake or change" rule]; there are many circumstances where change is desirable, but impossible, due to the rule. H. Goldman, Zoning Change: Flexibility v. Stability, 26 Md.L.Rev. 48, 51 (1966) [hereinafter Goldman]. The facts in one Maryland case illustrate exactly what the writer means. See MacDonald v. Board of County Comm'rs for Prince George's County, 238 Md. 549, 210 A.2d 325 (1965). In MacDonald the property in question was zoned single family residential but had never been developed. As such there could be no showing of a change in condition. The developers wanted to build high-rise apartments on the land. The zoning board decided this might be a better use for the land, but no one had been able to prove the original zoning was erroneous when passed. As the writer concluded, [t]he reason for the change [in MacDonald] was evident—ideas had changed. A more modern jurisdiction would have allowed the change had the proponents shown the amendment to be reasonable and not arbitrary or capricious; the Maryland court, not able to satisfy the "mistake or change" test, had no choice but to strike down the amendment, no matter how reasonable and desirable it appeared to be. Goldman at 52.

In contrast our rule on amending zoning ordinances is considered more liberal and flexible. Under our approach we give the original zoning ordinance no greater presumption of validity than the amendment. The same standards used to justify original zoning are used in determining the propriety of amendatory ordinances. Id. at 53–54. We expressed our view on this point in Keller v. City of Council Bluffs, 246 Iowa 202, 207–08, 66 N.W.2d 113, 116–17 (1954):

We are of the opinion the governing body of a municipality may amend its zoning ordinances anytime it deems circumstances and conditions warrant such actions, and such an amendment is valid if the procedural requirements of the statute are followed and it is not unreasonable or capricious nor inconsistent with the spirit and design of the zoning statute. The burden is upon the plaintiffs attacking the amendment to establish that the acts of the council were arbitrary, unreasonable, unjust and out of keeping with the spirit of the zoning statute. See also Iowa Code § 414.5 (municipality "may from time to time . . . amend, supplement, change, modify, or repeal" zoning ordinances).

This liberality and flexibility expressed in Keller is consistent with the rule that in legislative matters a municipality may not bind its successors. Hanna v. Rathje, 171 N.W.2d 876, 880 (Iowa 1969). Such a rule is necessary because city council members are "trustees for the public." Id. So the determination of when the public's interest requires a change in zoning must be within the discretion of the municipality. Anderson, § 4.27 at 291. Because of this discretion, courts reviewing zoning amendments should not substitute their judgment as to the wisdom or propriety of the municipality's action when the reasonableness of the amendments is fairly debatable. Anderson v. City of Cedar Rapids, 168 N.W.2d at 742.

Here we need to review the written reasons the city gave for enacting the 1985 amendment that downzoned the tract. Only after such a review can we determine whether circumstances and conditions warranted the downzoning.

The district court found that the city had relied on the written reasons in downzoning the tract, that the reasons were proper ones to consider, and that the reasons were "debatably reasonable." The court concluded it could not, therefore, strike down the amendatory ordinance. For reasons that follow, we think there is substantial evidence to support the district court's findings.

The Neuzils cite their own reasons why the 1985 downzoning amendment is unreasonable, arbitrary, and capricious. They include the following: 1. The tract has proximity to the largest employer—The University of Iowa Hospitals and Clinics—in Johnson County, which is within walking distance. 2. City utilities are available. 3. The size of the tract will permit large-scale development and preserve open space. 4. Housing on this tract will help reduce the need for private automobile transportation. The city bus service is one block away. 5. Public schools are in the vicinity. 6. There are three access streets to the tract. 7. The tract is adjacent to other multi-family dwellings. 8. The area has been zoned for multi-family use since 1962. 9. Prior to the 1985 rezoning, there were no changes in the area or environment since the adoption of the most recent Iowa City Zoning Ordinance. All these reasons are arguments for developing the tract with multi-family units. However, balanced against Neuzils' reasons are the city's reasons for downzoning the tract. All the city's reasons are statutorily recognized. Moreover, there is substantial evidence to support each one.

While the tract was originally zoned for multi-family dwellings, the actual development of the surrounding area is mostly single-family and duplex dwellings. So the challenged amendment seeks to place the tract in conformity with other land in the same area. See Iowa Code § 414.3 (municipality is required to give reasonable consideration to the character of the area).

The city found that the prior zoning—RM–12—would increase the traffic flow in the area past its current accommodation. According to the city's thinking, the downzoning would reduce the potential for such burdensome traffic increases. Traffic considerations are reasonable grounds, under the city's police power, for amending zoning ordinances. See Iowa Code § 414.3 (zoning ordinances should be designed to lessen congestion in the streets).

Additionally, the city found that downzoning would help maintain the current property values in the area—a consideration that bears a substantial relationship to the public's health, safety, welfare and comfort. * * * Finally, the city considered the environmental impact of the current zoning. Consideration included both aesthetic impact and flood-pollution consequences of the prior RM–12 zoning. These two considerations take into account the safety and security of the area as well as the general public's comfort and welfare. * * *

One fact that bears on our analysis is that the 1978 Comprehensive Plan contemplated limiting development of the tract at eight to sixteen dwellings per acre. As the city recognized in its written reasons, the 1985 downzoning amendment is consistent with what the city had been contemplating since 1978. So the Neuzils should not have been surprised that what was contemplated in 1978 occurred in 1985. What the city did in 1985 was in keeping with the spirit of the 1978 Comprehensive Plan.

What immediately becomes apparent from our analysis is that there is a difference of opinion between the Neuzils and the city. Differing opinions are the crux of the "fairly debatable" rule—"if there is some basis for the ordinance ... and there is room for two opinions, the challenged ordinance is valid." Anderson, § 3.20, at 138.

The Neuzils' reasons boil down to this: the 1985 downzoning amendment prohibited the most beneficial use of the tract. As we said, this is not enough to brand a zoning ordinance as unreasonable, capricious or discriminatory. Stone v. City of Wilton, 331 N.W.2d at 402. The Neuzils offered no proof, as the plaintiffs did in Kempf, that the tract could not be improved with any development that would be economically feasible. See Kempf v. City of Iowa City, 402 N.W.2d at 400.

IV. DISPOSITION.

The Neuzils' burden on appeal is a heavy one: to establish, as a matter of law, that the 1985 downzoning amendment was unreasonable, capricious or discriminatory. We think they failed to do so. Under the facts as found by the district court, we are convinced that the city acted within its authorized police power in downzoning the tract in 1985.

Accordingly, we vacate the decision of the court of appeals and affirm the judgment of the district court.

DECISION OF COURT OF APPEALS VACATED; DISTRICT COURT JUDGMENT AFFIRMED.

All justices concur except SCHULTZ, J., who dissents.

SCHULTZ, JUSTICE (dissenting).

The fundamental justification for amending a zoning ordinance is a change in conditions making the amendment reasonably necessary to protect the public interest. 8 E. McQuillin, The Law of Municipal Corporations § 25.67b, at 170 (3d rev. ed. 1976). Here, the trial court found that there was no significant change in the general location from the 1983–84 zoning ordinance to the 1985 downzoning. Under the facts of this case, I would conclude that the action of the city council was unreasonable and should be declared invalid.

From the time this property was annexed by the city in 1956 until 1985, the city has never zoned the property in a manner that would prevent the construction of multi-family residences. In 1962 the city commissioned a comprehensive zoning plan which affected the property but allowed multi-family dwellings. In the 1960s and 1970s the surrounding property was highly developed. In 1978 the property was rezoned and a new comprehensive plan adopted. Following extensive studies a new ordinance was adopted in 1983. Because of a defect it was readopted during the spring of 1985. While the property was downzoned during this period, multi-resident dwellings were still allowed.

At the insistence of a group of neighbors and over the recommendation of its planning and zoning commission, the city council, four months after its latest ordinance, rezoned the property to a type of district which disallows multi-dwelling construction. Neighbors also use the land for recreational purposes, and their representatives had previously attempted to have the same undeveloped property made into a city park.

Because of its location near the stadium and the hospital, this property is best used as multi-family dwellings. The object of zoning is to put property to its best use.

I am aware that zoning is not static and existing ordinances are subject to reasonable revision as the need appears and that ordinances may be amended any time circumstances and conditions warrant such action. * * *

What was the reason for the ordinance amendment? After this action was filed, the city set forth the purported reasons for the rezoning. Traffic, pollution and congestion are not new to the area and were present both four months and two years earlier when the city studied this tract. This rezoning procedure was instituted by neighbors and not by the city or its planning staff. The obvious reason for the rezoning was neighborhood pressure. While I do not challenge or condemn the political process, I do not believe that the city council acted reasonably under the circumstances. It ignored the best use of the property and the interest of the general public in having housing convenient to Iowa City's largest employer. It bowed to a group who has enjoyed the use of this property and wishes to dictate its further use at the owners' expense. Without a careful restudy of the property in the area, the council had no legitimate reason to make changes.

I would reverse the trial court.

FASANO v. BOARD OF COUNTY COMM'RS OF WASHINGTON COUNTY

Supreme Court of Oregon, In Banc, 1973.
264 Or. 574, 507 P.2d 23.

HOWELL, JUSTICE. The plaintiffs, homeowners in Washington county, unsuccessfully opposed a zone change before the Board of County Commissioners of Washington County. Plaintiffs applied for and received a writ of review of the action of the commissioners allowing the change. The trial court found in favor of plaintiffs, disallowed the zone change, and reversed the commissioners' order. The Court of Appeals affirmed, 489 P.2d 693 (1971), and this court granted review.

The defendants are the Board of County Commissioners and A.G.S. Development Company. A.G.S., the owner of 32 acres which had been zoned R–7 (Single Family Residential), applied for a zone change to P–R (Planned Residential), which allows for the construction of a mobile home park. The change failed to receive a majority vote of the Planning Commission. The Board of County Commissioners approved the change and found, among other matters, that the change allows for "increased densities and different types of housing to meet the needs of urbanization over that allowed by the existing zoning."

The trial court, relying on its interpretation of Roseta v. County of Washington, 254 Or. 161, 458 P.2d 405, 40 A.L.R.3d 364 (1969), reversed the order of the commissioners because the commissioners had not shown any change in the character of the neighborhood which would justify the rezoning. The Court of Appeals affirmed for the same reason, but added the additional ground that the defendants failed to show that the change was consistent with the comprehensive plan for Washington county.

According to the briefs, the comprehensive plan of development for Washington county was adopted in 1959 and included classifications in the county for residential, neighborhood commercial, retail commercial, general commercial, industrial park and light industry, general and heavy industry, and agricultural areas.

The land in question, which was designated "residential" by the comprehensive plan, was zoned R–7, Single Family Residential.

Subsequent to the time the comprehensive plan was adopted, Washington county established a Planned Residential (P–R) zoning classification in 1963. The P–R classification was adopted by ordinance and provided that a planned residential unit development could be established and should include open space for utilities, access, and recreation; should not be less than 10 acres in size; and should be located in or adjacent to a residential zone. The P–R zone adopted by the 1963 ordinance is of the type known as a "floating zone," so-called because the ordinance creates a zone classification authorized for future use but not placed on the zoning map until its use at a particular location is approved by the governing body. The R–7 classification for the 32 acres continued until April 1970 when the classification was changed to P–R to permit the defendant A.G.S. to construct the mobile home park on the 32 acres involved.

 The defendants argue that (1) the action of the county commissioners approving the change is presumptively valid, requiring plaintiffs to show that the commissioners acted arbitrarily in approving the zone change; (2) it was not necessary to show a change of conditions in the area before a zone change could be accomplished; and (3) the change from R–7 to P–R was in accordance with the Washington county comprehensive plan.

We granted review in this case to consider the questions—by what standards does a county commission exercise its authority in zoning matters; who has the burden of meeting those standards when a request for change of zone is made; and what is the scope of court review of such actions?

Any meaningful decision as to the proper scope of judicial review of a zoning decision must start with a characterization of the nature of that decision. The majority of jurisdictions state that a zoning ordinance is a legislative act and is thereby entitled to presumptive validity. This court made such a characterization of zoning decisions in Smith v. County of Washington, 241 Or. 380, 406 P.2d 545 (1965):

> "Inasmuch as ORS 215.110 specifically grants to the governing board of the county the power to amend zoning ordinances, a challenged amendment is a legislative act and is clothed with a presumption in its favor. Jehovah's Witnesses v. Mullen et al., 214 Or. 281, 292, 330 P.2d 5, 74 A.L.R.2d 347 (1958), appeal dismissed and cert. denied, 359 U.S. 436, 79 S.Ct. 940, 3 L.Ed.2d 932 (1959)." 241 Or. at 383, 406 P.2d at 547.

However, in *Smith* an exception to the presumption was found and the zoning held invalid. Furthermore, the case cited by the *Smith* court, Jehovah's Witnesses v. Mullen et al., supra, at least at one point viewed the contested zoning in that case as an administrative as opposed to legislative act.

At this juncture we feel we would be ignoring reality to rigidly view all zoning decisions by local governing bodies as legislative acts to be accorded a full presumption of validity and shielded from less than constitutional scrutiny by the theory of separation of powers. Local and small decision groups are simply not the equivalent in all respects of state and national legislatures. There is a growing judicial recognition of this fact of life:

> "It is not a part of the legislative function to grant permits, make special exceptions, or decide particular cases. Such activities are not legislative but administrative, quasi-judicial, or judicial in character. To place them in the hands of legislative bodies, whose acts as such are not judicially reviewable, is to open the door completely to arbitrary government." Ward v. Village of Skokie, 26 Ill.2d 415, 186 N.E.2d 529, 533 (1962) (Klingbiel, J., specially concurring).

The Supreme Court of Washington, in reviewing a rezoning decision, recently stated:

> "Whatever descriptive characterization may be otherwise attached to the role or function of the planning commission in zoning procedures, e.g., advisory, recommendatory, investigatory, administrative or legislative, it is manifest * * * that it is a public agency, * * * a principle [sic] and statutory duty of which is to conduct public hearings in specified planning and zoning matters, enter findings of fact—often on the basis of disputed facts—and make recommendations with reasons assigned thereto. Certainly, in its

role as a hearing and fact-finding tribunal, the planning commission's function more nearly than not partakes of the nature of an administrative, quasi-judicial proceeding, * * *." Chrobuck v. Snohomish County, 78 Wash.2d 858, 480 P.2d 489, 495–496 (1971).

Ordinances laying down general policies without regard to a specific piece of property are usually an exercise of legislative authority, are subject to limited review, and may only be attacked upon constitutional grounds for an arbitrary abuse of authority. On the other hand, a determination whether the permissible use of a specific piece of property should be changed is usually an exercise of judicial authority and its propriety is subject to an altogether different test. An illustration of an exercise of legislative authority is the passage of the ordinance by the Washington County Commission in 1963 which provided for the formation of a planned residential classification to be located in or adjacent to any residential zone. An exercise of judicial authority is the county commissioners' determination in this particular matter to change the classification of A.G.S. Development Company's specific piece of property. The distinction is stated, as follows, in Comment, Zoning Amendments—The Product of Judicial or Quasi–Judicial Action, 33 Ohio St.L.J. 130 (1972):

> " * * * Basically, this test involves the determination of whether action produces a general rule or policy which is applicable to an open class of individuals, interest, or situations, or whether it entails the application of a general rule or policy to specific individuals, interests, or situations. If the former determination is satisfied, there is legislative action; if the latter determination is satisfied, the action is judicial." 33 Ohio St.L.J. at 137.

We reject the proposition that judicial review of the county commissioners' determination to change the zoning of the particular property in question is limited to a determination whether the change was arbitrary and capricious.

In order to establish a standard of review, it is necessary to delineate certain basic principles relating to land use regulation.

* * *

In Oregon the county planning commission is required by ORS 215.050 to adopt a comprehensive plan for the use of some or all of the land in the county. Under ORS 215.110(1), after the comprehensive plan has been adopted, the planning commission recommends to the governing body of the county the ordinances necessary to "carry out" the comprehensive plan. The purpose of the zoning ordinances, both under our statute and the general law of land use regulation, is to "carry out" or implement the comprehensive plan. 1 Anderson, American Law of Zoning, § 1.12 (1968). Although we are aware of the analytical distinction between zoning and planning, it is clear that under our statutes the plan adopted by the planning commission and the zoning ordinances enacted by the county governing body are closely related; both are intended to be parts of a single integrated procedure for land use control. The plan embodies policy determinations and guiding principles; the zoning ordinances provide the detailed means of giving effect to those principles.

* * *

We believe that the state legislature has conditioned the county's power to zone upon the prerequisite that the zoning attempt to further the general welfare of the community through consciousness, in a prospective sense, of the factors mentioned above. In other words, except as noted later in this opinion, it must be proved that the change is in conformance with the comprehensive plan.

In proving that the change is in conformance with the comprehensive plan in this case, the proof at a minimum, should show (1) there is a public need for a change of the kind in question, and (2) that the need will be best served by changing the classification of the particular piece of property in question as compared with other available property.

* * *

Because the action of the commission in this instance is an exercise of judicial authority, the burden of proof should be placed, as is usual in judicial proceedings, upon the one seeking change. The more drastic the change, the greater will be the burden of showing that it is in conformance with the comprehensive plan as implemented by the ordinance, that there is a public need for the kind of change in question, and that the need is best met by the proposal under consideration. As the degree of change increases, the burden of showing that the potential impact upon the area in question was carefully considered and weighed will also increase. If other areas have previously been designated for the particular type of development, it must be shown why it is necessary to introduce it into an area not previously contemplated and why the property owners there should bear the burden of the departure.[12]

12. For example, if an area is designated by the plan as generally appropriate for residential development, the plan may also indicate that some high-density residential development within the area is to be anticipated, without specifying the exact location at which that development is to take place. The comprehensive plan might provide that its goal for residential development is to assure that residential areas are healthful, pleasant and safe places in which to live. The plan might also list the following policies which, among others, are to be pursued in achieving that goal:

1. High-density residential areas should be located close to the urban core area.

2. Residential neighborhoods should be protected from any land use activity involving an excessive level of noise, pollution or traffic volume.

3. High trip-generating multiple family units should have ready access to arterial or collector streets.

4. A variety of living areas and housing types should be provided appropriate to the needs of the special and general groups they are to serve.

5. Residential development at urban densities should be within planned sewer and water service areas and where other utilities can be adequately provided.

Under such a hypothetical plan, property originally zoned for single family dwellings might later be rezoned for duplexes, for garden apartments, or for high-rise apartment buildings. Each of these changes could be shown to be consistent with the plan.

Although we have said in *Roseta* that zoning changes may be justified without a showing of a mistake in the original plan or ordinance, or of changes in the physical characteristics of an affected area, any of these factors which are present in a particular case would, of course, be relevant. Their importance would depend upon the nature of the precise change under consideration.

By treating the exercise of authority by the commission in this case as the exercise of judicial rather than of legislative authority and thus enlarging the scope of review on appeal, and by placing the burden of the above level of proof upon the one seeking change, we may lay the court open to criticism by legal scholars who think it desirable that planning authorities be vested with the ability to adjust more freely to changed conditions. However, having weighed the dangers of making desirable change more difficult against the dangers of the almost irresistable pressures that can be asserted by private economic interests on local government, we believe that the latter dangers are more to be feared.

What we have said above is necessarily general, as the approach we adopt contains no absolute standards or mechanical tests. We believe, however, that it is adequate to provide meaningful guidance for local governments making zoning decisions and for trial courts called upon to review them. With future cases in mind, it is appropriate to add some brief remarks on questions of procedure. Parties at the hearing before the county governing body are entitled to an opportunity to be heard, to an opportunity to present and rebut evidence, to a tribunal which is impartial in the matter—i.e., having had no prehearing or ex parte contacts concerning the question at issue—and to a record made and adequate findings executed. Comment, Zoning Amendments—The Product of Judicial or Quasi–Judicial Action, 33 Ohio St.L.J. 130–143 (1972).

* * *

As there has not been an adequate showing that the change was in accord with the plan, or that the factors listed in ORS 215.055 were given proper consideration, the judgment is affirmed.

BRYSON, JUSTICE (specially concurring).

The basic facts in this case exemplify the prohibitive cost and extended uncertainty to a homeowner when a governmental body decides to change or modify a zoning ordinance or comprehensive plan affecting such owner's real property.

This controversy has proceeded through the following steps:

Although in addition we would require a showing that the county governing body found a bona fide need for a zone change in order to accommodate new high-density development which at least balanced the disruption shown by the challengers, that requirement would be met in most instances by a record which disclosed that the governing body had considered the facts relevant to this question and exercised its judgment in good faith. However, these changes, while all could be shown to be consistent with the plan, could be expected to have differing impacts on the surrounding area, depending on the nature of that area. As the potential impact on the area in question increases, so will the necessity to show a justification.

1.   The respondent opposed the zone change before the Washington County Planning Department and Planning Commission.

2.   The County Commission, after a hearing, allowed the change.

3.   The trial court reversed (disallowed the change).

4.   The Court of Appeals affirmed the trial court.

5.   We ordered reargument and additional briefs.

6.   This court affirmed.

The principal respondent in this case, Fasano, happens to be an attorney at law, and his residence is near the proposed mobile home park of the petitioner A.G.S. No average homeowner or small business enterprise can afford a judicial process such as described above nor can a judicial system cope with or endure such a process in achieving justice. The number of such controversies is ascending.

In this case the majority opinion, in which I concur, adopts some sound rules to enable county and municipal planning commissions and governing bodies, as well as trial courts, to reach finality in decision. However, the procedure is no panacea and it is still burdensome.

It is solely within the domain of the legislative branch of government to devise a new and simplified statutory procedure to expedite finality of decision.

Notes

1.   The Fasano doctrine was re-examined in a subsequent case and applied to a rezoning of a 600 acre tract for multi-family housing, Neuberger v. City of Portland, 37 Or.App. 13, 586 P.2d 351 (1978). On appeal, the Oregon Supreme Court modified the court of appeals decision, but adhered to the application of Fasano to the rezoning in issue, and devoted considerable attention to the question of which land use decisions might be legislative in nature and which would be treated as quasi-judicial. Neuberger v. City of Portland, 288 Or. 155, 603 P.2d 771 (1979), rehearing denied 288 Or. 585, 607 P.2d 722. The court stated:

> * * * [O]ur land use decisions indicate that when a particular action by a local government is directed at a relatively small number of identifiable persons, and when that action also involves the application of existing policy to a specific factual setting, the requirement of quasi-judicial procedures has been implied from the governing law.
>
> Although both of these factors are frequently present in the cases in which we have held or assumed that quasi-judicial functions were exercised, each is * * * a separate indicator of the possible need for adjudicatory procedures. The reasons, moreover, are different in each instance.
>
> When specific facts must be determined in order that pre-existing criteria may be applied, procedures similar to those used in adjudications are important in order to assure that factual determinations will be made correctly. When the requirement of such procedures is implied

because a relatively small number of persons is directly affected, even though the decision-maker is not entirely bound by pre-existing criteria but is empowered to exercise broad discretion the law may require a formal hearing procedure. * * *

A third consideration * * * is whether the process is bound to result in a decision. Although that factor is rarely discussed in the cases because in many contexts its presence is readily apparent, it was not so obvious in * * * the recent case of Henthorn v. Grand Prairie School Dist., 287 Or. 683, 601 P.2d 1243 (1979). In *Henthorn* the determination that the school board was required to make a decision on the basis of information produced at a hearing required by statute was important to our conclusion that the proceedings were quasi-judicial and, therefore subject to judicial review under the writ of review.

2. In Cooper v. Board of County Comm'rs of Ada County, 101 Idaho 407, 614 P.2d 947 (1980), the court held that a decision not to rezone 99 acres from low density residential (one unit per acre) to a density which would permit two to three units per acre, was a quasi-judicial decision, entitling the property owner to procedural due process, which, on the facts, the court found had been denied. Also see Golden v. City of Overland Park, 224 Kan. 591, 584 P.2d 130 (1978), where the city denied approval to a rezoning request from an office designation to permit a small shopping center, and the court also found the decision to be quasi-judicial and, on the facts, unreasonable.

3. The Supreme Court of Florida moved in the direction of Fasano and overruled some earlier cases in Board of County Comm'rs of Brevard County v. Snyder, 627 So.2d 469 (Fla.1993). In this case the owner of a half acre parcel located in a district zoned for single-family use applied for a rezoning to multi-family, intending to build four to six units. The planning director indicated he approved of the rezoning as it was consistent with the comprehensive plan, but several citizens were opposed because of potential increase in traffic and the rezoning was denied. The court held that although earlier cases had applied the fairly debatable rule in rezonings as well as initial zoning efforts, rezoning actions which have an impact on a limited number of persons where the decision can be viewed as policy application rather than policy setting, should be viewed as quasi-judicial. The court delineated the following procedure:

> Upon consideration, we hold that a landowner seeking to rezone property has the burden of proving that the proposal is consistent with the comprehensive plan and complies with all procedural requirements of the zoning ordinance. At this point, the burden shifts to the governmental board to demonstrate that maintaining the existing zoning classification with respect to the property accomplishes a legitimate public purpose. In effect the landowners' traditional remedies will be subsumed within this rule, and the board will now have the burden of showing that the refusal to rezone the property is not arbitrary, discriminatory, or unreasonable. If the board carries its burden, the application should be denied.

4. Compare with the above cases, South Gwinnett Venture v. Pruitt, 491 F.2d 5 (5th Cir.1974) where the entire court, sitting en banc, overturned

a panel decision and held "that local zoning is a quasi-legislative procedure, not subject to federal judicial consideration in the absence of arbitrary action. Moreover, we see no viable distinction between zoning board functions involved in the adoption of a comprehensive zoning plan and those exercised in reclassification of a piece of property under an existing plan * * *." This was in line with Higginbotham v. Barrett, 473 F.2d 745 (5th Cir.1973), in which the same court had stated that "the law is settled that the zoning of property, including the preparation of comprehensive land plans, involves the exercise of judgment which is legislative in character and is subject to judicial control only if arbitrary and without rational basis." The majority of the panel in the earlier version of South Gwinnett Venture v. Pruitt, 482 F.2d 389 (5th Cir.1973), certiorari denied 416 U.S. 901, 94 S.Ct. 1625, 40 L.Ed.2d 119 (1974), attempted to distinguish the legislative action of adopting a comprehensive zoning plan from "the adjudicative decision inherent in tract rezoning"—the latter situation deemed to require adherence to minimal standards of due process.

NOVA HORIZON, INC. v. CITY COUNCIL OF THE CITY OF RENO

Supreme Court of Nevada, 1989.
105 Nev. 92, 769 P.2d 721.

PER CURIAM:

Appellants are developers who planned to build a hotel/convention center (the Project) on land next to the Bally Grand in Reno. Prior to submitting an application for necessary approvals, appellants purchased the land in question. The plot consists of 2.9 acres, bordered on three sides by the Bally Grand. On August 29, 1984, appellants submitted to the Reno Planning Commission an application requesting:

1. a change of zoning, M–1 to C–3;

2. a Special Use Permit; and

3. acceptance of a tentative subdivision map,

to construct a twenty-eight story, 804–room hotel and casino. At that time, the property owned by appellants was zoned M–1 as defined and limited in Section 18.06.270 of the Reno Municipal Code. M–1 zoning allows commercial development but imposes height restrictions of sixty-five feet, which would not accommodate appellants' project as planned. Additionally, M–1 does not allow any residential use and the proposed project was planned to include the sale of 312 units on a time-share basis.

On November 7, 1984, the Reno Planning Commission, by a vote of four to three, recommended to the City Council that it approve the three separate requests. Appellants' application came before respondents on December 10, 1984. At that time, a public hearing was held wherein appellants presented their case and the community was given the opportunity to respond. After the conclusion of testimony, the City Council unanimously voted to deny all of appellants' requests.

* * *

We note, preliminarily, that the district court properly subjected the City's action to a substantial evidence standard of review. This court, in addressing the propriety of a district court ruling reversing a zone change approval by the appropriate governmental body, declared:

> Respondents recognize the general rule that a court is not empowered to substitute its judgment for that of a zoning board, in this case the board of county commissioners, when the board's action is supported by substantial evidence.

> * * *

> The lower court had before it the same evidence as the board. Its function was not to conduct a trial de novo, but only to ascertain as a matter of law if there was any substantial evidence before the board which would sustain the board's action. The function of this court at this time is the same as that of the lower court. [Citation omitted.]

> * * *

> Under the police power, zoning is a matter within sound legislative action and such legislative action must be upheld if the facts do not show that the bounds of that discretion have been exceeded.

McKenzie v. Shelly, 77 Nev. 237, 240–242, 362 P.2d 268, 269–70 (1961). In *Shelly,* we reversed the district court since the presumptive validity of the board's action was supported by substantial evidence and there was no showing that the board abused its discretion.

Numerous cases support the premise that zoning boards may not unreasonably or arbitrarily deprive property owners of legitimate, advantageous land uses. For example, the Supreme Court of Virginia affirmed a trial court decision holding an unduly restrictive zoning classification void. *Town of Vienna Council v. Kohler,* 218 Va. 966, 244 S.E.2d 542 (1978). The *Kohler* court concluded that "a denial of a rezoning request will not be sustained if under all the facts of the particular case, the denial is unreasonable, or is discriminatory, or is without substantial relationship to the public health, safety, morals and general welfare." *Id.* 244 S.E.2d at 548. *See also,* e.g., *Raabe v. City of Walker,* 383 Mich. 165, 174 N.W.2d 789 (1970) (invalidating rezoning of small enclave in midst of residential area to accommodate an industrial park); *City of Conway v. Housing Authority,* 266 Ark. 404, 584 S.W.2d 10 (1979) (City of Conway directed to rezone property, as the denial of the rezoning request was arbitrary and inconsistent with surrounding zoning); *Lowe v. City of Missoula,* 165 Mont. 38, 525 P.2d 551 (1974) (restrictive zoning impressed on landowner's property was so lacking in fact information as to constitute an abuse of discretion; rezoning held to be invalid). In the latter case, the Montana Supreme Court, quoting from an earlier case, stated:

> Under the guise of protecting the public or advancing its interest, the state may not unduly interfere with private business or prohibit

lawful occupations, or impose unreasonable or unnecessary restrictions upon them. Any law or regulation which imposes unjust limitations upon the full use and enjoyment of property, or destroys property value or use, deprives the owner of property rights.

In the instant case, the requested change in zoning was in conformity with the long-range development plans adopted by the City of Reno. The zone change was requested at the suggestion of the Reno City Planning staff and is consistent with the zoning of the surrounding property. Moreover, it appears that appellants may have invested substantial sums of money (allegedly over $1,200,000.00) in land acquisition and project development costs in anticipation of the City's approval of their application.

At the public hearing in which appellants' application was considered, only one person presented opposition to the project and his objections were basically rebuffed by members of the Reno City Council. Nevertheless, the Council unanimously denied approval to what was described as an architecturally "superior" project on the specified grounds that approval would violate a campaign promise against locating new casinos outside the "downtown area" and a similar pledge to diversification that would pay higher employee wages.

In determining whether the action of the Council concerning the zone change was without substantial evidentiary support and, consequently, an abuse of discretion, it is essential to first consider the effect of the City's master plan, as amended, and land use/transportation guide on the Council's latitude in zoning matters.

Chapter 278 of the Nevada Revised Statutes governs many aspects of planning and zoning. It not only provides for the formation and compensation of planning commissions and the adoption of master plans, it also provides for zoning in accordance with an adopted master plan. NRS 278.250(2) provides, in pertinent part: "2. The zoning regulations shall be adopted in accordance with the master plan for land use * * *." (Emphasis supplied.) This suggests that municipal entities must adopt zoning regulations that are in substantial agreement with the master plan, including a land-use guide if one is also adopted by the city council. Other jurisdictions have construed their statutes as requiring strict conformity between master plans and zoning ordinances, even to the point of requiring changes in zoning after a modification in a master plan. *See Baker v. City of Milwaukie,* 271 Or. 500, 533 P.2d 772 (1975); *Fasano v. Board of County Comm'rs,* 264 Or. 574, 507 P.2d 23 (1973). While such a strict view of the invariable application of a master plan on zoning matters may lend a high degree of predictability to prospective land uses and facilitate usage planning by land owners, we do not perceive the legislative intent to be so confining and inflexible. We therefore choose to view a master plan as a standard that commands deference and a presumption of applicability, rather than a legislative straightjacket from which no leave may be taken. In pertinent part, the Montana Supreme Court analyzed the issue as follows:

To require strict compliance with the master plan would result in a master plan so unworkable that it would have to be constantly changed to comply with the realities. The master plan is, after all, a plan. On the other hand, to require no compliance at all would defeat the whole idea of planning. Why have a plan if the local government units are free to ignore it at any time? The statutes are clear enough to send the message that in reaching zoning decisions, the local governmental unit should at least substantially comply with the comprehensive plan (or master plan).

Little v. Board of County Comm'rs, 631 P.2d 1282, 1293 (Mont.1981).

Having determined that master plans are to be accorded substantial compliance under Nevada's statutory scheme, and recognizing anew the general reluctance to judicially intervene in zoning determinations absent clear necessity, *Board of Comm'rs v. Dayton Dev. Co.,* 91 Nev. 71, 530 P.2d 1187 (1975), we turn now to the issue of respondents' zoning action in the instant case. It is clear on the record that no evidentiary basis exists for the Council's denial of appellants' zone change request. It is equally clear that no deference, let alone a presumptive applicability, was accorded Reno's master plan by the Council. In one instance, an expression of deference to a campaign promise was the stated basis for what was tantamount to a disregard for the master plan. The other expression offered as a specific basis for rejecting appellants' application was a pledge, presumably to constituents, to seek diversification in favor of higher employee wages. The latter point was equally untenable as a basis for zoning denial. Moreover, as noted above, the surrounding properties enjoyed the same zoning sought by appellants and no evidence, let alone reasoning, was presented to justify a denial of appellants' request for rezoning. We therefore are compelled to reverse the district court on this point.

We are not constrained to grant similar relief concerning appellants' request for a special use permit and acceptance of a tentative subdivision map. While the record provides no existing or prospective basis for denying the zone change, we are loathe to direct authorization for a project that may or may not be deserving of the Council's approval. The Council simply did not effectively address the effect of the impact of such a substantial project on the City of Reno. While it may be argued with considerable cogency from the record that appellants justified an approval of their entire application, and that it is unfair to subject them to further proceedings, we nevertheless conclude that it would be unwise and inappropriate for this court to accommodate an approval by forfeiture.

If appellants remain interested in the construction of their project, we will assume that, upon rehearing, the Council will exercise its judgment fairly and in accordance with the merits as reflected by the evidence and deliberations of record.

We realize that our ruling may appear to be inconsistent with our opinion in *City Council, Reno v. Travelers Hotel,* 100 Nev. 436, 683 P.2d

960 (1984), where we affirmed the issuance of a peremptory writ of mandamus requiring approval of a special use permit for a hotel-casino. In that case, however, rezoning was not an issue and the Council was able to focus directly on the project itself. Here, the only specified basis for rejecting appellants' application was essentially the project's location outside the downtown area, a reason which, if implemented, would constitute an inappropriate *de facto* amendment to the City's master plan and land use/transportation guide. We are simply unable to discern from the record that the Council adequately focused its attention on the merits of the project and its total impact on the community. Considerations of public health, safety and welfare demand both such a focused attention and the exercise of a fair and enlightened discretion by the Council based upon substantial evidence.

The judgment of the district court is reversed insofar as the zone change is concerned, and remanded with instructions to issue a peremptory writ of mandamus requiring respondents to grant appellants' application for zone change. The district court shall also modify its judgment to the extent of requiring respondents, upon application by appellants, to entertain anew the merits of appellants' application for special use permit and acceptance of tentative subdivision map, all in accordance with this opinion.

Notes

1. Compare with the Nevada decision Tate v. Miles, 503 A.2d 187 (Del.1986). In the latter case the planning commission held a hearing on a rezoning application and recommended approval to the county council; the council held a public hearing and subsequently enacted a rezoning ordinance with no findings or statement of reasons, merely stating that change was in accord with the comprehensive plan and promoted public welfare. The trial court gave the neighbors a summary judgment and the supreme court affirmed, stating that although under Delaware law rezoning is a legislative act, it "resembles" a judicial determination because a zoning decision must be supported by a record sufficient to withstand judicial challenge. With no reasons for the change in the record a court has no means to review the decision. The court held that a rezoning decision must be accompanied by findings and a statement of the reasons for the rezoning.

2. In addition to the question of the standard of review when rezoning is viewed as a quasi-judicial rather than a legislative act, other consequences may flow from the characterization of rezoning decisions. For example, in a judicial challenge to a city's decision not to rezone, may the plaintiff-property owner compel members of the city legislative body to testify as to their reasons or motivations for voting to deny the petition? In Wait v. City of Scottsdale, 127 Ariz. 107, 618 P.2d 601 (1980), the court held that the denial of a rezoning petition was a legislative act and that the motives of council members in denying the petition and the reasons they considered were beyond the scope of judicial inquiry. Similarly, in Sheffield Development Co. v. City of Troy, 99 Mich.App. 527, 298 N.W.2d 23 (1980), the court held that because rezoning was a legislative act, council members could not be compelled to answer questions regarding their motives in denying the

rezoning application. The court did state that the motives of legislators could be examined when the complaint alleges fraud, personal interest, or corruption.

3. The particular method of reviewing zoning decisions varies from state to state. Some enabling acts and some zoning ordinances prescribe the method of seeking review. Where statutes or ordinances are silent, injunction suits and certiorari are quite common. See, e.g., Platte Woods United Methodist Church v. City of Platte Woods, 935 S.W.2d 735 (Mo.App.1996). In recent years attorneys have sometimes sought to utilize the federal courts to review zoning decisions, relying on civil rights legislation or other, more novel, theories of federal jurisdiction. Refer back to Chapter V and the section on "Other Remedies." Consider the utility of the following examples:

a. Bodor v. East Coventry Twp., 325 F.Supp. 1102 (E.D.Pa.1971). Plaintiff sued to restrain the township officials from preventing him from establishing a seventy foot by twelve foot mobile home as a permanent residence on a four acre tract of land. "Plaintiffs' complaint raises the substantial constitutional issues of due process of law and equal protection under the law in that in order for Plaintiffs to avail themselves of the administrative remedies provided in the township's zoning ordinance and building code ordinance, Plaintiffs would allegedly have to pay a $750.00 filing fee. * * * Plaintiffs have alleged facts which, if proved, establish a concerted effort by the Board of Supervisors of East Coventry Township to preclude the review of their Zoning and Building Code Ordinances through the establishment of a prohibitive filing fee. Such an allegation sets forth a claim upon which relief can be granted."

b. City of Miami v. Woolin, 387 F.2d 893 (5th Cir.1968). The city ordinances prohibited erection of gasoline filling stations within 350 yards of a church, hospital, or school, and within 750 feet of another filling station. The court held that the equal protection clause of the Fourteenth Amendment rendered the ordinance unconstitutional and upheld a permanent injunction.

c. Minshew v. Smith, 380 F.Supp. 918 (N.D.Miss.1974). Plaintiffs, homeowners and adjacent property owners, sued the owner of a motel and several city officials for compensatory and punitive damages on a theory that the defendants conspired to achieve an illegal amendment of the zoning ordinance to allow the motel to expand into the adjacent residential zone. The court found for the plaintiffs and ordered compensatory damages (the motel had already built), but refused to award punitive damages.

d. Walker v. State of North Carolina, 262 F.Supp. 102 (W.D.N.C.1966), affirmed 372 F.2d 129 (4th Cir.1967), certiorari denied 388 U.S. 917, 87 S.Ct. 2134, 18 L.Ed.2d 1360 (1967). Petitioner remodeled his house without securing a building permit. He was arrested and charged with a misdemeanor, receiving a thirty-day jail sentence which was suspended on the condition that he comply with the building code and pay court costs. Petitioner appealed to the state supreme court which upheld the validity of the building code. Petitioner is now in federal district court seeking a writ of habeas corpus. "Petitioner has failed to show a violation of any of his federal constitutional rights, and, for this reason, his petition will be, and hereby is, dismissed."

e. Bob Layne Contractor, Inc. v. Bartel, 504 F.2d 1293 (7th Cir.1974). The developer of a subdivision which included restrictive covenants for residential use only subsequently vacated a portion of the plat because of a new highway and sought to turn the vacated portion into commercial property. Residents in the subdivision sued in state court to enforce the covenant. The developer brought this action in federal court alleging that the actions of the defendants to oppose the commercial rezoning and to enforce the covenant were a violation of the federal antitrust laws. A summary judgment for defendants was upheld.

f. DeFalco v. Dirie, 923 F.Supp. 473 (S.D.N.Y.1996). Real estate developers sued town officials and others for extortion under RICO (Racketeer Influenced and Corrupt Organizations), 18 U.S.C.A. § 1962 (c). The court held that the plaintiffs stated a cause of action based on municipal employees' activities in extorting money in return for necessary permits. The court also held that a municipality could be considered as an "enterprise" for purposes of bringing a RICO claim. Also see Manor Healthcare Corp. v. Lomelo, 929 F.2d 633 (11th Cir.1991), a suit against the mayor and president of the city council under § 1983 alleging that the defendants extorted $30,000 from a nursing home in a rezoning matter. The court held that the city was properly dismissed as a party because the city neither adopted nor ratified the mayor's bribery and extortion.

4. Use of § 1983 of Title 42, U.S.Code to review zoning decisions has grown more popular since the Supreme Court ruled that cities are subject to suit under that provision in Monell v. Department of Social Services of the City of New York, 436 U.S. 658, 98 S.Ct. 2018, 56 L.Ed.2d 611 (1978). However, § 1983 suits may have limitations. First, the complaint must allege deprivation of a constitutional right, which can be difficult for the disappointed property owner denied a rezoning; many federal courts have held that a zoning permit is not a property right. Second, the local legislators may have immunity. See T & M Homes, Inc. v. Township of Mansfield, 162 N.J.Super. 497, 393 A.2d 613 (1978); Gorman Towers, Inc. v. Bogoslavsky, 626 F.2d 607 (8th Cir.1980); Creative Environments, Inc. v. Estabrook, 491 F.Supp. 547 (D.Mass.1980); Robinson v. City of Raytown, 606 S.W.2d 460 (Mo.App.1980). However, in Dunmore v. City of Natchez, 703 F.Supp. 31 (S.D.Miss.1988), the court held that to the extent city officials were acting in a legislative capacity in denying a variance they were immune from personal liability, but to the extent that they may have participated in a conspiracy to deny a black female applicant a variance because of her race, they had no immunity.

5. Our emphasis in this chapter is on zoning districts and separation of land uses. Students should also be aware that sometimes zoning disputes turn on the interpretation of words in the ordinance. For example, many zoning ordinances prohibit the keeping of "livestock" in residential districts. Persons who keep exotic pets often find themselves embroiled in a dispute over the issue of whether their pet is "livestock." See, e.g., Barnes v. City of Anderson, 642 N.E.2d 1004 (Ind.App.1994) where the court considered if "Sassy" the Vietnamese pot-bellied pig was a household pet or "livestock." Sometimes the ordinance uses the term "wild animal" thus placing pet lions, tigers, and bears in jeopardy when neighbors complain. Another example is Saurer v. Board of Zoning Appeals, 629 N.E.2d 893 (Ind.App.1994) where the

court held that rusty trailers, building trusses, semi-trailers, hog roasters and tables kept outdoors in a rural area did not constitute "junk" under a zoning ordinance defining a junkyard as a lot for the storage or sale of junk, scrap metal, scrap vehicles, or scrap machinery. The court said that junk, like pornography, is difficult to define but that "we know them when we see them." Just because the items are unpleasant to view does not make them junk, and courts are not arbiters of aesthetics and good taste.

SECTION 6.   NONCONFORMING USES

At the time a city adopts a zoning ordinance or adds land through annexation, it is obvious that some of the land uses then existing will be inconsistent with the uses prescribed by the ordinance for those sections of the city. Typical of this is the neighborhood grocery store, drug store or gasoline station located in an area zoned as residential. From the beginning, such pre-existing uses have customarily been exempted from the operation of zoning ordinances for the reasons set forth in the first case in this section. This has been the traditional approach. It was no doubt thought that these uses would wither and die as time passed. In more recent times, planners have come to recognize that nonconforming uses, once legitimated by the zoning ordinance, tend to remain indefinitely. Some efforts to discourage this have been based on what is sometimes referred to as a "control approach," under which the use is regulated in various ways—a different form of nonconforming use will not be permitted (although some ordinances have administrative procedures which may allow this), the location of the use is not permitted to be changed within the area, the facility housing the use cannot be expanded, and a new and different product or form of service will not be allowed.[13] In the event the nonconforming use is destroyed by fire or a similar disaster, some ordinances have provided that the structure cannot be rebuilt to continue such use if more than a certain percentage of it has been destroyed. These efforts at controlling the nonconforming use have for the most part been unsuccessful in eliminating it or only mildly successful at best. Moreover, the existence of nonconforming uses sometimes provides a basis for requests for variances by property owners in the same general area. As a result of the problem presented by nonconforming uses, more recent zoning efforts have tended toward the amortization approach, which involves the forced termination of the nonconforming use at the end of a specific time period—in other words, a phasing-out process, which is justified on the theory that the property owner is thus given a reasonable period of time in which to plan for his eventual loss and thereby "amortize" his business over such period.

This section will present the salient considerations developed by the courts in dealing with nonconforming uses and related regulations and

13. For a detailed discussion, see 1 Anderson, American Law of Zoning §§ 6.30–6.50 (3d ed. 1986).

the legitimacy of efforts to dispose of such uses. In this connection, several questions most commonly arise in the various cases:

1. Was there an established use at the time of zoning? (In that regard, what if the site for the structure had been surveyed, or an architect employed, or the site graded, or the basement or foundation dug, or construction begun, and so on?) In short, what was the existing situation when zoning was instituted?[14] The question of change of position and good faith by the landowner often enters in.[15]

2. What is the extent of the nonconforming use, and will the terms of the ordinance permit expansion or a change of some sort with respect to such use?

3. Has there been a termination of the nonconforming use due to substantial destruction of the building in which it is housed, or abandonment of the use, or legislative action of one type or another (including the amortization process)?

4. Is the nonconforming use subject to termination as a nuisance through the granting of injunctive relief?

In connection with this latter question, some cases (particularly some of the earlier ones) removed noxious uses which amounted to nuisances or were nuisance-like in character. This was basically the reasoning and result of Hadacheck v. Sebastian[16] and Reinman v. Little Rock.[17]

Another consideration is the extent to which the elimination of the nonconforming use will result in substantial loss to the landowner. In a New York case, a sanction against the keeping of pigeons in a residential district was upheld even though the defendant had kept pigeons prior to zoning.[18]

A distinction may also be drawn between purely seasonal use and uses which last all year or for the bulk of the year. Along the same line, there are distinguishing features which courts may consider in connection with (a) nonconforming uses which do not involve a structure of any substance, such as a parking lot or used car lot, (b) nonconforming uses in temporary structures, (c) nonconforming uses in conforming structures (such as a retail business in a store building), and (d) nonconforming uses in nonconforming structures (such as a retail business in a dwelling house). Often, zoning ordinances will provide automatic relief to owners of vacant residential lots that become nonconforming due to increased minima in area requirements, or upzoning. But see Khan v. Zoning Bd. of Appeals of Village of Irvington, 87 N.Y.2d 344, 639 N.Y.S.2d 302, 662 N.E.2d 782 (1996) where the court refused to adopt a

---

14. See, for example, Griffin v. County of Marin, 157 Cal.App.2d 507, 321 P.2d 148 (Dist.Ct.App.1958) (grading the site establishes the nonconforming use).

15. See 1 Anderson, supra note 14, § 6.29.

16. 239 U.S. 394, 36 S.Ct. 143, 60 L.Ed. 348 (1915).

17. 237 U.S. 171, 35 S.Ct. 511, 59 L.Ed. 900 (1915).

18. People v. Miller, 304 N.Y. 105, 106 N.E.2d 34 (1952).

so-called "single and separate ownership" rule as matter of common law; this rule states that one who owns property in single and separate ownership prior to enactment of the ordinance rendering it nonconforming has a vested right to use the property for residential purposes.

On the general subject of the nonconforming use, see 1 Anderson, American Law of Zoning §§ 6.01–.71 (3d ed. 1986); 8A McQuillin, Municipal Corporations §§ 25.180–.212(a) (Rev. 3d ed. 1986); and Anderson, The Nonconforming Use—A Product of Euclidean Zoning, 10 Syracuse L.Rev. 214 (1959).

A. EXPANSION OR EXTENSION

STATE v. PERRY

Supreme Court of Errors of Connecticut, 1962.
149 Conn. 232, 178 A.2d 279.

SHEA, ASSOCIATE JUSTICE. The defendant was convicted, after a trial, to the court, of a violation of the zoning regulations of Stamford. He has appealed, claiming that the court erred in finding on all the evidence that he was guilty of the crime charged beyond a reasonable doubt.

The material facts are not disputed. The defendant is president of the Pickwick Ice Cream Company, which has manufactured ice cream for over twenty-five years on premises located on Newfield Avenue in Stamford. Prior to 1951 the premises were in an industrial zone. In that year, the property was rezoned to a commercial neighborhood zone, and the industrial use by the ice cream company became a nonconforming use. Before this change of zone, all of the property was used in connection with the ice cream business, either for manufacture or storage or for the parking of trucks. In January, 1959, the defendant brought to the property a large trailer which was later insulated and equipped with a blower unit. A rubber hose attached to the trailer was connected to pipes leading from the manufacturing plant. Through these pipes, ammonia, as a cooling agent, was conducted to the trailer to refrigerate it. The trailer was kept at a freezing temperature all of the time and was used to store materials connected with the production of ice cream. The company owned a tractor to which it could connect the trailer for transportation purposes. The trailer is roadworthy, has no foundation and may be moved within a few minutes by hooking it up to the tractor. The trailer is not permanently registered with the commissioner of motor vehicles. Temporary registrations have been issued for it, but the last one expired December 24, 1959. Since then, the trailer has remained on the premises, constantly hooked up to the plant. In February, 1959, the zoning enforcement officer in writing, requested the defendant to discontinue the use of the trailer.

The Stamford zoning regulations provide that a nonconforming use may be continued but may not be extended or expanded, or changed to a less restrictive use. Stamford Zoning Regs. § 9(A) (1951, as amended).[19] The intention of the regulations is to abolish nonconforming uses, or to reduce them to conformity, as speedily as justice will permit. This is in accordance with the policy of the law and the spirit of zoning. Town of Guilford v. Landon, 146 Conn. 178, 182, 148 A.2d 551; Salerni v. Scheuy, 140 Conn. 566, 570, 102 A.2d 528. It is apparent from the evidence that the defendant attempted to provide, through the use of the trailer, additional enclosed space for his freezing and storing operations. Had he attempted to add to the existing building or to erect a new building for these purposes, he could not have done so, because this would have constituted, beyond question, an extension of a nonconforming use. What he cannot do directly he has attempted to do indirectly by the importation of the trailer. The facts clearly show that the trailer, because of its makeup, location and long continued attachment to the pipes leading from the plant, is intended, designed and arranged to be used to expand, enlarge and extend the nonconforming use conducted in the building on the premises. This is a clear violation of the regulation. Beerwort v. Zoning Board of Appeals, 144 Conn. 731, 734, 137 A.2d 756; Burmore Co. v. Smith, 124 N.J.L. 541, 547, 12 A.2d 353; 2 Rathkopf, Law of Zoning and Planning (3d Ed.) p. 59–6. It is not a simple case of increasing the size of the defendant's business. Rather, it is an expansion and extension of the use of the premises by adding facilities for storage and the freezing of commodities where such accommodations had not previously existed. Grundlehner v. Dangler, 51 N.J.Super. 53, 59, 143 A.2d 192, modified on other grounds, 29 N.J. 256, 148 A.2d 806.

There is no error.

In this opinion the other Judges concurred.

Notes

1. There are many interesting cases involving the general subject-matter presented in State v. Perry. Generally speaking, there seems to be no right to expand or enlarge a nonconforming use regardless of whether the local ordinance prohibits it. See 1 Anderson, American Law of Zoning § 6.40 (3d ed. 1986). The theory behind this is readily apparent—the nonconforming use, as such, is contrary to the intent and purposes of zoning. Normally, however, zoning ordinances contain provisions which specifically apply.

The problems arise, however, in distinguishing between the extension or enlargement of a nonconforming use and its repair, or in determining whether the construction of a new building is permissible (—it usually is not—), or whether the addition of new equipment amounts to an extension, or whether some new service or product is such an addition as to constitute an extension, or whether an increase in the intensity of use or volume of

---

19. "Section 9—Non-conforming Uses A—Any building or use of land or building legally existing at the time of enactment of this regulation, or of any amendments thereto, or authorized lawful permit issued prior to the adoption of these regulations which does not conform to the provisions of these regulations for the Use Districts in which it is located, shall be designated a non-conforming use. Such use may be continued but may not be extended or expanded, or changed to a less restrictive use as listed in Section 5—Land Use Schedule."

business amounts to a violation. These are only a few of the multitude of problems which arise in regard to changes in nonconforming uses.

Consider these situations:

(a) Before the town adopted its zoning ordinance, Anthony had been removing and processing sand and gravel from the land in question and had developed an operation whereby he could load the ingredients for concrete on dump trucks and take the loaded material to the customer. Some years later, after zoning had made his use nonconforming, he erected more modern facilities which could be used in connection with more complicated vehicles. The wooden platform which had previously been used for loading and storing materials was replaced by a steel bin and accessories, and new small buildings and a heating plant were constructed. Where dump trucks had been serviced by the earlier arrangement, the new facilities serviced cement mixer trucks. The town sought an injunction. What result? See Seekonk v. Anthony, 339 Mass. 49, 157 N.E.2d 651 (1959).

(b) At the time of the zoning ordinance in 1948, the land in question was used as a used car lot and a store or warehouse for the storage and sale of second-hand furniture and other used articles. This was a nonconforming use. Over a twelve-year period, this developed "by some sort of 'creeping' process" into a "full-fledged junk yard and shop, where, among other things, large numbers of worn out and wrecked motor vehicles were junked and burned." Was this an enlargement and extension, or was it only the intensification of a pre-existing nonconforming use? (The latter, said the court, would be permissible, while the former would not be.) See Phillips v. Zoning Comm'r, 225 Md. 102, 169 A.2d 410 (1961). In Traveler Real Estate, Inc. v. Cain, 160 A.D.2d 1214, 555 N.Y.S.2d 217 (1990) the court held that a beauty parlor operating on the first floor of a two-story building could be denied a permit to install tanning beds on the second floor because that would be an expansion.

(c) At the time of the zoning ordinance defendant was using the property for outdoor storage of earthmoving equipment along with some repair and maintenance. Now defendant wishes to build a structure to enclose his operation. The Supreme Court of Minnesota, in a case of first impression, held that the structure would be an expansion or extension of the nonconforming use: "An addition to an existing building is clearly an extension or expansion of a prior nonconforming use. In our judgment, construction of a building where none existed before constitutes an expansion of a nonconforming use in the same manner as an addition to an existing building. Furthermore, the building will prolong the continuation of the nonconforming use and considerably lessen the likelihood that it will be eliminated in the foreseeable future." County of Freeborn v. Claussen, 295 Minn. 96, 203 N.W.2d 323 (1972). Also see Mossman v. City of Columbus, 234 Neb. 78, 449 N.W.2d 214 (1989) where the court interpreted a provision in the ordinance allowing alteration of nonconforming uses, only if no "structural alterations" were made, to prohibit a mobile home owner to replace his mobile home with another one.

(d) The purchasers of a nonconforming church building were denied permission to convert it into a single-family residence which would also be nonconforming because of lot frontage and area requirements. The town invoked a regulation which prohibited conversion of one nonconforming use to another nonconforming use. In Petruzzi v. Zoning Bd. of Appeals, 176 Conn. 479, 408 A.2d 243 (1979), the court held that the permit had been improperly denied because the church structure had preceded the enactment of the first zoning ordinance making its nonconformity a vested right. Also, the court noted that only interior alteration of the structure was involved. Also see Kopietz v. Zoning Bd. of Appeals, 211 Mich.App. 666, 535 N.W.2d 910 (1995) where the court reversed the denial of a permit to convert a nonconforming funeral home into a nonconforming bed-and-breakfast. The court held that the board abused its discretion by failing to make a determination whether the proposed nonconforming use moved in the direction of diminishing the nonconformity.

(e) An asphalt company sought permission to construct a 1000 barrel capacity asphalt storage tank to replace two 400 barrel underground tanks which had developed leaks. In Nu–Way Emulsions, Inc. v. City of Dalworthington Gardens, 610 S.W.2d 562 (Tex.Civ.App.1980), the court held that the proposal amounted to enlargement and alteration of a nonconforming use rather than repair of an existing use as alleged by the plaintiff. Cf. Feldman v. Zoning Hearing Bd. of City of Pittsburgh, 89 Pa.Cmwlth. 237, 492 A.2d 468 (1985) where the property owner sought to convert an auto repair shop into a convenience store/gas station; Stevens v. Town of Rye, 122 N.H. 688, 448 A.2d 426 (1982) involving conversion of an auto garage into a showroom for plumbing supplies and bath fixtures.

(f) Conversion of an existing nonconforming restaurant into a discotheque was held to be a substantial alteration of the use in Town of Belleville v. Parrillo's, Inc., 83 N.J. 309, 416 A.2d 388 (1980). The court stressed the factors of the changes in hours of operation, clientele, admission policies, facilities, and music. Similarly, conversion of a movie theater to live entertainment was held to be an impermissible expansion of a nonconforming use in Conforti v. City of Manchester, 141 N.H. 78, 677 A.2d 147 (1996). A little closer to the line, perhaps, is Marzocco v. City of Albany, 217 A.D.2d 872, 629 N.Y.S.2d 847 (1995) where the owner of a nonconforming tavern/restaurant catering to the gay population and featuring male strippers changed the character of his business to one offering topless female dancers as entertainment, then giving up his liquor license and establishing a "juice bar" offering totally nude female dancers and "erotic entertainment." The court found that a significant change in use was involved.

(g) A private care facility operated for about four years in a residential zone which permitted nursing homes, but excluded facilities that care for "insane or other mental cases." The facility cared for eight elderly people with mental problems as a nonconforming use. When the facility changed to one which cared for young people with mental problems the city charged the operator with violating the zoning ordinance. Although the city argued that young people with mental problems are more apt to be violent than elderly people with such infirmities and that the facility was expanding the nonconforming use, the court reasoned that the intensification was permissible because the nature and character of the use remained substantially the same. The court analogized the change as similar to a store which changes its inventory or a factory which changes its product. City of Jewell Junction v. Cunningham, 439 N.W.2d 183 (Iowa 1989).

2. In Hansen Brothers Enterprises, Inc. v. Board of Supervisors of Nevada County, 12 Cal.4th 533, 48 Cal.Rptr.2d 778, 907 P.2d 1324 (1996) the court held that the diminishing asset doctrine required that a mining company be allowed expand its rock quarrying and aggregate production into other areas of its property. The court said that under the diminishing asset doctrine quarrying cannot be limited to land actually excavated at the time of enactment of a restrictive ordinance because to do so would deprive the landowner of his use of the property as a quarry. Contra: Township of Fairfield v. Likanchuk's, Inc., 274 N.J.Super. 320, 644 A.2d 120 (App.Div. 1994) (diminishing asset doctrine not applicable unless owner can show that the entire tract was dedicated by the owner to the mining activity).

3. In Memory Gardens Cemetery, Inc. v. Village of Arlington Heights, 250 Ill.App.3d 553, 190 Ill.Dec. 238, 621 N.E.2d 107 (1993) a nonconforming cemetery sought a permit to construct an additional mausoleum. (Twelve mausoleums were already on the cemetery property.) After the city denied the permit the cemetery sought a declaratory judgment that it did not need a permit on the theory that a mausoleum in a cemetery is not a change in use. The plaintiffs put on the testimony of several expert witnesses who all defined a cemetery as including in-ground internment, mausoleum entombment, and inurnment of cremated remains. The court found, however, that under Illinois law, mausoleums are treated distinctly and thus the construction of a mausoleum would be an expansion or enlargement of a nonconforming use (although, apparently, internment of additional bodies in gravesites would not be an expansion or enlargement). Compare Town of Gardiner v. Blue Sky Entertainment Corp., 213 A.D.2d 790, 623 N.Y.S.2d 29 (1995) where the town sought to close down a nonconforming tourist camp that had been used for sky diving, parachuting, and other recreational aviation activities. The court held that an increase in the volume of skydivers, pilots, and campers was not an improper extension of the nonconforming use because there was no change in the nature of the use, just the volume.

B. DISCONTINUANCE

STATE EX REL. MOREHOUSE v. HUNT

Supreme Court of Wisconsin, 1940.
235 Wis. 358, 291 N.W. 745.

[A building which could accommodate 20 to 25 students, in the University Heights area of Madison, was used as a fraternity house before the district was zoned for single family residences. The fraternity in the early 1930's deeded the building to its mortgagee. It was then used as a rooming house for over two years. In 1934, it was leased to Dean Garrison of the law school "to be used for the purpose of residence only." Dean Garrison and his family lived in the structure for the initial two year lease period and then for three more years under successive one year leases. Two servants and a student who tended the furnace lived with the Garrisons. From September, 1935, Dean Garrison subleased some extra rooms as a separate apartment.

After Dean Garrison moved out the mortgagee-owner sought a nonconforming use permit permitting renewed use as a fraternity house. The building commissioner refused, but this was reversed by the board of zoning appeals, which wrote an elaborate decision.

Certiorari was brought by neighbors. The circuit judge reversed the zoning board.]

FOWLER, JUSTICE. * * * The case is certiorari. When certiorari is invoked to review the action of an administrative board, the findings of the board upon the facts before it are conclusive if in any reasonable view the evidence sustains them. Wisconsin Labor R. Board v. Fred Rueping L. Co., 228 Wis. 473, 493, 279 N.W. 673, 117 A.L.R. 398. Under this rule the appeal board's view of the facts, so far as they appear from its decision, must be accepted as final and conclusive upon the trial court and upon us. The statutory provision for review by certiorari of the board's action, to the effect that the court may take further evidence and may consider it in reaching its determination, may warrant the court's overriding the board's findings of fact if the additional evidence received shows them to be erroneous, but where as here the additional evidence is incompetent it cannot be given that effect however it might be if it were competent. The view of the board that the owner did not intend to abandon the right of use of the building as a fraternity house but that the use of it for a residence was intended to be only temporary until opportunity should arise to sell it for that purpose, must therefore be upheld and given whatever legal effect it has.

* * *

The quotations from the decision of the board above given show that the board concluded as fact that lapse for a year of the nonconforming use before resuming or adopting another lawful nonconforming use, was a reasonable time in which to resume or adopt a lawful nonconforming use; that lapse of the conforming use under either of the above situations is consistent with and does not constitute an abandonment of the nonconforming use, and that under the facts of the instant case the owner by leasing the premises to Dean Garrison and permitting him to use them as a one-family residence for one year did not intend to abandon or discontinue Class B use.

The question remains whether the owner's intent in respect above stated operates to avoid the language of the ordinance declaring that discontinuance of a nonconforming use prevents resumption of that use.

Although the letter of the ordinance is as stated the letter need not necessarily be applied. State ex rel. Schaetz v. Manders, supra. "The letter killeth but the spirit giveth life." If the resumption of the nonconforming use is within the spirit of the ordinance, although contrary to its letter, the spirit rather than the letter governs.

That mere cessation of a nonconforming use under the terms of a zoning ordinance does not destroy the right to continue it or prevent resumption of it was held in the Manders case, supra. Under the rule of that case, discontinuance involves more than mere cessation. It involves abandonment. Under that rule, had the owner kept the premises vacant, waiting opportunity to rent or sell to a fraternity, the nonconforming use would have continued. Under the reason of that rule, had the owner, under the finding of fact as to the owner's intention, employed a caretaker for the house this would not have operated as a discontinuance. * * *

* * * But the reservation of right to cancel the lease on sale of the premises is indicative of intent to sell for a fraternity house if opportunity arose. Putting in the lease for "residence only" indicates that the lessee should not turn the house into a tearoom or restaurant or a boardinghouse, but it does preclude the idea of making it a two-family residence, as later was done, to the knowledge and with the implied assent of the owner, and as might have been done forthwith without violating of the ordinance. Whether under all the circumstances the owner's acts constituted a "voluntary relinquishment or abandonment" of the right to devote the premises to a Class B use depends on whether the use of the building as a single-family residence for a year was a reasonable time under all the circumstances, to allow the owner to devote the premises to the Class B use of a two-family residence. The appeal board thought it was. This was a question for the board to decide and its decision should be sustained. * * *

* * * We are of opinion that the judgment of the circuit court should be reversed, and the record remanded with directions to enter judgment affirming the ruling of the board of zoning appeals. * * *

[The dissenting opinion of Wickhem, J., in which two other justices concurred, is not given.]

TOYS "R" US v. SILVA

Supreme Court, New York County, 1996.
167 Misc.2d 897, 639 N.Y.S.2d 881.

DAVID B. SAXE, Justice.

In this Article 78 proceeding, petitioner Toys "R" Us asks this court to reinstate a permit issued by the Department of Buildings of the City of New York ("DOB"), which authorized Toys "R" Us to construct and operate a three-story, 38,000–square foot retail toy store at Third Avenue and 80th Street in Manhattan. If this relief is granted, this court would be required to be set aside the determination of the Board of Standards and Appeals of the City of New York ("BSA"), which revoked the permit issued by the DOB.

I. OVERVIEW AND CHRONOLOGY

The premises are located at 1411–19 Third Avenue, at the northeast corner of Third Avenue and East 80th Street, and consist of the basement and first and second floors of a sixteen story building, with loading docks fronting along East 80th Street.

From the time the building was built in 1926, it served as a storage and warehouse facility, in accordance with a 1926 certificate of occupancy, and in accordance with the zoning regulation applicable to that area at that time. When Morgan Manhattan Storage and Warehouse Company ("Morgan Manhattan") purchased the premises in 1956, the building had been exclusively used and occupied as a warehouse, and it is uncontested that Morgan Manhattan continued to actively use and occupy the premises as a warehouse until August 1989.

It is similarly undisputed that, in reliance upon a contract of sale for the premises, Morgan Manhattan ceased warehouse operations, and emptied the warehouse, for the period of August 1989 to April 1991. It is even agreed that when it was apparent that the sale had fallen through, Morgan Manhattan attempted to reinstate sufficient use of the premises as a warehouse, so as to avoid losing treatment of the premises as a non-conforming use. This reinstatement of the non-conforming use was necessary in view of the 1961 Zoning Resolution which had rezoned the neighborhood in which the building is located, from a retail zoning district to a residential and commercial district. While the commercially-zoned portion, fronting on Third Avenue, does not present a problem for the petitioner, the portion of the building fronting on 80th Street (including the warehouse's loading docks), which is now in a residential zone, may only continue to be operated as a non-conforming use (warehouse or retail store) if the non-conforming use was not abandoned.

Since Morgan Manhattan still intended to sell the property, in "reinstating" the warehouse use it did not recommence full operations of the warehouse business, nor did it invite back former customers. Instead, a limited quantity of goods then being stored in other Morgan warehouses were transferred to the 80th Street facility, so as to reinstate use of the warehouse for storage.

The single disputed point is whether the actions taken and the use made of the warehouse, as recommenced in April of 1991, sufficed to protect its character as a non-conforming use.

If it failed to retain that character, the toy store may only be constructed in that portion of the premises fronting on Third Avenue, which is commercially zoned; but the portion along 80th Street, where the loading docks are located, will only be permitted to be used for residential premises.

In June of 1992, Chase Manhattan Bank ("Chase") acquired the premises from Morgan Manhattan by way of a deed in lieu of foreclosure.

In February 1993, counsel for Chase Manhattan Bank sent the DOB a letter requesting "informal advice" as to whether the non-conforming use of the subject premises could be continued by Chase Manhattan Bank or any successor owner. In response to this request, the DOB issued an informal opinion that the non-conforming use at the premises had been reestablished in April 1991 and could thus be lawfully continued.

In March of 1994, Toys "R" Us purchased a commercial condominium unit of the premises, consisting of the basement, and first and second floors, from a subsidiary of Chase.

In June of 1994, the petitioner filed with the DOB an application and plans to convert the basement, first and second floors of the premises to a retail toy store. The petitioner conceded that Morgan Manhattan discontinued the operation of the warehouse in August 1989, but asserted that Morgan Manhattan reestablished the non-conforming warehouse use in April 1991.

In August 1994, the DOB approved petitioner's application and plans for the proposed development and, in September 1994, issued a building permit, authorizing the conversion of the basement, first and second floors of the premises to a retail toy store.

On October 5, 1994, the DOB issued a letter officially denying a request for revocation of the building permit it had issued to Toys "R" Us.

In October of 1994, a coalition of neighborhood and block associations called "Neighbors–R–Us" challenged the grant of the building permit by way of an administrative appeal to the BSA.

On February 7, 1995, a public hearing was begun, and was continued on numerous occasions until July 18, 1995. The position of the neighborhood alliance was vigorously supported by a number of elected officials, whose statements were read into the record before the BSA. The BSA also reviewed hundreds of pages of submitted documents and heard testimony from all sides.

The BSA issued its decision on the appeal by a resolution dated July 18, 1995 in which it accepted the contention of the neighborhood alliance that warehouse use had been discontinued for a full two-year period, and therefore the right to continue the non-conforming use had been abandoned. The BSA overturned the DOB's ruling on the permit.

V. ISSUE AND ANALYSIS

The question for this Court to decide is whether, upon the entire record, the BSA's finding that there was a substantial discontinuance of the non-conforming use of the premises for a continuous two year period was arbitrary, capricious, or unreasonable.

The Regulation

Zoning Regulation section 52–61 specifically provides that,

If for a continuous period of two years either the non-conforming use of land with minor improvements is discontinued, or the active operation of *substantially* all the non-conforming uses in any building or other structure is discontinued, such land or building or other structure shall thereafter be used only for a conforming use. Intent to resume active operation shall not affect the foregoing (emphasis added).

In other words, in a residential district such as the 80th Street portion of the premises in question, an existing non-conforming warehouse use may be continued (or may be changed to a non-conforming retail store use), so long as the active operation of substantially all of the non-conforming warehouse use has not been discontinued for any continuous two year period. If however, the active operation of substantially all of the non-conforming warehouse use has been discontinued for a continuous period of two years, the premises may be used thereafter only for a conforming use.

It bears emphasis that a single word distinguishes this situation from those treated in this state's controlling case law: the word "substantially".

In the leading case of Marzella v. Munroe, 69 N.Y.2d 967, 516 N.Y.S.2d 647, 509 N.E.2d 342 [1987], the regulation under consideration (Village of Dobbs Ferry Code § 300–81B), stated that "an abandoned non-conforming use cannot be resumed", containing no further standard for guidance. The landowner's application for a permit to renovate was denied by the village building inspector, which decision was affirmed by the Zoning Board of Appeals, with the holding that the non-conforming use of the property had been abandoned and that under the Dobbs Ferry Code, an abandoned non-conforming use cannot be resumed. However, the Court annulled that determination, holding that "abandonment does not occur unless there has been a complete cessation of the non-conforming use" (Marzella, 69 N.Y.2d at 968, 516 N.Y.S.2d 647, 509 N.E.2d 342, supra). Therefore, any minimal non-conforming use is enough to protect the non-conforming use status.

Similarly, in Town of Islip v. P.B.S. Marina, Inc., 133 A.D.2d 81, 518 N.Y.S.2d 427 [2d Dept 1987], appeal denied 70 N.Y.2d 611, 523 N.Y.S.2d 495, 518 N.E.2d 6 [1987], the zoning ordinance at issue reads, "discontinuance of any non-conforming use for a period of one year or more terminates such non-conforming use ..." (Town of Islip, supra, at 82, 518 N.Y.S.2d 427, citing the Town of Islip Code s 68–15[B]). Therefore, where one mooring of a marina was leased, and was used at least twice each year, the Court held that the non-conforming use was not terminated (133 A.D.2d at 82, 518 N.Y.S.2d 427, supra; see also Baml Realty, Inc. v. State of New York, 35 A.D.2d 857, 314 N.Y.S.2d 1013 [3rd Dept 1970]; Daggett v. Putnam, 40 A.D.2d 576, 334 N.Y.S.2d 556 [4th Dept 1972]).

The "complete cessation" standard which is applied in all of the above mentioned cases, is not entirely applicable here. In each case cited, the respective town's zoning ordinance only speaks of a discontinuance without any further qualification; none use the word "substantial" or "substantially", as does the regulation in question.

Nevertheless, while the "complete cessation" standard cannot be directly applied, the policy underlying that standard must be applied here. As a rule, any community would prefer to extinguish any non-conforming uses. Nevertheless, zoning ordinances must be strictly construed against the zoning authority, since they are in derogation of the common law, and interfere with the free use of land by the property owner (Thomson Indus. v. Incorporated Vil. of Port Wash. N., 27 N.Y.2d 537, 539, 313 N.Y.S.2d 117, 261 N.E.2d 260).

Importantly, Zoning Resolution 52–61 uses the word "all", albeit with the modifier "substantially". If the law had instead provided for loss of non-conforming use status merely upon discontinuance of a substantial amount of the non-conforming use, the reasoning of the BSA would appropriately conform to the resolution. However, when a zoning resolution uses the word "all", some quantifiable, actual good faith use of the property for warehousing or storage cannot logically constitute a showing of a discontinuance of "all", or even "substantially all" of the active operation of the non-conforming uses. The BSA conceded that Morgan actually placed stored goods in the warehouse for the period in question; there was no finding of bad faith or fraud. Therefore, there clearly was some actual good faith in the use of the property for storage, constituting a continuation of the non-conforming uses.

Furthermore, if there is any question as to how much good faith usage of the property for a non-conforming use constitutes a sufficient amount, any ambiguity in the zoning ordinance must be resolved in favor of the property owner (Exxon Corp. v. Board of Stnds. & Appeals of the City of N.Y., 128 A.D.2d 289, 515 N.Y.S.2d 768 [1st Dept 1987], appeal denied 70 N.Y.2d 614, 524 N.Y.S.2d 676, 519 N.E.2d 622 [1988]).

It is important to recognize in this matter that the landowner had an absolute right to recommence using the property as a warehouse within the two year period, even if its purpose was simply to protect the property's status as a non-conforming use (and not to reinstate business operations). Unquestionably, the mere "intent to resume active operations" is insufficient to establish the resumption of a non-conforming use (Zoning Regulation § 52–61). And, given the absence of the "complete cessation" standard, a truly de minimus use—for instance, placing one box in a warehouse for one day—could constitute an insufficient showing, being instead merely a fraudulent attempt to avoid the effects of an abandonment of a non-conforming use. However, there is no reason why reinstatement of the use must mirror the extent of the use previously made of the premises. In other words, actual good faith use of the warehouse for storage of goods fulfills the requirement of continuation of a non-conforming use, even if the amount and type of use is far less than that made when a business was being operated in the premises.

The BSA did not find that the warehouse was closed, locked, and vacant, as the neighborhood groups would have it. Rather, it accepted the evidence which indicated that Morgan Manhattan had a full-time employee on-site, was storing some 19 or 20 crates or pallets of property, and had electricity running (albeit about 10% of the company's normal use while it was operating a full-scale business). It emphasized that these facts were insufficient to support the running of a "legitimate business operation" (see, BSA Resolution dated July 18, 1995, p. 8).

In contrast to the legal conclusion reached by the BSA, I hold that the proper construction of Zoning Resolution § 52–61, based on the facts as found by the BSA, requires the conclusion reached by the DOB: the non-conforming use was not abandoned for the full two year period. Active operation of the non-conforming uses does not require a full-scale business operation. A warehouse concededly being used for storage must satisfy that requirement.

* * *

For all the foregoing reasons, the petition is granted, and the determination of the respondent Board of Standards and Appeals is annulled. The DOB permits are reinstated, pursuant to the terms of the stipulation, as initially issued.

Notes

1. Compare with the principal case New Venture Realty, Ltd. v. Fennell, 210 A.D.2d 412, 620 N.Y.S.2d 99 (1994) where the court found that a light manufacturing nonconforming use in a residential zone was lost by abandonment because although the property was used for storage and sales of material, no actual manufacturing was conducted during the one-year period.

There is no uniformity of interpretation in situations in which the use has been discontinued and resumption of it is attempted. Some ordinances attempt to spell out specific time periods and provide that the use cannot be resumed after a given period of non-use has elapsed. A Wisconsin provision stated that if the nonconforming use were *"discontinued* for a period of 12 months, any future use of the building and premises shall conform to the ordinance." Did the word, "discontinued," mean a "voluntary abandonment" in the sense of an *intent* to discontinue? In State ex rel. Brill v. Mortenson, 6 Wis.2d 325, 96 N.W.2d 603 (1959), the Wisconsin court answered in the negative. Board of Zoning Adjustment v. Boykin, 265 Ala. 504, 92 So.2d 906 (1957), states, however, that "the word discontinuance, as used in a zoning ordinance, is equivalent to abandonment" and adds that "discontinuance results from the concurrence of an intent to abandon and some overt act or failure to act which carries the implication of abandonment." See 1 Anderson, American Law of Zoning § 6.60 (3d ed. 1986).

2. The construction by courts of "discontinued" as implying the requirement of an intent to abandon the nonconforming use is rather odd in view of the purpose of zoning. It exacerbates the problem caused by the nonconforming use and increases the difficulty in dealing with it. Some courts look at the fact of discontinuance and ignore the intent of the owner. Thus in City of Chicago v. Cohen, 49 Ill.App.3d 342, 7 Ill.Dec. 174, 364 N.E.2d 335 (1977), the nonconforming use was terminated even though the owner testified he had no intention of abandoning but rather was actively seeking a tenant during the six month period. Also see Martin v. Beehan, 689 S.W.2d 29 (Ky.App.1985) where the court found a nonconforming hotel abandoned despite intermittent attempts to sell the hotel over a ten-year period. The court said the intent of the owner was immaterial, as did the courts in Anderson v. City of Paragould, 16 Ark.App. 10, 695 S.W.2d 851

(1985), and Ka–Hur Enterprises, Inc. v. Zoning Bd. of Appeals of Provincetown, 40 Mass.App.Ct. 71, 661 N.E.2d 120 (1996).

. An unusual situation was presented in Sapakoff v. Town of Hague Zoning Bd. of Appeals, 211 A.D.2d 874, 621 N.Y.S.2d 215 (1995) where a nonconforming restaurant and bar was forfeited to the federal government under the drug laws, and the government sold the property at auction to Sapakoff who sought to reinstitute the nonconforming use. The court held that the two-year discontinuance provision was not tolled by virtue of the federal seizure and the permit to resume the previous use was revoked.

3. In Boles v. City of Chattanooga, 892 S.W.2d 416 (Tenn.App.1994) the court held that discontinuance of an adult-oriented establishment while a temporary restraining order was in effect was involuntary, and thus did not constitute discontinuance of a nonconforming use; and, in State ex rel. McArthur v. Board of Adjustment of City of Crestwood, 872 S.W.2d 651 (Mo.App.1994) the court held that the city could not terminate nonconforming use rights of six spaces in a mobile home park that had been vacant for a period of time, because the individual spaces were not lots or parcels, and thus the owner's inability to rent the individual spaces in the park was not a discontinuance.

4. Can a city treat a change of ownership as a discontinuance or termination-triggering event? In Village of Valatie v. Smith, 190 A.D.2d 17, 596 N.Y.S.2d 581 (1993) the court held that a provision in the village code terminating a nonconforming use upon a change in ownership of the property was unconstitutional on its face. The court stated: "[T]he provision at issue appears to run afoul of fundamental rule that zoning deals basically with land use rather than the person who owns or occupies the land." In Caserta v. Zoning Bd. of Appeals of City of Milford, 41 Conn.App. 77, 674 A.2d 855 (1996) the court held that after a change in ownership and an attempt by the new owner to reestablish a discontinued use, reference must be made to the previous owner's intent to reestablish the use. And, in Town of Lyons v. Bashor, 867 P.2d 159 (Colo.App.1993) the court held that the right to maintain a prior nonconforming use of two houses on one lot ran with the land (the lot was put up for sale after a court ordered dissolution of a marriage and had partitioned the land).

5. An exhaustive annotation on resumption of nonconforming uses after a break in continuity is found in 57 A.L.R.3d 279 (1974). Also see Eric J. Strauss and Mary M Giese, Elimination of Nonconformities: The Case of Voluntary Discontinuance, 25 The Urban Lawyer 159 (1993).

C. DESTRUCTION

MOFFATT v. FORREST CITY

Supreme Court of Arkansas, 1961.
234 Ark. 12, 350 S.W.2d 327.

McFADDIN, JUSTICE. This litigation involves the application of the Zoning Ordinance of Forrest City, Arkansas. Appellants, Mr. and Mrs. Louie Moffatt, purchased a home in the residential district of Forrest City in 1951. In 1954 they made additions to the home and began operating a meat market and meat processing plant in said additions; and, as business improved, they made other additions and enlargements to the meat market portion of the premises. In 1959, Forrest City adopted a zoning ordinance which classified the area in which the Moffatt premises are located as entirely residential. Moffatt's market was a nonconforming use. The Zoning Ordinance provided: "If a building occupied by a non-conforming use is damaged to the extent of 60 per cent or more of its reproduction value exclusive of foundations, such building may not be restored for any non-conforming use."

On July 20, 1960, there was a fire in which the Moffatt residence quarters were almost entirely destroyed, and the market portion was considerably damaged. When the Moffats undertook to repair the market in order to resume business, the municipality filed this suit in Chancery Court to enjoin them from any reconstruction. The city alleged that the building was more than 60 per cent destroyed, exclusive of foundations, and that because of the Zoning Ordinance the owners could not restore the property for use as a meat market, such being a nonconforming use. The Moffatts resisted the city's claim. There were several hearings in the Chancery Court, and the Chancellor personally viewed the premises. The Chancery decree sustained the city's claim and enjoined the reconstruction of the building, or any building on the premises, for use as a meat market. The Moffatts have appealed, urging two points:

I. The Appellants Were Entitled to the Application of the Rule of Strict Construction in Their Favor of the Zoning Ordinance.

II. The Appellee Did Not Sustain Its Burden of Proof by a Preponderance of the Evidence.

We agree with the appellants that a zoning ordinance is to be strictly construed in favor of the property holders, since the ordinance is in derogation of the common law and operates to deprive the owner of the property of a use which would otherwise be lawful. City of Little Rock v. Williams, 206 Ark. 861, 177 S.W.2d 924, and cases and authorities there cited; see, also City of West Helena v. Bockman, 221 Ark. 677, 256 S.W.2d 40. But even giving the Zoning Ordinance of Forrest City[20] a strict construction in favor of the property holders, we must decide the fact question: whether the building on the premises was damaged "to the extent of 60 per cent or more of its reproduction value exclusive of foundations."

The residence and the meat market were housed in one structure. This is shown by the plats and pictures in the transcript. Regardless of the fact that there were additions to the market side of the house, there was only one overall building; and appellants could not have successfully claimed that the market was one building and the residence was another. Such a theory was originally urged, but with becoming candor

---

20. Allowing the replacement of a structure for a nonconforming use necessarily depends on the wording of the particular ordinance involved. For general statements on this matter, see 58 Am.Jur. 1029, "Zoning" § 162; 101 C.J.S. Zoning § 197, p. 960; and Yokley on "Zoning Law and Practice", Second Edition, § 157.

appellants' learned counsel conceded: " * * * the cause was ultimately submitted on the theory that the market and the residence constituted one structure and that the issue before the Court was 60% destruction of it exclusive of foundations."

There was evidence that the total value of the building before the fire was approximately $15,000; and that to restore the building after the fire would cost approximately $12,000. Five witnesses—some of them building contractors—testified that the damage exceeded 60 per cent. Mr. Moffatt did not dispute the fact that the residence portion of the structure was a total loss; and there was other evidence that the residence portion was $^{10}\!/_{15}$ths of the total value. While there is evidence to the contrary, we cannot say that the preponderance of the evidence is contrary to the Chancellor's conclusions as to the percentage of damage.

Affirmed.

Notes

1. In Stanton v. Town of Pawleys Island, 317 S.C. 498, 455 S.E.2d 171 (1995) the court reversed the denial of a permit to repair a home that had been substantially damaged in a hurricane. The zoning ordinance prohibited ground level living quarters in coastal high hazard areas. Thus Stanton's house was nonconforming. The court held that, as a whole, the house was not more than 50% destroyed. Compare Pelham Esplanade v. Village of Pelham Manor Board of Trustees, 154 A.D.2d 599, 546 N.Y.S.2d 427 (1989) where the owner of two apartment buildings sought a permit to rebuild one of the buildings that had undergone fire damage greater than 50%. The court held that looking at the "apartment complex as a whole," less than 50% was destroyed and the owner was entitled to the permit.

2. In the absence of an ordinance such as the one in the principal case, the general rule is that a discontinuance of use caused by a fire on the premises does not amount to an abandonment and building may be repaired and the use resumed. See generally, 1 Anderson, American Law of Zoning §§ 6.55, 6.56, 6.59 (3d ed. 1986).

What about discontinuance of the use due to repair of the building, acts of war, government restrictions, foreclosure or condemnation actions, or injunctive relief granted by a court having equity powers? See Annot., 56 A.L.R.3d 138 (1974).

D. AMORTIZATION—USES AND LIMITATIONS

GRANT v. MAYOR & CITY COUNCIL OF BALTIMORE

Court of Appeals of Maryland, 1957.
212 Md. 301, 129 A.2d 363.

HAMMOND, JUDGE. From the beginning of zoning in Baltimore billboards were excluded prospectively from residential districts, although those already there were permitted to remain as nonconforming uses. Then in 1950 the City Council passed Ordinance 1101, approved April 5 of that year, requiring all outdoor advertising structures in residential districts to be removed not later than five years from the passage of the ordinance. In 1953 after full hearings and extended consideration, there was passed Ordinance 711 generally revising the zoning laws of the City. Paragraph 13(d) narrowed the exclusion of the 1950 ordinance, providing only that "Billboards and poster boards situated in Residential and Office Use Districts and Residential Use Districts shall be removed by April 5, 1955 * * * "that is, within five years of the passage of the 1950 ordinance.

The corporate appellants, signboard companies, and the individual appellants, owners of property leased for the use of billboards, ask us to reverse the chancellor who dismissed their bill that sought to declare the 1953 ordinance invalid and unconstitutional and to restrain the Mayor and City Council and the Building Inspection Engineer of Baltimore from enforcing it.

The Morton Company, Inc., or its corporate predecessors, had for many years been in the outdoor advertising business. In 1955 it had about sixteen hundred billboards in Baltimore and its environs, some nine hundred being within the city limits. Seventy-eight are in residential or residential and office use districts, all being nonconforming uses that have endured since the passage of the first zoning ordinance in 1931. Fourteen of these are illuminated. All of the thirty-eight leases for the nonconforming billboards were entered into after 1950. Most are for terms of one year; none, except one executed in 1952, has a term of over five years. Morton received about $45,000 a year gross from advertisers on the seventy-eight billboards. Its testimony was that billboard coverage is sold in "packages" of from fifteen to sixty boards for frequent repetition on main roads and so as to provide a network of coverage which is "almost inescapable" to a "captive audience". Removal of the nonconforming billboards would seriously diminish the adequacy of coverage and injure the business. After the filing of the bill, Donnelly Advertising Corporation of Maryland acquired the assets of Morton and was allowed to intervene in the case, as were several individual appellees who owned homes near billboards.

The individual appellants, Mr. and Mrs. Grant, and Samuel Cooper, each own a parcel of land in a residential district which has been leased for billboard use continuously since before the original Baltimore zoning ordinance of 1931. The Grant lease was for one year beginning November 1, 1953. There have been two one year extensions as the lease allowed. The rent is $200 a year. The Cooper lease was for one year beginning April 1, 1954, and there has been one extension for another year. The Grants bought their unimproved lot on the east side of Greenspring Avenue near Gordon Road in 1923. It has been leased for billboards since 1927. Cooper bought his lot, on which there is a house he rents out, in 1953, and he continued the leasing of part of the property for billboard use begun before 1931 by his predecessors in title. His rent is $35 a year.

The appellants urge that their rights to nonconforming uses are vested rights of property which the enforcement of paragraph 13(d) of Ordinance 711 of 1953 would take from them without compensation, contrary to Art. 3, Sec. 40 of the Constitution of Maryland, and so would deprive them of property without due process of law, Const. Declaration of Rights, Art. 19, as well as be discriminatory and a denial of the equal protection of the laws.

Nonconforming uses have been a problem since the inception of zoning. Originally they were not regarded as serious handicaps to its effective operation; it was felt they would be few and likely to be eliminated by the passage of time and restrictions on their expansion. For these reasons and because it was thought that to require immediate cessation would be harsh and unreasonable, a deprivation of rights in property out of proportion to the public benefits to be obtained and, so, unconstitutional, and finally a red flag to property owners at a time when strong opposition might have jeopardized the chance of any zoning, most, if not all, zoning ordinances provided that lawful uses existing on the effective date of the law could continue although such uses could not thereafter be begun. Nevertheless, the earnest aim and ultimate purpose of zoning was and is to reduce nonconformance to conformance as speedily as possible with due regard to the legitimate interests of all concerned, and the ordinances forbid or limit expansion of nonconforming uses and forfeit the right to them upon abandonment of the use or the destruction of the improvements housing the use. * * *

Nonconforming uses have not disappeared as hoped and anticipated because the general regulation of future uses and changes, with some existing uses uncontrolled, have put the latter in an entrenched position often with a value that is great—and grows—because of the artificial monopoly given it by the law. Indeed, there is general agreement that the fundamental problem facing zoning is the inability to eliminate the nonconforming use. City of Los Angeles v. Gage, 127 Cal.App.2d 442, 274 P.2d 34, 40.

* * *

The frustrations of the people as they were faced with nonconforming uses soon found their representatives in the lawmaking bodies trying other ways to get rid of them. Two tools resorted to were eminent domain and the law of nuisances. The effectiveness of eminent domain is restricted by the necessity that the purchase must be for public use, by the complexities of administrative procedures and by the high cost of reimbursing the property owners. The law of nuisances has limits that many times make its use fall short of the objective. Some courts will restrain only common law nuisances and even where the lawmakers have expanded the nuisance category, judicial enforcement seems often to have been restricted to uses that cause a material and tangible interference with the property or personal well-being of others, uses that are equivalent to or are likely to become common law traditional nuisances.

It has become apparent that if nonconforming uses are to be dealt with effectively it must be under the law of zoning, a law not limited in its controls to harmful and noxious uses in the common law sense. Many legislative bodies have come to the technique of statutes or ordinances that call for the cessation of the extraneous use after a tolerance or amortization period, varying in length with the nature of the use and of the structures devoted to the use, from one year to sixty years. Some of the jurisdictions that have enacted such provisions are cited below.[21] It has been said that the only positive method yet devised of eliminating nonconforming uses is to determine the normal useful remaining economic life of the structure devoted to the use and prohibit the owner from using it for the offending use after the expiration of that time. Crolly and Norton, Termination of Nonconforming Uses, 62 Zoning Bulletin 1, June 1952, cited in City of Los Angeles v. Gage, supra, 274 P.2d 34, 41.

Some Courts have refused to distinguish between laws requiring immediate cessation of nonconforming uses and those that demand cessation only after the expiration of a tolerance or amortization period, holding that the latter as well as the former are unconstitutional.[22]

Other Courts have held that nonconforming uses could be stopped after specified periods of time. * * *

* * *

The distinction between an ordinance that restricts future uses and one that requires existing uses to stop after a reasonable time, is not a

21. Colo.Stat.Ann. (Supp.1953) c. 45A, § 19 (county zoning); Ill.Rev.Stat.1953, c. 24, § 73–1 (city zoning); Kan.Gen.Stat.Ann. 1949, § 19–2919 (county zoning); Mass.Acts 1948, c. 214, § 9; Okl.Stat.Ann., tit. 19, c. 19A, § 863.16 (county zoning); Pa.Stat.Ann. Purdon, tit. 16, § 2033 (county zoning); Utah Code Ann.1943, § 19–24–18 (county zoning); Va.Code 1950, § 15–843 (city zoning); Chicago Zoning Ord., § 20 (1944); Cleveland, Ohio, Ord. § 1281–9(e) (1930); Bridgeport, Conn.; Los Angeles Mun.Code, § 12.123 B & C (1946); New Orleans, La., Zoning Ord.; Richmond, Va., Zoning Ord., Art. XIII, § 1 (1948); Seattle, Wash. See State ex rel. Miller v. Cain, 40 Wash.2d 216, 242 P.2d 505, 507; Wichita, Kan., Zoning Ord. § 24 (1948).

22. Cases so holding include: James v. City of Greenville, 227 S.C. 565, 88 S.E.2d 661; Town of Greenburgh v. General Outdoor Adv. Co., Sup., 109 N.Y.S.2d 826; Town of Somers v. Camarco, 308 N.Y. 537, 127 N.E.2d 327; City of Akron v. Chapman, 160 Ohio St. 382, 116 N.E.2d 697, 42 A.L.R.2d 1140; City of Corpus Christi v. Allen, 152 Tex. 137, 254 S.W.2d 759, 761. The South Carolina and New York cases do not discuss in any detail the possible dis-

tinctions between immediate cessation and termination after a period of amortization. The Ohio case is criticized in 67 Harvard Law Review 1283 as being inconsistent "with the general acceptance of amortization principles". The Ohio statute had the weakness of leaving the time for stopping the nonconforming use with the city council and thus, perhaps, was unduly harsh in not providing a definite tolerance period. Too, the decision of the council as to the choice of the use to be stopped and the time for the stopping could well have been actually discriminatory. In the Corpus Christi case the Supreme Court of Texas refused to end a nonconforming use under a two year amortization provision, finding the power attempted to be used would be unreasonable because any benefit to the city by its exercise would be small and the damage to the property owner would be heavy. The Court concluded its opinion, however, as follows: "Our conclusion is not to be construed as a holding that the ordinance in question may not, under other circumstances, be invoked to terminate a nonconforming use, not a nuisance nor injurious to the public health, morals, safety or welfare."

difference in kind but one of degree and, in each case, constitutionality depends on overall reasonableness, on the importance of the public gain in relation to the private loss. New York applies the rule of reasonableness to legislative efforts to end nonconforming uses—quite strictly as People v. Miller, 304 N.Y. 105, 106 N.E.2d 34, 35, shows. The Court said: "The decisions are sometimes put on the ground that the owner has secured a 'vested right' in the particular use—which is but another way of saying that the property interest affected by the particular ordinance is too substantial to justify its deprivation in light of the objectives to be achieved by enforcement of the provision. (Cf. Note, 41 Harv.L.Rev. 667; Note, 39 Yale L.J. 735, 740.) Every zoning regulation, because it affects property already owned by individuals at the time of its enactment, effects some curtailment of 'vested' rights, either by restricting prospective uses or by prohibiting the continuation of existing uses. A regulation of the latter variety, however, almost always imposes substantial loss and hardship upon the individual property owner—a loss much greater than that sustained by reason of a prospective use restriction only—and that factor underlies the rule that we are discussing."

There is no difference in kind, either, between limitations that prevent the adding to or extension of a nonconforming use, or provisions that the right to the use is lost if abandoned or if the structure devoted to the use is destroyed, or the denial of a right to substitute a new use for the old, all of which are common if not universal in zoning laws and all of which are established as constitutional and valid, on the one hand, and a requirement, on the other, that an existing nonconformance must cease after a reasonable time. The significance and effect of difference in degree in any given case depends on circumstances, environment and length of the period allowed for amortization.

We think that in requiring billboards to leave residential areas after a tolerance period of five years, the City Council has not over-stepped the line that divides the reasonable and constitutional from the arbitrary and invalid. Billboards are not nuisances per se—indeed, Ordinance 711 provides, as did predecessor ordinances, that a billboard may be erected in commercial and industrial zones as a matter of right, unless it is determined as a fact that it " * * * would menace the public health, safety, security or morals". * * *

* * *

Having determined the harm to the public welfare, the Council undoubtedly concluded that an equitable means of reconciling the conflicting interests of the public on the one hand, and those of advertising companies and those leasing land to them on the other, and thus the satisfaction of the requirements of due process, would be a five year amortization period. We cannot say that the remedy chosen was arbitrary, nor that the City Council was wrong in its conclusion that the effect for good on the community by the elimination of billboards within five years would far more than balance individual losses. Certainly that is the unanimous view of those expert in the field and of the forty civic and improvement associations which studied the problem and endorsed the ordinance. As we have noted, and as the report of the Planning Commission pointed out to the City Council, a number of States and municipalities have provisions requiring elimination of nonconforming uses in residential districts within stated periods of time, varying with the nature of the structures involved. That many lawmaking bodies throughout the country have adopted the same approach does not make the approach valid, but certainly the fact that after full consideration, they have followed the same course to meet the same problem, is some indication of the reasonableness of the course. Too, some support for the validity of the amortization method of eliminating nonconforming uses is found in the law reviews. Almost unanimously they commend the method as the best available and find it valid and constitutional.[23]

* * *

There would seem to be a clear basis for classifying billboards separate and apart from other signs and other advertising. The report of the Planning Commission to the City Council put billboards in a separate category for several reasons and recommended the continuance of other signs and other forms of advertising, because they were felt to be truly accessory to the buildings or other nonconforming uses which would be permitted to continue, and the Council agreed. Billboards are not accessory uses. There is no need to refer again to their many objectionable features. Many Courts have said that classification of billboards for purposes of regulation and prohibition is valid and constitutional. See Thomas Cusack Co. v. City of Chicago, 242 U.S. 526, 37 S.Ct. 190, 61 L.Ed. 472; Packer Corp. v. State of Utah, 285 U.S. 105, 52 S.Ct. 273, 76 L.Ed. 643; St. Louis Poster Advertising Co. v. City of St. Louis, 249 U.S. 269, 39 S.Ct. 274, 63 L.Ed. 599; Kelbro, Inc. v. Myrick, 113 Vt. 64, 30 A.2d 527; General Outdoor Advertising Co. v. Department of Public Works, 289 Mass. 149, 193 N.E. 799, supra. See also Murphy, Inc. v. Town of Westport, 131 Conn. 292, 40 A.2d 177, 156 A.L.R. 568. The validity of the classification would seem to destroy the argument of the appellants that the ordinances are discriminatory as to them.

There were many objections to the admissibility of evidence. Our consideration of the case has led us to the conclusion that if there were errors, they were not prejudicial in that the result reached by the chancellor, of which we approve, should have been reached whether or not the evidence objected to had been in the case. The decree will be affirmed.

Decree affirmed, with costs.

Note

See also Harbison v. City of Buffalo, 4 N.Y.2d 553, 176 N.Y.S.2d 598, 152 N.E.2d 42 (1958), where an amortization ordinance survived its first

23. 67 Harvard Law Review 1283; 53 Michigan Law Review 762; 35 Virginia Law Review 348; 102 Univ. of Pa. Law Review 91; 41 Columbia Law Review 457; 33 Dicta 93. See also annotation in 42 A.L.R.2d 1146.

encounter with the New York Court of Appeals. But, as stated by Anderson, Amortization of Nonconforming Uses—A Preliminary Appraisal of Harbison v. City of Buffalo, 10 Syracuse L.Rev. 44 (1958), " * * * the margin of success was narrow, the dimensions of approval were ambiguous, and the dissent was sharp and provocative." The majority opinion lists the following factual questions which must be answered in testing the period of amortization: Nature of the surrounding neighborhood, the value and condition of the improvements on the premises, the nearest area in which the user might relocate, the cost of relocation, and other reasonable costs which the user might sustain.

AKRON v. CHAPMAN

Supreme Court of Ohio, 1953.
160 Ohio St. 382, 116 N.E.2d 697, 42 A.L.R.2d 1140.

[In 1922 defendant's junkyard became a nonconforming use in a residential district, due to enactment of a zoning ordinance. In 1950, the city council by special ordinance declared that after January 1, 1951, use of defendant's land should conform to the residential classification specified in the zoning ordinance. The retroactive provision of the zoning ordinance is quoted in the opinion. Defendant continued to operate his junkyard after January 1, 1951. This is an action to close his business. The trial court found for the defendant; the court of appeals reversed and held for the city.]

LAMNECK, JUDGE. There is no claim of nuisance in this case. The sole issue is whether the city may terminate the lawful nonconforming use, which was in existence at the time of the passage of the zoning ordinance, after the use has been permitted to continue for an extended period.

The zoning ordinance passed in 1922 contains the following provision:

"A building, existing at the time of the passage of this ordinance, which does not conform to the regulations of the use district in which it is located may remain for a reasonable period and the existing use of such building may be continued or extended to any portion of such building which portion was arranged or designed for such use at the time of the passage of this ordinance, but a nonconforming use shall not be otherwise extended. A nonconforming use *shall be discontinued and removed when, in the opinion of the council, such use has been permitted to exist or continue for a reasonable time.*" (emphasis ours.)

The defendant contends:

1. The council of a municipality is prohibited by the Fourteenth Amendment to the United States Constitution and by Section 2, Article I of the Constitution of this state, from enacting a zoning ordinance which outlaws an existing lawful business, unless compensation is paid therefor.

2. If a council has that power, the enactment of the ordinance passed in January 1950, directed to him individually, is discriminatory and in violation of the same constitutional provisions.

Section 1, Article XIV, Amendments, United States Constitution, and Section 16, Article I, Ohio Constitution, both provide that no person shall be deprived of life, liberty or *property* without due process of law.

Section 2, Article I of the Ohio Constitution, provides that government is instituted for the equal protection and benefit of all citizens.

* * *

In the instant case, the 1950 ordinance does not order the defendant to raze the buildings now existing on his premises. We know of no zoning ordinance in this state intended to accomplish such a result unless the existing structures are a nuisance affecting the public health, safety, morals or general welfare or unless the city exercises its power of eminent domain. In State ex rel. Bruestle v. Rich, 159 Ohio St. 13, 110 N.E.2d 778, this court held that property may be taken for "the public welfare" or "for public use" to eliminate slum conditions and other conditions of blight, under the power of eminent domain, but in such cases the owners are entitled to adequate compensation. Zoning ordinances contemplate the gradual elimination of nonconforming uses within a zoned area, and, where an ordinance accomplishes such a result without depriving a property owner of a vested *property right,* it is generally held to be constitutional.

Thus the denial of the right to resume a nonconforming use after a period of nonuse has been upheld, as well as the denial of the right to extend or enlarge an existing nonconforming use. The denial of the right to substitute new buildings for those devoted to an existing nonconforming use and to add or extend such buildings has also been upheld. See 58 American Jurisprudence, 1026 and 1029, Sections 156, 158 and 162, and the Stegner case, supra.

But in the instant case no such situation exists. We are asked by the plaintiff herein to uphold the provision of a municipal ordinance, which in effect denies the owner of property the right to continue to conduct a lawful business thereon, which use was in existence at the time of the passage of the ordinance and has continued without expansion or interruption ever since. If we do this on the ground that the provision is a proper exercise of the police power, then the right to continue to conduct other lawful businesses, similarly established and conducted on zoned property, may likewise be denied by legislative fiat under the guise of a proper exercise of the police power.

In Turnpike Co. v. Parks, 50 Ohio St. 568, 579, 35 N.E. 304, 28 L.R.A. 769, it is stated:

"* * * it is very obvious that everything which takes the form of an enactment is not therefore to be deemed the law of the land, or due course or process of law. If this were so, then decrees and forfeitures in all possible forms, and acts confiscating the property of one person or class of persons, or a particular description of property, upon some view of public policy, where it could not be said to be taken for a public use, would be the law of the land."

In the case of Jones v. City of Los Angeles, 211 Cal. 304, 295 P. 14, an ordinance which prohibited the continuation of an existing lawful business within a zoned area was declared to be unconstitutional as being the taking of property without due process of law and being an unreasonable exercise of the police power. In that case, the city by ordinance provided that it should be unlawful to continue the operation of institutions in a certain area for the care and treatment of mentally ill persons. The court, however, upheld the ordinance as to new businesses in the zoned area.

We have examined the cases, cited in the plaintiff's brief, in support of its contention that the exercise of the power to terminate a lawful nonconforming use in existence at the time of the passage of a comprehensive zoning ordinance, where such use has continued for an extended period thereafter, is a proper exercise of the police power. Although some of these citations support the plaintiff's position, we are of the opinion that they are in conflict with the great weight of authority on the subject and not consistent with past pronouncements of this court. See 58 American Jurisprudence, 1021, Section 146 et seq.; State ex rel. v. Stegner, supra; and State ex rel. v. Arnold, supra.

What is property? It has been defined as not merely the ownership and possession of lands or chattels but the unrestricted right of their use, enjoyment and disposal. Anything which destroys any of these elements of property, to that extent destroys the property itself. The substantial value of property lies in its use. If the right of use is denied, the value of the property is annihilated and ownership is rendered a barren right. See Spann v. City of Dallas, 111 Tex. 350, 235 S.W. 513, 19 A.L.R. 1387, and O'Connor v. City of Moscow, 69 Idaho 37, 202 P.2d 401, 9 A.L.R.2d 1031.

The right to continue to use one's property in a lawful business and in a manner which does not constitute a nuisance and which was lawful at the time it was acquired is within the protection of Section 1, Article XIV, Amendments, Constitution of the United States, and Section 16, Article I of the Ohio Constitution, which provide that no person shall be deprived of life, liberty or property without due process of law.

The effect of the provisions of the 1922 ordinance and the 1950 ordinance, complained of in this case, is to deprive the defendant of a continued lawful use of his property and is in violation of the due process clauses of the state and federal Constitutions.

The judgment of the Court of Appeals must, therefore, be reversed, and that of the Court of Common Pleas affirmed.

Judgment reversed.

Notes

1. Is the key point in this case the fact that the ordinance was aimed solely at the defendant's property? Is the language and reasoning employed by the court subject to attack on other grounds? Is the court's definition of "property" entirely correct and appropriate? See the Note, Amortization: A Means of Eliminating the Nonconforming Use in Ohio, 19 Case W.Res.L.Rev. 1042, 1053–1054 (1968). Do you agree with the author of the Note or with the court? This same Note, incidentally, at pages 1057–1060, discusses amortization provisions with an eye to what language should withstand the scrutiny of courts.

2. For a case with similar facts as in the Akron case but an opposite result, see Collins v. City of Spartanburg, 281 S.C. 212, 314 S.E.2d 332 (1984). The court upheld an ordinance imposing a five-year amortization period on junkyards, auto wrecking yards and auto storage yards, balancing the large public gain from elimination of eyesores against the small private loss. Also see Neighborhood Committee on Lead Pollution v. Board of Adj. of City of Dallas, 728 S.W.2d 64 (Tex.App.1987) where the court upheld a six year amortization period for a lead smelting and plating operation. Under Texas law, the Board of Adjustment may determine the termination date for nonconforming uses, under the standard of examining the capital investment in the structure by the person owning the land at the time the use became nonconforming. Board of Adjustment of Dallas v. Patel, 882 S.W.2d 87 (Tex.App.1994).

3. Amortization provisions have become very popular in recent years. A clear majority of jurisdictions have followed the Grant case rationale while the Akron case represents the minority view. The reporters working on the Model Land Development Code, in the commentary to Article 4, have listed the cases upholding amortization (Model Land Development Code, pp. 170–172); however, they go on to suggest that the technique does not seem to work well in practice:

> Nevertheless, although the amortization technique has been supported by the courts, has been widely discussed in the literature, and has found its way into the text of a large number of zoning ordinances, very few uses of land of substantial significance have been eliminated as a result of amortization. In 1971 the American Society of Planning Officials polled its membership to determine the extent to which amortization was being used to eliminate nonconforming uses. Out of 489 cities and counties responding, 159 reported that their zoning ordinances contained amortization provisions, but only 27 communities reported use of the technique against buildings and structures. Where amortization has been used it has usually been against billboards or other uses involving a negligible capital investment. In general, most zoning administrators who were surveyed expressed dissatisfaction with the amortization technique. See Robert Scott, "The Effect of Nonconforming Land–Use Amortization," (Planning Advisory Service Report No. 280, May, 1972).

4. In Centaur, Inc. v. Richland County, 301 S.C. 374, 392 S.E.2d 165 (1990) the court upheld a two-year amortization period for sexually-oriented

business and limiting their relocation to sixteen specified areas in the
county.

SECTION 7. POPULAR INVOLVEMENT: THE INITIATIVE AND REFERENDUM AND ORDINANCES REQUIRING NEIGHBORHOOD CONSENT

A. CONSENT BY THE NEIGHBORS

VALKANET v. CITY OF CHICAGO

Supreme Court of Illinois, 1958.
13 Ill.2d 268, 148 N.E.2d 767.

[Plaintiffs asked for a declaratory judgment in the trial court that
they were entitled to a license to operate a home for the aged in an
apartment zone. The ordinance required consent by a majority of owners
on both sides of the street for the block in which a home for the aged
was to be located. Plaintiffs contended this requirement was invalid and
did not obtain such consent. The trial court found the requirement void
and the city appealed].

DAVIS, CHIEF JUSTICE. * * * From the complaint and the record of the
proceedings below, it appears that the plaintiffs' theory is that the
ordinance is void in that it is an illegal delegation of legislative power to
private individuals, a deprivation of property without due process of law,
and a denial of equal protection of the law.

The defendant contends that the restriction imposed on operating
such homes by section 136–6 is a reasonable and proper exercise of police
power, and that the consent provision for waiver of the restriction is
valid.

Unaided by brief and argument of plaintiffs, we have examined the
state of the law concerning the validity of "frontage consent" provisions,
and, like McQuillin, have found "a decided difference of judicial view and
sometimes of jurisdictional consistency as to the validity of municipal
legislation of this character, not entirely explainable by varying provisions of the ordinances or by differing statutory or charter grants of
authority." (8 McQuillin, Municipal Corporations, 3rd ed., p. 348.) * * *

An analysis of * * * [our] decisions reveals that we have sustained
frontage-consent provisions where the effect was to permit the waiver of
a prohibition of a structure, business, trade or occupation properly
subject to the police power, such as livery stables, saloons, garages and
billboards. Spies v. Board of Appeals, 337 Ill. 507, 513, 169 N.E. 220. Yet
we have consistently held that a municipality cannot deprive a citizen of
a valuable property right under the guise of prohibiting or regulating
some business or occupation which has no tendency to injure the public
health or morals, or interfere with the general welfare. Spies v. Board of
Appeals, 337 Ill. 507, 169 N.E. 220; People ex rel. Deitenbeck v. Village

of Oak Park, 331 Ill. 406, 163 N.E. 445; People ex rel. Friend v. City of Chicago, 261 Ill. 16, 103 N.E. 609.

The prevailing view concerning such consent provisions is illustrated by two leading decisions of the United States Supreme Court. The first, Eubank v. City of Richmond, 226 U.S. 137, 33 S.Ct. 76, 57 L.Ed. 156, held invalid an ordinance allowing two thirds of the abutting property owners in the block to establish a set-back line, on the ground that such enactment was, in effect, legislative action by the property owners without the benefit of any standard for the exercise of such power, and therefore an improper delegation of a legislative function. Cf. Gorieb v. Fox, 274 U.S. 603, 47 S.Ct. 675, 71 L.Ed. 1228. The second decision, Thomas Cusack Co. v. City of Chicago, 242 U.S. 526, 37 S.Ct. 190, 61 L.Ed. 472, involved a billboard ordinance in language similar to the ordinance before us. It absolutely prohibited billboards in certain districts, but permitted the restriction to be modified with the consent of the persons most affected. The court, at Thomas Cusack Co. v. City of Chicago, 242 U.S. 526, 531, 37 S.Ct. 190, 61 L.Ed. 472, 476, in distinguishing the Eubank case, said:

> "The one ordinance permits two thirds of the lot owners to impose restrictions upon the other property in the block, while the other permits one-half of the lot owners to remove a restriction from the other property owners. This is not a delegation of legislative power, but is, as we have seen a familiar provision affecting the enforcement of laws and ordinances."

While the Cusack decision has been criticized, (University of Illinois 1954 Law Forum, 309, 311–312,) it has been generally followed. And, even though it is impossible to lay down a hard-and-fast rule, we conclude that if an ordinance permits a certain percentage of the property owners to impose or create a restriction upon their neighbors' property by the device of consent provisions, such limitation constitutes an invalid delegation of legislative power, but if the consent provision merely waives or modifies a lawful and reasonable legislative restriction or prohibition, it is within constitutional limitations. (2 Metzenbaum, Law of Zoning, 2d ed., p. 1067; 8 McQuillin, Municipal Corporations, 3rd ed., page 348, sec. 25.151; 1 Yokley, Zoning Law, p. 201, sec. 89; Anno: 21 A.L.R.2d 551 et seq.) It follows that the consent provisions of section 136–6 of the code are not an invalid delegation of legislative power. However, this does not determine that its proscription of homes for the aged is a reasonable exercise of the police power. The cases in which we have upheld prohibitions that might be waived by consent provisions have dealt with uses the location of which have a strong tendency to injure public health or morals or affect the general welfare, and have the general characteristics of a nuisance, such as saloons, Swift v. People ex rel. Ferris Wheel Co., 162 Ill. 534, 44 N.E. 528, junk shops, Smolensky v. City of Chicago, 282 Ill. 131, 118 N.E. 410, garages, People ex rel. Busching v. Ericsson, 263 Ill. 368, 105 N.E. 315, and billboards, Thomas Cusack Co. v. City of Chicago, 267 Ill. 344, 108 N.E. 340, affirmed in 242 U.S. 526, 37 S.Ct. 190, 61 L.Ed. 472.

There is no showing in this record that homes for the aged are offensive to the health, morals and welfare of the community. The property in question is located in the "apartment house" use district which includes "boarding or lodging house, hotels, hospital home for dependents or nursing home." Defendant urges that such homes are properly subject to the police power, citing Father Basil's Lodge, Inc. v. City of Chicago, 393 Ill. 246, 65 N.E.2d 805 but in that case we merely held that a municipality had the power to regulate and license the establishment of homes for the aged for the purpose of protecting the health and safety of the occupants thereof. We refrained from passing upon the validity of the frontage-consent provisions of the ordinance, since we found such provisions to be severable and without application to the appellant.

The case most analogous to the facts here is State of Washington ex rel. Seattle Title Trust Co. v. Roberge, 278 U.S. 116, 49 S.Ct. 50, 73 L.Ed. 210. There an ordinance, similar to the one before us, prohibited erection of homes for the aged in a "first residence district" unless two thirds of the property owners within 400 feet of the proposed site gave their consent in writing. The court held this restriction violative of due process, State of Washington ex rel. Seattle Title Trust Co. v. Roberge, 278 U.S. 116, 121, 49 S.Ct. 50, 73 L.Ed. 210, 213, and stated: "Legislatures may not, under the guise of the police power, impose restrictions that are unnecessary and unreasonable upon the use of private property or the pursuit of useful activities. * * * The facts disclosed by the record make it clear that the exclusion of the new home from the first district is not indispensable to the general zoning plan. And there is no legislative determination that the proposed building and use would be inconsistent with public health, safety, morals or general welfare. The enactment itself plainly implies the contrary. The grant of permission for such building and use, although purporting to be subject to such consents, shows that the legislative body found that the construction and maintenance of the new home was in harmony with the public interest and with the general scope and plan of the zoning ordinance."

In its opinion the court also distinguished Thomas Cusack Co. v. City of Chicago, 242 U.S. 526, 37 S.Ct. 190, 61 L.Ed. 472, relied on by defendant, on the ground that the facts there were sufficient to warrant the conclusion that billboards were liable to endanger the safety and decency of the district involved and held that a home for the aged is clearly distinguishable "from such billboards or other uses which by reason of their nature are liable to be offensive." 278 U.S. 122, 73 L.Ed. 214.

Similar results have been reached in cases involving an "old ladies home," Women's Kansas City St. Andrew Society v. Kansas City, Mo., 58 F.2d 593, a church, State ex rel. Roman Catholic Bishop of Reno v. Hill, 59 Nev. 231, 90 P.2d 217, a retail store, Spies v. Board of Appeals, 337 Ill. 507, 169 N.E. 220, and a school, Concordia Collegiate Institute v. Miller, 301 N.Y. 189, 93 N.E.2d 632, 21 A.L.R.2d 544.

Defendant has not cited, nor have we found, any case upholding the exclusion of homes for the aged from a use district similar to the one in question, either by application of frontage-consent provisions or otherwise. Defendant, however, urges that Shepard v. City of Seattle, 59 Wash. 363, 109 P. 1067, is analogous to the case at bar. We cannot agree. The court there upheld an ordinance which declared insane asylums to be a public nuisance, and provided for their abatement as such, subject to the written consent of any property owner within 200 feet. Such ordinance, which contained a legislative finding that the proposed use is a public nuisance, is clearly inapposite here. State of Washington ex rel. Seattle Title Trust Co. v. Roberge, 278 U.S. 116, 122, 73 L.Ed. 210, 214.

In the case at bar there is neither legislative finding that the proposed use is a public nuisance, or that it is apt to be such when operated in an apartment-house-use district, nor satisfactory evidence tending to show that the maintenance of the home will work an injury, annoyance or inconvenience to any property owner. On the contrary, the general zoning plan of the city of Chicago declares a nursing home to be appropriate in an apartment-house-use district. The record fails to disclose a rational basis for subjecting homes for the aged to the requirement of frontage consents and is without evidence to support a conclusion that the proposed use has any different effect on the public health, welfare, safety and morals than the other permitted uses in the district.

Since we find no basis for the exercise of the police power in prohibiting the home for the aged in the apartment-house-use district, the ordinance as applied to this proposed use is an unconstitutional deprivation of property without due process of law. Spies v. Board of Appeals, 337 Ill. 507, 169 N.E. 220; State of Washington ex rel. Seattle Title Trust Co. v. Roberge, 278 U.S. 116, 49 S.Ct. 50, 73 L.Ed. 210. Accordingly, the judgment of the trial court is affirmed.

Judgment affirmed.

Notes

1. The student note referred to in the principal case, Consent Provisions in Modern Zoning Statutes, 1954 U.Ill.L.F. 309, discusses a number of cases relative to this subject including Eubank v. City of Richmond, 226 U.S. 137, 33 S.Ct. 76, 57 L.Ed. 156 (1912), and Thomas Cusack Co. v. City of Chicago, 242 U.S. 526, 37 S.Ct. 190, 61 L.Ed. 472 (1916), both of which are also discussed in the principal case. Do you think the distinction made in the Valkanet case as between set-back lines and billboards or as between the billboards and old folks' homes is a valid one? The distinction which places billboards in a separate class has been followed in a majority of cases.

2. In Town of Gardiner v. Stanley Orchards, Inc., 105 Misc.2d 460, 432 N.Y.S.2d 335 (1980), the court held invalid a provision in an ordinance which prohibited mobile homes unless all landowners within 500 feet consented in writing, and in Grendel's Den, Inc. v. Goodwin, 495 F.Supp. 761 (D.Mass. 1980), affirmed sub nom. Larkin v. Grendel's Den, 459 U.S. 116, 103 S.Ct. 505, 74 L.Ed.2d 297 (1982), the court struck down a state statute which

provided that no premises within 500 feet of a church or school could receive a liquor license if the church or school filed a written objection. In both cases the courts discussed the problem of delegating legislative authority to private landowners.

3. In Luger v. City of Burnsville, 295 N.W.2d 609 (Minn.1980) the court reversed a local decision to grant the property owner a variance "subject to letters of approval by all abutting property owners." The court indicated that a local zoning agency could not avoid the political implications of its decisions by such a transfer of power to the neighbors. Also, in Lakin v. City of Peoria, 129 Ill.App.3d 651, 84 Ill.Dec. 837, 472 N.E.2d 1233 (1984) the court held that requiring the applicant for a variance to obtain the consent of adjoining and abutting neighbors was an unconstitutional delegation of legislative authority.

B. THE INITIATIVE AND REFERENDUM PROCESS

CITY OF EASTLAKE v. FOREST CITY ENTERPRISES, INC.

Supreme Court of the United States, 1976.
426 U.S. 668, 96 S.Ct. 2358, 49 L.Ed.2d 132.

MR. CHIEF JUSTICE BURGER delivered the opinion of the Court.

The question in this case is whether a city charter provision requiring proposed land use changes to be ratified by 55% of the votes cast violates the due process rights of a landowner who applies for a zoning change.

The City of Eastlake, Ohio, a suburb of Cleveland, has a comprehensive zoning plan codified in a municipal ordinance. Respondent, a real estate developer, acquired an eight-acre parcel of real estate in Eastlake zoned for "light industrial" uses at the time of purchase.

In May 1971, respondent applied to the City Planning Commission for a zoning change to permit construction of a multifamily, high-rise apartment building. The Planning Commission recommended the proposed change to the City Council, which under Eastlake's procedures could either accept or reject the Planning Commission's recommendation. Meanwhile, by popular vote, the voters of Eastlake amended the city charter to require that any changes in land use agreed to by the Council be approved by a 55% vote in a referendum.[24] The City Council

---

24. As adopted by the voters, Art. VIII, § 3, of the Eastlake City Charter provides in pertinent part:

"That any change to the existing land uses or any change whatsoever to any ordinance * * * cannot be approved unless and until it shall have been submitted to the Planning Commission, for approval or disapproval. That in the event the city council should approve any of the preceding changes, or enactments, wheth-er approved or disapproved by the Planning Commission it shall not be approved or passed by the declaration of an emergency, and it shall not be effective, but it shall be mandatory that the same be approved by a 55% favorable vote of all votes cast of the qualified electors of the City of Eastlake at the next regular municipal election, if one shall occur not less than sixty (60) or more than one hundred and twenty (120) days after its passage,

approved the Planning Commission's recommendation for reclassification of respondent's property to permit the proposed project. Respondent then applied to the Planning Commission for "parking and yard" approval for the proposed building. The Commission rejected the application, on the ground that the City Council's rezoning action had not yet been submitted to the voters for ratification.

Respondent then filed an action in state court, seeking a judgment declaring the charter provision invalid as an unconstitutional delegation of legislative power to the people. While the case was pending, the City Council's action was submitted to a referendum, but the proposed zoning change was not approved by the requisite 55% margin. Following the election, the Court of Common Pleas and the Ohio Court of Appeals sustained the charter provision.

The Ohio Supreme Court reversed. 41 Ohio St.2d 187, 324 N.E.2d 740 (1975). Concluding that enactment of zoning and rezoning provisions is a legislative function, the court held that a popular referendum requirement, lacking standards to guide the decision of the voters, permitted the police power to be exercised in a standardless, hence arbitrary and capricious manner. Relying on this Court's decisions in Washington ex rel. Seattle Trust Co. v. Roberge, 278 U.S. 116, 49 S.Ct. 50, 73 L.Ed. 210 (1928), Thomas Cusack Co. v. Chicago, 242 U.S. 526, 37 S.Ct. 190, 61 L.Ed. 472 (1917), and Eubank v. Richmond, 226 U.S. 137, 33 S.Ct. 76, 57 L.Ed. 156 (1912), but distinguishing James v. Valtierra, 402 U.S. 137, 91 S.Ct. 1331, 28 L.Ed.2d 678 (1971), the court concluded that the referendum provision constituted an unlawful delegation of legislative power.

We reverse.

I

The conclusion that Eastlake's procedure violates federal constitutional guarantees rests upon the proposition that a zoning referendum involves a delegation of legislative power. A referendum cannot, however, be characterized as a delegation of power. Under our constitutional assumptions, all power derives from the people, who can delegate it to representative instruments which they create. See, e.g., The Federalist No. 39 (J. Madison). In establishing legislative bodies, the people can reserve to themselves power to deal directly with matters which might otherwise be assigned to the legislature. Hunter v. Erickson, 393 U.S. 385, 392, 89 S.Ct. 557, 561, 21 L.Ed.2d 616 (1969).

The reservation of such power is the basis for the town meeting, a tradition which continues to this day in some States as both a practical and symbolic part of our democratic processes. The referendum, similarly, is a means for direct political participation, allowing the people the final decision, amounting to a veto power, over enactments of represen-

otherwise at a special election falling on   mary election * * *."
the generally established day of the pri-

tative bodies. The practice is designed to "give citizens a voice on questions of public policy." James v. Valtierra, supra, 402 U.S., at 141, 91 S.Ct., at 1333.

In framing a state constitution, the people of Ohio specifically reserved the power of referendum to the people of each municipality within the State.

* * *

To be subject to Ohio's referendum procedure, the question must be one within the scope of legislative power. The Ohio Supreme Court expressly found that the City Council's action in rezoning respondent's eight acres from light industrial to high-density residential use was legislative in nature. Distinguishing between administrative and legislative acts, the court separated the power to zone or rezone, by passage or amendment of a zoning ordinance, from the power to grant relief from unnecessary hardship. The former function was found to be legislative in nature. * * *

II

The Ohio Supreme Court further concluded that the amendment to the city charter constituted a "delegation" of power violative of federal constitutional guarantees because the voters were given no standards to guide their decision. Under Eastlake's procedure, the Ohio Supreme Court reasoned, no mechanism existed, nor indeed could exist, to assure that the voters would act rationally in passing upon a proposed zoning change. This means that "appropriate legislative action [would] be made dependent upon the potentially arbitrary and unreasonable whims of the voting public." 41 Ohio St.2d, at 195, 324 N.E.2d, at 746. The potential for arbitrariness in the process, the court concluded, violated due process.

* * *

In basing its claim on federal due process requirements, respondent also invokes Euclid v. Ambler Realty Co., 272 U.S. 365, 47 S.Ct. 114, 71 L.Ed. 303 (1926), but it does not rely on the direct teaching of that case. Under *Euclid,* a property owner can challenge a zoning restriction if the measure is "clearly arbitrary and unreasonable, having no substantial relation to the public health, safety, morals, or general welfare." Id., at 395, 47 S.Ct., at 121. If the substantive result of the referendum is arbitrary and capricious, bearing no relation to the police power, then the fact that the voters of Eastlake wish it so would not save the restriction. * * *

But no challenge of the sort contemplated in Euclid v. Ambler Realty is before us. The Ohio Supreme Court did not hold, and respondent does not argue, that the present zoning classification under Eastlake's comprehensive ordinance violates the principles established in Euclid v. Ambler Realty. If respondent considers the referendum result itself to be unreasonable, the zoning restriction is open to challenge in state court, where the scope of the state remedy available to respondent would be determined as a matter of state law, as well as under Fourteenth Amendment standards. That being so, nothing more is required by the Constitution.

Nothing in our cases is inconsistent with this conclusion. Two decisions of this Court were relied on by the Ohio Supreme Court in invalidating Eastlake's procedure. The thread common to both decisions is the delegation of legislative power, originally given by the people to a legislative body, and in turn delegated by the legislature to a *narrow segment* of the community, not to the people at large. In Eubank v. Richmond, 226 U.S. 137, 33 S.Ct. 76, 57 L.Ed. 156 (1912), the Court invalidated a city ordinance which conferred the power to establish building setback lines upon the owners of two-thirds of the property abutting any street. Similarly, in Washington ex rel. Seattle Title Trust Co. v. Roberge, 278 U.S. 116, 49 S.Ct. 50, 73 L.Ed. 210 (1928), the Court struck down an ordinance which permitted the establishment of philanthropic homes for the aged in residential areas, but only upon the written consent of the owners of two-thirds of the property within 400 feet of the proposed facility.[25]

Neither *Eubank* nor *Roberge* involved a referendum procedure such as we have in this case; the standardless delegation of power to a limited group of property owners condemned by the Court in *Eubank* and *Roberge* is not to be equated with decisionmaking by the people through the referendum process. The Court of Appeals for the Ninth Circuit put it this way:

"A referendum, however, is far more than an expression of ambiguously founded neighborhood preference. It is the city itself legislating through its voters—an exercise by the voters of their traditional right through direct legislation to override the views of their elected representatives as to what serves the public interest." Southern Alameda Spanish Speaking Organization v. Union City, California, 424 F.2d 291, 294 (1970).

Our decision in James v. Valtierra, upholding California's mandatory referendum requirement, confirms this view. Mr. Justice Black, speaking for the Court in that case, said:

25. The Ohio Supreme Court also considered this Court's decision in Thomas Cusack Co. v. Chicago, 242 U.S. 526, 37 S.Ct. 190, 61 L.Ed. 472 (1917). In contrast to *Eubank* and *Roberge,* the *Cusack* Court *upheld* a neighborhood consent provision which permitted property owners to waive a municipal restriction prohibiting the construction of billboards. This Court in *Cusack* distinguished *Eubank* in the following way:

"[The ordinance in *Eubank*] left the establishment of the building line untouched until the lot owners should act and then * * * gave to it the effect of law. The ordinance in the case at bar absolutely prohibits the erection of any billboards * * * but permits this prohibition to be modified with the consent of the persons who are to be most affected by such modification." 242 U.S., at 531, 37 S.Ct. at 192. Since the property owners could simply waive an otherwise applicable legislative limitation, the Court in *Cusack* determined that the provision did not delegate legislative power at all. Ibid.

This procedure ensures that *all the people* of a community will have a voice in a decision which may lead to large expenditures of local governmental funds for increased public services * * *. 402 U.S., at 143, 91 S.Ct., at 1334 (emphasis added).

Mr. Justice Black went on to say that a referendum procedure, such as the one at issue here, is a classic demonstration of "devotion to democracy * * *." Id., at 141. As a basic instrument of democratic government, the referendum process does not, in itself, violate the Due Process Clause of the Fourteenth Amendment when applied to a rezoning ordinance.[26] Since the rezoning decision in this case was properly reserved to the people of Eastlake under the Ohio Constitution, the Ohio Supreme Court erred in holding invalid, on federal constitutional grounds, the charter amendment permitting the voters to decide whether the zoned use of respondent's property could be altered.

The judgment of the Ohio Supreme Court is reversed, and the case is remanded for further proceedings not inconsistent with this opinion.

Reversed and remanded.

[A dissenting opinion by MR. JUSTICE POWELL is omitted.]

MR. JUSTICE STEVENS, with whom MR. JUSTICE BRENNAN joins, dissenting.

* * *

A zoning code is unlike other legislation affecting the use of property. The deprivation caused by a zoning code is customarily qualified by recognizing the property owner's right to apply for an amendment or variance to accommodate his individual needs. The expectancy that particular changes consistent with the basic zoning plan will be allowed frequently and on their merits is a normal incident of property ownership. When the governing body offers the owner the opportunity to seek such a change—whether that opportunity is denominated a privilege or a right—it is affording protection to the owner's interest in making legitimate use of his property.

The fact that an individual owner (like any other petitioner or plaintiff) may not have a legal right to the relief he seeks does not mean

---

26. The fears expressed in dissent rest on the proposition that the procedure at issue here is "fundamentally unfair" to landowners; this fails to take into account the mechanisms for relief potentially available to property owners whose desired land use changes are rejected by the voters. First, if hardship is occasioned by zoning restrictions, *administrative* relief is potentially available. Indeed, the very purpose of "variances" allowed by zoning officials is to avoid "practical difficulties and unnecessary hardship." 8 E. McQuillan, Municipal Corporations § 25.159, p. 511 (3d ed. 1965). As we noted, *supra,* at 677, remedies remain available under the Ohio Supreme Court's

holding and provide a means to challenge unreasonable or arbitrary action. Euclid v. Ambler Realty Co., 272 U.S. 365, 47 S.Ct. 114, 71 L.Ed. 303 (1926).

The situation presented in this case is not one of a zoning action denigrating the use or depreciating the value of land; instead, it involves an effort to *change* reasonable zoning restriction. No existing rights are being impaired; new use rights are being sought from the City Council. Thus, this case involves an owner's seeking approval of a new use free from the restrictions attached to the land when it was acquired.

that he has no right to fair procedure in the consideration of the merits of his application. The fact that codes regularly provide a procedure for granting individual exceptions or changes, the fact that such changes are granted in individual cases with great frequency, and the fact that the particular code in the record before us contemplates that changes consistent with the basic plan will be allowed, all support my opinion that the opportunity to apply for an amendment is an aspect of property ownership protected by the Due Process Clause of the Fourteenth Amendment.

* * *

Although this Court has decided only a handful of zoning cases, literally thousands of zoning disputes have been resolved by state courts. Those courts have repeatedly identified the obvious difference between the adoption of a comprehensive citywide plan by legislative action and the decision of particular issues involving specific uses of specific parcels. In the former situation there is generally great deference to the judgment of the legislature; in the latter situation state courts have not hesitated to correct manifest injustice.

* * *

Specialists in the practice of zoning law are unhappily familiar with the potential for abuse which exists when inadequate procedural safeguards apply to the dispensation of special grants. The power to deny arbitrarily may give rise to the power to exact intolerable conditions.[27] The insistence on fair procedure in this area of the law falls squarely within the purpose of the Due Process Clause of the Fourteenth Amendment.

* * *

As the Justices of the Ohio Supreme Court recognized, we are concerned with the fairness of a provision for determining the right to make a particular use of a particular parcel of land. In such cases, the state courts have frequently described the capricious character of a decision supported by majority sentiment rather than reference to articulable standards. Moreover, they have limited statutory referendum procedures to apply only to approvals of comprehensive zoning ordinances as opposed to amendments affecting specific parcels. This conclu-

---

27. One expert on zoning matters has made the following comment:

"The freedom from accountability of the municipal governing body may be tolerable in those cases where the legislature is engaged in legislating but it makes no sense where the legislature is dispensing or refusing to dispense special grants. When the local legislature acts to pass general laws applicable generally it is performing its traditional role and it is entitled to be free from those strictures we place upon an agency that is charged with granting or denying special privileges to particular persons. When the municipal legislature crosses over into the role of hearing and passing on individual petitions in adversary proceedings it should be required to meet the same procedural standards we expect from a traditional administrative agency." R. Babcock, The Zoning Game 158 (1966). Compare this comment with the practice of another "zoning man." See United States v. Staszcuk, 517 F.2d 53, 56 (C.A.7 1975).

sion has been supported by characterizing particular amendments as "administrative" and revision of an entire plan as "legislative."

In this case the Ohio Supreme Court characterized the Council's approval of respondent's proposal as "legislative." I think many state courts would have characterized it as "administrative." The courts thus may well differ in their selection of the label to apply to this action, but I find substantial agreement among state tribunals on the proposition that requiring a citywide referendum for approval of a particular proposal like this is manifestly unreasonable. Surely that is my view.

* * *

I have no doubt about the validity of the initiative or the referendum as an appropriate method of deciding questions of community policy. I think it is equally clear that the popular vote is not an acceptable method of adjudicating the rights of individual litigants. The problem presented by this case is unique, because it may involve a three-sided controversy, in which there is at least potential conflict between the rights of the property owner and the rights of his neighbors, and also potential conflict with the public interest in preserving the city's basic zoning plan. If the latter aspect of the controversy were predominant, the referendum would be an acceptable procedure. On the other hand, when the record indicates without contradiction that there is no threat to the general public interest in preserving the city's plan—as it does in this case, since respondent's proposal was approved by both the Planning Commission and the City Council and there has been no allegation that the use of this eight-acre parcel for apartments rather than light industry would adversely affect the community or raise any policy issue of citywide concern—I think the case should be treated as one in which it is essential that the private property owner be given a fair opportunity to have his claim determined on its merits.

As Justice Stern points out in his concurring opinion, it would be absurd to use a referendum to decide whether a gasoline station could be operated on a particular corner in the city of Cleveland. The case before us is not that clear because we are told that there are only 20,000 people in the city of Eastlake. Conceivably, an eight-acre development could be sufficiently dramatic to arouse the legitimate interest of the entire community; it is also conceivable that most of the voters would be indifferent and uninformed about the wisdom of building apartments rather than a warehouse or factory on these eight acres. The record is silent on which of these alternatives is the more probable. Since the ordinance places a manifestly unreasonable obstacle in the path of every property owner seeking any zoning change, since it provides no standards or procedures for exempting particular parcels or claims from the referendum requirement, and since the record contains no justification for the use of the procedure in this case, I am persuaded that we should respect the state judiciary's appraisal of the fundamental fairness of this decisionmaking process in his case.

I therefore conclude that the Ohio Supreme Court correctly held that Art. VIII, § 3, of the Eastlake charter violates the Due Process Clause of the Fourteenth Amendment, and that its judgment should be affirmed.

Notes

1. On remand, the Ohio Supreme Court found no state constitutional issues in the case and dismissed the proceedings. Forest City Enterprises v. City of Eastlake, 48 Ohio St.2d 47, 356 N.E.2d 499 (1976). See Rosenberg, Referendum Zoning: Legal Doctrine and Practice, 53 Cincinnati L.Rev. 381 (1984). In Jurkiewicz v. Butler County Bd. of Elections 85 Ohio App.3d 503, 620 N.E.2d 146 (1993) the court held that a change of zoning to planned unit development was a legislative act and thus subject to referendum.

2. Two state courts, just prior to the Supreme Court decision in the principal case, considered the same issue and, following the lead of the Ohio Supreme Court, disapproved the use of the referendum for zoning amendments. O'Meara v. City of Norwich, 167 Conn. 579, 356 A.2d 906 (1975); Andover Development Corp. v. City of New Smyrna Beach, 328 So.2d 231 (Fla.App.1976).

3. In James v. Valtierra, 402 U.S. 137, 91 S.Ct. 1331, 28 L.Ed.2d 678 (1971), relied on in the principal case, the Court upheld a California constitutional provision which provided that no low-rent public housing project could be developed unless approved by referendum in the community.

4. By holding that the federal constitution does not inhibit mandatory referenda in zoning cases, the Court is essentially leaving the issue to state law and state court determination. A number of state courts have held that a zoning amendment is not subject to referendum because a zoning amendment is quasi-judicial or administrative in nature and is not a legislative act. The leading post–Eastlake decisions are Allison v. Washington County, 24 Or.App. 571, 548 P.2d 188 (1976); Leonard v. City of Bothell, 87 Wash.2d 847, 557 P.2d 1306 (1976). Also see Kelley v. John, 162 Neb. 319, 75 N.W.2d 713 (1956); West v. Portage, 392 Mich. 458, 221 N.W.2d 303 (1974); Forman v. Eagle Thrifty Drugs & Markets, Inc., 89 Nev. 533, 516 P.2d 1234 (1973); and Bird v. Sorenson, 16 Utah 2d 1, 394 P.2d 808 (Utah 1964). Compare Arnel Development Co. v. City of Costa Mesa, 28 Cal.3d 511, 169 Cal.Rptr. 904, 620 P.2d 565 (1980), where the court held that the enactment or amendment of a zoning ordinance is a legislative act even if it affects only a small area or a few landowners and is subject to the initiative and referendum provisions of the state constitution. On remand, the Court of Appeals found the initiative arbitrary and discriminatory as it was directed at one developer. 126 Cal.App.3d 330, 178 Cal.Rptr. 723 (1981).

On the other hand, a number of states find rezonings to be legislative. See State ex rel Hickman v. City Council of Kirksville, 690 S.W.2d 799 (Mo.App.1985); Florida Land Co. v. City of Winter Springs, 427 So.2d 170 (Fla.1983); Wright v. City of Lakewood, 43 Colo.App. 480, 608 P.2d 361 (1979), cf. Margolis v. District Ct., County of Arapahoe, 638 P.2d 297 (Colo.1981); Chynoweth v. City of Hancock, 107 Mich.App. 360, 309 N.W.2d 606 (1981); Jacobs, Visconsi & Jacobs Co. v. City of Burton, 108 Mich.App.

497, 310 N.W.2d 438 (1981); R. G. Moore Building Corp. v. Committee for the Repeal of Ordinance R (C)–88–13, 239 Va. 484. 391 S.E.2d 587 (1990).

5. In 1991 the Urban, State and Local Government Law Section of the American Bar Association approved a recommendation to the ABA House of Delegates regarding the problem reflected in the City of Eastlake situation. Part A of the recommendation was that the ABA recommend: "That all state legislatures adopt legislation prohibiting the use of the initiative/referendum in 'site specific' zoning cases." Part B urged state legislatures in states with initiative and referendum provisions to adopt legislation prohibiting general land-use policy proposals from being submitted for initiative or referendum unless the the proposal conforms with the comprehensive plan or amends such plan. For an explanation of the reasons for the proposals see 14 Urban, State and Local Law Newsletter, No. 3, Spring 1991 (American Bar Association). Apparently, at the House of Delegates meeting, August 12–13, 1991, the section report (No. 111) on site-specific zoning referenda and initiatives was withdrawn by the proponents. ABA, Summary of Action of the House of Delegates, 1991 Annual Meeting. Also see the DeVita case in note 7, infra.

6. A distinction is frequently made between use of the initiative to adopt a zoning ordinance and the use of a referendum to put a zoning ordinance or amendment to the electorate for approval or rejection. Many courts have held that an initiated zoning ordinance is improper because of conflict with the state zoning enabling legislation which usually requires notice and hearing prior to adoption of a zoning ordinance. See Annotation, Adoption of Zoning Ordinance or Amendment Thereto Through Initiative Process, 72 A.L.R.3d 991 (1976). A leading California case to that effect, Hurst v. Burlingame, 207 Cal. 134, 277 P. 308 (1929), was overruled in Associated Home Builders of the Greater Eastbay, Inc. v. City of Livermore, set forth in Section 3 of the previous chapter (in which the court upheld an initiated growth control ordinance). Similarly, in Oregon, a 1974 case holding the initiative process inapplicable to zoning, Tatum v. Clackamas County, 19 Or.App. 770, 529 P.2d 393 (1974), was overruled in Allison v. Washington County, 24 Or.App. 571, 548 P.2d 188 (1976). Ohio has long held that zoning ordinances or amendments are subject to initiative. Drockton v. Board of Elections, 16 Ohio Misc. 211, 240 N.E.2d 896 (1968). Missouri has held that rezoning cannot be accomplished by initiative, State ex rel. Childress v. Anderson, 865 S.W.2d 384 (Mo.App.1993). Also see Queen Creek Land & Cattle Corp. v. Yavapai County Bd. of Supervisors, 108 Ariz. 449, 501 P.2d 391 (1972). Cf. Kaiser Hawaii Kai Development Co. v. City and County of Honolulu, 70 Hawaii 480, 777 P.2d 244 (1989).

7. The California Supreme Court held, in DeVita v. County of Napa, 9 Cal.4th 763, 38 Cal.Rptr.2d 699, 889 P.2d 1019 (1995), that voters could amend a comprehensive plan by use of the initiative and could, in that amended plan, provide that any land use designations enacted by initiative can only be changed during the following 30 years by majority vote of the county electorate. The purpose and effect of the amended plan was to keep land designated as agricultural or open space in those categories for 30 years, unless voters agreed to change.

8. In Smith v. Town of St. Johnsbury, 150 Vt. 351, 554 A.2d 233 (1988) the court upheld a statute which provided that rezonings approved by a

supermajority of selectmen in an urban municipality could be overturned by a simple majority of voters in a referendum, but rezonings in rural municipalities required a supermajority in referendum elections.

9. On the implications of the Eastlake case for resolving the constitutional issues arising from housing discrimination, see Hogue, Eastlake and Arlington Heights: New Hurdles in Regulating Urban Land Use?, 28 Case West.Res.L.Rev. 41 (1977). The Arlington Heights case appears in the next chapter in the section dealing with housing discrimination.

SECTION 8. INTERGOVERNMENTAL ZONING CONFLICTS

BROWN v. KANSAS FORESTRY, FISH AND GAME COMM'N

Court of Appeals of Kansas, 1978.
2 Kan.App.2d 102, 576 P.2d 230.

FOTH, CHIEF JUDGE:

The issue presented in this appeal is whether, in the absence of any clear legislative direction one way or the other, a state agency must conform its land use to local zoning regulations. It is an issue which has not been squarely answered by the courts of this state.

The agency involved here is the state forestry, fish and game commission. In 1975 it purchased two lots in the middle of a twenty-three lot subdivision near Manhattan, Kansas, which had been zoned for single family residences. The commission intended to use the land for a public parking lot, complete with toilet facilities, for the convenience of its patrons using a fishing and recreation facility on the adjacent Big Blue River.

The plaintiffs own and reside on fourteen of the twenty-one other lots in the subdivision. They brought this action to enjoin the commission from its proposed use of its land, alleging that such use would violate both Riley county zoning regulations and certain restrictive covenants governing the subdivision. After a hearing, and upon the parties' stipulation that the commission's proposed use would violate the zoning regulations, the trial court temporarily enjoined the use. It further ordered that the injunction would be made permanent unless the commission promptly perfected an appeal or applied for rezoning. Rather than seek rezoning the commission elected to take this appeal.

In this court, as in the court below, the commission argues that it is exempt from local zoning regulations for two reasons. First it says that as an agency of the state itself, performing a governmental function, it is immune from regulation by a mere political subdivision in the absence of a legislative declaration to the contrary. Second, it relies on its possession of the power of eminent domain as indicating a legislative intent that its use of land not be subject to control by local authorities.

A concise review of the terms in which courts have traditionally analyzed conflicts between governmental agencies over land use regulations is found in City of Temple Terrace v. Hillsborough Ass'n, Etc., 322 So.2d 571 (Fla.App.1975), affirmed on opinion below, Hillsborough Ass'n, Etc., v. City of Temple Terrace, 332 So.2d 610 (Fla.1976). The Florida Court of Appeals there noted:

" * * * In deciding this type of case, the courts have used varying tests. One approach utilized by a number of courts is to rule in favor of the superior sovereign. Thus, where immunity from a local zoning ordinance is claimed by an agency occupying a superior position in the governmental hierarchy, it is presumed that immunity was intended in the absence of express statutory language to the contrary. E.g., Aviation Services, Inc. v. Board of Adjustment, 1956, 20 N.J. 275, 119 A.2d 761. A second test frequently employed is to determine whether the institutional use proposed for the land is 'governmental' or 'proprietary' in nature. If the political unit is found to be performing a governmental function, it is immune from the conflicting zoning ordinance. E.g., City of Scottsdale v. Municipal Court, 1962, 90 Ariz. 393, 368 P.2d 637. On the other hand, when the use is considered proprietary, the zoning ordinance prevails. E.g., Taber v. City of Benton Harbor, 1937, 280 Mich. 522, 274 N.W. 324. Where the power of eminent domain has been granted to the governmental unit seeking immunity from local zoning, some courts have concluded that this conclusively demonstrates the unit's superiority where its proposed use conflicts with zoning regulations. E.g., Mayor of Savannah v. Collins, 1954, 211 Ga. 191, 84 S.E.2d 454. Other cases are controlled by explicit statutory provisions dealing with the question of whether the operation of a particular governmental unit is subject to local zoning. E.g., Mogilner v. Metropolitan Plan Commission, 1957, 236 Ind. 298, 140 N.E.2d 220.

"When the governmental unit which seeks to circumvent a zoning ordinance is an arm of the state, the application of any of the foregoing tests has generally resulted in a judgment permitting the proposed use. This has accounted for statements of hornbook law to the effect that a state agency authorized to carry out a function of the state is not bound by local zoning regulations. 2 Anderson, American Law of Zoning § 9.06 (1968); 8 McQuillin, Municipal Corporations § 25.15 (1965)." (p. 574.)

* * *

There being no "explicit statutory provision" applicable here, the commission relies on the other three common tests: in its first argument it combines the "superior sovereign" with the "governmental-proprietary" test; in its second it asserts the "eminent domain" test. All have been subject to scholarly criticism as too simplistic, avoiding the kind of analysis needed for rational resolution of the complex issues posed by land use problems in a modern, urban-oriented society. See, Comment, "The Applicability of Zoning Ordinances to Governmental Land Use," 39

Tex.L.Rev. 316 (1961); Note, "Municipal Power to Regulate Building Construction and Land Use by Other State Agencies," 49 Minn.L.Rev. 284 (1964); Comment, "The Inapplicability of Municipal Zoning Ordinances to Governmental Land Uses," 19 Syracuse L.Rev. 698 (1968); Note, "Governmental Immunity From Local Zoning Ordinances," 84 Harv.L.Rev. 869 (1971).

Recent judicial pronouncements are increasingly in the same vein. Thus in State v. Kopp, 330 S.W.2d 882 (Mo.1960), the question was whether a city had to comply with county zoning ordinances in building a sewage disposal plant outside the city limits. The court viewed the question as one of legislative intent, "not to be resolved simply by applying the 'governmental vs. proprietary' test." (p. 887.) The court went on to find that the grant of eminent domain power to the city evinced a legislative intent that it not be subject to county zoning. Just two years later, however, the same court, in St. Louis County v. City of Manchester, 360 S.W.2d 638 (Mo.1962), found that a city's possession of eminent domain power did not grant automatic immunity from the county's zoning power in locating its disposal plant. Rather, the court sought to reconcile the two powers and held that the eminent domain statutes "do not purport to give the city the right to select the exact location in St. Louis County, and the public interest is best served in requiring it to be done in accordance with the zoning laws." (p. 642.) Missouri thus has abandoned as controlling both the governmental-proprietary and the eminent domain tests, looking instead to legislative intent and the public interest.

The Missouri court relied in part on City of Richmond v. County Board, 199 Va. 679, 101 S.E.2d 641 (1958), where a statute authorizing the city to establish a jail outside the city limits was held not to authorize a location in violation of the county's zoning regulation. Rather than rely on any automatic test, and specifically rejecting the "governmental-proprietary" test, the Virginia court also sought to reconcile the two enactments and give each full play. * * *

Pennsylvania has employed a similar analysis. In Wilkinsburg–Penn Jt. W.A. v. Churchill B., 417 Pa. 93, 207 A.2d 905 (1965), a municipal water authority sought to build a water tower in violation of borough zoning restrictions. When the borough refused a variance the authority brought suit to enjoin the borough from interfering with the proposed structure. The court viewed the question as one of statutory construction; the fact that the authority was given the power to determine its services "exclusively" did not make it immune from the zoning power of the borough. "The initial service decisions remain with the Authority, but they must be made within the framework of other applicable laws, unless the Legislature directs otherwise." (p. 101, 207 A.2d p. 909.) The two grants of authority—to build and to zone—could be reconciled. Should there be an improper exercise of the zoning power as to the authority's land use, the court said, it could be challenged in the same manner as other zoning decisions.

Later, in City of Pittsburgh v. Commonwealth, 468 Pa. 174, 360 A.2d 607 (1976), the same court decided a zoning dispute between the state's bureau of corrections and a city over the location of a pre-release center for women convicts. It commenced its analysis by observing:

"Resolving the conflict simply by saying that the 'state' agency must prevail because it is exercising the power of the sovereign overlooks that the zoning power the city seeks to exercise is also a sovereign power. Such a resolution ignores the interests the state seeks to promote by legislative grants of powers to municipalities. Interests such as those fostered by comprehensive land use planning statutes are too important not to be recognized as involving exercises of state power." (p. 180, 360 A.2d p. 610.)

The court resolved the question by again reconciling the grants of authority. The city's zoning, which would permit pre-release centers in other parts of the city, was held not to be arbitrary. Finding that "suitable alternatives exist to accommodate both the community's interest in maintaining the integrity of low-density, residential zoning and the needs of the Bureau" (p. 187, 360 A.2d p. 614), the court held that the state agency's use was subject to the city's zoning ordinance.

Pennsylvania's way in this area was indicated by the leading case in the new wave of intergovernmental zoning decisions, Rutgers v. Piluso, 60 N.J. 142, 286 A.2d 697 (1972). There the question was whether Rutgers, the state university, could build student housing units in excess of the maximum number permitted by a township zoning ordinance. * * *

After recognizing the three common tests (asserted by the commission here) and reviewing its own prior decisions, the court formulated its own test:

"The rationale which runs through our cases and which we are convinced should furnish the true test of immunity in the first instance, albeit a somewhat nebulous one, is the legislative intent in this regard with respect to the particular agency or function involved. That intent, rarely specifically expressed, is to be divined from a consideration of many factors, with a value judgment reached on an overall evaluation. All possible factors cannot be abstractly catalogued. The most obvious and common ones include [1] the nature and scope of the instrumentality seeking immunity, [2] the kind of function or land use involved, [3] the extent of the public interest to be served thereby, [4] the effect local land use regulation would have upon the enterprise concerned and [5] the impact upon legitimate local interests. * * * In some instances one factor will be more influential than another or may be so significant as to completely overshadow all others. No one, such as the granting or withholding of the power of eminent domain, is to be thought of as ritualistically required or controlling. And there will undoubtedly be cases, as there have been in the past, where the broader public interest is so important that immunity must be granted even though the local interests may be great. The point is that there is no precise formula or set of criteria which will determine every case mechanically and automatically." (pp. 152–53, 286 A.2d p. 702. Numbers inserted.)

The court went on to find that the state university performed an essential governmental function for the benefit of all the people of the state, and that the legislature would not intend its growth to be subject to restriction or control by local land use regulation. After observing that the same reasoning would generally be true of all state functions and agencies, the court added the following caveat:

> "It is, however, most important to stress that such immunity in any situation is not completely unbridled. Even when it is found to exist, it must not, as this court said in Washington Township v. Village of Ridgewood, supra, 26 N.J. [578] at 584–586, 141 A.2d 308, be exercised in an unreasonable fashion so as to arbitrarily override all important legitimate local interests. This rule must apply to the state and its instrumentalities as well as to lesser governmental entities entitled to immunity. For example, it would be arbitrary, if the state proposed to erect an office building in the crowded business district of a city where provision for off-street parking was required, for the state not to make some reasonable provision in that respect. And, at the very least, even if the proposed action of the immune governmental instrumentality does not reach the unreasonable stage for any sufficient reason, the instrumentality ought to consult with the local authorities and sympathetically listen and give every consideration to local objections, problems and suggestions in order to minimize the conflict as much as possible. * * *" (pp. 153–54, 286 A.2d p. 703.)

The test applied in *Rutgers* has come to be known as the "balancing of interests" test. In Kunimoto v. Kawakami, 56 Haw. 582, 545 P.2d 684 (1976), the state university of Hawaii was permitted to condemn land for a use which would violate Honolulu's zoning ordinances. The finding of immunity was based on the overriding statewide concern for higher education expressed in the Hawaii constitution and the university's enabling legislation. The court, however, expressly reserved the question of whether the "balancing of interest" test expounded in *Rutgers* would apply to other state projects.

In another state university case, City of Newark v. University of Delaware, 304 A.2d 347 (Del.Ch.1973), the court reached the same result—i.e., the university's immunity—by expressly following the *Rutgers* rationale. A legislative intent that the university be immune from local zoning was inferred from the vital role it plays in the state's public mission, although such immunity would not prevail if the university's action were shown to be unreasonable or arbitrary in a given instance.

Minnesota adopted a "balancing of interests" test in Town of Oronoco v. City of Rochester, 293 Minn. 468, 197 N.W.2d 426 (1972), at about the same time as and apparently quite independently of the

Rutgers decision, which was not cited. In that case the city's proposed sanitary landfill would violate a township zoning ordinance. The court recognized that under the "general rule" the city would be immune because it possessed eminent domain powers and would be exercising a governmental function. It declined to follow the general rule, saying:

"* * * However, the trend is to limit such freedom from regulation, a trend which we believe is well within the dictates of the public interest, principally because the pungent realities of urban sprawl and overpopulation have accentuated the need for land-use planning and control that serves as foundation for the exercise of police power in the area of zoning. Consequently, in order to support the principle of enlightened land-use control, we decline to adopt in Minnesota the general rule of governmental exemption from zoning regulation.

"The exigencies of the present matter, however, illustrate the core of wisdom in that general rule and the danger in too readily assuming enlightenment where none in fact may exist in the implementation of a particular local zoning policy. Therefore, we adopt a balancing-of-public-interests test for the resolution of conflicts which arise between the exercise by governmental agencies of their police power and their right of eminent domain. This is preferable to adherence to a less flexible 'general rule' based simply on the form of the opposing parties rather than the substance of their conflict." (p. 471, 197 N.W.2d p. 429. Footnotes omitted.)

Balancing the city's urgent need to replace its present disposal system against the marginal impact on the proposed area for the new facility, the court found immunity should prevail under the facts of that case.

The Florida Court of Appeals, in City of Temple Terrace v. Hillsborough Ass'n, Etc., supra, after describing the traditional tests in the language quoted above, rejected them one by one. It adopted in their stead the *Rutgers* "balancing of interests" test, justifying its decision by saying:

"The old tests were adopted at a time when state government was much smaller. The myriad of agencies now conducting the functions of the state have necessarily resulted in a diminution of centralized control. The decision of a person administering an outlying function of a state agency with respect to the site where this function should be performed is not necessarily any better than the decision of the local authorities on the subject of land use. The adoption of the balancing of interests test will compel governmental agencies to make more responsible land-use decisions by forcing them to consider the feasibility of other sites for the facility as well as alternative methods of making the use of the proposed site less detrimental to the local zoning scheme.

"Our burgeoning population and the rapidly diminishing available land make it all the more important that the use of land be intelligently controlled. This can only be done by a cooperative effort between interested parties who approach their differences with an open mind and with respect for the objectives of the other. When the state legislature is silent on the subject, the governmental unit seeking to use land contrary to applicable zoning regulations should have the burden of proving that the public interests favoring the proposed use outweigh those mitigating against a use not sanctioned by the zoning regulations of the host government." (322 So.2d at 578–79.)

In adopting the Court of Appeals opinion in that case as its own the Florida Supreme Court noted a further policy consideration:

"An ancillary benefit in resolving inter-governmental disputes results from our adoption of the City's view. By requiring state agencies to seek local approval for non-conforming uses, an administrative solution is always present in the form of zoning appeals. In contrast, if the state were not required to seek local approval, the city would always be forced to litigate its disagreement, as happened here. It serves the public's benefit to resolve these controversies in a way which does not mandate the most expensive and least expeditious way of settling intergovernmental disputes." (Hillsborough Ass'n, Etc. v. City of Temple Terrace, supra at 612, n. 3.)

Finally, among foreign cases, we note Matter of Suntide Inn Motel, 563 P.2d 125 (Okl.1977), cited to us by the commission at oral argument. It does not support the kind of automatic immunity urged on us by the commission. The issue in that case was whether the state department of corrections was required to have city planning commission approval for the location of a community treatment center. Three justices in the majority found that such approval was not necessary, basically because the state, as the superior sovereign, was not bound by local regulation in the absence of an express legislative declaration. Four justices dissented, urging that the *Rutgers* balancing test should be adopted, and that under such a test the state agency should seek local approval. * * *

Two justices were in between. They concurred in the finding of immunity, but only because they thought the result of balancing tipped in favor of the state agency. * * *

* * *

In our own analysis we start with the premise that the legislature has not spoken directly on the subject, any more than has our Supreme Court. * * * There is nothing in the statutes which says the commission is subject to local zoning, nor is there anything which grants it immunity.

We therefore regard the question as open in this state. Given the choice, we think this case aptly illustrates why the balancing of interests test better promotes the public's interest than any of the traditional mechanical tests.

* * * The real questions are where the decision-making authority should be lodged, and if a claim of arbitrariness is to be made who should have the presumption of reasonableness and who the burden of proof.

Dealing with the specifics of this case, we are not talking about establishing a public hunting or fishing facility in an area zoned for agriculture. The merits of such a case appear clear, at least on the surface. Here, we are dealing with an all-night parking lot with toilet facilities in the middle of a residential subdivision. The commission anticipates that the recreational facility will be used at a rate of 10,000 man days per year. At least some of those users will employ the proposed parking lot. The merits of this proposal are not nearly so clear. * * *

If we look at the factors suggested as relevant by the Rutgers court we find: (1) The instrumentality seeking immunity is a state agency, and its judgment is entitled to considerable deference. (2) The general function being performed—promoting recreation—is one of recognized public utility but hardly on a level of importance with public education. The specific use, providing parking space near but not in a recreation area, is of a more marginal public interest. (3) While there is public interest in the proposed use in that some people will find this parking lot more convenient than other available lots, the segment of the population affected is relatively small. (4) Regulation, if rezoning is refused, would have the effect of requiring the parking lot to be located in some area other than a residential subdivision. Such a move might make the lot less convenient, but would probably not substantially impair the usefulness of the recreation area. (5) The proposed use would, prima facie at least, have a substantial adverse impact on the surrounding householders and on the existing land use plan.

* * * [T]hese factors were not weighed on the basis of evidence either by a zoning body or by the court below, and our observations are based on a skimpy record and our own general knowledge. The commission simply asserted its immunity, without attempting to justify the reasonableness of its decision, while the court looked no further than the admitted violation of the zoning regulation.

It seems to us that, on balance, the initial decision on reasonableness in this case can be made more expeditiously and with greater discernment by the local zoning authority—here the county. That being so, we infer a legislative intent that the responsibility should be imposed on that body. If rezoning is arbitrarily denied, that decision can be reviewed by the courts at the commission's behest through normal channels. If, on the other hand, we were to hold that the commission's status as superior sovereign immunizes it from the normal zoning processes as it urges, then the burden of going forward with a lawsuit would fall on either the county or the affected landowners. In such a suit they would be required to show arbitrariness on the part of the commission. While it is true the landowners would have much the same burden if dissatisfied by an order *granting* rezoning, that would be because two administrative agencies at different levels have concurred in finding the proposed use appropriate. The zoning route strikes us as cheaper and faster, and it puts the local land use decision in local hands where, in this case, it belongs.

In this case the district court ordered the commission to seek rezoning. It can still do so. In our opinion that is the proper course for it to take, and the trial court properly so ordered.

Affirmed.

Notes

1. Two years after the principal case, the Supreme Court of Kansas was faced with the question of whether the state Board of Regents was required to obtain a building permit and follow city building codes in constructing a new facility at the University of Kansas Medical Center. In State ex rel. Schneider v. City of Kansas City, 228 Kan. 25, 612 P.2d 578 (1980), the court quoted extensively from the principal case, and then, enigmatically, stated: "Whatever may be the merits of such a balancing of interest approach to the use of land by a state agency under city or county zoning laws, we do not feel such a test would be feasible or practical as applied to local building codes and proposed construction by the Board of Regents."[28] Ten years later the Kansas court felt that the balancing test should apply to a state agency charged with the construction of prisons. In Herrmann v. Board of County Comm'rs, 246 Kan. 152, 785 P.2d 1003 (1990) the court held the agency not to be immune from local zoning, but found that the balancing test favored the construction of a correctional facility because a prison is a major project of compelling state interest; moreover, a federal court had ordered a new prison or, if the state failed, court-ordered release of felons.

2. The Temple Terrace case from Florida, relied on by the court in the principal case, dealt with the issue of whether a non-profit corporation performing what would otherwise be a state function in operating a home for the mentally retarded, was immune from a local zoning ordinance. The question of exclusion of group homes from certain zoning districts is treated extensively in the next chapter. See City of Muskegon Heights v. Moseler, 178 Mich.App. 609, 444 N.W.2d 145 (1989), reversed without opinion 433 Mich. 918, 448 N.W.2d 721 (1989).

3. Courts in many states have taken up the question of which test to use in resolving intergovernmental zoning conflicts. Although the superior sovereign and eminent domain tests still appear to prevail, the trend of decisions is clearly in the direction of the balancing of interests approach. See, e.g., City of Ames v. Story County, 392 N.W.2d 145 (Iowa 1986). The issue in this case is becoming very common—whether a city is subject to county regulations in locating a waste disposal facility. See City of Fargo v. Harwood Twp., 256 N.W.2d 694 (N.D.1977); City of Everett v. Snohomish

---

28. A similar case involving local building codes and a state university is Regents of Univ. of California v. City of Santa Monica, 77 Cal.App.3d 130, 143 Cal.Rptr. 276 (1978). Compare Varnado v. Southern University at New Orleans, 621 So.2d 176 (La. App.1993) holding that the university was bound by the local zoning ordinance as to the use of off-campus property.

County, 112 Wash.2d 433, 772 P.2d 992 (1989). But see City of Washington v. Warren County, 899 S.W.2d 863 (Mo.banc 1995) where the court espoused the eminent domain test and held that a city was immune from the county's zoning ordinance in connection with an airport; Macon–Bibb County Hospital Authority v. Madison, 204 Ga.App. 741, 420 S.E.2d 586 (1992), holding that the county hospital was immune from local zoning regulations as regards placement of roof signs on its medical center.

4. Several cases dealing with intergovernmental immunity involve the applicability of local zoning ordinances to construction of correctional facilities by state agencies. This type of public use is almost certain to provoke neighbors and local communities to protest and litigate the question. In Dearden v. City of Detroit, 403 Mich. 257, 269 N.W.2d 139 (1978), the court held that the state department of corrections was immune from local zoning ordinances, and to hold otherwise would thwart state policy to locate correctional facilities in community settings. To the same effect, see City of New Orleans v. State of Louisiana, 364 So.2d 1020 (La.1978); County Commissioners of Bristol v. Conservation Comm'n of Dartmouth, 380 Mass. 706, 405 N.E.2d 637 (1980); Lane v. Zoning Bd. of Adjustment of City of Talladega, 669 So.2d 958 (Ala.Civ.App.1995). With these cases, compare City of Pittsburgh v. Commonwealth of Pennsylvania, 468 Pa. 174, 360 A.2d 607 (1976) and Matter of Suntide Inn Motel, 563 P.2d 125 (Okl.1977) (overruled by Independent School Dist. No. 89 v. City of Oklahoma City, 722 P.2d 1212 (Okl.1986) (adopting balancing test)), both discussed in the principal case.

Also see City of Hattiesburg v. Region XII Comm'n on Mental Health and Retardation, 654 So.2d 516 (Miss.1995); Taylor v. State, Dept. of Rehabilitation and Correction, 43 Ohio App.3d 205, 540 N.E.2d 310 (1988) where the court held the state should make "reasonable efforts" to comply with local land use restrictions in siting correctional facilities, but need not follow local zoning procedures. And in City of Louisville Bd. of Zoning Adjustment v. Gailor, 920 S.W.2d 887 (Ky.App.1996) the court held that a private corporation seeking to construct and operate a correctional facility in downtown Louisville enjoyed the same immunity from local zoning regulations as a public entity. Contra to the Kentucky decision is Freedom Ranch, Inc. v. Board of Adjustment of City of Tulsa, 878 P.2d 380 (Okl.App.1994), cert. denied 513 U.S. 1043, 115 S.Ct. 636, 130 L.Ed.2d 543.

5. What if the intergovernmental dispute involves a "foreign" government? In Town of Groton v. Laird, 353 F.Supp. 344 (D.Conn.1972) the court stated that the Navy was exempt from the local zoning ordinance. In Township of Middletown v. N/E Regional Office, United States Postal Service, 601 F.Supp. 125 (D.N.J.1985) the court held that the Postal Service was not subject to local zoning laws. And, in U.S. Postal Service v. Town of Greenwich, Connecticut, 901 F.Supp. 500 (D.Conn.1995) the court held that the state building code could not be applied to a post office construction project under the Supremacy Clause. Compare Pan American Health Organization v. Montgomery County, 338 Md. 214, 657 A.2d 1163 (1995) where the court held the international health organization was not exempt from the local zoning rules. This problem is discussed in 3 Williams, American Land Planning Law § 81.01 (1986).

6. If the ultimate issue in zoning conflicts between various levels of state government is that of legislative intent, do you think the best solution might be a statute spelling out the proper relationships? Along this line see City and County of Denver v. Board of County Commissioners, 782 P.2d 753 (Colo.1989) discussing the 1974 Land Use Act which allows both state and local government to regulate land uses that might have an impact beyond the immediate scope of the project. The case involved site selection and construction of major water and sewage treatment systems.

In South Carolina, S.C. Code Ann. § 6–7–830 (Supp. 1991) provides: "All agencies, departments and subdivisions of this State that use real property, as owner or tenant, in any county or municipality in this State shall be subject to the zoning ordinance thereof." See City of Charleston v. South Carolina State Ports Authority, 309 S.C. 118, 420 S.E.2d 497 (1992) (ports authority had to obtain architectural approval by city board of architectural review before constructing a building).

7. Of course, a statutory solution might not be viable in heading off conflicts between two cities or two counties. Consider, for example, City of Kirkwood v. City of Sunset Hills, 589 S.W.2d 31 (Mo.App.1979) dealing with the issue of one municipality acquiring a municipal swimming pool in a neighboring town without complying with a zoning ordinance.

8. Another aspect of intergovernmental conflict is the question of regionalism versus local parochialism in land use decision making. If a city wants to put a landfill within its limits, but right up against a fine residential area in an adjacent municipality, what legal principles come into play? Is it a matter of comity?, of legal standing?, or something beyond the scope of land use law? Consider the following materials.

BOROUGH OF CRESSKILL v. BOROUGH OF DUMONT

Supreme Court of New Jersey, 1954.
15 N.J. 238, 104 A.2d 441.

VANDERBILT, C.J. From a decision of the Law Division of the Superior Court setting aside an amendment to its zoning ordinance the defendant Borough of Dumont appealed. We certified the borough's appeal on our own motion while it was pending in the Appellate Division.

The focal point of the action is Block 197 on the tax map of Dumont, which as a result of the challenged amendment to the zoning ordinance would be changed from an A and B residential zone to a D business district. Two separate complaints were filed, the first by three neighboring boroughs of Cresskill, Demarest and Haworth and by several residents of these boroughs as well as by several residents of Dumont. The second complaint was filed by William A. Wendland and Marjorie Wendland, his wife, who are property owners on the block in question.

The first complaint in effect charges that the amendatory ordinance is not in accordance with the comprehensive zoning plans in effect in the boroughs of Cresskill, Demarest, Dumont and Haworth in that it fails to take into consideration the physical, economic, and social conditions prevailing throughout the entire area of those four municipalities and the use to which the land in that region can and may be put most advantageously, and that regard was given solely to the political boundaries of the Borough of Dumont in utter disregard of the contiguous residential areas of the plaintiff boroughs. Lastly, the complaint charges that the amendment is invalid in that it represents "spot zoning" for the benefit of an individual property owner and thus constitutes a variance from the previously existing ordinance obtained without recourse to the Board of Adjustment of the Borough of Dumont, as prescribed by statute. The complaint filed by the Wendlands asserts that the amendatory ordinance is not in accordance with the comprehensive plan for zoning in Dumont, that the amendment will destroy the present character of the plaintiffs' lands, that it constitutes "spot zoning" and is an invalid attempt to grant a variance.

The defendant filed a separate answer to each complaint, claiming in each instance that the ordinance was a valid exercise of the zoning power. As to the first complaint, filed by the three boroughs and the individual plaintiffs, it claimed that neither the boroughs nor such individuals as were not residents of Dumont were proper parties, and that those plaintiffs who were residents of Dumont had no standing because their property rights were not affected. As to the complaint of the Wendlands, the defendant claimed that the action was not brought in good faith and that the complaint failed to state a claim on which relief could be granted. The cases were consolidated for trial.

* * *

The amendment to the zoning ordinance to change Block 197 to a "D Business District" had been under consideration by the Borough Council and the Planning Board of Dumont for three or four years, according to the mayor. On November 26, 1952, it was submitted to the planning board, which unanimously approved it. On December 9, 1952, it was adopted by a unanimous vote of the governing body of the borough at a meeting at which no objection was made by any residents of the borough, although representatives of the other three boroughs strenuously opposed it. Section 4 of the basic zoning ordinance of the borough adopted in 1942 provided that "D Business District is primarily intended for the conduct of commerce, general business and the sale of commodities and all such uses shall be permitted." The section then goes on to prohibit manufacturing, trucking, livery stables, slaughter houses and the like. It would appear, however, that such business activities as department and retail stores, theaters, motels, restaurants, garages and bowling alleys are permitted.

* * *

The trial judge held that the ordinance was invalid since it did not promote the public welfare, was not in accordance with any comprehensive plan, and did not promote any of the statutory purposes relating to zoning.

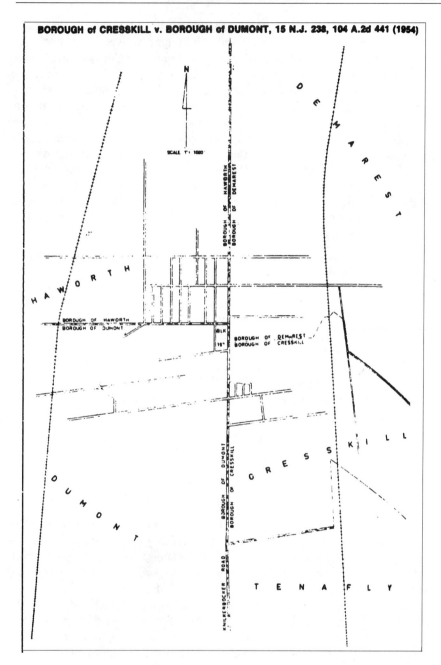

BOROUGH of CRESSKILL v. BOROUGH of DUMONT, 15 N.J. 238, 104 A.2d 441 (1954)

I.

The appellant first argues that the plaintiffs were not proper parties to the action and that therefore its motion to dismiss the complaint should have been granted. In this regard the appellant directs its attack primarily toward the three municipal plaintiffs and the individual plaintiffs who reside in the other boroughs. It is unnecessary, however, for us to decide this issue, because the Wendlands own property on Block 197, the very area affected by the amendatory ordinance. Clearly they have sufficient interest to bring this action. Speakman v. Mayor and Council of Borough of North Plainfield, 8 N.J. 250, 258, 84 A.2d 715 (1951), Menges v. Township of Bernards, 4 N.J. 556, 559, 73 A.2d 540 (1950). The fact that they did not testify is not significant, since they were parties plaintiff and all evidence produced on the plaintiffs' case inured to their benefit. It is therefore immaterial whether the municipal and remaining individual plaintiffs have adequate status to challenge the ordinance and the question is therefore reserved.

II.

The appellant also contends that the trial court erred in considering the property in adjoining municipalities, claiming that only property lying within the borough itself is to be taken into consideration by the borough authorities in their zoning. * * *

* * * Such a view might prevail where there are large undeveloped areas at the borders of two contiguous towns, but it cannot be tolerated where, as here, the area is built up and one cannot tell when one is passing from one borough to another. Knickerbocker Road and Massachusetts Avenue are not Chinese walls separating Dumont from the adjoining boroughs. At the very least Dumont owes a duty to hear any residents and taxpayers of adjoining municipalities who may be adversely affected by proposed zoning changes and to give as much consideration to their rights as they would to those of residents and taxpayers of Dumont. To do less would be to make a fetish out of invisible municipal boundary lines and a mockery of the principles of zoning. There is no merit to the defendant's contention. * * *

That comprehensive planning requires municipal officials to give consideration to adjoining and nearby properties in other municipalities is recognized not only by the decisions of our courts but also by various legislative enactments. As long ago as 1930, in defining the purposes of municipal planning the Legislature provided that municipal planning boards should give attention to "neighboring territory" and the "environs" of the municipality. * * * In the enactment of the new Municipal Planning Act, L.1953, c. 433, the foregoing section was repealed but its objectives as to the consideration of territory outside of the municipal boundaries was continued and enlarged. * * * Although the exercise of zoning powers is a constitutional responsibility of the municipalities, Article IV, Sec. VI, par. 2, supra, it is to be noted that the Legislature has also provided for both county planning boards, R.S. 40:27–1, and regional planning boards, R.S. 40:27–9, thus indicating its intention to extend planning beyond municipal lines.

III.

* * *

The Borough of Dumont, as we have seen, is predominantly a residential community composed largely of one-family dwellings, as are the contiguous boroughs. The area surrounding Block 197 is, of course, residential and has been so zoned for years. The mayor testified that 200 to 220 one-family dwellings are to be constructed on the property adjoining Block 197 on the west. There is not the slightest indication that the character of the neighborhood is changing. * * *

Here the very purpose of the ordinance was to permit the construction of a shopping center on this one block. The council has in effect granted the owner a zoning variance, clearly an action beyond its powers. It follows therefore that the ordinance must be set aside as "spot zoning" in violation of the comprehensive plan of the borough and contrary to the provisions of the zoning law.

The judgment below is affirmed. * * *

Notes

1. Can a local unit rule its provincial world and ignore the effects of its zoning upon "outsiders"? If not, how can these outside interests be heard and be protected? Note that these may be interests of immediate neighbors as in the Cresskill case, or wider metropolitan regional interests as in State ex rel. Anshe Chesed Congregation v. Bruggemeier, 97 Ohio App. 67, 115 N.E.2d 65 (1953), where a satellite village of 1,800 was required to take a metropolitan-wide synagogue with 5,000 members. Or there may be state-wide interest as in the case of zoning affecting the state highways or the state's public waters. Or the interests might be national, as where local zoning has impact on national defense activities, national parks or forests or national transportation routes. (See, e.g., MacDonald v. Board of County Comm'rs for Prince George's County, 238 Md. 549, 210 A.2d 325 (1965) which involved the national interest in protecting the view from Mt. Vernon from a proposed high-rise apartment building across the river in Maryland.)[29] Will the courts always act to protect such interest? If so, on what substantive legal basis? The statutory requirement of a "comprehensive plan"? Due process and its prolific offspring, "general welfare"? Equal protection? And what about party-in-interest rules on the procedural side? Are these such that interested outside groups, local units, the state or the federal government can intervene in local zoning proceedings and insist on judicial review? Would an administrative appeals procedure to a state agency or to a joint local-state board be a better solution?

2. In the Cresskill case neighbors complained of an affirmative act, an amendment changing existing zoning. Suppose a local unit is asked to change its zoning. Suppose the change would be of direct benefit to outsiders, but the requested change is refused. Do the outsiders have any standing to complain?

In Wrigley Properties, Inc. v. City of Ladue, 369 S.W.2d 397 (Mo.1963), a city which lay in the path of better residential development and represent-

---

29. Also see United States v. Board of Supervisors, 611 F.2d 1367 (4th Cir.1979), holding that the United States had standing to seek an injunction to restrain construction of high-rise office buildings across the Potomac from the capitol. The interest of the government was its proprietary interest in the capitol and protecting the symmetry of its skyline and the setting of its monuments. The gravamen of the complaint was the ultra vires action of defendant in granting a special use permit.

ing about the finest residential development in the entire St. Louis metropolitan area refused to change its residential zoning so as to authorize a 10–acre shopping center. The question, said the court, was fairly debatable. One of the reasons cited by the court as possibly sustaining the council's refusal to rezone was "that the proposed use as a shopping center appears to be *more for the benefit of other cities and towns than for the benefit of Ladue.*" (Emphasis supplied.) Compare this with Duffcon Concrete Products v. Cresskill, 1 N.J. 509, 64 A.2d 347, 9 A.L.R.2d 678 (1949), where the New Jersey court concluded that a densely settled suburb could properly exclude industry if it has some other place to go in the general area, but nevertheless, where the following general standard was announced:

> What may be the most appropriate use of any particular property depends not only on all the conditions, physical, economic and social, prevailing within the municipality and its needs, present and reasonably prospective, but also on the nature of the entire region in which the municipality is located and the use to which the land in that region has been or may be put most advantageously. The effective development of a region should not and cannot be made to depend upon the adventitious location of municipal boundaries, often prescribed decades or even centuries ago and based in many instances on considerations of geography, of commerce, or of politics that are no longer significant with respect to zoning.

See Haar, Regionalism and Realism in Land Use Planning, 105 U.Pa. L.Rev. 5 (1957), and Note, Zoning Against the Public Welfare: Judicial Limitations on Municipal Parochialism, 71 Yale L.J. 720 (1962).

3. On this question of regional considerations, what about the following: A town in the state of New York adopted a law which rezoned part of the town, including an area contiguous to the New Jersey border, from a residential district of one-acre plots to an "office park" district. At the time the law was passed, the land which was rezoned was "mostly wooded" and sloped up from a river. The new zoning provision made possible the construction of a large office-research complex. A municipal corporation of the State of New Jersey brought an action in federal court complaining with respect to the action taken by the adjoining New York community. The New Jersey community argued that it would be injured by reduction in revenues which would result from depreciation in the value of its property and by the need for additional expenditures "to provide for adequate traffic and other related expenses." It sought damages in excess of $10,000 and declaratory relief. The New York town moved for summary judgment alleging that the complaint failed to state a cause of action. Aside from the merits of the claim, does the New Jersey township have standing to sue? See Township of River Vale v. Town of Orangetown, 403 F.2d 684 (2d Cir.1968). Compare Orange Fibre Mills, Inc. v. City of Middletown, 94 Misc.2d 233, 404 N.Y.S.2d 296 (1978). Also see Village of Barrington Hills v. Village of Hoffman Estates, 81 Ill.2d 392, 43 Ill.Dec. 37, 410 N.E.2d 37 (1980), certiorari denied, 449 U.S. 1126, 101 S.Ct. 943, 67 L.Ed.2d 112 (1981), where the court held that one municipality had standing to challenge another's zoning decision to allow construction of an open-air music theatre near the residential areas in the plaintiff village, and City of Thornton v. Board of County Comm'rs, 42 Colo.App. 102, 595 P.2d 264 (1979), where the city was allowed standing to

challenge the county rezoning of property adjacent to city-owned land from agricultural to planned unit development. In Town of Mesilla v. City of Las Cruces, 120 N.M. 69, 898 P.2d 121 (1995) the court held that a town was a "person aggrieved" and had standing to challenge rezoning of the neighboring city that allegedly resulted in aesthetic and economic injury to the plaintiff town.

4. A common problem in recent years, involves the shopping center developer who secures relatively inexpensive undeveloped land near a city which is usually subject to less onerous county regulation and the developer proposes a "regional" shopping center which may have a harmful economic impact on city plans to either preserve or redevelop a viable downtown retail district or to establish a regional shopping center at a different location. Does the city have any basis for blocking the proposed development? Consider the following cases:

a. Save a Valuable Environment (SAVE) v. City of Bothell, 89 Wash.2d 862, 576 P.2d 401 (1978): The city rezoned a 141 acre farm to permit construction of a major regional shopping center. SAVE, a nonprofit environmental protection organization, challenged the rezoning as having a detrimental effect on both the environment and the economy of the area. After holding that SAVE had standing, the court stated:

> * * * Bothell may not act in disregard of the effects outside its boundaries. Where the potential exists that a zoning action will cause a serious environmental effect outside jurisdictional borders, the zoning body must serve the welfare of the entire affected community. If it does not do so it acts in an arbitrary and capricious manner. * * *
>
> The action was arbitrary and capricious [in this case] in that it failed to serve the welfare of the community as a whole. Specifically, adverse environmental effects and potentially severe financial burdens on the affected community have been completely disregarded. * * *
>
> We do not hold that a city proposing a rezone which will affect neighboring jurisdictions must engage in inter-jurisdictional planning. It is clear, however, that such coordinated planning is desirable and might have avoided the result in this case.

b. Carmel Estates, Inc. v. Land Conservation and Development Commission, 51 Or.App. 435, 625 P.2d 1367 (1981). The Board of County Commissioners approved rezoning 26.5 acres of agricultural land for the construction of a shopping center halfway between the cities of Sandy and Gresham. The city of Sandy and the Metropolitan Service District challenged the proposed rezoning as inconsistent with several goals of the existing comprehensive plan, most particularly the goal prohibiting conversion of agricultural land to urban uses without a showing of necessity. In the report of the hearing officer (which was adopted by the Commission), after stating that to allow this development would frustrate the very purpose of urban growth boundaries and render the plan useless in controlling urban sprawl, the following comment appears:

> According to the testimony, this development would seriously frustrate urban-level utilization of lands in Sandy. Mr. Roger Jordan, city manager, testified that '* * * a development of this magnitude only three or

four miles away from our incorporated boundaries, when we have made all the investments to accommodate growth within our boundaries, would have a drastic effect.' * * * Mr. Jack Hammond, the city attorney stated that a consultant hired by the city found that [the proposed] shopping center would reduce retail sales in Sandy by 17.7 percent * * * In response to this undisputed evidence, the Board of County Commissioners found:

"The City of Sandy has presented argument that it will suffer economic injury because of increased competition to its existing and planned commercial enterprises. The Board has weighed the detriment to the city against the public benefit of the proposed uses and finds that the proposed uses outweigh the detriment to the City of Sandy." Findings, p. 6.

This finding ignores applicable law. Proof that rural development will injure a city is proof of a Goal 14 violation. Cities and counties are not in competition for urban developments. Cities are the housing, employment, shopping, and service centers and providers. * * * The whole point of Goal 14 is that rural lands are not available to satisfy the state's housing, shopping, nonresource employment, and other non-farm and non-forest related needs.

5. Sometimes the shopping center dispute involves two cities which are vying for the large shopping center so as to increase the tax base. This problem is typified by the case of City of Rohnert Park v. Harris, 601 F.2d 1040 (9th Cir.1979), cert. denied sub nom. City of Rohnert Park v. Landrieu, 445 U.S. 961, 100 S.Ct. 1647, 64 L.Ed.2d 236 (1980). Here two towns, seven miles apart, each wanted to develop a regional shopping center. When one of the towns lined up a developer and anchor tenants, the other town sued alleging violation of antitrust laws, HUD regulations (selling urban renewal land at under market value to the developer) and the federal administrative procedure act. The court found no cause of action. In the next section of this chapter the antitrust problems of cities in the context of zoning and development decisions are examined in more detail. As you will see, the shopping center problem dominates this area of law.

A Note on Federal Preemption

Normally, we do not think of the federal government setting out to override local land use regulations, and indeed that issue is rarely discussed in the formulation of federal law or regulations. However, in recent years more and more instances appear of conflict—or apparent conflict—between local land use ordinances and federal statutes or regulations. Cataloging all such conflicts is impossible. Some of the recent examples will suffice to alert the land use attorney to the problem.

1. The Federal Railway Safety Act has been held to preempt all local railroad safety legislation (except state law in an area where the Secretary of Transportation has not issued a regulation or order, and stricter state law is necessary). CSX Transportation, Inc. v. City of Plymouth, 86 F.3d 626 (6th Cir.1996). In this case the court held that a local ordinance prohibiting trains from obstructing streets for more than five minutes was preempted by the federal act. The reasoning was that compliance with the local ordinance

would require railroads to schedule shorter, more frequent trains, with a concomitant effect on train traffic accident rates. Many communities where railroads still operate have ordinances like the one held preempted.

2. In Payless Shoesource, Inc. v. Town of Penfield, New York, 934 F.Supp. 540 (W.D.N.Y.1996), the court considered the application of a town sign ordinance that required all commercial signs in a particular area to be either yellow, red, or white. The owner of a retail shoe store claimed that the sign ordinance conflicted with a federally registered trademark. The trademarked sign was yellow with two orange-colored "O"s. The court held that the sign ordinance was not preempted by the federal Lanham Act provision prohibiting a state or one of its subdivisions from requiring "alteration" of a federally registered mark.

3. Local regulation of television satellite dishes and antennas was specifically preempted by FCC regulation 47 C.F.R. § 25.104 et seq. This specific preemption came about as a result of widespread aesthetic concerns, particularly in suburban communities, when satellite receiving dishes became popular in the 1970's and thereafter. See Loschiavo v. City of Dearborn, 33 F.3d 548 (6th Cir.1994), holding that the FCC regulation precluding enforcement of zoning restrictions regulating satellite dishes created a private right of action under § 1983. In 1995 Congress undertook an important revision of the Communications Act of 1934, resulting in the Telecommunications Act of 1996. One section of the 1996 act has generated much discussion of local zoning and the siting of wireless communication towers (mostly for cellular telephone service providers) Section 704 (a) of the act provides that "nothing in this Act shall limit or affect the authority of a State or local government instrumentality thereof over decisions regarding the placement, construction, and modification of personal wireless service facilities." The section then goes on to provide several paragraphs of limitations on local powers, including prohibition of discrimination among providers of wireless services, requirements of prompt action in handling siting requests, and restriction on local regulations based on allegedly harmful effects of radio frequency emissions. See the website, http://www.fcc.gov/wtb/tower.html.

Some recent cases have begun to address the rights of telecommunications providers in local zoning disputes and zoning moratoria. A number of these cases and analysis of the 1996 act can be found in Robert A. Heverly, Dealing with Towers, Antennas, and Satellite Dishes, Land Use Law, Nov. 1996, p. 3. In particular, see Bell Atlantic Mobile Systems, Inc. v. Zoning Hearing Bd. of Twp. of O'Hara, ___ Pa.Cmwlth. ___, 676 A.2d 1255 (1996); Sprint Spectrum v. City of Medina, 924 F.Supp. 1036 (W.D.Wa.1996). In Woodmoor Improvement Ass'n v. Brenner, 919 P.2d 928 (Colo.App.1996), a homeowner presented a proposal to install a satellite dish to the architectural committee of the homeowners' association which approved his plan after specifying some fencing and screening of the dish. Subsequently the association sued to enforce the restrictive covenant prohibiting outside antennas or aerials. The court held for the homeowner; the case turned on the issue of the authority of the architectural committee to approve the proposal and the doctrine of detrimental reliance.

4.   The federal Fair Housing Amendments Act, 42 U.S.C.A. § 3604 (f) (1) makes it unlawful to discriminate in the sale or rental, or to otherwise make unavailable or deny, a dwelling to any buyer or renter because of a handicap. The U.S. Court of Appeals for the Sixth Circuit held, in Larkin v. State of Michigan Dept. of Social Services, 89 F.3d 285 (6th Cir.1996), that the federal act preempted the Michigan zoning enabling act provision that prohibited the location of group homes within a radius of 1500 feet from an existing group home, a provision designed to preclude excessive concentration of group homes in one location. More information on this problem is presented in Chapter VIII, in the section on group homes.

5.   The National Manufactured Housing and Safety Standards Act, 42 U.S.C.A. §§ 5401–5426 has been held to preempt city ordinances imposing greater safety requirements for mobile or manufactured homes. Scurlock v. City of Lynn Haven, Florida, 858 F.2d 1521 (11th Cir.1988).

6.   The Stewart B. McKinney Homeless Assistance Act, 42 U.S.C.A. § 11301 et seq. requires federal agencies to make surplus and underutilized federal property available to lease to organizations wishing to to provide housing for homeless persons. This act was held to preempt local zoning ordinances in United States v. Village of New Hempstead, New York, 832 F.Supp. 76 (S.D.N.Y.1993).

7.   CERCLA (Comprehensive Environmental Response, Compensation and Liability Act) has been held to preempt conflicting state or local regulation ("conflict preemption"). See, e.g., United States v. Denver, 100 F.3d 1509 (10th Cir.1996). This case pitted a local zoning restriction on maintenance of hazardous waste in industrial zones against an EPA order requiring the owner of a site in the city to do on-site solidification of soils contaminated with radioactive waste.

8.   In Condor Corp. v. City of St. Paul, 912 F.2d 215 (8th Cir.1990) the plaintiff argued that the denial of a conditional permit to operate a heliport in the city was preempted by Federal Aviation Administration regulations on siting of heliports. The court found the argument to be "specious."

9.   Sometimes the federal government acts to head off a preemption issue. For example, in PL 104–59 Congress amended the federal highway laws to add a provision that the federal designation of a scenic byway does not preempt state criteria for the designation of scenic byways under state law.

SECTION 9.   THE APPLICATION OF ANTITRUST LAW TO ZONING AND DEVELOPMENT DECISIONS

Zoning and development restrictions frequently have an anti-competitive impact. A municipal decision to allow a shopping center or an apartment complex can inhibit similar development on other property. Such decisions, of course, are the essence of the police power. Recall the Bartram case where the court discussed the city's decision to provide for shopping facilities away from the downtown area. The impact of such a decision can lead to economic decline of the downtown. Many downtowns in this country exhibit the effects of malling. Conversely, if a city decides to rehabilitate its downtown by providing favorable zoning advantages and financial assistance for a new hotel/convention center, outlying hotels and motels may suffer. The policy behind the antitrust laws is to favor competition and disfavor monopoly. Can landowners or competitors challenge zoning decisions under the antitrust laws?

JUSTER ASSOCIATES v. CITY OF RUTLAND, VERMONT

United States Court of Appeals, Second Circuit, 1990.
901 F.2d 266.

WINTER, CIRCUIT JUDGE:

This antitrust action pits developers who are seeking permits necessary to begin construction of a new shopping mall against the owners of an existing mall who possess permits allowing them to double its size. The novel aspect of this not-unusual scenario is that the existing mall is accusing its as-yet non-existent competitor of monopolistic practices.

Two New York partnerships that wish to expand their shopping mall in Rutland, Vermont have sued the City of Rutland and several prospective developers of a new shopping center in the Rutland area, claiming that the City and the developers have conspired to restrain trade and to monopolize the market of leasing space in violation of federal antitrust laws, see 15 U.S.C.A. §§ 1, 2, 15, 26 (1988); that they have tortiously interfered with the plaintiffs' business relationships; and that they have deprived plaintiffs of property interests without due process in violation of 42 U.S.C.A. § 1983 (1982) ("Section 1983"). Chief Judge Billings granted judgment on the pleadings and dismissed the complaint. Because the complaint fails to allege antitrust injuries and because the defendants are immune from antitrust liability under the *Noerr–Pennington* doctrine, we affirm.

BACKGROUND

Plaintiff Juster Associates, a New York limited partnership, owns the Rutland Mall in the Town of Rutland, Vermont ("Town of Rutland" or "the Town"). Plaintiff Juster Development Company ("JDC"), a New York general partnership, proposes to develop an extension of the Rutland Mall with Juster Associates on JDC's adjoining land. Juster Associates and JDC (collectively "Juster") possess the licenses and permits necessary to expand the mall to double its current size.

Defendant City of Rutland ("City of Rutland" or "the City") is a municipal corporation. Defendant Finard–Zamias Associates ("FZA") is a developer that has applied for a land-use permit under Vermont law, Vt.Stat.Ann. tit. 10, §§ 6001–6092 (1984) ("Act 250"), regarding its proposed development of a regional shopping center in the Town of Rutland adjacent to the City of Rutland. Defendants William Finard, Damian Zamias, and Steven Mosites are partners in FZA (collectively "the Developers").

Act 250 requires, inter alia, that shopping center developers obtain approval for their projects from the state-appointed District Environmental Commission ("Commission"). Vt.Stat.Ann. tit. 10, § 6086 (1984 & Supp.1989). That the Commission takes into account the views of major municipalities in granting or denying approval to projects is not seriously disputed by the parties. There is also no question that the City of Rutland has played an active role with regard to the Juster and FZA developments in an effort to protect what it perceives as its interests. In fact, the City of Rutland was granted party status before the Commission in proceedings concerning both Juster's and FZA's applications.

On September 27, 1988, the City of Rutland and the Developers, acting through their Vermont corporation Finard–Zamias Rutland Development Company ("FZR"), entered into an agreement regarding the Developers' proposed new regional shopping center. The agreement noted the Developers' need for the cooperation and assistance of the City to satisfy various permit requirements of Act 250 and provided for the payment of direct and indirect impact fees by FZR to the City. In particular, FZR agreed to offset any adverse impact on the City's municipal services or tax base through one of three means: (1) payment of impact fees, (2) investment of at least $10 million in non-residential real estate in the City, or (3) adoption, with legislative approval, of a gross-receipts user fee. FZR also agreed to provide other long-term support to the Rutland community, including housing assistance, public transportation, regional promotional activities, and cultural and social activities. In return, FZR gained access to the City's water supply and sewage facilities at most-favored customer rates, obtained assurances that the City would improve transportation routes and traffic control around the development, and won the active support of the City in FZA's Act 250 permit proceedings. Finally, FZR agreed to refrain either from actively recruiting tenants for the regional shopping center from the City's central business district or from actively promoting relocation of existing businesses from within the City limits.

Meanwhile, the City had unsuccessfully opposed Juster in Act 250 proceedings regarding Juster's proposed expansion of the Rutland Mall. Juster, which is thus now armed with the necessary permits to expand its mall, filed this complaint on January 23, 1989. On April 17, 1989, the City filed a motion for judgment on the pleadings under Fed.R.Civ.P. 12(c), and the other defendants filed a motion for dismissal under Fed.R.Civ.P. 12(b)(6). The district court granted both motions. Juster appeals.

DISCUSSION

We affirm the judgment for two reasons. First, with regard to the claims under Sections 1 and 2 of the Sherman Act, the complaint's allegations that Juster has suffered damage because the City of Rutland has subsidized or otherwise aided the Developers in their attempt to build their shopping center do not constitute an antitrust injury. Second, assuming *arguendo* that the agreement between the City and the Developers restricts competition, they are immune from liability under the antitrust laws.

* * *

We turn first to Juster's claims under Sections 1 and 2 of the Sherman Act, 15 U.S.C.A. §§ 1, 2 (1988). To prevail on such claims, Juster must assert "injury of the type the antitrust laws were intended to prevent and that flows from that which makes defendants' acts unlawful." *Brunswick Corp. v. Pueblo Bowl–O–Mat, Inc.,* 429 U.S. 477, 489, 97 S.Ct. 690, 697, 50 L.Ed.2d 701 (1977). Juster has not alleged such an injury.

As we stated in *R.C. Bigelow, Inc. v. Unilever N.V.,* 867 F.2d 102, 109 (2d Cir.), *cert. denied,* 493 U.S. 815, 110 S.Ct. 64, 107 L.Ed.2d 31 (1989), the mere fact of increased competition and reduced profits resulting from an agreement between other parties does not constitute an antitrust injury to a plaintiff. *See also Cargill, Inc. v. Monfort of Colorado, Inc.,* 479 U.S. 104, 116, 107 S.Ct. 484, 498, 93 L.Ed.2d 427 (1986). Juster may thus well be "in a worse position than [it] would have been" had the challenged agreement not been executed, *Brunswick,* 429 U.S. at 486, 97 S.Ct. at 696, but that fact does not by itself establish an antitrust injury. To hold otherwise would be to "divorce[ ] antitrust recovery from the purposes of the antitrust laws," *id.* at 487, 97 S.Ct. at 697, which were "enacted for 'the protection of *competition,* not *competitors,*'" *id.* at 488, 97 S.Ct. at 697 (quoting *Brown Shoe Co. v. United States,* 370 U.S. 294, 320, 82 S.Ct. 1502, 1521, 8 L.Ed.2d 510 (1962) (emphasis in original)).

We have applied these principles to a claim similar to Juster's and have found no antitrust injury. In *Eastway Constr. Corp. v. City of New York,* 762 F.2d 243 (2d Cir.1985), *cert. denied,* 484 U.S. 918, 108 S.Ct. 269, 98 L.Ed.2d 226 (1987), we upheld against an antitrust challenge an agreement between New York City and a private consortium of banks that denied the plaintiff construction company access to low-cost mortgage lending. Stating that the plaintiff had failed even to allege, much less to show, any anticompetitive effects on consumers from its exclusion from the lending market by contract between New York and the consortium, we affirmed the district court's grant of summary judgment to the defendants. *See id.* at 251.

The agreement in this case presents even less of an arguable antitrust injury than did the agreement in *Eastway.* Here, the agreement between the City and the Developers provided for payment of impact fees by the Developers to the City and support by the Developers for various public projects in the City. This portion of the agreement raises the Developers' costs and in no way injures competition. In fact, it doesn't even injure Juster. In exchange, the Developers gained access, at most-favored customer rates, to the water and sewage facilities of the City, as well as a promise of improvements in transportation routes to the regional shopping center. Although access to these municipal facilities and the promise of improvements no doubt aid the Developers, they do so by making their project more attractive to consumers than it would otherwise be. This is not an injury to competition, no matter how injurious it may be to Juster as a competitor.

Finally, the City pledged its support for the Developers in the Act 250 permit proceedings. This support is no more than part of a not-unusual bargain struck between a municipality and a developer for the purpose of controlled growth of commercial real estate. The Developers have no market share whatsoever at present, and the alternative to negotiating with the City is to attempt to obtain a permit without the City's support. Without that support, of course, they might fail, a result beneficial to Juster as a competitor but hardly in the interests of consumers. The agreement attacked by Juster is thus a vehicle by which competitors can challenge existing firms. Were courts to strike down such agreements, potential new entrants to a market would find entry more difficult, and consumers would suffer. Juster's claim is thus designed to enhance barriers to entry of new competitors, a result that would stand antitrust law on its head.

Even if one reads the complaint to allege that Juster is at a disadvantage because the City of Rutland is subsidizing the new mall, still no antitrust harm has been alleged. Such a disadvantage would derive solely from the fact that subsidization reduces the costs and increases the attractiveness of the new mall, therefore allowing it to compete more effectively with Juster. Although Juster's concern is understandable, we perceive no harm to consumers in the decision of the City's taxpayers to subsidize more attractive shopping conditions or lower prices to shoppers at the Developers' mall in order to ameliorate the taxpayers' concerns about the impact of new development on their municipality.

Having held that the City of Rutland's support for the Developers' proposed regional shopping center does not create any antitrust injury, we also address the City's and Developers' claim that they are immune from liability under the antitrust laws. We reach the issue of immunity because the district court based its rulings partially on the fact that the Developers have not yet entered the market and expressly left open the possibility that Juster may bring another antitrust suit once the Developers enter the market and gain some market power. The Developers are apprehensive that further litigation concerning their agreement with the City will occur when they enter the market. To foreclose a further challenge to that agreement, we address the Developers' claim of immunity.[30]

* * *

30. The City is immune from antitrust liability for damages under the Local Government Antitrust Act, 15 U.S.C.A. §§ 34–36 (1988) ("LGAA"). The LGAA provides that "[n]o damages, interest on damages, costs, or attorney's fees may be recovered under [the antitrust laws] from any local government, or official or employee thereof acting in an official capacity." 15 U.S.C.A. § 35(a). Because "local government" includes "a city," 15 U.S.C.A. § 34(1)(A),

Central to the agreement between the Developers and the City was the Developers' desire for the City's support in the Act 250 proceedings regarding their application. The City's views were important to the Commission, and it was formally a party to the FZA Act 250 proceedings. Whether gaining support from the City was essential or merely helpful, seeking it was within the realm of conduct protected by the First Amendment and thus immunized by the *Noerr–Pennington* doctrine. We believe, therefore, that the activities of the Developers and the City in negotiating their agreement are immunized from anti-trust liability.

The Supreme Court's decision in *Allied Tube & Conduit Corp. v. Indian Head, Inc.,* 486 U.S. 492, 108 S.Ct. 1931, 100 L.Ed.2d 497 (1988), in which it distinguished "anticompetitive political activity that is immunized despite its commercial impact from anticompetitive commercial activity that is unprotected despite its political impact," *id.* at 507–08 n. 10, 108 S.Ct. at 1941 n. 10, does not preclude application of the *Noerr–Pennington* doctrine in the instant matter. In *Allied Tube,* members of the steel industry packed an annual meeting of the National Fire Protection Association with new members solely to vote against a new type of electrical conduit that posed an economic threat to steel conduit. *See id.* at 495–97, 108 S.Ct. at 1937. The Supreme Court, in holding that this action was not immune under *Noerr–Pennington,* stated that "this is itself a case close to the line" between anticompetitive political activity and anticompetitive commercial activity, and it cautioned that its decision "depends on the context and nature of the activity." *See id.* at 508 n. 10, 108 S.Ct. at 1941 n. 10. If the activity in *Allied Tube,* which involved influencing a private organization's position on a potentially public issue, was close to the line, then the activities of the Developers and the City in this case, which involved the City's direct support as a party to the Act 250 proceedings, falls on the side of the line protected by *Noerr–Pennington* immunity.

The Supreme Court's recent decision in *Federal Trade Comm'n v. Superior Court Trial Lawyers Ass'n,* 493 U.S. 411, 110 S.Ct. 768, 107 L.Ed.2d 851 (1990), also does not alter this conclusion. In *Superior Court,* the Court held that a boycott by trial lawyers in private practice who acted as court-appointed counsel for indigent defendants was not immune from antitrust liability. In doing so, the Court reviewed its decisions in *Noerr* and *Allied Tube,* distinguishing the former from *Superior Court* on the grounds that the restraint of trade effected by the boycott in *Superior Court* "was the *means* by which respondents sought to obtain favorable legislation." *Superior Court,* 110 S.Ct. at 776 (emphasis in original). By contrast, the Court noted, the restraint of trade in *Noerr* "was the intended *consequence* of public action." *Id.* (emphasis in original). The activity at issue in this case is within the ambit of the protection afforded by *Noerr* because, like *Noerr,* the claimed restraint of trade is the consequence of the governmental action.

Rutland is obviously immune from suit for
damages.

Juster's remaining arguments are wholly without merit. The Section 1983 claim was properly dismissed because it failed to state any deprivation of a constitutionally protected property interest. As Chief Judge Billings held, Juster has failed to identify contractually established business relationships that will be disrupted as a result of defendants' conduct. Juster's interests in possible future relationships with tenants at the Rutland Mall do not constitute property interests of the sort protected by the Constitution, for Juster cannot claim to have "a legitimate claim of entitlement" to these benefits. *Board of Regents v. Roth,* 408 U.S. 564, 577, 92 S.Ct. 2701, 2709, 33 L.Ed.2d 548 (1972).

Finally, Juster's state-law claim of tortious interference with business relationships was properly dismissed because Juster failed to allege more than the possibility that it may face legitimate competition. *See Giroux v. Lussier,* 126 Vt. 555, 561, 238 A.2d 63, 67 (1967). The actions it complains of in this claim are virtually identical to the conduct made the basis of its antitrust claims, discussed *supra.* There is nothing tortious about competition.

Affirmed.

Notes

1. Also see Mason City Center Associates v. City of Mason City, Iowa, 671 F.2d 1146 (8th Cir.1982) where a developer brought an antitrust action against the city for conspiring with the plaintiff's competitors to prevent the development of a regional shopping center on the edge of the city. The alleged conspiracy was based upon an agreement the city had entered into with another developer to redevelop the downtown shopping area, an agreement that was approved by the electorate in a referendum. Another interesting case is Jacobs, Visconsi & Jacobs Co. v. City of Lawrence, Kansas, 715 F.Supp. 1000 (D.Kan.1989). The plaintiffs, a mall developer and owners of property at the edge of the city, sought rezoning to develop a suburban shopping mall. The initial response of planning staff was to promote the downtown area as the only shopping district. An advisory election resulted in voters opposing a downtown mall in 1987. Then two other developers proposed suburban shopping malls. The city commission denied rezonings for suburban shopping centers in 1988. The plaintiffs sought to have some of the city commissioners recuse because of their ownership of downtown property or involvement with the downtown retail district. The commissioners refused and the developer sued.

2. Interest in using the antitrust laws to challenge municipal decisions affecting competition was spurred by a case in Illinois in the mid–1980's. In Unity Ventures v. County of Lake, 631 F.Supp. 181 (N.D.Ill.1986) a developer sued the county and the Village of Grayslake alleging that they conspired to frustrate his development by withholding sanitary sewer extensions and choosing to direct development into a portion of the county other than where the plaintiff sought to develop. A jury awarded the plaintiff $9,500,000 which was trebled to $28,500,000 under the antitrust statute. The federal court entered a judgment n.o.v. which was affirmed in 841 F.2d 770 (7th Cir.1988), cert. denied, 488 U.S. 891, 109 S.Ct. 226, 102 L.Ed.2d 216 (1988). A subsequent attempt by the municipalities to recover attorneys' fees was

denied, 894 F.2d 250 (7th Cir.1990). The size of the original verdict in this case sent land use lawyers scurrying to the treatises on antitrust law and it appeared that the 1990's would see steady litigation in this vein. See Deutsch & Butler, Recent Limits on Municipal Antitrust Liability, Land Use Law (Jan. 1987) p. 3.

However, in 1991 the Supreme Court decided, in City of Columbia v. Omni Outdoor Advertising, Inc., 499 U.S. 365, 111 S.Ct. 1344, 113 L.Ed.2d 382 (1991), that local governments should be immune from federal antitrust liability under the Parker v. Brown (317 U.S. 341, 63 S.Ct. 307, 87 L.Ed. 315) doctrine immunizing states from antitrust liability. In this case a billboard company established that it was closed out of the market in Columbia, South Carolina because a rival company had, in cahoots with the city council, sponsored zoning ordinances prohibiting new billboard construction, thus preserving to itself 95% of the market. The majority opinion held that a "conspiracy" exception to the Parker doctrine would not be recognized because such an exception would swallow up the Parker rule and cause a spate of lawsuits against municipal officials. A dissent by Justice Stevens stated: "Today the Court acknowledges the anticompetitive consequences of this and similar agreements but decides that they should be exempted ... because it fears that enunciating a rule that allows the motivations of public officials to be be probed may mean that innocent public officials may be harassed with baseless charges. The holding evidences an unfortunate lack of confidence in our judicial system and will foster the evils the Sherman Act was designed to eradicate."

Also, Congress enacted the Local Government Antitrust Act, 15 U.S.C.A. §§ 34–36 providing that no damages, costs or attorney's fees may be recovered under the antitrust laws against local governments or their officials or employees. After these developments would you bring an antitrust action?

3. Where private parties lobby the city to deny rezoning to a potential competitor, the doctrine of Noerr–Pennington immunity may apply. This doctrine holds that anti-competitive intent should give way to free speech guarantees in seeking favorable legislation. In Miracle Mile Associates v. City of Rochester, 617 F.2d 18 (2d Cir.1980), the immunity was recognized where one shopping center developer extensively petitioned federal and state agencies to make certain that a competitor complied with all environmental regulations, and in Westborough Mall, Inc. v. City of Cape Girardeau, 532 F.Supp. 284 (E.D.Mo.1981), remanded 693 F.2d 733 (8th Cir.1982), the immunity was applied where one shopping center developer successfully convinced the city to give it favorable zoning treatment vis-a-vis a competitor.

4. Noerr–Pennington immunity is subject to an exception known as the sham exception where attempts to influence the legislative process are a "mere sham to cover what is actually nothing more than an attempt to interfere directly with the business relations of a competitor." The sham exception was applied in a case where an existing shopping center conspired with several property owners to stop, or delay as long as possible, construction of a competing shopping center. The defendants, among other activities, filed court appeals from every local decision, knowing they lacked standing to do so, effectively delaying the new center for five years. Landmarks

Holding Corp. v. Bermant, 664 F.2d 891 (2d Cir.1981). The Noerr–Pennington immunity and sham exception are intricately entwined with the subject matter of the following note:

A Note on SLAPP (Strategic Lawsuits Against Public Participation)

In a 1996 book, *SLAPPs: Getting Sued for Speaking Out* (Temple Univ. Press) by Professors George W. Pring and Penelope Canan, who coined the term SLAPP suit, the authors describe how "both individuals and groups are now being routinely sued in multimillion-dollar damage actions for such 'All–American' political activities as circulating a petition, writing a letter to the editor, testifying at a public hearing, reporting violations of law, lobbying for legislation, peacefully demonstrating, or otherwise attempting to influence government action." Most of the cases that involve SLAPPs are land use disputes. A number of states have enacted anti-SLAPP legislation, and even without legislation, such doctrines as malicious prosecution, sanctions for frivolous lawsuits, and other civil procedure provisions are encountered. The following case is but one example of the SLAPP problem.

HOMETOWN PROPERTIES, INC. v. FLEMING

Supreme Court of Rhode Island, 1996.
680 A.2d 56.

LEDERBERG, JUSTICE.

In this case we construe for the first time the provisions of G.L.1956 chapter 33 of title 9, as enacted by P.L.1993, chs. 354, 448, an act entitled "Limits on Strategic Litigation Against Public Participation" (the anti-SLAPP statute or the act). The plaintiffs, Hometown Properties, Inc., Homevest, Inc., Charles H. Gifford, III, Michael L. Baker, and Edward B. Mancini (collectively referred to as "Hometown" or "plaintiffs") brought suit against Nancy Hsu Fleming (Fleming or defendant), claiming that Fleming's communications with various state and federal governmental officials constituted both tortious interference with contractual relations and defamation. Invoking the provisions of the act, Fleming moved to dismiss Hometown's action as "strategic litigation against public participation" or a SLAPP suit and argued that the suit attempted to abridge her rights to free speech and to petition government for the redress of grievances. Fleming sought this Court's review of the Superior Court's denial of her motion to dismiss Hometown's suit. For the reasons stated below, we grant certiorari, quash the decision of the motion justice, and remand this case to the Superior Court with directions to enter summary judgment for the defendant.

FACTS AND PROCEDURAL HISTORY

The plaintiffs are the owners of a landfill in North Kingstown, Rhode Island. On or about November 21, 1991, and February 17, 1992, a number of North Kingstown residents, Fleming among them, participated in meetings with Louise Durfee (Durfee), then director of the Rhode Island Department of Environmental Management (DEM). The meetings focused on two issues: alleged ground-water contamination caused by landfills, specifically plaintiffs' landfill, and DEM's proposed rules and regulations concerning landfills. Following these meetings, Fleming wrote a letter to Durfee and posted copies to various state and federal officials. The letter, dated April 12, 1992, stated, inter alia:

> We take this opportunity to express our appreciation for your continued consideration of our efforts to close and clean up the Hometown/Homevest landfill.

> * * *

> In letters to you and in meetings with you, we have developed the following understandings:

> * * *

> 5. There are clear statements by the EPA and other experts that the Landfill contains hazardous waste, that the Landfill continues to contaminate offsite groundwater exceeding Maximum Contamination Levels, that the Landfill should be closed and cleaned-up, and that onsite monitoring wells were never purposely placed to detect concentrations of leachate.

> 6. The Landfill is on track to being declared a Superfund site.

> 7. The Town expert has documented a three-year history of groundwater contamination, levels of contamination that would have never been detected were the Town to have relied on the onsite wells for the protection of its Citizen's drinking water.

> * * *

> 9. The Owners of the Landfill have consistently refused to contribute to the Town's effort to monitor the groundwater, and has [sic], as a matter of fact, vigorously resisted monitoring activities by your own office.

The letter went on to comment on the proposed new "Rules and Regulations For Groundwater Quality." In response, Hometown, through its counsel, informed Fleming by letter that if she did not "(a) provide to us the specific facts and documents on which your statements were based or (b) confirm to us in writing that you will promptly furnish to Louise Durfee, and the other officials to whom your April 12 letter was copied, the retraction which is enclosed," then Hometown would "have no alternative but to pursue the formal legal remedies available."

Fleming did not retract her statements, and on December 2, 1992, Hometown filed a complaint in the Superior Court, alleging defamation and tortious interference with contractual relations and seeking compensatory and punitive damages. * * *

Subsequent to the Superior Court's denial of Fleming's first motion to dismiss, the General Assembly, on July 24, 1993, enacted the anti-SLAPP statute, P.L.1993, ch. 448, § 1. The act applied retroactively to all actions that had "not been fully adjudicated on, or subsequent to, the effective date" of the act, and allowed a party to such an action to file a "special motion to dismiss a claim" within sixty days of the effective date of the act. Public Laws 1993, ch. 448, § 2.

On September 17, 1993, relying on the anti-SLAPP statute, Fleming filed a second motion to dismiss and a motion to stay discovery. Hometown objected to Fleming's motions, arguing that the anti-SLAPP statute was unconstitutional and, in the alternative, that Fleming had failed to demonstrate that the anti-SLAPP statute would protect her from liability. Fleming's second motion to dismiss was not decided, but was passed on by the motion justice. On February 24, 1994, the Attorney General filed a notice of intervention pursuant to Rule 24(d) of the Superior Court Rules of Civil Procedure and G.L.1956 §§ 9–30–11 and 9–33–3.

Fleming filed a third motion to dismiss on May 25, 1994. Accompanying her memorandum in support of the motion, Fleming submitted various scientific reports and government documents attached to her affidavit that avowed that the disputed statements were made in response to a request for public comment on the proposed DEM landfill rules and regulations. She further averred that her statements were supported by and derived from the documents attached to her affidavit.

After oral argument on the third motion, the motion justice, on August 4, 1994, denied Fleming's motion. In her decision, the motion justice declined to address the constitutionality of the act. Instead, she presumed that the anti-SLAPP statute was constitutional but determined that she could not rule as a matter of law that Fleming was entitled to immunity under its provisions. The motion justice stated that she was "not satisfied that defendant has demonstrated that she falls within the class of defendants defined" in the anti-SLAPP statute. In addition, the motion justice rejected Fleming's argument that she was entitled to protection under the so-called "Noerr–Pennington" doctrine developed by the United States Supreme Court. Because Hometown's complaint included "allegations of the tort of libel," the motion justice determined that Noerr–Pennington was inapplicable, and she relied, instead, on the Supreme Court's rulings in McDonald v. Smith, 472 U.S. 479, 105 S.Ct. 2787, 86 L.Ed.2d 384 (1985) (holding that the petition clause does not provide absolute immunity to defendants charged with libel), and White v. Nicholls, 44 U.S. (3 How.) 266, 11 L.Ed. 591 (1845) (defining malice as "falsehood and the absence of probable cause").

* * *

NOERR–PENNINGTON DOCTRINE AND THE "SHAM" EXCEPTION

The United States Supreme Court developed the Noerr–Pennington doctrine in the context of antitrust litigation in order to protect the legitimate exercise of the constitutional right to petition the government after retributive civil claims were brought by parties harmed by petitioning activity. Professional Real Estate Investors, Inc. v. Columbia Pictures Industries, Inc., 508 U.S. 49, 56, 113 S.Ct. 1920, 1926, 123 L.Ed.2d 611,

621 (1993) (citing Eastern Railroad Presidents Conference v. Noerr Motor Freight, Inc., 365 U.S. 127, 81 S.Ct. 523, 5 L.Ed.2d 464 (1961)).

This Court has adopted the Noerr–Pennington premise and has applied its protection to common-law tort claims. * * *

We have also adopted the Supreme Court's position that petitioning activity that amounts to "a mere sham" is not immune under Noerr–Pennington. Eastern Railroad Presidents Conference v. Noerr Motor Freight, Inc., 365 U.S. 127, 144, 81 S.Ct. 523, 533, 5 L.Ed.2d 464, 475 (1961). Consequently, sham petitioning activities that "are not genuinely aimed at procuring favorable government action" but constitute inappropriate uses of governmental process, are not protected under the doctrine. * * *

PETITIONING ACTIVITY PROTECTED UNDER THE ANTI-SLAPP STATUTE

The General Assembly enacted the anti-SLAPP statute in 1993. P.L.1993, chs. 354, 448. Like the Noerr–Pennington doctrine, the anti-SLAPP statute was adopted in order to protect valid petitioning activities. This purpose is evinced by § 9–33–1 of the act, which states:

> The legislature finds and declares that full participation by persons and organizations and robust discussion of issues of public concern before the legislative, judicial, and administrative bodies and in other public fora are essential to the democratic process, that there has been a disturbing increase in lawsuits brought primarily to chill the valid exercise of the constitutional rights of freedom of speech and petition for the redress of grievances; that such litigation is disfavored and should be resolved quickly with minimum cost to citizens who have participated in matters of public concern. P.L. 1993, ch. 448, § 1.

As enacted in 1993, § 9–33–2(a) of the anti-SLAPP statute provided:

> In any case in which a party asserts that the civil claims * * * against said party are based on said party's lawful exercise of its right of petition or of free speech * * * in connection with a matter of public concern, said party may bring a special motion to dismiss. * * * The court shall grant such special motion if the moving party by the preponderance of the evidence shall demonstrate to the satisfaction of the court (a) that the claim * * * subject to the motion is an action involving petition or free speech * * * and (b) that said moving party did not engage in a course of tortious conduct toward the party against whom such special motion is made. In making its determination, the court shall consider the pleadings and supporting and opposing affidavits stating the facts upon which the liability or defense is based.

* * *

In 1995 the General Assembly amended § 9–33–2 (P.L.1995, ch. 386, § 1). As amended, the provisions of § 9–33–2 are nearly identical to the Supreme Court's articulation of the constitutionally derived conditional immunity afforded to nonsham petitioning activity under Noerr–Pennington. Specifically, § 9–33–2(a) now provides:

> Conditional immunity.—(a) A party's exercise of his or her right of petition or of free speech under the United States or Rhode Island Constitutions in connection with a matter of public concern shall be conditionally immune from civil claims, counterclaims, or cross-claims. Such immunity will apply as a bar to any civil claim, counterclaim, or cross-claim directed at petition or free speech * * * except if said petition or free speech constitutes a sham. Petition or free speech constitutes a sham only if it is not genuinely aimed at procuring favorable government action, result or outcome, regardless of ultimate motive or purpose. Petition or free speech will be deemed to constitute a sham as defined in the previous sentence only if it is both:

> (1) objectively baseless in the sense that no reasonable person exercising the right of speech or petition could realistically expect success in procuring such government action, result, or outcome, and

> (2) subjectively baseless in the sense that it is actually an attempt to use the governmental process itself for its own direct effects. Use of outcome or result of the governmental process shall not constitute use of the governmental process itself for its own direct effects.

* * *

The most significant modification made by the 1995 amendment changed the most equivocal language of the anti-SLAPP statute. Specifically, Public Law 1995, ch. 386, replaced the requirement that a party's petitioning activity not amount to "tortious conduct" with the requirement that such activity not constitute sham petitioning. The amendment defines "sham petitioning" in accordance with the test articulated by the Supreme Court in Professional Real Estate Investors. We are of the opinion that by adopting the sham petitioning definition, the General Assembly intended to remove the ambiguity inherent in the 1993 statute by defining what it intended by the term "tortious conduct."

Our conclusion in this regard is consistent with precedent as well as with the legislative purpose set forth in § 9–33–1. In Cove Road, we emphasized that "the right to petition governmental bodies for the redress of grievances is 'among the most precious of the liberties safeguarded by the Bill of Rights.' " 674 A.2d at 1236 (quoting United Mine Workers of America v. Illinois State Bar Association, 389 U.S. 217, 222, 88 S.Ct. 353, 356, 19 L.Ed.2d 426, 430 (1967)). The Supreme Court has long recognized the "preferred place given in our scheme to the great, the indispensable democratic freedoms secured by the First Amendment" and that it is "in our tradition to allow the widest room for discussion, the narrowest range for its restriction." Thomas v. Collins, 323 U.S. 516, 530, 65 S.Ct. 315, 322–23, 89 L.Ed. 430, 440, reh'g denied, 323 U.S. 819, 65 S.Ct. 557, 89 L.Ed. 650 (1945). By enacting the anti-SLAPP statute, the General Assembly intended to secure the vital role of open discourse on matters of public importance, and we shall construe the statute in the manner most consistent with that intention. Hence, we reject Hometown's posture that simply by its inclusion of a defamation count in its complaint against Fleming, it can circumvent the General Assembly's clear design that conditional immunity apply to all legitimate petitioning activity that becomes the subject of a punitive civil claim.

* * *

We conclude, on the basis of our application of the sham test to Fleming's activities, that the motion justice erred in ruling that she could not "rule as a matter of law that the defendant did not engage in tortious conduct toward the plaintiffs." In her affidavit, Fleming presented detailed averments that her statements were based upon various scientific studies and reports. Hometown submitted no opposing affidavit or other evidence to challenge Fleming's statements but relied solely on the assertions in its pleadings. On the basis of the record before us, it is clear that Fleming did not engage in sham activity that was "objectively baseless in the sense that no reasonable person exercising the right of speech or petition could realistically expect success in procuring [favorable] government action, result, or outcome." Section 9–33–2(a)(1). The anti-SLAPP statute and our holding today are consistent with the independence and individualism that led this state's earliest settlers "to create a free community of seekers after the Truth and a haven for those persecuted elsewhere for their conscientious beliefs," William G. McLoughlin, Rhode Island, A History, ch. 1 at 10 (1978), and they resonate with the expression inscribed on the Rhode Island statehouse dome: "Rara temporum felicitas ubi sentire quae velis et quae sentias dicere licet."[31]

Therefore, for the reasons stated above, we grant the petition for certiorari and quash the decision of the Superior Court, to which we remand this matter with our direction to enter summary judgment in favor of the defendant.

Notes

1. Some other SLAPP cases of interest are Opinion of the Justices (SLAPP Suit Procedure), 138 N.H. 445, 641 A.2d 1012 (1994) where the court held invalid a portion of the state statute permitting dismissal of a SLAPP suit before discovery is completed because it violated the state constitutional right to a jury trial, and Gordon v. Marrone, 202 A.D.2d 104, 616 N.Y.S.2d 98 (1994), awarding an environmental group (The Nature Conservancy) $10,000 in attorney's fees for having to defend a SLAPP suit challenging the group's tax exemption brought by a developer who had been opposed by the group. Also see Alexandra D. Lowe, The Price of Speaking Out, ABA Journal (Sept. 1996) p. 48.

31. Translated from the Latin: "Rare felicity of the times when it is permitted to think what you wish and to say what you think."

2. Another interesting case is Creek v. Village of Westhaven, 80 F.3d 186 (7th Cir.1996). A developer filed a civil rights action against the village and a homeowners association for their actions, including a lawsuit, to delay and prevent the developer from building a rent-subsidized apartment complex. The developer alleged that the actions of the village and the association were unlawful attempts to discriminate on racial grounds. The court remanded for a trial and, in the opinion, held that the municipality did not share any First Amendment protection the homeowners association might have for having filed a suit to invalidate the federal approval of rent support for the project, and that the village would have to establish its own independent immunity. The court added that even if municipalities have First Amendment rights, they do not have the right to foment discrimination based on race.

Chapter VIII

ZONING AND DISCRIMINATION

The institution of zoning may be said to be inherently discriminatory because it is exclusionary by nature. The heart of the zoning process is to separate land uses by districts, which necessarily means that all uses will be excluded from a particular district except those which are specifically or conditionally permitted. If the zoning ordinance makes no provision for a specific use or for its inclusion as a conditional use, then the use is excluded from the entire jurisdiction.

Obviously, this situation presents several important considerations. An initial and basic issue is whether a zoning ordinance must provide, at least in one or more districts, for any or every type of land use that may be desired. If that question is answered in the affirmative, zoning would not prove to be a useful technique in eliminating or confining certain undesirable or troublesome land uses, such as boiler factories, rendering plants, other types of heavy industry, or automobile junkyards. If the answer is in the negative, however, and a city need not provide for every kind of land use, then carried to the extreme this could give rise to other serious legal considerations. To put it another way, if a city need not permit every type of land use, can it exclude all or practically all forms of land use except the very highest or most desirable? In such a situation, what legal principles can be applied to control the use of zoning to prevent discrimination resulting from economic disparities which, either obviously or inferentially, may include racial discrimination or which, in effect, may preserve racial segregation? What legal principles may be applied, and to what extent, to zoning limitations on opportunities for federally subsidized housing for persons of low and moderate incomes or relative to privately financed housing for persons of that status?

A more subtle form of exclusion results or may result from traditional zoning regulations that do not exclude uses, but which have an exclusionary effect through their impact on the cost of housing and the appearance of the community. These requirements include minimum lot size requirements, minimum house sizes, extraordinary setback requirements, and for that matter, subdivision exactions which affect the economics of land development and thereby create market limitations.

Inquiry is appropriate as to the point at which the cumulative effect of unusual and expensive subdivision exactions, minimum zoning requirements and costs attributable to building code regulations may so promote segregated housing patterns as to amount to a misuse of the police power. (On all of this, generally, see Wright, exclusionary Land Use Controls and the Taking Issue, 8 Hastings Const.L.Q. 545 (1981).)

The exclusionary effects of zoning and land use controls in general has become one of the most discussed issues of the past decade, although the question has been around for much longer than that as illustrated by articles extending back to the early and middle 1950's. The issue has heightened and become an increasing point of litigation in roughly the past ten to fifteen years as what might be called nontraditional constitutional considerations of a civil rights nature have increasingly been raised in state and federal litigation. This chapter is intended to provide some insight into these difficult problems which constitute some of the most complex and sophisticated issues existing in the field of land use control. Basic principles of our society are involved, and the cases involving exclusionary uses of the police power probe not only its scope but also its relationship to the concept of equal protection of the law.

Although the answers to the questions raised are by no means readily available, since this is an area of the law which continues to ferment, these issues present some of the most important and exciting land use concerns since the advent of zoning.

SECTION 1. EXCLUSIONARY ZONING

A. THE "SINGLE–FAMILY" PROBLEM

Zoning, from the point of view of the average citizen, created a hierarchy of districts, culminating in the single-family residential district. This "highest" district was to be protected, not only from commercial and industrial incursions, but also from structures which might house more than one family, such as duplexes, townhouses, and apartments. Also, the single-family dwelling was understood to exclude mobile homes and manufactured housing. In carrying out this view of zoning, which originates in Justice Sutherland's opinion in the Euclid case (where he denounced apartments as parasitic nuisances in the single-family districts), cities and towns had to carefully define "single-family" in order to insure protection for this highest zoning district. In the course of doing this, a legal problem soon emerged—to what extent could a definition of family be applied to unusual personal living arrangements in structures which were clearly built as single-family houses. We begin the study of discrimination and exclusionary zoning by looking at how the courts have treated zoning ordinances which, by definition, excluded non-traditional living arrangements from the single-family zone.

VILLAGE OF BELLE TERRE v. BORAAS

Supreme Court of the United States, 1974.
416 U.S. 1, 94 S.Ct. 1536, 39 L.Ed.2d 797.

Mr. Justice Douglas delivered the opinion of the Court.

Belle Terre is a village on Long Island's north shore of about 220 homes inhabited by 700 people. Its total land area is less than one square mile. It has restricted land use to one-family dwellings excluding lodging houses, boarding houses, fraternity houses, or multiple dwelling houses. The word "Family" as used in the ordinance means, "One or more persons related by blood, adoption or marriage, living and cooking together as a single housekeeping unit, exclusive of household servants. A number of persons but not exceeding two (2) living and cooking together as a single housekeeping unit though not related by blood, adoption, or marriage shall be deemed to constitute a family."

Appellees (Dickmans) are owners of a house in the village and leased it in December, 1971 for a term of 18 months to Michael Truman. Later Bruce Boraas became a colessee. Then Anne Parish moved into the house along with three others. These six are students at nearby State University at Stony Brook and none is related to the other by blood, adoption, or marriage. When the village served the Dickmans with an "Order to Remedy Violations" of the ordinance, the owners plus three tenants thereupon brought this action under 42 U.S.C.A. § 1983 for an injunction declaring the ordinance unconstitutional. The District Court held the ordinance constitutional and the Court of Appeals reversed, one judge dissenting. 2 Cir., 476 F.2d 806. The case is here by appeal, 28 U.S.C.A. § 1254(2); and we noted probable jurisdiction, 414 U.S. 907, 94 S.Ct. 234, 38 L.Ed.2d 145.

* * *

The present ordinance is challenged on several grounds: that it interferes with a person's right to travel; that it interferes with the right to migrate to and settle within a State; that it bars people who are uncongenial to the present residents; that the ordinance expresses the social preferences of the residents for groups that will be congenial to them; that social homogeneity is not a legitimate interest of government; that the restriction of those whom the neighbors do not like trenches on the newcomers' rights of privacy; that it is of no rightful concern to villagers whether the residents are married or unmarried; that the ordinance is antithetical to the Nation's experience, ideology and self-perception as an open, egalitarian, and integrated society.

We find none of these reasons in the record before us. It is not aimed at transients. Cf. Shapiro v. Thompson, 394 U.S. 618, 89 S.Ct. 1322, 22 L.Ed.2d 600. It involves no procedural disparity inflicted on some but not on others such as was presented by Griffin v. Illinois, 351 U.S. 12, 76 S.Ct. 585, 100 L.Ed. 891. It involves no "fundamental" right guaranteed by the Constitution, such as voting, Harper v. Virginia State

Board, 383 U.S. 663, 86 S.Ct. 1079, 16 L.Ed.2d 169; the right of association, NAACP v. Alabama ex rel. Patterson, 357 U.S. 449, 78 S.Ct. 1163, 2 L.Ed.2d 1488; the right of access to the courts, NAACP v. Button, 371 U.S. 415, 83 S.Ct. 328, 9 L.Ed.2d 405; or any rights of privacy, cf. Griswold v. Connecticut, 381 U.S. 479, 85 S.Ct. 1678, 14 L.Ed.2d 510; Eisenstadt v. Baird, 405 U.S. 438, 453–454, 92 S.Ct. 1029, 1038–1039, 31 L.Ed.2d 349. We deal with economic and social legislation where legislatures have historically drawn lines which we respect against the charge of violation of the Equal Protection Clause if the law be "reasonable, not arbitrary" (quoting F.S. Royster Guano Co. v. Virginia, 253 U.S. 412, 415, 40 S.Ct. 560, 561, 64 L.Ed. 989) and bears "a rational relationship to a [permissible] state objective." Reed v. Reed, 404 U.S. 71, 76, 92 S.Ct. 251, 254, 30 L.Ed.2d 225.

It is said, however, that if two unmarried people can constitute a "family," there is no reason why three or four may not. But every line drawn by a legislature leaves some out that might well have been included. That exercise of discretion, however, is a legislative not a judicial function.

It is said that the Belle Terre ordinance reeks with an animosity to unmarried couples who live together. There is no evidence to support it; and the provision of the ordinance bringing within the definition of a "family" two unmarried people belies the charge.

The ordinance places no ban on other forms of association, for a "family" may, so far as the ordinance is concerned, entertain whomever they like.

The regimes of boarding houses, fraternity houses, and the like present urban problems. More people occupy a given space; more cars rather continuously pass by; more cars are parked; noise travels with crowds.

A quiet place where yards are wide, people few, and motor vehicles restricted are legitimate guidelines in a land use project addressed to family needs. This goal is a permissible one within Berman v. Parker, supra. The police power is not confined to elimination of filth, stench, and unhealthy places. It is ample to lay out zones where family values, youth values, and the blessings of quiet seclusion, and clean air make the area a sanctuary for people.

* * *

Reversed.

MR. JUSTICE MARSHALL, dissenting.

This case draws into question the constitutionality of a zoning ordinance of the incorporated village of Belle Terre, New York, which prohibits groups of more than two unrelated persons, as distinguished from groups consisting of any number of persons related by blood, adoption or marriage, from occupying a residence within the confines of the township. Appellees, the two owners of a Belle Terre residence, and

976 ZONING AND DISCRIMINATION Ch. 8

three unrelated student tenants challenged the ordinance on the grounds that it establishes a classification between households of related and unrelated individuals, which deprives them of equal protection of the laws. In my view, the disputed classification burdens the students' fundamental rights of association and privacy guaranteed by the First and Fourteenth Amendments. Because the application of strict equal protection scrutiny is therefore required, I am at odds with my brethren's conclusion that the ordinance may be sustained on a showing that it bears a rational relationship to the accomplishment of legitimate governmental objectives.

* * *

When separate but equal was still accepted constitutional dogma, this Court struck down a racially restrictive zoning ordinance. Buchanan v. Warley, 245 U.S. 60, 38 S.Ct. 16, 62 L.Ed. 149 (1917). I am sure the Court would not be hesitant to invalidate that ordinance today. The lower federal courts have considered procedural aspects of zoning, and acted to insure that land use controls are not used as means of confining minorities and the poor to the ghettos of our central cities. These are limited but necessary intrusions on the discretion of zoning authorities. By the same token, I think it clear that the First Amendment provides some limitation on zoning laws. It is inconceivable to me that we would allow the exercise of the zoning power to burden First Amendment freedoms, as by ordinances that restrict occupancy to individuals adhering to particular religious, political or scientific beliefs. Zoning officials properly concern themselves with the uses of land—with, for example, the number and kind of dwellings to be constructed in a certain neighborhood or the number of persons who can reside in those dwellings. But zoning authorities cannot validly consider who those persons are, what they believe, or how they choose to live, whether they are Negro or white, Catholic or Jew, Republican or Democrat, married or unmarried.

My disagreement with the Court today is based upon my view that the ordinance in this case unnecessarily burdens appellees' First Amendment freedom of association and their constitutionally guaranteed right to privacy. Our decisions establish that the First and Fourteenth Amendments protect the freedom to choose one's associates. NAACP v. Button, 371 U.S. 415, 430, 83 S.Ct. 328, 336, 9 L.Ed.2d 405 (1963). Constitutional protection is extended not only to modes of association that are political in the usual sense, but also to those that pertain to the social and economic benefit of the members. The selection of one's living companions involves similar choices as to the emotional, social, or economic benefits to be derived from alternative living arrangements.

The freedom of association is often inextricably entwined with the constitutionally guaranteed right of privacy. The right to "establish a home" is an essential part of the liberty guaranteed by the Fourteenth Amendment. Meyer v. Nebraska, 262 U.S. 390, 399, 43 S.Ct. 625, 626, 67 L.Ed. 1042 (1923); Griswold v. Connecticut, 381 U.S. 479, 495, 85 S.Ct. 1678, 1687, 14 L.Ed.2d 510 (1965). And the Constitution secures to an individual a freedom "to satisfy his intellectual and emotional needs within the privacy of his own home." Stanley v. Georgia, 394 U.S. 557, 564–565, 89 S.Ct. 1243, 1248, 22 L.Ed.2d 542 (1969); see Paris Adult Theatre I v. Slaton, 413 U.S. 49, 66–67, 93 S.Ct. 2628, 2640–2641, 37 L.Ed.2d 446 (1973). Constitutionally protected privacy is, in Mr. Justice Brandeis' words, "as against the government, the right to be let alone * * * the right most valued by civilized man." Olmstead v. United States, 277 U.S. 438, 478, 48 S.Ct. 564, 572, 72 L.Ed. 944 (1928) (dissenting opinion). The choice of household companions—of whether a person's "intellectual and emotional needs" are best met by living with family, friends, professional associates or others—involves deeply personal considerations as to the kind and quality of intimate relationships within the home. That decision surely falls within the ambit of the right to privacy protected by the Constitution.

The instant ordinance discriminates on the basis of just such a personal lifestyle choice as to household companions. It permits any number of persons related by blood or marriage, be it two or twenty, to live in a single household, but it limits to two the number of unrelated persons bound by profession, love, friendship, religious or political affiliation or mere economics who can occupy a single home. Belle Terre imposes upon those who deviate from the community norm in their choice of living companions significantly greater restrictions than are applied to residential groups who are related by blood or marriage, and comprise the established order with the community. The town has, in effect, acted to fence out those individuals whose choice of lifestyle differs from that of its current residents.

This is not a case where the Court is being asked to nullify a township's sincere efforts to maintain its residential character by preventing the operation of rooming houses, fraternity houses or other commercial or high-density residential uses. Unquestionably, a town is free to restrict such uses. Moreover, as a general proposition, I see no constitutional infirmity in a town limiting the density of use in residential areas by zoning regulations which do not discriminate on the basis of constitutionally suspect criteria. This ordinance, however, limits the density of occupancy of only those homes occupied by unrelated persons. It thus reaches beyond control of the use of land or the density of population, and undertakes to regulate the way people choose to associate with each other within the privacy of their own homes.

* * *

A variety of justifications have been proffered in support of the village's ordinance. It is claimed that the ordinance controls population density, prevents noise, traffic and parking problems, and preserves the rent structure of the community and its attractiveness to families. As I noted earlier, these are all legitimate and substantial interests of government. But I think it clear that the means chosen to accomplish these purposes are both over-and under-inclusive, and that the asserted goals could be as effectively achieved by means of an ordinance that did not discriminate on the basis of constitutionally protected choices of lifestyle. The ordinance imposes no restriction whatsoever on the number of persons who may live in a house, as long as they are related by marital or sanguinary bonds—presumably no matter how distant their relationship. Nor does the ordinance restrict the number of income earners who may contribute to rent in such a household, or the number of automobiles that may be maintained by its occupants. In that sense the ordinance is under-inclusive. On the other hand, the statute restricts the number of unrelated persons who may live in a home to no more than two. It would therefore prevent three unrelated people from occupying a dwelling even if among them they had but one income and no vehicles. While an extended family of a dozen or more might live in a small bungalow, three elderly and retired persons could not occupy the large manor house next door. Thus the statute is also grossly over-inclusive to accomplish its intended purposes.

There are some 220 residences in Belle Terre occupied by about 700 persons. The density is therefore just above three per household. The village is justifiably concerned with density of population and the related problems of noise, traffic, and the like. It could deal with those problems by limiting each household to a specified number of adults, two or three perhaps, without limitation on the number of dependent children. The burden of such an ordinance would fall equally upon all segments of the community. It would surely be better tailored to the goals asserted by the township than the ordinance before us today, for it would more realistically restrict population density and growth and their attendant environmental costs. Various other statutory mechanisms also suggest themselves as solutions to Belle Terre's problems—rent control, limits on the number of vehicles per household, and so forth, but, of course, such schemes are matters of legislative judgment and not for this Court. Appellants also refer to the necessity of maintaining the family character of the village. There is not a shred of evidence in the record indicating that if Belle Terre permitted a limited number of unrelated persons to live together, the residential, familial character of the community would be fundamentally affected.

By limiting unrelated households to two persons while placing no limitation on households of related individuals, the village has embarked upon its commendable course in a constitutionally faulty vessel. Cf. Marshall v. United States, 414 U.S. 417, 94 S.Ct. 700, 38 L.Ed.2d 618 (1974) (dissenting opinion). I would find the challenged ordinance unconstitutional. But I would not ask the village to abandon its goal of providing quiet streets, little traffic, and a pleasant and reasonably priced environment in which families might raise their children. Rather, I would commend the town to continue to pursue those purposes but by means of more carefully drawn and even-handed legislation.

I respectfully dissent.

[A dissenting opinion by Justice Brennan is omitted.]

Notes

1. Also see Palo Alto Tenants Union v. Morgan, 321 F.Supp. 908 (N.D.Cal.1970), affirmed 487 F.2d 883 (9th Cir.1973), certiorari denied 417 U.S. 910, 94 S.Ct. 2608, 41 L.Ed.2d 214 (1974).

2. In 1977, the Supreme Court was faced with another "single-family" case. In Moore v. City of East Cleveland, Ohio, 431 U.S. 494, 97 S.Ct. 1932, 52 L.Ed.2d 531 (1977), the ordinance contained a complex definition of family which had the effect of making Mrs. Moore's occupancy of her dwelling along with her son and two grandsons (who were first cousins) illegal. In a plurality opinion by Justice Powell, the Court distinguished Belle Terre by noting that the earlier case affected only unrelated individuals while the East Cleveland ordinance forbade the living together of certain categories of relatives. The Court thus gave "close scrutiny" to the ordinance because of the governmental intrusion into the "family" and found that the city could offer no acceptable justification for such intrusion. The city's argument that the objectives of the ordinance were to avoid overcrowding, traffic congestion and undue burdens on the school system was found by the Court to have, at best, a tenuous relationship to the definition of family and the effect of the ordinance on Mrs. Moore.

Justice Powell explained the Belle Terre case in the following statement:

The city argues that our decision in Village of Belle Terre v. Boraas, 416 U.S. 1, 94 S.Ct. 1536, 39 L.Ed.2d 797 (1974), requires us to sustain the ordinance attacked here. Belle Terre, like East Cleveland, imposed limits on the types of groups that could occupy a single dwelling unit. Applying the constitutional standard announced in this Court's leading land-use case, Village of Euclid v. Ambler Realty Co., 272 U.S. 365, 47 S.Ct. 114, 71 L.Ed. 303 (1926), we sustained the Belle Terre ordinance on the ground that it bore a rational relationship to permissible state objectives.

But one overriding factor sets this case apart from *Belle Terre*. The ordinance there affected only *unrelated* individuals. It expressly allowed all who were related by "blood, adoption, or marriage" to live together, and in sustaining the ordinance we were careful to note that it promoted "family needs" and "family values." 416 U.S., at 9, 94 S.Ct., at 1541. East Cleveland, in contrast, has chosen to regulate the occupancy of its housing by slicing deeply into the family itself. This is no mere incidental result of the ordinance. On its face it selects certain categories of relatives who may live together and declares that others may not. In particular, it makes a crime of a grandmother's choice to live with her grandson in circumstances like those presented here.

When a city undertakes such intrusive regulation of the family, neither *Belle Terre* nor *Euclid* governs; the usual judicial deference to the legislature is inappropriate. "This Court has long recognized that freedom of personal choice in matters of marriage and family life is one of the liberties protected by the Due Process Clause of the Fourteenth Amendment." * * * Of course, the family is not beyond regulation.

* * * But when the government intrudes on choices concerning family living arrangements, this Court must examine carefully the

importance of the governmental interests advanced and the extent to which they are served by the challenged regulation.

3. After Belle Terre, would you expect the state courts to accept restrictive zoning ordinance definitions of "family" so as to exclude from the single-family district living arrangements other than the traditional family? Consider the following materials.

McMINN v. TOWN OF OYSTER BAY

Court of Appeals of New York, 1985.
66 N.Y.2d 544, 498 N.Y.S.2d 128, 488 N.E.2d 1240.

SIMONS, JUDGE.

Plaintiffs are the owners and tenants of a four-bedroom house in Massapequa in the Town of Oyster Bay, Long Island, which is in violation of the Town zoning ordinance. They commenced this action against defendants, the Town of Oyster Bay, the Town Council and its supervisor and building inspector, for a declaration that that portion of the ordinance restricting "single-family" housing to any number of persons related by blood, marriage or adoption or to two persons not so related but both of whom are 62 years of age or older violates the due process and equal protection clauses of the State Constitution (N.Y. Const., art. I, §§ 6, 11) and Human Rights Law § 296 (Executive Law § 296). Plaintiffs also sought an injunction against further enforcement of the ordinance. Following a trial, Supreme Court concluded that the age requirement for defining two unrelated individuals as a family violated the State constitutional guarantee of equal protection of the laws and that the ordinance also violated Executive Law § 296(5) to the extent it prohibited occupancy of a single-family house by two individuals on the ground of marital status but that the ordinance was in all other respects valid (111 Misc.2d 1046, 445 N.Y.S.2d 859). The combined effect of these rulings was to find the ordinance constitutional insofar as it restricted occupancy of a single-family home to any number of persons related by blood, marriage or adoption or two unrelated persons. On cross appeals, the Appellate Division modified the judgment and declared that the challenged portion of the ordinance was facially unconstitutional under the due process clause of our State Constitution insofar as it prohibits occupancy of one-family homes by persons unrelated by blood, marriage or adoption and that it was constitutional insofar as it limits occupancy of one-family homes to a single housekeeping unit (105 A.D.2d 46, 482 N.Y.S.2d 773).

* * *

Plaintiffs Robert and Joan McMinn purchased their house in 1973. It is in a D Residence district. On June 1, 1976, they leased the house to four unrelated young men between the ages of 22 and 25 who had grown up in the area and wanted to remain near their families but not reside with them. Shortly after the tenants moved in, a criminal information was filed against the McMinns in District Court, Nassau County, charging them with violating the zoning ordinance because the house was occupied by more than one family. The McMinns and the tenants then commenced this action seeking declaratory and injunctive relief and the criminal proceedings have been adjourned pending its disposition. In their complaint, plaintiffs assert only State constitutional and statutory claims and expressly reserve the right to litigate all Federal claims in a Federal forum pursuant to *England v. Medical Examiners,* 375 U.S. 411, 84 S.Ct. 461, 11 L.Ed.2d 440. They contend that the restrictive definition of "family" contained in the ordinance is facially invalid under Executive Law § 296 and the due process and equal protection clauses of the State Constitution (N.Y. Const., art. I, §§ 6, 11) or, in the alternative, that it violated these statutory and constitutional provisions as applied to them.

* * *

Indisputably, this ordinance was enacted to further several legitimate governmental purposes, including preservation of the character of traditional single-family neighborhoods, reduction of parking and traffic problems, control of population density and prevention of noise and disturbance. The dispute centers on whether the means the local legislature has chosen, the challenged ordinance and more specifically the definition of "family" contained in it, are reasonably related to the achievement of these legitimate purposes.

Manifestly, restricting occupancy of single-family housing based generally on the biological or legal relationships between its inhabitants bears no reasonable relationship to the goals of reducing parking and traffic problems, controlling population density and preventing noise and disturbance (*see, Moore v. East Cleveland,* 431 U.S. 494, 499–500, 97 S.Ct. 1932, 1935–1936, 52 L.Ed.2d 531; *id.,* at p. 520, n. 16, 97 S.Ct. at p. 1946, n. 16 [Stevens, J., concurring]; *City of Santa Barbara v. Adamson,* 27 Cal.3d 123, 164 Cal.Rptr. 539, 544, 610 P.2d 436, 441; *State v. Baker,* 81 N.J. 99, 405 A.2d 368, 373). Their achievement depends not upon the biological or legal relations between the occupants of a house but generally upon the size of the dwelling and the lot and the number of its occupants. Thus, the definition of family employed here is both fatally overinclusive in prohibiting, for example, a young unmarried couple from occupying a four-bedroom house who do not threaten the purposes of the ordinance and the underinclusive in failing to prohibit occupancy of a two-bedroom home by 10 or 12 persons who are related in only the most distant manner and who might well be expected to present serious overcrowding and traffic problems.

Nor is the ordinance's restrictive definition of family saved by the desire to preserve the character of the traditional single-family neighborhood in Oyster Bay. That is a legitimate governmental objective (*see, Group House v. Board of Zoning & Appeals,* 45 N.Y.2d 266, 271, 408 N.Y.S.2d 377, 380 N.E.2d 207; *City of White Plains v. Ferraioli,* 34 N.Y.2d 300, 305, 357 N.Y.S.2d 449, 313 N.E.2d 756; *see also, Village of Belle Terre v. Boraas,* 416 U.S. 1, 9, 94 S.Ct. 1536, 1541, 39 L.Ed.2d 797; *and see generally, Validity of Ordinance Restricting Number of Unrelated*

Persons Who Can Live Together in Residential Zone, Ann., 12 A.L.R.4th 238), but a municipality may not seek to achieve it by enacting a zoning ordinance that "limit[s] the definition of family to exclude a household which in every but a biological sense is a single family" (*City of White Plains v. Ferraioli, supra,* 34 N.Y.2d at p. 306, 357 N.Y.S.2d 449, 313 N.E.2d 756). Zoning is "intended to control types of housing and living and not the genetic or intimate internal family relations of human beings" (*City of White Plains v. Ferraioli, supra,* at p. 305, 357 N.Y.S.2d 449, 313 N.E.2d 756) and if a household is "the functional and factual equivalent of a natural family" (*Group House v. Board of Zoning & Appeals, supra,* 45 N.Y.2d at p. 272, 357 N.Y.S.2d 449, 313 N.E.2d 756), the ordinance may not exclude it from a single-family neighborhood and still serve a valid purpose. This ordinance, by limiting occupancy of single-family homes to persons related by blood, marriage or adoption or to only two unrelated persons of a certain age, excludes many households who pose no threat to the goal of preserving the character of the traditional single-family neighborhood, such as the households involved in *White Plains* and *Group House,* and thus fails the rational relationship test.

* * *

Defendants contend that the scope of protection accorded under the due process clause of our State Constitution is coextensive with the protection provided by the due process clause of the 14th Amendment and that the challenged portion of the ordinance would survive Federal due process scrutiny under *Village of Belle Terre v. Boraas,* 416 U.S. 1, 94 S.Ct. 1536, 39 L.Ed.2d 797, *supra.* Because the ordinance challenged in this case contains age limitations making it more restrictive than the *Belle Terre* ordinance and because the Supreme Court did not state in either *Belle Terre* or *Moore v. East Cleveland,* 431 U.S. 494, 97 S.Ct. 1932, 52 L.Ed.2d 531, *supra* what definition of family is minimally necessary to survive Federal due process scrutiny, those decisions are not determinative of whether the ordinance before us would withstand Federal constitutional analysis. We have no need to consider the issue, however, for it is clear that the definition of family contained in this ordinance is incompatible with our prior decisions in *White Plains* and *Group House.* Although those cases did not involve an explicit adjudication of the homeowner's constitutional rights, they also cannot reasonably be interpreted as relying upon the public policy favoring establishment of group homes found in the Social Services Law (Social Services Law § 374–c). Quite the contrary, in each case the court expressly disavowed any reliance on the homeowner's assertion that enforcement of the restrictive definitions of family contained in the challenged ordinance would contravene the State's Social Services Law and the public policy embodied in it (*see, Group House v. Board of Zoning & Appeals,* 45 N.Y.2d 266, 271, 408 N.Y.S.2d 377, 380 N.E.2d 207, *supra; City of White Plains v. Ferraioli,* 34 N.Y.2d 300, 306, 357 N.Y.S.2d 449, 313 N.E.2d 756, *supra; cf. Crane Neck Assn. v. New York City/Long Is. County Servs. Group,* 61 N.Y.2d 154, 472 N.Y.S.2d 901, 460 N.E.2d

1336). Thus, the reasoning employed in *White Plains* and *Group House* is equally applicable to the constitutional issue raised on this appeal and provides ample support for the conclusion reached today.

Accordingly, in view of our holding that the definition of family in article I, § 1 of the Building Zone Ordinance of the Town of Oyster Bay is facially unconstitutional under the due process clause of the New York State Constitution (art. I, § 6), the order of the Appellate Division should be affirmed, with costs.

KAYE, JUDGE (concurring).

[Concurring opinion omitted.]

Note

Also see Baer v. Town of Brookhaven, 73 N.Y.2d 942, 540 N.Y.S.2d 234, 537 N.E.2d 619 (1989) where the court struck down a prohibition against more than four unrelated persons in the single family district. The defendants were five elderly women sharing a house.

CITY OF LADUE v. HORN

Missouri Court of Appeals, 1986.
720 S.W.2d 745.

CRANDALL, JUDGE.

Defendants, Joan Horn and E. Terrence Jones, appeal from the judgment of the trial court in favor of plaintiff, City of Ladue (Ladue), which enjoined defendants from occupying their home in violation of Ladue's zoning ordinance and which dismissed defendants' counterclaim. We affirm.

The case was submitted to the trial court on stipulated facts. Ladue's Zoning Ordinance No. 1175 was in effect at all times pertinent to the present action. Certain zones were designated as one-family residential. The zoning ordinance defined family as: "One or more persons related by blood, marriage or adoption, occupying a dwelling unit as an individual housekeeping organization." The only authorized accessory use in residential districts was for "[a]ccommodations for domestic persons employed and living on the premises and home occupations." The purpose of Ladue's zoning ordinance was broadly stated as to promote "the health, safety, morals and general welfare" of Ladue.

In July, 1981, defendants purchased a seven-bedroom, four-bathroom house which was located in a single-family residential zone in Ladue. Residing in defendants' home were Horn's two children (aged 16 and 19) and Jones's one child (age 18). The two older children attended out-of-state universities and lived in the house only on a part-time basis. Although defendants were not married, they shared a common bedroom, maintained a joint checking account for the household expenses, ate their meals together, entertained together, and disciplined each other's children. Ladue made demands upon defendants to vacate their home because their household did not comprise a family, as defined by Ladue's zoning ordinance, and therefore they could not live in an area zoned for single-family dwellings. When defendants refused to vacate, Ladue sought to enjoin defendants' continued violation of the zoning ordinance. Defendants counterclaimed, seeking a declaration that the zoning ordinance was constitutionally void. They also sought attorneys' fees and costs. The trial court entered a permanent injunction in favor of Ladue and dismissed defendants' counterclaim. Enforcement of the injunction was stayed pending this appeal.

* * *

Capsulated, defendants' attack on Ladue's ordinance is three-pronged. First, the zoning limitations foreclose them from exercising their right to associate freely with whomever they wish. *Roberts v. United States Jaycees,* 468 U.S. 609, 104 S.Ct. 3244, 82 L.Ed.2d 462 (1984). Second, their right to privacy is violated by the zoning restrictions. *Stanley v. Georgia,* 394 U.S. 557, 89 S.Ct. 1243, 22 L.Ed.2d 542 (1969). Third, the zoning classification distinguishes between related persons and unrelated persons. *United States Dept. of Agriculture v. Moreno,* 413 U.S. 528, 93 S.Ct. 2821, 37 L.Ed.2d 782 (1973). Defendants allege that the United States and Missouri Constitutions grant each of them the right to share his or her residence with whomever he or she chooses. They assert that Ladue has not demonstrated a compelling, much less rational, justification for the overly proscriptive blood or legal relationship requirement in its zoning ordinance.

Defendants posit that the term "family" is susceptible to several meanings. They contend that, since their household is the "functional and factual equivalent of a natural family," the ordinance may not preclude them from living in a single-family residential Ladue neighborhood. *See, e.g., McMinn v. Town of Oyster Bay,* 66 N.Y.2d 544, 498 N.Y.S.2d 128, 488 N.E.2d 1240 (Ct.App.1985). Defendants argue in their brief as follows:

> The record amply demonstrates that the private, intimate interests of Horn and Jones are substantial. Horn, Jones, and their respective children have historically lived together as a single family unit. They use and occupy their home for the identical purposes and in the identical manners as families which are biologically or maritally related.

To bolster this contention, defendants elaborate on their shared duties, as set forth earlier in this opinion. Defendants acknowledge the importance of viewing themselves as a family unit, albeit a "conceptual family" as opposed to a "true non-family," in order to prevent the application of the ordinance.

The fallacy in defendants' syllogism is that the stipulated facts do not compel the conclusion that defendants are living as a family. A man and woman living together, sharing pleasures and certain responsibilities, does not *per se* constitute a family in even the conceptual sense. To approximate a family relationship, there must exist a commitment to a permanent relationship and a perceived reciprocal obligation to support and to care for each other. *See, e.g., State ex rel. Ellis v. Liddle,* 520 S.W.2d 644, 650 (Mo.App.1975). Only when these characteristics are present can the conceptual family, perhaps, equate with the traditional family. In a traditional family, certain of its inherent attributes arise from the legal relationship of the family members. In a non-traditional family, those same qualities arise in fact, either by explicit agreement or by tacit understanding among the parties.

While the stipulated facts could arguably support an inference by the trial court that defendants and their children comprised a non-traditional family, they do not compel that inference. Absent findings of fact and conclusions of law, we cannot assume that the trial court's perception of defendants' familial status comported with defendants' characterization of themselves as a conceptual family. In fact, if a finding by the trial court that defendants' living arrangement constituted a conceptual family is critical to a determination in defendants' favor, we can assume that the court's finding was adverse to defendants' position. Ordinarily, given our deference to the decision of the trial court, that would dispose of this appeal. We decline, however, to restrict our ruling to such a narrow basis. We therefore consider the broader issues presented by the parties. We assume, *arguendo,* that the sole basis for the judgment entered by the trial court was that defendants were not related by blood, marriage or adoption, as required by Ladue's ordinance.

We first consider whether the ordinance violates any federally protected rights of the defendants. Generally, federal court decisions hold that a zoning classification based upon a biological or a legal relationship among household members is justifiable under constitutional police powers to protect the public health, safety, morals or welfare of the community. *See* P. Rohan, Zoning and Land Use Controls, § 3.04[2][a] (1986).

* * *

In *Village of Euclid v. Ambler Realty Co.,* 272 U.S. 365, 47 S.Ct. 114, 71 L.Ed. 303 (1926) and in *Nectow v. City of Cambridge,* 277 U.S. 183, 48 S.Ct. 447, 72 L.Ed. 842 (1928), the United States Supreme Court also established the due process parameters of permissible legislation. The ordinance in question must have a "foundation in reason" and bear a "substantial relation to the public health, the public morals, the public safety or the public welfare in its proper sense." *Nectow,* 277 U.S. at 187–88, 48 S.Ct. at 448 (quoting *Euclid,* 272 U.S. at 395, 47 S.Ct. at 121).

In the *Village of Belle Terre v. Boraas,* 416 U.S. 1, 94 S.Ct. 1536, 39 L.Ed.2d 797 (1974), the court addressed a zoning regulation of the type at issue in this case. The court held that the Village of Belle Terre ordinance involved no fundamental right, but was typical of economic and social legislation which is upheld if it is reasonably related to a permissible governmental objective. *Id.* at 7–8, 94 S.Ct. at 1540. The challenged zoning ordinance of the Village of Belle Terre defined family as:

> One or more persons related by blood, adoption or marriage, living and cooking together as a single housekeeping unit [or] a number of persons but not exceeding two (2) living and cooking together as a single housekeeping unit though not related by blood, adoption, or marriage * * *.

The court upheld the ordinance, reasoning that the ordinance constituted valid land use legislation reasonably designed to maintain traditional family values and patterns.

The importance of the family was reaffirmed in *Moore v. City of East Cleveland,* 431 U.S. 494, 97 S.Ct. 1932, 52 L.Ed.2d 531 (1977), wherein the United States Supreme Court was confronted with a housing ordinance which defined a "family" as only certain closely related individuals. Consequently, a grandmother who lived with her son and two grandsons was convicted of violating the ordinance because her two grandsons were first cousins rather than brothers. The United States Supreme Court struck down the East Cleveland ordinance for violating the freedom of personal choice in matters of marriage and family life. The court distinguished *Belle Terre* by stating that the ordinance in that case allowed all individuals related by blood, marriage or adoption to live together; whereas East Cleveland, by restricting the number of related persons who could live together, sought "to regulate the occupancy of its housing by slicing deeply into the family itself." *Id.* at 498, 97 S.Ct. at 1935. The court pointed out that the institution of the family is protected by the Constitution precisely because it is so deeply rooted in the American tradition and that "[o]urs is by no means a tradition limited to respect for the bonds uniting the members of the nuclear family." *Id.* at 504, 97 S.Ct. at 1938.

Here, because we are dealing with economic and social legislation and not with a fundamental interest or a suspect classification, the test of constitutionality is whether the ordinance is reasonable and not arbitrary and bears a rational relationship to a permissible state objective. *Belle Terre,* 416 U.S. at 7–8, 94 S.Ct. at 1540. "[E]very line drawn by a legislature leaves some out that might well have been included. That exercise of discretion, however, is a legislative, not a judicial, function." *Id.* at 8, 94 S.Ct. at 1540. (footnote omitted).

Ladue has a legitimate concern with laying out guidelines for land use addressed to family needs. "It is ample to lay out zones where family values, youth values, and the blessings of quiet seclusion and clean air make the area a sanctuary for people." *Id.* at 9, 94 S.Ct. at 1541. The question of whether Ladue could have chosen more precise means to effectuate its legislative goals is immaterial. Ladue's zoning ordinance is rationally related to its expressed purposes and violates no provisions of the Constitution of the United States. Further, defendants' assertion that they have a constitutional right to share their residence with whomever they please amounts to the same argument that was made and found unpersuasive by the court in *Belle Terre.*

We next consider whether the Ladue ordinance violates any rights of defendants protected by the Missouri Constitution. Defendants rely on several Missouri cases which they allege have "expanded the definition of 'family.' "We disagree with defendants' conclusion.

In *State ex rel. Ellis v. Liddle,* 520 S.W.2d 644 (Mo.App.1975), the zoning ordinance divided the term "family" into two distinct categories, as follows:

> First, "one or more persons related by blood, marriage, or adoption living together in one dwelling unit" in a "common household" including servants, guests, boarders, roomers or lodgers. The ordinance places no limitation on the number of such persons occupying the dwelling unit. Second, persons "not related by blood, marriage, or adoption". Such occupancy may not exceed 10 persons in any one dwelling unit.

Id. at 650. Given this definition, the court permitted the operation of a group home for six to eight juvenile boys and two "teaching parents" in a single-family residential neighborhood in Maryville, Missouri. The court stated that it was clear that, *"both under the specific terms of the ordinance* and under common law" (emphasis added), the operation of the group home did no violence to the single-family residence requirement.

In *City of Vinita Park v. Girls Sheltercare, Inc.,* 664 S.W.2d 256 (Mo.App.1984), this court allowed the use of a single-family residence as a girls' group home operated by the Juvenile Court of St. Louis County in the City of Vinita Park. The Vinita Park Zoning Ordinance defined family as "[o]ne or more persons related by blood or marriage occupying a premises and living as a single housekeeping unit." *Id.* at 258. The housing ordinance contained a more expansive definition of family:

> [A]n individual or married couple and the children thereof and no more than two other persons related directly to the individual or married couple by blood or marriage and not more than three persons not related by blood or marriage living together as a single housekeeping unit in a dwelling unit.

Id. at 259 n. 1.

The court stated that, although the group did not "conform to the letter of either of the *ordinances* which defines family," it did conform to "the spirit of the *ordinances.*" *Id.* at 259. (emphasis added). After addressing the "family" issue, the court addressed what it referred to as the "pivotal issue" of the case concerning what limitations there are on the power of a municipality to zone public uses. The court held that "the leasing of the premises pursuant to the statutory authority for the county and juvenile court to establish a group home is a governmental function (use) and thereby immune from the City of Vinita Park's zoning ordinance." *Id.* at 262.

In both of these cases, the reviewing court looked to the definition of family as set forth in the ordinance. Defendants' argument that these cases "expand" the definition of family is unpersuasive. The clear implication of these cases is that the appellate court will give deference to a zoning ordinance, particularly when there is no overriding governmental interest or statutory authority to negate the legislative prerogative to define family based upon biological or legal relationships.

For purposes of its zoning code, Ladue has in precise language defined the term family. It chose the definition which comports with the historical and traditional notions of family; namely, those people related by blood, marriage or adoption. That definition of family has been upheld in numerous Missouri decisions. *See, e.g., London v. Handicapped Facilities Board of St. Charles County,* 637 S.W.2d 212 (Mo.App.1982) (group home not a "family" as used in restrictive covenant); *Feely v. Birenbaum,* 554 S.W.2d 432 (Mo.App.1977) (two unrelated males not a "family" as used in restrictive covenant); *Cash v. Catholic Diocese,* 414 S.W.2d 346 (Mo.App.1967) (nuns not a "family" as used in a restrictive covenant).

Decisions from other state jurisdictions have addressed identical constitutional challenges to zoning ordinances similar to the ordinance in the instant case. The reviewing courts have upheld their respective ordinances on the ground that maintenance of a traditional family environment constitutes a reasonable basis for excluding uses that may impair the stability of that environment and erode the values associated with traditional family life.[1]

The essence of zoning is selection; and, if it is not invidious or discriminatory against those not selected, it is proper. *Town of Durham v. White Enterprises, Inc.,* 115 N.H. 645, 348 A.2d 706 (1975). There is no doubt that there is a governmental interest in marriage and in preserving the integrity of the biological or legal family. There is no concomitant governmental interest in keeping together a group of unrelated persons, no matter how closely they simulate a family. Further, there is no state policy which commands that groups of people may live under the same roof in any section of a municipality they choose.

---

1. *See, e.g., City of White Plains v. Ferraioli,* 34 N.Y.2d 300, 357 N.Y.S.2d 449, 313 N.E.2d 756 (1974) (married couple, their two children and 10 foster children not a family under city's ordinance); *Rademan v. City and County of Denver,* 186 Colo. 250, 526 P.2d 1325 (1974) (two married couples living as a "communal family" not a family); *Town of Durham v. White Enterprises, Inc.,* 115 N.H. 645, 348 A.2d 706 (1975) (student renters not a family); *Prospect Gardens Convalescent Home, Inc. v. City of Norwalk,* 32 Conn.Sup. 214, 347 A.2d 637 (1975) (nursing home employees living together not a family). *See generally* Annot., 12 A.L.R.4th 238 (1985). A number of jurisdictions have found restrictive zoning ordinances invalid. *See, e.g., City of Des Plaines v. Trottner,* 34 Ill.2d 432, 216 N.E.2d 116 (1966) (ordinance with restrictive definition of family violates authority delegated by state legislature in the enabling statute); *City of Santa Barbara v. Adamson,* 27 Cal.3d 123, 164 Cal.Rptr. 539, 610 P.2d 436 (1980) (zoning ordinance limiting the number of unrelated persons who could live together, but not related persons, did not further legislative goals); *Charter Township of Delta v. Dinolfo,* 419 Mich. 253, 351 N.W.2d 831 (1984) (restrictive definition of family not rationally related to achieving township's goals).

The stated purpose of Ladue's zoning ordinance is the promotion of the health, safety, morals and general welfare in the city. Whether Ladue could have adopted less restrictive means to achieve these same goals is not a controlling factor in considering the constitutionality of the zoning ordinance. Rather, our focus is on whether there exists some reasonable basis for the means actually employed. In making such a determination, if any state of facts either known or which could reasonably be assumed is presented in support of the ordinance, we must defer to the legislative judgment. We find that Ladue has not acted arbitrarily in enacting its zoning ordinance which defines family as those related by blood, marriage or adoption. Given the fact that Ladue has so defined family, we defer to its legislative judgment.

The judgment of the trial court is affirmed.

PUDLOWSKI, P.J., and KAROHL, J., concur.

Notes

1. The New York and Missouri cases clearly depict the "battle line" over the issue of single-family definitions. Which approach do you find more sound? Do you detect in this problem the perennial dispute concerning judicial activism versus judicial deference to legislative authority? Another case like the Ladue case is Zavala v. City of Denver, 759 P.2d 664 (Colo. 1988).

2. In City of Santa Barbara v. Adamson cited in the footnote by the Missouri court, the California Supreme Court struck down an ordinance which defined family to include as many as five unrelated people living together as a single housekeeping unit. The court based its decision primarily upon the provision in the California constitution protecting privacy. The facts in Adamson are somewhat unusual:

> The record shows that appellants are three residents of a house in a single-family zone where the minimum lot-size is one acre. They and other individuals form a group of 12 adults who live in a 24–room, 10–bedroom, 6–bathroom house owned by appellant Adamson. The occupants are in their late 20's or early 30's and include a business woman, a graduate biochemistry student, a tractor-business operator, a real estate woman, a lawyer, and others. They are not related by blood, marriage, or adoption.

> They moved into the house after Adamson acquired it on December 1, 1977. On February 9, 1978, following warnings, the city attorney sued for a temporary restraining order, preliminary injunction, and permanent injunction. A restraining order was issued on March 7, 1978; a preliminary injunction on March 29, 1978.

> Appellants' household illustrates the kind of living arrangements prohibited by the ordinance's rule-of-five. (Section 28.04.230, subd. 2, supra.) They chose to reside with each other when Adamson made it known she was looking for congenial people with whom to share her house. Since then, they explain, they have become a close group with social, economic, and psychological commitments to each other. They share expenses, rotate chores, and eat evening meals together. Some

have children who regularly visit. Two (not including Adamson) have contributed over $2,000 each to improving the house and defraying costs of this lawsuit. Emotional support and stability are provided by the members to each other; they enjoy recreational activities such as a trip to Mexico together; they have chosen to live together mainly because of their compatibility.

Regarding physical environment, the house has 6,231 square feet of space and is hidden from the street by trees and a fence. It has off-street parking for at least 12 cars. Appellants have built a wall around part of the property and a new, private driveway to help isolate them from neighbors' houses. There is no evidence of overcrowding though, after appellants had arrived, some neighbors did notice a larger number of cars parked on the property and an understandable increase in the number of residents.

3.   Another case, similar to the Adamson case, also rejected the Belle Terre rationale and found that an ordinance containing a restrictive definition of family violated the state constitutional provision recognizing the right of privacy. See State v. Baker, 81 N.J. 99, 405 A.2d 368 (1979). Also see City of Chula Vista v. Pagard, 115 Cal.App.3d 785, 171 Cal.Rptr. 738 (1981), where a claim of religious freedom to live communally was at issue; Holy Name Hospital v. Montroy, 153 N.J.Super. 181, 379 A.2d 299 (1977), where the court found that four nuns sharing a house constituted a harmless voluntary family; Children's Home of Easton v. City of Easton, 53 Pa. Cmwlth. 216, 417 A.2d 830 (1980), where the court held that a proposed foster home was the functional equivalent of a biological family and thus distinguishable from Belle Terre.

4.   In Borough of Glassboro v. Vallorosi, 117 N.J. 421, 568 A.2d 888 (1990) the New Jersey Supreme Court struck down a single-family definition that was applied to a group of ten college sophomores leasing a house. The court noted that the ordinance was adopted after "a rowdy weekend celebration by Glassboro State College students." Because the students planned to live in the house for three years and shared housekeeping duties, the court found that they were the functional equivalent of a family.

Compare College Area Renters and Landlord Ass'n v. City of San Diego, 43 Cal.App.4th 677, 50 Cal.Rptr.2d 515 (1996). Here the court held that an attempt by the city to restrict the number of unrelated occupants in apartments under a sliding scale relating to square footage, off-street parking, and number of bathrooms violated the state constitution's equal protection provision. Owner-occupied overcrowded housing was exempted from the ordinance, enacted to deal with the problem of "mini dorms" in neighborhoods near college campuses. Another "mini dorm" case is Kirsch v. Prince George's County, 331 Md. 89, 626 A.2d 372, cert. denied 510 U.S. 1011, 114 S.Ct. 600, 126 L.Ed.2d 565 (1993) (zoning ordinance restricting rental to student groups but not other groups of similar size violates Equal Protection Clause).

The Michigan Court of Appeals, on the other hand, upheld an ordinance in Ann Arbor limiting occupancy of single-family houses to not more than six unrelated individuals. Stegeman v. City of Ann Arbor, 213 Mich.App. 487, 540 N.W.2d 724 (1995). Perhaps college students in Michigan are different than a religious commune, because an earlier Michigan Supreme Court case, Charter Twp. of Delta v. Dinolfo, 419 Mich. 253, 351 N.W.2d 831 (1984) held that a ban against more than six unrelated individuals occupying a single-family house denied due process and was arbitrary as applied to members of The Work of Christ Community living together in a house. Also see Unification Theological Seminary v. City of Poughkeepsie, 201 A.D.2d 484, 607 N.Y.S.2d 383 (1994).

5. In the Wall Street Journal, Jan. 7, 1981, p. 21, an article describes the building of a new type of house in California, called a tandem house, containing two private areas of equal size with a bedroom and bathroom flanking a common area of living room, dining room and kitchen. This house is designed for buyers called "mingles" or "couplets" who may be unrelated persons (neither a traditional nor alternative family) who could not individually afford to buy a house and who by combining assets can share a house. The tandem house is obviously designed to meet the problem of inflationary mortgage and building costs. Should zoning ordinance definitions of family be allowed to inhibit such real estate marketing devices as the tandem house?

6. The single-family problem is important not only in the context presented in this section—the traditional family as opposed to alternative styles of living—but is also an essential ingredient in the problem presented in a later section, exclusion of group homes and institutional uses in the single-family zoning district.

B. EXCLUSION BY LARGE LOT REQUIREMENTS

The local zoning ordinance may prescribe a minimum area for industrial, commercial or residential use. In this section we look at cases involving such restrictions for residential use. In prescribing such minimal requirements the local legislative body may have in mind:

1. The need for a sufficiently fat real estate levy to pay pro rata costs of schools and municipal services;

2. Aesthetics, in the sense of an attractive estate type of neighborhood for pleasant living with substantial green space;

3. Protection of agricultural land from premature subdivision into small lots;

4. Development of a "snob appeal" neighborhood for the "right" people, or otherwise expressed, "preservation of the character of the neighborhood;"

5. Public health, especially where absence of public sewer and heavy soil requires a substantial area for effective private sewage disposal;

6. Danger from fire;

7. Traffic control and off-street parking;

8. Topography, i.e., the irregularities of the terrain.

Which of these reasons is valid as a basis for sustaining minimum area requirements? For a case upholding a three-acre minimum in the "finest residential development of the entire metropolitan area" of St. Louis, in which evidence under most of the headings just given was reviewed, see Flora Realty & Inv. Co. v. City of Ladue, 362 Mo. 1025, 246 S.W.2d 771 (1952), appeal dismissed 344 U.S. 802, 73 S.Ct. 41, 97 L.Ed. 626 (1952). This is only one of numerous such cases.

Unlike most of the cases alleging that a zoning ordinance is exclusionary because no provision is made for a particular use, the cases in this section, and the one which follows raise the exclusionary zoning problem because the particular requirement allegedly raises the cost of housing or renders economically infeasible housing types which might be within the means of low and moderate income families. Should the courts, or do the courts, apply different legal standards to this type of exclusion?

SIMON v. NEEDHAM

Supreme Judicial Court of Massachusetts, 1942.
311 Mass. 560, 42 N.E.2d 516, 141 A.L.R. 688.

RONAN, J. This is a petition filed in the Land Court in accordance with G.L. (Ter.Ed.) c. 240, sec. 14A and c. 185, sec. 1(j½), both as inserted by St.1934, c. 263, to determine the validity and extent of a zoning by-law which prescribed a minimum area of one acre for house lots in the residential district in which the petitioner's land was located. The judge of the Land Court made a written decision which included findings of fact and rulings of law. He ordered the petition dismissed. The petitioner excepted to certain rulings, to the refusal to give the rulings requested by him, and to the order dismissing the petition.

Needham is a suburb of Boston located twelve miles from the center of Boston, having an area of about eight thousand one hundred sixty-two acres, and a population of approximately thirteen thousand which has been steadily increasing for the last twelve years. It is essentially a residential community with a few manufacturing plants. It has two local business centers and also a small business district containing a number of garages in the northeasterly part of the town where a main traffic route intersects one of the principal highways of the town. A branch line of a railroad having five stations serves the town as do also three bus lines.

The land now owned by the petitioner has been in a single residence district since the adoption of a zoning by-law by the town in 1925. There was no minimum house lot area for the district until 1931, when an area of seven thousand square feet was established. This area was increased in 1939 to ten thousand square feet. The by-law contains a provision authorizing the board of appeals to permit the use of a smaller lot in certain instances. This by-law was amended on July 21, 1941, by dividing the single residence zone into two districts, A and B. All the building lots in district A, which included nearly all of the south side of the town, were required to be at least an acre in area. This new district then comprised one hundred eighty-nine lots, thirty-three of them having an area of less than an acre and others having an area of many acres. The petitioner's land was located in district A.

Early in June, 1941, the petitioner entered into an agreement to purchase a triangular parcel of land, which was bounded on each side by a public highway, and contained about twenty-four and one-half acres. He had a plan prepared showing the subdivision of this parcel into fifty-eight lots, varying in area from thirteen thousand five hundred to twenty-seven thousand square feet, and submitted the plan at a hearing before the planning board, which took the matter under advisement. He then recorded this plan and a later plan in the registry of deeds. The transfer of the land to him was recorded later in July, 1941. The planning board on August 19, 1941, disapproved the plan submitted to it because the lots did not comply with the by-law as amended.

The petitioner's lot is covered with a small growth of pine, scrub oak and birches and is suitably adapted for the construction of dwellings. It is located in a stretch of rolling country side, which comprises undeveloped woodland, tillage and pasture land, except for swamp land where the land slopes down to the Charles River. The Charles River and Sabrina Lake districts are the sites of country estates, with expensive buildings and large acreages. The land in question is about three quarters of a mile distant from these districts.

There was evidence tending to show a steady demand for new homes in the town. During the four years commencing with January 1, 1937, more than four hundred fifty permits have been issued by the building inspector for the construction of dwellings. There was also evidence that the value of the petitioner's land had been diminished by reason of the requirement that the area of house lots should be at least an acre.

The issue presented for decision is whether the town had the power to prescribe this minimum area for lots in the residential district in which the petitioner's land is located.

A city or town is expressly empowered to adopt zoning ordinances or by-laws "For the purpose of promoting the health, safety, convenience, morals or welfare of its inhabitants" and to "regulate * * * the size and width of lots." G.L. (Ter.Ed.) c. 40, sec. 25, as appearing in St.1933, c. 269, sec. 1. Municipalities have the right to determine whether the public interests demand an exercise of the power and, if so, to select the measures that are necessary for the protection of such interests. A city or town is justified in asserting the power where the interests of the public require such action and where the means employed are reasonably necessary for the accomplishment of the purpose. The authority of the respondent town to regulate the size of house lots is not challenged, but its authority to fix the area at a minimum of an acre is assailed. * * *

The physical characteristics of the district itself, considered in conjunction with those of the town, strongly indicate that the district is admirably suited for one family residences. Its nearness to Boston and other densely populated areas makes it available for residential purposes for those who desire the advantages of the quiet and beauty of rural surroundings. The evidence shows a steady demand for homes in the town, and that the development of different areas for the construction of homes has already begun and will probably continue. The establishment of a neighborhood of homes in such a way as to avoid congestion in the streets, to secure safety from fire and other dangers, to prevent overcrowding of land, to obtain adequate light, air and sunshine, and to enable it to be furnished with transportation, water, light, sewer and other public necessities, which when established would tend to improve and beautify the town and would harmonize with the natural characteristics of the locality, could be materially facilitated by a regulation that prescribed a reasonable minimum area for house lots. The area was to be determined not only in the light of present needs of the public but also with a view to the probable requirements of the public that would arise in the immediate future from the normal development of the land. The advantages enjoyed by those living in one-family dwellings located upon an acre lot might be thought to exceed those possessed by persons living upon a lot of ten thousand square feet. More freedom from noise and traffic might result. The danger from fire from outside sources might be reduced. A better opportunity for rest and relaxation might be afforded. Greater facilities for children to play on the premises and not in the streets would be available. There may perhaps be more inducement for one to attempt something in the way of the cultivation of flowers, shrubs and vegetables. There may be other advantages accruing to the occupants of the larger lots. The benefits derived by those living in such a neighborhood must be considered with the benefit that would accrue to the public generally who resided in Needham by the presence of such a neighborhood. In the four towns that adjoin Needham the minimum area restrictions for some residential lots have been fixed in one at twenty thousand square feet, in two others at forty thousand square feet, and in the fourth at an acre. Of eight other towns within a short distance from Needham, six have prescribed a minimum area of forty thousand square feet for house lots, and two others have fixed the minimum area as an acre. Such evidence is not decisive that the imposition of a restriction of an area of an acre is reasonable and proper, but it is persuasive that many other communities when faced with an apparently similar problem have determined that the public interest was best served by the adoption of a restriction in some instances identical and in others nearly identical with that imposed by the respondent town. * * *

There may be a difference of opinion as to the real advantages that will accrue from the larger lots and whether they are such as to lead one to the conclusion that the adoption of the acre area will result in a real and genuine enhancement of the public interests. It seems to us that a belief that such a result may be realized in this instance is not unreasonable. * * *

The planning board of the town reported, at the special town meeting that adopted the amendment, recommending the passage of the amendment on the ground that the town was receiving more than $60,000 in taxes from district A, that on account of the small amount of municipal service required by the district a tax profit of nearly $50,000 or $2 on the tax rate had resulted, and there would be a much higher tax rate if the district was developed with low cost houses. The expense that might be incurred by a town in furnishing police and fire protection, the construction and maintenance of public ways, schoolhouses, water mains and sewers and other public conveniences might be considered as an element, more or less incidentally involved, in the adoption of a zoning by-law that will promote the health, safety, convenience, morals or welfare of the inhabitants of the town without imposing any unreasonable and arbitrary burden upon the landowners. A zoning by-law cannot be adopted for the purpose of setting up a barrier against the influx of thrifty and respectable citizens who desire to live there and who are able and willing to erect homes upon lots upon which fair and reasonable restrictions have been imposed, nor for the purpose of protecting the large estates that are already located in the district. The strictly local interests of the town must yield if it appears that they are plainly in conflict with the general interests of the public at large, and in such instances the interest of "the municipality would not be allowed to stand in the way." * * * We assume in favor of the petitioner that a zoning by-law cannot be used primarily as a device to maintain a low tax rate. It does not appear that it was so used here. It cannot be assumed that the voters in following the recommendations of the board were activated by the reasons mentioned by the board. See Duffey v. Hopkinton, 236 Mass. 5, 127 N.E. 540; Sheldon v. School Committee of Hopedale, 276 Mass. 230, 177 N.E. 94. These reasons dealt with merely one phase of a subject under discussion at the town meeting. We do not know what other considerations were advanced for the passage of the amendment. The citizens of the town were undoubtedly familiar with the locality and with all the material factors involved in the necessity, character and degree of regulation that should be adopted in the public interest. The action of the voters is not to be invalidated simply because someone presented a reason that was unsound or insufficient in law to support the conclusion for which it was urged. * * *

The ruling dismissing the petition necessarily included an implied ruling that the by-law was valid. There was no error in refusing the rulings requested. The petitioner properly does not now contend that any rights accrued to him by filing his plans of the subdivision of the land in the registry of deeds without securing their approval by the planning board. We cannot quite pronounce the instant by-law invalid when applied to the petitioner's land in all the circumstances disclosed by this record. We make no intimation that, if the lots were required to be larger than an acre or if the circumstances were even slightly different, the same result would be reached. It will be time enough to determine that question when it is presented.

Exceptions overruled.

Notes

1. Compare the more recent case of Aronson v. Town of Sharon, 346 Mass. 598, 195 N.E.2d 341 (1964), in which the Massachusetts Supreme

Judicial Court invalidated the zoning of a district as a rural single residential district with each lot to contain not less than 100,000 square feet and to have a width of not less than 200 feet. Sharon was a residential town with one small industry and two business centers which were four and five miles from the site. The nearest school was over three miles away and a national highway was about seven miles away by road. There was no sewer system and water service was not extended to most areas zoned as "Single Residence District Rural," but was available on a public road abutting the site. Much of the area involved was inaccessible by road. There were no large country estates and little residential development in the district. It was argued that "all that has made Sharon beautiful" could be best carried out by the lot size requirements and that the zoning would encourage leaving land in the natural state and thus provide "amenities that are fundamental to mental and physical health." But the court felt that "however worthy the objectives, the by-laws attempts to achieve a result which properly should be the subject of eminent domain." It regarded the square foot requirement on these lots as being unreasonably large. Simon v. Needham, said the Massachusetts court, stated certain advantages of living upon an acre lot as compared with one of 10,000 square feet. But: "While initially an increase in lot size might have the effects there noted, the law of diminishing returns will set in at some point. As applied to the petitioners' property, the attainment of such advantages does not reasonably require lots of 100,000 square feet. Nor would they be attained by keeping the rural district undeveloped, even though this might contribute to the welfare of each inhabitant. Granting the value of recreational areas to the community as a whole, the burden of providing them should not be borne by the individual property owner unless he is compensated." Also see Wilson v. Town of Sherborn, 3 Mass.App.Ct. 237, 326 N.E.2d 922 (1975).

2. But consider also the case of County Comm'rs of Queen Anne's County v. Miles, 246 Md. 355, 228 A.2d 450 (1967), in which the Maryland Court of Appeals upheld a county zoning ordinance providing for five residential zones, one of which covered a substantial land area and imposed a five-acre minimum lot size. The ordinance was attacked on the basis that "the properties were so zoned in order that they could be disposed of only to 'substantial' people, of 'more than ample' financial resources." The court noted that "there were many criteria considered in the decision" including the fact that many historical sites were located in the area. Other testimony, which the court cited, was to the effect that it was desirable to attract persons "of means" to the community; that tourists could be attracted in this manner; that it was a reasonable use of zoning for a rural county to employ in an otherwise urbanized area to preserve the desired character of the county; and that it would contribute to the health and safety of the county by minimizing the sanitation problems, reducing the traffic and channeling the denser population growth into locations nearer the centers of public service, the established towns, etc. The court stated:

> We agree that if the primary purpose or effect of the ordinance is to benefit private interests, rather than the public welfare, the legislation cannot be held valid merely because some of its incidental effects may be for the general good. On the other hand, if the ordinance has a substantial relationship to the general welfare of the community in that

it can fairly be taken as a reasonable effort to plan for the future within the framework of the County's economic and social life, it is not unconstitutional because under it some persons may suffer loss and others be benefited. Courts of other states have had occasion to balance these factors; the decisions, as we read them, turn on the various economic, physical and sociological factors involved in the particular case.

After reviewing a number of these cases, the Maryland court concluded that the ordinance was fair and reasonable and not arbitrary or capricious. The court further concluded that the ordinance did not treat like properties in ways which were unjustifiably dissimilar.

3. The Miles case was noted in 28 Md.L.Rev. 90 (1968), which states that minimum lot requirements of large size (up to five acres) have more often than not been upheld as a valid exercise of the police power. The note quotes, however, from Bilbar Const. Co. v. Board of Adjustment, 393 Pa. 62, 141 A.2d 851, 858 (1958), to this effect: "[M]inimum lot areas may not be ordained so large as to be exclusionary in effect and, thereby, serve a private rather than the public interest." The note reiterates that not too many cases have struck down minimum lot requirements and states that those which have done so have generally considered the desire to keep down the cost of local government as being the chief motivating factor for such exclusionary zoning.

In County of Ada v. Henry, 105 Idaho 263, 668 P.2d 994 (1983) the court upheld a county ordinance requiring an 80–acre minimum lot size. A dissenting judge said: "It is a strange West which we now have where a man of industrious nature is by a bureaucratic ordinance deprived of the right to build his own house on a ten-acre tract. And for what reason? Because it has been thought better that the law should be that a single dwelling be not erected on less than 80 acres! The proposition is basically so monstrous as to be undeserving of further comment."

4. Out of this morass, the obvious problem for anyone seeking to create valid minimum lot requirements is to determine how maximum the minimum requirements may be in the light of the situation at hand. The problem for a lawyer is at what point the minimum ceases to have justification under the police power. You should attempt to identify the various factors which may enter into consideration. Obviously, a three or four-acre minimum might be excessive in one set of circumstances and not excessive in another. Also, it is apparent that how the particular situation strikes the court, or the effect of the particular socio-economic views of the members of the court, is something which may enter in but is not easily catalogued.

NATIONAL LAND AND INVESTMENT CO. v. KOHN

Supreme Court of Pennsylvania, 1965.
419 Pa. 504, 215 A.2d 597.

["Sweetbriar," an 85 acre residential development tract, was worth $260,000 when the lot minimum was one acre. Now that the minimum for the residential area of which "Sweetbriar" is a part has been changed to four acres, the most optimistic estimate is $175,000. The zoning amendment was held unconstitutional by the trial court. The Supreme Court first disposed of a variety of procedural questions to get to the substance of the constitutional issue. Part of the court's analysis of that issue is set out below. Two judges dissented.]

ROBERTS, JUSTICE. * * * Easttown Township has an area of 8.2 square miles devoted almost exclusively to residential use * * * The township finds itself in the path of a population expansion approaching from two directions. From the east, suburbs closer to the center of Philadelphia are reaching capacity and residential development is extending further west to Easttown. In addition, a market for residential sites is being generated by the fast growing industrial-commercial complex in the King of Prussia–Valley Forge area to the north of Easttown Township.

Easttown's vital statistics provide a good indication of its character. At present, about 60% of the township's population resides in an area of about 20% of the township. The remaining 40% of the population occupies the balance of about 80% of its area. Privately imposed restrictions limit lot areas to four, five and ten acre minimums on approximately 10% of the total area of the township, consisting of land located in the southern and western sections. Of the total 5,157 acres in the township, some 898, or about 17%, have been restricted by the new zoning ordinance to minimum lots of two acres. Approximately 1,565 acres composing about 30% of the township are restricted by the zoning ordinance to lots of four acres minimum area. About 5% of the population live in the areas zoned for two and four acre sites which together constitute about 47% of the township. Some 1,835 acres, representing about 35% of the township, remain unaffected by the new zoning and continue, under the township's original zoning classification, to be zoned for building sites with a minimum area of one acre.

* * *

U.S. Census figures show that Easttown's population grew from 2,307 in 1920 to 6,907 in 1960. As of April, 1963, the population estimate was 8,400. Public school population through the sixth grade grew from 498 in the school year 1955–56 to 1,052 in the school year 1963–64 and, as projected, will be about 1,680 in 1969–70.

New residential construction from 1951 through the first eight months of 1963, a twelve year period, consisted of 1,149 units at an estimated cost of about $21,000,000, with an average of 100 building permits annually. At this rate of growth, allowing four persons per housing unit in Easttown, its population, related to new residences, would grow under the previous one acre minimum zoning at the rate of about 400 persons per annum.

* * *

The task of considering the Easttown Township zoning ordinance and passing upon the constitutionality of its four acre minimum area requirement as applied to appellees' property is not an easy one. In the span of years since 1926 when zoning received its judicial blessing, the art and science of land planning has grown increasingly complex and sophisticated. The days are fast disappearing when the judiciary can look at a zoning ordinance and, with nearly as much confidence as a professional zoning expert, decide upon the merits of a zoning plan and its contribution to the health, safety, morals or general welfare of the community. This Court has become increasingly aware that it is neither a super board of adjustment nor a planning commission of last resort * * * The zoning power is one of the tools of government which, in order to be effective, must not be subjected to judicial interference unless clearly necessary. For this reason, a presumption of validity attaches to a zoning ordinance which imposes the burden to prove its invalidity upon the one who challenges it. * * *

While recognizing this presumption, we must also appreciate the fact that zoning involves governmental restrictions upon a landowner's constitutionally guaranteed right to use his property, unfettered, except in very specific instances, by governmental restrictions. The time must never come when, because of frustration with concepts foreign to their legal training, courts abdicate their judicial responsibility to protect the constitutional rights of individual citizens. Thus, the burden of proof imposed upon one who challenges the validity of a zoning regulation must never be made so onerous as to foreclose, for all practical purposes, a landowner's avenue of redress against the infringement of constitutionally protected rights.

The oft repeated, although ill defined, limitation upon the exercise of the zoning power requires that zoning ordinances be enacted for the health, safety, morals or general welfare of the community. * * *

We turn, then, to the question of the constitutionality of four acre minimum in the factual context of the instant case. Quite obviously, appellees will be deprived of part of the value of their property if they are limited in the use of it to four acre lots. When divided into one acre lots as originally planned, the value of "Sweetbriar" for residential building was approximately $260,000. When the four acre restriction was imposed, the number of available building sites in "Sweetbriar" was reduced by 75% and the value of the land, under the most optimistic appraisal, fell to $175,000. The four acre minimum greatly restricts the marketability of this tract because, with fewer potential lots, the cost of improvements such as curbing, streets and other facilities is thus greater on each lot. In addition, each building lot being larger, the cost per lot is automatically increased. The desire of many buyers not to be burdened with the upkeep of a four acre lot also makes "Sweetbriar," so restricted, less desirable. Although there was some evidence in the record that lots of four acres or more could eventually be sold it is clear that there is not a readily available market for such offerings.

Against this deprivation of value, the alleged public purposes cited as justification for the imposition of a four acre minimum area requirement upon appellees' land must be examined. Appellants contend that the four acre minimum is necessary to insure proper sewage disposal in the township and to protect township water from pollution. * * *

We can not help but note also that the Second Class Township Code provides for establishing sanitary regulations which can be enforced by a "sanitary board" regardless of the zoning for the area. The Code also provides for the installation and maintenance of sewer systems but the township has made no plans in this regard. In addition, under the township subdivision regulations, the zoning officer may require lots larger than the minimum permitted by the zoning ordinance if the result of percolation tests upon the land show that a larger land area is needed for proper drainage and disposal of sewage. These legislatively sanctioned methods for dealing with the sewage problem compel the conclusion that a four acre minimum is neither a necessary nor a reasonable method by which Easttown can protect itself from the menace of pollution.

sewage

In addition to the alleged problem of sewage disposal as justifying the four acre minimum, appellants cite the inadequacy of township roads and the burden which continued one acre zoning for the entire township would impose upon that road system.

inadequate roads

* * *

According to the experts produced for both sides, Easttown's present road network as a whole is capable, with normal maintenance and improvement, of serving a population up to 13,000. This is 4,600 more than the population of the township in April, 1963. On the basis of the former one acre zoning, resulting in a population increase of 400 persons per year, that figure would not be reached until after 1972 or later.

It can be seen, therefore, that the restriction to four acre lots, so far as traffic is concerned, is based upon possible future conditions. Zoning is a tool in the hands of governmental bodies which enables them to more effectively meet the demands of evolving and growing communities. It must not and can not be used by those officials as an instrument by which they may shirk their responsibilities. Zoning is a means by which a governmental body can plan for the future—it may not be used as a means to deny the future. * * *

It is not difficult to envision the tremendous hardship, as well as the chaotic conditions, which would result if all the townships in this area decided to deny to a growing population sites for residential development within the means of at least a significant segment of the people.

The third justification for rezoning, and one urged upon us most assiduously, deals with the preservation of the "character" of this area. The photographic exhibits placed in the record by appellants attest to the fact that this is an area of great beauty containing old homes surrounded by beautiful pasture, farm and wood land. It is a very desirable and attractive place in which to live.

Preservation of Character

Involved in preserving Easttown's "character" are four aspects of concern which the township gives for desiring four acre minimum zoning. First, they cite the preservation of open space and the creation of a "greenbelt" which, as most present day commentators impress upon us, are worthy goals. While in full agreement with these goals, we are convinced that four acre minimum zoning does not achieve the creation of a greenbelt in its technical sense and, to the limited extent that open space is so preserved, such zoning as is here involved is not a permissible means to that end.

* * *

If the preservation of open spaces is the township objective, there are means by which this can be accomplished which include authorization for "cluster zoning" or condemnation of development rights with compensation paid for that which is taken. A four acre minimum acreage requirement is not a reasonable method by which the stated end can be achieved.

Next, the township urges us to consider the historic sites in the township and the need to present them in the proper setting. We are unmoved by this contention since it appears to be purely and simply a makeweight. First, an examination of the map of historical sites in the township demonstrates that the overwhelming majority of such sites, located in areas of dense population, can hardly be provided with proper settings by four acre zoning elsewhere in the township. * * *

Closely related to the goal of protecting historic monuments is the expressed desire to protect the "setting" for a number of old homes in Easttown, some dating back to the early days of our Commonwealth. Appellants denominate this goal as falling within the ambit of promoting the "general welfare". Unfortunately, the concept of the general welfare defies meaningful capsule definition and constitutes an exceedingly difficult standard against which to test the validity of legislation. However, it must always be ascertained at the outset whether, in fact, it is the public welfare which is being benefited or whether, disguised as legislation for the public welfare, a zoning ordinance actually served purely private interests.

There is no doubt that many of the residents of this area are highly desirous of keeping it the way it is, preferring, quite naturally, to look out upon land in its natural state rather than on other homes. These desires, however, do not rise to the level of public welfare. This is purely a matter of private desire which zoning regulations may not be employed to effectuate.

* * *

The fourth argument advanced by appellants, and one closely analogous to the preceding one, is that the rural character of the area must be preserved. If the township were developed on the basis of this zoning, however, it could not be seriously contended that the land would retain its rural character—it would simply be dotted with larger homes on larger lots.

Appellants point to the fact that the surrounding townships have similar low density zoning provisions. Although the zoning of the surrounding area is frequently a relevant consideration in assessing the validity of a zoning regulation * * * it is not controlling on the issue presented. This is particularly so when we are dealing with a unique zoning classification such as is involved here. With most zoning classifications, there can be little question as to their suitability in any political subdivision; the only issue concerns their placement. With these classifications, the surrounding zoning is particularly relevant. As the classification itself becomes more questionable, however, similar classifications in surrounding districts become of less significance in supporting the validity of the restriction.

* * *

The township's brief raises (but, unfortunately, does not attempt to answer) the interesting issue of the township's responsibility to those who do not yet live in the township but who are part, or may become part, of the population expansion of the suburbs. Four acre zoning represents Easttown's position that it does not desire to accommodate those who are pressing for admittance to the township unless such admittance will not create any additional burdens upon governmental functions and services. The question posed is whether the township can stand in the way of the natural forces which send our growing population into hitherto undeveloped areas in search of a comfortable place to live. We have concluded not. A zoning ordinance whose primary purpose is to prevent the entrance of newcomers in order to avoid future burdens, economic and otherwise, upon the administration of public services and facilities can not be held valid. Of course, we do not mean to imply that a governmental body may not utilize its zoning power in order to insure that the municipal services which the community requires are provided in an orderly and rational manner.

The brief of the appellant-intervenors creates less of a problem but points up the factors which sometime lurk behind the espoused motives for zoning. What basically appears to bother intervenors is that a small number of lovely old homes will have to start keeping company with a growing number of smaller, less expensive, more densely located houses. It is clear, however, that the general welfare is not fostered or promoted by a zoning ordinance designed to be exclusive and exclusionary. * * *

In light of the foregoing, therefore, we are compelled to conclude that the board of adjustment committed an error of law in upholding the constitutionality of the Easttown Township four acre minimum requirement as applied to appellees' property. We therefore affirm the order of the Court of Common Pleas of Chester County.

Order affirmed.

Notes

1. The Wall Street Journal for August 15, 1966, reported that to avoid the expense of further litigation the town and the builder in the principal case finally compromised on two-acre lots.

2. Compare, with the Kohn case, Bilbar Const. Co. v. Board of Adjustment, 393 Pa. 62, 141 A.2d 851 (1958), which notes that minimum lot areas cannot be so large as to be exclusionary and thereby serve private interests, but finds a one-acre requirement to be reasonable. This was in the same township.

3. See also, Board of County Supervisors v. Carper, 200 Va. 653, 107 S.E.2d 390 (1959), in which a two-acre minimum lot requirement was imposed on about two-thirds of a rapidly growing county. The Virginia court viewed the practical effect of the restriction as preventing low-income people from living in that part of the county and stated that this purpose bore no relation to a valid exercise of the police power. Apparently, it was intended to funnel the low-income population into the eastern one-third of the county "where the cost of operating government would be more economical."

4. The Pennsylvania court returned to the problem of large lot zoning in Appeal of Kit–Mar Builders, Inc., 439 Pa. 466, 268 A.2d 765 (1970). In this case the developer contracted to purchase 140 acres contingent on rezoning to permit one acre homesites, the existing zoning requiring two acre lots on roadways and three acre lots in the interior. The rezoning was denied on grounds of sewerage problems and the developer appealed. Justice Roberts again wrote the majority opinion, striking down the two and three acre restrictions, and reaffirming National Land: "We once again reaffirm our past authority and refuse to allow the township to do precisely what we have never permitted—keep out people, rather than make community improvements. * * * [C]ommunities must deal with the problems of population growth. They may not refuse to confront the future by adopting zoning regulations that effectively restrict population to near present levels." Justice Bell wrote a concurring opinion and two justices dissented. Justice Roberts keyed his opinion to a judicial stand against exclusionary zoning practices. *Quaere:* Is a decision striking down two acre zoning to favor a developer who desires one acre sites a judicial blow against exclusionary zoning? Should not the real issue be whether the community is making provisions for low and moderate income housing? And further, if a community does provide in its zoning for a variety of housing types, then why does it matter that some zones are set aside for one, two, or five acre lots? Consider these questions in connection with the materials on inclusionary zoning in Section 2 infra.

5. The Pennsylvania cases to 1970 are discussed in Comment, 16 Vill.L.Rev. 507 (1970). Developments from 1970 to 1980 are discussed, inter alia, in Martin v. Township of Millcreek, 50 Pa.Cmwlth. 249, 413 A.2d 764 (1980), a case dealing with a ten acre minimum in a rural township. In Hock v. Board of Supervisors of Mount Pleasant Twp., 154 Pa.Cmwlth. 101, 622 A.2d 431 (1993) the court struck down a three-acre minimum in a rural township enacted to preserve prime farmland and to maintain the rural character of the area. But see Reimer v. Board of Supervisors of Upper Mount Bethel Twp., 150 Pa.Cmwlth. 323, 615 A.2d 938 (1992) where a similar lot size minimum was upheld on the basis of concern about ground water pollution, the water table and sewage facilities.

6. See Senior v. Zoning Commission, 146 Conn. 531, 153 A.2d 415 (1959) (four acre minimum upheld for a town having the highest per capita

income in the U.S.); Franmor Realty Corp. v. Old Westbury, 280 App.Div. 945, 116 N.Y.S.2d 68 (1952) (two acre minimum per single family residence upheld); and Gignoux v. Kings Point, 199 Misc. 485, 99 N.Y.S.2d 280 (1950) (40,000 square foot minimum per single family residence upheld). In the first case, to the claim that zoning limited ownership and use of land to the wealthy, the court replied that there were other zones in the town with smaller minima. Various other factors were noted including topography, proximity to urban areas, character of existing residences and absence of commerce and industry.

7. Coke and Liebman, Political Values and Population Density Control, 37 Land Econ. 347 (1961) conclude:

Large minimum lot size requirements have become an important focus of the suburban political process because they are thought to be instrumental in achieving three values: amenity, tax base, and neighborhood homogeneity. Realization of the tax base and homogeneity values depend in large part upon the correctness of the assumption that larger lots result in higher priced homes. The results of this study cast considerable doubt upon the wisdom of making the assumption. The correlation between lot size and selling price is so low that a municipality cannot automatically assure itself of expensive residential areas simply by adopting large lot zoning policies.

YBARRA v. TOWN OF LOS ALTOS HILLS

United States Court of Appeals, Ninth Circuit, 1974.
503 F.2d 250.

Before KILKENNY and WALLACE, CIRCUIT JUDGES, and SOLOMON, DISTRICT JUDGE.

OPINION

SOLOMON, DISTRICT JUDGE.

Appellants challenge the constitutionality of a large-lot zoning ordinance of the City of the Town of Los Altos Hills ["Los Altos" or "the town"], a California suburban community. The trial court held that the zoning ordinance was constitutional and dismissed the action. We affirm.

Appellants are two Mexican–Americans and the Confederacion de la Raza Unida, an unincorporated association of Mexican–American organizations. Neither of the named individual appellants are residents of Los Altos, but both qualify for federally assisted low-income housing. They brought this action on their own behalf and on behalf of all other persons of Mexican descent whose incomes qualify them for federally assisted housing.

In December, 1970, appellants obtained an option to buy certain lots in Los Altos. They paid a nominal amount for the option but agreed to pay $14,000 per acre if the option were exercised. The option could only be exercised if the land were rezoned for multifamily dwellings and if the Federal Housing Administration approved a low-income housing project for that land.

The zoning ordinance provides that a housing lot shall contain not less than one acre and that no lot shall be occupied by more than one primary dwelling unit. Appellants have not applied for a zoning variance to allow construction of their proposed multifamily project.

Appellants brought this action against the town, its city manager, and the members of the town council. Appellants allege that the zoning ordinance prevents them from constructing a housing project and assert that the ordinance violates the supremacy, due process, and equal protection clauses of the United States Constitution. They seek declaratory and injunctive relief.

* * *

Appellants' principal contention is that the Los Altos zoning ordinance denies them equal protection of the laws. They assert that the ordinance discriminates against Mexican–Americans and the poor and that the town must show a compelling state interest to justify discrimination against "suspect classifications" based on ethnic background and wealth.

Appellants' evidence at trial showed that in Santa Clara County, in which Los Altos is located, there is a high statistical correlation between being Mexican–American and being poor. Mexican–Americans form only 2.1% of the town's population but comprise 17.59% of the county's population.

The trial court found that the ordinance prevented poor people from living in Los Altos. He also found that if Mexican–Americans did not live there, it was because of the poverty and not because of their race. Appellants concede that the ordinance does not bar wealthy Mexican–Americans from living in Los Altos. We agree that discrimination against the poor does not become discrimination against an ethnic minority merely because there is a statistical correlation between poverty and ethnic background.

Appellants also assert that they need not show racial discrimination to void the ordinance and that it is sufficient to show that the ordinance discriminates against the poor. They argue that the town must show a compelling interest to justify the ordinance because wealth is a suspect classification. *See* Harper v. Virginia Board of Elections, 383 U.S. 663, 86 S.Ct. 1079, 16 L.Ed.2d 169 (1966); Griffin v. Illinois, 351 U.S. 12, 76 S.Ct. 585, 100 L.Ed. 891 (1956).

In San Antonio School District v. Rodriguez, 411 U.S. 1, 93 S.Ct. 1278, 36 L.Ed.2d 16 (1973), the court discussed the conditions under which poverty becomes a suspect classification under the equal protection clause:

"The individuals, or groups of individuals, who constituted the class discriminated against in our prior cases shared two distinguishing characteristics: because of their impecunity they were completely unable to pay for some desired benefit, and as a consequence, they sustained an absolute deprivation of a meaningful opportunity to enjoy that benefit. 411 U.S. at 20, 93 S.Ct. at 1290."

In our view these two criteria set forth the threshold requirements before a court using traditional tests may consider whether the classification is constitutionally impermissible.

Appellants meet the first criterion because the ordinance prevents them from living in Los Altos because of their poverty. They failed to meet the second criterion because they did not show that they had no "meaningful opportunity" to obtain low-cost housing. The evidence showed that no poor people live or work in Los Altos. Appellants failed to show that adequate low-cost housing was unavailable elsewhere in Santa Clara County in areas accessible to appellants' jobs and social services. In these circumstances the town need not show a compelling interest to justify a zoning ordinance which discriminates against the poor.

Since there is no suspect classification requiring a strict standard of review, the town need only show that the ordinance bears a rational relationship to a legitimate governmental interest. Id. at 40, 93 S.Ct. 1278. Here the ordinance is rationally related to preserving the town's rural environment. See Village of Belle Terre v. Boraas, 416 U.S. 1, 94 S.Ct. 1536, 39 L.Ed.2d 797 (1974). The ordinance does not violate the equal protection clause.

Appellants allege that the ordinance violates Section 65302 of the California Government Code, which requires towns to adopt housing plans which "make adequate provision for the housing needs of all economic segments of the community." We believe that the section requires a town to provide housing for its residents but does not require it to provide housing for non-residents, even though the non-residents may live in the broader urban community of which the town is a part.

Appellants' other contentions are without merit. The ordinance does not conflict with the National Housing Act, 42 U.S.C.A. §§ 1401 et seq., and does not violate the supremacy clause. James v. Valtierra, 402 U.S. 137, 140, 91 S.Ct. 1331, 28 L.Ed.2d 678 (1971). The ordinance is not arbitrary and does not deny appellants due process. See Village of Euclid v. Ambler Realty Co., 272 U.S. 365, 47 S.Ct. 114, 71 L.Ed. 303 (1926).

The judgment of the district court dismissing the action is affirmed.

Notes

1. Is the legal principle to be gleaned from the preceding cases that large lot zoning is definitely exclusionary in regard to low income groups, but such exclusion is constitutionally legitimate as long as housing opportunities for lower income groups are provided elsewhere in the region? If you think otherwise, then what is the principle? An intermediate appellate court in New York, in Robert E. Kurzius, Inc. v. Incorporated Village of Upper Brookville, 67 A.D.2d 70, 414 N.Y.S.2d 573 (1979), reversed 51 N.Y.2d 338, 434 N.Y.S.2d 180, 414 N.E.2d 680 (1980), struck down a five acre minimum on the ground that the housing needs of low and moderate income persons were not being met within the village. The Court of Appeals rejected that

reasoning, stating: "There was no proof that persons of low or moderate incomes were foreclosed from housing in the *general region* because of an unavailability of properly zoned land." (Emphasis supplied.)

2. The *Ybarra* case should be compared with such housing cases as Village of Arlington Heights v. Metropolitan Housing Development Corp., infra, United States v. City of Black Jack, Missouri, infra, and Hills v. Gautreaux, infra.

C. EXCLUSION BY BUILDING SIZE REQUIREMENTS

LIONSHEAD LAKE, INC. v. TOWNSHIP OF WAYNE

Supreme Court of New Jersey, 1952.
10 N.J. 165, 89 A.2d 693, appeal dismissed 344 U.S.
919, 73 S.Ct. 386, 97 L.Ed. 708 (1953).

VANDERBILT, C.J. The plaintiff, the owner and developer of a large tract of land in the defendant township, commenced this action in lieu of a prerogative writ challenging the validity of the defendant's zoning ordinance in fixing the minimum size of dwellings and in placing certain of its properties in a residential district. On the plaintiff's motion the trial court entered summary judgment in its favor on the first count, setting aside the provisions of the ordinance fixing the minimum size of dwellings, Lionshead Lake, Inc. v. Wayne Tp., 8 N.J.Super. 468, 73 A.2d 287 (Law Div.1950). On appeal this judgment was reversed by the Appellate Division of the Superior Court because of the existence of a factual question and the case was remanded for trial, Lionshead Lake, Inc. v. Wayne Tp., 9 N.J.Super. 83, 74 A.2d 609 (App.Div.1950).

The Township of Wayne is the most extensive municipality in Passaic County. It covers 25.34 square miles in comparison with the 23.57 square miles of Newark. It has a population of 11,815 in comparison with Newark's 437,857. Only 12% of the total area of the township has been built up. Included within its borders are several sizeable lakes (the one located within the plaintiff's development, e.g., having an area of about 145 acres) and as a result a considerable number of its residences have been built for summer occupancy only. Although a political entity, it is in fact a composite of about a dozen widely scattered residential communities, varying from developments like the plaintiff's where the average home costs less than $10,000 to more expensive sections where the homes cost from $35,000 to $75,000. It has but little business or industry.

On July 12, 1949, four years after the plaintiff had commenced the development of its Lionshead Lake properties and after over a hundred houses had been constructed there, the defendant adopted a revised zoning ordinance dividing the entire township into four districts; residence districts A and B, a business district and an industrial district, the last two comprising but a very small proportion of the township's total area. In section 3 of the ordinance pertaining to residence A districts it was provided that:

"(d) Minimum Size of Dwellings:

Every dwelling hereafter erected or placed in a Residence A District shall have a living-floor space, as herein defined

of not less than 768 square feet for a one story dwelling;

of not less than 1000 square feet for a two story dwelling having an attached garage;

of not less than 1200 square feet for a two story dwelling not having an attached garage."

These minimum size requirements for dwellings were made applicable to residence B districts by section 4(d) of the ordinance, to business districts by section 5(c), and to industrial districts by section 6(b) 1, the result being that the same minimum size requirements for dwellings prevail throughout the entire township.

Within the entire township only about 70% of all the existing dwellings meet the minimum requirements of the ordinance; in some sections of the township as few as 20% of the existing dwellings comply with the ordinance requirements, in others (among them the plaintiff's Lionshead Lake development) only about 50% are above the prescribed minimum, while in other areas the percentage of compliance is far greater, reaching 100% in some of the more exclusive sections. The low percentage of compliance in certain areas is not particularly significant, however, for the reason that the township is as yet substantially undeveloped. Compliance with the requirements of the ordinance in the future will undoubtedly result in the nonconforming houses comprising but a small minority even in those areas where they are now in the majority. There was testimony to the effect that to build a house for year-round occupancy having the minimum 768 square feet of living space would cost from $10,000 to $12,000, if mass produced, and that only about 30% of the population were financially able to afford such homes. The plaintiff's witness who so testified, a builder and developer, was hardly qualified, however, to express an opinion as to the financial ability of present and potential residents of the township and his opinion as to construction costs was considerably out of line with that of the defendant's expert who testified that homes complying with the ordinance could be and were being built at a cost of $8,500 to $9,200 if for year-round occupancy and $7,500 to $8,200 if for seasonal use only.

To meet the plaintiff's attack on the reasonableness of the ordinance the defendant produced a recognized public health expert, who testified that the living-floor space in a dwelling had a direct relation to the mental and emotional health of its occupants and that he had developed scientific standards for different size families: 400 square feet for one person, 750 square feet for two persons, 1,000 square feet for three persons, 1,150 square feet for four persons, 1,400 square feet for five persons, and 1,550 square feet for six persons. These the witness considered as desirable goals rather than legal standards. He conceded that the housing standards prescribed by the agencies of the Federal

Government are below those written into the ordinance, as are those of the New Jersey Code of Minimum Construction Requirements for One and Two Family Dwellings, prepared by the Department of Economic Development, Division of Planning and Engineering (1946), which, however, does not have the force of law but is merely advisory.

After considering this and other evidence the trial court concluded that the minimum size requirements of the ordinance were not reasonably related to the public health, were arbitrary and unreasonable, and not within the police powers of the defendant. Accordingly, judgment was entered on the first count of the complaint in favor of the plaintiff setting aside the minimum size of dwelling requirements with respect to the residence A and residence B districts in which the plaintiff's property is located. The plaintiff failed to introduce any proof in support of the second count of its complaint in which it objected to the placing of its property in a residential zone. The court therefore granted the defendant's motion for a dismissal thereof with prejudice, but subsequently declined to enter formal judgment to that effect. On the petition of the defendant we granted certification to review the judgment of the trial court with respect to the first count and its refusal to enter judgment with respect to the second count.

* * *

Thus not only has the Constitution conferred on the Legislature very broad powers to pass enabling acts with respect to zoning but the Legislature in a like effort to make effective its constitutional power in this respect has given the municipalities similar broad powers expressed in considerably greater detail than in the Constitution. To the traditional presumption with respect to the validity of every legislative act there has been added, moreover, the constitutional mandate to construe such legislation liberally in favor of the municipalities. These constitutional and statutory changes have in effect adopted the reasoning of the dissenting opinion in Brookdale Homes, Inc. v. Johnson, 126 N.J.L. 516, 19 A.2d 868 (E. & A.1941) and rendered inapplicable the decision of the majority of the Court of Errors and Appeals holding invalid an ordinance imposing minimum restrictions on the size of dwellings to protect the character of a community and property values therein, Id., 123 N.J.L. 602 (Sup.Ct.1940), affirmed o.b. 126 N.J.L. 516 (E. & A.1941). We are bound by these changes in our organic law and accordingly this court in Schmidt v. Board of Adjustment of the City of Newark, 9 N.J. 405, 88 A.2d 607 (1952), has held that so long as the zoning ordinance was reasonably designed, by whatever means, to further the advancement of a community as a social, economic and political unit, it is in the general welfare and therefore a proper exercise of the zoning power. The underlying question before us is whether in the light of these constitutional and legislative provisions the zoning ordinance of the defendant township is arbitrary and unreasonable. That question, moreover, must be answered in the light of the facts of this particular case. We must bear in mind, finally, that a zoning ordinance is not like the law of the

Medes and Persians; variances may be permitted, the zoning ordinance may be amended, and if the ordinance proves unreasonable in operation it may be set aside at any time.

In Duffcon Concrete Products, Inc. v. Borough of Cresskill, 1 N.J. 509, 513, 64 A.2d 347, 9 A.L.R.2d 678 (1949) we said:

"What may be the most appropriate use of any particular property depends not only on all the conditions, physical, economic and social, prevailing within the municipality and its needs, present and reasonably prospective, but also on the nature of the entire region in which the municipality is located and the use to which the land in that region has been or may be put most advantageously."

The Township of Wayne is still for the most part a sparsely settled countryside with great natural attractions in its lakes, hills and streams, but obviously it lies in the path of the next onward wave of suburban development. Whether that development shall be "with a view of conserving the value of property and encouraging the most appropriate use of land throughout such municipality" and whether it will "prevent the overcrowding of land or buildings" and "avoid undue concentration of population" depends in large measure on the wisdom of the governing body of the municipality as expressed in its zoning ordinance. It requires as much official watchfulness to anticipate and prevent suburban blight as it does to eradicate city slums.

Has a municipality the right to impose minimum floor area requirements in the exercise of its zoning powers? Much of the proof adduced by the defendant township was devoted to showing that the mental and emotional health of its inhabitants depended on the proper size of their homes. We may take notice without formal proof that there are minimums in housing below which one may not go without risk of impairing the health of those who dwell therein. One does not need extensive experience in matrimonial causes to become aware of the adverse effect of overcrowding on the well-being of our most important institution, the home. Moreover, people who move into the country rightly expect more land, more living room, indoors and out, and more freedom in their scale of living than is generally possible in the city. City standards of housing are not adaptable to suburban areas and especially to the upbringing of children. But quite apart from these considerations of public health which cannot be overlooked, minimum floor-area standards are justified on the ground that they promote the general welfare of the community and, as we have seen in Schmidt v. Board of Adjustment of the City of Newark, 9 N.J. 405, 88 A.2d 607 (1952), supra, the courts in conformance with the constitutional provisions and the statutes hereinbefore cited take a broad view of what constitutes general welfare. The size of the dwellings in any community inevitably affects the character of the community and does much to determine whether or not it is a desirable place in which to live. It is the prevailing view in municipalities throughout the State that such minimum floor-area standards are necessary to protect the character of the community. A survey made by the Department of Conservation and Economic Development in 1951 disclosed that 64 municipalities out of the 138 reporting had minimum dwelling requirements. In the light of the Constitution and of the enabling statutes, the right of a municipality to impose minimum floor-area requirements is beyond controversy.

With respect to every zoning ordinance, however, the question remains as to whether or not in the particular facts of the case and in the light of all of the surrounding circumstances the minimum floor-area requirements are reasonable. Can a minimum of living floor space of 768 square feet for a one-story building; of 1,000 square feet for a two-story dwelling having an attached garage; and of 1,200 square feet for a two-story dwelling not having an attached garage be deemed unreasonable in a rural area just beginning to change to a suburban community? It is significant that the plaintiff admits that of the 100 houses in its development 30 met the minimum requirements when constructed and 20 more by voluntary additions of the owners to meet their individual needs have been enlarged to conform to the minimum requirements of the ordinance, and while the litigation has been pending 20 others have been constructed conforming to the ordinance. If some such requirements were not imposed there would be grave danger in certain parts of the township, particularly around the lakes which attract summer visitors, of the erection of shanties which would deteriorate land values generally to the great detriment of the increasing number of people who live in Wayne Township the year round. The minimum floor area requirements imposed by the ordinance are not large for a family of normal size. Without some such restrictions there is always the danger that after some homes have been erected giving a character to a neighborhood, others might follow which would fail to live up to the standards thus voluntarily set. This has been the experience in many communities and it is against this that the township has sought to safeguard itself within limits which seem to us to be altogether reasonable.

* * *

The judgment on the first count of the plaintiff's complaint is reversed. Judgment shall be entered with prejudice in favor of the defendant on the second count of the complaint.

JACOBS, J. (concurring). [Only a part of the concurring opinion is given.]

* * * The plaintiff's purpose apparently was to resume the construction of structures, discontinued upon the adoption of the ordinance, containing 484 square feet of living space. The record contains photographs of these tiny structures described at one point as "doll houses"; perhaps the following excerpt from Jonathan Swift's Verses on Blenheim, though in other context, is not inappropriate:

Thanks, sir, cried I, 'tis very fine. But where d'ye sleep, or where d'ye dine? I find, by all you have been telling, That 'tis a house, but not a dwelling.

It seems to me that the lower court's striking down of the township's ordinance was clearly erroneous. See Thompson v. City of Carrollton, supra, where an ordinance prescribing a minimum of 900 square feet was sustained; Dundee Realty Co. v. Omaha, 144 Neb. 448, 13 N.W.2d 634 (1944) where an ordinance providing for 1,000 square feet minimum for one-story dwellings and 1,200 square feet minimum for more than one-story dwellings was likewise sustained; and Flower Hill Building Corp. v. Village of Flower Hill, supra, where the court declined to declare that an 1,800 square feet minimum was invalid on its face. Admittedly the township's ordinance was entitled to the benefit of the presumption of validity and reasonableness. Lumund v. Board of Adjustment of the Borough of Rutherford, 4 N.J. 577, 586, 73 A.2d 545 (1950); Guaclides v. Englewood Cliffs, 11 N.J.Super. 405, 411, 78 A.2d 435 (App.Div.1951). It constituted important legislative action representing the governing body's best judgment as to what zoning restrictions were required to promote the health, morals and general welfare of the community as a whole. Decent respect for its problems and sincerity required that its action remain unimpaired in the absence of clear showing that it was arbitrary, unreasonable, or beyond the authority of the general Zoning Act. Cf. Ogden v. Saunders, 25 U.S. (12 Wheat.) 213, 270, 6 L.Ed. 606, 625 (1827). I find no such showing in the record.

A witness for the plaintiff testified that at the time of the adoption of the ordinance the cost of a house containing 768 square feet of living space, if mass produced, would approximate $9,500 to $10,500. On the other hand, another witness testified "that a year round one-family home, containing 768 square feet in area complying in all respects with the building code of the Township of Wayne would presently cost between $8,500 and $9,200." Applications for permits filed by the plaintiff since the passage of the ordinance indicated that it was constructing such houses at even lesser stated costs. The record contains nothing to indicate the buying power of residents of Passaic County where Wayne Township is located, although the May 10, 1952, issue of Sales Management (at page 414) estimates that Passaic County has an average effective buying income per annum of $6,000 per family, and represents the forty-ninth highest county in the United States. In the light of the foregoing I find no basis for the suggestion that the minimum in the ordinance is unreasonably high; in any event it is clearly within the broad range which should be allowed in the interests of social progress. Cf. Schmidt v. Board of Adjustment, Newark, 9 N.J. 405, 416, 88 A.2d 607 (1952).

The further suggestion has been advanced that the ordinance is defective in that it does not differentiate between various sections of the township and is not related to the number of occupants of the dwelling. This ignores the fact that the ordinance prescribes only *minimum* footage which is small enough to be applicable throughout the entire community. If any neighborhood ought to have a higher minimum, perhaps it will be dealt with in a later ordinance; in the meantime no harm is done to it by any of the present restrictions. Similarly, perhaps some later ordinance will attempt to deal with the complex subject of relating minimum living space to actual occupants; in the meantime the prescribed minimum is sufficiently low to be applied generally. No matter what may be the size of the particular family the 786 feet minimum will be a significant step forward when contrasted with the plaintiff's "doll houses." Mathematical precision in the ordinance need not be attained; it is sufficient that its comprehensive provisions are reasonably calculated to achieve ends which are within the broad ambit of proper modern day zoning. Cf. Duffcon Concrete Products, Inc. v. Borough of Cresskill, 1 N.J. 509, 64 A.2d 347, 9 A.L.R.2d 678 (1949); Guaclides v. Englewood Cliffs, supra. * * *

[Dissenting opinion of Oliphant, J. is not given.]

Note

This case was debated pro and con in the following series of articles: Haar, The Wayne Township Case: Zoning for Minimum Standards, 66 Harv.L.Rev. 1051 (1953); Nolan and Horack, How Small A House?—Zoning for Minimum Space Requirements, 67 Harv.L.Rev. 967 (1954); and Haar, Wayne Township: Zoning for Whom?—In Brief Reply, 67 Harv.L.Rev. 986 (1954). Haar's first article dissects the case pointing out in detail what he regarded to be defects in the court's reasoning and difficulties presented by the result. Professor Haar regarded the case as pointing up the need for regional planning to provide standards for the courts to follow in weighing individual zoning provisions. Professors Nolan and Horack disagreed somewhat sharply with Professor Haar's evaluation of the case. They felt that Haar's charge that zoning had been misused in this way to create economic segregation and permit the domination of real estate interests over legitimate planning was not supported by the facts or record in the case. After an extensive exploration of the facts, record and the opinion, Nolan and Horack concluded that the decision was justified and well-founded. Haar responded, again expressing his point of view, and stating his opposition to the social and economic stratification which he felt the decision encouraged.

It is impossible to discuss these articles at depth in this note due to the extent to which each side details its views. The debate is commended to the student as an excellent "high level" confrontation between some leading authorities in the land use field. Certainly, as he reads, the student should take note not only of the effort by these able scholars to express their own views of the case and its validity or error, but also the socio-economic arguments employed and the way in which they are applied. You should ask yourself to what extent these scholars differ in (a) their underlying philosophy as to land use planning; (b) the extent to which and manner in which they would apply their philosophy to this case; (c) the proposals which they advance as solutions; (d) the extent to which these proposals reflect underlying socio-economic attitudes or values; and (e) what are and how do you rank the conflicting values which are at stake.

See also Crolly and Norton, Zoning for Minimum House Size, Zoning Bull. 1 (No. 65, Nov. 1952); Williams, Zoning and Housing Policies, 10 J. Housing 94 (1953); and Williams, Planning Law and the Supreme Court, Zoning Digest (March–April 1961). Other scholars have, sometime later, referred back to the principal case in a related context. See, Williams and Wacks, Segregation of Residential Areas Along Economic Lines: Lionshead Lake Revisited, 1969 Wis.L.Rev. 827.

HOME BUILDERS LEAGUE OF SOUTH JERSEY, INC. v. TOWNSHIP OF BERLIN

Supreme Court of New Jersey, 1979.
81 N.J. 127, 405 A.2d 381.

SCHREIBER, J.

At issue in this case is the validity of provisions in a municipal zoning ordinance which impose minimum floor area requirements for residential dwellings irrespective of the number of occupants living in the home and unrelated to any other factor, such as frontage or lot size. The challenge was initiated when the Home Builders League of South Jersey, Inc. (League) and three builders, Award Homes, Inc., Lincoln Property Co., N.E., Inc., and Chiusano Bros., Inc., filed a complaint in lieu of prerogative writ in the Superior Court seeking invalidation of the floor area minima in the zoning ordinances of four municipalities in Camden County—Voorhees Township, Berlin Township, and the Boroughs of Pine Hill and Stratford. The New Jersey Public Advocate, the Senior Citizens Advocate Center, the Gray Panthers of South Jersey, and the South Jersey Tenants Organization were permitted to intervene as plaintiffs. At the conclusion of an extended trial the trial court found defendants' "nonoccupancy based" floor area minima to be unrelated to the public health, safety or welfare and hence an arbitrary, capricious and unreasonable exercise of the municipal zoning power. Defendants were given 90 days to amend their ordinances to provide for occupancy-related floor area standards. 157 N.J.Super. 586, 385 A.2d 295 (Law Div.1978).

Only Voorhees Township appealed. Plaintiff-intervenors filed a cross-appeal because of the trial court's "failure to declare occupancy-based floor space requirements greater than the minimum necessary to protect the public health, safety and general welfare unreasonable *per se,* irrational, arbitrary and void." Before the case was heard in the Appellate Division, we granted direct certification on our own motion, pursuant to R. 2:12–1. 77 N.J. 503, 391 A.2d 482 (1978). We now affirm, albeit for slightly different reasons from those given by the trial court.

* * *

Voorhees Township is located within the Philadelphia–Camden area, less than 15 miles southeast of Camden. It is a developing municipality. Its population grew from 3784 in 1960 to 6214 in 1970, and 7320 in 1976. The Camden County Planning Board has projected an increase in population to 23,458 by 1990, and the Township's master plan estimates population at full development to be 37,627. Voorhees Township is linked to the Philadelphia–Camden urban center by a number of highways and the PATCO Hi–Speed rail line. The Township's area is 7345 acres. In 1970, there were 3899 acres of vacant developable land (exclusive of (1) land with slopes greater than 12%; (2) wetlands; (3) qualified farmlands; and (4) public lands), or about 53% of the Township's total area.

The Voorhees Township Zoning Ordinance establishes a number of residential zones, each with different lot area, frontage, and floor area minima. They may be summarized as follows:

Zone	Minimum Lot Size (sq. ft.)	Minimum Frontage (ft.)	Minimum Floor Area (sq. ft.)
R.R. (rural)—single family houses	43,560	200	1,600
R–100A—single family houses	15,000	100	
up to 3 bedrooms			1,600
each additional bedroom			400
RD–2—single family houses	12,500	90	
60% of subdivision			1,200
20% of subdivision			1,351
20% of subdivision			1,501
R–100—single family houses	12,500	100	1,200
R–75—single family houses	9,375	75	1,100
T.C. (Township Center)			
apartments	10,000	100	none
townhouses:	1,000	none	
2 bedrooms			1,200
3 bedrooms			1,350
4 bedrooms			1,500
Avian—single family houses	1,000		
85% of subdivision		20	
15% of subdivision		10	
1–4 rooms			none
5 rooms			1,200
each additional room			150
P.U.D. (planned unit development)			
apartments	flexible	flexible	750
townhouses:	flexible	flexible	
1–2 bedrooms			1,200
3 bedrooms			1,350
4 bedrooms			1,500
single family houses	10,000	flexible	1,200

———

The minimum floor area requirements in the different zones are not strictly comparable: in the R.R., R–100, R–75, T.C. and Avian zones, the minima are expressed in terms of gross floor area, while the R–100A and RD–2 requirements are for "minimum living area," which is defined as "the living space in any house, exclusive of porches, attached sheds and garages." The P.U.D. minima are stated in terms of "habitable floor area," which is defined as gross floor area less garages, open patios, basements and unfinished attics.

The R–75 and R–100 zones are virtually fully developed. In the Avian section, where the eased restrictions are apparently the result of prior litigation, the room count excludes bath and powder rooms. The Avian district is the only one in which some single family houses may be constructed irrespective of a minimum floor area. Finally, the lot size requirement in the R–100A zone and the frontage requirement in RD–2 allow for some variation in any proposed subdivision.

* * *

In support of its contention that the municipality has the authority to enact a provision setting forth floor space minima for residences, Voorhees relies upon two provisions in the Municipal Land Use Law. N.J.S.A. 40:55D–65(b) provides that a zoning ordinance may regulate the "size of buildings," "the percentage of lot" that may be occupied, and for these purposes "may specify floor area ratios and other ratios and regulatory techniques governing the intensity of land use and the provision of adequate light and air." Second, N.J.S.A. 40:55D–62(a) states that "[t]he zoning ordinance shall be drawn with reasonable consideration to the character of each district and its peculiar suitability for particular uses and to encourage the most appropriate use of land."

Even though N.J.S.A. 40:55D–65(b) might be read literally to include the power to impose minimum floor space (regulation of the size of a building), the end result must not be contrary to the general welfare and in fact must further the public health, safety, morals or general welfare. Almost inevitably restrictions on the use of land will have both salutary and detrimental effects. A provision which has some beneficial effect will not automatically be deemed valid and consonant with the general welfare. Attention must also be directed toward the detrimental effects that a particular provision has. A provision which has some relationship to promotion of the general welfare or any subpart thereof, such as public health, safety, or any of the other purposes designated in the Municipal Land Use Law, N.J.S.A. 40:55D–2, would be upheld if it does not at the same time promote ends which are contrary to the general welfare. Where, however, a zoning provision, in addition to promoting legitimate zoning goals, also has effects contrary to the general welfare, closer scrutiny of the provision and its effects must be undertaken. The fact that a provision may have some adverse effect is not determinative. Rather, the court is required to decide whether a proper legislative goal is being achieved in a manner reasonably related to that goal.

Consider, for example, minimum lot size. Such a restriction may be closely related to the goals of public health and safety, as well as preserving the characteristics of a neighborhood. Thus, such a restriction may be valid despite the exclusionary impact resulting from increased housing costs due to minimum lot size. Compare Fischer v. Tp. of Bedminster, 11 N.J. 194, 93 A.2d 378 (1952) (upholding validity of five-acre minimum lot size) with Schere v. Tp. of Freehold, 119 N.J.Super. 433, 292 A.2d 35 (App.Div.), certif. den. 62 N.J. 69, 299 A.2d 67 (1972), cert. den. 410 U.S. 931, 93 S.Ct. 1374, 35 L.Ed.2d 593 (1973) (invalidating minimum lot restriction of slightly less than one acre). Where, however, these adverse consequences become too predominant, the zoning provision cannot stand, despite the fact that it bears some relationship to legitimate zoning purposes.

Minimum floor area requirements bear a direct relationship to the cost of a house. The larger the house, the more likely its cost will be greater. Living in a more spacious house will be more expensive due to higher taxes, mortgage payments, and expenses for heat, maintenance, and insurance. * * *

* * * If the Township's sole purpose in setting up the minima was to provide for more costly residences so as to exclude lower or moderate income persons, we would strike down this direct form of economic segregation. See, e.g., Lefcoe, "The Public Housing Referendum Case, Zoning, and the Supreme Court," 59 Calif.L.Rev. 1384, 1438–1439 (1971); Sager, "Tight Little Islands: Exclusionary Zoning, Equal Protection, and the Indigent," 21 Stan.L.Rev. 767, 781 (1969); Williams, "Planning Law and Democratic Living," 20 Law & Contemp.Prob. 317, 343 (1955); Haar, "Zoning for Minimum Standards: The Wayne Township Case," 66 Harv.L.Rev. 1051, 1055 (1953).

A limitation on a person's right to expend whatever amount he desires to construct a house—unrelated to appropriate purposes such as health, safety or welfare—would transgress constitutional due process standards. See Brookdale Homes, Inc. v. Johnson, 123 N.J.L. 602, 606, 10 A.2d 477 (Sup.Ct.1940), aff'd o.b. 126 N.J.L. 516, 19 A.2d 868 (E. & A.1941). (The holding in *Brookdale Homes* that an ordinance imposing minimum restrictions on the size of dwellings to protect the character of a community and property values therein was invalid was overruled in Lionshead Lake, Inc. v. Tp. of Wayne, 10 N.J. 165, 172, 89 A.2d 693 (1952), app. dism. 344 U.S. 919, 73 S.Ct. 386, 97 L.Ed. 708 (1953).) The few cases which touch on the validity of zoning ordinances prescribing minimum dollar cost of houses have indicated them to be unreasonable. See Stein v. City of Long Branch, 2 N.J.Misc. 121 (Sup.Ct), app. dism. 100 N.J.L. 413, 126 A. 924 (E. & A.1924); County Comm'rs v. Ward, 186 Md. 330, 46 A.2d 684 (1946); Appeal from Ordinance, Borough of Speers, 28 Wash.Co. 221 (Pa.Quar.Sess.1948).

We have acknowledged that zoning restrictions and limitations may have some economic effect in elevating the cost of a house, but nothing in the Municipal Land Use Law sanctions such economic segregation in and of itself as a proper zoning goal. We hold that when it is shown that a municipality has adopted as part of its zoning ordinance a minimum size living area provision which is on its face unrelated to any other factor, it will be presumed to have acted for improper purposes. The burden is then on the municipality to establish that a valid basis does exist. * * * We hasten to add that the establishment of such a basis does not terminate the judicial inquiry. At that point it must be determined whether the provision furthers or is contrary to the general welfare. It is then that the court must weigh and balance, as previously discussed, the exclusionary and salutary effects of the provision.

The bases which Voorhees has advanced are that the minima will (1) promote public health and safety and (2) maintain the nature of residential neighborhoods and conserve property values.

A. PUBLIC HEALTH AND SAFETY

We agree with the trial court's factual findings that minimum floor area requirements are not *per se* related to public health, safety or morals. The record contains substantial evidence in this respect. Dr. Eric Mood, Associate Clinical Professor of Public Health in the Department of Epidemiology and Public Health in the Yale School of Medicine, testified that the Voorhees floor space requirements were not related to and did not serve the public health, safety and welfare. In his opinion such criteria could be so related only if they were based on occupancy. The same opinion was expressed by John Rahenkamp, who has been engaged in land planning for years, and Alan Mallach, who heads a consulting firm which works principally in the area of housing.

* * *

The ratio of occupants to space obviously can affect public health, family stability and emotional well being. 2 N. Williams, American Planning Law § 63.01 at 626 (1974). This interrelationship is found in standards fixed by the American Public Health Association which set a minimum residency requirement of 150 square feet for one person and 100 square feet for each additional occupant. These criteria are currently recommended by the U.S. Department of Housing and Urban Development (HUD). HUD has always prescribed occupancy-based standards in relation to space.

We have previously adverted to the different area minima in Voorhees' various residential zones. Since the minima necessary for public health, safety and morals in the R.R., RD–2 and other zones are unquestionably the same, it follows that the Township was not considering health, safety and morals when it enacted these provisions. As the trial court aptly commented, "It is ridiculous to suggest that an 1,100 square foot house may be 'healthful' in one part of town and not another." 157 N.J.Super. at 601, 385 A.2d at 302.

Nor can minimum floor areas be utilized to prevent over-crowding. In the absence of some relationship between living areas and the number of occupants, unless there is a ratio between the space and inhabitants, obviously the problem is not being alleviated. This is not to say that there is not a minimum below which any residence may not go without the risk of impairing the health of an inhabitant. * * *

B.   CHARACTER OF THE NEIGHBORHOOD AND CONSERVING PROPERTY VALUES

The trial court mistakenly held that preservation of the character of a neighborhood and conservation of property values are no longer proper zoning purposes because of the repeal of N.J.S.A. 40:55–32 which had expressly referred to these objectives. Although the new statute omits the language that

> [s]uch regulations shall be made with reasonable consideration, among other things, to the character of the district and its peculiar suitability for particular uses, and with a view of conserving the value of property and encouraging the most appropriate use of land throughout such municipality[,] [N.J.S.A. 40:55–32, repealed by L.1975, c. 291, § 80]

it does state that

> [t]he zoning ordinance shall be drawn with reasonable consideration to the character of each district and its peculiar suitability for particular uses and to encourage the most appropriate use of land. [N.J.S.A. 40:55D–62(a)]

Although the phrase "conserving the value of property" does not appear in the existing statute, we have no doubt that the Legislature did not intend to deny the legitimacy of that consideration. It is intertwined with the character of a district. N.J.S.A. 40:55D–62(a). Conservation of the value of property is subsumed within the express purposes of promoting the "general welfare," the "well-being of neighborhoods," and a "desirable visual environment." N.J.S.A. 40:55D–2(a), (e) and (i).[2] See Pascack Ass'n, Ltd. v. Mayor of Washington Tp., supra, 74 N.J. at 483–484, 379 A.2d 6, holding that maintaining the character of a fully developed, predominantly single family residential community constitutes an appropriate desideratum of zoning. All of these goals are laudable and permissible. However, the method selected to attain them must be reasonable.

Whether the size of a house alone has relevance to the quality or property value of neighboring homes is a troublesome question. This is brought into sharp focus when the decision in Lionshead Lake, Inc. v. Tp. of Wayne, supra, is compared with the expert testimony in this case. The experts testified without exception that smaller houses do not because of their size cause a decrease in the value of adjacent dwellings or adversely affect the character of the neighborhood. They pointed out that aesthetic qualities are best maintained through the use, *inter alia,*

---

2. Aesthetic considerations are apparently now expressly authorized in the zoning statute. See the concurring opinion of Justice Jacobs in *Lionshead Lake,* supra, 10 N.J. at 176, 89 A.2d at 698, where he wrote that provisions in the zoning ordinance "were influenced in considerable part by aesthetic considerations" which he believed to be "entirely proper." See also Westfield Motor Sales Co. v. Town of Westfield, 129 N.J.Super. 528, 535–539, 324 A.2d 113 (Law Div.1974).

of lot size, setbacks, side yards, lot coverage ratios, topographical and landscaping requirements.

Williams and Wacks have expressed a similar thought:

"Increasing the size of houses has nothing to do with improving the appearance of an area. Topography has a lot to do with it, and the presence of trees has even more. (Landscaping and maintenance obviously are also important.) Perhaps most important of all is lot size, and particularly lot size in relation to house size; in fact, the present appearance of both the central plain and Lionshead Lake strongly suggests that an increase in house size can actually detract from the appearance of an area, unless lot sizes are increased proportionately. [Williams & Wacks, "Segregation of Residential Areas Along Economic Lines: Lionshead Lake Revisited," 1969 Wis. L.Rev. 827, 846]"

Professor Haar has written:

Certainly beauty has no relation to size. The ordinance, moreover, contains no guarantee of design or site planning. In addition, if the initial cost of building to meet the minimum size requirement is high, a family budget may not permit the additions to exteriors, such as planting and painting, which may be aesthetically desirable. [Haar, supra, 66 Harv.L.Rev. at 1057–1058]

The majority opinion in Lionshead Lake, Inc. v. Tp. of Wayne, supra, although referring to the fact that there are minima in housing below which the health of the occupants might be impaired, rested its conclusion in upholding several minimum living areas in the zoning ordinance on the protection of land values generally and of the character of the community.[3] *Lionshead* recognized that

> [w]ith respect to every zoning ordinance, however, the question remains as to whether or not in the particular facts of the case and in the light of all of the surrounding circumstances the minimum floor-area requirements are reasonable. [10 N.J. at 174, 89 A.2d at 698]

The opinion did not discuss the impact of economic segregation, although Justice Oliphant in dissent referred to that factor when he wrote:

"Zoning has its purposes, but as I conceive the effect of the majority opinion it precludes individuals in those income brackets who could not pay between $8,500 and $12,000 for the erection of a house on a lot from ever establishing a residence in this community as long as the 768 square feet of living space is the minimum requirement in the zoning ordinance. A zoning provision that can produce this effect

---

3. Some commentators have interpreted *Lionshead* as resting on public health grounds. See, e.g., 2 R. Anderson, American Law of Zoning, § 8.06 at 22 (2d ed. 1976); 6 P. Rohan, Zoning and Land Use Controls, § 42.05[2][b] at 79–82 (1978). If that were its basis, it would certainly no longer be sound. See Kirsch Holding Co. v. Borough of Manasquan, supra.

certainly runs afoul of the fundamental principles of our form of government. [10 N.J. at 181, 89 A.2d at 701]"

Shortly after *Lionshead,* the Court acknowledged in Pierro v. Baxendale, 20 N.J. 17, 118 A.2d 401 (1955), that when conditions change, the dangers of economic segregation may warrant a reexamination of *Lionshead.* In that case Justice Jacobs wrote on behalf of the majority:

"We are aware of the extensive academic discussion following the decisions in the *Lionshead* and *Bedminster* cases, supra, and the suggestion that the very broad principles which they embody may intensify dangers of economic segregation which even the more traditional modes of zoning entail. * * * In the light of existing population and land conditions within our State these [municipal zoning] powers may be fairly exercised without in anywise endangering the needs or reasonable expectations of any segments of our people. If and when conditions change, alterations in zoning restrictions and pertinent legislative and judicial attitudes need not be long delayed." [20 N.J. at 29, 118 A.2d at 407–409]

We have experienced that change in conditions which has been reflected in pertinent legislative and judicial attitudes. Zoning which excludes low and moderate income families for fiscal purposes has been condemned as contrary to the general welfare. * * * As we have stated previously, once it is demonstrated that the ordinance excludes people on an economic basis without on its face relating the minimum floor area to one or more appropriate variables, the burden of proof shifts to the municipality to show a proper purpose is being served. This was a burden Wayne was not called upon to meet and Voorhees is. It is a burden which Voorhees has failed to meet.

In conclusion we hold that on its face the Voorhees zoning ordinance prescribes minimum floor areas for residences which are unrelated to legitimate zoning purposes. Voorhees has not directed our attention to anything in the ordinance which ties these requirements to public health or safety or preservation of the character of the neighborhood. Rather, the ordinance appears to be directed solely toward economic segregation. Under these circumstances and in the absence of proofs showing a connection between the minima and the legitimate purposes of zoning (public health, safety and welfare), such as would be established by an occupancy relationship, the provisions must fall.

The judgment declaring invalid those provisions of the Voorhees Township zoning ordinance requiring that residential units contain minimum area floor space is affirmed. We perceive no reason to stay the effectiveness of our adjudication of invalidity.

Notes

1. Considering this case in the light of the Lionshead Lake decision, what modifications were made by the New Jersey court to that case as authority and what is left of it?

2. Also see Appeal of Medinger, 377 Pa. 217, 104 A.2d 118 (1954), where the court struck down a sliding scale minimum scheme with greater square footage required in higher zoning districts than in lower residential districts. The plaintiffs in that case desired to construct a replica of a colonial farmhouse using authentic materials painstakingly acquired over many years. In Frischkorn Constr. Co. v. Lambert, 315 Mich. 556, 24 N.W.2d 209 (1946), the court struck down a requirement of a minimum number of cubic feet for each house noting that compliance would do no more than irrationally expand attic space and not increase usable living space. Compare Foremost Life Ins. Co. v. Waters, 125 Mich.App. 799, 337 N.W.2d 29 (1983) upholding a 720 square foot minimum for mobile homes.

3. Consider this comment from Babcock, Classification and Segregation Among Zoning Districts, 1954 U.Ill.L.F. 186, 201–203:

> The control of house size has raised the cry of "economic segregation," amounting to snobbery or "aesthetics." There *is* economic segregation in such minimum controls, but this should not shock us unless we are shocked by the entire principle of zoning. Zoning is full of examples of "economic segregation," none of which appear to disturb the critics or the courts.

> The basic character of a zoning ordinance is classification, and, if you wish, segregation. The two-family residence is kept out of the single-family area, the corner grocery is kept out of both districts. It is apparent that such segregation does impose economic hardship upon individuals who may wish to augment their income by converting their house to two apartments or by erecting a store on the front of their living quarters. They are thereby kept out of a neighborhood they might otherwise occupy. Indeed, in the absence of pertinent decisions on the subject in Illinois, it is to such established practices that the proponent of these *new* standards must turn for precedent.

> The history of zoning ordinances is the history of an attempt to divide the municipality into districts not simply on the basis of *use* classifications but of other standards more akin to house and lot size than to use of land. Thus there are numerous Illinois ordinances in which residential districts have different yard and setback provisions. The use of these controls on a sliding scale appears to eliminate any rationale as a health or fire safety measure. The justification for a sliding scale of minimum yard provisions cannot be based alone upon providing adequate open spaces for recreation or fire safety. If so, the space should increase in direct ratio to an increase in density of occupancy; yet just the opposite ratio is customarily established. The justification for minimum setbacks varying with the district has no exclusive basis in providing adequate traffic vision; otherwise the same setback would be applicable to all districts. Indeed, even the exclusion of two-family dwellings from single-family areas, though looked upon generally as a health and fire safety measure, has an apparent element of this same concept of protection to the existing character of a neighborhood.

> The issue must, it would appear, be faced, first, on the basis of whether there *is* a relationship between relative uniformity of size of

house and lot within a particular area *and* the preservation of property values and the tax base in that area; and second, if this relationship does exist, whether this "conservation" is a reasonable exercise of the police power, or simply a segregation scheme, at its best economic and at its worst racial in its implications.

There is much opinion (but few if any facts) that there is a clear relationship between the maintenance of adequate tax values and the maintenance of uniform standards of house size in a particular area. Certainly there is evidence that an area of large homes puts into the community far more in taxes than it takes out in cost of services. If such a relationship does exist it is hard to see where classification by maintenance of those standards has any less relationship to the 'public health, welfare, comfort, and morals' than the old customary classifications of districts by yards, setbacks, and, indeed, in some of its forms, height. * * *

Compare, Williams, Planning Law in the Supreme Court, Zoning Digest 107 (April 1961):

> * * * The whole value structure of American democracy was heavily influenced by, and in fact was a natural outgrowth of, a particular type of society, widely prevalent in the colonial settlements along the Atlantic seaboard and recurring regularly on later frontiers and elsewhere: a small town or rural society where there were no great inequalities and everyone knew everyone else, so that mutual acquaintance and respect had a chance to develop. These values not only survived but had substantial influence in modifying the great social differences which arose in the nineteenth century. When the crisis of the Civil War came, the eventual result was the official restatement of these values in the thirteenth, fourteenth, and fifteenth amendments. There are of course all sorts of current complications in this connection. Among them, the current suburbanization of the nation raises a new set of problems. To the extent that the strong trend toward "homogeneous"—i.e. segregated—residential areas becomes the prevailing pattern, there is at least a substantial possibility of a gradual erosion of the living habits and attitudes that form the basis of such values. In a democratic society, committed to moving towards these ideals, serious questions are raised when the powers of government are used to exclude a minority from access to decent living conditions; and the situation is not improved when it is a small, relatively well-to-do minority trying to exclude the majority of the population. * * *

4. See generally, on this subject, an annotation on the validity and construction of zoning regulations prescribing minimum floorspace or cubic content of the residence in 96 A.L.R.2d 1409 (1964). The annotation provides a good summary of the cases to that date and states that regulations on minimum floorspace or cubic content have generally been upheld as a valid exercise of the police power, although in some cases the regulations have been held invalid on the basis that they bear no relation to a reasonable exercise of the power. Some assaults have been based on the question of whether enforcement of such regulations amounted to a taking of private property without compensation.

5. Although the courts discuss the lack of relationship between minimum house size and the number of occupants and hint that regulations limiting occupancy might pass muster, do you think that a regulation limiting the number of persons who can live in a dwelling would be valid? Consider College Area Renters and Landlord Association v. City of San Diego, 42 Cal.App.4th 543, 50 Cal.Rptr.2d 515 (1996). In this case the city sought to alleviate problems caused by "mini dorms" described as apartments where several students lived in a small area. The regulation provided:

> It shall be unlawful for an owner of real property in the R–1–5000 zone and located within the area designated on Map C–841 on file in the office of the City Clerk to rent, lease or allow to be occupied or subleased, for any form of consideration, any one-family dwelling unit, or portion thereof, in violation of any of the following development regulations:
>
> 1. No such dwelling unit shall be occupied by more persons, over the age of eighteen (18), than is permitted by the most restrictive of the following regulations:
>
> a. Two (2) persons for each 70 square feet of shared bedroom area, plus one (1) additional person for each additional 50 square feet of bedroom area in bedrooms shared by more than two (2) persons, as provided for in Uniform Housing Code section 503; or
>
> b. Four (4) persons for each full or three-quarter bathroom and two (2) persons for each half bathroom; or
>
> c. One (1) person for each usable off-street parking space on the premises, developed, located and maintained in accordance with the provisions of Division 8 of this Article, plus one additional person; provided, however, that not more than two (2) parking spaces may be in tandem, nor more than one (1) curb cut per front yard, street side yard or alley be allowed for determining occupancy limits based on parking restrictions.
>
> 2. No such dwelling or portion thereof, may be rented if it does not have at least one room, other than a bedroom, with a minimum of 120 square feet of habitable net floor space.

The court found that the regulation violated equal protection because of the distinction between owner-occupied and rented dwellings.

D. EXCLUSION OF COMMERCE AND INDUSTRY

McDERMOTT v. VILLAGE OF CALVERTON PARK
Supreme Court of Missouri, En Banc, 1970.
454 S.W.2d 577.

[In their petition the McDermotts directed a three-pronged attack on the constitutionality and the validity of the Village's zoning ordinance, Ordinance No. 77. That ordinance, while it divided the municipality into four districts, restricted the use of land and buildings in all such districts to one-family dwellings, save for public parks and other uses not here material. Relying in the main on the decision of the Supreme Court in City of Moline Acres v. Heidbreder, Mo., 367 S.W.2d 568, the trial court held that under our zoning enabling statutes, §§ 89.010 to 89.140, inclusive, RSMo 1959, V.A.M.S., the Village did not have the statutory power and authority to adopt a zoning ordinance which restricted the use of all land and buildings to one-family dwellings, and declared Ordinance No. 77 invalid. Defendants' appeal followed.

* * *

Plaintiff's property comprises about 2½ acres, and fronts 280 feet on the west side of North Florissant Road between Connolly Drive and Barto Drive, in the Village of Calverton Park. It was subdivided into 19 lots in 1925. The McDermotts acquired the tract in June, 1946. On January 15, 1953, the Village adopted Ordinance No. 77. As stated the use of the land and buildings in all of the four districts into which the municipality is thereby divided is restricted by the ordinance to one-family dwellings, the differences in the zoning districts being the size of the lots, building lines, and building materials. On January 8, 1963, the McDermotts entered into a contract for the sale of their property to Larry Witzer or assigns for $58,500, conditioned upon the rezoning of the tract for the commercial use of the property as a shopping center, "at the expense of the seller"; and the procurement of all necessary building permits, based upon the purchaser's plans, which "shall be obtained by buyer at his expense." Thereafter, on May 27, 1967, the McDermotts as owners and William Goodman as their real estate agent filed with the Village an application for a change of zoning. The Board of Trustees of the Village denied the application on September 23, 1963. On January 21, 1964, the McDermotts filed with the Village's Building Commissioner an application for a building permit for the construction of a shopping center on their property, accompanied by a set of plans, which application the Building Commissioner denied. This action followed, instituted by the McDermotts on February 8, 1964.][4]

HOLMAN, JUDGE.

* * *

Our first task is to re-examine the case of City of Moline Acres v. Heidbreder, supra, in which a zoning ordinance that placed all of the village in one district zoned for single-family dwellings was held to be invalid. Defendants have devoted a substantial portion of their brief in pointing out factual distinctions between that case and the one before us, and contend that Moline Acres is not here applicable. While these cases have many distinguishing features we think Moline Acres, unless overruled, would control the decision in the case before us. This because Moline Acres held that our zoning statutes did not give to a municipality the power to adopt a one-use district zoning ordinance encompassing the whole town; that the village had no authority to adopt such a zoning

---

4. This statement of facts is taken from the decision in the case by the Missouri Court of Appeals, McDermott v. Village of   Calverton Park, 447 S.W.2d 837 (Mo.App. 1969).

ordinance. While Calverton Park had four districts, all were restricted to a single use, i.e., "one-family dwellings," and hence we consider the Moline Acres case to be applicable.

We have carefully re-examined Moline Acres and have concluded that it is not sound and should therefore no longer be followed. We have read and reread the applicable statutes and find nothing therein to indicate a legislative intent that, *under all circumstances,* a municipality must provide for more than one use in its zoning ordinance. We recognize that a comprehensive plan of zoning would, in most cities, particularly isolated ones, require commercial zoning districts in order for the needs of the residents to be conveniently supplied. However, St. Louis County, which completely surrounds (except for the portion fronting on the Mississippi River) the large City of St. Louis, is in a rather unique situation. Many people who work in St. Louis City live in the County. That fact, coupled with its own growth, has caused a vast number of cities and villages to be formed in the County, many of which are primarily for residential purposes rather than commercial or manufacturing. Those are often referred to as "bedroom" municipalities. Many of those cities are completely surrounded by other cities and most of the others border on one or more cities. * * *

The purpose for zoning is to promote health, safety, morals, and the general welfare. Section 89.020, supra. Certainly, where commercial and professional services are conveniently available elsewhere, none of those purposes would be enhanced by multiple-use zoning as compared to one-family dwelling use. Moreover, § 89.040 provides that the zoning should be "designed to lessen congestion in the streets; to secure safety from fire, panic and other dangers; to promote health and the general welfare; to provide adequate light and air; to prevent the overcrowding of land; to avoid undue concentration of population * * *." Under circumstances such as exist in Calverton Park all of those objectives are promoted by the one-family dwelling requirement and would be more likely to be accomplished than would be the case if there were multiple-use zoning. Furthermore, the "comprehensive plan" required by that section "shall be made with reasonable consideration, among other things, to the character of the district and its peculiar suitability for particular uses, and with a view to conserving the values of buildings and encouraging the most appropriate use of land throughout such municipality." Those requirements can be met by a one-use zoning ordinance such as we have in this case. We see nothing therein which would require multiple-use zoning.

As heretofore stated, we find nothing in any of the statutes which would preclude one-use zoning.

There do not appear to be many cases that have considered this question. The case of Valley View Village v. Proffett, 6th Cir., 221 F.2d 412, and Connor v. Township of Chanhassen, 249 Minn. 205, 81 N.W.2d 789, support our view. The contrary view is indicated in Dowsey v. Village of Kensington, 257 N.Y. 221, 177 N.E. 427, 86 A.L.R. 642, and

Gundersen v. Village of Bingham Farms, 372 Mich. 352, 126 N.W.2d 715. The Gunderson case followed the Moline Acres case. While we regret that situation, we cannot permit it to restrain us from making what we consider to be a correct decision at this time.

As indicated, we rule that Ordinance No. 77 is not invalid as a matter of law.

* * *

The question for our decision is whether the public interest and welfare is sufficient to outweigh the financial detriment to plaintiff. If the question is fairly debatable we cannot interfere and the ruling of the Board of Trustees must prevail.

We have concluded that, at the very least, the question is fairly debatable. It would appear to be contrary to the general welfare of the inhabitants to rezone this property for unnecessary commercial use in a village so obviously suitable for exclusive one-family dwellings. When we consider that no resident except plaintiff would receive a benefit, and that there would be the various detriments which we have heretofore outlined, it could hardly be said that the decision of the trustees was so arbitrary and unreasonable that it would infringe upon the rights of plaintiff under the various constitutional provisions mentioned.

* * *

The judgment is reversed and the cause is remanded with directions to the trial court to enter a judgment in accordance with the views herein expressed.

Note

Also see Cadoux v. Planning and Zoning Commission, 162 Conn. 425, 294 A.2d 582 (1972), certiorari denied 408 U.S. 924, 92 S.Ct. 2496, 33 L.Ed.2d 335 (1972), and the annotation in 54 A.L.R.3d 1282. In addition to the New York (Dowsey v. Village of Kensington) and Michigan (Gunderson v. Village of Bingham Farms) cases cited in the principal case for the view that single use zoning is invalid, see Hobart v. Collier, 3 Wis.2d 182, 87 N.W.2d 868 (1958) and Matthews v. Board of Zoning Appeals of Greene County, 218 Va. 270, 237 S.E.2d 128 (1977). The Gunderson case in Michigan was modified when a later court explained that towns had to have a minimum of two zones, and in Countrywalk Condominiums, Inc. v. Oakland Circuit Court City of Orchard Lake Village, 221 Mich.App. 19, ___ N.W.2d ___ (1997) the court upheld a zoning scheme allowing only single-family, professional offices, and local business. The total exclusion of apartments and condominiums was justified on the basis of an overburdened traffic system.

The Missouri courts have continued to follow the Calverton Park case. See, e.g., Clarkson Valley Estates, Inc. v. Village of Clarkson Valley, 630 S.W.2d 151 (Mo.App.1982).

GENERAL BATTERY CORP. v. ZONING HEARING BD. OF ALSACE TWP.

Commonwealth Court of Pennsylvania, 1977.
29 Pa.Cmwlth. 498, 371 A.2d 1030.

MENCER, JUDGE.

Nestled in the picturesque setting of a well-known valley, Alsace Township, Berks County, is in many ways removed from the metropolitan activities of the nearby City of Reading. The township's inhabitants enjoy a harmonious mix of rural and suburban uses in their "bedroom community" close to the city. It is not surprising, then, that they seek to perpetuate their township's seclusion. One method they have chosen is zoning: The Alsace Township zoning ordinance makes no provision for industry or industry-related uses anywhere in the township.

This ordinance has been attacked by General Battery Corporation (General Battery). General Battery, which generates waste as an incident of its lead-smelting operations in Muhlenberg Township, was denied a permit to construct waste disposal facilities on land it owned in an R–2 rural farm zone of Alsace Township. It appealed to the Alsace Township Zoning Hearing Board (Board), contending, *inter alia*, that the zoning ordinance embodied an unreasonable exercise of police power. The Board disagreed, and General Battery appealed to the Court of Common Pleas of Berks County. Without taking additional evidence, the court held the ordinance invalid. The Alsace Township Board of Supervisors appealed to this Court.

* * *

Initially, we note that, while a party challenging a zoning ordinance must overcome its presumed validity, the presumption is overcome by showing a total exclusion of an otherwise legitimate use. Appeal of Green & White Copter, Inc., 25 Pa.Cmwlth. 445, 360 A.2d 283 (1976). Within this context, a legitimate use is one which is not so particularly objectionable and undesirable that its prohibition appears prima facie to be designed to protect the public interest. Beaver Gasoline Company v. Osborne Borough, 445 Pa. 571, 285 A.2d 501 (1971); *Green & White Copter,* supra; see, *Exton Quarries,* supra note 1. Thus, an activity "generally known to give off noxious odors, disturb the tranquility of a large area by making loud noises, have the obvious potential of poisoning the air or the water of the area, or similarly have clearly deleterious effects upon the general public" is not a legitimate use of land under this rule.

Once the presumption of validity is overcome, the burden of proof shifts to the municipality to establish the legitimacy of the prohibition by evidence establishing what interest is sought to be protected. *Beaver,* supra.

We hold that the total exclusion of industrial waste disposal facilities in Alsace Township shifts the burden of proof to the municipality. In this connection, we note the comprehensive role of an active and proficient department of this Commonwealth which has been entrusted with the duty of controlling and supervising the type of activity with which we are concerned. Under the authority of the Pennsylvania Solid Waste Management Act, the Pennsylvania Department of Environmental Resources is given broad power to regulate waste disposal systems. In addition, the Department is authorized to use a wide variety of methods to protect and preserve the quality of our water. Under these circumstances, we conclude that waste disposal facilities do not have the obvious potential for polluting air or water or otherwise creating uncontrollable health or safety hazards. Nor do common knowledge and experience suggest other clearly deleterious effects which would inevitably be visited upon the public in general. We therefore conclude that waste disposal facilities under the diligent control of the Department do not embody a use, the total exclusion of which appears prima facie to be designed to protect the public health, safety and welfare. Concomitantly, the burden shifts to Alsace Township to justify the exclusionary zoning ordinance.

We hold that Alsace Township has not carried its burden. In particular, we are unpersuaded that the township has established that by excluding the activity in issue it endeavored to protect those public interests which zoning statutes permit municipalities to protect. Before the Board, the township sought by cross-examination of General Battery's witnesses to establish that the specific disposal facility contemplated, a landfill with a liner and a system of tanks designed to protect against the possible leaching into the soil of compounds produced in General Battery's lead-smelting operations, might have detrimental effects. However, this evidence, dealing as it does with the application of the ordinance to General Battery's proposed use of its land, is not dispositive on the issue of the ordinance's facial invalidity. Obviously, a zoning ordinance may be invalid as a whole, although not in relation to specific property. *Exton Quarries,* supra note 1; *accord, Girsh Appeal,* supra note 1. We conclude that whether a possibility exists that General Battery's activity might have detrimental effects does not justify a total exclusion of all industrial waste disposal facilities.

Nor can we consider as other than specious the township's attitude that the prohibition protects township inhabitants from industrial waste generated in another municipality. Clearly, *where* the waste is generated has very little bearing on whether its disposal is harmful. See Lutz v. Armour, 395 Pa. 576, 151 A.2d 108 (1959). Having been unable to conclude that whatever effects might issue from waste disposal operations would be so prejudicial to the public health, safety and welfare as to support the total exclusion of those facilities, we decline to derive such prejudice from the origin of the waste to be disposed of.

We therefore hold that the Board committed an error of law when it concluded that Alsace Township had established a public interest in support of its total exclusion of industrial waste disposal facilities. We agree with the court below that the zoning ordinance is invalid.

Order affirmed.

Notes

1. In Beaver Gasoline Co. v. Zoning Hearing Board of Borough of Osborne, 445 Pa. 571, 285 A.2d 501 (1971), the court was confronted with an ordinance that created two residential zones and one commercial zone. The commercial zone specifically excluded gasoline service stations, resulting in a total ban on such uses in the borough. The court dealt with the problem of the opponent of a zoning classification having the burden of proof to establish invalidity by stating:

> In situations involving the total prohibition of otherwise legitimate land uses, which, by common experience, appear to be as innocuous as the land use here contested, the applicant has met his burden of overcoming the presumption of constitutionality by showing the total ban. Thereafter, if the municipality is to sustain the validity of the ban, it must present evidence to establish the public purpose served by the regulation. It is not inconceivable, of course, that the municipality could establish the validity of a total ban, but it is its responsibility to do so. In the instant case, the municipality offered no evidence to establish the validity of the regulation and has, consequently failed to show that the regulation bears a relationship to the public health, safety, morals and general welfare.

In Lambros, Inc. v. Town of Ocean Ridge, Fla., 392 So.2d 993 (Fla.App. 1981), the court rejected the Pennsylvania rule and held that the burden of proof remained with the property owner to establish that the ordinance (excluding all commercial use after an amortization period) was arbitrary.

Pennsylvania courts have regularly taken the position that the zoning power does not usually permit total exclusion of a particular use. In addition to the principal case and Beaver Gasoline, see Exton Quarries, Inc. v. Zoning Board of Adjustment, 425 Pa. 43, 228 A.2d 169 (1967) and Sullivan v. Board of Supervisors of Lower Makefield Twp., 22 Pa.Cmwlth. 318, 348 A.2d 464 (1975).

In Eveline Twp. v. H & D Trucking Co., 181 Mich.App. 25, 448 N.W.2d 727 (1989) the court held the local ordinance totally prohibited commercial port facilities within the township and was, therefore, unconstitutional.

2. In Marcus Associates, Inc. v. Town of Huntington, 45 N.Y.2d 501, 410 N.Y.S.2d 546, 382 N.E.2d 1323 (1978), the court upheld a zoning ordinance which limited the number of uses and the size of uses in the only zoning district designated for industrial uses. The property owner argued that the ordinance was invalid because its purpose was to preserve the character of the district for "blue chip" industry, which exceeded the municipal power under the zoning enabling legislation. The court stated that the language of the enabling legislation "indicates that population density may be regulated in any setting, whether industrial or residential."

SECRET DESIRES LINGERIE, INC.
v. CITY OF ATLANTA

Supreme Court of Georgia, 1996.
266 Ga. 760, 470 S.E.2d 879.

THOMPSON, JUSTICE.

On October 4, 1993, the City of Atlanta enacted an ordinance to regulate lingerie modeling studios. Appellants challenged the constitutionality of the ordinance, seeking declaratory and injunctive relief. Following a trial, the superior court upheld the constitutionality of the ordinance. This appeal followed.

Appellants assert the City did not rely upon relevant evidence of the undesirable secondary effects of lingerie modeling studios when it enacted the ordinance and that, therefore, the ordinance cannot pass constitutional muster. We agree.

When a governing body enacts an ordinance regulating adult entertainment establishments because of their purported undesireable secondary effects, it must rely upon specific evidence showing a correlation between such establishments and the undesirable secondary effects the governing body seeks to control. Chambers v. Peach County, 266 Ga. 318, 320, 467 S.E.2d 519 (1996). The governing body can rely on evidence in the form of studies performed by other governmental units. City of Renton v. Playtime Theatres, 475 U.S. 41, 51, 106 S.Ct. 925, 930–31, 89 L.Ed.2d 29 (1986); Discotheque v. City Council of Augusta, 264 Ga. 623, 624, 449 S.E.2d 608 (1994). It can rely on evidence in the form of its own formal studies, see World Famous Dudley's v. City of College Park, 265 Ga. 618, 619, 458 S.E.2d 823 (1995), and it may rely on evidence not contained in formal studies. See Parker v. Whitfield County, 265 Ga. 829, 463 S.E.2d 116 (1995) (county relied upon studies of other communities as well as formal and informal meetings between members of the board, county sheriff's department, county residents and commissioners of other counties). The studies need not be perfect, World Famous Dudley's v. City of College Park, supra, but they must be considered before the ordinance is passed in order for the ordinance to be considered as one enacted for the purpose of combating the undesirable secondary effects of sexually explicit businesses. Chambers v. Peach County, supra. In a lawsuit challenging the constitutionality of an ordinance regulating adult business establishments, the governing body must be able to offer evidence of the studies it relied upon in enacting the ordinance. Id. If it cannot do so, the ordinance cannot be deemed constitutional.

At trial, the City introduced the testimony of three of its vice squad officers who opined that there is a correlation between lingerie modeling studios and prostitution. But the City did not even show that members of the city council were aware of the officers' conclusions, much less that the ordinance was enacted on the basis of those conclusions. And the ordinance itself sheds no light on this issue.

Compare World Famous Dudley's v. City of College Park, supra, in which the preamble of an ordinance regulating adult business establishments recited that it was based on the experiences of certain cities.

The City is unable to point to any evidence demonstrating that it considered specific studies of the pernicious secondary effects of lingerie modeling studios before enacting the ordinance. Although the trial court found that the City had knowledge of the police officers' conclusions prior to the enactment of the ordinance, the trial court's finding is clearly erroneous. There is not a scintilla of evidence demonstrating that the police officers (or their superiors) alerted the city council to the problems they uncovered.

The trial court erred in upholding the constitutionality of the ordinance. Chambers v. Peach County, supra.

Judgment reversed.

All the Justices concur, except FLETCHER, P.J., and HUNSTEIN, J., who dissent.

FLETCHER, PRESIDING JUSTICE, dissenting.

The trial court found that the City of Atlanta had knowledge of the secondary effects of lingerie modeling studios "prior to and at the time" the city council enacted the challenged ordinance. Because this factual finding is not clearly erroneous and the city's ordinance does not violate free speech, I dissent.

* * *

The police officers testified that they had investigated complaints of criminal activity in lingerie modeling studios; had seen acts of prostitution, simulated sex, and public indecency in the establishments; and had arrested one patron for engaging in sexual intercourse with an employee. The officers explained the difficulties they encountered in making arrests and their discussions with their supervisors about how best to curtail the crimes occurring in lingerie modeling shops and other adult entertainment establishments. This testimony shows that the city did not need to collect studies from other cities; it could rely on its own relevant experience in passing the ordinance to prevent crime. After two days of testimony, the trial court found that "acts of public indecency have been taking place in such establishments for several years" and the city was "aware of criminal activities taking place in lingerie modeling studios prior to and at the time the ordinance was enacted." A review of the record shows that the trial court was not clearly erroneous in finding the city relied on its own experience in enacting the ordinance.

In reversing, the majority opinion ignores the rationale for evaluating city ordinances to determine if they impermissibly infringe on free speech. Instead, it collapses federal first amendment law to a single test: whether the city council relied on "specific studies" of secondary effects before enacting the ordinance. Just as a governing body is not required to consider a "study" before adopting regulations that restrict leafletting at a state park or seeking an injunction that restricts demonstrations on public streets and sidewalks outside facilities offering abortions, a city is not required under either the United States Constitution or the Georgia Constitution to consider a "study" before enacting an ordinance that regulates lingerie modeling studios. All the first amendment requires is that a city rely on evidence that it reasonably believes is relevant to its important governmental interests. This court should not require more.

We have never addressed whether lingerie modeling is expressive conduct entitled to the protection of the free speech clause of the United States and Georgia Constitutions. Assuming that it is, this court must determine whether the law furthers an important government interest, the government interest is unrelated to the suppression of speech, and the incidental restriction of speech is no greater than is essential to further the government interest. The Atlanta ordinance meets this test. First, the trial court found that acts of public indecency had occurred in lingerie modeling establishments for years and that the city was aware of these criminal activities in enacting the ordinance. Second, the city's interest in preventing crime is unrelated to the suppression of expressive conduct. Third, the restrictions in the ordinance are no greater than is essential to further the city's interest in crime prevention. Unlike the total ban on private modeling sessions that was challenged in Quetgles, [264 Ga. at 708, 450 S.E.2d 677] the challenged ordinance here merely imposes reasonable regulations. The ordinance requires each establishment to obtain a license and employee permits, prohibits locking devices that hinder police inspection, and establishes reasonable closing hours. Because the city's ordinance does not restrict protected expression in violation of the federal or state constitutions, the trial court properly concluded that the ordinance was constitutional. Therefore, I would affirm.

I am authorized to state that JUSTICE HUNSTEIN joins in this dissent.

Notes

1. Some commercial or industrial uses may be considered so "obnoxious" that total exclusion will be upheld. See, e.g., Wigginess Inc. v. Fruchtman, 482 F.Supp. 681 (S.D.N.Y.1979), upholding a zoning ordinance provision prohibiting the operation of adult physical culture establishments offering massages by members of the opposite sex to their customers, and Northend Cinema, Inc. v. City of Seattle, 90 Wash.2d 709, 585 P.2d 1153 (1978), certiorari denied sub nom. Apple Theatre, Inc. v. City of Seattle, 441 U.S. 946, 99 S.Ct. 2166, 60 L.Ed.2d 1048 (1979), upholding a zoning ordinance prohibiting "adult movie" theaters in all neighborhoods but the downtown district. Compare Fox Valley Reproductive Health Care Center, Inc. v. Arft, 446 F.Supp. 1072 (E.D.Wis.1978) and Bossier City Medical Suite, Inc. v. City of Bossier City, 483 F.Supp. 633 (W.D.La.1980), dealing with the issue of exclusion of an abortion clinic. Some of these cases, of course, raise constitutional issues, such as freedom of speech and denial of equal protection. See, e.g. Genusa v. City of Peoria, 475 F.Supp. 1199 (C.D.Ill.1979), modified 619 F.2d 1203 (7th Cir.1980).

An important case relating the exclusionary zoning issue to the First and Fourteenth Amendments is Young v. American Mini Theatres, Inc., 427 U.S. 50, 96 S.Ct. 2440, 49 L.Ed.2d 310 (1976), which upheld a Detroit zoning ordinance requiring dispersal of adult theaters and bookstores. The ordinance involved in that case is much like the one in the Northend Cinema case, supra, and has become a much-utilized device in larger cities plagued with complaints about the detrimental effects of sex-oriented businesses on both residential and commercial neighborhoods. See Annotation, Validity of "War Zone" Ordinances Restricting Location of Sex–Oriented Businesses, 1 A.L.R.4th 1297 (1980). However, courts do sometimes strike down locational zoning for adult businesses. See Topanga Press, Inc. v. City of Los Angeles, 989 F.2d 1524 (9th Cir.1993). And some adult business ordinances falter on the definitions that trigger restrictions. For example, in Triplett Grille, Inc. v. City of Akron, 816 F.Supp. 1249 (N.D.Ohio 1993) the ordinance was struck down as overbroad because it applied to performances which included nudity of any kind, not just erotic entertainment. Also see Barnes v. Glen Theatre, Inc., 501 U.S. 560, 111 S.Ct. 2456, 115 L.Ed.2d 504 (1991), and City of Renton v. Playtime Theatres, 475 U.S. 41, 106 S.Ct. 925, 89 L.Ed.2d 29 (1986), the source of the secondary effects doctrine discussed in the principal case.

2.   The cases discussed above involve uses which at least some citizens in the community wish to exclude either for reasons of protecting public morals or the prevention of the detrimental effect of sex-oriented businesses. What about exclusions which may be based on aesthetics or lack of enthusiasm for the kind of business involved? Some state courts have considered the validity of zoning ordinances which exclude fast food or carry out restaurants from the retail business district. In Frost v. Village of Glen Ellyn, 30 Ill.2d 241, 195 N.E.2d 616 (1964), and La Salle Nat. Bank v. City of Park Ridge, 74 Ill.App.3d 647, 30 Ill.Dec. 587, 393 N.E.2d 623 (1979), the courts found such exclusions invalid. Also see A. Copeland Enterprises v. City of New Orleans, 372 So.2d 764 (La.App.1979). On bowling alleys and billiard rooms, see the annotation in 100 A.L.R.3d 252 (1980). Exclusion of video game parlors was upheld in Marshfield Family Skateland, Inc. v. Town of Marshfield, 389 Mass. 436, 450 N.E.2d 605 (1983) (contra as to pinball machines, People v. Palazzolo, 62 Mich.App. 140, 233 N.W.2d 216 (1975)). An intermediate appellate court in Connecticut upheld a town's prohibition of ice cream vending trucks in Blue Sky Bar v. Town of Stratford, 4 Conn.App. 261, 493 A.2d 908 (1985) affirmed 203 Conn. 14, 523 A.2d 467 (1987). A federal court, on the other hand, found a city's denial of a permit to operate a fortune telling and palmistry business violated substantive due process. Marks v. City Council of City of Chesapeake, Va., 723 F.Supp. 1155 (E.D.Va.1988).

3.   Sometimes, the exclusionary zoning argument involves the friction between an older, precisely worded zoning ordinance and a commercial proposal which does not quite fit the legislative mold. See, e.g., Edgemont Bank & Trust Co. v. City of Belleville, 85 Ill.App.3d 665, 40 Ill.Dec. 928, 407 N.E.2d 159 (1980), where the court held invalid a zoning classification which prohibited use of property for a walk-up banking facility in a light commercial zone.

4. In Uni–Worth Enterprises, Inc. v. City of Cleveland, 412 F.Supp. 349 (N.D.Miss.1976), the court enjoined enforcement of the zoning ordinance to the extent it disallowed the plaintiff's business of replacing automobile windshields at the customers' homes (in residential zones). The court found that, as applied to plaintiff, the ordinance was an interference with interstate commerce.

E. EXCLUSION OF APARTMENTS, CONDOMINIUMS AND TIME–SHARES

APPEAL OF GIRSH

Supreme Court of Pennsylvania, 1970.
437 Pa. 237, 263 A.2d 395.

ROBERTS, JUSTICE. By agreement dated July 13, 1964, appellant contracted to purchase a 17½ acre tract of land, presently zoned R–1 Residential, in Nether Providence Township, Delaware County. Appellant agreed to pay a minimum of $110,000 (later changed by agreement to $120,000) for the property. He further agreed to request the Township Board of Commissioners to change the R–1 Residential zoning classification so that a high-rise apartment could be built on the property and to pay $140,000 if this request were granted.

Nether Providence is a first-class township with a population of almost 13,000 persons and an area of 4.64 square miles. Approximately 75% of the Township is zoned either R–1 or R–2 Residential, which permit the construction of single-family dwelling units on areas not less than 20,000 and 14,000 square feet, respectively. Multi-unit apartment buildings, although not *explicitly* prohibited, are not provided for in the ordinance. The Township contains the customary commercial and industrial districts, as well as two areas where apartments have been permitted and constructed only after variances were secured.

After the Board refused to amend the zoning ordinance, appellant sought a building permit to construct two nine-story luxury apartments, each containing 280 units. The permit was refused since the R–1 Residential classification does not permit multiple dwellings. Appellant appealed to the Zoning Board of Adjustment and announced that he would attack the constitutionality of the zoning ordinance in lieu of seeking a variance. The Zoning Board sustained the ordinance and denied relief. The Court of Common Pleas of Delaware County affirmed, and appellant took this appeal. We hold that the failure of appellee-township's zoning scheme to provide for apartments is unconstitutional and reverse the decree of the court below.

Initially, it is plain that appellee's zoning ordinance indeed makes no provision for apartment uses. Appellee argues that nonetheless apartments are not explicitly *prohibited* by the zoning ordinance. Appellee reasons that although only single-family residential uses are provided for, nowhere does the ordinance say that there shall be no apartments. In theory, an apartment use by variance is available, and appellee urges that this case thus is different from prior cases in which we severely questioned zoning schemes that did not allow given uses in an *entire* municipality. See Exton Quarries, Inc. v. Zoning Board of Adjustment, 425 Pa. 43, 228 A.2d 169 (1967); Ammon R. Smith Auto Co. Appeal, 423 Pa. 493, 223 A.2d 683 (1966); Norate Corp. v. Zoning Board of Adjustment, 417 Pa. 397, 207 A.2d 890 (1965).

Appellee's argument, although perhaps initially appealing, cannot withstand analysis. It is settled law that a variance is available *only* on narrow grounds, i.e., "where the property is subjected to an unnecessary hardship, unique or peculiar to itself, and where the grant thereof will not be contrary to the public interest. The reasons to justify the granting of a variance must be 'substantial, serious and compelling.' " Poster Advertising Company, Inc. v. Zoning Board of Adjustment, 408 Pa. 248, 251, 182 A.2d 521, 523 (1962). In light of this standard, appellee's land-use restriction in the case before us cannot be upheld against constitutional attack because of the *possibility* that an *occasional* property owner may carry the heavy burden of proving sufficient hardship to receive a variance. To be constitutionally sustained, appellee's land-use restriction must be reasonable. If the failure to make allowance in the Township's zoning plan for apartment uses is unreasonable, that restriction does not become any the more reasonable because once in a while, a developer may be able to show the hardship necessary to sustain a petition for a variance. At least for the purposes of this case, the failure to provide for apartments anywhere within the Township must be viewed as the legal equivalent of an explicit total prohibition of apartment houses in the zoning ordinance.

Were we to accept appellee's argument, we would encourage the Township in effect to spot-zone a given use on variance-hardship grounds. This approach distorts the question before us, which is whether appellee must provide for apartment living as part of its *plan* of development. Cf. Eves v. Zoning Board of Adjustment, 401 Pa. 211, 164 A.2d 7 (1960).

By emphasizing the possibility that a given land owner *could* obtain a variance, the Township overlooks the broader question that is presented by this case. In refusing to allow apartment development as part of its zoning scheme, appellee has in effect decided to zone *out* the people who would be able to live in the Township if apartments were available. Cf. National Land and Investment Co. v. Easttown Twp. Board of Adjustment, 419 Pa. 504, 532, 215 A.2d 597, 612 (1965): "The question posed is whether the township can stand in the way of the natural forces which send our growing population into hitherto undeveloped areas in search of a comfortable place to live. We have concluded not. A zoning ordinance whose primary purpose is to prevent the entrance of newcomers in order to avoid future burdens, economic and otherwise, upon the administration of public services and facilities can not be held valid."

We emphasize that we are not here faced with the question whether we can compel appellee to zone *all* of its land to permit apartment development, since this is a case where *nowhere* in the Township are apartments permitted. Instead, we are guided by the reasoning that controlled in *Exton Quarries, supra.* We there stated that "The constitutionality of zoning ordinances which totally prohibit legitimate businesses * * * from an entire community should be regarded with particular circumspection; for unlike the constitutionality of most restrictions on property rights imposed by other ordinances, the constitutionality of total prohibitions of legitimate businesses cannot be premised on the fundamental reasonableness of allocating to each type of activity a particular location in the community." 425 Pa. at 58, 228 A.2d at 179. In *Exton Quarries* we struck down an ordinance which did not allow quarrying anywhere in the municipality, just as in *Ammon R. Smith Auto Co. Appeal, supra,* we did not tolerate a total ban on flashing signs and in *Norate Corp., supra,* we struck down a prohibition on billboards everywhere in the municipality. Here we are faced with a similar case, but its implications are even more critical, for we are here dealing with the crucial problem of population, not with billboards or quarries. Just as we held in *Exton Quarries, Ammon R. Smith,* and *Norate* that the governing bodies must make some provision for the use in question, we today follow those cases and hold that appellee cannot have a zoning scheme that makes no reasonable provision for apartment uses.

Appellee argues that apartment uses would cause a significant population increase with a resulting strain on available municipal services and roads, and would clash with the existing residential neighborhood. But we *explicitly* rejected both these claims in *National Land, supra:* "Zoning is a tool in the hands of governmental bodies which enables them to more effectively meet the demands of evolving and growing communities. It must not and can not be used by those officials as an instrument by which they may shirk their responsibilities. Zoning is a means by which a governmental body can plan for the future—it may not be used as a means to deny the future. * * * Zoning provisions may not be used * * * to avoid the increased responsibilities and economic burdens which time and natural growth invariably bring." 419 Pa. at 527–528, 215 A.2d at 610. Cf. Delaware County Community College Appeal, 435 Pa. 264, 254 A.2d 641 (1969); O'Hara's Appeal, 389 Pa. 35, 131 A.2d 587 (1957). That reasoning applies equally here. Likewise we reaffirm our holding in *National Land* that protecting the character—really the aesthetic nature—of the municipality is not sufficient justification for an exclusionary zoning technique. 419 Pa. at 528–529, 215 A.2d at 610–611.

This case presents a situation where, no less than in *National Land,* the Township is trying to "stand in the way of the natural forces which send our growing population into hitherto undeveloped areas in search of a comfortable place to live." Appellee here has simply made a decision that it is content with things as they are, and that the expense or change in character that would result from people moving in to find "a comfortable place to live" are for someone else to worry about. That decision is unacceptable. Statistics indicate that people are attempting to move away from the urban core areas, relieving the grossly over-crowded conditions that exist in most of our major cities. Figures show that most jobs that are being created in urban areas, including the one here in question, are in the suburbs. New York Times, June 29, 1969, p. 39 (City Edition). Thus the suburbs, which at one time were merely "bedrooms" for those who worked in the urban core, are now becoming active business areas in their own right. It follows then that formerly "outlying," somewhat rural communities, are becoming logical areas for development and population growth—in a sense, suburbs to the suburbs. With improvements in regional transportation systems, these areas also are now more accessible to the central city.

In light of this, Nether Providence Township may not permissibly choose to only take as many people as can live in single-family housing, in effect freezing the population at near present levels. Obviously if every municipality took that view, population spread would be completely frustrated. Municipal services must be provided *somewhere*, and if Nether Providence is a logical place for development to take place, it should not be heard to say that it will not bear its rightful part of the burden.[5] Certainly it can protect its attractive character by requiring apartments to be built in accordance with (reasonable) setback, open space, height, and other light-and-air requirements,[6] but it cannot refuse to make any provision for apartment living. The simple fact that someone is anxious to build apartments is strong indication that the location of this township is such that people are desirous of moving in, and we do not believe Nether Providence can close its doors to those people.

It is not true that the logical result of our holding today is that a municipality must provide for all types of land use. This case deals with the right of people to *live on land,* a very different problem than whether appellee must allow certain industrial uses within its borders.[7] Apart-

---

5. Perhaps in an ideal world, planning and zoning would be done on a *regional* basis, so that a given community would have apartments, while an adjoining community would not. But as long as we allow zoning to be done community by community, it is intolerable to allow one municipality (or many municipalities) to close its doors at the expense of surrounding communities and the central city.

6. As appellants indicate, the apartments here in question would cover only 2.7 acres of a 17.7 acre tract, would be located far back from the road and adjacent properties, and would be screened by existing high trees. Over half of the trees now on the tract would be saved.

It should be pointed out that much of the opposition to apartment uses in suburban communities is based on fictitious emotional appeals which insist on categorizing all apartments as being equivalent to the worst big-city tenements. See Babcock and Bossel-

man, Suburban Zoning and the Apartment Boom, 111 U.Pa.L.Rev. 1040, 1051–1072 (1963), wherein the authors also convincingly refute the arguments that apartments necessarily will: not "pay their own way"; cut off light and air; become slums; reduce property values; be destructive to the "character of the community"; and bring in "low-class" people.

7. Even in the latter case, if the Township instituted a total ban on a given use, that decision would be open to at least considerable question under our decision in *Exton Quarries,* supra.

In addition, at least hypothetically, appellee could show that apartments are not appropriate on the site where appellant wishes to build, but that question is not before us as long as the zoning ordinance in question is fatally defective on its face. Appellee could properly decide that apartments are more appropriate in one part of the Township than in another, but it can-

ment living is a fact of life that communities like Nether Providence must learn to accept. If Nether Providence is located so that it is a place where apartment living is in demand, it must provide for apartments in its plan for future growth; it cannot be allowed to close its doors to others seeking a "comfortable place to live."

The order of the Court of Common Pleas of Delaware County is reversed.

BELL, C.J., files a concurring opinion.

JONES, J., files a dissenting opinion in which COHEN and POMEROY, JJ., join.

BELL, CHIEF JUSTICE (concurring).

This case poses for me a very difficult problem. One of the most important rights, privileges and powers which (at least until recently) has differentiated our Country from Communist and Socialist Countries, is the right of ownership and the concomitant use of property. The only limitation or restriction thereof was "sic utere tuo ut alienum non laedas"—a right to use one's property in any way and manner and for any purpose the owner desires, except and unless it injures the property of another, or endangers or seriously affects the health or morals or safety of others.

Then along came zoning with its desirable objectives. However, desirable or worthwhile objectives have too often been carried to an unfair or unwise or unjustifiable extreme, or an extreme which makes the Act or Ordinance illegal or unconstitutional.

This Ordinance cannot be sustained under the theory or unwitting pretense that it is necessary for, or has a substantial relationship to the protection of the health or morals or safety of the people of that Township, and, as Justice Roberts points out, it cannot and should not be legalized or Constitutionalized under the theory of "general welfare" or "public interest or worthy objectives." Furthermore, Courts, Legislators, zoning bodies and most of the public have forgotten or rendered meaningless Article I, Section 1, of the Constitution of Pennsylvania, which provides: "All men are born equally free and independent, and have certain inherent and indefeasible rights, among which are those of * * * acquiring, possessing and protecting property * * *."

I believe that a County or Township can "reasonably" regulate the location, size, height, setbacks, light and air requirements, etc. of apartment houses or buildings, but that neither a County nor a Township can *totally prohibit* all apartment houses or buildings. Cf. Exton Quarries Inc. v. Zoning Board of Adjustment, 425 Pa. 43, 228 A.2d 169. Whether an ordinance which makes no provision for, or authorization of, apartment houses is equivalent to a total prohibition thereof raises (at least, for me) a difficult question. However, I have come to the conclusion that the present zoning ordinance (1) *in practical effect* amounts to a prohibi-

not decide that apartments can fit in *no* part of the Township.

tion of apartment houses, and (2) cannot be saved or legalized by a right to a variance which is grantable only upon proof of (a) unnecessary hardship upon and which is unique or peculiar to the property involved, as distinguished from the hardship arising from the impact of the zoning ordinance upon the entire district, and (b) where the proposed variance will not be contrary to the public safety, health, morals or general welfare: DiSanto v. Zoning Board of Adjustment, 410 Pa. 331, 189 A.2d 135; Sheedy v. Zoning Board of Adjustment, 409 Pa. 655, 187 A.2d 907; Brennen v. Zoning Board of Adjustment, 409 Pa. 376, 187 A.2d 180; Joseph B. Simon & Co. v. Zoning Board of Adjustment, 403 Pa. 176, 168 A.2d 317.

For these reasons, I concur in the Opinion of the Court.

JONES, JUSTICE (dissenting).

* * *

The principles governing the disposition of cases involving a constitutional attack on a zoning ordinance have been oft-repeated in our case law. "The test of constitutionality of a zoning ordinance is whether it bears a substantial relation to the health, safety, morals or general welfare of the public: [Citing authority]. One who challenges the constitutionality of a zoning ordinance has no light burden and it is settled that before a zoning ordinance can be declared unconstitutional it must be shown that its provisions are clearly arbitrary and unreasonable, having no substantial relation to the public health, safety, morals or general welfare. If the validity of the legislative judgment is fairly debatable, the legislative judgment must be allowed to control: * * * "

* * *

I turn now to appellant's second contention, *viz.,* that the zoning ordinance permitting only single-family dwellings is unconstitutional as applied to the Duer Tract in particular. Appellant's first argument under this heading is that the ordinance has no relation to the public health, safety and welfare. I cannot agree. The proposed apartment complex would be the largest of its kind in Delaware County, housing an estimated 1,600 persons, and would increase the population of the township by 13%. We cannot refute the conclusion that such a large and rapid increase in population would place a strain on the township's limited municipal services and rural roads. Furthermore, except for the railroad tracks, the area surrounding the Duer Tract is composed exclusively of single-family dwellings. The proposed apartment towers would be incompatible with the existing residential neighborhood and would introduce a structure completely out of proportion to any other building in the township. Furthermore, the complex would present a density problem in this area of the township. The First Class Township Code specifically empowers local municipalities to zone for density; I conclude that the ordinance in question is a proper application of that power.

* * *

Therefore, I would hold that the Township is *not* constitutionally required to provide for multiple-unit apartment buildings in its zoning ordinance and that the ordinance in question is not unconstitutional as applied to the Duer Tract.

I dissent.

COHEN and POMEROY, JJ., join in this dissenting opinion.

Notes

1. Does the court's decision in the Girsh case fail to take into account the role of land values and market forces in affecting types of housing? How can a court in reviewing allegedly exclusionary zoning practices mandate housing for low and moderate income families? If a court is unable to give affirmative relief, is the community decision to exclude what, in reality, amounts to high priced apartments really arbitrary? In this connection, consider the Mt. Laurel case, infra, and see Slade, Mt. Laurel: A View From the Bridge, 27 Land Use & Zoning Digest No. 6, p. 15 (1975).

2. Recall the language Justice Sutherland used in the Euclid case when referring to apartments: " * * * [V]ery often the apartment house is a mere parasite, constructed in order to take advantage of the open spaces and attractive surroundings created by the residential character of the district. Moreover, the coming of one apartment house is followed by others * * *." Not only have attitudes about multi-family dwellings changed a great deal since 1926, the economics of development in the inflation-ridden 1980's have forced developers out of single-family development into some form of multi-family development. On the other hand, the prejudice Justice Sutherland exhibited toward mingling of apartment houses and single-family dwellings in the same district is still very much evident today.

3. In Berger v. Board of Supervisors of Whitpain Twp., 31 Pa.Cmwlth. 386, 376 A.2d 296 (1977), the court found a township zoning ordinance invalid in not allowing, as a matter of right, townhouse development; citing Girsh, the court said: " * * * the ordinance which fails entirely to provide for a needed and desired kind of residential use is exclusionary and as a consequence unconstitutional." In Application of Friday, 33 Pa.Cmwlth. 256, 381 A.2d 504 (1978), the court struck down a total exclusion of apartments despite the municipality's argument that it was not in the path of population expansion and that it was a participant in a regional planning effort. The Pennsylvania courts have not limited their holdings on exclusionary zoning to total exclusion of multi-family housing. In Township of Willistown v. Chesterdale Farms, Inc., 462 Pa. 445, 341 A.2d 466 (1975), the supreme court invalidated a zoning ordinance which permitted multi-family dwellings on 80 acres out of a total of 11,589 acres in the township, calling the ordinance an example of "tokenism" and "selective admission." Then, in Surrick v. Zoning Hearing Board of Township of Upper Providence, 476 Pa. 182, 382 A.2d 105 (1977), the supreme court announced a three part test for defining exclusionary zoning:

> The initial inquiry must focus upon whether the community in question is a logical area for development and population growth. * * * The community's proximity to a large metropolis and the community's and

region's projected population growth figures are factors which courts have considered in answering this inquiry. * * *

Having determined that a particular community is in the path of urban-suburban growth, the present level of development within the particular community must be examined. Population density data and the percentage of total undeveloped land and the percentage available for the development of multi-family dwellings are factors highly relevant to this inquiry.

* * *

Assuming that a community is situated in the path of population expansion and is not already highly developed, this Court has, in the past, determined whether the challenged zoning scheme effected an exclusionary result or, alternatively, whether there was evidence of a "primary purpose" or exclusionary intent to zone out the natural growth of population.

For a case applying the three factors, see Appeal of Abcon, Inc., 35 Pa. Cmwlth. 589, 387 A.2d 1303 (1978). In that case the court found that the township was not practicing de jure exclusion of townhouses because one of the seven residential districts did inferentially permit such development. However, when applying the Surrick factors the court found de facto exclusion in that Horsham Township, eight miles from the Philadelphia city limits, is a likely area for development and population growth, that only 124 acres or 1.16% of the total land area is zoned for multi-family housing, and that while no evidence of exclusionary intent is shown, the exclusionary impact is clear. Compare, H & R Builders, Inc. v. Borough Council, 124 Pa.Cmwlth. 88, 555 A.2d 948 (1989).

4. In Zelvin v. Zoning Board of Appeals of Town of Windsor, 30 Conn.Sup. 157, 306 A.2d 151 (1973), the court refused to hold unconstitutional a zoning amendment which had the effect of halting all apartment development. After noting the Girsh case, the court distinguished that case by pointing out that previous development of apartments in Windsor had been allowed to the extent that 19% of the total number of dwelling units in the town were in multi-family structures. Also see Moss v. Town of Winchester, 365 Mass. 297, 311 N.E.2d 555 (1974).

5. For an unusual case where a developer tried to attack a zoning ordinance as exclusionary because it permitted garden apartments but excluded high-rise luxury apartments, see Swiss Village Associates v. Municipal Council of Twp. of Wayne, 162 N.J.Super. 138, 392 A.2d 596 (1978).

McHENRY STATE BANK v. CITY OF McHENRY

Appellate Court of Illinois, Second District, 1983.
113 Ill.App.3d 82, 68 Ill.Dec. 615, 446 N.E.2d 521.

[The plaintiff bank was trustee of property having on it a seventeen unit apartment building which the beneficial owner, Peter Tutera, wanted to convert to condominiums. It was in an area zoned R–4 for multiple family dwellings. There was a minimum lot requirement of 2500 square feet per dwelling, and this property was non-conforming in only having 1882 square feet per dwelling. Condominiums were permitted only in R–5 and R–5A districts having larger square feet requirements. The city would not permit the conversion, denied rezoning and denied an area variance. The trial court granted defendant's motion to dismiss.]

HOPF, JUSTICE:

* * *

A zoning ordinance is presumed valid and a party attacking the ordinance must prove by clear and convincing evidence that the classification is arbitrary, unreasonable and without a substantial relationship to the public welfare. * * *

Plaintiff has challenged the facial validity of the ordinance, consequently we are required to review the ordinance itself.

Under the ordinance, condominiums are only permitted in districts R–5 and R–5A, and are the only permitted uses in those districts. Other residential zoning districts permit cumulative zoning; however, R–5 and R–5A do not. There further appears to be a wide disparity between the minimum lot requirements in the districts which permit condominiums as opposed to requirements in those zoned districts which permit apartments.

According to the city's zoning ordinance in general the city council may grant a variation in zoning only where the physical surroundings of the property would result in particular hardship if the zoning ordinance is applied strictly; the conditions on which the petition is based are unique; the petitioner's purpose is not solely financial gain; the alleged hardship has not been created by the present owner; granting the variation will not be materially detrimental to the public welfare or surrounding properties, and; the proposed variation will not impair an adequate supply of light and air to adjacent property, substantially increase fire hazards or traffic, endanger the public safety, or substantially impair the value of neighboring property. As one can see by simple review of the variations standards, procuring a variation is not compatible with apartment conversion.

Condominiums and condominium conversions are lawful operations (Ill.Rev.Stat.1981, ch. 30, pars. 301 *et seq.*), and they should not be prohibited entirely by a zoning ordinance unless doing so has a substantial relationship to the public welfare. *Village of Cahokia v. Wright* (1973), 11 Ill.App.3d 124, 296 N.E.2d 30, *aff'd* (1974), 57 Ill.2d 166, 311 N.E.2d 153; *High Meadows Park, Inc. v. City of Aurora* (1969), 112 Ill.App.2d 220, 250 N.E.2d 517.

Though condominiums are not prohibited entirely under the city's zoning ordinance, as condominium zones within the ordinance are provided, the practical effect of restricting condominiums to only condominium zones does constitute an impermissible discrimination against the conversion of existing apartment dwellings into condominium units. A disparate treatment of condominiums and apartments is constitutional only if there would be some basis for distinction. (*Village of Cahokia v. Wright* (1973) 11 Ill.App.3d 124, 296 N.E.2d 30, *aff'd* (1974), 57 Ill.2d 166, 311 N.E.2d 153.) Where no real difference exists between groups treated differently and there is no basis for the disparity of classification, the ordinance is invalid. If a zoning ordinance permits certain uses of property but excludes other uses which are not significantly different, the ordinance cannot be sustained. *City of Chicago v. Sachs* (1953), 1 Ill.2d 342, 115 N.E.2d 762.

A conversion of an apartment building into a condominium complex does not basically involve a change in the use of the property, but only a change in the ownership. (*Maplewood Village Tenants Association v. Maplewood Village* (1971), 116 N.J.Super. 372, 282 A.2d 428; *Bridge Park Co. v. Borough of Highland Park* (1971), 113 N.J.Super. 219, 273 A.2d 397.) The statute enabling a municipality to enact zoning ordinances is directed to the regulation of the use of the property. See Ill.Rev.Stat.1981, ch. 24, par. 11–13–1.

There appears to be no Illinois case precisely on this point, however a municipality should not be permitted to use its zoning power for the purpose of precluding condominiums or condominium conversions. *Maplewood Tenants Association v. Maplewood Village* (1971), 116 N.J.Super. 372, 282 A.2d 428; *Bridge Park Co. v. Borough of Highland Park* (1971), 113 N.J.Super. 219, 273 A.2d 397.

* * *

The plaintiff has made out a *prima facie* case that the city by restricting condominium use to a non-cumulative lower density zoning district has discriminated against the conversion of apartment buildings to condominiums in other zoning areas. The statute enabling a municipality to enact zoning ordinances is directed against the use of the property. (Ill.Rev.Stat.1981, ch. 24, par. 11–13–1.) The city may not use its zoning powers to differentiate between condominiums and apartments based solely on the form of ownership. *Maplewood Village Tenants Association v. Maplewood Village* (1971), 116 N.J.Super. 372, 282 A.2d 428; *Bridge Park Co. v. Borough of Highland Park* (1971), 113 N.J.Super. 219, 273 A.2d 397.

In the present posture of the case there has been no evidence of a distinction between use contemplated by the plaintiff for his apartment building in Zone R–4 and the permissible condominium use of R–5 and R–5A. In the absence of evidence showing any distinction between these uses, or that the zoning classifications bore any real and substantial relationship to the public health, safety or welfare (*City of Champaign v. Roseman* (1958), 15 Ill.2d 363, 155 N.E.2d 34), the case must be remanded for further proceedings.

The judgment of the trial court of McHenry County is reversed and this case is remanded for further proceedings.

Reversed and Remanded.

Van Deusen and Lindberg, JJ., concur.

Notes

1. In Boland v.City of Great Falls, 275 Mont. 128, 910 P.2d 890 (1996) the court upheld a rezoning to allow construction of a condominium complex on land previously zoned for single-family dwellings. The neighbors' allegation of impermissible spot zoning was dismissed by the court because the prior zoning allowed townhouses, which the court concluded were generally similar to the proposed condos. The court also held that the entire neighborhood would benefit from the elimination of eyesores on the undeveloped property.

2. Most courts faced with the question of zoning ordinances which purport to discriminate against the condominium form of ownership have found such restrictions invalid, usually on the theory that the form of ownership or title-holding is not a legitimate zoning consideration. The problem of conversion of existing apartments to condominiums, however, involves a different set of problems. The existing structure remains the same (perhaps even refurbished and aesthetically more appealing), but the existing stock of rental housing is diminished. Many cities have sought to regulate such conversions. In City of Miami Beach v. Rocio Corp., 404 So.2d 1066 (Fla.App.1981) the court held that the city ordinance was preempted by state law. The California Supreme Court upheld a city ordinance which required a special use permit for conversion of apartments to condominiums, Griffin Development Co. v. City of Oxnard, 39 Cal.3d 256, 217 Cal.Rptr. 1, 703 P.2d 339 (1985). Also see, Leavenworth Properties v. City and County of San Francisco, 189 Cal.App.3d 986, 234 Cal.Rptr. 598 (1987); Claridge House One, Inc. v. Borough of Verona, 490 F.Supp. 706 (D.N.J.1980), affirmed 633 F.2d 209 (3d Cir.1980); Hornstein v. Barry, 560 A.2d 530 (D.C.App.1989); Bannerman v. City of Fall River, 391 Mass. 328, 461 N.E.2d 793 (1984); Annotation, Validity and Construction of Law Regulating Conversion of Rental Housing to Condominiums, 21 A.L.R.4th 1083 (1983); Judson, Defining Property Rights: The Constitutionality of Protecting Tenants from Condominium Conversion, 18 Harv.Civ.Rts.Civ.Lib.L.Rev. 179 (1983). Also see the material concerning gentrification in the Section on Housing Discrimination, infra.

3. In City of Portsmouth v. Schlesinger, 140 N.H. 733, 672 A.2d 712 (1996) the court considered the problem of whether a developer who sought to convert existing housing units to condominium ownership could be assessed an "impact fee" of $2.5 million in exchange for a rezoning. The developer made two payments and then stopped, leaving a balance of $1.7 million on its promissory note to the city. In a suit to collect, the developers asserted that the exaction was illegal and ultra vires. The city argued that the defense could not be raised because the developers did not timely appeal the original rezoning. When the case was originally heard in the federal district court, that court ruled for the developers. On appeal, the U.S. Court of Appeals for the First Circuit certified the question of timeliness to the New Hampshire Supreme Court. That court ruled that the defense was properly raised. Subsequently the First Circuit affirmed the original district court judgment for the developers. See 82 F.3d 547 (1st Cir.1996).

JACKSON COURT CONDOMINIUMS
v. CITY OF NEW ORLEANS

United States Court of Appeals, Fifth Circuit, 1989.
874 F.2d 1070.

JERRE S. WILLIAMS, CIRCUIT JUDGE:

Jackson Court Condominiums, Inc., the former owner of a condominium complex, sued the City of New Orleans after the Council of the City of New Orleans (hereafter "the City Council" or "the Council") passed a moratorium on the establishment of time-share condominiums in residential areas. The Council then refused to grant the company an exemption from the moratorium under a waiver provision. The $3.5 million suit alleges equal protection violations, both substantive and procedural due process violations, various state law claims, and an unconstitutional taking. The district court granted summary judgment for the city, and Jackson Court filed a timely appeal. We find the district court's ruling correct and affirm its judgment.

FACTUAL AND PROCEDURAL BACKGROUND

In the early 1980's time-share condominiums were a rapidly growing phenomenon and developers began to build or create them in New Orleans. The City Council of New Orleans became concerned that this phenomenon would have a deleterious effect on the city's historic neighborhoods.

As a result, in December 1980, the City Council passed an ordinance asking the City Planning Commission to make a comprehensive zoning study of time-sharing and transient vacation rentals. At the same time it embarked on a program of creating moratoriums on time-shares, first in the Vieux Carré district, nine months later in the Faubourg Marigny district, and finally on October 22, 1981, it passed Ordinance 8344 M.C.S. which created a city-wide moratorium on time-shares within certain zoning classification areas.[8] This moratorium contained a provision allowing the Council to grant a waiver to a covered party if it could demonstrate that it would experience undue hardship and the time-share would not adversely affect the character of the neighborhood.

* * *

Jackson Court purchased the apartments with the intent of transforming them into luxury time-share condominiums, and to that end invested $1.2 million in the property. A map which Jackson Court prepared for trial shows 40 properties in the neighborhood of Jackson Court, 29 of which were non-transient residential uses, six of which were community uses, four of which were small-scale commercial and business uses, and one of which was a boarding house.

---

8. The moratorium included a prohibition on new time-share plans in the single family residential, two-family residential, multiple-family residential, medical service, general office, and special industrial zoning districts.

Jackson Court eventually applied for a waiver from the provisions of the city-wide time-share moratorium, and had a hearing before the City Council on April 15, 1982. The day prior to the hearing, Jackson Court had filed a condominium declaration (which contained provisions permitting time-sharing) with the Conveyance Office of the Parish of Orleans and had registered with the City of New Orleans. The City Council refused Jackson Court's application for a waiver in a 6–1 vote. * * *

After the waiver denial Jackson Court used the apartment complex as a set of luxury apartments rather than as a time-share complex. Eventually, Jackson Court lost ownership of its property at a foreclosure sale instituted by a mortgage creditor.

Jackson Court first filed suit in state court, requesting injunctive relief and claiming that Ordinance 8344, the city-wide moratorium of October 1981, was in violation of Louisiana state law, local procedural law, and the city charter. Jackson Court further claimed that its due process and equal protection rights had been violated. The relief was denied. On appeal the Circuit Court of Appeals of the State of Louisiana found the issue moot as Jackson Court had ceased to be owner of the property in question. The Supreme Court of Louisiana denied certiorari.

Jackson Court then brought a 42 U.S.C.A. § 1983 suit in federal court. Initially New Orleans was given summary judgment on the basis of *res judicata*. This decision was reversed and remanded on appeal. *Jackson Court Condos v. City of New Orleans,* 793 F.2d 1288 (5th Cir.1986) (unpublished). On remand, the district court again granted summary judgment for the City of New Orleans, finding that it had no jurisdiction over the case under 42 U.S.C.A. § 1983 because Jackson Court did not state any valid claims of deprivation of constitutionally secured rights. *Jackson Court Condominiums, Inc. v. City of New Orleans,* 665 F.Supp. 1235 (E.D.La.1987). This decision is the subject of the appeal.

Five issues are raised: 1) Did the City of New Orleans deny Jackson Court procedural due process when passing the moratorium on time-shares or when rejecting its application for a waiver? 2) Was Jackson Court denied substantive due process in either of these actions? 3) Did these actions violate Jackson Court's right to equal protection? 4) Did Ordinance 8344, the moratorium, or 8585, creating a permanent ban, effect an unconstitutional taking of property? 5) Was Jackson Court unfairly denied a jury trial? Because we affirm the district court's summary judgment ruling on the four constitutional claims, we find the district court was correct in finding no jurisdiction and hence dismissing the case, along with some pendant state claims which we do not consider here. The jury trial issue therefore is moot. We examine the other four issues in order.

* * *

II. SUBSTANTIVE DUE PROCESS CLAIMS

A. *The Moratorium*

Jackson Court claims that it was denied substantive due process when the City Council passed the city-wide moratorium on time-share arrangements in RM–1 and RM–2 residential districts. The applicable standard here was established in *Shelton.* "We hold that the outside limit upon a state's exercise of its police power and zoning decisions is that they must have a rational basis." *Shelton,* 780 F.2d at 482. The key to such an inquiry is whether the question is "at least debatable." *Id.* at 483. Those challenging a legislative decision "must convince the court that the legislative facts on which the classification is apparently based could not reasonably be conceived to be true by the governmental decisionmaker." *Id.* at 479, *quoting Vance v. Bradley,* 440 U.S. 93, 110–11, 99 S.Ct. 939, 949, 59 L.Ed.2d 171 (1979).

The preamble to Ordinance 8344, which established the temporary moratorium, states that the City Council had called upon the City Planning Commission to study time-share plans and that "[t]he proliferation of time-share plans throughout the city prior to the consideration of the recommendations of the City Planning Commission might threaten the character of residential neighborhoods." This preamble adequately delineated reasons for the Council's action. We upheld a similar moratorium against a substantive due process attack in *Schafer v. City of New Orleans:*

> Interim development controls such as this moratorium have been found to play an important role in municipal planning. They aid in "bridging the gap between planning and its implementation into legal measures." They may, as here, be used to preserve the status quo while study of the area and its needs is completed.

Schafer, 743 F.2d at 1090.

Certainly the protection of residential integrity is a legitimate objective of a zoning regulation. *Penn Central Transportation Co. v. City of New York,* 438 U.S. 104, 98 S.Ct. 2646, 57 L.Ed.2d 631 (1978); *New Orleans v. Dukes,* 427 U.S. 297, 96 S.Ct. 2513, 49 L.Ed.2d 511 (1976). The City of New Orleans was concerned that the implementation of time-share arrangements in residential neighborhoods would increase the noise, littering, and vandalism which might be associated with transient users. This was a legitimate concern of the city and was debatable. Therefore the moratorium reaches the threshold established in *Shelton* for substantive due process.

* * *

III. THE EQUAL PROTECTION CLAIM

Jackson Court also claims that it was denied its Fourteenth Amendment equal protection rights by the moratorium and the denial of its waiver application.

First, it claims that because the city-wide moratorium denied the right to establish time-share arrangements in RM–2 districts but not other transient uses (such as boarding houses) it violated the equal protection clause. This claim is disposed of easily. As the district court correctly pointed out, as long as a classification is rationally related to a legitimate state objective, a legislature is allowed to attack a perceived problem piecemeal. *Katzenbach v. Morgan,* 384 U.S. 641, 657, 86 S.Ct. 1717, 1727, 16 L.Ed.2d 828 (1966); *Railway Express Agency v. New York,* 336 U.S. 106, 110, 69 S.Ct. 463, 466, 93 L.Ed. 533 (1949). Zoning classifications (at least in the absence of a classification affecting fundamental personal rights or based upon inherently suspect distinctions such as race, religion, or alienage) are subject to the same rational basis analysis utilized in due process claims. *Horizon Concepts, Inc. v. City of Balch Springs,* 789 F.2d 1165, 1167 (5th Cir.1986); *cf. City of New Orleans v. Dukes,* 427 U.S. 297, 303, 96 S.Ct. 2513, 2516–17, 49 L.Ed.2d 511 (1976). Under-inclusivity alone is not sufficient to state an equal protection claim. This ordinance was rationally related to a legitimate state objective. Hence, the moratorium by itself did not violate the equal protection clause.

* * *

IV. The Taking Claim

Jackson Court alleges that by establishing the moratorium and later the permanent ban on time-share developments in RM–1 and RM–2 areas the City of New Orleans effected a taking for which Jackson Court must be compensated under the eminent domain provisions of the Fifth Amendment. A taking may be shown if a zoning ordinance does not substantially advance legitimate state interests or denies an owner economically viable use of his land. *Agins v. City of Tiburon,* 447 U.S. 255, 261, 100 S.Ct. 2138, 2141, 65 L.Ed.2d 106 (1980). As we have already decided, the moratorium and later prohibition certainly advanced a legitimate government interest. So the inquiry here must be limited to the second criterion; whether the ordinance sufficiently intruded upon the owner's economically viable use of his land to constitute a "taking." The Fifth Amendment prohibition against taking without compensation does not guarantee the most profitable use of property, *Goldblatt v. Town of Hempstead,* 369 U.S. 590, 592, 82 S.Ct. 987, 989, 8 L.Ed.2d 130 (1962), and a diminution in value, standing alone, does not establish a taking. *Penn Central Transportation Co. v. City of New York,* 438 U.S. 104, 131, 98 S.Ct. 2646, 2663, 57 L.Ed.2d 631 (1978). The taking issue in these contexts is resolved by focusing on the uses the regulations permit. *Id.* at 131, 98 S.Ct. at 2663.

The district court found that "[n]owhere in the Complaint or Amended Complaint does Jackson Court allege that it has been deprived of all viable economic use of its property." *Jackson Court,* 665 F.Supp. at 1242. Jackson Court urges us to overturn the district court's grant of summary judgment to the City of New Orleans, claiming that this was an incorrect finding. The court's statement was in fact erroneous,

Jackson Court in its complaint did allege total loss of the property solely as a result of the Council's action. Jackson Court did state a facially valid taking claim in its complaint. This error on the part of the district court, however, fell far short of being fatal. The district court did find that Jackson Court's claim of total deprivation was essentially an urged factual conclusion, not supported by any facts Jackson Court asserted in its pleadings.

> [I]n fact, Jackson Court alleges that the property was being utilized as an apartment building at the time of purchase and there is nothing to indicate that the property could no longer be utilized as such. Rather, Jackson Court's allegation is essentially that it was deprived of what it perceived to be the most profitable expectation of its property.

Id. at 1242.

In order to avoid summary judgment the party opposing the summary judgment "may not rest upon the mere allegations of his pleading * * * but must set forth the specific facts showing that there is a genuine issue for trial." *Anderson v. Liberty Lobby,* 477 U.S. 242, 250–51, 106 S.Ct. 2505, 2511, 91 L.Ed.2d 202 (1986), *quoting First National Bank of Arizona v. Cities Service Co.,* 391 U.S. 253, 88 S.Ct. 1575, 20 L.Ed.2d 569 (1968). "[T]here is no issue for trial unless there is sufficient evidence favoring the nonmoving party for a jury to return a verdict for that party." *Anderson,* 477 U.S. at 250–51, 106 S.Ct. at 2511. The district court found that Jackson Court failed to meet this standard. The record supports that decision.

During the earlier state district court proceeding the president of Jackson Court, Pierre Villere, stated that he was aware of the City Council's initial decision to explore limitations on time-share arrangements in May of 1981, three months prior to purchase of the property. When asked about what actions he took after he learned of the October 1981 moratorium he stated that he and his associates knew "that there would have to be other alternative uses to the property in the event that time-sharing did not turn out to be financially feasible." Jackson Court seems to rely upon the business failure while renting the property as apartments as establishing a fact question as to whether there was a taking of constitutional dimension from the viable economic use of its property. The record shows, however, that Jackson Court took a knowledgeable risk in purchasing the property and failed. It was the market, rather than the City, which deprived Jackson Court of that potential use. There is no evidence to indicate that the city's action was the sole cause of the bankruptcy. This was a typical business failure, perhaps abetted somewhat by zoning, which is not at all uncommon when risky choices are made by the business.

We have held that refusal to rezone may in limited circumstances totally deprive the owner of economic value in his property. In *Hernandez v. City of Lafayette,* 643 F.2d 1188, 1197 (5th Cir., Unit A, 1981), *cert.*

denied, 455 U.S. 907, 102 S.Ct. 1251, 71 L.Ed.2d 444 (1982) we found the taking claim strong enough to avoid summary judgment because the shape, location, and encumbrances on the land made it unsuitable for residential development, for which it was then zoned. The present controversy is not at all analogous because Jackson Court's property had previously been operated as leased apartments and could still theoretically have been used as apartments or as condominiums without the time-share feature.

Jackson Court also argues that two other cases support its taking claim: *Wheeler v. City of Pleasant Grove,* 664 F.2d 99 (5th Cir. Unit B Dec.1981), *cert. denied,* 456 U.S. 973, 102 S.Ct. 2236, 72 L.Ed.2d 847 (1982) and *A.A. Profiles, Inc. v. City of Fort Lauderdale,* 850 F.2d 1483 (11th Cir.1988). Neither is persuasive. In each of those cases a municipal body approved the projects proposed by a property owner. Subsequently, after great expenditure and reliance on the city's approval, in each case the municipality then passed an ordinance which prohibited the property owner from pursuing the project. No such reversal of policy after a commitment occurred in the instant case.

The district court also found that Jackson Court's taking claim was premature even assuming it valid because Jackson Court had not sought compensation under state law. Under *Williamson County Regional Planning Commission v. Hamilton Bank,* 473 U.S. 172, 194–97, 105 S.Ct. 3108, 3120–22, 87 L.Ed.2d 126 (1985) an aggrieved party is required to seek not only administrative relief before alleging a taking claim but must also first seek compensation under state law if the state has provided an adequate process for obtaining compensation. Louisiana recognizes a cause of action for such a taking without formal condemnation, i.e. "inverse condemnation." *See Reymond v. State Department of Highways,* 255 La. 425, 231 So.2d 375, 383 (1970); *Trustees of Pomeroy v. Town of Westlake,* 357 So.2d 1299 (La.App. 3d Cir.), *cert. denied,* 359 So.2d 205 (La.1978); La. Const. art. 1, § 4; La.Rev.Stat.Ann. § 19.102 (West 1979). *But see A.A. Profiles,* 850 F.2d at 1486–87, n. 3 (although Florida recognized inverse condemnation, the Eleventh Circuit concluded that zoning matters were entirely distinct from the availability of inverse condemnation suits in the context of the exercise of eminent domain power under Florida law). We need not and do not address this issue because the grant of summary judgment can be upheld on the basis of the facts and pleadings as not constituting a taking.

Conclusion

We uphold the district court's summary judgment in favor of the city on Jackson Court's substantive and procedural due process claims, the equal protection claim, and the taking claim. We therefore do not examine the trial court's denial of Jackson Court's request for jury trial.

AFFIRMED.

F. EXCLUSION OF MOBILE HOMES

TOWN OF GLOCESTER v. OLIVO'S
MOBILE HOME COURT, INC.

Supreme Court of Rhode Island, 1973.
111 R.I. 120, 300 A.2d 465.

KELLEHER, JUSTICE. The defendant corporation is the owner and operator of a mobile home park located in the town of Glocester on land which is situated on the easterly side of Chopmist Hill Road just north of the junction of that highway and Pound Road. The parcel contains approximately 38 acres. In this action, the town seeks to enjoin the corporation from violating a provision found in both its licensing and zoning ordinances which limits the number of mobile homes that can be parked in such a facility to 30. The defendant filed an answer which in essence challenges the constitutionality of the 30–unit limitation and asked that the town be restrained from interfering with "its right" to operate a mobile home park containing more than 30 units. A hearing was held before a justice of the Superior Court. The trial justice, in upholding the limitation, alluded to the public health problems which are not found in "conventional habitation." Judgment was entered ordering the defendant to reduce the number of units parked on its premises to 30 and to obtain the requisite license. This appeal ensued and to put it in its proper focus, we will set out just a few of the pertinent facts found in the record. * * *

In May, 1965, the council made several substantial changes in its mobile home ordinance. All mobile homes had to be located in a park. The maximum number of mobile homes that could be serviced at any given time in any park was 30. About five months later, in October, 1965, the town council reinforced its restrictive efforts relative to the immobilized mobile home by enacting a zoning ordinance in which the use of mobile homes was prohibited except that any mobile home park then in existence could continue and expand so long as its expansion did not exceed the 30–unit limitation found in the licensing ordinance. There were at that time three such parks in the town. Any potential mobile home park operator who might wish to locate in Glocester now found himself in the same zoning category as the manufacturer of fertilizer, the distiller of tar, or the owner of a commercial piggery.

* * *

The common law permitted one to use his property in a manner and for such purposes as he chose so long as he did not maintain a nuisance or injure others. This right, however, has been made subject to regulations, restrictions and control by the state through the legitimate exercise of its police power. The test of legitimacy is the existence of a reasonable relationship between the exercise of this power and the public health, safety, morals and general welfare. A zoning limitation which is not so related represents a confiscation of private property without just compensation. See Goldstein v. Zoning Board of Review, 101 R.I. 728, 227 A.2d 195 (1967); Buckminster v. Zoning Board of Review, 69 R.I. 396, 33 A.2d 199 (1943); Robinson v. Town Council, 60 R.I. 422, 199 A. 308 (1938). When measured by these standards, the limitation of 30 mobile homes as applied to Olivo is patently unconstitutional. We have made this determination realizing full well that a duly enacted ordinance carries with it a presumption of constitutionality which will disappear only on a contrary showing beyond a reasonable doubt. City of Providence v. Stephens, 47 R.I. 387, 133 A. 614 (1926). However, such a principle does not permit us to adopt an ostrich-like stance by burying our heads in the sand and ignoring the obvious.

* * *

The restrictive steps taken by the Glocester Town Council give us an opportunity to examine the motives of those who call their mobile house a home. We are told that "Recent population increases, coupled with the apparent inability of the United States housing industry to overcome problems of tight money, galloping costs, and labor shortages, have resulted in a serious undersupply of new single family dwellings in the low to middle price ranges. These conditions have caused a rapid expansion of the mobile home industry. Derived from this is a demand for more mobile home parks, whose expansion has been frustrated by public pressure, municipal policies, and zoning restrictions which attempt to keep mobile homes and mobile home parks out of a given area." Van Iden, Zoning Restrictions Applied to Mobile Homes, 20 Clev.St. L.Rev. 196 (1970). It is believed that today one out of every five new single-family dwellings is a mobile home and that this fraction will increase. Note, The Community and the Park Owner Versus the Mobile Home Park Resident: Reforming the Landlord–Tenant Relationship, 52 B.U.L.Rev. 810 (1972). It is obvious that a mobile home park can no longer be primarily classified as a gathering place for a group of nomads who wander hither, thither and yon over the highways and byways. We cannot assume that an occupant of a mobile home poses any greater threat to the public safety than the other inhabitants of a municipality who might live in a more conventional type of residence. Many years ago, this court observed that a gasoline filling station was not a nuisance *per se*. Sundlun v. Zoning Board of Review, 50 R.I. 108, 145 A. 451 (1929). Today, the same sentiments can be expressed about a mobile home park.

The municipality's contention, that its limitation of 30 units constitutes an effort to lessen congestion, seems to be a diplomatic way of expressing its real concern, that of finding some way to maintain the population of its schools at a point where a stable tax rate can be preserved. We do not believe that a zoning ordinance was ever intended to fulfill such a function. Rhode Island, like its sister states, has witnessed the exodus from the cities to the suburbs. Our state is often described as the "City–State." A motorist may, because of our modern expanded system of highways, travel from one end of Rhode Island to its extreme opposite end in the matter of just one hour. Glocester is a pleasant rural area. By automobile, it lies just about 25 minutes to the west of our capital city, Providence. Its 1965 zoning ordinance sets up four zones—agricultural, residential, commercial and industrial. The bulk of the town is zoned for agriculture. The commercial classification is subdivided into two categories—neighborhood commercial and highway commercial. Most commercial establishments are to be found along United States Route 44. Even though the council provided an industrial zoning classification, the zoning map, which is part of the ordinance, shows that no part of the town has been zoned industrial.

The 30–mobile home limit might be considered as one type of exclusionary zoning.[9]

Even though we have stated that the location and use of a mobile home is subject to a valid exercise of the police power, the limitation of 30 mobile homes found in the Glocester zoning ordinance and its licensing counterpart, at least as it applies to Olivo's property, fails to satisfy the requisite constitutional standards.

* * *

The defendant's appeal is sustained. The judgment appealed from is vacated and the case is remanded to the Superior Court for entry of judgment in accordance with this opinion.

Notes

1. Compare the case of Clark v. County of Winnebago, 817 F.2d 407 (7th Cir.1987). The property owner sought to have a portion of his land rezoned to "Mobile Home District." When his request was denied, he brought a due process challenge in federal court on the theory that the requirements for the mobile home district were discriminatory and that the ordinance unconstitutionally discriminated between site-built homes and mobile homes. The court upheld the ordinance, stating: "There was testimony at trial that, despite advances in the mobile home industry, distinctions between mobile homes and site-built homes still exist with respect to design, construction, and general appearance. While some mobile homes may compare favorably with conventional homes, zoning classifications necessarily require that generalizations be made. Mathematical certainty is not required

9. Strictly speaking, the council's actions did not amount to true exclusionary zoning because it permitted the three mobile home parks to continue to operate. An ordinance which in effect barred trailer or mobile home parks from an entire New Jersey municipality has been upheld. Vickers v. Township Committee of Gloucester Township, 37 N.J. 232, 181 A.2d 129 (1962). A contrary position has been taken in Michigan in Gust v. Canton Township, 342 Mich. 436, 70 N.W.2d 772 (1955). A compilation of diverse judicial views expressed on the validity of zoning regulations which exclude mobile home parks can be found in 42 A.L.R.3d 598. In Steel Hill Development, Inc. v. Town of Sanbornton,

469 F.2d 956 (C.A. 1st Cir.1972), the constitutionality of a zoning amendment which changed the minimum lot size from three-fourths of an acre to three and in some instances to six acres was upheld. The court made it clear that its approval of the zoning enactment was limited to the facts as established by the record before it. In fact, Chief Judge Coffin expressed concern whether the amendment came about because the inhabitants of Sanbornton desired to keep "outsiders" beyond their borders. Population growth, he said, " * * * has to go somewhere, unwelcome as it may be, and in that case we do not think it should be channelled by the happenstance of what town gets its veto in first."

for the ordinance to pass constitutional muster, so long as there is a reasonable basis for the classification chosen."

2. Because of the general recognition that manufactured housing is an essential method of meeting the housing needs of low and moderate income residents, courts have begun to question the validity of total exclusion of mobile homes or mobile home parks from the entire community. See, e.g., In re Shore, 524 Pa. 436, 573 A.2d 1011 (1990); Guy v. Brandon Twp., 181 Mich.App. 775, 450 N.W.2d 279 (1989); Taylor v. Shaw and Cannon Co., 236 Va. 15, 372 S.E.2d 128 (1988); Jensen's, Inc. v. City of Dover, 130 N.H. 761, 547 A.2d 277 (1988); Borough of Malvern v. Jackson, 108 Pa.Cmwlth. 248, 529 A.2d 96 (1987), settlement stipulation approved 521 Pa. 570, 559 A.2d 489 (1989). In Stahl v. Upper Southampton Twp. Zoning Hearing Bd., 146 Pa.Cmwlth. 659, 606 A.2d 960 (1992), appeal denied 533 Pa. 639, 621 A.2d 584 (1993), the court found a de facto exclusion of mobile home parks where the ordinance permitted such parks with minimum 9,000 square foot lots, density requirements of three units per acre, and a requirement that the park be in single ownership.

3. Congress, in P.L. 93–383, provided the basis for federal regulation of construction standards for manufactured homes. See 42 U.S.C.A. § 5401 et seq.and 24 C.F.R. § 3280 et seq. The federal certification of manufactured homes along with changes in style (such as pitched roofs and non-metal siding) and the advent of double-wide and triple-wide homes have contributed to more widespread acceptance of manufactured housing in communities around the country. See Colorado Manufactured Housing Ass'n v. Pueblo County, 857 P.2d 507 (Colo.App.1993); Tennessee Manufactured Housing Ass'n v. Metropolitan Government of Nashville, 798 S.W.2d 254 (Tenn.App. 1990); compare Duggins v. Walnut Cove, 63 N.C.App. 684, 306 S.E.2d 186 (1983).

4. Not all mobile home parks are low and moderate income neighborhoods. The New York Times, Dec. 13, 1990, p. B 1, contains an illustrated article about the Point Dume Club in Malibu, California, a 297 unit mobile home park where units sell for as much as $300,000 and may have a Maserati or Rolls–Royce parked in the driveway. One insurance company that insures mobile homes has estimated that the percentage of mobile home owners with incomes above $40,000 increased from 2% in 1981 to 10% in 1990 to 15% in 1993. See Kevin Sack, Mobile Homes Go Upscale: One Pet Per Plot, Please, N.Y. Times, Feb. 23, 1997, p. E 3.

5. The bulk of the litigation involving zoning and mobile homes or manufactured housing deals with the issue of whether such dwellings can be confined to parks or special districts and excluded from single-family zones. The next case and notes following it take up this issue.

DUCKWORTH v. CITY OF BONNEY LAKE

Supreme Court of Washington, En Banc, 1978.
91 Wash.2d 19, 586 P.2d 860.

STAFFORD, JUSTICE.

This is an appeal from a summary declaratory judgment holding unconstitutional a portion of the Bonney Lake zoning ordinance.

* * *

The Duckworths own a city lot which is zoned R.S. (single family residence). On October 28, 1976, the City issued the Duckworths a building permit authorizing them to place a 24′ x 64′ mobile home on their lot. The mobile home has a living area of approximately 1500 sq. ft. and was manufactured in compliance with state and federal construction safety standards for such homes. See RCW 43.22.340–.420; 42 U.S.C.A. 5401, 5402, 5403; 24 C.F.R. 280.01 et seq. Such compliance with state and federal construction safety standards is deemed compliance with local building code standards of safety for mobile homes. The Duckworths planned to place the mobile home upon a permanent foundation and attach it to existing utilities.

On November 16, 1976, following delivery of the mobile home, the Duckworths were notified that the City had revoked their building permit. According to the City, the zoning code authorized the Duckworths to place their mobile home only in the R.D. zone because mobile homes could be placed only in "designated" areas and the R.D. zone was the only area so "designated" vis-a-vis R.S. and R.D. zones.

* * *

DID THE TRIAL COURT ERR IN HOLDING UNCONSTITUTIONAL A ZONING ORDINANCE THAT DISTINGUISHES BETWEEN MOBILE HOMES AND CONVENTIONAL HOMES FOR THE PURPOSE OF PLACING THEM IN DIFFERENT AREAS?

The Duckworths challenged as unconstitutional the City's use of its *legislative* power to exclude mobile homes from the R.S. zone and to restrict their location to the R.D. zone. On this issue, the trial court ruled the City had the burden of proof to demonstrate that the exclusion of mobile homes from the R.S. zone was a reasonable exercise of its police power. Further, the trial court determined the City had failed to meet its burden and thus the exclusion was unconstitutional. In the context of a summary judgment, the trial court's determination was erroneous.

The power of the City to plan for its physical development through zoning stems from RCW 35.63.080 which provides in part:

> "*For this purpose the council* * * * in such measure as is deemed reasonably necessary or requisite in the interest of health, safety, morals and the general welfare * * * by general ordinances * * * *may regulate and restrict the location and the use of buildings, structures and land for residence* * * * and other purposes; the * * * construction and design of buildings * * * and the subdivision and development of land."

(Italics ours.)

Municipal zoning ordinances enacted pursuant to such statutory authority will be held constitutional as a valid exercise of the police power if they bear a substantial relation to the public health, safety, morals or general welfare. Two inquiries must be made when measuring such legislative enactments against the permissible bounds of the police power.

The initial inquiry is whether the legislation tends to promote the public health, safety, morals or welfare. * * * If it does, the wisdom, necessity and policy of the law are matters left exclusively to the legislative body. * * *

The second inquiry is whether the legislation bears a reasonable and substantial relation to accomplishing the purpose established by the first inquiry. * * *

The two inquiries cannot be made in a vacuum. The public interest to be promoted or the evil to be corrected and the relationship of the legislation to this public purpose must be determined. To this end the court necessarily engages in certain presumptions. * * * If the court can reasonably conceive of a state of facts which would warrant the legislation, those facts will be presumed to exist. Further, it will be presumed that the legislation was passed with reference to those facts. * * *

These rules are more than mere rules of judicial convenience. They establish the line of demarcation between legislative and judicial functions. * * *

In examining the validity of the City's zoning code, we first observe that the purpose of zoning is not to increase or decrease the value of any *particular* lot or tract. Rather it is to benefit the *community generally* by the intelligent planning of land uses without unreasonable discrimination. The "general purpose" of zoning is to stabilize uses, conserve property values, preserve neighborhood characters, and promote orderly growth and development. McNaughton v. Boeing, supra, 68 Wash.2d at 661, 414 P.2d 778. See also B. Hodes & G. Roberson, The Law of Mobile Homes 190 (3d ed. 1974). As Charles S. Rhyne states in Municipal Law (1957) at page 943:

> "Zoning stabilizes the uses of land and furnishes a protection to residential neighborhoods which will cause them to maintain themselves in a decent and sanitary way and protects the civic and social values of the American home. Thus, residential * * * districts may be established and all nonconforming and conflicting uses excluded therefrom so long as the classification is reasonably related to the welfare, health, and safety of those living in the district."

(Footnotes omitted.)

We recognize that rapid increase in the number of mobile homes presents a complex zoning and planning problem. As with every new use, mobile homes must be provided for. But, any provision made must be by zoning regulations designed to fit the community's *total* need. We are also cognizant that increased mobile home use has developed in a climate of municipal and neighborhood hostility which originally impeded efforts to effect reasonable and rational accommodations between the mobile homes and more conventional residential uses. R. Anderson, 2 American Law of Zoning, § 14.01, p. 547 (2d ed. 1976).

Generally speaking, however, most municipal efforts to *totally exclude* mobile homes from a community have been found unconstitutional as an unreasonable exercise of police power. American Law of Zoning, § 14.04 at 558–62; Annot., *Use of trailer or similar structure for residence purposes as within limitation of restrictive covenant, zoning provision, or building regulation,* 96 A.L.R.2d 232, § 3[a], p. 237 (1964). However, and in recognition of differing needs, it is well settled that while such homes may not be *totally excluded,* they may be classified separately from other residential uses for purposes of regulation. American Law of Zoning, § 14.01, p. 550 and § 14.05, pp. 562–566; 96 A.L.R.2d, supra at 232, § 3[b] at 238. As so regulated, mobile homes may be restricted to certain zones and excluded from others. The Law of Mobile Homes, supra, at p. 189; American Law of Zoning, supra, § 14.05, pp. 562–66. It is also generally accepted that these types of restrictions upon use have several reasonable bases.

First, mobile homes tend to stunt growth potential of the land and have an adverse effect upon the development potential of a neighborhood. American Law of Zoning, supra, § 14.01, p. 550, § 14.05, p. 563. Quite apart from whether mobile homes are less beautiful or more attractive than conventional dwellings, they do not look like conventional homes. This difference in appearance has persuaded many municipalities that mobile homes in conventional home neighborhoods will depress property values. In this regard it is generally recognized that the exterior architectural appeal and functional plan of a structure should not be so at variance with either the exterior architectural appeal or functional plan of the structures already constructed or in the course of construction, in the immediate neighborhood, as to cause substantial depreciation in the property value of the neighborhood. See State v. Wieland, 269 Wis. 262, 69 N.W.2d 217, cert. denied, 350 U.S. 841, 76 S.Ct. 81, 100 L.Ed. 750 (1955). In short, the very fact of structural difference may make mobile homes an architectural and economic depreciating factor in a conventional residential neighborhood whereas the effect will be quite the contrary if located in a mobile home zone. The difference in appearance and its recognized potential effect upon an existing neighborhood of conventional homes is a legitimate and significant factor to consider in enacting zoning laws. American Law of Zoning, supra, § 14.01, p. 548.

A second reason for separate classification of mobile homes is that they commonly have minimum storage capacity. This conceivably may encourage an overflow of the miscellany of children's vehicles, toys and various tools. If these storage problems are not addressed by the individual owner, the result to the community may be increased clutter or the mushrooming of sheds and other temporary shelters.

Space limitations also may generate other municipal concerns. In discussing planned development controls for mobile homes, Frederick H. Blair, Jr. recognizes that mobile homes also generally lack garage space and thus may require additional municipal planning for parking to meet the needs of the owners, their neighbors, and their guests without interference with normal movement of traffic. F. Blair, Regulation of Modular Housing with Special Emphasis on Mobile Homes, pp. 78–80 (1971).

It has also been recognized that while the need for municipal services may be similar for both conventional housing and mobile homes, these needs generally vary in degree. Thus, requiring that different types of housing be maintained in separate zones cannot be deemed unreasonable or without a rational relationship to the differing needs for municipal services. See American Law of Zoning, supra, § 14.05, p. 563; see also McKie v. County of Ventura, 38 Cal.App.3d 555, 113 Cal.Rptr. 143 (1974).

Finally, considerations of attractiveness and beauty in the sense of surrounding conventional architecture are also appropriate municipal concerns when planning for the general welfare. See Lionshead Lake, Inc. v. Wayne Twp., 10 N.J. 165, 177, 89 A.2d 693 (1952). While we have indicated that aesthetic considerations alone may not support invocation of the police powers, the fact that aesthetics play a part in adoption of zoning ordinances does not affect its validity if the regulation finds reasonable justification in serving a generally recognized ground for exercise of the police power. Polygon Corp. v. Seattle, 90 Wash.2d 59, 70, 578 P.2d 1309 (1978); Department of Ecology v. Pacesetter Constr. Co., 89 Wash.2d 203, 571 P.2d 196 (1977). See 6 McQuillin, Municipal Corporations, §§ 24.15, 24.16, p. 476 et seq. (rev.vol. 1969).

In sum, it is generally recognized that where a municipality provides an adequate area for mobile home development, as was done in the instant case, mobile homes may be excluded from conventional residential districts. As we have said, a municipality may exclude them from conventional residential districts because as a nonconventional use they tend to lower, adversely affect, or at least stunt the growth potential of the surrounding land. Regulation of Modular Housing, with Special Emphasis on Mobile Homes, supra at 62; American Law of Zoning, supra, § 14.05, p. 563. This problem does not derive from aesthetics alone. Economic concerns as well as concerns for orderliness, adequate parking and the proper supply of municipal services are also legitimate bases for regulation. See Berman v. Parker, 348 U.S. 26, 75 S.Ct. 98, 99 L.Ed. 27 (1954).

A city which is systematically planned and developed to include all types of living units in an orderly pattern offers greater attractiveness to the home seeker than one which is allowed to develop in a haphazard way. If zoning regulations stabilize the value of property, promote the permanency of home surroundings, and add to the happiness and comfort of the citizens, they most certainly promote the general welfare. See Cady v. Detroit, 289 Mich. 499, 286 N.W. 805 (1939); State ex rel. Carter v. Harper, 182 Wis. 148, 196 N.W. 451 (1923). * * *

* * *

With the foregoing considerations in mind, we hold that a set of facts can be conceived which reasonably might have prompted the City to enact the challenged zoning code. * * * Moreover, the zoning code tends to promote the health, safety and welfare of the City's residents.

More specifically, it tends to correct a conceivable evil and to promote the City's interest in orderly growth and development.

We also conclude that the City's zoning code bears a reasonable and substantial relation to accomplishing these presumed purposes. It is neither fanciful nor merely aesthetic. On the contrary, it is reasonable in application and has a real relation to the public health, safety and general welfare. Within the limits of the few uncontroverted facts before us on summary judgment, we hold that the City may constitutionally exercise its police power to exclude mobile homes from the R.S. zone.

DID THE TRIAL COURT ERR BY HOLDING THAT THE CITY ABUSED ITS POLICE POWER IN ENACTING THE CHALLENGED ORDINANCE?

As we have indicated, a city may constitutionally exercise its police power and regulate land uses by providing separate areas for mobile homes and conventional housing. We now must consider whether the trial court correctly determined *on summary judgment* that the City abused its power by enacting the challenged land use restrictions. In this respect, the trial court determined that the City failed to prove the challenged provisions were a reasonable exercise of its power. On appeal, the Duckworths maintain that the trial court correctly placed the burden of proof upon the City citing State ex rel. Wenatchee Cong. of Jehovah's Witnesses v. Wenatchee, 50 Wash.2d 378, 383, 312 P.2d 195 (1957). We disagree.

In *Wenatchee,* we held that the government has the burden of demonstrating the reasonableness of its *administrative* actions. State ex rel. Wenatchee Cong. of Jehovah's Witnesses v. Wenatchee, supra at 383, 312 P.2d 195. A different rule applies in the *legislative* setting. The burden of establishing invalidity of a *legislative* enactment rests heavily on the party asserting its unconstitutionality. Moreover, every presumption will be indulged in favor of constitutionality. * * *

Nevertheless, the Duckworths suggest that we should abandon our adherence to the foregoing rule governing the burden of proof for legislative acts and apply the *Wenatchee* rule to the City's zoning code. In this respect, the Duckworths rely on authority from Michigan and Pennsylvania.

Although Michigan at one time apparently did follow our *administrative* rule on burden of proof, it has now abandoned it in favor of the one recognized by us, when a potential housing use is not *totally* excluded. See Kropf v. Sterling Heights, 391 Mich. 139, 215 N.W.2d 179 (1974). Moreover, the Pennsylvania courts also will shift the burden of proof and negate any presumption of validity attaching to a zoning enactment *only if* the challenging party first shows a *total exclusion* of an otherwise legitimate use. General Battery Corp. v. Zoning Hearing Bd., 29 Pa.Cmwlth. 498, 371 A.2d 1030 (1977). Here, we are not concerned with the *total* prohibition of mobile homes. Thus, neither the Michigan nor the Pennsylvania rules are applicable. We see no reason for changing the longstanding presumption of validity followed by this and most other courts.

* * *

If reasonable minds can differ concerning whether a particular zoning restriction has a substantial relationship to the public health, safety or general welfare, *no* abuse of discretion is established and the legislative act must stand. Lutz v. Longview, supra; 8A McQuillin, Municipal Corporations, § 25.279 (3d ed. 1977). After reviewing the very limited uncontroverted facts and considering the nature of the pleadings, we can only conclude that the Duckworths failed to meet *their* burden of proving the City acted arbitrarily or capriciously.

IS AN ASSERTED HOUSING SHORTAGE A REASON TO OVERTURN THE ZONING ORDINANCE?

The Duckworth brief alludes to an asserted housing shortage as a reason for overturning the ordinance. The issue is not properly before us on summary judgment. Nothing in the pleadings or in the uncontroverted facts support this assertion. We also reject the argument because a shortage, if in fact it exists, is not a valid reason for overturning a zoning ordinance. Lower Merion Twp. v. Gallup, 158 Pa.Super. 572, 46 A.2d 35 (1946).

CONCLUSION

Because of the summary nature of this proceeding and the fact that we are limited to the few *uncontroverted material facts* revealed in the pleadings and by the City's limited factual concessions, we hold that the trial court erred in holding the challenged portion of the City's ordinance unconstitutional.

The cause is remanded for trial and determination on the merits in a manner consistent with this opinion

Notes

1. In Cannon v. Coweta County, 260 Ga. 56, 389 S.E.2d 329 (1990), the Supreme Court of Georgia held that a per se exclusion of manufactured homes from single-family districts was unconstitutional. The court questioned the trial court's acceptance of the county argument that manufactured homes adversely affect the local tax base and that manufactured homes adversely affect the value of nearby site-built homes. In a footnote the court suggested that a local government could regulate manufactured homes in such ways as requiring attachment to a permanent foundation, appropriate lot sizes, and aesthetic standards. Compare, Grant v. County of Seminole, Fla., 817 F.2d 731 (11th Cir.1987).

2. An excellent source, even though several years old, for finding the statutes, regulations and cases dealing with mobile homes is Hodes and Roberson, The Law of Mobile Homes (3rd ed., 1974). Also, several reports prepared by the American Society of Planning Officials deal with mobile homes. Particularly useful is Planning Advisory Service Report No. 265, Modular Housing, Including Mobile Homes: A Survey of Regulatory Prac-

tices and Planners' Opinions (1971). Also see, Jaffe, Mobile Homes in Single–Family Neighborhoods, Land Use Law (June 1983), p. 4.

3. Note that the court in the Duckworth case did not address the issue of whether a "mobile home" can be construed to be a "single-family dwelling" and thus be permitted in the single-family residential district. A number of cases touch on this issue, which turns out to be a difficult one for courts. A series of cases in just two states well illustrates this difficulty. See Columbia County v. Kelly, 25 Or.App. 1, 548 P.2d 163 (1976); Clackamas County v. Dunham, 30 Or.App. 595, 567 P.2d 605 (1977) reversed 282 Or. 419, 579 P.2d 223 (1978) for the Oregon approach, and Courtland Twp. v. Cole, 66 Mich.App. 474, 239 N.W.2d 630 (1976); Robinson Twp. v. Knoll, 70 Mich.App. 258, 245 N.W.2d 709 (1976), affirmed, vacated, and remanded 410 Mich. 293, 302 N.W.2d 146 (1981); North Cherokee Village Membership v. Murphy, 71 Mich.App. 592, 248 N.W.2d 629 (1976) for the Michigan approach. Also see, Hansman v. Oneida County, 123 Wis.2d 511, 366 N.W.2d 901 (1985) (modular home permanently attached to a foundation held not to be a mobile home) and Fischer v. Driesen, 446 N.W.2d 84 (Iowa App.1989) (double-wide manufactured home set on concrete and steel piers held not to violate restrictive covenant against trailers).

4. In California a statute, Cal.Govt.Code § 65852.3 provides:

(a) A city, including a charter city, county, or city and county, shall allow the installation of manufactured homes certified under the National Manufactured Housing Construction and Safety Standards Act of 1974 (42 U.S.C.A. Sec. 5401 et seq.) on a foundation system, pursuant to Section 18551 of the Health and Safety Code, on lots zoned for conventional single-family residential dwellings. Except with respect to architectural requirements, a city, including a charter city, county, or city and county, shall only subject the manufactured home and the lot on which it is placed to the same development standards to which a conventional single-family residential dwelling on the same lot would be subject, including, but not limited to, building setback standards, side and rear yard requirements, standards for enclosures, access, and vehicle parking, aesthetic requirements, and minimum square footage requirements. Any architectural requirements imposed on the manufactured home structure itself, exclusive of any requirement for any and all additional enclosures, shall be limited to its roof overhang, roofing material, and siding material. These architectural requirements may be imposed on manufactured homes even if similar requirements are not imposed on conventional single-family residential dwellings. However, any architectural requirements for roofing and siding material shall not exceed those which would be required of conventional single-family dwellings constructed on the same lot. At the discretion of the local legislative body, the city or county may preclude installation of a manufactured home in zones specified in this section if more than 10 years have elapsed between the date of manufacture of the manufactured home and the date of the application for the issuance of a permit to install the mobilehome in the affected zone. In no case may a city, including a charter city, county, or city and county, apply any development standards which will have the effect of precluding manufactured homes from being installed as permanent residences.

Also see 30A Maine Rev.Stat.Ann. § 4358, and Paladac v. City of Rockland, 558 A.2d 372 (Me.1989). A number of states have adopted statutes similar to the one in California. In Tennessee Manufactured Housing Ass'n v. Metropolitan Govt. of Nashville, 798 S.W.2d 254 (Tenn.App.1990), the court construed a statute providing " ... no power or authority granted by this Code to regulate zoning or land use planning shall be used to exclude the placement of a residential dwelling on land designated for residential use solely because the dwelling is partially or completely constructed in a manufacturing facility; provided, however, that the term 'residential dwelling' as used in this part shall not apply to factory-manufactured mobile homes constructed as a single self-contained unit and mounted on a single chassis ... " The court held that the proviso did not apply to a double-wide manufactured home, reasoning that the word "and" in the proviso was intended as a conjunctive; thus a double-wide home was not one on a single chassis.

5. In Ettinger v. City of Lansing, 215 Mich.App. 451, 546 N.W.2d 652 (1996), the court upheld a zoning ordinance that permitted mobile homes in residential single-family districts but excluded mobile home parks in most such districts. The property owner unsuccessfully relied on a Michigan statute providing: "A local government ordinance shall not be designed as exclusionary to mobile homes generally whether the mobile homes are located inside or outside of mobile home parks or seasonal mobile home parks."

6. In recent years, cities with financial problems have looked differently at mobile homes for taxation purposes. Instead of considering the mobile home as a vehicle, subject only to personal property taxation, some communities have begun taxing mobile homes as real property. See Koester v. Hunterdon County Bd. of Taxation, 79 N.J. 381, 399 A.2d 656 (1979). A study conducted in New Jersey as a result of this case disclosed that some 40 states tax mobile homes as personal property. See Wall Street Journal, Nov. 26, 1980, p. 23. If a city taxes a mobile home as real estate, can it or should it continue to treat it differently than a traditional house for zoning purposes? In re Plaster, 101 B.R. 696 (Bkrtcy.Okl.1989) held that a mobile home used as the debtor's residence was personalty rather than realty under the Bankruptcy Code.

G. EXCLUSION OF INSTITUTIONAL USES AND GROUP HOMES

CITY OF WHITE PLAINS v. FERRAIOLI

Court of Appeals of New York, 1974.
34 N.Y.2d 300, 357 N.Y.S.2d 449, 313 N.E.2d 756.

BREITEL, CHIEF JUDGE.

In an action by the City of White Plains to enforce its zoning ordinance and enjoin use of a single-family house as a "group home" for 10 foster children, defendants, Abbott House, Inc. and the owners of the house, appeal. Abbott House, a private agency licensed by the State to care for neglected and abandoned children, leases the house in an "R–2" single-family zone. The city contends that the group home is not a single-family use, but either a philanthropic institution, allowed only by special permit, or a boarding house, wholly excluded from an "R–2" zone. The city obtained summary judgment in the courts below.

The issue is a narrow one: whether the "group home," consisting of a married couple and their two children, together with 10 foster children, qualifies as a single "family" unit, under the ordinance. It is concluded that the group home, set up in theory, size, appearance and structure to resemble a family unit, fits within the definition of family, for purposes of a zoning ordinance. Hence, the order of the Appellate Division should be reversed and summary judgment granted to defendants.

Abbott House as noted, is a not-for-profit membership corporation licensed by the State to care for neglected and abandoned children. In 1971, legislation was enacted permitting so-called "authorized agencies" like Abbott House to establish "group homes," under strict State regulation and inspection, where from 7 to 12 foster children might live in a simulated family atmosphere (Social Services Law, § 374–c, Consol. Laws, c. 55; L.1971, ch. 677). The group home concept is relatively new; instead of being institutionalized, neglected or abandoned youngsters are divided into small groups and placed in homes with an adult couple, approximating a normal family environment. In this way, it is thought, the children obtain many of the benefits of home life. Siblings may be kept together. Whatever other advantages there are to the group home, it is also less costly than institutionalized care. Abbott House also operates a traditional dormitory-style institution elsewhere in the State which houses over 100 children.

The particular group home in this case consists of an adult couple, the Seards, their two children, and 10 foster children. Of the 10, there are seven siblings, the Bell children ranging in age from 7 to 13, and three unrelated youngsters. The Seards are paid a salary to care for the children and all household expenses are paid by Abbott House, with substantial funding to it by the City of New York. Abbott House has a five-year lease on a house owned by the Ferraiolis who are also defendants. The children, natural and foster, live together as if they were brothers and sisters and the Seards were their common parents. The household is maintained as a family would be in a single housekeeping unit with kitchen facilities.

The Ferraioli house is in an R–2 zone of the city where the principal permitted uses are as a "Single family dwelling for one housekeeping unit only," fire houses, police stations, public schools and churches. As an accessory use, a resident family may include up to two roomers. Welfare uses, including philanthropic institutions, are special uses permitted in R–2 districts or other residential districts only at the discretion of the zoning board of appeals. Abbott House has not sought permission from the board. Rooming houses are permitted in certain residential districts of the city, but not in an R–2 zone.

The zoning ordinance defines a family:

A "family" is one or more persons limited to the spouse, parents, grandparents, grandchildren, sons, daughters, brothers or sisters of the owner or the tenant or of the owner's spouse or tenant's spouse living together as a single housekeeping unit with kitchen facilities.

It is significant that the group home is structured as a single housekeeping unit and is, to all outward appearances, a relatively normal, stable, and permanent family unit, with which the community is properly concerned. If that be true, the group home is no less qualified to occupy the Ferraioli house than are any of the neighboring families in their respective homes.

The group home is not, for purposes of a zoning ordinance, a temporary living arrangement as would be a group of college students sharing a house and commuting to a nearby school * * *. Every year or so, different college students would come to take the place of those before them. There would be none of the permanency of community that characterizes a residential neighborhood of private homes. Nor is it like the so-called "commune" style of living. The group home is a permanent arrangement and akin to a traditional family, which also may be sundered by death, divorce, or emancipation of the young. Neither the foster parents nor the children are to be shifted about; the intention is that they remain and develop ties in the community. The purpose is to emulate the traditional family and not to introduce a different "life style."

Of course, the Supreme Court of the United States, in the recent *Belle Terre* case, has held that it is a proper purpose of zoning to lay out districts devoted to "family values" and "youth values." Hence, toward that end those uses which conflict with a stable, uncongested single family environment may be restricted. High density uses, for example, may be restricted; so too those uses which are associated with occupancy by numbers of transient persons may be limited. By requiring single family use of a house, the ordinance emphasizes and ensures the character of the neighborhood to promote the family environment. The group home does not conflict with that character and, indeed, is deliberately designed to conform with it.

Thus the city has a proper purpose in largely limiting the uses in a zone to single-family units. But if it goes beyond to require that the relationships in the family unit be those of blood or adoption, then its definition of family might be too restrictive (see Kirsch Holding Co. v. Borough of Manasquan, 59 N.J. 241, 250, 281 A.2d 527; City of Des Plaines v. Trottner, 34 Ill.2d 432, 216 N.E.2d 116 [per Schaeffer, J.]; Boston–Edison Protective Assn. v. Paulist Fathers, 306 Mich. 253, 10 N.W.2d 847). Zoning is intended to control types of housing and living and not the genetic or intimate internal family relations of human beings.

Whether a family be organized along ties of blood or formal adoptions, or be a similarly structured group sponsored by the State, as is the group home, should not be consequential in meeting the test of the zoning ordinance. So long as the group home bears the generic character of a family unit as a relatively permanent household, and is not a framework for transients or transient living, it conforms to the purpose of the ordinance (see Planning & Zoning Comm. v. Synanon Foundation, 153 Conn. 305, 308, 216 A.2d 442). Moreover, in no sense is the group home an institutional arrangement, which would be another matter. Indeed, the purpose of the group home is to be quite the contrary of an institution and to be a home like other homes.

In short, an ordinance may restrict a residential zone to occupancy by stable families occupying single-family homes, but neither by express provision nor construction may it limit the definition of family to exclude a household which in every but a biological sense is a single family. The minimal arrangement to meet the test of a zoning provision, as this one, is a group headed by a householder caring for a reasonable number of children as one would be likely to find in a biologically unitary family.
* * *

Defendants contend, and the issue raised is not without trouble, that the zoning ordinance, if it prohibits a group home use in an R–2 district, absolutely or without a special permit, contravenes the State's Social Services Law. That law, as discussed above, authorizes licensed agencies to establish group homes in appropriate neighborhoods (Social Services Law, § 374–c). In somewhat analogous circumstances, courts have held local zoning ordinances void as contrary to State policy when they restricted an "agency boarding home," a day care center, and a center for delinquent youths (Abbott House v. Village of Tarrytown, 34 A.D.2d 821, 312 N.Y.S.2d 841; Matter of Unitarian Universalist Church v. Shorten, 63 Misc.2d 978, 980–981, 314 N.Y.S.2d 66 [Meyer, J.]; Nowack v. Department of Audit & Control, 72 Misc.2d 518, 520, 338 N.Y.S.2d 52). Certainly, by constitutional provision and State policy, the care of neglected and abandoned children is a paramount concern (N.Y.Const., art. VII, § 8, subd. 2; Matter of Wiltwyck School v. Hill, 11 N.Y.2d 182, 193, 227 N.Y.S.2d 655, 182 N.E.2d 268). Since it is concluded, however, that a group home is a family, this broader question need not now be resolved by this court.

* * *

Accordingly, the order of the Appellate Division should be reversed, with costs, and summary judgment granted to defendants dismissing the complaint.

CITY OF CLEBURNE, TEXAS v. CLEBURNE LIVING CENTER

Supreme Court of the United States, 1985.
473 U.S. 432, 105 S.Ct. 3249, 87 L.Ed.2d 313.

JUSTICE WHITE delivered the opinion of the Court.

A Texas city denied a special use permit for the operation of a group home for the mentally retarded, acting pursuant to a municipal zoning ordinance requiring permits for such homes. The Court of Appeals for the Fifth Circuit held that mental retardation is a "quasi-suspect" classification and that the ordinance violated the Equal Protection Clause because it did not substantially further an important governmental purpose. We hold that a lesser standard of scrutiny is appropriate, but conclude that under that standard the ordinance is invalid as applied in this case.

I

In July, 1980, respondent Jan Hannah purchased a building at 201 Featherston Street in the city of Cleburne, Texas, with the intention of leasing it to Cleburne Living Centers, Inc. (CLC), for the operation of a group home for the mentally retarded. It was anticipated that the home would house 13 retarded men and women, who would be under the constant supervision of CLC staff members. The house had four bedrooms and two baths, with a half bath to be added. CLC planned to comply with all applicable state and federal regulations.

The city informed CLC that a special use permit would be required for the operation of a group home at the site, and CLC accordingly submitted a permit application. In response to a subsequent inquiry from CLC, the city explained that under the zoning regulations applicable to the site, a special use permit, renewable annually, was required for the construction of "[h]ospitals for the insane or feeble-minded, or alcoholic [sic] or drug addicts, or penal or correctional institutions." The city had determined that the proposed group home should be classified as a "hospital for the feebleminded." After holding a public hearing on CLC's application, the city council voted three to one to deny a special use permit.

* * *

III

Against this background, we conclude for several reasons that the Court of Appeals erred in holding mental retardation a quasi-suspect classification calling for a more exacting standard of judicial review than is normally accorded economic and social legislation. First, it is undeniable, and it is not argued otherwise here, that those who are mentally retarded have a reduced ability to cope with and function in the everyday world. Nor are they all cut from the same pattern: as the testimony in this record indicates, they range from those whose disability is not immediately evident to those who must be constantly cared for.[10] They

---

10. Mentally retarded individuals fall into four distinct categories. The vast majority—approximately 89%—are classified as "mildly" retarded, meaning that their IQ is between 50 and 70. Approximately 6% percent are "moderately" retarded, with IQs between 35 and 50. The remaining two categories are "severe" (IQs of 20 to 35) and "profound" (IQs below 20). These last two categories together account for about 5% of the mentally retarded population. App. 39 (testimony of Dr. Philip Roos).

Mental retardation is not defined by reference to intelligence or IQ alone, however. The American Association on Mental Deficiency (AAMD) has defined mental retardation as " 'significantly subaverage general intellectual functioning existing concur-

are thus different, immutably so, in relevant respects, and the states' interest in dealing with and providing for them is plainly a legitimate one.[11] How this large and diversified group is to be treated under the law is a difficult and often a technical matter, very much a task for legislators guided by qualified professionals and not by the perhaps ill-informed opinions of the judiciary. Heightened scrutiny inevitably involves substantive judgments about legislative decisions, and we doubt that the predicate for such judicial oversight is present where the classification deals with mental retardation.

Second, the distinctive legislative response, both national and state, to the plight of those who are mentally retarded demonstrates not only that they have unique problems, but also that the lawmakers have been addressing their difficulties in a manner that belies a continuing antipathy or prejudice and a corresponding need for more intrusive oversight by the judiciary. Thus, the federal government has not only outlawed discrimination against the mentally retarded in federally funded programs, see § 504 of the Rehabilitation Act of 1973, 29 U.S.C.A. § 794, but it has also provided the retarded with the right to receive "appropriate treatment, services, and habilitation" in a setting that is "least restrictive of [their] personal liberty." Developmental Disabilities Assistance and Bill of Rights Act, 42 U.S.C.A. §§ 6010(1), (2). In addition, the government has conditioned federal education funds on a State's assurance that retarded children will enjoy an education that, "to the maximum extent appropriate," is integrated with that of non-mentally retarded children. Education of the Handicapped Act, 20 U.S.C.A. § 1412(5)(B). The government has also facilitated the hiring of the mentally retarded into the federal civil service by exempting them from the requirement of competitive examination. See 5 CFR § 213.3102(t) (1984). The State of Texas has similarly enacted legislation that acknowledges the special status of the mentally retarded by conferring certain rights upon them, such as "the right to live in the least restrictive setting appropriate to [their] individual needs and abilities," including "the right to live ... in a group home." Mentally Retarded

---

rently with deficits in adaptive behavior and manifested during the developmental period.' "Brief for AAMD et al. as *Amici Curiae* 3 (quoting AAMD, Classification in Mental Retardation 1 (H. Grosman ed. 1983)). "Deficits in adaptive behavior" are limitations on general ability to meet the standards of maturation, learning, personal independence, and social responsibility expected for an individual's age level and cultural group. *Id.*, at 4, n. 1. Mental retardation is caused by a variety of factors, some genetic, some environmental, and some unknown. *Id.*, at 4.

11. As Dean Ely has observed:

"Surely one has to feel sorry for a person disabled by something he or she can't do

anything about, but I'm not aware of any reason to suppose that elected officials are unusually unlikely to share that feeling. Moreover, classifications based on physical disability and intelligence are typically accepted as legitimate, even by judges and commentators who assert that immutability is relevant. The explanation, when one is given, is that *those* characteristics (unlike the one the commentator is trying to render suspect) are often relevant to legitimate purposes. At that point there's not much left of the immutability theory, is there?" J. Ely, Democracy and Distrust 150 (1980) (footnote omitted). See also *id.*, at 154–155.

Persons Act of 1977, Tex.Rev.Civ.Stat.Ann., Art. 5547–300, § 7 (Vernon Supp.1985).

* * *

Doubtless, there have been and there will continue to be instances of discrimination against the retarded that are in fact invidious, and that are properly subject to judicial correction under constitutional norms. But the appropriate method of reaching such instances is not to create a new quasi-suspect classification and subject all governmental action based on that classification to more searching evaluation. Rather, we should look to the likelihood that governmental action premised on a particular classification is valid as a general matter, not merely to the specifics of the case before us. Because mental retardation is a characteristic that the government may legitimately take into account in a wide range of decisions, and because both state and federal governments have recently committed themselves to assisting the retarded, we will not presume that any given legislative action, even one that disadvantages retarded individuals, is rooted in considerations that the Constitution will not tolerate.

Our refusal to recognize the retarded as a quasi-suspect class does not leave them entirely unprotected from invidious discrimination. To withstand equal protection review, legislation that distinguishes between the mentally retarded and others must be rationally related to a legitimate governmental purpose. This standard, we believe, affords government the latitude necessary both to pursue policies designed to assist the retarded in realizing their full potential, and to freely and efficiently engage in activities that burden the retarded in what is essentially an incidental manner. The State may not rely on a classification whose relationship to an asserted goal is so attenuated as to render the distinction arbitrary or irrational. See *Zobel v. Williams,* 457 U.S. 55, 61–63, 102 S.Ct. 2309, 2313–2314, 72 L.Ed.2d 672 (1982); *United States Department of Agriculture v. Moreno,* 413 U.S. 528, 535, 93 S.Ct. 2821, 2826, 37 L.Ed.2d 782 (1973). Furthermore, some objectives—such as "a bare ... desire to harm a politically unpopular group," *Moreno,* 413 U.S., at 534, 93 S.Ct., at 2826—are not legitimate state interests. See also *Zobel, supra,* 457 U.S., at 63, 102 S.Ct., at 2314. Beyond that, the mentally retarded, like others, have and retain their substantive constitutional rights in addition to the right to be treated equally by the law.

IV

We turn to the issue of the validity of the zoning ordinance insofar as it requires a special use permit for homes for the mentally retarded. We inquire first whether requiring a special use permit for the Featherston home in the circumstances here deprives respondents of the equal protection of the laws. If it does, there will be no occasion to decide whether the special use permit provision is facially invalid where the mentally retarded are involved, or to put it another way, whether the city may never insist on a special use permit for a home for the mentally retarded in an R–3 zone. This is the preferred course of adjudication since it enables courts to avoid making unnecessarily broad constitutional judgments. * * *

The constitutional issue is clearly posed. The City does not require a special use permit in an R–3 zone for apartment houses, multiple dwellings, boarding and lodging houses, fraternity or sorority houses, dormitories, apartment hotels, hospitals, sanitariums, nursing homes for convalescents or the aged (other than for the insane or feeble-minded or alcoholics or drug addicts), private clubs or fraternal orders, and other specified uses. It does, however, insist on a special permit for the Featherston home, and it does so, as the District Court found, because it would be a facility for the mentally retarded. May the city require the permit for this facility when other care and multiple dwelling facilities are freely permitted?

It is true, as already pointed out, that the mentally retarded as a group are indeed different from others not sharing their misfortune, and in this respect they may be different from those who would occupy other facilities that would be permitted in an R–3 zone without a special permit. But this difference is largely irrelevant unless the Featherston home and those who would occupy it would threaten legitimate interests of the city in a way that other permitted uses such as boarding houses and hospitals would not. Because in our view the record does not reveal any rational basis for believing that the Featherston home would pose any special threat to the city's legitimate interests, we affirm the judgment below insofar as it holds the ordinance invalid as applied in this case.

The District Court found that the City Council's insistence on the permit rested on several factors. First, the Council was concerned with the negative attitude of the majority of property owners located within 200 feet of the Featherston facility, as well as with the fears of elderly residents of the neighborhood. But mere negative attitudes, or fear, unsubstantiated by factors which are properly cognizable in a zoning proceeding, are not permissible bases for treating a home for the mentally retarded differently from apartment houses, multiple dwellings, and the like. It is plain that the electorate as a whole, whether by referendum or otherwise, could not order city action violative of the Equal Protection Clause, *Lucas v. Forty-Fourth General Assembly of Colorado,* 377 U.S. 713, 736–737, 84 S.Ct. 1459, 1473–1474, 12 L.Ed.2d 632 (1964), and the City may not avoid the strictures of that Clause by deferring to the wishes or objections of some fraction of the body politic. "Private biases may be outside the reach of the law, but the law cannot, directly or indirectly, give them effect." *Palmore v. Sidoti,* 466 U.S. 429, 433, 104 S.Ct. 1879, 1882, 80 L.Ed.2d 421 (1984).

Second, the Council had two objections to the location of the facility. It was concerned that the facility was across the street from a junior high school, and it feared that the students might harass the occupants of the Featherston home. But the school itself is attended by about 30 mentally retarded students, and denying a permit based on such vague, undifferentiated fears is again permitting some portion of the community to validate what would otherwise be an equal protection violation. The other objection to the home's location was that it was located on "a five hundred year flood plain." This concern with the possibility of a flood, however, can hardly be based on a distinction between the Featherston home and, for example, nursing homes, homes for convalescents or the aged, or sanitariums or hospitals, any of which could be located on the Featherston site without obtaining a special use permit. The same may be said of another concern of the Council—doubts about the legal responsibility for actions which the mentally retarded might take. If there is no concern about legal responsibility with respect to other uses that would be permitted in the area, such as boarding and fraternity houses, it is difficult to believe that the groups of mildly or moderately mentally retarded individuals who would live at 201 Featherston would present any different or special hazard.

Fourth, the Council was concerned with the size of the home and the number of people that would occupy it. The District Court found, and the Court of Appeals repeated, that "[i]f the potential residents of the Featherston Street home were not mentally retarded, but the home was the same in all other respects, its use would be permitted under the city's zoning ordinance." App. 93; 726 F.2d, at 200. Given this finding, there would be no restrictions on the number of people who could occupy this home as a boarding house, nursing home, family dwelling, fraternity house, or dormitory. The question is whether it is rational to treat the mentally retarded differently. It is true that they suffer disability not shared by others; but why this difference warrants a density regulation that others need not observe is not at all apparent. At least this record does not clarify how, in this connection, the characteristics of the intended occupants of the Featherston home rationally justify denying to those occupants what would be permitted to groups occupying the same site for different purposes. Those who would live in the Featherston home are the type of individuals who, with supporting staff, satisfy federal and state standards for group housing in the community; and there is no dispute that the home would meet the federal square-footage-per-resident requirement for facilities of this type. See 42 CFR § 442.447 (1984). In the words of the Court of Appeals, "The City never justifies its apparent view that other people can live under such 'crowded' conditions when mentally retarded persons cannot." 726 F.2d, at 202.

In the courts below the city also urged that the ordinance is aimed at avoiding concentration of population and at lessening congestion of the streets. These concerns obviously fail to explain why apartment houses, fraternity and sorority houses, hospitals and the like, may freely locate in the area without a permit. So, too, the expressed worry about fire hazards, the serenity of the neighborhood, and the avoidance of danger to other residents fail rationally to justify singling out a home such as 201 Featherston for the special use permit, yet imposing no such restrictions on the many other uses freely permitted in the neighborhood.

The short of it is that requiring the permit in this case appears to us to rest on an irrational prejudice against the mentally retarded, including those who would occupy the Featherston facility and who would live under the closely supervised and highly regulated conditions expressly provided for by state and federal law.

The judgment of the Court of Appeals is affirmed insofar as it invalidates the zoning ordinance as applied to the Featherston home. The judgment is otherwise vacated.

It is so ordered.

[A concurring opinion by Justice Stevens, concurred in also by Chief Justice Burger, has been omitted. Justice Marshall wrote a lengthy dissent supporting heightened scrutiny for distinctions based on mental retardation; he was joined by Justices Brennan and Blackmun.]

Notes

1. The group home is an outgrowth of the principle of deinstitutionalization or normalization which is based on the policy of rejecting the large custodial institution as a method of dealing with those members of society who are dependent, such as the mentally handicapped, juvenile delinquents and neglected or orphaned children. The group home is designed to provide an environment which approximates that of normal society, which perforce includes the idea of family living. The public and private organizations which promote and operate group homes frequently seek locations in single-family zoning districts; often, a clash between local government or nearby neighbors and the proposed group home results in litigation. Because so many local governments have demonstrated hostility to the location of group homes in single-family districts, since the late 1970's, state legislation has become increasingly common as a device for preempting local zoning ordinances which may be restrictive of group homes. For an overview of this problem, see Comment, 24 Kan.L.Rev. 677 (1976); Kressel, The Community Residence Movement: Land Use Conflicts and Planning Imperatives, 5 N.Y.U.Rev.L. & Soc.Change 137 (1975); Lippincott, A Sanctuary for People: Strategies for Overcoming Zoning Restrictions on Community Homes for Retarded Persons, 31 Stan.L.Rev. 767 (1979); Hopperton, A State Legislative Strategy for Ending Exclusionary Zoning of Community Homes, 19 Urb. L.Ann. 47 (1980).

2. The majority of cases dealing with zoning of group homes has favored their location in single-family districts. In most of the cases the courts utilize the approach of defining the word family so as to include the surrogate family implicit in the group home concept. See, e.g., Oliver v. Zoning Comm'n of Town of Chester, 31 Conn.Sup. 197, 326 A.2d 841 (1974) permitting a state-supervised group home for eight or nine employable adult retarded persons and two house-parents in the single-family district. In Eichlin v. Zoning Hearing Bd. of New Hope Borough, ___ Pa.Cmwlth. ___, 671 A.2d 1173 (1996) the court held that eight unrelated HIV-infected persons were the functional equivalent of a family. However, the courts are not always willing to treat every type of group home as a family situation.

In Planning and Zoning Commission of Town of Westport v. Synanon Foundation, Inc., 153 Conn. 305, 216 A.2d 442 (1966), the zoning ordinance provided for "one family per lot." The evidence showed that anywhere from eleven to thirty-four people were living on the premises. The court reversed a lower court decision denying an injunction, stating:

> The only remaining question is whether the phrase "one family," which is left undefined in the Westport zoning ordinance, is broad enough to encompass the group of persons residing at the premises leased by the defendant. The trial court concluded that the use of this property as found was not excluded by the zoning ordinance. The applicable provision of the ordinance, which is a permissive rather than a prohibitory ordinance, allows "[o]ne detached dwelling for occupancy by one family per lot." Westport Zoning Regs., c. 3, § 1(B)(1) (1958, as amended). Obviously the use of this dwelling was not by one family, under any definition, since the trial court found that it was occupied over a long period of time by an everchanging aggregate of individuals. Such a group of individuals, who were sleeping, cooking, eating, working, and carrying on other activities at these premises, cannot be interpreted to come within the meaning of the word "family," either according to common usage or under the dictionary definitions, and the trial court's conclusion to the contrary, in the absence of a controlling definition in the ordinance, cannot be sustained. City of Schenectady v. Alumni Ass'n of Union Chapter, Delta Chi Fraternity, Inc., 5 A.D.2d 14, 15, 168 N.Y.S.2d 754; Cassidy v. Triebel, 337 Ill.App. 117, 127, 85 N.E.2d 461; 101 C.J.S. Zoning § 143. Indeed, if these occupants were held to constitute "one family," it is difficult to imagine any group or organization which would not be considered one family, and the phrase 'occupancy by one family per lot' would be rendered superfluous, in conflict with the well-established rule that, whenever feasible, the language of an ordinance will be construed so that no clause is held superfluous, void, or insignificant.

The same type of reasoning was used by the Supreme Court of Ohio in holding that a foster home with an average of seven foster children was not an integrated family unit and could not locate in a single-family zoning district. Carroll v. Washington Twp. Zoning Comm'n, 63 Ohio St.2d 249, 408 N.E.2d 191 (1980). Also see Civitans Care, Inc. v. Board of Adj., 437 So.2d 540 (Ala.Civ.App.1983). And, in Northern Maine General Hosp. v. Ricker, 572 A.2d 479 (Me.1990) the court held that a prerelease center for adult inmates could be excluded from a single-family district that permitted group homes because it was significantly more objectionable than other types of group homes.

3.   Some courts have avoided the "single-family" problem by finding a group home to be a permitted educational facility in the single-family district, e.g., Fitchburg Housing Auth. v. Board of Zoning Appeals, 380 Mass. 869, 406 N.E.2d 1006 (1980); Campbell v. City Council of Lynn, 415 Mass. 772, 616 N.E.2d 445 (1993), or a permitted community center, e.g., Appeal of Fleming, 44 Pa.Cmwlth. 641, 405 A.2d 1309 (1979).

4.   Some group home cases do not involve local hostility through the zoning ordinance but rather a conflict with restrictive covenants limiting use

of the proposed group home to single-family dwelling purposes. Here again, the courts generally read the covenants so as to permit the group home. See, e.g., Bellarmine Hills Ass'n v. Residential Systems Co., 84 Mich.App. 554, 269 N.W.2d 673 (1978); Jayno Heights Landowners Ass'n v. Preston, 85 Mich.App. 443, 271 N.W.2d 268 (1978); Malcolm v. Shamie, 95 Mich.App. 132, 290 N.W.2d 101 (1980); Crowley v. Knapp, 94 Wis.2d 421, 288 N.W.2d 815 (1980); Annotation, 71 A.L.R.3d 693 (1976). In Berger v. State, 71 N.J. 206, 364 A.2d 993 (1976), the court dealt with both a covenant and a restrictive zoning ordinance and also discussed a state statute favoring establishment of group homes. In Clem v. Christole, Inc., 548 N.E.2d 1180 (Ind.App.1990), the court held that a state statute invalidating restrictive covenants which prohibit group homes constituted a taking.

5. Another approach to the group home problem is reflected in cases which find that state-operated or state-sponsored group homes are immune from local zoning ordinances. Refer back to the material on intergovernmental immunity in the previous chapter and in particular, see Hillsborough Ass'n for Retarded Citizens v. City of Temple Terrace, 332 So.2d 610 (Fla.1976); Township of South Fayette v. Commonwealth, 477 Pa. 574, 385 A.2d 344 (1978); City of Baltimore v. State Dept. of Health and Mental Hygiene, 38 Md.App. 570, 381 A.2d 1188 (1978); Region 10 Client Management, Inc. v. Town of Hampstead, 120 N.H. 885, 424 A.2d 207 (1980). Compare Brownfield v. State, 63 Ohio St.2d 282, 407 N.E.2d 1365 (1980).

6. In some cases the zoning ordinance is not exclusionary as to group homes, but such uses may require a special use permit or exception, or may be a conditional use in the single-family district. As to the standards to be applied in such cases, see Warren County Probation Ass'n v. Warren County Zoning Hearing Bd., 50 Pa.Cmwlth. 486, 414 A.2d 398 (1980). Also see State v. City of Bellingham, 25 Wash.App. 33, 605 P.2d 788 (1979); Ayers v. Porter County Plan Comm'n, 544 N.E.2d 213 (Ind.App.1989).

7. More than one half of the states have adopted legislation since 1970 designed to overcome zoning barriers to establishment of group homes. The legislation is not uniform and the approach varies from state to state. Typically, the statutes may apply only to certain types of group homes, e.g., those for the developmentally disabled, and may impose maximum residency limits in language such as "up to six [or eight] persons." See Hopperton, A State Legislative Strategy for Ending Exclusionary Zoning of Community Homes, 19 Urban L.Ann. 47 (1980). Also see Adams County Ass'n for Retarded Citizens, Inc. v. City of Westminster, 196 Colo. 79, 580 P.2d 1246 (1978); State ex rel. Thelen v. City of Missoula, 168 Mont. 375, 543 P.2d 173 (1975). In Garcia v. Siffrin Residential Ass'n, 63 Ohio St.2d 259, 407 N.E.2d 1369 (1980), the court held the state statute permitting group homes in single-family districts could not operate to preempt a local home rule zoning ordinance excluding such uses.

8. One unusual case involving group homes is People v. St. Agatha Home for Children, 47 N.Y.2d 46, 416 N.Y.S.2d 577, 389 N.E.2d 1098 (1979), cert. denied 444 U.S. 869, 100 S.Ct. 145, 62 L.Ed.2d 94 (1979), where the plaintiffs charged the operators of a group home with operating a non-secure juvenile detention facility in violation of the criminal provisions of the zoning ordinance. The court held that the burden of proof requisite in a

criminal proceeding had not been met and that the group home was operating under county aegis and was, therefore, immune from the city zoning ordinance.

9. The Fair Housing Amendments Act of 1988 (FHAA), P.L. 100–430 makes discrimination against the handicapped in the sale, lease, or construction of multi-family units a prohibited practice. In Baxter v. City of Belleville, Ill., 720 F.Supp. 720 (S.D.Ill.1989) the court enjoined a city from refusing a special permit to remodel a building to house AIDS patients. In the same vein, see Association of Relatives and Friends of AIDS Patients v. Regulations and Permits Admn., 740 F.Supp. 95 (D.Puerto Rico 1990); Support Ministries for Persons with AIDS, Inc. v. Village of Waterford, New York, 808 F.Supp. 120 (N.D.N.Y.1992); Familystyle of St. Paul, Inc. v. City of St. Paul, 728 F.Supp. 1396 (D.Minn.1990). In Hill v. Community of Damien of Molokai, 121 N.M. 353, 911 P.2d 861 (1996) the court held that a group home for AIDS patients did not violate a restrictive covenant specifying single-family residential uses, and that even if the residents did not constitute a "family" and violated the covenant, the covenant would violate the Fair Housing Act. In United States v. City of Taylor, Michigan, 798 F.Supp. 442 (E.D.Mich.1992) the court found intentional discrimination against the proposed residents of an adult foster care home for 12 elderly disabled persons, and a violation of the Fair Housing Act.

In Epicenter of Steubenville, Inc. v. City of Steubenville, 924 F.Supp. 845 (S.D.Ohio 1996) the court held that a city ordinance imposing a one-year moratorium against new adult care facilities violated the FHAA. However, the Fair Housing Act does not provide a way to get around the separation of uses in a zoning ordinance. In Brandt v. Village of Chebanse, 82 F.3d 172 (7th Cir.1996) the court upheld denial of a variance for an apartment building with handicapped-accessible units to locate in a single-family residential district. The court found that because a permit had been previously denied for a similar non-accessible project, the denial in this case was not based on discrimination against the handicapped. Compare, however, Larkin v. State of Michigan Dept. of Social Services, 89 F.3d 285 (6th Cir.1996), where the court held that a Michigan statute prohibiting location of group homes within 1500 feet of existing group homes was preempted by the federal act. And in Association for Advancement of the Mentally Handicapped v. City of Elizabeth, 876 F.Supp. 614 (D.N.J.1994) the court held that a city ordinance and the authorizing provision of the state enabling act that automatically denied conditional use permits for group homes for developmentally disabled persons on certain conditions violated the FHAA.

CITY OF EDMONDS v. OXFORD HOUSE, INC.

Supreme Court of the United States, 1995.
514 U.S. 725, 115 S.Ct. 1776, 131 L.Ed.2d 801.

JUSTICE GINSBURG delivered the opinion of the Court.

The Fair Housing Act (FHA or Act) prohibits discrimination in housing against, *inter alios*, persons with handicaps. Section 3607(b)(1) of the Act entirely exempts from the FHA's compass "any reasonable local, State, or Federal restrictions regarding the maximum number of occupants permitted to occupy a dwelling." 42 U.S.C.A. § 3607(b)(1). This case presents the question whether a provision in petitioner City of Edmonds' zoning code qualifies for § 3607(b)(1)'s complete exemption from FHA scrutiny. The provision, governing areas zoned for single-family dwelling units, defines "family" as "persons [without regard to number] related by genetics, adoption, or marriage, or a group of five or fewer [unrelated] persons." Edmonds Community Development Code (ECDC) § 21.30.010 (1991).

The defining provision at issue describes who may compose a family unit; it does not prescribe "*the* maximum number of occupants" a dwelling unit may house. We hold that § 3607(b)(1) does not exempt prescriptions of the family-defining kind, i.e., provisions designed to foster the family character of a neighborhood. Instead, § 3607(b)(1)'s absolute exemption removes from the FHA's scope only total occupancy limits, i.e., numerical ceilings that serve to prevent overcrowding in living quarters.

I

In the summer of 1990, respondent Oxford House opened a group home in the City of Edmonds, Washington for 10 to 12 adults recovering from alcoholism and drug addiction. The group home, called Oxford House—Edmonds, is located in a neighborhood zoned for single-family residences. Upon learning that Oxford House had leased and was operating a home in Edmonds, the City issued criminal citations to the owner and a resident of the house. The citations charged violation of the zoning code rule that defines who may live in single-family dwelling units. The occupants of such units must compose a "family," and family, under the City's defining rule, "means an individual or two or more persons related by genetics, adoption, or marriage, or a group of five or fewer persons who are not related by genetics, adoption, or marriage." Edmonds Community Development Code (ECDC) § 21.30.010. Oxford House–Edmonds houses more than five unrelated persons, and therefore does not conform to the code.

Oxford House asserted reliance on the Fair Housing Act, 102 Stat. 1619, 42 U.S.C.A. § 3601 et seq., which declares it unlawful "[t]o discriminate in the sale or rental, or to otherwise make unavailable or deny, a dwelling to any buyer or renter because of a handicap of . . . that buyer or a renter." § 3604(f)(1)(A). The parties have stipulated, for purposes of this litigation, that the residents of Oxford House–Edmonds "are recovering alcoholics and drug addicts and are handicapped persons within the meaning" of the Act.

Discrimination covered by the FHA includes "a refusal to make reasonable accommodations in rules, policies, practices, or services, when such accommodations may be necessary to afford [handicapped] person[s] equal opportunity to use and enjoy a dwelling." § 3604(f)(3)(B). Oxford House asked Edmonds to make a "reasonable accommodation" by allowing it to remain in the single-family dwelling it had leased. Group homes for recovering substance abusers, Oxford urged, need 8 to

12 residents to be financially and therapeutically viable. Edmonds declined to permit Oxford House to stay in a single-family residential zone, but passed an ordinance listing group homes as permitted uses in multifamily and general commercial zones.

Edmonds sued Oxford House in the United States District Court for the Western District of Washington seeking a declaration that the FHA does not constrain the City's zoning code family definition rule. Oxford House counterclaimed under the FHA, charging the City with failure to make a "reasonable accommodation" permitting maintenance of the group home in a single-family zone. The United States filed a separate action on the same FHA-"reasonable accommodation" ground, and the two cases were consolidated. Edmonds suspended its criminal enforcement actions pending resolution of the federal litigation.

On cross-motions for summary judgment, the District Court held that ECDC § 21.30.010, defining "family," is exempt from the FHA under § 3607(b)(1) as a "reasonable ... restrictio[n] regarding the maximum number of occupants permitted to occupy a dwelling." App. to Pet. for Cert. B–7. The United States Court of Appeals for the Ninth Circuit reversed; holding § 3607(b)(1)'s absolute exemption inapplicable, the Court of Appeals remanded the cases for further consideration of the claims asserted by Oxford House and the United States. Edmonds v. Washington State Building Code Council, 18 F.3d 802 (1994).

The Ninth Circuit's decision conflicts with an Eleventh Circuit decision declaring exempt under § 3607(b)(1) a family definition provision similar to the Edmonds prescription. See Elliott v. Athens, 960 F.2d 975 (1992). We granted certiorari to resolve the conflict, and we now affirm the Ninth Circuit's judgment.

The sole question before the Court is whether Edmonds' family composition rule qualifies as a "restrictio[n] regarding the maximum number of occupants permitted to occupy a dwelling" within the meaning of the FHA's absolute exemption. 42 U.S.C.A. § 3607(b)(1). In answering this question, we are mindful of the Act's stated policy "to provide, within constitutional limitations, for fair housing throughout the United States." § 3601. * * *

* * *

A

Congress enacted § 3607(b)(1) against the backdrop of an evident distinction between municipal land use restrictions and maximum occupancy restrictions.

Land use restrictions designate "districts in which only compatible uses are allowed and incompatible uses are excluded." D. Mandelker, Land Use Law § 4.16, pp. 113–114 (3d ed.1993) (hereinafter Mandelker). These restrictions typically categorize uses as single-family residential, multiple-family residential, commercial, or industrial. See, e.g., 1 E. Ziegler, Jr., Rathkopf's The Law of Zoning and Planning § 8.01, pp. 8–2 to 8–3 (4th ed.1995); Mandelker § 1.03, p. 4; 1 E. Yokley, Zoning Law and Practice § 7–2, p. 252 (4th ed.1978).

Land use restrictions aim to prevent problems caused by the "pig in the parlor instead of the barnyard." Village of Euclid v. Ambler Realty Co., 272 U.S. 365, 388, 47 S.Ct. 114, 118, 71 L.Ed. 303 (1926). In particular, reserving land for single-family residences preserves the character of neighborhoods, securing "zones where family values, youth values, and the blessings of quiet seclusion and clean air make the area a sanctuary for people." Village of Belle Terre v. Boraas, 416 U.S. 1, 9, 94 S.Ct. 1536, 1541, 39 L.Ed.2d 797 (1974); see also Moore v. City of East Cleveland, 431 U.S. 494, 521, 97 S.Ct. 1932, 1947, 52 L.Ed.2d 531 (1977) (Burger, C.J., dissenting) (purpose of East Cleveland's single-family zoning ordinance "is the traditional one of preserving certain areas as family residential communities"). To limit land use to single-family residences, a municipality must define the term "family"; thus family composition rules are an essential component of single-family residential use restrictions.

Maximum occupancy restrictions, in contradistinction, cap the number of occupants per dwelling, typically in relation to available floor space or the number and type of rooms. . . . These restrictions ordinarily apply uniformly to all residents of all dwelling units. Their purpose is to protect health and safety by preventing dwelling overcrowding.

* * *

Section 3607(b)(1)'s language—"restrictions regarding the maximum number of occupants permitted to occupy a dwelling"—surely encompasses maximum occupancy restrictions. But the formulation does not fit family composition rules typically tied to land use restrictions. In sum, rules that cap the total number of occupants in order to prevent overcrowding of a dwelling "plainly and unmistakably," see A.H. Phillips, Inc. v. Walling, 324 U.S. 490, 493, 65 S.Ct. 807, 808, 89 L.Ed. 1095 (1945), fall within § 3607(b)(1)'s absolute exemption from the FHA's governance; rules designed to preserve the family character of a neighborhood, fastening on the composition of households rather than on the total number of occupants living quarters can contain, do not.

B

Turning specifically to the City's Community Development Code, we note that the provisions Edmonds invoked against Oxford House, ECDC §§ 16.20.010 and 21.30.010, are classic examples of a use restriction and complementing family composition rule. These provisions do not cap the number of people who may live in a dwelling. In plain terms, they direct that dwellings be used only to house families. Captioned "USES," ECDC § 16.20.010 provides that the sole "Permitted Primary Us[e]" in a single-family residential zone is "[s]ingle-family dwelling units." Edmonds itself recognizes that this provision simply "defines those uses permitted in a single family residential zone." Pet. for Cert. 3.

A separate provision caps the number of occupants a dwelling may house, based on floor area:

> "Floor Area. Every dwelling unit shall have at least one room which shall have not less than 120 square feet of floor area. Other habitable rooms, except kitchens, shall have an area of not less than 70 square feet. Where more than two persons occupy a room used for sleeping purposes, the required floor area shall be increased at the rate of 50 square feet for each occupant in excess of two." ECDC § 19.10.000 (adopting Uniform Housing Code s 503(b) (1988)).

This space and occupancy standard is a prototypical maximum occupancy restriction.

Edmonds nevertheless argues that its family composition rule, ECDC § 21.30.010, falls within § 3607(b)(1), the FHA exemption for maximum occupancy restrictions, because the rule caps at five the number of unrelated persons allowed to occupy a single-family dwelling. But Edmonds' family composition rule surely does not answer the question: "What is the maximum number of occupants permitted to occupy a house?" So long as they are related "by genetics, adoption, or marriage," any number of people can live in a house. Ten siblings, their parents and grandparents, for example, could dwell in a house in Edmonds' single-family residential zone without offending Edmonds' family composition rule.

Family living, not living space per occupant, is what ECDC § 21.30.010 describes. Defining family primarily by biological and legal relationships, the provision also accommodates another group association: five or fewer unrelated people are allowed to live together as though they were family. This accommodation is the peg on which Edmonds rests its plea for § 3607(b)(1) exemption. Had the City defined a family solely by biological and legal links, § 3607(b)(1) would not have been the ground on which Edmonds staked its case. * * * It is curious reasoning indeed that converts a family values preserver into a maximum occupancy restriction once a town adds to a related persons prescription "and also two unrelated persons."

Edmonds additionally contends that subjecting single-family zoning to FHA scrutiny will "overturn Euclidian zoning" and "destroy the effectiveness and purpose of single-family zoning." Brief for Petitioner 11, 25. This contention both ignores the limited scope of the issue before us and exaggerates the force of the FHA's antidiscrimination provisions. We address only whether Edmonds' family composition rule qualifies for § 3607(b)(1) exemption. Moreover, the FHA antidiscrimination provisions, when applicable, require only "reasonable" accommodations to afford persons with handicaps "equal opportunity to use and enjoy" housing. §§ 3604(f)(1)(A) and (f)(3)(B).

* * *

The parties have presented, and we have decided, only a threshold question: Edmonds' zoning code provision describing who may compose a "family" is not a maximum occupancy restriction exempt from the FHA under § 3607(b)(1). It remains for the lower courts to decide whether Edmonds' actions against Oxford House violate the FHA's prohibitions against discrimination set out in §§ 3604(f)(1)(A) and (f)(3)(B). For the reasons stated, the judgment of the United States Court of Appeals for the Ninth Circuit is

Affirmed.

Justice THOMAS, with whom Justice SCALIA and Justice KENNEDY join, dissenting. [Dissenting opinion omitted.]

Note

In Elliott v. City of Athens, 960 F.2d 975 (11th Cir.1992) (the case the Court rejects in the principal case) the court held that the maximum occupancy exemption in the Fair Housing Act applied to the city ordinance permitting a maximum of four unrelated individuals in the single-family district, and denial of a permit for a group home for recovering alcoholics did not violate the act.

CULP v. CITY OF SEATTLE

Court of Appeals of Washington, Division 1, 1979.
22 Wash.App. 618, 590 P.2d 1288.

WILLIAMS, JUDGE.

* * *

The facts are that Friends Services, Inc., sought to establish a home for retarded children in the Madison Park area of Seattle. It applied for a permit to build a facility there housing up to 12 children to be supervised by a professional staff. There is some dispute as to how the proposed facility would be operated, but it is clear that Friends Services will supply a professional staff, at least one of whom will be in residence at all times. The site for the proposed facility is within a zone classified as "Single Family Residence High Density Zone," Seattle zoning code § 26.16 and a children's resident home is permitted only as a conditional use when authorized by the Board. Seattle zoning code, § 26.12.030.

After a public hearing, an examiner approved the conditional use permit. A neighborhood group appealed to the Seattle Board of Adjustment. The Board confirmed the issuance with the condition that "someone will live in the dwelling unit and that the complete staff will not be rotated at all times." The neighborhood group then obtained review by certiorari to the superior court. The court decided that the facility would not meet the requirements of a children's resident home and vacated the permit. Friends Services' appeal followed.

* * *

The guidelines established by the Seattle zoning code for the proposed facility require that it be a children's resident home which is defined as:

> A *dwelling unit* occupied by a family which provides full-time supervision for from seven to twelve children unrelated to the resident family.

Seattle zoning code § 26.06.040.

A "Family" is defined as:

> Any number of related persons, or not to exceed eight nonrelated persons, or not to exceed a total of eight related and nonrelated, nontransient persons living as a single, nonprofit housekeeping unit as distinguished from a group occupying a club; *boarding, lodging, or rooming house; fraternity, sorority, or group student house.*

Seattle zoning code § 26.06.070.

The issue on appeal is whether the staff of the facility as proposed by Friends Services constitutes a "family" within this definition. Friends Services argues that only one staff member need be a nontransient resident of the children's home for the "family" requirement to be satisfied. The remainder of the staff need not live on the premises. The neighborhood group argues that the definition of family requires that all the staff live on the premises as a nontransient, single housekeeping unit. This is a question of law for the court to decide. * * *

It should be noted that the code provides not only for a children's resident home, but, also, for a children's institution which is defined as:

> An establishment consisting of one or more *buildings* organized and maintained for the group care and supervision of thirteen or more children, but not including *hospitals.*

Seattle zoning code § 26.06.040.

It is apparent that the scheme of the code is to differentiate between a dwelling occupied by a family which takes in and cares for children and one which is occupied by children supervised by a staff. The former is compatible with the traditional notion of a family; the latter is compatible with the traditional notion of an institution. The framers of the code recognized the distinction and allowed land in a single family resident zone to be used for the former. A staff operated institution such as that proposed by Friends Services does not fit. There is not the stability and continuity of living and sharing which a family unit affords.

The trial court's order vacating the permit is affirmed.

ANDERSEN, ACTING CHIEF JUDGE (concurring).

I concur that the decision of the trial court should be affirmed.

Boards of adjustment have considerable discretion. That discretion is not unlimited, however. What the Seattle Board of Adjustment did here was to try to stretch the meaning of the Seattle Zoning Code past what the Seattle City Council intended when it enacted that code.

The problem with stretching the definitions of the words "family" and "home" in the zoning code to achieve that which is felt to be socially desirable (that is, to allow special housing for retarded citizens to be established in single family residential neighborhoods) is that once stretched, the definition may also accommodate that which may not necessarily be so socially desirable, such as mini-prisons, for example.

As the learned trial judge pointed out in his oral decision, if the Seattle City Council, as the legislative branch of that city's government, considers it appropriate that homes such as are here at issue be established in residential neighborhoods, then the straightforward way of doing this is to amend the city's zoning ordinance to so provide.

RINGOLD, JUDGE (dissenting).

I would hold that the facility as proposed by Friends Services and the condition imposed by the Board satisfies the definition of "family" and therefore reverse the trial court.

* * *

The majority creates an impossible morass when it attempts to define "family" as * * * "[a relationship] compatible with the traditional notion of a family." The word is used to designate many relationships. * * *

It is, however, not necessary for us to indulge in etymology to discover the meaning of "family" as used by the drafters of the Zoning Code because they define it as *any* number of related and nonrelated persons. One person will suffice. Moreover, nothing in the ordinance defining "family" requires that all members of the staff reside at the proposed facility. It requires only that a number of them, as few as one or as many as eight, reside there.

A children's resident home need only be occupied by a "family" which provides "full-time supervision" for 7 to 12 children. Families use relatives, friends, babysitters, and tutors to provide some regular supervisory function. To hold that all persons performing some regular function in any family setting must actually reside in the house would lead to unreasonable and illogical consequences which should be avoided. * * *

Friends Services indicated to the Board that its staff arrangements included staff persons living at the proposed facility as their place of residence. This was sufficient to support the grant of the conditional use permit. The condition imposed by the Board is consistent with the Zoning Code requirements for a children's resident home.

My interpretation of the relevant provisions of the Zoning Code would require us to reverse the trial court's decision and reinstate the conditional use permit as granted by the Board. If the future operation of the children's resident home were found to be in violation of the Zoning Code or the terms of the conditional use permit, appropriate action could then be pursued before the proper municipal body.

Notes

1. Does the principal case clearly differentiate a group home from an institution? Should such a distinction be made? For purposes of evaluating a

zoning ordinance for its validity insofar as it may exclude a particular use from the single-family district, some attention should be paid to whether the proposed use is going to be operated as a family. On the other hand, the point where a group home turns into an institution may be difficult to discern.

In Taylor Home of Charlotte,Inc. v. City of Charlotte, 116 N.C.App. 188, 447 S.E.2d 438 (1994) neighbors succeeded in stopping a proposed group home for persons with full-blown AIDS. The court approved the local board interpretation of the state enabling legislation for group homes and the city ordinance to define group homes as "sheltered living arrangements primarily for rehabilitation." The court stated: "The Board interpreted that language to require that the residents of a group home be such that some day they could live normal lives. The Board found as a fact that that 'a dictionary commonly defines "rehabilitation" to mean the restoring of a handicapped or delinquent person to a useful life through education and therapy.' " Compare "K" Care, Inc. v. Town of Lac du Flambeau, 181 Wis.2d 59, 510 N.W.2d 697 (1993) where the court considered whether the denial of a permit to construct a facility for elderly residents violated the Fair Housing Act. The town argued that the federal statute only applied to discrimination against the handicapped and by definition the federal act was inapplicable to a home for the elderly. The court held: "We conclude that the proposed residents of the new facility ... are handicapped within the meaning of the FHA. These residents obviously suffer from physical and mental impairments that substantially limit one or more major life activities. They are unable to eat, bathe, walk or use a toilet without assistance. In short, they are no longer able to live independently." Also see City of St. Joseph v. Preferred Family Healthcare, 859 S.W.2d 723 (Mo.App.1993) where the court found that persons recovering from alcohol and drug abuse were not mentally or physically handicapped within the meaning of the federal Rehabilitation Act of 1973, § 504 (29 U.S.C.A. § 794). Also see Daniel R. Mandelker, Zoning Discrimination Against Group Homes Under the Fair Housing Act, Land Use Law (Nov. 1994) p. 3.

2. Consider Arkansas Release Guidance Foundation v. Hummel, 245 Ark. 953, 435 S.W.2d 774 (1969). The nonprofit corporation acquired two apartment houses in the apartment district to be used as a "halfway house" for the rehabilitation of recently paroled felons during their transition to the free world. The zoning classification permitted institutions of an "educational, religious or philanthropic nature." In a suit by the foundation for a declaratory judgment the court found that in considering the "overall purpose of zoning ordinances in general" the proposed halfway house was not an institution of educational, religious, or philanthropic nature.

Compare with this case, Abbott House v. Village of Tarrytown, 34 A.D.2d 821, 312 N.Y.S.2d 841 (1970) and State ex rel. Ellis v. Liddle, 520 S.W.2d 644 (Mo.App.1975), two intermediate appellate court cases allowing foster home type juvenile facilities in a group home setting within single family zoning districts.

3. In Pemberton Township v. State, 171 N.J.Super. 287, 408 A.2d 832 (1979) the court enjoined location of a group home for juvenile delinquents in a residential area because it was an "institutional use" and thus did not

come under the group home statute which defined group home as one operated by the state department of youth and family services (the proposed home was to be operated by the state department of corrections). On appeal the injunction was dissolved. 178 N.J.Super. 346, 429 A.2d 360 (1981).

4. What if group homes are specifically permitted in some zoning districts, but excluded from the single-family district? A rational approach to this problem would focus on whether the purpose and clientele of the group home requires a surrogate family setting. Courts seldom discuss this issue. See, e.g., Residential Management Systems v. Jefferson County Plan Comm'n, 542 N.E.2d 227 (Ind.App.1989).

H. EXCLUSION OF RELIGIOUS INSTITUTIONS AND PRIVATE SCHOOLS

STATE EX REL. LAKE DRIVE BAPTIST CHURCH v. VILLAGE OF BAYSIDE

Supreme Court of Wisconsin, 1961.
12 Wis.2d 585, 108 N.W.2d 288.

[Mandamus to compel rezoning to permit plaintiff to build a church. The lower court dismissed the action. Bayside, which grew from 553 residents in 1953, when the village was incorporated, to about 3,000 in 1958, is principally residential. In the first half of 1954, the village board indicated it would agree to the construction of the church but wanted to see plans. In mid–1954 the church incorporated, choosing its name in expectation that it would build on the proposed Lake Drive site. In July, 1954, the village adopted a zoning ordinance which excluded churches from the entire village. In 1956, this ordinance was amended and churches were permitted at several locations but, in spite of the recommendation of its planning consultant and its planning commission, the village board refused to rezone plaintiff's land so that a church could be built on it.]

FAIRCHILD, JUSTICE.

* * * With respect to use of land in residence districts for a church, zoning ordinances fall into three types: (1) Permitting churches in all; (2) permitting a church only upon special permit, after hearing; and (3) excluding churches, often, if not usually, from districts where residential use is itself restricted to certain types of dwellings.

It appears that most zoning ordinances fall into the first two types.[12] The first presents no constitutional problem. Many of the cases on this subject arise from denials of permits under the second type of ordinance. Standards in ordinances of the second type appear to be vaguely defined or omitted, and that fact has given rise to some difficulty. A practical advantage of this method is that it permits administrative determination on a case-by-case basis of the suitability of particular sites for church use. We are urged to decide the matter before us on the principle that

---

12. "Regulation of the Location of Churches by Municipal Zoning Ordinances"   (1956–1957), 23 Brooklyn Law Review, 185, 186.

only the first or possibly the second type of ordinance is valid. Several courts, in considering whether to set aside a denial of a permit under an ordinance of the second type, have said that an ordinance of the third type would be invalid.[13]

The supreme court of Texas had an ordinance of the third type before it, and held it invalid.[14]

The supreme court of Florida held a similar ordinance valid.[15] The court noted that the church bought the property with knowledge of the zoning restrictions; there were sites available in districts where churches would be permitted; church use would cause the value of the surrounding property to depreciate, and give rise to a genuine traffic problem. The court also pointed out that churches are now customarily used for many activities besides worship services and prayer meetings.

A California court of appeal held an ordinance of the third type valid. The court noted that the record did not indicate that the church could not be built in a district where churches would be permitted.[16] The following reference to that decision was made by the supreme court of the United States:

13. "The law is well settled that the building of a church may not be prohibited in a residential district." Dictum in Board of Zoning Appeals v. Decatur, Indiana Co. of Jehovah's Witnesses, 233 Ind. 83, 91, 117 N.E.2d 115, 119 (1954).

"It is well established in this country that a zoning ordinance may not wholly exclude a church or synagogue from any residential district. Such a provision is stricken on the ground that it bears no substantial relation to the public health, safety, morals, peace, or general welfare of the community." Dictum in Diocese of Rochester v. Planning Board, 1 N.Y.2d 508, 522, 136 N.E.2d 827, 834 (1956).

"Since a city cannot legally exclude a church from a residential district by a zoning ordinance, it cannot legally accomplish the same result by denying permits unless the reasons for refusing the permits are based on valid evidence showing that to permit a church would be detrimental to the health, the safety, the morals or the general welfare of the community." Congregation Committee, North Fort Worth Congregation, Jehovah's Witnesses v. Halton City, 287 S.W.2d 700, 704 (Tex.Civ.App. 1956).

"We seriously question the constitutionality of any enactment that seeks flatly to prohibit the erection of churches in residential districts." State ex rel. Synod of Ohio v. Joseph, 139 Ohio St. 229, 240, 39 N.E.2d 515, 520 (1942).

This court citing the foregoing Ohio case has said: "The majority of courts, on constitutional grounds, refuse to uphold the exclusion of churches by zoning. Appellants' argument as to the value of religious institutions to society might be well advanced if we had a zoning ordinance before us." Hall v. Church of the Open Bible, 4 Wis.2d 246, 249, 89 N.W.2d 798 (1958).

See Bassett, Zoning (1936 ed.), p. 200; 2 Metzenbaum, Zoning (2d ed.), pp. 1461–1464; 2 Yokley, Zoning Law and Practice (2d ed.), pp. 110–112, sec. 222.

See Anno. Zoning Regulations—Churches, 74 A.L.R.2d 377.

14. In Sherman v. Simms, 143 Tex. 115, 119, 183 S.W.2d 415, 417 (1944), the court said: "To exclude churches from residential districts does not promote the health, the safety, the morals or the general welfare of the community, and to relegate them to business and manufacturing districts could conceivably result in imposing a burden upon the free right to worship and, in some instances, in prohibiting altogether the exercise of that right. An ordinance fraught with that danger will not be enforced."

15. Miami Beach United Lutheran Church v. Miami Beach, 82 So.2d 880 (Fla. 1955).

16. Corporation of the Presiding Bishop of the Church of Jesus Christ of Latter-Day Saints v. Porterville, 338 U.S. 805, 70 S.Ct. 78, 94 L.Ed. 487 (1949). (Appeal dismissed.)

"When the effect of a statute or ordinance upon the exercise of First-amendment freedoms is relatively small and the public interest to be protected is substantial, it is obvious that a rigid test requiring a showing of imminent danger to the security of the nation is an absurdity. We recently dismissed for want of substantiality an appeal in which a church group contended that its First-amendment rights were violated by a municipal zoning ordinance preventing the building of churches in certain residential areas."[17]

Most of the decisions on this subject appear to involve denials of a special permit to build a church under the second type of ordinance. In a number, the denial has been set aside, sometimes with an accompanying statement that there is no valid basis for exclusion.[18]

In a few cases, denials under the second type of ordinance have been upheld.[19]

It is clear enough that a church has some attributes which tend to make it less desirable to its next-door neighbor than a one-family dwelling. It entails substantial gatherings of people, resulting disturbance, and the problem of parking automobiles. In a case where we permitted enforcement of a private covenant preventing the use of property for a church, we said:

> Conceding the social value of churches, it is nevertheless true that churches, like other places of assembly, produce noise, congestion, and traffic hazards. The exclusion of uses which create such conditions in an area planned as residential cannot be said to be against public policy.[20]

This court has recognized that the protection of property values is an objective upon which a zoning ordinance may be grounded. In the same decision, it referred to the general rule that zoning power may not be exercised for purely aesthetic considerations, but suggested great doubt whether this rule is still the law. Whether restriction of use of a district to strictly residential uses will protect property values is the type of question upon which the decision of the municipal board is accepted unless shown to be unreasonable.

17. American Communications Ass'n v. Douds, 339 U.S. 382, 397, 70 S.Ct. 674, 94 L.Ed. 925 (1950).

18. Board of Zoning Appeals v. Decatur, Indiana Co. of Jehovah's Witnesses, 233 Ind. 83, 117 N.E.2d 115 (1954); Community Synagogue v. Bates, 1 N.Y.2d 445, 154 N.Y.S.2d 15, 136 N.E.2d 488 (1956); Diocese of Rochester v. Planning Board, 1 N.Y.2d 508, 154 N.Y.Supp.2d 849, 136 N.E.2d 827 (1956); State ex rel. Anshe Chesed Congregation v. Bruggemeier, 97 Ohio App. 67, 115 N.E.2d 65 (1953); Young Israel Organization v. Dworkin, 105 Ohio App. 89, 133 N.E.2d 174 (1956).

19. Milwaukie Co. of Jehovah's Witnesses v. Mullen, 214 Or. 281, 330 P.2d 5, 74 A.L.R.2d 347 (1958) (denial based on traffic congestion); Galfas v. Ailor, 81 Ga. App. 13, 57 S.E.2d 834 (1950) (denial based on traffic problem); West Hartford Methodist Church v. Zoning Board of Appeals, 143 Conn. 263, 121 A.2d 640 (1956) (denial based on substantial injury to surrounding homes).

20. Hall v. Church of the Open Bible, 4 Wis.2d 246, 249, 89 N.W.2d 798 (1958).

A church, however, is not to be viewed merely as the owner of property complaining against a restriction on its use. It may also challenge an ordinance as an unwarranted burden upon, or interference with, the freedom of the adherents of the church to worship after the manner of their faith. We are familiar with the constitutional protection of freedom of religion from governmental interference.

An ordinance which excludes a church from a particular district must pass two tests:

> (1) Can it reasonably be said that use for a church would have such an effect on the area that exclusion of such use will promote the general welfare, and

> (2) Does the exclusion impose a burden upon freedom of worship which is not commensurate with the promotion of general welfare secured?

The United States supreme court has said of religious freedom, protected by the First amendment:

> "Thus the amendment embraces two concepts—freedom to believe and freedom to act. The first is absolute but, in the nature of things, the second cannot be. Conduct remains subject to regulation for the protection of society. The freedom to act must have appropriate definition to preserve the enforcement of that protection. In every case the power to regulate must be so exercised as not, in attaining a permissible end, unduly to infringe the protected freedom."[21]

The test is whether a regulation is an *undue infringement*. Any restriction upon the opportunity to build a house of worship is at least a potential burden upon the freedom of those who would like to worship there. Whether the burden is slight or substantial will depend upon circumstances. In a community where adequate and accessible building sites are available in all districts, it might be a negligible burden to exclude churches from some of them. There must be many circumstances under which a religious group could demonstrate that an exclusion from a particular area would be a substantial burden.

The Bayside ordinance, since 1956, has excluded churches from "A," "B," and "C" districts, where one-family dwellings are permitted, has permitted dwellings, churches, and other institutions in several "E" districts, and has confined "D" districts to dwellings and certain business uses. We conclude that the exclusion of churches, of itself, does not render the ordinance invalid. To determine invalidity would require determination that the "E" districts do not afford reasonably suitable, accessible, and available sites as compared with those in other districts. While there was testimony questioning the suitability of sites in the "E" districts, and the court found that some of the land was overpriced, we

21. Cantwell v. Connecticut, 310 U.S. (1940).
296, 303, 60 S.Ct. 900, 84 L.Ed. 1213

do not find it necessary, in this case, to decide whether, as to a church first coming upon the scene after passage of the 1956 amendment, the exclusion of churches from all but "E" districts was an undue burden.

3. *Invalidity with respect to "C" districts.* The Bayside ordinance permits schools and municipal buildings in "C" districts, but excludes churches. Permitted schools are not limited to public schools. Some, at least, of the attributes of a church which annoy neighbors, are also characteristic of schools. It is at least arguable that it is arbitrary and capricious to exclude churches while permitting schools. Exclusion of churches has been held invalid where an ordinance permitted dwellings, schools, colleges, public libraries, public museums and art galleries, parks, etc., and farms and greenhouses[22] and where an ordinance permitted homes, municipal buildings, railroad stations, public schools, and clubhouses.[23] This court has upheld exclusion of private and parochial high schools from a district where public high schools are permitted,[24] but considered it necessary to point out that while all high schools would present detrimental effects, public high schools presented certain advantages which the zoning authority could have considered compensating. In any event, little attention has been given to this issue in the briefs of the parties here, and we do not decide it. [The court then stated that the 1954 Bayside ordinance which excluded churches from the entire village had been clearly unconstitutional.]

5. *Presumption of validity.* "Under well-established rules, where a municipal body enacts regulations pursuant to authority expressly granted, all presumptions are in favor of its validity, and any person attacking it must make the fact of its invalidity clearly appear."[25] Cases like the present, however, raise not only the questions usually raised by restriction upon an owner's right to use his property, but the additional question of whether religious freedom is being unduly impaired. We conclude that it is the duty of a court to give the closest scrutiny to the question whether the exclusion of a church from a district is justified.

The supreme court of Oregon has commented critically on a tendency "to cloak petitioning churches with a species of judicial favoritism under the zoning laws."[26] It seems to us that the courts must be sensitive to any claim that an undue burden is put upon freedom of worship. This is true both because of the importance of this freedom, and because of the real possibility that an overgenerous reliance upon the presumption of validity may cloak discriminatory action against a religious group which is too small a minority in the community to have an effective voice.

22. Ellsworth v. Gercke, 62 Ariz. 198, 156 P.2d 242 (1945).

23. North Shore Unitarian Society v. Plandome, 200 Misc. 524, 109 N.Y.S.2d 803 (1951).

24. State ex rel. Wisconsin Lutheran H.S. Conference v. Sinar, 267 Wis. 91, 65 N.W.2d 43 (1954).

25. State ex rel. Newman v. Pagels, 212 Wis. 475, 479, 250 N.W. 430 (1933).

26. Milwaukie Co. of Jehovah's Witnesses v. Mullen, 214 Or. 281, 316, 330 P.2d 5, 74 A.L.R.2d 347, 369 (1958).

6. *Vested rights.* Plaintiff argues that its action in reliance upon favorable intimations of the village board gave it a property right to construct a church on its site, or estopped the village board from preventing it. Counsel cites Rosenberg v. Whitefish Bay, 199 Wis. 214, 225 N.W. 838 (1929), and subsequent decisions. Plaintiff accepted the land (as a gift), chose its name, and prepared its first plans after the board manifested a favorable attitude and before the 1956 amendment. The record does not disclose the extent of any expenditure during that period, and we do not find that the principle of the Rosenberg Case is applicable.

7. *Arbitrary action of the board.* As we have heretofore noted, the Bayside ordinance of 1954 excluded churches from the village and therefore could not have prevented plaintiff from building on its site. Assuming that the 1956 amendment, by providing that churches might be erected in certain districts, made valid the parts of the ordinance excluding churches from other districts, was it arbitrary and capricious not to include plaintiff's site in a district where plaintiff could proceed with its building? While plaintiff's prior relationship with the village board and its various activities in reliance thereon are insufficient to give plaintiff a so-called "vested" right to build, they do provide strong equitable considerations for favorable zoning if at all reasonable.

In reaching the conclusion that the action of the village board was arbitrary and capricious, we have been persuaded by the following propositions: (a) Plaintiff is entitled to the benefit of equitable considerations arising out of its actions in reliance on the board's indication of agreement. (b) The board rejected not only its own original view, but the recommendation of the consultant it employed, and the repeated recommendation of the village plan commission. (c) It appears that the property is better suited for a church than for residences. (d) Any traffic hazard could be readily eliminated by the village. (e) The fact that other owners combined their lots in Pelham Heath has little significance. [The court then found the site was suitable for a church; that there would be no adverse effects on other lots; that traffic adjustments could easily be made and that the village was not morally committed to keep the zoning unchanged.]

* * *

Judgment reversed, cause remanded with directions to enjoin enforcement of the Bayside zoning ordinance against construction of a church on plaintiff's site, and to issue a peremptory writ of mandamus commanding the building inspector to issue the building permit applied for.

[The concurring and dissenting opinions which follow have been drastically edited.]

HALLOWS, JUSTICE (concurring). I concur with the result of the court's opinion and much of its reasoning. However, I would reverse also on the ground the exclusion of churches from residential districts is invalid and particularly the exclusion of churches from the "C" district which permits schools and municipal buildings as well as residences is invalid because such classification is arbitrary, unreasonable, and capricious.

* * *

Considering the nature of the zoning power of a municipality, I cannot agree the exercise of that power to exclude churches of itself does not render an ordinance invalid. The zoning power may only be exercised to promote the health, safety, morals, and general welfare of the community. * * *

The majority rule in this country is that churches may not, either by the express or implied language of the zoning ordinance, validly be excluded from residential areas as an absolute and an invariable rule. * * *

The church in our society has long been identified with family and residential life. Churches traditionally have been and should be located in that part of the community where people live. They should be easily and conveniently located to the home. Churches are not supermarkets, manufacturing plants, or commercial establishments and should not be restricted to such areas. How can the exclusion of churches from a residential area promote public morals or the general welfare? To so hold is a failure to understand the purpose and the influence of churches. * * *

It is true, in State ex rel. Wisconsin Lutheran H.S. Conference v. Sinar, 267 Wis. 91, 65 N.W.2d 43 (1954), we held an ordinance which excluded private high schools from a classification which included public schools was a valid classification. The arguments and the reasoning of the dissenting opinion in the Sinar Case appeal to this writer as being valid. Perhaps the Sinar Case can be distinguished in that it dealt with schools and not churches, but that is of little consequence because I do not see the validity of the distinction between a public school and a private school in the same land-use district. A year after the Sinar Case was decided, a California court came to the opposite conclusion in holding a zoning ordinance could not exclude a private elementary school from an area where public schools were permitted. The Roman Catholic Welfare Corp. of San Francisco v. Piedmont, 45 Cal.2d 325, 289 P.2d 438, 439 (1955). * * *

CURRIE, JUSTICE (dissenting). I am in full accord with the holding of the opinion of the court written by MR. JUSTICE FAIRCHILD that zoning ordinances which exclude churches from residence districts do not violate the First amendment of the United States constitution as incorporated into the Fourteenth amendment, if suitable and sufficient locations for churches are provided in other use districts.

* * *

However, I must respectfully dissent from the holding of the opinion of the court that the zoning of the particular tract of land owned by the relator was arbitrary and capricious. * * *

Inasmuch as the avoidance of traffic congestion in residence areas, and protection against depreciation of surrounding property values, are a sufficient basis to support the exercise of the police power to exclude churches from residence-use districts, it is not proper for a court to second-guess the municipal legislative body as to whether a church to be built in some particular location in a residence-use district would produce such harmful results. Therefore, in the instant case it is entirely immaterial what motives prompted the majority of the village board to vote not to include relator's property in a class "E" district so long as the motive was not to discriminate against a church as such.

* * *

The trial court's memorandum opinion, findings of fact, and conclusions of law, make it clear that the trial court found that the village board's action did not discriminate against the relator's property on grounds of religion. Such finding is not against the great weight and clear preponderance of the evidence, and, therefore, is conclusive upon this court.

I would affirm the judgment below.

Notes

1. See Mooney v. Orchard Lake, 333 Mich. 389, 53 N.W.2d 308 (1952); Diocese of Rochester v. Planning Board of Brighton, 1 N.Y.2d 508, 154 N.Y.S.2d 849, 136 N.E.2d 827 (1956); Annot., 74 A.L.R.2d 377 (1960), 62 A.L.R.3d 197 (1975); Church, Regulations excluding Churches from Residential Districts, 1962 Wis.L.Rev. 358; Comment, Churches and Zoning, 70 Harv.L.Rev. 1428 (1957); Reynolds, Zoning the Church: The Police Power Versus the First Amendment, 64 Boston U.L.Rev. 767 (1984). Also see Kola Tepee v. Marion County, 99 Or.App. 481, 782 P.2d 955, rev. denied 309 Or. 441, 789 P.2d 5 (1990), where a proposed church was excluded from a district zoned exclusively for agricultural use, and Cornerstone Bible Church v. City of Hastings, 740 F.Supp. 654 (D.Minn.1990), where a church was ordered to vacate a commercial building under a zoning ordinance that allowed churches in residential, but not commercial, districts.

2. Where a community decides to regulate church location by a special use permit, particular care should be taken in drafting the standards to be applied by the local administrators. Thus in State ex rel. Anshe Chesed Congregation v. Bruggemeier, 97 Ohio App. 67, 115 N.E.2d 65 (1953), the ordinance provided for a permit to build a church "when such location will substantially serve the public convenience and welfare and will not substantially and permanently injure the appropriate use of neighboring property." The court in overruling the denial of a permit for a very large church stressed the absence of any reference in the standard to traffic and safety. The court also said: "It must be observed that a village, which is contiguous to and a part of a great metropolitan area from which it derives its very

existence, cannot arbitrarily refuse within reasonable limits to contribute its share to the general welfare of the community as a whole." Compare Jewish Reconstructionist Synagogue of North Shore, Inc. v. Incorporated Village of Roslyn Harbor, 38 N.Y.2d 283, 379 N.Y.S.2d 747, 342 N.E.2d 534 (1975), where the court held that religious institutions have a preeminent status under the First Amendment and that status makes freedom of religion the dominant factor in considering the application of zoning restrictions which are detrimental to the religious institution. In this case the court held that a 100 foot setback ordinance could not be applied so as to exclude the institution. In a subsequent proceeding in the same case the court further held that the village could not require the synagogue to pay the costs of a transcript of the variance proceeding nor the cost of renting a hall for the hearing, 40 N.Y.2d 158, 386 N.Y.S.2d 198, 352 N.E.2d 115 (1976). But the "preeminent status" argument did not seem to sway the federal court in Holy Spirit Ass'n for the Unification of World Christianity v. Town of New Castle, 480 F.Supp. 1212 (S.D.N.Y.1979), where the court held that the town might make a limited inquiry into the bona fides of the institution's beliefs without violating its First Amendment rights.

3. Did the Wisconsin court in the principal case in effect reverse the normal presumption of constitutionality? Is it saying that zoning which excludes churches will be presumed invalid until the local unit meets the burden of showing insubstantial impairment of religious freedom? On the presumption of constitutionality generally, the ordinary assumption is that the presumption applies with equal strength for federal, state and local legislation. See Pacific States Box & Basket Co. v. White, 296 U.S. 176, 186, 56 S.Ct. 159, 163, 80 L.Ed. 138, 101 A.L.R. 853 (1935).

Congress, in the Religious Freedom Restoration Act of 1993, 42 U.S.C.A. § 2000bb, et seq., provided that government shall not substantially burden a person's exercise of religion, even if the burden results from a rule of general applicability unless the government demonstrates that application of the burden is in furtherance of a compelling governmental interest and is the least restrictive means of furthering that interest. This statute was enacted in response to the Supreme Court's holding in the "Indian Peyote" case, Employment Div. v. Smith, 494 U.S. 872, 110 S.Ct. 1595, 108 L.Ed.2d 876 (1990), that a facially neutral rule applies to religiously motivated conduct. In Flores v. City of Boerne, 73 F.3d 1352 (5th Cir.1996), the court upheld the validity of RFRA in a case challenging the inclusion of portions of a Roman Catholic cathedral in the city's historic district. The Supreme Court granted certiorari in the case late in 1996, and on June 25, 1997, the Court struck down the Act as exceeding the powers of Congress (1997 WL 345322). Although RFRA is no longer a factor in evaluating the validity of zoning ordinances as applied to religious uses, the First Amendment free exercise clause is still applicable.

4. As the principal case suggests, most zoning ordinances establish a policy of finding churches compatible with the single-family residential district (albeit with some protection for surrounding residences by way of conditional use permits or some similar device). See, e.g., Christian Gospel Church, Inc. v. San Francisco, 896 F.2d 1221 (9th Cir.1990). However, ancillary religious institutions such as convents or monasteries pose different problems. See Diakonian Soc'y v. City of Chicago Zoning Bd. of Appeals, 63

Ill.App.3d 823, 20 Ill.Dec. 634, 380 N.E.2d 843 (1978). Also see Missionaries of Our Lady of La Salette v. Village of Whitefish Bay, 267 Wis. 609, 66 N.W.2d 627 (1954) which involved the single family provisions of an ordinance as applied to three priests and two lay brothers living in a house owned by a religious order. Application of Laporte, 2 A.D.2d 710, 152 N.Y.S.2d 916, affirmed Laporte v. City of New Rochelle, 2 N.Y.2d 921, 161 N.Y.S.2d 886, 141 N.E.2d 917 (1957), considered *sixty* student members of a religious order as constituting a single family group where they occupied a Roman Catholic college building as a residence. The dissenting judge in the appellate division opinion pointed out that this was really a college dormitory not a one-family dwelling. In Damascus Community Church v. Clackamas County, 45 Or.App. 1065, 610 P.2d 273 (1980), appeal dismissed 450 U.S. 902, 101 S.Ct. 1336, 67 L.Ed.2d 326 (1981), the court held that a permit for a church in a residential area did not authorize establishment of an ancillary, full-time parochial school. Accord: Abram v. City of Fayetteville, 281 Ark. 63, 661 S.W.2d 371 (1983); Seward Chapel, Inc. v. City of Seward, 655 P.2d 1293 (Alaska 1982); Rhema Christian Center v. District of Columbia Bd. of Zoning Adj., 515 A.2d 189 (D.C.App.1986), subsequent decision, Towles v. District of Columbia Bd. of Zoning Adj., 578 A.2d 1128 (D.C.App.1990). Contra: Alpine Christian Fellowship v. County Comm'rs of Pitkin County, 870 F.Supp. 991 (D.Colo.1994).

In St. John's Evangelical Lutheran Church v. City of Hoboken, 195 N.J.Super. 414, 479 A.2d 935 (1983), the city sought to prevent the church from operating a shelter for 30 to 50 homeless persons on the ground that such a shelter is not a customary ancillary use. The court granted an injunction in favor of the church. Contra are First Assembly of God of Naples, Florida, Inc. v. Collier County, 20 F.3d 419, (11th Cir.1994), modified, 27 F.3d 526, cert. denied 513 U.S. 1080, 115 S.Ct. 730, 130 L.Ed.2d 634 (1995); Daytona Rescue Mission, Inc. v. City of Daytona Beach, 885 F.Supp. 1554 (M.D.Fla.1995) (the court in this case also held that RFRA did not protect the church from a neutral and generally applicable zoning code). However, in Jesus Center v. Farmington Hills Zoning Bd. of Appeals, 215 Mich.App. 54, 544 N.W.2d 698 (1996) the court held that RFRA was applicable to a homeless shelter operated by a church on weekends; homeless persons were bussed to the church from poor neighborhoods in the region. Also see Western Presbyterian Church v. Board of Zoning Adjustment of District of Columbia, 862 F.Supp. 538 (D.D.C.1994).

In Needham Pastoral Counseling Center, Inc. v. Board of Appeals of Needham, 29 Mass.App. 31, 557 N.E.2d 43, rev. denied 408 Mass. 1103, 560 N.E.2d 121 (1990), the court found that a proposed 864 square foot addition to a church building for offices and counseling rooms for a psychological counseling center with a spiritual component was more like a mental health clinic than a religious activity, and that the building permit was properly denied.

See Shelley R. Saxer, When Religion Becomes a Nuisance: Balancing Land Use and Religious Freedom When Activities of Religious Institutions Bring Outsiders into the Neighborhood, 84 Kentucky L. J. 507 (1996).

5. In State v. Cameron, 100 N.J. 586, 498 A.2d 1217 (1985), the New Jersey Supreme Court held that an ordinance which excludes churches and

similar places of worship from the single-family district was unconstitutionally vague as applied to a minister who held weekly services in his home for 25 people. Also see, Farhi v. Commissioners of the Borough of Deal, 204 N.J.Super. 575, 499 A.2d 559 (1985). Compare City of Colorado Springs v. Blanche, 761 P.2d 212 (Colo.1988). In LeBlanc–Sternberg v. Fletcher, 104 F.3d 355 (2d Cir.1996) the court upheld a district court's array of relief in a long dispute between groups of Orthodox Jews and the Village of Airmont, New York. The plaintiffs claimed that the zoning code of the village was discriminatory in purposefully inhibiting the rights of home worship and other religious expression. The district court opinion is in 922 F.Supp. 959 (S.D.N.Y.1996) and a previous appellate opinion is 67 F.3d 412 (2d Cir.1995), dealing with the federal government cause of action based on the Fair Housing Act.

6.   In Cochise County v. Broken Arrow Baptist Church, 161 Ariz. 406, 778 P.2d 1302 (App.1989), the church built a metal building containing 5,000 square feet with a concrete floor to contain a printing press and literature distribution center; there was no sanctuary in the building. The church neglected to obtain a permit and the trial court granted an injunction against occupying the building finding it a public nuisance. On appeal the court held that the building was obviously a manufacturing facility and not a church, and affirmed the injunction.

7.   In Love Church v. City of Evanston, 671 F.Supp. 515 (N.D.Ill.1987) the court held that an ordinance requiring churches to obtain a special permit was a violation of equal protection because meeting halls, theatres and schools were not required to obtain special permits.

STATE EX REL. WISCONSIN LUTHERAN HIGH SCHOOL CONFERENCE v. SINAR

Supreme Court of Wisconsin, 1954.
267 Wis. 91, 65 N.W.2d 43, appeal dismissed 349 U.S.
913, 75 S.Ct. 604, 99 L.Ed. 1248 (1955).

BROWN, JUSTICE.

* * *

[T]he common council of Wauwatosa adopted a zoning ordinance whose provisions, material to this action, are as follows:

"5. That Section 14.03(1) of said Zoning Code defines 'A' Residence District Regulations as follows:

(1) Use: No building or premises shall be used and no building shall be hereafter erected or altered within any 'A' Residence District, unless otherwise provided in this ordinance, except for the following uses:

"(a) Single Family Dwellings.

* * *

"(e) Public Schools and Private Elementary Schools."

* * * Reference to sec. 14.03(1)(e) of the ordinance discloses that the erection of public high schools is permitted and the erection of private schools above the elementary rank is forbidden in the "A" residence district. The defendant inspector relied on this prohibition in refusing to issue a building permit to the plaintiff.

The power to zone is granted to cities in order to promote the "health, safety, morals or the general welfare of the community." Sec. 62.23(7)(a), Stats., supra. We have recognized that the term "general welfare" includes considerations of public convenience, and general prosperity. State ex rel. Carter v. Harper, supra. The means adopted to promote these ends must, of course, bear a reasonable relation to the declared purpose. Id., 182 Wis. at page 152, 196 N.W. 451, 33 A.L.R. 269; Nectow v. City of Cambridge, 277 U.S. 183, 48 S.Ct. 447, 72 L.Ed. 842. Appellants have made it abundantly clear that respondent's projected school has many features which seriously impair the social and economic benefits to the entire community which the zoning law is designed to preserve and promote. It will add to the congestion of the surrounding streets. Athletic events will bring noisy crowds and if the contests are held at night, there will be bright lights to interfere with the peace and comfort of the neighborhood. The school property will be taken from the tax roll, thus increasing the financial burden of the city's taxpayers. The presence of the school will lessen the taxable value of nearby homes and will deter the building of new homes in the area. Other detriments are easily thought of. But, as respondent points out, each such discordant feature attends the presence of a public school to an equal degree.

Respondent submits, therefore, that there is no difference in the effect on the community between the permitted public high school and the prohibited private one and hence the ordinance's discrimination between them is unreasonable, not founded on a difference in fact material to the object sought to be attained by building ordinances, and is a measure which denies to respondent the equal protection of the laws and deprives it of property without due process of law, contrary to the provisions of the Fourteenth Amendment of the United States Constitution. Therefore, it asserts, so far as this case is concerned, the ordinance is void.

" * * * [A] classification to be valid must always rest on a difference which bears a fair, substantial, natural, reasonable, and just relation to the object, act, or persons in respect to which it is proposed. * * * "12 Am.Jur. p. 153, sec. 481, Const.Law. Respondent cites Catholic Bishop of Chicago v. Kingery, 371 Ill. 257, 20 N.E.2d 583, and City of Miami Beach v. State ex rel. Lear, 128 Fla. 750, 175 So. 537. These are cases whose facts are practically identical with the present one. In them the respective courts held that there was no substantial difference between public and private schools in relation to the object sought to be accomplished by the zoning ordinance and therefore, in so far as it prohibited the presence of a private school while allowing a public one, it was void. If these decisions were controlling authority upon us we would necessarily affirm the learned trial court for we can not distinguish them from ours in any material respect. But their authority is persuasive, only, and it fails to persuade.

The subject of public education and the establishment and operation of public schools is a governmental function of this state. Art. X, Wis.Const. Chapters 36 to 42, Stats. The City School Plan, secs. 40.50 to 40.60, Stats., has made the city the municipal entity for the administration of school affairs of those cities which have come under it, as the city of Wauwatosa has done. State ex rel. Board of Education v. City of Racine, 205 Wis. 389, 236 N.W. 553 (1931). In the performance of other governmental functions we do not restrict the behavior of persons or the use of property to the same extent that we do when only private interests are pursued and the fact that the standards are different commonly raises no suspicion that an illegal discrimination is thereby imposed or that the difference between municipality and citizen is insufficient to support separate classifications. For example, who considers he has a right to ignore speed laws because they need not be observed by the fire department responding to a call? Sec. 85.40(5), Stats. Nor is the state controlled by a building requirement which an individual must observe. City of Milwaukee v. McGregor, 140 Wis. 35, 121 N.W. 642 (1909). It may be that the essential differences between government and governed are so great that the two are in different classes per se at any time when governmental functions are involved and no ordinance is void by reason of discrimination, alone, merely because it gives a preference to the government, acting in its governmental capacity, which it withholds from private corporations or individuals.

However, we decide the present appeal on the narrower ground that tangible differences material to the classifications of the ordinance can be readily pointed out which sustain the distinction made by the ordinance between the schools. To begin with, the term "public" is the antithesis of "private." The public school is not a private one. They serve different interests and are designed to do so. The private school is founded and maintained because it is different. Is that difference material to the purpose of zoning? In many respects the two schools perform like functions and in probably all respects concerning noise, traffic difficulties and the other objectionable features already mentioned they stand on an equality, so that in several of the objects of zoning ordinances,—the promotion of health, safety and morals, as laid down by sec. 62.23(7)(a), Stats., and developed by respondent's brief, we may not say that the two schools differ. But when we come to "the promotion of the general welfare of the community",—"Ay, there's the rub." The public school has the same features objectionable to the surrounding area as a private one, but it has, also, a virtue which the other lacks, namely, that it is located to serve and does serve that area without discrimination. Whether the private school is sectarian or commercial, though it now complains of discrimination, in its services it discriminates and the public school does not. Anyone in the district of fit age and educational qualifications may attend the public high school. It is his right. He has no comparable right to attend a private school. To go there he must meet additional standards over which the public neither has nor should have control. The private school imposes on the community all the disadvantages of the public school but does not compensate the community in the same manner or to the same extent. If the private school does not make the same contribution to public welfare this difference may be taken into consideration by the legislative body in framing its ordinances. If education offered by a school to the residents of an area without discrimination is considered by the council to compensate for the admitted drawbacks to its presence there, that school may be permitted a location which is denied to another school which does not match the offer, and we can not say that such a distinction is arbitrary or unreasonable or that such discrimination between the two schools lacks foundation in a difference which bears a "fair, substantial, reasonable and just relation;" to the promotion of the general welfare of the community, which is the statutory purpose of zoning laws in general and of the ordinance in question.

While we have not found any decisions sustaining the public v. private distinction between schools in zoning cases and respondent has found two to the contrary, supra, it has not been difficult to find supporting examples in other activities. Thus, an ordinance permitted only municipal parks in a residence district. A property owner set up a bathing beach ostensibly run as a private club but actually open to the public. He asserted that it was a park and that there was an illegal discrimination by the ordinance which permitted a municipal park but not a private one. The court said: " * * * There is nothing unreasonable in the classification that makes a distinction between municipally owned and privately owned playgrounds and parks. * * * " McCarter v. Beckwith, 247 App.Div. 289, 285 N.Y.S. 151, 154 (1936). The decision was affirmed without opinion, 272 N.Y. 488, 3 N.E.2d 882, and was denied certiorari 299 U.S. 601, 57 S.Ct. 194, 81 L.Ed. 443.

* * *

Even more persuasive is our own leading case on zoning ordinances, State ex rel. Carter v. Harper, supra. The ordinance there under consideration contained a provision which allowed a public service corporation, upon a finding of public necessity and convenience to erect buildings and put its property to use in its business in any zone. We said, 182 Wis. at page 162, 196 N.W. at page 456:

" * * * It must be apparent that an ordinance enacted pursuant to state authority, which prevents the erection of buildings or the conduct of business deemed inimical to public interest, need not also prohibit the erection of buildings or the conduct of business which is essential to the comfort and convenience of the public, and which the duly constituted authority of the state determines to be necessary for the public service which a public utility is required to render. * * * "

The private corporation, because affected by the public interest, was enabled to conduct activities in zones where similar industries not so affected were forbidden to operate. If such preferential treatment of a mere private corporation did not invalidate the ordinance because of the public interest in the utility, how much stronger is the position of the appellants whose contention rests on an ordinance which gives the preference to the public,—the municipality,—itself! We consider the authority very strong in support of the conclusion which we have already reached independently, that no unconstitutional or otherwise illegal discrimination appears in the Wauwatosa zoning ordinance by reason of its exclusion of private high schools from "A" residence zones while accepting public schools of the same rank. Consequently, the refusal of appellant building inspector to issue a building permit for the erection of respondent's private high school was proper and must be sustained.

Orders and judgment reversed. Cause remanded with directions to quash the writ of mandamus.

[Two justices dissented. Steinle, J.'s dissenting opinion is not given.]

Notes

1. The California court (3 judges dissenting) disagreed with the Sinar holding. Roman Catholic Welfare Corp. v. City of Piedmont, 45 Cal.2d 325, 289 P.2d 438 (1955). It relied on Catholic Bishop of Chicago v. Kingery, 371 Ill. 257, 20 N.E.2d 583 (1939), where the Illinois court stated: " * * * [S]uch a [Catholic] school, conducted in accordance with the educational requirements established by State educational authorities, is promotive of the general welfare." These would seem to be the better reasoned cases. It may be argued, among other things, that private schools, in this day of overcrowded public schools, serve a useful public purpose. But most important, where is the public interest served under the police power when public schools and private elementary schools are permitted in an area but private high schools are denied admittance? To compress the exclusion of private high schools within the power to regulate for the health, safety, morals and welfare of the community, within such a context, is to strain at a gnat and develop a mental hernia in the process. See Annot., 74 A.L.R.3d 14 (1976).

The Michigan Court of Appeals, in Lutheran High School Ass'n of Greater Detroit v. City of Farmington Hills, 146 Mich.App. 641, 381 N.W.2d 417 (1985), appeal denied 425 Mich. 870 (1986), held that a parochial high school was not immune from the local zoning ordinance and that the city did not act improperly in denying a variance to build a gymnasium (apparently, public high schools are not subject to the zoning ordinance). Also see Cornell University v. Bagnardi, 68 N.Y.2d 583, 510 N.Y.S.2d 861, 503 N.E.2d 509 (1986); Father Ryan High School, Inc. v. City of Oak Hill, 774 S.W.2d 184 (Tenn.App.1988).

2. The Town of Yorktown is an area consisting of fine homes. Its zoning permitted public elementary and high schools and private and parochial elementary and high schools. A school was defined as an institution "offering a comprehensive curriculum of study similar to that of a public school." Also permitted were accessory uses customarily incidental and subordinate to school use. Wiltwyck School for Boys is financed by public and private funds. It accepts free of charge about 100 delinquent, maladjust-

ed or emotionally disturbed boys between ages 8 and 12, who are found to have potential for rehabilitation. The boys receive instruction in regular grammar school subjects by teachers employed by the City of New York. In addition, the school has a many faceted program of other activities—singing, sports, art, counseling, etc. After Wiltwyck had purchased 113 acres as a site for a new "school" in Yorktown, the town amended its zoning so as to prohibit any "charitable institution" unless it was using land prior to the date of the amendment. The majority of the appellate division said Wiltwyck was a charitable institution and properly excluded. In an elaborate dissent, Justice Kleinfeld disagreed saying that in his judgment Wiltwyck was a "school" permitted by the ordinance. He also said that if this was not so then the exclusion of Wiltwyck was invalid as being contrary to clearly enunciated state policy: "The town by its * * * Zoning Ordinance, and * * * its officials by their decisions construing it, have effectively thwarted and subverted the State's fundamental public policy to provide for the support and welfare of delinquent and neglected children. For if Yorktown may bar W[iltwyck], so may every other municipality in the State." Wiltwyck School for Boys, Inc. v. Hill, 14 A.D.2d 198, 219 N.Y.S.2d 161 (1961), reversed 11 N.Y.2d 182, 227 N.Y.S.2d 655, 182 N.E.2d 268 (1962). And see an excellent Comment, Zoning Against the Public Welfare: Judicial Limitations on Municipal Parochialism, 71 Yale L.J. 720 (1962).

3.   Schools are not the only use which may involve the validity of a zoning ordinance which distinguishes between publicly owned and privately owned facilities. The issue has also arisen in connection with "recreational" uses. Compare Town of Los Altos Hills v. Adobe Creek Properties, Inc., 32 Cal.App.3d 488, 108 Cal.Rptr. 271 (1973) with Kramer v. Government of the Virgin Islands, 479 F.2d 350 (3d Cir.1973). The two cases, decided the same day, "look" in different directions on the issue. The California intermediate appellate court found a legitimate basis for distinguishing between public and private recreational facilities, while the U.S. Court of Appeals held that a drive-in theater was properly allowed in a "recreational use" zone. Also see Town of Huntington v. Park Shore Country Day Camp of Dix Hills, Inc., 47 N.Y.2d 61, 416 N.Y.S.2d 774, 390 N.E.2d 282 (1979), where the court disallowed a commercial tennis camp in a zone which permitted non-profit recreational facilities.

CHICAGO v. SACHS

Supreme Court of Illinois, 1953.
1 Ill.2d 342, 115 N.E.2d 762.

KLINGBIEL, JUSTICE.   The city of Chicago brought a quasi-criminal proceeding in the municipal court of Chicago against Rogers Park Playschool, Inc., charging that it violated the Municipal Code in operating a prekindergarten play school in an area zoned as an apartment-house district. The court found defendant guilty, and imposed a fine of $100. Defendant appeals directly to this court, the trial court having certified that the validity of an ordinance is involved.

Defendant's school accepts children between three and five years of age, and has an enrollment of approximately thirty. Five instructors are employed, and the children are taught and guided in the use of materials, and in music, art and group activities. The school is located in an area designated as an apartment-house district. Under the terms of the ordinance, uses permissible in such districts include grade or high school, apartment house, boarding or lodging house, hotel, hospital, home for dependents or nursing home, boarding school, vocational school, college or university, club, fraternity or sorority house, and a number of other specified uses. A prekindergarten or nursery school is not explicitly mentioned in the ordinance, however, and plaintiff contends that since it is not the kind of school expressly permitted under the ordinance the judgment of the municipal court must be affirmed. Defendant insists, first, that as the ordinance allows grade schools it should be construed to permit, by implication, nursery schools as well. It is secondly urged that if the use of the premises for such purpose is not permissible under the zoning ordinance the latter is unreasonable, arbitrary and void.

Examination of the ordinance reveals that it expressly lists the sole uses to which property in the area may be devoted. It goes into much detail and was apparently intended to be specific. We cannot conclude, therefore, that a use not specified is nevertheless permitted by implication. Nor does a nursery school, or prekindergarten school, fall within the commonly understood meaning of the term "grade school." The accepted definition of grade school is "A school divided into successive grades" (Webster's New International Dictionary, 2nd ed.) and defendant's school is not so divided.

The remaining issue, therefore, is whether the ordinance is applied to the use in question is arbitrary, unreasonable and void. Cities have the power, through proper zoning ordinances, to impose reasonable restraints upon the use of private property. But in exercising such power they must employ classifications which bear a substantial relation to the public health, safety, or welfare. If such a relationship is not present the ordinance will be declared invalid. Catholic Bishop of Chicago v. Kingery, 371 Ill. 257, 20 N.E.2d 583. Even though a zoning ordinance might well be valid in its general aspects, it may, when applied to a particular piece of property and a particular set of acts, to be so arbitrary and unreasonable as to result in confiscation of the property. Johnson v. Village of Villa Park, 370 Ill. 272, 18 N.E.2d 887. In cases of that kind the ordinance, as applied to the designated real estate, is void. Such is the situation in the case at bar. Under this ordinance defendant's property might be used for a grade school, high school, boarding school, vocational school, college, or university. We fail to see how a prekindergarten or nursery school is more detrimental to public health, safety, or welfare than is a grade school, for example, or, indeed, how it can be considered objectionable at all in an apartment-house district. In any event, the possibility of noise and disturbance, suggested in plaintiff's brief, would be equally present in the operation of other schools permitted by the ordinance, and cannot afford any basis for a difference of treatment.

We have recently observed that a zoning ordinance cannot "effect an arbitrary discrimination against the class on which it operates by omitting from its coverage persons and objects similarly situated. Statutory classifications can only be sustained where there are real differences between the classes, and where the selection of the particular class, as distinguished from others, is reasonably related to the evils to be remedied by the statute or ordinance." Ronda Realty Corp. v. Lawton, 414 Ill. 313, 111 N.E.2d 310, 312. Similarly, an ordinance cannot be sustained which permits designated uses of property while excluding other uses not significantly different. As applied to defendant's property under the present circumstances, the ordinance is capricious and unreasonable, and is therefore invalid.

The judgment of the municipal court of Chicago is reversed.

SEIDITA v. BOARD OF ZONING APPEALS OF CITY OF SCRANTON

Commonwealth Court of Pennsylvania, 1979.
41 Pa.Cmwlth. 340, 399 A.2d 156.

MacPHAIL, JUDGE.

Christoforo A. Seidita applied to the Zoning Board of the City of Scranton (Board) for a special exception to use certain premises as a day care center for young children. The Board denied Seidita's application. Seidita appealed to the Court of Common Pleas of Lackawanna County, which, without taking further testimony, held that the Board's denial of the special exception constituted "an indefensible abuse of discretion and an error of law." The Court also held that Seidita was entitled to the exception unless there was persuasive proof that the health, safety and morals of the community would be affected. Finding no such proof, the Court reversed the Board.

* * *

The premises in question lie in an R–2 residential district under the terms of the zoning ordinance in question. There is no doubt that the intended use of the premises is not a "permitted use" in R–2 districts. Seidita claims that the intended use is a special use exception within the ordinance's definition of "appropriate public uses." That term is defined as follows:

> "*Use Class 17. Appropriate Public Uses.* Includes public and quasi-public uses of a welfare, educational, religious, recreation and cultural nature, and dormitories, fraternities, and religious homes accessory to such uses, radio and television transmission or receiving towers; and essential public utilities that require enclosure within a building, except for telephone central office buildings and telephone booths.

> "Such Public Uses permitted by the Board as a Special Use shall be appropriate to the character of the District in which it is proposed and to the area which it will serve. Such appropriate Public Uses shall have adequate access, shall provide off-street parking and

loading as specified in section 6.100, shall provide necessary land-scaping and screening to protect adjoining areas, and shall comply with the following lot, yard and building regulations. * * * "

"Appropriate public uses" are permitted in all of the zoning districts under the terms of the ordinance. Seidita contends, and the lower court found, that the proposed children's day care center is an "appropriate public use."

The Board and James Douglass (Appellants) contend that the Board's refusal to grant the special exception was correct. They point to the fact that "use class 12" of the ordinance specifically provides for "nurseries for the day care of young children" as a special use in R–3 districts but not in R–2 districts. In School Lane Hills, Inc. v. East Hempfield Township Zoning Hearing Board, 18 Pa.Cmwlth. 519, 336 A.2d 901 (1975), we considered a similar problem. In that case the landowners wanted to use a part of their premises as a rehabilitation center under "an appropriate public use" exception set forth in the township zoning ordinance. While we agreed that a rehabilitation center may very well promote the "welfare" of a community, we held that since a rehabilitation center also fits the definition of a "sanitarium," which in turn is a "hospital" (a use not allowed by right or by way of special exception in the district where the use was proposed), the court below was precluded from finding that "hospitals" were intended to fall within the scope of "appropriate public uses." Accordingly, we found that a rehabilitation center could not be permitted as a special use. We are of the opinion that that decision controls the instant case. Even if the day care center fits the definition of an "appropriate public use," neither the Board nor this Court could permit it in an R–2 district, since provision is made for such use as a special exception in R–3 districts (but not in R–2 districts).

We find no merit in Seidita's argument that there is some distinction between a "day care center for young children" and "nurseries for the day care of young children." Webster's New Collegiate Dictionary (1976) defines "nursery" as "a place where children are temporarily cared for in their parent's absence." This definition accurately describes Seidita's proposed day care center.

In summary, we find no abuse of discretion and no error of law by the Board. Accordingly, the order of the Court of Common Pleas of Lackawanna County must be reversed.

* * *

CRUMLISH, JR., JUDGE, dissenting.

I respectfully dissent.

I would affirm the trial court's decision to order the zoning board to issue a special use permit to Appellee for a Children's Day Care Center. A careful scrutiny of the City of Scranton's zoning ordinance leads me to the inescapable conclusion that such a proposed use is permissible as an appropriate public use under Use Class 17 of the ordinance. In my opinion, the operation of a day care center fits precisely within the permissible uses set forth under Use Class 17 which "includes public and quasi-public uses of a welfare, educational * * * nature." The ordinance's further requirement that such public uses be "appropriate to the character of the District in which it is proposed" is clearly satisfied in the instant case since the record reveals that the building Appellee proposes to use as a day care center was originally constructed by the Scranton School District and used as a public school for over 50 years and thereafter as a parochial school for many years. The recommendation of the City Planning Commission that Appellee's application for a special use permit be granted lends further support to my belief that the proposed use complies with the standards of the ordinance and would not adversely affect the character of the community.

While I wholeheartedly agree with the trial court's concern that the zoning board's decision denying Appellee's request is an unwarranted and unreasonable intermeddling with his ownership of the property, I am more deeply concerned with the ramifications of today's decision upon a modern society where day care centers provide an essential and needed public service to a parent who, because of outside controlling influences, is obliged to work so that he or she may adequately support and rear his or her family in a manner which will improve a much needed and too-often ignored obligation. The quality of Appellee's service would be guaranteed by the Department of Public Welfare whose approval and licensure would be a prerequisite for operation. I believe the Board's denial of Appellee's special use permit was properly held to have been an abuse of discretion.

Notes

1. Compare with the principal case Kern v. Zoning Hearing Bd. of Twp. of Tredyffrin, 68 Pa.Cmwlth. 396, 449 A.2d 781 (1982). Also see Cohen v. City of Des Plaines, 742 F.Supp. 458 (N.D.Ill.1990), where day care centers were allowed to operate in church buildings but not elsewhere; the court found a denial of equal protection and an establishment clause violation. The Seventh Circuit reversed, 8 F.3d 484 (1993), cert. denied 512 U.S. 1236, 114 S.Ct. 2741, 129 L.Ed.2d 861 (1994). In City of Little Rock v. Infant–Toddler Montessori School, Inc., 270 Ark. 697, 606 S.W.2d 743 (1980), the Arkansas Supreme Court reversed a lower court finding that a proposed Montessori school for children one to three years in age was an "educational institution with curriculum equivalent to a public elementary school" which could locate as a matter of right under the zoning ordinance in the single-family district. The majority opinion stated: "The ages and accompanying capabilities of children as young as one year old are also evidence that the curriculum does not rise to the level of public elementary education." A dissenting opinion disagreed: "The Infant–Toddler Montessori School has a curriculum which includes instruction in language development, math, science, geography, botany, zoology, reading, and motor development. * * * The educational structure and method used are comparable to those of the beginning grades of the public elementary schools." Compare Hartman v. City of Columbia, 268 S.C. 44, 232 S.E.2d 15 (1977), where the court found a

day care center to be the equivalent of a school. Accord: City of Richmond Heights v. Richmond Heights Presbyterian Church, 764 S.W.2d 647 (Mo. banc 1989).

2. In DeSisto College, Inc. v. Town of Howey–In–The–Hills, 706 F.Supp. 1479 (M.D.Fla.1989), the court held that a college for learning disabled students was not a school within the meaning of the zoning ordinance. Compare Visionquest National, Ltd. v. Pima County Bd. of Adj. Dist. No. 1, 146 Ariz. 103, 703 P.2d 1252 (App.1985), where the court held that a facility for juvenile offenders on a ranch was a private school. But see Visionquest National, Ltd. v. Board of Supervisors of Honey Brook Twp., 524 Pa. 107, 569 A.2d 915 (1990).

3. Residential zoning permits "public and parochial schools." A missionary seminary was held not to be a "school" within the meaning of this ordinance. Only grammar and high schools to serve residents of the neighboring area were intended. Yanow v. Seven Oaks Park Inc., 11 N.J. 341, 94 A.2d 482, 36 A.L.R.2d 639 (1953). Is this justified? How does it correspond to the reasoning in the above cases?

4. See In re O'Hara's Appeal, 389 Pa. 35, 131 A.2d 587 (1957), where a Roman Catholic high school to serve 1,200 to 1,600 pupils was ordered into a fine residential area by a court holding that denial of a special use permit was arbitrary and unreasonable.

5. For a note on preschools, day schools and summer camps, see Annot., 64 A.L.R.3d 1087 (1975). And consider Langbein v. Board of Zoning Appeals, 135 Conn. 575, 67 A.2d 5 (1949). A zoning ordinance permitted "schools" in a residential district. Mr. Borman applied for a permit to operate a summer day "school" for boys and girls between 5 and 14 years of age. Proposed activities included swimming, arts, crafts, boating, hiking, basketball, volleyball, softball, tetherball, badminton, horseshoes, story telling, photography, croquet, fishing and free play. The Connecticut court said Mr. Borman was entitled to a permit under the ordinance. Also see Mandelstam v. City Com'n of South Miami, 539 So.2d 1139 (Fla.App.1988) (gymnastics school).

6. In Church of God of Louisiana, Inc. v. Monroe–Ouachita Regional Planning Comm'n, 404 F.Supp. 175 (W.D.La.1975), the court found denial of a special exception for a day-care center to be operated by a black church to be racially discriminatory and found no compelling governmental interest to justify the discrimination.

I. HOUSING DISCRIMINATION

(1) Racial Exclusion

UNITED STATES v. CITY OF BLACK JACK, MISSOURI

United States Court of Appeals, Eighth Circuit, 1974.
508 F.2d 1179, certiorari denied 422 U.S. 1042,
95 S.Ct. 2656, 45 L.Ed.2d 694 (1975).

[In 1970 the Black Jack area was unincorporated, and was under the St. Louis County master plan. The plan designated 67 acres for multi-family housing, only 15 of which had been developed. In 1969, the Inter–Religious Center for Urban Affairs obtained an option on 12 acres for the purpose of creating housing for low and moderate income persons living in economically depressed and deteriorated areas of St. Louis. In 1970, the area residents succeeded in having Black Jack incorporated as a city. After its incorporation, an ordinance was passed prohibiting the construction of any new multiple-family dwellings and making existing ones nonconforming uses. The United States brought an action to enjoin enforcement of the ordinance under Title VIII of the Civil Rights Act of 1968, 42 U.S.C.A. § 3601 et seq. The District Court held the plaintiff had failed to establish a racially discriminatory purpose or effect and it dismissed the case. Further facts appear in the opinion.]

HEANEY, CIRCUIT JUDGE.

* * *

The racial composition of Black Jack and the surrounding area was set forth by the District Court in its opinion, and is not contested by the parties:

"Statistical information submitted shows that at the relevant time the area which is now the City of Black Jack was virtually all white, with a black population of between 1% and 2%. The area of St. Louis County north of Interstate Highway 270, which includes Black Jack, is approximately 99% white. * * *

"The virtually all-white character of Black Jack was in marked contrast to the racial composition of other parts of the St. Louis area. In 1970, the pupil population of the City of St. Louis School District was 65.6% black. * * * In 1970, the Kinloch School District, which is only two miles from the nearest boundary of the Hazelwood School District [of which Black Jack is a part], had 1,245 students, all of whom were black.

"The percentage of blacks in St. Louis County has increased only slightly overall from 4.1% in 1950 to 4.8% in 1970. During the same period, the percentage of blacks in the City of St. Louis more than doubled from 17.9% to 40.9%.

"Between 1950 and 1970, the population of the city declined * * * [by] 27%, while the population of the county more than doubled * * *. From 1960 to 1970, there were approximately 102,-298 new housing starts in the county, and 15,348 in the city, a ratio of almost 7 to 1. During the same period, the city had a net decrease of 24,548 housing units, while the county had a net increase of 84,169. * * *

"The concentration of blacks in the city and in pockets in the county is accompanied by the confinement of a disproportionate number of them in overcrowded or substandard accommodations. The 1970 census reveals that in St. Louis city and county approximately 40% of the black families, as compared with 14% of the white families, lived in overcrowded units. * * * "

United States v. City of Black Jack, Missouri, supra, 372 F.Supp. at 325.

The District Court further found that the average cost of a home in the City of Black Jack in 1970 was approximately $30,000, and that the average income of Black Jack families is approximately $15,000 per year. It found that Park View Heights was designed to meet the housing needs of families making between $5,528 and $10,143 per year.

* * *

We turn then to the merits of the decision below. Congress has declared that the purpose of the Fair Housing Act of 1968 is "to provide, within constitutional limitations, for fair housing throughout the United States." 42 U.S.C.A. § 3601. The Act was passed pursuant to congressional power under the Thirteenth Amendment to eliminate the badges and incidents of slavery. In construing the Civil Rights Act of 1866, also founded on that power, the Supreme Court has declared that

> * * * when racial discrimination herds men into ghettos and makes their ability to buy property turn on the color of their skin, then it too is a relic of slavery.

Jones v. Mayer Co., 392 U.S. 409, 442–443, 88 S.Ct. 2186, 2205, 20 L.Ed.2d 1189 (1968).

Title VIII is designed to prohibit "all forms of discrimination, sophisticated as well as simple-minded." Williams v. Matthews Co., 499 F.2d 819, 826 (8th Cir.1974). Just as Congress requires

> * * * the removal of artificial, arbitrary, and unnecessary barriers to employment when the barriers operate invidiously to discriminate on the basis of racial or other impermissible classification[,]

Griggs v. Duke Power Co., 401 U.S. 424, 430–431, 91 S.Ct. 849, 853, 28 L.Ed.2d 158 (1971), such barriers must also give way in the field of housing. The discretion of local zoning officials, recently recognized in Village of Belle Terre v. Boraas, 416 U.S. 1, 94 S.Ct. 1536, 39 L.Ed.2d 797 (1974), must be curbed where "the clear result of such discretion is the segregation of low-income Blacks from all White neighborhoods." Danks v. Pork, 341 F.Supp. 1175, 1180 (N.D.Ohio, 1972), aff'd in part & rev'd in part without opinion, 473 F.2d 910 (6th Cir.1973).

The burden of proof in Title VIII cases is governed by the concept of the "prima facie case." Williams v. Matthews Co., supra 499 F.2d at 826. To establish a prima facie case of racial discrimination, the plaintiff need prove no more than that the conduct of the defendant actually or predictably results in racial discrimination; in other words, that it has a discriminatory effect. See id.; United Farmworkers of Florida Housing Project, Inc. v. City of Delray Beach, 493 F.2d 799, 808 (5th Cir.1974); Hawkins v. Town of Shaw, Mississippi, 461 F.2d 1171, 1172 (5th Cir. 1972) (en banc); Kennedy Park Homes Ass'n v. City of Lackawanna, supra 436 F.2d at 114; Dailey v. City of Lawton, Oklahoma, 425 F.2d 1037, 1039 (10th Cir.1970); Norwalk CORE v. Norwalk Redevelopment Agency, 395 F.2d 920, 931 (2d Cir.1968). The plaintiff need make no showing whatsoever that the action resulting in racial discrimination in housing was racially motivated.[27] See Williams v. Matthews Co., supra 499 F.2d at 826; United Farmworkers of Florida Housing Project, Inc. v. City of Delray Beach, supra 493 F.2d at 808; Kennedy Park Homes Ass'n v. City of Lackawanna, supra 436 F.2d at 114; Citizens Committee for Faraday Wood v. Lindsay, supra 362 F.Supp. at 658; Banks v. Park, supra 341 F.Supp. at 1180. Effect, and not motivation, is the touchstone, in part because clever men may easily conceal their motivations, but more importantly, because

> * * * [w]hatever our law was once, * * * we now firmly recognize that the arbitrary quality of thoughtlessness can be as disastrous and unfair to private rights and the public interest as the perversity of a willful scheme.

Hobson v. Hansen, 269 F.Supp. 401, 497 (D.D.C.1967), aff'd sub nom. Smuck v. Hobson, 132 U.S.App.D.C. 372, 408 F.2d 175 (1969) (en banc).

Once the plaintiff has established a prima facie case by demonstrating racially discriminatory effect, the burden shifts to the governmental defendant to demonstrate that its conduct was necessary to promote a compelling governmental interest.

Must be compelling St. interest

The District Court concluded that the ordinance had no discriminatory effect. It based this conclusion on its finding that, because Park View Heights was designed to meet the needs of families earning between $5,000 and $10,000 per year—a class including 32 percent of the black population in the metropolitan area and 29 percent of the white population—the ordinance had no measurably greater effect on blacks than on whites. The court's conclusion was in error. It failed to take into account either the "ultimate effect" or the "historical context" of the City's action. See United Farmworkers of Florida Housing Project, Inc. v. City of Delray Beach, supra 493 F.2d at 810; Kennedy Park Homes Ass'n v. City of Lackawanna, supra 436 F.2d at 112. The ultimate effect of the ordinance was to foreclose 85 percent of the blacks living in the metropolitan area from obtaining housing in Black Jack, and to foreclose

27. The United States contends that the ordinance ought also be enjoined because it was enacted for the purpose of excluding blacks. There is evidence in the record to support that contention. Opposition to Park View Heights was repeatedly expressed in racial terms by persons whom the District Court found to be the leaders of the incorporation movement, by individuals circulating petitions, and by zoning commissioners themselves. Racial criticism of Park View Heights was made and cheered at public meetings. The uncontradicted evidence indicates that, at all levels of opposition, race placed a significant role, both in the drive to incorporate and the decision to rezone. We agree with the Tenth Circuit's conclusion that improper purpose may be shown circumstantially:

* * * If proof of a civil right violation depends on an open statement by an official of an intent to discriminate, the Fourteenth Amendment offers little solace to those seeking its protection. In our opinion it is enough for the complaining parties to show that the local officials are effectuating the discriminatory designs of private individuals. * * *

Dailey v. City of Lawton, 425 F.2d 1037, 1039 (10th Cir.1970).

Nevertheless, we do not base our conclusion that the Black Jack ordinance violates Title VIII on a finding that there was an improper purpose.

them at a time when 40 percent of them were living in substandard or overcrowded units.

The discriminatory effect of the ordinance is more onerous when assessed in light of the fact that segregated housing in the St. Louis metropolitan area was

> * * * in large measure the result of deliberate racial discrimination in the housing market by the real estate industry and by agencies of the federal, state, and local governments. * * *

United States v. City of Black Jack, Missouri, supra 372 F.Supp. at 326.

Black Jack's action is but one more factor confining blacks to low-income housing in the center city, confirming the inexorable process whereby the St. Louis metropolitan area becomes one that "has the racial shape of a donut, with the Negroes in the hole and with mostly Whites occupying the ring." Mahaley v. Cuyahoga Metropolitan Housing Authority, 355 F.Supp. 1257, 1260 (N.D.Ohio, 1973), rev'd, 500 F.2d 1087 (6th Cir.1974). See also Crow v. Brown, 332 F.Supp. 382, 384 (N.D.Ga., 1971), aff'd per curiam, 457 F.2d 788 (5th Cir.1972). Park View Heights was particularly designed to contribute to the prevention of this prospect so antithetical to the Fair Housing Act. The Board of Directors of the Park View Housing Corporation was one-half white and one-half black. Affirmative measures were planned to assure that members of the black community would be aware of the opportunity to live in Park View Heights. There was ample proof that many blacks would live in the development, and that the exclusion of the townhouses would contribute to the perpetuation of segregation in a community which was 99 percent white.

It having been established that the ordinance had a discriminatory effect, it follows that the United States had made out a prima facie case under Title VIII, and the burden shifted to the City to demonstrate that a compelling governmental interest was furthered by that ordinance. We turn to that question. The City asserted primarily the following governmental interests to justify the ban on further apartments:

Cities response →

(1) Road and traffic control;

(2) Prevention of overcrowding of schools;

(3) Prevention of devaluation of adjacent single-family homes.

Several other interests were also alluded to in the record, including exclusion of apartments where there were already too many and where there was no need for them.

In determining whether any of these rise to the level of a compelling governmental interest, we must examine: first, whether the ordinance in fact furthers the governmental interest asserted; second, whether the public interest served by the ordinance is constitutionally permissible[28]

---

28. This portion of the analysis is essentially a qualitative one. For example, Shapiro v. Thompson, supra 394 U.S. at 629–631, 89 S.Ct. 1322, 22 L.Ed.2d 600, held that it was constitutionally impermissible for a state to inhibit migration by needy persons

and is substantial enough to outweigh the private detriment caused by it;[29] and third, whether less drastic means are available whereby the stated governmental interest may be attained. See Shapiro v. Thompson, 394 U.S. 618, 637, 89 S.Ct. 1322, 22 L.Ed.2d 600 (1969); Note, Exclusionary Zoning and Equal Protection, 84 Harv.L.Rev. 1645, 1651 (1971).

We need not go beyond the first step in the inquiry, for we find that there is no factual basis for the assertion that any one of the three primary interests asserted by the City is in fact furthered by the zoning ordinance, and we find that the other asserted interests—at least on the facts of this case—are clearly not substantial in relation to the housing opportunities foreclosed. To paraphrase the Supreme Court in Shapiro v. Thompson, supra at 638, 89 S.Ct. 1322, we conclude that the City does not use and has no need to use the ordinance for the governmental purposes suggested.

* * *

We hold that Zoning Ordinance No. 12 of the City of Black Jack violates Title VIII, because it denies persons housing on the basis of race, in violation of § 3604(a), and interferes with the exercise of the right to equal housing opportunity, in violation of § 3617. The remedy for this violation of the Fair Housing Act is provided in § 3615:

> * * * any law of a State, a political subdivision, or other such jurisdiction that purports to require or permit any action that would be a discriminatory housing practice under this subchapter shall to that extent be invalid.

We, therefore, reverse and remand with instructions to the District Court to enter a permanent injunction upon receipt of this Court's order, enjoining the enforcement of the ordinance. The mandate of this Court shall be issued forthwith.

Reversed and remanded.

Note

The sponsors of the project in the principal case also sued the City of Black Jack. In Park View Heights Corp. v. City of Black Jack, 467 F.2d 1208 (8th Cir.1972) (pre-dating the principal case), the court found the zoning ordinance to be exclusionary, ordered reclassification of all land zoned for multi-family use prior to the offending ordinance to a multi-family designation, ordered affirmative action to permit the construction of the particular project, and, after the principal case, approved a consent settlement of $450,000 damages. The affirmative action portion of the decree was further

---

into the state, because such migration was a constitutional right. That case further held that limiting payment of welfare benefits to those who had "contributed" to the state in the past through taxes was constitutionally impermissible. Id. at 633, 89 S.Ct. 1322.

29. This portion of the analysis is essentially quantitative. For example, preservation of the public peace and welfare by avoiding racial conflict was held insufficient to validate a zoning ordinance restricting racial integration in Buchanan v. Warley, 245 U.S. 60, 38 S.Ct. 16, 62 L.Ed. 149 (1917).

litigated, and in Park View Heights Corp. v. City of Black Jack, 454 F.Supp. 1223 (E.D.Mo.1978), the district court denied injunctive relief requiring the city to ensure construction of the project and additional damages because the project had become economically infeasible due to inflation and new property standards established by HUD. The Eighth Circuit Court of Appeals reversed, 605 F.2d 1033 (8th Cir.1979), holding that notwithstanding the earlier damage settlement and the present economic infeasibility of the project, the city is subject to a continuing, enforceable duty to affirmatively promote moderately priced, interracial housing equivalent to that which would have been built but for the racially discriminatory zoning. In February, 1982, a consent decree was entered which permanently enjoins the city from engaging in discriminatory actions depriving persons of equal access to housing. At one point during the protracted Black Jack litigation, a local woman with a large number of children ran for mayor, campaigning in Ku Klux Klan regalia; she lost in the primary.

VILLAGE OF ARLINGTON HEIGHTS v. METROPOLITAN HOUSING DEVELOPMENT CORP.

Supreme Court of the United States, 1977.
429 U.S. 252, 97 S.Ct. 555, 50 L.Ed.2d 450.

Mr. Justice Powell delivered the opinion of the Court.

In 1971 respondent Metropolitan Housing Development Corporation (MHDC) applied to petitioner, the Village of Arlington Heights, Ill., for the rezoning of a 15-acre parcel from single-family to multiple-family classification. Using federal financial assistance, MHDC planned to build 190 clustered townhouse units for low-and moderate-income tenants. The Village denied the rezoning request. MHDC, joined by other plaintiffs who are also respondents here, brought suit in the United States District Court for the Northern District of Illinois. They alleged that the denial was racially discriminatory and that it violated, *inter alia,* the Fourteenth Amendment and the Fair Housing Act of 1968, 82 Stat. 81, 42 U.S.C.A. § 3601 et seq. Following a bench trial, the District Court entered judgment for the Village, 373 F.Supp. 208 (1974), and respondents appealed. The Court of Appeals for the Seventh Circuit reversed, finding that the "ultimate effect" of the denial was racially discriminatory, and that the refusal to rezone therefore violated the Fourteenth Amendment. 517 F.2d 409 (1975). We granted the Village's petition for certiorari, 423 U.S. 1030, 96 S.Ct. 560, 46 L.Ed.2d 404 (1975), and now reverse.

* * *

The planned development did not conform to the Village's zoning ordinance and could not be built unless Arlington Heights rezoned the parcel to R-5, its multiple-family housing classification. Accordingly, MHDC filed with the Village Plan Commission a petition for rezoning, accompanied by supporting materials describing the development and specifying that it would be subsidized under § 236. The materials made clear that one requirement under § 236 is an affirmative marketing plan designed to assure that a subsidized development is racially integrated. MHDC also submitted studies demonstrating the need for housing of this type and analyzing the probable impact of the development. To prepare for the hearings before the Plan Commission and to assure compliance with the Village building code, fire regulations, and related requirements, MHDC consulted with the Village staff for preliminary review of the development. The parties have stipulated that every change recommended during such consultations was incorporated into the plans.

During the spring of 1971, the Plan Commission considered the proposal at a series of three public meetings, which drew large crowds. Although many of those attending were quite vocal and demonstrative in opposition to Lincoln Green, a number of individuals and representatives of community groups spoke in support of rezoning. Some of the comments, both from opponents and supporters, addressed what was referred to as the "social issue"—the desirability or undesirability of introducing at this location in Arlington Heights low-and moderate-income housing, housing that would probably be racially integrated.

Many of the opponents, however, focused on the zoning aspects of the petition, stressing two arguments. First, the area always had been zoned single-family, and the neighboring citizens had built or purchased there in reliance on that classification. Rezoning threatened to cause a measurable drop in property value for neighboring sites. Second, the Village's apartment policy, adopted by the Village Board in 1962 and amended in 1970, called for R–5 zoning primarily to serve as a buffer between single-family development and land uses thought incompatible, such as commercial or manufacturing districts. Lincoln Green did not meet this requirement, as it adjoined no commercial or manufacturing district.

At the close of the third meeting, the Plan Commission adopted a motion to recommend to the Village's Board of Trustees that it deny the request. The motion stated: "While the need for low and moderate income housing may exist in Arlington Heights or its environs, the Plan Commission would be derelict in recommending it at the proposed location." Two members voted against the motion and submitted a minority report, stressing that in their view the change to accommodate Lincoln Green represented "good zoning." The Village Board met on September 28, 1971, to consider MHDC's request and the recommendation of the Plan Commission. After a public hearing, the Board denied the rezoning by a 6–1 vote.

* * *

[The Seventh Circuit Court of Appeals] first approved the District Court's finding that the defendants were motivated by a concern for the integrity of the zoning plan, rather than by racial discrimination. Deciding whether their refusal to rezone would have discriminatory effects was more complex. The court observed that the refusal would have a disproportionate impact on blacks. Based upon family income, blacks constituted 40% of those Chicago area residents who were eligible to become tenants of Lincoln Green, although they composed a far lower percentage of total area population. The court reasoned, however, that under our decision in James v. Valtierra, 402 U.S. 137, 91 S.Ct. 1331, 28 L.Ed.2d 678 (1971), such a disparity in racial impact alone does not call for strict scrutiny of a municipality's decision that prevents the construction of the low-cost housing.

There was another level to the court's analysis of allegedly discriminatory results. Invoking language from Kennedy Park Homes Assn. v. City of Lackawanna, 436 F.2d 108, 112 (C.A.2 1970), cert. denied, 401 U.S. 1010, 91 S.Ct. 1256 (1971), the Court of Appeals ruled that the denial of rezoning must be examined in light of its "historical context and ultimate effect." 517 F.2d, at 413. Northwest Cook County was enjoying rapid growth in employment opportunities and population, but it continued to exhibit a high degree of residential segregation. The court held that Arlington Heights could not simply ignore this problem. Indeed, it found that the Village had been "exploiting" the situation by allowing itself to become a nearly all-white community. Id., at 414. The Village had no other current plans for building low-and moderate-income housing, and no other R–5 parcels in the Village were available to MHDC at an economically feasible price.

Against this background, the Court of Appeals ruled that the denial of the Lincoln Green proposal had racially discriminatory effects and could be tolerated only if it served compelling interests. Neither the buffer policy nor the desire to protect property values met this exacting standard. The court therefore concluded that the denial violated the Equal Protection Clause of the Fourteenth Amendment.

* * *

Our decision last Term in Washington v. Davis, 426 U.S. 229, 96 S.Ct. 2040, 48 L.Ed.2d 597 (1976), made it clear that official action will not be held unconstitutional solely because it results in a racially disproportionate impact. "Disproportionate impact is not irrelevant, but it is not the sole touchstone of an invidious racial discrimination." Id., at 242. Proof of racially discriminatory intent or purpose is required to show a violation of the Equal Protection Clause. * * *

* * * In making its findings on this issue, the District Court noted that some of the opponents of Lincoln Green who spoke at the various hearings might have been motivated by opposition to minority groups. The court held, however, that the evidence "does not warrant the conclusion that this motivated the defendants." 373 F.Supp., at 211.

On appeal the Court of Appeals focused primarily on respondents' claim that the Village's buffer policy had not been consistently applied and was being invoked with a strictness here that could only demonstrate some other underlying motive. The court concluded that the buffer policy, though not always applied with perfect consistency, had on several occasions formed the basis for the Board's decision to deny other rezoning proposals. "The evidence does not necessitate a finding that Arlington Heights administered this policy in a discriminatory manner." 517 F.2d, at 412. The Court of Appeals therefore approved the District Court's findings concerning the Village's purposes in denying rezoning to MHDC.

We also have reviewed the evidence. The impact of the Village's decision does arguably bear more heavily on racial minorities. Minorities constitute 18% of the Chicago area population, and 40% of the income groups said to be eligible for Lincoln Green. But there is little about the sequence of events leading up to the decision that would spark suspicion. The area around the Viatorian property has been zoned R–3 since 1959, the year when Arlington Heights first adopted a zoning map. Single-family homes surround the 80–acre site, and the Village is undeniably committed to single-family homes as its dominant residential land use. The rezoning request progressed according to the usual procedures. The Plan Commission even scheduled two additional hearings, at least in part to accommodate MHDC and permit it to supplement its presentation with answers to questions generated at the first hearing.

The statements by the Plan Commission and Village Board members, as reflected in the official minutes, focused almost exclusively on the zoning aspects of the MHDC petition, and the zoning factors on which they relied are not novel criteria in the Village's rezoning decisions. There is no reason to doubt that there has been reliance by some neighboring property owners on the maintenance of single-family zoning in the vicinity. The Village originally adopted its buffer policy long before MHDC entered the picture and has applied the policy too consistently for us to infer discriminatory purpose from its application in this case. Finally, MHDC called one member of the Village Board to the stand at trial. Nothing in her testimony supports an inference of invidious purpose.

In sum, the evidence does not warrant overturning the concurrent findings of both courts below. Respondents simply failed to carry their burden of proving that discriminatory purpose was a motivating factor in the Village's decision. This conclusion ends the constitutional inquiry. The Court of Appeals' further finding that the Village's decision carried a discriminatory "ultimate effect" is without independent constitutional significance.

Respondents' complaint also alleged that the refusal to rezone violated the Fair Housing Act of 1968, 42 U.S.C.A. § 3601 et seq. They continue to urge here that a zoning decision made by a public body may, and that petitioners' action did, violate § 3604 or § 3617. The Court of Appeals, however, proceeding in a somewhat unorthodox fashion, did not decide the statutory question. We remand the case for further consideration of respondents' statutory claims.

Reversed and remanded.

[Concurring and dissenting opinions are omitted.]

Notes

1. See in connection with the preceding cases, Wright, Constitutional Rights and Land Use Planning: The New and the Old Reality, 1977 Duke L.J. 841. Also see United States v. Wagner, 930 F.Supp. 1148 (N.D.Tex. 1996). In this case the federal government sued several homeowners in a subdivision who had filed a lawsuit in state court seeking to prevent a neighbor from selling a house for use as a group home for mentally retarded children. The trial court held that the neighbors violated the Fair Housing Act and awarded damages to the intervening homeowner who had tried to sell for a group home ($7,500 for emotional distress and $8,000 in punitive damages). Also, the attorney for the homeowner was awarded over $46,000 in attorney's fees and expenses for the intervention in the federal suit to establish the FHA violation (he had already been awarded more than $3,500 for defending in the state court lawsuit).

2. The net effect of the Arlington Heights decision was to alert attorneys that a statistical showing of discriminatory impact of land use decisions discouraging subsidized multi-family housing would not be enough to invoke the equal protection clause of the Fourteenth Amendment. However, as the Black Jack, Missouri case indicates and as the closing paragraph of Arlington Heights suggests, a statistical presentation might be sufficient to establish a violation of the Fair Housing Act. This distinction was taken up by the Seventh Circuit upon the remand of the Arlington Heights case. In Metropolitan Housing Development Corp. v. Village of Arlington Heights, 558 F.2d 1283 (7th Cir.1977), certiorari denied 434 U.S. 1025, 98 S.Ct. 752, 54 L.Ed.2d 772 (1978), the court held that Arlington Heights had a statutory obligation under the Fair Housing Act to refrain from zoning policies that had the effect of foreclosing construction of low-cost housing within its boundaries. On the issue of what conduct on the part of a city is sufficient to prove a violation of the Fair Housing Act, the court said:

> We turn now to determining under what circumstances conduct that produces a discriminatory impact but which was taken without discriminatory intent will violate section 3604(a). Four critical factors are discernible from previous cases. They are: (1) how strong is the plaintiff's showing of discriminatory effect; (2) is there some evidence of discriminatory intent, though not enough to satisfy the constitutional standard of Washington v. Davis; (3) what is the defendant's interest in taking the action complained of; and (4) does the plaintiff seek to compel the defendant to affirmatively provide housing for members of minority groups or merely to restrain the defendant from interfering with individual property owners who wish to provide such housing. We shall examine each of these factors separately.

> 1. There are two kinds of racially discriminatory effects which a facially neutral decision about housing can produce. The first occurs when that decision has a greater adverse impact on one racial group than on another. The second is the effect which the decision has on the community involved; if it perpetuates segregation and thereby prevents interracial association it will be considered invidious under the Fair Housing Act independently of the extent to which it produces a disparate effect on different racial groups. * * *

The fact that the conduct complained of adversely affected white as well as nonwhite people, however, is not by itself an obstacle to relief under the Fair Housing Act. See United States v. City of Black Jack, 508 F.2d 1179 (8th Cir.1974), cert. denied, 422 U.S. 1042, 95 S.Ct. 2656, 45 L.Ed.2d 694 (1975); Kennedy Park Homes Assoc., Inc. v. City of Lacka-wanna, 436 F.2d 108 (2d Cir.1970), cert. denied, 401 U.S. 1010, 91 S.Ct. 1256, 28 L.Ed.2d 546 (1971). In both of these cases, local zoning ordinances prevented the construction of low-income housing projects which would not have been limited to nonwhite people. Both courts nonetheless found a racially discriminatory effect.

* * *

2. The second factor which appears to have been important in previous Fair Housing Act cases which focused on the discriminatory effect of the defendant's conduct was the presence of some evidence of discriminatory intent. In three cases this evidence was insufficient to independently support the relief which the plaintiff sought. * * * In another case the court found the defendant liable on both a discriminatory intent and a discriminatory impact theory. * * *

These courts did not address the role that evidence of intent ought to play in determining whether liability should be imposed because of discriminatory impact. But it is evident that the equitable argument for relief is stronger when there is some direct evidence that the defendant purposefully discriminated against members of minority groups because that evidence supports the inference that the defendant is a wrongdoer. Thus, the absence of any such evidence in this case is a factor buttressing the Village's contention that relief should be denied.

We conclude, however, that this criterion is the least important of the four factors that we are examining. By hypothesis, we are dealing with a situation in which the evidence of intent constitutes an insufficient basis on which to ground relief. If we were to place great emphasis on partial evidence of purposeful discrimination we would be relying on an inference—that the defendant is a wrongdoer—which is at best conjectural. In addition, the problems associated with requiring conclusive proof of discriminatory intent which we earlier discussed remain troublesome in any attempt to weigh partial evidence of intent.

* * *

3. The third factor which we find to be important is the interest of the defendant in taking the action which produces a discriminatory impact. If the defendant is a private individual or a group of private individuals seeking to protect private rights, the courts cannot be overly solicitous when the effect is to perpetuate segregated housing. * * * Similarly, if the defendant is a governmental body acting outside the scope of its authority or abusing its power, it is not entitled to the deference which courts must pay to legitimate governmental action. * * * On the other hand, if the defendant is a governmental body acting within the ambit of legitimately derived authority, we will less readily find that its action violates the Fair Housing Act. * * *

4. The final criterion which will inform the exercise of our discretion is the nature of the relief which the plaintiff seeks. The courts ought to be more reluctant to grant relief when the plaintiff seeks to compel the defendant to construct integrated housing or take affirmative steps to ensure that integrated housing is built than when the plaintiff is attempting to build integrated housing on his own land and merely seeks to enjoin the defendant from interfering with that construction. To require a defendant to appropriate money, utilize his land for a particular purpose, or take other affirmative steps toward integrated housing is a massive judicial intrusion on private autonomy. By contrast, the courts are far more willing to prohibit even nonintentional action by the state which interferes with an individual's plan to use his own land to provide integrated housing.

The Court of Appeals remanded the case to the District Court. In 1978, MHDC and the Village of Arlington Heights reached a settlement which provided for construction of low-cost housing on an alternate 26 acre site in an unincorporated area abutting the village. A nearby suburb, Mount Prospect, and a civic association sought intervention to protest the approval of a consent decree. The Seventh Circuit upheld the consent decree. Metropolitan Housing Development Corp. v. Village of Arlington Heights, 616 F.2d 1006 (7th Cir.1980). Also see Creek v. Village of Westhaven, 80 F.3d 186 (7th Cir.1996).

The analysis by the Seventh Circuit court has proven to be the prevailing approach, and the Supreme Court apparently adopted the analysis in Town of Huntington, New York v. Huntington Branch, NAACP, 488 U.S. 15, 109 S.Ct. 276, 102 L.Ed.2d 180 (1988) (per curiam opinion).

3. Other important cases involving racially discriminatory zoning practices are Kennedy Park Homes Ass'n v. City of Lackawanna, N.Y., 436 F.2d 108 (2d Cir.1970), certiorari denied 401 U.S. 1010, 91 S.Ct. 1256, 28 L.Ed.2d 546 (1971); Joseph Skillken & Co. v. City of Toledo, 380 F.Supp. 228 (N.D.Ohio 1974), reversed 528 F.2d 867 (6th Cir.1975), vacated and remanded 429 U.S. 1068, 97 S.Ct. 800, 50 L.Ed.2d 786 (1977), after remand 558 F.2d 350 (6th Cir.1977), certiorari denied 434 U.S. 985, 98 S.Ct. 611, 54 L.Ed.2d 479 (1977), rehearing denied 434 U.S. 1051, 98 S.Ct. 904, 54 L.Ed.2d 805 (1978); Resident Advisory Bd. v. Rizzo, 564 F.2d 126 (3d Cir.1977), certiorari denied 435 U.S. 908, 98 S.Ct. 1457, 55 L.Ed.2d 499 (1978); United States v. City of Parma, Ohio, 494 F.Supp. 1049 (N.D.Ohio 1980); United States v. City of Birmingham, 538 F.Supp. 819 (E.D.Mich.1982). Also see Scott v. Greenville County, 716 F.2d 1409 (4th Cir.1983), holding that a developer who was denied a permit to build low-income housing which complied with all existing zoning regulations could sue the county for damages under Section 1983.

4. Is the import of the above cases that no city can make a zoning decision which is unfavorable to a developer of low income housing? May a city defend a negative decision by showing good faith use of traditional zoning principles plus no racially discriminatory motive plus other nearby opportunities for low income housing? For authority that the answer to the first question is no and the answer to the second question is yes, see Confederacion de la Raza Unida v. City of Morgan Hill, 324 F.Supp. 895

(N.D.Cal.1971) and Ybarra v. Town of Los Altos Hills, 503 F.2d 250 (9th Cir.1974). Compare Southern Alameda Spanish Speaking Organization v. City of Union City, California, 424 F.2d 291 (9th Cir.1970).

Obviously, not every impediment placed in the path of the developer of racially integrated, low-income housing is a violation of equal protection or the Fair Housing Act. Not every denial of a building permit or refusal to rezone land for higher density development can be shown to be a case of exclusionary zoning based on race. See Cowart v. City of Ocala, 478 F.Supp. 774 (M.D.Fla.1979), where the developer failed to modify his plan to comply with local ordinances, resulting in official withdrawal of approval of the project and denial of a building permit. Also see Des Vergnes v. Seekonk Water Dist., 601 F.2d 9 (1st Cir.1979), vacated 454 U.S. 807, 102 S.Ct. 81, 70 L.Ed.2d 76 (1981); Angell v. Zinsser, 473 F.Supp. 488 (D.Conn.1979); Lake Bluff Housing Partners v. City of South Milwaukee, 197 Wis.2d 157, 540 N.W.2d 189 (1995). Also see Brandt v. Village of Chebanse, Illinois, 82 F.3d 172 (7th Cir.1996) where the court held that the Fair Housing Act was not applicable to a developer who wanted a variance to build four-unit apartment buildings with the first floor apartments wheelchair accessible. The court noted that developers are required to make apartments accessible to the handicapped:

> So what Brandt proposes to build is essentially the minimum required by federal law. If such a proposal obliges a government to waive its single-family zoning rules, then four (or more) unit buildings can be erected anywhere a developer pleases. Those who find zoning laws unjustifiable limitations on the use of property would be cheered; but it is unlikely that the Fair Housing Act was designed to abolish single-family zoning for all developers who comply with the requirement that first-floor apartments be accessible to handicapped tenants.

5. The Fair Housing Act and the concomitant development of the discriminatory effect doctrine, and the Fourteenth Amendment suit alleging discriminatory intent, are not the only legal remedies available to rectify alleged acts of local officials which result in housing discrimination. A conspiracy theory under 42 U.S.C.A. § 1985(3) was recognized by a federal court in Fralin & Waldron, Inc. v. County of Henrico, Virginia, 474 F.Supp. 1315 (E.D.Va.1979). In that case the developers optioned a tract of land which was zoned to permit medium density residential development. After making extensive preparations to build a low-to moderate-income housing project, the county officials downzoned the land to exclude the type of project that was planned. The plaintiffs asked for injunctive and monetary relief and the court, in denying defendants' motion to dismiss, found sufficient allegations of conspiracy to deny constitutional rights. The court also discussed the extent of immunity which some of the individual defendants might claim under the civil rights statutes.

6. Virtually all the cases litigating the issue of housing discrimination under the Fair Housing Act involve municipal defendants and challenges to land use policies on the ground of their discriminatory intent or discriminatory effect. Does the Fair Housing Act apply to a private landlord who takes some action regarding his property which has the effect of reducing the available housing stock for minority persons within the community? See the

case of Dreher v. Rana Management, Inc., 493 F.Supp. 930 (E.D.N.Y.1980), where tenants sued the landlord under the Fair Housing Act to enjoin conversion of the building into housing for college students. The plaintiffs alleged that 90 percent of the occupants were black and that after conversion 90 percent of the occupants would be white, thus reducing the housing stock available to black persons in the community. The court granted defendants' motion for a summary judgment.

A Note on Gentrification

In many cities the process of gentrification—rehabilitation of buildings in certain neighborhoods which opens housing opportunities to upscale tenants but, at the same time, displaces minorities and lower income residents—has resulted in conflict and litigation. Especially where the gentrifiers obtain government subsidies either by way of HUD grants or rehabilitation tax credits, representatives of the lower income displacees have tried to enjoin the subsidies. The case law in this area is not consistent; often the issue of standing is involved. Also the extent of HUD authority may be in question. City government generally endorses gentrification because it upgrades neighborhoods and fattens the tax base. On the other hand, the potential displacees frequently have some political voice in local government, and some cities have ordinances regulating gentrification. Following are some authorities which address the problems:

1. Law review articles: McDougall, Gentrification: The Class Conflict over Urban Space Moves into the Courts, 10 Fordham Urb.L.J. 177 (1981); LeGates & Hartman, Gentrification–Caused Displacement, 14 The Urban Lawyer 31 (1982); Henig, Neighborhood Response to Gentrification: Conditions of Mobilization, 17 Urb.Affairs Q. 343 (1982); Bryant & McGee, Gentrification and the Law: Combatting Urban Displacement, 25 Wash. U.J.Urb. & Contemp.L. 43 (1983); Cohen, San Francisco's Neighborhood Commercial Special Use District Ordinance: An Innovative Approach to Commercial Gentrification: 13 Golden Gate U.L.Rev. 367 (1983); Marcuse, To Control Gentrification: Anti–Displacement Zoning and Planning for Stable Residential Districts, 13 N.Y.U.Rev. of Law & Social Change 931 (1984); Marcuse, Gentrification, Abandonment, and Displacement: Connections, Causes, and Policy Responses in New York City, 28 Wash.U.J.Urb. & Contemp.L. 195 (1985).

2. Cases which touch on the problem of gentrification: Angell v. Zinsser, 473 F.Supp. 488 (D.Conn.1979); Alschuler v. Department of Housing and Urban Development, 515 F.Supp. 1212 (N.D.Ill.1981), affirmed and remanded 686 F.2d 472 (7th Cir.1982); Business Ass'n of University City v. Landrieu, 660 F.2d 867 (3d Cir.1981); Wicker Park Historic District Preservation Fund v. Pierce, 565 F.Supp. 1066 (N.D.Ill.1982); Munoz–Mendoza v. Pierce, 711 F.2d 421 (1st Cir.1983); NAACP v. Harris, 567 F.Supp. 637 (D.Mass.1983); Sansom Committee v. Lynn, 735 F.2d 1552, 1553 (3d Cir. 1984), cert. denied 469 U.S. 1017, 105 S.Ct. 431, 83 L.Ed.2d 358 (1984); Latinos Unidos De Chelsea v. Secretary of Housing, 799 F.2d 774 (1st Cir.1986).

GAUTREAUX v. CHICAGO HOUSING AUTHORITY

United States Court of Appeals, Seventh Circuit, 1974.
503 F.2d 930, affirmed sub nom. Hills v. Gautreaux, 425
U.S. 284, 96 S.Ct. 1538, 47 L.Ed.2d 792 (1976).

MR. JUSTICE CLARK:[30]

Appellants, black tenants in and applicants for public housing, brought these consolidated cases separately in 1966 against the Chicago Housing Authority (CHA) and the Secretary of Housing and Urban Development (HUD) respectively, charging that CHA had intentionally violated 42 U.S.C.A. § 1981 and § 1982 in maintaining existing patterns of residential separation of races by its tenant assignment and site selection procedures, contrary to the Equal Protection Clause of the Fourteenth Amendment; and that HUD had "assisted in the carrying on * * * of a racially discriminatory public housing system within the City of Chicago" in violation of the Fifth Amendment. Appellants sought an injunction against CHA restraining such practices and requiring CHA to remedy the past effects of its unconstitutional site-selection and tenant-assignment procedures by building any future public housing units in predominantly white areas. This appeal grows out of the decision of the district court on remand for a determination of appropriate relief pursuant to separate findings that both CHA and HUD were responsible for de jure segregation in the public housing program in Chicago. In 1969 the District Court found with the appellants on the merits and since that time has devoted its efforts to effectuating this ruling. After some four years of hearings, several judgment orders and four appeals, the District Court on the last remand called on the parties to propose a "comprehensive plan" to remedy past effects of the public housing segregation indulged in by CHA and HUD, including "alternatives which are not confined in their scope to the geographic boundary of the City of Chicago." HUD proposed, and the District Court, after an evidentiary hearing, ordered a plan under which HUD would "cooperate" with CHA in the latter's efforts to increase the supply of public housing units but eliminated any relief not confined to the geographic boundary of the City of Chicago and refused to impose any specific affirmative obligations upon HUD beyond its "best efforts." 363 F.Supp. 690 (1973). The appellants contend that a metropolitan area remedial plan including housing in suburban areas, as well as those within the limits of Chicago, is necessary to remedy the past effects of said unconstitutional public housing segregation policy and attain that racial balance required by the Fourteenth Amendment. Given the eight years tortuous course of these cases, together with the findings and judgment orders of the District Court and the opinions of this Court (now numbering five), we believe the relief granted is not only much too little but also much too late in the

---

30. Associate Justice Tom C. Clark of the Supreme Court of the United States   (Ret.) is sitting by designation.

proceedings. In effect, appellants, having won the battle back in 1969, have now lost the war. We are fully aware of the many difficult and sensitive problems that the cases have presented to the able District Judge and we applaud the care, meticulous attention and the judicious manner in which he has approached them. With his orders being ignored and frustrated as they were, he kept his cool and courageously called the hand of the recalcitrant. Perhaps in the opinion on remand on the third appeal, 457 F.2d 124 (7th Cir.1972), the repetition of a statement in the opinion on remand in the second appeal, 448 F.2d 731 that: "It may well be that the District Judge, in his wise discretion, will conclude that little equitable relief above the entry of a declaratory judgment and a simple 'best efforts' clause, will be necessary * * * "led the beleaguered District Judge to limit any plan to the boundaries of the City of Chicago and the "best efforts" of CHA and HUD. This is to be regretted and we trust that upon remand the matter will be expedited to the end that the segregated public housing system which has resulted from the action of CHA and HUD will be disestablished, and the deficiency in the supply of dwelling units will be corrected as rapidly as possible and in the manner indicated in this opinion.

We shall not burden this opinion with the details of the eight-year delay that has thus far deprived the appellants of the fruits of the District Court's judgment entered on July 1, 1969. In addition the unconstitutional action of CHA has stripped thousands of residents of the City of Chicago of their Fifth and Fourteenth Amendment rights for a score of years. Indeed, anyone reading the various opinions of the District Court and of this Court quickly discovers a callousness on the part of the appellees towards the rights of the black, underprivileged citizens of Chicago that is beyond comprehension. As far back as 1954, the District Court found that CHA had continuously refused to permit black families to reside in four public housing projects built before 1944; and that as far back as 1954 CHA has imposed a black quota on the four projects to the end that at the beginning of 1968 black tenants only occupied between 1 percent to 7 percent of the 1,654 units in the projects. The non-white population of Chicago at that time was 34.4 percent. In 64 public housing sites, having 30,848 units (other than the four above mentioned), the tenants were 99 percent black. All during this period Illinois law required that CHA secure prior approval of new sites for public housing from the City Council of the City of Chicago, but the District Court found that CHA set up a preclearance arrangement under which the alderman in whose ward a site was proposed would receive an informal request from CHA for clearance. The alderman, the Court found, to whom sites in the white neighborhoods were submitted, vetoed the sites and the City Council rejected 99½ percent of the units proposed for white sites while only 10 percent were refused in black areas. Moreover, the Court found that during this period about 90 percent of the waiting list of some 13,000 applicants to CHA for occupancy in its projects were black. These findings were neither challenged nor appealed. Furthermore, as early as July 1, 1969, a judgment order was entered herein, requiring CHA to build 700 new housing units in predominantly white areas and requiring 75 percent of all future units built by CHA to be constructed in such areas. This judgment also ran against the City Council of the City of Chicago (not then a party) on the basis of notice. Finally, CHA was directed by the District Court to "affirmatively administer its public housing system * * * to the end of disestablishing the segregated public housing system which has resulted from CHA's unconstitutional site selection and tenant assignment procedures * * * [and] use its best efforts to increase the supply of Dwelling Units as rapidly as possible * * *". 304 F.Supp. 736 (1969). No appeal was taken from this judgment.

Appellants and the District Court waited patiently for a year and a half but CHA submitted no sites for family dwellings to the City Council. The appellants contacted CHA and were advised that CHA had no intention to submit sites prior to the Chicago mayoralty election of April, 1971. The parties then asked for and were given informal hearings, so as to prevent publicity, and finally the District Court modified its "best efforts" provision in the July 1, 1969 judgment order so as to affirmatively require CHA to submit sites for no fewer than 1500 units to the City Council for approval on or before September 20, 1970. This order was appealed by CHA and affirmed 436 F.2d 306, cert. den. 402 U.S. 922, 91 S.Ct. 1378, 28 L.Ed.2d 661 (1971).

Meanwhile, in the separate suit against HUD filed simultaneously with the one against CHA (and now consolidated), the District Court had dismissed all four counts. On appeal this Court held that HUD had violated the due process clause of the Fifth Amendment and reversed with directions to enter a summary judgment for the appellants. This Court found that HUD had approved and funded family housing sites chosen by CHA in black areas of Chicago. HUD's explanation was "it was better to fund a segregated housing system" than deny housing altogether. This Court found that in the sixteen years (1950–1966) HUD spent nearly $350 million on such projects "in a manner which perpetuated a racially discriminatory housing system in Chicago"; that its excuse of community and local government resistance has not been accepted as viable and that this Court was "unable to avoid the conclusion that the Secretary's past actions constituted racial discriminatory conduct in their own right." Gautreaux v. Romney, 448 F.2d 731 (7th Cir.1971).

During the progress of this litigation, HUD was conferring with the City of Chicago concerning grants under the Model Cities Program (established by the Demonstration Cities and Metropolitan Development Act of 1966, 42 U.S.C.A. § 3301 et seq.). A $38 million grant was made for the calendar year 1970. However, for the 1971 calendar year HUD required a "letter of intention" signed by the Mayor of Chicago, the Chairman of CHA and the Regional Administrator of HUD, indicating how Chicago's large housing deficiency would be met. Under this letter CHA was to acquire sites for 1700 units within a specified timetable. HUD approved $26 million and had released $12 million when the opinion in *Romney,* supra came down. Appellants then sought an injunction from the District Court restraining further payments by HUD under the Model Cities Program unless and until sites in predominantly white areas for 700 dwelling units had been certified to the City Council for approval (at the time only 288 had been approved). The District Court granted this relief but on appeal the order was reversed. 457 F.2d 124 (7th Cir.1972). On remand the District Court entered a summary judgment against HUD, consolidated the cases and entered an order calling for each of the parties to file suggestions for a "comprehensive plan" to remedy the past effects of the public housing segregation, including "alternatives which are not confined in their scope to the geographic boundary of the City of Chicago."

HUD proposed a "best efforts" judgment order under which it would "cooperate" with CHA in the latter's efforts to increase the supply of housing units in accordance with the earlier judgment order against CHA and reported in 304 F.Supp. 736. Its proposed relief was confined to the geographic boundaries of the City of Chicago. Its "best thinking" was that the letter of intention previously mentioned and signed by the Mayor, the Regional Administrator of HUD and CHA should be carried out. This letter only covered the matter of the relocation housing deficiency of 4300 units and did not spell out any "comprehensive plan to remedy the past effects". Appellants' proposed plan provided a mechanism by which CHA could supply remedial housing in suburban areas as well as within Chicago and required HUD to administer its programs affirmatively to ensure that the order was carried out. At the hearing the appellants introduced evidence of the need for a metropolitan plan and the unreliability of HUD's "best efforts." HUD offered evidence of the lack of funds then available and CHA offered no evidence. On December 8, 1972, Bradley v. Milliken, 484 F.2d 215 (6th Cir.1973) came down, holding that a remedial plan involving suburban school districts in the metropolitan area of Detroit was necessary to disestablish existing segregation. Appellants then requested a *"Bradley* plan" order. On September 11, 1973, the District Court sustained the HUD proposal and this appeal resulted.

* * *

2. A METROPOLITAN PLAN IS NECESSARY AND EQUITABLE

After careful consideration and reflection we are obliged to conclude that on the record here it is necessary and equitable that any remedial plan to be effective must be on a suburban or metropolitan area basis. This could entail additional time but not under proper management since the intra-city portion of the plan may proceed without any further delay. In the meanwhile the suburban or metropolitan phases of the plan can be perfected (new parties, if necessary, etc.) and effectuated without delaying or interfering with the intracity phase of the comprehensive plan. There are only five housing authorities (in addition to CHA) involved, and while voluntary cooperation is not indicated, a Court order directing that those not volunteering were to be made parties might help. On the record here we are not able to discuss—much less pass upon—the validity of any specific metropolitan plan. We leave that for the district court on remand.

Our decision in regard to the necessity and equity of suburban or metropolitan area action is predicated on the following:

The equitable factors which prevented metropolitan relief in Milliken v. Bradley are simply not present here. There is no deeply rooted tradition of local control of public housing; rather, public housing is a federally supervised program with early roots in federal statutes. See 42 U.S.C.A. § 1401 et seq.; Gautreaux v. Romney, 448 F.2d 731, 737–740 (7th Cir.1971). There has been a federal statutory commitment to non-discrimination in housing for more than a century, 42 U.S.C.A. § 1982, and the Secretary of HUD is directed to administer housing programs "in a manner affirmatively to further the policies" of non-discrimination, 42 U.S.C.A. § 3608(d)(5). In short, federal involvement is pervasive.

Similarly, the administrative problems of building public housing outside Chicago are not remotely comparable to the problems of daily bussing thousands of children to schools in other districts run by other local governments. CHA and HUD can build housing much like any other landowner, and whatever problems arise would be insignificant compared to restructuring school systems as proposed in Milliken v. Bradley.

In Milliken v. Bradley, the Chief Justice emphasized that there was no evidence of discrimination by the suburban school districts affected. Here, although the record was not made with the Supreme Court's *Milliken* opinions in mind, there is evidence of suburban discrimination. Plaintiff's Exhibit 11 indicates that of twelve suburban public housing projects, ten were located in or adjacent to overwhelmingly black census tracts. And although the case was not limited to public housing, it is not irrelevant that we recently took judicial notice of widespread residential segregation "in Chicago and its environs." Clark v. Universal Builders, Inc., 501 F.2d 324, p. 335 (7th Cir.1974). We went on to hold that a prima facie showing had been made that this segregation had discriminatory effects throughout the metropolitan area.

Finally, the possibility of metropolitan relief has been under consideration for a long time in this case. While they disagree as to what relief the District Court should order, the parties are in agreement that the metropolitan area is a single relevant locality for low rent housing purposes and that a city-only remedy will not work.

* * *

In addition to CHA's and HUD's strong, positive statements as to the necessity for a metropolitan plan here, the appellants also offered the testimony of a recognized demographer who estimated that a continuance of present trends in black and white census tracts would lead to at least a 30 percent black occupancy in every census tract in Chicago by the year 2000. The District Judge himself added support to this thesis; however his prediction was 1984:

> "[E]xisting patterns of racial separation must be reversed if there is to be a chance of averting the desperately intensifying division of Whites and Negroes in Chicago. On the basis of present trends of Negro residential concentration and of Negro migration into and White migration out of the central city, the President's Commission on Civil Disorders estimates that Chicago will become 50% Negro by 1984. By 1984 it may be too late to heal racial divisions." (296 F.Supp. 907, 915).

If this prediction comes true it will mean that there will be no "general Public Housing Area" left in Chicago on which CHA could build desegregated public housing. In the ten-year period 1960–1970 the population of the City of Chicago declined by 183,000 people, a decrease of 505,000 whites and an increase of 322,000 blacks. The expert demographer further testified that by providing desegregated housing opportunities in the suburban areas, the rate of white exodus from the city would diminish. There was no testimony to the contrary. In fact "White flight" has brought on the same condition in most of our metropolitan cities, such as Indianapolis, Indiana. See United States v. Board of School Commissioners, 332 F.Supp. 655, 676 (S.D.Ind.1971); also as to Atlanta, Georgia; Calhoun v. Cook, 332 F.Supp. 804, 805 (N.D.Ga.1971). Like conditions—but aggravated—exist in Washington, D.C. and Cleveland, Ohio.

The realities of "White flight" to the suburbs and the inevitability of "resegregation" by rebuilding the ghettos as CHA and HUD were doing in Chicago must therefore be considered in drawing a comprehensive plan. The trial judge back in 1969 ordered scattered-site, low-rise housing—despite much criticism—but the experts now agree that such requirements are mandatory. His warning that "By 1984 it may be too late to heal racial divisions," rather than a cliche, is a solemn warning as to the interaction of "White flight" and "black concentration." It is the most serious domestic problem facing America today. As Assistant Secretary Simmons further advises:

> "As Whites have left the cities, jobs have left with them. After 1960, three-fifths of all new industrial plants constructed in this country were outside of central cities. In some cases as much as 85% of all new industrial plants located outside central cities were inaccessible to Blacks and other minorities who swelled ghetto populations." (Pls.' Exh. 9, p. 3).

These words also convey a solemn warning, i.e., we must not sentence our poor, our underprivileged, our minorities to the jobless slums of the ghettos and thereby forever trap them in the vicious cycle of poverty which can only lead them to lives of crime and violence.

By way of concluding, we have carefully read the records in these cases and find no evidence that the suburban or metropolitan area should not be included in a comprehensive plan. All of the parties, the

Government officials, the documentary evidence, the sole expert and the decided cases agree that a suburban or metropolitan area plan is the *sine qua non* of an effective remedy. In fact the Judge himself recognized its importance in his original judgment order by authorizing housing units to be provided in suburban Cook County on a voluntary basis. See 304 F.Supp. at 739. Furthermore, in his order of December 23, 1971, calling for the preparation by the parties of a "comprehensive plan", he wisely included the following paragraph:

> "3. In the preparation of such plan or plans, the parties are requested to provide the Court with as broad a range of alternatives as seem to the parties feasible as a partial or complete remedy for such past effects, including, if the parties deem it necessary or appropriate to provide full relief, alternatives which are not confined in their scope to the geographic boundary of the City of Chicago."

In light of all of these considerations we can but conclude that the District Court's finding as to not including in a comprehensive plan of relief areas outside the City of Chicago, i.e., the suburban or metropolitan area, was clearly erroneous.

3. ACTION ON REMAND

The judgment order of September 11, 1973, is reversed and the causes are remanded for further consideration in the light of this opinion, to wit: the adoption of a comprehensive metropolitan area plan that will not only disestablish the segregated public housing system in the City of Chicago which has resulted from CHA's and HUD's unconstitutional site selection and tenant assignment procedures but will increase the supply of dwelling units as rapidly as possible.

It is so ordered.

TONE, CIRCUIT JUDGE (dissenting).

[Dissenting opinion omitted.]

ORDER
On Rehearing

MR. JUSTICE CLARK.

On rehearing, we affirm our view that the trial judge should not have refused to "consider the propriety of metropolitan area relief." His conclusion that the only factual basis for plaintiffs' request was the opinion of an urbanologist ignores much of the record and, in particular, the statements of the parties themselves to the effect that "only metropolitan-wide solutions will do."

The requested relief does not go "far beyond the issues of this case," as the trial judge suggests. Rather, it is reasonable to conclude from the record that defendants' discriminatory site selection within the City of Chicago may well have fostered racial paranoia and encouraged the "white flight" phenomenon which has exacerbated the problems of achieving integration to such an extent that intra-city relief alone will not suffice to remedy the constitutional injuries. The extra-city impact of defendants' intra-city discrimination appears to be profound and far-reaching and has affected the housing patterns of hundreds of thousands of people throughout the Chicago metropolitan region.

It is in this sense, we believe, that the Supreme Court requires a showing that "there has been a constitutional violation within one district that produces a significant segregative effect in another district." Milliken v. Bradley, 418 U.S. at 745, 94 S.Ct. at 3127. We therefore reaffirm our remanding of this case for additional evidence and for further consideration of the issue of metropolitan area relief in light of this opinion and that of the Supreme Court in Milliken v. Bradley. In the meantime, intra-city relief should proceed apace without further delay.

A majority of the judges in regular active service not having requested that a vote be taken on the suggestion for an *en banc* rehearing, and a majority of the panel having voted to deny a rehearing,

It is ordered that the petition of the appellees for a rehearing in the above-entitled appeal be, and the same is hereby denied.

TONE, CIRCUIT JUDGE, adheres to his prior dissent.

Notes

1. The Seventh Circuit was affirmed in an 8–0 opinion by Justice Stewart in Hills v. Gautreaux, 425 U.S. 284, 96 S.Ct. 1538, 47 L.Ed.2d 792 in April, 1976. A consent decree settled the case in 1981. See 33 Land Use Law No. 9, at 4 (1981).

2. Since the time of Gautreaux, the concept of scatter-site public housing has been generally accepted. In some cities high rise public housing projects have been demolished. On the other hand, through the 1980's very little federal money was budgeted for public housing; instead, HUD and Congress opted for subsidies for private developers of housing and programs akin to vouchers for eligible recipients to secure housing in the private sector. In the late 1990's, Congress seems inclined to reduce the federal financial commitment to local housing authorities even more. See, Hall v. Housing Authority of Louisville, 660 S.W.2d 674 (Ky.App.1983); Strykers Bay Neighborhood Council v. City of New York, 695 F.Supp. 1531 (S.D.N.Y. 1988); Citizens Committee for Faraday Wood v. Lindsay, 507 F.2d 1065 (2d Cir.1974), cert. denied 421 U.S. 948, 95 S.Ct. 1679, 44 L.Ed.2d 102 (1975). Also see Spallone v. United States, 493 U.S. 265, 110 S.Ct. 625, 107 L.Ed.2d 644 (1990).

(2) The Problem of Standing

WARTH v. SELDIN

Supreme Court of the United States, 1975.
422 U.S. 490, 95 S.Ct. 2197, 45 L.Ed.2d 343.

MR. JUSTICE POWELL delivered the opinion of the Court.

Petitioners, various organizations and individuals resident in the Rochester, N.Y., metropolitan area, brought this action in the District

Court for the Western District of New York against the town of Penfield, an incorporated municipality adjacent to Rochester, and against members of Penfield's Zoning, Planning, and Town Boards. Petitioners claimed that the town's zoning ordinance, by its terms and as enforced by the defendant board members, respondents here, effectively excluded persons of low and moderate income from living in the town, in contravention of petitioners' First, Ninth, and Fourteenth Amendment rights and in violation of 42 U.S.C.A. §§ 1981, 1982, and 1983. The District Court dismissed the complaint and denied a motion to add petitioner Housing Council in the Monroe County Area, Inc., as party-plaintiff and also a motion by petitioner Rochester Home Builders Association, Inc., for leave to intervene as party-plaintiff. The Court of Appeals for the Second Circuit affirmed, holding that none of the plaintiffs, and neither Housing Council nor Home Builders Association, had standing to prosecute the action. * * *

* * * The complaint identified Metro–Act as a not-for-profit New York corporation, the purposes of which are "to alert ordinary citizens to problems of social concern; * * * to inquire into the reasons for the critical housing shortage for low and moderate income persons in the Rochester area and to urge action on the part of citizens to alleviate the general housing shortage for low and moderate income persons." Plaintiffs Vinkey, Reichert, Warth, and Harris were described as residents of the city of Rochester, all of whom owned real property in and paid property taxes to that city. Plaintiff Ortiz, "a citizen of Spanish/Puerto Rican extraction," also owned real property in and paid taxes to Rochester. Ortiz, however, resided in Wayland, N.Y., some 42 miles from Penfield where he was employed. The complaint described plaintiffs Broadnax, Reyes, and Sinkler as residents of Rochester and "persons fitting within the classification of low and moderate income as hereinafter defined * * *." Although the complaint does not expressly so state, the record shows that Broadnax, Reyes, and Sinkler are members of ethnic or racial minority groups: Reyes is of Puerto Rican ancestry; Broadnax and Sinkler are Negroes.

Petitioners' complaint alleged that Penfield's zoning ordinance, adopted in 1962, has the purpose and effect of excluding persons of low and moderate income from residing in the town. In particular, the ordinance allocates 98% of the town's vacant land to single-family detached housing, and allegedly by imposing unreasonable requirements relating to lot size, setback, floor area, and habitable space, the ordinance increases the cost of single-family detached housing beyond the means of persons of low and moderate income. Moreover, according to petitioners, only 0.3% of the land available for residential construction is allocated to multifamily structures (apartments, townhouses, and the like), and even on this limited space, housing for low-and moderate-income persons is not economically feasible because of low density and other requirements. Petitioners also alleged that "in furtherance of a policy of exclusionary zoning," the defendant members of Penfield's Town, Zoning, and Planning Boards had acted in an arbitrary and discriminatory manner: they had delayed action on proposals for low-and moderate-cost housing for inordinate periods of time; denied such proposals for arbitrary and insubstantial reasons; refused to grant necessary variances and permits, or to allow tax abatements; failed to provide necessary support services for low-and moderate-cost housing projects; and had amended the ordinance to make approval of such projects virtually impossible.

* * *

Petitioners further alleged certain harm to themselves. The Rochester property owners and taxpayers—Vinkey, Reichert, Warth, Harris, and Ortiz—claimed that because of Penfield's exclusionary practices, the city of Rochester had been forced to impose higher tax rates on them and others similarly situated than would otherwise have been necessary. The low-and moderate-income, minority plaintiffs—Ortiz, Broadnax, Reyes, and Sinkler—claimed that Penfield's zoning practices had prevented them from acquiring, by lease or purchase, residential property in the town, and thus had forced them and their families to reside in less attractive environments. * * *

* * * [W]e turn first to the claims of petitioners Ortiz, Reyes, Sinkler, and Broadnax, each of whom asserts standing as a person of low or moderate income and, coincidentally, as a member of a minority racial or ethnic group. We must assume, taking the allegations of the complaint as true, that Penfield's zoning ordinance and the pattern of enforcement by respondent officials have had the purpose and effect of excluding persons of low and moderate income, many of whom are members of racial or ethnic minority groups. We also assume, for purposes here, that such intentional exclusionary practices, if proved in a proper case, would be adjudged violative of the constitutional and statutory rights of the persons excluded.

But the fact that these petitioners share attributes common to persons who may have been excluded from residence in the town is an insufficient predicate for the conclusion that petitioners themselves have been excluded, or that the respondents' assertedly illegal actions have violated their rights. Petitioners must allege and show that they personally have been injured, not that injury has been suffered by other, unidentified members of the class to which they belong and which they purport to represent. Unless these petitioners can thus demonstrate the requisite case or controversy between themselves personally and respondents, "none may seek relief on behalf of himself or any other member of the class." * * *

no standing

* * *

We find the record devoid of the necessary allegations. As the Court of Appeals noted, none of these petitioners has a present interest in any Penfield property; none is himself subject to the ordinance's strictures; and none has ever been denied a variance or permit by respondent officials. * * * Instead, petitioners claim that respondents' enforcement of the ordinance against third parties—developers, builders, and the like—has had the consequence of precluding the construction of housing suitable to their needs at prices they might be able to afford. * * *

Here, by their own admission, realization of petitioners' desire to live in Penfield always has depended on the efforts and willingness of third parties to build low-and moderate-cost housing. The record specifically refers to only two such efforts: that of Penfield Better Homes Corp., in late 1969, to obtain the rezoning of certain land in Penfield to allow the construction of subsidized cooperative townhouses that could be purchased by persons of moderate income; and a similar effort by O'Brien Homes, Inc., in late 1971. But the record is devoid of any indication that these projects, or other like projects, would have satisfied petitioners' needs at prices they could afford, or that, were the court to remove the obstructions attributable to respondents, such relief would benefit petitioners. Indeed, petitioners' descriptions of their individual financial situations and housing needs suggest precisely the contrary— that their inability to reside in Penfield is the consequence of the economics of the area housing market, rather than of respondents' assertedly illegal acts. In short, the facts alleged fail to support an actionable causal relationship between Penfield's zoning practices and petitioners' asserted injury.

* * *

The petitioners who assert standing on the basis of their status as taxpayers of the city of Rochester present a different set of problems. These "taxpayer-petitioners" claim that they are suffering economic injury consequent to Penfield's allegedly discriminatory and exclusionary zoning practices. Their argument, in brief, is that Penfield's persistent refusal to allow or to facilitate construction of low-and moderate-cost housing forces the city of Rochester to provide more such housing than it otherwise would do; that to provide such housing, Rochester must allow certain tax abatements; and that as the amount of tax-abated property increases, Rochester taxpayers are forced to assume an increased tax burden in order to finance essential public services.

"Of course, pleadings must be something more than an ingenious academic exercise in the conceivable." United States v. SCRAP, 412 U.S., at 688, 93 S.Ct. 2405, 37 L.Ed.2d 254. We think the complaint of the taxpayer-petitioners is little more than such an exercise. Apart from the conjectural nature of the asserted injury, the line of causation between Penfield's actions and such injury is not apparent from the complaint. Whatever may occur in Penfield, the injury complained of—increases in taxation—results only from decisions made by the appropriate Rochester authorities, who are not parties to this case.

* * *

We turn next to the standing problems presented by the petitioner associations—Metro–Act of Rochester, Inc., one of the original plaintiffs; Housing Council in the Monroe County Area, Inc., which the original

plaintiffs sought to join as a party-plaintiff; and Rochester Home Builders Association, Inc., which moved in the District Court for leave to
intervene as plaintiff. There is no question that an association may have
standing in its own right to seek judicial relief from injury to itself and
to vindicate whatever rights and immunities the association itself may
enjoy. * * *

* * * The association must allege that its members, or any one of
them, are suffering immediate or threatened injury as a result of the
challenged action of the sort that would make out a justiciable case had
the members themselves brought suit. * * * So long as this can be
established, and so long as the nature of the claim and of the relief
sought does not make the individual participation of each injured party
indispensable to proper resolution of the cause, the association may be
an appropriate representative of its members, entitled to invoke the
court's jurisdiction.

[The Court found that none of the associations had standing because
the interests of their members were not directly affected by the challenged policies of the town.]

* * *

* * * It is the responsibility of the complainant clearly to allege
facts demonstrating that he is a proper party to invoke judicial resolution of the dispute and the exercise of the court's remedial powers. We
agree with the District Court and the Court of Appeals that none of the
petitioners here has met this threshold requirement. Accordingly, the
judgment of the Court of Appeals is

Affirmed.

[Four Justices dissented. The dissenting opinions are omitted.]

Notes

1. The principal case was a severe deterrent to the movement to seek
broad relief in the federal courts against allegedly exclusionary zoning
policies. What the Court seemed to require to satisfy the standing principle,
was a developer ready, willing and able to undertake construction of subsidized housing and also ready, willing and able to undertake costly and
lengthy litigation, as in the Arlington Heights case, supra. In the Arlington
Heights opinion, the Court addressed the standing issue again, stating:

Here there can be little doubt that MHDC meets the constitutional
standing requirements. The challenged action of the petitioners stands
as an absolute barrier to constructing the housing MHDC had contracted to place on the Viatorian site. If MHDC secures the injunctive relief it
seeks, that barrier will be removed. An injunction would not, of course,
guarantee that Lincoln Green will be built. MHDC would still have to
secure financing, qualify for federal subsidies, and carry through with
construction. But all housing developments are subject to some extent to
similar uncertainties. When a project is as detailed and specific as
Lincoln Green, a court is not required to engage in undue speculation as
a predicate for finding that the plaintiff has the requisite personal stake

in the controversy. MHDC has shown an injury to itself that is "likely to be redressed by a favorable decision." * * *

Clearly MHDC has met the constitutional requirements, and it therefore has standing to assert its own rights. Foremost among them is MHDC's right to be free of arbitrary or irrational zoning actions. See Euclid v. Ambler Realty Co., 272 U.S. 365, 47 S.Ct. 114, 71 L.Ed. 303 (1926); Nectow v. City of Cambridge, 277 U.S. 183, 48 S.Ct. 447, 72 L.Ed. 842 (1928); Village of Belle Terre v. Boraas, 416 U.S. 1, 94 S.Ct. 1536, 39 L.Ed.2d 797 (1974). But the heart of this litigation has never been the claim that the Village's decision fails the generous *Euclid* test, recently reaffirmed in *Belle Terre.* Instead it has been the claim that the Village's refusal to rezone discriminates against racial minorities in violation of the Fourteenth Amendment. As a corporation, MHDC has no racial identity and cannot be the direct target of the petitioners' alleged discrimination. In the ordinary case, a party is denied standing to assert the rights of third persons. * * * [Here] we have at least one individual plaintiff who has demonstrated standing to assert these rights as his own.

Respondent Ransom, a Negro, works at the Honeywell factory in Arlington Heights and lives approximately 20 miles away in Evanston in a 5–room house with his mother and his son. The complaint alleged that he seeks and would qualify for the housing MHDC wants to build in Arlington Heights. Ransom testified at trial that if Lincoln Green were built he would probably move there, since it is closer to his job.

The injury Ransom asserts is that his quest for housing nearer his employment has been thwarted by official action that is racially discriminatory. If a court grants the relief he seeks, there is at least a "substantial probability," * * * that the Lincoln Green project will materialize, affording Ransom the housing opportunity he desires in Arlington Heights. His is not a generalized grievance. Instead, as we suggested in *Warth,* supra, at 507, 508 n. 18, it focuses on a particular project and is not dependent on speculation about the possible actions of third parties not before the court. * * * Unlike the individual plaintiffs in *Warth,* Ransom has adequately averred an "actionable causal relationship" between Arlington Heights' zoning practices and his asserted injury.

2. In Strykers Bay Neighborhood Council v. City of New York, 695 F.Supp. 1531 (S.D.N.Y.1988), the court found no standing to challenge a city decision to reallocate land set aside for low-income housing to luxury apartments. However, in Comer v. Cisneros, 37 F.3d 775 (2d Cir.1994) the court held that low-income minority residents of Buffalo did have standing to bring a class action on behalf of former, current, and future minority residents of public housing projects and applicants for federal housing assistance in the suburbs.

3. On the use of class actions in exclusionary zoning and housing discrimination cases, compare Joseph Skillken & Co. v. City of Toledo, 380 F.Supp. 228 (N.D.Ohio 1974), reversed 528 F.2d 867 (6th Cir.1975), vacated and remanded 429 U.S. 1068, 97 S.Ct. 800, 50 L.Ed.2d 786 (1977), after remand 558 F.2d 350 (6th Cir.1977), certiorari denied 434 U.S. 985, 98 S.Ct.

611, 54 L.Ed.2d 479, rehearing denied 434 U.S. 1051, 98 S.Ct. 904, 54 L.Ed.2d 805 (1978), with Suffolk Housing Services v. Town of Brookhaven, 69 A.D.2d 242, 418 N.Y.S.2d 452 (1979).

4. The rationale in Warth v. Seldin has been rejected by some state courts insofar as it would preclude nonresidents from challenging the exclusionary housing practices of a community. See Home Builders League v. Township of Berlin, 81 N.J. 127, 405 A.2d 381 (1979) and Stocks v. City of Irvine, 114 Cal.App.3d 520, 170 Cal.Rptr. 724 (1981).

(3) Discrimination Based on Age

COLONY COVE ASSOCIATES v. BROWN

California Court of Appeal, 1990.
220 Cal.App.3d 195, 269 Cal.Rptr. 234.

BOREN, ASSOCIATE JUSTICE.

Respondent, owner of a mobile home park, enacted a park rule restricting residency to senior citizens, age 55 or older. Respondent then sought to evict appellants, tenants in the park, because appellants' children, minors born after the park's enactment of its age restriction, were not "grandfathered" as were their parents, who had resided in the park prior to the rule. Appellants appeal following summary judgments granted in unlawful detainer actions brought by respondent. We hold that the enforcement of the mobile home park's senior citizen, age 55 or older, resident restriction does not run afoul of constitutional proscriptions, relevant state statutes, or the Fair Housing Amendments Act of 1988.

* * *

I. CONSTITUTIONAL CONCERNS

In *Schmidt v. Superior Court* (1989) 48 Cal.3d 370, 256 Cal.Rptr. 750, 769 P.2d 932, the Supreme Court held that a mobile home park rule limiting residence to adults 25 years or older was not unconstitutional. The *Schmidt* court assumed arguendo the existence of state action such as to warrant applying constitutional concerns to private conduct (*id.* at pp. 388–389, fn. 14, 389, 256 Cal.Rptr. 750, 769 P.2d 932), and concluded that the mobile home park rule was not, as or when applied, either irrational or arbitrary and did not violate the constitutional rights to equal protection or familial privacy. (*Id.* at pp. 390–391, 256 Cal.Rptr. 750, 769 P.2d 932.)

In sustaining the constitutionality of the mobile home park rule, the court reasoned as follows: "[A]lthough the constitutional right of 'familial privacy' undoubtedly encompasses a parent's right to live with his or her child (see, e.g., *Moore* [*v. East Cleveland* (1977)] 431 U.S. 494, 500–506 [97 S.Ct. 1932, 1936–1939, 52 L.Ed.2d 531]), the mobile home park's 25–years–or–older policy at issue here does not, of course, purport to compel the separation of parent and child or to preclude the family from living together in an entire city (cf., e.g., *Moore, supra,* 431 U.S.

494 [97 S.Ct. 1932]; *Molino v. Mayer and Council of Bor. of Glassboro* (1971) 116 N.J.Super. 195 [281 A.2d 401]) or neighborhood (cf. [*City of Santa Barbara v.*] *Adamson* [1980] 27 Cal.3d 123 [164 Cal.Rptr. 539, 610 P.2d 436]), but simply denies the family access to a limited number of housing units. In *Bynes v. Toll* (2d Cir.1975) 512 F.2d 252, 254–256, the Second Circuit upheld a state university regulation excluding married students with children from university housing, explaining that the students' unquestioned constitutional right to procreate and to bring up their children did not mean that the university was 'constitutionally mandated to provide them campus housing to perform their protected prerogatives' (512 F.2d at p. 255), and, on similar grounds, courts of other states which have considered the validity of age-based housing regulations comparable to the rule at issue here—in the absence of a legislative measure barring such age restrictions—uniformly upheld the general constitutional validity of such rules. [Citations.] Particularly in light of the distinct characteristics of mobile home parks—e.g., the generally greater percentage of older residents, the smaller size of the units, the more substantial potential lack of privacy and the greater expense that might have to be incurred in rendering such a park safe for children residents—we agree with the conclusion of the above cited cases that such an age-based regulation is neither irrational nor arbitrary or otherwise vulnerable to constitutional attack." (*Schmidt v. Superior Court, supra,* 48 Cal.3d at pp. 389–390, 256 Cal.Rptr. 750, 769 P.2d 932, fns. omitted.)

The reasoning in *Schmidt* is particularly compelling here in the context of not merely an adult-only but a senior citizen age restriction rule. In view of the recognized desirability of special living environments and services providing communal educational and recreational facilities which meet the physical and social needs of senior citizens (see Civ.Code, §§ 51.2, subd. (a) and 51.3, subd. (a); cf. *Huntington Landmark Adult Community Assn. v. Ross* (1989) 213 Cal.App.3d 1012, 1018–1019, 261 Cal.Rptr. 875), respondent's age-based discrimination is "neither irrational nor arbitrary or otherwise vulnerable to constitutional attack." (*Schmidt v. Superior Court, supra,* 48 Cal.3d at p. 390, 256 Cal.Rptr. 750, 769 P.2d 932.)

II. State Statutory Provisions

Relevant California statutes do not preclude the establishment and enforcement of a senior citizen age qualification rule in a private mobile home park. In analyzing relevant state statutes, *Schmidt v. Superior Court, supra,* 48 Cal.3d 370, 256 Cal.Rptr. 750, 769 P.2d 932 held that a private mobile home park rule which limited residence in the park to persons 25 years or older, as permitted by Civil Code section 798.76,[31] did not violate the broad antidiscrimination policy embodied in the Unruh

---

31. Civil Code section 798.76 provides as follows:

"The management may require that a purchaser of a mobile home which will remain in the park, comply with any rule or regulation limiting residence to adults only."

Civil Rights Act (Civ.Code, § 51 et seq.), even though the park rule operated to exclude families with children younger than 25 years of age. Most significantly, the amendments to the Unruh Act which address age-based discrimination in housing, Civil Code sections 51.2 and 51.3,[32] reflect a legislative intent specifically to exclude mobile home parks from the reach of the act. * * *

The amendments to the Unruh Act were enacted in response to a prior judicial expression of the appropriateness of age-based discrimination favoring senior citizens. In *Marina Point, Ltd. v. Wolfson* (1982) 30 Cal.3d 721, 180 Cal.Rptr. 496, 640 P.2d 115, where the court held the general provisions of the Unruh Act prohibited an ordinary apartment complex from adopting a rule which excluded all families with children from the complex, the court emphasized that the age-based exclusionary policy which it proscribed was distinguishable from "the age-limited admission policies of retirement communities or housing complexes reserved for older citizens." (*Id.* at p. 742, 180 Cal.Rptr. 496, 640 P.2d 115.) As the court observed, "In light of the public policy reflected by [legislation allowing for adults-only housing in mobile home parks (Civ. Code, § 798.76)], age qualifications as to a housing facility reserved for older citizens can operate as a reasonable and permissible means under the Unruh Act of establishing and preserving specialized facilities for those particularly in need of such services or environment. [Citations.] Such a specialized institution designed to meet a social need differs fundamentally from the wholesale exclusion of children from an apartment complex otherwise open to the general public." (*Id.* at pp. 742–743, 180 Cal.Rptr. 496, 640 P.2d 115, fns. omitted.)

With the declared intent "to clarify the holdings in *Marina Point, Ltd. v. Wolfson[, supra]*" (Civ.Code, § 51.2, subd. (b)), and another related decision, the Legislature enacted Civil Code sections 51.2 and 51.3. (See *Schmidt v. Superior Court, supra,* 48 Cal.3d at pp. 383–384, 256 Cal.Rptr. 750, 769 P.2d 932.) * * *

III. THE FAIR HOUSING AMENDMENTS ACT OF 1988

The contention that the Fair Housing Amendments Act of 1988 (Pub.L. No. 100–430 (Sept. 13, 1988) 102 Stat. 1619, 1988 U.S.Code Cong. & Admin.News, No. 8), effective March 1989, invalidates respon-

---

32. Civil Code section 51.2 provides, in pertinent part, as follows: "(a) Section 51 shall be construed to prohibit a business establishment from discriminating in the sale or rental of housing based upon age. Where accommodations are designed to meet the physical and social needs of senior citizens, a business establishment may establish and preserve such housing for senior citizens, pursuant to Section 51.3 of the Civil Code."

Civil Code section 51.3 provides, in pertinent part, as follows: "(a) The Legislature finds and declares that this section is essential to establish and preserve specially de-signed accessible housing for senior citizens. There are senior citizens who need special living environments and services, and find that there is an inadequate supply of this type of housing in the state. [¶](b) The Legislature finds and declares that different age limitations for senior citizens housing are appropriate in recognition of the size of a development in relationship to the community in which it is located. [¶](c) For the purposes of this section, the following definitions apply: * * * [¶](4) 'Dwelling unit' or 'housing' means any residential accommodation other than a mobile home."

dent's adults-only policy and proscribes eviction proceedings on familial status grounds is unavailing. In applying federal legislation to the present situation (see *Gulf Offshore Co. v. Mobil Oil Corp.* (1981) 453 U.S. 473, 477–478, 101 S.Ct. 2870, 2874–2875, 69 L.Ed.2d 784), it is apparent that the Fair Housing Amendments Act makes it generally unlawful to discriminate in the sale or rental of housing or to make a "dwelling" otherwise unavailable on the basis of "familial status," as well as on the previously forbidden grounds of race, color, religion, sex or national origin. (42 U.S.C.A. § 3604.) The definition of the term "dwelling" in the Fair Housing Act includes mobile home sites. (See, e.g., *United States v. Warwick Mobile Homes Estates, Inc.* (4th Cir.1976) 537 F.2d 1148; *United States v. Grooms* (M.D.Fla.1972) 348 F.Supp. 1130, 1133.) The term "familial status" is defined as families which include children under the age of 18. (42 U.S.C.A. § 3602(k).)

While the amendment to the Fair Housing Act thus generally bars discrimination in mobile home housing against families with children under 18, it also, however, creates an exception for "housing for older persons" in which discrimination on the basis of familial status is not prohibited. (42 U.S.C.A. § 3607(b)(1).) "Housing for older persons" is legislatively defined to include, in part, housing which is (1) "intended for, solely occupied by, persons 62 years of age or older," or (2) "intended and operated for occupancy by at least one person 55 years of age or older per unit." (42 U.S.C.A. § 3607(b)(2)(B) and (b)(2)(C).)

In determining whether "housing for older persons" qualifies within the meaning of the latter category involving "occupancy by at least one person 55 years of age or older per unit," the amendment to the Fair Housing Act requires that "the Secretary [of Housing and Urban Development (HUD)] shall develop regulations which include at least the following requirements: (i) the existence of significant facilities and services specifically designed to meet the physical or social needs of older persons, or if the provision of such facilities and services is not practicable, that such housing is necessary to provide important housing opportunities for older persons; and (ii) that at least 80 percent of the units are occupied by at least one person 55 years of age or older per unit; and (iii) the publication of, and adherence to, policies and procedures which demonstrate an intent by the owner or manager to provide housing for persons 55 years of age or older." (42 U.S.C.A. § 3607(b)(2)(C)(i to iii).)

The amendment further contains a "grandfather clause" in section 3607(b)(3)(A). That section provides that housing will not be disqualified as "housing for older persons" merely because "persons residing in such housing as of September 13, 1988," do not meet the requirements under either the 62 or 55 years of age or older categories, so long as any new occupants meet the age requirements under either of those two categories, as specified in section 3607(b)(2)(B) or (b)(2)(C).

* * *

It is sufficient for our purpose in reviewing the grant of a motion for summary judgment that the mobile home park, as indicated by its age restriction regulation, was "intended and operated for occupancy by at least one person 55 years of age or older per unit." (42 U.S.C.A. § 3607(b)(2)(C).) Moreover, as a matter of law, to the extent that units in the park are occupied by persons not in that category, "The act also contains a 'grandfather clause,' providing that persons under the applicable age limits who were residing in housing when the federal act was enacted will not disqualify the housing from the statutory exemption for housing for older persons so long as the applicable age requirements are applied to all new occupants. (42 U.S.C.A. § 3607(b)(3).)" (*Schmidt v. Superior Court, supra,* 48 Cal.3d at p. 375, fn. 4, 256 Cal.Rptr. 750, 769 P.2d 932.) Accordingly, there were no triable issues of material fact, and summary judgment was appropriate. (See *AARTS Productions, Inc. v. Crocker National Bank* (1986) 179 Cal.App.3d 1061, 1064–1065, 225 Cal.Rptr. 203; Code Civ.Proc., § 437c, subd. (c).)

* * *

IV. Conclusion

We are aware of the plight of young couples with children who seek affordable housing. We also recognize the unique difficulties which arise when a mobile home owner is forced to vacate a mobile home park rental space. The Legislature has also acknowledged the critical importance of adequate housing for families. (See Health & Saf.Code, §§ 50001, 50003, 50003.3, 50004; Gov.Code, § 65913; *Marina Point, Ltd. v. Wolfson, supra,* 30 Cal.3d at p. 743, 180 Cal.Rptr. 496, 640 P.2d 115.) Discrimination against children in housing is at odds with fundamental notions of humanity. "A society that sanctions wholesale discrimination against its children in obtaining housing engages in a suspect activity. Even the most primitive society fosters the protection of its young; such a society would hardly discriminate against children in their need for shelter * * *." (*Marina Point, Ltd. v. Wolfson, supra,* 30 Cal.3d at p. 744, 180 Cal.Rptr. 496, 640 P.2d 115.)

Nonetheless, as discussed above, our legislative bodies have also addressed the competing interests and housing needs of older persons in our society. Consistent with our constitutional and legislative analysis, appellants' legitimate housing needs cannot be satisfied by the present attack upon legislation which provides for the establishment of senior citizen mobile home parks.

Disposition

The judgments are affirmed. Respondent's request for sanctions is denied.

Lucas, P.J., and Ashby, J., concur.

Notes

1. Another case which gives a full discussion of the reasons for allowing mobile home parks dedicated to the elderly is Taxpayers Ass'n of Weymouth Twp., Inc. v. Weymouth Twp., 80 N.J. 6, 364 A.2d 1016 (1976), appeal dismissed 430 U.S. 977, 97 S.Ct. 1672, 52 L.Ed.2d 373 (1977). Also

see Seifred v. Zabel, 369 N.W.2d 571 (Minn.App.1985); Metro. Dade County Fair Housing and Employment Appeals Bd. v. Sunrise Village Mobile Home Park, Inc., 485 So.2d 865 (Fla.App. 3 Dist.1986).

2.   A leading case contrary to the position of allowing zoning for the elderly is Hinman v. Planning and Zoning Comm'n, 26 Conn.Sup. 125, 214 A.2d 131 (1965). The court ruled that a rural town of less than 5,000 population did not have authority under the enabling act to create a new zoning classification (Senior Citizen Planned Community District) for development on tracts of 400 or more acres. In New York, the courts have allowed such zoning. See Maldini v. Ambro, 36 N.Y.2d 481, 369 N.Y.S.2d 385, 330 N.E.2d 403 (1975), appeal dismissed 423 U.S. 993, 96 S.Ct. 419, 46 L.Ed.2d 367 (1975); Campbell v. Barraud, 58 A.D.2d 570, 394 N.Y.S.2d 909 (1977); Apfelbaum v. Town of Clarkstown, 104 Misc.2d 371, 428 N.Y.S.2d 387 (1980); but see the unusual case of Central Management Co. v. Town Bd. of Oyster Bay, 47 Misc.2d 385, 262 N.Y.S.2d 728 (1965), where the town board rejected a proposed high rise apartment building for the elderly because it was to be built in an area remote from medical and shopping facilities on a plot of land which was virtually an island between two expressways, and the court held that the board could not take into account the age of the proposed residents and the rejection was thus arbitrary.

3.   Prior to the decision in the principal case, the California legislature passed a resolution (S.J.R. 1, 1989) requesting that the President and the Congress amend the Fair Housing Act Amendments of 1988 to clarify the rules concerning mobile home parks for the elderly. The resolution states that most California mobile home parks have adults-only restrictions and that the HUD regulations are ambiguous as to what is required for a mobile home park to operate with age restrictions without violating the act. The resolution also notes that the cost of senior citizen housing in mobile home parks might be increased by the cost of installation of facilities to meet the physical or social needs of the residents as stated in the act. Federal courts have been reluctant to find exceptions for elder residences that lack special facilities. In Lanier v. Fairfield Communities, Inc., 776 F.Supp. 1533 (M.D.Fl.1990) the court held that the exception was not available where the residential community was two miles from the nearest shopping and medical facilities, provided no transportation, no emergency call buttons, and no congregate dining or health facilities. Also see Park Place Home Brokers v. P–K Mobile Home Park, 773 F.Supp. 46 (N.D.Ohio 1991) (off-site facilities and services could not be considered in determining whether the mobile home park could claim the exemption); Hooker v. Weathers, 990 F.2d 913 (6th Cir.1993) (burden of proof is on the owner of the residences to establish the older persons exemption). In 1995 Congress amended the act to strike out the section requiring significant facilities to serve the elderly as a condition for exemption, P.L. 104–76, § 2.

4.   Perhaps the most controversial part of the Fair Housing Act Amendments of 1988 is the rule against discrimination in the rental of apartment housing on the basis of familial status (i.e., children under 18). The Congressional intent is clearly to prohibit adults-only apartment buildings, a widespread practice across the nation. This provision, which became effective in March, 1989, will undoubtedly promote a great deal more litigation than the adults-only mobile home park. See, e.g., United States v. Tropic Seas, Inc.,

887 F.Supp. 1347 (D.Haw.1995). Also, federal courts have seen a number of cases brought under the provision in the Fair Housing Act Amendments prohibiting discrimination in housing on the basis of handicap. See, e.g., Larkin v. State of Michigan Dept. of Social Services, 89 F.3d 285 (6th Cir.1996). Also see James Brooke, Young Unwelcome in Retirees' Haven, N.Y. Times, Feb. 16, 1997, p. 10.

5. In Betsey v. Turtle Creek Associates, 736 F.2d 983 (4th Cir.1984), the court found a violation of the Fair Housing Act where an adults-only rental policy had a disparate racial impact on minority tenants.

6. See Helen L. Edmonds and Dwight H. Merriam, Zoning and the Elderly: Issues for the 21st Century, Land Use Law (Mar. 1995), p. 3.

SECTION 2. INCLUSIONARY ZONING

In exclusionary zoning cases where the nature of the issue is exclusion of a particular use from the community as a whole or from the single-family residential zoning district, the remedy to be applied by a court is rather easy to state. Usually the developer-plaintiff will be granted an injunction to allow the particular use desired. However, where the allegations of exclusionary zoning are directed at the community's failure to make provision for housing all segments of the population in need of housing, the remedies available to a court raise important legal and social questions. Does the concept of exclusionary zoning in the constitutional sense imply a duty of *inclusionary* zoning—affirmative action on the part of the community to meet the legitimate needs of all segments of the population? If the answer to this question is yes, then how is court to ensure that the duty is met? These troubling questions are addressed in the following materials.

A. THE DUTY TO PROVIDE LOW–COST HOUSING OPPORTU- NITIES

SOUTHERN BURLINGTON COUNTY NAACP v. TOWNSHIP OF MOUNT LAUREL

Supreme Court of New Jersey, 1975.
67 N.J. 151, 336 A.2d 713.
Appeal dismissed 423 U.S. 808, 96 S.Ct. 18, 46 L.Ed.2d 28 (1975).

HALL, J. This case attacks the system of land use regulation by defendant Township of Mount Laurel on the ground that low and moderate income families are thereby unlawfully excluded from the municipality. The trial court so found, 119 N.J.Super. 164 (Law Div. 1972), and declared the township zoning ordinance totally invalid. Its judgment went on, in line with the requests for affirmative relief, to order the municipality to make studies of the housing needs of low and moderate income persons presently or formerly residing in the community in substandard housing, as well as those in such income classifications presently employed in the township and living elsewhere or reasonably expected to be employed therein in the future, and to present a plan of affirmative public action designed "to enable and encourage the satisfaction of the indicated needs." Jurisdiction was retained for judicial consideration and approval of such a plan and for the entry of a final order requiring its implementation.

The township appealed to the Appellate Division and those plaintiffs, not present or former residents, cross-appealed on the basis that the judgment should have directed that the prescribed plan take into account as well a fair share of the regional housing needs of low and moderate income families without limitation to those having past, present or prospective connection with the township. * * *

The implications of the issue presented are indeed broad and far-reaching, extending much beyond these particular plaintiffs and the boundaries of this particular municipality.

There is not the slightest doubt that New Jersey has been, and continues to be, faced with a desperate need for housing, especially of decent living accommodations economically suitable for low and moderate income families. The situation was characterized as a "crisis" and fully explored and documented by Governor Cahill in two special messages to the Legislature—A Blueprint for Housing in New Jersey (1970) and New Horizons in Housing (1972).

Plaintiffs represent the minority group poor (black and Hispanic)[33] seeking such quarters. But they are not the only category of persons barred from so many municipalities by reason of restrictive land use regulations. We have reference to young and elderly couples, single persons and large, growing families not in the poverty class, but who still cannot afford the only kinds of housing realistically permitted in most places—relatively high-priced, single-family detached dwellings on sizeable lots and, in some municipalities, expensive apartments. We will, therefore, consider the case from the wider viewpoint that the effect of Mount Laurel's land use regulation has been to prevent various categories of persons from living in the township because of the limited extent of their income and resources. In this connection, we accept the representation of the municipality's counsel at oral argument that the regulatory scheme was not adopted with any desire or intent to exclude prospective residents on the obviously illegal bases of race, origin or believed social incompatibility.

---

33. Plaintiffs fall into four categories: (1) present residents of the township residing in dilapidated or substandard housing; (2) former residents who were forced to move elsewhere because of the absence of suitable housing; (3) nonresidents living in central city substandard housing in the region who desire to secure decent housing and accompanying advantages within their means elsewhere; (4) three organizations representing the housing and other interests of racial minorities. The township originally challenged plaintiffs' standing to bring this action. The trial court properly held (119 N.J.Super. at 166) that the resident plaintiffs had adequate standing to ground the entire action and found it unnecessary to pass on that of the other plaintiffs. The issue has not been raised on appeal. We merely add that both categories of nonresident individuals likewise have standing. N.J.S.A. 40:55–47.1; cf. Walker v. Borough of Stanhope, 23 N.J. 657 (1957). No opinion is expressed as to the standing of the organizations.

As already intimated, the issue here is not confined to Mount Laurel. The same question arises with respect to any number of other municipalities of sizeable land area outside the central cities and older built-up suburbs of our North and South Jersey metropolitan areas (and surrounding some of the smaller cities outside those areas as well) which, like Mount Laurel, have substantially shed rural characteristics and have undergone great population increase since World War II, or are now in the process of doing so, but still are not completely developed and remain in the path of inevitable future residential, commercial and industrial demand and growth. Most such municipalities, with but relatively insignificant variation in details, present generally comparable physical situations, courses of municipal policies, practices, enactments and results and human, governmental and legal problems arising therefrom. It is in the context of communities now of this type or which become so in the future, rather than with central cities or older built-up suburbs or areas still rural and likely to continue to be for some time yet, that we deal with the question raised.

Extensive oral and documentary evidence was introduced at the trial, largely informational, dealing with the development of Mount Laurel, including the nature and effect of municipal regulation, the details of the region of which it is a part and the recent history thereof, and some of the basics of housing, special reference being directed to that for low and moderate income families. The record has been supplemented by figures, maps, studies and literature furnished or referred to by counsel and the *amici,* so that the court has a clear picture of land use regulation and its effects in the developing municipalities of the state.

This evidence was not contradicted by the township, except in a few unimportant details. Its candid position is that, conceding its land use regulation was intended to result and has resulted in economic discrimination and exclusion of substantial segments of the area population, its policies and practices are in the best present and future fiscal interest of the municipality and its inhabitants and are legally permissible and justified. It further asserts that the trial court was without power to direct the affirmative relief it did.

I

THE FACTS * * *

[At this point Judge Hall presents an extensive physical description and history of the growth and development of the township.]

* * *

All this affirmative action for the benefit of certain segments of the population is in sharp contrast to the lack of action, and indeed hostility, with respect to affording any opportunity for decent housing for the township's own poor living in substandard accommodations, found largely in the section known as Springville (R–3 zone). The 1969 Master Plan Report recognized it and recommended positive action. The continuous official reaction has been rather a negative policy of waiting for dilapidated premises to be vacated and then forbidding further occupancy. An earlier non-governmental effort to improve conditions had been effectively thwarted. In 1968 a private non-profit association sought to build subsidized, multi-family housing in the Springville section with funds to be granted by a higher level governmental agency. Advance municipal approval of the project was required. The Township Committee responded with a purportedly approving resolution, which found a need for "moderate" income housing in the area, but went on to specify that such housing must be constructed subject to all zoning, planning, building and other applicable ordinances and codes. This meant single-family detached dwellings on 20,000 square foot lots. (Fear was also expressed that such housing would attract low income families from outside the township.) Needless to say, such requirements killed realistic housing for this group of low and moderate income families.

The record thoroughly substantiates the findings of the trial court that over the years Mount Laurel "has acted affirmatively to control development and to attract a selective type of growth" (119 N.J.Super. at 168) and that "through its zoning ordinances has exhibited economic discrimination in that the poor have been deprived of adequate housing and the opportunity to secure the construction of subsidized housing, and has used federal, state, county and local finances and resources solely for the betterment of middle and upper-income persons." (119 N.J.Super. at 178.)

There cannot be the slightest doubt that the reason for this course of conduct has been to keep down local taxes on *property* (Mount Laurel is not a high tax municipality) and that the policy was carried out without regard for non-fiscal considerations with respect to *people,* either within or without its boundaries. This conclusion is demonstrated not only by what was done and what happened, as we have related, but also by innumerable direct statements of municipal officials at public meetings over the years which are found in the exhibits. The trial court referred to a number of them. 119 N.J.Super. at 169–170. No official testified to the contrary.

This policy of land use regulation for a fiscal end derives from New Jersey's tax structure, which has imposed on local real estate most of the cost of municipal and county government and of the primary and secondary education of the municipality's children. The latter expense is much the largest, so, basically, the fewer the school children, the lower the tax rate. Sizeable industrial and commercial ratables are eagerly sought and homes and the lots on which they are situate are required to be large enough, through minimum lot sizes and minimum floor areas, to have substantial value in order to produce greater tax revenues to meet school costs. Large families who cannot afford to buy large houses and must live in cheaper rental accommodations are definitely not wanted, so we find drastic bedroom restrictions for, or complete prohibition of, multi-family or other feasible housing for those of lesser income.

This pattern of land use regulation has been adopted for the same purpose in developing municipality after developing municipality. Almost every one acts solely in its own selfish and parochial interest and in effect builds a wall around itself to keep out those people or entities not adding favorably to the tax base, despite the location of the municipality or the demand for varied kinds of housing. There has been no effective intermunicipal or area planning or land use regulation. * * *

II

THE LEGAL ISSUE

The legal question before us, as earlier indicated, is whether a developing municipality like Mount Laurel may validly, by a system of land use regulation, make it physically and economically impossible to provide low and moderate income housing in the municipality for the various categories of persons who need and want it and thereby, as Mount Laurel has, exclude such people from living within its confines because of the limited extent of their income and resources. Necessarily implicated are the broader questions of the right of such municipalities to limit the kinds of available housing and of any obligation to make possible a variety and choice of types of living accommodations.

We conclude that every such municipality must, by its land use regulations, presumptively make realistically possible an appropriate variety and choice of housing. More specifically, presumptively it cannot foreclose the opportunity of the classes of people mentioned for low and moderate income housing and in its regulations must affirmatively afford that opportunity, at least to the extent of the municipality's fair share of the present and prospective regional need therefor. These obligations must be met unless the particular municipality can sustain the heavy burden of demonstrating peculiar circumstances which dictate that it should not be required so to do.

We reach this conclusion under state law and so do not find it necessary to consider federal constitutional grounds urged by plaintiffs. We begin with some fundamental principles as applied to the scene before us.

Land use regulation is encompassed within the state's police power. Our constitutions have expressly so provided since an amendment in 1927. That amendment, now Art. IV, § 6, par. 2 of the 1947 Constitution, authorized legislative delegation of the power to municipalities (other than counties), but reserved the legislative right to repeal or alter the delegation (which we take it means repeal or alteration in whole or in part). The legislative delegation of the zoning power followed in 1928, by adoption of the standard zoning enabling act, now found, with subsequent amendments, in N.J.S.A. 40:55–30 to 51.

It is elementary theory that all police power enactments, no matter at what level of government, must conform to the basic state constitutional requirements of substantive due process and equal protection of the laws. These are inherent in Art. I, par. 1 of our Constitution, the requirements of which may be more demanding than those of the federal Constitution. * * *

* * *

It is plain beyond dispute that proper provision for adequate housing of all categories of people is certainly an absolute essential in promotion of the general welfare required in all local land use regulation. Further the universal and constant need for such housing is so important and of such broad public interest that the general welfare which developing municipalities like Mount Laurel must consider extends beyond their boundaries and cannot be parochially confined to the claimed good of the particular municipality. It has to follow that, broadly speaking, the presumptive obligation arises for each such municipality affirmatively to plan and provide, by its land use regulations, the reasonable opportunity for an appropriate variety and choice of housing, including, of course, low and moderate cost housing, to meet the needs, desires and resources of all categories of people who may desire to live within its boundaries. Negatively, it may not adopt regulations or policies which thwart or preclude that opportunity.

* * *

We turn to application of these principles in appraisal of Mount Laurel's zoning ordinance, useful as well, we think, as guidelines for future application in other municipalities.

The township's general zoning ordinance (including the cluster zone provision) permits, as we have said, only one type of housing—single-family detached dwellings. This means that all other types—multi-family including garden apartments and other kinds housing more than one family, town (row) houses, mobile home parks—are prohibited. Concededly, low and moderate income housing has been intentionally excluded. While a large percentage of the population living outside of cities prefers a one-family house on its own sizeable lot, a substantial proportion do not for various reasons. Moreover, single-family dwellings are the most expensive type of quarters and a great number of families cannot afford them. Certainly they are not pecuniarily feasible for low and moderate income families, most young people and many elderly and retired persons, except for some of moderate income by the use of low cost construction on small lots.

As previously indicated, Mount Laurel has allowed some multi-family housing by agreement in planned unit developments, but only for the relatively affluent and of no benefit to low and moderate income families. And even here, the contractual agreements between municipality and developer sharply limit the number of apartments having more than one bedroom. * * *

Mount Laurel's zoning ordinance is also so restrictive in its minimum lot area, lot frontage and building size requirements, earlier detailed, as to preclude single-family housing for even moderate income families. Required lot area of at least 9,375 square feet in one remaining regular residential zone and 20,000 square feet (almost half an acre) in the other, with required frontage of 75 and 100 feet, respectively, cannot be called small lots and amounts to low density zoning, very definitely increasing the cost of purchasing and improving land and so affecting the cost of housing. As to building size, the township's general requirements of a minimum dwelling floor area of 1,100 square feet for all one-story houses and 1,300 square feet for all of one and one-half stories or higher is without regard to required minimum lot size or frontage or the number of occupants (see Sente v. Mayor and Municipal Council of City of Clifton, 66 N.J. 204, 208–209, 330 A.2d 321 (1974)). In most aspects these requirements are greater even than those approved in Lionshead Lake, Inc. v. Township of Wayne, supra, 10 N.J. 165, 89 A.2d 693, almost 24 years ago and before population decentralization, outer suburban development and exclusionary zoning had attained today's condition. See also Williams and Wacks, Segregation of Residential Areas Along Economic Lines: Lionshead Lake Revisited, 1969 Wis.L.Rev. 827. Again it is evident these requirements increase the size and so the cost of housing. The conclusion is irresistible that Mount Laurel permits only such middle and upper income housing as it believes will have sufficient taxable value to come close to paying its own governmental way. * * *

Without further elaboration at this point, our opinion is that Mount Laurel's zoning ordinance is presumptively contrary to the general welfare and outside the intended scope of the zoning power in the particulars mentioned. A facial showing of invalidity is thus established, shifting to the municipality the burden of establishing valid superseding reasons for its action and non-action. We now examine the reasons it advances.

* * *

[Judge Hall rejected the reasons advanced by the defendant, which were primarily fiscal and ecological.]

* * *

We have earlier stated that a developing municipality's obligation to afford the opportunity for decent and adequate low and moderate income housing extends at least to " * * * that municipality's fair share of the present and prospective regional need therefor." Some comment on that conclusion is in order at this point. Frequently it might be sounder to have more of such housing, like some specialized land uses, in one municipality in a region than in another, because of greater availability of suitable land, location of employment, accessibility of public transportation or some other significant reason. But, under present New Jersey legislation, zoning must be on an individual municipal basis, rather than regionally. So long as that situation persists under the present tax structure, or in the absence of some kind of binding agreement among all the municipalities of a region, we feel that every municipality therein must bear its fair share of the regional burden. (In this respect our holding is broader than that of the trial court, which was limited to Mount Laurel-related low and moderate income housing needs.)

The composition of the applicable "region" will necessarily vary from situation to situation and probably no hard and fast rule will serve to furnish the answer in every case. Confinement to or within a certain county appears not to be realistic, but restriction within the boundaries of the state seems practical and advisable. (This is not to say that a developing municipality can ignore a demand for housing within its boundaries on the part of people who commute to work in another state.) Here we have already defined the region at present as "those portions of Camden, Burlington and Gloucester Counties within a semicircle having a radius of 20 miles or so from the heart of Camden City." The concept of "fair share" is coming into more general use and, through the expertise of the municipal planning adviser, the county planning boards and the state planning agency, a reasonable figure for Mount Laurel can be determined, which can then be translated to the allocation of sufficient land therefor on the zoning map. See generally, New Jersey Trends, ch. 27, Listokin, Fair Share Housing Distribution: An Idea Whose Time Has Come?, p. 353. We may add that we think that, in arriving at such a determination, the type of information and estimates, which the trial judge (119 N.J.Super. at 178) directed the township to compile and furnish to him, concerning the housing needs of persons of low and moderate income now or formerly residing in the township in substandard dwellings and those presently employed or reasonably expected to be employed therein, will be pertinent.

There is no reason why developing municipalities like Mount Laurel, required by this opinion to afford the opportunity for all types of housing to meet the needs of various categories of people, may not become and remain attractive, viable communities providing good living and adequate services for all their residents in the kind of atmosphere which a democracy and free institutions demand. They can have industrial sections, commercial sections and sections for every kind of housing from low cost and multi-family to lots of more than an acre with very expensive homes. Proper planning and governmental cooperation can prevent over-intensive and too sudden development, insure against future suburban sprawl and slums and assure the preservation of open space and local beauty. We do not intend that developing municipalities shall be overwhelmed by voracious land speculators and developers if they use the powers which they have intelligently and in the broad public interest. Under our holdings today, they can be better communities for all than they previously have been.

III

THE REMEDY

As outlined at the outset of this opinion, the trial court invalidated the zoning ordinance *in toto* and ordered the township to make certain studies and investigations and to present to the court a plan of affirmative public action designed "to enable and encourage the satisfaction of the indicated needs" for township related low and moderate income housing. Jurisdiction was retained for judicial consideration and approval of such a plan and for the entry of a final order requiring its implementation.

We are of the view that the trial court's judgment should be modified in certain respects. We see no reason why the entire zoning ordinance should be nullified. Therefore we declare it to be invalid only to the extent and in the particulars set forth in this opinion. The township is granted 90 days from the date hereof, or such additional time as the trial court may find is reasonable and necessary to allow, to adopt amendments to correct the deficiencies herein specified. It is the local function and responsibility, in the first instance at least, rather than the court's, to decide on the details of the same within the guidelines we have laid down. If plaintiffs desire to attack such amendments, they may do so by supplemental complaint filed in this cause within 30 days of the final adoption of the amendments.

We are not at all sure what the trial judge had in mind as ultimate action with reference to the approval of a plan for affirmative public action concerning the satisfaction of indicated housing needs and the entry of a final order requiring implementation thereof. Courts do not build housing nor do municipalities. That function is performed by private builders, various kinds of associations, or, for public housing, by special agencies created for that purpose at various levels of government. The municipal function is initially to provide the opportunity through appropriate land use regulations and we have spelled out what Mount Laurel must do in that regard. It is not appropriate at this time, particularly in view of the advanced view of zoning law as applied to housing laid down by this opinion, to deal with the matter of the further extent of judicial power in the field or to exercise any such power. See, however, Pascack Ass'n v. Mayor and Council of the Township of Washington, 131 N.J.Super. 195, 329 A.2d 89 (Law Div.1974), and cases therein cited, for a discussion of this question. The municipality should first have full opportunity to itself act without judicial supervision. We trust it will do so in the spirit we have suggested, both by appropriate zoning ordinance amendments and whatever additional action encouraging the fulfillment of its fair share of the regional need for low and moderate income housing may be indicated as necessary and advisable. (We have in mind that there is at least a moral obligation in a municipality to establish a local housing agency pursuant to state law to provide housing for its resident poor now living in dilapidated, unhealthy quarters.) The portion of the trial court's judgment ordering the preparation and submission of the aforesaid study, report and plan to it for further action is therefore vacated as at least premature. Should Mount Laurel not perform as we expect, further judicial action may be sought by supplemental pleading in this cause.

The judgment of the Law Division is modified as set forth herein. No costs.

[Two concurring opinions are omitted.]

SOUTHERN BURLINGTON COUNTY NAACP v. TOWNSHIP OF MOUNT LAUREL (MT. LAUREL II)

Supreme Court of New Jersey, 1983.
92 N.J. 158, 456 A.2d 390.

WILENTZ, C.J.

This is the return, eight years later, of *Southern Burlington County N.A.A.C.P. v. Township of Mount Laurel,* 67 *N.J.* 151, 336 A.2d 713 (1975) (*Mount Laurel I*). We set forth in that case, for the first time, the doctrine requiring that municipalities' land use regulations provide a realistic opportunity for low and moderate income housing. The doctrine has become famous. The *Mount Laurel* case itself threatens to become infamous. After all this time, ten years after the trial court's initial order invalidating its zoning ordinance, Mount Laurel remains afflicted with a blatantly exclusionary ordinance. Papered over with studies, rationalized by hired experts, the ordinance at its core is true to nothing but Mount Laurel's determination to exclude the poor. Mount Laurel is not alone; we believe that there is widespread noncompliance with the constitutional mandate of our original opinion in this case.

To the best of our ability, we shall not allow it to continue. This Court is more firmly committed to the original *Mount Laurel* doctrine than ever, and we are determined, within appropriate judicial bounds, to make it work. The obligation is to provide a realistic opportunity for housing, not litigation. We have learned from experience, however, that unless a strong judicial hand is used, *Mount Laurel* will not result in housing, but in paper, process, witnesses, trials and appeals. We intend by this decision to strengthen it, clarify it, and make it easier for public officials, including judges, to apply it.

* * *

There are a number of municipalities around the State that have responded to our decisions by amending their zoning ordinances to provide realistic opportunities for the construction of low and moderate income housing. Further, many other municipalities have at least recognized their obligation to provide such opportunities in their ordinances and master plans. Finally, state and county government agencies have responded by preparing regional housing plans that help both the courts and municipalities themselves carry out the *Mount Laurel* mandate. Still, we are far from where we had hoped to be and nowhere near where we should be with regard to the administration of the doctrine in our courts.

* * *

The constitutional basis for the *Mount Laurel* doctrine remains the same. The constitutional power to zone, delegated to the municipalities subject to legislation, is but one portion of the police power and, as such, must be exercised for the general welfare. When the exercise of that power by a municipality affects something as fundamental as housing, the general welfare includes more than the welfare of that municipality and its citizens: it also includes the general welfare—in this case the housing needs—of those residing outside of the municipality but within the region that contributes to the housing demand within the municipality. Municipal land use regulations that conflict with the general welfare thus defined abuse the police power and are unconstitutional. In particular, those regulations that do not provide the requisite opportunity for a fair share of the region's need for low and moderate income housing conflict with the general welfare and violate the state constitutional requirements of substantive due process and equal protection. * * *

No one has challenged the *Mount Laurel* doctrine on these appeals. Nevertheless, a brief reminder of the judicial role in this sensitive area is appropriate, since powerful reasons suggest, and we agree, that the matter is better left to the Legislature. We act first and foremost because the Constitution of our State requires protection of the interests involved and because the Legislature has not protected them. We recognize the social and economic controversy (and its political consequences) that has resulted in relatively little legislative action in this field. We understand the enormous difficulty of achieving a political consensus that might lead to significant legislation enforcing the constitutional mandate better than we can, legislation that might completely remove this Court from those controversies. But enforcement of constitutional rights cannot await a supporting political consensus. So while we have always preferred legislative to judicial action in this field, we shall continue—until the Legislature acts—to do our best to uphold the constitutional obligation that underlies the *Mount Laurel* doctrine. That is our duty. We may not build houses, but we do enforce the Constitution.

We note that there has been some legislative initiative in this field. We look forward to more. The new Municipal Land Use Law explicitly recognizes the obligation of municipalities to zone with regional consequences in mind, *N.J.S.A.* 40:55D–28(d); it also recognizes the work of the Division of State and Regional Planning in the Department of Community Affairs (DCA), in creating the State Development Guide Plan (1980) (SDGP), which plays an important part in our decisions today. Our deference to these legislative and executive initiatives can be regarded as a clear signal of our readiness to defer further to more substantial actions.

The judicial role, however, which could decrease as a result of legislative and executive action, necessarily will expand to the extent that we remain virtually alone in this field. In the absence of adequate legislative and executive help, we must give meaning to the constitutional doctrine in the cases before us through our own devices, even if they are relatively less suitable. That is the basic explanation of our decisions today.

Our rulings today have several purposes. First, we intend to encourage voluntary compliance with the constitutional obligation by defining it more clearly. We believe that the use of the State Development Guide Plan and the confinement of all *Mount Laurel* litigation to a small group of judges, selected by the Chief Justice with the approval of the Court, will tend to serve that purpose. Second, we hope to simplify litigation in this area. While we are not overly optimistic, we think that the remedial use of the SDGP may achieve that purpose, given the significance accorded it in this opinion. Third, the decisions are intended to increase substantially the effectiveness of the judicial remedy. In most cases, upon determination that the municipality has not fulfilled its constitutional obligation, the trial court will retain jurisdiction, order an immediate revision of the ordinance (including, if necessary, supervision of the revision through a court appointed master), and require the use of effective affirmative planning and zoning devices. The long delays of interminable appellate review will be discouraged, if not completely ended, and the opportunity for low and moderate income housing found in the new ordinance will be as realistic as judicial remedies can make it. We hope to achieve all of these purposes while preserving the fundamental legitimate control of municipalities over their own zoning and, indeed, their destiny.

* * *

II.

RESOLUTION OF THE ISSUES

A. *Defining the Mount Laurel Obligation*

In *Oakwood v. Madison,* this Court held that it was sufficient in *Mount Laurel* litigation for courts to look to the *"substance "*of challenged zoning ordinances and to the existence of *"bona fide* efforts" by municipalities to meet their obligations. * * * It was hoped that this test would adequately protect the constitutional rights of lower income persons while at the same time minimizing the role of the courts in this area. Unfortunately, experience has taught us that this formulation is too vague to provide adequate guidance for either trial courts or municipalities. As the *Mount Laurel II* and *Mahwah* cases demonstrate, the *Madison* test does not ensure sufficient judicial scrutiny of zoning ordinances. Even those that plainly fail to meet the requisites of the *Mount Laurel* doctrine may pass the test of *Madison.*

Therefore, proof of a municipality's bona fide attempt to provide a realistic opportunity to construct its fair share of lower income housing shall no longer suffice. Satisfaction of the *Mount Laurel* obligation shall be determined solely on an objective basis: if the municipality has *in fact* provided a realistic opportunity for the construction of its fair share of low and moderate income housing, it has met the *Mount Laurel* obligation to satisfy the constitutional requirement; if it has not, then it has failed to satisfy it. Further, whether the opportunity is "realistic" will depend on whether there is in fact a likelihood—to the extent economic conditions allow—that the lower income housing will actually be constructed. Plaintiff's case will ordinarily include proof of the municipality's fair share of the regional need and defendant's proof of its satisfaction. Good or bad faith, at least on this issue, will be irrelevant. The numberless approach encouraged in *Madison,* where neither plaintiffs nor defendants are required to prove a fair share number, is no longer acceptable.

* * *

In order to meet their *Mount Laurel* obligations, municipalities, at the very least, must remove all municipally created barriers to the construction of their fair share of lower income housing. Thus, to the extent necessary to meet their prospective fair share and provide for their indigenous poor (and, in some cases, a portion of the region's poor), municipalities must remove zoning and subdivision restrictions and exactions that are not necessary to protect health and safety. * * *

Once a municipality has revised its land use regulations and taken other steps affirmatively to provide a realistic opportunity for the construction of its fair share of lower income housing, the *Mount Laurel* doctrine requires it to do no more. For instance, a municipality having thus complied, the fact that its land use regulations contain restrictive provisions incompatible with lower income housing, such as bedroom restrictions, large lot zoning, prohibition against mobile homes, and the like, does not render those provisions invalid under *Mount Laurel.* Obviously, if they are otherwise invalid—for instance if they bear no reasonable relationship to any legitimate governmental goal—they may be declared void on those other grounds. But they are not void because of *Mount Laurel* under those circumstances. * * *

[U]nless removal of restrictive barriers will, without more, afford a realistic opportunity for the construction of the municipality's fair share of the region's lower income housing need, affirmative measures will be required.

There are two basic types of affirmative measures that a municipality can use to make the opportunity for lower income housing realistic: (1) encouraging or requiring the use of available state or federal housing subsidies, and (2) providing incentives for or requiring private developers to set aside a portion of their developments for lower income housing. Which, if either, of these devices will be necessary in any particular municipality to assure compliance with the constitutional mandate will be initially up to the municipality itself. Where necessary, the trial court overseeing compliance may require their use. We note again that least-cost housing will not ordinarily satisfy a municipality's fair share obligation to provide low and moderate income housing unless and until it has attempted the inclusionary devices outlined below or otherwise has proven the futility of the attempt.

* * *

The implication of the observation that lower income housing cannot be built without subsidies is that if the *Mount Laurel* principle requires municipalities to provide a realistic opportunity for such housing through their land use regulations but leaves them free to prevent subsidies through non-action, that obligation is a charade. *Mount Laurel* was never intended to produce the perfect model of a just zoning ordinance; it was intended to provide a realistic opportunity for the construction of lower income housing.

We do not suggest that a municipality would be required to create a housing authority to meet its *Mount Laurel* obligation. We do, however, expect municipal officials in appropriate cases to do more than pass land use regulations conforming to *Mount Laurel I*. Where appropriate, municipalities should provide a realistic opportunity for housing through other municipal action inextricably related to land use regulations.

* * *

Satisfaction of the *Mount Laurel* obligation imposes many financial obligations on municipalities, some of which are potentially substantial. By contrast, a tax abatement for a low or moderate income housing project will have only a minimal effect on the public fisc. Thus viewed, the asserted fiscal reasons justifying the failure to provide a tax abatement may be nothing more than a red herring. The direct and immediate financial impact of a tax abatement agreement between the municipality and the developer may be unimportant when compared with increases in municipal and school district costs caused by the advent of lower income housing. The trial court in a *Mount Laurel* case, therefore, shall have the power to require a municipality to cooperate in good faith with a developer's attempt to obtain a subsidy and to require that a tax abatement be granted for that purpose pursuant to applicable New Jersey statutes where that abatement does not conflict with other municipal interests of greater importance.

There are several inclusionary zoning techniques that municipalities must use if they cannot otherwise assure the construction of their fair share of lower income housing. Although we will discuss some of them here, we in no way intend our list to be exhaustive; municipalities and trial courts are encouraged to create other devices and methods for meeting fair share obligations.

The most commonly used inclusionary zoning techniques are incentive zoning and mandatory set-asides. The former involves offering economic incentives to a developer through the relaxation of various restrictions of an ordinance (typically density limits) in exchange for the construction of certain amounts of low and moderate income units. The latter, a mandatory set-aside, is basically a requirement that developers include a minimum amount of lower income housing in their projects.

Incentive zoning is usually accomplished either through a sliding scale density bonus that increases the permitted density as the amount of lower income housing provided is increased, or through a set bonus for participation in a lower income housing program. *See* Fox & Davis, 3 *Hastings Const.L.Q.* 1015, 1060–62 (1977).

Incentive zoning leaves a developer free to build only upper income housing if it so chooses. Fox and Davis, in their survey of municipalities using inclusionary devices, found that while developers sometimes profited through density bonuses, they were usually reluctant to cooperate with incentive zoning programs; and that therefore those municipalities that relied exclusively on such programs were not very successful in actually providing lower income housing. *Id.* at 1067.

Sole reliance on "incentive" techniques (or, indeed, reliance exclusively on any one affirmative device) may prove in a particular case to be insufficient to achieve compliance with the constitutional mandate.

A more effective inclusionary device that municipalities must use if they cannot otherwise meet their fair share obligations is the mandatory set-aside. According to the Department of Community Affairs, as of 1976 there were six municipalities in New Jersey with mandatory set-aside programs, which varied from a requirement that 5 percent of developments in a certain zone be composed of low and moderate income units (Cherry Hill, Camden County) to a requirement that between 15 and 25 percent of all PUDs be reserved for low and moderate income housing (East Windsor, Mercer County). * * *

The use of mandatory set-asides is not without its problems: dealing with the scarcity of federal subsidies, maintaining the rent or sales price of lower income units at lower income levels over time, and assuring developers an adequate return on their investments. Fox and Davis found that the scarcity of federal subsidies has greatly undermined the effectiveness of mandatory set-asides where they are triggered only when a developer is able to obtain such subsidies. Fox & Davis, *supra,* 3 *Hastings Const.L.Q.* at 1065–66. Where practical, a municipality should use mandatory set-asides even where subsidies are not available.

* * *

In addition to the mechanisms we have just described, municipalities and trial courts must consider such other affirmative devices as zoning substantial areas for mobile homes and for other types of low cost housing and establishing maximum square footage zones, *i.e.,* zones where developers cannot build units with *more* than a certain footage or build anything other than lower income housing or housing that includes a specified portion of lower income housing. In some cases, a realistic opportunity to provide the municipality's fair share may require over-zoning, *i.e.,* zoning to allow for *more* than the fair share if it is likely, as it usually is, that not all of the property made available for lower income housing will actually result in such housing.

Although several of the defendants concede that simply removing restrictions and exactions is unlikely to result in the construction of lower income housing, they maintain that requiring the municipality to use affirmative measures is beyond the scope of the courts' authority. We disagree. * * * If it is plain, and it is, that unless we require the use of affirmative measures the constitutional guarantee that protects poor people from municipal exclusion will exist "only on paper," then the only "appropriate remedy" is the use of affirmative measures.

The specific contentions are that inclusionary measures amount to a taking without just compensation and an impermissible socio-economic use of the zoning power, one not substantially related to the use of land. Reliance is placed to some extent on *Board of Supervisors v. DeGroff Enterprises, Inc.*, 214 *Va.* 235, 198 *S.E.*2d 600 (1973), to that effect. We disagree with that decision. We now resolve the matter that we left open in *Madison*. * * * We hold that where the *Mount Laurel* obligation cannot be satisfied by removal of restrictive barriers, inclusionary devices such as density bonuses and mandatory set-asides keyed to the construction of lower income housing, are constitutional and within the zoning power of a municipality.

* * *

The contention that generally these devices are beyond the municipal power because they are "socio-economic" is particularly inappropriate. The very basis for the constitutional obligation underlying *Mount Laurel* is a belief, fundamental, that excluding a class of citizens from housing on an economic basis (one that substantially corresponds to a socio-economic basis) distinctly disserves the general welfare. That premise is essential to the conclusion that such zoning ordinances are an abuse of the zoning power and are therefore unconstitutional.

It is nonsense to single out inclusionary zoning (providing a realistic opportunity for the construction of lower income housing) and label it "socio-economic" if that is meant to imply that other aspects of zoning are not. Detached single family residential zones, high-rise multi-family zones of any kind, factory zones, "clean" research and development zones, recreational, open space, conservation, and agricultural zones, regional shopping mall zones, indeed practically any significant kind of zoning now used, has a substantial socio-economic impact and, in some cases, a socio-economic motivation. It would be ironic if inclusionary zoning to encourage the construction of lower income housing were ruled beyond the power of a municipality because it is "socio-economic" when its need has arisen from the socio-economic zoning of the past that excluded it.

Looked at somewhat differently, having concluded that the constitutional obligation can sometimes be satisfied only through the use of these inclusionary devices, it would take a clear contrary constitutional provision to lead us to conclude that that which is necessary to achieve the constitutional mandate is prohibited by the same Constitution. In other words, we would find it difficult to conclude that our Constitution both requires and prohibits these measures.

* * *

As the cost of ordinary housing skyrockets for purchasers and renters, mobile homes become increasingly important as a source of low cost housing. The evidence clearly supports a finding that mobile homes are significantly less expensive than site-built housing. * * * Therefore, subject to the qualifications noted hereafter, we rule that municipalities that cannot otherwise meet their fair share obligations must provide zoning for low-cost mobile homes as an affirmative device in their zoning ordinances.

* * *

Lest we be misunderstood, we do *not* hold that every municipality must allow the use of mobile homes as an affirmative device to meet its *Mount Laurel* obligation, or that any ordinance that totally excludes mobile homes is *per se* invalid. Insofar as the *Mount Laurel* doctrine is concerned, whether mobile homes must be permitted as an affirmative device will depend upon the overall effectiveness of the municipality's attempts to comply: if compliance can be just as effectively assured without allowing mobile homes, *Mount Laurel* does not command them; if not, then assuming a suitable site is available, they must be allowed.

* * *

There may be municipalities where special conditions such as extremely high land costs make it impossible for the fair share obligation to be met even after all excessive restrictions and exactions, *i.e.,* those not essential for safety and health, have been removed and all affirmative measures have been attempted. In such cases, *and only in such cases,* the *Mount Laurel* obligation can be met by supplementing whatever lower income housing can be built with enough "least cost" housing to satisfy the fair share. Least cost housing does not, however, mean the most inexpensive housing that developers will build on their own; it does not mean $50,000–plus single family homes and very expensive apartments. Least cost housing means the least expensive housing that builders can provide after removal by a municipality of *all* excessive restrictions and exactions and after thorough use by a municipality of all affirmative devices that might lower costs. Presumably, such housing, though unaffordable by those in the lower income brackets, will be inexpensive enough to provide shelter for families who could not afford housing in the conventional suburban housing market. At the very minimum, provision of least cost housing will make certain that municipalities in "growth" areas of this state do not "grow" only for the well-to-do.

The form that "least cost" housing will take can vary with the particular characteristics of individual municipalities. Municipalities that must resort to "least cost" housing to meet their *Mount Laurel* obligations should, if appropriate, zone significant areas for housing that most closely approaches lower income housing, *e.g.,* mobile homes. Furthermore, "overzoning" for such housing will greatly increase the likelihood that some of these units, even if not "lower income," will be affordable by those close to the top of the moderate income bracket. * * *

It is important for us to emphasize here that unless it meets the stringent "least cost" requirements set out above, middle income housing will not satisfy the *Mount Laurel* obligation. This is so despite claims by some defendant-municipalities that the provision of such middle income housing will allow less expensive housing to "filter down" to lower income families. The problem with this theory is that the housing that has been built and is now being built in suburbs such as Mount Laurel is rapidly *appreciating* in value so that none of *it* will "filter down" to poor people. Instead, if the only housing constructed in municipalities like Mount Laurel continues to be middle and upper income, the only "filter down" effect that will occur will be that housing on the fringes of our inner cities will "filter down" to the poor as more of the middle class leave for suburbs, thereby exacerbating the economic segregation of our cities and suburbs. * * *

The remedies permitted herein upon judgment of non-compliance go beyond what had previously been allowed by this Court in *Mount Laurel* cases. They were clearly anticipated by the Court, however, in *Madison,* where we explicitly approved and adopted remedies far beyond our actions in *Mount Laurel I.* * * *

In short, there being a constitutional obligation, we are not willing to allow it to be disregarded and rendered meaningless by declaring that we are powerless to apply any remedies other than those conventionally used. We intend no discourse on the history of judicial remedies, but suspect that that which we deem "conventional" was devised because it seemed perfectly adequate in view of the obligation it addressed. We suspect that the same history would show that as obligations were recognized that could not be satisfied through such conventional remedies, the courts devised further remedies, and indeed the history of Chancery is as much a history of remedy as it is of obligation. The process of remedial development has not yet been frozen.

We should be clear as to what is new here and what is conventional and about the extent of remedial change, regardless of the labels used. The use of a master to aid in resolution of a dispute is not new. Indeed, here it is not a remedy at all but a method of aiding the parties in complying with a court order.

When the court orders that an ordinance be amended, it does very little different from ordering that a variance be granted, actions taken by our courts in New Jersey for many years. It does very little different from declaring that a zoning ordinance is invalid on equal protection grounds, the effect of that often being not simply to allow a plaintiff to use his property in a manner not permitted by the ordinance, but to give the same right to an entire class. The ordinance is effectively amended to permit a use explicitly excluded, or in some cases to exclude one explicitly permitted. Sometimes the action of the court comes even closer to ordering, indeed declaring, that an ordinance has been changed, *see*

West Point Island Ass'n v. Township Committee of Dover Twp., 54 *N.J.* 339, 255 A.2d 237 (1969), where this Court, in effect, affirmed the decision of a trial court ordering a municipality to take certain action, which action could be taken only by the adoption of a resolution that the municipality had not adopted. As noted above, we did not hesitate, in *Madison,* to order amendment of the municipal zoning ordinance. Similarly, in *Lusardi v. Curtis Point Property Owners Ass'n,* 86 *N.J.* 217, 430 A.2d 881 (1981), relying on the judiciary's power to regulate zoning in the public interest, we effectively modified an ordinance that conflicted with the state's policy of affording recreational opportunities on the Atlantic seafront for as many citizens as possible.

The scope of remedies authorized by this opinion is similar to those used in a rapidly growing area of the law commonly referred to as "institutional litigation" or "public law litigation."

* * *

CONCLUSION

We have reexamined the *Mount Laurel* doctrine and we have found it correct. We have reaffirmed the judiciary's commitment to the enforcement of the constitutional right and its resulting remedy. We have found it necessary to rectify the ineffective administration of this doctrine in our courts. We have simplified the scope of litigation; the *Mount Laurel* obligation is to provide a realistic opportunity for housing, not litigation. We have substituted as a remedy the plans for growth in the State Development Guide Plan for the concept of developing municipalities, directed lower courts to dispose of the *Mount Laurel* litigation on a one-stop basis, and provided for the assignment of three judges to manage the cases statewide on a uniform basis. We have required municipalities to take affirmative action to comply with *Mount Laurel* and refocused the litigation on the question of whether low and moderate income housing will be built.

As we said at the outset, while we have always preferred legislative to judicial action in this field, we shall continue—until the Legislature acts—to do our best to uphold the constitutional obligation that underlies the *Mount Laurel* doctrine. That is our duty. We may not build houses, but we do enforce the Constitution.

The provision of decent housing for the poor is not a function of this Court. Our only role is to see to it that zoning does not prevent it, but rather provides a realistic opportunity for its construction as required by New Jersey's Constitution. The actual construction of that housing will continue to depend, in a much larger degree, on the economy, on private enterprise, and on the actions of the other branches of government at the national, state and local level. We intend here only to make sure that if the poor remain locked into urban slums, it will not be because we failed to enforce the Constitution.

In *Mount Laurel,* we reverse the trial court and remand (but affirm as to the builder's remedy); in both *Chester* and *Franklin,* we affirm the trial court in part but reverse and remand for limited further proceedings described herein; in *Clinton,* we reverse the Appellate Division and remand; in *Mahwah,* we reverse the trial court and remand; and in the Middlesex County cases, we reverse the judgment of the Appellate Division and remand. In all cases the remand is to the trial court for further proceedings consistent with this opinion.

Notes

1. What results would you expect to see after the decision in *Mount Laurel II?* Until 1985, not much happened except more litigation. The weaknesses of judicial rather than legislative oversight remained until the state legislature passed the "Fair Housing Act", N.J.Laws 1985, ch. 222. This statute created an administrative agency called The Council on Affordable Housing (COAII) with power to define housing regions and the regional needs for low and moderate income housing. The Council also has rulemaking power to establish criteria for determination of fair share obligations of municipalities. The Act was challenged by a number of municipalities, realtors, and other interested parties and was upheld in an opinion which has come to be known as *Mount Laurel III.* The case is Hills Development Co. v. Township of Bernards, 103 N.J. 1, 510 A.2d 621 (1986). In addition to upholding the Act the decision praises the legislative approach, especially insofar as it seems to provide for more consistency than the judicial approach of granting builders' remedies.

2. Time will tell if the "Fair Housing Act" will actually result in a measurable increase in affordable housing opportunities. An article in the New York Times, Feb. 24, 1986, p. A 1, reported that the first large Mount Laurel developments in New Jersey (with homes priced between $27,000 and $58,000) attracted mostly young, first-time, suburbanite home buyers and retired people, divorced people and renters. At most, ten percent of the buyers can be said to have migrated from the urban centers to take advantage of housing opportunities.

3. New Hampshire found the first Mt. Laurel case persuasive, and in Britton v. Town of Chester, 134 N.H. 434, 595 A.2d 492 (1991), the court struck down a two-acre minimum lot size restriction, and found that the ordinance had the effect of limiting the total area of the town available for affordable housing to 1.73% of the land in the town. The court said the ordinance violated the state zoning enabling legislation delegating zoning power for the "general welfare of the community." The court also approved of a builder's remedy as in Mt. Laurel II, but less drastic; the court ordered the town to revise its zoning ordinance, and face a builder's remedy if it did not do so.

HOLMDEL BUILDERS ASSOCIATION v. TOWNSHIP OF HOLMDEL

Supreme Court of New Jersey, 1990.
121 N.J. 550, 583 A.2d 277, certiorari denied sub. nom Morris Indus.
Builders, Inc. v. Township of South Brunswick, 507 U.S. 1031,
113 S.Ct. 1848, 123 L.Ed.2d 472 (1993).

HANDLER, J.

In 1975, this Court held that developing municipalities are constitutionally required to provide a realistic opportunity for the development of low- and moderate-income housing. Southern Burlington County NAACP v. Mount Laurel Township, 67 N.J. 151, 336 A.2d 713, cert. denied, 423 U.S. 808, 96 S.Ct. 18, 46 L.Ed.2d 28 (1975) (Mt. Laurel I). In the years following, many municipalities failed to comply with the clear mandate of Mt. Laurel I. The failure to provide the necessary opportunity for affordable housing led to a new legal challenge. We clarified and reaffirmed the constitutional mandate set forth in Mt. Laurel I, imposing an affirmative obligation on every municipality to provide its fair share of affordable housing. Southern Burlington County NAACP v. Mount Laurel Township, 92 N.J. 158, 456 A.2d 390 (1983) (Mt. Laurel II). We enumerated several possible approaches by which municipalities could comply with the constitutional obligation, including lower-income density bonuses and mandatory set-asides. We stressed that "municipalities and trial courts are encouraged to create other devices and methods for meeting fair share obligations." Id. at 265–66, 456 A.2d 390. Subsequently, the Legislature codified the Mt. Laurel doctrine, including its available compliance measures, by enacting the Fair Housing Act, L.1985, c. 222; N.J.S.A. 52:27D–301 to–329 (FHA). We have since upheld the constitutionality of the FHA. Hills Dev. Co. v. Bernards Township, 103 N.J. 1, 25, 510 A.2d 621 (1986).

The cases that comprise this appeal arise out of attempts by several municipalities to comply with their obligation to provide a realistic opportunity for the construction of affordable housing under our ruling in Mt. Laurel II and the provisions of the FHA. The Townships of Chester, South Brunswick, Holmdel, Middletown, and Cherry Hill all adopted ordinances to provide for low-and moderate-income housing. The ordinances, in varying forms, impose fees on developers as a condition for development approval. The fees are dedicated to an affordable-housing trust fund to be used in satisfying the municipality's Mt. Laurel obligation.

Several builders' associations initiated suits challenging those ordinances, claiming that each was an ultra vires act, exceeding the authority of the zoning and police powers and the Fair Housing Act; an invalid tax in violation of the uniform property taxation requirement of the New Jersey Constitution; a taking without just compensation in violation of both the United States and New Jersey Constitutions; and a denial of due process and equal protection in violation of both the United States and New Jersey Constitutions. Plaintiff New Jersey Builders Association sought a refund of the monies paid into the Chester Township affordable-housing trust fund plus accrued interest.

The trial courts in each case except Cherry Hill ruled that the ordinance at issue was facially unconstitutional because it imposed an unauthorized tax on a select group of individuals. The trial court in Chester also held that the New Jersey Builders Association lacked standing to seek a refund on behalf of its members. The courts did not address the due-process, equal-protection, and taking claims. In each case except Cherry Hill, they granted summary judgment to plaintiffs. In denying plaintiff's summary-judgment motion in Cherry Hill, the trial court ruled that the ordinance was constitutional and within the scope of municipal power. We denied the unsuccessful defendants' motions for direct certification.

Defendants, and Cherry Hill as intervenor, appealed the grants of summary judgment on the substantive issues, and plaintiff New Jersey Builders Association cross-appealed on the standing issue. Consolidating the cases on appeal, the Appellate Division affirmed each case except Holmdel. The Appellate Division concluded that mandatory provisions for "in lieu" development fees are unauthorized revenue-raising devices. Holmdel Builders Ass'n v. Township of Holmdel, 232 N.J.Super. 182, 193, 556 A.2d 1236 (App.Div.1989). As such, it deemed mandatory development fees invalid taxes. It agreed with the trial courts that shifting a public responsibility to a limited segment of the community violates the State Constitution's rule of uniform taxation. Id. at 193–94, 556 A.2d 1236. The court further concluded that ordinances requiring mandatory set-asides are valid only if accompanied by zoning incentives, such as a density bonus, that bear a reasonable relationship to the cost incurred in constructing the mandatory-set-aside housing. Id. at 201, 556 A.2d 1236. The court ruled that a voluntary provision allowing a developer to choose between constructing affordable housing or paying an "in lieu" development fee into an affordable-housing trust fund is valid provided that the fee bears a reasonable relationship to the benefits conferred by the density bonus. Ibid. With respect to the cross-appeal, the Appellate Division determined that a trade organization does not have standing to seek a refund on behalf of its members. Id. at 204, 556 A.2d 1236.

Accordingly, the Appellate Division ruled that the ordinances of the Townships of Chester and South Brunswick, which require payment of a mandatory development fee, were invalid because they imposed an unauthorized tax. Middletown Township's ordinance was held invalid because one section imposed a mandatory development fee, while another section required a mandatory set-aside without providing a compensating benefit. The court concluded that the voluntary nature of Holmdel's ordinance and its optional provision for an increase in density, giving the developer a compensating benefit, was facially valid; it remanded the Holmdel case for a plenary hearing with respect to the validity of Holmdel's ordinance as applied. The Appellate Division did not rule on intervenor Cherry Hill's ordinance.

* * *

This appeal raises two major substantive issues. One is whether there is statutory authority, derived from the FHA, the Municipal Land Use Law (MLUL), N.J.S.A. 40:55D–1 to–129, and the general police power of government, N.J.S.A. 40:48–2, that enables a municipality to impose affordable-housing development fees as a condition for development approval. That issue raises the related questions whether the development-fee ordinances constitute an impermissible taking of property or violate substantive due process or equal protection. The second major issue is whether affordable-housing development fees are an unconstitutional form of taxation. Finally, if these ordinances are invalid, the appeal presents the issue whether a trade organization has standing to seek a refund on behalf of its members.

* * *

In sum, the Townships of Chester and South Brunswick have enacted ordinances that impose a mandatory development fee on all new non-inclusionary developments as a condition for development approval. Their ordinances do not give developers a density bonus in exchange for the development fee. Middletown Township's ordinance imposes a mandatory development fee on all new commercial development as a condition for development approval. Non-inclusionary residential developers may choose between constructing the affordable housing or paying an in-lieu fee. Density bonuses do not accompany any of the options. Holmdel Township enacted an ordinance that gives developers a density bonus if they contribute to an affordable-housing trust fund. Cherry Hill Township's ordinance imposes a mandatory development fee on all new commercial developments and non-inclusionary residential developments of a sufficient size.

* * *

Any inquiry into the validity of development-fee ordinances must inevitably consider the complex factors that contribute to the persistent and substantial shortage of low-and moderate-income housing (hereafter, lower-income or affordable housing). This inquiry necessarily begins with our seminal decisions in Mt. Laurel I and Mt. Laurel II.

The core of those decisions is that every municipality, not just developing municipalities, must provide a realistic, not just a theoretical, opportunity for the construction of lower-income housing. We realized that the solution to the shortage of affordable housing could not "depend on the inclination of developers to help the poor, [but rather must rely] on affirmative inducements to make the opportunity real." Id., 92 N.J. at 261, 456 A.2d 390. The principal mode of compliance suggested in Mt. Laurel II was mandatory set-asides. We flatly rejected claims that such inclusionary measures amount to a taking without just compensation and an impermissible socio-economic use of the zoning power, concluding that "the builder who undertakes a project that includes a mandatory set-aside voluntarily assumes the financial burden, if there is one, of that condition." Id. at 267 n. 30, 456 A.2d 390. However, we never envisaged mandatory set-asides as the exclusive solution for the dearth of lower-income housing. In Mt. Laurel II, we encouraged municipalities "to create other devices and methods for meeting fair share obligations." 92 N.J. at 265–66, 456 A.2d 390.

The solutions proposed in Mt. Laurel II to meet the critical shortage of affordable housing were strongly influenced by the Court's perception of the causes of that shortage. We noted that the flight of industry and commerce from urban to suburban areas is largely responsible for the social ill that the Mt. Laurel doctrine is intended to address. * * *

The phenomenon of unfettered non-residential development has exacerbated the need for lower-income housing, and has generated widespread efforts to link such needed residential development to non-residential development. Thus, nationwide, municipalities have attempted to shift the externalities of development to non-inclusionary developers. See, e.g., Alterman, "Evaluating Linkage and Beyond: Letting the Windfall Genie Out of the Exactions Bottle," 34 Wash. U.J. Urb. & Contemp. L. 3, 7 (1988).

The broad concept of linkage describes any of a wide range of municipal regulations that condition the grant of development approval on the payment of funds to help finance services and facilities needed as a result of development. In the context of developing affordable housing, linkage refers to any scheme that requires developers to mitigate the adverse effects of non-residential development upon the shortage of housing either indirectly, by contributing to an affordable-housing trust fund, or directly, by actually constructing affordable housing. See A. Mallach, Inclusionary Housing Programs: Policies and Practices (1985). The idea of linking community housing goals with non-residential real estate development has inspired new governmental efforts to address the lower-income housing crisis. See Smith, "From Subdivision Improvement Requirements to Community Benefit Assessments and Linkage Payments: A Brief History of Land Development Exactions," 50 Law & Contemp. Probs. 5 (1987); Gallogly, "Opening the Door for Boston's Poor: Will 'Linkage' Survive Judicial Review?", 14 Environmental Affairs 447 (1987).

Affordable-housing linkage ordinances are the most recent phenomenon in this area. See, e.g., Connors & High, "The Expanding Circle of Exactions: From Dedication to Linkage," 50 Law & Contemp. Probs. 69 (1987). Such ordinances link or couple the right to engage in non-residential development to the provision of affordable housing. The ordinances at issue in this appeal are all examples of linkage. Each requires certain developers to help finance the construction of affordable housing either as a condition for receiving permission to build or in order to obtain some type of density bonus. Only Holmdel's ordinance gives developers the option of actually constructing affordable-housing units.

The linkage trend has gained momentum during the past decade. See Symposium: Land–Use, Zoning, and Linkage Requirements Affecting the Pace of Urban Growth, 20 Urban Lawyer 513 (1988); Bauman & Ethier, "Development Exactions and Impact Fees: A Survey of American Practices," 50 Law & Contemp. Probs. 51 (1987). The fairness and legality of linkage have inspired much debate among legal scholars, the business community, and the judiciary. Proponents, including amicus curiae Princeton Township, forcefully argue that by attracting new residents to an area, commercial developments increase the need for housing in general and thus for affordable housing. To the extent that the additional need for housing is not met with increased supply, housing prices will be pushed upward, exacerbating both the need for, and unattainability of, lower-income housing. Therefore, it is appropriate for municipalities to charge commercial developers with a portion of the responsibility for creating more affordable-housing units. Gruen, "The Economics of Requiring Office–Space Development to Contribute to the Production and/or Rehabilitation of Housing," in D. Porter, Downtown Linkages (1985); cf. Surenian, "Mount Laurel II and the Fair Housing Act," 319–23 (NJICLE 1987) (advocating linkage fees in theory but cautioning against fees in practice due to "ineffectiveness of bureaucracy" and propensity of municipalities to evade fair-share obligations). In addition, linkage advocates stress the need to consider the effect of all development on the finite supply of land. Land must be viewed as an essential but exhaustible resource; any land that is developed for any purpose reduces the supply of land capable of being used to build affordable housing. See Major, "Linkage of Housing and Commercial Development: The Legal Issues," 15 Real Estate L.J. 328, 331 (1987). The scarcity of land as a resource bears on the opportunity and means to provide affordable housing. See Hills Dev. Co. v. Bernards Township, supra, 103 N.J. at 61, 510 A.2d 621; Tocco v. New Jersey Council on Affordable Hous., 242 N.J.Super. 218, 221, 576 A.2d 328 (App.Div.), certif. denied, 122 N.J. 403, 585 A.2d 401 (1990).

Amicus curiae the Public Advocate argues that commercial developers ought not be exempt from the financial burden of Mt. Laurel compliance because their projects, like those of multifamily residential developers, consume land, water, and sewerage capacity that could otherwise be devoted to or held for the satisfaction of the municipality's lower-income-housing obligation. This Court has implicitly recognized that unrestrained nonresidential development can itself deepen the shortage of affordable housing. Mt. Laurel II, supra, 92 N.J. at 210 n. 5, 456 A.2d 390.

* * *

Plaintiffs argue that linkage fees constitute an impermissible form of exactions because they seek to require developers to provide for off-site public needs that have not been caused by their developments and furnish them no benefits. See Divan Builders v. Planning Bd. of Wayne Township, 66 N.J. 582, 598, 334 A.2d 30 (1975) (developer "could be compelled only to bear that portion of the cost [of off-site improvements] which bears a rational nexus to the needs created by and benefits conferred upon, the subdivision"); New Jersey Builders Ass'n v. Mayor of Bernards Township, 108 N.J. 223, 237, 528 A.2d 555 (1987) (municipal authority to charge developers limited "only to improvements the need for which arose as a direct consequence of the particular subdivision or development under review"); see also N.J.S.A. 40:55D–42 (developer can be required "to pay his pro rata share of the cost of providing only reasonable and necessary street improvements and water, sewerage and drainage facilities" located off-site). Because we have uniformly required a strong nexus between development and off-site improvements, plaintiffs contend that the development fees are prohibited. Although the Appellate Division found that N.J.S.A. 40:55D–42 does not specifically govern the development-fee ordinances at issue in this case, it determined that the development fees were variant forms of off-site exactions and invalid. 232 N.J.Super. at 198, 556 A.2d 1236.

In the context of off-site improvements, an exaction generally requires developers to supply or finance public facilities or amenities made necessary by proposed development. See Smith, supra, 50 Law & Contemp. Probs. 5. We have traditionally required a strong, almost but-for, causal nexus between off-site public facilities and private development in order to justify exactions. That nexus achieves two ends. First, it ensures that a developer pays for improvement that is necessitated by the development itself, Divan Builders, supra, 66 N.J. at 601, 334 A.2d 30, or is a "direct consequence" of the development, New Jersey Builders Ass'n, supra, 108 N.J. at 237, 528 A.2d 555. Second, it protects a developer from paying a disproportionate share of the cost of improvements that also benefit other persons. Longridge Builders, Inc. v. Planning Bd. of Princeton Township, 52 N.J. 348, 350, 245 A.2d 336 (1968); see also N.J.S.A. 40:56–27 (special assessments may be imposed on property owners only for unique or special benefits); Meglino v. Township Comm. of the Township of Eagleswood, 103 N.J. 144, 161, 510 A.2d 1134 (1986) (special assessments in excess of benefit to particular properties violate both enabling legislation and takings clause); McNally v. Township of Teaneck, supra, 75 N.J. 33, 43, 379 A.2d 446 (1977) (same).

Those commentators who believe that affordable-housing linkage measures are essentially a type of exaction for off-site improvements generally assume that a similar causal link is required and exists between new commercial space and an increased demand for lower-income housing. See Merriam & Andrews, "Defensible Linkage," 54 J. Am. Plan. A. 199 (1988); Bosselman & Stroud, "Mandatory Tithes: The Legality of Land Development Linkage," 17 Land Use and Envtl. L. Rev. 151 (1986). We do not believe, however, that the development-fee ordinances before us must be founded on a stringent nexus between commercial construction and the need for affordable housing. We find a sound basis to support a legislative judgment that there is a reasonable relationship between unrestrained nonresidential development and the need for affordable residential development. We do not equate such a reasonable relationship with the strict rational-nexus standard that demands a but-for causal connection or direct consequential relationship between the private activity that gives rise to the exaction and the public activity to which it is applied. Rather, the relationship is to be founded on the actual, albeit indirect and general, impact that such nonresidential development has on both the need for lower-income residential development and on the opportunity and capacity of municipalities to meet that need. Inclusionary zoning itself is based on that relationship. Such zoning measures are designed to reach all land development, to address the potential diminishment of affordable housing, and to encourage within the municipality, the region, and the state the creation of affordable housing. Such governmental measures are thus not analogous to specific off-site infrastructure improvements occasioned by a particular development.

We conclude that the rational-nexus test is not apposite in determining the validity of inclusionary zoning devices generally or of affordable-housing development fees in particular. * * *

Plaintiffs present related claims that the development-fee ordinances violate constitutional standards pertaining to the taking of property, due process, and equal protection. These contentions need not be addressed on their merits in view of our determination that municipal inclusionary zoning measures consisting of development fees for lower-income housing must be adopted in accordance with duly promulgated administrative regulations. We nevertheless observe that insofar as those contentions are addressed to the facial validity of the development-fee ordinances in these cases, they do not have merit.

The claims based on alleged violations of due process and equal protection standards by development-fee ordinances do not project new or additional substantive considerations. Because plaintiffs do not allege that they are a member of a suspect class, * * *

Further, central to those several claims is the allegation that development fees are confiscatory. The Appellate Division, believing that the fees were unfair or confiscatory, concluded that those constitutional violations would be rectified if developers received compensatory benefits. 232 N.J.Super. at 201, 556 A.2d 1236.

In response to similar claims in Mt. Laurel II that mandatory set-asides were confiscatory, this Court stated that "the builder who undertakes a project that includes a mandatory set-aside voluntarily assumes the financial burden, if there is any, of that condition." 92 N.J. at 267 n. 30, 456 A.2d 390. A developer may be made to bear the economic burdens of providing affordable housing so long as those burdens are not excessive and the project remains profitable. See id. at 279 n. 37, 456 A.2d 390 (a twenty-percent set-aside may be a "reasonable minimum"); N.J.A.C. 5:92–8.4(c); see also In re Egg Harbor Assocs., supra, 94 N.J. at 358, 464 A.2d 1115 (specific plan for inclusionary zoning involving a 20% set-aside is "neither arbitrary nor unreasonable," nor an unconstitutional taking). In Mt. Laurel II, we suggested that "[w]here practical, a municipality should use mandatory set-asides even where [federal] subsidies are not available," 92 N.J. at 268, 456 A.2d 390, and that mandatory set-asides would be legitimate as long as developers were assured "an adequate return on their investments," ibid.; no density bonuses, compensatory benefits, or subsidies were specifically required.

Since initial authority for promulgating development-fee regulations lies with COAH, we do not reach the question of when, if ever, compensatory benefits might have to accompany mandatory development fees. As long as the measures promulgated are not confiscatory and do not result in an inadequate return of investment, there would be no constitutional injury. We leave it to COAH to determine initially the level at which fees might become confiscatory.

Plaintiffs' remaining major contention is that the affordable-housing development fees are a form of taxation and, as such, exceed delegated municipal revenue-raising authority in violation of the state constitutional command that all property taxes be levied uniformly. N.J. Const. of 1947 art. VIII, § 1, para. 1.

* * *

In Mt. Laurel II, however, we determined that mandatory set-asides as a form of inclusionary zoning were not analogous to a tax. We viewed them as legitimate regulatory measures suitably addressed to the broad goals of zoning. Development fees, to reiterate, perform an identical function.

The Appellate Division also concluded that shifting the public responsibility for providing affordable housing to developers would violate the constitutional rule of uniformity in real property taxation. 232 N.J.Super. at 193–94, 556 A.2d 1236. If development fees are property taxes, arguably they may be constitutionally vulnerable because they apply to newly developed lands, exempting property that has already been developed, and therefore may lack the requisite uniformity. See New Jersey State League of Municipalities v. Kimmelman, 105 N.J. 422, 522 A.2d 430 (1987) (statute prohibiting newly-constructed single-family dwellings from being added to tax-assessment list until certificate of occupancy issued violated constitution). Nevertheless, the putative tax effect of any development fee scheme may turn on the nature and extent to which the property is burdened. Cf. Prowitz v. Ridgefield Park Village, 237 N.J.Super. 435, 568 A.2d 114 (App.Div.1989) (property tax assessment must account for affordable-housing requirements that limit resale value of units), certif. granted, 121 N.J. 666, 583 A.2d 350 (1990).

Although we do not regard development fees as a form of taxation, we stress that mandatory set-asides do not transgress the uniformity provision by imposing the responsibility of addressing the municipality's affordable-housing problems on developers of residential property. Ordinances that impose that responsibility on developers of commercial property and non-inclusionary residential property stand on the same footing.

In sum, because the development fees are a form of inclusionary zoning and similar to other land-use and related exactions, they are regulatory measures, not taxes.

* * *

We determine that under the FHA, as well as the zoning power of the MLUL and the police power, municipalities with the approval of

COAH can impose reasonable fees on the development of commercial and non-inclusionary residential property as inclusionary-zoning measures to provide lower-income housing. Such development fees may be enacted by ordinance and, subject to the approval and certification of COAH, may be included as part of a municipality's housing element and fair-share obligation under the FHA. Because the FHA does not provide sufficient guidance, the effectuation of such authority appropriately requires the promulgation of rules by COAH that will provide the standards and guidelines for the imposition and use of such development fees. We are satisfied that regulatory measures for development fees to be used for affordable housing adopted pursuant to valid rules can address constitutional concerns relating to due process, equal protection, the taking of property, or invalid taxation. In view of the grounds for our decision in this case, contentions based on those concerns need not be further addressed. Because of the absence of enabling administrative regulations, we hold that the current development-fee ordinances were not validly adopted.

The judgment of the Appellate Division is affirmed in part and reversed in part.

Notes

1. For a general view of the problems discussed in the Holmdel case, see Johnston, Schwartz, Wandeseforde–Smith & Caplan, Selling Zoning: Do Density Bonus Incentives for Moderate–Cost Housing Work?, 36 Wash. U.J.Urb. & Contemp.L. 45 (1989). In Villager Pond, Inc. v. Town of Darien, 56 F.3d 375 (2d Cir.1995) the developer of a condominium sued the town for damages in regard to an "exaction" of two units in the development to be conveyed to the town for low and moderate income people. The court rejected the argument that the developer had a property interest in receiving his zoning permits under the Dolan v. City of Tigard case, but remanded to the trial court for a determination of the developer's property interest.

2. Not long after Mount Laurel I the New York Court of Appeals, in Berenson v. Town of New Castle, 38 N.Y.2d 102, 378 N.Y.S.2d 672, 341 N.E.2d 236 (1975), held that zoning ordinances must give consideration to regional housing needs. After remand, the trial court found that the town was not meeting its fair share of regional housing needs and ordered, inter alia, that the town make provision for 3,500 units of multi-family housing by the year 1987. The town appealed the order, with the following result:

BERENSON v. TOWN OF NEW CASTLE

Supreme Court of New York, Appellate Division, 1979.
67 A.D.2d 506, 415 N.Y.S.2d 669.

GULOTTA, JUSTICE.

The plaintiffs have secured a declaratory judgment invalidating the zoning ordinance of the Town of New Castle to the extent that it fails to make adequate provision for multi-family housing. (At the time this action was commenced, the ordinance totally excluded multi-family residential housing from the list of permitted uses. A subsequent amendment, examined in proposal form at the trial and enacted prior to Special Term's decision, purports to provide for 100–150 units of multi-family housing, as a permitted use, in the central business district of Chappaqua.) The issue on appeal is *not* whether the Town of New Castle may permissibly exclude multi-family housing from within its borders. The town now concedes that its total exclusion was improper and contends that the interim amendment of its zoning ordinance "is just the beginning of a process of experimentation in accommodating alternative housing forms including multi-family housing." Rather, the issue before us is whether the far-reaching remedial provisions of the judgment may be sustained. We hold that, for the most part, they may not.

* * *

* * * That there does exist an unmet local and regional need for multi-family housing is not seriously contested by the town on appeal, and this finding is amply supported by the evidence. However, instead of merely declaring the ordinance unconstitutional and remanding the matter to the Town Board for passage of an amended zoning ordinance which would pass judicial muster, Special Term went further and awarded the plaintiffs comprehensive affirmative relief. Finding that the town had not merely "failed" to consider local and regional housing needs, but, on the contrary, had "continuously and actively opposed any planning or program that would suggest the assumption by it of any responsibility to meet local or regional housing needs", and that compliance with the standards for local government land use control would not be promoted if made to depend upon repetitive litigation of the basic substantive issues, Special Term promulgated "judicially established housing goals" by declaring that the construction of 3,500 units of multi-family housing over the next 10 years was "the most conservative estimate of what will be required of New Castle * * * to supply its own needs * * * [and] its share of the regional needs", and directed the town to amend its zoning ordinance, land use regulations and planning policies to accommodate the needed housing. The town was given six months within which to comply, and in the absence of timely and satisfactory compliance, Special Term decreed that the traditional presumption of validity attending zoning ordinances would be suspended and applications for rezoning would be granted on an *ad hoc* basis to individual developers whose proposals meet the judicially established housing goals, unless the town is able to establish compelling reasons for denial. Special Term also declared that the zoning ordinance was unconstitutional as it applied to the plaintiffs' property and directed the town to rezone that property for multi-family housing at a density of eight units per acre within six months. In its decision, Special Term stated that a building permit should be issued to the plaintiffs upon the advent of rezoning. To all of this broad, comprehensive relief the town objects, and rightfully so.

* * *

* * * Zoning and land use regulations were deemed to be legislative functions, to be exercised by and within the particular expertise of the *local* legislative body. Thus, with the single exception of discriminatory zoning of similarly situated parcels, in which case the obvious remedy was to treat like parcels alike, a judicial declaration that a zoning ordinance was invalid as applied to a particular piece of property was never accompanied by a declaration which actually rezoned that property or placed it within a particular use classification. * * *

More recently, however, court challenges to exclusionary zoning on behalf of those excluded from the community have come into being, spawned by tremendous economic and social changes and the deterioration of city life. These challenges have not been prompted by the mere growth of the suburbs as attractive, affluent, mainly white collar bedroom communities, for those have been with us for many years. Rather, the critical factor appears to have been the relatively recent flight of blue collar jobs to the suburbs, where housing for the employer, but not his employees, was willingly provided. Moreover, while the early judicial challenges to such exclusionary practices were brought by plaintiff-developers who wished to put their property to a more profitable, higher density use, it was soon recognized that the developers' rights could not realistically be separated from the rights of others, then nonresidents, " 'in search of a comfortable place to live' "(Concord Township Appeal, 439 Pa. 466, 474, n. 6, 268 A.2d 765, 768, n. 6) and the cases were decided accordingly. In these cases, the relief sought was generally a declaration of the unconstitutionality of the zoning ordinance and the relief, when granted, consisted of such a declaration and, in some of cases, in a departure from past practices, a direction, in effect, rezoning the plaintiff's land * * *.

[At this point the court reviewed the Pennsylvania and New Jersey exclusionary zoning cases.]

* * *

Turning back now to the case at bar, Special Term found, on the basis of the evidence adduced at the trial that "the most conservative estimate of what will be required of New Castle over the next ten years to supply its own needs for multi-family housing and to meet its share of the regional needs for such housing is not less than 3,500 multi-family housing units," a figure which the court determined was not speculative, but rather "a realistic planning goal that recognized the minimum needs established by the evidence." As previously noted, since it deemed the town to be resistant to the voluntary assumption of its responsibilities in this respect and considered a one-time detailed mandate of specified changes in the zoning ordinance to be superior to expensive and repetitive litigation to achieve zoning relief on a parcel by parcel basis, Special Term simply directed the town to amend its ordinance and accessory regulations to provide for the construction of at least 3,500 units of multi-family housing by the end of 1987. In our opinion, this mandate is unsupported by the evidence, contrary to law, and contrary to sound principles of planning.

As respects the evidence adduced at the trial, it is readily apparent that this case contains a most peculiar incongruity. Although the amended complaint does not challenge the town's ordinance as exclusionary with respect to low and moderate income housing (which, in fact, it certainly is), and plaintiffs themselves do not purport either to represent low and moderate income persons seeking housing within the town or to be interested in building multi-family housing affordable by such persons, evidence as to the housing needs of this particular income group (persons having an annual income of less than $10,000 in 1970, which by reason of inflation, translates into $14,613 in 1977) abounds in the record. Indeed, evidence as to the present housing needs of the town's residents and workers was quantified only as to this income group, although evidence as to regional housing needs was introduced both as to this lower income group and the population in general. As for the number of units it ordered to be provided, Special Term did not ascribe its 3,500 figure to any particular evidence or expert witness, but it is clear from the record that it was taken from the testimony of two particular experts, Levy and Raymond. Although one witness worked forward and the other backward, both estimated a "fair share" for the town to be about 3,500 units, based on a projected growth of the population of Westchester County, the number of housing units required to be constructed to keep pace with such growth, and New Castle's fair share of such units, figured on the basis of its percentage of the remaining land in the county suitable for such development. *However, neither estimate was geared to the needs of lower income groups in particular.* In fact, Levy's "target figure" was not meant to include only multi-family units, while Raymond admitted that it was preferable to satisfy present needs first, as future needs might change during the period between the advent of rezoning and completion of the finished units.

There was also evidence in the case (not relied on by Levy or Raymond) that the Tri–State Regional Planning Commission had estimated a housing deficit, based on the 1970 census, of over 2,000,000 units in the tri-state region, over 60,000 units in Westchester County, and about 6,000 units in the 13 communities of Northern Westchester, of which New Castle is a part. These figures were based exclusively on the needs of families earning less than $10,000 in 1970 and took into account those units necessary to replace housing which was presently substandard, overcrowded (more than 1.01 persons per room) or cost-imbalanced (rent being 25% or more of the family's income), as well as new units which would be necessary for those who wished to reside closer to their employment. However, the figures themselves are inherently inflated, as the categories of substandard, overcrowded and cost-imbalanced housing often overlap; they do not distinguish between single-and multi-family dwellings; and, more importantly, the appropriate remedy for the problem described is not necessarily the construction of new housing, since the emphasis today is on the rehabilitation of existing units and on rent subsidies. Moreover, the data is now more than eight years old, and the estimated shortfall of 6,000 units was calculated with reference to all 13 communities of Northern Westchester, most of which have similarly made little or no provision for multi-family or "least-cost" housing, but have not been joined as defendants in this action (cf. Urban League of Greater New Brunswick v. Mayor, 142 N.J.Super. 11, 359 A.2d 526).

In point of fact then, the multi-family housing quota of 3,500 units, adopted by Special Term as New Castle's "fair share" of regional housing needs is a highly abstract and speculative number, to which the trial court ultimately gave more weight than did its proponents, Levy and Raymond. Further, the court apparently failed to appreciate that the figure itself was referable to the housing market in general, both as to income groups and the type of housing (single-or multi-family) to be provided, and was not directly referable to the needs of the low income groups with which the court was primarily concerned. *The use of a "fair share" goal has never been judicially approved in the context of the housing needs of the population at large.* Its *raison d'etre* lies in the housing needs of the low and moderate income groups whose "circumstances of * * * economic helplessness * * * to find adequate housing * * * [combined with] the wantonness of foreclosing them therefrom by [exclusionary] zoning", impelled the New Jersey Supreme Court to adopt the "fair share" doctrine in the first instance (Pascack Assn. v. Mayor & Council of Township of Washington, Bergen County, 74 N.J. 470, 480, 379 A.2d 6, 11). Moreover, Special Term's judgment cannot and does not insure that any of the multi-family units to be constructed will be anything other than luxury condominiums, with which the market may already be saturated. While not sufficient to save the zoning ordinance from invalidation, the town's contention that multi-family rental housing (the type most affordable by persons of low and moderate income) cannot be constructed today even *with* governmental subsidies unless the land is publicly owned or figured at zero cost is not without some merit, especially if we are talking about providing lower income housing in sizeable quantities. Indeed, the New Jersey Supreme Court's subsequent focus upon "least-cost" housing as opposed to *low-income* housing is attributable to its recognition that it will be virtually impossible to provide large amounts of newly constructed housing for the economically less fortunate in the foreseeable future (Oakwood at Madison v. Township of Madison, 72 N.J. 481, 371 A.2d 1192 supra).

Aside from these evidentiary and practical problems, it is also abundantly clear that Special Term's declaration of a specific, mandatory "fair share" quota for the Town of New Castle is unsupported by case law and contrary to the public policy considerations embodied therein. It will be recalled that the "fair share" doctrine in Pennsylvania never encompassed the judicial specification of a particular number of higher density units to be built or the acreage to be devoted to such usage, and that even in New Jersey, where the doctrine is most highly developed, the Supreme Court has thus far refused to require judicial prescription of a mandatory "fair share" unit quota, concluding in essence, that such a course would be both inappropriate and impracticable. Nor is the decision of the Court of Appeals on the prior *Berenson* appeal (38 N.Y.2d 102, 378 N.Y.S.2d 672, 341 N.E.2d 236, supra) authority for the adoption of a "fair share" unit quota. Quite to the contrary, in holding that New Castle could validly exclude multi-family housing if its neighboring communities provided a sufficient number of such units, or the land upon which they could be built, to satisfy their own, New Castle's, and the regional needs, the Court of Appeals impliedly held that New Castle per se did not have to bear any "fair share" of any such housing burden. On the other hand, however, we cannot be blind to the fact that were the regional and local needs already being satisfied elsewhere, it is unlikely that we would be presented with the instant lawsuit, as the desire of developers and builders such as the plaintiffs to maximize their profits through more intensive land usage is, after all, dependent upon a market demand for that type of development. In any event, by holding that the courts had no choice, in the absence of meaningful regional planning, but to "assess the reasonableness of what the locality has done" (Berenson v. Town of New Castle, 38 N.Y.2d 102, 111, 378 N.Y.S.2d 672, 682, 341 N.E.2d 236, 243, supra), the Court of Appeals in our view, merely intended to have Special Term determine whether New Castle's exclusion of multi-family dwellings was reasonable in light of present and foreseeable local and regional needs. We do not perceive that the court intended that a finding of unreasonableness, i.e., that there was an *unmet* local or regional need for multi-family housing which the town had ignored by excluding such housing, would authorize the court to go even further and remedy the deficiency by specific judicial fiat.

Although we therefore, find that Special Term erred in mandating a "fair share" unit goal, there is little doubt but that the record establishes an unsatisfied local and regional need for multi-family housing on the part of what we shall simply call the less affluent residents of the New York City metropolitan area. Indeed, the town does not argue to the contrary. And while multi-family zoning cannot insure that such units will actually be built, or that, if built, they will be affordable by families of modest means, the absence of such zoning, as noted by Special Term, surely precludes any such construction.

As a court of law, we cannot provide any lasting solution for the complex problems posed by cases such as this, but we can and must in appropriate cases require a developing municipality such as the Town of New Castle to cease its policy of immunizing itself from the ordinary incidents of growth and "confront the challenge of population growth with open doors" (Golden v. Planning Bd. of Town of Ramapo, 30 N.Y.2d 359, 379, 334 N.Y.S.2d 138, 153, 285 N.E.2d 291, 302, supra). The zoning ordinance thus having been properly declared unconstitutional for failure to make adequate provision for multi-family housing, the judgment should be modified so as to delete the 3,500 unit requirement, but direct that the matter be remanded to the Town Board to remedy its zoning deficiency within six months. Further, Special Term should retain jurisdiction for the purpose of allowing the plaintiffs to challenge the sufficiency of any amended ordinance by supplemental pleadings in this case. It is our expectation that the town will now set about its task with the utmost good faith. However, we feel compelled to note that the interim amendment here, characterized by one of plaintiffs' witnesses as having been drawn with such care as might be exercised if the town had to accept a leper colony into its midst, was not such a good-faith effort. Allegedly designed to provide 100–150 units of multi-family housing in the central business district of Chappaqua (an inadequate number in any event), plaintiffs presented uncontroverted proof that this estimated yield was based solely on spatial capacity and, as a general matter, could not be realized without the conversion of existing commercial space into residential space or the construction of a second floor on the tops of one-story commercial buildings, there being so little vacant land left to develop; as a practical matter, it was stated, the construction of no more than 27 units was realistically possible.

* * *

Judgment of the Supreme Court, Westchester County, entered December 30, 1977, modified, on the law, by deleting the third, fourth, fifth and sixth decretal paragraphs thereof and substituting therefor provisions (1) remanding the matter to the Town Board to remedy its zoning deficiency within a period of six months, (2) directing the Town Board to rezone plaintiffs' property for multi-family use and (3) directing that Special Term retain jurisdiction for the purpose of allowing plaintiffs to challenge the sufficiency and validity of any amended ordinance by supplemental pleadings in this case. As so modified, judgment affirmed, with costs to respondents payable by appellant.

* * *

SHAPIRO, JUSTICE (concurring in part and dissenting in part).

With one exception, I concur in the scholarly and comprehensive opinion of my brother MR. JUSTICE GULOTTA.

The amended zoning ordinance enacted by the Town of New Castle in response to the caveat of Berenson v. Town of New Castle, 38 N.Y.2d 102, 378 N.Y.S.2d 672, 341 N.E.2d 236, was a derisive mockery, verging on contempt. * * *

* * *

In a case such as this where the dilatory tactics of the town have prevented the plaintiffs from proceeding with their building project for more than five years, two strikes should be out. The conduct of the town fathers exhibits a flagrant and intentional and malicious policy of disregard for the law which was clearly intended to impede, if not entirely defeat, the rights of the plaintiffs. Thus, the zoning ordinance should be declared invalid with no period of grace. If there is no zoning until the town fathers shoulder their proper responsibilities—so be it. They should not be given leisure time to reform. Enough is enough.

Notes

1. The earlier decision in the Berenson case rejected a facial attack on the zoning ordinance, Berenson v. Town of New Castle, 38 N.Y.2d 102, 378 N.Y.S.2d 672, 341 N.E.2d 236 (1975).

2. The New York courts have, since the Berenson decision, continued to insist that fair share problems are for the legislature, and attempts to obtain judicial relief have, for the most part, failed. See, e.g., Suffolk Housing Services v. Town of Brookhaven, 70 N.Y.2d 122, 517 N.Y.S.2d 924, 511 N.E.2d 67 (1987) and Asian Americans for Equality v. Koch, 72 N.Y.2d 121, 531 N.Y.S.2d 782, 527 N.E.2d 265 (1988). Also see Strykers Bay Neighborhood Council v. City of New York, 695 F.Supp. 1531 (S.D.N.Y.1988); Spallone v. United States, 493 U.S. 265, 110 S.Ct. 625, 107 L.Ed.2d 644 (1990).

FERNLEY v. BOARD OF SUPERVISORS OF SCHUYLKILL TOWNSHIP

Supreme Court of Pennsylvania, 1985.
509 Pa. 413, 502 A.2d 585.

HUTCHINSON, JUSTICE.

Appellants, owners of 245 acres of undeveloped land in Schuylkill Township in Chester County, appeal a * * * decision of the Board of Supervisors of Schuylkill Township denying appellants' application for a curative amendment which challenged the total prohibition of multi-family dwellings contained in the Township's zoning ordinance on exclusionary grounds and sought the establishment of a new residential district in which appellants could construct garden apartments, townhouses and quadraplexes. We now reverse Commonwealth Court and hold that Schuylkill Township's zoning ordinance is impermissibly exclusionary because it totally prohibits the construction of multi-family dwellings.

* * *

On this appeal, appellants challenge Commonwealth Court's conclusion that the zoning ordinance's absolute prohibition of multi-family housing is not unconstitutionally exclusionary because Schuylkill Township is not a logical area for growth and development, and, therefore, no one has been excluded. In reaching its conclusion, Commonwealth Court employed the "fair share" analysis first announced in *Surrick v. Zoning Hearing Board,* 476 Pa. 182, 382 A.2d 105 (1977), which, until its decision, had been applied only in cases involving zoning regulations which partially, not totally, ban a particular type of housing stock. We are now confronted with the question of whether a fair share analysis must be employed to assess the exclusionary impact of zoning regulations which totally prohibit a basic type of housing. We hold that the fair share analysis is inapplicable to this Schuylkill Township zoning ordinance which absolutely prohibits apartment buildings.

The "fair share" test, enunciated in *Surrick, supra,* was judicially developed as a means of analyzing zoning ordinances which effect a partial ban that amounts to a *de facto* exclusion of a particular use, as distinguished from those ordinances which provide for a total or *de jure* exclusion. The *de facto* exclusionary doctrine "was intended to foster regional growth by requiring communities located on the fringes of the metropolitan areas to absorb the 'increased responsibility' and 'economic burdens' which time and natural growth invariably bring." * * *

Cases involving *de facto* or partially exclusionary zoning turn on the question of whether the provision for a particular use in the ordinance at issue reasonably accommodates the immediate and projected demand for that use. In these cases certain factors influencing population growth become relevant to the question of whether a zoning ordinance which already allows a particular and basic type of housing stock in designated areas is nevertheless impermissibly exclusionary because the amount of housing of that type permitted under the ordinance is unfairly limited when compared to the immediate and projected demand for it.

Considerations underpinning the fair share principle are irrelevant when the challenged zoning regulation totally excludes a basic form of housing such as apartments. It is true that demand for apartments often derives from the pressure of regional population growth. *See, e.g., Appeal of Girsh*, 437 Pa. at 244, 263 A.2d at 398 (township could not be permitted to "choose to only take as many people as can live in single-family housing, in effect freezing population at near present levels"). Similarly, permitting any type of new construction within a municipality will, ordinarily, result in an increase in that community's population.

However, demand for housing is not necessarily correlated to population growth. Regardless of projected growth patterns, there may be many families who presently desire to make their home in Schuylkill Township but who are effectively zoned out of the community because they cannot afford to purchase either a single-family house or a duplex. Accordingly, Schuylkill Township's contention that its zoning ordinance does not exclude anyone because population projections show little or no growth in the community is untenable. Because the Township has failed to establish that the total exclusion of apartments serves a legitimate public purpose, the zoning ordinance is unconstitutional insofar as it fails to provide for apartments or for other types of multi-family housing.

We must next determine the judicial relief to which appellants are entitled. Appellants contend that they are entitled to definitive relief, *i.e.,* automatic and total approval of their development plan. Conversely, the appellee argues that appellants' remedy is limited to the additional development rights provided them under the amendment passed by the Township in 1975 for the purpose of curing any constitutional infirmity created by the total ban on multi-family housing contained in the zoning ordinance as originally enacted.

* * *

[The Court then holds that a governing body may not totally prohibit the proposed development of a person successfully challenging the ordinance, and cannot subject the project to unreasonable restrictions. It may subject the developer to reasonable restrictions provided for in its ordinance.]

Therefore, we reverse the Commonwealth Court's order and remand the record to the Court of Common Pleas for approval of appellants' proposed development unless the appellee can show that appellants' plan is incompatible with the site or reasonable, pre-existing health and safety codes and regulations relating to lands, structures or their emplacement on lands which the court determines apply to the development plan. *See* Section 1011(2) of the Pennsylvania Municipalities Code, 53 P.S. § 11011(2); *Ellick v. Board of Supervisors,* 17 Pa.Commonwealth at 413–17, 333 A.2d at 246–49.

Reversed and remanded to Common Pleas for proceedings consistent with this opinion.

* * *

NIX, CHIEF JUSTICE, concurring.

I am satisfied that on this record the challenged zoning ordinance is constitutionally flawed under either the "total exclusion" theory announced in the *Appeal of Girsh,* 437 Pa. 237, 263 A.2d 395 (1970), or the "fair share" principle followed in *Surrick v. Zoning Hearing Board of Township of Upper Providence,* 476 Pa. 182, 382 A.2d 105 (1977).

In these instances where there is a successful challenge to an unconstitutional zoning ordinance it is imperative for this Court to mandate that, subject to reasonable modifications, the township or municipality must ultimately adopt the underlying development plan. Not only does such policy guard against any possible retaliation against the litigant who opposed the zoning board, but it also serves to deter the passage of unconstitutional zoning ordinances.

* * *

Naturally, it is for the municipality to decide whether apartments are more appropriate in one part of the township than in another, *Appeal of Girsh, supra,* 437 Pa. at 246 n. 6, 263 A.2d at 399 n. 6. As we stated in *Appeal of Girsh, supra,* "Certainly [the township] can protect its attractive character by requiring apartments to be built in accordance with (reasonable) setback, open space, height, and other light-and-air requirements, but it cannot refuse to make any provision for apartment living." *Id.* at 245, 263 A.2d at 399 (footnote omitted). Thus, it is appropriate that the developer's plan in the instant case be approved subject to "certain reasonable restrictions."

Accordingly, I would reverse the Commonwealth Court's order and remand the case to the Court of Common Pleas to consider any adjustments which may be required to make the proposed plan compatible with the overall zoning plan of the Township.

McDERMOTT, JUSTICE, concurring and dissenting.

I agree that the challenged zoning ordinance is unconstitutional. However, that is the only thing in the majority opinion with which I can agree.

* * *

In the present case, the Board of Supervisors concluded as a matter of law that Schuylkill Township was not a logical area for growth and development. This conclusion was based upon findings of fact such as the following: the township is less accessible to major employment centers than other municipalities in the region; the projected population growth for the township by 1980 is less than 1,000 people; other municipalities in the region will have more rapid population increases than will Schuylkill Township; there are no specific plans to increase employment in the township, although such plans do exist on a county-wide basis; the Delaware Valley (consisting of Bucks, Chester, Delaware, Montgomery and Philadelphia counties in Pennsylvania and Burlington, Camden, Gloucester, and Mercer counties in New Jersey) will experience no population growth between 1978 and 2000; the township is outside the Philadelphia metropolitan area; and, there is no need for high density housing in the township.

* * *

Although we have not precisely defined the concept of a logical area for growth, our prior decisions have made it clear that a municipality may not stand in isolation. The municipality and the region surrounding it must be studied as a whole. *See Appeal of Elocin, Inc.*, 501 Pa. 348, 461 A.2d 771 (1983), *Appeal of M.A. Kravitz Co., Inc.*, 501 Pa. 200, 460 A.2d 1075 (1983). Among the factors to be analyzed are the following: the distance, both in miles and in driving time, from major urban areas; the accessibility of public transportation including regional high-speed rail lines; the proximity of industrial parks, corporate headquarters, and other sources of employment opportunity; the distance from major highways; and population trends in both the municipality and in surrounding municipalities that might logically and realistically be considered to be part of the region.

In this case the board and the lower courts focused so narrowly on Schuylkill Township as to ignore all the evidence in the record that demonstrated that the area surrounding this enclave is constantly growing. That evidence established that Schuylkill Township is less than one hour's driving time from center city Philadelphia and that it is on the edge of the Philadelphia Standard Metropolitan Statistical Area. Furthermore, it is located within minutes of the Pennsylvania Turnpike, the Schuylkill Expressway, the King of Prussia office and retail complex, and the developing high-technology corridor along Route 202. There are large industrial parks and regional headquarters of major corporations located in nearby townships. A township in such a region cannot be said to be in an area of no growth or one that will be immune from suburban expansion.

On the issue of prior development within the township the Board of Supervisors made no factual findings. However, the record indicates that as of 1965 apparently 70% of the township was either farm land or was undeveloped. Approximately 17% was residential consisting mostly of houses built in the 1930's and 1940's. Industrial and commercial areas accounted for less than 1% of the township's land.

On this record I would conclude that the zoning ordinance of Schuylkill Township as it existed in April of 1975, fostered an unconstitutional exclusion.

* * *

ZAPPALA, JUSTICE, concurring and dissenting.

I join with the Court in ruling that the zoning ordinance challenged in this case is invalid.

* * *

I disagree with the Majority, however, as to the remedy applicable upon this finding of a violation. The Majority cites language from *Casey v. Zoning Hearing Board of Warwick Township,* 459 Pa. 219, 328 A.2d 464 (1974), to the effect that a successful litigant is entitled to relief which recognizes the propriety of his challenge, rewards his efforts in testing the legality of the ordinance, and prevents "retributive" action by the municipality which would correct the illegality but leave the challenger unbenefitted. To proceed directly from this unobjectionable language to the statement that "[a]ccordingly, *Casey* governs the instant litigation and mandates that appellants be permitted to develop their property *as proposed,* subject to reasonable restrictions, *regardless of how that land is currently zoned,*" at 589 (emphasis added), is to "answer" the question presented by avoiding it.

* * *

McDERMOTT, J., joins in the dissenting portion of this concurring and dissenting opinion.

Notes

1. The Fernley case was followed in Borough of Malvern v. Jackson, 108 Pa.Cmwlth. 248, 529 A.2d 96 (1987), remanded 521 Pa. 570, 559 A.2d 489 (1989) and H & R Builders, Inc. v. Borough Council of Norwood, 124 Pa.Cmwlth. 88, 555 A.2d 948 (1989).

2. Where a fully developed city has been found in violation of the Fair Housing Act or guilty of racially discriminatory zoning practices under the Equal Protection clause, the problem of fashioning judicial relief is almost as

great as in cases involving developing municipalities. See United States v. City of Parma, Ohio, 494 F.Supp. 1049 (N.D.Ohio 1980).

B. LEGISLATIVE APPROACHES

BOARD OF APPEALS OF HANOVER v. HOUSING APPEALS COMMITTEE IN DEPT. OF COMMUNITY AFFAIRS

Supreme Judicial Court of Massachusetts, 1973.
363 Mass. 339, 294 N.E.2d 393.

TAURO, CHIEF JUSTICE.

This is a reservation and report by a Superior Court judge without decision of two suits in equity brought by (1) the board of appeals of the town of Hanover (Hanover board) and (2) the board of appeals of the town of Concord (Concord board). * * * The bills present similar questions concerning the constitutional validity and the substantive and procedural effects of G.L. c. 40B, §§ 20–23, inserted by St.1969, c. 774, § 1 (c. 774). The cases are, therefore, decided together.

* * *

The bills present three issues for resolution concerning the powers and procedures of the boards of appeals and the committee under G.L. c. 774. We must determine:

(a) whether c. 774 confers power upon both the committee and the boards to override zoning regulations which hamper the construction of low and moderate income housing;

(b) whether such power to override zoning regulations, if it exists, is constitutional; and

(c) whether such power to override zoning regulations, if it exists, was properly exercised by the committee in the instant cases.

* * *

The boards argue that the Legislature did not intend to grant the power to override local zoning by-laws or ordinances to any authority when it enacted c. 774. Thus, their respective decisions to deny comprehensive permits in these cases were reasonable and consistent with local needs because neither they nor the committee had authority to issue comprehensive permits for a use of land not permitted under local zoning by-laws. The boards contend that the Legislature's purpose in enacting c. 774 was merely to provide a streamlined procedure for processing applications for the necessary local approvals of construction of low or moderate income housing. Where previously an applicant was forced to negotiate with various local agencies or officials before gaining their approval, c. 774's new time limits expedited the process by allowing the applicant to apply for and obtain a comprehensive permit from a single agency, the board of appeals. The committee argues, to the contrary, that the text, history, and context of c. 774 indicate that the

Legislature intended to confer to both the board and the committee the power to override any local requirements and regulations, including zoning by-laws, which prevented the construction of low and moderate income housing when such housing is deemed "consistent with local needs."

* * *

Examination of the subsequent legislative history of c. 774 as redrafted by the Committee on Ways and Means (renumbered House Bill No. 5581) discloses neither a change of purpose nor a change of method on the part of the Legislature. The redrafted bill had the same title as the Urban Affairs Committee bill, "An Act providing for the construction of low or moderate income housing in cities and towns and for relief from local restrictions hampering such construction." Since the title to a statute may be considered in its construction, Silverman v. Wedge, 339 Mass. 244, 245, 158 N.E.2d 668, the identical titles suggest that no major change of substance was intended by the redrafting of the Committee on Ways and Means. Moreover, records of the legislative debate reveal that both proponents and opponents of the redrafted bill realized that the bill would grant the power to override local zoning regulations which hampered the construction of low and moderate income housing. The House Journal indicates that opposition to the bill was based on the bill's incursion into the municipalities' power to exercise a veto over low and moderate income housing. In both the House and the Senate, opponents of the bill attempted unsuccessfully to amend the bill in a way which would have stripped the legislation of its primary effect by excluding the bill's applicability to any city or town which refused to accept it. * * * Clearly, such an amendment would not have been necessary if local zoning powers were to remain inviolate under the new law because city councils and town meetings already had the power to prevent any nonconforming use.

* * *

We have often stated that a construction of a statute which would completely negate legislative intent should be avoided. Assessors of Newton v. Pickwick Ltd., Inc., 351 Mass. 621, 625, 223 N.E.2d 388. The boards' interpretation of this statute would have exactly this effect. Streamlining local permit procedures could not possibly serve the statute's clear purpose of promoting the construction of low and moderate income housing if the cities and towns retained the unlimited power to enforce restrictive zoning ordinances or by-laws which prevented the construction of such housing. Therefore, we hold that c. 774 confers on boards of appeals and the Housing Appeals Committee the power to override local "requirements and regulations," including zoning ordinances or by-laws, which are not "consistent with local needs."

Does c. 774 Violate the Home Rule Amendment?

We must now determine whether the grant of such power is constitutional. * * *

Thus, municipalities can pass zoning ordinances or by-laws as an exercise of their independent police powers but these powers cannot be exercised in a manner which frustrates the purpose or implementation of a general or special law enacted by the Legislature in accordance with § 8's provisions. The adoption of the Home Rule Amendment has not altered the Legislature's supreme power in zoning matters as long as the Legislature acts in accordance with § 8. Chapter 774 is a proper exercise of the powers reserved to the Legislature by § 8 because it is a general law which applies to two or more municipalities. It is in addition to the Legislature's continuing exercise of such reserve power in its numerous amendments to G.L. c. 40A, which is the basic enabling statute for zoning by-laws and ordinances. Therefore, the statute's grant of power to boards of appeals and to the committee to override local zoning ordinances or by-laws which would otherwise frustrate the statute's objective of providing for the critical regional need for low and moderate income housing does not violate the Home Rule Amendment.

Does the Boards' or Committee's Exercise of their Power to Override Local Zoning Regulations Deemed Inconsistent with Local Needs Constitute Spot Zoning?

The amici curiae argue that when the committee exercises its power to override local zoning by-laws deemed inconsistent with local needs, it engages in illegal spot zoning because its act singles out a particular parcel of property in a community for treatment different from that given to similar surrounding land indistinguishable from it in character.

However, we have frequently held that a spot zoning violation involves more than a mere finding that a parcel of property is singled out for less restrictive treatment than that of surrounding land of a similar character. If we accepted the amici curiae's test for spot zoning, the State could never exercise its undoubted power to override local zoning ordinances or by-laws for legitimate public purposes because there would always be a disparity of treatment between the area where the local ordinance or by-law is ignored and the rest of that zoning area where it is enforced. Moreover, zoning variances and amendments would also be subject to serious challenge on spot zoning grounds if the test were merely one of dissimilar treatment of similar parcels of property.

* * *

Thus, the central question posed by this spot zoning challenge is whether the difference of treatment accorded by c. 774 serves the public welfare or merely affords an economic benefit to the owner of the land receiving special treatment. We decided in the *Lamarre* case that zoning changes affording special treatment to encourage the construction of multi-family residences in cities with housing shortages promote the public welfare. 324 Mass. p. 546, 87 N.E.2d 211. We followed this decision in Henze v. Building Inspector of Lawrence, Mass., 269 N.E.2d 711, where we held that the need for low and moderate income housing justified a zoning reclassification of a parcel of land from a one and two-family residential district to a multi-family residential district.[34] We think these decisions are dispositive of the spot zoning challenge. Chapter 774 reflects the Legislature's judgment that the special treatment accorded to a site proposed for the construction of low and moderate income housing and necessitated by exclusionary zoning practices serves the general welfare by promoting the construction of badly needed housing units in the suburbs. The statute's "consistent with local needs" standard and its provisions for judicial review of the board's and committee's decisions insure that special treatment will be allowed only when it serves the public interest. Thus, we hold that the exercise of c. 774's power to override local zoning by-laws and ordinances deemed inconsistent with local needs does not constitute spot zoning.

Is c. 774 Unconstitutionally Vague?

The boards contend that c. 774 improperly delegates legislative authority to an administrative agency and is void for vagueness because its provisions fail to provide standards sufficient to guide administrative action and to limit the exercise of untrammeled discretion. See Smith v. Board of Appeals of Fall River, 319 Mass. 341, 344, 65 N.E.2d 547. These constitutional claims of "void for vagueness" and unlawful delegation of legislative authority are closely related. The principal question posed by both claims is whether the statute is so vague "that men of common intelligence must necessarily guess at its meaning and differ as to its application." * * *

[The court found the statute contained sufficient standards and was not unduly vague.]

* * *

We have reviewed the committee's decisions on the Hanover and the Concord applications "upon consideration of the entire record" and conclude that both decisions were supported by substantial evidence.

In conclusion, c. 774 represents the Legislature's attempt to satisfy the regional need for housing without stripping municipalities of their power to zone. By creating a "consistent with local needs" criterion which expands the scope of relevant local needs considered by the local boards to include the regional need for low and moderate income housing, the Legislature has given the boards the power to override the local exclusionary zoning practices in order to encourage the construction of such housing in the suburbs. By fixing a ceiling on the extent to which a board must override local zoning regulations, the Legislature has clearly delineated that point where local interests must yield to the

---

34. Most State and Federal courts have rejected spot zoning claims where the zoning change contributed to the public welfare by promoting the construction of multiple dwellings in communities that have housing shortages. See Wolpe v. Poretsky, 81 U.S.App.D.C. 67, 154 F.2d 330, cert. den. 329 U.S. 724, 67 S.Ct. 69, 91 L.Ed. 627; Malafronte v. Planning & Zoning Bd. of Milford, 155 Conn. 205, 230 A.2d 606; Hedin v. County Commrs. of Prince Georges County, 209 Md. 224, 120 A.2d 663; Burford v. Austin, 379 S.W.2d 671 (Tex.Civ.App.). See also Anderson, Am.Law of Zoning, § 5.06, pp. 248–249.

general public need for housing. This ceiling establishes the minimum share of responsibility that each community must shoulder in order to alleviate the housing crisis that confronts the Commonwealth.

As we noted in Simon v. Needham, 311 Mass. 560, 42 N.E.2d 516, the municipality's power to control its character and land usages by its zoning regulations is not unlimited. * * *

The legislative reports which prompted c. 774's passage demonstrated how local restrictive zoning regulations have set up, in fact if not intentionally, a barrier against the introduction of low and moderate income housing in the suburbs. Moreover, this barrier exists at a time when our housing needs for the low and moderate income groups cannot be met by the "inner cities." This housing crisis demands a legislative and judicial approach[35] that requires "the strictly local interests of the town" to yield to the regional need for the construction of low and moderate income housing. Chapter 774 represents the Legislature's use of its own zoning powers to respond to this problem.

The Legislature's zoning power may be used "where the interests of the public require such action and where the means employed are reasonably necessary for the accomplishment of the purpose." Simon v. Needham, 311 Mass. 560, 562, 42 N.E.2d 516, 517. Within these broad limits, the General Court is the sole judge as to how and when the power is to be exercised as long as it acts in accordance with the powers

---

35. Although comprehensive legislation seems the most rational and efficient way of combatting exclusionary zoning practices by the suburbs, some courts, in States where the Legislature has not acted to remedy the problem, have struck down restrictive zoning requirements on substantive due process and equal protection grounds. See Girsh Appeal, 437 Pa. 237, 263 A.2d 395 (1970) (Pennsylvania Supreme Court held that the failure to provide for apartments anywhere in a particular town was unconstitutional denial of due process even though multi-family residences were not expressly prohibited). The court emphasized that in examining whether a particular zoning regulation promoted the general welfare, it would consider the external effects of the regulation on other cities as well as the internal effects on the particular city's welfare. "Perhaps in an ideal world, planning and zoning would be done on a regional basis, so that a given community would have apartments, while an adjoining community would not. But as long as we allow zoning to be done community by community, it is intolerable to allow one municipality (or many municipalities) to close its doors at the expense of surrounding communities and the central city." p. 245, fn. 4, 263 A.2d p. 399. See also County Supervisors of Fairfax County, Virginia v. Carper, 200 Va. 653, 107 S.E.2d 390 (Virginia Su-

preme Court of Appeals invalidated a two acre minimum lot size requirement because its effect was to exclude low income groups from the area).

However, many State courts have upheld restrictive zoning regulations (e.g., minimum lot size requirements) despite their exclusionary impact on low and moderate income groups on the ground that these regulations have a rational relationship to the local community's general welfare. These courts refused to consider the external effects of exclusionary zoning practices on other cities because they were not considered relevant to the determination of whether the local community's general welfare was advanced. See Zygmont v. Planning & Zoning Commn. of Greenwich, 152 Conn. 550, 210 A.2d 172; Honeck v. County of Cook, 12 Ill.2d 257, 146 N.E.2d 35; Flora Realty & Inv. Co. v. Ladue, 362 Mo. 1025, 246 S.W.2d 771, app. dism. 344 U.S. 802, 73 S.Ct. 41, 97 L.Ed. 626; Bilbar Constr. Co. v. Easttown Township Bd. of Adjustment, 393 Pa. 62, 141 A.2d 851.

For a discussion of recent legislative and judicial attacks against exclusionary zoning, see 7 Harv.J. on Legislation, 246; 22 Syracuse L.Rev. 465; Notes, 84 Harv.L.Rev. 1645; 69 Univ. of Mich.L.Rev. 339; 23 Stanford L.Rev. 767.

reserved to it by § 8 of the Home Rule Amendment. Our responsibility in examining the Legislature's exercise of its zoning power is limited to the determination of whether the legislation adopts a reasonable means to serve a legitimate public purpose. Our analysis of c. 774's legislative history and text leads us to conclude that the Legislature's adoption of an administrative mechanism designed to supersede, when necessary, local restrictive requirements and regulations, including zoning by-laws and ordinances, in order to promote the construction of low and moderate income housing in cities and towns is a constitutionally valid exercise of the Legislature's zoning power which was properly implemented in the proceedings before us.

In each case, a decree shall be entered in the Superior Court affirming the decision of the Housing Appeals Committee.

So ordered.

Notes

1.   In 1975, Massachusetts amended its enabling act to provide, *inter alia,* "zoning ordinances or by-laws may also provide for special permits authorizing increases in the permissible density of population or intensity of a particular use in a proposed development; provided that the petitioner or applicant shall, as a condition for the grant of said permit, provide certain open space, housing for persons of low or moderate income, traffic or pedestrian improvements, or other amenities." See Iodice v. City of Newton, 397 Mass. 329, 491 N.E.2d 618 (1986); Bonan v. City of Boston, 398 Mass. 315, 496 N.E.2d 640 (1986); Zoning Bd. of Appeals of Greenfield v. Housing Appeals Comm., 15 Mass.App.Ct. 553, 446 N.E.2d 748 (1983).

2.   Also see Cal.Govt.Code § 65580 et seq., a 1980 statute which deals with planning for the housing needs of the community and the region, including the fair share concept. Of special interest is § 65589 which states, in part: "Nothing in this article shall require a city * * * to * * * expend local revenues for the construction of housing, housing subsidies, or land acquisition." Other relevant California statutes to consider are Cal.Govt. Code § 65302.8, § 65863.6, § 65913.1, § 65913.2, and § 66412.2.

3.   Rhode Island has amended its zoning enabling legislation to provide, in R.I. Gen. L. § 45–24–30, that the purposes of zoning ordinances include:

* * *

(8) Promoting a balance of housing choices, for all income levels and groups, to assure the health, safety and welfare of all citizens and their rights to affordable, accessible, safe and sanitary housing.

(9) Providing opportunities for the establishment of low and moderate income housing.

* * *

(16) Providing opportunities for reasonable accommodations in order to comply with the Rhode Island Fair Housing Practices Act, the United States Fair Housing Amendments Act of 1988 (FHAA), the

Rhode Island Civil Rights of Individuals with Handicaps Act, and the Americans with Disabilities Act of 1990 (ADA).

4. In addition to the principal case, see Floyd v. New York State Urban Development Corp., 41 A.D.2d 395, 343 N.Y.S.2d 493 (1973), affirmed 33 N.Y.2d 1, 347 N.Y.S.2d 161, 300 N.E.2d 704 (1973), upholding the power of the Urban Development Corporation, a public entity, to override the zoning regulations of local municipalities.

5. Not very many states have enacted legislation comparable to that in Massachusetts and New York, probably for the reason that local municipal control of zoning is so entrenched and agencies like those created in those two states smack of regional government, a highly controversial political notion.

C. THE VALIDITY OF INCLUSIONARY ORDINANCES

BOARD OF SUPERVISORS OF FAIRFAX COUNTY v. DeGROFF ENTERPRISES, INC.

Supreme Court of Virginia, 1973.
214 Va. 235, 198 S.E.2d 600.

HARMAN, JUSTICE.

The question presented by this appeal is the validity of amendment 156 (the amendment) to the Fairfax County Zoning Ordinance (ordinance) which became effective on September 1, 1971.

When the amendment, which consists of 39 typewritten pages, is stripped of detail, it requires the developer of fifty or more dwelling units in five zoning districts (RT–5, RTC–5, RT–10, RTC–10 and RM–2G) to commit himself, before rezoning or site plan approval to build at least 15% of these dwelling units as low and moderate income housing within the definitions promulgated from time to time by the Fairfax County Housing and Redevelopment Authority (FCHRA) and the United States Department of Housing and Urban Development (HUD). Under the amendment the housing units designated as low and moderate income units can be sold or rented only to persons of low and moderate income as defined by FCRHA and HUD regulations and the sale or rental price for such units cannot exceed the amount established as price guidelines by those agencies.

After a lengthy hearing the trial court found the amendment invalid on the grounds that the Board of Supervisors exceeded its authority under the zoning enabling act, Code § 15.1–486 et seq., that the amendment constituted an improper delegation of legislative authority, and that the amendment was arbitrary and capricious.

The hearing before the trial court clearly demonstrated both a demand and an urgent need for housing units for low and moderate income families in Fairfax County. Indeed, the uncontroverted evidence indicates that the need then existed there for 10,500 such dwelling units.

The Board of Supervisors of Fairfax County (Board) on the basis of this need, would have us hold the amendment valid on the ground that it "facilitates 'creation of a convenient * * * and harmonious community' and is essential to the 'health, safety, * * * [and] general welfare of the public.' "In support of this proposition the Board cites Code § 15.1–489 in which these purposes for zoning ordinances are enumerated.

That a problem exists in the need for low and moderate income housing has been recognized for many years. In 1937, in an effort to help meet this need, the Congress passed the United States Housing Act, Act of Sept. 1, 1937, c. 896, 50 Stat. 888.

The following year the General Assembly, to implement the low income housing provisions of this federal act, passed the Housing Authority Law, Acts of Assembly, 1938, c. 310, which now appears, as amended, as Code § 36–1 et seq. In Mumpower v. Housing Authority, 176 Va. 426, 11 S.E.2d 732 (1940), we considered the Housing Authorities Law and found it to be a constitutionally valid exercise of the police power. In doing so we recognized that slum eradication and the erection of low income public housing was "a matter of vital concern to the public and to the State." Id. at 437, 11 S.E.2d at 735.

Today, as a part of the nationwide effort to solve the housing problem upon which billions of dollars of public funds have been expended, redevelopment and housing authorities exist in most, if not all, of the urban areas of the Commonwealth and in many of the non-urban areas.

Thus it would appear that providing low and moderate income housing serves a legitimate public purpose. The question, then, becomes whether this public purpose can be accomplished by the amendment to the ordinance which rests upon the police power.

The principles of zoning law are well settled in Virginia. This court, speaking through Mr. Justice I'Anson, in Board of Supervisors v. Carper, 200 Va. 653, 107 S.E.2d 390 (1959), summarized these established principles as follows:

> "The general principles applicable to a judicial review of the validity of zoning ordinances are well settled. The legislative branch of a local government in the exercise of its police power has wide discretion in the enactment and amendment of zoning ordinances. Its action is presumed to be valid so long as it is not unreasonable and arbitrary. The burden of proof is on him who assails it to prove that it is clearly unreasonable, arbitrary or capricious, and that it bears no reasonable or substantial relation to the public health, safety, morals, or general welfare. The court will not substitute its judgment for that of a legislative body, and if the reasonableness of a zoning ordinance is fairly debatable it must be sustained. * * * The exercise of the police power is subject to the constitutional guarantee that no property shall be taken without due process of law and where the police power conflicts with the Constitution the latter is supreme, but courts will not restrain the exercise of such power

except when the conflict is clear." West Bros. Brick Co. v. City of Alexandria, supra, 169 Va. at page 281, 192 S.E. at page 885.

" * * * '[T]he purpose of zoning is in general twofold: to preserve the existing character of an area by excluding prejudicial uses, and to provide for the development of the several areas in a manner consistent with the uses for which they are suited. The regulations should be related to the character of the district which they affect; and should be designed to serve the welfare of those who own and occupy land in those districts.' See also I Yokley, Zoning Law and Practice, § 10, pp. 12, 13." 200 Va. at 660, 107 S.E.2d at 395.

In Carper we held invalid a zoning ordinance which had as its purpose the exclusion of low and middle income groups from the western areas of Fairfax County. The effect of this decision is to prohibit socio-economic zoning. We conclude that the legislative intent was to permit localities to enact only traditional zoning ordinances directed to physical characteristics and having the purpose neither to include nor exclude any particular socio-economic group.

* * *

More recently in Fairfax County v. Columbia Pike Ltd., 213 Va. 437, 192 S.E.2d 778 (1972), we followed our earlier holding in Mooreland v. Young, 197 Va. 771, 91 S.E.2d 438 (1956), that the zoning enabling act does not authorize the governing body of a county to control compensation for the use of lands or the improvements thereon.

When the amendment is measured by these legal standards, we find it deficient.

The amendment, in establishing maximum rental and sale prices for 15% of the units in the development, exceeds the authority granted by the enabling act to the local governing body because it is socio-economic zoning and attempts to control the compensation for the use of land and the improvements thereon.

Of greater importance, however, is that the amendment requires the developer or owner to rent or sell 15% of the dwelling units in the development to persons of low or moderate income at rental or sale prices not fixed by a free market. Such a scheme violates the guarantee set forth in Section 11 of Article 1 of the Constitution of Virginia, 1971, that no property will be taken or damaged for public purposes without just compensation.

Affirmed.

Note

Refer back to Mt. Laurel II, where the court specifically rejects the reasoning of the Virginia court. Which decision makes more sense? Do you see a parallel between mandatory set-asides in the housing field and the dispute over affirmative action in the employment area?

Chapter IX

AESTHETIC REGULATIONS
AND PRESERVATION
OF RESOURCES

As we have seen in the previous chapters, zoning started out as a tool for segregating inconsistent land uses in the city and for regulating the height and size of structures and their placement on lots. As zoning became both acceptable and fashionable, the legal approval extended to zoning was seen as a convenient source of power to accomplish public objectives which had nothing to do with separating uses or regulating building bulk. In many respects the development was much like the expansion of federal regulation which took place in Congress in the twentieth century acting under the Commerce Clause of Article I of the Constitution. The zoning power was something of an empty vessel receptive to many land use regulations to accomplish multiple purposes. In this chapter, several different types of land use regulations are examined. Some of the cases deal with provisions in zoning ordinances, and many of the opinions talk in terms of zoning and the police power. However, the subject matter of the regulations is not, strictly speaking, consonant with the concept of zoning, and thus the editors feel that this material belongs in a separate chapter.

SECTION 1. AESTHETICS AND
ARCHITECTURAL
CONTROL

Until the mid 1950's courts would state almost routinely that aesthetic considerations in land use regulation, especially zoning, were not a sufficient basis for exercising the police power. This attitude was probably reflective of the notion that the law could not tolerate restrictions based on something as indefinable as aesthetic sense, as beauty, after all, lies in the eye of the beholder. However, when Justice Douglas wrote in 1954 in Berman v. Parker, which is reproduced in Chapter V, supra that taking property for urban renewal was taking for a public use, and that aesthetic considerations formed a part of the valid public interest, state appellate courts began to reexamine the question of whether aesthetics were a legitimate basis for public regulation. The impact of Berman v. Parker is illustrated by the Wisconsin decision in State ex rel. Saveland Park Holding Corp. v. Wieland, which is reproduced in this chapter. Since 1954, the attitude of courts has shifted quite substantially on the issue. The main developments have come in two areas: Regulation of signs and billboards and regulation of the appearance of structures.

In considering the cases and materials in this chapter, a number of considerations must be taken into account. Among others, these include the particular policy of a jurisdiction as manifested in its statutes or judicial attitudes and how high aesthetic, environmental and related considerations rank on the scale of values in that jurisdiction; whether such concerns are or should be legitimately included within the police power without regard to whether tradition would exclude them unless joined with some other "legitimate" police power concern; whether the upholding and enforcement of such values, even if considered a valid police power exercise, so deprive an owner of his property rights as to constitute a taking which should require compensation; and whether the judicial or statutory approval of such considerations would ultimately permit the aesthetic sensibilities of a few individuals to force others to conform to their particular ideas to the point of oppression.

A. REGULATION OF SIGNS AND BILLBOARDS

STATE v. DIAMOND MOTORS, INC.

Supreme Court of Hawaii, 1967.
50 Hawaii 33, 429 P.2d 825.

LEVINSON, JUSTICE. In 1957 the City and County of Honolulu enacted Ordinance No. 1557 which was codified, after the adoption in 1959 of the Charter of the City and County of Honolulu, as Article 26 (Signs Regulations) of Chapter 13 (Regulations Promoting General Welfare) of the Revised Ordinances of Honolulu 1961. The ordinance is comprehensive in nature and provides for the regulation and control of outdoor signs, the location, erection, maintenance and use of signs, and penalties for the violation thereof. It prohibits, among other things, the erection and the maintenance in industrial districts of ground signs exceeding 75 square feet in area or exceeding 16 feet in height from the ground.[1]

---

1. Findings and declarations contained in the ordinance include the following:

"(a) That the people of the City have a primary interest in controlling the erection, location and maintenance of outdoor signs in a manner designed to protect the public health, safety and morals and to promote the public welfare; and

"(b) That the rapid economic development of the City has resulted in a great increase in the number of businesses with a marked increase in the number and size of signs advertising such business activities; and

* * *

"(g) That the natural beauty of landscape, view and attractive surroundings

Appellant Alexander is the owner of a ground sign 40 feet high and more than 75 square feet in area, which he installed in 1965 upon the premises of appellant Diamond Motors, Inc., located in an industrial district on the main highway between Honolulu International Airport and downtown Honolulu and the Waikiki beach area. As provided in the ordinance, the City's Building Superintendent gave written notice to appellants to correct the violation by appropriately reducing the area and height of the sign within 20 days. Appellants failed to make the corrections.

Each of the appellants was, thereafter, charged by an information filed August 25, 1965 with a violation of the ordinance and, upon a consolidated trial by jury, was found guilty as charged. * * *

Appellants assert: (1) that the ordinance, including its application to appellants, is based exclusively upon aesthetic considerations; (2) that legislation based exclusively upon aesthetic considerations is outside the scope of police powers and therefore invalid; and (3) that application of the ordinance to appellants constitutes a taking of private property without the payment of compensation in violation of the Fifth Amendment to the Constitution of the United States and Article I, Section 18 of the Constitution of the State of Hawaii.

Appellee disputes the first assertion and argues that the ordinance was enacted for a number of purposes, among which was the preservation of aesthetics as a means to the end of protecting and promoting the general welfare of the people of the City and County of Honolulu, particularly by protecting and promoting the tourist trade and thereby the economic well-being of the City and County of Honolulu.

Appellee's answering brief admittedly "does not extend to supporting the proposition that aesthetics alone is a proper objective for the exercise of the City's police power." Perhaps, the "weight of authority" in other jurisdictions persuaded the City to present the more traditional arguments because it felt that it was safer to do so. However, the brief of The Outdoor Circle as amicus curiae presents, as we think, a more modern and forthright position.

We accept beauty as a proper community objective, attainable through the use of the police power. We are mindful of the reasoning of

of the Hawaiian Islands, including the City, constitutes an attraction for tourists and visitors; and

"(h) That a major source of income and revenue of the people of the City is derived from the tourist trade; and

"(i) That the indiscriminate erection and maintenance of large signs seriously detract from the enjoyment and pleasure of the natural scenic beauty of the City which in turn injuriously affect the tourist trade and thereby the economic well-being of the City; and

"(j) That it is necessary for the promotion and preservation of the public health, safety and welfare of the people of the City that the erection, construction, location, maintenance of signs be regulated and controlled. (Sec. 13–26.1 R.O. 1957)."

Permissible ground signs on any lot or parcel of land in industrial districts are limited by the ordinance to "One ground sign, lighted or unlighted, not exceeding 75 square feet in area, relating to businesses conducted on the premises, and not exceeding 16 feet in height from the ground."

most courts that have upheld the validity of ordinances regulating outdoor advertising and of the need felt by them to find some basis in economics, health, safety, or even morality. See Thomas Cusack Co. v. City of Chicago, 242 U.S. 526, 37 S.Ct. 190, 61 L.Ed. 472 (1917). We do not feel so constrained.

Hawaii's constitution provides:

> The State shall have power to conserve and develop its natural beauty, objects and places of historic or cultural interest, sightliness and physical good order, and for that purpose private property shall be subject to reasonable regulation. (Article VIII, Section 5.)

Appellants argue that this constitutional provision has no application to this case because the offending sign is located in an industrial area. We do not agree. The natural beauty of the Hawaiian Islands is not confined to mountain areas and beaches. The term "sightliness and physical good order" does not refer only to junk yards, slaughter houses, sanitation, cleanliness, or incongruous business activities in residential areas as appellants argue.

* * *

Cromwell v. Ferrier, 19 N.Y.2d 263, 225 N.E.2d 749 (New York 1967) upheld the constitutionality of a town zoning ordinance which was a comprehensive and detailed plan for regulation of signs in the township. The court said:

> " * * * Advertising signs and billboards, if misplaced, often are egregious examples of ugliness, distraction, and deterioration. They are just as much subject to reasonable controls, including prohibition, as enterprises which emit offensive noises, odors, or debris. The eye is entitled to as much recognition as the other senses, but, of course, the offense to the eye must be substantial and be deemed to have material effect on the community or district pattern. * * * "(p. 755.)

Oregon City v. Hartke, 240 Or. 35, 400 P.2d 255, decided in 1965, in holding that an ordinance wholly excluding automobile wrecking yards from Oregon City was a valid exercise of the police power, said:

> " * * * there is a growing judicial recognition of the power of a city to impose zoning restrictions which can be justified solely upon the ground that they will tend to prevent or minimize discordant and unsightly surroundings. This change in attitude is a reflection of the refinement of our tastes and the growing appreciation of cultural values in a maturing society. The change may be ascribed more directly to the judicial expansion of the police power to include within the concept of 'general welfare' the enhancement of the citizen's cultural life." (pp. 46–47, 400 P.2d p. 261.)

> "We join in the view 'that aesthetic considerations alone may warrant an exercise of the police power.' "(p. 49, 400 P.2d p. 262.)

* * *

We hold that the application of the ordinance to appellants constituted a regulation for the public welfare under the City's police power in a legitimate field for legitimate aesthetic reasons and that it does not constitute a taking of private property without the payment of compensation. Cromwell v. Ferrier, supra, 19 N.Y.2d 263, 225 N.E.2d 749 (New York 1967).

The remaining question raised by appellants is whether the application of the ordinance to appellants is an arbitrary, discriminatory and unreasonable deprivation and denial of due process and equal protection in violation of the Fifth and Fourteenth Amendments to the Constitution of the United States and Article I, Section 4 of the Constitution of the State of Hawaii.

Appellants argue that "the arbitrary limitation of height and size of signs cannot be considered reasonably necessary and appropriate for the accomplishment of the aesthetic objective set forth in the * * * Ordinance, which seeks to eliminate the 'indiscriminate erection and maintenance of large signs which seriously detract from the enjoyment and pleasure of the natural scenic beauty' of the community."

The City has said through its legislative body that the limitations placed by the ordinance on height and size of signs are necessary. Classifications are obviously required. The burden is upon the appellants to show that the limitations and classifications are unreasonable. State v. Safeway Stores, Inc., 106 Mont. 182, 76 P.2d 81. The record does not so show. Appellants say that whether a classification violates the equal protection clause of the Fourteenth Amendment to the Constitution of the United States is a judicial question. It was incumbent on them in invoking the protection of the Fourteenth Amendment "to show with convincing clarity" that the ordinance created against them the discrimination of which they complain. Corporation Comm'n of Oklahoma v. Lowe, 281 U.S. 431, 50 S.Ct. 397, 74 L.Ed. 945. They have not done so.

* * *

The judgments are affirmed.

MAYOR AND CITY COUNCIL OF BALTIMORE v. MANO SWARTZ, INC.

Court of Appeals of Maryland, 1973.
268 Md. 79, 299 A.2d 828.

SINGLEY, JUDGE. For the second time we have before us an attack on the validity of Ordinance No. 663 of the Mayor and City Council of Baltimore (the City), approved 1 November 1965, now Baltimore City Code Art. 1, § 39 (1966) (the Ordinance), which was designed to regulate signs in the central business district of Baltimore.

There was testimony that the City had been so successful in limiting the size and design of signs in agreements for the sale of sites in the Charles Center renewal area that a decision was made to endeavor to achieve uniformity in the whole of the downtown district.

In City of Baltimore v. Charles Center Parking, 259 Md. 595, 271 A.2d 144 (1970), we affirmed a decree of the Circuit Court of Baltimore City which had found arbitrary and discriminatory and violative of Article 23 of Maryland's Declaration of Rights and of the Fourteenth Amendment to the Constitution of the United States § 1(e)(4) of the Ordinance, which had made unlawful the painting of a sign on an exterior wall of a building. We concluded that this result was mandated by the fact that § 1(j) of the Ordinance permitted billboards and poster boards, subject to zoning regulations, in the same area where painted signs were prohibited, particularly since the City offered no testimony which would support a rational distinction between painted signs and billboards.

In that case, we addressed ourselves to a narrow issue—the validity of § 1(e)(4)—and expressed no opinion as regards the validity of the Ordinance as a whole. The assault mounted in this case is of wider scope.

On 30 October 1970, just before the expiration of the five-year moratorium contained in § 1(g) of the Ordinance, Mano Swartz, Inc., and nine other firms doing business in the central business district (Swartz) filed a bill of complaint in the Circuit Court of Baltimore City against the City and the City's Director of Construction and Building Inspection seeking to enjoin the enforcement of § 1(e)(1) which proscribes signs projecting more than 12 inches "from the primary surface of the building to which it is attached * * * "and § 1(e)(4) which prohibits roof top signs.

Filed with the bill of complaint was the text of the Ordinance: * * *

(a) A Commission on Signs is created. It shall have three members appointed as of January 1, 1966, under the provisions of Article IV, Section 6, of the City Charter. One of the three members shall represent the retail merchants in the area defined in this section. Another member shall represent the sign industry. The third member of the Commission shall be a representative of the public at large. * * *

(b) The Commission may retain technical advisors, amongst which shall be included an architect, a graphic artist and a sign designer.

* * *

(d) The Commission, after public notice and hearing may adopt and promulgate rules and regulations establishing standards and requirements for commercial signs, billboards, and other advertising structures and devices within the area described in this section. Any such rules and regulations shall be designed and intended to provide for beauty, attractiveness, esthetics, and symmetry in the commercial signs, billboards, and other advertising structures and devices, and to relieve conditions of gaudiness and drabness in certain portions of the defined area.

* * *

The Ordinance had as its sole purpose the achievement of an aesthetically pleasing result, and we have held this not to be a permissible use of the police power, Feldstein v. Kammauf, 209 Md. 479, 484–489, 121 A.2d 716 (1956); Goldman v. Crowther, 147 Md. 282, 302–309, 128 A. 50 (1925); Byrne v. Maryland Realty Co., 129 Md. 202, 211, 98 A. 547 (1916); see, 1 Anderson, American Law of Zoning § 7.21 at 520–21 (1968); 2 Metzenbaum, The Law of Zoning 1577–1578 (2d ed. 1955); 1 Rathkopf, The Law of Zoning and Planning 11–1 (3d ed. 1972); 16 Am.Jr.2d Constitutional Law § 292 at 569 (1964).

While aesthetic goals may legitimately serve as an additional legislative purpose, if health, morals or safety or other ends generally associated with the concept of public welfare are being served, * * * they cannot be the only purpose of regulation, Byrne v. Maryland Realty Co., supra, 129 Md. at 211, 98 A. 547.

The City might well have prevailed had the legislative intent been the elimination of signs or pennants which distracted motorists, Kenyon Peck, Inc. v. Kennedy, 210 Va. 60, 168 S.E.2d 117 (1969) or the promotion of highway safety, Stevens v. City of Salisbury, 240 Md. 556, 567–568, 214 A.2d 775 (1965); see E.B. Elliott Adv. Co. v. Metropolitan Dade County, 425 F.2d 1141 (5th Cir.1970), petition for cert. dismissed, 400 U.S. 805, 91 S.Ct. 12, 27 L.Ed.2d 35; Village of Larchmont v. Sutton, 30 Misc.2d 245, 217 N.Y.S.2d 929 (1961); *approved and followed in,* Village of Larchmont v. Levine, Sup., 225 N.Y.S.2d 452 (1961). The fact that another result might have been one which was aesthetically pleasing would not necessarily have imported an element of constitutional infirmity.

The effort to eliminate what was referred to in argument before us as "visual pollution" by controlling signs and billboards through the exercise of the zoning power has been slowly developing, General Outdoor Adv. Co. v. Indianapolis, 202 Ind. 85, 172 N.E. 309, 72 A.L.R. 453 (1930); Opinion of the Justices to the Senate, 333 Mass. 773, 128 N.E.2d 557, 561 (1955); People v. Sterling, 128 Misc. 650, 220 N.Y.S. 315 (1927); State ex rel. Saveland Park Holding Corp. v. Wieland, 269 Wis. 262, 69 N.W.2d 217, 222 (1955); 58 Am.Jur. Zoning § 30 at 959 (1948); 1 Anderson, American Law of Zoning, supra, § 7.21 at 520–23; 1 Rathkopf, Law of Zoning and Planning, supra, at 11–9, 11–22; 1 Yokely, Zoning Law and Practice § 2–4 at 28 (3d ed. 1965); Dukeminier, Zoning for Aesthetic Objectives: A Reappraisal, 20 Law & Contemp.Prob. 218 (1955); Masotti & Selfon, Aesthetic Zoning and the Police Power, supra, 46 J.Urban L. 773, 779–86; Note, 47 Cornell L.Rev. 647, 651–652 (1962); Annot., Aesthetic Objectives or Considerations as Affecting Validity of Zoning Ordinance, 21 A.L.R.3d 1222, 1225 (1968). The principal difficulty is that other forms of pollution, stench and noise and the like, can be measured by more nearly objective standards. If beauty, however, lies in the eyes of the beholder, so does the tawdry, the gaudy and the vulgar—and courts have traditionally taken a gingerly approach to legislation which circumscribes property rights by applying what amount to subjective standards, which may well be those of an idiosyncratic group. See discussion in, General Outdoor Advertising Co. v. Department of Public Works, supra, 193 N.E. at 815–816; Cromwell v. Ferrier, 19 N.Y.2d 263,

279 N.Y.S.2d 22, 225 N.E.2d 749, 755, 21 A.L.R.3d 1212 (1967); Dukeminier, Zoning for Aesthetic Objectives: A Reappraisal, 20 Law & Contemp.Prob., supra, at 224–229 (1955); Michelman, Toward a Practical Standard for Aesthetic Regulation, 15 Prac.Law. 36 (1969); Norton, Police Power, Planning and Aesthetics, 7 Santa Clara Law. 171, 183–185 (1967); Note, Aesthetic Considerations in Land Use Planning, 35 Albany L.Rev. 126, 131 (1970); Note, Zoning for Aesthetics—A Problem of Definition, 32 U.Cin.L.Rev. 367, 373 (1963).

We think Justice Cardozo had it about right when, speaking for the New York Court of Appeals in People v. Rubenfeld, 254 N.Y. 245, 172 N.E. 485, 486–487 (1930), he observed, by way of dicta:

> "The organs of smell and hearing, assailed by sounds and odors too pungent to be borne, have been ever favored of the law * * * more conspicuously, it seems, than sight, which perhaps is more inured to what is ugly or disfigured * * *. Even so, the test for all the senses, for sight as well as smell and hearing, has been the effect of the offensive practice upon the reasonable man or woman of average sensibilities * * *. One of the unsettled questions of the law is the extent to which the concept of nuisance may be enlarged by legislation so as to give protection to sensibilities that are merely cultural or aesthetic." [citations omitted]

Our predecessors recognized that this problem had long existed when in Byrne v. Maryland Realty Co., supra, 129 Md. at 211, 98 A. 547, they cited with approval the language of the Mississippi court which rejected an attempt through the exercise of the police power to exclude a market from a residential area in Quintini v. City of Bay St. Louis, 64 Miss. 483, 1 So. 625, 628 (1887):

> "The law can know no distinction between citizens because of the superior cultivation of the one over the other. It is with common humanity that courts and legislatures must deal; and that use of property which in all common sense and reason is not a nuisance to the average man cannot be prohibited because repugnant to some sentiment of a particular class."

Until now, only a minority of jurisdictions can be said to have validated regulatory schemes which were primarily or solely concerned with aesthetic considerations, Stone v. City of Maitland, 446 F.2d 83, 89 (5th Cir.1971); City of St. Paul v. Chicago, St. Paul, Minneapolis & Omaha Ry. Co., 413 F.2d 762, 767–768 (8th Cir.1969); Sunad, Inc. v. Sarasota, 122 So.2d 611, 614 (Fla.1960); State ex rel. Civello v. New Orleans, 154 La. 271, 97 So. 440, 444–445, 33 A.L.R. 260 (1923); Naegele Outdoor Adv. Co. v. Village of Minnetonka, 281 Minn. 492, 162 N.W.2d 206, 212 (1968); Cromwell v. Ferrier, supra, 225 N.E.2d at 753–755; People v. Stover, 12 N.Y.2d 462, 240 N.Y.S.2d 734, 191 N.E.2d 272, 274–276 (1963), appeal dismissed, 375 U.S. 42, 84 S.Ct. 147, 11 L.Ed.2d 107; United Advertising Corp. v. Metuchen, 42 N.J. 1, 198 A.2d 447, 449 (1964); Oregon City v. Hartke, 240 Or. 35, 400 P.2d 255, 262–263 (1965); State ex rel. Carter v. Harper, 182 Wis. 148, 196 N.W. 451, 454–456, 33

A.L.R. 269 (1923); 1 Anderson, American Law of Zoning, supra §§ 7.15, 7.22 at 508, 526 and cases cited therein; Annot., Aesthetic Objectives or Considerations as Affecting Validity of Zoning Ordinance, supra, 21 A.L.R.3d, § 4(a) at 1235 and cases cited therein.

* * *

We do not wish to be understood as saying that aesthetic considerations cannot play a proper role in the zoning process, because they do. It has long been recognized that the police power may rightly be exercised to preserve an area which is generally regarded by the public to be pleasing to the eye or historically or architecturally significant. * * *

In Footnote 88 to his article, Maryland Zoning—The Court and Its Critics, 27 Md.L.Rev. 39, 53 (1967), George W. Liebmann concludes, and we think quite rightly, that our case law and statutes have followed the approach urged by Ernst Freund, Standards of American Legislation 115–16 (1917):

"[I]t is undesirable to force by law upon the community standards of taste which a representative legislative body may happen to approve of, and compulsion with that end in view would be justly resented as inconsistent with a traditional spirit of individualism. But it is a different question whether the state may not protect the works of nature or the achievements of art or the associations of history from being wilfully marred. In other words, emphasis should be laid upon the character of the place as having an established claim to consideration and upon the idea of disfigurement as distinguished from the falling short of some standard of beauty."

Because the purpose of the Ordinance was not the preservation or protection of something which was aesthetically pleasing, but rather was intended to achieve by regulation an aesthetically pleasing result, with no thought of enhancing the public welfare, we shall not disturb the result reached below.

Decree affirmed, costs to be paid by appellants.

METROMEDIA, INC. v. CITY OF SAN DIEGO

Supreme Court of the United States, 1981.
453 U.S. 490, 101 S.Ct. 2882, 69 L.Ed.2d 800.

[The City of San Diego enacted an ordinance which, in effect banned all off-site billboards while allowing on-site advertising signs. The California Supreme Court upheld the ordinance, 26 Cal.3d 848, 610 P.2d 407 (1980), although the court also held that removal of some existing billboards after the expiration of an amortization period would require compensation under the Federal Highway Beautification Act.]

JUSTICE WHITE announced the judgment of the Court and delivered an opinion in which JUSTICE STEWART, JUSTICE MARSHALL and JUSTICE POWELL join.

This case involves the validity of an ordinance of the city of San Diego, Cal., imposing substantial prohibitions on the erection of outdoor advertising displays within the city.

* * *

Early cases in this Court sustaining regulation of and prohibitions aimed at billboards did not involve First Amendment considerations. See Packer Corporation v. Utah, 285 U.S. 105, 52 S.Ct. 273, 76 L.Ed. 643 (1932); St. Louis Poster Advertising Co. v. St. Louis, 249 U.S. 269, 39 S.Ct. 274, 63 L.Ed. 599 (1919); Cusack Co. v. City of Chicago, 242 U.S. 526, 37 S.Ct. 190, 61 L.Ed. 472 (1917). Since those decisions, we have not given plenary consideration to cases involving First Amendment challenges to statutes or ordinances limiting the use of billboards, preferring on several occasions summarily to affirm decisions sustaining state or local legislation directed at billboards.

Suffolk Outdoor Advertising Co. v. Hulse, 439 U.S. 808, 99 S.Ct. 66, 58 L.Ed.2d 101 (1978), involved a municipal ordinance that distinguished between off-site and on-site billboard advertising, prohibiting the former and permitting the latter. We summarily affirmed a judgment sustaining the ordinance, thereby rejecting the submission, repeated in this case, that prohibiting off-site commercial advertising violates the First Amendment. The definition of "billboard," however, was considerably narrower in *Suffolk* than it is here: "A sign which directs attention to a business, commodity, service, entertainment, or attraction sold, offered or existing elsewhere than upon the same lot where such sign is displayed." This definition did not sweep within its scope the broad range of noncommercial speech admittedly prohibited by the San Diego ordinance. Furthermore, the New York ordinance, unlike that in San Diego, contained a provision permitting the establishment of public information centers in which approved directional signs for businesses could be located. This Court has repeatedly stated that although summary dispositions are decisions on the merits, the decisions extend only to "the precise issues presented and necessarily decided by those actions." Mandel v. Bradley, 432 U.S. 173, 176, 97 S.Ct. 2238, 2240, 53 L.Ed.2d 199 (1977); see also Hicks v. Miranda, 422 U.S. 332, 345, n. 14, 95 S.Ct. 2281, 2290, 45 L.Ed.2d 223 (1975); Edelman v. Jordan, 415 U.S. 651, 671, 94 S.Ct. 1347, 1359, 39 L.Ed.2d 662 (1974). Insofar as the San Diego ordinance is challenged on the ground that it prohibits noncommercial speech, the *Suffolk* case does not directly support the decision below.

The Court has summarily disposed of appeals from state-court decisions upholding state restrictions on billboards on several other occasions. Markham Advertising Co. v. Washington, 393 U.S. 316, 89 S.Ct. 553, 21 L.Ed.2d 512 (1969), and Newman Signs, Inc. v. Hjelle, 440 U.S. 901, 99 S.Ct. 1205, 59 L.Ed.2d 449 (1979), both involved the facial validity of state billboard prohibitions that extended only to certain designated roadways or to areas zoned for certain uses. The statutes in both instances distinguished between on-site commercial billboards and off-site billboards within the protected areas. Our most recent summary action was Lotze v. Washington, 444 U.S. 921, 100 S.Ct. 257, 62 L.Ed.2d 177 (1979), which involved an "as applied" challenge to a Washington prohibition on off-site signs. In that case, appellants erected, on their own property, billboards expressing their political and social views. Although billboards conveying information relating to the commercial use of the property would have been permitted, appellants' billboards were prohibited, and the state courts ordered their removal. We affirmed a judgment rejecting the First Amendment challenge to the ordinance. * * *

Billboards are a well-established medium of communication, used to convey a broad range of different kinds of messages. As Justice Clark noted in his dissent below:

> "The outdoor sign or symbol is a venerable medium for expressing political, social and commercial ideas. From the poster or 'broadside' to the billboard, outdoor signs have played a prominent role throughout American history, rallying support for political and social causes." 164 Cal.Rptr., at 533–534, 610 P.2d, at 430–431.

The record in this case indicates that besides the typical commercial uses, San Diego billboards have been used

> "to publicize the 'City in motion' campaign of the City of San Diego, to communicate messages from candidates for municipal, state and national offices, including candidates for judicial office, to propose marriage, to seek employment, to encourage the use of seat belts, to denounce the United Nations, to seek support for Prisoners of War and Missing in Action, to promote the United Crusade and a variety of other charitable and socially-related endeavors and to provide directions to the traveling public."

But whatever its communicative function, the billboard remains a "large, immobile, and permanent structure which like other structures is subject to * * * regulation." 164 Cal.Rptr., at 522, 610 P.2d, at 419. Moreover, because it is designed to stand out and apart from its surroundings, the billboard creates a unique set of problems for land-use planning and development.

* * *

As construed by the California Supreme Court, the ordinance restricts the use of certain kinds of outdoor signs. That restriction is defined in two ways: first, by reference to the structural characteristics of the sign; second, by reference to the content, or message, of the sign. Thus, the regulation only applies to a "permanent structure constituting, or used for the display of, a commercial or other advertisement to the public." 164 Cal.Rptr., at 513, n. 2, 610 P.2d, at 410. Within that class, the only permitted signs are those (1) identifying the premises on which the sign is located, or its owner or occupant, or advertising the goods produced or services rendered on such property and (2) those within one of the specified exemptions to the general prohibition, such as temporary political campaign signs. To determine if any billboard is prohibited by the ordinance, one must determine how it is constructed, where it is located, and what message it carries.

Thus, under the ordinance (1) a sign advertising goods or services available on the property where the sign is located is allowed; (2) a sign on a building or other property advertising goods or services produced or offered elsewhere is barred; (3) noncommercial advertising, unless within one of the specific exceptions, is everywhere prohibited. The occupant of property may advertise his own goods or services; he may not advertise the goods or services of others, nor may he display most noncommercial messages.

* * *

* * * [I]n Central Hudson v. Public Service Comm'n, 447 U.S. 557, 100 S.Ct. 2343, 65 L.Ed.2d 341 (1980), we held that: "The Constitution * * * accords a lesser protection to commercial speech than to other constitutionally guaranteed expression. The protection available for a particular commercial expression turns on the nature both of the expression and of the governmental interests served by its regulation." Id., at 562–563, 100 S.Ct., at 2349–2350 (citation omitted). We then adopted a four-part test for determining the validity of government restrictions on commercial speech as distinguished from more fully protected speech. (1) The First Amendment protects commercial speech only if that speech concerns lawful activity and is not misleading. A restriction on otherwise protected commercial speech is valid only if it (2) seeks to implement a substantial governmental interest, (3) directly advances that interest, and (4) reaches no farther than necessary to accomplish the given objective. Id., at 563–566, 100 S.Ct., at 2350–2351.

Appellants agree that the proper approach to be taken in determining the validity of the restrictions on commercial speech is that which was articulated in *Central Hudson,* but assert that the San Diego ordinance fails that test. We do not agree.

There can be little controversy over the application of the first, second, and fourth criteria. There is no suggestion that the commercial advertising at issue here involves unlawful activity or is misleading. Nor can there be substantial doubt that the twin goals that the ordinance seeks to further—traffic safety and the appearance of the city—are substantial governmental goals. It is far too late to contend otherwise with respect to either traffic safety, Railway Express Agency, Inc. v. New York, 336 U.S. 106, 69 S.Ct. 463, 93 L.Ed. 533 (1949), or esthetics, see Penn Central Transportation Co. v. New York City, 438 U.S. 104, 98 S.Ct. 2646, 57 L.Ed.2d 631 (1978); Village of Belle Terre v. Boraas, 416 U.S. 1, 94 S.Ct. 1536, 39 L.Ed.2d 797 (1974); Berman v. Parker, 348 U.S. 26, 33, 75 S.Ct. 98, 102, 99 L.Ed. 27 (1954). Similarly, we reject appellants' claim that the ordinance is broader than necessary and, therefore, fails the fourth part of the *Central Hudson* test. If the city has a sufficient basis for believing that billboards are traffic hazards and are unattractive, then obviously the most direct and perhaps the only effective approach to solving the problems they create is to prohibit them. The city has gone no farther than necessary in seeking to meet its ends. Indeed, it has stopped short of fully accomplishing its ends: It has not prohibited all billboards, but allows on-site advertising and some other specifically exempted signs.

The more serious question, then, concerns the third of the *Central Hudson* criteria: Does the ordinance "directly advance" governmental interests in traffic safety and in the appearance of the city? It is asserted that the record is inadequate to show any connection between billboards and traffic safety. The California Supreme Court noted the meager record on this point but held "as a matter of law that an ordinance which eliminates billboards designed to be viewed from the streets and highways reasonably relates to traffic safety." 164 Cal.Rptr., at 515, 610 P.2d, at 412. Noting that "billboards are intended to, and undoubtedly do, divert a driver's attention from the roadway," ibid., and that whether the "distracting effect contributes to traffic accidents invokes an issue of continuing controversy," ibid., the California Supreme Court agreed with many other courts that a legislative judgment that billboards are traffic hazards is not manifestly unreasonable and should not be set aside. We likewise hesitate to disagree with the accumulated, common-sense judgments of local lawmakers and of the many reviewing courts that billboards are real and substantial hazards to traffic safety.[2] There is nothing here to suggest that these judgments are unreasonable. As we said in a different context, Railway Express Agency, Inc. v. People of New York, 336 U.S. 106, 109, 69 S.Ct. 463, 465, 93 L.Ed. 533 (1949):

> "We would be trespassing on one of the most intensely local and specialized of all municipal problems if we held that this regulation had no relation to the traffic problem of New York City. It is the judgment of the local authorities that it does have such a relation. And nothing has been advanced which shows that to be palpably false."

We reach a similar result with respect to the second asserted justification for the ordinance—advancement of the city's esthetic interests. It is not speculative to recognize that billboards by their very nature, wherever located and however constructed, can be perceived an

2. See E.B. Elliott Advertising Co. v. Metropolitan Dade County, 425 F.2d 1141, 1152 (C.A.5 1970); Markham Advertising Co. v. Washington, 73 Wash.2d 405, 439 P.2d 248, 258 (1968); New York State Thruway Authority v. Ashley Motor Court, 10 N.Y.2d 151, 218 N.Y.S.2d 640, 642, 176 N.E.2d 566, 568 (1961); Ghaster Properties, Inc. v. Preston, 176 Ohio St. 425, 200 N.E.2d 328, 337 (1964); Newman Signs, Inc. v. Hjelle, 268 N.W.2d 741, 757 (N.D. 1978); Lubbock Poster Co. v. City of Lubbock, 569 S.W.2d 935, 939 (Tex.Civ.App. 1978); State v. Lotze, 92 Wash.2d 52, 593 P.2d 811, 814 (1979); Inhabitants, Town of Boothbay v. National Advertising Co., 347 A.2d 419, 422 (Me.1975); Stuckey's Stores, Inc. v. O'Cheskey, 93 N.M. 312, 600 P.2d 258, 267 (1979); In re Opinion of the Justices, 103 N.H. 268, 169 A.2d 762, 764 (1961); General Outdoor Advertising Co. v. Dept. of Public Works, 289 Mass. 149, 193 N.E. 799, 813–814 (1935). But see John Donnelly & Sons v. Campbell, 639 F.2d 6, 11 (C.A.1 1980); State ex rel. Dept. of Transportation v. Pile, 603 P.2d 337, 343 (Okla.1979); Metromedia, Inc. v. City of Des Plaines, 26 Ill.App.3d 942, 326 N.E.2d 59, 62 (1975).

"esthetic harm."[3] San Diego, like many other States and municipalities, has chosen to minimize the presence of such structures. Such esthetic judgments are necessarily subjective, defying objective evaluation, and for that reason must be carefully scrutinized to determine if they are only a public rationalization of an impermissible purpose. But there is no claim in this case that San Diego has as an ulterior motive the suppression of speech, and the judgment involved here is not so unusual as to raise suspicions in itself.

It is nevertheless argued that the city denigrates its interest in traffic safety and beauty and defeats its own case by permitting on-site advertising and other specified signs. Appellants question whether the distinction between on-site and off-site advertising on the same property is justifiable in terms of either esthetics or traffic safety. The ordinance permits the occupant of property to use billboards located on that property to advertise goods and services offered at that location; identical billboards, equally distracting and unattractive, that advertise goods or services available elsewhere are prohibited even if permitting the latter would not multiply the number of billboards. Despite the apparent incongruity, this argument has been rejected, at least implicitly, in all of the cases sustaining the distinction between off-site and on-site commercial advertising. We agree with those cases and with our own decisions in Suffolk Outdoor Advertising Co. v. Hulse, 439 U.S. 808, 99 S.Ct. 66, 58 L.Ed.2d 101 (1978); Markham Advertising Co. v. Washington, 393 U.S. 316, 89 S.Ct. 553, 21 L.Ed.2d 512 (1969); Newman Signs, Inc. v. Hjelle, 440 U.S. 901, 99 S.Ct. 1205, 59 L.Ed.2d 449 (1979).

In the first place, whether on-site advertising is permitted or not, the prohibition of off-site advertising is directly related to the stated objectives of traffic safety and esthetics. This is not altered by the fact that the ordinance is under-inclusive because it permits on-site advertising. Second, the city may believe that off-site advertising, with its periodically changing content, presents a more acute problem than does on-site advertising. See *Railway Express*, supra, 336 U.S. at 110, 69 S.Ct. at 465. Third, San Diego has obviously chosen to value one kind of commercial speech—on-site advertising—more than another kind of commercial speech—off-site advertising. The ordinance reflects a decision by the city that the former interest, but not the latter, is stronger than the city's interests in traffic safety and esthetics. The city has decided that in a limited instance—on-site commercial advertising—its

---

3. See John Donnelly & Sons v. Campbell, supra, 639 F.2d at 11–12; E.B. Elliott Advertising Co. v. Metropolitan Dade County, supra, 425 F.2d at 1152; Newman Signs, Inc. v. Hjelle, supra, 268 N.W.2d at 757; Markham Advertising Co. v. Washington, supra, 439 P.2d at 259; Stuckey's Stores, Inc. v. O'Cheskey, supra, 600 P.2d at 267; Suffolk Outdoor Advertising Co. v. Hulse, 43 N.Y.2d 483, 402 N.Y.S.2d 368, 370, 373 N.E.2d 263, 265 (1977); John Donnelly & Sons, Inc. v. Outdoor Advertising Bd., 369 Mass. 206, 339 N.E.2d 709, 717 (1975); Cromwell v. Ferrier, 19 N.Y.2d 263, 279 N.Y.S.2d 22, 26, 225 N.E.2d 749, 753 (1967); State v. Diamond Motors, Inc., 50 Haw. 33, 429 P.2d 825, 827 (Haw.1967); United Advertising Corp. v. Metuchen, 42 N.J. 1, 198 A.2d 447, 449 (1964); In re Opinion of the Justices, supra, 169 A.2d at 764. But see State ex rel. Dept. of Transportation v. Pile, supra, 603 P.2d at 342; Sunad, Inc. v. Sarasota, 122 So.2d 611, 614–615 (Fla.1960).

interests should yield. We do not reject that judgment. As we see it, the city could reasonably conclude that a commercial enterprise—as well as the interested public—has a stronger interest in identifying its place of business and advertising the products or services available there than it has in using or leasing its available space for the purpose of advertising commercial enterprises located elsewhere. See Railway Express v. New York, supra, 336 U.S., at 116, 69 S.Ct., at 468 (Jackson, J., concurring); Bradley v. Public Utilities Comm'n, 289 U.S. 92, 97, 53 S.Ct. 577, 579, 77 L.Ed. 1053 (1933). It does not follow from the fact that the city has concluded that some commercial interests outweigh its municipal interests in this context that it must give similar weight to all other commercial advertising. Thus, off-site commercial billboards may be prohibited while on-site commercial billboards are permitted.

The constitutional problem in this area requires resolution of the conflict between the city's land-use interests and the commercial interests of those seeking to purvey goods and services within the city. In light of the above analysis, we cannot conclude that the city has drawn an ordinance broader than is necessary to meet its interests, or that it fails directly to advance substantial government interests. In sum, insofar as it regulates commercial speech the San Diego ordinance meets the constitutional requirements of *Central Hudson,* supra.

It does not follow, however, that San Diego's general ban on signs carrying noncommercial advertising is also valid under the First and Fourteenth Amendments. The fact that the city may value commercial messages relating to on-site goods and services more than it values commercial communications relating to off-site goods and services does not justify prohibiting an occupant from displaying its own ideas or those of others.

As indicated above, our recent commercial speech cases have consistently accorded noncommercial speech a greater degree of protection than commercial speech. San Diego effectively inverts this judgment, by affording a greater degree of protection to commercial than to noncommercial speech. There is a broad exception for on-site commercial advertisements, but there is no similar exception for noncommercial speech. The use of on-site billboards to carry commercial messages related to the commercial use of the premises is freely permitted, but the use of otherwise identical billboards to carry noncommercial messages is generally prohibited. The city does not explain how or why noncommercial billboards located in places where commercial billboards are permitted would be more threatening to safe driving or would detract more from the beauty of the city. Insofar as the city tolerates billboards at all, it cannot choose to limit their content to commercial messages; the city may not conclude that the communication of commercial information concerning goods and services connected with a particular site is of greater value than the communication of noncommercial messages.

Furthermore, the ordinance contains exceptions that permit various kinds of noncommercial signs, whether on property where goods and services are offered or not, that would otherwise be within the general ban. A fixed sign may be used to identify any piece of property and its owner. Any piece of property may carry or display religious symbols, commemorative plaques of recognized historical societies and organizations, signs carrying news items or telling the time or temperature, signs erected in discharge of any governmental function, or temporary political campaign signs. No other noncommercial or ideological signs meeting the structural definition are permitted, regardless of their effect on traffic safety or esthetics.

Although the city may distinguish between the relative value of different categories of commercial speech, the city does not have the same range of choice in the area of noncommercial speech to evaluate the strength of, or distinguish between, various communicative interests. See Carey v. Brown, 447 U.S. 455, 462, 100 S.Ct. 2286, 2291, 65 L.Ed.2d 263 (1980); Police Department of Chicago v. Mosley, 408 U.S. 92, 96, 92 S.Ct. 2286, 2290, 33 L.Ed.2d 212 (1972). With respect to noncommercial speech, the city may not choose the appropriate subjects for public discourse: "To allow a government the choice of permissible subjects for public debate would be to allow that government control over the search for political truth." *Consolidated Edison Co.,* supra, 447 U.S., at 538, 100 S.Ct., at 2333. Because some noncommercial messages may be conveyed on billboards throughout the commercial and industrial zones, San Diego must similarly allow billboards conveying other noncommercial messages throughout those zones.[4]

Finally, we reject appellee's suggestion that the ordinance may be appropriately characterized as a reasonable "time, place and manner" restriction. The ordinance does not generally ban billboard advertising as an unacceptable "manner" of communicating information or ideas; rather, it permits various kinds of signs. Signs that are banned are banned everywhere and at all times. We have observed that time, place

---

4. Because a total prohibition of outdoor advertising is not before us, we do not indicate whether such a ban would be consistent with the First Amendment. But see Schad v. Borough of Mount Ephraim, 452 U.S. 61, 101 S.Ct. 2176, 68 L.Ed.2d 671, on the constitutional problems created by a total prohibition of a particular expressive forum, live entertainment in that case. Despite Justice Stevens' insistence to the contrary, post, at 1, 2, and 10, n. 14, we do not imply that the ordinance is unconstitutional because it "does not abridge enough speech."

Similarly, we need not reach any decision in this case as to the constitutionality of the federal Highway Beautification Act of 1965, Pub.L. 89–285, 79 Stat. 1028, 23 U.S.C.A. § 131. That Act, like the San Diego ordinance, permits on-site commercial billboards in areas in which it does not permit billboards with noncommercial mes-

sages. 23 U.S.C.A. § 131(c). However, unlike the San Diego ordinance, which prohibits billboards conveying noncommercial messages throughout the city, the federal law does not contain a total prohibition of such billboards in areas adjacent to the Interstate and primary highway systems. As far as the Federal Government is concerned, such billboards are permitted adjacent to the highways in areas zoned industrial or commercial under state law or in unzoned commercial or industrial areas. 23 U.S.C.A. § 131(d). Regulation of billboards in those areas is left primarily to the States. For this reason, the decision today does not determine the constitutionality of the federal statute. Whether, in fact, the distinction is constitutionally significant can only be determined on the basis of a record establishing the actual effect of the Act on billboards conveying noncommercial messages.

and manner restrictions are permissible if "they are justified without reference to the content of the regulated speech * * * serve a significant governmental interest, and * * * leave open ample alternative channels for communication of the information." Virginia Pharmacy Board v. Virginia Consumer Council, 425 U.S. 748, 771, 96 S.Ct. 1817, 1830, 48 L.Ed.2d 346 (1976). Here, it cannot be assumed that "alternative channels" are available, for the parties stipulated to just the opposite: "Many businesses, politicians and other persons rely upon outdoor advertising because other forms of advertising are insufficient, inappropriate and prohibitively expensive." A similar argument was made with respect to a prohibition on real estate "For Sale" signs in Linmark Associates, Inc. v. Willingboro, 431 U.S. 85, 97 S.Ct. 1614, 52 L.Ed.2d 155 (1977), and what we said there is equally applicable here:

> "Although in theory sellers remain free to employ a number of different alternatives, in practice [certain products are] not marketed through leaflets, sound trucks, demonstrations, or the like. The options to which sellers realistically are relegated * * * involve more cost and less autonomy than * * * signs * * * are less likely to reach persons not deliberately seeking sales information * * * and may be less effective media for communicating the message that is conveyed by a * * * sign. * * * The alternatives, then, are far from satisfactory." 431 U.S., at 93, 97 S.Ct., at 1618.

It is apparent as well that the ordinance distinguishes in several ways between permissible and impermissible signs at a particular location by reference to their content.

* * *

Because the San Diego ordinance reaches too far into the realm of protected speech, we conclude that it is unconstitutional on its face. The judgment of the California Supreme Court is reversed and the case remanded to that court.

JUSTICE BRENNAN, with whom JUSTICE BLACKMUN joins, concurring in the judgment.

Believing that "a total prohibition of outdoor advertising is not before us," * * *, the plurality does not decide "whether such a ban would be consistent with the First Amendment." Instead, it concludes that San Diego may ban all billboards containing commercial speech messages without violating the First Amendment, thereby sending the signal to municipalities that bifurcated billboard regulations prohibiting commercial messages but allowing noncommercial messages would pass constitutional muster. * * * I write separately because I believe this case in effect presents the total ban question, and because I believe the plurality's bifurcated approach itself raises serious First Amendment problems and relies on a distinction between commercial and noncommercial speech unanticipated by our prior cases.

* * *

* * * In the case of billboards, I would hold that a city may totally ban them if it can show that a sufficiently substantial governmental interest is directly furthered by the total ban, and that any more narrowly drawn restriction, i.e., anything less than a total ban, would promote less well the achievement of that goal.

Applying that test to the instant case, I would invalidate the San Diego ordinance. The city has failed to provide adequate justification for its substantial restriction on protected activity. * * * First, although I have no quarrel with the substantiality of the city's interest in traffic safety, the city has failed to come forward with evidence demonstrating that billboards actually impair traffic safety in San Diego. Indeed, the Joint Stipulation of Facts is completely silent on this issue. Although the plurality hesitates "to disagree with the accumulated, common sense judgments of local lawmakers and of the many reviewing courts that billboards are real and substantial hazards to traffic safety," ante, at 17, I would not be so quick to accept legal conclusions in other cases as an adequate substitute for evidence *in this case* that banning billboards directly furthers traffic safety. Moreover, the ordinance is not narrowly drawn to accomplish the traffic safety goal. Although it contains an exception for signs "not visible from any point on the boundary of the premises," App. to Juris. Statement 111a, billboards not visible from the street but nevertheless visible from the "boundary of the premises" are not exempted from the regulation's prohibition.

Second, I think that the city has failed to show that its asserted interest in aesthetics is sufficiently substantial in the commercial and industrial areas of San Diego. I do not doubt that "[i]t is within the power of the [city] to determine that the community should be beautiful," Berman v. Parker, 348 U.S. 26, 33, 75 S.Ct. 98, 102, 99 L.Ed. 27 (1954), but that power may not be exercised in contravention of the First Amendment. * * *

It is no doubt true that the appearance of certain areas of the city would be enhanced by the elimination of billboards, but "it is not immediately apparent as a matter of experience" that their elimination in all other areas as well would have more than a negligible impact on aesthetics. See John Donnelly & Sons v. Campbell, 639 F.2d 6, 23 (C.A.1 1980), petition for cert. filed (Mar. 19, 1981) (Pettine, J., concurring in the judgment.) The Joint Stipulation reveals that

> "[s]ome sections of the City of San Diego are scenic, some blighted, some containing strips of vehicle related commercial uses, some contain new and attractive office buildings, some functional industrial development and some areas contain older but useful commercial establishments." Joint Stipulation § 8, App. to Juris. Statement 121a.

A billboard is not *necessarily* inconsistent with oil storage tanks, blighted areas, or strip development. Of course, it is not for a court to impose its own notion of beauty on San Diego. But before deferring to a city's judgment, a court must be convinced that the city is seriously and comprehensively addressing aesthetic concerns with respect to its environment. Here, San Diego has failed to demonstrate a comprehensive coordinated effort in its commercial and industrial areas to address other obvious contributors to an unattractive environment. In this sense the ordinance is underinclusive. See Erznoznik v. City of Jacksonville, 422 U.S. 205, 214, 95 S.Ct. 2268, 2275, 45 L.Ed.2d 125 (1975). Of course, this is not to say that the city must address all aesthetic problems at the same time, or none at all. Indeed, from a planning point of view, attacking the problem incrementally and sequentially may represent the most sensible solution. On the other hand, if billboards alone are banned and no further steps are contemplated or likely, the commitment of the city to improving its physical environment is placed in doubt. By showing a comprehensive commitment to making its physical environment in commercial and industrial areas more attractive, and by allowing only narrowly tailored exceptions, if any, San Diego could demonstrate that its interest in creating an aesthetically pleasing environment is genuine and substantial. This is a requirement where, as here, there is an infringement of important constitutional consequence.

I have little doubt that some jurisdictions will easily carry the burden of proving the substantiality of their interest in aesthetics. For example, the parties acknowledge that a historical community such as Williamsburg, Va. should be able to prove that its interests in aesthetics and historical authenticity are sufficiently important that the First Amendment value attached to billboards must yield. And I would be surprised if the Federal Government had much trouble making the argument that billboards could be entirely banned in Yellowstone National Park, where their very existence would so obviously be inconsistent with the surrounding landscape. I express no view on whether San Diego or other large urban areas will be able to meet the burden. But San Diego failed to do so here, and for that reason I would strike down its ordinance.

* * *

[Dissenting opinions by CHIEF JUSTICE BURGER, JUSTICE REHNQUIST and JUSTICE STEVENS are omitted.]

Notes

1. A staggering amount of case law exists in the area of sign regulations. For a thorough discussion and analysis of the leading cases, see 4 Williams, American Land Planning Law §§ 118.01–127.02 (1988). In the early years courts were sometimes quite inventive in conjuring up non-aesthetic reasons to justify regulation of billboards and other signs. See, e.g., City of Passaic v. Paterson Bill Posting, Advertising and Sign Painting Co., 72 N.J.L. 285, 62 A. 267 (1905), where the court said:

> In cases of fire they [signs] often cause their spread and constitute barriers against their extinction; and in cases of high wind, their temporary character, frail structure and broad surface render them liable to be blown down and to fall upon and injure those who may

happen to be in their vicinity. The evidence shows and common observation teaches us that the ground in the rear thereof is being constantly used as privies and dumping ground for all kinds of waste * * * that behind [them] the lowest form of prostitution and other acts of immorality are frequently carried on, almost under public gaze; they offer shelter and concealment for the criminal while lying in wait for his victim * * *

The trend of decision today is in the frank recognition of the aesthetic justification for sign regulation, and the more recent cases tend to follow the reasoning of the Diamond Motors case. However, the Mano Swartz case should serve as a caution to the quick assumption that sign regulation is presumptively valid under the police power. In connection with the Mano Swartz case, see Montgomery County v. Citizens Bldg. & Loan Ass'n, Inc., 20 Md.App. 484, 316 A.2d 322 (1974), and Donnelly Advertising Corp. v. City of Baltimore, 279 Md. 660, 370 A.2d 1127 (1977), where the court distinguished Mano Swartz and upheld sign regulations in the Old Baltimore urban renewal district. In the course of the opinion the court also held that the company was not entitled to compensation for two billboards located near Interstate 40 because their removal was dictated by the ordinance and not by the Highway Beautification Act. Also see Metromedia, Inc. v. Mayor and City Council of Baltimore, 538 F.Supp. 1183 (D.Md.1982) which held that the city restrictions against outdoor advertising signs in an urban renewal area were justified constitutionally by the city's interests in traffic safety and aesthetics, but the ordinance was invalid in its discrimination against noncommercial messages.

2. Do you agree with the manner in which the Court in Metromedia disposed of the argument dealing with the difference between regulation of signs (location, size, setbacks, etc.) and prohibition of all off-site signs? Do you agree with the principle that cities may rationally distinguish between off-site signs, totally prohibiting such signs, and on-site signs? Are not many on-site signs just as distracting and aesthetically offensive as billboards? Is the decision to ban billboards while allowing on-site signs really a political decision in the sense that local governments cannot get away with ordering all local businesses to remove on-site signs? How can a city meet the burden of proof, outlined in Justice Brennan's concurring opinion? For a case upholding regulation of *all* signs to a size of under four square feet, see People v. Goodman, 31 N.Y.2d 262, 338 N.Y.S.2d 97, 290 N.E.2d 139 (1972). Compare City of Fayetteville v. S & H, Inc., 261 Ark. 148, 547 S.W.2d 94 (1977), where a majority of the court held that a sign ordinance requiring removal of non-conforming signs after an amortization period was an unconstitutional taking, to the extent that the signs were in connection with an ongoing business and were not in themselves traffic hazards. A plurality of the court opined that the device of amortization was itself invalid. In a later case, City of Fayetteville v. McIlroy Bank & Trust Co., 278 Ark. 500, 647 S.W.2d 439 (1983), the court upheld the same ordinance and approved the amortization scheme.

3. Since the decision in Metromedia, courts have continued to uphold sign ordinances which do not differentiate between commercial and noncommercial speech. Some courts, however, have gone beyond Metromedia and have held content-neutral sign ordinances invalid as violative of the first

amendment. Prior to Metromedia, Martin v. Wray, 473 F.Supp. 1131 (E.D.Wis.1979) and Farrell v. Township of Teaneck, 126 N.J.Super. 460, 315 A.2d 424 (1974)[5] struck down ordinances which banned political signs in residential zones. More recently, see City of Antioch v. Candidates' Outdoor Graphic Service, 557 F.Supp. 52 (N.D.Cal.1982), holding that an ordinance which imposed a year-round ban on political signs except for 60 days prior to an election was unconstitutional because it was not the least drastic means of protecting visual amenities and aesthetics. Also, compare Abel v. Town of Orangetown, 724 F.Supp. 232 (S.D.N.Y.1989) (upholding ordinance prohibiting candidates from posting signs on public property) with Klein v. Baise, 708 F.Supp. 863 (N.D.Ill.1989) (enjoining enforcement of a state law prohibiting advertising on bus shelters on behalf of a political candidate). In Macdonald Advertising Co. v. City of Pontiac, 916 F.Supp. 644 (E.D.Mich. 1995) the court found that a city ordinance requiring billboards to obtain special permits was invalid insofar as there were not standards to guide the discretion of the local government and that the absence of standards constituted a prior restraint on freedom of speech under the First Amendment. And, in Village of Schaumburg v. Jeep Eagle Sales Corp., 285 Ill.App.3d 481, 221 Ill.Dec. 679, 676 N.E.2d 200 (1996) the court held that a local sign ordinance that prohibited display of more than three "official" flags at any one business violated the automobile dealer's First Amendment rights in that the ordinance permitted an unlimited number of "banners."

4.   A federal judge in Florida thrice struck down content-neutral bans on portable signs despite city arguments of traffic safety and aesthetics. See Signs, Inc. of Florida v. Orange County, Florida, 592 F.Supp. 693 (M.D.Fla. 1983); All American Sign Rentals, Inc. v. City of Orlando, 592 F.Supp. 85 (M.D.Fla.1983); Harnish v. Manatee County, Florida, 597 F.Supp. 601 (M.D.Fla.1984). The Eleventh Circuit Court of Appeals reversed the latter case, upholding the county's aesthetic interest, 783 F.2d 1535 (11th Cir. 1986).

5.   In Daugherty v. City of East Point, 447 F.Supp. 290 (N.D.Ga.1978), the court struck down, on First Amendment grounds an ordinance prohibiting "For Sale" signs, designed to stabilize racial transition in residential neighborhoods. A completely different First Amendment problem was presented in the city of Vero Beach, Florida, where the ordinance prohibits rooftop signs and the city attorney interpreted the ordinance to apply to a 14-foot high blue neon cross erected by a local church. If the Vero Beach case goes to litigation, how do you think a court would resolve the dispute?

6.   An unusual sign case is presented in Supersign of Boca Raton, Inc. v. City of Fort Lauderdale, 766 F.2d 1528 (11th Cir.1985), where the court upheld a local sign ordinance provision which prohibited advertising signs on watercraft and certain vehicles. Also see Solomon v. City of Gainesville, 763 F.2d 1212 (11th Cir.1985), striking as unconstitutionally vague, a city

---

5. Also see two subsequent New Jersey cases, State v. J. & J. Painting, 167 N.J.Super. 384, 400 A.2d 1204 (1979), holding that the commercial speech doctrine did not require that defendants be allowed to place temporary advertising signs on the lawns of houses they were in process of painting or roofing, and State v. Miller, 83 N.J. 402, 416 A.2d 821 (1980), holding that free speech protected defendant's political expression in placing a large sign in his front yard welcoming prospective residents to "this flood hazard area."

ordinance prohibiting signs or graphics with obscene words or illustrations. The plaintiff was the owner of a pizza parlor whose sign depicted a reproduction of Leonardo da Vinci's famous anatomical illustration. And see City of Ladue v. Gilleo, 512 U.S. 43, 114 S.Ct. 2038, 129 L.Ed.2d 36 (1994) where the Court held that application of the zoning ordinance sign provisions to a homeowner who placed a notebook-size sheet of paper in her window protesting the Gulf War, was a denial of her First Amendment right of free speech.

7. Many of the cases after Metromedia present the similar situation of billboard companies challenging city restrictions. Some of these cases worth consulting include Nat'l Advertising Co. v. City of Rolling Meadows, 789 F.2d 571 (7th Cir.1986); Naegele Outdoor Advertising, Inc. v. City of Durham, 844 F.2d 172 (4th Cir.1988); Rzadkowolski v. Village of Lake Orion, 845 F.2d 653 (6th Cir.1988); National Advertising Co. v. City of Orange, 861 F.2d 246 (9th Cir.1988); Ackerley Communications of Mass., Inc. v. City of Somerville, 878 F.2d 513 (1st Cir.1989); Major Media of Southeast, Inc. v. City of Raleigh, 621 F.Supp. 1446 (E.D.N.C.1985) cert. denied 479 U.S. 1102, 107 S.Ct. 1334, 94 L.Ed.2d 185 (1987); Jackson v. City Council of Charlottesville, Virginia, 659 F.Supp. 470 (W.D.Va.1987) affirmed in part 840 F.2d 10 (4th Cir.1988); National Advertising Co. v. Town of Babylon, 703 F.Supp. 228 (E.D.N.Y.1989) affirmed in part 900 F.2d 551 (2d Cir.1990).

A Note on the Federal Highway Beautification Act

On October 22, 1965, the Federal Highway Beautification Act took effect. Some of the political and interpretive problems under this act are commented on by Netherton and Markham in Roadside Development and Beautification: Legal Authority and Methods 11–15 (Highway Research Board, 1966):

Public Policy and the Highway Beautification Act of 1965

Major efforts were made by both the Administration and the Congress to define the public policy on which the Highway Beautification Act of 1965 was based, and not since the mid–1950's, when the present multi-billion dollar highway program was launched, has as voluminous a legislative history been produced for a Federal-aid highway law. Commencing with the President's Message on Natural Beauty in February, 1965, the formulation of policy was continued in a White House Conference on Natural Beauty in May, Congressional hearings in July and August, legislative debates leading to enactment of a law in October, and a series of special briefings for state officials, industry and non-governmental groups in November and December.

It is therefore ironical that despite this background the governmental agencies responsible for enacting and administering this law, the industries and groups affected by it, and the general public were, at the close of 1965, still uncertain about the policy of the law and the extent to which they favored it. Strong minority views in Congress apparently remained unreconciled by perfecting amendments to the original bill, and affected industries and organizations adopted a wait-and-see attitude toward features of the new program on which they had reservations. To some degree this atmosphere was also reflected by the remark of the President, upon signing the Highway Beautification Act: "This bill does not represent everything that we wanted. It does not represent what we need. It does not represent what the national interest requires. But it is a first step, and there will be other steps."[6]

Examining the policy of the highway beautification law first in its most basic terms, a starting point is provided by the President's statement that:

"In a nation of continental size, transportation is essential to the growth and prosperity of the national economy. But that economy, and the roads that serve it, are not ends in themselves. They are meant to serve the real needs of the people of this country. And those needs include the opportunity to touch nature and see beauty, as well as rising income and swifter travel. Therefore, we must make sure that the massive resources we now devote to roads also serve to improve and broaden the quality of American life."[7]

It is evident that in 1965 the Administration proposed and the Congress agreed to the addition of a new dimension to the national Federal-aid highway policy. This new dimension extended the public interest to include what the President called "a new conservation * * * to protect the countryside, save it from destruction, and restore what has been destroyed * * *. [T]his new conservation must not be just the classic conservation of protection and development, but a creative conservation of restoration and innovation."[8] It clearly implied that henceforth highways should be viewed not only as facilities of transportation but as features of the community and environment, and that environmental quality ranked with engineering quality in roadbuilding.

To this end, the legislation of 1965 requires that by 1968 the states must establish "effective control" over roadside advertising signs and junkyards or else suffer the penalty of a reduction in their Federal-aid funds. This constitutes a major change in Federal-aid policy since use of financial penalties was considered and rejected by Congress in 1958 in favor of securing state implementation of the national policy on roadside advertising by increasing the financial aid to states which enacted controls.

The authority for this step is hardly open to question since other features of the Federal-aid highway program have utilized this device. Nor was the wisdom of this device seriously objectionable to the states in view of the general recognition that development of the roadsides inevitably and significantly affected the efficiency and safety of the roadway. Moreover, six years of effort to secure voluntary action by the states to implement the advertising control policy and the failure of states to use funds authorized for special landscaping and scenic enhancement under the Federal aid law of 1940, was persuasive evidence that stronger measures were needed.

More open to question were some of the policy changes contained in the substance of the control standards prescribed for roadside advertising and

---

6. White House Press Release, "Remarks of the President at the Signing Ceremony of the Highway Beautification Act", October 22, 1965.

7. House Report 1084, 89th Cong., 1st Session, "Highway Beautification Act of 1965," September 22, 1965, p. 2.

8. Statement by the President in A Report on Natural Beauty To The President from the Secretaries of Interior, Agriculture, Commerce, H.E.W., the Administrator of HHFA and Director of Office of Equal Opportunity, October 1, 1965.

junkyards. Initial Administration proposals regarding control of roadside land use visualized use of state police power, yet in its committee reports and debates Congress declared roadside advertising and junkyards were legitimate business enterprises which should be spared financial hardship as much as possible by receiving compensation for the removal of signs by state order. References made to safety objectives, it was declared, were "in no sense to be construed as a brief for the use of the police power."[9] Deference to the interests of the roadside advertising and junkyard industries to operate in commercial and industrial areas also appeared in the law's provision that junkyards might continue to operate in industrial areas and billboards might continue to use commercial and industrial areas under a program of "effective control".

These provisions of the beautification law were promptly hailed by the billboard industry, which editorialized that: "For the first time, it is an admission by a governmental body that outdoor advertising can legitimately conduct business in commercial and industrial areas of this country. And it will help to weed out the fly-by-night operators who have been the bane of the industry."[10]

This interpretation dramatizes one of the major problems of policy-making for it involves the distinction between what the law requires public agencies to do in connection with regulation of private land use, and what a bountiful sovereign chooses to do as an act of generosity. Litigation over the constitutionality of state laws implementing the national policy of 1958 for control of advertising along Interstate highways emphasized this distinction. And all four state supreme courts which passed on this legislation made clear their view that "the use prohibited by these statutes is in substance and effect a use of the public highway for advertising purposes. To hold that such a nonconforming use should be protected would in effect lead to the absurd result of recognizing such use, before its statutory prohibition, as creating a vested property interest in the highway."[11] To argue that Congress in the Highway Beautification Act of 1965 recognized any legal rights of private landowners and their lessees thus disregards not only the state supreme court decisions on the 1958 roadside advertising control legislation, but also runs contrary to legal doctrine which underlies other features of modern highway programs such as control of highway access.

The evident intention of Congress to define the public interest in highway beautification in such a way that hardship on roadside industry and landowners would be minimized led to further changes in Federal highway policy. While excepting commercial and industrial areas from the prohibitory features of effective billboard control, the law did make permitted structures in these areas subject to standards for size, spacing and lighting to be promulgated by the Secretary of Commerce. However, prior to enactment of this bill, the Secretary of Commerce advised the Congress of his intention

---

9. House of Representatives, Report No. 1084, 89th Cong., 1st Sess., September 22, 1965, p. 4.

10. Editorial entitled "Seize the Moment," in Pennsylvania Outdoor News, November 1965, p. 2.

11. Ghaster Properties, Inc. v. Preston, 176 Ohio St. 425, 200 N.E.2d 328 (1964). See also: Opinion of the Justices, 169 A.2d 762 (N.H.1961), Moore v. Ward, 377 S.W.2d 881 (Ky.1964), Fuller v. Fiedler, Memo.Op., Dane County Cir.Ct., May 22, 1961, and 19 Wis.2d 422, 120 N.W.2d 700 (1963).

that "such regulations insofar as they are consistent with the purposes of this act, shall be helpful to the advertising industry, and that, for instance, standards of size which may be adopted would be insofar as possible consistent with standard size billboards in customary use."[12] The presence of this statement in the legislative history of the beautification law raises a question as to the extent that standards of control for outdoor advertising should, in effect, be those developed by the advertising industry for promotion of practices it may desire, as opposed to those which existing local zoning and public desires may call for.

A similar question arises with respect to the Federal law's requirement that states pay just compensation to landowners and billboard owners when signs lawfully placed prior to the establishment of controls are removed. The law's legislative history makes it clear that Congress felt that "equity and fairness" required that those who lose their signs should receive compensation for the economic distress which regulation may cause. By so providing, however, it would seem that Congress is voluntarily extending the concept of public responsibility for the economic consequences of the highway program to new limits, building upon precedents established earlier in authorizing use of Federal aid funds for payment of the cost of relocating utility facilities and displaced persons. In these earlier cases, however, the policy of Congress was limited to authorizing payment when required by state law; here the payment appears as a mandatory feature of Federal aid.

The Highway Beautification Act of 1965 further expanded the scope of the public interest to include the special needs of the motoring public for information regarding automotive services and accommodations during travel. As substantial segments of the Interstate System have been opened for use, experience with controlled-access highway travel has convinced many that additional information facilities were needed. Therefore, the 1965 legislation authorized state highway departments to maintain maps, and permit directories and advertising pamphlets to be made available to motorists at information centers in safety rest areas adjacent to the highway.

One further provision representing an addition to Federal-aid policy, which Congress considered to be among the most important features of the 1965 act, related to exercise of administrative authority delegated to the Secretary of Commerce. Under the law, the Secretary was called upon, in conjunction with the states, to take certain actions, including the designation of commercial and industrial zones and unzoned areas being used for commercial or industrial purposes, and promulgation of standards for certain aspects of outdoor advertising control and the screening of junk-yards within areas where their continued presence was permitted. In the event that the Secretary and a state failed to agree on one of these matters the determination of the Secretary overrode that of the state. Thus, for the protection of all concerned, Congress provided that any state affected by the controls required under the act was entitled to a "day in court"—the right to judicial review of any determination by the Secretary that a state has failed to effectively control roadside advertising or junkyards. Preliminary to judicial

12. House of Representatives, Report   22, 1965, p. 5.
No. 1048, 89th Cong., 1st Sess., September

review, administrative procedures (involving notice, hearing, written records and orders) prescribed in the law must be complied with.

Statutory provision for state suits against the Secretary of Commerce to determine eligibility for funds apportioned under the Federal-aid program is unprecedented in the historic Federal–State partnership for highway construction. Only once before has a state resorted to judicial processes to settle its differences with the Federal government over such a matter, and in this case the state's standing to sue without specific statutory authorization was open to serious question. Little can be ventured as to the effect of this new statutory right of the states since no experience yet exists with respect to it. Certainly, however, subordination of the Secretary's administrative judgment to that of the courts for determination of a state's eligibility for Federal aid even on a limited range of issues opens the possibility for development of a new dimension to the working relationship of the states and Federal government in the Federal-aid highway program, and adds a quasi-judicial character to the administrative functions of the Secretary of Commerce under this program. * * *

————

The 1978 amendments to the Highway Beautification Act, are very specific in requiring compensation for removal of certain signs. To put the problem in perspective, as of Sept. 30, 1977, 463,724 billboards had been removed from along federal highways under the act, leaving 265,-952. Compensation for the average billboard in 1978 was $1,500. The Federal Highway Administration estimated that about $40 million a year for 10 years would be necessary to complete removal of all billboards along federal highways. In 1978 Congress appropriated $18 million for sign removal. See Charlton, The Billboard Act is Taking Effect, Ever So Slowly, N.Y. Times, Mar. 26, 1978, p. 18E.

B. THE APPEARANCE OF STRUCTURES AND OTHER AESTHETIC REGULATIONS

STATE EX REL. SAVELAND PARK HOLDING CORP. v. WIELAND

Supreme Court of Wisconsin, 1955.
269 Wis. 262, 69 N.W.2d 217, certiorari denied
350 U.S. 841, 76 S.Ct. 81, 100 L.Ed. 750.

[The lower court issued a preemptory writ of mandamus commanding defendant to issue a building permit on the ground that the ordinance under which such permit had been refused was unconstitutional and void.]

CURRIE, JUSTICE. The sole issue on this appeal is the constitutionality of ordinance No. 129 of the village of Fox Point, adopted by the village board of said village on July 23, 1946.

Sec. 1 of such ordinance provides as follows:

"No building permit for any structure for which a building permit is required shall be issued unless it has been found as a fact by the Building Board by at least a majority vote, after a view of the site of the proposed structure, and an examination of the application papers for a building permit, which shall include exterior elevations of the proposed structure, that the exterior architectural appeal and functional plan of the proposed structure will, when erected, not be so at variance with either the exterior architectural appeal and functional plan of the structures already constructed or in the course of construction in the immediate neighborhood or the character of the applicable district established by Ordinance No. 117 [the general zoning ordinance of the village], or any ordinance amendatory thereof or supplementary thereto, as to cause a substantial depreciation in the property values of said neighborhood within said applicable district."

Subsequent sections of the ordinance provide that the Building Board shall consist of three residents of the village, two of whom shall be architects, and provide a method of appeal from the decision of the Building Board to the Board of Appeals of the village.

On this appeal it is conceded that relator's application for a building permit disclosed compliance with all provisions of the general zoning ordinance of the village, and the sole reason why the defendant building inspector refused to grant the permit was the failure of the Building Board to make the necessary finding prescribed by sec. 1 of ordinance No. 129 as a prerequisite to the issuance of the permit.

The village of Fox Point was incorporated in 1926. It consists of approximately two and one-half square miles, and the entire area has been zoned for residential use only. There is, however, a small business district and a relatively small institutional district permitting churches, lodges, and municipal buildings, but the vast majority of the territory in the village is devoted to residence purposes. The village has developed into a highly desirable residential village, almost entirely built up of single family residences.

The learned trial court held the ordinance unconstitutional on the following three grounds: (1) that the preservation of property values is not by itself a proper objective for the exercise of the police power in enacting a zoning ordinance; (2) that the ordinance essentially is concerned with aesthetics which also is not a proper basis for exercise of the police power; and (3) that the standards prescribed in the ordinance for governing the action and decision of the Building Board are so indefinite as to subject applicants for building permits to the unlimited and arbitrary discretion of such board.

* * *

We have no difficulty in arriving at the conclusion that the protection of property values is an objective which falls within the exercise of the police power to promote the "general welfare", and that it is immaterial whether the zoning ordinance is grounded solely upon such objective or that such purpose is but one of several legitimate objectives. Anything that tends to destroy property values of the inhabitants of the village necessarily adversely affects the prosperity, and therefore the general welfare, of the entire village. Just because, in the particular case now before us, property values in a limited area only of the village are at stake does not mean that such threatened depreciation of property values does not affect the general welfare of the village as a whole. If relator is permitted to erect a dwelling house on its land of such nature as to substantially depreciate the value of surrounding property, there is danger that this same thing may be repeated elsewhere within the village, thus threatening property values throughout the village.

The learned trial court held that the objective of the ordinance is grounded largely upon aesthetic considerations, which are insufficient to justify the exercise of the police power. While the ordinance does use the term "architectural appeal", a building permit is only authorized to be withheld in those cases where the architectural appeal of the proposed structure is so at variance with that of structures already constructed, or being constructed, "as to cause a substantial depreciation in the property values" in the immediate neighborhood. This court pointed out in Jefferson County v. Timmel, 261 Wis. 39, 61, 51 N.W.2d 518 (1952), that while the general rule is that the zoning power may not be exercised for purely aesthetic considerations, such rule was undergoing development. In view of the latest word spoken on the subject by the United States supreme court in Berman v. Parker, 348 U.S. 26, 75 S.Ct. 98, 99 L.Ed. 27 (1954), this development of the law has proceeded to the point that renders it extremely doubtful that such prior rule is any longer the law.

In Berman v. Parker the United States supreme court had before it the question of the constitutionality of an Act of Congress providing for slum clearance in the District of Columbia under which appellants' property was included within the boundaries of the district to be condemned for slum clearance purposes, although it was used for store purposes and in no sense constituted slum housing. Appellants urged that the act, insofar as it permitted its property to be taken for such purpose, could not be justified under the police power, but was in violation of the "due process" clause of the Fifth Amendment. The court in a unanimous opinion by Mr. Justice Douglas declared, 75 S.Ct. at pages 102, 103:

> "The concept of the public welfare is broad and inclusive. See Day–Brite Lighting, Inc. v. State of Missouri, 342 U.S. 421, 424, 72 S.Ct. 405, 407, 96 L.Ed. 469. The values it represents are spiritual as well as physical, aesthetic as well as monetary. It is within the power of the legislature to determine that the community should be beautiful as well as healthy, spacious as well as clean, well-balanced as well as carefully patrolled. In the present case, the Congress and its authorized agencies have made determinations that take into account a wide variety of values. It is not for us to reappraise them. *If those who govern the District of Columbia decide that the Nation's*

capitol should be beautiful as well as sanitary, there is nothing in the Fifth Amendment that stands in the way. "(Emphasis supplied.)

While the court in Berman v. Parker, supra, was dealing with the "due process" clause of the Fifth Amendment, which restricts the power of Congress, and it is the "due process" clause of the Fourteenth Amendment which is applicable to state action, we consider such distinction to be immaterial in considering the scope of the police power and its exercise to promote the general welfare.

We now come to the last issue presented, *viz.*, whether the standards set by ordinance No. 129 for governing the functioning of the Building Board of the village are so indefinite as to subject applicants for buildings permits to the arbitrary discretion of such board. It will be recalled that the ordinance specifically provides for an appeal from the decision of the Building Board to the village Board of Appeals, and, of course, timely court review by certiorari will always lie from the decision of the Board of Appeals.

In order for a building permit to be refused under the ordinance the Building Board must find, as a fact, that the exterior architectural appeal and the proposed plan of structure when erected shall not be so at variance with those of structures already constructed, or in the course of construction, "in the immediate neighborhood" * * * "as to cause a *substantial* depreciation in the property values of said *neighborhood.*" The two words of the ordinance which have been singled out as being most objectionable from the standpoint of indefiniteness are "*neighborhood*"and "*substantial* ".

While several cases are cited in which courts have been called upon to define the term "*neighborhood* "we consider the decision of the Iowa court in Youtzy v. City of Cedar Rapids, 150 Iowa 53, 129 N.W. 351 (1911), as being the most helpful. That case involved the taking of land by condemnation, and complaint was made by the appellant land owner that witnesses had been permitted to testify as to sale prices of lands which were so far removed as to not be located in the neighborhood of the property being condemned. The Iowa court, in its opinion, conceded that property to be used by way of comparison or illustration "should be in the same neighborhood or so nearly similar to the one in question that knowledge of the former, and of its value, will afford some degree of aid to the intelligent and fair-minded juror in estimating the value of the latter." It then proceeded to define "*neighborhood* ", and stated:

> "The term neighborhood is one of quite indefinite meaning, and it may well be that in some cases the trial court will permit the inquiry to take a wider territorial range than it could allow in others. Certainly this court cannot attempt to fix a standard of measurement, and say as a matter of law that the similar property concerning which inquiry may be found within a given number of feet, yards, or blocks of the property condemned. Counsel for appellant argues, in effect, that, as the word has been used in cases of this class, 'neighborhood' has reference only to adjoining property, but

we think that this cannot be. The reasonable proposition is that the trial court is vested with discretion to draw the line in each case as shall seem just under all the circumstances developed by the testimony, and that, unless abuse of such discretion is shown, its ruling will not be held reversible error."

While the court in Youtzy v. Cedar Rapids, supra, was defining the term *"neighborhood"* as used in a rule of the common law, instead of a statute or ordinance, we consider the foregoing quotation equally applicable to its use in the instant case in ordinance No. 129. Clearly *"neighborhood "*, as used in the ordinance, does extend further than adjoining property and may vary according to existing conditions. For example, in a section of the village where the average building lot comprises several acres, the limits of the neighborhood might well be held to extend farther than in the case of an area in the village where building lots average less than an acre each in area.

Although it is impossible for this court in this decision to establish, in terms of measurement of feet, the radius of the largest permissible area which would qualify as a neighborhood under the ordinance, there is undoubtedly in each case a point beyond which a court could hold as a matter of law, that certain property was not in the same neighborhood as applicant's property, and that it would be an abuse of discretion if the Building Board determined otherwise. In case of a court review some effect necessarily would have to be accorded the adjective *"immediate"* preceding the word *"neighborhood"* where the latter first appears in the ordinance.

Just because some discretion is necessarily accorded the board to determine the limits of a neighborhood, as applied to a particular applicant's property, does not render the ordinance void. City of Milwaukee v. Ruplinger, 155 Wis. 391, 145 N.W. 42 (1914), and Pinkerton v. Buech, 173 Wis. 433, 181 N.W. 125 (1921). In the first mentioned of said two cases, this court upheld an ordinance of the plaintiff city which prohibited anyone from carrying on a junk shop in the city without a license, and further provided [155 Wis. 391, 145 N.W. 43] " 'all applications for license under this ordinance shall be made to the mayor who may grant or refuse to grant such license as to him may seem best for the good order of the city.' " The court held the ordinance granting to the mayor the power to grant or refuse licenses " *'as to him may seem best for the good order of the city' "* set a sufficiently definite standard, and held the ordinance constitutional. In the Pinkerton case the constitutionality of a statute providing for the licensing of private detectives was upheld which required the approval of the application by the fire and police commission of the city and a finding by the secretary of state that the applicant was *"of good character, competency and integrity."*

Turning now to the word *"substantial"* which has also been attacked by relator as being too indefinite, we find that the Washington supreme court in In re Krause's Estate, 173 Wash. 1, 21 P.2d 268, 270 (1933), held that the term *"substantially"* was not so indefinite as to render a contract employing it to be unenforceable. The particular contract provided " 'neither party shall have the right to make a new will as to property which has pursuant hereto been *substantially* benefited by the other party'," with respect to which the court stated:

"Substantial" as an adjective means something worthwhile as distinguished from something without value, or merely nominal.

This court is frequently required to apply the wording of section 227.20(1)(d), Stats., "unsupported by substantial evidence in view of the entire record", in cases involving review of determinations by administrative agencies under our uniform Administrative Procedure Act. We do not recall of any litigant ever having raised the question that the word "substantial" therein rendered such quoted portion of the statute indefinite and void.

Determining whether or not a proposed structure will *"substantially"* depreciate property values in the area is simply the reverse of the common question that must be answered in the assessing of benefits resulting from a public improvement in levying a special assessment against the benefited property. There the question must be determined whether or not the public improvement benefits property, and if so what property and to what extent.

It is our considered judgment that ordinance No. 129 constitutes a valid exercise of the police power of the village of Fox Point, and its provisions are not so indefinite or ambiguous as to subject applicants for building permits to the uncontrolled arbitrary discretion or caprice of the Building Board.

Judgment reversed and cause remanded with directions to quash the proceedings.

Note

Compare the case of Waterfront Estates Development, Inc. v. City of Palos Hills, 232 Ill.App.3d 367, 173 Ill.Dec. 667, 597 N.E.2d 641 (1992) where the court found that the ordinance creating the city's appearance commission was an overbroad delegation of authority, and that the ordinance was unconstitutionally vague. The defendant unsuccessfully argued that the appearance commission only acted in an advisory capacity making recommendations to the city council.

STATE EX REL. STOYANOFF v. BERKELEY

Supreme Court of Missouri, Division No. 2, 1970.
458 S.W.2d 305.

PRITCHARD, COMMISSIONER. Upon summary judgment the trial court issued a peremptory writ of mandamus to compel appellant to issue a residential building permit to respondents. The trial court's judgment is that the below-mentioned ordinances are violative of Section 10, Article I of the Constitution of Missouri, 1945, V.A.M.S., in that restrictions placed by the ordinances on the use of property deprive the owners of their property without due process of law. Relators' petition pleads that they applied to appellant Building Commissioner for a building permit to allow them to construct a single family residence in the City of Ladue, and that plans and specifications were submitted for the proposed residence, which was unusual in design, "but complied with all existing building and zoning regulations and ordinances of the City of Ladue, Missouri."

It is further pleaded that relators were refused a building permit for the construction of their proposed residence upon the ground that the permit was not approved by the Architectural Board of the City of Ladue. Ordinance 131, as amended by Ordinance 281 of that city, purports to set up an Architectural Board to approve plans and specifications for buildings and structures erected within the city and in a preamble to "conform to certain minimum architectural standards of appearance and conformity with surrounding structures, and that unsightly, grotesque and unsuitable structures, detrimental to the stability of value and the welfare of surrounding property, structures and residents, and to the general welfare and happiness of the community, be avoided, and that appropriate standards of beauty and conformity be fostered and encouraged." It is asserted in the petition that the ordinances are invalid, illegal and void, "are unconstitutional in that they are vague and provide no standard nor uniform rule by which to guide the architectural board," that the city acted in excess of statutory powers (§ 89.020, RSMo 1959, V.A.M.S.) in enacting the ordinances, which "attempt to allow respondent to impose aesthetic standards for buildings in the City of Ladue, and are in excess of the powers granted the City of Ladue by said statute."

Relators filed a motion for summary judgment and affidavits were filed in opposition thereto. Richard D. Shelton, Mayor of the City of Ladue, deponed that the facts in appellant's answer were true and correct, as here pertinent: that the City of Ladue constitutes one of the finer suburban residential areas of Metropolitan St. Louis, the homes therein are considerably more expensive than in cities of comparable size, being homes on lots from three fourths of an acre to three or more acres each; * * * It is then pleaded that relators' description of their proposed residence as " 'unusual in design' is the understatement of the year. It is in fact a monstrosity of grotesque design, which would seriously impair the value of property in the neighborhood."

The affidavit of Harold C. Simon, a developer of residential subdivisions in St. Louis County, is that he is familiar with relators' lot upon which they seek to build a house, and with the surrounding houses in the neighborhood; that the houses therein existent are virtually all two-story houses of conventional architectural design, such as Colonial, French Provincial or English; and that the house which relators propose to construct is of ultramodern design which would clash with and not be in conformity with any other house in the entire neighborhood. It is Mr. Simon's opinion that the design and appearance of relators' proposed residence would have a substantial adverse effect upon the market values of other residential property in the neighborhood, such average market value ranging from $60,000 to $85,000 each.

As a part of the affidavit of Russell H. Riley, consultant for the city planning and engineering firm of Harland Bartholomew & Associates, photographic exhibits of homes surrounding relators' lot were attached. * * * In substance Mr. Riley went on to say that the City of Ladue is one of the finer residential suburbs in the St. Louis area with a minimum of commercial or industrial usage. The development of residences in the city has been primarily by private subdivisions, usually with one main lane or drive leading therein (such as Lorenzo Road Subdivision which runs north off of Ladue Road in which relators' lot is located). The homes are considerably more expensive than average homes found in a city of comparable size. The ordinance which has been adopted by the City of Ladue is typical of those which have been adopted by a number of suburban cities in St. Louis County and in similar cities throughout the United States, the need therefor being based upon the protection of existing property values by preventing the construction of houses that are in complete conflict with the general type of houses in a given area. The intrusion into this neighborhood of relators' unusual, grotesque and nonconforming structure would have a substantial adverse effect on market values of other homes in the immediate area. According to Mr. Riley the standards of Ordinance 131, as amended by Ordinance 281, are usually and customarily applied in city planning work and are: "(1) whether the proposed house meets the customary architectural requirements in appearance and design for a house of the particular type which is proposed (whether it be Colonial, Tudor English, French Provincial, or Modern), (2) whether the proposed house is in general conformity with the style and design of surrounding structures, and (3) whether the proposed house lends itself to the proper architectural development of the City; and that in applying said standards the Architectural Board and its Chairman are to determine whether the proposed house will have an adverse affect on the stability of values in the surrounding area."

Photographic exhibits of relators' proposed residence were also attached to Mr. Riley's affidavit. They show the residence to be of a pyramid shape, with a flat top, and with triangular shaped windows or doors at one or more corners.

* * *

Section 89.020 provides: "For the purpose of promoting health, safety, morals or the general welfare of the community, the legislative body of all cities, towns, and villages is hereby empowered to regulate and restrict the height, number of stories, and size of buildings and other structures, the percentage of lot that may be occupied, the size of yards, courts, and other open spaces, the density of population, the preservation of features of historical significance, and the location and use of buildings, structures and land for trade, industry, residence or other purposes." Section 89.040 provides: "Such regulations shall be made in accordance with a comprehensive plan and designed to lessen congestion in the streets; to secure safety from fire, panic and other dangers; to promote health *and the general welfare;* to provide adequate light and air; to prevent the overcrowding of land; to avoid undue concentration of population; to preserve features of historical significance; to facilitate the adequate provision of transportation, water, sewerage, schools, parks, and other public requirements. *Such regulations shall be made with reasonable consideration, among other things, to the character of the district and its peculiar suitability for particular uses, and with a view to conserving the values of buildings and encouraging the most appropriate use of land throughout such municipality."* (Italics added.)

Relators say that "Neither Sections 89.020 or 89.040 nor any other provision of Chapter 89 mentions or gives a city the authority to regulate architectural design and appearance. There exists no provision providing for an architectural board and no entity even remotely resembling such a board is mentioned under the enabling legislation." Relators conclude that the City of Ladue lacked any power to adopt Ordinance 131 as amended by Ordinance 281 "and its intrusion into this area is wholly unwarranted and without sanction in the law." As to this aspect of the appeal relators rely upon the 1961 decision of State ex rel. Magidson v. Henze, Mo.App., 342 S.W.2d 261. That case had the identical question presented. An Architectural Control Commission was set up by an ordinance of the City of University City. In its report to the Building Commissioner, the Architectural Control Commission disapproved the Magidson application for permits to build four houses. It was commented that the proposed houses did not provide for the minimum number of square feet, and "In considering the existing character of this neighborhood, the Commission is of the opinion that houses of the character proposed in these plans are not in harmony with and will not contribute to nor protect the general welfare of this neighborhood" (loc. cit. 264). The court held that § 89.020, RSMo1949, V.A.M.S., does not grant to the city the right to impose upon the landowner aesthetic standards for the buildings he chooses to erect.

As is clear from the affidavits and attached exhibits, the City of Ladue is an area composed principally of residences of the general types of Colonial, French Provincial and English Tudor. The city has a comprehensive plan of zoning to maintain the general character of buildings therein. The Magidson case, supra, did not consider the effect of § 89.040, supra, and the italicized portion relating to the character of the district, its suitability for particular uses, and the conservation of the values of buildings therein. These considerations, sanctioned by statute, are directly related to the general welfare of the community. That proposition has support in a number of cases cited by appellant. State ex rel. Carter v. Harper, Building Commissioner, 182 Wis. 148, 196 N.W. 451, 454, quotes Chicago B. & Q. Ry. Co. v. People of State of Illinois ex rel. Drainage Commissioners, 200 U.S. 561, 26 S.Ct. 341, 50 L.Ed. 596, 609, " 'We hold that the police power of a state embraces regulations designed to promote the public convenience or the general prosperity, as well as regulations designed to promote the public health, the public morals or the public safety.' " In Marrs v. City of Oxford (D.C.D.Kan.) 24 F.2d 541, 548, it was said, "The stabilizing of property values, and giving some assurance to the public that, if property is purchased in a residential district, its value as such will be preserved, is probably the most cogent reason back of zoning ordinances." See also People v. Calvar Corporation et al., Sup., 69 N.Y.S.2d 272, 279 (aff'd 286 N.Y. 419, 36 N.E.2d 644); Kovacs v. Cooper, Judge, 336 U.S. 77, 69 S.Ct. 448, 93 L.Ed. 513, 526; Wulfsohn v. Burden, 241 N.Y. 288, 150 N.E. 120, 122[3], 43 A.L.R. 651; and Price et al. v. Schwafel (Cal.), 92 Cal.App.2d 77, 206 P.2d 683, 685. The preamble to Ordinance 131, quoted above in part, demonstrates that its purpose is to conform to the dictates of § 89.040, with reference to preserving values of property by zoning procedure and restrictions on the use of property. This is an illustration of what was referred to in Deimeke v. State Highway Commission, Mo., 444 S.W.2d 480, 484, as a growing number of cases recognizing a change in the scope of the term "general welfare." In the Deimeke case on the same page it is said, "Property use which offends sensibilities and debases property values affects not only the adjoining property owners in that vicinity but the general public as well because when such property values are destroyed or seriously impaired, the tax base of the community is affected and the public suffers economically as a result."

Relators say further that Ordinances 131 and 281 are invalid and unconstitutional as being an unreasonable and arbitrary exercise of the police power. It is argued that a mere reading of these ordinances shows that they are based entirely on aesthetic factors in that the stated purpose of the Architectural Board is to maintain "conformity with surrounding structures" and to assure that structures "conform to certain minimum architectural standards of appearance." The argument ignores the further provisos in the ordinance: " * * * and that unsightly, grotesque and unsuitable structures, *detrimental to the stability of value and the welfare of surrounding property, structures, and residents,* and *to the general welfare and happiness of the community,* be avoided, and that appropriate standards of beauty and conformity be fostered and encouraged." (Italics added.) Relators' proposed residence does not descend to the " 'patently offensive character of vehicle graveyards in close proximity to such highways' " referred to in the Deimeke case, supra (444 S.W.2d 484). Nevertheless, the aesthetic factor to be taken into account by the Architectural Board is not to be considered alone. Along with that inherent factor is the effect that the proposed residence would have upon the property values in the area. In this time of burgeoning urban areas, congested with people and structures, it is certainly in keeping with the ultimate ideal of general welfare that the Architectural Board, in its function, preserve and protect existing areas in which structures of a general conformity of architecture have been erected. The area under consideration is clearly, from the record, a fashionable one. In State ex rel. Civello v. City of New Orleans, 154 La. 271, 97 So. 440, 444, the court said, "If by the term 'aesthetic considerations' is meant a regard merely for outward appearances, for good taste in the matter of the beauty of the neighborhood itself, we do not observe any substantial reason for saying that such a consideration is not a matter of general welfare. The beauty of a fashionable residence neighborhood in a city is for the comfort and happiness of the residents, and it sustains in a general way the value of property in the neighborhood." See also People v. Stover, 12 N.Y.2d 462, 240 N.Y.S.2d 734, 191 N.E.2d 272, 274[3]; State ex rel. Saveland Park Holding Corp. v. Wieland, 269 Wis. 262, 69 N.W.2d 217, 222; Reid v. Architectural Board of Review of the City of Cleveland Heights, 119 Ohio App. 67, 192 N.E.2d 74, 77; and Oregon City v. Hartke, 240 Or. 35, 400 P.2d 255, 261, for pronouncements of the principle that aesthetics is a factor to be considered in zoning matters.

* * * The denial by appellant of a building permit for relators' highly modernistic residence in this area where traditional Colonial, French Provincial and English Tudor styles of architecture are erected does not appear to be arbitrary and unreasonable when the basic purpose to be served is that of the general welfare of persons in the entire community.

In addition to the above-stated purpose in the preamble to Ordinance 131, it establishes an Architectural Board of three members, all of whom must be architects. Meetings of the Board are to be open to the public, and every application for a building permit, except those not affecting the outward appearance of a building, shall be submitted to the Board along with plans, elevations, detail drawings and specifications, before being approved by the Building Commissioner. The Chairman of the Board shall examine the application to determine if it conforms to proper architectural standards in appearance and design and will be in general conformity with the style and design of surrounding structures and conducive to the proper architectural development of the city. If he so finds, he approves and returns the application to the Building Commissioner. If he does not find conformity, or has doubt, a full meeting of the Board is called, with notice of the time and place thereof given to the applicant. The Board shall disapprove the application if it determines the proposed structure will constitute an unsightly, grotesque or unsuitable structure in appearance, detrimental to the welfare of surrounding property or residents. If it cannot make that decision, the application shall be returned to the Building Commissioner either with or without suggestions or recommendations, and if that is done without disapproval, the Building Commissioner may issue the permit. If the Board's disapproval is given and the applicant refuses to comply with recommendations, the Building Commissioner shall refuse the permit. Thereafter provisions are made for an appeal to the Council of the city for review of the decision of the Architectural Board. Ordinance 281 amends Ordinance 131 only with respect to the application initially being submitted to and considered by all members of the Architectural Board.

Relators claim that the above provisions of the ordinance amount to an unconstitutional delegation of power by the city to the Architectural Board. It is argued that the Board cannot be given the power to determine what is unsightly and grotesque and that the standards, "whether the proposed structure will conform to proper architectural standards in appearance and design, and will be in general conformity with the style and design of surrounding structures and conducive to the proper architectural development of the City * * * "and "the Board shall disapprove the application if it determines that the proposed structure will constitute an unsightly, grotesque or unsuitable structure in appearance, detrimental to the welfare of surrounding property or residents * * *," are inadequate. * * * Ordinances 131 and 281 are sufficient in their general standards calling for a factual determination of the suitability of any proposed structure with reference to the character of the surrounding neighborhood and to the determination of any adverse effect on the general welfare and preservation of property values of the community. Like holdings were made involving Architectural Board ordinances in State ex rel. Saveland Park Holding Corp. v. Wieland, 269 Wis. 262, 69 N.W.2d 217, and Reid v. Architectural Board of Review of the City of Cleveland Heights, 119 Ohio App. 67, 192 N.E.2d 74, supra.

The judgment is reversed.

Notes

1. Do the two principal cases indicate that aesthetic considerations alone may not be sufficient to sustain the police power, and that support for architectural review boards must be also found in the general welfare aspect of the police power as used to sustain property values? On the point of whether aesthetic considerations affect the validity of the zoning ordinance see the annotation in 21 A.L.R.3d 1222, and on architectural design regulations, see the annotation in 41 A.L.R.3d 1397.

2. In Guinnane v. San Francisco City Planning Comm'n, 209 Cal. App.3d 732, 257 Cal.Rptr. 742 (1989), the court upheld the denial of a permit for a four-story house with five bedrooms, five bathrooms, and parking for two cars. Although the proposed house was in conformance with all the zoning and building regulations, the permit was denied because the height, length, bulk, and area of the planned house would not be in character with the surrounding residences which were significantly smaller. The court rejected the argument that there were no specific standards to guide the planning commission, stating that this was the type of decision properly left to the sound discretion of the agency.

In most jurisdictions courts require the issuance of permits when all requirements of the ordinance have been met.

3. Not all of the modern cases support the validity of architectural review. In City of West Palm Beach v. State ex rel. Duffey, 158 Fla. 863, 30 So.2d 491 (1947), the court struck down a self-executing provision of the ordinance which provided that the "completed appearance of every new building or structure must substantially equal that of the adjacent buildings or structures in said subdivision, in appearance, square foot area, and height." The court held that the words "substantially equal" and "appearance" were unduly vague. A leading case which disapproved an architectural

review board similar to the ones approved in the principal cases was
Pacesetter Homes v. Village of Olympia Fields, 104 Ill.App.2d 218, 244
N.E.2d 369 (1968). Cf. Reid v. Architectural Bd. of Review of City of
Cleveland Heights, 119 Ohio App. 67, 192 N.E.2d 74 (1963). One commentator attempted to reconcile the Illinois holding with the Wisconsin, Missouri
and Ohio cases by pointing out that the ordinance in the Illinois case did not
explicitly mention as a standard the protection of property values. See
Henley, Beautiful as Well as Sanitary—Architectural Control by Municipalities in Illinois, 59 Ill.Bar J. 39 (1970). A New Jersey case disapproved
architectural review boards on the ground that the state enabling act did not
authorize such regulations. See Piscitelli v. Township Committee of Scotch
Plains, 103 N.J.Super. 589, 248 A.2d 274 (1968). However, that court relied
primarily on the Missouri case overruled in Stoyanoff.

4. Although the caselaw on architectural review boards is sparse, the
use of such boards, particularly in suburban, predominantly residential
communities is spreading. A recent publication will probably spur the use of
such boards even more. The American Institute of Architects, Committee on
Design Publication, Design Review Boards: A Handbook for Communities
(1974), offers a legal analysis of the problem plus a model ordinance
(annotated) drafted by Prof. George Lefcoe. In 1968, when the A.I.A. began
its research project on design review boards, it counted 221 such boards. The
number operating today is unknown.

Also consider that there are probably many sets of restrictive covenants
requiring architectural committee review of proposed dwellings. For one
example, see Catalina Square Improvement Comm. v. Metz, 630 S.W.2d 324
(Tex.App.1982) involving a dispute over replacement of a wood shingle roof
with a composite roof.

5. In an article entitled, "Billboards, Glass Houses, and the Law,"
which appeared in the April, 1966, edition of Harper's Magazine, Richard F.
Babcock, member of the Illinois Bar, stated at page 30:[13]

> Artistic creativeness is a function of the individual, and we social
> scientists, concerned with the place of grace in urban design, will have
> either to choose government by a Borgia or, if we insist upon a
> government of burghers, to declare design off-limits, for the politicians.
> The rub is that if we opt for the dictator we may get Dr. Goebbels rather
> than a Renaissance prince. So my choice, even at the cultural level, is to
> go for democracy but insist that design is not the function of govern-
> ment, except in the following limited area:

> First, we should be heartened by the evidence that a representative
> government is concerned enough to encourage the untried and the
> different in design and in any of the other arts. This is a different breed
> of cat from a command by government, municipal or federal, that design
> must conform to the established order. Nor do I regard as inconsistent
> with my thesis governmental efforts to preserve, by eminent domain or
> by regulation, those features of the man-made landscape that by any
> definition are landmarks of our heritage. And I do not regard as difficult
> the distinction that must be made between a thousand homogeneous

suburbs and a Beacon Hill; a Galena, Illinois; portions of San Antonio; or the unique nineteenth-century square in Woodstock, Illinois. I am even ready to concede that from this exception it must logically follow that we must be prepared to preserve one or perhaps two postwar suburbs * * * which proves beyond question my devotion to logic if not to beauty!

Second, government cannot abdicate its duty to select which natural amenities shall be shielded from any scheme of man. (The only issue here is whether government must pay or can achieve the result by regulation.) The government, local and national, must play the dominant role in any debate over whether any construction shall be permitted along the Chicago lakefront; whether a hydroelectric project on the Hudson River should be constructed irrespective of the consequences to historic landmarks and natural beauty; whether the Allagash River in Maine or the Dinosaur Area or the Redwoods or the Dunes shall be preserved or sacrificed for the economic best interest of the country; and whether the public view of San Francisco Bay shall be spoiled.

Third, government can and should identify those circumstances where design in the private sector will have a demonstrable impact upon public services. Government must prescribe the perimeters of the choices allowed the designer in such cases. If, for example, one accepts the premise that building bulk and density do have an impact on the efficiency of public services such as streets, sanitation, and schools, then one can more readily accept regulation designed to protect these facilities that may limit freedom of choice by the designer.

Finally, the government should offer incentives to the builder to provide more open space than would otherwise be required. The Chicago zoning ordinance grants a bonus in the form of additional permitted floor area to the builder who will provide greater open space at ground level. Some suburban ordinances will permit a greater number of dwelling units per acre to the developer who clusters his houses, thereby creating more usable common open space. (Both are examples of what baseball vice presidents call the "natural trade." The developer gets increased gross revenues, the city gets additional open space.)

Beyond these limits I fear to go in the regulation of design.

PEOPLE v. STOVER

Court of Appeals of New York, 1963.
12 N.Y.2d 462, 240 N.Y.S.2d 734, 191 N.E.2d 272, appeal dismissed
375 U.S. 42, 84 S.Ct. 147, 11 L.Ed.2d 107 (1963).

FULD, JUDGE. The defendants, Mr. and Mrs. Stover, residents of the City of Rye since 1940, live in a 2½-story 1-family dwelling, located in a pleasant and built-up residential district, on the corner of Rye Beach and Forest Avenues. A clothesline, filled with old clothes and rags, made its first appearance in the Stovers' front yard in 1956 as a form of "peaceful protest" against the high taxes imposed by the city. And, during each of the five succeeding years, the defendants added another clothesline to mark their continued displeasure with the taxes. In 1961, therefore, six lines, from which there hung tattered clothing, old uniforms, underwear, rags and scarecrows, were strung across the Stovers' yard—three from the porch across the front yard to trees along Forest Avenue and three from the porch across the side yard to trees along Rye Beach Avenue.

In August of 1961, the city enacted an ordinance prohibiting the erection and maintenance of clotheslines or other devices for hanging clothes or other fabrics in a front or side yard abutting a street (General Ordinances, § 4–3.7). However, the ordinance provides for the issuance of a permit for the use of such clotheslines if there is "a practical difficulty or unnecessary hardship in drying clothes elsewhere on the premises" and grants a right of appeal to the applicant if a permit is denied.[14]

Following enactment of the ordinance, Mrs. Stover, the record owner of the property, applied for a permit to maintain clotheslines in her yard. Her application was denied because, she was advised, she had sufficient other property available for hanging clothes and she was directed to remove the clotheslines which were in the yards abutting the streets. Although no appeal was taken from this determination and no permit ever issued, the clotheslines were not removed. Relying upon the ordinance, the city thereupon charged the defendants with violating its provisions. They were tried and convicted and their judgments of conviction have been affirmed by the County Court of Westchester County. Upon the trial the defendant Webster Stover disputed the sufficiency of the evidence to connect him with the erection or maintenance of the clotheslines but he does not do so here, urging instead that the ordinance, as it has been applied to him and his wife, is unconstitutional both as an interference with free speech and as a deprivation of property without due process.[15]

It is a fair inference that adoption of the ordinance before us was prompted by the conduct and action of the defendants but we deem it clear that, if the law would otherwise be held constitutional, it will not be stricken as discriminatory or invalid because of its motivation. Cf. Town of Hempstead v. Goldblatt, 9 N.Y.2d 101, 211 N.Y.S.2d 185, 172 N.E.2d 562, affirmed 369 U.S. 590, 82 S.Ct. 987, 8 L.Ed.2d 130. Our

14. The full text of the ordinance reads in this way (General Ordinance, § 4–3.7):

"*Clothes lines.* No clothes lines, drying racks, poles or other similar devices for hanging clothes, rags or other fabrics shall be erected or maintained in a front yard or side yard abutting a street. If there is a practical difficulty or unnecessary hardship in drying clothes elsewhere on the premises, a permit shall be issued by the City Clerk permitting the use of said front or side yard for such purpose upon approval of and a finding by the Building Inspector that drying of clothes elsewhere on the premises would create a practical difficulty or unnecessary hardship. If a permit is denied, the applicant may appeal to the Board of Appeals of this city. The provisions of this section shall be applicable to existing conditions."

15. We merely note that the proof of Mr. Stover's participation is more than ample to support the conviction. He not only acknowledged, at a public hearing before the Rye City Council, that he had erected the lines as a protest against his taxes and was leaving them there "until he got some action on his assessment" but he alleged the same thing in a complaint in a declaratory judgment action which he and his wife had instituted against the city.

problem, therefore, is to determine whether the law violates First Amendment rights or otherwise exceeds the police power vested in a city on the ground that it was enacted without regard to considerations of public health, safety and welfare.

The People maintain that the prohibition against clotheslines in front and side yards was "intended to provide clear visibility at street corners and in driving out of driveways, and thus avoid and reduce accidents; to reduce distractions to motorists and pedestrians; and to provide greater opportunity for access in the event of fires". Although there may be considerable doubt whether there is a sufficiently reasonable relationship between clotheslines and traffic or fire safety to support an exercise of the police power, it is our opinion that the ordinance may be sustained as an attempt to preserve the residential appearance of the city and its property values by banning, insofar as practicable, unsightly clotheslines from yards abutting a public street. In other words, the statute, though based on what may be termed aesthetic considerations, proscribes conduct which offends sensibilities and tends to debase the community and reduce real estate values.

There are a number of early decisions, both in this State * * * and elsewhere * * *, which hold that aesthetic considerations are not alone sufficient to justify exercise of the police power. But since 1930 this court has taken pains repeatedly to declare that the issue is an open and "unsettled" one in New York. People v. Rubenfeld, 254 N.Y. 245, 248–249, 172 N.E. 485, 486–487; see, also, Perlmutter v. Greene, 259 N.Y. 327, 332, 182 N.E. 5, 6, 81 A.L.R. 1543; New York State Thruway Auth. v. Ashley Motor Ct., Inc., 10 N.Y.2d 151, 156–157, 218 N.Y.S.2d 640, 642–643, 176 N.E.2d 566, 568–569. In addition, we have actually recognized the governmental interest in preserving the appearance of the community by holding that, whether or not aesthetic considerations are in and of themselves sufficient to support an exercise of the police power, they may be taken into account by the legislative body in enacting laws which are also designed to promote health and safety. * * * "Aesthetic considerations", this court wrote in Dowsey v. Village of Kensington, 257 N.Y. 221, 230, 177 N.E. 427, 430, supra, "are, fortunately, not wholly without weight in a practical world."

Once it be conceded that aesthetics is a valid subject of legislative concern, the conclusion seems inescapable that reasonable legislation designed to promote that end is a valid and permissible exercise of the police power. If zoning restrictions "which implement a policy of neighborhood amenity" are to be stricken as invalid, it should be, one commentator has said, not because they seek to promote "aesthetic objectives" but solely because the restrictions constitute "unreasonable devices of implementing community policy." Dukeminier, Zoning for Aesthetic Objectives: A Reappraisal, 20 Law & Contemp.Prob. 218, 231. Consequently, whether such a statute or ordinance should be voided should depend upon whether the restriction was "an arbitrary and irrational method of achieving an attractive, efficiently functioning, prosperous community—and *not* upon whether the objectives were primarily aesthetic." Dukeminier, loc. cit. And, indeed, this view finds support in an ever-increasing number of cases from other jurisdictions which recognize that aesthetic considerations alone may warrant an exercise of the police power. * * *

Cases may undoubtedly arise, as we observed above, in which the legislative body goes too far in the name of aesthetics, cf. Matter of Mid–State Adv. Corp. v. Bond, 274 N.Y. 82, 8 N.E.2d 286; Dowsey v. Village of Kensington, 257 N.Y. 221, 177 N.E. 427, supra; Dukeminier, Zoning for Aesthetic Objectives: A Reappraisal, 20 Law & Contemp.Prob. 218, 231, but the present, quite clearly is not one of them. The ordinance before us is in large sense regulatory rather than prohibitory. It causes no undue hardship to any property owner, for it expressly provides for the issuance of a permit for clotheslines in front and side yards in cases where there is practical difficulty or unnecessary hardship in drying clothes else-where on the premises. Moreover, the ordinance imposes no arbitrary or capricious standard of beauty or conformity upon the community. It simply proscribes conduct which is unnecessarily offensive to the visual sensibilities of the average person. It is settled that conduct which is similarly offensive to the senses of hearing and smell may be a valid subject of regulation under the police power, see, e.g., People v. Rubenfeld, 254 N.Y. 245, 172 N.E. 485, supra, and we perceive no basis for a different result merely because the sense of sight is involved.

Nor is there any warrant or justification for a charge—which seems to have been abandoned on this appeal—that the ordinance is being enforced solely against the defendants or that there is a pattern of discrimination consciously being practiced against them. As the court below noted, the building superintendent testified, without contradiction, that all applications for permits were checked and investigated, that other applications for permits had been denied and that the defendants were the only persons who refused to remove clotheslines violative of the ordinance.

* * *

[The balance of the majority opinion, in which the court discusses the contention of the defendants that their freedom of speech had been denied them, is omitted. The court concluded that the prohibition against clotheslines had no necessary relationship to the dissemination of ideas or opinions.]

The judgment appealed from should be affirmed.

VAN VOORHIS, JUDGE (dissenting).

My concern in this case is not with limitation of free speech nor whether aesthetic considerations are enough in themselves to justify zoning regulations in prescribed instances, but with the extent to which a municipality can go in restricting the use of private property. The ordinance whose validity is now being upheld prohibits the erection and maintenance of clotheslines in a front or side yard abutting a street. Exceptions may be granted, and we were told upon the argument that 26 exceptions have been allowed in Rye, with the practical result that this ordinance is enforced against few others, if any, than the appellants. Even if that be held not to undermine the ordinance, it seems to me to exceed zoning powers for municipalities such as this to dictate to owners of houses and lots where they may put their clotheslines. The validity of ordinances may be tested in court according to whether the exercise of power delegated to the municipality is reasonable or arbitrary. People ex rel. City of Olean v. Western N.Y. & Pa. Traction Co., 214 N.Y. 526, 108 N.E. 847; Commissioners of Palisades Interstate Park v. Lent, 240 N.Y. 1, 147 N.E. 228. In the case last cited it was said that "What is reasonable is in large part tested by what is ordinary usage and common experience." 240 N.Y. p. 8, 147 N.E. p. 230. What has happened here is that these defendants conceived the unusual idea of hanging what the majority opinion describes as "tattered clothing, old uniforms, underwear, rags and scarecrows" across their yard as a form of protest against the amount of their taxes. The city, at the instance of other residents in the area, fought back by adopting this ordinance from the operation of which almost every other property owner applying for a permit has been excepted. Although the origin of this dispute is evidently political in nature, the validity of this ordinance is sought to be upheld entirely on the basis of aesthetic considerations, e.g., that the eye is offended by what hangs from these clotheslines. No cases have been cited from this or any other jurisdiction holding that a municipal corporation or political subdivision can direct house and lot owners where they shall hang their clothes. Aesthetic considerations, in a certain sense, underlie all zoning, usually in combination with other factors with which they are interwoven. Lot area, setback and height restrictions, for example, are based essentially on aesthetic factors. Occasionally public safety considerations are blended with aesthetics, such as the tendency of billboards to distract the attention of automobile drivers or of high hedges to block their view at street intersections. Aesthetic factors are given effect, in such cases, but have been limited to specific situations and not extended to anything which offends the taste of the neighbors or of the local legislature. One may assume, for example, that a clothesline ordinance would be invalid which permitted the hanging of white but not red blankets, or allowed shirts to be put out to dry after washing but not underwear. Probably, at least until the next step in zoning law, a municipality would be held unauthorized to direct house owners what colors their homes should be painted, or what kinds of trees or shrubbery they should be allowed to grow and where they should be planted. Nevertheless if they can be told where to hang their clothes in their yards, these items would be but a small step beyond the present holding, or to prescribe what architectural designs should be adopted so as to harmonize with the designs of the neighbors. To direct by ordinance that all buildings erected in a certain area should be one-story ranch houses would scarcely go beyond the present ruling as a question of power, or to lay down the law that they should be all of the same color, or of different colors, or that each should be of one or two or more color tones as might suit the aesthetic predilections of the city councillors or zoning boards of appeal.

This ordinance is unrelated to the public safety, health, morals or welfare except insofar as it compels conformity to what the neighbors like to look at. Zoning, important as it is within limits, is too rapidly becoming a legalized device to prevent property owners from doing whatever their neighbors dislike. Protection of minority rights is as essential to democracy as majority vote. In our age of conformity it is still not possible for all to be exactly alike, nor is it the instinct of our law to compel uniformity wherever diversity may offend the sensibilities of those who cast the largest numbers of votes in municipal elections. The right to be different has its place in this country. The United States has drawn strength from differences among its people in taste, experience, temperament, ideas, and ambitions as well as from differences in race, national or religious background. Even where the use of property is bizarre, unsuitable or obstreperous it is not to be curtailed in the absence of overriding reasons of public policy. The security and repose which come from protection of the right to be different in matter of aesthetics, taste, thought, expression and within limits in conduct are not to be cast aside without violating constitutional privileges and immunities. This is not merely a matter of legislative policy, at whatever level. In my view, this pertains to individual rights protected by the Constitution.

Aesthetic factors have always played an important part in zoning, as they have in the licensing of television and radio. Theatre and entertainment, as well as other forms of music, art, philosophy and literature are closely involved in aesthetics, which are not a veneer but are fundamental to the human mind and spirit. Nor are aesthetics confined to landscape gardening, tract development or architectural design. The avoidance by courts, sometimes seemingly to the point of evasion, of sustaining the constitutionality of zoning solely on aesthetic grounds has had its origin in a wholesome fear of allowing government to trespass through aesthetics on the human personality. In this instance, hanging tattered clothing, underwear, rags and scarecrows on a clothesline can scarcely be regarded as articulating a protest against excessive taxation, but to prohibit it by law upon the ground that it offends the aesthetic sensibilities of the neighbors or of the public officials of the municipality means—unless well defined and effectively enforced limits are placed upon this power to rule aesthetics by government—opening the door to the invasion by majority rule of a great deal of territory that belongs to the individual human being. It was once said of a famous lady of history that she had so much taste, and all of it so bad. Individual taste, good or bad, should ordinarily be let alone by government.

In authorizing the regulation of setback lines, yard areas, height of buildings and many permitted uses, the dominant factor has often been and should be aesthetic. But it is important not to allow general or unlimited power in government to regulate aesthetics in zoning or other departments of municipal administration. Extending aesthetic factors to the regulation of clotheslines suggests that zoning power, in the future, may extend to many other types of regulation also, since municipal boards and councils are being authorized in large degree to impose their ideas of aesthetics, and may be expected to do so on an expanding scale to placate the wishes of other property owners who constitute a large segment of the electorate. Unless clotheslines create traffic or health hazards, it seems to me that they should not be interfered with by law in suburban or rural areas. More important than this, however, does it seem that extensions of categories of local legislation for purely aesthetic purposes should be defined and limited, and, if they are to be enlarged, it should not be under reasoning which sets no ascertainable bounds to what can be done or attempted under this power.

The judgments of conviction of appellants should be reversed and the charges against them dismissed.

Notes

1. In City of Smyrna v. Parks, 240 Ga. 699, 242 S.E.2d 73 (1978), the court upheld a prohibition against chain link fences in front yards, finding that, in addition to aesthetic objectives, the ordinance was a safety measure in that fire fighters would be able to enter premises more easily when faced with a wood fence. Also see People v. Tolman, 110 Cal.App.3d Supp. 6, 168 Cal.Rptr. 328 (1980), upholding an ordinance prohibiting parking of vehicles over three tons on residential streets, as applied to a homeowner who had parked a 7½ ton truck tractor in front of her home continuously for ten years prior to enactment of the ordinance. Compare State v. Piemontese, 282 N.J.Super. 307, 659 A.2d 1385 (1995) where the court held that an ordinance requiring property owners to keep lawns, hedges and bushes from becoming "overgrown and unsightly" was vague and overly broad.

2. The theory of the Stover case does not necessarily mean that all aesthetic regulations in New York are free from attack. In Sackson v. Zimmerman, 103 A.D.2d 843, 478 N.Y.S.2d 354 (1984) the court held that a purely aesthetic regulation must be supported by a showing that the offense to the eye has a substantial and material effect on the community. The court struck down application of a local ordinance which applied an inordinate setback on a property owner to preserve neighbors' views of nearby mansions which would be obstructed by the presence of a smaller house.

Tennessee and North Carolina have joined the ranks of the states which hold that purely aesthetic considerations are within the police power. See State v. Smith, 618 S.W.2d 474 (Tenn.1981) and State v. Jones, 305 N.C. 520, 290 S.E.2d 675 (1982).

3. Good discussions of the problem of zoning for aesthetic purposes and the development of the concept can be found in Newsom, Zoning for Beauty, 3 Land Use Controls Q. 33 (No. 3, 1969); Comment, Zoning, Aesthetics and the First Amendment, 64 Colum.L.Rev. 81 (1964); and Note, Aesthetic Zoning: A Current Evaluation of the Law, 18 U.Fla.L.Rev. 430 (1965). As both the Florida note writer and the Wisconsin court in the Wieland case point out, Berman v. Parker, 348 U.S. 26, 75 S.Ct. 98, 99 L.Ed. 27 (1954), changed things as far as zoning for aesthetics was concerned. The Supreme Court had said that the legal concept of the public welfare included aesthetic values, as well as monetary values. Before that, aesthetic zoning had paraded under the guise of elevating the commercial worth of the property involved.

While many jurisdictions may consider aesthetics, there must be some other sustaining purpose present. Typical of this line of cases is Farley v. Graney, 146 W.Va. 22, 119 S.E.2d 833 (1960), stating that the great weight of authority is to the effect that aesthetic considerations alone will not justify the exercise of the police power for zoning purposes, but that these considerations may be given due weight along with other factors. This is the majority rule, but it seems unlikely to represent the trend. Over the long haul, Berman v. Parker is more likely to prevail.

PARKING ASSOCIATION OF GEORGIA, INC. v. CITY OF ATLANTA, GEORGIA

Supreme Court of Georgia, 1994.
264 Ga. 764, 450 S.E.2d 200.

THOMPSON, JUSTICE.

The City of Atlanta enacted a zoning ordinance aimed specifically at surface parking lots with 30 or more spaces in several downtown and midtown zoning districts. The ordinance requires minimum barrier curbs and landscaping areas equal to at least ten percent of the paved area within a lot, ground cover (shrubs, ivy, pine bark or similar landscape materials) and at least one tree for every eight parking spaces. Its stated purpose is to improve the beauty and aesthetic appeal of the City, promote public safety, and ameliorate air quality and water run-off problems. All costs of compliance with the ordinance are to be borne by the landowners; however, no landowner is required to reduce the number of parking spaces by more than three percent.

Plaintiffs, an association of companies managing or owning surface parking lots in the affected areas, as well as individual owners of affected parking lots, brought suit against the City seeking declaratory and injunctive relief on the grounds that the ordinance is unconstitutional and void. The superior court ruled in favor of the City and denied injunctive relief. Plaintiffs appealed.

* * *

Plaintiffs failed to present clear and convincing evidence that the ordinance presents a significant detriment. Plaintiffs may experience a loss of profits due to a reduction in the number of available parking spaces and the costs of compliance; however, a zoning ordinance does not exceed the police power simply because it restricts the use of property, diminishes the value of property, or imposes costs in connection with the property. * * * A loss of at most three percent of plaintiffs' parking spaces does not constitute a significant deprivation. * * *

Plaintiffs also failed to present clear and convincing evidence that the ordinance is unsubstantially related to the public health, safety, morality and welfare. The ordinance was designed to regulate aesthetics, crime, water run-off, temperature and other environmental concerns. The means adopted have a real and substantial relation to the goals to be attained.

An ordinance is not unreasonable even if designed only to improve aesthetics. * * *

Plaintiffs failed to meet either prong of this state's balancing test. The ordinance is constitutional and valid.

Plaintiffs assert the ordinance constitutes an unconstitutional denial of equal protection because it only applies to paved parking lots with 30 or more spaces in downtown and midtown zoning districts. We disagree.

A zoning ordinance does not offend the equal protection clauses of the State and Federal Constitutions if "it has some fair and substantial relation to the object of the legislation and furnishes a legitimate ground of differentiation. [Cit.]" Bailey Investment Co. v. Augusta–Richmond County Board of Zoning Appeals, 256 Ga. 186, 187, 345 S.E.2d 596 (1986). The larger lots have a far greater impact upon aesthetics, water run-off, temperature, pedestrian traffic and other health, safety and environmental concerns; the affected districts have the greatest concentration of parking lots. Thus, the ordinance rationally differentiates between larger and smaller parking lots and between affected and unaffected zoning districts. " 'If the validity of the legislative classification for zoning purposes be fairly debatable, the legislative judgment must be allowed to control.' " DeKalb County v. Chamblee Dunwoody Hotel Partnership, 248 Ga. 186, 190, 281 S.E.2d 525 (1981) (quoting Euclid v. Ambler Realty Co., 272 U.S. 365, 388, 47 S.Ct. 114, 118, 71 L.Ed. 303 (1926)).

Judgment affirmed.

All the Justices concur, except HUNT, C.J., and SEARS and CARLEY, JJ., who dissent.

SEARS, JUSTICE, dissenting.

I disagree with the majority's application of the significant detriment test to this case. That test is essentially the same as the "economically viable use" test employed by the United States Supreme Court. See Ziegler, Rathkopf's The Law of Zoning and Planning, § 6.08[1]. The significant detriment test looks to the land as a whole to evaluate a takings claim, as well as to factors to consider such as " 'the suitability of the subject property for the zoned purposes,' " Guhl v. Holcomb Bridge Road Corp., 238 Ga. 322, 323, 232 S.E.2d 830 (1977), and "the character of the neighborhood, the zoning, and the use of properties nearby," Ziegler, § 6.08[1], at 6–34. Although that test and some of its factors are well-suited to rezoning cases, they are not well-suited to cases such as this one in which a local government has sought to extract a benefit for the public from only a portion of a whole parcel of property. In such cases, courts have established an exception to the "economically viable use" or "significant detriment" takings standard. [A] regulation may be held a taking, even though the owner is afforded an economically viable use of the property, under benefit-extraction taking analysis when the burden imposed by [the] regulation is found to be one that, as a matter of fairness and justice, should be borne by the public as a whole.

Ziegler, § 6.08[1], 6–29, n. 4. This line of taking analysis reflects the traditional distinction, often noted in commentary and court decisions, between regulation that performs an arbitration or harm prevention function, where the result sought to be achieved distinctly relates to some problem involving or generated by a private owner's activity or proposed use, and regulation that simply secures a public benefit ... at the unfair expense of private owners who are simply convenient targets of opportunity for extracting the benefit. Id. at § 6.10[1], 6–91, 6–92.

Extractions for the public benefit are generally upheld if the two requirements are met: First, that the extraction is closely related to a particular problem generated by the owner's use of his land, 1 Ziegler at § 6.10[1], [6][c]; Nollan v. California Coastal Comm'n, 483 U.S. 825, 835–840, 107 S.Ct. 3141, 3147–3150, 97 L.Ed.2d 677 (1987); Dolan v. City of Tigard, 512 U.S. 374 , 114 S.Ct. 2309, 129 L.Ed.2d 304 (1994); and second, that the extraction represents the property owner's proportion of the particular problem, 1 Ziegler at § 6.10[1], [6][c]; Nollan, 483 U.S. at n. 4, 835–36, 107 S.Ct. at n. 4, 3147–48; Dolan, 512 U.S. at ___, 114 S.Ct. at 2319, 129 L.Ed.2d at 320. A host of courts have applied these standards both before and after Nollan. See 1 Ziegler, § 6.10. A significant feature of the benefit-extraction analysis is that an extraction may constitute a taking under it even though it would not under the "economically viable use" or "significant detriment" test. * * *

Finally, in analyzing whether an extraction is an expense that in fairness and justice should be paid for by the public as a whole, I would consider the nature of the governmental interest at stake. For instance, if, in fact, an extraction would actually promote nothing more than the aesthetics of the community, rather than a more compelling public interest such as the public safety, I would weigh that factor against the local government.

As the benefit-extraction analysis test that I propose has not previously been utilized in this state, I would remand this case to the trial court for it to resolve the case using this analysis.

I am authorized to state that Chief Justice HUNT and Justice CARLEY join in this dissent.

C. UNDERGROUND UTILITIES

On May 5, 1968, the St. Louis Post Dispatch printed excerpts from an article in the National Civic Review which extolled the virtues of burying power lines and telephone lines. The article pointed out that the cost of undergrounding utility wires in an average residential subdivision in southern California was only about $130 per lot in 1966. It was further reported Southern California Edison Company had, in 1966, undergrounded more than 18,000 homes. Although the cost of undergrounding utility wires is usually passed on by the subdivider to the homeowner, in some communities the cost may be split between the utility and the homeowner and the city. In Minnesota and North Dakota and other areas served by the Northern States Power Company the cost of undergrounding to all-electric homes is borne entirely by the utility.

The greatest obstacle to utilization of the police power by cities to require underground utility wires is the question of cost. Also, a problem may arise over the jurisdiction a municipality may exercise over a state-regulated utility.

UNION ELECTRIC CO. v. CITY OF CRESTWOOD
Supreme Court of Missouri, Division No. 2, 1973.
499 S.W.2d 480.

FINCH, JUSTICE. The issue presented herein is whether a municipal ordinance which prohibits thereafter any aboveground construction of utility transmission lines is valid. The trial court upheld the ordinance. We reverse.

The pertinent facts are these: Union Electric Company (UE) is an electric utility company serving a considerable area, including the City of St. Louis and the numerous municipalities located in St. Louis County. * * *

* * *

Sometime in 1968, officials of Crestwood had a conference with officials of UE relative to the possibility of placing all UE lines underground, but UE discouraged the idea on the basis of the additional cost involved. Subsequently, and before UE started construction of the proposed 138KV line, the Board of Aldermen of the City of Crestwood passed its Ordinance No. 1119, the ordinance here in question. This ordinance prohibited future aboveground construction of transmission lines in the City of Crestwood and made violation of the ordinance a misdemeanor. This declaratory judgment suit by UE followed adoption of that ordinance.

UE's petition in that action asserted that (1) the ordinance is ultra vires in that it exceeds the authority of the city and invades the field of regulation of utility companies which the state has vested in and reserved to the Public Service Commission; (2) the additional cost of placing these lines underground would be so much greater that it would prevent UE from performing its statutory duty to render adequate and safe service at a reasonable cost; (3) the ordinance exceeds the police power of the city in that it does not reasonably relate to the health, safety and welfare of the public; and (4) the ordinance results in a partial taking of UE's vested property and contract rights as granted to it by the existing 20-year franchise.

* * *

The validity of the foregoing conclusion is demonstrated by the evidence in this case. It disclosed that to construct the 1.8 miles of 138KV line aboveground would cost $217,000, and the 34KV line would cost $84,300. However, to place these underground for the 1.8 miles

located in Crestwood, the cost would increase to $1,560,000 and $496,-
600, respectively. If Crestwood had the right by its ordinance to specify
how UE should design and install its transmission lines or to require it
to spend this substantially greater sum in constructing said lines, then
other municipalities would have like authority. The record shows that
UE serves the City of St. Louis and 99 municipalities in St. Louis
County. In addition, it operates elsewhere, although that is not detailed
in this record. If 100 such municipalities each had the right to impose its
own requirements with respect to installation of transmission facilities, a
hodgepodge of methods of construction could result and costs and
resulting capital requirements could mushroom. As a result, the supervision and control by the Public Service Commission with respect to the
company, its facilities, its method of operation, its service, its indebtedness, its investment, and its rates which the General Assembly obviously
contemplated would be nullified. As the New Jersey court observed,
"chaos would result" and neither UE nor the Public Service Commission
could be assured that the company would be able to and would furnish
uniform, adequate and reasonable service to all customers.[16]

We conclude and hold that Ordinance No. 1119 invades the area of
regulation vested in the Public Service Commission by the General
Assembly and hence that Crestwood, in adopting that ordinance, exceeded its authority. For this reason, the ordinance is invalid, and we so hold.

* * *

In view of the conclusions hereinabove set out, we deem it unnecessary to consider and decide the other contentions advanced by UE as
reasons for declaring Ordinance No. 1119 invalid.

16. While not a part of the record on appeal or dispositive of this case, it is of interest to note, and we take judicial notice of the fact, that the Public Service Commission has taken action to establish a comprehensive statewide plan with reference to what shall be done with respect to undergrounding of electric transmission and distribution lines of certificated electric utility companies in this state.

On March 3, 1970, in Case No. 16,926, the Commission entered an order directing its Staff to immediately undertake an investigation of all factors relative to the undergrounding of electric transmission and distribution lines, and on completion of the investigation to report its findings and recommendations concerning "(1) the desirability of a uniform statewide tariff for the underground construction of electric distribution and transmission lines, (2) the economic feasibility of underground construction of electric distribution and transmission lines as opposed to overhead construction of such lines in light of the comparative costs of their construction and maintenance, and (3) the establishment of undergrounding priorities with ac-

companying guidelines to aid in future analysis and determination of such priorities."

Thereafter, the order was amended on September 22, 1970, to provide that the investigation should proceed in phases. It specified that Phase I should relate to underground distribution systems in new residential subdivisions, including the power lines from substations to said subdivisions, and Phase II was to relate to underground distribution systems in high density commercial areas.

Thereafter, on June 28, 1971, the Commission adopted General Order No. 52—Section I, which was thereafter amended on October 26, 1971, requiring undergrounding of electrical distribution systems in new residential subdivisions, and directing certificated electric companies to file tariffs to cover said undergrounding directed by that General Order. Thus, action relative to Phase I has already been implemented, with other reports and possible subsequent action to follow.

Judgment reversed.

Notes

1. Does the principal case suggest that the city officials of Crestwood had read the article in the St. Louis Post Dispatch in 1968, but that the supreme court judges had not? Is the essence of the case that undergrounding of utilities can only be accomplished by statewide regulation or special enabling legislation? Some evidence of the effect of the case is found in statutes later adopted in other states, undoubtedly through the efforts of the regulated utilities.

2. A number of cases have held that in the absence of clear legislative intent to preempt municipal authority to regulate streets and utility lines, zoning regulations which require undergrounding of utilities are valid. Kahl v. Consolidated Gas, Elec. Light & Power Co., 191 Md. 249, 60 A.2d 754 (1948); Benzinger v. Union Light, Heat & Power Co., 293 Ky. 747, 170 S.W.2d 38 (1943); Arizona Public Serv. Co. v. Town of Paradise Valley, 125 Ariz. 447, 610 P.2d 449 (1980). In Central Maine Power Co. v. Waterville Urban Renewal Auth., 281 A.2d 233 (Me.1971), the court recognized the aesthetic significance of requiring undergrounding in a renewal area, and held that the utility could be compelled to bear the cost. Also see Sleepy Hollow Lake, Inc. v. Public Serv. Comm'n, 43 A.D.2d 439, 352 N.Y.S.2d 274 (1974), which upheld the state agency order to underground utilities, which order was allegedly based solely on aesthetic and environmental preservation grounds. On the other hand, requiring a landowner to reinstall electric wiring underground in the course of a redevelopment project was held to be a taking in Redevelopment Authority of Oil City v. Woodring, 498 Pa. 180, 445 A.2d 724 (1982). And, in Bright Development v. City of Tracy, 20 Cal.App.4th 783, 24 Cal.Rptr.2d 618 (1993) the court held that a developer could not be required to bear the cost of placing off-site utilities underground in order to receive approval of his subdivision plat.

3. Where the state has clearly preempted utility regulation, as the court found in the principal case, then municipal authority to compel undergrounding may be limited to the use of subdivision exactions requiring the developer to pay the cost of undergrounding, if the utility is equipped to install underground lines. Some of the cases finding state preemption are Village of Carthage v. Central New York Tel. & Tel. Co., 185 N.Y. 448, 78 N.E. 165 (1906); In re Public Serv. Elec. and Gas Co., 35 N.J. 358, 173 A.2d 233 (1961); Cleveland Elec. Illuminating Co. v. City of Painesville, 10 Ohio App.2d 85, 226 N.E.2d 145 (1967). See 7 McQuillan, Municipal Corporations § 24.588 (3d Ed.1968).

4. Quite apart from the movement to place utility wires underground, based solely on aesthetic considerations, what about a reverse problem? When public parks or other open spaces are considered as routes for highways or other public works allegedly inconsistent with park purposes, can citizens successfully prevent the undertaking? For a classic example of this problem see the lengthy litigation involving the struggle of citizens of Memphis, Tennessee, to prevent the construction of Interstate Highway 40 through Overton Park in Memphis: Citizens to Preserve Overton Park, Inc. v. Volpe, 309 F.Supp. 1189 (W.D.Tenn.1970), 432 F.2d 1307 (6th Cir.1970),

401 U.S. 402, 91 S.Ct. 814, 28 L.Ed.2d 136 (1971); after remand Citizens to Preserve Overton Park, Inc. v. Volpe, 335 F.Supp. 873 (W.D.Tenn.1972), affirmed sub nom. Citizens to Preserve Overton Park, Inc. v. Brinegar, 494 F.2d 1212 (6th Cir.1974), certiorari denied sub nom. Citizens to Preserve Overton Park, Inc. v. Smith, 421 U.S. 991, 95 S.Ct. 1997, 44 L.Ed.2d 481 (1975). Early in 1981, newspaper reports indicated that the city had finally abandoned the completion of Interstate 40 through Memphis. Also see Coalition for Responsible Regional Development v. Brinegar, 518 F.2d 522 (4th Cir.1975). For an overview of the several legal theories that can be raised in such cases, see Annot., Construction of Highway Through Park as Violation of Use to which Park Property May Be Dedicated, 60 A.L.R.3d 581 (1974).

SECTION 2. PRESERVATION OF NATURAL RESOURCES

A. RESTRICTIONS ON REMOVAL OF EXPLOITABLE RESOURCES

EXTON QUARRIES, INC. v. ZONING BD. OF ADJUSTMENT OF WEST WHITELAND TWP.

Supreme Court of Pennsylvania, 1967.
425 Pa. 43, 228 A.2d 169.

[Exton had acquired substantial acreage for quarrying limestone. It had removed 40 to 50 tons to test its quality during 1952–1955. In 1957, the township zoned the property "I—Industrial", which was the least restricted classification under its new zoning ordinance. Quarrying, however, was a specifically prohibited use under that classification, as were certain other uses of various kinds. Similar nuisance-like uses were also excluded. Exton argued that there was no statutory authority for a township to enact a complete ban on quarries. Exton's argument was sustained, and the township appealed.]

ROBERTS, JUSTICE.

* * *

The essence of Exton's non-constitutional challenge to section 701(3) is that, under 53 P.S. § 67001, once having designated an industrial district in its zoning laws, it was compelled thereafter to employ its power "to restrict and regulate * * * the use of land" in accordance with the industrial designation. This means, appellees argue, that since quarrying is an industrial use of land, the township's power "to restrict and regulate" does not encompass the ability to absolutely prohibit any particular industrial uses. * * *

In dealing with Exton's non-constitutional challenge to the prohibition of quarrying, it is appropriate that we first consider simply the language of the Enabling Act. We believe that the pertinent phrase—"to regulate and restrict * * * the location and use of buildings, structures and land for trade, industry, residence or other purposes"—considered by itself does not compel the conclusion that Exton seeks to establish. Indeed, the most striking aspect of this language—especially in view of the inclusion of the words "other purposes"—is the generality and flexibility of the powers granted. It must be borne in mind that the power granted extends to both *location* and *use*. Exton's argument might have far greater force if the statutory language included only the word "location" and not the word "use." Then we might be persuaded that once a township has been divided into districts for trade, industry and residence, the zoning power could not be further utilized to regulate and restrict the uses within a municipality. But with the employment of the phrase "location and use", we would find it difficult to attach to the statutory term "use" the independent significance which we must assume the Legislature intended. * * *

In contributing to our consideration that the Enabling Act does authorize township-wide bans on selected uses of land, we have also considered opinions of courts of other jurisdictions construing statutes similar to ours. In Duffcon Concrete Prods., Inc. v. Borough of Cresskill, 1 N.J. 509, 64 A.2d 347, 9 A.L.R.2d 678 (1949) the highest court of New Jersey held that a municipality was authorized to prohibit all heavy industrial uses by virtue of a statute empowering it "to regulate and restrict * * * the location and use and extent of use of buildings and structures and land for trade, industry, residence, or other purposes." In Oregon City v. Hartke, 240 Or. 35, 400 P.2d 255 (1965) the court held that a township might prohibit certain uses under a grant of statutory power "to create or divide the city into districts within some of which it shall be lawful and within others of which it shall be unlawful to * * * carry on certain trades or callings" and to "regulate, restrict and segregate the location of industries." On the other hand, most cases which have struck down, as not authorized, municipality-wide prohibitions of selected uses have done so on the basis of far more narrowly drawn enabling statutes.[17] Thus the prohibition of slaughter houses in Mayor & Council of Mount Airy v. Sappington, 195 Md. 259, 73 A.2d 449 (1950) was based on a zoning statute which only authorized the municipality to "make reasonable regulations in regard to buildings to be erected in said town and grant building permits for the same; to establish five districts in said town and regulate the kind of materials used in the erection of buildings within such districts, with special

17. The court in Oregon City v. Hartke, 240 Or. 35, 400 P.2d 255 (1965) while upholding a prohibition of certain uses under a broad grant of powers, see text supra, observed that: "The statute in question should be distinguished from those which enable towns to regulate and restrict one particular item, e.g., billboard advertising or the sale of liquor. Cases construing the latter type of statutes as preventing total exclusion of the item cannot be controlling in the instant case where only one of many uses of land has been prohibited." Id. at 259 n. 4. See Blancett v. Montgomery, 398 S.W.2d 877, 10 A.L.R.3d 1220 (Ky.1966) (prohibition of exploration for gas and oil in municipality of 355.18 acres upheld on basis of statute similar to Act of May 1, 1933, P.L. 103, art. XX, § 2003, added by the Act of July 10, 1947, P.L. 1481, § 47, 53 P.S. § 67003).

reference to the prevention and suppression of fires." It is true that in Suburban Ready–Mix Corp. v. Village of Wheeling, 25 Ill.2d 548, 185 N.E.2d 665 (1962) and People ex rel. Trust Co. of Chicago v. Village of Skokie, 408 Ill. 397, 97 N.E.2d 310 (1951) the Illinois Supreme Court has expressed the view that the Illinois Legislature did not grant its municipalities the power to ban from their borders any lawful businesses.[18] The Illinois court's expressions however were not part of a considered analysis of the enabling statutes and in neither case was lack of legislative authorization the sole ground upon which the prohibiting ordinances were struck down nor did the court cite the language of any enabling act.

* * *

The constitutionality of zoning ordinances which totally prohibit legitimate businesses such as quarrying from an entire community should be regarded with particular circumspection; for unlike the constitutionality of most restrictions on property rights imposed by other ordinances, the constitutionality of total prohibitions of legitimate businesses cannot be premised on the fundamental reasonableness of allocating to each type of activity a particular location in the community. We believe this is true despite the possible existence outside the municipality of sites on which the prohibited activity may be conducted, since it is more probable than not that, as the operator of the prohibited business is forced to move further from the property he owns, his economic disadvantage will increase to the point of deprivation. Moreover, if one municipality may, with only moderate justification, totally prohibit an undesired use of land, it is not unlikely that surrounding municipalities will do the same—thus increasing the distance to an alternative site and the concomitant economic disadvantage. Thus the possible availability of alternative sites somewhere outside the municipality on which the totally banned business may be conducted does not make permissible the deprivation within the township of property rights imposed by a municipality-wide ban of a particular kind of business. For these reasons, we believe that a zoning ordinance which totally excludes a particular business from an entire municipality must bear a more substantial relationship to the public health, safety, morals and general welfare than an ordinance which merely confines that business to a certain area in the municipality.

* * *

18. As Judge Schaefer pointed out in his concurring opinion in the *Suburban* case, the view taken by the Illinois court puts it in the position of requiring that every municipality in the state must provide for every use somewhere within its borders. In Mutual Supply Co. Appeal, 366 Pa. 424, 430, 77 A.2d 612, 615 (1951) this Court said that prohibition of industrial uses within a township would not "ipso facto" be a legal defect and cited to this effect the leading case of Duffcon Concrete Prods., Inc. v. Borough of Cresskill, 1 N.J. 509, 64 A.2d 347, 9 A.L.R.2d 678 (1949). Interestingly enough, the Illinois court in Village of Spillertown v. Prewitt, 21 Ill.2d 228, 171 N.E.2d 582 (1961) held that a densely populated municipality had the power, even in the absence of specific statutory authority, to prohibit strip mining by virtue of a grant to it of general police powers.

Appellant urges as a basis for sustaining a prohibition of quarrying in West Whiteland, that quarrying interferes with public health, safety, morals and general welfare because of the dust, noise, vibrations, and excess truck traffic produced. It asserts, in addition, as a basis for the prohibition that a quarry will interfere with the township's water supply and create a large pit in the township which will not only be unaesthetic but also a danger to children in the area. Appellant also relies on the testimony of a planning expert who prepared a comprehensive plan for the township *subsequent* to the enactment of the ordinance prohibiting quarrying.

Several of the bases alleged by the township in support of township wide prohibition of quarrying can, we think, be disposed of easily. The township's reliance on the increase in truck traffic, for instance, is hardly reasonable absent a showing, which does not appear on the record, that quarrying operations will involve any greater increase in truck traffic than other industrial uses which are permitted. The township's assertion that quarrying will disturb the underground water supply in West Whiteland, though found as a fact by the Board, is not supported by competent evidence. The only testimony which the township produced to support this statement was given by witnesses unqualified in geology and the thrust of this testimony was contradicted by Exton's witness, head of the geology department of Bryn Mawr College. The contention that creation of the quarrying pit would be a danger to children is not a consideration which merits much weight. The danger to children could be so easily reduced by erection of proper fencing—a regulation which we see no reason why a township could not impose under its zoning powers, not to speak of its other powers—that it hardly supports prohibition of quarrying. The unaesthetic aspects of a quarry pit are insufficient of themselves to support its prohibition.

Among the other justifications for the prohibition of quarrying were creation of dust, noise and vibration. An air pollution expert testifying for the township suggested that an operation of the size proposed to be constructed by Exton would if *uncontrolled* put into the air at least a ton of dust per hour and if *controlled* about a ton of dust per day. Properly controlled dust would tend not to settle, and on a normal day such controlled dust could be seen for about "a mile or more." No evidence appears of record as to what effect the dust produced might have on health, nor did the air pollution expert indicate the extent to which quarrying and the other uses specifically prohibited in the ordinance would create greater amounts of harmful dust than an increase of permitted industry or those other pollution producing uses permitted in the township, although it is admitted by the expert that such other uses would add pollutants to the air. Given these facts, in addition to the fact that according to the official zoning map of the township attached to the 1957 ordinance, a substantial fraction of the township land is located more than a mile from any cluster of residential development, we fail to see how creation of dust by quarrying bears a sufficiently substantial relationship to the public health, safety, morals and general welfare to justify its prohibition.

As to the noise and vibration from the blasting associated with quarrying, the testimony offered by appellant was from non-expert witnesses who resided anywhere from ½ to 1½ miles from operating quarries. These witnesses stated that blasting and vibration from operations in these quarries shook their houses and was an unpleasant experience. The record does not faintly suggest, however, any reason to suppose that such blasting occurs during sleeping hours; indeed the record suggests that blasting would occur during the day and at most on one or two occasions a week. Nor does this record suggest by any competent evidence that the level of noise or vibration from the blasting as well as other aspects of the quarrying operation would have a defined effect on health. While we can appreciate the great desirability of quiet and tranquility, this does not raise it to a consideration of constitutional significance. Moreover, even assuming the substantial relationship to public health of quiet in an area closely located to a hospital or to general welfare where noise would interfere with the efficient operation of a school, we fail to see how a township, which according to its zoning map contains one area of over three square miles in which no schools or hospitals are located and in which there are less than 100 residences, and other buildings, could constitutionally prohibit quarrying throughout its borders on the grounds of the noise and vibration.

Nor do we believe that appellant's reliance on the testimony of a planning consultant can support the constitutionality of the zoning ordinance. The planning consultant testified that in a study prepared for the township *subsequent* to the enactment of the prohibition of quarrying, he had advised its exclusion because West Whiteland was primarily a residential community, that people were moving in rapidly "looking for the amenities of country life", that quarrying was a "nuisance", that he had never seen one that was not "somewhat of a problem in terms of either vibration or pollution or noise, * * * [or] danger," that anywhere a quarry was placed in West Whiteland Township industrial zone there would be a problem of excessive truck traffic, that a quarry would be harmful aesthetically, that a quarry would "do a great deal of damage to the township", that he "equated" vibration with the mental health of the community—although he denied being an expert on vibration and never professed to be an expert in mental health and admitted he himself had not suffered an apparent health problem during the time he lived close enough to a quarry to feel vibrations,—and finally that because of the unaesthetic aspects of quarrying it was an activity which would inhibit the development nearby of residences and certain kinds of industry. In light of our previous discussion of traffic, dust and vibration, we believe that the consultant's testimony consisted in reality of no more than a series of epithets based solidly on only one objection relevant to West Whiteland Township as a whole—that this quarry was unaesthetic and conflicted with his projected plans. Such an objection, as this Court has stated, is not sufficient in and of itself to sustain the constitutionality of a zoning restriction on the use of private property.

* * *

Judgment affirmed.

[A concurring opinion is omitted.]

COHEN, JUSTICE (dissenting).

* * *

In my opinion the regulation herein involved did not amount to an "arbitrary, unnecessary or unreasonable intermeddling with the private ownership of property * * *." And the cavalier fashion by which the majority opinion disposes of every legislative objective in enacting the zoning ordinance in question fails to convince me that I am wrong. The legislative objectives of the zoning ordinance prohibiting quarrying were to:

(1) Control traffic on an already congested highway;

(2) Prevent the expulsion of dust in great quantities into the atmosphere;

(3) Protect the surrounding property owners or users (including elementary school children) from the dangers of blasting;

(4) Protect the water supply of the surrounding property owners and users;

(5) Protect the township roads from deterioration from over use by heavily laden trucks and from sink holes resulting;

(6) Eliminate the noise emanating from blasting and rock crushing; and

(7) Prevent the creation of a large hole in the middle of the township.

To my way of thinking, these considerations amount to very legitimate public purposes and are certainly so reasonably related to health, safety, morals and general welfare that a casual brushing aside and disregard of the merit of each of them will not appease me. The majority are content to supply their own solution to each of the problems presented by diminishing the record (by finding incompetent the township's testimony with regard to the underground water supply), by suggesting legislation which the township chose not to enact (in particular, the fencing of the quarry to protect children), or by superficial treatment (such as concluding that because the record does not indicate that blasting will occur during sleeping hours it will not disturb the community).

* * *

The danger of the majority's rationalizations is that while it superficially recognizes that there are standards by which to test the constitutionality of zoning legislation, it meticulously avoids their application by substituting its judgment for that of the zoning board. In effect, this decision has made our Court a zoning board—and a poor one at that.

* * *

Finally, as an example of the majority opinion's disregard for the appropriate burden of proof in an attack on the constitutionality of a zoning ordinance, I cite its discussion of the problem of dust expulsion. One of the legislative objectives behind the ordinance was to prevent the expulsion of great quantities of dust into the air. Since this problem was one of the factors that led to the enactment of the ordinance which is cloaked with a presumption of constitutionality, the burden is upon Exton to prove that the amount of dust expelled into the air by its quarrying activities would not be excessive. The majority, however, reverse the burden and conclude that because the township presented no evidence as to the effect of the dust on health or as to the relative increase in air pollution caused by permissible uses of the land, there is no justification for the ordinance on that ground.

Notes

1.   Another case striking down a zoning provision which amounted to a total prohibition on the removal of earth products is Beard v. Town of Salisbury, 378 Mass. 435, 392 N.E.2d 832 (1979). Compare Lane County v. Bessett, 46 Or.App. 319, 612 P.2d 297 (1980).

2.   Refer back to Goldblatt v. Town of Hempstead, Hadacheck v. Sebastian, and the Consolidated Rock Products cases in Chapter V. Also refer back to the section on exclusion of commerce and industry in Chapter VII. Comparing those materials with the principal case, can you conclude that the crucial factor in deciding the validity of regulations forbidding the removal of earth products is the nature of surrounding uses? Does this factor differ from the approach studied in Chapter II in connection with nuisance cases? See Willis v. Menard County Bd. of Comm'rs, 55 Ill.App.3d 26, 12 Ill.Dec. 832, 370 N.E.2d 636 (1977).

3.   For the relationship between a zoning ordinance and a separate earth removal ordinance, see Goodwin v. Board of Selectmen of Hopkinton, 358 Mass. 164, 261 N.E.2d 60 (1970).

4.   A general approach to the problems presented in the principal case and the above notes can be found in Bosselman, The Control of Surface Mining: An Exercise in Creative Federalism, 9 Nat.Res.J. 137 (1969) and American Society of Planning Officials, Land Use Control in the Surface Extraction of Minerals (Planning Advisory Service Report No. 153 1961).

5.   The Federal Surface Mining Act, 30 U.S.C.A. § 1201 et seq., requires surface miners to restore land to its prior condition and original contour, and also regulates the impact of surface mining on the surrounding environment with special regard to water quality and soil conditions. Several pre-enforcement suits were filed challenging the constitutionality of the statute, and two federal district courts in Indiana and Virginia found the statute invalid in part. In the Virginia case, Virginia Surface Mining and Reclamation Ass'n, Inc. v. Andrus, 483 F.Supp. 425 (W.D.Va.1980), the

district court held that although the act was within the commerce power of Congress, it interfered with an integral governmental function of the state under the doctrine of National League of Cities v. Usery, 426 U.S. 833, 96 S.Ct. 2465, 49 L.Ed.2d 245 (1976), and thus violated the Tenth Amendment. The court also held that the act was a taking of property insofar as the impossibility of restoring steep slope mines to the original contours would make it impossible to mine coal physically and economically. The Supreme Court reversed unanimously. In Hodel v. Virginia Surface Mining and Reclamation Ass'n. Inc., 452 U.S. 264, 101 S.Ct. 2352, 69 L.Ed.2d 1 (1981), and Hodel v. State. of Indiana, 452 U.S. 314, 101 S.Ct. 2376, 69 L.Ed.2d 40 (1981), Justice Marshall found the statute facially valid. On the taking issue, he stated:

The District Court held that two of the Act's provisions violate the Just Compensation Clause of the Fifth Amendment. First, the court found that the steep-slope provisions discussed above effect an uncompensated taking of private property by requiring operators to perform the "economically and physically impossible" task of restoring steep-slope surface mines to their approximate original contour. 483 F.Supp., at 437. The court further held that, even if steep-slope surface mines could be restored to their approximate original contour, the value of the mined land after such restoration would have "been diminished to practically nothing." Ibid. Second, the court found that § 522 of the Act effects an unconstitutional taking because it expressly prohibits mining in certain locations and "clearly prevent[s] a person from mining his own land or having it mined." Id., at 441. Relying on this Court's decision in Pennsylvania Coal Co. v. Mahon, 260 U.S. 393, 43 S.Ct. 158, 67 L.Ed. 322 (1922), the District Court held that both of these provisions are unconstitutional because they "depriv[e] [coal mine operators] of any use of [their] land, not only the most profitable." 483 F.Supp., at 441.

We conclude that the District Court's ruling on the "taking" issue suffers from a fatal deficiency: neither appellees nor the court identified any property in which appellees have an interest that has allegedly been taken by operation of the Act. By proceeding in this fashion, the court below ignored this Court's oft-repeated admonition that the constitutionality of statutes ought not be decided except in an actual factual setting that makes such a decision necessary. * * *

Because appellees' taking claim arose in the context of a facial challenge, it presented no concrete controversy concerning either application of the Act to particular surface mining operations or its effect on specific parcels of land. Thus, the only issue properly before the District Court and, in turn, this Court, is whether the "mere enactment" of the Surface Mining Act constitutes a taking. See Agins v. Tiburon, 447 U.S. 255, 260, 100 S.Ct. 2138, 2141, 65 L.Ed.2d 106 (1980). The test to be applied in considering this facial challenge is fairly straightforward. A statute regulating the uses that can be made of property effects a taking if it "denies an owner economically viable use of his land * * *." Agins v. Tiburon, supra, at 260, 100 S.Ct., at 2141. See Penn Central Transp. Corp. v. New York City, 438 U.S. 104, 98 S.Ct. 2646, 57 L.Ed.2d 631 (1978). The Surface Mining Act easily survives scrutiny under this test.

First, the Act does not, on its face, prevent beneficial use of coal bearing lands. Except for the proscription of mining near certain locations by § 522(e), the Act does not categorically prohibit surface coal mining; it merely regulates the conditions under which such operations may be conducted. The Act does not purport to regulate alternative uses to which coal bearing lands may be put. Thus, in the posture in which the case comes before us, there is no reason to suppose that "mere enactment" of the Surface Mining Act has deprived appellees of economically viable use of their property.

Moreover, appellees cannot at this juncture legitimately raise complaints in this Court about the manner in which the challenged provisions of the Act have been or will be applied in specific circumstances, or about their effect on particular coal mining operations. There is no indication in the record that appellees have availed themselves of the opportunities provided by the Act to obtain administrative relief by requesting either a variance from the approximate original contour requirement of § 515(d) or a waiver from the surface mining restrictions in § 522(e). If appellees were to seek administrative relief under these procedures, a mutually acceptable solution might well be reached with regard to individual properties, thereby obviating any need to address the constitutional questions. The potential for such administrative solutions confirms the conclusion that the takings issue decided by the District Court simply is not ripe for judicial resolution.

Also see Keystone Bituminous Coal Ass'n v. DeBenedictis, 480 U.S. 470, 107 S.Ct. 1232, 94 L.Ed.2d 472 (1987).

B. CONSERVATION OF FORESTS, TREES, AND AGRICULTURAL LAND

HOOD VIEW NEIGHBORHOOD ASS'N v. BOARD OF COUNTY COMM'RS OF CLACKAMAS COUNTY

Court of Appeals of Oregon, 1979.
43 Or.App. 869, 604 P.2d 447.

ROBERTS, JUDGE.

Plaintiffs in this writ of review proceeding appeal from an order of the trial court affirming the county commissioners' approval of a preliminary plat for companion subdivisions totaling 92 homesites on 479 acres of land between the cities of Sherwood and Wilsonville in Clackamas County. Plaintiffs' dispositive contention is that the plat does not conform to the Agricultural Lands Goal (Goal #3) of the statewide planning goals adopted by the Land Conservation and Development Commission (LCDC). We reverse.

* * *

Goal #3 provides in relevant part:

"Agricultural lands shall be preserved and maintained for farm use, consistent with existing and future needs for agriculture products, forest and open space. These lands shall be inventoried and preserved by adopting exclusive farm use zones pursuant to ORS ch. 215. Such minimum lot sizes as are utilized for any farm use zones shall be appropriate for the continuation of the existing commercial agricultural enterprise within the area.

* * *

"AGRICULTURAL LAND—in western Oregon is land of predominantly Class I, II, III and IV soils * * * as identified in the Soil Capability Classification System of the United States Soil Conservation Service, and other lands which are suitable for farm use taking into consideration soil fertility, suitability for grazing, climatic conditions, existing and future availability of water for farm irrigation purposes, existing land use patterns, technological and energy inputs required, or accepted farming practices. Lands in other classes which are necessary to permit farm practices to be undertaken on adjacent or nearby lands, shall be included as agricultural land in any event."

* * *

It is not disputed that the land in question is predominantly composed of the soil classes named in Goal #3. Therefore, the land is agricultural within the meaning of Goal #3.

Relying on Meeker v. Board of Comm'rs, 36 Or.App. 699, 585 P.2d 1138 (1978), defendants contend that the requirements of Goal #3 are met by the five-acre lots in the proposed subdivisions. In *Meeker* we noted that there is no statewide minimum lot size for the preservation of agricultural lands. 36 Or.App. at 707, 585 P.2d 1138. In that case we approved the division of an 82–acre parcel of land in Clatstop County into seven parcels where the Board of County Commissioners had determined in extensive findings that a large farm unit would not be economically viable and that smaller units would facilitate greater agricultural usage.

In the time since plaintiffs brought this appeal, the Supreme Court has reviewed *Meeker* and agreed that the subdivision was permissible under the unique facts of the case. 287 Or. 665, 601 P.2d 804 (1979). Defendants here argue that because there is no statewide minimum lot size, the Board's determination that agricultural use would be maximized by the proposal is controlling.

However, in *Meeker* the Board's extensive findings allowed the reviewing courts to determine the basis for its decision and to decide that there was evidence to support the finding that the purposes of Goal #3 were indeed met. Unlike those findings, the relevant finding by the Board in this case, as follows, is conclusory and does not give us enough information to determine whether the purposes of Goal #3 could be met by the developer's proposal.

"1. The proposed subdivision conforms with the applicable goals and guidelines of the Land Conservation and Development Commission in the following respects:

a. Agricultural use of those portions of the subject property which are agricultural lands will be maximized by the development of small farms such as contemplated by the proposal."

* * *

Because the Board's findings on the Goal #3 issue are insufficient for purposes of review and because the plat failed to comply with the county's subdivision ordinance, we reverse.

Reversed.

Notes

1. "Agricultural" zoning may be of two general types, zoning which restricts land to agricultural uses and zoning which permits a wide variety of mixed uses in order to placate farm landowners and get them to drop their opposition to the ordinance. Exclusive agricultural zoning has been little tested in the courts. One case upholding an agricultural zoning district with a requirement of 160 acre minimum lot sizes is Wilson v. County of McHenry, 92 Ill.App.3d 997, 48 Ill.Dec. 395, 416 N.E.2d 426 (1981). Also see Codorus Township v. Rodgers, 89 Pa.Cmwlth. 79, 492 A.2d 73 (1985); Barancik v. County of Marin, 872 F.2d 834 (9th Cir.1988), cert. denied 493 U.S. 894, 110 S.Ct. 242, 107 L.Ed.2d 192 (1989).

Sometimes areas are set aside in exclusive agricultural districts awaiting subdividers who are willing to comply with local requirements. As such subdividers appear, the zoning ordinance is amended so as to create residential spots within the agricultural district. See Goldstein, Land Use Control Problems in Waukesha County, Wisconsin, 146 et seq. (Thesis, Univ. of Wis. Law Library, 1955), who reports almost 200 such amendments. See also Cutler, Legal and Illegal Methods for Controlling Community Growth on the Urban Fringe, 1961 Wis.L.Rev. 370, 396. The other side of this coin can be seen in the case, Green v. Bourbon County Joint Planning Comm'n, 637 S.W.2d 626 (Ky.1982), where the court suggested that a planning assumption that parcels over five acres were agricultural and thus not to be considered subdivisions was erroneous.

2. In Hansen v. Chelan County, 81 Wash.App. 133, 913 P.2d 409 (1996) the appellate court held that a county's refusal to issue a special permit for a golf course on land zoned agricultural was arbitrary because under the agricultural zoning other uses permitted outright would have as great an effect on agricultural uses (the ordinance permitted residential development in the agricultural zone). In Hopewell Twp. Bd. of Supervisors v. Golla, 499 Pa. 246, 452 A.2d 1337 (1982) the court held an agricultural preservation ordinance to be unconstitutional and discriminatory in that owners of large tracts were treated differently under the ordinance. Also, consider the impact of the following case:

GRAND LAND COMPANY v. TOWNSHIP OF BETHLEHEM

Superior Court of New Jersey, Appellate Division, 1984.
196 N.J.Super. 547, 483 A.2d 818, petition for certiorari
denied 101 N.J. 253, 501 A.2d 924 (1985).

FURMAN, J.A.D.

Environmental Defense Fund, intervenor below, appeals from a judgment striking down a Bethlehem Township Zoning ordinance amendment as invalid zoning. * * * Plaintiff Grand Land Company (Grand Land) cross-appeals from the dismissal of its claim for damages for an unlawful taking of its property.

Grand Land is the owner of approximately 155 acres in the Musconetcong River valley within the township, which it acquired in 1972 when zoned for exclusive industrial use. Unsuccessful in marketing the property for industrial use, Grand Land has leased it for agricultural use. About 100 of the 155 acres are actively farmed. By zoning ordinance amendment in 1979, the property was part of approximately 1250 acres within the industrial zone which was rezoned A–25 for agricultural use. Other permitted uses within the A–25 zone are one-family dwellings "as part of a farming operation," churches, municipal structures, private or public schools, public parks, public or private golf courses, "essential services" and single-family dwellings on one and a half acres minimum size lots, not more than one lot to be subdivided in any given year, and subject to the following requirements:

> For each one, 1½ acre building lot at least 25 or more acres of land devoted to farming or agricultural use shall remain. For each 26.5 acres, only one (1) building lot shall be permitted.

Bethlehem Township is designated on the State Development Guide Plan partly as a limited growth area and partly as an agricultural area. The Musconetcong River valley within the township is prime agricultural soil, about 85% actively farmed and designated on the State plan as an agricultural area. Approximately 800 acres of the valley within the township remain zoned for exclusive industrial use but are predominately in pre-existing, non-conforming agricultural use. A relatively small wedge-shaped area of approximately 300 acres is zoned for single family residential use on five acre minimum lots. Most of the balance of the township's 27.37 square miles is wooded and mountainous on the steeply sloped Musconetcong Mountain, sparsely developed and with limited public highway access. The mountain area is zoned for residential use on one and a half acre, three acre and five acre minimum size lots.

In a careful opinion below Judge D'Annunzio reviewed the sharp decline in acreage in agricultural use in recent years and the legislative response with its aim to preserve farmland and to encourage agricultural, horticultural and related uses. He recognized that zoning for exclusive agricultural use may be valid under the Municipal Land Use Law,

N.J.S.A. 40:55D–1 *et seq.,* and that Bethlehem Township is not a growth area with low and moderate income housing obligations under *So. Burlington Cty., N.A.A.C.P. v. Mount Laurel Tp., (Mount Laurel II),* 92 *N.J.* 158, 215, 456 *A.*2d 390 (1983). He rejected Grand Land's cause of action for damages for an unlawful taking because its property was not zoned into inutility but, rather, was zoned for a "reasonable use." Focusing upon the permissible uses and restrictions in the A–25 zone, he held them to be invalid as "a weak attempt to preserve agriculture" and an unreasonable exclusion of residential housing opportunity. He ordered that single family dwellings on one and a half acre lots "are permitted uses" in the A–25 zone, without the condition that 25 acres be set aside for agricultural use.

On appeal we need not and do not decide whether an exclusive agricultural zone may be valid under the Municipal Land Use Law, specifically *N.J.S.A.* 40:55D–2. Such a zoning enactment is not challenged in this litigation; the A–25 zone permits residential, as well as agricultural, use. Like Judge D'Annunzio, we view as decisive whether residential use in the A–25 zone was unreasonably restricted, without justification under applicable statutory and decisional zoning law and without reasonable relation to any valid zoning objective.

Before dealing with that decisive issue, we express agreement with a preliminary ruling below. Under *Mount Laurel II* Bethlehem Township was not obligated to provide a realistic opportunity for a fair share of its region's low and moderate income housing needs; nor is there any evidence in the record of housing needs of indigenous poor on whose behalf the township would have the obligation to provide a realistic opportunity for "decent housing."

In the A–25 zone, residential use on one and a half acre lots is permissible by subdivision of both a building lot and a 25 acre lot which must remain in agricultural use; or, alternatively, by subdivision of a single one and a half acre lot conditional upon reservation of 25 acres of the property prior to subdivision, not necessarily adjoining, in continuing agricultural use.

That zoning restriction is palpably indefensible and without authority in the Municipal Land Use Law or decisional law. In this state a municipality is barred from conditioning subdivision approval upon an involuntary reservation of land within a subdivision for a public purpose, such as a school or park, *Midtown Properties, Inc. v. Madison Tp.,* 68 *N.J.Super.* 197, 210, 172 *A.*2d 40 (Law Div.1961), aff'd o.b. 78 *N.J.Super.* 471, 189 *A.*2d 226 (App.Div.1963). *A fortiori,* in our view, subdivision approval for a residential building lot may not be conditioned upon reservation of adjoining or nearby land for a private use, as in the A–25 zone under challenge before us, precluding any other use permitted by ordinance or, it appears, by variance, *N.J.S.A.* 40:55D–70. We conclude that the restriction on residential use in the A–25 zone is invalid zoning beyond the powers delegated to municipalities under the Municipal Land Use Law.

* * *

Finally, we are constrained to reverse the zoning revision imposed by the judgment below that single family dwellings on one and a half acre minimum size lots are permitted uses without condition in the A–25 zone. The revision so ordered would drastically alter Bethlehem Township's zoning plan. The township should have the opportunity to adopt a comprehensive revised zoning ordinance upon a review of current housing and other needs, in furtherance of relevant zoning objectives, *N.J.S.A.* 40:55D–2. Meanwhile, the zoning ordinance amendment establishing the A–25 zone is null and void; the zoning ordinance in effect prior to that amendment is to govern the designated A–25 areas pending adoption of any zoning revision.

We affirm in part and reverse in part in accordance herewith.

Notes

1.   Exclusive agricultural zoning has real estate tax implications. Suppose that for the years such zoning is in force, the assessor values the land as agricultural land and does not include any value due to subdivision potential. Then, one day after the agricultural land is ripe or overripe for subdivision, the exclusive agricultural zoning is repealed and housing development is permitted. In your opinion could some kind of "yield" tax be established requiring the farm owner who sells for subdivision development to pay a sum approximately equal to the taxes he saved because of the zoning?

2.   In zoning outlying areas "farming" is often designated a permitted use. Many of these ordinances are loosely drafted. See, for example, Johnson v. Debaun, 206 Misc. 806, 135 N.Y.S.2d 217 (1954), which raised the question whether the extensive raising of pigs to be sold soon after birth is among the "usual accessories" to a farm. The court answered this question in the negative and in doing so thought that farmers could have done a better job of drafting the ordinance than was actually done by the non-farmer draftsman. Compare DeCoster v. Franklin County, 497 N.W.2d 849 (Iowa 1993) where the court held that the owner of a 160–acre farm devoted to hog ranching could erect a holding basin for sewage and waste generated in the hog confinement buildings; a state statute exempts from local zoning, land, farm buildings and structures which are primarily adapted for use for agricultural purposes. In De Benedetti v. River Vale, 21 N.J.Super. 430, 91 A.2d 353 (1952), the expansion of part-time chicken raising to full-time, including construction of additional chicken housing facilities, was held permitted in a Residence A District under a proviso in the ordinance as follows: "Nothing herein contained shall prevent or prohibit persons in this district engaged in farming of any type from re-constructing, enlarging or erecting additional buildings in the normal course of such business."

And see Columbia Twp. Bd. of Zoning Appeals v. Otis, 104 Ohio App.3d 756, 663 N.E.2d 377, appeal denied 74 Ohio St.3d 1457, 656 N.E.2d 951 (1995) where the court held a statute restricting local government regulation of agricultural uses was inapplicable to prevent a cease and desist order entered against the owner of a 23 acre farm who was offering theme hayrides complete with a sound system, lights in the woods, and a lounge area in the barn with game machines and sales of hot dogs and coffee. In Little v. Winborn, 518 N.W.2d 384 (Iowa 1994) the court held that rezoning of agricultural property from "agricultural protection district" to "agricultural" in order to allow the owner to use his property for a shooting range was invalid spot zoning. In Stillwater Twp. v. Rivard, 547 N.W.2d 906 (Minn.App.1996) the court remanded an appeal for a trial on the issue of whether a zoning ordinance which permitted "farming or other agricultural purposes," without defining agriculture, precluded the owner of a 24–acre horse farm from retail sales of horses, tack, feed, and wood shavings.

3. For helpful material on rural zoning in general and exclusive agricultural zoning in particular, see Solberg, The Why and How of Rural Zoning, (U.S.D.A., Agr.Info.Bull. No. 196, 1958); Rural Zoning in the United States: Analysis of Enabling Legislation (U.S.D.A.Misc.Publ. No. 1232 (1972)); Mich.Farm Bureau, The Use of Zoning to Retain Essential Agricultural Lands (1976).

Regulations to conserve the soil or the forests are not usually viewed as akin to zoning. In fact, there has been little use made of such restrictions. Otte and Vlasin, Districts That Manage Resources, 1963 Yearbook of Agriculture 424, 431, note that although all American states have passed enabling legislation and around 3,000 soil conservation districts have been created and although most jurisdictions authorize these districts to enact land use regulations by use of the local referendum device, the power to do so has seldom been employed. For a brief history of soil conservation districts, see Beuscher, Law and the Farmer (3rd ed. 1959). Also see 16 U.S.C.A. § 1501 et seq., for the framework of the federal rural environmental conservation program.

MINDEL v. TOWNSHIP COUNCIL OF TWP. OF FRANKLIN

Superior Court of New Jersey, Law Division, 1979.
167 N.J.Super. 461, 400 A.2d 1244.

IMBRIANI, J.S.C.

It is incredible in this day and age that a court should be called upon by a municipality to deny an owner the right to farm his land. But here is such a case. If the municipality is upheld, the result will be to compel the owner to either build residential housing units or suffer his land to lie fallow.

The property is located in an area that now is essentially rural in nature. Many farms dot the area. The township seeks to change the character to one that will be suburban. The beginnings are already present. Nearby is a growing municipal office complex, several churches, schools, a restaurant and a postoffice. Several residential subdivisions have already been built and others are planned.

In 1966 plaintiff, a dentist and investor purchased two parcels of vacant land separated by a road. One contains 13½ acres and lies in a R–

20 residential zone, which neither permits nor prohibits farming. The other contains 4.4 acres and lies in a R–40 residential zone, which permits farming.

Both parcels are leased to a crop farmer. He plants only corn and soy beans. He keeps no animals. The township seeks to restrain him from farming the larger tract because it is not a permitted use.

* * *

It is charged that the township's true motive for prohibiting farming in certain zones is to avoid the loss of tax revenues on vacant lands. And in fact, in a February 3, 1976 report to the board of adjustment concerning the property in question, the township planner stated that "the only practical difference between the proposal and the property as it exists now is in its tax status."

The township argues that plaintiff's use of his land for crop farming is inconsistent with its master plan, which anticipates greater population density in this area of the community where it has built costly sewerage, water and road facilities. It calculates that the minimum economic density for such urban services is one residential dwelling unit per half acre. Farming would not be sufficiently intensive to earn the municipality a fair return on its capital investment. It argues that the "proximity of the subject property to the Township's center district [i.e., a municipal office complex exists and is being expanded] demand[s] urban compatibility."

The township obviously cannot compel plaintiff to develop his land. So it seeks to eliminate the statutory tax incentive to farm and compel plaintiff to choose between not using his land at all or developing it more intensively.

* * *

As a result of the Farmland Assessment Act municipal governments, in designing a zoning scheme, may no longer be parochial. They must consider the "interests of all the people in New Jersey." While the State properly applied its zoning power in the past to assist and be compatible with our growing population and expansion of commercial development, it became clear to the Legislature in the 1960s that a change of policy was needed. Open spaces had to be preserved while the State formulated necessary programs. The change could not occur overnight. Time was needed. Time could be obtained either by outright purchases of such lands (which patently involved unacceptable costs) or by providing tax incentives to induce owners to withhold development of their vacant and open lands. The latter approach was adopted.

* * *

The township argues that *Mt. Laurel* compels a municipality to provide its fair share of housing, which is what defendant seeks to accomplish. It notes that farming is already permitted in 72% of the township. But it is one thing to provide sufficient areas within a municipality where housing for the poor and middle class is permitted and something entirely different to compel an owner under the guise of a zoning regulation to build housing units. The former is permissible. But the latter is not.

The proofs show a great demand for farmland in this area. Local farmers actively bid against each other whenever farmlands become available. Cultivation here fills this demand.

Adverse impact on adjoining owners from farming is minimal. Active cultivation that may result in dust and noise from farm machinery will occur only two to four days a year. There are no chickens, pigs or animals that some may find distasteful.

The benefits from continued farming are enormous. And this without detriment to the health, safety or welfare of the public. On the other hand, the evidence demonstrates that the only respect in which farming of this land is offensive is that it is not more economically lucrative to the Township.

Since plaintiff is not a farmer, but an investor, it is likely that, as the surrounding community develops, market forces will take their natural course and the land will probably become more valuable. Normally its residential development value will far surpass its value as a farm. At some point he, or his heirs, will most likely sell the land. Then the township will most likely see development of the property consistent with its master plan. Of course, during the interim, plaintiff assumes the risk the state adopts a policy or program designating his lands for open spaces forever.

In the meantime, however, the reduced tax assessment provided by the Farmland Assessment Act will have served its purpose, which is to induce property owners to defer development of their lands. This delay will provide the Legislature with additional time to provide for open space by means of Conservation Easements, Green Acres projects, and other means. * * *

* * *

The specific facts of this case convince this court that the strict application of the township zoning ordinance to plaintiff's land is unreasonable and arbitrary.

The benefits to both the public and plaintiff from farming are clear. What harm or evil would befall the township if this land was to be farmed rather than lie fallow? Other than the loss of some tax revenues, this court can perceive none. Farming is a temporary use. No permanent buildings or structures will be built that will impede or prevent a conversion to residential use whenever the owner so desires. The use could be changed at any time.

Here we must seek to balance the application of two strong policies of the state. One to preserve open spaces, as expressed in the Farmland Assessment Act, and the other to permit a municipality to design its own zoning scheme. If no conflict exists, each statute shall be upheld and applied. But where a conflict appears, as here, then the court must uphold that policy which will do least violence to public policy as expressed in both statutes. In this case to permit farming will uphold the purposes of the Farmland Assessment Act without, as the court has noted, harming or doing violence to the purposes of the zoning statutes.

* * *

This holding is limited to the facts in the present matter. This decision does not say that farming must be allowed anywhere throughout the municipality. The township is free to defend its zoning ordinance where different types of farming or different neighborhood characteristics result in measurable detriment to overriding zoning considerations.

Notes

1. In Borough of Kinnelon v. South Gate Associates, 172 N.J.Super. 216, 411 A.2d 724 (1980), the court held that the New Jersey Farmland Assessment Act did not preempt municipal power to prohibit, restrict or condition the use of property for commercial farming or timbering operations where appropriate under the land use enabling legislation. The court stated that to the extent the opinion in the principal case indicated otherwise, it was disapproved. Also see Save Centennial Valley Ass'n, Inc. v. Schultz, 284 N.W.2d 452 (S.D.1979).

2. A number of states have statutes which are referred to as farmland protection acts. See Burgess–Jackson, The Ethics and Economics of Right-to-Farm Statutes, 9 Harv.J.L. & Pub.Pol'y 480 (1986). In Jerome Twp. v. Melchi, 184 Mich.App. 228, 457 N.W.2d 52 (1990) the court held that the state right to farm statute could not protect the farmer retroactively and that the land was zoned residential prior to the adoption of the act; the result was that the farmer's commercial apiary was declared a nuisance. And in Wellington Farms, Inc. v. Township of Silver Spring, ___ Pa.Cmwlth. ___, 679 A.2d 267 (1996) the court held that the state's farmland protection statute did not immunize the farm from a zoning provision prohibiting the slaughtering of poultry not raised on site.

Although there is no uniformity in these statutes the general thrust is to insulate farmers from nuisance actions brought by newly arrived residential subdivision residents. In a different vein is a very interesting Maine statute, Maine Rev.Stat.Ann., Title 7, Section 51, *et seq.* Originally adopted in 1988, and revised in 1989, this statute allows farmers to register their farmland with the state. If the farm is registered, the statute prohibits abutting landowners from engaging in "inconsistent development or use." This phrase is defined to include residential buildings, schools, campgrounds, and commercial food establishments. (The legislative findings suggested that the use of chemicals on farms poses a danger to humans in close proximity.)

3. In most states, the use of the zoning power to preserve land in agriculture has not been viewed as workable. Yet prime agricultural land has been disappearing at an alarming rate. Roughly some 22 million acres were converted from agriculture to other uses in the 1960's and 8 million acres were converted from 1967–1975. Much of this land has been lost to urban

sprawl. To combat the trend, most states have utilized the tax power to provide incentives for keeping land in agricultural uses. One state, Vermont, has come up with a tax approach that provides disincentives to land speculation. At this point, consider the following tax approaches to conservation of farmland:

a. Preferential assessment—agricultural land is taxed on the basis of its value as farmland instead of its potential value for development. Such statutes are found in Arkansas, Colorado, Delaware, Florida, Indiana, Iowa, New Mexico, South Dakota, and Wyoming. See, e.g., Town of St. John v. State Bd. of Tax Comm'rs, 665 N.E.2d 965 (Ind.Tax Ct.1996).

b. Deferred taxation—agricultural land is taxed on the basis of its value as farmland, but when the owner finally sells, the taxing agency recoups the differential between farm basis and development basis for the past three or more years. Such schemes are utilized in Alabama, Connecticut, Hawaii, Illinois, Kentucky, Louisiana, Maine, Maryland, Minnesota, Montana, New Hampshire, New York, North Carolina, Oregon, Rhode Island, Texas, and Virginia.

c. Restrictive agreements—the landowner agrees with the taxing agency to keep land as agricultural open space for a specified period. Ten years is typical. Taxes will be based on farm value. If the owner wants to sell prior to the end of the term he must pay the differential as in b., above, plus a penalty tax. California, Hawaii, Maine, Pennsylvania, and Vermont have some form of this device.

On the question of whether preferential assessment accomplishes the purpose of preservation of agricultural land, see Roberts, The Big Giveaway Called Differential Assessment: Some Thoughts on the Integration of Tax and Land Use Policy, 2 Urban L. & Policy 65 (1979). The article concludes that preferential assessment does not prevent conversion of farmland to other uses and thus makes no economic sense, even though this approach might make political sense. Also see Myers, Open Space Taxation and State Constitutions, 33 Vand.L.Rev. 837 (1980); Henke, Preferential Property Tax Treatment of Farmland, 53 Or.L.Rev. 117 (1974); Adamson, Preferential Land Assessment in Virginia, 10 U.Richmond L.Rev. 111 (1970).

4. Many other approaches to farmland preservation have been utilized or advocated in addition to zoning and tax incentives. For a critical survey of the field, see Batie and Looney, Preserving Agricultural Lands: Issues and Answers, 1 Agricultural L.J. 600 (1980). Also see Myers, The Legal Aspects of Agricultural Districting, 55 Indiana L.J. 1 (1979); Peterson and McCarthy, Farmland Preservation by Purchase of Development Rights; The Long Island Experiment, 26 De Paul L.Rev. 447 (1977); Delogu, Comprehensive State and Local Government Land Use Control Strategy to Preserve the Nation's Farmland is Unnecessary and Unwise, 34 U.Kan.L.Rev. 519 (1986). On the purchase of development rights, also see Louthan v. King County, 94 Wash.2d 422, 617 P.2d 977 (1980). In California, voters in Napa County amended the comprehensive plan by initiative and provided in the plan that land designated agricultural or open space could not be changed for 30 years without a majority vote of the county electorate. This use of the initiative was upheld in DeVita v. County of Napa, 9 Cal.4th 763, 38 Cal.Rptr.2d 699, 889 P.2d 1019 (1995).

5. The other side of the coin, in seeking to conserve agricultural land, is to try to reduce urban sprawl. For an example of this approach, see Freilich and Ragsdale, A Legal Study of the Control of Urban Sprawl in the Minneapolis–St. Paul Metropolitan Region (Twin Cities Metropolitan Council Rpt. 1974).

———

Do any of the theories given to justify conservation of natural resources or forest land or agricultural land in the rural areas of the country have any application within the city? In at least one area some development has occurred in that a few cities have utilized the police power to conserve trees. This type of regulation can take two forms: Restrictions on cutting of trees, analogous to the restrictions on removal of earth products, and affirmative tree planting requirements, analogous to subdivision exactions studied in Chapter VI.

Some cities spend considerable amounts of tax money in tree planting programs. In 1969, for example, New York City reportedly spent $750,000 to plant 5,000 trees; also, private corporations have spent money to plant trees in downtown areas. In 1955 the Richfield Oil Co. spent some $20,000 to plant 13 trees in downtown Los Angeles. Advocates of such plantings point out that trees are the only asset a city has which increases in value over time rather than depreciates (although others point out that eventually trees can become a liability when removal is necessary). Some land use enabling legislation authorizes cities to require "landscaping" in connection with subdivision exactions, but there is no reliable estimate on how many cities use the power to require subdividers to plant trees as a condition of subdivision approval. For a model landscaping ordinance, see 2A Matthews and Matthews, Municipal Ordinances § 40.57 (1973). Also, refer back to the Georgia Parking Association case earlier in this chapter.

If a city can use the police power (via subdivision regulations) to require tree planting, can the same power be used to prevent destruction of trees on privately owned land? The law is clear that the police power can be used to require private owners to destroy diseased trees (the Dutch Elm disease epidemic has engendered much legislation) and even healthy trees may be ordered destroyed because they pose a danger to other public interests. Miller v. Schoene, 276 U.S. 272, 48 S.Ct. 246, 72 L.Ed. 568 (1928). If the police power can be used to destroy trees, no reason would seem to prevent use of the power to conserve individual trees. However, American communities apparently have not done much along that line. In England, however, trees are taken more seriously. The Civic Amenities Act of 1967 (since repealed and reenacted as part of the Town and Country Planning Act of 1971) provides affirmatively for requiring tree plantings in connection with land development and negatively for tree preservation orders which, at risk of heavy penalty (£250 or double the value of the tree), prevent destruction of trees.

In at least one state, Hawaii, statutory recognition of tree preservation has been undertaken. A 1975 statute, Hawaii Rev.Stat. § 58–1 et seq., commands each county to establish an arborist advisory committee to advise and recommend protective ordinances and review all actions deemed to endanger exceptional trees. Section 58–4 authorizes counties to enact protective regulations and to seek injunctions against removal or destruction of exceptional trees. Exceptional trees are defined as "a tree or stand or grove of trees with historic or cultural value, or which by reason of its age, variety, location, size, esthetic quality, or endemic status has been designated by the county committee as worthy of preservation."

In Southland Addition Homeowner's Ass'n v. Board of Adjustments, 710 S.W.2d 194 (Tex.App.1986) the court held that a desire to preserve trees was a sufficient special circumstance to authorize the grant of a variance, and in Schwalbach v. Forest Lawn Memorial Park, 687 S.W.2d 551 (Ky.App.1985), the court ruled for the owner of a large tree which deposited leaves, twigs and seeds in the plaintiff's gutters clogging them. The opinion discusses and adopts the so-called Massachusetts rule, which allows the owner of land the liberty to grow trees regardless of the extension of boughs or roots onto adjoining land.

On the other side of the coin, can trees be regarded as a nuisance? In County of Westchester, v. Town of Greenwich, Connecticut, 76 F.3d 42 (2d Cir.1996) a county in New York brought an action against the Connecticut city and several landowners to obtain a prescriptive easement along a runway approach to the county airport and have the landowners' trees cut as a public nuisance. In an earlier decision, the federal court certified to the Connecticut Supreme Court the question as to whether avigation and clearance easements could be obtained by prescription. 986 F.2d 624 (2d Cir.1993). The Connecticut court held that the New York county could not have acquired an easement by prescription because its use of the airspace above the property owners' lands was not sufficiently adverse under either federal or state law. County of Westchester v. Town of Greenwich, 227 Conn. 495, 629 A.2d 1084 (1993). On the nuisance issue the court found for the landowners, quoting the trial judge's statement:

> If normally unobjectionable land use such as growing trees can be transformed into an "unreasonable" activity by the act of building an airport that lacks the necessary property rights for full operation, then there would be no reason for airports to ever bother paying for property rights beyond those needed for the the land the airport actually occupies, because the airports could acquire the air easements they needed without cost by bringing nuisance suits against any landowner whose property contained structures blocking, or threatening to block, the airports' runways' clear zones.

In Sea Island Scenic Parkway Coalition v. Beaufort County Bd. of Adjustments and Appeals, 316 S.C. 231, 449 S.E.2d 254 (1994) the court held that the board acted arbitrarily in deciding to permit the developer of a supermarket to remove over half of the protected live oak trees on the property, citing a provision in the zoning ordinance that "endangered or valued trees will not be normally permitted [to be removed]."

Frequently, restrictive covenants contain provisions relating to trees. See Annotation, Validity, Construction, and Effect of Restrictive Covenants as to Trees and Shrubbery, 13 A.L.R.4th 1346 (1982).

C. COASTLINE REGULATIONS

1972 marks the beginning of widespread programs to treat coastal areas as a special problem of land use control. Concern about the coastline was sparked by several events and developments. In some states, on the east coast, large industrial complexes such as oil refineries were proposed in coastal areas with fragile eco-systems; in the extreme southeast (southern Florida) and to some extent in the northeast coastal sections, rapid shoreline urbanization was seen as a problem; on the west coast, scenic values and wild coastline areas were threatened by residential development.

The Coastal Zone Management Act of 1972, 16 U.S.C.A. § 1451 et seq., was the congressional response to the concerns that were voiced. The legislative findings and declaration of policy are of some interest:

§ 1451. Congressional findings

The Congress finds that—

(a) There is a national interest in the effective management, beneficial use, protection, and development of the coastal zone;

(b) The coastal zone is rich in a variety of natural, commercial, recreational, industrial, and esthetic resources of immediate and potential value to the present and future well-being of the Nation;

(c) The increasing and competing demands upon the lands and waters of our coastal zone occasioned by population growth and economic development, including requirements for industry, commerce, residential development, recreation, extraction of mineral resources and fossil fuels, transportation and navigation, waste disposal, and harvesting of fish, shellfish, and other living marine resources, have resulted in the loss of living marine resources, wildlife, nutrient-rich areas, permanent and adverse changes to ecological systems, decreasing open space for public use, and shoreline erosion;

(d) The coastal zone, and the fish, shellfish, other living marine resources, and wildlife therein, are ecologically fragile and consequently extremely vulnerable to destruction by man's alterations;

(e) Important ecological, cultural, historic, and esthetic values in the coastal zone which are essential to the well-being of all citizens are being irretrievably damaged or lost;

(f) Special natural and scenic characteristics are being damaged by ill-planned development that threatens these values;

(g) In light of competing demands and the urgent need to protect and to give high priority to natural systems in the coastal zone, present state and local institutional arrangements for planning and regulating land and water uses in such areas are inadequate; and

(h) The key to more effective protection and use of the land and water resources of the coastal zone is to encourage the states to exercise their full authority over the lands and waters in the coastal zone by assisting the states, in cooperation with Federal and local governments and other vitally affected interests, in developing land and water use programs for the coastal zone, including unified policies, criteria, standards, methods, and processes for dealing with land and water use decisions of more than local significance.

§ 1452.   Congressional declaration of policy

The Congress finds and declares that it is the national policy (a) to preserve, protect, develop, and where possible, to restore or enhance, the resources of the Nation's coastal zone for this and succeeding generations, (b) to encourage and assist the states to exercise effectively their responsibilities in the coastal zone through the development and implementation of management programs to achieve wise use of the land and water resources of the coastal zone giving full consideration to ecological, cultural, historic, and esthetic values as well as to needs for economic development, (c) for all Federal agencies engaged in programs affecting the coastal zone to cooperate and participate with state and local governments and regional agencies in effectuating the purposes of this chapter, and (d) to encourage the participation of the public, of Federal, state, and local governments and of regional agencies in the development of coastal zone management programs. With respect to implementation of such management programs, it is the national policy to encourage cooperation among the various state and regional agencies including establishment of interstate and regional agreements, cooperative procedures, and joint action particularly regarding environmental problems.

The federal act does not seek to regulate any coastal areas directly. The thrust of the statute is to provide encouragement and funds for the states and territories covered by the act to develop and implement coastal management plans. The coverage is quite broad, some thirty states (all states touching on a coast plus those touching on the Great Lakes) and American Samoa, Guam, Puerto Rico and the Virgin Islands are included.

Also see the Coastal Barrier Resources Act, 16 U.S.C.A. § 3505 which prohibits the federal government from subsidizing development on barrier islands along the Atlantic and Gulf coasts; in particular, the act prevents federal spending for flood insurance or seawalls, airports, bridges, roads and sewers in undeveloped areas of the islands.

Although all of the states covered by the Coastal Zone Management have adopted coastal zone plans, the most stringent state regulations can be found in California, where voters adopted an initiative measure creating the California Coastal Zone Conservation Commission endowed with power to require a permit for any development in the area extending 1,000 yards landward from the mean high tide line. Cal.Public Resources Code § 27100 et seq. See Ausness, Land Use Controls in Coastal Areas, 9 Cal.West.L.Rev. 391 (1973). Facial attacks on state coastal zone regulation have not succeeded in the courts. One leading case is CEEED v. California Coastal Zone Conservation Comm'n, 43 Cal.App.3d 306, 118 Cal.Rptr. 315 (1974) where the court rejected ultra vires, due process, separation of powers, and takings arguments put forth to challenge the California statute. Also see State v. Superior Court of Orange County, 12 Cal.3d 237, 115 Cal.Rptr. 497, 524 P.2d 1281 (1974) and Klitgaard & Jones, Inc. v. San Diego Coast Regional Comm'n, 48 Cal.App.3d 99, 121 Cal.Rptr. 650 (1975).

In Liberty v. California Coastal Comm'n, 113 Cal.App.3d 491, 170 Cal.Rptr. 247 (1980), the court held that the Commission could condition a permit for a restaurant upon building adequate parking facilities to handle the probable increase in traffic to be generated by the applicant's activities, but that a condition requiring the parking facilities to be dedicated for free public parking until 5:00 p.m. daily was a disguised taking of private property for public use.

In Pacific Legal Foundation v. California Coastal Commission, 129 Cal.App.3d 44, 180 Cal.Rptr. 858 (1982) an intermediate appellate court struck down commission regulation requiring dedication of public access to beach areas as a condition of granting a permit for development. The state supreme court vacated the decision on grounds of lack of ripeness, 33 Cal.3d 158, 188 Cal.Rptr. 104, 655 P.2d 306 (1982). Also see Whalers' Village Club v. California Coastal Commission, 173 Cal.App.3d 240, 220 Cal.Rptr. 2 (2 Dist. 1985). In Lee County v. Morales, 557 So.2d 652 (Fla.App.1990) the court held that downzoning of commercially zoned lots on a barrier island was consistent with coastal protection, and reversed an award of $66,590 for a temporary taking.

Recall that in the Nollan case, reproduced in Chapter VI, the Supreme Court was dealing with the issue of whether the Commission could condition a permit on dedication of private beachfront, and found that there was no clear nexus between the condition and the regulatory mission. And, of course, in the Lucas case, in Chapter V, the Supreme Court held that application of the South Carolina coastal regulation was a taking of Lucas' property.

D. REGULATION OF BEACHES AND RECREATION AREAS

STATE EX REL. THORNTON v. HAY
Supreme Court of Oregon, 1969.
254 Or. 584, 462 P.2d 671.

GOODWIN, JUSTICE. William and Georgianna Hay, the owners of a tourist facility at Cannon Beach, appeal from a decree which enjoins them from constructing fences or other improvements in the dry-sand area between the sixteen-foot elevation contour line and the ordinary high-tide line of the Pacific Ocean.

The issue is whether the state has the power to prevent the defendant landowners from enclosing the dry-sand area contained within the legal description of their ocean-front property.

The state asserts two theories: (1) the landowners' record title to the disputed area is encumbered by a superior right in the public to go upon and enjoy the land for recreational purposes; and (2) if the disputed area is not encumbered by the asserted public easement, then the state has power to prevent construction under zoning regulations made pursuant to ORS 390.640.

The defendant landowners concede that the State Highway Commission has standing to represent the rights of the public in this litigation, ORS 390.620, and that all tideland lying seaward of the ordinary, or mean high-tide line is a state recreation area as defined in ORS 390.720.[19]

The land area in dispute will be called the dry-sand area. This will be assumed to be the land lying between the line of mean high tide and the visible line of vegetation.

The vegetation line is the seaward edge of vegetation where the upland supports vegetation. It falls generally in the vicinity of the sixteen-foot-elevation contour line, but is not at all points necessarily identical with that line. Differences between the vegetation line and the sixteen-foot line are irrelevant for the purposes of this case.

* * *

The only issue in this case, as noted, is the power of the state to limit the record owner's use and enjoyment of the dry-sand area, by whatever boundaries the area may be described.

The trial court found that the public had acquired, over the years, an easement for recreational purposes to go upon and enjoy the dry-sand area, and that this easement was appurtenant to the wet-sand portion of the beach which is admittedly owned by the state and designated as a "state recreation area."

Because we hold that the trial court correctly found in favor of the state on the rights of the public in the dry-sand area, it follows that the state has an equitable right to protect the public in the enjoyment of those rights by causing the removal of fences and other obstacles.

It is not necessary, therefore, to consider whether ORS 390.640 would be constitutional if it were to be applied as a zoning regulation to

---

19. ORS 390.720 provides:

"Ownership of the shore of the Pacific Ocean between ordinary high tide and extreme low tide, and from the Oregon and Washington state line on the north to the Oregon and California state line on the south, excepting such portions as may have been disposed of by the state prior to July 5, 1947, is vested in the State of Oregon, and is declared to be a state recreation area. No portion of such ocean shore shall be alienated by any of the agencies of the state except as provided by law."

lands upon which the public had not acquired an easement for recreational use.

In order to explain our reasons for affirming the trial court's decree, it is necessary to set out in some detail the historical facts which lead to our conclusion.

The dry-sand area in Oregon has been enjoyed by the general public as a recreational adjunct of the wet-sand or foreshore area since the beginning of the state's political history. The first European settlers on these shores found the aboriginal inhabitants using the foreshore for clam-digging and the dry-sand area for their cooking fires. The newcomers continued these customs after statehood. Thus, from the time of the earliest settlement to the present day, the general public has assumed that the dry-sand area was a part of the public beach, and the public has used the dry-sand area for picnics, gathering wood, building warming fires, and generally as a headquarters from which to supervise children or to range out over the foreshore as the tides advance and recede. In the Cannon Beach vicinity, state and local officers have policed the dry sand, and municipal sanitary crews have attempted to keep the area reasonably free from man-made litter.

Perhaps one explanation for the evolution of the custom of the public to use the dry-sand area for recreational purposes is that the area could not be used conveniently by its owners for any other purpose. The dry-sand area is unstable in its seaward boundaries, unsafe during winter storms, and for the most part unfit for the construction of permanent structures. While the vegetation line remains relatively fixed, the western edge of the dry-sand area is subject to dramatic moves eastward or westward in response to erosion and accretion. For example, evidence in the trial below indicated that between April 1966 and August 1967 the seaward edge of the dry-sand area involved in this litigation moved westward 180 feet. At other points along the shore, the evidence showed, the seaward edge of the dry-sand area could move an equal distance to the east in a similar period of time.

Until very recently, no question concerning the right of the public to enjoy the dry-sand area appears to have been brought before the courts of this state. The public's assumption that the dry sand as well as the foreshore was "public property" had been reinforced by early judicial decisions. See Shively v. Bowlby, 152 U.S. 1, 14 S.Ct. 548, 38 L.Ed. 331 (1894), which affirmed Bowlby v. Shively, 22 Or. 410, 30 P. 154 (1892). These cases held that landowners claiming under federal patents owned seaward only to the "high-water" line, a line that was then assumed to be the vegetation line.

* * *

Recently, however, the scarcity of oceanfront building sites has attracted substantial private investments in resort facilities. Resort owners like these defendants now desire to reserve for their paying guests the recreational advantages that accrue to the dry-sand portions of their deeded property. Consequently, in 1967, public debate and political activity resulted in legislative attempts to resolve conflicts between public and private interests in the dry-sand area:

> ORS 390.60 "(1) The Legislative assembly hereby declares it is the public policy of the State of Oregon to forever preserve and maintain the sovereignty of the state heretofore existing over the seashore and ocean beaches of the state from the Columbia River on the North to the Oregon–California line on the South so that the public may have the free and uninterrupted use thereof.

> "(2) The Legislative Assembly recognizes that over the years the public has made frequent and uninterrupted use of lands abutting, adjacent and contiguous to the public highways and state recreation areas and recognizes, further, that where such use has been sufficient to create easements in the public through dedication, prescription, grant or otherwise, that it is in the public interest to protect and preserve such public easements as a permanent part of Oregon's recreational resources.

> "(3) Accordingly, the Legislative Assembly hereby declares that all public rights and easements in those lands described in subsection (2) of this section are confirmed and declared vested exclusively in the State of Oregon and shall be held and administered in the same manner as those lands described in ORS 390.720.

> " * * * ."

The state concedes that such legislation cannot divest a person of his rights in land, Hughes v. Washington, 389 U.S. 290, 88 S.Ct. 438, 19 L.Ed.2d 530 (1967), and that the defendants' record title, which includes the dry-sand area, extends seaward to the ordinary or mean high-tide line. Borax Consolidated Ltd. v. Los Angeles, supra.

The landowners likewise concede that since 1899 the public's rights in the foreshore have been confirmed by law as well as by custom and usage. Oregon Laws 1899, p. 3, provided:

> That the shore of the Pacific ocean, between ordinary high and extreme low tides, and from the Columbia river on the north to the south boundary line of Clatsop county on the south, is hereby declared a public highway, and shall forever remain open as such to the public.

The disputed area is *sui generis*. While the foreshore is "owned" by the state, and the upland is "owned" by the patentee or record-title holder, neither can be said to "own" the full bundle of rights normally connotated by the term "estate in fee simple." 1 Powell, Real Property § 163, at 661 (1949).

In addition to the *sui generis* nature of the land itself, a multitude of complex and sometimes overlapping precedents in the law confront ed the trial court. Several early Oregon decisions generally support the trial court's decision, i.e., that the public can acquire easements in private land by long-continued use that is inconsistent with the owner's exclusive possession and enjoyment of his land. A citation of the cases could end the discussion at this point. But because the early cases do not agree on the legal theories by which the results are reached, and because this is an important case affecting valuable rights in land, it is appropriate to review some of the law applicable to this case.

One group of precedents relied upon in part by the state and by the trial court can be called the "implied-dedication" cases. The doctrine of implied dedication is well known to the law in this state and elsewhere. See cases collected in Parks, The Law of Dedication in Oregon, 20 Or.L.Rev. 111 (1941). Dedication, however, whether express or implied, rests upon an intent to dedicate.[20] In the case at bar, it is unlikely that the landowners thought they had anything to dedicate, until 1967, when the notoriety of legislative debates about the public's rights in the dry-sand area sent a number of ocean-front landowners to the offices of their legal advisers.

A second group of cases relied upon by the state, but rejected by the trial court, deals with the possibility of a landowner's losing the exclusive possession and enjoyment of his land through the development of prescriptive easements in the public.

In Oregon, as in most common-law jurisdictions, an easement can be created in favor of one person in the land of another by uninterrupted use and enjoyment of the land in a particular manner for the statutory period, so long as the user is open, adverse, under claim of right, but without authority of law or consent of the owner. Feldman et ux. v. Knapp et ux., 196 Or. 453, 476, 250 P.2d 92 (1952); Coventon v. Seufert, 23 Or. 548, 550, 32 P. 508 (1893). In Oregon, the prescriptive period is ten years. ORS 12.050. The public use of the disputed land in the case at bar is admitted to be continuous for more than sixty years. There is no suggestion in the record that anyone's permission was sought or given; rather, the public used the land under a claim of right. Therefore, if the public can acquire an easement by prescription, the requirements for such an acquisition have been met in connection with the specific tract of land involved in this case.

The owners argue, however, that the general public, not being subject to actions in trespass and ejectment, cannot acquire rights by prescription, because the statute of limitations is irrelevant when an action does not lie.

20. Because of the elements of public interest and estoppel running through the cases, intent to dedicate is sometimes "presumed" instead of proven. But conceptually, at least, dedication is founded upon an intent to dedicate. Security and Investment Co. of Oregon City v. Oregon City, 161 Or. 421, 433, 90 P.2d 467 (1939); City of Clatskanie v. McDonald, 85 Or. 670, 674, 167 P. 560 (1917); Portland Ry., L. & P. Co. v. Oregon City, 85 Or. 574, 582, 166 P. 932 (1917); Harris v. St. Helens, 72 Or. 377, 386, 143 P. 941 (1914); Parrott v. Stewart, 65 Or. 254, 259, 132 P. 523 (1913); Lownsdale v. City of Portland, 1 Or. 397, 405 (1861). See, also, Nicholas v. Title & Trust Co., 79 Or. 226, 154 P. 391 (1916); Kuck v. Wakefield, 58 Or. 549, 555, 115 P. 428 (1911). Additional cases are collected in Parks, The Law of Dedication in Oregon, 20 Or.L.Rev. 111 (1941).

While it may not be feasible for a landowner to sue the general public, it is nonetheless possible by means of signs and fences to prevent or minimize public invasions of private land for recreational purposes. In Oregon, moreover, the courts and the Legislative Assembly have both recognized that the public can acquire prescriptive easements in private land, at least for roads and highways. See, e.g., Huggett et ux. v. Moran et ux., 201 Or. 105, 266 P.2d 692 (1954), in which we observed that counties could acquire public roads by prescription. And see ORS 368.405, which provides for the manner in which counties may establish roads. The statute enumerates the formal governmental actions that can be employed, and then concludes: "This section does not preclude acquiring public ways by adverse user."

Another statute codifies a policy favoring the acquisition by prescription of public recreational easements in beach lands. See ORS 390.610. While such a statute cannot create public rights at the expense of a private landowner the statute can, and does, express legislative approval of the common-law doctrine of prescription where the facts justify its application. Consequently, we conclude that the law in Oregon, regardless of the generalizations that may apply elsewhere,[21] does not preclude the creation of prescriptive easements in beach land for public recreational use.

Because many elements of prescription are present in this case, the state has relied upon the doctrine in support of the decree below. We believe, however, that there is a better legal basis for affirming the decree. The most cogent basis for the decision in this case is the English doctrine of custom. Strictly construed, prescription applies only to the specific tract of land before the court, and doubtful prescription cases could fill the courts for years with tract-by-tract litigation. An established custom, on the other hand, can be proven with reference to a larger region. Ocean-front lands from the northern to the southern border of the state ought to be treated uniformly.

The other reason which commends the doctrine of custom over that of prescription as the principal basis for the decision in this case is the unique nature of the lands in question. This case deals solely with the dry-sand area along the Pacific shore, and this land has been used by the public as public recreational land according to an unbroken custom running back in time as long as the land has been inhabited.

21. See, e.g., Sanchez v. Taylor, 377 F.2d 733, 738 (10th Cir.1967), holding that the general public cannot acquire grazing rights in unfenced land. Among other reasons assigned by authorities cited in Sanchez v. Taylor are these: prescription would violate the rule against perpetuities because no grantee could ever convey the land free of the easement; and prescription rests on the fiction of a "lost grant," which state of affairs cannot apply to the general public.

The first argument can as well be made against the public's acquiring rights by express dedication; and the second argument applies equally to the fictional aspects of the doctrine of implied dedication. Both arguments are properly ignored in cases dealing with roads and highways, because the utility of roads and the public interest in keeping them open outweighs the policy favoring formal over informal transfers of interests in land.

A custom is defined in 1 Bouv.Law Dict., Rawle's Third Revision, p. 742 as "such a usage as by common consent and uniform practice has become the law of the place, or of the subject matter to which it relates."

In 1 Blackstone, Commentaries *75–*78, Sir William Blackstone set out the requisites of a particular custom.

Paraphrasing Blackstone, the first requirement of a custom, to be recognized as law, is that it must be ancient. It must have been used so long "that the memory of man runneth not to the contrary." Professor Cooley footnotes his edition of Blackstone with the comment that "long and general" usage is sufficient. In any event, the record in the case at bar satisfies the requirement of antiquity. So long as there has been an institutionalized system of land tenure in Oregon, the public has freely exercised the right to use the dry-sand area up and down the Oregon coast for the recreational purposes noted earlier in this opinion.

The second requirement is that the right be exercised without interruption. A customary right need not be exercised continuously, but it must be exercised without an interruption caused by anyone possessing a paramount right. In the case at bar, there was evidence that the public's use and enjoyment of the dry-sand area had never been interrupted by private landowners.

Blackstone's third requirement, that the customary use be peaceable and free from dispute, is satisfied by the evidence which related to the second requirement.

The fourth requirement, that of reasonableness, is satisfied by the evidence that the public has always made use of the land in a manner appropriate to the land and to the usages of the community. There is evidence in the record that when inappropriate uses have been detected, municipal police officers have intervened to preserve order.

The fifth requirement, certainty, is satisfied by the visible boundaries of the dry-sand area and by the character of the land, which limits the use thereof to recreational uses connected with the foreshore.

The sixth requirement is that a custom must be obligatory; that is, in the case at bar, not left to the option of each landowner whether or not he will recognize the public's right to go upon the dry-sand area for recreational purposes. The record shows that the dry-sand area in question has been used, as of right, uniformly with similarly situated lands elsewhere, and that the public's use has never been questioned by an upland owner so long as the public remained on the dry sand and refrained from trespassing upon the lands above the vegetation line.

Finally, a custom must not be repugnant, or inconsistent, with other customs or with other law. The custom under consideration violates no law, and is not repugnant.

Two arguments have been arrayed against the doctrine of custom as a basis for decision in Oregon. The first argument is that custom is unprecedented in this state, and has only scant adherence elsewhere in the United States. The second argument is that because of the relative brevity of our political history it is inappropriate to rely upon an English doctrine that requires greater antiquity than a newly-settled land can muster. Neither of these arguments is persuasive.

The custom of the people of Oregon to use the dry-sand area of the beaches for public recreational purposes meets every one of Blackstone's requisites. While it is not necessary to rely upon precedent from other states, we are not the first state to recognize custom as a source of law. See Perley et ux'r v. Langley, 7 N.H. 233 (1834).

On the score of the brevity of our political history, it is true that the Anglo–American legal system on this continent is relatively new. Its newness has made it possible for government to provide for many of our institutions by written law rather than by customary law.[22] This truism does not, however, militate against the validity of a custom when the custom does in fact exist. If antiquity were the sole test of validity of a custom, Oregonians could satisfy that requirement by recalling that the European settlers were not the first people to use the dry-sand area as public land.

Finally, in support of custom, the record shows that the custom of the inhabitants of Oregon and of visitors in the state to use the dry sand as a public recreation area is so notorious that notice of the custom on the part of persons buying land along the shore must be presumed. In the case at bar, the landowners conceded their actual knowledge of the public's long-standing use of the dry-sand area, and argued that the elements of consent present in the relationship between the landowners and the public precluded the application of the law of prescription. As noted, we are not resting this decision on prescription, and we leave open the effect upon prescription of the type of consent that may have been present in this case. Such elements of consent are, however, wholly consistent with the recognition of public rights derived from custom.

Because so much of our law is the product of legislation, we sometimes lose sight of the importance of custom as a source of law in our society. It seems particularly appropriate in the case at bar to look to an ancient and accepted custom in this state as the source of a rule of law. The rule in this case, based upon custom, is salutary in confirming a public right, and at the same time it takes from no man anything which he has had a legitimate reason to regard as exclusively his.

---

22. The English law on customary rights grew up in a small island nation at a time when most inhabitants lived and died without traveling more than a day's walk from their birthplace. Most of the customary rights recorded in English cases are local in scope. The English had many cultural and language groups which eventually merged into a nation. After these groups developed their own unique customs, the unified nation recognized some of them as law. Some American scholars looking at the vast geography of this continent and the freshness of its civilization, have concluded that there is no need to look to English customary rights as a source of legal rights in this country. See, e.g., 6 Powell, Real Property § 934, note 5, at 362 (1949). Some of the generalizations drawn by the text writers from English cases would tend to limit customary rights to specific usages in English towns and villages. See Gray, The Rule Against Perpetuities §§ 572–588 (1942). But it does not follow that a custom, established in fact, cannot have regional application and be enjoyed by a larger public than the inhabitants of a single village.

For the foregoing reasons, the decree of the trial court is affirmed.

DENECKE, JUSTICE (specially concurring).

I agree with the decision of the majority; however, I disagree with basing the decision upon the English doctrine of "customary rights." In my opinion the facts in this case cannot be fitted into the outlines of that ancient doctrine. 6 Powell, Real Property 362, § 934, n. 5 (1968); 2 Thompson, Real Property, 463, § 369, n. 50 (1961); Gray, The Rule Against Perpetuities, ch. 17 (4th ed. 1942); 15 Harv.L.Rev. 329, 332 (1903).

In my opinion the doctrine of "customary rights" is useful but only as an analogy. I am further of the opinion that "custom," as distinguished from "customary rights," is an important ingredient in establishing the rights of the public to the use of the dry sands.

I base the public's right upon the following factors: (1) long usage by the public of the dry sands area, not necessarily on all the Oregon beaches, but wherever the public uses the beach; (2) a universal and long held belief by the public in the public's right to such use; (3) long and universal acquiescence by the upland owners in such public use; and (4) the extreme desirability to the public of the right to the use of the dry sands. When this combination exists, as it does here, I conclude that the public has the right to use the dry sands.

Admittedly, this is a new concept as applied to use of the dry sands of a beach; however, it is not new as applied to other public usages. In Luscher v. Reynolds, 153 Or. 625, 56 P.2d 1158 (1936) we held that regardless of who owns the bed of a lake, if it is capable of being boated, the public has the right to boat it.

> " * * * There are hundreds of similar beautiful, small inland lakes in this state well adapted for recreational purposes, but which will never be used as highways of commerce in the ordinary acceptation of such terms. As stated in Lamprey v. State, 52 Minn. 181, 53 N.W. 1139, 18 L.R.A. 670, 38 Am.St.Rep. 541, quoted with approval in Guilliams v. Beaver Lake Club, supra [90 Or. 13, 175 P. 437], 'To hand over all these lakes to private ownership, under any old or narrow test of navigability, would be a great wrong upon the public for all time, the extent of which cannot, perhaps, be now even anticipated.' Regardless of the ownership of the bed, the public has the paramount right to the use of the waters of the lake for the purpose of transportation and commerce." 153 Or. at 635–636, 56 P.2d at 1162.

In Collins v. Gerhardt, 237 Mich. 38, 211 N.W. 115, 116 (1926), the defendant was wading Pine River and fishing. The plaintiff, who owned the land on both sides and the bed of Pine River, sued defendant for trespass. The court held for the defendant:

> "From this it follows that the common-law doctrine, viz., that the right of fishing in navigable waters follows the ownership of the soil, does not prevail in this state. It is immaterial who owns the soil

in our navigable rivers. The trust remains. From the beginning the title was impressed with this trust for the preservation of the public right of fishing and other public rights which all citizens enjoyed in tidal waters under the common law. * * *." 237 Mich. at 48, 211 N.W. at 118.

These rights of the public in tidelands and in the beds of navigable streams have been called "jus publicum" and we have consistently and recently reaffirmed their existence. Corvallis Sand & Gravel Co. v. State Land Board, 250 Or. 319, 335–337, 439 P.2d 575 (1968); Smith Tug & Barge Co. v. Columbia–Pac. Towing, 250 Or. 612, 638, 443 P.2d 205 (1968). The right of public use continues although title to the property passes into private ownership and nothing in the chain of title reserves or notifies anyone of this public right. Winston Bros. Co. v. State Tax Comm., 156 Or. 505, 510–511, 62 P.2d 7 (1937).

In a recent treatise on waters and water rights the authors state:

"The principle that the public has an interest in tidelands and banks of navigable waters and a right to use them for purposes for which there is a substantial public demand may be derived from the fact that the public won a right to passage over the shore for access to the sea for fishing when this was the area of substantial public demand. As time goes by, opportunities for much more extensive uses of these lands become available to the public. The assertion by the public of a right to enjoy additional uses is met by the assertion that the public right is defined and limited by precedent based upon past uses and past demand. But such a limitation confuses the application of the principle under given circumstances with the principle itself.

"The law regarding the public use of property held in part for the benefit of the public must change as the public need changes. The words of Justice Cardozo, expressed in a different context nearly a half-century ago are relevant today in our application of this law: 'We may not suffer it to petrify at the cost of its animating principle.' "1 Clark (ed-in-chief), Waters and Water Rights, at 202 (1967).

Notes

1. What difference does it make if a court recognizes public rights in beaches to be based on custom rather than acquired by prescription? In City of Daytona Beach v. Tona–Rama, Inc., 294 So.2d 73 (Fla.1974), the court rejected the prescriptive rights doctrine in favor of the custom doctrine pointing out that the right of customary use of the dry sand area of beaches by the public does not create any interest in the land itself. Thus, by utilizing the custom doctrine, the court was able to hold that the defendant could build a 176 foot high observation tower next to its pier because the tower would not interfere with the customary use of the beach.

2. California and Texas follow the prescriptive rights/implied dedication approach. Gion v. Santa Cruz, 2 Cal.3d 29, 84 Cal.Rptr. 162, 465 P.2d 50

(1970) and County of Los Angeles v. Berk, 26 Cal.3d 201, 161 Cal.Rptr. 742, 605 P.2d 381 (1980); Seaway Co. v. Attorney General, 375 S.W.2d 923 (Tex.Civ.App.1964) and Moody v. White, 593 S.W.2d 372 (Tex.Civ.App.1979); Arrington v. Mattox, 767 S.W.2d 957 (Tex.App.1989). Hawaii utilizes the custom doctrine. In re Ashford, 50 Hawaii 314, 440 P.2d 76 (1968).

Custom as a source of law in Hawaii presents some unusual property law problems. Prior to western influences in Hawaii, property rights were based on a feudal system. In the nineteenth century, bowing to western pressures, King Kamehameha III instituted a new property system, based on English law, granting one-third of the land to the government, one-third to the chiefs and commoners, and reserving one-third to himself. Because the previous system included the customary practices of the people to use land, trails, and access freely, the king decreed that land granted in fee simple was subject to the customary gathering rights of tenants. In recent years the Hawaiian courts have been called upon to define the scope of customary rights. In Create 21 Chuo, Inc. v. Southwest Slopes, Inc., 81 Hawai'i 512, 918 P.2d 1168 (1996) the court held that customary public access rights to archaeological sites are encumbrances on title. Also see Public Access Shoreline Hawaii v. Hawaii County Planning Comm'n, 79 Hawai'i 425, 903 P.2d 1246 (1995). A local title company, Perfect Title Co., specializes in tracing land ownership using nineteenth century Hawaiian Kingdom law, leading to charges that many property sales in Hawaii are suspect. See Rob Perez, Title Claims Block Isle Land Deals, Honolulu Star–Bulletin, Jan. 8, 1997.

3.   The Maryland Supreme Court carefully considered both doctrines in Department of Natural Resources v. Mayor and Council of Ocean City, 274 Md. 1, 332 A.2d 630 (1975), but upon strict application of the prescription and implied dedication doctrines refused to find a public right in a beach area. Compare State ex rel. Haman v. Fox, 100 Idaho 140, 594 P.2d 1093 (1979), where the court also examined both doctrines, rejected the prescriptive rights/implied dedication approach, and held that although Idaho would recognize the custom doctrine, the requisite elements had not been shown.

4.   In 1981 the New Jersey Constitution was amended to require the state to follow certain procedures to claim any land which had not been overflowed by tides for 40 years prior to the amendment, or lose any such claims. In 1982 a new state agency, the Tidelands Resource Council, announced plans to prepare detailed maps of tidelands and assert state claims, an announcement which caused thousands of homeowners along the coast to be concerned about their titles. See, Janson, Landowners on Jersey Coast Wonder if They Really Are, N.Y. Times, Jun. 7, 1982, p. B 1. By the end of 1982, the Council had prepared 713 maps and filed state tideland claims. See Dickinson v. Fund for Support of Free Public Schools, 95 N.J. 65, 469 A.2d 1 (1983) and City of Jersey City v. Tidelands Resource Council, 95 N.J. 100, 469 A.2d 19 (1983), both cases upholding the Council's procedures. Also see Brancasons, Inc. v. State, 8 N.J.Tax 413 (1985), affirmed 210 N.J.Super. 570, 510 A.2d 279 (1986).

5.   In Pigorsh v. Fahner, 386 Mich. 508, 194 N.W.2d 343 (1972), the court rejected an argument that public rights in Lake Michigan authorized an easement across private lands for access to the lake. Compare Tucci v. Salzhauer, 40 A.D.2d 712, 336 N.Y.S.2d 721 (1972), affirmed 33 N.Y.2d 854,

352 N.Y.S.2d 198, 307 N.E.2d 256 (1973). See generally, Nat'l Ass'n of Attorneys General, Legal Issues in Beach Access (1975).

Beach access cases cause difficult problems. In Mackall v. White, 85 A.D.2d 696, 445 N.Y.S.2d 486 (1981), leave to appeal denied 56 N.Y.2d 503, 450 N.Y.S.2d 1025, 435 N.E.2d 1100 (1982), the court held that subdivision approval could not be conditioned upon dedication of public beachfront access. However, in Matthews v. Bay Head Improvement Ass'n, 95 N.J. 306, 471 A.2d 355 (1984), the New Jersey Supreme Court held that a nonprofit association owning beachfront property was required to permit public access to the extent reasonably necessary for recreational swimming. Compare Bell v. Town of Wells, 557 A.2d 168 (Me.1989), where the court held that an owner of intertidal land subject to an easement for public fishing, fowling and navigation did not have to allow public recreational use.

BOROUGH OF NEPTUNE CITY v. BOROUGH OF AVON–BY–THE–SEA

Supreme Court of New Jersey, 1972.
61 N.J. 296, 294 A.2d 47.

HALL, J. The question presented by this case is whether an ocean-front municipality may charge non-residents higher fees than residents for the use of its beach area. The Law Division sustained an amendatory ordinance of defendant Borough of Avon–By–The–Sea (Avon) so providing. 114 N.J.Super. 115, 274 A.2d 860 (1971). The challenge came from plaintiffs Borough of Neptune City, an adjacent inland municipality, and two of its residents. We granted plaintiffs' motion to certify their appeal to the Appellate Division before argument in that tribunal. R. 2:12–2. The question posed is of ever increasing importance in our metropolitan area. We believe that the answer to it should turn on the application of what has become known as the public trust doctrine.

Avon, in common with other New Jersey municipalities bordering on the Atlantic Ocean, is a seasonal resort-oriented community. The attraction to the influx of temporary residents and day visitors in the summer months is, of course, the ocean beach for bathing and associated recreational pleasures and benefits. See Kirsch Holding Co. v. Borough of Manasquan, 59 N.J. 241, 243–244, 281 A.2d 513 (1971). According to the stipulation of facts, Avon's year-round population of 1850, resident within its approximately seven square block area, is increased in the summertime to about 5500 people (not counting day visitors), with the seasonal increase living in four hotels, 40 rooming and boarding houses and innumerable rented and owned private dwellings.

* * *

Years ago Avon's beach, like the rest of the New Jersey shore, was free to all comers. As the trial court pointed out, "with the advent of automobile traffic and the ever-increasing number of vacationers, the beaches and bathing facilities became overcrowded and the beachfront municipalities began to take steps to limit the congestion by regulating the use of the beach facilities and by charging fees." 114 N.J.Super. at

117, 274 A.2d at 861. It also seems obvious that local financial considerations entered into the picture. Maintenance of beach fronts is expensive and adds substantially to the municipal tax levy if paid for out of property taxes. Not only are there the costs of lifeguards, policing, cleaning, and the like, but also involved are capital expenses to prevent or repair erosion and storm damage through the construction of jetties, groins, bulkheads and similar devices. (Construction of the latter is generally aided in considerable part, as it has been in Avon, by state and other governmental funds.) In addition, the seasonal population increase requires the expansion of municipal services and personnel in the fields of public safety, health and order. On the other hand, the values of real estate in the community, both commercial and residential, are undoubtedly greater than those of similar properties in inland municipalities by reason of the proximity of the ocean and the accessibility of the beach. And commercial enterprises located in the town are more valuable because of the patronage of large numbers of summer visitors. (Avon does not have, in contrast with many other shore communities, extensive boardwalk stores and amusements.)

Legislative authority to municipalities to charge beach user fees, for revenue purposes, was granted by two identical statutes—the first, L.1950, c. 324, p. 1083, N.J.S.A. 40:92–7.1 applicable only to boroughs, and the second, L.1955, c. 49, p. 165, N.J.S.A. 40:61–22.20, applicable to all municipalities. * * *

Until 1970 Avon's ordinance, adopted pursuant to the quoted statute, made no distinction in charges as between residents and non-residents. The scheme then and since is that of registration and issuance of season, monthly or daily, identification badges for access to and use of the beach area east of the boardwalk. (The boardwalk is open and free to all.) The amounts of money involved are substantial. In 1969, 32,741 badges of all categories were issued and the revenue from beachfront operations totalled $149,758.15, which went into the borough's general revenues.

The distinction between residents and non-residents was made by an amendment to the ordinance in 1970, the enactment which is attacked in this case. It was accomplished by making the rate for a monthly badge the same as that charged for a full season's badge ($10.00), by restricting the sale of season badges to residents and taxpayers of Avon and the members of their immediate families, and also apparently by substantially increasing the rates for daily badges (from $1.00 and $1.25 to $1.50 and $2.25). A "resident" is defined as any person living within the territorial boundaries of the borough for not less than 60 consecutive days in the particular calendar year. The result is considerably higher charges for non-residents under the definition than for permanent residents, taxpayers and those staying 60 days or more. Residents of Neptune City, for example, using the beach daily, would pay twice as much for the season (two monthly badges) as residents of Avon.

Plaintiffs attacked the ordinance on several grounds, including the claim of a common law right of access to the ocean in all citizens of the state. This in essence amounts to reliance upon the public trust doctrine, although not denominated by plaintiffs as such. Avon, although inferentially recognizing some such right, defended its amendatory ordinance on the thesis, accepted by the trial court, that its property taxpayers should nevertheless not be called upon to bear the expense, above non-discriminating beach user fees received, of the cost of operating and maintaining the beachfront, claimed to result from use by non-residents and that consequently the discrimination in fees was not irrational or invidious. All recognized that an oceanfront municipality may not absolutely exclude non-residents from the use of its dedicated beach, including, of course, land seaward of the mean high water mark; a trial court decision, Brindley v. Lavallette, 33 N.J.Super. 344, 348–349, 110 A.2d 157 (Law Div.1954), had so held, although not by reliance upon the public trust doctrine. We approve that holding.

Avon's proofs, based on 1969 figures, sought to show a deficit of about $50,000 between user fees received in that year and the costs of operation and maintenance of the beach. The cost figures were derived from estimates of the portions of budgetary line items said to be attributable to the beach as well as from projections on an annual basis of expected future capital expenses. Plaintiffs urge that some of these allocations are unsound. Moreover, there was no showing that the same costs would not be incurred even if only residents (under the definition) used the beach, nor was it demonstrated that the 1970 discriminatory fee schedule closed the alleged financial gap.

We prefer, however, not to treat the case on this basis, but rather, as we indicated at the outset, to approach it from the more fundamental viewpoint of the modern meaning and application of the public trust doctrine.

That broad doctrine derives from the ancient principle of English law that land covered by tidal waters belonged to the sovereign, but for the common use of all the people. Such lands passed to the respective states as a result of the American Revolution. For recent dissertations on the history, development and modern connotations of the doctrine, see generally 1 Waters and Water Rights (Clark ed. 1967), §§ 36.3, 36.4, pp. 190–202; Sax, "The Public Trust Doctrine in Natural Resource Law: Effective Judicial Intervention," 68 Mich.L.Rev. 471 (1970); Note, "The Public Trust in Tidal Areas: A Sometime Submerged Traditional Doctrine," 79 Yale L.J. 762 (1970); and with particular reference to New Jersey, Note, Jaffee, "State Citizen Rights Respecting Greatwater Resource Allocation: From Rome to New Jersey," 25 Rutgers L.Rev. 571 (1971).

A succinct statement of the principle is found in the leading case of Illinois Central Railroad Company v. State of Illinois, 146 U.S. 387, 435, 13 S.Ct. 110, 111, 36 L.Ed. 1018, 1036 (1892):

"It is the settled law of this country that the ownership of and dominion and sovereignty over lands covered by tide waters, within the limits of the several states, belong to the respective states within which they are found, with the consequent right to use or dispose of any portion thereof, when that can be done without substantial impairment of the interest of the public in the waters, and subject always to the paramount right of Congress to control their navigation so far as may be necessary for the regulation of commerce with foreign nations and among the states. This doctrine has been often announced by this court * * *."

The original purpose of the doctrine was to preserve for the use of all the public natural water resources for navigation and commerce, waterways being the principal transportation arteries of early days, and for fishing, an important source of food. * * *

It is safe to say, however, that the scope and limitations of the doctrine in this state have never been defined with any great degree of precision. That it represents a deeply inherent right of the citizenry cannot be disputed. Two aspects should be particularly mentioned, one only tangentially involved in this case and the latter directly pertinent. The former relates to the lawful extent of the power of the legislature to alienate trust lands to private parties; the latter to the inclusion within the doctrine of public accessibility to and use of such lands for recreation and health, including bathing, boating and associated activities. Both are of prime importance in this day and age. Remaining tidal water resources still in the ownership of the State are becoming very scarce, demands upon them by reason of increased population, industrial development and their popularity for recreational uses and open space are much heavier, and their importance to the public welfare has become much more apparent. Cf. New Jersey Sports & Exposition Authority v. McCrane, 61 N.J. 1, at 55, 292 A.2d 545, at 579 (1972) (concurring and dissenting opinion of Hall, J.). All of these factors mandate more precise attention to the doctrine.

Here we are not directly concerned with the extent of legislative power to alienate tidal lands because the lands seaward of the mean high water line remain in state ownership, the municipality owns the bordering land, which is dedicated to park and beach purposes, and no problem of physical access by the public to the ocean exists. * * *

* * *

We have no difficulty in finding that, in this latter half of the twentieth century, the public rights in tidal lands are not limited to the ancient prerogatives of navigation and fishing, but extend as well to recreational uses, including bathing, swimming and other shore activities. The public trust doctrine, like all common law principles, should not be considered fixed or static, but should be molded and extended to meet changing conditions and needs of the public it was created to benefit. The legislature appears to have had such an extension in mind in enacting N.J.S.A. 12:3–33, 34, previously mentioned. Those sections, generally speaking, authorize grants to governmental bodies of tide-flowed lands which front upon a public park extending to such lands, but only upon condition that any land so granted shall be maintained as a public park for public use, resort and recreation. Cf. Martin v. City of Asbury Park, 114 N.J.L. 298, 176 A. 172 (E. & A. 1935).

Other states have readily extended the doctrine, beyond the original purposes of navigation and fishing, to cover other public uses, and especially recreational uses. In Massachusetts, it was held many years ago that "it would be too strict a doctrine to hold that the trust for the public, under which the state holds and controls navigable tide waters and the land under them, beyond the line of private ownership, is for navigation alone. It is wider in its scope, and it includes all necessary and proper uses, in the interest of the public." Home for Aged Women v. Commonwealth, 202 Mass. 422, 89 N.E. 124, 129 (1909). Wisconsin, where the doctrine covers all navigable waters, has long held that it extends to all public uses of water including pleasure boating, sailing, fishing, swimming, hunting, skating and enjoyment of scenic beauty. Representative modern cases are Hixon v. Public Service Commission, 32 Wis.2d 608, 146 N.W.2d 577, 582 (1966); Muench v. Public Service Commission, 261 Wis. 492, 53 N.W.2d 514, 520 (1952), affirmed on rehearing 261 Wis. 492, 55 N.W.2d 40 (1952). Courts in several other states have recently recognized the vital public interest in the use of the sea shore for recreational purposes and have, under various theories consistent with their own law, asserted the public rights in such land to be superior to private or municipal interests. See, e.g., State ex rel. Thornton v. Hay, 254 Or. 584, 462 P.2d 671 (1969); Gion v. City of Santa Cruz, 2 Cal.3d 29, 84 Cal.Rptr. 162, 465 P.2d 50 (1970); Gewirtz v. City of Long Beach, 69 Misc.2d 763, 330 N.Y.S.2d 495 (Sup.Ct., Nassau Cty.1972). Modern text writers and commentators assert that the trend of the law is, or should be, in the same direction. 1 Waters and Water Rights, supra, § 36.4(B), pp. 200–202; Sax, supra, 68 Mich.L.Rev. at 556, 565; Note, supra, 79 Yale L.J. at 777–778, 784–785; Note, Jaffee, supra, 25 Rutgers L.Rev., at 608 n. 226, 690, 701.

We are convinced it has to follow that, while municipalities may validly charge reasonable fees for the use of their beaches, they may not discriminate in any respect between their residents and non-residents. The Avon amendatory ordinance of 1970 clearly does so by restricting the sale of season badges to residents, as defined in the ordinance, resulting in a lower fee to them. In addition the fee for daily badges, which would be utilized mostly by non-residents, may have been as well discriminatorily designed with respect to the amount of the charge. Since we cannot tell what fee schedule the municipality would have adopted when it passed this ordinance in 1970 if it had to do so on the basis of equal treatment for all, we see no other course but to set aside the entire amendatory enactment.

We recognize, however, that Avon has operated under the present schedule since 1970 and that the present beach season is about half over. Other oceanfront municipalities may well have similar enactments. Also

Avon very likely has operated its budget and financial affairs on the basis of the beach user fees expected to be collected under the present schedule in reliance upon the trial court decision. To attempt now to turn the clock back to the non-discriminatory schedule (with considerably lower charges) specified in the pre-amendment ordinance would only create hopeless practical confusion and some unfairness to the municipality and its taxpayers. We therefore determine that the judgment to be entered pursuant to this opinion should operate prospectively only and become effective on January 1, 1973.

We ought also to say that we fully appreciate the burdens, financial and otherwise, resting upon our oceanfront municipalities by reason of the attraction of the sea and their beaches in the summer season to large numbers of people not permanently resident in the community. The rationale behind N.J.S.A. 40:61–22.20 certainly is that such municipalities may properly pass on some or all of the financial burden, as they decide, by imposing reasonable beach user fees, which we have held here must be uniform for all. We think it quite appropriate that such municipalities may, in arriving at such fees, consider all additional costs legitimately attributable to the operation and maintenance of the beachfront, including direct beach operational expenses, additional personnel and services required in the entire community, debt service of outstanding obligations incurred for beach improvement and preservation, and a reasonable annual reserve designed to meet expected future capital expenses therefor. They may also, we think, very properly regulate and limit, on a first come, first served basis, the number of persons allowed on the beach at any one time in the interest of safety.

The judgment of the Law Division is reversed and the cause is remanded to that tribunal for the entry of a judgment consistent with this opinion. No costs.

For reversal: CHIEF JUSTICE WEINTRAUB and JUSTICES JACOBS, HALL, and SCHETTINO—4.

For affirmance: JUSTICES FRANCIS and MOUNTAIN—2.

FRANCIS, J. (dissenting). I cannot agree with the result reached by the majority.

It is undisputed that anciently and currently the sovereign—here the State of New Jersey—owns the fee title to the portion of the ocean beach front seaward of the mean high water mark. Nor can it be denied that the beach area landward of the mean high water mark is owned by the upland title holder. I agree that the people have the right to use and enjoy the ocean in common, and that the right includes use in common of the beach area seaward of the mean high water mark; such is the public trust doctrine. In the absence of some unusual circumstance, or some reasonable regulation by the State, it is undoubtedly true that no person using *that strip* as an incident of his temporary enjoyment of the ocean can be considered a trespasser. Reference has been made to the fact that in the past agencies of the State have either given or sold certain riparian grants purporting to convey to the upland owner title to the land for a specified distance seaward of the mean high water mark. It has been suggested that the land described in such grants (at least the portion thereof remaining in its natural state) would be subject to the common public right to use and enjoy the strip between the mean high water mark and the ocean. But that problem is not before us now.

However, the majority opinion here states views upon a subject of serious consequence to ocean front communities and to the owners private or public, of beach front land above the mean high water mark. The basic question may be couched in these terms: Since the people generally have the common right to use and enjoy the ocean and the portion of the beach below the mean high water mark, of what utility is that right if access from the upland does not exist or is refused by the upland owner? Although the majority opinion disclaims any positive ruling on the subject, it seems to imply that exercise of the common right carries with it by way of implementation, the right to use and enjoy *any* beach upland for purposes of recreation and access to the ocean.

In my view, the common right is not so pervasive. Of course, generally speaking, reasonable access to the ocean and to the land strip which is in the public domain cannot be denied, but the law does not require that such access be without limitation or qualification. In localities where ocean front municipalities do not own or operate public beaches, and all ocean front property is in private ownership, such municipalities, as a legitimate *exercise of their right of eminent domain,* could provide for reasonable public access. For example, we are told that in some out of state communities where title to the public roads terminates at high or low water mark, the beach for the width of the road is regarded as subject to an easement of way for members of the public to the longitudinal strip of beach front seaward of the mean high water mark and into the ocean. But, whatever the technical situation in those places, it does not mean in this State that privately owned beach area upland of the mean high water mark is subject to public use. In my judgment a private owner could legally fence in his entire beach area upland of the mean high water mark, if he was moved to do so.

Communities like Avon which have only a few blocks of ocean front are aware that their publicly owned and maintained beaches risk over-crowding to the detriment of local residents and taxpayers unless some reasonable limitations are imposed on use by non-residents. In my view it is neither arbitrary nor invidiously discriminatory for the local governing body which owns, operates and maintains a public beach in the interest of its residents to charge a higher daily, weekly or monthly fee to non-residents who seek the privilege of using the beach. Avon has the right, I think, to fence in its beach to the mean high water mark, if it wishes and restrict the use thereof to its own residents and taxpayers with or without an admission fee. If it wishes to open this upland beach (owned by it) to use by non-residents, I see nothing in N.J.S.A. 40:92–7.1 or N.J.S.A. 40:61–22.20 which prohibits the municipality from imposing reasonable limits on the invitation by means of a charge of higher use fees to the non-residents. Accordingly, I see no merit in the contention that the inequality between the fees Avon charges for use of its upland beach to its own residents and taxpayers, and those charged to non-residents, renders illegal the fees imposed upon the non-residents.

For the reasons stated, I would affirm the judgment of the trial court. JUSTICE MOUNTAIN joins in this dissent.

Notes

1. The court extended the holding of the principal case to cover dry sand beaches in Van Ness v. Borough of Deal, 78 N.J. 174, 393 A.2d 571 (1978). In Hyland v. Borough of Allenhurst, 78 N.J. 190, 393 A.2d 579 (1978), the court held that members of the public must be allowed to use municipal toilet facilities, but have no right to use changing facilities. Also see Gewirtz v. City of Long Beach, 69 Misc.2d 763, 330 N.Y.S.2d 495 (Sup.Ct. Nassau Cty. 1972), affirmed 45 A.D.2d 841, 358 N.Y.S.2d 957 (1974), leave to appeal denied 35 N.Y.2d 644, 364 N.Y.S.2d 1025, 324 N.E.2d 370 (1974).

2. For a leading case on the use of the zoning power to prevent a landowner from developing his beachfront property, see McCarthy v. City of Manhattan Beach, 41 Cal.2d 879, 264 P.2d 932 (1953).

3. Once the public beach is established, how extensive is the right of public use? Does it extend to nude bathing? See Williams v. Hathaway, 400 F.Supp. 122 (D.Mass.1975) where the plaintiffs attacked a regulation promulgated by the Secretary of the Interior banning public nude bathing at a remote beach within the Cape Cod National Seashore. The court found that the long-established custom of nude bathing at that particular site gave the plaintiffs a limited constitutional right which could be asserted in nude bathing, but that the right was out-balanced by the Secretary's interest in preserving the beach from environmental harm which was escalating by virtue of a large increase in the number of people using the beach with increased traffic, parking and litter. Compare MacDonald v. Newsome, 437 F.Supp. 796 (D.N.C.1977), dealing with the rights of surfers.

STATE v. McILROY

Supreme Court of Arkansas, 1980.
268 Ark. 227, 595 S.W.2d 659, certiorari denied 449
U.S. 843, 101 S.Ct. 124, 66 L.Ed.2d 51 (1980).

HICKMAN, JUSTICE.

W.L. McIlroy and his late brother's estate, owners of 230 acres in Franklin County, sought a chancery court declaration that their rights as riparian landowners on the Mulberry River were, because the stream was not a navigable river, superior to the rights of the public.

McIlroy joined as defendants the Ozark Society, a conservationist group, and two companies that rent canoes for use on the Mulberry and other Ozark Mountain streams. The State of Arkansas, intervening, claimed the Mulberry was a navigable stream and the stream bed the property of the state, not the McIlroys.

The Ozark Society and the other defendants generally claimed that the Mulberry was a navigable stream but that even if the court found otherwise, a public easement in the Mulberry should be recognized. The defendants also argued that the public had acquired a prescriptive easement in the river and that the act admitting Arkansas into the Union placed the Mulberry in the public domain.

The chancellor declared the Mulberry was not a navigable stream. He found the McIlroys owned it as riparian property owners with the incidental right to prevent the public from using the stream (the McIlroys owned land on both sides of the Mulberry.) He declined to enjoin the Ozark Society from the publication of "The Mighty Mulberry," a brochure proclaiming the Mulberry as an excellent stream for canoeing.

* * *

The Mulberry River, located in northwest Arkansas, heads up in the Ozark Mountains and flows in a westerly direction for about 70 miles until it joins the Arkansas River. It could best be described as an intermediate stream, smaller than the Arkansas River, the lower White and Little Red Rivers and other deep, wide rivers that have been used commercially since their discovery. But neither is it like the many small creeks and branches in Arkansas that cannot be regularly floated with canoes or flatbottomed boats for any substantial period of time during the year. The Mulberry is somewhere in between. It is a stream that for about 50 or 55 miles of its length can be floated by canoe or flatbottomed boat for at least six months of the year. Parts of it are floatable for longer periods of time. The Mulberry is a typical rock-bottomed Ozark Mountain stream, flowing with relatively clear water and populated by a variety of fish. Small-mouth bass favor such a stream and populate the Mulberry.

For most of its distance it is a series of long flat holes of water interrupted by narrower shoals. These shoals attract the canoeists. McIlroy describes the stream as following a tortuous course; canoeists find it an exciting stream testing the skill of an experienced canoeist. Watergaps, affairs of wire or boards erected across the stream to hold cattle, have at times been erected but, according to W.L. McIlroy, they go down with the first rise of water. It is not a stream easily possessed. In recent years, the Mulberry has claimed the lives of several canoeists.

Annually, since 1967, the Ozark Society has sponsored for its members one or more float trips on the Mulberry River. These trips take them through McIlroy's property, which is located about 23 miles up the river from where the Mulberry enters the Arkansas. McIlroy said he had a confrontation with Ozark Society members in 1975 when about 600 people put in at a low water bridge on his property. The bridge, near Cass, serves a county road, and is undisputably a public bridge. Canoeists and fishermen have regularly used it as an access place to the river.

Although we are aware of the general characteristics of the river, we must here only determine the navigability of the Mulberry as it flows through the appellees' property. The chancellor faced this issue and ruled the river non-navigable. We reverse his decision and hold that the Mulberry River is navigable. While our decision will be a precedent for this river and should be used by the public and landowners as such, of necessity the judgment is directed only to the parties to this lawsuit.

This is essentially a lawsuit about the river as it passes through McIlroy's property. W.L. McIlroy testified that just below the bridge is a long hole of water, perhaps the longest on that stretch of the river, which is about 100 feet wide; it narrows to a shoal. He said a man could wade the water almost any time of the year. He claimed the river could sometimes not be canoed for an entire year. He said dry spots usually existed for six to eight months of the year. He denied seeing a canoe before 1974. However, from 1947 to 1971, McIlroy was in California. During that time he would spend only a week or so a year in Arkansas.

The great preponderance of the evidence conflicts with McIlroy's estimate of the river. It is floatable for at least six months of the year. According to a pamphlet, "The Float Streams of Arkansas," published by an Arkansas state agency, the floating season is October through June. This is for a course from a point considerably upstream from McIlroy's property to the river's mouth, a distance of about 50 miles. Numerous canoeists testified they had floated the Mulberry through the Cass area, mostly in the spring of the year. It was not disputed, however, that at times, usually in the summer months, the Mulberry could not be floated.

The evidence by testimony and exhibits demonstrates conclusively that the Mulberry had been used by the public for recreational purposes for many years. It has long been used for fishing and swimming and is today also popular among canoeists.

* * *

The facts presented prove that the Mulberry River at the point in question is capable of recreational use and has been used extensively for recreational purposes. We must now decide whether such a stream is navigable.

Determining the navigability of a stream is essentially a matter of deciding if it is public or private property. See, State v. Korrer, 127 Minn. 60, 148 N.W. 617, supp. op. 127 Minn. 60, 148 N.W. 1095 (1914). Navigation in fact is the standard modern test of navigability, and, as embroidered by the federal courts, controls when navigation must be defined for federal purposes—maritime jurisdiction, regulation under the Commerce Clause, and title disputes between the state and federal governments. See, Hitchings v. Del Rio Woods Recreation & Park District, 55 Cal.App.3d 560, 127 Cal.Rptr. 830 (1976); Day v. Armstrong, 362 P.2d 137 (Wyo.1961). Otherwise, the state may adopt their own definitions of navigability. Donnelly v. United States, 228 U.S. 243, 33 S.Ct. 449, 57 L.Ed. 820 (1913).

While navigation in fact is widely regarded as the proper test of navigability, St. Louis, Iron Mountain & Southern Railroad Co. v.

Ramsey, 53 Ark. 314, 13 S.W. 931 (1890), it is a test which should not be applied too literally. For example, it has been said a stream need not be navigable at all its points or for the entire year to be navigable. Economy Light & Power Co. v. United States, 256 U.S. 113, 41 S.Ct. 409, 65 L.Ed. 847 (1921). The real issue in these cases is the definition of navigation in fact.

Arkansas has adopted the standard definition of navigability. Lutesville Sand & Gravel Co. v. McLaughlin, supra. That test, which was similar to the general test used by the federal courts, defines navigability in terms of a river's potential for commercial usefulness; that is, whether the water could be used to remove the products of the surrounding land to another place. * * *

Therefore, a river is legally navigable if actually navigable and actually navigable if commercially valuable.

* * *

Since that time no case presented to us has involved the public's right to use a stream which has a recreational value, but lacks commercial adaptability in the traditional sense. Our definition of navigability is, therefore, a remnant of the steamboat era.

However, many other states have been presented with this same problem. Back in 1870, the Massachusetts Supreme Court found a stream navigable that could only be used for pleasure. The stream was about two feet deep at low water. The court stated:

> If water is navigable for pleasure boating, it must be regarded as navigable water though no craft has ever been upon it for the purpose of trade or agriculture. Attorney General v. Woods, 108 Mass. 436, 440 (1870).

In Ohio, the court recently was faced with this problem and decided to change its definition of navigation. The Ohio court said:

> We hold that the modern utilization of our water by our citizens requires that our courts, in their judicial interpretation of the navigability of such waters, consider their recreational use as well as the more traditional criteria of commercial use. State ex rel. Brown v. Newport Concrete Co., 44 Ohio App.2d 121, 127, 336 N.E.2d 453, 457, 73 Ohio Ops.2d 124 (1975).

Applying a "public trust" to the Little Miami River, the Ohio court found that the State of Ohio " * * * holds these waters in trust for those Ohioans who wish to use the stream for all legitimate uses, be they commercial, transportational, or recreational." State ex rel. Brown v. Newport Concrete Co., supra.

Michigan reached a similar conclusion in 1974. Navigability in Michigan was significantly affected by whether logs had been, or could be, floated down a stream. That "floatable test" had been used by the Michigan court until it was confronted with the same problem that we have. Michigan readily admitted that its definition needed to be changed:

We therefore hold that members of the public have the right to navigate and to exercise the incidents of navigation in a lawful manner at any point below high water mark on waters of this state which are capable of being navigated by oar or motor propelled small craft. Kelley ex rel. MacMullen v. Hallden, 51 Mich.App. 176, 214 N.W.2d 856, 864 (1974).

For examples of other states that have adopted similar definitions of navigation, see: People v. Mack, 19 Cal.App.3d 1040, 97 Cal.Rptr. 448 (1971); Lamprey v. State, 52 Minn. 181, 53 N.W. 1139 (1893); Luscher v. Reynolds, 153 Or. 625, 56 P.2d 1158 (1936).

* * * There is no doubt that the segment of the Mulberry River that is involved in this lawsuit can be used for a substantial portion of the year for recreational purposes. Consequently, we hold that it is navigable at that place with all the incidental rights of that determination.

* * *

Reversed.

FOGLEMAN, C.J., concurs in part and dissents in part.

I cannot join in the court's new definition of navigability, even though I concur in the reversal of the decree in this case. * * *

The test of navigability is the means of determining the property rights of riparian owners. As such it is a rule of property. To repudiate this rule of property by judicial decision will have the effect of invalidating titles that were acquired in reliance upon the rule and such a change, if desirable, should be brought about by legislation, which operates only prospectively and cannot upset titles already vested. * * *

* * * The prohibition against the taking, appropriation or damaging of private property without just compensation is binding on all branches of government. The judicial branch is no more vested with the power to take, appropriate or damage the established property rights of individuals without compensating them than is the executive branch. And yet the apparent effect of this decision accomplishes that very result. I submit that, insofar as titles vested under the test of navigability applied up until this very date, the change of the test is a violation of due process of law under both the state and federal constitutions, as well as of Art. 2, §§ 22 and 23 of the Arkansas constitution. Judicial submission to public clamor is not in keeping with constitutional government.

* * *

I find that the record discloses that the public has acquired an easement to use of the Mulberry River across the lands of the appellees by prescription just as fully as they would have acquired an easement for vehicular traffic across their riparian lands by adverse use for more than seven years after appellees should have known that the public use was adverse. That such an easement may be acquired by prescription was recognized in Buffalo River Conservation & Recreation Council v. National Park Service, 558 F.2d 1342 (8 Cir., 1977), in reliance upon

Clinton Chamber of Commerce v. Jacobs, 212 Ark. 776, 207 S.W.2d 616
(1948); Howard v. State, 47 Ark. 431, 2 S.W. 331; Patton v. State, 50
Ark. 53, 6 S.W. 227; McClain [McLain] v. Keel, 135 Ark. 496, 205 S.W.
894.

* * *

The chancellor held that canoeing constituted only an occasional
trespass and that the right to use the stream had been asserted or
brought home to the landowner within the period of limitations. I
respectfully disagree. It is true that McIlroy and others denied knowing
of the use being made of the stream for as long as 7 years. The absence
of W.M. McIlroy from the area during the early use of the stream by
canoeists will explain his professed ignorance of the facts to some extent.
There is evidence from which it might be said that the use which began
about 1952 was permissive. That use steadily increased, and must have
been obvious to anyone who observed the stream from the McIlroy farm.
A use that originates as a permissive use may be treated as adverse and
becomes an absolute right to a passageway, not only when it continues
openly for 7 years after the landowner has knowledge that the use is
adverse to his interest, but also when the usage continues for 7 years
after the facts and circumstances of the prior usage are such that the
landowner would be presumed to know the usage was adverse. * * * I
think that it was shown by a clear preponderance of the evidence that
the owners of the McIlroy lands should be presumed to have known that
a passageway on the Mulberry River was being used by the public
adversely to them and under a claim of right.

Since I cannot agree to the taking and appropriating by judicial fiat
of vested property rights of riparian owners on streams which are
nonnavigable under the test applied in Arkansas for a century, I must
dissent from the majority opinion, but I would reverse the decree on the
ground that a prescriptive easement has been acquired by adverse use.

PEOPLE EX REL. YOUNGER v.
COUNTY OF EL DORADO

California Court of Appeal, 1979.
96 Cal.App.3d 403, 157 Cal.Rptr. 815.

PARAS, ASSOCIATE JUSTICE

May a county ban all rafting and boating on a section of a navigable
river highly suited to and much used for such recreational activities?
Under the circumstances here presented it may not.

The South Fork of the American River in El Dorado County between
Chili Bar Dam and Salmon Falls, a distance of about 20 miles, is in
question. Because of its location, flow, lack of obstructions, and the
variety of challenges presented by its "runs," it is one of the two most
popular whitewater rafting areas in California. When dam construction
on the Stanislaus River is completed, there will be no comparable river

for rafting in the state. The popularity of this segment of river has increased dramatically in recent years. In 1975, 30 commercial rafting organizations spent approximately 21,000 commercial user days navigating the river. Private user days amounted to about 14,000.

The raft trip usually takes two days. Most of the land on both sides of the river is privately owned and access to the water is limited. Property owners along the river complain of noise, litter, pollution and unsanitary conditions caused by the rafters, as well as of trespassing and fire danger during overnight stops.

On August 10, 1976, the El Dorado County Board of Supervisors adopted an ordinance making it unlawful "to float, swim or travel in said waterway by any artificial means." Fishing or swimming "in a lawful manner," use of the public areas, and exercise of property rights by private owners were declared exempt. Violation of the ordinance was pronounced a misdemeanor punishable by a fine of up to $500 or six months in jail, or both.

* * *

The ordinance is neither a permissible special-use area designation or a reasonable sanitation and pollution control measure. On its face, it is an absolute prohibition against boating by the public. The record shows that the affected section of the river is not a significant fishing stream, and partly because of restricted access, fishing is light. Swimming in whitewater areas without such artificial means as lifejackets is obviously neither popular nor safe. Thus the ordinance effectively bans virtually all public use of the river.

However laudable its purpose, the exercise of police power may not extend to total prohibition of activity not otherwise unlawful. (Frost v. City of Los Angeles (1919) 181 Cal. 22, 183 P. 342, (ban on supplying water less pure than purest available); San Diego T. Assn. v. East San Diego (1921) 186 Cal. 252, 200 P. 393 (ban on operation of hospitals treating infectious or contagious diseases within city limits).) Courts are especially sensitive to infringements upon constitutional rights under the guise of exercise of police power. (See Scrutton v. County of Sacramento (1969) 275 Cal.App.2d 412, 421, 79 Cal.Rptr. 872.) The public's right of access to navigable streams is a constitutional right. (Cal. Const., art. X, § 4; Marks v. Whitney (1971) 6 Cal.3d 251, 98 Cal.Rptr. 790, 491 P.2d 374.)

The trial court relied on an Attorney General's opinion that an ordinance banning motorboat operations on a portion of the American River in Sacramento County established a special-use area (45 Ops.Cal. Atty.Gen. 122 (1965)). Its reliance was misplaced. While we express no opinion as to the correctness of the analysis or conclusion in that opinion, we distinguish a situation in which exclusion of power boats from an area better suited to "non-power" uses (id., at p. 123) protects the environment and fosters other recreational uses from the present situation in which *all* forms of "travel by artificial means" are excluded from an area ideally suited to such activity. The El Dorado County ordinance is not a special-use area designation; it is virtually a no-use area designation.

While obviously effective to eliminate pollution and sanitation problems, the ordinance goes too far. The county contends use prohibition is the only way to eliminate pollution and sanitation problems. But the logical extension of this hypothesis is the prohibition of all industry, agriculture, and even human habitation, the effect of which would be to eliminate pollution entirely. The public has a right to use the river; it has no right to pollute the river. Reasonable regulation is in order; use prohibition is not. The problems of pollution and sanitation in our increasingly crowded state are difficult and complex, calling for imaginative and sophisticated solutions. But total prohibition of access is an impermissible solution. The ordinance is invalid because it denies the constitutional right of the public to use of and access to a navigable stream.

The judgment is reversed with directions to enter judgment for plaintiffs enjoining enforcement of the ordinance in question.

Notes

1. Compare with the principal cases People v. Emmert, 198 Colo. 137, 597 P.2d 1025 (1979), where the court held that, despite a provision in the state constitution that unappropriated water of every natural stream is the property of the people, land underlying non-navigable streams was owned by the proprietors of adjoining lands, and canoeists were trespassers.

Also see Bott v. Commission of Natural Resources, 415 Mich. 45, 327 N.W.2d 838 (1982) where the court applied the "floating log" theory of navigability and held that the owner of all the land surrounding a 35 acre lake could exclude riparian owners of a nearby lake which was connected to the lake in question by small creeks.

2. In the arid western states the ownership of stream beds is a very complex issue. In 1994 Arizona enacted a statute to address the problem, 37 Ariz. Rev. Stat. § 1101 et seq. The statutory purpose set forth is:

> [T]o establish an administrative procedure for the necessary fact-finding efforts and the determination of the extent of this state's ownership of the beds of watercourses located in this state. This act is designed to confirm the titles currently held by private parties and political subdivisions to those lands located in watercourses, other than the Colorado river, that are determined not to have been navigable at the time of statehood, to confirm this state's ownership in public trust of lands located in the beds of watercourses determined to have been navigable at statehood and to acknowledge the state's ethical and equitable obligations to deal fairly with those citizens of this state who have in good faith acquired leases or title, paid taxes, improved land and otherwise acted in justifiable reliance on this state's failure to assert its claims for over seventy years. * * *

3. One effect of finding public rights in a stream is to call into question the common law principle of title to riparian lands and title to the riverbed

itself. As the dissent in the McIlroy case suggests, the effect of redefining navigability could affect ownership of oil, gas and other minerals and sand and gravel dredging operations. Traditionally in the United States, the ability to use a stream commercially has determined its navigability. See generally, Bonelli Cattle Co. v. Arizona, 414 U.S. 313, 94 S.Ct. 517, 38 L.Ed.2d 526 (1973), overruled Oregon v. Corvallis Sand and Gravel Co., 429 U.S. 363, 97 S.Ct. 582, 50 L.Ed.2d 550 (1977); United States v. Willow River Power Co., 324 U.S. 499, 65 S.Ct. 761, 89 L.Ed. 1101 (1945); In re River Queen, 275 F.Supp. 403 (W.D.Ark.1967), affirmed 402 F.2d 977 (8th Cir. 1968). Water rights can be acquired by prescriptive use, as the dissent suggests. The case of Buffalo River Conservation and Recreation Council v. National Park Serv., 558 F.2d 1342 (8th Cir.1977) takes the prescriptive rights approach. Moreover, support for the dissent's "taking" argument can be found in the implications which may be drawn from Kaiser Aetna v. United States, 444 U.S. 164, 100 S.Ct. 383, 62 L.Ed.2d 332 (1979), in which the water was found to be navigable, but because it had been artificially made navigable after being in private ownership, the public was held to be excluded until just compensation was paid to the owners.

What do you think of this solution to the title problems resulting from the McIlroy case? Statutorily define navigable waters in the traditional sense and vest title to beds of non-navigable streams in the riparian owners. Then, grant the public an easement for recreational use in all waters having value for recreational purposes. Preserve all other constitutional, statutory and common law rights and remedies of landowners (including the right to sue for trespass or nuisance).

Index

References are to Pages

1289

NUISANCES—Cont'd
Power plants, 147
Private nuisances, 43
Psychic injuries, 66–67, 108–114
Public nuisances, 43
Quarries, 134–137
Race tracks, 67–71
Recreational uses, 76, 132–133
Rendering plants, 58–60
Residential uses,
    Exclusively, 109–112
    Predominantly, 110, 113
    Recreational, 74–77
    Rural, 67–77
    Rururban fringe, 77–96
Rural residential use, 67–77
Rururban fringe, 77–96
Salvage yards, 96–101
Self-help, 133
Sic utere tuo ut alienum non laedas, 47
Sign, 132
Spite fence, 129–132
State-federal conflicts, 146–151
Storm drain, 133
Substantial harm, 47
Supermarkets, 106–107
Television interference, 141–142
Trespasses, compared with, 151–152
Ultrahazardous activities, 150
U.S. (federal) common law, 146–147
Zoned areas,
    Generally, 134–141
    Conforming uses, 134–140
    Nonconforming uses, 141

OFFICIAL MAP
Generally, 740–753
Amendment, invalidity of, 751
Constitutionality, 742–748
Described and defined, 740–742
Establishing building or set-back lines, other methods, 741
Exhausting administrative remedies, 741
Hardship cases or provisions, 740
Marketability of land, effect on, 740–753
Master plan, comparison with, 740–741
Title encumbrance, 753

OIL AND GAS
Waste, 42

OPEN LANDS
Agricultural zoning, 1246–1256
Environmental controls on, 548–558
Flood plains, 541–548
Highway beautification and scenic easements, 1208–1212
Nuisances, 51–77
Open spaces, 548–558
Preservation, 548–558
Shorelands, 508–516
View protection, 561–565
Wildlife preserves, 315, 501–508

OPEN SPACE
Agreements on, 1256
Cluster plan, 859–870
Protection of view, 561–565

PARKS
See Dedication for Public Use, Schools and parks

PIGGERIES
As nuisance, 74–77

PLANNING
See also, Master Plan; Zoning
Generally, 263–288
Background, 263–268
Enabling acts, 288–292
Environmental considerations, 310–316
Failure to plan, 771, 797–799
Federal legislation, 309–310
Houston, 771
Interstate compacts, 323–331
Local planning agency, 289–295
Master plan, 288–309
Official map, 740–753
Planning profession,
    History of, 272–278
    Legal status, 278–288
Regional, 321–323
State, 310–321
Zoning, relation to, 800–812
Zoning versus planning, 796–799

POLICE POWER
Basic rule, 333–338
Constitutional considerations, 333–338
Flood plains, 541–548
Hillsides, 548–557
Historic development, 332–338
Historic districts, 566–575
Official map, relation to, 740–742
Reservations of use, 635–640
Subdivision regulations, relation to, 654–655
Taking, 338–384
Zoning, relation to, 788–796

PREEMPTION
Federal legislation, 955–957

PRIVATE CONTROLS
See Easements; Equitable Servitudes; Restrictive Covenants

PRIVATE PROPERTY
Aesthetics, protection of, 1217–1225
Duty not to interfere with neighbors, 17, 44
Police power, effect on, 332–338
Takings legislation, 488–491
Theory of right to own, 1–2

PROPERTY
Equitable servitude or restrictive covenant as, 186–193
Police power, effect on, 332–338

†